The New York
Botanical Garden
Illustrated Encyclopedia
of Horticulture

The New York Botanical Garden Illustrated Encyclopedia of Horticulture

Thomas H. Everett

Volume 1
A-Be

Garland Publishing, Inc.
New York & London

Library of Congress Cataloging in Publication Data

Everett, Thomas H
    The New York Botanical Garden illustrated encyclopedia of horticulture.

    1. Horticulture—Dictionaries. 2. Gardening—Dictionaries. 3. Plants, Ornamental—Dictionaries. 4. Plants, Cultivated—Dictionaries. I. New York (City). Botanical Garden. II. Title.
SB317.58.E94   635.9′03′21   80-65941
ISBN 0-8240-7231-6

PHOTO CREDITS

Black and White
Agri-Plast Company: Ringing (part c), p. 96. W. Atlee Burpee Company: *Arabis caucasica*, p. 215. A. B. Graf: *Adenanthera pavonina*, p. 50; *Agalmyla parasitica*, p. 74: *Aiphanes caryotaefolia*, p. 93; *Astelia nervosa*, p. 282; *Astroloba skinneri*, p. 292; *Averrhoa carambola*, p. 311. The New York Botanical Garden: *Ageratum houstonianum* (Dwarf variety), p. 85; *Aglaeonema nitidum curtisii*, p. 87; To Air Layer (parts e & f), p. 95; *Albuca fastigiata*, p. 101; *Alocasia watsoniana*, p. 118; *Aloe variegata*, p.124; *Amarcrinum*, p. 136; *Amorphophallus bulbifer*, p. 145; *Amorphophallus titanum* (2 pictures), p. 145; *Amsonia tabernaemontana*, p. 148; *Antennaria rosea*, p. 182; Snapdragons in a border of mixed annuals, p. 192; double-flowered snapdragon, p. 193; *Antirrhinum molle*, p. 194; *Apios americana*, p. 199; *Ardisia polycephala*, p. 232; *Aristolochia grandiflora*, p. 245; *Armeria juniperifolia*, p. 248; Tropical arp, 251; *Artemisia frigida*, p. 257; *Astilbe arendsii*, p. 288; *Rhododendron* (Azalea) *Calendulaceum*, p. 315; Tropical bamboo, p. 338. United States National Arboretum: Rhododendron (Azalea) Glenn Dale hybrid 'Witchery', p. 323. University of California, Berkeley: Young apple tree correctly pruned, p. 205. Other photographs by Thomas H. Everett.

Color
Harold Frisch: *Anemone coronaria, Anemone pulsatilla.* The New York Botanical Garden: *Actaea pachypoda, Actaea rubra* (fruits), *Aesculus hippocastanum* (flowers), *Agave angustifolia marginata, Aletris farinosa, Aquilegia jonesii, Aquilegia* long-spurred hybrid, *Arethusa bulbosa, Argemone polyanthemos, Asarum caudatum, Asclepias tuberosa,* Azalea (*Rhododendron japonicum* hybrids, *Rhododendron nudiflorum, Rhododendron viscosum, Rhododendron canadense*). Other photographs by Thomas H. Everett.

Published by Garland Publishing, Inc.
136 Madison Avenue, New York, New York 10016

Printed in the United States of America

This work is dedicated to the honored memory of the distinguished horticulturists and botanists who most profoundly influenced my professional career: Allan Falconer of Cheadle Royal Gardens, Cheshire, England; William Jackson Bean, William Dallimore, and John Coutts of the Royal Botanic Gardens, Kew, England; and Dr. Elmer D. Merrill and Dr. Henry A. Gleason of The New York Botanical Garden.

Foreword

According to Webster, an encyclopedia is a book or set of books giving information on all or many branches of knowledge generally in articles alphabetically arranged. To the horticulturist or grower of plants, such a work is indispensable and one to be kept close at hand for frequent reference.

The appearance of *The New York Botanical Garden Illustrated Encyclopedia of Horticulture* by Thomas H. Everett is therefore welcomed as an important addition to the library of horticultural literature. Since horticulture is a living, growing subject, these volumes contain an immense amount of information not heretofore readily available. In addition to detailed descriptions of many thousands of plants given under their generic names and brief description of the characteristics of the more important plant families, together with lists of their genera known to be in cultivation, this Encyclopedia is replete with well-founded advice on how to use plants effectively in gardens and, where appropriate, indoors. Thoroughly practical directions and suggestions for growing plants are given in considerable detail and in easily understood language. Recommendations about what to do in the garden for all months of the year and in different geographical regions will be helpful to beginners and will serve as reminders to others.

The useful category of special subject entries (as distinct from the taxonomic presentations) consists of a wide variety of topics. It is safe to predict that one of the most popular will be Rock and Alpine Gardens. In this entry the author deals helpfully and adequately with a phase of horticulture that appeals to a growing group of devotees, and in doing so presents a distinctly fresh point of view. Many other examples could be cited.

The author's many years as a horticulturist and teacher well qualify him for the task of preparing this Encyclopedia. Because he has, over a period of more than a dozen years, written the entire text (submitting certain critical sections to specialists for review and suggestions) instead of farming out sections to a score or more specialists to write, the result is remarkably homogeneous and cohesive. The Encyclopedia is fully cross referenced so that one may locate a plant by either its scientific or common name.

If, as has been said, an encyclopedia should be all things to all people, then the present volumes richly deserve that accolade. Among the many who call it "friend" will be not only horticulturists ("gardeners," as our author likes to refer to them), but growers, breeders, writers, lecturers, arborists, ecologists, and professional botanists who are frequently called upon to answer questions to which only such a work can provide answers. It seems safe to predict that it will be many years before lovers and growers of plants will have at their command another reference work as authoritative and comprehensive as T. H. Everett's Encyclopedia.

John M. Fogg, Jr.
Director Emeritus, Arboretum of the Barnes Foundation
Emeritus Professor of Botany, University of Pennsylvania

Preface

The primary objective of *The New York Botanical Garden Illustrated Encyclopedia of Horticulture* is a comprehensive description and evaluation of horticulture as it is known and practiced in the United States and Canada by amateurs and by professionals, including those responsible for botanical gardens, public parks, and industrial landscapes. Although large-scale commercial methods of cultivating plants are not stressed, much of the content of the Encyclopedia is as basic to such operations as it is to other horticultural enterprises. Similarly, although landscape design is not treated on a professional level, landscape architects will find in the Encyclopedia a great deal of importance and interest to them. Emphasis throughout is placed on the appropriate employment of plants both outdoors and indoors, and particular attention is given to explaining in considerable detail the how- and when-to-do-it aspects of plant growing.

It may be useful to assess the meanings of two words I have used. Horticulture is simply gardening. It derives from the Latin *hortus*, garden, and *cultura*, culture, and alludes to the intensive cultivation in gardens and nurseries of flowers, fruits, vegetables, shrubs, trees, and other plants. The term is not applicable to the extensive field practices that characterize agriculture and forestry. Amateur, as employed by me, retains its classic meaning of a lover from the Latin *amator*; it refers to those who garden for pleasure rather than for financial gain or professional status. It carries no implication of lack of knowledge or skills and is not to be equated with novice, tyro, or dabbler. In truth, amateurs provide the solid basis upon which American horticulture rests; without them the importance of professionals would diminish. Numbered in millions, amateur gardeners are devotees of the most widespread avocation in the United States. This avocation is serviced by a great complex of nurseries, garden centers, and other suppliers; by landscape architects and landscape contractors; and by garden writers, garden lecturers, Cooperative Extension Agents, librarians, and others who dispense horticultural information. Numerous horticultural societies, garden clubs, and botanical gardens inspire and promote interest in America's greatest hobby and stand ready to help its enthusiasts.

Horticulture as a vocation presents a wide range of opportunities which appeal equally to women and men. It is a field in which excellent prospects still exist for capable entrepreneurs. Opportunities at professional levels occur too in nurseries and greenhouses, in the management of landscaped grounds of many types, and in teaching horticulture.

Some people confuse horticulture with botany. They are not the same. The distinction becomes more apparent if the word gardening is substituted for horticulture. Botany is the science that encompasses all systematized factual knowledge about plants, both wild and cultivated. It is only one of the several disciplines upon which horticulture is based. To become a capable gardener or a knowledgeable plantsman or plantswoman (I like these designations for gardeners who have a wide, intimate, and discerning knowledge of plants in addition to skill in growing them) it is not necessary to study botany formally, although such study is likely to add greatly to one's pleasure. In the practice of gardening many botanical truths are learned from experience. I have known highly competent gardeners without formal training in botany and able and indeed distinguished botanists possessed of minimal horticultural knowledge and skills.

Horticulture is primarily an art and a craft, based upon science, and at some levels perhaps justly regarded as a science in its own right. As an art it calls for an appreciation of beauty and form as expressed in three-dimensional spatial relationships and an ability to translate aesthetic concepts into reality. The chief materials used to create gardens are living plants, most of which change in size and form with the passing of time and often show differences in color and texture and in other ways from season to season. Thus it is important that designers of gardens have a wide familiarity with the sorts of plants that lend themselves to their purposes and with plants' adaptability to the regions and to the sites where it is proposed to plant them.

As a craft, horticulture involves special skills often derived from ancient practices passed from generation to generation by word of mouth and apprenticeship-like contacts. As a technology it relies on this backlog of empirical knowledge supplemented by that acquired by scientific experiment and investigation, the results of which often serve to explain rather than supplant old beliefs and practices but sometimes point the way to more expeditious methods of attaining similar results. And from time to time new techniques are developed that add dimensions to horticultural practice; among such of fairly recent years that come to mind are the manipulation of blooming season by artificial daylength, the propagation of orchids and some other plants by meristem tissue culture, and the development of soilless growing mixes as substitutes for soil.

One of the most significant developments in American horticulture in recent decades is the tremendous increase in the number of different kinds of plants that are cultivated by many more people than formerly. This is particularly true of indoor plants or houseplants, the sorts grown in homes, offices, and other interiors, but is by no means confined to that group. The relative affluence of our society and the freedom and frequency of travel both at home and abroad has contributed to this expansion, a phenomenon that will surely continue as avid collectors of the unusual bring into cultivation new plants from the wild and promote wider interest in sorts presently rare. Our garden flora is also constantly and beneficially expanded as a result of the work of both amateur and professional plant breeders.

It is impracticable in even the most comprehensive encyclopedia to describe or even list all plants that somewhere within a territory as large as the United States and Canada are grown in gardens. In this Encyclopedia the majority of genera known to be in cultivation are described, and descriptions and often other pertinent information about a complete or substantial number of their species and lesser categories are given. Sorts likely to be found only in collections of botanical gardens or in those of specialists may be omitted.

The vexing matter of plant nomenclature inevitably presents itself when an encyclopedia of horticulture is contemplated. Conflicts arise chiefly between the very understandable desire of gardeners and others who deal with cultivated plants to retain long-familiar names and the need to reflect up-to-date botanical interpretations. These points of view are basically irreconcilable and so accommodations must be reached.

As has been well demonstrated in the past, it is unrealistic to attempt to standardize the horticultural usage of plant names by decree or edict. To do so would negate scientific progress. But it is just as impracticable to expect gardeners, nurserymen, arborists, seedsmen, dealers in bulbs, and other amateur and professional horticulturists to keep current with the interpretations and recommendations of plant taxonomists; particularly as these sometimes fail to gain the acceptance even of other botanists and it is not unusual for scientists of equal stature and competence to prefer different names for the same plant.

In practice time is the great leveler. Newly proposed plant names accepted in botanical literature are likely to filter gradually into horticultural usage and eventually gain currency value, but this sometimes takes several years. The complete up-to-dateness and niceties of botanical naming are less likely to bedevil horticulturists than uncertainties concerned with correct plant identification. This is of prime importance. Whether a tree is labeled *Pseudotsuga douglasii, P. taxifolia,* or *P. menziesii* is of less concern than that the specimen so identified is indeed a Douglas-fir and not some other conifer.

After reflection I decided that the most sensible course to follow in *The New York Botanical Garden Illustrated Encyclopedia of Horticulture* was to accept almost in its entirety the nomenclature adopted in *Hortus Third* published in 1976. By doing so, much of the confusion that would result from two major comprehensive horticultural works of the late twentieth century using different names for the same plant is avoided, and it is hoped that for a period of years a degree of stability will be attained. Always those deeply concerned with critical groups of plants can adopt the recommendations of the latest monographers. Exceptions to the parallelism in nomenclature in this Encyclopedia and *Hortus Third* are to be found in the CACTACEAE for which, with certain reservations but for practical purposes, as explained in the Encyclopedia entry Cactuses, the nomenclature of Curt Backeburg's *Die Cactaceae*, published in 1958–62, is followed; and the ferns, where I mostly accepted the guidance of Dr. John T. Mickel of The New York Botanical Garden. The common or colloquial names employed are those deemed to have general acceptance. Cross references and synonymy are freely provided.

The convention of indicating typographically whether or not plants of status lesser than species represent entities that propagate and persist in the wild or are sorts that persist only in cultivation is not followed. Instead, as explained in the Encyclopedia entry Plant Names, the word variety is employed for all entities below specific rank and if in Latin form the name is written in italic, if in English or other modern language, in Roman type, with initial capital letter, and enclosed in single quotation marks.

Thomas H. Everett
Senior Horticulture Specialist
The New York Botanical Garden

Acknowledgments

I am indebted to many people for help and support generously given over the period of more than twelve years it has taken to bring this Encyclopedia to fruition. Chief credit belongs to four ladies. They are Lillian M. Weber and Nancy Callaghan, who besides accepting responsibility for the formidable task of filing and retrieving information, typing manuscript, proofreading, and the management of a vast collection of photographs, provided much wise council; Elizabeth C. Hall, librarian extraordinary, whose superb knowledge of horticultural and botanical literature was freely at my disposal; and Ellen, my wife, who displayed a deep understanding of the demands on time called for by an undertaking of this magnitude, and with rare patience accepted inevitable inconvenience. I am also obliged to my sister, Hette Everett, for the valuable help she freely gave on many occasions.

Of the botanists I repeatedly called upon for opinions and advice and from whom I sought elucidation of many details of their science abstruse to me, the most heavily burdened have been my friends and colleagues at The New York Botanical Garden, Dr. Rupert C. Barneby, Dr. Arthur Cronquist, and Dr. John T. Mickel. Other botanists and horticulturists with whom I held discussions or corresponded about matters pertinent to my text include Dr. Theodore M. Barkley, Dr. Lyman Benson, Dr. Ben Blackburn, Professor Harold Davidson, Dr. Otto Degener, Harold Epstein, Dr. John M. Fogg, Jr., Dr. Alwyn H. Gentry, Dr. Alfred B. Graf, Brian Halliwell, Dr. David R. Hunt, Dr. John P. Jessop, Dr. Tetsuo Koyama, Dr. Bassett Maguire, Dr. Roy A. Mecklenberg, Everitt L. Miller, Dr. Harold N. Moldenke, Dr. Dan H. Nicolson, Dr. Pascal P. Pirone, Dr. Ghillean Prance, Don Richardson, Stanley J. Smith, Ralph L. Snodsmith, Marco Polo Stufano, Dr. Bernard Verdcourt, Dr. Edgar T. Wherry, Dr. Trevor Whiffin, Dr. Richard P. Wunderlin, Dr. John J. Wurdack, Yuji Yoshimura, and Rudolf Ziesenhenne.

Without either exception or stint these conferees and correspondents shared with me their knowledge, thoughts, and judgments. Much of the bounty so gleaned is reflected in the text of the Encyclopedia but none other than I am responsible for interpretations and opinions that appear there. To all who have helped, my special thanks are due and are gratefully proferred.

I acknowledge with much pleasure the excellent cooperation I have received from the Garland Publishing Company and most particularly from its President, Gavin Borden. To Ruth Adams, Geoffrey Braine, Nancy Isaac, Carol Miller, and Melinda Wirkus, I say thank you for working so understandingly and effectively with me and for shepherding my raw typescript through the necessary stages.

How to Use This Encyclopedia

A vast amount of information about how to use, propagate, and care for plants both indoors and outdoors is contained in the thousands of entries that compose *The New York Botanical Garden Illustrated Encyclopedia of Horticulture*. Some understanding of the Encyclopedia's organization is necessary in order to find what you want to know.

Arrangement of the Entries

Genera

The entries are arranged in alphabetical order. Most numerous are those that deal with taxonomic groups of plants. Here belong approximately 3,500 items entered under the genus name, such as ABIES, DIEFFENBACHIA, and JUGLANS. If instead of referring to these names you consult their common name equivalents of FIR, DUMB CANE, and WALNUT, you will find cross references to the genus names.

Bigeneric Hybrids & Chimeras

Hybrids between genera that have names equivalent to genus names—most of these belonging in the orchid family—are accorded separate entries. The same is true for the few chimeras or graft hybrids with names of similar status. Because bigeneric hybrids frequently have characteristics similar to those of their parents and require similar care, the entries for them are often briefer than the regular genus entries.

Families

Plant families are described under their botanical names, with their common name equivalents also given. Each description is followed by a list of the genera accorded separate entries in this Encyclopedia.

Vegetables, Fruits, Herbs, & Ornamentals

Vegetables and fruits that are commonly cultivated, such as broccoli, cabbage, potato, tomato, apple, peach, and raspberry; most culinary herbs, including basil, chives, parsley, sage, and tarragon; and a few popular ornamentals, such as azaleas, carnations, pansies, and poinsettias, are treated under their familiar names, with cross references to their genera. Discussions of a few herbs and some lesser known vegetables and fruits are given under their Latin scientific names with cross references to the common names.

Other Entries

The remaining entries in the Encyclopedia are cross references, definitions, and more substantial discussions of many subjects of interest to gardeners and others concerned with plants. For example, a calendar of gardening activity, by geographical area, is given under the names of the months and a glossary of frequently applied species names (technically, specific epithets) is provided in the entry Plant Names. A list of these general topics, which may provide additional information about a particular plant, is provided at the beginning of each volume of the Encyclopedia.

Cross References & Definitions

The cross references are of two chief types: those that give specific information, which may be all you wish to know at the moment:
Boojam Tree is *Idria columnaris*.
Cobra plant is *Darlingtonia californica*.
and those that refer to entries where fuller explanations are to be found:
Adhatoda. See Justicia.
Clubmoss. See Lycopodium and Selaginella.

Additional information about entries of the former type can, of course, be found by looking up the genus to which the plant belongs—*Idria* in the case of the boojam tree and *Darlingtonia* for the cobra plant.

ORGANIZATION OF THE GENUS ENTRIES

Pronunciation

Each genus name is followed by its pronunciation in parentheses. The stressed syllable is indicated by the diacritical mark ´ if the vowel sound is short as in man, pet, pink, hot, and up; or by ˋ if the vowel sound is long as in mane, pete, pine, home, and fluke.

Genus Common Names
Family Common Names
General Characteristics

Following the pronunciation, there may be one or more common names applicable to the genus as a whole or to certain of its kinds. Other names may be introduced later with the descriptions of the species or kinds. Early in the entry you will find the common and botanical names of the plant family to which the genus belongs, the number of species the genus contains, its natural geographical distribution, and the derivation of its name. A description that stresses the general characteristics of the genus follows, and this may be supplemented by historical data, uses of some or all of its members, and other pertinent information.

Identification of Plants

Descriptions of species, hybrids, and varieties appear next. The identification of unrecognized plants is a fairly common objective of gardeners; accordingly, in this Encyclopedia various species have been grouped within entries in ways that make their identification easier. The groupings may bring into proximity sorts that can be adapted for similar landscape uses or that require the same cultural care, or they may emphasize geographical origins of species or such categories as evergreen and deciduous or tall and low members of the same genus. Where the description of a species occurs, its name is designated in ***bold italic.*** Under this plan, the description of a particular species can be found by referring to the group to which it belongs, scanning the entry for the species name in bold italic, or referring to the opening sentences of paragraphs which have been designed to serve as lead-ins to descriptive groupings.

Gardening & Landscape Uses
Cultivation
Pests & Diseases

At the end of genus entries, subentries giving information on garden and landscape uses, cultivation, and pests or diseases or both are included, or else reference is made to other genera or groupings for which these are similar.

General Subject Listings

The lists below organize some of the Encyclopedia entries into topics which may be of particular interest to the reader. They are also an aid in finding information other than Latin or common names of plants.

PLANT ANATOMY AND TERMS USED IN PLANT DESCRIPTIONS

All-America Selections
Alternate
Annual Rings
Anther
Apex
Ascending
Awl-Shaped
Axil, Axillary
Berry
Bloom
Bracts
Bud
Bulb
Bulbils
Bulblet
Bur
Burl
Calyx
Cambium Layer
Capsule
Carpel
Catkin
Centrals
Ciliate
Climber
Corm
Cormel
Cotyledon
Crown
Deciduous
Disk or Disc
Double Flowers
Drupe
Florets
Flower
Follicle
Frond
Fruit
Glaucous
Gymnosperms
Head
Hips
Hose-in-Hose

Inflorescence
Lanceolate
Leader
Leaf
Leggy
Linear
Lobe
Midrib
Mycelium
Node
Nut and Nutlet
Oblanceolate
Oblong
Obovate
Offset
Ovate
Palmate
Panicle
Pedate
Peltate
Perianth
Petal
Pinnate
Pip
Pistil
Pit
Pod
Pollen
Pompon
Pseudobulb
Radials
Ray Floret
Rhizome
Runners
Samara
Scion or Cion
Seeds
Sepal
Set
Shoot
Spore
Sprigs
Spur
Stamen
Stigma
Stipule

Stolon
Stool
Style
Subshrub
Taproot
Tepal
Terminal
Whorl

GARDENING TERMS AND INFORMATION

Acid and Alkaline Soils
Adobe
Aeration of the Soil
Air and Air Pollution
Air Drainage
Air Layering
Alpine Greenhouse or Alpine House
Amateur Gardener
April, Gardening Reminders For
Aquarium
Arbor
Arboretum
Arch
Asexual or Vegetative Propagation
Atmosphere
August, Gardening Reminders For
Balled and Burlapped
Banks and Steep Slopes
Bare-Root
Bark Ringing
Baskets, Hanging
Bed
Bedding and Bedding Plants
Bell Jar
Bench, Greenhouse
Blanching
Bleeding
Bog
Bolting
Border
Bottom Heat
Break, Breaking
Broadcast
Budding
Bulbs or Bulb Plants

Gardening Terms and Information (Continued)

State Agricultural Experimental Stations
Stock or Understock
Straightedge
Strawberry Jars
Strike
Stunt
Succession Cropping
Sundials
Syringing
Thinning or Thinning Out
Tillage
Tilth
Tools
Top-Dressing
Topiary Work
Training Plants
Tree Surgery
Tree Wrapping
Trenching
Trowels
Tubs
Watering
Weeds and Their Control
Window Boxes

FERTILIZERS AND OTHER SUBSTANCES RELATED TO GARDENING

Algicide
Aluminum Sulfate
Ammonium Nitrate
Ammonium Sulfate
Antibiotics
Ashes
Auxins
Basic Slag
Blood Meal
Bonemeal
Bordeaux Mixture
Calcium Carbonate
Calcium Chloride
Calcium Metaphosphate
Calcium Nitrate
Calcium Sulfate
Carbon Disulfide
Chalk
Charcoal
Coal Cinders
Cork Bark
Complete Fertilizer
Compost and Composting
Cottonseed Meal
Creosote
DDT
Dormant Sprays
Dried Blood
Fermate or Ferbam
Fertilizers
Fishmeal
Formaldehyde
Fungicides
Gibberellic Acid
Green Manuring
Growth Retardants
Guano
Herbicides or Weed-Killers
Hoof and Horn Meal

Hormones
Humus
Insecticide
John Innes Composts
Lime and Liming
Liquid Fertilizer
Liquid Manure
Manures
Mulching and Mulches
Muriate of Potash
Nitrate of Ammonia
Nitrate of Lime
Nitrate of Potash
Nitrate of Soda
Nitrogen
Orchid Peat
Organic Matter
Osmunda Fiber or Osmundine
Oyster Shells
Peat
Peat Moss
Permanganate of Potash
Potassium
Potassium Chloride
Potassium-Magnesium Sulfate
Potassium Nitrate
Potassium Permanganate
Potassium Sulfate
Pyrethrum
Rock Phosphate
Rotenone
Salt Hay or Salt Marsh Hay
Sand
Sawdust
Sodium Chloride
Sprays and Spraying
Sulfate
Superphosphate
Trace Elements
Urea
Urea-Form Fertilizers
Vermiculite
Wood Ashes

TECHNICAL TERMS

Acre
Alternate Host
Annuals
Antidessicant or Antitranspirant
Biennals
Binomial
Botany
Chromosome
Climate
Clone
Composite
Conservation
Cross or Crossbred
Cross Fertilization
Cross Pollination
Cultivar
Decumbent
Dicotyledon
Division
Dormant
Endemic
Environment
Family

Fasciation
Fertility
Fertilization
Flocculate
Floriculture
Genus
Germinate
Habitat
Half-Hardy
Half-Ripe
Hardy Annual
Hardy Perennial
Heredity
Hybrid
Indigenous
Juvenile Forms
Juvenility
Legume
Monocotyledon
Monoecious
Mutant or Sport
Mycorrhiza or Mycorhiza
Nitrification
Perennials
pH
Plant Families
Photoperiodism
Photosynthesis
Pollination
Pubescent
Saprophyte
Self-Fertile
Self-Sterile
Species
Standard
Sterile
Strain
Terrestrial
Tetraploid
Transpiration
Variety

TYPES OF GARDENS AND GARDENING

Alpine Garden
Artificial Light Gardening
Backyard Gardens
Biodynamic Gardening
Bog Gardens
Botanic Gardens and Arboretums
Bottle Garden
City Gardening
Colonial Gardens
Conservatory
Container Gardening
Cutting Garden
Desert Gardens
Dish Gardens
Flower Garden
Fluorescent Light Gardening
Formal and Semiformal Gardens
Greenhouses and Conservatories
Heath or Heather Garden
Herb Gardens
Hydroponics or Nutriculture
Indoor Lighting Gardening
Japanese Gardens
Kitchen Garden
Knot Gardens

The New York
Botanical Garden
Illustrated Encyclopedia
of Horticulture

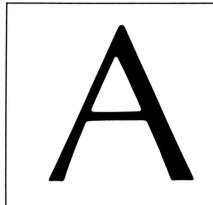

A

AARON'S BEARD is *Hypericum calycinum*.

ABACA or Manila-Hemp is *Musa textilis*.

ABELE or White Poplar is *Populus alba*.

ABELIA (Ab-èlia). The honeysuckle family CAPRIFOLIACEAE includes several genera that contain attractive shrubs. Here belong the beauty bush, bush honeysuckles, weigelas, viburnums, and snowberries, as well as *Abelia*. The last consists of about thirty species, mostly natives of eastern temperate Asia, but one is a native of the Himalayas and two are natives of Mexico. The genus is named in honor of Dr. Clarke Abel, a physician and the author of a book describing a journey made into China in 1817 by a British embassy that he served.

Abelias are small- to medium-sized flowering shrubs with deciduous, semi-evergreen, or evergreen foliage. Those cultivated are decidedly ornamental. A few are hardy in the north, but most require milder climates. The genus, which is closely related to and was at one time included in *Linnaea*, has undivided, sometimes toothed, short-stalked leaves, usually opposite but occasionally in threes, and white, pink, or purplish blooms with two- to five-parted calyxes long-persistent after the corollas fall, and cylindrical, funnel- or bell-shaped corollas with five spreading lobes. There are four stamens in pairs. The one-seeded fruits, technically achenes, are capped by the persistent calyxes. The fruits differ from those of the closely related beauty bush (*Kolkwitzia*) in not being bristly. Abelias bloom freely. The flowers are sometimes solitary, but more commonly occur in clusters, in leaf axils or at the end of short branches. Often the clusters are aggregated in terminal panicles of considerable size.

The most common and attractive sorts are hybrids. Hardiest is glossy abelia (*A. grandiflora*); its parents are two Chinese species, *A. chinensis* and *A. uniflora*. This familiar and useful shrub is hardy in the vicinity of New York City and survives

outdoors in sheltered locations as far north as Boston, Massachusetts. Handsome and free-blooming, it attains a height of 5 feet and in mild climates is evergreen or semi-evergreen. Where cold winters are the rule it is deciduous. Not its least attractive feature is its beautiful glossy foliage. The leaves are ovate, 1 inch to 2 inches long or slightly longer and shallowly-toothed. They are dark green with paler undersides and are almost hairless except near the bases of the midribs beneath. The faintly fragrant flowers are in clusters of two to four or more rarely are solitary, in the leaf axils and at the ends of short shoots. They are white blushed with pink, and on the same plant these flowers have from two to five conspicuous purplish-bronze sepals and bell-shaped corollas ¾ inch long, with spreading lobes. The insides of their throats are hairy. This shapely and graceful shrub blooms from midsummer to fall. Dwarf varieties, up to 3 feet tall are offered as *A. g. prostrata* and *A. g.* 'Sherwood'. The hybrid *A.* 'Edward Goucher' raised by Edward Goucher of the United States Department of Agriculture, has as parents *A. grandiflora* and *A. schumannii*. Because *A. grandiflora* is itself a hybrid, *A.* 'Edward

Abelia grandiflora

Goucher' has ancestry involving three species. In habit it is intermediate between its parents, but its flowers more closely resemble those of *A. grandiflora*. They are borne in late summer and fall. This semi-evergreen, slightly less hardy than *A. grandiflora*, survives at least as far north as New York City.

Hardy species, kinds not of hybrid origin, are *A. englerana* and *A. graebnerana*, both deciduous, early summer bloomers, and Chinese. The former is 3 to 6 feet tall and hardy as far north as Boston, Massachusetts. It has slender spreading branches and shoots slightly hairy when young. Lanceolate-elliptic to elliptic-ovate, the pointed, slightly-toothed, shiny leaves are ¾ inch to 1½ inches long and somewhat hairy on the veins below and along the margins. Borne in clusters at the ends of short shoots, from the previous year's branches, the rose-pink to purplish-pink blooms are slightly over ½ inch long and have two sepals. The corolla is tubular with a swollen base and an expanded, bell-shaped upper part. Like the former, *A. graebnerana* has flowers with just two sepals. It is 4 to 10 feet tall and has pointed, few-toothed, oblong-ovate leaves 1½ to 2 inches long. The upper sides of the leaves sometimes have scattered hairs. Less free flowering and somewhat less hardy than *A. englerana*, it has flowers at the ends of short shoots along shoots of the previous year's growth. They are 1 inch long, bell-shaped, and pink with yellow throats. This species is hardy about as far north as Philadelphia, Pennsylvania.

Tender species, kinds other than hybrids, not generally hardy north of Virginia, include some Chinese sorts and, in cultivation, one species from Mexico and one species from the Himalayas. Among the Chinese species is *A. schumannii*, a parent of *A.* 'Edward Goucher'. It is semi-evergreen or deciduous and has 1-inch-long, slightly-toothed, ovate leaves, hairy above when young, hairy below on the midribs, and densely-hairy along the margins. Its slender, purplish stems, hairy when young, arch gracefully and form a 5- to 6-foot tall bush. Rose-pink and 1 inch long or somewhat longer, the flowers are hairy on their outsides, and solitary in the leaf axils of the short current season's shoots that develop from the stems of the previous year's growth. They have two sepals and funnel-shaped corollas with spreading lobes. They appear throughout summer and fall. The stalks (filaments) of the stamens are hairy.

Other tender Chinese abelias include *A. chinensis*, a spreading, deciduous shrub, 3 to 6 feet in height. It has minute, red-downy young shoots and toothed, ovate leaves ¾ inch to 1½ inches long with scattered hairs above and on the midribs beneath. Its ½-inch-long, fragrant, white blooms, hairy inside their corolla tubes, have protruding stamens and five pinkish sepals about ¼ inch long. They are terminal and axillary in dense clusters at the ends of the stems. Parent of the popular *A. grandiflora*, and the one from which its tendency to evergreenness derives, *A. uniflora* is a native of China. Up to 6 feet tall

Abelia chinensis

Abelia chinensis

and of arching spreading habit, it has long-pointed, ovate leaves, slightly toothed and 1 inch to 2 inches long. They are glossy and hairless above, paler and hairy on their midribs beneath. The white-tinged-pink, bell-shaped flowers, about 1 inch long, produced in early summer, are solitary or in twos or threes; they come from the axils of upper leaves, and have orange throats. About 1 inch long and up to 1 inch across the face of the bloom, they are broadly tubular. The sepals vary from two to four, the smaller number being more usual. It is probably not hardy north of Virginia.

The only Himalayan abelia, *A. triflora* does not live up to its English reputation of being "the hardiest of the Abelias" in the United States. In eastern North America it cannot be considered hardy north of Virginia. Upright in habit, it attains a height of 12 feet. It has reflexed bristly hairs on its young shoots, and deciduous, lanceolate to ovate-lanceolate leaves, the lower ones usually with a few coarse teeth. All the leaves are somewhat hairy on both surfaces and at their margins. They are 1½ to 3 inches long by ⅓ to 1 inch wide. The fragrant, erect blooms develop in early summer in 2-inch-wide clusters at the ends of short shoots. They are blush-pink and have slender, cylindrical corolla tubes about ⅝ inch long that expand into a flat, five-lobed face ½ inch in diameter. There are five, persistent, reddish, very narrow-linear sepals feathered with long, silky hairs. The sepals are a little over to a little under ½ inch long. This is a very beautiful shrub.

The Mexican *A. floribunda*, a handsome evergreen, is tenderer than the abelias just discussed. It blooms in early summer. Up to 10 feet in height, but often lower, it has reddish, downy young shoots. Its glossy, rich green, broadly-pointed-ovate leaves are ¾ inch to 1½ inches long, shallowly-toothed, and hairy along their margins and

Abelia floribunda

to some extent on the midribs beneath. The slender funnel-shaped flowers are solitary from leaf axils near the ends of short twigs. They are pendulous and 1½ to 2 inches long, and may occur in groups of two or three. They have five sepals.

Garden and Landscape Uses. The cultivated abelias must be accounted among the most beautiful and useful flowering shrubs. Easy to grow, they have an undefinable quality of choiceness that characterizes really good plants, a quality that implies more than abundance of bloom or brilliance of color. Indeed on the latter count abelias do not rate particularly high. As for flower color, theirs is a muted contribution to the landscape. They may be used effectively wherever shrubs are appropriate, as single specimens, in groups with others of their kind or with other shrubs, in foundation plantings, and as informal screens and hedges. The evergreen and semievergreen abelias, such as *A. grandiflora*, associate very well with azaleas and bloom when the azaleas are without flowers. As a group they respond to well-drained soils enriched with compost, leaf mold, or peat moss. They succeed in sun or light shade. Not only the corollas of the flowers, but also their calyxes, which remain long after the corollas fall, are decorative, as also is the foliage.

Cultivation. Abelias are usually propagated by summer cuttings or by cuttings of ripened shoots in the fall. Both root readily. Nonhybrids are also easy to grow by sowing seeds in spring in sandy peaty soil. These germinate within a few weeks and the seedlings usually begin to bloom in their third year. Established plants require very little care. Pruning of those that bloom in early summer is done as soon as the flowers fade, of those that flower from midsummer to fall in early spring. Even if rather severe pruning is necessary because of winter killing of the shoots, as is likely with *A. grandiflora* at the northern limits of its hardiness range, new shoots that bloom their first season develop freely. Other attentions that encourage good growth are mulching with compost or peat moss and applying a complete garden fertilizer each spring. In general, these shrubs are remarkably free of pests and diseases. They adapt well to city conditions.

ABELIOPHYLLUM (Abelio-phýllum) — White-Forsythia. A native shrub of Korea, the only species of *Abeliophyllum* belongs in the olive family OLEACEAE, as does *Forsythia*, which it rather resembles. Like *Forsythia*, it blooms in late winter or very early spring before its leaves develop, but its flowers are white, not yellow, and its leaves resemble those of *Abelia*, a fact recognized in the choice of its generic name, since *Abeliophyllum* is a combination of a modification of *Abelia*, and the Greek *phyllon*, a leaf.

The multi-branched white-forsythia (*A. distichum*) is 2 to 3 feet tall and bears blooms profusely in finger-shaped clusters along the quadrangular shoots of the previous year's growth. The bisexual flowers are about ½ inch across and have four spreading petals joined at their bases to form a corolla tube, two stamens, and a compressed fruit winged all around. The pointed, short-stalked leaves are opposite, lobeless, and without teeth. They are ¾ inch to 2 inches long and have hairs on both sides. The white-forsythia is hardy in southern New England. It was not introduced to cultivation in America or Europe until 1924.

Abeliophyllum distichum

Garden Uses and Cultivation. The best use for this unusual and pleasing shrub is to plant it where it will be seen when it blooms. Because in cold climates winter excursions around the garden are usually at a minimum, good sense dictates that the white-forsythia can be with best advantage located near a path to a front door or close by an equally well winter-traversed way. For best effect it should be backed by evergreens. It needs full sun and grows well in any ordinary, well-drained garden soil. Little pruning is needed. Such as is, may be done immediately after the flowers fade. Propagation is easy by summer cuttings of leafy shoots, by hardwood cuttings taken at leaf fall, by layering, and by seeds sown in sandy peaty soil. Cut branches brought indoors in winter and stood in water force into flower easily and well.

ABELMOSCHUS (Abel-móschus). By some authorities this genus of the mallow family MALVACEAE, is named *Laguna*, by others it is included in *Hibiscus*. It consists of from six to twenty species, again depending upon the botanical authority followed, and inhabits southern and southeastern Asia, Indonesia, and islands of the Pacific to Australia. Its name is derived indirectly

from the Arabic name *abu'l misk*, father of musk, for *A. moschatus*.

The chief distinguishing characteristic of *Abelmoschus* is the large calyx that splits down one side and falls with the petals and stamens, to which it is joined at its base. The perennials, biennials, and annuals included are roughly hairy, and have stalked leaves with palmately (in handlike fashion) angled, lobed, or divided blades, with margins that are usually toothed. The flowers are in terminal racemes with a very small bractlike leaf at the base of each flower stalk, or are solitary from the leaf axils. The calyx is five toothed. The funnel-shaped corollas consist of five petals, folded spirally in bud. They are longer than the stamens. Generally the petals are yellow with bases that are purple or maroon-red, more rarely white or pinkish. The many stamens are joined in a column. The style has five short branches. The fruits are capsules.

Okra or gumbo (*A. esculentus* syn. *Hibiscus esculentus*) is the most familiar cultivated kind. An annual up to 7 feet tall, this well-known vegetable has stout, erect stems; large, lobed, or divided leaves; and purple- or red-centered, yellow or white flowers, with petals 1½ to 2 inches long. The blooms are succeeded by slender, five-angled pods up to 8 inches long. Only the young pods are used for food. Okra, a native of tropical Asia, is widely cultivated throughout the world in regions with long hot summers.

As ornamentals, two variable species are cultivated. The musk-mallow (*A. moschatus* syn. *Hibiscus abelmoschus*) is an annual or a biennial 6 to 10 feel tall or taller, with long-stalked leaves with blades up to 8 inches in length that are variously lobed or divided and toothed. The flowers, from the upper leaf axils, are yellow with dark purple centers, and have petals 2½ to 4 inches long. The fruits, up to 3½ inches in length, and round or slightly angled, contain musk-scented seeds used in perfumery. The perennial *A. manihot* (syn. *Hibiscus manihot*) differs in its seed pods being strongly five-angled and in the number of the bracts, usually not more than six, which form the involucre immediately below the flower; also the fruits tend to be shorter, up to 2¼ inches in length. Its stems are hollow. The long-stalked leaves have broad blades up to 1½ feet in diameter that are three- to seven-lobed or cleft, and toothed. Yellow or whitish, with small purple-red centers, the flowers are in the leaf axils and terminal racemes. They are 1¾ to 3 inches or more long.

Garden and Landscape Uses and Cultivation. The ornamental species discussed are used for variety in mixed flower beds and borders, to fill gaps at the fronts of shrubberies, and to plant in naturalistic fashion in informal areas. They grow without difficulty in ordinary soil in full sun,

but are not winter hardy in the north. Both kinds, however, flower the first year from seeds sown in spring and are often treated as annuals. Seeds may be sown where the plants are to remain and the seedlings thinned to 1½ to 2 feet apart, or plants can be started early indoors and set in the garden after all danger of frost has gone. For the cultivation of okra see Okra or Gumbo.

ABIES (A-bies)—Fir. This very important group of conifers contains many highly ornamental firs as well as many of great commercial significance as suppliers of lumber and other products. Belonging to the pine family PINACEAE, the genus *Abies* has for its name its ancient Latin one. It contains fifty species and is widely distributed in temperate parts of the northern hemisphere, occurring from sea level up to the limits at which trees grow in the higher latitudes, and in mountains further south. Its southernmost limits are just inside the Tropic of Cancer in Guatemala in the New World, and in North Africa in the Old.

Firs resemble spruces (*Picea*), and the two are often confused. They are pyramidal evergreens with the formal aspect of the conventional Christmas tree. But firs and spruces are easily told apart. The seed-bearing cones of the fir are lateral on the branchlets and always upright, those of the spruce are usually at the ends of branchlets and always pendent. As soon as their seeds ripen, fir cones break up and fall to pieces. Spruce cones remain intact after shedding their seeds and eventually drop whole from the tree. Another simple difference, observable at all seasons, is the manner in which the leaves are seated on the shoots. Those of spruces are on little cushions, or pegs, that remain attached to the shoots when the leaves fall, or if green leaves are pulled off, they come off with the leaves, with small shred of bark attached. It is these basal pegs that give the rough, grater-like character to spruce shoots that have shed their foliage. Fir leaves are seated not on pegs but directly on the branchlets. When they fall or are pulled off they break away cleanly leaving flat round marks on smooth shoots. Upon drying, the leaves of spruces fall from the branches, those of firs remain attached for a long time. Even from a distance, it is usually possible to distinguish firs from spruces. The branches of firs are usually strictly horizontal; or on young trees, they are angled slightly upward. Those of spruces generally angle downward.

Firs are among the stateliest coniferous trees. They have solitary, tapered trunks and branches in more or less distinct whorls (tiers). On young trees, the bark is smooth and thin, on old specimens often thick and furrowed. On lateral branches and branchlets the leaves are linear to linear-lanceolate and most commonly are ranked in two spreading rows, but sometimes they point toward the shoot tips and overlap. They are usualy flat with a longitudinal central groove on their upper side, in a few species they are quadrangular. The undersides commonly are marked with two longitudinal white lines. The leaves of leading shoots are never two-ranked, but spread in all directions. When bruised, the foliage of firs gives off an aromatic, often turpentine-like odor. The flowers, unrecognizable as such except under the hand lens or the microscope of a botanist, are in cones. Male and female cones grow on the same tree. The former are catkin-like and develop from the undersides of the branchlets. The latter are egg-shaped to cylindrical-ovoid, have many woody scales, and contain the seeds.

Fir lumber is not hard, strong, or very durable, but that of many species is exploited for a variety of purposes when those qualities are not important, for pulp, wood wool, lightly constructed structures, interior trim and, because their wood is inodorous, packing boxes for butter, lard, and other foods. Among the species used for such purposes are the red fir, noble fir, alpine fir, cascade fir, and balsam fir in America, the silver fir and Nordmann fir in Europe and nearby Asia, and in the Orient the momi fir, Saghalin fir, and Siberian fir. The wood of the silver fir is much used as sounding boards for musical instruments, and Strasbourg turpentine, used in artists' paints and varnishes is obtained from this species. The balsam fir supplies the resin called Canada balsam and in eastern North America is a favorite and most satisfactory Christmas tree. Balsam pillows are made from its fragrant leaves. As Christmas trees, firs are much superior to spruces. A cut fir, installed even in a superheated apartment as a holiday decoration will not cover all beneath it with a gentle rain of green needles after the first few days, as all too often happens with spruces.

The three best native American firs for gardens are the white fir, red fir, and noble fir. Enthusiastic gardeners sometimes try other kinds. They find it difficult to resist the temptation to dig from their mountain homes such beautiful plants when small and transfer them to lowland gardens, where in most cases they promptly die or, even worse, linger as pathetic caricatures of their kind. The fact must be faced that many firs prosper only in regions of long cold winters and cool summers, in unpolluted, constantly humid air. The balsam fir (A. balsamea), the Southern balsam fir (A. fraseri), and the alpine fir (A. lasiocarpa) are best enjoyed in their native wilds. Attempts to tame them, unless conditions that closely duplicate those to which they are accustomed can be provided, are doomed to failure.

The white fir, or Colorado fir (A. concolor), is indigenous from Colorado to

Abies concolor

New Mexico. Exceptionally, it attains 250 feet in height, but more usually does not exceed 150 feet. Its trunk is sometimes 6 feet in diameter. The white fir has short branches and resinous buds, and forms a narrow, rather stiff, well-foliaged spire. Its young shoots are hairless. Its flat leaves, 1¾ to 3¼ inches in length, are longer than those of most firs and have faint glaucous lines on both surfaces. When young they are pale blue-green, but they gradually change to dull green. Their upper surfaces are not grooved, but slightly convex. The leaves form two rows angling upward and outward from the shoots, or sometimes stand almost vertically. The seed cones are 3 to 5 inches long and about 1¼ inches in diameter. When young, they are purple or greenish; at maturity, they are brown.

The red fir (A. magnifica) differs from the white fir in having mostly definitely four-sided leaves, keeled (with a longitudinal ridge) and with faint whitish lines on their upper sides and two pale bands beneath. Its cylindrical cones, 6 to 9 inches long and 3 to 5 inches broad, are tapered slightly at their apexes, and in summer are violet-purple. They turn brown at maturity. The red fir is conspicuously slender with rusty-hairy young shoots and resinous buds. The leaves on the upper sides of the middle parts of the shoots curve upward from bases pressed tightly against the shoots. It shares these characteristics only with the noble fir, from which it is distinguished by its quadrangular leaves marked on their upper sides with a keel instead of a groove. The red fir, a native of the mountains from California to Oregon, thrives better in the Northeastern and North Central states than many West Coast trees, but is less hardy than the white fir and noble fir. It succeeds in sheltered locations in southern New England. As a native, it attains a maximum height of 200 feet or more and may have a trunk diameter of 10 feet. Variety A. m. shastensis is

distinct in having reflexed bracts that protrude beyond the scales of the cones. The cones of A. m. xanthocarpa, a high alpine variety, are golden-yellow during their growing period. Other varieties are A. m. argentea with bluish-white foliage; A. m. glauca, with deep glaucous bluish-green leaves; and the low-growing A. m. prostrata.

The noble fir A. procera (syn. A. nobilis) is as tall or taller than, and is generally similar to the red fir, but it has flatter leaves, 1¼ inches or less long, grooved above, and set more densely and irregularly along the shoots. The leaves are sometimes slightly notched at their tips. They have two grayish bands on the lower surface, fine grayish lines above. Those on the upper sides and toward the centers of the shoots are curved like those of the red fir. The young shoots are clothed in rusty red hairs. The buds are resinous. The cones are 4½ to 10 inches long, cylindrical, green at first, becoming purplish-brown at maturity.

Firs native to Europe, among the best for landscape planting, are the Greek fir (A. cephalonica) and the Spanish fir (A. pinsapo. Their common names indicate the lands to which they are indigenous. The Greek fir is hardy in southern New England, the Spanish fir, not reliably so in climates harsher than that of Long Island, New York. These handsome, stiffly-pyramidal trees, up to 100 feet tall, have resinous buds. Their foliage is arranged in a manner unusual among firs; their flattened, usually curved leaves radiating at right angles around the shoots. The leaves of the Greek fir narrow gradually into sharp, stiff points and are about 1 inch long; those of the Spanish fir, up to ¾ inch long, thick and rigid, are bluntish or end in short points. The cones of the Greek fir are cylindrical, about 6 inches long by 1½ inches wide and have protruding, yellow-

Abies cephalonica

brown reflexed bracts; those of the Spanish fir are a little shorter and a little broader, and their bracts are concealed by the cone scales. The Spanish fir is found wild only on limestone soils.

A desirable species from the Caucasus and Black Sea regions, the Nordmann fir (**A. nordmanniana**) is sometimes 225 feet tall as a native. It has nonresinous buds and lustrous young shoots with scattered hairs. The leaves on the lower parts of the branchlets spread in two rows at nearly right angles or point slightly forward.

Abies nordmanniana

Fruiting cones of *Abies nordmanniana*

Those above spread in various directions, and point toward the tips of the branchlets. They clothe the shoots densely. They are 1 inch to 1¼ inches long, notched at their tips, glossy green, grooved down the centers on the top sides, and have two whitish bands underneath. The cones, 6 inches long by 2 inches wide, are cylindrical and dark reddish-brown. They have slightly protruding, reflexed bracts. It is similar to the cascade fir (*A. amabilis*) of western North America, but its winter buds are not resinous and its foliage does not smell of orange peel when bruised. Varieties of the Nordmann fir are *A. n. au-*

rea, with leaves, especially young ones, of golden-brown, and *A. n. tortifolia*, which has sickle-shaped, twisted leaves.

Eastern Asian firs are by far the most numerous as to species. Not all firs from eastern Asia are in cultivation and not all are likely to give satisfaction as garden plants. Five, three from Japan and two from Korea, are among the best firs for American gardens. One of the most decorative is **A. veitchii**. In its native Japan, this slender, stiffly-pyramidal tree is about 80 feet tall. It has resinous buds, and branchlets covered with short hairs. The crowded leaves are arranged similarly to those of the Nordmann fir, but are softer, and the upper ones are not pressed against the shoots as tightly as those of *A. nordmanniana*. They are notched at their apexes, about 1 inch long, and have two chalk-white bands on their undersides. They point forward. Those on the lower parts of the shoots are in two rows. The cones, bluish-purple when young, but brown at maturity, are about 3 inches long. They have slightly protruding, reflexed bracts.

Abies veitchii

Varieties are *A. v. nikkoensis*, distinguished by its cones being not more than 2 inches long, and *A. v. olivacea*, the cones of which are green when young and grayish-brown later. This fir and its varieties are hardy in southern Canada.

Another beautiful, not quite as hardy Japanese fir is the Nikko fir (**A. homolepis**). It grows up to 100 feet tall and survives in most of New England and in Nova Scotia. Its hairless shoots are deeply grooved, its buds resinous. The leaves spread at right angles from the twigs; those from the lower sides spread more or less horizontally, whereas the leaves along the center of the shoot rise upward and outward to form a V-shaped depression between their rows. They are lustrous, dark green,

Abies homolepis

grooved down their centers, marked beneath with two prominent white bands, and about 1 inch long. The cylindrical cones, slightly narrowed above and below, are 4½ inches long by 1½ inches broad. When young they are purple. Varieties are *A. h. scottiae*, a dwarf form, *A. h. tomomi*, which branches sparingly and has shorter leaves than the typical species, and *A. h. umbellata*, the young cones of which are green. The Momi fir (**A. firma**) of southern Japan grows up to 150 feet tall. Broadly pyramidal, it has massive, spreading branches, and slightly resinous buds. Its barely-grooved branchlets are always hairy in the grooves when the trees are young, but only occasionally on older specimens.

Abies firma (foliage)

The leaves are rigid and spread to form a marked V-shaped depression between their rows on the upper sides of the shoots. They are up to 1½ inches long, bright lustrous green above, and have two rather indistinct grayish bands on their undersides. Those of young trees terminate in a pair of hard, sharp points. On older trees, the leaf ends are blunt and slightly notched. The cones, 4 to 5 inches long and 1½ to 1¾ inches wide, are pale green when young. The bracts protrude from between the cone scales, but are not reflexed. This is the least hardy of the Japanese firs discussed above. In exceptionally severe winters it suffers some injury in the vicinity of New York City.

Korean firs that have proven satisfactory in cultivation, *A. koreana* and *A. holophylla*, the former known as the Korean fir the latter the needle fir, are both hardy in southern New England. Both have slightly resinous buds. The Korean fir is up to 60 feet in height, has shoots that are sparingly-hairy at first, but naked later, and leaves that spread outward and upward from the shoots, but not in definite rows. They are broadest toward their notched or pointed tips, glossy dark green, with two intensely white bands beneath, about ¾ inch in length, and are crowded along the branchlets. They spread upward and outward. The cones of this species are about 2½ inches long by about 1 inch wide and are flattened at their ends. They are violet-purple before they mature and have slightly exerted, reflexed bracts. The needle fir is closely related to the Nikko fir (*A. homolepis*) and has leaves with two grayish bands beneath arranged in the same fashion, but its branchlets are very slightly grooved and its cones are green when young. When mature the cones are 5 to 6 inches long with bracts that are concealed by the cone scales. In the wild, the needle fir attains a height of 100 to 150 feet.

Other sorts include these: *A. alba*, the silver fir of central and southern Europe, up to 150 feet tall, has hairy twigs, small nonresinous buds, and leaves in comblike rows, which are dark green above and white-striped beneath. Its cones, up to 5½ inches long, have exserted, reflexed bracts. *A. a. columnaris* is narrowly-columnar. *A. a. compacta* is dwarf and bushy with short leaves. *A. a. pendula* has drooping branches. *A. a. tortuosa*, dwarf and compact, has crowded branches. *A. amabilis*, the Cascade fir, native from British Columbia and Alberta to Oregon, is up to 250 feet tall, has pale or silvery-white bark, foliage that smells of orange when bruised, very resinous buds, gray-hairy, young shoots, leaves arranged like those of *A. nordmanniana*, up to 1¼ inches long and with squared or notched apexes, and cones 3½ to 6 inches long, which are purple before maturity. *A. balsamea*, the balsam fir, which is notoriously unamenable to cultivation outside its home territory, although its dwarf varieties are more accommodating, is indigenous from Labrador to Minnesota, Iowa, and West Virginia. It is up to 75 feet tall, has very resinous, reddish buds, short-hairy branchlets, and leaves in comblike rows or spreading upward with a V-shaped parting down the centers of the shoots. They are up to 1 inch long, slightly notched

at their tips, and are dark, lustrous green with a few grayish lines near the ends above and two gray bands beneath. The cones, violet-purple when young, are up to 4 inches long by 1¾ inches wide. *A. b. hudsonia* is a dwarf, spreading variety with dark green, broader and shorter leaves. *A. b. nana* has dark green leaves less than ¼ inch long. It forms a rounded bush. *A. b.*

Abies balsamea nana

phanerolepis has smaller cones with protruding bracts. *A. b. variegata* has foliage variegated with white. *A. bracteata* (syn. *A. venusta*), the bristlecone fir of California, adapted only for regions of mild winters, grows up to 150 feet tall, has hairless shoots, spindle-shaped, nonresinous buds, leaves up to 2 inches long that spread horizontally in two rows, and cones 3 to 4 inches long, with protruding bracts tipped with rigid spines. *A. chensiensis*, native of China, where it exceeds 200 feet in height, has slightly resinous buds, hairless branchlets, leaves up to 1½ inches long spreading or angling upward in two rows with a V-shaped space between, and cones 2 to 3 inches long and one-half as wide. *A. cilicica*, the Cilician fir, native to Syria and Asia Minor and plentiful in the Antitaurus Mountains along with the cedar of Lebanon, is very like *A. nordmanniana*, but has narrower, less crowded leaves and larger cones with concealed bracts. *A. delavayi* (syn. *A. fabri*), a variable Chinese species of wide natural distribution, is up to 130 feet tall and has more or less hairy shoots, densely-resinous buds, leaves up to 1¼ inches long, dark green above and with two white bands beneath, in two rows with a V-shaped space between, and dark blue or violet, barrel-shaped cones up to 4 inches long, with protruding often reflexed bracts. *A. d. faxoniana* (syn. *A. faxoniana*) has young shoots with red-brown shaggy hairs and leaves that spread almost horizontally. *A. d. forrestii* (syn. *A. forrestii*) has young shoots bright rusty-red that are

Abies delavayi forrestii (fruiting cones)

hairless or slightly hairy. *A. d. georgei* has red-brown, densely-hairy young shoots, and cones with especially long reflexed bracts. *A. fargesii* resembles *A. delavayi* and is perhaps only a variety of it. A native of China, it has hairless shoots, leaves that spread horizontally in two or more rows, and red-brown or purple cones with protruding, spreading bracts. *A. fraseri*, the Southern balsam fir, native to the Allegheny Mountains, is very like *A. balsamea*, but has shorter leaves conspicuously notched at their ends. *A. f. prostrata* is a low, spreading variety. *A. kawakamii*, of Taiwan, is very like Japanese *A. mariesii*, but has longer, narrower leaves and cones 2 to 3 inches long. *A. lasiocarpa*, the alpine or Rocky Mountain fir, indigenous from New Mexico to Alaska, is sometimes 150 feet tall; it has silver-gray or whitish bark, small resinous buds, shoots with short red hairs, crowded leaves that spread forward and upward, which are up to 1½ inches long and have whitish lines above and two broad pale bands beneath, and cylindrical, dark purple, downy cones, 2 to 4 inches long and about 1½ inches wide. *A. l. arizonica*, the cork fir, has thick corky bark and cones smaller than those of its typical species. *A. l. beissneri* is a dwarf variety with distorted branches and twisted leaves. *A. l. compacta* is dense and dwarf. *A. mariesii*, a Japanese, usually is not very satisfactory in cultivation, at least in eastern North America. It differs from *A. veitchii* chiefly in its shoots being more densely-hairy, and its cones larger. *A. nephrolepis*, of China, Korea, and Siberia, is very like *A. sibirica*, but has more hairy shoots, leaves up to 1 inch long, and smaller cones. *A. numidica*, the Algerian fir, up to 100 feet tall, has hairless shoots, nonresinous or very slightly resinous buds, and leaves up to ¾ inch long, with whitish lines on their upper surfaces near the tips, and two white bands on the undersides, those lowest on the shoots spreading horizontally, the others directed upward or on vigorous branchlets backward. The cones are cylindrical, 5 to 7 inches long, about

1½ inches wide, with their scales concealing the bracts. *A. pindrow*, native to the Himalayas, 200 feet tall and narrowly-pyramidal, has large resinous buds, smooth hairless shoots, and crowded leaves up to 2½ inches long, which end in two sharp points. The lower leaves on the shoots spreading horizontally or downward, the others irregularly upward and forward, to cover the shoots, and cones up to 7 inches long and 2½ inches wide, violet-purple when young, with short bracts completely hidden by the cone scales. *A. p. brevifolia* has reddish-brown rather than gray shoots and shorter, rigid leaves. *A. p. intermedia* may be a hybrid between *A. pindrow* and *A. spectabilis*, its shoots and buds are like the former, its leaf arrangement is like the latter. *A. recurvata* is from western China where it grows 120 feet tall, has lustrous, hairless shoots and very resinous buds, and its sharp-pointed leaves, up to 1½ inches long, are recurved on the upper rows, on the lower ones in comblike ranks. The spreading leaves are lustrous green or bluish-green above, paler or glaucous beneath; the cones, 2 to 4 inches long and violet-purple when young, occur in clusters; their bracts are concealed by the scales. *A. sachalinensis*, the Saghalin fir, a native of northern Japan, the Kurile Islands, and Saghalin Island, attains a height of 120 feet, has whitish bark, small resinous buds, and young shoots furrowed, with hairs in the depressions. Its leaves resemble those of *A. veitchii*, but are narrower, 1¾ inches long, notched at their tips, with two indistinct pale bands beneath, each of seven to eight lines of stomata, and cones about 3½ inches long by 1½ inches wide, with very large reflexed bracts. *A. s. mayriana* has leaves less than 1 inch long. *A. s. nemorensis* has cones 2½ inches long with bracts hidden by the scales. *A. sibirica*, up to 100 feet in height, is similar to the Saghalin fir, but has minutely-downy shoots without furrows and leaves 1½ inches long with four to five lines of stomata in each pale band on their undersides. *A. spectabilis*, the Himalayan fir, grows 150 to 200 feet tall, is broadly pyramidal, has resinous buds and furrowed shoots, with pubescence in the depressions. The leaves, arranged like those of *A. homolepis*, are up to 2½ inches long and notched at their tips, with two white bands beneath. The cones are like those of *A. pindrow*, but larger. Hardy only in mild climates. *A. s. brevifolia* has leaves 1¼ inches long. *A. squamata*, the flaky fir, with bark that peels in thin, papery flakes, native of western China at altitudes up to 14,000 feet, which is higher than any other fir grows. It is 120 feet tall, has very resinous buds, hairy-red-brown shoots, crowded, sharp-pointed, erect and curved leaves, and violet cones 2 inches long or a little longer, with slightly exserted bracts. *A. sutchuenensis* resembles *A. fargesii*, but

has shorter, more erect leaves with yellowish stalks, and its cone bracts are concealed by the scales.

Garden and Landscape Uses. When in perfect condition, no conifers are more beautiful or more imposing than firs, but alas, they are not for every garden. For best development they need pure air, cool, humid summers, and well-drained, but not dry, fertile soil. In North America most kinds can be grown successfully in the Pacific Northwest. Those best adapted for less humid areas in the Northeastern and North Central states are the white fir, Nikko fir, and the Nordmann fir.

As ornamentals firs are generally less tolerant of adverse environments than are many spruces (*Picea*). They are usually most decorative when young. As they approach the half-century mark, they often become thin-topped and lose lower limbs. This detracts from their beauty. Firs do not thrive where exposed to strong winds. This may seem strange when one considers their native habitats, but in the northlands and mountains, where they are at home, they stand closely together and shelter each other, or as solitary specimens, they are likely to develop asymmetrical tops usually unacceptable in ornamentals. When used for landscaping, they should be sheltered, perhaps by a planting of pines or other wind-tolerant conifers or by a nearby slope or hill. Firs should not be planted near the sunny sides of buildings because reflected heat can harm them. In suitably sheltered places they can be used with good effects singly, in groups, and as avenue trees. They are appropriate backgrounds for rock gardens.

Cultivation. If the location is suitable the care of firs is not demanding, but if the site is not appropriate, few cultural practices are likely to help. Firs can be transplanted without undue difficulty even when they are comparatively big. A permanent mulch of organic material such as peat moss, compost, pine needles, or wood chips is of benefit. In dry weather, periodic deep soakings are helpful. Whenever possible firs should be raised from seeds. When this is not practicable, as for instance with horticultural varieties, they may be veneer grafted onto seedling understocks in a greenhouse in winter or very early spring, or in some cases, they may be increased by cuttings planted under mist or in a propagating bench in a very humid greenhouse in summer. Grafting scions and cuttings must be made from leading shoots. If they are made from lateral branches, they grow asymmetrically usually without ever developing a leading shoot. Sow seeds in sandy peaty soil in a protected bed outdoors or in a cold frame, or in pots or flats in a cool greenhouse. Under favorable conditions, the seeds germinate in a few weeks, but often the percentage of germination is not high, and because fir

seeds usually do not remain viable more than a year or two it is important to obtain them as fresh as possible. Since young seedlings are sensitive to strong sun, they should be lightly shaded.

Diseases and Pests. Firs are subject to many diseases but rarely are these serious in ornamental plantings. Needle and twig blight and leaf-cast sometimes affect foliage and are controlled with copper fungicides, cankers occasionally develop on trunks and branches, rusts infect forest trees more often than those planted for ornament. The chief insect pests are spruce spider mites, caterpillars, scale insects, bagworms, and aphids.

ABROMA (Ab-ròma). A close relative of the chocolate tree, *Abroma* is included with it in *Theobroma* by some botanists. It belongs in the sterculia family STERCULIACEAE. Those who recognize *Abroma* as a separate genus accept two or three species, which are natives of Madagascar, tropical Asia, and Australia. The name comes from the Greek *a*, not, and *broma*, food. It alludes to its members, which unlike the chocolate tree, do not supply food, but instead are reported to be mildly poisonous.

Abromas are evergreen trees or shrubs with hairy, lobeless or palmately (in hand-fashion) lobed leaves. They have dull purple blooms with a five-cleft calyx and a corolla with five hooded petals that narrow below to shafts or claws, a stamen tube with two or three anthers, five elongated petal-like staminodia (aborted stamens), and one style.

Approximately 10 feet tall, *A. fastuosum* has soft-hairy foliage. Its lower leaves are three- to five-lobed, its upper ones ovate and lobeless and its flowers are deep chocolate-purple. It is indigenous to tropical Asia and Australia.

Garden and Landscape Uses and Cultivation. Abromas are easily grown outdoors in the humid tropics and in tropical greenhouses. They have attractive foliage

Abroma fastuosum

and interesting blooms. They prosper in any reasonably fertile soil and may be propagated by seeds and by cuttings of firm, but not hard shoots.

ABROMEITIELLA (Abrom-eitiélla). The South American genus *Abromeitiella* consists of five species of the pineapple family BROMELIACEAE, that commonly perch on rocks or grow in the ground; they do not, as do most bromeliads, perch on trees. Its name commemorates Johannes Abromeit, a German professor of botany of the late nineteenth and early twentieth centuries.

Abromeitiellas form low cushions of many to very numerous rosettes of small, stiff, fleshy leaves. Their flowers, which are small and of insignificant decorative appeal, have three each sepals and petals, six stamens, and a style with a three-lobed stigma. The fruits are capsules.

Rare in cultivation, but occasionally included in choice collections of succulent plants, *A. brevifolia* and *A. chlorantha* are natives of Argentina; *A. chlorantha* also occurs in Bolivia. The former has 1-inch-long, spineless, triangular leaves and greenish flowers. The leaves of the latter are about the same size, but differ in being tipped with a sharp spine. Its flowers are greenish.

Abromeitiella brevifolia

Abromeitiella chlorantha

Garden Uses and Cultivation. These are easy-to-grow collectors' items. In warm, semidesert regions, such as parts of southern California, they are appropriate for rock gardens. As greenhouse plants, they grow satisfactorily in pans (shallow pots) of well-drained soil of a type appropriate for cactuses and other succulents. They need sun, low humidity, and a night temperature in winter of 50 to 55°F with higher temperatures required by day and in other seasons. The soil should be kept moist throughout the year but allowed to nearly dry out before watering. Propagation is easy by division or seeds.

ABRONIA (Ab-rònia)—Sand-Verbena. The genus *Abronia* of the four o'clock family NYCTAGINACEAE consists of about twenty-five, usually low, trailing annuals and perennials commonly grown as annuals. It is a native of western North America and supplies a few species that are cultivated in gardens, the most popular being the pink sand-verbena. The name comes from the Greek *abros*, graceful.

Abronias are mostly glandular-pubescent. They have opposite, stalked, thickish leaves, the individuals of each pair being a different size. The bisexual flowers are in verbena-like, stalked clusters of few to many that are terminal or arise from the leaf axils and are backed with an involucre or collar of five to eight, thin, dry bracts. They are fragrant and white, pink, red, or yellow. They have no true petals. The petal-like parts of the flower, four to five in number, joined at their bases to form a slender tube, and notched at their ends, are sepals. Each flower has four or five stamens of unequal length. The leathery, more or less top-shaped fruits are winged or ribbed.

The pink sand-verbena (**A. umbellata**) is highly variable and is divided by botanists into several intergrading subspecies or varieties based chiefly on details of the wings of the fruits. It is a more or less sticky-pubescent perennial, with slender, prostrate stems up to 3 feet long and little or freely branched. Its ovate to lanceolate-oblong, slender-stalked leaves are 1 inch to 3 inches long and often irregular in outline. The flowers are ten to fifteen together in heads with stalks 2 to 6 inches long; they are rose-pink or rarely white. The fruits have four or five wings. The pink sand-verbena is a native of the coast of California. The plant previously known as *A. alba* is *A. umbellata alba*. It has white to pink flowers.

The yellow sand-verbena (**A. latifolia**), native of seashores from California to British Columbia, is a perennial with thick, fleshy roots, much-branched prostrate stems 1 foot to 3 feet long, and succulent, stout-stalked, sticky, round to ovate leaves ½ inch to 2 inches in length and in width. Its flowers are yellow, its fruits five-winged.

Distinguished by its dark red to red-purple flowers, *A. maritima* occurs along the coast of southern California. A perennial, it has fleshy roots, much-branched, prostrate stems 1 foot to 3 feet in length, and ovate to ovate-oblong thick, sticky leaves. Its fruits are mostly five-winged.

A desert annual, *A. villosa* is indigenous from California and Nevada, to Colorado, Arizona, and Baja California. Its prostrate or ascending stems are up to 1½ feet long, hairy, and usually sticky. The leaves, ovate to nearly round and sparingly glandular, have stalks that, like those of the flower clusters, are sticky. The blooms are purplish-rose-pink. The fruits have three to four wings. The long hairs on the stems and flowers distinguish this species from *A. umbellata*. Another annual denizen of deserts from California to Nevada is *A. pogonantha*. It has prostrate or ascending, much-branched sticky, hairy stems up to 1½ feet long and oblong-ovate to nearly round leaves. Its flowers are white to rose-pink. Its fruits have two, or sometimes three, wings.

Abronia villosa

Garden Uses. Sand-verbenas are attractive plants for flower beds, rock gardens and hanging baskets. Except in very mild climates they are invariably treated as annuals and with little trouble make colorful displays of bloom throughout the summer. Many are pleasantly scented, their fragrance becoming more intense in the evening. Their flowers are quite charming when cut and last well in water. These plants grow in any ordinary porous garden soil, with a preference for soils that are sandy. They need full sun.

Cultivation. Seeds may be sown in spring where the plants are to remain or in a greenhouse in a temperature of 60 to 65°F earlier. In mild climates, they may be sown outdoors in fall for flowering the following summer. Germination is hastened if the husks surrounding the seeds are removed or the seeds are soaked in water for twenty-four hours before sowing. Seedlings from outdoor sowings are thinned to about 9 inches apart, those from indoor sowings are transplanted 2 inches apart in flats of porous soil and are grown in a sunny greenhouse in a night temperature of 50 to 55°F and day temperatures five to ten degrees higher until planting out time, after all danger of frost has passed. Indoor seeding is done about ten weeks before the plants are to be transferred to the garden, where they are set 9 inches to 1 foot apart. Summer care is minimal. The taller kinds may require staking. Brushwood inserted among them gives satisfactory support. The perennial sand-verbenas are also easily increased by cuttings, but because seeds give satisfactory results this means of propagation is not often used.

ABROPHYLLUM (Abro-phýllum). One or two species of tender shrubs of eastern Australia constitute *Abrophyllum* of the saxifrage famiy SAXIFRAGACEAE, or according to botanists who segregate escallonias and their kin, to the escallonia family ESCALLONIACEAE. The generic name is from the Greek *abros*, delicate, and *phyllon*, a leaf, and refers to the foliage.

A tall, handsome shrub with alternate, pointed, slightly-toothed, elliptic to ovate-lanceolate leaves up to 9 inches long, *A. ornans* has small, yellow flowers in branching clusters at the ends of the shoots or from the axils of the upper leaves. Their calyxes are five-lobed, and there are five each petals and stamens. The fruits are egg-shaped berries.

Garden Uses and Cultivation. Planted to some extent as an ornamental in southern California and climatically similar regions, this species succeeds in ordinary, not over-rich, well-drained soil. It is propagated by cuttings and seeds.

ABRUS (Ab-rus)—Rosary-Pea or Crab's Eye. A dozen New and Old World species of the pea family LEGUMINOSAE belong here. The name is from the Greek *abros*, delicate, and alludes to the appearance of the foliage. One species, the rosary-pea or crab's eye, is fairly commonly cultivated outdoors in warm regions, sometimes in greenhouses.

The genus *Abrus* has pinnate leaves of numerous small leaflets, small pealike flowers in racemes from the leaf axils, and short seed pods. The rosary-pea (*A. precatorius*) attains a height of 10 feet or more and is slightly hairy. Its leaves have five to fifteen pairs of leaflets each up to ½ inch long. The tiny flowers, red, purple, or rarely white, in racemes 1 to 3 inches long, are succeeded by flat, broad, hairy pods up to 1½ inches long. These contain very beautiful ovoid seeds ¼ inch more or less long, that are brilliant glossy scarlet over most of their surface, but for about one-third of their length from one end, are shining jet black. The seeds are displayed and remain attached to the pods for a long

Abrus precatorius

time, dropping one by one. Beautiful the seeds may be, but dangerous too. They contain abrin, one of the most toxic of poisons, in such amounts that a single seed well chewed and swallowed is sufficient to kill a person. Broken seeds are especially toxic in contact with wounds.

These deadly seeds are used freely in the tropics for making rosaries, necklaces, purses, rattles, greeting cards, etc. Handcraft articles incorporating them and commonly sold to tourists are potentially dangerous, especially in the hands of children. Seeds with their coats broken are more surely poisonous than unbroken ones, but all can be deadly, not only to human beings, but to animals too. Interestingly, the roots of this vine are used in place of licorice, but are inferior to it, and in India the leaves are used for making a tea.

Garden Uses and Cultivation. Because of the poisonous character of the seeds, which are attractive to children, careful consideration of the possible risks involved should be given before planting this vine. It grows without difficulty in ordinary soil in sunny locations in tropical climates and is naturalized in southern Florida. In greenhouses, it thrives in well-drained soil kept fairly moist in a minimum temperature of 60°F and a highly humid atmosphere. It requires full sun, but a little light shade in summer is desirable. This vine is easily raised from seeds and can be propagated by cuttings taken in spring and inserted in a propagating bed in a warm greenhouse.

ABSINTHIUM or Common wormwood is *Artemisia absinthium*.

ABUTILON (A-bù-til-on) — Flowering-Maple. This genus is not related to true maples (*Acer*), but is a botanical cousin of hibiscuses, mallows, hollyhocks, cotton, and okra. A simple study of the flowers reveals the general similarity of structure

and form that prompts botanists to include all these in the mallow family MALVACEAE.

Abutilons occur as natives in the tropics and subtropics of the Old World and the New. They number more than 100 species. Those commonly cultivated are South American species and their hybrids. The common name flowering-maple refers to the maple-like leaves of many abutilons. The botanical name is derived from the Arabic for a kind of mallow.

Flowering-maples are not flamboyant. Their flowers, of muted rather than brilliant hues, are often partly concealed by the foliage and do not appear in great numbers at any one time. These plants do, however, bloom for many weeks or months, chiefly from spring through fall, and afford a range of extraordinarily pleasing flower colors. A few varieties have beautifully variegated foliage. The flowers when cut, last well in water and are useful for arrangements and for corsages.

The genus *Abutilon* consists of shrubs and herbaceous plants with alternate, long-stalked, sometimes lobed leaves. The flowers are solitary, axillary, and pendulous. They have five-parted, sometimes highly colored calyxes and, typically, five obovate petals that form a bell-shaped or, in some kinds, a wheel-shaped, yellow, orange, pink, red, or white bloom, usually beautifully marked with a network of darker veins. The stamens are joined in a column around the branched style, with the anthers clustered at its apex. The fruits are wheel-shaped or star-shaped capsules. For the plant previously named *A. vitifolium* see Corynabutilon.

Chinese jute, a coarse, lustrous, grayish fiber, much like jute and used to a considerable extent in the Orient for making rugs, is a commercial product of the weedy-looking *A. theophrasti* (syn. *A. avicennae*). This, an annual herbaceous native of southeastern Asia, is naturalized in North America.

Abutilon theophrasti

Species of abutilons in cultivation can be grouped as those with markedly lobed leaves and those in which the foliage is slightly or not lobed. Both have toothed leaf edges. To the former group belongs *A. striatum*, a native of Guatemala, which is a tall shrub or a small tree. Its nearly hairless leaves are three- to seven-lobed with the central lobe at least twice as long as the palm of the leaf and narrowed at its base. The leaves, up to 6 inches long and nearly 6 inches wide, have stalks 1 inch to 5 inches long. The solitary, long-stalked blooms, 1¼ to 1¾ inches long, have orange petals veined with crimson that do not spread widely. The 1-inch-long calyxes have lanceolate, densely-downy lobes. Several presumed variations of this species are grown as *A. s. thompsonii*. Most have leaves mottled with yellow. In one variety, *A. s. t. flore-pleno*, the flowers are double; they have more than the usual five petals. In another, perhaps more correctly *A. s. spurium* than a variety of *A. s. thompsonii*, the foliage is pubescent.

Native to Brazil, Uruguay, and Argentina, *A. pictum* has sparsely-hairy leaves about 3 inches long, with usually only three, more rarely five, lobes; the lateral lobes are often small, and the middle lobe is not longer and usually shorter than the palm of the leaf and broadened toward its base. The yellow or orange, usually solitary flowers, on slender stalks up to 2½ inches long, are veined with crimson. They are about 1¼ inches long and have deeply-lobed, 1-inch-long, downy calyxes. This species is not infrequently misnamed *A. striatum*.

A showy species with lobeless leaves, *A. insigne* has 2-inch-wide, pendulous blooms with flaring petals of white very heavily overlain with a net of purple and red veins. The young stems are brown-hairy, the leaves are pointed and heart-shaped, 3 to 6 inches in length and pubescent on their undersides. It is native to Colombia.

Slender, pendulous branches are responsible for the distinctive drooping habits of *A. megapotamicum* (syn. *A. vexillarium*) and its variegated-leaved variety, *A. m. variegatum*. These are the most popular flowering-maples whose leaves are not strongly lobed, being narrowly-ovate to somewhat arrow-shaped, slender-pointed, and 2 to 4 inches long. Sometimes suspicions of a lobe appear on each coarsely-toothed margin. The attractive, pendulous flowers are solitary, axillary, and lemon-yellow with red calyxes. The rather globose and rigid, 1-inch-long calyx narrows at its mouth from where the corolla lobes (petals) spread like a ballet dancer's skirt, with the hemline about 1 inch in diameter. The stamens and pistil protrude. In *A. m. variegatum*, the foliage is blotched yellow. South America is the home of *A. megapotamicum*.

Abutilon megapotamicum variegatum

Hybrid flowering-maples, collectively referred to *A. hybridum*, are by far the most commonly grown. Their ancestry is not well known, but it undoubtedly involves several species and probably mutations. They have variously shaped, lobed or lobeless, toothed, hairy or hairless leaves, in some varieties variegated with yellow or white. Their broadly-bell-shaped or sometimes flatter flowers have conspicuous, usually pubescent, calyxes. To this group

Abutilon hybridum

belongs the popular *A. h. savitzii*, a compact grower with handsome, grayish-green, white-margined leaves, and sometimes a few all-white ones. Another beautiful variegated variety is the taller 'Souvenir de Bonn', with white-bordered leaves and salmon-colored flowers veined with crimson. Numerous other varieties of *A. hybridum* have been given horticultural names and are listed and described in the catalogs of dealers.

A hybrid of known ancestry quite distinct from those included in *A. hybridum* is **A. milleri**. Its parents are *A. megapotamicum*

Abutilon hybridum savitzii

Abutilon hybridum 'Souvenir de Bonn'

and *A. pictum*. The offspring has many characteristics of the first-named parent. Its shoots are slender, its leaves, sometimes slightly three-lobed, but not markedly so, are toothed. They are ovate-lanceolate, up to 6 inches long and about 3 inches wide. The yellow-veined-with-red blooms, solitary from the leaf axils, are 1½

Abutilon milleri

inches long. The column of stamens and style is exposed to view. There are several forms of this hybrid.

Garden and Landscape Uses. In climates with little or no frost, abutilons are satisfactory permanent outdoor plants. They are easy-to-grow, useful shrubs for beds and borders, and they bloom for extended periods. Occasional trimming, best done in late winter, helps keep them shapely and to size. Another popular use, especially for erect-growing kinds with variegated foliage, is as bedding plants; like geraniums, young plants are set out in late spring and are taken up before winter. They provide pleasing displays throughout the summer. For this purpose also, specimens trained in tree form, as standards to use the common horticultural term for plants so grown, are attractive and give more height than specimens grown in bush form; of course they need to be underplanted with lower plants of the same or different kinds. Abutilons with pendulous stems show to fine advantage in hanging baskets; the more erect kinds can also be so used.

As indoor plants, abutilons are fine for greenhouses and window gardens. For the latter use, the bushy hybrids are especially appropriate but the more vinelike and pendulous-stemmed kinds are also useful. In greenhouses and conservatories, all kinds of abutilons are easily cultivated and can be displayed to advantage in pots, tubs, hanging baskets, and ground beds. The vinelike *A. megapotamicum*, *A. milleri*, and other vigorous, long-stemmed kinds are especially lovely when trained to pillars or to wires stretched a few inches below the greenhouse roof.

Abutilon megapotamicum variegatum in a hanging pot

Cultivation. Where abutilons grow permanently outdoors, they make few demands on the time or skill of gardeners. About all that is needed is to prune them sometimes, usually in late winter or spring, at the beginning of a new season's growth, and in the case of lax-stemmed kinds, to keep their shoots tied to wires, stakes, or other supports. To increase vigor an occasional application of fertilizer is helpful, and in prolonged periods of dry weather, watering will be necessary. Pruning consists of cutting out thin, misplaced, and obviously over-crowded branches and shortening others as may be needed to shape the plant and keep it tidy.

Indoor cultivation of flowering-maples is not difficult. They thrive without undue care provided the place where they grow is not over-hot and they receive good light. Full sun is desirable, but they stand light shade during the height of summer. Fairly young specimens are more desirable than old ones, which tend to develop hard stems and branches, unproductive of good foliage and flowers, and often become leggy and unsightly. Abutilons are easy to propagate. It is advisable to root cuttings each spring or in August to have young plants coming along to replace those that have served their purpose and should be discarded. They are also easy to raise from spring-sown seeds, but the progeny is likely to show considerable variation in color of flowers and other details. Young plants are encouraged to branch by pinching out the tips of their shoots occasionally, say when the rooted cutting is 4 to 6 inches high and once or twice more when the primary and secondary branches of the young plant are 4 to 6 inches long. Old plants that are being kept over winter should be pruned fairly severely in late winter by cutting out very weak branches entirely and shortening the stronger ones. At the same time, remove the plant from its pot, loosen the roots, shake out as much old soil as reasonably possible, and repot into a fresh soil mixture in as small a pot as the roots will comfortably fit. Immediately following this treatment, water with special care and spray the stems and foliage with water two or three times a day to stimulate new growth. More generous watering is resumed as soon as roots have penetrated the new soil.

Abutilons succeed indoors in a variety of soils. For small plants not yet in the pots in which they are to bloom, a porous, fertile mixture that contains an abundance of peat moss or other decayed organic matter and that is not pressed too firmly about the roots is preferred. This encourages stem and foliage growth and, in a suitable environment, the young plant rapidly increases in size. During this period it is important to repot the plant into a larger pot whenever its roots tend to become crowded.

When the plant is transferred to the container in which it is to bloom, usually some time from April to June, a heavier, leaner soil, one that contains a higher proportion of loam and less sand and organic matter than for the earlier pottings is better and it should be packed more firmly. Good drainage must be provided. This heavier, but porous, soil and firmer potting encourage flower production and rather short-jointed, stocky growth. They offset, to some extent, a natural tendency toward the production of loose, straggling shoots, which can no longer be controlled by pinching once the plants come into bloom. Too generous fertilizing favors stem and leaf growth at the expense of flowers, but starvation or semistarvation brings its troubles too, as unsatisfactory growth, pale foliage, and extra susceptibility to harm by insect pests. Abutilons are "hungry" plants, and once their final pots are well filled with healthy roots fertilization, discreet but regular, is necessary. Applications of dilute liquid fertilizer every week or two in summer are usually beneficial. The appearance of the plants will suggest the need for these. If growth tends to be too lush, fertilization should be suspended for a while. From spring through fall, the soil must never become dry. In winter, when the plants are semi-resting, it should be less moist, but never completely dry. A night temperature in winter of 45 to 50°F is adequate. An increase of five to ten degrees during the day is appropriate. With the coming of spring, both night and day temperatures may with advantage be increased by about five degrees. In summer, the plants may be placed outdoors.

Tree or standard abutilons are developed by allowing the main stem of a young plant to grow without interruption while removing all the side shoots as soon as they are big enough to be picked out by finger and thumb. This is continued until the stem attains a suitable height, usually 2½ to 3 feet or over. Then its tip is pinched and several side branches are allowed to develop. These, and the branches that develop from them, are in turn pinched when 4 or 5 inches long, and this is repeated until a head of the desired size is attained. The heads of standards 1 year old or more are pruned back each spring to their established size.

ACACIA (Acà-cia)—Wattle, Mimosa. Its name pronounced with its second "c" like "sh," this vast genus inhabits the tropics, subtropics, and to some extent warm-temperate regions of many parts of the world. It includes evergreen and deciduous plants, many thorny, and frequently trees and shrubs, but rarely climbers or herbaceous plants. By far the best known horticulturally are the Australian yellow-flowered evergreens called wattles. These are freely planted as ornamentals in California, the Mediterranean region, and other places that enjoy warm, dry climates. Gum arabic is a product of *Acacia nilotica tomentosa*.

The 750 to 800 species of *Acacia* belong to the pea family LEGUMINOSAE. The name, the Greek one for the gum arabic tree, alludes to the thorny character of that species. The derivation is from the Greek *akis*, a sharp point. The plants named false-acacia and rose-acacia belong to the genus *Robinia*. The three-horned-acacia is *Gleditsia triacanthos*.

Acacias have leaves twice-pinnate, or in one large group mostly Australian and including many of the most familiar kinds, reduced to flattened, modified leafstalks that have the appearance of undivided leaves and are technically phyllodes. Some acacias with phyllodes may even when large bear some leaves with reduced pinnate or bipinnate leaf blades attached to the tips of the phyllodes. When raised from seeds, all the phyllode-bearing acacias first produce leaves with divided blades. This characteristic becomes less pronounced as successive leaves with broader leafstalks develop, and finally in most cases, only true phyllodes are produced. The numerous, individually small, yellow or less commonly whitish flowers are in stalked, solitary, paired, or clustered cylindrical spikes or else in small globose heads, solitary, clustered, or in racemes from the leaf axils. They are generally very numerous and showy. Each tiny flower has a lobed, toothed, or fringed calyx or none, five petals or none, many stamens, responsible for the typical fuzzy appearance of the flower heads, and one style.

Leaves of young seedling acacia with phyllodes (flattened stalks) and pinnate blades

The fruits are stalked or stalkless pods. Some species of *Acacia* are sources of commercial products including the finest gum arabic, cutch used in tanning and employed in dyeing the original khaki cloth, other dyestuffs, and cassie flowers used in perfumery. Several species yield high quality lumber. The shittimwood of the Bible, from which it is believed the Ark of the Covenant was made, is a product of *A. seyal*. Australian acacias or wattles are the

most important group cultivated for ornament. They can conveniently be divided into two chief groups, those that have, except as young seedlings, undivided leaves (phyllodes) and those with more or less lacy, bipinnate leaves with many leaflets.

Wattles with lacy, twice-pinnate foliage, fewer in number than those with undivided leaves, and with flowers, according to the species, in small spherical heads or cylindrical spikes, include some of the most lovely. Outstanding are the Cootamundra wattle, the green, black, and silver wattles and the weeping acacia or hairy wattle. Cootamundra or silver wattle (*A. baileyana*), in Europe usually called mimosa, is an attractive small tree or shrub. This has shoots and foliage that are hairless. The leaves, 1 inch to 2 inches long, and spiraled around the branches, are usually gray-glaucous. Each has four, six, or rarely eight primary divisions of about twenty ¼-inch-long leaflets. In branchless racemes longer than the leaves, which come from the upper leaf axils and are presented as though in terminal panicles, the myriad spherical flower heads are displayed in later winter. The ½-inch-wide seed pods are 1½ to 4 inches in length.

Acacia baileyana

The purple-leaf acacia (*A. b. purpurea*) has lavender to purple new shoots. The silver-green acacia *A. dealbata* (syn. *A. decurrens dealbata*) has hairy shoots and silvery-gray to pale green foliage. A tree 50 feet tall or taller, this acacia has leaves 3 to 6 inches long divided into thirteen to twenty-five first divisions each of which has thirty to forty pairs of leaflets. The yellow flowers, profusely borne in spring, are in branchless racemes. Green wattle (*A. decurrens*), beautiful and hairless or somewhat hairy and 15 to 30 feet fall, has angled branchlets, and leaves with generally eight to fifteen pairs or more of primary divisions, but occasionally only five or six. Each of these has thirty to forty pairs of narrow leaflets up to ⅓ inch long. The yellow flowers are in spherical heads, the pubescent seed pods are 3 to 4 inches long. A shrub up to approximately 12 feet tall, or sometimes a small tree, *A. drummondii* has

minutely-downy shoots and leaves up to about 2 inches long with two to four pairs of main divisions each with two to six pairs of leaflets up to ⅓ inch long. The lemon-yellow flowers are in cylindrical spikes ½ inch to 1¼ inches long, ⅓ to ½ inch in diameter. Black acacia or black wattle *A. mearnsii* (syn. *A. d. mollis*) is a tree 20 to 40 feet tall or sometimes taller. It has leaves with up to twenty or often fewer pairs of primary divisions, each with up to sixty pairs of crowded leaflets up to ⅛ inch long. The spherical heads of pale yellow flowers come in panicles in summer. The 2- to 4-inch-long seed pods are up to ¼ inch wide. Bronzy young foliage is a characteristic of *A. pruinosa*, sometimes called the frosty acacia. It is a tree up to about 60 feet tall with a head about two-thirds as broad as its height. The leaves, 3 to 4 inches long, are of two to four pairs of major divisions each with up to about twenty-four pairs of leaflets ½ to ¾ inch long. The cream to yellow, fragrant, globular heads of bloom are in racemes. Black acacia or hairy wattle (*A. pubescens*) is a beauty, with pendulous branches and softly-pubescent shoots and foliage. Of shrub or small tree dimensions, it has leaves of ten to twelve chief divisions, each with twenty pairs or so of small leaflets. Its great quantities of golden-yellow, globular flower heads in large terminal panicles are displayed in spring. The cedar wattle (*A. terminalis* syn. *A. elata*) is a beautiful tree, in its native Australia favoring shaded ravines, and 60 to 90 feet tall. In California it can attain a height of 25 feet in as little as three years. Despite this phenomenal growth it is long-lived. The young shoots of the cedar wattle are clothed with yellow down. Its approximately 1-foot-long leaves are of two to six pairs of primary divisions 5 to 7 inches in length and each of eight to thirteen pairs of pointed-lanceolate, pubescent, dark green leaflets up to 2 inches long and a little more than ¼ inch in width. The flower heads are in branched racemes displayed in sprays over 1 foot long and two-thirds wide.

Wattles, with undivided leaves (phyllodes) and flowers in tiny globular heads, include the following kinds: Kangaroo-thorn (*A. armata*) is a shrub 6 to 10 feet tall or sometimes taller, and about as wide as high, with drooping branchlets and slender, ¼-inch-long spines. Its sharp-pointed leaves, oblong to half-ovate, ½ to 1 inch long and ⅛ to ¼ inch wide, are carried with their straightest margin against the shoot. The solitary or sometimes paired heads of yellow flowers on stalks ½ to ¾ inch long are ⅓ inch in diameter. Broom wattle (*A. calamifolia* syn. *A. pulverulenta*), a shrub up to 10 feet in height, has slightly mealy-coated, hairless shoots. Its threadlike, scattered leaves, 2 to 4 inches long and not more than ⅛ inch wide, ter-

Acacia armata

minate in short, recurved points. Up to ⅜ inch in diameter, the heads of bloom are in axillary racemes of four or fewer, or may be solitary. Called knife leaf acacia, **A. cultriformis** is a silvery-gray, glaucous-foliaged, hairless shrub or multiple-trunked small tree. It has slender, angled shoots and closely-set, obliquely-obovate-lanceolate leaves ½ to 1 inch long that have been described as looking like blades of paring knives stuck into the stems. The heads of yellow blooms are in racemes of ten to twenty in terminal, leafy panicles. Blue-leaved wattle or blue wattle (**A. cyanophylla**) is a tall shrub or multi-trunked tree 20 to 30 feet tall with a head 20 to 40 feet wide. It has long, glaucous branchlets, pendulous when heavy with bloom, and bluish, linear to oblanceolate leaves varying greatly in size and proportions. They are from 6 inches to 1 foot long, from less than ¼ inch to 1½ inches wide. The abundant, orange-yellow flower heads, ¼ to ½ inch in diameter, are in terminal and axillary racemes up to 3 inches long, often presented in leafy, terminal panicles or in

Acacia cyanophylla

small clusters from the leaf axils. Solitary or clustered, the heads of bloom of **A. cyclopis** make less effective floral displays than those of many acacias, but the species is esteemed for its resistance to drought and its usefulness for screening. Attaining heights of 20 to 30 feet and about two-thirds as wide as tall, this acacia has dark green leaves up to 3½ inches long by up to 1 inch wide. Another drought-resister, the shrubby **A. decora**, is 5 to 8 feet tall or sometimes taller, and about as wide as tall. It has angled, glaucous, sometimes slightly-downy shoots and bluish, curved, linear to narrowly-lanceolate or oblanceolate, one-veined, 1- to 2-inch-long leaves. The yellow flowers, less than ¼ inch in diameter, are in axillary racemes 1 inch to 2 inches long often forming leafy panicles. Black or blackwood acacia (**A. melanoxylon**) in cultivation makes a densely-foliaged, pyramidal tree rarely more than 40 feet in height, though it is usually lower. In Australia, where its lumber is highly esteemed as the best of all acacia woods for pianos, cabinets, and other fine furniture, it attains heights of 80 to 100 feet. The straight to somewhat sickle-shaped, lanceolate to oblanceolate leaves are 2½ to 4½ inches long and up to more than 1 inch wide. They have three to six longitudinal veins. Cream-to straw-colored flower heads in racemes considerably shorter than the leaves come from the leaf axils. A fast-grower, blackwood acacia is better suited for large than small areas. The seed pods are much curled. Weeping acacia or weeping myall (**A. pendula**), one of the earliest acacias to display its blooms, is very lovely and well suited for restricted areas. A willowy tree with pendulous branches, in its native land it is 20 to 40 feet high. In cultivation it rarely much exceeds the least of these dimensions and may attain a width of 15 feet. Its heavy, violet-scented wood is prized in Australia for fine furniture and tobacco pipes. Often curved, the linear to lanceolate, pointed leaves of the weeping myall are 2 to 3 inches long. The yellow flower heads, under ¼ inch in diameter, are in axillary racemes of seven or fewer that have very short, downy stalks and are often plentifully displayed in leafy, cylindrical panicles. Pearl acacia (**A. podalyriaefolia**) is a shrub 10 to 20 feet tall, more or less as broad as tall, its young shoots clothed with soft, gray down. Very distinctive, its usually pubescent, glaucous-bluish-gray, satiny leaves are ovate to oblong, 1 inch to 1¾ inches long and ½ to 1 inch wide. Excellent for small landscapes where larger acacias would be disproportionate, pearl acacia is one of the first to bloom. Its showy, golden-yellow flower heads ⅓ to ½ inch wide are in branchless axillary racemes longer than the leaves. Golden wattle (**A. pycnantha**) is a small, hairless, usually short-lived tree with more or less drooping branchlets. Its blunt, lus-

trous leaves, sickle-shaped to lanceolate, oblong-lanceolate, or broadly-obovate, 2½ to 6 inches long by ½ inch to a little more than 1 inch wide, have a prominent midvein. Bright yellow and very showy, the exceedingly fragrant flower heads, about ⅓ inch in diameter, are in branched or branchless racemes 2 to 3 inches long. So abundant are they that their weight often bends the branches. The everblooming acacia (**A. retinodes**) earns its popular sobriquet from its habit of blooming, although not profusely, through much of

Acacia retinodes

the year. It is sometimes misidentified as *A. floribunda*. One of the species hardiest to cold, this is a quick-growing shrub or tree up to 20 feet or sometimes taller, about as wide as high. It has curved, linear-lanceolate, yellowish-green leaves 3 to 6 inches long and up to ¼ inch wide, narrowed to their bases. The fragrant, yellow flower heads, ¼ inch in diameter, are in axillary panicles up to 3 inches long. A wide-spreading tree or shrub 15 to 30 feet high, **A. saligna** has dark green, pendulous, pointed-linear leaves 3 to 9 inches long or longer and ¼ to 1 inch wide. The flower heads, in axillary racemes 1 inch to 3 inches long, are displayed in slender cylindrical panicles about 1 foot in length.

Wattles with undivided leaves (phyllodes) and flowers in cylindrical spikes much longer than they are wide include a number of popular kinds. One of the most common is the Sydney wattle (**A. longifolia**). This is a tall, billowy bush or tree

Acacia longifolia

20 feet tall or sometimes taller. It has angled, hairless or nearly hairless shoots and oblong-lanceolate to oblanceolate leaves 3 to 6 inches long up to ¾ inch wide, with three to five longitudinal veins. The spikes of bright yellow flowers are 1 inch to 2½ inches long and ¼ to ½ inch in diameter. With pointed-linear-lanceolate leaves up to ¼ inch wide, which are mostly near the ends of the shoots, A. l. floribunda has spikes of paler yellow blooms. Intermediates between this and A. longifolia are common. The Sydney wattle is often misidentified as A. latifolia. The species to which this name rightly belongs differs in its leaves being 1½ to 2 inches wide. Star acacia (A. verticillata) is a graceful, wide shrub or small tree with more or less hairy shoots and prickle-pointed leaves, which are solitary and scattered or in whorls (circles of more than two). They have one vein and are ½ to ¾ inch long and not more than ⅛ inch wide. The yellow flowers, in spikes ½ to 1 inch long, are so plentiful that they often hide the leaves.

Acacia verticillata

The cassie or sweet acacia (**A. farnesiana**), also called huisache, opopanax, and popinac, is cultivated in France and elsewhere for its flowers, which are used in perfumery. Now widely naturalized in many warm, dry regions, its original provenance is not known with certainty, but in all probability is American. In any case it occurs spontaneously in parts of the southwestern United States and Mexico. A much-branched, deciduous, thorny shrub or tree 8 to 15 feet tall and often 15 feet wide, it has zigzagged shoots, feathery, green foliage, and nearly orange-yellow, solitary, single flower heads on stalks from the leaf axils. The leaves are of five to eight pairs of primary divisions each of ten to twenty-five pairs of tiny leaflets. Very similar and possibly not botanically distinct

from A. farnesiana, the Chilean **A. cavenia** is a thorny shrub or tree up to 20 feet high, known in its native country as espino-cavan.

The koa (**A. koa**) is a magnificent native of the Hawaiian Islands. When grown under forest conditions it may have a trunk without limbs for 50 feet or more topped by a large head of wide-spreading branches. It has sickle-shaped leaves (phyllodes) 5 to 6 inches long by 1 inch to 2 inches wide. Its yellow flowers are in small, spherical heads. The attractive wood of koa is called Hawaiian-mahogany.

Garden and Landscape Uses. Acacias, less frequently planted than formerly, in part because of their comparatively short lives and in part because of the availability in California, Arizona, and elsewhere where acacias were so abundantly popular of a greater diversity of trees and shrubs, are still among the most lovely ornamental trees and shrubs for such parts. They are greatly admired by visitors and are employed usefully as screens, hedges, wind-

Acacia farnesiana

Acacia cavenia

breaks, and in many decorative ways by landscape architects and home gardeners. The flowers of many are useful for cutting. Some kinds, such as A. dealbata, A. longifolia, A. melanoxylon, and A. elata, grow at extraordinary rates.

Among the most popular, A. verticillata and A. longifolia withstand wind well and are adapted for planting in beach areas; A. armata and A. cultriformis make good barrier hedges. Others suitable for hedges and screens are A. cyanophylla, A. cyclopis, A. decora, and A. dealbata. Those acacias with more or less pendulous branches can be used to excellent advantage on slopes and banks. Unless ample space is available and the location is surely suitable be wary of planting blackwood acacia. It has rampant roots capable of lifting pavements and this makes it difficult to grow other plants nearby. Drought resistant A. farnesiana succeeds in desert areas and prospers in alkaline soils. Others that tolerate alkaline

Acacia farnesiana

soils include *A. cyclopis* and *A. retinodes.* Some acacias will stand light frost, but most are not happy with temperatures appreciably below 20°F. In addition to their outdoor uses in climates that meet their needs, acacias are beautiful for pot and tub cultivation in conservatories and greenhouses.

Cultivation. The chief requirements of acacias are pruning and training to the forms they are to assume. If the top of the main stem is cut off early they branch and form shrubs or multi-trunked trees. By retaining the leading shoot, and judiciously and early cutting off the lower branches and keeping the main shoot tied to a stake, single-trunked, tree-form specimens are achieved. Routine pruning later consists of periodically cutting out enough branches to admit sufficient light and air to the interiors to discourage branches from dying back and to reduce the likelihood of storm damage. When grown as hedges such species as *A. armata, A. cyclopis, A. decora, A. farnesiana,* and *A. verticillata* may be sheared regularly to maintain strict effects or pruned less frequently and less formally. Watering may be needed regularly during the first summer following planting but not afterward. Once established, the deep, searching roots are usually capable of finding sufficient moisture. When you water, soak deeply at well-spaced intervals, not frequently and shallowly. The latter practice delays deep-rooting and sure anchorage. Acacias are readily propagated from seeds and cuttings. Prior to sowing pour hot water over the seeds and leave them to soak for twenty-four to forty-eight hours. Sow outdoors in May or earlier indoors. Transplant the seedlings to small pots and successively to larger containers until they are big enough to be planted outdoors. Acacias do not transplant readily from the open ground. Cuttings made from firm but not hard side shoots may be rooted under mist or in a greenhouse propagating bench.

Greenhouse cultivation is usually restricted to a few kinds, the most important, *A. armata, A. baileyana, A. dealbata, A. drummondii, A. longifolia, A. pendula, A. pubescens, A. retinodes,* and *A. verticillata.* For their satisfactory cultivation they must be housed from fall to late spring in a well-ventilated, sunny greenhouse or conservatory where the night temperature is kept between 40 and 50°F whenever weather permits. Day temperatures should not be more than five to ten degrees higher. In spring after the flowers fade prune back severely all previous year's shoots of specimens you do not want to increase in size. Shorten the shoots of plants you want to grow larger less severely. From then on provide rather warmer conditions and on sunny days spray the tops lightly with water to encourage new growth. When the new growth is ½ to 1 inch long, repot into larger containers specimens in need of

more root room. Be sure the soil is an agreeable one that permits the ready passage of water through it. A mixture of approximately equal parts of good topsoil, peat moss, and coarse sand or perlite, with some dried cow manure and bonemeal added, is satisfactory. As soon as the danger of frost is over, put the acacias in a sunny place outdoors with their containers buried to their rims in a bed of sand, cinders, wood chips, sawdust, or some similar material, there to be left until the threat of fall frost gives warning of the need to return them to the greenhouse. At no time must the soil be allowed to dry out. Soak at intervals as needed to keep it moderately moist. Biweekly applications of dilute liquid fertilizer from spring to fall to specimens that have filled their containers with roots are highly beneficial. Chief pests are caterpillars, mealybugs, and scale insects.

ACAENA (Ac-aèna)—New Zealand Bur or Bidi-Bidi. The usually more or less woody perennials that comprise this group of perhaps 100 species belong in the rose family ROSACEAE. Cultivated acaenas are mostly trailers, but others are shrubs up to 3 feet tall. Most are natives of the southern hemisphere, others of California, Mexico, Central America, and Hawaii. Their name is from the Greek *akaina,* a thorn, and alludes to the spines of the flower and fruiting heads.

Acaenas have alternate, pinnate leaves with an odd number of leaflets and conspicuous stipules (leafy appendages at the bases of the leafstalks) that are joined to the leafstalks. The small, inconspicuous flowers, each with three to five sepals, no petals, one to ten or rarely thirty to forty stamens, and usually a solitary pistil with a divided, feathery stigma, are in interrupted spikes of dense globular or cylindrical heads. Their calyx tubes have barbed or hooked bristly spines. The fruits (commonly called seeds) are embedded in hard fleshy tissue.

In gardens acaenas are admired chiefly for their attractive foliage and typical mat-forming growth, although the flower heads of the New Zealand bur or bidi-bidi (*Acaena microphylla*), and to a lesser extent, of some other acaenas, are decorative.

An endemic New Zealander, *A. microphylla,* which is up to 2 inches tall, forms dense mats of grayish- to pinkish-bronze. The evergreen leaves, not exceeding 2 inches in length and often smaller have seven to thirteen leaflets each less than ¼ inch long. Its heads of bloom are rich crimson and have long spines. The New Zealand *A. inermis* is similar with leaves with sometimes slightly longer leaflets and up to 4 inches long, but with nonspiny flower heads. From the same country comes *A. buchananii,* distinguished by its lovely silvery, whitish-green foliage and small yellowish-green, spiny, globular flower heads.

This is a low, compact trailer with rooting stems, and leaves up to ¾ inch long that when young are densely-hairy. Each leaf has eleven to thirteen leaflets. Another species with small blue-gray, silky-hairy leaves, each with seven to nine leaflets, and creamy-yellow flower heads, is grown in gardens as *A. glauca,* but is correctly named *A. caesiiglauca.*

Other New Zealanders deserving of consideration are *A. novae-zealandiae, A. anserinifolia,* and *A. glabra.* With silky-hairy leaves of five or seven coarsely-toothed leaflets, *A. novae-zealandiae* has comparatively large, spherical, purplish flower heads with long spines. The leaves of the quite rampant, stem-rooting *A. anserinifolia* (syn. *A. sanguisorbae*) are 2 to 6 inches long and consist of seventeen to twenty-one coarsely-toothed leaflets up to ¾ inch long. Its slender-stalked, globular, spiny flower heads are purplish. A vigorous trailer, *A. glabra* has leaves up to 1¼ inches long, with seven to eleven green or brownish-green, coarsely-toothed leaflets, sometimes reddish beneath, and up to ½ inch long. Its globular flower heads are green or reddish-purple.

South American acaenas include the variable *A. ovalifolia,* which resembles the New Zealand *A. microphylla,* but has larger leaves. They are up to 4 inches long and have seven to eleven toothed leaflets more or less hairy on their undersides. The flower heads are purplish. This species inhabits temperate South America and the Falkland Islands. From Chile and Patagonia comes *A. pinnatifida.* With leaves up to 9 inches long and flower stems that may exceed 18 inches, it has erect stems and leaves of seven to eleven deeply-pinnately-divided leaflets. Its cylindrical flower spikes have purplish spines. Also from Patagonia, *A. sericea* is about 3 inches tall and has creeping stems and leaves of seven to eleven toothed leaflets that are silky-hairy beneath. Its green flower heads are cylin-

Acaena buchananii

drical. Fernlike *A. myriophylla*, a native of Chile, is 6 inches to 1 foot in height and has leaves, silky on their undersides, with seven or nine deeply cut leaflets and small green flower heads in interrupted spikes. The silvery-leaved *A. argentea*, from Chile and Peru, has creeping stems and largish leaves of usually nine toothed leaflets. Its flower heads are dark purple. Not known ever to have been in cultivation, the tiny lili-wai (*A. exigua*), which inhabits swamps high in the mountains of Hawaii, might prove a fascinating challenge to skilled and curious gardeners.

Acaena myriophylla

Garden Uses. Horticulturally acaenas can be most usefully employed in rock gardens and similar places. The smaller ones are attractive for decorating crevices between flagstone and brick paving laid on soil or sand, and for planting in dry walls. They serve satisfactorily to mask ground that would otherwise be bare after the foliage of such bulbs as crocuses and colchicums has died. They are quite excellent for chinks between vertical rocks. Acaenas prosper best in light shade. In climates where they grow well it may be necessary to restrain the more vigorous from invading the territories of weaker neighbors. This is easily done by pulling out the offending portions. There is no doubt that these plants are most satisfactory where winters are considerably milder than that of New York City. Yet a few kinds, notably *A. glauca*, *A. buchananii*, *A. microphylla*, *A. novae-zealandiae*, and *A. pinnatifida*, have proven satisfactory at The New York Botanical Garden and in other gardens near the city when planted in sheltered locations and protected over winter with a covering of cut branches of evergreens. Even if they are killed back in winter, they are likely to grow strongly again in spring.

Cultivation. A rather sparse diet such as is supplied by a sandy soil not too filled with organic matter agrees with acaenas.

Perfect drainage they must have. Planting is best done in spring, the young plants being set 4 to 8 inches apart. Until the plants cover the ground, weeds must be kept down but afterward acaenas are well able to take care of themselves. They need essentially no routine care except, in climates where they are on the borderline of hardiness, some light winter protection. They seem to resent overhead watering and, at least where summers are very hot, prosper better under moraine conditions in rock gardens than where they are sprinkled. Propagation is very easily achieved by division and cuttings; and they are easily grown from seed.

ACALYPHA (Acályph-a)—Chenille Plant or Red-hot-cat-tail, Joseph's Coat or Copper Leaf. Very few of the 450 herbaceous and shrubby, tropical, subtropical, and temperate region species of *Acalypha* of the spurge family EUPHORBIACEAE are cultivated. Those that are, are highly attractive warm-climate ornamental shrubs. The name is the ancient Greek one for the nettle.

Acalyphas have alternate, toothed, long-stalked leaves, and petal-less, unisexual flowers usually with both sexes on the same plant. They are in terminal or axillary spikes or racemes and have four-parted calyxes, eight to sixteen stamens, and three styles with fringed stigmas. The fruits are small capsules.

Most cultivated kinds are grown for the beauty of their foliage. The chenille plant or red-hot-cat-tail (*A. hispida* syn. *A. sanderi*) has attractive flowers. This native of the East Indies attains a maximum height of about 15 feet and has green, obovate leaves up to 8 inches long and very conspicuous, decorative, pendulous, cylindri-

Acalypha hispida

cal spikes of female flowers up to 1½ feet long and 1 inch wide. They look like strips of plush or chenille, brilliant crimson in the typical species, creamy-white in the variety *A. h. alba*. Variety *A. h. ramosa* is distinguished by its branched flower spikes.

Acalypha hispida alba

Joseph's coat and copper leaf are names applied to *A. wilkesiana* of the South Sea Islands, and its varieties. These attain heights up to 15 feet and are much branched. Their inconspicuous flowers are in slender spikes up to 8 inches long. They are great favorites because of their handsome and varied foliage. In typical *A. wilkesiana* the coarsely-toothed, elliptic or ovate leaves, 5 to 8 inches long, are bronzy-green mottled with copper- or purple-red.

Acalypha wilkesiana

The leaves of *A. w. macafeeana* are red marked with crimson and bronze, those of *A. w. macrophylla* are russet-brown. Green leaves marked with orange and red are characteristic of *A. w. musaica*. The foliage of *A. w. triumphans* is spotted with crimson, green, and brown. The obovate leaves of *A. w. obovata* are bronzy-green with narrow rosy-pink margins. Variety *A. w.* 'Ceylon' has curiously twisted, coarsely-toothed, maroon leaves with bright pink margins.

Acalypha wilkesiana 'Ceylon'

Usually considered to be a distinct species, but perhaps only a variation of *A. wilkesiana*, the New Guinean *A. godseffiana* is a dense shrub with heart-shaped to narrowly-ovate, coarsely-toothed, green leaves with cream margins. Its greenish-yellow flower spikes are shorter than the leaves. In variety *A. g. heterophylla* the leaves are much dissected and often of different shapes, with varying degrees of dissection appearing on the same plant.

Acalypha godseffiana

Garden and Landscape Uses. In the tropics and frost-free subtropics acalyphas, both those grown for their blooms and those for their foliage, are among the most common and useful shrubs. They are planted in beds and as single specimens and also as attractive hedges. In more northern climates they may be planted in summer flower beds with other warm-cli-

mate plants for temporary tropical effects. As greenhouse plants the colored-leaved kinds and the kinds with showy flowers are esteemed.

Cultivation. Outdoors acalyphas make good growth in any fertile, reasonably moist, well-drained soil. For pot cultivation loamy, rich earth that drains easily is most suitable; it should be coarse rather than finely sifted. Pruning, or in the case of young plants, pinching out the tips of the shoots, is done to control size and achieve shapeliness and bushiness. Major pruning is generally done in late winter or early spring, at the beginning of the growing season. Acalyphas are gross feeders; fertilizing regularly and keeping the plants watered sufficiently in dry weather encourages lush foliage. Cuttings root readily at any time, but when plants are needed for summer bedding and greenhouse decoration they are usually made and inserted in late summer or fall or in late winter, depending on the size of the plants needed for the following summer's display. For their best growth indoors a humid atmosphere and a minimum night temperature of 60°F is needed. From spring through fall it is better that the minimum night temperature be 70°F, and at all seasons day temperatures may exceed those maintained at night by five to fifteen degrees.

Magnificent specimens of the chenille plant may be had in bloom in greenhouses in summer in 8- or 9-inch pots from cuttings rooted the previous August and grown on without pinching their main stems. Any laterals that develop are removed as soon as they are large enough to grasp between finger and thumb. Such plants must be grown under humid, constantly tropical conditions; until they are planted in their final pots they must be transplanted successively to larger pots as soon as their roots fill the containers they are in, and they must be watered with dilute liquid fertilizer two or three times a week once their final pots are filled with roots. Any check to their continuous rapid growth is detrimental. Well-grown specimens in a single season attain heights of 3 to 4 feet and are loaded with drooping tassels of bloom reaching well below the rim of the pot.

Pests. Mealybugs, red spider mites, and scale insects are the most troublesome pests.

ACAMPE (Acám-pe). A dozen or so African and Asian species of the orchid family ORCHIDACEAE belong here. None is especially ornamental, nor likely to interest other than specialists. The name, applied in reference to the brittle blooms, is from the Greek *akampe*, inflexible.

Robust, evergreen epiphytes, plants that perch on trees or other plants without taking nourishment from them, or more rarely that grow on rocks, acampes have much

the aspect of vandas. They have thick, leathery, two-ranked leaves, from the axils of which come close heads or dense, cylindrical racemes of waxy, fragrant flowers. The blooms have approximately equal-sized sepals and petals, the latter narrower than the former, and a lip of similar length. A hybrid between *Acampe* and *Vanda* is *Vancampe*.

The four kinds treated here are similar in habit. Indigenous from the Malay Peninsula to the Himalayas, the summer-flowering *A. longifolia* is about 2 feet tall. It has erect, often branched stems, and rigid, up-pointing, tongue-shaped leaves, broadest toward their apexes, and up to 8 inches long. The densely-crowded, sometimes branched, erect racemes of fleshy, cupped blooms that do not open widely and are up to ¾ inch wide, are up to 4 inches in length. Marked with crimson spots and narrow crossbars, the sepals and petals are basically light yellow. The lip is white sparsely spotted with purple. Unlike those of *A. longifolia*, the thick, stiff leaves of *A. dentata* of India arch outward and downward. About ½ inch in diameter, the brown-blotched, yellowish-white flowers with white- and purple-streaked lips, are in loose panicles or racemes occasionally up to 1 foot long. They appear mostly in summer. Similar in color and arrangement, the flowers of *A. multiflora* are about ½ inch wide. The plant, up to 1 foot in height, has tongue-shaped leaves up to 1 foot long and about 2 inches wide. It blooms in fall and early winter, and is native from southern China to northern India and the Himalayas. From it *A. papillosa*, indigenous from Burma to the Himalayas, is differentiated by leaves less than 6 inches long and its blooms being in rarely branched, dense, headlike racemes usually about 1½ inches long. About ½ inch wide, the blooms are mainly deep yellow spotted with brown, but the lip, longer than the sepals, is white with a rose-red midrib.

Acampe papillosa

Garden Uses and Cultivation. These orchids are unlikely to interest nonspecialists. Because their roots need excellent aeration acampes usually thrive better in hanging baskets than pots. They respond to the same environments and attention as tropical vandas. For further information see Orchids.

ACANTHACEAE —Acanthus Family. This is a family of approximately 250 genera and ten times as many species of dicotyledons that are widely distributed in the tropics and subtropics. Most sorts are herbaceous plants or subshrubs. They have opposite, undivided leaves and asymmetrical, four- or five-parted flowers usually solitary or in spikelike inflorescences sometimes with large, showy bracts. There are two or four, or rarely five stamens and a style, usually long, with two stigmas. The fruits are dry capsules.

Familiar cultivated plants that belong here include *Acanthus, Anisacanthus, Aphelandra, Asystasia, Barleria, Chamaeranthemum, Crossandra, Dicliptera, Dyschoriste, Elytraria, Eranthemum, Fittonia, Graptophyllum, Gymnostachyum, Hemigraphis, Hygrophila, Hypoestes, Justicia, Lankesteria, Mackaya, Megaskepasma, Odontonema, Pachystachys, Peristrophe, Pseuderanthemum, Ruspolia, Ruttya, Sanchezia, Schaueria, Stenandrum, Strobilanthes, Thunbergia, Whitfieldia, Xantheranthemum,* and *Xanthosoma.*

ACANTHEPHIPPIUM (Acanth-ephíppium). The fifteen species of *Acanthephippium* of the orchid family ORCHIDACEAE constitute a genus native from tropical Asia to Fiji. The derivation of the name, which is often misspelled *Acanthophippium,* is unexplained. Related to the better-known *Calanthe,* acanthephippiums usually grow in the ground. Only rarely do they perch on rocks or trees. Although quite attractive they are not frequent in orchid collections.

Acanthephippiums have conspicuous, often furrowed, cylindrical to conical pseudobulbs with broad, pleated leaves at their apexes. The erect, leafless racemes of generally strongly fragrant flowers develop from the bases or sides of the old pseudobulbs at about the time the new growths that will become the next pseudobulbs appear. Urn-shaped to cup-shaped, they have three broad, fleshy sepals that form a tube around the two narrower petals and the lip, which is affixed to the top of a short, thick column.

Native of southern China, India, and Ceylon, *A. bicolor* has egg-shaped pseudobulbs about 2 inches long, each with several elliptic-lanceolate leaves up to 1 foot long and about 4 inches wide. The racemes of up to six cup-shaped, fragrant blooms are about 2 inches in length. They are predominantly yellow streaked with red or reddish-brown. The lip is bright lemon-yellow. Similar, but of sturdier habit, Himalayan *A. sylhetense* has cream to

rather murky yellow blooms spotted and streaked with dull purple. With pseudobulbs up to 10 inches tall by 2 inches thick and irregularly conical, *A. javanicum* is a native of Borneo, Java, Sumatra, and Malaya. Its pseudobulbs have usually three or four short-stalked leaves up to 2 feet long by 6 inches wide, sometimes suffused with purple on their undersides. The racemes, from the sides rather than the bases of the pseudobulbs, are up to 5 inches long. The strongly fragrant, about 2-inch-long blooms are predominantly yellowish to pinkish spotted and lined with red-purple. The lip is white spotted with red.

Garden Uses and Cultivation. These are for the keen collector of orchids. They require humid, tropical conditions and essentially the same care as *Phaius.* For further information see Orchids.

ACANTHOCALYCIUM (Acantho-calýcium). Six natives of the high lands in Argentina, related to *Echinopsis* and by some botanists included in *Lobivia,* constitute *Acanthocalycium* of the cactus family CACTACEAE. The name comes from the Greek *akantha,* a thorn, and *kalyx,* the calyx of a flower. Its meaning is apparent.

Acanthocalyciums are small- to medium-sized globular or cylindrical cactuses that differ from *Echinopsis* and *Lobivia* only in minor floral characteristics. The ovaries and perianth tubes of the flowers are clothed with woolly, sharp-pointed, recurved scales.

Its stems globular to cylindrical and up to 2 feet tall by 6 inches thick, *A. spiniflorum* (syns. *Echinopsis spiniflora, Echinocactus spiniflorus*) has seventeen to twenty-two slightly notched ribs with closely-spaced spine clusters. There are ten to twenty needle-like, reddish-brown to yellowish, or whitish spines with reddish bases and apexes in each cluster. There are three or less somewhat thicker central spines. Nearly 1½ inches long and wide, the funnel-shaped blooms are pink. Spherical with a flattened or depressed top, *A. klimpelianum* (syns. *Echinopsis klimpeliana, Lobivia klimpeliana*), some 4 inches in diameter, has about nineteen straight ribs. Spaced ¾ inch apart, the clusters of dark-tipped, brownish, grayish, or nearly black spines are of six to ten radials and two centrals up to 1¼ inches long. The white flowers come from the sides of the plant, are funnel-shaped, approximately 1¼ inches long. Spherical to cylindrical and up to 8 inches tall and 4½ inches in diameter, pale green to olive-green *A. violaceum* (syn. *Echinopsis violacea*) has about fifteen, somewhat notched ribs. The stiff, bristly, needle-like, yellow spines deepen in color toward their apexes. They are up to 1¼ inches long, and occur in clusters of a dozen or more, spaced ½ to ¾ inch apart. The three or four central spines are somewhat longer. Carried near the centers of the plants, the 3-inch-long, trumpet-shaped, light violet-colored flowers are about 2 inches in diameter.

Acanthocalycium spiniflorum

Garden Uses and Cultivation. These are choice collectors' cactuses suitable for rock gardens in dry, warm climates and for greenhouses and sunny windows. They are perhaps a little less robust than most species of *Echinopsis*, but serve the same purposes and in general respond to the same conditions and care. For more information see Cactuses.

ACANTHOCEREUS (Acantho-cèreus). The trailing, clambering, or sometimes erect night-blooming cactuses that make up this genus of the cactus family CACTACEAE have jointed stems with usually three, but sometimes as many as seven ribs, the larger numbers generally on young shoots. The group is native from Florida to Texas and South America. There are eight species. The name is from the Greek *akantha*, a thorn, and *Cereus*, another genus of cactuses.

In *Acanthocereus* the areoles (positions from which the spines come) are woolly and give rise to clusters of stiff spines. The solitary, funnel-shaped blooms are white or greenish. They have long perianth tubes, many wide-spreading perianth segments (petals), and scaly ovaries. The stamens are shorter than the petals and are erect. The style is four-lobed. Numerous black seeds are contained in dark red fruits.

Native from southern Florida to Texas and northern South America, *A. pentagonus* has arching or clambering stems 6 to 20 feet long that frequently bend to the ground and root at their ends. They are 1¼ to 3¼ inches in diameter and have three to five shallowly-scalloped angles. The areoles are commonly up to 2 inches apart. Each has one to several central spines up to 2 inches long, and six to twelve smaller radials. The larger numbers are from the older areoles. The blooms are 6 to 8 inches long. Their perianth tubes and ovaries have prominent areoles with brown hairs and spines. The inner perianth segments (petals) are white, the outer green. The red, oblongish fruits are edible. A native of Mexico and Cuba, *A. baxaniensis* is sometimes confused with *A. pentagonus*. It commonly has stems with four, broad, winglike ribs and spine clusters of one to three centrals up to 1¼ inches long and five or more radials about ½ inch long. The 10-inch-long flowers have white inner petals and brownish-green outer ones.

A native of Guatemala, *A. horridus* (syn. *A. horribilis*) has somewhat thicker stems, with broad, flangelike, deeply-undulated ribs. From each areole come one or two stout central spines up to 3 inches long and one to six radial spines up to ½ inch in length. The blooms, up to 8 inches long, have white inner petals and brown or greenish outer ones. The stamens are white, the style creamy-white. The fruits, under 1½ inches long, are red with white-felted areoles. An erect species, with forking,

conspicuously three-winged stems 6 to 9 feet tall, *A. pitaja* (syn. *A. columbianus*) is a native of Colombia. Each of its areoles have one or two very stout central spines, up to about 2 inches long, and five to eight very short radial spines. The broad-throated blooms, some 10 inches in length, are white.

Garden and Landscape Uses and Cultivation. These easy-to-grow plants have the general adaptabilities and requirements of many desert cactuses. For more information see Cactuses.

ACANTHOLIMON (Acantho-lìmon) — Prickly-Thrift. Prickly-thrifts belong to the plumbago family PLUMBAGINACEAE. There are about 150 species, natives of semi-deserts, deserts, and stony places in mountains from the Mediterranean region to the Himalayas. The name, from the Greek *akantha*, a spine, and the related genus *Limonium*, alludes to the prickly foliage.

Evergreen, subshrubby, tufted, low perennials compose *Acantholimon*. They form compact hummocks of short stems and much-crowded, rigid, slender, sharp-pointed, needle-like leaves that are cylindrical or slightly three-angled. The pink, lavender-pink, or white, sea-lavender-like or thriftlike blooms, with persistent papery bracts, usually at their bases, are displayed in crowded heads, spikes, or short racemes. They have tubular, ten-ribbed, lobed calyxes, five petals joined at their bases, five stamens, and five separate styles. The fruits are little utricles (one-seeded, bladder-like seed pods).

Dark green, densely compact, and with prickle-pointed leaves, *A. glumaceum* forms mounds 4 to 6 inches tall, often considerably wider. Its bright, rose-pink blooms are hoisted above the foliage in narrow, rather one-sided spikes of nine or fewer blooms ½ to ¾ inch wide. This is native to Armenia. A native of Asia Minor, *A. venustum* differs in having less densely compact tufts of slightly wider, stiff leaves, and bigger bright pink blooms in spikes of twelve to twenty.

Garden Uses and Cultivation. Prickly-thrifts, considered choice additions to rock gardens, revel in warm, sunny locations and faultlessly-drained, dryish, sandy or limestone soils. They are also appropriate for alpine greenhouses. They grow slowly and are none too hardy, and not reliably so in the region of New York City. Propagation is by slow-to-germinate seeds sown in sharply-drained, sandy soil, kept just moist, but not saturated, in a cold frame or cool greenhouse. Cuttings are taken in summer. Cuttings root slowly and often with difficulty in propagating beds in cold frames or greenhouses. Layering affords the surest means of multiplication. This is done in spring, and the daughter plants are not removed from the parent until the following spring. Established specimens of prickly-thrifts should be left undisturbed. All that is desirable is a shallow top dressing of suitable, sandy soil spread around them occasionally, and in cold climates the protection afforded by a light winter covering of branches of pines or other evergreens.

ACANTHOLOBIVIA (Acantho-lobívia). Two species of cactuses of the cactus family CACTACEAE that much resemble *Lobivia* and by some authorities are included there constitute *Acantholobivia*. The generic name alludes to a characteristic of the fruits. It comes from the Greek *akantha*, a spine, and the name of the related genus.

Natives at high altitudes in Peru, acantholobivias differ from *Lobivia* in having spiny fruits. Sometimes included in choice collections, *A. tegeleriana* (syn. *Lobivia tegeleriana*) has plant bodies about 4 inches in diameter, with about sixteen notched ribs and clusters of about twelve spines up to 2 inches long. The orange to pinkish-orange, funnel-shaped blooms are 1½ inches in length, the greenish fruits about 1 inch in diameter. The blooms open at night.

Garden Uses and Cultivation. These are as for *Lobivia*. For additional information see Cactuses.

Acantholimon glumaceum

Acantholimon glumaceum, young plant

ACANTHOPANAX (Acanthó-panax)—Five-Leaf-Aralia. As a group the deciduous or rarely evergreen shrubs and small trees that constitute this eastern and southern Asian and Philippine Island genus of the aralia family ARALIACEAE are of secondary horticultural importance. Except in botanical gardens and similar collections only one is at all commonly planted. Yet they can serve usefully, particularly in difficult situations. Comprising fifty species, *Acanthopanax* has a name derived from the Greek *akantha*, a spine, and *Panax* another genus of *Araliaceae*. The plant known as *A. ricinifolia* is *Kalopanax pictus*.

Generally conspicuously prickly, acanthopanaxes have alternate leaves digitately (in finger-fashion) divided into separate leaflets, or more rarely only lobed. The small, dull flowers may be all of one sex or a mixture of unisexual and bisexual blooms on individual plants. They are in umbels often arranged in large panicles, have minutely-toothed calyxes, usually five but sometimes only four petals, the same number of stamens, and two to five styles. The fruits are black or black-purple berries, generally about ¼ inch in diameter, containing five or fewer seeds, and tipped with the persistent styles.

Five-leaf-aralia (**A. sieboldianus** syns. *A. pentaphyllus*, *Aralia pentaphylla*) is the most frequently cultivated and most useful. Native to Japan and China, this is a spiny shrub 6 to 10 feet tall with slim, arching branches and attractive, hairless foliage. It has slender-stalked leaves with blades rounded in outline and up to 2½ inches across that consist of usually five, but sometimes three or seven rather thin, ovate-oblong to oblong-obovate, stalkless, toothed leaflets. Solitary, terminating stalks 2 to 4 inches long, the 1-inch-wide umbels of greenish-white blooms originate from shoots of the previous year's growth. Because so far as is known only female plants are in cultivation in North America the fruits are not seen here. A rare variety, *A. s. variegatus*, with white-margined leaves is described. Differing from *A. sieboldianus* in having thinner leaves, and flowers with two styles separate nearly to their bases instead of five to seven joined nearly to their tops, **A. spinosus** is endemic to Japan. Plants cultivated under this name are frequently *A. sieboldianus*.

Of decorative worth because of their long-lasting foliage and abundant displays of black fruit in fall, **A. divaricatus** is native to Japan and **A. simonii** to China. The former is a loose-branched shrub up to 12 feet tall, with stems with a few paired spines much broadened at their bases. Its leaves are hairy, especially beneath, and have five or rarely three ovate to oblong-obovate, short-stalked leaflets 2 to 4½ inches long, with double-toothed margins. The yellow-anthered, brownish-purple flowers, with those of the terminal umbels bi-

sexual, are crowded in spherical heads about 1 inch in diameter that are in terminal panicles at the ends of leafy shoots. They have two styles. Bushy and not exceeding 5 feet in height, the Chinese *A. simonii* has hairless branches with down-pointing, hooked spines. Its leaves, bristly-hairy on both surfaces, have five, or on the uppermost only three, short-stalked leaflets, with the center one of the largest and up to 6 inches long by 2 inches wide. The leaflets are coarsely-bristle-toothed and often have a few prickles. The umbels of blooms, on stalks up to 2 inches long, are in terminal clusters. The nearly related **A. henryi** of China is distinguishable from *A. simonii* by its young shoots having rough hairs, and the undersides of its leaves being downy instead of bristly hairy.

With showy black fruit and leaves that hang long into fall, **A. lasiogyne** is too large and vigorous for any but large landscapes. This native of China becomes 15 to 20 feet tall and as broad with a graceful habit. It has leaves with three leaflets, stalkless or nearly stalkless, and slightly-toothed above their middles or toothless. They are obovate to obliquely-ovate, and 1½ to 2 inches long. The white flowers have two spreading styles. The Chinese **A. wardii** is closely similar to *A. lasiogyne*. It differs in its flowers having hairless instead of hairy calyxes, and in individual stalks longer than those of *A. lasiogyne*. Another vigorous Chinese, **A. senticosus**, has densely-bristly or sometimes prickly, sparingly-branched, erect stems. Its slender-stalked leaves are of five, or less commonly of three, short-stalked, elliptic-obovate to oblong, sharply-toothed leaflets 2½ to 4½ inches long, with scattered hairs. The purplish-yellow flowers, in spherical umbels about 1½ inches wide are solitary or a few occur together on slender stalks. Variety *A. s. inermis* is nearly or entirely without prickles and has larger leaves and umbels.

Garden and Landscape Uses. The acanthopanaxes described here are all deciduous, and are hardy in southern New England. Hardier even further north are *A. sieboldianus*, and the extremely cold-tolerant *A. senticosus*. By far the most useful and perhaps most attractive species is *A. sieboldianus*. This has good-looking foliage and thrives in poor, even dryish soil, in considerable shade as well as in sun. It prospers under city conditions, and can be sheared to form a good hedge. Planted fairly closely together all kinds form effective barriers and screens, and stand some shade, but are generally better satisfied with sunny locations. None is fussy so far as soil is concerned.

Cultivation. The only care needed is to thin out crowded, and shorten gangly branches occasionally. This is best done in late winter or spring. When grown as a formal hedge *A. sieboldianus* needs shear-

ing once or twice a year. Propagation is by summer cuttings under mist or in a greenhouse or cold frame propagating bed, by leaf cuttings, by transplanting rooted portions of established plants, by layering, and by seeds.

ACANTHOPHIPPIUM See Acanthephippium.

ACANTHOPHOENIX (Acanthophoè-nix)—Barbel Palm. Two species belong in this genus, both natives of the Mascarene Islands in the Indian Ocean. They are in the palm family PALMAE. The generic name is from the Greek *akantha*, a spine, and *Phoenix*, another genus of palms, and refers to certain similarities of appearance.

Barbel palms are stately. They have solitary, ringed, spiny trunks up to 60 feet in height, and beautiful crowns of long, gracefully curved pinnate leaves consisting of numerous leaflets each with a prominent midrib. The pendulous flower clusters have two main branches, many secondary branches, and two flat spathes up to 2 feet long that fall early. Each cluster includes male and female flowers, the former the more numerous. The black fruits are ¼ to ½ inch long. The sheathing leaf-stalks are spiny.

The red barbel palm (**Acanthophoenix rubra**) is so called because in its young stages its leaves have conspicuous red mid-veins. At that time they are especially beautiful. The leaves, which attain a length of 12 feet on mature plants, have their central stalks bristly-hairy as also is the lower portion of the midrib of each leaflet. This species is native of Reunion Island. The yellow barbel palm (**A. crinita**) is similar, but perhaps not quite as strong a grower. On young plants its leaves are yellow-green. They have fuzzy-hairy stalks with a few spines on the sheathing basal portions. The flower clusters and spathes are shorter than those of the red barbel palm. The yellow barbel palm inhabits Reunion and Mauritius islands.

Garden and Landscape Uses. These very tall and lovely palms are suitable for planting as single specimens or in groups. They succeed in southern Florida and in humid tropical lands and are elegant for large greenhouses.

Cultivation. Barbel palms thrive in full sun in any fairly good garden soil. Indoors they need a minimum winter temperature of 60 to 65°F, a humid atmosphere, shade from strong sun, and rich, porous soil kept always moist but never waterlogged. Well-rooted specimens are improved by giving them dilute liquid fertilizer at weekly or biweekly intervals from spring through fall. They are easily propagated by seeds sown in sandy peaty soil in a temperature of 80°F. The seeds take up to three months or sometimes longer to germinate. For further information see Palms.

ACANTHOPHYLLUM. This genus is apparently not cultivated. The plant sometimes grown as *Acanthophyllum spinosum* is *Dianthus petraeus noeanus.*

ACANTHORHIPSALIS (Acantho-rhípsalis). Included by many botanists in *Rhipsalis,* the South American genus *Acanthorhipsalis* comprises five species of epiphytic (tree-perching) plants. It belongs in the cactus family CACTACEAE. Its name, alluding to the relationship and its spiny character, is derived from the Greek *akantha,* a prickly plant, and the name of the closely allied genus *Rhipsalis.*

These cactuses are bushy. They have angled, winged, or flat, spiny stems and many small white, purple, or red flowers that open during the day. The fruits are berries.

A native of Peru, **A. micrantha** has branches up to about 8 inches long mostly with three crenated angles. The closely-set areoles each has a cluster of three to ten spines about ½ inch long. About 1 inch in length, the flowers are purple.

Garden Uses and Cultivation. These are as for *Rhipsalis.* For more information see Cactuses.

ACANTHORRHIZA. See Cryosophila.

ACANTHOSTACHYS (Acantho-stáchys). Most of the members of the pineapple family BROMELIACEAE are sufficiently look-alike to be easily recognizable as such. A few, the Spanish-moss (*Tillandsia usneoides*) for example, fit less obviously into the pattern. Among these mavericks is the only species of *Acanthostachys,* a native of southern Brazil, Argentina, and Paraguay. The generic name, derived from the Greek *akantha,* a spine, and *stachys,* a spike, alludes to the appearance of the flower and fruiting heads.

Not infrequently grown by bromeliad fanciers, **A. strobilacea** is best adapted for hanging baskets or elsewhere where its long, drooping, reedy leaves can be displayed effectively. It forms spidery-look-

ing rosettes of few rigid, tapering, spine-margined, olive-green to brownish, scurfy leaves 1 foot to 3 feet long by not more than ½ inch wide, channeled along their upper sides, and ending in a sharp point. The quill-like flower stalks, their lower parts sheathed by the bases of the leaves, come from the centers of the rosettes and are up to 1 foot long. Each terminates in a flower head that suggests a slender pine cone or miniature pineapple. The heads, 1 inch to 2 inches long, are of orange or red bracts with yellow flowers in their axils. From immediately beneath each flower head sprout few leaflike bracts of different lengths, the longest sometimes more than 1 foot long. The blooms have three each sepals and petals, six stamens, and a three-parted style. The fruits are separate berries in a conelike head. One of the hardier bromeliads, this survives outdoors in southern California. For cultivation see Bromeliads or Bromels.

ACANTHUS (Acán-thus)—Bear's Breech. About a score slightly tender and tender herbaceous perennials and small shrubs make up *Acanthus.* Natives chiefly of the Mediterranean region, they belong in the acanthus family ACANTHACEAE. The generic name is from the Greek *akantha,* a spine. It refers to the prickle-toothed edges of the leaves of some kinds.

Acanthuses are stately plants grown for the decorative appeal of their ornamental foliage as well as for their attractive blooms. The simple beauty of acanthus leaves inspired the ancients to conventionalize their forms as decorations for the capitals of Corinthian and other columns. It is thought that these architectural embellishments are based on the foliage of *A. spinosissimus* and *A. mollis.* In most cultivated kinds (*A. montanus* is an exception), the foliage is all or nearly all basal. Often the large, variously cut and toothed leaves reach upward and arch outward in almost fountain-like fashion. In some kinds the lobes or teeth of the leaves are spine-tipped. The flowers are in stiffly-erect spikes with conspicuous, leafy, spiny, more or less colored bracts interspersed. The calyx is four-parted with two of its lobes larger than the others. The corolla, dull white or somewhat dingy pink or purple, consists of a broad tube and one large three-lobed lip. There are four thick-stalked stamens with hairy anthers. The fruits are four-seeded capsules. Acanthus blooms are densely clustered in spikes up to 1½ feet long.

The hardiest kinds stand considerable cold but are not reliable in climates harsher than that of Washington, D.C. Even there, they benefit from some winter protection. One of the finest and hardiest is *A. mollis latifolius,* which differs from the species *A.*

Acanthostachys strobilacea (flowers)

Acanthostachys strobilacea

Acanthus mollis latifolius

Acanthus mollis

mollis, a native of Italy, in being larger and more robust. In bloom *A. mollis* attains a height of 3 to 4 feet and has heart-shaped, mostly basal, wavy-margined leaves about 2 feet long by 1 foot wide. They are not spiny. The pubescent flower spikes have white or pink blooms and deeply-toothed bracts. In addition to *A. m. latifolius* there are varieties *A. m. candelabrum,* with large leaves and purple and white flowers, and *A. m. niger,* with glossy foliage and purplish-white blooms. Another kind with spineless, wavy-edged leaves is *A. balcan-*

Acanthus balcanicus

icus (syn. *A. longifolius*) of Dalmatia. Its bright green, all basal leaves are 2 to 3 feet long and proportionately narrower than those of *A. mollis.* Its flower spikes, which attain heights of 3 to 4½ feet, have purple-pink flowers and oval, spiny, slender-pointed reddish bracts.

Differing from the above are species that have the margins of their leaves furnished with spine-tipped teeth. Best known is *A. spinosissimus* of southern Europe. This has deeply-pinnately-cut, hairy, lanceolate leaves and flower spikes 3 to 4 feet tall. The blooms are purplish.

Two lower-growing species with spiny-edged leaves are *A. caroli-alexandri,* of Greece, and *A. perringii,* of the mountains of Asia Minor. The former is 9 inches to 1½ feet tall and forms a loose rosette of all basal, lanceolate, pinnately-divided leaves less than 1½ feet long and up to 4 inches wide. Its white or pinkish flowers are in dense spikes. The leaves of the latter are stalkless, lanceolate, deeply-toothed, and up to 6 inches long. Its spikes of rose-pink blooms are interspersed with spiny bracts.

A tropical species of much merit is *A. montanus,* native to West Africa. It differs from the other acanthuses discussed in being a shrub with definite stems and is 3 feet tall or somewhat taller. Its glossy, alternate leaves, up to about 1 foot long by 6 inches broad, are pinnately-lobed and have spiny edges. In terminal spikes 6 to 10 inches long, the attractive flowers are white stained with purple.

Acanthus montanus

Garden and Landscape Uses. As garden ornamentals in regions of moderately mild winters acanthuses serve rather specially because of the ornamental qualities of their foliage as well as the dignified, if muted, values of their displays of bloom. The larger ones are well adapted for associating with architectural features and are seen to good advantage near walls, steps, and the like, and on terraces. They are also admirable for lawn beds and other isolated groupings and for massing boldly on banks and other places where their splendid

leaves show to good effect. The smaller *A. caroli-alexandri* and *A. perringii* are appropriate for rock gardens but the latter, unlike other acanthuses, objects to really hot summers. West African *A. montanus,* as may be expected, revels in heat and humidity and makes itself thoroughly at home either outdoors or in greenhouses where such conditions obtain. It is a good decorative, evergreen shrub.

Cultivation. Acanthuses luxuriate in deep, fertile, well-drained soil and, almost all, in full sun. An exception to the last is *A. montanus,* which seems to prefer that the fullest intensity of really strong sun be tempered with a little shade, but certainly not too much. They abhor soils that are excessively wet in winter and if allocated to such, promptly express their dissatisfaction by dying. In the north they should be protected over winter with a thick layer of branches of evergreens, salt hay, or other material that will prevent the ground from freezing too deeply and modify the ill effects of alternate freezing and thawing. A spring application of a complete fertilizer stimulates vigorous growth. Propagation of the nonshrubby kinds is by very careful division, best done in spring, and by seeds sown in a temperature of 60 to 65°F. Cuttings provide an easy way of increasing *A. montanus.* When grown in greenhouses it should be pruned back hard and repotted in late winter and spring. First-year plants may be allowed to develop a single stem without pinching. In succeeding years, as a result of the annual pruning they will branch and carry more than one flower spike.

ACCENT PLANTS. Plants used in garden and landscape design to provide strong emphasis by contrasting sharply in form with their surroundings are called accent plants. The contrast may be accentuated by other differences such as those of height, type, and texture or color of foliage. Usually the characteristics upon which the effects depend are stable rather than transitory. Form may be natural or artificially produced by pruning, shearing, or shaping in other ways, or by grafting, training, or employing some other horticultural skill. Examples of plants the natural forms of which recommend them for use as accents are Alberta spruce (*Picea glauca albertiana*), Italian cypress (*Cupressus sempervirens*), Irish yew (*Taxus baccata stricta*), and Lombardy poplar (*Populus nigra italica*), all of which supply strong vertical lines; mugo pine (*Pinus mugo mugo*), boxwood (*Buxus sempervirens*), and *Thuja occidentalis globosa,* which are naturally more or less globular and compact; and some plants of distinctive, but less formal outline such as Pfitzer's juniper (*Juniperus chinensis pfitzeriana*) and Hick's yew (*Taxus media hicksii*). Weeping trees and shrubs with pendulous branches are effective as accents. Examples are Sargent's weeping hemlock (*Tsuga canadensis pendula*), weeping cherry (*Prunus subhirtella*), and weeping willow (*Salix babylonica*).

By pruning or shearing, many shrubs and trees, evergreen and deciduous, can be shaped formally as accents. Especially susceptible to such treatment are arborvitaes, certain barberries, boxwoods, thujas, and yews among evergreens, and such deciduous kinds as certain barberries, privets, and hawthorns. The shaping may be done to achieve such forms as pyramids or cones or globes, which are natural in some other plants, or to develop frankly artificial

(d) Sargent's weeping hemlock

(g) Mullein (*Verbascum*)

Accent plants: (a) Italian cypress

(e) Weeping cherry

(h) Boxwoods accent the boundaries of this vista

(b) Lombardy poplar

(f) Foxgloves (*Digitalis*)

(c) Boxwood

forms, as is done in topiary. Standards, plants with a single tall stem or trunk topped with a head of branches, developed by grafting or training, lend themselves well for use as accents. Examples of plants often trained in this way include fuchsias, geraniums, lantanas, *Catalpa bignonioides nana* (often misnamed *C. bungei*), and weeping mulberry (*Morus alba pendula*).

Properly used, to frame a view, terminate an axis, complement an architectural feature, or define an area, as for example by placement at the ends of flower borders, accent plants can be satisfying and charming. Their tasteless and indiscrimi-

nate uses, unfortunately not uncommon, produce landscape abominations. This is especially true of strictly formal shapes. Discretion and restraint must guide the use of accent plants. Too few rather than too many is a good rule. Their overabundance defeats their prime purpose, that of accentuating a particular feature of landscape design. Too many are likely to produce uneasy, restless, or incongruous effects.

ACER (À-cer)—Maple, Box-Elder. This splendid genus includes some of the best known and useful trees of temperate climates. Surely everyone is familiar with at least one kind. Certain species, such as the sugar maple in North America, the sycamore maple in Great Britain, and the Japanese maple in Japan, are especially beloved by the peoples of the lands they inhabit and this is reflected in their literature, poetry, and arts. Except for oaks no other group of hardy trees of such importance includes so many kinds. True, there are more than twice as many willows, but many are shrubs, often of extremely lowly stature, and the vast majority have no horticultural, arboricultural, or commercial significance. The reverse is true of maples.

The genus *Acer*, together with *Dipteronia*, forms the maple family ACERACEAE. Its name is the ancient Latin one for maples, of which there are more than 200 species. A few are shrubs, most are trees, and the great majority are deciduous. Maples occur as natives throughout most of the temperate zone and in some tropical mountains of the northern hemisphere. By far the greatest number are Asian, but several American and a few European maples excel in size and magnificence.

Maples are usually easily recognizable. They have opposite, stalked leaves, commonly lobed and more or less hand-shaped, and in some kinds consisting of three to seven distinct leaflets arranged pinnately. The flowers, in clusters or racemes, appear in spring before or with the leaves. They are bisexual or unisexual, sometimes both on the same tree, but often individual trees bear one sex only. The small flowers have five or rarely four sepals, and the same number of petals, or sometimes none. There are four to ten, usually eight, stamens and two styles or stigmas. The fruits are very characteristic. Technically samaras, they are commonly called keys. Each consists of a compressed, bony nutlet with an elongated, membranous wing. The nutlets are joined in pairs and the wings diverge at angles characteristic of the species, or are sometimes parallel.

Of American maples probably the first to come to mind is the sugar maple or rock maple (**A. saccharum**), the foliage of which in fall sets New England and other northeastern hillsides ablaze with brilliant yellows, scarlet, and deeper reds. The sugar maple served the colonists, and Indians for untold centuries before them, as a source of a nutritious sugar obtained from its sap.

Acer saccharum

It still is exploited for this. It is also valued for its lumber, called hard maple, much esteemed for furniture, flooring, bowling alleys, and many other purposes. The especially handsomely-grained woods called bird's-eye maple and fiddle-back maple are of this species. The sugar maple, native from eastern Canada to Georgia and Texas, attains a height of 120 feet. Its leaves, from 3 to 6 inches broad, are green above, paler

on their undersides, three- to five-lobed, and at their bases, heart-shaped. The greenish-yellow flowers without petals expand with the leaves. They have long, slender, hairy, individual stalks, and are in almost stalkless, axillary and terminal clusters. The wings of the hairless fruits diverge, but slightly. Several distinct varieties are recognized. One of the best, the sentry maple *A. s.* 'Temple's Upright' has a narrow, compact, columnar head. It

Acer saccharum 'Temple's Upright'

grows rather slowly. Variety *A. s. conicum* has a dense, conical crown of upright branches. In *A. s. glaucum* the underside of the foliage is glaucous. The leaves of *A. s. rugelii* have usually three toothless lobes, those of *A. s. schneckii* are densely-hairy on the veins beneath, and the black maple *A. s. nigrum* (syn. *A. nigrum*), with black instead of gray bark, has leaves pubescent beneath. This is indigenous from Canada to South Dakota, Missouri, West Virginia, and Kentucky. Its lumber, for all practical purposes identical with that of the sugar maple is also called hard maple. The chalk maple *A. s. leucoderme* (syn. *A. leucoderme*) ranges from North Carolina to Georgia and Louisiana. Exceptionally 45 feet tall, but usually not over 25 feet, it has light gray bark and three- to five-lobed leaves up to 3 inches across and pubescent on their undersides. In fall they become scarlet. Its slender-stalked, petal-less, yellow flowers are followed by fruits with wings that spread at an angle of about 120 degrees. This maple is hardy in southern New England.

The silver maple or white maple (**A. saccharinum**) is quite different. Its greenish-yellow flowers appear well before the leaves. They are in nearly stalkless, lateral clusters and are without petals. The fruits, pubescent when young, have large, widely-spreading wings. The long-stalked leaves have five, coarsely-toothed, sharp-pointed,

Acer saccharinum

Acer saccharinum (flowers)

deep lobes. They are green above. Their undersides are silvery-white, very apparent when a breeze flutters them. In fall they turn yellow. The silver maple grows to a height of 120 feet and has an oval or rounded, wide-spreading head with often somewhat pendulous branches. Its limbs are brittle and much subject to storm breakage. The lumber of silver maple, called soft maple, is used for furniture, flooring, interior trim, and other purposes. It is inferior in appearance and wearing quality to that of sugar maple and black maple. Silver maple is native over most of eastern and central North America. Its best known variety is Wier's weeping maple (*A. s. laciniatum*), which has pendulous branches, and leaves cleft deeply into narrow segments. A slightly different form of the same variety is called Skinner's weeping maple. In *A. s. pyramidale* the upright branches form a narrow, pyramidal head. The foliage of *A. s. lutescens*, bronze when young, becomes yellow later. Other varieties are *A. s. aureum*, with leaves variegated with yellow, and *A. s. tripartitum*, in which the leaves are divided almost to their bases into three broad lobes.

The third great maple of eastern North America is the red, scarlet, or swamp maple (**A. rubrum**). This beautiful, picturesque tree favors wet soils and meadows

Acer rubrum

and is abundant from Newfoundland to Florida and Texas. It attains a height of 120 feet and has its upper trunk and branches covered with steel-gray bark. In earliest spring, long before the leaves appear, every branch and twig is decorated with quite conspicuous clusters of usually red flowers. The males have bright yellow stamens that contrast sharply with the red petals, but trees with female flowers are more showy because their blooms are commonly more intensely red, last longer, and are succeeded by bright red fruits. The wings of the fruits diverge to form an angle of about 60 degrees. The leaves of red maple are shining green above, glaucous beneath, and hairy along the veins on their undersides. They are long-stalked, 2 to 4 inches long, and have three to five short, toothed lobes. This maple assumes fall garb earlier than most. Its changing color flags the first approach of fall. In New England its foliage begins to redden before the end of August, usually on a branch or two at first, followed by a gradual flushing until the entire tree is uniformly brilliant red. Although less brittle than silver maple, the branches of red maple are rather weak and subject to storm damage. The lumber, like that of silver maple is called soft maple. It has the same uses as silver maple. Among the best of several varieties is the columnar red maple (*A. r. columnare*), which has a narrow, erect head, and grows more rapidly than the columnar sugar maple. Other varieties are *A. r. drummondii*, with five-lobed leaves, pubescent on their undersides, *A. r. globosum*, of dwarf, compact growth, *A. r. magnificum*, the leaves of which in fall are bright red with green veins, *A. r. schlesingeri*, which colors in fall a full month before the typical species, *A. r. tomentosum*, with five-lobed leaves pubescent beneath, and *A. r. trilobum*, the leaves of which are pubescent beneath and three-lobed near their tips. Nurserymen have given names to many superior and supposedly superior strains of red maple

they have selected and propagated vegetatively. Here belong varieties named 'Armstrong', 'Bowhall', 'Doric', 'Gerling', 'Scanlon', and 'Tilford'. They are described in catalogs.

Acer rubrum columnare

The Oregon or big-leaf maple (*A. macrophyllum*), native from Alaska to California, has the largest leaves of any maple. They are 8 inches to 1 foot across, three- to five-lobed, and when young pubescent. In fall they turn bright yellow or orange. The tree is round-headed, up to 100 feet tall, and has pendulous clusters of small, fragrant, yellow flowers. The hairy fruits have wings diverging at right angles. Excellent for the Pacific Coast region, it, unfortunately, is not well suited to eastern conditions. It is hardy about as far north as Pennsylvania.

Acer macrophyllum (flowers and foliage)

The box-elder (*A. negundo*) has very un-maple-like foliage. Highly variable, this native throughout most of North America is extremely hardy to cold and drought. A

rapid grower, it does not rank highly as a tree for gardens or landscapes except in parts of the Middle West and other regions where torrid, dry summers and cold winters strictly limit the kinds of trees that can be grown. The box-elder has a wide-spreading, open crown up to 70 feet in height, and ashlike leaves of three to five or rarely more toothed or lobed leaflets up to 4 inches long. Its yellow-green, petalless flowers appear before the leaves, the males in pendulous clusters, the females in drooping racemes. The sexes are on separate trees. The fruits are glabrous. Their wings, often incurved, diverge at an angle of 60 degrees or less. The box-elder has weak branches and is subject to storm damage. Variety *A. n. californicum* has leaves of three leaflets as also does *A. n. texanum*. Those of the latter are almost hairless when mature, whereas those of the former are densely-pubescent. There are several variegated- and colored-leaved varieties of box-elder. Best known and most attractive is *A. n. variegatum*, the leaflets of which are margined with a broad white band. The leaves of *A. n. aureo-marginatum* are bordered with yellow, those of *A. n. aureo-variegatum* are spotted yellow, and those of *A. n. auratum* are uniformly yellow.

Smaller American maples include the Florida maple (*A. barbatum* syn. *A. floridanum*), which is used as a street tree in parts of the southeast. At its best about 50 feet tall, it has a dense, rounded head, light-colored, whitish bark that resembles that of beech trees, and three-lobed leaves up to 3 inches across and glaucous on their undersides. The wings of the fruits are spreading or sometimes close together. Native from Virginia to Florida and Texas, it is not hardy in the north. The striped maple or moosewood (*A. pensylvanicum*) is the sole American representative, the others are Asian, of a group of maples with thin, smooth bark marked with longitudinal stripes, alternately near-white and olive-green. Moosewood reaches a maximum height of about 40 feet and has large, long-stalked, three-lobed, bright green leaves that become clear yellow in fall. Its flowers are in drooping racemes up to 6 inches long. The wings of the fruits spread at a wide angle and each pair forms a crescent. Variety *A. p. erythrocladum* is especially pleasing in winter when its twigs, almost as brilliantly red as those of red-stemmed dogwoods (*Cornus*), are displayed to best advantage. Moosewood is native from Quebec to Wisconsin and Georgia. It inhabits moist woodlands. Rarely much over 25 feet in height, the mountain maple (*A. spicatum*) is very colorful in fall when its coarsely-toothed, three-lobed or slightly five-lobed leaves turn scarlet, yellow, and orange. It makes a good show with its fruits, which in summer are usually bright red. The mountain maple is native from Labrador to Saskatchewan, Iowa, and Georgia. Its greenish-yellow flowers, in dense, upright, hairy, slender spikes 3 to 6 inches long, are succeeded by fruits with wings that angle up to 45 degrees. Its yellowish-green leaves are pubescent beneath.

The Rocky Mountain maple (*A. glabrum*) enjoys a much wider natural range than its common name suggests. It is indigenous from Montana and South Dakota to New Mexico and California, and variety *A. g. douglasii* from Alaska to Oregon and Wyoming. About 25 feet in height, **A. glabrum** has three- or five-lobed, double-toothed leaves up to 5 inches across, lustrous dark green above and paler beneath, that become bright yellow in fall. Its greenish-yellow flowers are in raceme-like clusters. The wings of its fruits, often pink in summer, are incurved, and close together or slightly divergent. Variety *A. g. douglasii* has three-lobed leaves and fruits slightly bigger than those of the typical species. In *A. g. tripartitum* the leaves are smaller than those of the species and are usually three-parted. Bright red fruits are a delightful feature of *A. g. rhodocarpum*.

The vine maple (**A. circinatum**) is a beautiful native of the Pacific Coast, closely related to, and looking somewhat like, the Japanese maple (*A. palmatum*), from which it differs in having flowers with white or nearly white petals and leaves divided only to their middles that when young are hairy on their undersides. Its blooms, in drooping clusters, are among the prettiest and most ornamental of any maple. Their petals contrast effectively with the purple sepals. The vine maple commonly has several often more or less reclining and twisting trunks from near the ground. It forms a wide-spreading shrub or tree occasionally 35 feet tall but usually lower. Its bright green, seven- to nine-lobed leaves have double-toothed margins. In fall the foliage becomes brilliant orange and red. The fruits are handsome. Red in summer, they have wings that spread almost horizontally. The wood of this species is exceedingly tough and was used by the Indians to make frames (bows) for fishnets. The vine maple is hardy as far north as southern New England.

The most popular European species for planting in North America is the Norway maple (**A. platanoides**). It is used freely as a street and shade tree, sometimes in places where other species would be more satisfactory. Hardy in New England and adjacent Canada, it forms a rounded, densely-foliaged head that casts heavy shade, and produces great mats of soil-depleting feeding roots just beneath the ground surface. The combination of heavy shade and severe root competition often makes it impossible for other plants to survive beneath old specimens of this tree. In its favor is its adaptability to difficult con-

ditions, such as city environments, and its ability to withstand pruning, even severe cutting back, an accommodation of special importance where space is limited and the size of the crown must be controlled. The Norway maple is a quick grower, which endears it to impatient planters. At its biggest about 100 feet tall, this beautiful tree, native of Europe from Norway south and in western Asia, in spring is conspicuous because of its quite showy, erect, many-flowered, flattish clusters of greenish-yellow blooms, which appear with the leaves.

Acer platanoides

The fruits are pendulous and have wings that spread nearly horizontally. The bright green, five-lobed leaves, toothed and glabrous except for tufts of hair in the vein axils on the undersides, are heart-shaped at their bases, and 3 to 5 inches across. They change to yellow in fall. The leaf-stalks exude milky sap when broken, which affords an easy way of distinguishing this tree from the sugar maple, which it somewhat resembles. Many varieties of Norway maple have been described. Among the best and most distinct are *A. p. schwedleri*, with leaves bright red at first, but gradually changing as spring advances to a somewhat darker green than those of the typical species. Variety *A. p.* 'Crimson

Acer platanoides schwedleri

King' (syn. *A. p.* 'Goldsworth Purple') is similar, but its foliage remains dark red through the summer. The leaves of *A. p. albo-marginatum* are conspicuously margined with white, those of *A. p. aureo-marginatum* are edged with yellow, and *A. p. variegatum* has white-spotted leaves. A narrow, columnar head characterizes *A. p. columnare* in contrast to the head of *A. p. globosum*, which is compact and rounded. The small, twiggy *A. p. laciniatum* is very distinctive with a columnar head and leaves with clawlike lobes. Another variety, *A. p. lorbergii*, has light green leaves divided almost to their bases, with the points of the lobes turned upward. The leaves of *A. p. palmatifidum* are also divided almost to their bases, but the points of lobes are in the same plane as the main body of the leaf. The leaves of *A. p. rubrum* become dark red in late summer. In recent years nurserymen have selected and propagated superior strains of Norway maple. These, described in trade catalogs, have been given varietal names such as 'Cleveland', 'Charles F. Irish', 'Almira', and 'Olmsted'.

Acer platanoides globosum

The sycamore maple (**A. pseudoplatanus**) is the most massive European species. In England called sycamore and in Scotland plane, it is quite different from the trees called by those names in North America, which belong in the genus *Platanus*. Maples (*Acer*) have opposite leaves, planes (*Platanus*) alternate ones. The sycamore maple attains heights of 100 feet or more, has a trunk of great girth, and an immense, spreading head. Its leaves are five-lobed, coarsely-toothed, and 4 to 7 inches across. Of thicker texture than those of the Norway maple, they are glabrous except along the veins on their dull-glaucous undersides. The yellowish-green flowers, in drooping, cylindrical racemes or panicles, develop well after the foliage. The fruits have wings that diverge at an angle of about 60 degrees. Except that it has smaller leaves that assume no bright color before they drop and that it is much hardier, the sycamore maple has much the aspect of the Oregon maple (*A. macrophyllum*). The fruits of the Oregon maple are covered with yellow bristly hairs, those of the sycamore maple are hairless. The syc-

Acer pseudoplatanus

Acer pseudoplatanus (flowers)

Acer pseudoplatanus (fruits)

Acer pseudoplatanus variegatum

amore maple is hardy in southern New England. Among the most noteworthy of many varieties of sycamore maple are *A. p. variegatum*, with leaves beautifully variegated with white; *A. p. brilliantissimum*, with foliage coral-pink when it first unfolds; *A. p. corstorphinense*, with leaves bright yellow when young; *A. p. worleei*, with rich yellow leaves with reddish stalks; *A. p. erythrocarpum*, with smaller leaves and bright red fruits; *A. p. leopoldii*, with young foliage dark rosy-pink variegated with yellowish-pink; *A. p. purpureum*, with leaves rich purple beneath; and *A. p. to-*

mentosum, with more coarsely-toothed leaves, green and pubescent beneath. The sycamore maple and its varieties are among the most satisfactory trees for seaside planting. They withstand salt spray, winter gales, and intense summer sun very much better than most other trees.

The hedge maple (**A. campestre**) of Europe and western Asia may be 50 feet or more tall, but usually is considerably lower. Round-headed and with neat foliage, it has leaves 2 to 4 inches across. This is attractive, especially useful for screening, and adaptable for tall, sheared hedges. Its three- to five-lobed leaves are dull green above and pubescent beneath. Like the Norway maple their stalks contain milky sap. The greenish flowers are few together in erect clusters. The wings of the fruits spread horizontally. Without brilliant fall color, the leaves turn yellowish before dropping. There are several varieties, the best of which are *A. c. compactum*, a dense, low bush usually broader than high; *A. c. postelense*, with young foliage golden-yellow; *A. c. pulverulentum*, with leaves thickly dotted and blotched with white; *A. c. schwerinii*, with purple young foliage; and *A. c. variegatum*, with leaves edged with white. The hedge maple is hardy in New England.

Two species of southern Europe closely related to the hedge maple are the Montpelier maple (*A. monspessulanum*) and *A.*

opalus. The first is native also to western Asia. Both are hardy about as far north as southern New England. In mild climates **A. monspessulanum** is evergreen or semi-evergreen. Even where it loses its foliage in winter the leaves remain green until late in the fall. It attains a height of 25 to 30 feet, forms a dense, rounded head, and has three-lobed leaves up to 3 inches across, lustrous above, and glabrous except for axillary tufts of hairs on the veins beneath. The juice of the leafstalks is not milky. The greenish-yellow flowers, in drooping clusters, are succeeded by reddish fruits with wings that meet or overlap. Up to 45 feet tall, **A. opalus** has shallowly five-lobed, irregularly-toothed leaves, dark glossy green above, paler beneath, and when young downy on their undersides. The yellow flowers, many together in drooping clusters in early spring, are ornamental. The fruits have wings at right angles. Variety *A. o. tomentosum* (syn. *A. o. neapolitanum* has much larger leaves, felty-hairy beneath and with hairy stalks. In variety *A. o. obtusatum* the leaves are larger than those of the type, have more rounded lobes, are downy beneath, and have hairy stalks. The wings of the fruits are larger than those of the last-mentioned variety. Another worthwhile native of southern Europe and western Asia is **A. tataricum**. Up to 30 feet in height and reliably hardy in New England, this has bright red fruits in summer, and foliage that turns yellow to red in fall. Round-headed, it has bright green, broad-ovate, double-toothed leaves up to 4 inches long, glabrous above, when young pubescent on the veins beneath. On young trees the leaves are sometimes lobed. The greenish-white flowers are in upright clusters. The wings of the fruits are nearly parallel. This does best in fairly moist soil.

The maples of eastern Asia total more than one-half of the known species of the genus. Not all are cultivated and not all are of sufficient merit to be of horticultural interest. They include, however, a number of really fine kinds that succeed well in North America and are admirably adapted for gardens. Predominantly small trees, none equals in size the largest species of America and Europe. Most popular is the Japanese maple (**A. palmatum**), cultivated in horticultural varieties ranging from low shrubs to trees 25 feet or so tall. These,

Acer palmatum

mostly developed by Japanese gardeners as a result of centuries of breeding and selection, exhibit very diverse foliage characteristics. The hardier ones live in southern New England, but the more tender variegated kinds may not survive there. In its native Japan and Korea *A. palmatum* is occasionally 50 feet tall, but usually considerably lower. It is round-headed, often broader than tall, with seven- or five-lobed leaves up to 3½ inches long and 3½ inches wide. The lobes are double-toothed, ovate-lanceolate, and extend two-thirds of the way to the base of the blade. Except for tufts in the vein axils beneath, they are hairless. The foliage is green, but as fall approaches it becomes yellow, purplish, or bronzy. The small, purple flowers, borne in spring, are in nearly erect, few-flowered clusters. The narrow wings of the fruits spread widely, each pair forming a broad crescent. Horticultural varieties of Japanese maple, far more commonly cultivated than the typical species, are numerous. For convenience they are divided into groups based on how finely the leaves are dissected. Within the groups classification is based on foliage color and other character-

istics. Group I includes kinds with leaves deeply five- to nine-lobed and coarsely-double-toothed or incised. Here belong *A. p. atropurpureum*, with dark red-purple leaves; *A. p. sanguineum*, with smaller leaves of a lighter reddish-purple; *A. p. versicolor*, with white-spotted, bright green leaves; *A. p. aureum*, with yellow foliage; and *A. p. roseo-marginatum*, with small, deeply-cut leaves with pink margins. Group II has larger leaves with usually seven broad, evenly double-toothed lobes. Included here are *A. p. rubrum*, with leaves deep red when young, but becoming almost green later; *A. p. reticulatum*, with greenish-yellow leaves with green veins and margins; and *A. p. tricolor*, with leaves spotted with red, pink, and white. Group III has leaves divided nearly to their bases into narrow lobes with few or no teeth. Dark green-leaved *A. p. linearilobum* and a variant of it with red-purple leaves called *A. p. l. atropurpureum* (syn. *A. p. atrolineare*) belong here. Group IV has leaves divided to their bases into five to nine lobes that are again deeply lobed. Green-leaved *A. p. dissectum* is typical, as are *A. p. d. atropurpureum*, with deep red leaves, and *A. p. fredericii-guilelmii*, with green leaves speckled with white and pink. Group V, with very short-stalked, green leaves, includes *A. p. sessilifolium*. Unfortunately the identification and naming of varieties of Japanese maples is much confused, and bewilderment is increased by the practice of

Acer palmatum dissectum

Acer palmatum dissectum (foliage)

growers who raise plants from seeds and apply to the seedlings the names of established varieties. The latter do not, of course, breed true from seeds and should be propagated vegetatively.

Closely related to *A. palmatum*, as hardy, and sometimes called Japanese maple, is the fullmoon maple (**A. japonicum**), which differs from *A. palmatum* in having the stalks of its young leaves and the stalks and ovaries of its flowers hairy. These

Acer japonicum

Acer japonicum (flowers)

stalks in *A. palmatum* are hairless. The fullmoon maple, native of Japan, is there occasionally 50 feet tall, but is more commonly 30 feet or lower. Its roundish leaves, 2 to 5 inches long, have seven to eleven sharply-toothed, pointed-ovate or lanceolate lobes. The undersides are hairy along the veins. When unfolding, the leaves are silky-hairy, but they soon lose most of the hairs. They are green, and in fall turn bright red. The flowers are purple. The fruits have wings that spread almost horizontally. Varieties are *A. j. aureum*, with yellow foliage, and *A. j. aconitifolium*, with leaves divided almost to their bases into nine to eleven lobes that are again lobed. This last is called fernleaf maple.

Acer japonicum aconitifolium

Acer japonicum aureum

One of the tallest orientals is the painted maple (*A. truncatum*) of Japan, China, and Korea. Up to 60 feet tall it has five- or seven-lobed, toothless leaves 3 to 6 inches across, glabrous except for axillary tufts of hair on the veins beneath. The leaves turn bright yellow in fall. The greenish-yellow flowers are in erect clusters. The fruits are glabrous, with wings that, except in *A. t. connivens,* in which they spread at a very small angle or are parallel and almost touching, spread horizontally. Variety *A. t. marmoratum* has leaves spotted and blotched with white, *A. t. dissectum* has leaves with five primary lobes again deeply-lobed, *A. m. tricuspis* has smaller, three-lobed or sometimes lobeless leaves. This species and its varieties are hardy in southern New England.

The Amur maple (*A. ginnala*) is another interesting, extremely hardy species indigenous to Japan and the nearby mainland. About 20 feet tall, densely-branched, and round-headed, this graceful tree or tall shrub has firm-textured, double-toothed, three-lobed leaves up to 3 inches long, and lustrous above. They turn brilliant scarlet in fall. The center lobe of each leaf is much longer than the two side ones. The panicles of very fragrant, yellowish-white flowers are succeeded by conspicuous red fruits with nearly parallel wings. Variety *A. g. semenowii*, native of Turkestan, has smaller,

sometimes five-lobed leaves, and fruits with more widely divergent wings. The paperbark maple (*A. griseum*) has remarkably beautiful cinnamon-brown bark that peels in thin papery sheets after the manner of the river birch (*Betula nigra*), so that the trunk is always decorated with curls of colorful separating bark. This attains a height of about 25 feet, is densely-branched, and has an upright-branched, rounded head. Its branchlets are woolly. Its leaves are of three separate, blunt-toothed leaflets, the central one 2 to 2½ inches long, the side ones shorter. In fall the foliage changes to orange and red. The pendulous flowers are solitary or a few occur together on downy stalks. The fruits have wings that diverge at an angle of 60 to 90 degrees.

Acer griseum

Acer griseum (peeling bark)

It is hardy in New England. Closely related to the paperbark maple and about as hardy, *A. maximowiczianum* (syn. *A. nikoense*) of China and Japan is a rather slow grower that eventually may be 45 feet tall. It does not have the peeling bark of the paperbark maple, but is round-headed and has leaves of three separate, slightly-toothed leaflets that are brilliant red or purple in fall. The center leaflet is somewhat larger

than the lateral ones. The pendulous flowers, usually in threes, are yellow and about ½ inch in diameter. The fruits have wings from nearly parallel to widely divergent. It is hardy in southern New England.

The hornbeam maple (*A. carpinifolium*) is very distinctive. A native of Japan, it has bright green foliage that turns a warm brownish-yellow in fall and usually several trunks from near ground level that form a vase-shaped head. Reported to reach 50 feet in its homeland, in cultivation in America and Europe it is rarely more than one-half that height. Its leaves are very different from those of any other species in cultivation and bear an extraordinary resemblance of those of hornbeam (*Carpinus*). They are ovate-oblong, 2 to 4 inches long by about one-half as wide, without lobes, and are short-stalked. Their margins are double-toothed and from the midrib spread about twenty pairs of pinnate, parallel veins. When young, the foliage is densely covered with silky hairs that gradually fall so that by autumn the leaves are almost hairless. The green flowers are in clusters or racemes on slender stalks, the females have petals, but the males have not. The wings of the fruits form crescents. This tree is easily distinguished from hornbeams, even when not in flower or fruit, by its opposite leaves (or in winter, opposite leaf buds). It is hardy in southern New England. Another elegant Japanese is *A. argutum*. This native of woodlands attains a height of about 25 feet, and has attractive light green, five- or rarely seven-lobed, slender-stalked leaves with opposite, long-pointed, double-toothed lobes. Their undersides, especially along the whitish veins, are downy. The flowers are greenish-yellow and expand before the foliage. The males have four stamens and are in short racemes. The females are slender-stalked and in much longer, pendulous racemes. The wings of the fruits spread horizontally. This is hardy in southern New England.

The Manchurian maple (*A. mandshuricum*), from Siberia, Manchuria, and Korea, is hardy in New England. About 30 feet tall, but often lower and shrublike in cultivation, it resembles the box-elder (*A. negundo*) of North America. Like the box-elder, it grows rapidly, but is not as subject as the box-elder to storm damage. Its leaves have three oblong to oblong-lanceolate, blunt-toothed leaflets, dark green above, glaucous beneath, and pubescent along the veins. The greenish-yellow flowers are in terminal three- to five-flowered clusters. They appear before the foliage. The fruits have wings that spread at right angles or more widely.

Other kinds are *A. barbinerve*, a native of Manchuria and 25 feet tall, has five-lobed, coarsely double-toothed leaves 2 to 3½ inches long, yellowish-green flowers, and fruits with wings spreading at an angle of 90 to 120 degrees. **A. buergerianum**, the trident maple, is a small tree with lustrous leaves 1½ to 3½ inches long, of three usually obscurely-toothed, triangular, forward-pointing lobes, pale beneath, dark green above. A native of China and Japan, its male flowers are in clusters, its females in racemes. The wings of its fruits are

Acer buergeranum

Acer buergeranum (fruits and leaves)

closely parallel. **A. capillipes** of Japan, is 30 to 40 feet tall, has white-striped bark and red-veined, usually red-stalked, double-toothed, three-lobed leaves, with the central, triangular, pointed lobe the largest. The greenish-white flowers are in drooping racemes. The wings of the fruits spread at 120 degrees or more. **A. cappadocicum**, the coliseum maple, up to 60 feet tall and native from the Caucasus to northern India, has hairless leaves, 3 to 6 inches long, with five to seven long-pointed lobes, and stalks that when broken exude milky sap. Its flowers, in erect clusters, are greenish-yellow. The wings of its fruits spread at a wide angle. It differs from the closely-related Norway maple (*A. platanoides*) in its leaf margins not being toothed. *A. c. rubrum* has leaves reddish at first, green later. *A. c. tricolor* has young leaves blood-red bespeckled with pink. *A. c. tricaudatum* has smaller three-lobed leaves. **A.**

cissifolium has bright green leaves with three leaflets, toothed, and up to 3 inches long, that turn yellow, orange, and scarlet in fall. The flowers are in drooping racemes. The wings of the fruits are slightly divergent. This native of Japan attains a height of about 60 feet. **A. crataegifolium**, the hawthorn maple, up to 30 feet tall, has white-striped bark, and oblong-ovate bluish-green, pinnate-veined, unevenly-toothed leaves about 3 inches long, often with one or two pairs of lobes at their bases. The greenish-yellow blooms are in few-flowered erect racemes. The wings of the fruits spread in opposite directions. It is a native of Japan. *A. c. veitchii* has leaves variegated with pink or white. **A. davidii** of China, up to 50 feet in height, has whitish-striped bark and pinnate-veined, ovate, toothed leaves up to 6 inches long, and except on young plants, not lobed. In fall the foliage becomes yellow, red, and purple. The unisexual, yellowish flowers are in pendulous racemes. The wings of the fruits spread nearly oppositely. **A. diabolicum**, of Japan, a round-headed tree up to 30 feet in height, has five-lobed, broadly-ovate, toothed leaves up to 6 inches across. The flowers are yellow, the males in drooping clusters, the females in racemes. The fruits have bristly nutlets and broad wings, parallel and almost touch-

Acer diabolicum (fruits and leaves)

ing. Variety *A. d. purpurascens* has purplish flowers and fruits. Its young leaves are purplish. **A. dieckii**, a natural hybrid between the Norway maple (*A. platanoides*) and *A. lobelii* that attains 60 feet in height, has five- or sometimes seven-lobed, dark lustrous green, essentially toothless leaves with tufts of brown hair in the vein axils beneath and stalks that exude milky sap when broken. The flowers are yellow, the wings of the fruits widely divergent. **A. grosseri** is a tall shrub or small tree of China, with whitish-striped bark and toothed, ovate leaves 2 to 5 inches long, without lobes or with two short side lobes. The fruits have wings that diverge in nearly opposite directions. *A. g. hersii* dif-

fers in having leaves with pointed lateral lobes about one-half as long as the center lobe. **A. micranthum** is a graceful tall shrub or small tree of Japan with five- or sometimes seven-lobed leaves about 3 inches long. The lobes are slender-pointed and sharply double-toothed. In fall the foliage turns yellow. The greenish-white flowers are in slender racemes. The wings of the fruits are nearly horizontal. **A. miyabei**, up to 35 feet tall, round-headed, with slightly-corky branches, has three- or five-lobed leaves up to 6 inches across. They are downy beneath, especially on the veins and have shallow lobes. The leafstalks contain milky sap. In fall the foliage turns yellow. The clusters of yellow flowers have wings that spread in opposite directions or are deflexed. This tree is indigenous to Japan. There is a hybrid between this and the hedge maple (*A. campestre*). **A. pseudosieboldianum**, similar to *A. sieboldianum* but with nine- to eleven-lobed, double-toothed leaves, has purple flowers on glabrous stalks. It is native to eastern Asia. **A. rufinerve**, indigenous to Japan, attains a height of 40 feet and has three-lobed, double-toothed leaves 2½ to 4½ inches long, with rusty hairs along the veins beneath.

Acer rufinerve (fruits and leaves)

The center lobe is larger than the lateral lobes. The flowers are in erect racemes. In fall the foliage turns red. The wings of the fruits diverge at from 90 to 120 degrees. The leaves of *A. r. albo-limbatum* are spotted or margined with white. **A. sieboldianum**, a tall shrub or small tree of Japan, has seven- to nine-lobed, toothed leaves up to 3 inches in diameter, and hairy-stalked, yellowish flowers in drooping clusters. The wings of the fruits spread almost horizontally. The foliage of this maple, which is closely related to *A. japonicum*, turns red in fall. *A. s. microphyllum* has smaller leaves. **A. trautvetteri**, up to 45 feet tall, is a native of the Caucasus. It has deeply five-lobed, dark green leaves, 4 to 8 inches wide, slightly glaucous beneath and with tufts of hair in the vein axils. The flowers are in erect, pyramidal clusters. The fruits, pubescent when young, have closely parallel or overlapping wings. *A. triflorum*, native to Korea and Manchuria, is up to 40 feet tall and has leaves of three toothless or few-toothed, ovate to lanceolate leaflets up to 3½ inches long. The flowers are in groups of three. The fruits have very hairy nutlets and wings that diverge at 90 degrees or more. *A. truncatum*, of China, is a 25 foot-tall, round-headed tree with five- or sometimes seven-lobed leaves up to 4½ inches across. Like the shoots, when young the leaves are purplish. Their stalks contain milky juice. The greenish-yellow flowers are in upright clusters. The wings of the fruits are approximately at right angles. In fall the foliage becomes purplish-red. *A. tschonoskii* is a shrub or small tree of Japan, with five- or rarely seven-lobed leaves 2 to 4 inches in diameter; the lobes are triangular and slender-pointed. The veins on their undersides are hairy. The greenish-white flowers are in racemes. The fruits have incurved wings that diverge at 90 degrees.

Garden and Landscape Uses. Maples include some of the very best trees for landscaping. Those of first importance as large and medium-sized shade trees include Norway maple (*A. platanoides*), black maple (*A. saccharum nigrum*), sycamore maple (*A. pseudoplatanus*), sugar maple (*A. saccharum*), and for particular regions, big-leaf maple (*A. macrophyllum*), Florida maple (*A. barbatum*), and box-elder (*A. negundo*). For seaside planting the sycamore maple (*A. pseudoplatanus*), is especially useful. Small trees, of special value for home gardens and other places where space is limited include hedge maple (*A. campestre*), hornbeam maple (*A. carpinifolium*), Amur maple (*A. ginnala*), chalk maple (*A. saccharum leucoderme*), paperbark maple (*A. griseum*), vine maple (*A. circinatum*), and *A. argutum*. Several of the smaller species such as mountain maple (*A. spicatum*), moosewood (*A. pensylvanicum*), vine maple (*A. circinatum*), Amur maple (*A. ginnala*), and Japanese maple (*A. palmatum*) thrive in part shade. If in sunny locations these commonly do best where their trunks are shaded. The hedge maple, as its common name indicates, is useful for tall hedges and screens. It, like box-elder (*A. negundo*) and Montpelier maple (*A. monspessulanum*), prospers in dry soils, whereas red maple (*A. rubrum*), silver maple (*A. saccharinum*), and *A. tataricum* are partial to moist locations.

Many American and oriental maples are highly esteemed for their brilliant colored fall foliage, and some, such as Amur maple (*A. ginnala*), red-fruited sycamore maple (*A. pseudoplatanus erythrocarpum*), and *A. tataricum* have colorful fruits. The beautiful variegated and colored-leaved varieties of hedge maple (*A. campestre*), Norway maple (*A. platanoides*), sycamore maple (*A. pseudoplatanus*), sugar maple (*A. saccharum*), Japanese maple (*A. palmatum*), and full-

moon maple (*A. japonicum*) provide accents of color in green landscapes. Varieties of Japanese maple and fullmoon maple are especially appropriate for Japanese gardens and rock gardens. Variegated- and colored-leaved maples are very effective when grown in large tubs for terrace decoration and for forcing into early leaf in large conservatories.

Cultivation. Maples are easy to grow. They have many fibrous roots, transplant well even when large, and adapt themselves to ordinary garden soil, but succeed best in fertile, reasonably moist ones. Pruning as a routine practice is not needed but may be done with impunity when necessary. Summer, after the foliage is fully developed is the best season to prune, since cuts made during the dormant season are likely to ''bleed'' (exude sap) copiously in spring. This loss is not nearly as serious as it appears (fermentation of the often slightly sugary exudate may cause a bubbling or frothing that looks ominous, but does little or no harm to the tree), but nevertheless it is messy, unpleasant, and quite unnecessary. Because the feeding roots of maples are near the soil surface it is harmful to dig or cultivate deeply beneath or immediately around the trees. A far better plan is to keep the areas mulched or planted with groundcovers. Root competition and shade, however, often combine to make impossible the growth of groundcovers. One of the toughest covers for such places is *Euonymus radicans coloratus*. If this fails no other is likely to succeed. Alternatives to organic mulches or living groundcovers are mulches of crushed stone or gravel and various types of paving such as Belgian blocks (granite blocks once popular for street paving), and bricks.

Seeds, sown as soon as ripe, are satisfactory for raising species of maples, but not for perpetuating horticultural varieties. These must be propagated vegetatively. Seeds of some kinds germinate in summer as soon as they ripen, others do not germinate until the following spring and must be exposed to low temperatures for a period before they will grow. They may be stratified at 35 to 40°F for about three months and then sown, or, as soon as they are ripe they may be sown in a cold frame or in outdoor beds protected from disturbance by animals or birds. Common vegetative methods of increase are budding and grafting onto seedling understocks of the species to which the variety belongs or a closely related one. Commercially, budding is most commonly employed because this produces saleable plants faster than grafting. Budding is done in July and August. The best method of grafting is by using the whip and tongue graft on understocks that have been established in pots for a year. Alternatively, the side graft may be employed. Grafting is done in a greenhouse in winter. Unfortunately, incompatibilities between understocks and scions

are common and these are not fully understood, so the selection of a suitable understock is often a matter of trial and error. A fairly recent development is the propagation of maples from cuttings. Those of the Japanese maple (*A. palmatum*) and its varieties, as well as some other kinds, root successfully under mist. The best results are had from tip cuttings made from actively growing shoots, preferably taken from young stock plants. Maple cuttings may also be rooted under polyethylene plastic film, shaded from direct sun. There is evidence to suggest that maples raised from cuttings may be less tolerant of harsh winters and periods of drought than grafted specimens.

Many maples, particularly Japanese maples (varieties of *A. palmatum* and *A. japonicum*), suffer from scorching of the foliage in summer when more water is lost from the leaves than is replaced by the roots. This may be, and often is, because the ground is too dry and there is not sufficient water available to meet the needs of the tree, but that is not always the only cause of the trouble. With Japanese maples and sometimes others, the basic problem seems to be incompatibility between understock and graft or perhaps mechanical obstruction at the graft union that prevents the passage of sufficient water up the conducting vessels of the trunk. An obvious way of minimizing such trouble, in addition to making sure that the ground is kept moist at all times, is by locating the trees where they receive a little shade during the hottest part of the day, and where they are not subject to sweeping winds.

In large tubs the variegated and colored-leaved varieties of box-elder (*A. negundo*), sycamore maple (*A. pseudoplatanus*), Japanese maple (*A. palmatum*), and other kinds succeed in any fertile, porous soil. The containers must be well drained. If the trees are to be forced into early growth in a greenhouse, they should be planted in their containers sufficiently in advance to permit them to become well established before forcing begins. Until then, in cold climates, the plants should be kept outdoors with their tubs packed around with sawdust, leaf mold, peat moss or other material that will prevent the root balls from freezing solid. At no time must the soil be dry. In February or March the plants are brought into a greenhouse where the night temperature is about 50°F and the day temperature a little higher. The branches are sprayed frequently with water to soften the buds and encourage new growth. Forced plants may be put outdoors after all danger of frost has passed. If they are kept watered and fertilized regularly through the summer they can be forced again the following year. Tub-grown plants should be top-dressed with rich soil at the beginning of each growing season. Every few years they are likely to need re-tubbing.

ACERACEAE —Maple Family. Two genera and possibly 2,000 species compose the dicotyledonous family ACERACEAE. By far the most important of its elements, the maples constitute the genus *Acer*. The other genus included is *Dipteronia*. Members of this family are trees and shrubs with opposite, usually undivided, often lobed and toothed, usually palmately-veined leaves. More rarely, as in the box-elder, the leaves are pinnate. The small flowers are in clusters of racemes, usually have four or five each sepals and petals, and rarely are without petals. There are four to ten stamens and two styles. The fruits are pairs of winged fruits called samaras. The only commonly cultivated sorts are members of the genus *Acer*.

ACERANTHUS DIPHYLLUS is *Epimedium diphyllum*.

ACERIPHYLLUM. See Mukdenia.

ACEROLA is *Malpighia punicifolia*.

ACHENE. Dry fruits the walls or shells of which do not split to release the single seeds they contain are called achenes. An achene is one mature, fertilized ovary. Fruits of the daisy family COMPOSITAE are achenes.

ACHILLEA (Achil-lèa)—Yarrow or Milfoil. The genus *Achillea*, of the daisy family COMPOSITAE, is confined in the wild to the northern hemisphere. It consists of 200 species of mostly herbaceous perennials and a few subshrubs. Its name is derived from that of the Greek god Achilles, who was believed to have utilized these plants for healing wounds.

Achilleas mostly have deeply once- to thrice-divided leaves, but in some kinds they are merely toothed. Their flower heads are ordinarily small and many occur together in dense, more or less flat-topped clusters, but sometimes are solitary. The blooms are white, pink, red, or yellow and have bisexual disk florets and female ray florets. The genus is closely related to *Anthemis*, from which it is distinguished by its fruits (commonly called seeds) being compressed and without distinct ribs. Most kinds have smaller and more numerous flower heads than *Anthemis*, but in some they are fairly large. Because *Achillea* is not as well understood botanically as could be wished, and because its species hybridize readily, correct identification is not always easy. Kinds other than those here discussed are likely to be found in botanical gardens and other special collections. But most of those are to be avoided by discriminating gardeners, for the genus *Achillea* is rich in weedy species with dingy flowers.

Common yarrow or milfoil (**A. millefolium**) is well known. It is a frequent inhabitant (one hesitates to say weed because in some swards it serves usefully) in lawns where, as the result of mowing, it forms dense mats of little ferny leaves that remain green through droughts long after its companion grasses have turned brown. This species is also familiar as a weed of roadsides and waste places and in its more colorful pink- and red-flowered varieties as a cultivated occupant of gardens. Yarrow was long used medicinally, principally for staunching bleeding but also as a tea to stem fevers, purify the blood, and dispel melancholy. In earlier days it was dedicated to Satan and was known by such names as Devil's-nettle and Devil's-plaything. Native to North America, Europe, and Asia, the common yarrow presents slightly different forms in different geographical areas, but these are not sufficiently distinct to be of horticultural interest. It is an erect, aromatic, deep-rooted, herbaceous perennial, up to 3 feet in height, and is thinly- to densely-furnished with silky or woolly hairs. Its leaves are pinnately-dissected into numerous fine segments and are distinctly fernlike. They are up to 6 inches long by 1 inch wide and bright green. Those on the upper parts of the stems are stalkless, the lower ones are stalked. Typically, the broad clusters of small flower heads are flat or flattish, but sometimes they are round-topped. Each little head has about five white or pinkish ray florets and is up to ⅓ inch across. Va-

Achillea millefolium

rieties of the common yarrow sometimes cultivated in flower gardens are *A. m.* 'Cerise Queen', *A. m.* 'Fire King', *A. m. kelwayi*, *A. m. rosea*, and *A. m. rubra*, all with pink or red blooms.

Achillea millefolium rubra

Tall, white-flowered achilleas include the sneezeweed (*A. ptarmica*), *A. sibirica*, and their varieties. These exceed 1 foot in height and have much-branched, erect stems. The leaves of *A. ptarmica*, a native of Europe, are linear, narrowed at their bases and pointed at their tips; they are shallowly toothed in contrast to those of the Asian *A. sibirica*, which are linear, at least six times as long as wide, and deeply-cleft into oblong divisions that are again toothed. Favored garden varieties are *A. ptarmica* 'Boule de Neige', *A. p.* 'The Pearl', *A. p.* 'Snowball', and *A. sibirica* 'Perry's White', all with double flowers. A kind similar to *A. ptarmica*, but with round-ended, blunt leaves that broaden at their bases and clasp the stem, is *A. lingulata*, a native of eastern Europe.

Dwarf, white-flowered kinds of merit are *A. clavennae* and *A. umbellata*, natives of Europe. Tufted plants, the former is about 6 inches tall, the latter somewhat shorter. Both have ovate, silvery-gray, pinnately-divided leaves. The basal ones of *A. clavennae* exceed 1½ inches in length and have segments comparatively widely spaced, those of *A. umbellata* usually are under 1 inch long with their divisions close together. Both have clusters of several daisy-like flower heads atop erect stems.

Achillea umbellata

Variety *A. u. argentea* has more silvery foliage than *A. umbellata*. Differing in that its leaves are not pinnate *A. ageratifolia*, of Greece, has silvery hairy leaves, toothed, often deeply so, and up to 1½ inches long.

Variety *A. a. aizoon*, sometimes misidentified as *Anthemis aizoon*, has toothless or only slightly-toothed leaves.

The principal tall yellow achilleas are the Caucasian *A. filipendulina* (syn. *A. eupatorium*), an unidentified species that travels in gardens under the misnomer *A. clypeolata*, and their varieties and hybrids. Typically, *A. filipendulina* is a stout, erect, leafy plant, 2½ to 5 feet in height, with linear, pinnately-lobed and toothed leaves, and flat or slightly convex, tight clusters, 5 inches or more in diameter, of numerous bright yellow flower heads. The plant cultivated as *A. clypeolata* is 1½ to 2 feet tall and has gray, pinnately-cut leaves with the divisions again lobed or toothed. Its bright yellow flower heads are crowded in clusters 2½ inches or less wide. Known in gardens as *A. taygetea*, although quite different from the botanical species of that name, an attractive hybrid between the garden plants called *A. clypeolata* and *A. millefolium* is commonly grown. It is 1½ to 2 feet tall and has gray, pinnately-divided leaves and clusters, 1½ to 2 inches across, of pale yellow flower heads. A group of excellent garden plants has arisen from crossing *A. clypeolata* (of gardens) with *A. filipendulina*. These bear fancy names such as 'Coronation Gold', 'Moonshine', and 'Gold Plate'. Variety *A.* 'Schwefelblute' (syn. *A.* 'Flowers of Sulphur') of unknown garden origin is 2 feet tall, has dull green, pinnately-lobed leaves and clusters of sulfur-yellow flower heads 1½ to 3 inches in diameter.

Yellow-flowered and low, *A. tomentosa* and *A. chrysocoma* deserve the serious attention of gardeners, especially rock gardeners. They are very similar, the chief technical differences being that the scales of the involucre (collar of bracts below the flower head) is distinctly margined with

Achillea filipendulina

Achillea taygetea of gardens

Achillea tomentosa

dark brown in *A. chrysocoma* and not in *A. tomentosa*; also the leaves of *A. chrysocoma* are more densely covered with silky hairs. Both are spreading, mat-forming plants with numerous small ferny leaves, twice-pinnately-divided and consisting of slender segments. Their flower heads are crowded into more or less flat-topped clusters. Variety *A. t. aurea* has flowers deeper yellow than is typical of the species, *A. t. nana* is very low. Similar, but with pale lemon-yellow blooms, *A. lewisii* (syn. *A.* 'King Edward') is a hybrid between *A. tomentosa* and *A. clavennae*. Another hybrid,

Achillea ageratifolia

A. kolbiana, has as parents *A. tomentosa* and *A. umbellata,* and is intermediate between them.

Garden and Landscape Uses. Common yarrow as a flowering plant legitimately belongs in herb gardens and collections of plants once used medicinally, and nowhere else. Its pink- and red-flowered varieties are appropriate for flower borders and semiwild landscapes. It should be mentioned that there is no better plant than the common yarrow (*A. millefolium*) for forming lawns on banks and other areas too dry for regular lawn grasses. When repeatedly mown it makes a fine sod that stands traffic well.

Other tall-growing achilleas deserve accommodation in plantings of herbaceous perennials and supply useful flowers for cutting. The dwarfs are admirable for rock gardens and similar places. All need full sun and prosper in well-drained soils. They are especially adaptable to sandy soil.

Cultivation. With the exception of double-flowered and other horticultural varieties, achilleas are easily raised from seeds sown in sandy, well-drained soil. All are readily increased by division in spring or early fall. Provided they have sharply drained soil and full sun no difficulties attend their cultivation and no special care is required. They abhor wet, stagnant soil.

ACHIMENANTHA (Achimen-ántha). This is the correct botanical name of plants previously known as *Eucodonopsis.* It belongs to hybrids between *Achimenes* and *Smithiantha* of the gesneria family GESNERIACEAE. The hybrid *A. naegelioides* (syn. *Eucodonopsis achimenoides*) is sometimes cultivated. Garden uses and cultivation are as for the parent genera.

ACHIMENES (Achímen-es). A renascence of interest among gesneriad fanciers has resulted in increased attention being given to *Achimenes,* a genus of the gesneria family GESNERIACEAE, that attained great popularity in the latter half of the nineteenth century and later was almost forgotten by gardeners. The group consists of fifty species, natives of the American tropics, and many hybrids. The meaning of the name is obscure. Hybrids between *Achimenes* and *Smithiantha* are named *Achimenantha.*

Achimenes belong to a small group of genera of the gesneria family that has scaly rhizomes. These worm- or caterpillar-like reproductive organs consist of a short piece of stem, with many closely-spaced scales that are modified leaves. They develop plentifully underground and sometimes above ground in the leaf axils or even among the flowers. Achimenes are non-hardy, deciduous, herbaceous perennials. They are mostly hairy and have twos, threes, or fours of generally toothed, short-stalked leaves; the leaves of the twos are equal to markedly different in size. The

Common yarrow as a lawn plant:
(a) Digging clumps from an established lawn

(b) Dividing clumps into small pieces

(c) Planting divisions about 6 inches apart

(d) The result, a close turf a year later

blooms occur singly, in pairs, or on several-flowered stalks from the leaf axils. They have a deeply five-lobed calyx from which emerges, straight or at an angle, the tubular to nearly bell-shaped corolla with five spreading lobes (petals). The base of the corolla tube may be swollen or developed as a spur. There are four stamens, their anthers joined as a square, and a long style terminated with a two-lobed, cup-shaped or mouth-shaped stigma. The ovary is surrounded by a cup-shaped disk. The fruits are capsules. Botanists group achimenes according to the forms of their stigmas. The plant sometimes called *A. tubiflora* is *Sinningia tubiflora.*

White flowers are borne by *A. longiflora alba* (identical with blue-flowered *A. longiflora* except for the color of its blooms). Species with predominantly white blooms include the following: *A. candida,* native from Mexico to Panama, has rather puny, creamy-white to sometimes pinkish flowers nearly ½ inch wide and slightly longer, patched with yellow, lined with red, flecked with reddish-brown. They have mouth-shaped stigmas. It has sprawling stems 6 inches to 1½ feet long and sharply-toothed leaves up to 2 to 2½ inches long by 1½ inches wide; those of the pairs are sometimes unequal in size. Blooms with large, white or lavender-tinged, fringed or toothed

petals and cup-shaped stigmas distinguish *A. glabrata* from all other achimenes discussed here. Up to 1½ feet tall, this Mexican native has hairless or only slightly hairy, toothed, lanceolate to ovate leaves up to 3 inches long by 1¼ inches wide. The flowers are solitary in the leaf axils, up to 2 inches long and about 1½ inches wide. A native of Guatemala, *A. misera* is 6 to 9 inches tall and has densely-hairy stems and pairs of shallowly-toothed, equal-sized leaves about 1 inch long by ¾ inch wide. Solitary or several together, the small white

Achimenes misera

flowers are hairy on their outsides. An identifying characteristic is the presence of three pits on the underside of the corolla tube corresponding with three small protrusions inside. The stigmas are mouth-shaped.

Blue-, lavender-, purple-, and violet-flowered sorts include the following: *A. ehrenbergii* (syn. *A. lanata*), of Mexico, has the stems and under surfaces of its foliage conspicuously clothed with white, woolly hairs. Up to 1½ feet tall, it has opposite, scallop-margined leaves up to 6 inches long and 3 inches wide. The nodding blooms, on white-woolly stalks, are solitary or paired in the leaf axils. They have a corolla about 1¾ inches long with a pouched or somewhat bell-shaped tube without a basal spur. The flower face is

Achimenes ehrenbergii

oblique to the tube and is up to 1½ inches across. The blooms, lavender with yellow or orange markings in the throat, have two-lobed stigmas. A variable native from Mexico to Panama, *A. longiflora* is hairy and 1½ to 2 feet tall. It has sharp-pointed, sharp-toothed, ovate leaves up to 5 inches long by up to 2½ inches wide, sometimes suffused with purple on their undersides.

Achimenes longiflora

They are opposite or in circles of three or four. The corolla, set erectly in the calyx, is up to 2½ inches long, has a slender,

scarcely-widening, spurless tube, and blue to violet-blue lobes (petals) of unequal size that spread to give a face very oblique to the corolla tube and 1¼ to 1¾ inches across. The stigma is two-lobed. Variety *A. l. major* has especially large, richly colored blooms. A handsome hybrid of *A. longiflora* is *A. andersonii*. It has blue flowers with cream-colored and yellow centers. *A. andrieuxii* in appearance suggests an African-violet. From 3 to 4 inches high, it has woolly stems and ovate leaves with 1-inch-long stalks and 4-inch-long blades. The

Achimenes andersonii

white-throated, violet, spurred blooms are ½ inch wide, and slightly over ½ inch long. It is native to Mexico. *A. cettoana* is a Mexican with reddish-brown, 1-foot-long, freely-branched stems. Its leaves, in circles of three or four, are linear-lanceolate, about 2½ inches long by ½ inch wide. The solitary violet to blue-violet blooms have corolla tubes 1 inch to 1½ inches long, deeply-notched petals, with a pale spot on the lower petal. *A. grandiflora* attains a height of 2 feet. Native to Mexico, it has opposite, sharply-pointed, toothed, ovate, somewhat hairy leaves 1½ to 6 inches in length by 1¼ to 3½ inches wide, pale or tinged red on their undersides. The violet-purple blooms, solitary from the leaf axils, have slender corolla tubes 1 inch to 1¾ inches long that angle from the calyx and have a short basal spur. The blooms, about 1½ inches across their faces, have two-lobed stigmas. *A. patens*, of Mexico, is easily identified by the long spurs of its flowers, which considerably exceed the sepals in length. From 6 inches to 1-foot tall, it has pointed, ovate-lanceolate to ovate, coarsely-toothed, hairy leaves 1 inch to 4½ inches long by up to 1½ inches wide, and those of each pair are somewhat different sizes. The solitary blooms have corollas with tubes ½ to ¾ inch long, scarcely widening from bottom to top and erupting at an angle from the calyx. They are reddish-violet and suffused in the throat with yellow sprinkled with violet. The face of the bloom, somewhat oblique to the corolla tube and approximately 1¼ inches across,

Achimenes andrieuxii

is violet. The petals are minutely-toothed. The stigma is two-lobed.

Flowers of red, orange, and related hues are borne by the following achimenes: *A. antirrhina* (syn. *A. atrosanguinea*), native to Mexico, has downy stems 1 foot to 1½ feet in height and pairs of somewhat unequal-sized, moderately-long-stalked, sharply-toothed, oblong-ovate leaves with blades up to 2½ inches long by 1½ inches wide.

Achimenes antirrhina

The solitary blooms are rich reddish-orange with red dots in their orange to yellow throats. The corollas have funnel-shaped tubes, are 1½ inches long, and have spreading petals. The face of the bloom is about 1 inch wide. The stigmas are mouth-shaped. *A. erecta* (syn. *A. coc-*

Achimenes erecta

cinea) a native of Jamaica and from Mexico to Peru, is 6 inches to 18 inches tall. It has ovate to elliptic, few-toothed leaves, up to 2½ inches long by 1¼ inches wide, but often smaller, in twos or threes. The brilliant red to rose-red blooms have spurless corollas with a narrowly-cylindrical tube emerging straight from the calyx, ½ to ¾ inch long. The blooms are about ½ inch across. They have a two-lobed stigma. *A. skinneri* (syn. *A. hirsuta*), endemic to Guatemala and perhaps southern Mexico, is 1 foot to 3 feet tall. It has opposite, long-pointed, ovate leaves 1¾ to somewhat more than 3 inches long by up to 2¾ inches wide, purplish on their undersides, those of each pair approximately equal in size, hairy, and sharply-toothed. The flowers are borne singly or in pairs on stalks with bracts. Their rose-pink corolla tubes, yellowish in their throats and inserted obliquely in the calyx, are about 1½ inches long, somewhat swollen at the base, and expanding upward. The nearly symmetrical face of the bloom, of rounded, rosy-lavender to rose-pink, minutely-toothed petals is about 1 inch across. The stigma is two-lobed.

Yellow-flowered *A. flava* has more or less trailing stems up to 1½ feet in length and brief-stalked, pointed, coarsely-toothed, ovate leaves, those of each pair are unequal in size, the largest being up to 3 inches long by 1½ inches wide. They are hairy on the veins beneath. The bright yellow flowers with maroon dots inside are four or fewer on a stem. They are about ¾ inch long by about ½ inch wide. It is a native of Mexico.

Garden varieties and hybrids include many lovely kinds, some scarcely differing from natural species, others the exact ancestry of which is neither recorded nor apparent. Available kinds are listed and described in the catalogs of specialist dealers. They include, with white flowers, 'Ambroise Verschaffelt', 'Dainty Queen', and

Achimenes flava

'Margarita'. With pink blooms, 'Adele Delahaute', 'Little Beauty', and 'Peach Blossom'. With blue flowers, 'Galatea' and 'Valse Bleu'. With purple flowers, 'Masterpiece', 'Mauve Queen', and 'Purple King'. With lavender to magenta blooms, 'Camillo Brozzonii', 'Loveliness', and 'Vivid'; with red or orange-red flowers, 'Burnt Orange', 'Crimson Glory', and 'Master Ingram' (syn. 'Cardinal Velvet').

Garden Uses. Achimenes are delightful for greenhouses and, where the atmosphere is not too arid, considerable success is had with them in windows. Amateurs also cultivate them with more or less success under artificial lights. They may be accommodated in pots, pans (shallow pots), and hanging baskets.

Cultivation. Start achimenes into growth in successive batches from February to May to ensure a long season of bloom. First shake the rhizomes free from the old soil in which they have been dry and dormant. Separate them and space them 1 inch apart in flats or pans containing approximately 2 inches of peat moss or vermiculite. Cover them to a depth of about ½ inch with the same material. Water, and

place in a temperature of 65 to 70°F. As soon as new shoots are 2 inches tall, transplant into the receptacles in which they are to bloom. These may be pots or pans (shallow pots) 6 to 8 inches in diameter or smaller containers for weak growers. Or they may be transplanted to hanging baskets. Allow six plants to a 6-inch pot or pan, about ten to one 8 inches across. Use fertile, porous, nourishing soil with very generous proportions of leaf mold, rich compost, or peat moss. See that good drainage is provided. Do not pack the soil too much. It should yield a little when pressed firmly with the fingers. Put the planted containers in a greenhouse or an equivalent place where the night temperature is 60 to 65°F, and by day is five to ten or even fifteen degrees higher depending upon the brightness of the weather.

Water cautiously at first, and then more freely as growth develops and roots penetrate the soil. It is important to maintain a humid atmosphere, and experience amply demonstrates that these plants do better near the glass of the greenhouse than when far from it. Pinching out the tips of the shoots when they are 3 or 4 inches high causes branching and makes for more bushy specimens furnished to their bases with foliage. Neat staking is required. After the containers are fairly well filled with roots, begin a program of applying dilute liquid fertilizer, first at biweekly intervals, later more frequently. In summer airy, but not drafty, dry conditions are appreciated and until blooms appear daily misting the foliage with water is beneficial. Some shade from strong sun is needed but not more than necessary to keep the foliage from yellowing or scorching.

After blooming is over gradually dry the plants off in preparation for dormancy by gradually increasing the intervals between waterings and finally withholding water entirely. Then turn the pots or pans on their sides under a greenhouse bench or

Start achimenes into new growth at the end of their resting season: (a) Remove the plants from their pots and shake them free of soil

(b) Separate the rhizomes and plant them, whole or broken into pieces, in peat moss or vermiculite

(c) When new shoots are 2 inches tall transplant to the containers in which the plants are to bloom

store them elsewhere in a temperature of 50 to 55°F, where they can be kept dry until the following late winter or spring. Propagation of achimenes is easy by breaking the rhizomes into small pieces for planting, by summer cuttings, and by seeds. It is even possible to rub the scales off tubers and sow them like seeds. Each will give a new plant identical with the parent.

ACHLYS (Àch-lys)—Deer Foot or Vanilla Leaf. One of the two species of *Achlys* of the barberry family BERBERIDACEAE is a native from California to British Columbia, the other a native of Japan. They are perennial herbaceous plants with branching, creeping rootstocks and long-stalked leaves each of three leaflets. Their insignificant flowers, in short, dense spikes, are bisexual and without sepals or petals. They have six to thirteen long-stalked stamens, and a stalkless, broad stigma. The name is that of *Achlys*, the Greek god of the night.

The American species, the deer foot or vanilla leaf (*A. triphylla*), is a hairless plant with a solitary, nearly round leaf up to 1 foot in height that has a stalk approximately as long as the blade, and stalkless, fan-shaped, coarsely-toothed leaflets 2 to 6 inches long. The flower spikes are 1 inch to 2 inches long. The fruits are reddish. This plant is a native of moist woodlands.

Garden Uses and Cultivation. The deer foot is sometimes planted in woodland gardens and rock gardens and is appropriate for native plant gardens. It is best accommodated in dampish woodsy soil where it receives some shade. Propagation is by seeds and careful division of the rootstocks in early spring.

ACHRAS. The species formerly named *Achras sapota* is *Manilkara zapota*, the one formerly named *A. zapota* is *Pouteria mammosa*.

ACHYRANTHES. For plants cultivated under this name see Alternanthera and Iresine.

ACID AND ALKALINE SOILS. Soils are designated as acid, neutral, or alkaline depending upon their hydrogen ion concentration. This is expressed in terms of pH on a scale ranging from pH 0, the most acid, to pH 14, the most alkaline. The neutral point is pH 7. Practically no plants will grow in soil under pH 3.5 or over pH 9. Most have a decidedly more restricted range of tolerance. For practical purposes, pH 5.5 is considered strongly acid, pH 6 medium acid, pH 6.5 slightly acid, pH 7.5 slightly alkaline, pH 8 alkaline, and pH 8.5 strongly alkaline. The vast majority of garden plants succeed in slightly acid to slightly alkaline soils. A lesser number, especially many belonging in the heath family ERICACEAE require acid soil for their well-being; soil with a pH range of 4.5 to

5.5 is usually best. Examples are blueberries, heathers, heaths, mountain-laurel, and rhododendrons including azaleas, *Arctostaphylos, Enkianthus,* and *Pieris.* Some plants, notably those that grow as natives in limestone regions, alkali deserts, and salt marshes, require alkalinity and are intolerant of acidity. These, except for certain rock garden plants such as saxifragas, are less commonly cultivated outside their native regions and regions similar to them than are acid soil plants. Conditions under which plants grow in the wild show their tolerance of a particular pH range but do not necessarily indicate their preference for it. Species often grow where they do because they are unable to meet the competition of more successful kinds occupying areas that otherwise would be acceptable. Gardeners eliminate competition by weeding and in other ways, securing the locations for the exclusive use of the plants they want to grow. As a result many plants are satisfied under cultivation with soils distinctly different in acidity and other characteristics from those they are restricted to as wildlings.

Except for the common practice of liming to decrease acidity (old-time gardeners called it sweetening the soil), it is usually impractible to alter the pH of the soil over large tracts. This is, however, often accomplished successfully in small, local areas such as parts of rock gardens, bog gardens, native plant gardens, and heather gardens, and for pot plants. In the main when dealing with areas of considerable size it is more satisfactory and surely simpler to select plants adapted to the land than to undertake to modify the soil to suit finicky growers.

The use of lime to decrease acidity or achieve alkalinity is discussed under Lime and Liming. Alkalinity can be decreased and acidity increased by draining and leaching, as is done with alkali soils in the West, by adding large amounts of organic matter such as peat moss and oak leaf mold that have a fairly low pH, and by applying aluminum sulfate or agricultural sulfur. The amounts of these needed to effect a given change depend on the character of the soil. Less is necessary on sandy soil, more on clayey ones, than on medium loams. To illustrate, a sandy soil of pH 6 will be reduced to approximately pH 5 by the application of one-half pound of aluminum sulfate to 10 square feet. To achieve the same result on a loamy soil takes twice as heavy an application, on a clay soil one up to seven times as heavy. Sulfur, which acts more slowly than aluminum sulfate, is generally preferred. This because the latter, used in considerable amounts, results in a buildup in the soil of soluble aluminum in quantities toxic to plants. Moreover, the amount of sulfur needed to achieve the same result is one-third to one-half that of aluminum sulfate.

Installing special beds of acid soil for particular plants is often more practicable in small areas, such as parts of rock gardens, than attempting to modify the existing soil. This is particularly true where the native soil is alkaline or clayey. To make such beds, excavate to a depth of 8 inches or more. Make sure the bottoms of the excavations drain freely. If they do not the beds will act as basins to hold water, some of which may seep in from adjacent land and in alkaline areas neutralize acidity. Fill the excavations with a mixture consisting of acid peat moss, leaf mold, and nonalkaline, preferably sandy soil. Such soil is likely to be obtainable from under a well-established stand of pines or other trees. If it is not sandy, add coarse sand to the mixture. Usually there is little lateral movement of water in reasonably level ground beds made in the way described, and where the surrounding soil is not more than slightly alkaline, the beds are likely to retain their character for a considerable time. In more definitely alkaline regions it is better to have the beds raised 8 inches to 1 foot above the level of the surrounding soil. In any case changes may occur, and almost surely will, if the subsurface or adjacent soil is medium to strongly alkaline, and so occasional tests must be made to check the pH. Be careful not to use alkaline water for watering plants in acid-soil beds or if you must do so modify it before use by adding small amounts of white vinegar or other acid, or counteract its alkalizing effect by occasional applications of sulfur to the soil.

To determine the pH values of soils simple tests are available. You may have these done through your County Cooperative Extension Service or you can do them yourself with one of the testing kits sold by garden supply dealers. If you want to maintain a soil pH different from that of the surrounding area repeat the test from time to time to detect changes that indicate the need for further application of a corrective agent.

It cannot be too strongly emphasized that gardeners in the past have tended to overemphasize the importance of soil pH, to the extent that a wide variety of disappointments and failures due to other causes were blamed on a too acid or too alkaline condition. This in turn frequently fostered a belief that the one key to success was to change the pH, and other needed procedures were neglected.

ACIDANTHERA (Acid-anthèra). By some botanists included in nearly related *Gladiolus,* from which it chiefly differs in the perianth tube of the flower being straight or nearly so instead of curved, *Acidanthera* of the iris family IRIDACEAE consists of somewhat more than thirty species and is native from tropical Africa to South Africa. Its name, derived from the Greek *akis,* a point, and *anthera*, an anther, has obvious meaning.

These plants, like gladioluses, have bulblike organs called corms and more or less sword-shaped leaves. The flowers, in spikes, have a perianth with a long, slender tube and six nearly equal lobes commonly called petals, although more correctly they are tepals. There are three stamens and a three-branched style. The fruits are capsules.

A native of Ethiopia, Tanzania, and Malawi, *A. bicolor* (syn. *Gladiolus callianthus*) is about 2 feet tall and has mostly three or four linear leaves 6 inches to 1¼ feet long. Its loose flower spikes of up to twelve very fragrant, creamy-white blooms are conspicuously blotched with blackish-purple on the bases of their three lower petals. Like great butterflies, they are 2½ to 3 inches in diameter and have perianth tubes 3 to 4½ inches long. Variety *A. b. murieliae* is more robust and up to 3 feet or more tall; it has blooms that may exceed 4 inches in diameter and perianth tubes 4 to 5½ inches long. Variety *A. b.* 'Zwanenberg' is similar to *A. b. murieliae*, but blooms about three weeks earlier.

Garden and Landscape Uses and Cultivation. These are as for *Gladiolus*.

Acidanthera bicolor

ACINETA (Acin-èta). Fifteen species compose this genus of the orchid family Orchidaceae. Native from Mexico to northern South America, *Acineta* is allied to *Peristeria*. The name, alluding to the lips of the flowers, comes from the Greek *akinetos*, not moving.

Acinetas are robust evergreens or partial evergreens that in the wild commonly perch on trees (epiphytes) and more rarely on rocks. They have quite large, strongly vertically furrowed, egg-shaped to cylindrical pseudobulbs, each surmounted with two, three, or sometimes four, long leaves. From the bases of the pseudobulbs in due season hang long, thick, leafless stalks with, at their ends, crowded racemes of beautiful, often fragrant, more or less

cupped, fleshy blooms that look somewhat like those of stanhopeas. They never open fully.

The largest flowered kind, its blooms up to 3 inches long or longer, and in racemes with stems 2 feet or so in length, is *A. superba*. It has pseudobulbs sometimes 5 inches long, and leaves 1½ to 2 feet in length by about 2¾ inches wide. Heavily fragrant, the flowers have red-spotted yellowish, reddish, or brown sepals and petals, and a pouched, three-lobed, yellow to brown lip that is spotted purple, which has a two-lobed, purple-black projection from a callus on its surface. Similar in habit, *A. chrysantha* has flowers 2 inches or a little more in width, with generally bright yellow sepals, red-spotted yellow petals, and a golden-yellow three-lobed lip, marked reddish-brown or red, which has an erect, blunt, fleshy horn near its base. The smaller *A. barkeri* has fragrant blooms about 1½ inches in diameter usually ten to fifteen, but sometimes twenty or more in each raceme. They are bright yellow with the bases of the petals commonly sparingly spotted with red, and the three-lobed lip with a red patch. The middle lobe of the lip is much smaller than the two incurving ones that flank it.

Garden Uses and Cultivation. Because these beautiful orchids send their flower stems downward from the bottoms of the pseudobulbs they are completely unsuited for pot cultivation. Suspended open baskets that permit the stalks to grow between the slats of their bottoms are the best containers, and when planting no impediments such as crocks must be positioned

where they can impede the lengthening flower stems. The general cultivation needed is that appropriate for stanhopeas. Plenty of warmth and humidity is appropriate during the season of active growth, but following the full development and maturing of the new pseudobulbs a decided rest where the night temperature is about 60°F and, by day only moderately higher, is required. During the resting season, which may last for about a month, the soil is kept decidedly drier than at other times, but never completely dry. See *Orchids* for further information.

Acineta, unidentified species

Acineta, unidentified species

ACINOS (Ácin-os). This genus of ten species has at times been included in the nearly related *Calamintha* and *Satureja*. It differs from the former in that its flowers have curved calyx tubes pouched at their bases, from the latter in that the calyx tubes are tubular and thirteen-veined rather than bell-shaped and ten-veined. Its members are aromatic annuals, herbaceous perennials, and subshrubs of the mint family LABIATAE. The name *Acinos* is an adaptation of the Greek *akinos,* for a plant of this genus.

Acinoses have opposite, toothed leaves, and axillary clusters of small, asymmetrical, tubular flowers that have two-lipped calyxes, and tubular two-lipped corollas with a three-lobed lower lip. There are four stamens. The fruits are of four seedlike nutlets. The genus inhabits Europe, the Mediterranean region, and temperate Asia.

Except that *A. alpinus* (syns. *Satureja alpina*, *Calamintha alpina*) is perennial and woodier than the annual *A. thymoides* (syns. *A. arvensis*, *Satureja acinos*, *Calamintha acinos*) these species are much alike. They are 6 to 8 inches tall, much-branched, and have ovate or elliptic leaves about ½ inch long. Their flowers are purple-blue; those of *A. alpinus* have corolla tubes at least two-and-one-half times as long as the calyxes; those of *A. thymoides* have corolla tubes not more than twice the lengths of the calyxes. The lower lips of the corollas are deeply-cleft, the upper have three very small teeth. All are natives of Europe, with *A. thymoides* naturalized in North America.

Garden Uses and Cultivation. Appropriate for herb gardens, rock gardens and similar developments, these plants grow without difficulty in well-drained, not too fertile soils, in full sun. Light shearing after flowering, unless seeds are wanted, may be done to keep the plants shapely. Propagation is very easy by seeds, and in the case of the hardy perennial *A. alpinus* by summer cuttings in a shaded cold frame or cool greenhouse propagating bed.

ACIPHYLLA (Aci-phýlla). The genus *Aciphylla* of the carrot family UMBELLIFERAE is chiefly confined in the wild to New Zealand, but also represented in Australia. The name is from the Greek *akis*, a point, and *phyllon*, a leaf, and alludes to the formidably pointed leaves. The group consists of thirty-five species of herbaceous perennials mostly with rosettes of stiff, once-, twice- or thrice-pinnate leaves with sheathing bases. The flowers, in umbels arranged in long erect spikes or panicles, are carried well above the foliage. Individual plants have all male flowers or mostly females with a few males interspersed. The Maoris obtained a fragrant gum, which they greatly esteemed, from *A. squarrosa*.

In New Zealand these plants are called spaniards. One, *A. colensoi*, attains a height in bloom of 2 to 8 feet and has spiny leaves 1 foot to 2 feet long and ½ to ¾ inch wide that form yucca-like hemispheres of swordlike blades. The umbels of small, yellowish flowers are in narrow leafy racemes. The leaves of *A. squarrosa*, another New Zealander, are not more than ⅛ inch wide and the plant is smaller than *A. colensoi*, although its flower spikes may attain as great a height. Its blooms are whitish. Akin to *A. squarrosa*, the New Zealander *A. glaucescens* forms a tussock of glaucous or grayish-green, sharp-pointed, twice- or thrice-pinnate leaves from 1 foot to 3 feet or more long, with fine-toothed margins. The flowering stalks are 3 to 6 feet tall. Not exceeding 1½ feet in height, *A. monroi* has less rigid leaves than the aciphyllas so far mentioned and its umbels of flowers are in loose, broad panicles. They are yellowish. It is a native of alpine and subalpine places in the South Island of New Zealand.

Aciphylla glaucescens

Garden and Landscape Uses and Cultivation. Aciphyllas are hardy only where winters are mild. Undoubtedly their preference is for cool summers. Very well-drained, gritty soil with reasonable belowground moisture, and a sunny location, are likely the best growing conditions. Propagation is by seed.

ACKAMA (Ack-àma)—Makamaka. Three species of small trees, one each native of New Zealand, Australia, and New Guinea, are the only members of *Ackama* of the cunonia family CUNONIACEAE. It is closely related to *Weinmannia*, but differs in having its flowers in panicles instead of racemes and in other details. The derivation of the name is unknown.

Called makamaka in its native New Zealand, *A. rosaefolia* is an attractive tree up to 40 feet tall. Its minute, unisexual flowers, with many occurring together in much-branched panicles, make no particular show, but its foliage is decidedly attractive. The leaves, 3 to 10 inches in length, have three to eight pairs of nar-rowly-oblong to elliptic, stalkless or shortly-stalked, toothed leaves with large and conspicuous appendages (stipules) at their bases. This plant, sometimes planted in southern California and other essentially frost-free climates, is propagated by seeds and cuttings. It seems to find any ordinary, well-drained garden soil agreeable.

ACMENA (Ac-mèna)—Lillypilly. By some botanists *Acmena* is included in *Eugenia*, but the consensus is that it should be treated as a separate genus. It consists of a dozen or more species of nonhardy trees, or perhaps sometimes shrubs, wild from southern China, to Malaysia, the Philippine Islands, and Australia, and belongs in the myrtle family MYRTACEAE. Its members strongly resemble small-flowered species of *Syzygium*, from which they differ in the technical details of their anthers and fruits.

Acmenas have opposite, undivided, aromatic leaves. Their small flowers have four each sepals and tiny petals, the latter unite into a cap that drops when the blooms open. There are numerous, radiating, white to pink stamens, and one style. The fruits are globose, one-seeded berries with a conspicuous depressed scar left by the fallen calyx lobes at their apexes.

The lillipilly (*A. smithii* syns. *A. floribunda*, *Eugenia elliptica*), a native of Australia, is an evergreen tree from 60 to 100 feet tall. It has glossy, ovate to oblong-lanceolate, short-stalked leaves 1½ to 3½ inches long by one-third to one-half as wide. The fuzzy-looking white flowers are in terminal clusters 2 to 4 inches wide. Purple, or purple and white, the fruits, ¼ to ½ inch in diameter, are edible.

Acmena smithii

Garden and Landscape Uses and Cultivation. The lillipilly is a good ornamental for warm, essentially frostless climates, interesting because of its excellent foliage as well as for its displays of flowers and fruits. It responds to fertile, reasonably moist soil and sunny locations, but will stand part-day shade. Propagation is by seeds and by cuttings made from firm, but not hard shoots, planted in a greenhouse propagating bench.

ACNISTUS (Ac-nístus)—Wild-Tree-Tobacco. The genus *Acnistus* of the nightshade family SOLANACEAE is a native of tropical America. One of its fifty species is planted in Florida and other warm-climate areas as an ornamental. The derivation of the name is not known.

Acnistuses have alternate, undivided, lobeless and toothless leaves, and smallish, stalked blooms in axillary, stalkless clusters. The flowers have five-toothed calyxes, and narrowly-bell-shaped, usually five-lobed, corollas. The stamens generally number five. There is a slender style tipped with a slightly two-lobed stigma. The fruits are nearly spherical, many-seeded berries.

A fast-growing evergreen tree up to 30 feet in height, *A. arborescens* is a native of Central America and tropical South America. It has short-stalked, elliptic to elliptic-ovate leaves 2 to 7 inches long borne chiefly toward the ends of the shoots. The flower clusters come mostly from parts of the stems just below the foliage. The blooms have greenish-white corollas about ½ inch long and protruding stamens. They are succeeded by ½-inch-wide yellow or orange-yellow berries, which are attractive to birds.

Garden and Landscape Uses and Cultivation. The wild-tree-tobacco is suitable for adding interest and variety to plantings. It favors open locations and is believed to prefer rather heavy (somewhat clayey) soil. Seeds and cuttings are the means of propagation.

ACOELORRHAPHE (Acoelorrhà-phe). The Everglade palm or silver-saw palm seems to be the only one of this genus of possibly eight species of American palms cultivated. It is a native of southern Florida and Cuba and other West Indian islands and of Central America from Mexico to Honduras. In Florida it frequently inhabits the banks of slightly saline streams. The name *Acoelorrphaphe*, from the Greek *a*, without, *koilos*, hollow, and possibly *rhapis*, a needle, is not of obvious application. The genus belongs in the palm family PALMAE.

The everglade palm (*A. wrightii* syn. *Paurotis wrightii*) forms a clump of several to many erect, slender, bamboo-like stems up to 40 feet tall and is more or less clothed with old leaf bases, and stiff, almost round leaves 2 to 3 feet or sometimes more in diameter. The leaves are light glossy green above, silvery beneath, and divided to below their middles into as many as fifty narrow, bilobed segments. Their stalks are furnished with hooked, yellow-brown teeth. In bloom this palm is quite beautiful. It has many long, slender, erect or arching flower clusters carried well above the foliage. The pale green branches of the clusters are clothed with short hairs and at their bases are enclosed in tubular light green sheaths. The flowers are in threes. The globose, shining black fruits are ¼ to almost ½ inch in diameter.

Garden and Landscape Uses. One of the most attractive native American palms, the everglade palm is well adapted for decorative landscape planting. A special virtue is its tolerance of brackish water. At its best it presents a handsome mass of dense foliage from the ground up to a height of 20 to 40 feet that makes an excellent background or screen. It is also effective in isolated clumps on lawns. This palm thrives in sun or part-shade and is suitable for growing in greenhouses in pots or tubs.

Cultivation. A rich, moist to almost wet soil suits the everglade palm best. In greenhouses it succeeds where a minimum winter night temperature of 55°F is maintained with a rise of five or ten degrees during the day permitted. At other seasons the minimum night temperature may be higher. Indoors a humid atmosphere and shade from strong summer sun are necessary. From spring through fall watering should be copious, but rather less water is needed in winter. Well-rooted specimens benefit from regular applications of dilute liquid fertilizer from spring through fall. It is important that the containers be well drained and the soil porous. Propagation can be by very carefully dividing the plants, but recovery from the operation is uncertain and slow and a far better method is to rely upon fresh seeds sown in sandy, peaty soil in a temperature of 75 to 80°F. For further information see Palms.

ACOKANTHERA (Acok-ánthera)—Bushman's Poison, Winter Sweet. Some botanists include this genus of the dogbane family APOCYNACEAE in the closely related *Carissa*. Considered separately *Acokanthera* consists of fifteen species of shrubs and small trees of Africa and Arabia differing from *Carissa* in the clusters of flowers being truly lateral, in the stamens being joined to the corolla tube near its top, and in their anthers being often protruded. A most important difference is that carissas are benign plants, whereas acokantheras contain highly toxic milky sap. The sap of some acokantheras has been used as arrow poisons. The name, alluding to the pointed anthers, derives from the Greek *akok*, a point, and *anthera*, anther.

Acokantheras have opposite, leathery leaves and in clusters from the leaf axils small, white to pinkish fragrant flowers. Each has four or five sepals, a corolla with a slender tube and four or five spreading lobes (petals) overlapping to the left. There are four or five stamens. The fruits are technically berries.

Acokanthera oblongifolia

The winter sweet (*A. oblongifolia* syn. *Carissa spectabilis*) and the Bushman's poison (*A. oppositifolia* syn. *Carissa acokanthera*) both have ovate to ovate-ellipitic leaves up to 4 or 5 inches long by, in *A. oppositifolia*, up to 2 inches wide; those of *A. oblongifolia* are narrower. The many-flowered, flattish-topped clusters of white or pinkish, sweetly fragrant flowers are borne freely mostly at the ends of the shoots in the winter sweet; they are more elongated and chiefly from the axils of the leaves in Bushman's poison. Individual blooms of winter sweet are about ¾ inch wide; those of the Bushman's poison about ½ inch wide. The corolla tube is about equal in length to the diameter of the bloom. The purplish-black, one-seeded berries are about 1 inch long; those of the winter sweet are ellipsoid, those of the Bushman's poison spherical.

Acokanthera oppositifolia

Garden and Landscape Uses and Cultivation. These are highly effective ornamentals for outdoor cultivation in warm, essentially frost-free climates and in conservatories and greenhouses. They succeed in sun or part-day shade in ordinary well-drained soils and require no special care. In greenhouses winter night temperatures of 50 to 55°F are satisfactory with an increase, depending upon the brightness of the weather, of five to fifteen degrees by day. A moderately humid atmosphere is desirable. Pruning to shape and repotting when needed should receive attention in late winter or early spring. Propagation is easy by seeds and cuttings.

ACONITE or Monkshood. See Aconitum. For winter-aconite see Eranthis.

ACONITUM (Acon-ìtum)—Aconite, Monkshood, Wolfsbane. Aconites, monkshoods, or wolfsbanes are old-fashioned, hardy herbaceous perennials beloved for their summer and fall displays of bloom. Although casual inspection would scarcely lead one to suppose so, they belong in the buttercup family RANUNCULACEAE. The name is an ancient classical Greek one for some poisonous plant. In the wild *Aconitum* is restricted to temperate parts of the northern hemisphere. It is a complex entity containing probably more than 100 species. Besides its attractiveness as a source of decoratives *Aconitum* includes species from which are obtained important drugs. Many kinds contain virulent poisonous alkaloids, which are concentrated in their roots. The chief source of medicinal aconite is *A. napellus*. Decoctions of this species were given criminals in ancient times.

Aconites are clump-forming plants, with either much-branched perennial roots or thick, carrot- or turnip-shaped tuberous ones renewed each year at the ends of slender branches from the main tubers. The stems are rigid and erect or lax, more or less trailing, and vinelike. Usually they are branched in their upper parts. The leaves are alternate, palmately (in the fashion of the fingers of a wide-spread hand) veined, and usually lobed and toothed. In racemes or raceme-like panicles, the markedly asymmetrical flowers are very distinctive. Their showiest parts are petal-like sepals, of which there are five. The uppermost and biggest, forms a tall helmet or hood. There are two lateral, round- to kidney-shaped ones and a lower pair, narrower and less conspicuous. Beneath the hood are two small, spurlike petals, and there are sometimes up to three other minute ones. The stamens are numerous. There are two to five pistils that develop into podlike seed vessels called follicles. All kinds exhibit much variation, and many relatively minor variants have been described as species. The modern tendency is to group these into fewer and more easily recognizable entities.

Erect, rigid, few-branched or branchless stems, thickish, leathery leaves, and rich blue-purple blooms with sometimes white interiors, borne in fall, characterize *A. carmichaelli,* a native of China. It is 2 to 5 feet tall or sometimes taller, and has leaves with roundish blades, 2 to 6 inches wide, and cleft nearly, but not quite to their

bases into three primary lobes, each usually lobed and toothed. The blooms are crowded in wandlike panicles up to 8 inches long, with sometimes short branches. They have broad, rounded helmets approximately 1 inch tall, and hairless stamens. This species is often grown as *A. fischeri.* The Asian species to which that name rightly belongs does not seem to be cultivated. The plant known to gardeners as *A. wilsonii* is a tall variant of *A. carmichaelii,* which has looser panicles of blooms. Its correct name is *A. c. wilsonii.*

Leaves divided completely to their bases distinguish **A. napellus** and **A. variegatum** from *A. carmichaelii.* Both are highly variable natives of Europe, the first is naturalized in North America. They differ in the helmets of the flowers of *A. napellus* being usually broader than tall, the reverse being generally true of *A. variegatum,* and in the seeds of the former being winged on three angles, but not on their sides, whereas those of the latter are winged on only one angle and have transverse wings on their sides. Erect, with leafy stems 3 to 4 feet tall and pubescent in their upper parts, *A. napellus* has slightly hairy leaves, 2 to 4 inches across, divided into three primary divisions that are three-lobed and toothed. The flowering portion of the stem is often much-branched and has its terminal portion distinctly longer than the laterals. The many blooms are in crowded racemes up to 6 inches long or sometimes longer. They are violet or blue, pubescent in their outsides, and have hemispherical helmets about ¾ inch tall. The fruits are usually of three follicles. The stems of *A. variegatum* are 3 to 4½ feet tall, slender, and hairless and usually freely-branched above. The leaves, from 2 to 4½ inches wide, are cleft into five to seven broad, lobed, and toothed segments. The flower-bearing portion of the stem is nearly always loosely branched, with the terminal part usually not longer than the laterals. The blooms, blue, white, or variegated, occur few together in the

Aconitum napellus

racemes, and have helmets, twice as tall as wide, ½ to ¾ inch high.

A popular hybrid between *A. napellus* and *A. variegatum* is **A. bicolor** (syn. *A. stoerkianum*). This has flowers similar to those of its first-named parent, and foliage similar to that of the second. It originated in Europe, and does not produce viable seeds. About 3 feet in height and practically hairless, it has leaves 2 to 4 inches wide, cleft to their bases into five- to seven-lobed, toothed divisions. The flowering portions of the stem have short, ascending branches with few-flowered racemes of blooms, hairless on their outsides, often white and purple, and with strongly forward-arching helmets 1 inch tall.

The stems of **A. henryi** are slender in their upper parts and often semitwining, and much more flexuous than those of the aconites treated above. Its leaves, which generally resemble those of *A. carmichaelii,* but are thinner, are cleft nearly or quite to their bases into three to five major divisions. Its blooms are similar to those of *A. carmichaelii,* but more loosely disposed, and appear in summer rather than fall. This species and slight variants of it are

Aconitum carmichaelii

Aconitum carmichaelii

often grown as *A. autumnale, A. californicum,* and *A. napellus* 'Spark's Variety'. It has stems 3 to 6 feet tall, branching freely above, and leaves 2 to 6 inches wide and rounded in outline. Its dark bluish-purple flowers, with helmets ¾ to 1 inch long, are nearly or quite hairless on their outsides.

The eastern North American *A. uncinatum* is a weak-stemmed semiclimber 2 to 5 feet tall. Its many leaves, rounded to kidney-shaped in outline, and slashed nearly to their bases into generally three, but sometimes five major divisions, are mostly lobed and toothed. They are 2 to 4½ inches wide. The rich blue flowers, with helmets about ¾ inch tall, and slightly longer, have pubescent stalks, and occur few together in short terminal and lateral racemes. Variety *A. u. acutidens,* more commonly cultivated than the species, has the lobes of its leaves more distinctly wedge-shaped at their bases and with more pointed lobes and teeth.

Native from the Dakotas to British Columbia and California, *A. columbianum* is 1 foot to 5 feet tall. Its usually rigid, erect stems are sometimes weak and semiclimbing or trailing. Its thin leaves are deeply-cleft, not quite to their bases, into usually five, but sometimes three, lobed and pointed-toothed divisions. In outline they are more or less five-sided and are 2 to 5 inches across. The stalks that carry the purplish to blue blooms, are pubescent. The hoods, which are taller than they are wide, are up to 1 inch long. This is a very variable species.

Yellow- or yellowish-flowered aconites are less popular than the blue- and purple-flowered aconites, chiefly because their colors are not clear, and they are less ornamental. Two Europeans, both with scaly, bulblike roots, are occasionally grown. The specific designation of *A. vulparia,* derived from the Latin *vulpes,* a fox, alludes to its former use for poisoning foxes and wolves. In gardens it is sometimes misidentified as *A. lycoctonum* (syn. *A. septentrionale*), which usually has blue, rarely yellow, blooms, and does not appear to be cultivated. With erect stems frequently branched in their flowering parts., **A. vulparia** is 2 to 6 feet

tall. Its roundish or roundish-kidney-shaped leaves are slashed into five to nine divisions, three-lobed at their ends, and toothed. Their upper sides are dark green and hairless; they are paler beneath. The leafstalks and veins beneath are hairy. The basal leaves are long-stalked and up to 9 inches across, upward the leaves become gradually smaller and the lengths of their stalks diminish. The pale yellow flowers, in rather crowded, terminal, spikelike racemes, have round-topped, cylindrical helmets narrowed at their middles; they are about ¾ inch tall. The sepals do not persist about the young fruits, which consist of three little podlike follicles.

Very finely divided foliage distinguishes the pale yellow-flowered *A. anthora* from the aconites considered here. It has erect stems 1 foot to 3 feet tall and leaves divided to their bases into five to seven parts, deeply-once- and twice-cleft into very narrow, linear segments. The leaves are roundish in outline. The lowest ones are long-stalked and up to 6 inches across; above they are gradually reduced in size and stalk length. The flowers, in spikelike racemes, have rounded helmets about ¾ inch long with a short visor-like projection. The sepals are persistent around the fruits, which consist of five little pods (follicles).

Garden and Landscape Uses. The cultivated aconites are excellent furnishings for perennial flower beds. They are seen at their best in fairly massive groups set behind lower-growing neighbors. Two virtues are especially endearing, they bloom in late summer and fall, and tolerate, indeed for their best performance insist upon, a certain amount of shade. They will grow

in full sun, but of really heavy shade they are intolerant. They are not plants for infertile or dry land. They give of their best only in encouraging earth with a goodly organic content that is not lacking in fertility and is reasonably retentive of moisture without ever being for long periods wet. In addition to their value as border perennials aconites can be used effectively in less formal settings. They are good cut flowers. It may be well to repeat the warning that the roots, and to a lesser extent other parts, of these plants, are deadly if eaten. Because of this aconites must never be planted near vegetable gardens, children's gardens, or anywhere any possibility exists that they may be inadvertently eaten by animals or humans.

Cultivation. Aconites resent root disturbance. So long as they are prospering it is unwise to transplant them. Routine care consists of fertilizing each spring, keeping down weeds, staking, watering very thoroughly during dry periods, cutting and removing the tops after they are killed by frost, and where winters are cold, giving a winter covering of branches of evergreens, salt hay, or some other loose, insulating material. Propagation is by division, and by seeds sown in a cold frame or outdoors as soon as they are ripe.

ACORUS (Ácor-us)—Sweet Flag. At first glance these plants look more like grasses or iris than kin of calla-lilies, philodendrons, and skunk-cabbage, yet it is there that their relationship lies. They are members of the arum family, ARACEAE. There are two species of *Acorus,* natives of northern hemisphere temperate and subtropical

Aconitum vulparia

Aconitum vulparia

regions. The name is derived from the Greek *akoros*, used by Theophrastus for some plant with an aromatic rhizome.

Bog or shallow-water plants with creeping rhizomes, from which arise erect fans or parallel-veined, stalkless leaves, acoruses have flattened flower stalks with one seemingly lateral spadix (flower spike) with a leaflike spathe (bract) arising from its base and continuing in the same direction as the flower stalk. The minute flowers are bisexual, the fruits berry-like.

The sweet flag (*A. calamus*) is native from Nova Scotia and Quebec to Alberta, Minnesota, Colorado, Florida, and Texas, and also a native of Europe and Aisa. Up to 6 feet long and about 1 inch wide, but often smaller, its leaves are clustered at their bases. The spathes are 8 inches to 2 feet long. All parts, especially the rhizomes, are sweetly aromatic. The rootstocks yield the drug calamus, used medicinally as a carminative, stimulant, and tonic. They are also used for flavoring and are sometimes candied. Variety *A. c. variegatus*, with its younger leaves striped vertically with deep yellow, is cultivated. The much smaller *A. gramineus*, a native of eastern and central Asia, is less hardy.

Acorus calamus variegatus

Usually under 1 foot in height, it has tufts of narrow, pointed, erect leaves, a spadix 1 inch to 2 inches in length, and narrow, inconspicuous, spathes 3 to 8 inches long. Variety *A. g. variegatus* has leaves striped longitudinally with creamy-white. The dwarf *A. g. pusillus* is not more than about 3 inches tall.

Garden Uses and Cultivation. These plants are for watersides, wet places and moist soils, in sun or part-shade, and *A. gramineus* and its variety for pot culture in greenhouses, dish gardens, and terrariums. They grow well even where the surface is covered with up to 2 inches of water. Their display value depends entirely on their foliage; their flowers are not decorative. The sweet flag (*A. calamus*) is deciduous and very hardy. The evergreen *A. gramineus* is much more tender. A re-

Acorus gramineus variegatus

tentive soil containing a generous proportion of organic matter is to their liking. Planting is best done in spring or early fall. Propagation is easy by division at almost any time, but spring, just prior to the beginning of new growth, is generally best. Fresh seeds freed of surrounding pulp and sown before they have an opportunity to dry, germinate readily in constantly moist or wet soil.

ACRE. An acre, one six-hundred-and-fortieth of a square mile, contains 43,560 square feet or 4,840 square yards. One square acre has sides almost exactly 209 feet long. A plot 100 by 100 feet is approximately one-quarter of an acre, one 66 by 33 feet is precisely one-sixteenth of an acre. This modern acre is based on an ancient one defined as the amount of land that could be plowed in one day with a yoke of oxen. The metric unit of land measurement, the hectare contains almost exactly two and one-half (actually 2.471) acres.

ACRIDOCARPUS (Acrido-càrpus). Fifty species compose *Acridocarpus* of the malpighia family, MALPIGHIACEAE. Natives of Africa, Arabia, and Malagasy (Madagascar), they have a name alluding to a fanciful resemblance of their fruits to the insect, derived from the Greek *akris*, a locust, and *karpos*, fruit.

Trees, shrubs, and woody vines, with alternate or rarely opposite, undivided leaves that are often glandular on their undersides, the sorts of this genus have yellow flowers usually in racemes or panicles, but less often in branched, flattish clusters. Each bloom has a deeply five-lobed calyx, five unequal petals, ten stamens, and two styles. The fruits are samaras.

An attractive climber, *A. natalitius* of South Africa has blunt, oblong to obovate, rather pebble-surfaced leaves with a prominent midrib. The flowers, in terminal racemes, are rich yellow, 1¼ to 1½ inches in diameter.

Garden and Landscape Uses and Cultivation. Acridocarpuses are suitable for outdoor landscaping in the subtropics and

tropics and for greenhouses where the night temperature in winter is 50 to 55°F and that by day five to fifteen degrees higher. Porous, fertile soil is needed. Prune as needed to control size and shape immediately after flowering. Propagation is by seeds, cuttings, and layers.

ACROCLINIUM. For plants previously known by this name see Helipterum.

ACROCOMIA (Acrocò-mia) — Gru-Gru Palm, Corozo. Thirty species of bisexual, feather-leaved palms constitute *Acrocomia*. They are natives of South and Central America, Mexico, and the West Indies, and belong in the palm family PALMAE. The name comes from the Greek *akros*, top, and *kome*, a tuft. It alludes to the manner in which the foliage is borne. Several species are cultivated for ornament in the warmest parts of the United States and in the tropics. Some are known by the common name corozo, although they are distinct from the palm genus *Corozo*.

Acrocomias have solitary trunks that at least on young plants and commonly on mature ones are armed with numerous long, sharp prickles. Their leaves have many long, narrow leaflets with the undersides of their midribs usually prickly. The leafstalk and its extension that is the central axis of the leaf are also prickly and usually hairy. The flower clusters are axillary and have many stiff branches bearing female flowers below and male flowers above. The latter have six stamens. The fruits, which are sometimes hairy or prickly, are 1 inch to 1½ inches in diameter, thin-shelled, and contain one seed. Each flower cluster has two spathes or bracts, the larger, inner one woody and usually prickly, the outer one smaller and falling early. In some species the lower parts of the leaf-stalks remain attached to the trunk for many years after the leaves have fallen and when they finally drop leave a scarred, but not prickly trunk; in others the dead leaves fall intact leaving horizontal scars alternated with rows of long-persistent, stout

Acridocarpus natalitius

spines encircling the trunk. The palm previously named *A. crispa* and *A. armentalis* is *Gastrococos crispa*.

Like many palms, gru-grus are used by man. In markets in its native territory the edible seeds of *A. mexicana* are sold. Those of the Puerto-Rican corozo (*A. media*) have the flavor of coconut, and are also eaten. The fruits of some kinds provide food for cattle and hogs and oil is extracted from those of others and used for cooking and making soap. Since ancient times *A. vinifera* has been used by the Indians to make an intoxicating beverage. This, the coyol, is native to Central America.

Acrocomia media

A native of Martinique, **A. aculeata** is extremely spiny and attains 50 feet in height. Its stout trunk is cylindrical or somewhat thickened above, the leaves, green on both sides, fall away cleanly leaving an abundance of stout prickles, but not

Acrocomia aculeata

Acrocomia (trunk)

stubs or "boots" of the bases of old leafstalks. The largest spathe is 3 feet long or longer, covered with brown felty hairs and a few spines. The trunks of **A. hospes** and **A. mexicana** retain the bases of the leafstalks long after the leaves have fallen. The former is found only in cultivation, its native habitat is unknown. It is sometimes mistakenly called *A. sclerocarpa*, a name without botanical validity. Growing up to 25 feet tall or taller, *A. hospes* has a comparatively slender trunk, often bent near its summit. Its leaves curve and have numerous slender leaflets. The main spathe is cylindrical, long, and narrow. The fruits are broadly-pear-shaped, mostly about 1½ inches long. Usually lower, *A. mexicana* may under very favorable circumstances attain a height of 30 feet. The dead leaves form a brown shag that hangs around the trunk for a considerable time. The leaves, up to 12 feet or longer, have comparatively broad leaflets the longest of which may measure 3 feet. They are glaucous-blue and pubescent beneath. The main spathes are relatively short and broad. The fruits are flattened-globose and about 1½ inches across. Native to Argentina and Paraguay, *A. totai* as known in cultivation is up to 45 feet tall, but it is reported that in the wild it sometimes is much taller. It has a cylindrical trunk encircled with rows of conspicuous prickles, and a loose crown of long, arching and erect leaves with numerous hairless leaflets up to 2 feet long by ¾ inch wide that are green on both surfaces. The largest spathe of the inflorescence, up to 4 feet long, is felted with reddish hairs and is prickly only near its apex. The spherical, smooth fruits about 1¼ inches in diameter are a commercial source of palm oil.

Garden and Landscape Uses. Although young specimens are not among the most attractive palms, older and mature ones are of pleasing form and decidedly ornamental. Their many leaves arch gracefully to form shapely crowns. Their prickly

trunks are, of course, undesirable in some locations, and this is probably one reason why they are not more often planted for ornament.

Cultivation. Gru-gru palms grow satisfactorily in any ordinary garden soil that is reasonably moist. They may be propagated by seeds sown in sandy peaty soil kept moist in a temperature of 80 to 85°F or by suckers carefully removed with as many roots attached as possible, and potted. The newly potted suckers should be kept in a very warm, humid atmosphere and shaded from strong sun until they are well rooted. Until then the soil should be kept moist, but not wet and the foliage lightly sprayed with water several times a day. In greenhouses most kinds need a minimum winter night temperature of 60 to 65°F, with an increase of five or ten degrees by day, but *A. totai* and *A. mexicana* succeed under cooler conditions, say with a winter minimum night temperature of 50 to 55°F. For further information see *Palms*.

ACRODON (Ac-ròdon). Two or three species from South Africa are recognized, one of which is cultivated outdoors in California and other warm, dry regions and, by fanciers of succulents, in greenhouses. These plants belong in the carpetweed family AIZOACEAE and are of the *Mesembryanthemum* relationship. They are low-growing and have three-angled leaves with one or two small teeth near the tips of the keels. The flowers are daisy-like in appearance but not botanical structure. Unlike daisies, the flower heads of which are composed of many tiny flowers called florets, the flowers of *Acrodon* are solitary blooms with many petals and stamens. They have five stigmas. The name is from the Greek *akros*, at the end, and *odon*, a tooth. It alludes to the toothed apexes of the leaves.

Charming **A. bellidiflorus** (the specific epithet means daisy-like) forms 3-inch-tall clumps of glaucous, dark green foliage, and has glistening white- and- pink-striped

Acrodon bellidiflorus

blooms about 1¾ inches across, with feathery stigmas. They are borne freely and, if periods of dryness are alternated with periods of watering, more than once a year. The leaves are up to 3 inches long by up to ¼ inch wide; they are spreading and recurved. This species grows rather slowly, but spreads satisfactorily.

Garden Uses and Cultivation. A good plant for dryish soils and full sun, *A. bellidiflorus* is excellent for rock gardens and similar places. In greenhouses it may be grown in pans (shallow pots). Porous soil is essential and best if low in fertility. Propagation is very easily accomplished by cuttings. Indoors a minimum winter temperature of 45 to 50°F is satisfactory. Watering must always be done with care, especially in winter.

ACRONYCHIA (Acron-ýchia). This genus of fifty species of the rue family RUTACEAE is little cultivated. A native from tropical Asia to Australia, its name comes from the Greek *akron*, a tuft, and *onyx*, a claw, and alludes to the hooked tips of the petals. Acronychias have opposite or alternate leaves. Their flowers, in clusters or panicles, have their parts in fours or multiples of four.

Known in its native Australia as scrub-ash and scrub-yellow-wood, *Acronychia baueri* seems worthy of more flattering colloquial recognition. A tree up to 60 feet tall, it has opposite, obovate leaves up to 4 inches long, and tiny flowers, hairy on their outsides. The fruits are hard and about ½ inch in diameter. This species, the wood of which in its homeland is esteemed for handles of mallets and chisels, is reported to be planted in southern California.

ACROSTICHUM (Acrós-tichum). Three or four similar species, the number depending upon the interpretations of different botanists, of large ferns that in the wild inhabit brackish swamps and mangrove thickets in the tropics and subtropics throughout the world constitute *Acrostichum* of the pteris family PTERIDACEAE. The name, from the Greek *akros*, outer, and *stichos*, a row, is of obscure application.

Acrostichums have short, stout, erect rootstocks partially supported by thick stilt roots, and very large, thick, leathery, pinnate fronds (leaves) with stalked, toothless or obscurely-toothed leaflets. Clusters of spore capsules may be produced on the backs of all leaflets of fertile fronds or only on their upper ones. They cover the entire surface evenly.

Typical of the genus and of widespread natural distribution, *A. aureum* has erect fronds from 3 to 9 feet long with the leaf-stalks accounting for approximately one-third of their length. The leaflets are oblong, those of the biggest fronds may be 1½ feet long or longer by 4 inches wide.

On their undersides their mid-veins are conspicuously raised, on their upper sides they are depressed. Only the upper leaflets, which characteristically are somewhat smaller than the sterile leaflets and are stalkless, bear spores. From the last, **A. daneaefolium** (syn. *A. excelsum*) of the American tropics differs in having more spreading fronds 5 to 13 feet in length, with all or most of the leaflets of the fertile fronds bearing spores.

Acrostichum daneaefolium

Garden and Landscape Uses and Cultivation. In the humid tropics and subtropics acrostichums may be grown in swampy, especially brackish, soils. They are sometimes cultivated for their bold, imposing effects in large greenhouses and conservatories where winter night temperatures of 60 to 65°F are maintained, and shade from strong sun and a humid atmosphere are provided. They succeed in large pots or tubs kept with a few inches of their bases in water so that the soil is constantly moistened from below. Coarse, fertile earth that contains an abundance of organic matter is to the liking of these ferns. When needed, repotting is done in early spring. Well-rooted specimens are encouraged to retain their vigor and health by applications of dilute liquid fertilizer made at weekly intervals from spring to fall, but less frequently in winter. Propagation is by spores. For more information see Ferns. For the plant previously named *A. crinitum* see Elaphoglossum.

ACTAEA (Act-aèa)—Baneberry, Cohosh. Inhabitants of rich woods in temperate parts of the northern hemisphere, members of this genus belong in the buttercup family RANUNCULACEAE. There are about seven species, erect, deciduous herbaceous plants with large, twice- or thrice-divided leaves with lobed and toothed leaflets and dense, terminal racemes of small white blooms. The name *Actaea* is from the Greek *aktaia*, a name originally

applied to the elder (*Sambucus*). The flowers have three to five, early deciduous, petal-like sepals, four to ten smaller petals, many stamens, and a stalkless two-lobed stigma. The fruits are attractively colored, well-displayed berries containing several seeds. These plants have somewhat the appearance of bugbane (*Cimicifuga*), but differ markedly in their fruits, which in the latter genus are dry capsules that split to release the seeds.

The unwary must be careful of the too casual application of what may appear to be obvious names to the two species native to eastern North America. A complicating factor is that there is a red-fruited variety of the white baneberry and a white-fruited variety of the red baneberry. Fortunately the two differ in ways other than berry color. The white baneberry (*A. pachypoda* syn. *A. alba*) is 1¼ to 2½ feet tall, with leaves usually hairless on their undersides. The stigmas of the flowers are wider than the ovaries. The nearly spherical berries have decidedly thick stalks. Typically they are white and porcelain-like, with the persistent stigma forming a purplish spot at the end. The red-fruited variety of *A. pachypoda* is most easily distinguished from the next species by its stout berry stalks. The white baneberry is native from southeastern Canada to Georgia, Louisiana, and Oklahoma. The red baneberry (*A. rubra*) differs from the white baneberry chiefly in its leaves commonly being hairy on the veins beneath, in the stigma not being as broad as the ovary, and in the stalks of the berries being very slender. Also, the berries are ellipsoid and, in the typical species, red. In variety *A. r. neglecta* (which, with the result of confusing nomenclature further, has been named *A. alba* by some botanists) the berries are white. The red

Actaea rubra

baneberry is native from Labrador to Newfoundland, Alaska, New Jersey, Indiana, Iowa, and Arizona. Herb Christopher or black baneberry (*A. spicata*), native from western Europe to Japan, is similar to the red baneberry, but has oblong-cylindrical, shining purplish-black berries. Its flowers are white or bluish.

Garden and Landscape Uses and Cultivation. Baneberries are attractive in foliage and bloom and handsome in fruit. They are adapted for shaded informal areas and woodland plantings and, the American kinds, for native plant gardens. They are also useful for flower borders not exposed to strong sun. They are at their best in deep, fertile soil that contains an abundance of organic matter and is never excessively dry. Propagation is easy by division in spring. Seeds, taken from the berries and freed from surrounding pulp, give satisfactory results if sown in fall in a cold frame or outdoor bed protected from disturbance. The seed bed should be shaded and kept uniformly and moderately moist. Seeds not sown in the fall in which they ripen are unlikely to germinate well.

ACTINEA. See Hymenoxys.

ACTINELLA. See Hymenoxys.

ACTINIDIA (Actin-ídia)—Tara Vine, Silver Vine, Kiwi Berry or Chinese-Gooseberry or Yang-Tao. Eastern Asia is home to this genus of thirty-six species of hardy and nonhardy, hairy or hairless, perennial woody vines belonging to the actinidia family ACTINIDIACEAE (which was previously included in the dillenia family DILLENIACEAE). The generic name, alluding to the styles, which spread like the spokes of a wheel, comes from the Greek *aktis*, a ray.

Actinidias have alternate, long-stalked, undivided, toothed or toothless leaves, with those of some kinds decidedly ornamental. The cupped, white, yellow, or reddish flowers, unisexual on separate plants or more rarely unisexual and bisexual on the same plant, are solitary or in clusters from the leaf axils. They generally have five each sepals and petals, and numerous stamens with purple or yellow anthers. The many-seeded, usually edible fruits are juicy berries. Those of the Chinese-gooseberry or yang-tao, by New Zealanders renamed kiwi berry, are cultivated in that country as a crop for domestic use and export. A peculiarity of *Actinidia polygama* and *A. kolomikta* is that they attract cats, and put them into such a frenzy that they sometimes tear the plants to pieces.

The bower actinidia or tara vine (*A. arguta*), a vigorous, densely-foliaged, deciduous twiner up to 30 feet tall, is native from Japan, Korea, and China to Siberia. It has red-stalked, lustrous, broadly-ovate to ovate-oblong, bristly-toothed leaves 3 to 4½ inches long, and inconspicuous white and brownish, fragrant, purple-anthered blooms about ¾ inch across, mostly in threes. Its sweet, greenish-yellow, oblong to egg-shaped fruits, about 1 inch in diameter and without decorative

appeal, may be eaten raw or after preserving. A close relative of *A. arguta* is *A. purpurea* of southwestern China. It differs chiefly in its longer, narrower leaves, usually smaller blooms, and in the fruits being longer and dark purple.

Beautiful variegated foliage, green generously splashed with white or pink at the leaf ends or with occasional leaves wholly white or pink, distinguishes hardy *A. kolomikta*. Male plants, especially if growing in limy soil, are likely to be better variegated than females. A native of northeastern Asia and Japan, *A. kolomikta* is a slender climber 10 to 20 feet tall. Its irregularly-toothed, ovate-oblong leaves are 3 to 6 inches long. The fragrant, yellow-anthered blooms, ½ to ¾ inch wide, are solitary, or in twos or threes. The egg-shaped fruits are sweet, yellowish, and about 1 inch long.

Actinidia kolomikta

Silver vine (*A. polygama*) is hardy, and up to 20 feet in height. A native of China and Japan, it has broadly-elliptic to ovate-

Actinidia polygama

oblong leaves 3 to 5 inches long that are variegated with silvery-white or yellowish blotches, or occasionally are entirely white or yellowish, and are bristly along their stalks and veins. About ¾ inch wide, the fragrant blooms, usually in threes, have yellow anthers. The yellow, egg-shaped, 1½-inch-long fruits are edible but bitter. It is distinguished from *A. kolomikta* by the pith of its stems being white and continuous rather than brown and divided into crosswise, separate plates.

Kiwi berry, Chinese-gooseberry, or yang-tao (*A. chinensis*) of China is not hardy north of Philadelphia. A most handsome species in foliage and flower, it is a vigorous twiner 30 to 40 feet tall, with young shoots and foliage shaggy with velvety, red hairs.

Actinidia chinensis

These account for much of its beauty. The broadly-heart-shaped leaves, clothed on their undersides with stellate (starlike) white hairs, and with bristly margins, are 5 to 8 inches long. In small clusters, the 1½- to 2-inch-wide blooms, at first white, change to buff-yellow as they age. Having somewhat the flavor of gooseberries, the brown, oblongish to egg-shaped, fuzzy-surfaced fruits, 2½ to 3½ inches in length, contain tasty, translucent, pale green flesh at the center of which are embedded tiny purple seeds. The fruits are peeled, sprinkled with sugar, and eaten raw, or before they are absolutely ripe, are stewed or made into preserves.

Other actinidias sometimes cultivated are *A. callosa*, *A. coriacea*, and *A. lanceolata*. The very variable *A. callosa* ranges in the wild from Taiwan to China, India, and Malaysia. Up to about 20 feet in height, it has firm, hairless, obovate to ovate-lanceolate leaves from 2 to 4½ inches long, variously toothed, lustrous dark green above, and pale on their undersides. The many-stamened, yellow-anthered, white, or rarely yellowish flowers are about ¾ inch wide. Varieties with foliage exhibiting varying degrees of hairiness occur. The second species *A. coriacea* differs in its red or reddish, yellow-anthered flowers, which are solitary or in clusters of up to four on separate, leafless branchlets or along leafless parts of the shoots. The leathery, distantly-glandular-toothed, ovate-oblong leaves are 3 to 4 inches long, and hairless. It is native to southwestern China. Very distinct *A. lanceolata* of China attains heights up to 60 feet. It has firm, lanceolate to ovate-lanceolate leaves with wedge-shaped bases, and minutely-toothed margins. They are up to 3 inches long, and have dark green, hairless or sparsely-short-hairy upper surfaces, and undersides slightly glaucous, and clothed with minute, white, stellate (star-shaped) hairs. The greenish flowers, less than ½ inch wide, have yellow anthers and are in clusters of three to six. Less than ½ inch long, the egg-shaped fruits are brown.

A hydrid between *A. arguta* and *A. chinensis*, intermediate between its parents, is *A. fairchildii*. This, the only known hybrid in the genus, was raised in the United States.

Garden and Landscape Uses. Actinidias are splendid vines for arbors, trellises, and screens, and the kiwi berry for its edible fruits, which, as is usually true of other species, are borne by unisexual female plants, and then only if a male vine to supply pollen is nearby. With the exception of the kiwi berry and possibly *A. coriacea*, the species described above are hardy in the north, and most well into New England. They succeed in soils of ordinary garden quality in full sun or part shade.

Cultivation. No difficulty ordinarily attends the growing of actinidias unless it be where space is limited and their exuberance must be restrained. This may be done by pruning in late winter or spring. Seeds supply an easy method of obtaining new plants, and summer cuttings made from firm, but not woody shoots can be rooted in a greenhouse propagating bed, preferably with slight bottom heat, or under mist. The cutting method permits plants of known sex to be raised, which is an advantage when the kiwi berry is grown for its fruit, and also when it is desired to propagate especially handsome male individuals of variegated-leaved species.

ACTINIDIACEAE—Actinidia Family. Formerly included in the dillenia family DILLENIACEAE, the ACTINIDIACEAE contains three genera and 350 species of dicotyledons, natives of eastern and tropical Asia and to Australia. They are vines or climbing shrubs, with undivided leaves, and usually in axillary clusters, small, bisexual or unisexual flowers with five-parted calyxes and corollas, ten or more stamens, and five or more styles. The fruits are berries or capsules. The only genus of horticultural importance is *Actinidia*. The fruit marketed as kiwi fruit or kiwi berry is a product of *A. chinensis*.

ACTINIOPTERIS (Actini-ópteris). One species of fern of the pteris family PTERIDACEAE, native from South Africa to India, is the only member of *Actiniopteris*. Its name, from the Greek *aktis*, a ray, and *pteris*, a fern, alludes to the appearance of its fronds (leaves).

Elegant, and with short creeping rhizomes, *A. australis* (syn. *A. radiata*) has densely-clustered, three-times-parted, fan-shaped leaves, each part of which is again deeply divided into very slender, linear, hairless, firm segments. The general effect is that of fronds of a very tiny fan-leaved palm, with stalks 2 to 6 inches long, and deeply slashed, semicircular blades 1 inch to 1½ inches across. The fertile fronds rise above those without spores. The long, linear clusters of spore capsules, on longitudinal veins joining the vein tips, are covered by the rolled-under leaf margins.

Garden Uses and Cultivation. This unusual fern, which has been likened to a tiny edition of the fan palm *Livistona australis*, is of interest to collectors. It needs tropical or subtropical temperatures, in greenhouses a winter night minimum of 60°F is desirable, and thrives in a humid atmosphere, with shade from strong sun. Peaty soil containing an abundance of broken crocks or crushed brick, coarse sand, and some fine charcoal is to its liking. Drainage must be very sharp. To ensure this it is advisable to fill the pots to two-thirds or one-half their depth with crocks. At all times the earth should be damp, but never for long periods wet. Spores are by far the best way of securing new plants; increase can also be had by very careful division in late winter but this is somewhat risky. Following the operation the newly potted divisions should be kept in a very humid atmosphere at a temperature of 70 to 75°F, and watering should be done with great caution to avoid stagnating the soil. Additional information is given under Ferns.

ACTINOMERIS ALTERNIFOLIA is *Verbesina alternifolia*.

ACTINOPHLOEUS. See Ptychosperma.

ACTINOSTROBUS (Actinó-strobus). Endemic to western Australia and not frequently cultivated, the only two species of *Actinostrobus* belong to the cypress family CUPRESSACEAE. They differ from the nearly related *Callitris*, in their cones being encircled at their bases by closely-pressed bracts and in the shapes of the cone scales. The name, from the Greek *aktis*, a ray, and *strobos*, a cone, alludes to the arrangement of the scales of the cones.

These are densely-branched, evergreen shrubs with, on young plants, juvenile-type, alternate, needle-like, three-ranked leaves ¼ to ½ inch long in whorls (circles) of three; on older specimens the adult-type, scalelike leaves are about ⅛ inch long. Male and female cones are borne on the same plant. The spherical to egg-shaped

Actinidia fairchildii

fruiting cones are of six woody scales each with one or two triangular, three-winged seeds.

From 4 to 8 feet in height, *A. pyramidalis* (syn. *Callitris actinostrobus*) has upright branches with fine sprays of foliage, the scalelike leaves spreading at their tips, their lower parts pressed to the shoots. The egg-shaped cones are about ½ inch long and ½ inch wide at their bases. Somewhat smaller than the last and with more slender branchlets and smaller leaves, *A. acuminatus* also differs in technical characteristics of its stamens.

Garden and Landscape Uses and Cultivation. In mild, dry, frost-free or nearly frost-free climates these may be used as general-purpose evergreens. They respond to conditions and care appropriate for *Callitris*.

ACTINOTUS (Actinòt-us)—Flannel Flower. Of this group of fifteen species of Australian, Tasmanian, and New Zealand herbaceous plants of the carrot family UMBELLIFERAE one is sometimes cultivated. The name comes from the Greek *aktinotos*, rayed, and alludes to the involucres or collars of bracts associated with the flowers.

The flannel flower (*Actinotus helianthi*) is a white- woolly-haired perennial, usually grown as an annual. Erect, it attains a height of about 2 feet and has twice- to thrice-pinnately parted leaves; the leaflets are linear-oblong. The tiny velvety flowers are clustered in tight heads surrounded by white-woolly, petal-like bracts somewhat remindful of those of edelweiss (*Leontopodium*). The spread of the bracts is up to 2½ inches.

Garden Uses and Cultivation. Attractive for adding a touch of the unusual to sunny beds and borders, the flannel flower is without merit for cutting because it soon wilts in water. Seeds are sown in porous soil in a greenhouse in a temperature of 60 to 65°F eight to ten weeks before the young plants are to be transplanted to the garden, which may be done as soon as danger of frost is past and the weather is warm and settled. The seedlings are transplanted 2 inches apart in well-drained flats and grown in full sun in a night temperature of 55°F and day temperatures five to ten degrees higher. After a period of a week or two of being hardened they are planted about 9 inches apart in the garden. Alternatively, seeds can be sown in early spring where the plants are to remain, and the seedlings thinned sufficiently to prevent crowding. This plant needs perfectly drained, preferably sandy soil, and full sun.

ADA (A-da). There are only two species of this genus of the orchid family ORCHIDACEAE, both natives of Colombia. The name, a complimentary one, presumably honors an unidentified lady. In the wild, adas grow perched on trees or rocks rather than in the ground. They form clusters of flattened, oblong-ovoid pseudobulbs 3 to 4 inches long, the older ones furrowed, from the apexes of which come one or two evergreen leaves. The bright cinnamon-red or rich orange-red flowers, in usually recurved or nodding racemes on stalks with sheathing bracts are bell-shaped. There are hybrids between *Ada* and *Odontoglossum* named *Adaglossum*, and between *Ada* and *Cochlioda* named *Adioda*.

Commonest in cultivation, **Ada aurantiaca** has pointed, linear-strap-shaped leaves 6 inches to 1 foot long. Its arching flower stems are up to about 1½ feet long, and toward their tops, quite close together, are up to a dozen or more blooms 1 inch to 1½ inches long. They have pointed, linear-lanceolate sepals, and shorter, narrower petals, with a depressed line down their centers on their insides, those of the petals streaked with purple.

Ada aurantiaca

About one-half as long as the sepals, the pointed, narrowly-oblong lip has two short keels on its underside. The column is very short. The summer-blooming *A. lehmannii* differs from *A. aurantiaca* in being stiffer and having shorter, more erect flower stems, with racemes of up to eight 1-inch-long blooms. They have lips about three-quarters as long as the sepals, white with a narrow, fleshy, orange-colored band down the center.

Garden Uses and Cultivation. These brightly-colored orchids succeed under cool greenhouse conditions agreeable to odontoglossums that come from high elevations. For more information see Orchids.

ADAGLOSSUM (Ada-glòssum). This is the name of the orchid hybrid the parents of which are *Ada* and *Odontoglossum*.

ADAM-AND-EVE or Putty Root is *Aplectrum hyemale*.

ADAM'S NEEDLE. See Yucca.

ADANSONIA (Adan-sònia)—Baobab or Monkey Bread, Bottle Tree. This remarkable genus consists of about a dozen species of grotesque trees of almost ridiculous appearance, natives of hot, dry, regions of Africa, Madagascar, and northern Australia. They are chiefly not forest inhabitants, but grow in open grassy plains without protection from sun and wind. Consequently, they are water misers, and their structure is such that much of the moisture they obtain is conserved. To this end their trunks and stubby branches are abnormally thick, obese is not too strong a word to describe them, and serve as reservoirs. For like reason the roots strike deeply into the earth and the foliage is sparse; leaves transpire water, and baobabs cannot afford to lose too much.

The genus *Adansonia* is closely related to *Bombax* and belongs in the bombax family BOMBACACEAE. Its name honors the French botanist Michel Adanson, who traveled in Senegal between 1749 and 1753 and gave the first accurate account of this vegetable curiosity. Baobabs are occasionally planted as curiosities in southern Florida and in Hawaii and not uncommonly as shade trees in other parts of the tropics. They have leaves of several separate leaflets arranged digitately (like the fingers of a hand), large, solitary, hanging, five-petaled blooms, and woody, gourdlike fruits containing mealy pulp in which are embedded many seeds. The flowers are white, with obovate petals. The numerous stamens are joined into a tube that surrounds the style.

The African baobab or monkey bread (*A. digitata*), indigenous from the Sudan to the Transvaal and from Cape Verde to Abyssinia, is best known. It grows up to 75 feet tall and has an enormous barrel-like

Adansonia digitata, young tree at Fairchild Tropical Garden, Miami, Florida

Adansonia digitata

ADDER'S. This word is used as part of the
common names of these plants: adder's-
mouth (*Malaxis*), adder's-tongue (*Erythronium*), adder's-tongue fern (*Ophioglossum*).

ADENANDRA (Aden-ándra). Endemic to
South Africa, *Adenandra* of the rue family
RUTACEAE consists of small evergreen
shrubs related to *Diosma*. It comprises
twenty-five species. Its name, from the
Greek *aden*, a gland, and *aner*, male, alludes to the anthers having glands at their
tips.

Adenandras have alternate or rarely opposite, small, toothless leaves, gland-dot-
ted and commonly with a pair of glands at
the bottom of the leafstalk. The flowers,
solitary or in umbel-like racemes, terminate the stems. They have five-parted calyxes, five short-shafted, spreading petals,
and five stamens each tipped with a stalked
gland and alternating with the same number of gland-tipped staminodes (nonfunctional stamens). The short style is tipped
with a five-lobed stigma. The fruits are
capsules consisting of five sections (carpels).

From 2 to 3 feet tall and hairless, *A. fragrans* (syn. *Diosma fragrans*) has alternate,
slender-linear-oblong, minutely-toothed,
aromatic leaves ¾ to 1¼ inches long, and
with sticky stalks. In terminal clusters, the

Adenandra fragrans

trunk and short, fat, tapering branches.
Usually the girth of the trunk does not exceed 60 feet, but there is a record of one
specimen that measured 85 feet around its
trunk at 3 feet above the ground. Because,
when leafless, the branches look like roots,
some Africans, not entirely unreasonably,
believed that this tree grew upside down.
Trunk and branches contain but little woody
tissue, they consist largely of water storage
cells. Each leaf has three to seven glossy
leaflets about 5 inches long. The delightfully fragrant flowers, suspended on long
stalks, face downward; they are 5 to 7
inches in diameter and have pure white
petals that soon bend back. The stamens
have purplish anthers and are exceeded in
length by the seven- to ten-pointed stigma
that tips the long style. Like fat sausages
tapering at their ends, the fruits are 6 to 10
inches in length. Their pulp serves as food
for animals and humans and from it is
made a lemonade-like beverage. Natives of
Africa use the leaves as a vegetable. The
bark supplies an excellent strong fiber used
for cordage, fishnets, sacking, and rough
garments. Old baobabs often have hollow
trunks or they are hollowed by natives and
used for storing grain, as water reservoirs,

and for shelter. The baobab is a slow-growing tree that may live for over 1,000 years;
a calculation of an extreme age of 5,000
years has been made, but is probably an
exaggeration.

The Australian baobab or bottle tree (*A.
gregori*) grows 30 to 40 feet tall and usually
has a trunk not more than 60 feet in girth.
It is generally similar to the African species
and, like it, supplies useful fiber from its
bark and edible fruits and seeds. A beverage is prepared from a white gum that
exudes from the bark and is fermented to
give a highly intoxicating drink. This species exists in millions in both arid and humid parts of northern Australia. Water that
collects in the hollows formed at the bases
of its branches remains through the dry
summer and provides welcome, and sometimes life-saving supplies for birds, aborigines, and travelers.

**Garden and Landscape Uses and Culti-
vation.** In tropical climates these trees are
planted as specimens and for shade. In the
continental United States they can only be
expected to survive outdoors in extreme
southern Florida. They are easily satisfied
as to soil, provided it is of fair depth, and
are propagated by seed.

¾-inch-wide, fragrant pink flowers have
stalks up to 2 inches in length, but often
very much shorter. Its shoots erect and
slender, *A. uniflora* (syn. *Diosma uniflora*)
attains heights of 2 to 3 feet and has narrow leaves up to ½ inch long that taper to
both ends. Its solitary, short-stalked flowers are white with a center line of deep
pink down each petal. They have purplish-
brown anthers, and are 1 to 1½ inches in
diameter. A narrower-leaved variety is *A.
u. linearis*.

**Garden and Landscape Uses and Culti-
vation.** These are as for *Diosma*.

ADENANTHERA (Aden-anthèra) — Bead Tree, Red-Sandalwood Tree or Peacock Flower Fence. Here is another of the many tropical genera of the pea family LEGUMINOSAE. This ranges from Asia to Australia and islands of the Pacific. It consists of eight species of trees that, depending to a large extent upon climate, are more or less deciduous. The name comes from the Greek *aden*, a gland, and *anthera*, a flower, and alludes to there being glands on the anthers. The popular name bead tree refers to a use to which the bright red or red and black seeds are put. The best known species is the red-sandalwood tree or peacock flower fence, the source of Circassian seeds used as beads and for other decorative and useful purposes. In Hawaii they are made into leis.

The genus *Adenanthera* has leaves twice- or thrice-pinnate. They have numerous small leaflets. Their tiny golden to pale yellow flowers, in spikelike racemes, are not pea-like. They have five similar petals and ten stamens that protrude slightly or not at all. The pods, slender and flattened, become much twisted when they open to display and discharge the seeds.

The red-sandalwood tree (*A. pavonina*) becomes 50 to 80 feet tall under the most favorable circumstances, but in many parts

Adenanthera pavonina

of the tropics where it is planted it does not exceed 25 or 30 feet. It has large, twice-divided leaves with blunt leaflets 1 inch to 2 inches long. The primary divisions of the leaves are opposite, but the leaflets of those divisions are alternate, a somewhat unusual arrangement. The fragrant, creamy-yellow flowers are minute and in long, dense, slender spikes clustered at the ends of the branches and solitary from near to the bases of the leaves. The tiny petals spread in starlike fashion to reveal the stamens. Each seed pod contains up to a dozen brilliant red, lens-shaped, extremely hard seeds. So uniform are these in weight that they were, and perhaps still are in the Orient to some extent, used to weigh gold and silver. Each seed weighs nearly four grains. The wood of the red-sandalwood

tree is hard and is esteemed for cabinet-making and building. It serves as a substitute for true sandalwood (*Santalum album*) but upon exposure its color changes to purple. From it is obtained a red dye used by Hindus to mark religious symbols on their foreheads. The red-sandalwood is native in the tropics of the Old World.

Garden and Landscape Uses and Cultivation. In the tropics and subtropics the red-sandalwood is planted for shade and ornament for which purpose it is attractive. It succeeds in any reasonably good soil and in Puerto Rico has become naturalized in moist limestone regions. It is propagated by seed.

ADENIA (Ad-ènia). Widely distributed through the tropics and subtropics of the Old World, *Adenia* belongs to the passion flower family PASSIFLORACEAE. The ninety-two species include herbaceous plants and shrubs, often with tuberous roots. Some are succulents notable for their thick, gouty stems or trunks. These appear to be the only kinds cultivated. The name from the Greek *aden*, a gland, alludes to the glands on the leafstalks and flowers. Included in *Adenia* are plants previously known as *Echinothamnus*, *Machadoa*, *Modecca*, and *Ophiocaulon*. Some kinds are reported to be extremely poisonous if eaten.

Adenias have long, slender, or short, stout branches, usually with tendrils, those of the succulent kinds often becoming woody. Their alternate, often glaucous, stalked leaves are undivided, but often lobed in finger-fashion (palmately) or pinnately, or are divided into separate leaflets. There are two glands at the top of the leafstalk. The usually chiefly yellow, unisexual flowers are in long- or short-stalked clusters or sometimes solitary from the leaf axils. Generally only one sex occurs on each plant, less often both, or rarely male, female, and bisexual blooms. They have tubular, four- or five-lobed calyxes, and four or five petals sometimes fringed. Males have four or five stamens, sometimes the same number of glands, and sometimes a rudimentary ovary. Females have four or five staminodes (nonfunctional stamens), a stalked or stalkless ovary, a three-branched style or none, and kidney-shaped, dilated, or headlike stigmas. The fruits are many-seeded, spherical to egg-shaped, dry or pulpy, often berry-like capsules.

The most frequently cultivated *A. glauca*, a native of South Africa, has a large tuberous, more or less conical stem or trunk up to 3 feet in height, or in the wild sometimes subterranean. The tendril-bearing, long, slender stems have thick, grayish, glaucous, or purplish-gray leaves deeply cleft into five elliptic to obovate lobes. The flowers, clustered in the leaf axils, are yellow sometimes marked with red or purple. Egg-shaped, the fruits change from pale

green to yellow or rich orange as they ripen. The variable South African *A. fruticosa* has trunks, sometimes divided above into stout branches, 3 to 6 feet tall by more than 2 feet in diameter at the base, tapering upward. From near their tops come

Adenia fruticosa in the Botanic Garden, Stellenbosch, South Africa

slender stems that may attain a length of 20 feet. These have tendrils, and leaves typically rounded in outline, very deeply cleft into three or five elliptic lobes, but varying in shape and size. Much like the species described above, *A. spinosa* of South Africa differs in its up to 6-feet-tall trunk being brighter green, and in having elliptic, lobeless leaves. The very different and variable *A. globosa* of East Africa has a huge, subspherical or lumpy, boulder-like green trunk that may be 3 feet high and over 6 feet wide. From its top come numerous long, arching or ascending, strongly-thorny stems bearing tiny, narrow-lanceolate, lobeless leaves that soon fall. The flowers are greenish to creamy-yellow and fragrant, the fruits somewhat three-angled. It resembles *A. ballyi* of East Africa, which has a more gray-green trunk than the last, and bigger flowers and fruits. It differs also in technical characteristics.

Other kinds include the African *A. aculeata*, which is very tall and vining; prickly or not, the prickles often forked. The ovate-elliptic to roundish leaves may be lobeless or lobed halfway to the base. *A. firingalavensis*, of Madagascar, has a trunk 2 to 6 feet tall from which sprout usually very long, vining stems. The leaves are heart-shaped to orbicular, lobed or not. *A. keramanthus*, of East Africa, is distinct from all the others considered here in being a shrub with thick, erect, few-branched stems clothed with fine hairs. It has no tendrils. Its ovate to rounded, densely-hairy leaves are not lobed. *A. pechuelii*, native to southwest Africa, has a large, stubby, grayish-green trunk from the top of which sprout a multitude of short, much-branched shoots. *A. venenata* of Africa has a trunk up to 6 feet tall and 2 feet in diameter from which sprout short or long stems. Its lustrous leaves are conspicuously three- to five-lobed.

Garden Uses and Cultivation. The botanical curiosities described here are attractive and ordinarily easily cultivated plants for collectors of choice succulents. They may be planted outdoors in warm desert and semidesert regions, but generally are better adapted for greenhouses devoted to cactuses and other succulents. They are satisfactory in pots amply large to afford generous root room, or beds. Very well-drained, sandy soil suits them. It should be nearly dry during the fairly long season of winter dormancy, moderately moist at other times, but always permitted to become dryish before being soaked. Frequent dilute applications of liquid fertilizer do much to stimulate vigorous growth. Propagation is easy from seed. Most species root readily, although some root rather slowly, from cuttings made from moderately firm shoots. Good light, with perhaps just sufficient shade in summer to lightly moderate the strongest sun, is needed. Indoors a winter night temperature of 50 to 55°F with increases by day of up to fifteen degrees gives good results. For more information see Succulents.

ADENIUM (Adèn-ium)—Desert-Rose, Impala-Lily. Fifteen thick-stemmed, rather fleshy-leaved, succulents of tropical and subtropical Africa and Arabia constitute *Adenium* of the dogbane family APOCYNACEAE. The name is derived from Aden, where some members of the genus are natives. Adeniums contain abundant milky sap, reputed to be poisonous.

Sometimes called desert-rose, *A. obesum* is most commonly cultivated. This native of East Africa is a smooth, succulent shrub up to 6 feet in height, with stout, fleshy, gouty, grayish-green, branching stems. The leaves are clustered toward the tips of

the branches and are arranged spirally. From 1½ to 4 inches long, they are markedly obovate or spoon-shaped, dark glossy green above, with a whitish or pink midvein, and paler beneath. Their ends are indented or bayed inward and have a short point at the termination of the mid-vein. Under desert conditions the leaves may be deciduous during the dry season, but where continuous moisture is available they are evergreen. The very handsome blooms, borne profusely in oleander-like clusters from the branch ends, face boldly outward and make a brave show. They are funnel-form, with five, broad, wide-spreading corolla lobes (petals). They open in succession to provide a long season of bloom. Each flower is 2 inches long and 2 to 2½ inches across, bright rose-pink and paler toward the inner parts of the petals than at their margins. The inside of the corolla tube is yellowish with a few red longitudinal stripes. This plant closely resembles *Pachypodium*, but differs in not being spiny. The impala-lily (*A. o. multiflorum*), of the Transvaal, which grows up to 10 feet in height and has a swollen trunk and thick branches, bears spirally arranged, fleshy, dark green leaves. Its flowers are white with pink margins to the petals. This plant is relished by monkeys and elephants. Similar to *A. obesum*, but with smaller flowers and bluish-green, pointed long-obovate leaves is *A. somalense* of East Africa and Aden.

Garden and Landscape Uses. For sunny locations in warm desert and semidesert regions where little or no frost is experienced adeniums are handsome ornamentals that can be used attractively in home and other landscapes. They bloom for an extended period. They are effective in tubs and are beautiful greenhouse plants esteemed by collectors of succulents.

Cultivation. The most important requirement is soil that is porous and drains perfectly so that there is never danger of stagnant moisture about the roots. Water should be given to container-grown spec-

imens only when the soil approaches complete dryness and there is obvious need for it; then the earth should be saturated. Little or no fertilization is required. At all seasons the plants should be exposed to full sun. In greenhouses a minimum winter night temperature of 50°F is adequate with a few degrees increase by day. From spring through fall temperatures should be higher. Propagation is easy by cuttings planted in sand or other medium that permits the free passage of water and air, and by seeds sown in well-drained sandy soil where the temperature is 60 to 70°F.

Adenium somalense

ADENOCALYMMA ALLIACEUM is *Pseudocalymma alliaceum*.

ADENOCARPUS (Aden-ocárpus). Of the twenty species of *Adenocarpus* of the pea family, LEGUMINOSAE, none is hardy in the North. They are shrubs or small trees allied to *Cytisus* and *Genista*, but differ in having glandular ovaries and seed pods. They are natives of the Mediterranean region, Canary Islands, and high mountains of Africa. The name is from the Greek *aden*, a gland, and *karpos*, fruit. It alludes to the glandular seed pods.

These plants are deciduous or partially evergreen, with small leaves of three leaflets often folded together. In terminal racemes, the pea-shaped, yellow flowers have two-lipped calyxes with the upper lip of two separate lobes and the lower of three more or less joined. The standard petal is round-spatula-shaped and longer than the wing petals. The keel is almost as long as the standard. The stalkless, flattened, linear to oblong, many-seeded pods are typically warty and sticky-glandular.

Of rather gaunt appearance, *A. decorticans* is a deciduous shrub or tree up to 25 feet high with spreading branches and very crowded, hairy leaves up to 1 inch long, with slender leaflets sparingly hairy on both surfaces, up to ¾ inch long, and

Adenium obesum

Adenium obesum

with margins usually rolled inward. The golden-yellow flowers, in erect racemes 1¼ to 2¼ inches long, are followed by seed pods up to 2 inches long. It is a native of Spain. The closely related deciduous *A. complicatus* is 1 foot to 3 feet tall. Its leaflets are lanceolate to obovate-oblong and are hairy beneath and smooth on their upper sides. The yellow-streaked-with-red flowers are in terminal racemes. The seed pods are sparingly glandular and up to 1¼ inches long. This species is a native of southern Europe.

Evergreen or nearly evergreen species are *A. foliolosus* and *A. viscosus* (syn. *A. frankenioides*) both of the Canary Islands. Much branched *A. foliolosus* is 4 to 6 feet tall. It has hairy young shoots, and crowded, small, hairy leaves. The yellow flowers, with hairy standard petals, are in dense terminal racemes. They have calyxes with very long lower lips with teeth of equal size. When young the seed pods are glandular, later they are smooth. Up to 3 feet in height and with pubescent young shoots, *A. viscosus* has crowded leaves with folded, hairy, linear-oblong leaflets and short, compact racemes of yellow flowers, with the standard petal hairy at its apex. The center tooth of the lower calyx lip is longer than the others. The seed pods are sticky-glandular.

Garden and Landscape Uses and Cultivation. Attractive and showy plants for dryish, well-drained soils in full sun in warm-temperate and subtropical climates where dry or dryish summers are the rule, kinds of *Adenocarpus* may be planted with good effects in borders, beds, and rock gardens, and are satisfactory on slopes. They have the same uses and need the same care as brooms (*Cytisus*). Little or no pruning is needed. Propagation is by seeds and summer cuttings. Young specimens should be grown in containers until they are planted permanently. They do not transplant well from the open ground.

ADENOPHORA (Aden-óphora) — Ladybell. This genus of *Campanula* relatives is not widely cultivated and the kinds grown are often incorrectly identified. A native of temperate parts of Europe and Asia, *Adenophora* comprises sixty species. It belongs in the bellflower family CAMPANULACEAE. The name, from the Greek *aden*, a gland, and *phoreo*, bearing, alludes to the cushion-like or cuplike gland seated on top of the ovary and encircling the base of the style. The presence of this gland distinguishes *Adenophora* from *Campanula*.

Ladybells are hardy herbaceous perennials with much of the aspect of slender campanulas. They have fleshy roots and upright or more or less sprawling, generally branched stems. The basal leaves often differ in shape from those on the stems. The nodding or seminodding flowers are in raceme-like groupings along the stems

and branches. They have five-cleft calyxes, bell-shaped, five-lobed corollas, five stamens with stalks expanded and usually fringed with hairs at their bases, and three stigmas. The fruits are capsules.

The following species may be cultivated: *A. confusa*, of China, and 1 foot to 1½ feet tall, has stems without branches or branched near their tops. Its basal leaves are kidney-shaped and toothed. Those on the stems are narrowly-ovate to elliptic, finely-toothed, up to 1½ inches long and about 1 inch wide. Lilac-blue, the broadly-bell-shaped blooms are up to ¾ inch long. Their corollas are lobed to about one-third the way to their bases. *A. coronopifolia*, of Manchuria, 1 foot to 2 feet tall or sometimes taller, has more or less sprawling stems, upright, slender branches with stalkless or short-stalked, sparingly-toothed to almost toothless, linear-lanceolate leaves 3 to 4 inches long and about ¼ inch wide. The basal leaves are broadly-heart-shaped, with round-toothed margins. In raceme clusters of up to ten, the lilac-blue to purplish-blue, 1-inch-long flowers have calyxes one-quarter as long as the corollas. The latter are lobed to about one-third of their lengths. *A. polymorpha*, of Russia and eastern Asia, has stout, branched stems up to 3 feet high. In rather distantly spaced whorls (circles of more than two) its pointed, lanceolate to broadly-lanceolate, coarsely-sharp-toothed leaves are about 2 inches long by ½ inch wide. The small, blue to lilac-blue flowers have very shallowly-lobed corollas.

Garden and Landscape Uses and Cultivation. Ladybells may be used like campanulas in perennial beds and less formal areas. They prefer porous, fairly fertile soil and full sun or a little part-day shade. Established plants resent root disturbance. Do not attempt to transplant them unless absolutely necessary and do not expect to secure increase by dividing them. Propagation is best accomplished by seed and is simple to achieve. Sow the seeds in a cold frame in May or as soon as they are ripe, or in pots indoors in late winter or spring.

ADENOSTOMA (Adenó-stoma)—Chamiso or Greasewood, Ribbon Bush or Red Shank. Two evergreen shrubs, natives of dry chaparral soils in California and Baja California, are the only species of *Adenostoma*. They belong in the rose family ROSACEAE. The name derives from the Greek *aden*, a gland, and *stoma*, a mouth, and alludes to the five glands in the mouth of the corolla tube.

Adenostomas are heathlike in aspect and more or less resinous. They have alternate or clustered, rigid, linear, small leaves and many white flowers crowded in terminal clusters. They are attractive in bloom. The flowers are small, with obconical calyx tubes, five each sepals and petals. There are ten to fifteen stamens in

groups of two or three alternating with the petals, and a solitary style. The small, dry, one-seeded fruits (achenes) are enclosed by the persistent calyx.

The chamiso or greasewood (*A. fasciculatum*) attains a height of 1½ to 12 feet. It has reddish bark that shreds with age and leaves up to ⅓ inch long; they are in groups or bundles and are somewhat resinous and fragrant. The panicles of the almost stalkless flowers are 1½ to 4½ inches long and consist of tiny green-tubed blooms. The variety *A. f. obtusifolium* is distinguished by its pubescent shoots and blunter leaves. The name greasewood is also applied to other plants, some of no horticultural importance. The other species, the ribbon bush or red shank, *A. sparsifolium*, differs in having its leaves alternate and scattered along the shoots rather than clustered and its fragrant flowers on distinct stalks. It attains a height of 6 to 20 feet or rarely more.

Garden Uses and Cultivation. In their home territories and other warm, semidesert regions these shrubs are planted as ornamentals. They need well-drained soil, full sun, and are propagated by cuttings and by seeds sown in spring. The chamiso is hardier than the ribbon bush; it withstands several degrees of frost.

ADHATODA. See Justicia.

ADIANTUM (Adián-tum) — Maidenhair Fern. Maidenhair ferns are delightful and favorite ornamentals. The genus *Adiantum* they compose includes at least 200 species, and in addition many varieties. The group is chiefly tropical and warm-subtropical with the greatest concentration of species in South America. It occurs also in other warm parts of the world, less abundantly in temperate regions. Its name, alluding to the fronds repelling rather than being wetted by water, is from the Greek *adiantos*, unwetted. The genus belongs in the pteris family PTERIDACEAE.

Maidenhair ferns have creeping, or short, ascending rhizomes and fronds (leaves) with polished, very dark to nearly black stalks. Their usually broad blades are often delicately, pinnately-divided into many small segments. Less commonly they are once-pinnate or palmately-divided or are undivided. The leaf segments are without conspicuous mid-veins, and characteristically are of thin texture. The clusters of spore capsules are at or near the ends of freely forking veins and are covered by a folded-under piece of the leaf margin.

Most frequently cultivated of nonhardy maidenhair ferns are the delta maidenhair (*A. raddianum* syn. *A. cuneatum*) and its varieties. This native of the American tropics has a dense rootstock of very short, much-branched, creeping rhizomes. From this arise thickly clustered fronds with triangular to long-triangular or lanceolate-

Adiantum raddianum

ovate blades 6 inches to 1 foot long and two to four times or more divided into wedge-shaped, lozenge-shaped, or nearly round segments that rarely have spreading basal lobes and toothed margins. The color of the leaflet stalks extends well along the mostly five- or six-times-forked veins of the blades. The veins end at a sinus (cleft between the lobes) of the segment margins. Numerous varieties of delta maidenhair are grown and from time to time new ones are introduced to cultivation. Some are so similar that they can be distinguished from others only with difficulty.

Adiantum raddianum fritz-luthii

There are kinds with crested or ruffled frond segments, kinds with smaller than normal, and others with larger than normal frond segments, kinds with much dissected or skeletonized segments, kinds with segments that are united. A few varieties have variegated foliage, and there are sterile varieties that bear no spores. Available varieties are described in the catalogs of specialists.

Differing from *A. raddianum* in having darker green fronds with few, more distantly spaced, mostly three- to five-forked veins that end at the sinuses of its small, irregularly lobed frond segments, and in the basal lobes of the segments spreading,

A. excisum is native to Chile and Bolivia. Erect, it has fronds with twice- to thrice-pinnate blades about 10 inches long by 4 inches wide. In gardens it has been grown as *A.* 'Hawaiian Dwarf'.

Adiantum raddianum 'Kensington Gem'

Southern maidenhair or Venus' hair (***A. capillus-veneris***) is a native of warm-temperate and subtropical regions throughout the world, including the United States from Virginia to Missouri, Florida, Texas, and New Mexico. It is distinguishable from the delta maidenhair by the veins ending in the teeth of the frond segments rather than at their sinuses, and from the brittle maidenhair by the color of the segment stalks not continuing along the veins. This is variable. Typically its fronds have blades two or three times pinnately-divided into coarsely-lobed, roundish to angular-ovate segments that rarely overlap; they are from ½ to 1 inch long, and up to 1¼ inches wide. Varieties are *A. c. fimbriatum*, with chiefly once- or twice-pinnate fronds the few segments of which are more or less deformed or skeletonized, and have fringed or deeply lobed or toothed margins; *A. c. imbricatum*, the fronds of which have overlapping, broad segments with frilled margins; *A. c. mairisii*, which has mostly thrice-divided, broader triangular fronds than the

Adiantum raddianum 'Ocean Spray'

typical species; and *A. c.* 'Scintilla', which has skeletonized frond segments and mostly thrice-pinnate fronds. Much like *A. c. mairisii*, from which it differs most noticeably in the more compact, narrower blades of its fronds, and in their segments being fewer and more shallowly-lobed and more wedge-shaped, ***A. bellum*** is a native of Bermuda.

The brittle maidenhair (***A. tenerum***) is often confused with *A. raddianum* and *A. capillus-veneris*. A popular kind, it is native from Florida to Mexico, Peru, and the West Indies. Helpful distinguishing characteristics of this species are the usually present disklike enlargement at the ends of the stalks of the leaf segments. Also the color of the stalks do not continue into the blades of the segments or do so only briefly before it ends abruptly instead of being long continued. The blades of the fronds are triangular to ovate, three- or four-times-pinnate, 1½ to nearly 3 feet long, and one-half to three-quarters as broad as their lengths. The segments, mostly ½ to ¾ inch long, vary in shape.

Adiantum tenerum

Sterile segments are finely-toothed. The outstanding *A. t. farleyense* has fronds with large, deeply-lobed and relobed, ruffled, overlapping segments. Only rarely does this produce spores. They reproduce true to type. Similar variants are *A. t. fergusonii*, in which many of the segments are united; *A. t.* 'Marsha's Pride', with smaller, mostly twice-pinnate fronds; *A. t.* 'Lady Moxham', which has stouter fronds with larger, more frilled leaflets; and *A. t. gloriosum*, which has pink-tinged fronds. Other varieties are grown by specialists.

Handsome and variable ***A. trapeziforme***, of the American tropics, has short, creeping rhizomes, and fronds with up to four-times-pinnate, triangular blades up to 1½ feet long and wide. They have mainly oblongish to lozenge-shaped, toothed segments from slightly less than ½ inch to a little over 1 inch wide, and two to two-and-one half times as long as their width. The lower segments are often triangular. The color of the stalks of the segments is not carried into the blades. The maidenhair *A. cultratum* differs from *A. trapeziforme* in having long-creeping, more slender rhizomes, and shorter-stalked frond segments two-and-one-half to three times as long as they are wide. The somewhat similar *A. anceps* and *A. peruvianum* have more ovate frond segments than those of *A. trapeziforme* and *A. cultratum*. A native of Ecuador and Peru, *A. anceps* has fronds with long-pointed segments. The segment ends of *A. peruvianum*, a native of Ecuador and Bolivia, are rounded to blunt-pointed. Yet another species *A. pentadactylon*, has the general aspect of *A. trapeziforme*. It differs in that the color of the stalks of the segments is continued into the blades. In *A. p. sanctae-catharinae* (syns. *A. sanctae-catharinae*, *A. catharinae*) the frond segments are oblong-lozenge-shaped to lozenge-shaped-ovoid and much shorter-pointed than those of *A. pentadactylon*. A variant of *A. p. sanctae-catharinae*, *A. p. funckii* (syn. *A. funckii*) has more drooping fronds and more divided, longer-pointed segments.

Native to North America and temperate Asia, the deciduous *A. pedatum*, as its name implies, has pedate fronds. This means that they fork from the tip of the leafstalk and each division again forks one or more times to give the somewhat general effect of a palmate rather than a pinnate leaf. This species has short, creeping rhizomes and broad-ovate to kidney-shaped leaf blades up to 1 foot long; the blades are generally broader than long, with the major divisions pinnate. The asymmetrical-triangular segments are ½ to ¾ inch long, about one-half as wide as long, and sometimes deeply-cleft and -toothed. The compact, very dwarf *A. p. imbricatum* is sometimes misnamed *A. aleuticum*. The kind to which that name is correctly applied seems not to differ significantly from *A. pedatum*.

Adiantum pedatum

The tropical American *A. patens* differs from *A. pedatum* in the ribs of its fronds being paler and the upper edges of its frond segments being round-toothed rather than sharper-toothed or cleft.

Western North America from Oregon to Mexico is home to *A. jordanii*, a deciduous species that seems not to take well to cultivation. It has fronds with triangular-ovate blades up to three-times-pinnately-divided into scarcely-cleft, finely-toothed segments. The leaf blades are up to 1 foot long by approximately 6 inches wide. An evergreen natural intermediate hybrid between *A. pedatum* and *A. jordanii*, *A. tracyi*, has bluish-green foliage. It apparently does not produce viable spores. This has proven satisfactory in West Coast gardens.

Other sorts are these: *A. caudatum*, a native of tropical Africa and Asia, has pendent, slender-linear pinnate fronds 1 foot to 1½ feet long by about 1¾ inches wide that frequently develop plantlets at their

Adiantum caudatum

tips. *A. concinnum*, of Venezuela, Peru, and the West Indies, has twice- or thrice-pinnate, triangular to lanceolate-oblong fronds, with some of the segments covering the ribs of the blade. *A. cristatum*, of the West Indies, differs from *A. fructuosum* chiefly in its fronds having stalks with small hard bumps, with blades three-times-pinnate at their bases. *A. diaphanum* has roots with small tubers, and 1-foot-long fronds, with one- to three-times-pinnate blades 6 inches in length. It has somewhat the aspect of *A. hispidulum*, but with fronds

Adiantum diaphanum

less harsh to the touch and with hairless stalks. It is native to New Zealand, Australia, islands of the Pacific, and China. *A. formosum*, of Australia and New Zealand, has fronds with triangular, finely-divided blades up to four-times-pinnate and 2 feet long by 1½ feet wide, with hairy ribs. *A. fructuosum*, native to the American tropics, has fronds 2 to 3 feet tall with hairy stems and ribs, and twice-pinnate blades with the divisions that bear the final segments linear-lanceolate. *A. hispidulum*, of Asia, Australia, New Zealand and islands of the Pacific, is naturalized in the southern United States. It has reddish fronds with hairy stalks, and blades pedately divided in the fashion of those of *A. pedatum*, but with fewer, usually eight to ten, linear divisions. The segments are sparingly-

Adiantum hispidulum

white-hairy. *A. latifolium*, a native of tropical America and the West Indies, resembles *A. fructuosum*, but has long cordlike rhizomes. *A. macrophyllum*, which ranges from Mexico to South America, has few-branched rhizomes and fronds that have once-pinnate, ovate-oblong blades 6 inches to 1 foot long by two-thirds as wide as their lengths, with three to eight pairs of long-triangular segments sometimes lobed at their bases. *A. monochlamys*, of Japan, in aspect resembles *A. capillus-veneris*, but has on each frond segment only one or rarely two clusters of spore cases. *A. poiretii* has fronds of loosely-arranged, long-stalked segments and resembles *A. raddianum*, from which it differs in the teeth of its sterile fronds being much less obvious. *A. polyphyllum*, of Colombia and Venezuela, has very broadly-ovate frond blades 1¼ to 2½ feet long, with parts of the blade up to four-times-pinnate. The segments are more or less lozenge-shaped to broadly-triangular. *A. pulverulentum*, a native of tropical America and the West Indies resembles *A. fructuosum*, but differs in having only one or rarely two spore-case clusters on each frond segment. *A. reniforme*, of the Canary Islands and Madeira, is unique among cultivated maidenhairs in having fronds each of a single, undivided, roundish to kidney-shaped blade.

Garden and Landscape Uses. Because of their grace and delicacy maidenhair ferns are universally admired, where they are hardy, for outdoor planting, and as greenhouse plants. The cut fronds of some kinds, especially those of the delta maidenhair and its varieties, are much used by florists. Other than in terrariums these ferns are not satisfactory houseplants; their need for high atmospheric humidity mitigates against this. Outdoors, maidenhair ferns are adapted for sites shaded from strong sun and shielded from drying winds.

Adiantum polyphyllum

Adiantum pulverulentum

Adiantum reniforme

Sheltered nooks, crannies, and hollows where the air lies still and humid and the soil is well-drained are to their liking. They may be used to good effect on the banks of still or running water, in woodland gardens and rock gardens, and kinds appropriate for the purpose, in native plant gardens. Soil, loose and highly organic, and for some kinds, such as *A. reniforme, A. hispidulum,* and the southern maidenhair, of a limestone nature, is needed. It should be always damp, but not saturated. The roots of maidenhairs must have adequate air as well as moisture.

By far the hardiest species, the deciduous *A. pedatum* lives outdoors as far north as Quebec, Ontario, and Alaska. It requires a period of decided winter cold and does not prosper in warm climates. The next most cold-resistant, the southern maidenhair withstands four or five degrees of frost without harm and, although its foliage is killed may recover from short exposure to temperatures as low as 0°F. Other kinds are frost-tender, and some of the tropicals, such as *A. trapeziforme* for their best growth demand minimum winter night greenhouse temperatures of about 60°F with decidedly warmer conditions by day. Other greenhouse maidenhairs are satisfied with 55 or even 50°F night temperatures in winter, and daytime increases of five to fifteen degrees. In the warmest parts of the United States such as southern California and southern Florida the delta maidenhair lives permanently outdoors.

Cultivation. In environments such as are described above maidenhair ferns are generally easy to manage. Their chief enemies are slugs, snails, sowbugs, aphids, and occasionally scale insects. Strict hygiene (including the suppression of all weeds and the removal of accumulations of dead leaves and other vegetation and debris that can be used as hiding places) does much to forestall the ravages of the first three of the pests mentioned. Baits may also be used. Spraying with, or with pot specimens dipping the foliage in, a rotenone or pyrethrum insecticide or even fairly thick soapsuds eliminates aphids. To control scale insects all foliage is cut off at ground level and the cut ends that remain are sprayed with an insecticide recommended for the control of scale. Watering must be done without battering the fronds with a strong stream or heavy downpour. Soil in pots and baskets should be soaked without wetting the foliage. Where overall application is necessary use a fine mist. Outdoors in warm climates misting on dry days does much to prevent desiccation of the foliage.

In greenhouses maidenhair ferns may be planted in rockeries or grown in pots or hanging baskets in a mixture of one-half peat moss or leaf mold, one-quarter loamy topsoil, one-quarter coarse sand or perlite, with scatterings of chopped charcoal and perhaps some dried cow manure added.

The addition of crushed limestone or oyster shells for kinds known to prefer limestone soils is beneficial. Repot as soon as new growth begins in late winter or spring. In years when repotting is not needed, carefully pick away some of the surface soil and replace it with new. Good usable specimens can be had in pots 4 or 5 inches in diameter, much larger ones in containers up to 10 inches in diameter. Containers for maidenhairs must be well drained. Press the soil about the roots firmly with the fingers but do not ram it with a potting stick. Nonhardy maidenhairs can be kept in foliage the year around but most benefit from a period of dormancy, usually observed in winter. This is initiated by gradually withholding water until the fronds dry, and then removing the plants to a somewhat cooler but fairly humid place and turning the pots on their sides. The rest may last for two to three months. During it the soil must not be allowed to become absolutely parched. If it does the roots will die. Delta maidenhairs that are needed in full foliage in winter may be rested in summer by forcing them to go dormant by withholding water. When in leaf maidenhairs must be watered generously and the atmosphere kept very humid. Weekly or biweekly applications of decidedly weak liquid fertilizer benefit specimens that have filled their containers with roots. It is a good plan to keep the pots of such plants standing in wide saucers of shallow water. This not only keeps the soil moist by capillary attraction but denies slugs, snails, and sowbugs access to the plants. Strong sun is ruinous to maidenhairs, but good light, including weak sunshine, is necessary. The foliage of specimens grown in too heavy shade is sparse and weak. The most satisfactory method of propagation is by spores, but division is also practicable. This is done in spring at the very first signs of new growth. The rootstocks are cut with a sharp knife into sizable pieces and potted individually in pots just large enough to hold them comfortably. Then they are put into a greenhouse with a somewhat higher-than-normal temperature until new roots are well developed. If the maximum number of propagations are needed, with a stream of water wash away as much of the old soil as possible, cut the rootstocks into single growths with roots attached, and lay these in flats on a layer of moist sand or peat moss in a propagating case where the temperature is 70 to 75°F. When they have developed good roots pot the separations individually into 2½-inch pots. For further information see Ferns.

ADINA (Adìn-a). This group of twenty tropical and subtropical Asian and African species is little known in cultivation. It belongs in the madder family RUBIACEAE and consists of trees and shrubs with undivided, toothless, deciduous or evergreen leaves, and flowers in spherical heads, solitary or in panicles. The flowers have corollas with angled tubes and five lobes (petals). There are five stamens inserted at the mouth of the corolla. The slender style is longer than the stamens and ends in a headlike stigma. The fruits are capsules containing many winged seeds. The name comes from the Greek *adinos*, clustered, and alludes to the dense-headed flowers.

Native to China, *Adina rubella* is an attractive shrub 5 to 10 feet in height, with slender reddish-brown, pubescent branchlets, and pointed, elliptic to oblong, nearly stalkless leaves, lustrous green above, and paler and slightly pubescent on their veins beneath. Its very fragrant, lavender-pink or purplish flowers are in solitary, long-stalked heads that arise from the leaf axils and resemble those of the button bush (*Cephalanthus occidentalis*). They are produced over a long period in summer.

Adina rubella

Adina rubella

One species, *A. cordifolia*, of tropical and subtropical Asia, is sometimes grown in Puerto Rico and other warm lands. It is a tree up to 40 feet in height, with pubescent twigs, and opposite, pointed-broad-ovate, long-stalked leaves with blades 3 to

6 inches long, rounded or heart-shaped at their bases. The undersurfaces of the leaves are gray-pubescent. The globular heads of yellow flowers, 1 inch or more in diameter, are on slender stalks, shorter than those of the leaves. One or more arise from each leaf axil.

A large, handsome forest tree that in its native Africa grows along rivers and streams, *A. microcephala* is widespread and is esteemed for its hard, heavy, oily lumber, which is adapted for massive construction such as bridge building, and for furniture making and general carpentry. It is said to be resistant to termites and was used for dugout canoes. A variety, *A. m. galpinii* (syn. *A. galpinii*), is a common tree in parts of South Africa. Its wood is called African teak or Cape teak, and it is valued for similar purposes to that of the species. This kind and its variety are evergreens. Their leaves, in whorls of four, are lanceolate, and 6 to 12 inches long. The pale mauve, scented flowers are in solitary, long-stalked, axillary heads ¾ to 1 inch across.

Native to the Philippines, *A. garciae* has stalked, elliptic leaves about 3 inches long, and flowers in panicles. A native of China and Indochina, *A. pilulifera* (syn. *A. globiflora*) is a shrub or tree up to 30 feet tall, with pointed elliptic leaves 3 to 4 inches long, and greenish-yellow flowers in long-stalked, solitary, axillary heads about ½ inch across. Indigenous to China, Taiwan, and Japan, *A. racemosa* is a deciduous tree, up to 30 feet tall, with glabrous branchlets and glossy, pointed-ovate leaves slightly pubescent beneath and up to 4½ inches long. The pinkish flowers are in solitary, axillary, long-stalked heads.

Garden and Landscape Uses and Cultivation. The tropical and subtropical adinas described above are suitable for outdoor cultivation only in frost-free climates similar to those of their homelands. They are little known in cultivation. Very worthy of the attention of gardeners is the unusual flowering shrub, *A. rubella*. This attractive species is hardy in sheltered locations near New York City. It thrives in any ordinary garden soil in full sun. No regular pruning is necessary, but any needed may be done in spring before new growth begins. Propagation is very easily accomplished by leafy cuttings in summer, and by hardwood cuttings.

ADIODA (Adi-òda). This is the name of orchid hybrids the parents of which are *Ada* and *Cochlioda*.

ADLUMIA (Adlùm-ia) — Climbing-Fumitory, Mountain Fringe, Allegheny Vine. This genus of two species, one North American and one Korean, belongs in the fumitory family FUMARIACEAE and thus is kin with the bleeding heart (*Dicentra*) and with *Corydalis*. Its name commemorates

Major John Adlum, an American horticulturist, who died in 1836. Only one species is cultivated, the American *Adlumia fungosa* (syn. *A. cirrhosa*), which inhabits woods, mostly in the mountains, from Ontario to Michigan, North Carolina, and Indiana. It is an attractive biennial vine, with three- or four-pinnate leaves that have all the delicacy of ferns fronds. During its first year this plant forms only basal foliage, but in its second season it develops stems up to 10 feet long that climb by means of slender prehensile leafstalks. The leaves that aid in climbing are greatly elongated and have much smaller leaflets than the basal leaves of the previous year. The pretty, asymmetrical, white to purplish flowers resemble those of bleeding hearts (*Dicentra*). They are ½ inch long or longer and in pendulous clusters from the leaf axils.

Adlumia fungosa

Garden Uses and Cultivation. This delightful native is a plant for lightly shaded wild gardens, woodland paths, and similar places where the soil is moderately moist and contains an abundance of organic matter such as leaf mold or compost, where the air is relatively cool and humid, and where shelter from wind and light shade from strong sun are afforded. It is easily raised from seeds sown in early spring and if the site is favorable usually reproduces itself spontaneously once it is established. Supports, such as light brushwood, must be provided.

ADOBE. This is a name used in desert parts of North America for certain deflocculated clay and silt soils that characteristically are sticky and impervious to water when wet, and when dry become hard and compact. Some such are used for making sun-dried adobe bricks. As garden soils they are difficult to work. See Soils and their Management.

ADOBE-LILY is *Fritillaria pluriflora*.

ADONIDIA. See Veitchia.

Acacia longifolia

Abutilon hybridum variety

Acalypha hispida

Acanthus balcanicus

Acer saccharum, in brilliant fall color

Acer saccharum (sugar maple, fall foliage)

Achillea clypeolata hybrid

Aechmea species

Actaea pachypoda

Aeonium species

Actaea rubra (fruits)

Aeschynanthus pulcher

Adenium obesum

Aerides odorata alba

ADONIS (Adòn-is)—Pheasant's Eye. This group of twenty species of annuals and herbaceous perennials includes several of garden worth. They belong in the buttercup family RANUNCULACEAE and are natives of Europe and temperate Asia. Their name is that of the god favored by Venus and from whose blood, according to fable, the adonis flower sprung.

Adonises are erect, have alternate, finely-dissected leaves, and solitary, terminal, red or yellow flowers with five to eight sepals, five to sixteen petals, and many stamens and pistils. The fruits (achenes) are grouped in rounded or elongated heads. Adonises differ from the closely related buttercups (*Ranunculus*) in having petals without nectar pits.

Among the perennials the spring adonis (*Adonis vernalis*) is one of the best known. Native from Europe to the Caucasus, it sends up numerous, mostly unbranched stems clothed with delicate ferny foliage, and in spring is topped with upturned suns of golden, many-rayed blooms 2 to 3 inches across. The leaves are without stalks, the lowermost reduced to scales. The plant grows 6 inches to 1½ feet high. Differing from *A. vernalis* in that its lower leaves are

stalked and not merely represented by scales, *A. pyrenaica* of the Pyrenees has smaller, more brilliant golden flowers. It is robust and has mostly branched stems. This is one of the most attractive of the adonis tribe. The mountains of India to Japan is the range of a species closely resembling the Pyrenean species. This, *A. chrysocyathus*, has lovely golden blooms fully 1¾ inches in diameter. An attractive species from Russia, *A. volgensis*, resembles *A. vernalis*, but has branched stems. The outsides of its sepals are hairy. Blooming earlier than the spring adonis, and even hardier, very lovely *A. amurensis* is the first of all adonises to bloom. It regularly displays its bright yellow flowers before the last snows have vanished and well before it has had time to develop much foliage. The flowers, 1½ to 2 inches across, are deep yellow globes that nestle comfortably against attractive collars of green. The leaves have stalks almost as long as the blades, and three major divisions again much divided. The stems are usually branched. This attains a height of 8 inches to 1½ feet. There is a rare, white-flowered variation (*A. a. alba*), and a much commoner double-flowered kind that has green-

centered golden flowers. The last, a Japanese variety named 'Fukuju-Kai', does not set seeds. The species *A. amurensis* is a native of northeastern Asia.

Annual adonises include the summer adonis or pheasant's eye (*A. aestivalis*), which is 1 foot to 1½ feet tall and sparingly branched, with flat, crimson flowers 1 inch to 1½ inches across. In variety *A. a. citrina* the blooms are yellow. The autumn adonis or flos adonis (*A. annua* syn. *A. autumnalis*) is an annual that blooms in summer and fall. Its stems are branched and its flowers, rarely exceeding ¾ inch in diameter and not opening wide, are deep red with darker centers. This native of Europe and Asia is naturalized or occurs as a garden escape in parts of the United States. It is up to 2 feet tall, but is less attractive than *A. aestivalis*. The annual *A. flammea*, a native of central Europe, is similar to the fall adonis. Its scarlet blooms 1½ inches across quite often have a black spot at the base of each petal. An especially lovely annual from Syria, *A. aleppica* has 1½- to 2-inch-wide, flat, blood-red flowers in summer and fall. It grows to a height of about 1½ feet and resembles *A. aestivalis*.

Garden and Landscape Uses. Perennial adonises are useful and reliably hardy plants for rock gardens, naturalized plantings, and perennial beds in sun or light shade. The annuals, appropriate for flower beds and borders and for cutting, need full sun.

Cultivation. Adonises are easy to grow in any ordinary garden soil; they must be kept fairly moist, but not wet, however. The spring adonis, and probably some others, is appreciative of lime in the soil. It is better that the perennials, once established, remain undisturbed for as long as possible for they are likely to suffer temporary setbacks following transplanting. This often happens, too, after the plants are divided. (*A. amurensis* seems less prone than others to suffer from this operation), and so seed is often recommended as a means of propagation. Seeds, however, germinate slowly. They should be sown as soon as possible after they are ripe in a cold frame in porous, moderately moist soil. If carefully done, division in early fall or early spring is satisfactory. Each division should have a fair amount of roots and these must not dry while they are out of the ground.

ADOXA (Adóx-a)—Musk Root. The only species of this genus, the musk root constitutes the moschatel family ADOXACEAE. It has no close relatives, but shows an affinity to the saxifrage family SAXIFRAGACEAE and the aralia family ARALIACEAE. Its botanical name is from the Greek *adoxos*, insignificant. The common name refers to its musky odor. The musk root (*Adoxa moschatellina*) is sometimes cultivated in wild gardens. Its natural distribution ex-

Adonis vernalis

tends throughout the colder parts of the northern hemisphere, where it grows in woodlands and on moist banks; in North America it is found as far south as New York, Iowa, Illinois, Wisconsin, and Minnesota. This plant, of frail appearance, has scaly rootstocks and long-stalked basal leaves thrice-divided into three-parted leaflets. Its inconspicuous, small, greenish or yellowish flowers are in globose heads about ⅓ inch in diameter atop slender stems with two leaves smaller and shorter stalked than the basal ones. The plant is 4 to 8 inches tall.

Garden Uses and Cultivation. The musk root is of interest only to collectors of native or woodland plants. It succeeds in moist soil that contains an abundance of humus, in shade. Propagation is by seeds sown in similar earth, kept evenly moist, in a shaded cold frame.

ADOXACEAE—Moschatel Family. This family contains only the genus *Adoxa*. Its characteristics are given under the previous entry.

ADROMISCHUS (Adrom-íschus). Many attractive plants are included in this genus of succulents, closely related to *Cotyledon*, from which *Adromischus* differs in its blooms being usually tubular and in racemes rather than more bell-shaped and in panicles. They resemble the blooms of *Haworthia*. The genus is entirely South African and consists of fifty species. Its name comes from the Greek *adros*, strong, and *miskos*, a flower, and alludes to the sturdy flower stalks. It belongs in the orpine family CRASSULACEAE.

Species of *Adromischus* are small, evergreen, herbaceous plants or shrublets. They have mostly alternate leaves and, often, from the stems, aerial roots that soon wither but remain attached. These, it is thought, serve to absorb dew. The leaves vary much in size and shape according to species; they may be roundish and flat, sausage, or clubshaped. In a few kinds the whitish to reddish flowers are solitary. More commonly they are in clusters or spikes from the ends of the branches. They appear in summer.

One of the more popular kinds, *A. cristatus* has a short, eventually branching

Adromischus cristatus

stem from which sprout curled, red aerial roots, and short-stalked, paddle-shaped, plump, green leaves, rounded on both surfaces and with broad crinkle-edged ends. The flowers are greenish or whitish-red. Another commonly grown species, frequently misnamed *A. cooperi* (the plant to which this name rightly belongs does not seem to be in cultivation) is *A. festivus*. It has very short stems, and erect, wedge-shaped leaves rounded on both surfaces and about 1 inch long at the flattened and usually somewhat crinkled apex, and ¾ inch wide. They are gray-green and usually conspicuously flecked or mottled with reddish-brown. Fancifully, they are likened to plovers' eggs.

Adromischus festivus

Other kinds cultivated include the following: *A. alveolatus* has tuberous roots, short stems, and rough-surfaced, elliptic leaves, concave on their upper sides and up to 1¼ inches long and ¾ inch wide. Its flowers, a little more than ½ inch long are on stalks up to 7 inches long. *A. clavifolius* has stems plentifully clothed with reddish to gray aerial roots. From 1 inch to 3 inches long the leaves are cylindrical, flattened and somewhat waved at their apexes. The ½-inch-long flowers have very short individual stalks, and are in ones, twos, or threes from the nodes of the up to 1-foot-long common flowering stalks. *A. herrei* is a shrublet up to 4 inches tall with spiraled, ovate to broad-spindle-shaped, fleshy leaves, greenish or reddish, wrinkled, and coated with wax. *A. maculatus* has stems up to 4 inches long, and obovate-wedge-shaped, brown-spotted leaves up to 2¾ inches long by 1½ inches wide. Rising to heights up to 1¼ feet, the flowering stems carry ½ inch-long, stalkless flowers. *A. marianae*, a tiny clump-forming shrub, has leaves about ¾ inch long and ½ inch wide, flat or hollowed and often furrowed on their upper sides, their undersides are rounded. They are gray-green with paler margins and brownish-gray markings. The green flowers have red tips. *A. poellnitzianus* is little branched. Its short stems

Adromischus poellnitzianus

have many reddish aerial roots about ⅓ inch long or a little longer. The alternate, pale green leaves, cylindrical with flattened, wavy-margined ends, broaden from the base upward. They are more or less in rosettes and are 1 inch to 1¼ inches long. The flowers, on stems 1 foot tall or taller, are white with red tips. *A. saxicola* has few stems and alternate, linear-oblong leaves that narrow equally at both ends, are without markings, but are often pinkish or reddish toward their apexes. The flowers are mauve to purple, with pale margins to the petals. *A. triflorus* has opposite, obovate leaves approximately 2 inches long by 1 inch wide an on stems up to 8 inches high, ½-inch-long flowers, mostly in threes from each node. *A trigynus*, sometimes misidentified as *A. maculatus*, is an attractive species with alternate or nearly opposite, light to dark green to brownish-red leaves mottled on both sides with darker, variously-sized spots. The stem is short, the leaves nearly round to obovate. The purple-brown blooms are on stalks 9 inches to 1½ feet long.

Garden Uses and Cultivation. These are attractive plants for those who maintain collections of succulents outdoors in warm, mild climates or in greenhouses. Being easy to grow they are amenable to window garden cultivation. They require the same care as cotyledons, that is detailed under Succulents. New plants are raised with great ease from cuttings, single leaf cuttings, and from seeds.

AECHMEA (Aech-mèa). The "ch" in *Aechmea* is given the sound of "k." The name is that of a genus of about 150 species of the pineapple family BROMELIACEAE. Chiefly tropical South American, and indigenous nowhere except in the Americas, these plants are usually epiphytes (tree-perchers that take no nourishment from the trees they grow on), but some kinds grow in the ground or on rocks and others occur either on trees or in the ground. The name *Aechmea* is from the Greek *aichme*, a point, and alludes to the pointed sepals.

Aechmeas are stemless plants with rosettes, often swollen at their bases, of leathery, evergreen, linear to sword-shaped or oblong leaves generally with spiny margins. The leaf surfaces are often scurfy. In most kinds the rosettes produce a flower spike or panicle from the center, die after blooming once, and are replaced by sucker growths from their bases. A few kinds develop lateral flower stalks from the leaf axils and have permanent rosettes that bloom for many successive years. Usually, but by no means always, the flower spikes or panicles are displayed well above the foliage. The flowering stalks have several to many bracts, which are sometimes highly colored. The blooms have three separate or united, usually sharp-pointed sepals, separate or joined, three separate petals with at the bottom of each a pair of scales or ligules, and a style shorter than the stamens ending in a three-lobed stigma. The fruits are usually long-lasting, frequently brightly colored berries.

Cultivated aechmeas are very numerous. In the collections of fanciers and in the catalogs of specialist dealers references to species, varieties, and some very fine hybrids in addition to those now to be described will be found: *A. angustifolia*, from Central America to Brazil, has rosettes of spiny-edged, stiffish, channeled, sometimes arching, gray-green leaves 1¼ to 2 feet long by 1½ to 2½ inches wide. They

Aechmea angustifolia

have brown, scurfy scales on their undersides. The yellow blooms in long, narrow panicles with many short branches and small, purplish-red bracts, are succeeded by white berries some of which turn bright blue. Those that remain white do not contain fertile seeds. *A. aquilega* (syn. *Gravisia aquilega*), of northeastern South America, Trinidad, and Costa Rica, grows both as an epiphyte and as a terrestrial. Its funnel-form rosettes consist of up to thirty channeled, white-scaly, green or coppery-green leaves up to 3 feet in length. Attaining a height of 3 to 5 feet, the flowering stalk terminates in a narrow panicle with orange to light crimson bracts enclosing yellowish-orange flowers. *A. blumenavii*, a comparatively cold-hardy native of southern

Aechmea aquilega

Brazil, has purple-tipped, green leaves rarely more than 1 foot to 1½ feet long. Its panicles of flowers have pink stalks, pink bracts, and yellow blooms. They are decorative for many weeks. *A. bracteata* (syn. *A. schiedeana*) is a robust, strikingly handsome native from Mexico to Colombia. In its homelands its urn-shaped rosettes of viciously-toothed, apple-green, leathery leaves attain lengths of 3 to 4 feet. They form suckers that clump, 3 to 6 feet across.

Aechmea bracteata

The branched flowering stalks have showy, long-lasting, brilliant red bracts and yellow flowers. It grows well in the ground. *A. bromeliifolia*, widely distributed in Cen-

Aechmea bromeliifolia

tral and South America, has a tubular rosette of strap-shaped leaves with green upper surfaces, paler undersides. The flowers, greenish-yellow at first, changing to black, are partially embedded in a growth of white-woolly hairs. *A. calyculata* of Brazil and Argentina has tubular rosettes of toothed, channeled leaves up to 2 feet long, about 1½ inches wide. The bright yellow flowers are in short, tight, cylindrical heads topping 1-foot-long, red stalks. It is comparatively cold tolerant. *A. caudata*, of Brazil, has rosettes of rigid, arch-

Aechmea caudata variegata

ing leaves 1½ to 3½ feet long by 4 to 5 inches wide. The bright yellow flowers are in compact, branched, yellow-bracted, pyramidal heads that terminate long, mealy stalks. Variety *A. c. variegata* has foliage

Aechmea bromeliifolia

with longitudinal creamy strips. *A. chantinii* is a widely dispersed, variable species of the Amazon region. One of the most beautiful bromeliads, it has rosettes of spreading or more upright, dark green, olive-green, deep red, or nearly black leaves boldly or sometimes less strikingly cross-banded with silver or pinkish-gray. Its erect flowering stalks terminate in stiff-branched panicles of yellow and red blooms succeeded by white fruits that may become pale blue. The drooping bracts vary from orange to red or lavender. The plant known

Aechmea chantinii

as *A. amazonica*, its leaves green with silver bands, its bracts red, its flower orange, is a variant of this species. *A. dealbata* is a Brazilian, with tubular rosettes of few about 2 feet-long, dark green leaves cross-banded on their purplish-brown undersides with silvery bars. It has compact flower heads 3 to 4 inches long, their flowers pink. The brownish bracts are dusted with whitish powder. *A. distichantha*, a variable native from Brazil to Argentina, is 1½ to 2 feet in height. It does well grown as a terrestrial. It has rosettes of stiff, erect or arching, sharp-pointed, gray leaves and pink-stalked, open-branched panicles of violet-blue flowers and bright pink bracts. *A. d. canaliculata*, 1 foot tall or a little taller, has rosettes of erect, narrow leaves deeply-channeled in their lower parts. *A. d. schlumbergeri*, robust, is 2 to 3 feet tall. *A. fasciata* (syn. *Billbergia rhodocyanea*), one of the most commonly grown and handsomely-bloomed bromeliads, is native to Brazil. It has medium-sized, ample rosettes of broad, arching leaves, green and silvery-cross-banded or sometimes entirely dusted with silvery scales. The leaf margins have blackish spines. The blue flowers are in very long-lasting, tight, conical spikes held above the craters of the rosettes. They have many, showy, spreading, triangular, salmon-pink bracts. *A. f. albo-marginata* has leaves bordered with ivory-white. *A. f. purpurea* has foliage

flushed with dark purple. *A. f. variegata* has longitudinal bands of ivory-white throughout the leaf. *A. fosterana* is a beautiful native of Brazil that has tubular rosettes up to 2 feet tall of light green to reddish-green leaves with zigzag bands of purple-brown mottlings and green spines. The panicle of rich yellow flowers is ornamented with crimson bracts. *A. fulgens* in its native Brazil perches on trees or grows in the ground. It has rosettes of green leaves up to 1 foot long or somewhat longer by 2 to 3 inches wide. The flowering stalks terminate in a broad, pyramidal panicle, bractless or with very small bracts and flowers with bright red, berry-like bases and blue petals. After the petals fade the red fruits are decorative for many months. *A. f. discolor* forms wide rosettes of leaves with deep green upper surfaces and rich, glossy purple or violet undersides with a dusting of faint striping of whitish scales. Its flowers have dark purple petals, and its berries are red. *A. lamarchei* (syn. *A. lagenaria*), of Brazil, has rosettes of glossy, arching and spreading, strap-shaped leaves with purplish-red teeth. They are about 1½ feet long. Unlike other aechmeas here described the rosettes terminate stout stems. Its flowers are in conelike spikes topping stalks with showy, erect, bright rose-red bracts. The yellowish petals and white sepals become jet black within two or three

Aechmea fulgens discolor

days of opening. *A. lueddemanniana* is a Central American that in the wild grows both on trees and in the ground. Its spreading and arching, mottled, metallic-green and bronzy leaves are in rosettes that may have a spread of 3 feet. The erect flowering stalks terminate in dense, cylindrical spikes of lavender blooms succeeded by white berries that change to intense purple and remain attractive for several months. *A. l. marginata* 'Mend' has leaves with a broad central longitudinal band of green and quite broad pink margins. *A. l.*

Aechmea fasciata

rubra has rich bronzy-red foliage. *A. l. variegata* is distinguished by its leaves being marked longitudinally with grass-green, chartreuse, and carmine. ***A. mariae-reginae***, of Costa Rica, perches on trees or grows on the ground. It has open rosettes of broad, light green leaves 2 to 3 feet in length margined with strong spines. The

Aechmea mariae-reginae

flowers have bright red, berry-like bases and blue-tipped white petals that become pink with age. They are in vertical ranks on the stiffly-erect, dense, poker-like spikes, with, draping from below the bases of the poker head, 4-inch-long, watermelon-pink bracts of great loveliness. In its homeland the flowers of this species are much used as decorations at fiesta time. The blooms are succeeded by long-lasting, red-tipped berries. ***A. mexicana*** is a common native of Mexico and Central America. Its rosettes, up to 3 feet across, are of arching and spreading, strap-shaped leaves that in full sun assume in their upper one-thirds bright pink or red tones. The tiny, pink flowers are in erect, pyramidal panicles, with white-fuzzy stalks and white-fuzzy bases to the blooms. They are succeeded by dense clusters of pearly berries that last for months. ***A. miniata discolor*** of Brazil has rosettes

Aechmea miniata discolor

of spreading leaves 1 foot to 1½ feet long, olive-green above, shiny maroon on their undersides. The blue flowers, their berry-like lower parts changing to bright red, long-lasting fruits, are in loose panicles. ***A. nudicaulis***, a variable species native from Mexico to Panama, has typically narrow, tubular, few-leaved rosettes of gray-green or grayish-brownish-green leaves edged with black teeth. The flowering stalk, spreading more or less horizontally from the mouth of the funnel of foliage, is red and terminates in a narrow spikelike panicle of yellow flowers. In *A. n. aureo-rosea* the floral bracts are bright crimson, the flowers red with yellow-tipped petals. *A.*

Aechmea nudicaulis aureo-rosea

n. cuspidata has brownish to greenish leaves with irregular, grayish cross bands. Its floral bracts are small. *A. n. striatifolium* has leaves marked longitudinally with cream-colored stripes. ***A. orlandiana*** is a Brazilian

Aechmea orlandiana

of unusual appearance. In its wild state occurring both on trees and in the ground, it has rosettes of light green leaves conspicuously marked with zigzags of deep chocolate-brown and margined with stout, brown teeth. Plants grown in bright light develop maroon blotches at the leaf ends.

The lower leaves, 1 foot to 1½ feet long, are inclined to droop. The flowering stalks have salmon-scarlet bracts and compact panicles of white and pale yellow flowers. ***A. pectinata*** is a Brazilian that grows on trees and on the ground, often so near the sea that it is splashed by spray. It has handsome, symmetrical, rigid rosettes up to 2 feet across of many spreading, channeled leaves 3 to 4 inches wide that become reddish or red toward their apexes and margins. The greenish flowers are in tight, cone-shaped heads 2½ inches in diameter lifted on long stalks high above the foliage. The bracts are green. It is a shy bloomer. ***A. penduliflora*** grows on the

Aechmea penduliflora

ground and on trees from Costa Rica to Brazil. Of medium size, it has rich apple-green leaves that become pink on plants grown in strong light. The inconspicuous yellow flowers are in loose pyramidal pan-

Aechmea penduliflora

icles, succeeded by green-tipped, ivory-white berries nearly ½ inch long that change as they mature to bright porcelain-blue. ***A. phanerophlebia*** is Brazilian. Its heavily spine-toothed, stiff leaves, 1½ to 2 feet long by 1½ inches wide, are in erect, cylindrical to urn-shaped rosettes with some outer leaves spreading or drooping. The blue-petaled flowers and collars of rose-pink bracts form heads lifted above the foliage on slender stalks. *A. pineliana* is of medium size. Native of Brazil, it has rosettes of slender, pinkish-gray or coppery-tinged leaves that in good light become rich pink. They are 1 foot to 1½ feet long by about 1¼ inches wide. The flowers

Aechmea pineliana

are yellow, in tight, cone-shaped heads carried on erect stalks well above the foliage. The bracts are red. *A. p. minuta* differs from the species in its smaller size and more attractive silvery-bronze to greenish-silver coloring. *A. racinae* is aptly called Christmas jewels. Native in Brazilian rain forests, this small species produces, usually in midwinter, pendent flowering stems 1 foot long or longer ending in red-stalked racemes of yellow and black flowers peeping from brilliant red ovaries and succeeded by long-lasting, brilliant, orange-colored berries. Its strap-shaped leaves are soft and glossy. It needs partial shade. *A.*

Aechmea racinae

ramosa is a popular and handsome Brazilian, impressive with its rosettes of ascending-spreading, minutely-toothed, strap-shaped leaves 2 to 3 feet long by 2 inches

wide and varying in color in individual plants from green to yellow-green or a decidedly rosy-pink. Lifted well above the foliage, the red- or orange-stalked, narrowly-pyramidal, loosely-branched panicles of yellow flowers are succeeded by long-lasting, greenish-yellow berries. *A. recurvata* is a sun-loving, fairly cold-resistant native of Brazil. It has urn-shaped rosettes up to about 10 inches in diameter of rigid, narrowly-triangular, spreading, toothed leaves, the inner becoming brilliant red at flowering time. The purplish flowers are in crowded, egg-shaped heads at the ends of fairly short, stout stalks. *A. tillandsioides* is a somewhat variable native from Mexico to Brazil. Typically it has rosettes of glossy, arching, strap-shaped leaves 1¼ to 1½ feet long by 2 inches wide and margined with straight, brown spines. The erect flowering stalks, shorter than the leaves, have showy, crimson bracts and radiating branches with white flowers succeeded by blue berries. *A. t. amazonas* has larger panicles of bloom. *A. t. kienastii* is smaller and has shorter, fewer-branched panicles. *A. triangularis* is a Brazilian, with cylindrical rosettes of channeled leaves margined with black spines. The flowering stalk, decorated with rich rose-red, showy bracts, terminates in a tight, blue-black, poker-like or conelike head from which peek the short-lived blooms. It is native to

Aechmea tillandsioides kienastii

Brazil. *A. weilbachii*, of Brazil, is medium-sized. Its thin leaves, 1 foot to 1½ feet long by 1½ inches wide, are apple-green and have inconspicuous spines. The arching, dull red flowering stalk, up to 1½ feet long, terminates in loose, more or less cylindrical panicles up to 6 inches long. The lower parts of the blooms are orange-red and berry-like. The petals are lilac-colored, but soon become black. The berries are red. Variety *A. w. leodiensis* has lustrous foliage tinged with bronzy-pink.

Garden and Landscape Uses. Aechmeas are among the most popular bromeliads, outdoors in humid tropical and warm sub-

tropical regions and as greenhouse plants and houseplants. Among their numerous species, varieties, and hybrids are sorts for many uses, sizes ranging from small neat plants not more than a few inches across to giants 6 feet or even more in diameter. They come in many handsome colors of foliage and bloom, often with leaves striped, barred, or otherwise variegated, and with undersides differing in hue from the upper surfaces. Not only do they display great variety of foliage but the coloring and forms of their flowers and bracts vary tremendously. Not the least of their attractions are the often colorful, long-lasting, berry-like fruits.

From among this great variety can be selected kinds for many particular purposes, to be used as striking solitary specimens, to adorn the trunks, branches, and crotches of trees, the terrestrials as underplantings in lightly shaded ground beds beneath trees and shrubs. Aechmeas associates with good effect with other warm-climate tree-perchers (epiphytes) appreciating dappled shade and reasonably humid surroundings.

Cultivation. Given environments fairly well to their liking, aechmeas accommodate with enthusiasm and are accounted among the easiest of bromeliads to grow. Indoors they succeed best where the night temperature in winter is between 55 and 60°F, increased by five to fifteen degrees by day or even somewhat higher. A humid atmosphere, light shade from strong sun, and a rooting mixture kept always moist, but not soggy, which is loose and contains a preponderance of coarse organic matter such as osmunda fiber, coarse leaves, and bark chips such as are used for orchids suits aechmeas. Propagation is easy by offsets and seeds. For more information see Bromeliads and Bromels.

Aechmea weilbachii

AEGLE (Aè-gle)—Bael Fruit. There is only one species of this genus. The plant sometimes called *Aegle sepiaria* is *Poncirus trifoliata*. The bael fruit (*A. marmelos*) of India is a more or less spiny tree of the rue family

RUTACEAE. Its name is that of one of three sisters, the Hesperides, who according to Greek mythology, guarded a tree that bore golden apples.

Growing in the tropics up to 40 feet, but in the continental United States not more than 20 feet, the bael fruit has long, slender, sometimes drooping branches and slender-stalked leaves of three narrowly-ovate leaflets, the central one larger than the others. The margins of the leaflets are wavy or are furnished with irregular small teeth. The leaflets are 1¼ to 5 inches long. The flowers, in hairy clusters, have a four- or five-toothed calyx, the same number of narrow, greenish-white petals, and numerous stamens. They are succeeded by globose to pear-shaped, greenish-yellow fruits 2 to 6 inches in diameter and covered with hard yellow or grayish shells, which at first are hairy. They contain aromatic, sweet, orange pulp and many seeds. The bael fruit, which is related to oranges, lemons, and grapefruits, is not much grown in the United States, but is popular in India and other parts of tropical Asia. There the blooms are used in perfumes and the fruits, bark, and roots in medicines. The wood and shells of the fruits are made into various small objects. The tree is of religious significance and is commonly planted in temple gardens. Its leaves are used in the worship of the Hindu god Siva.

Garden and Landscape Uses and Cultivation. The bael tree is occasionally planted in Florida and Hawaii, chiefly as an unusual producer of edible fruits, which may be eaten raw or used in preserves and beverages. It grows in ordinary soil and presents no special problems. It is usually propagated by seed.

AEGLOPSIS (Aeglóp-sis). Five African species, relatives of *Citrus* and belonging to the rue family RUTACEAE, compose *Aeglopsis*. The name derives from that of the related genus *Aegle,* and the Greek *opsis,* similar to.

Trees or shrubs with undivided leaves, and blooms in few- to many-flowered axillary panicles, aeglopsises belong to the group of *Citrus* relatives that have hard-shelled fruits. Their flowers have four- or five-parted calyxes, four or five petals, two or three times as many stamens as petals, and a short style. The globose to somewhat pear-shaped fruits are large and filled with a mucilaginous, aromatic juice.

A shrub or small tree with solitary, strong spines. *A. chevalieri* inhabits tropical West Africa. Much-branched, it has elliptic, short-stalked leaves 2 to 4½ inches long, which are about two-thirds as long as they are wide. In panicles up to eight, but sometimes more, the white flowers are ¾ to 1 inch wide. They have five, sometimes four, petals. The yellowish to bright orange-brown fruits are 2 to 4 inches in diameter.

Garden and Landscape Uses and Cultivation. This species flowers and fruits freely while still small. It succeeds in southern Florida, and is grown for interest and as an understock for *Balsamocitrus* and *Aegle.* It may be expected to prosper under the general circumstances that suit oranges, with warmer conditions perhaps appreciated.

AEGOPODIUM (Aegopòd-ium) — Goutweed or Bishop's Weed. Of the seven species of *Aegopodium* that inhabit Europe and temperate Asia only one is cultivated, and the discriminating gardener may well have reservations about admitting that to his plantings. Unless carefully controlled, it can become a pestiferous weed. Despite this, like so many other rampant growers, in a carefully chosen site it can serve usefully. This genus belongs in the carrot family UMBELLIFERAE. Its name is derived from the Greek *aix,* a goat, and *podion,* a little foot, and probably refers to the shape of the leaflets. The kind cultivated is the goutweed or bishop's weed (*A. podagraria*), a native of Europe, hardy, and naturalized in North America. It is most commonly cultivated in its variegated-leaved variety. *A. p. variegatum,* which differs from the typical kind in having clear white-edged leaves.

The goutweed is 1 foot tall or slightly taller and spreads aggressively by creeping, underground rootstocks. Its long-stalked leaves are twice thrice-divided into ovate or elliptic toothed leaflets. The flowers are tiny, white or yellowish, and in flat, compound umbels, 1½ to 3 inches wide, carried above the foliage in early summer.

Garden Uses and Cultivation. Let the unwary gardener beware of planting this determined spreader close to choice plants of lesser vigor; it can be disastrous if admitted to a rock garden. The goutweed roots deeply and once established is difficult to eradicate. If used with discretion it can serve well as a groundcover and for edgings where few other plants will grow and where there is no danger of it crowding out less vigorous plants. The variegated-leaved variety is a less vigorous spreader than the green-leaved variety, but not much. It sometimes partly reverts to the green-foliaged type; when this occurs the reverted portions should be weeded out promptly. The goutweed is increased by division in early fall or spring. It grows best in rather moist soil and part-shade.

AEONIUM (Aeòn-ium). Succulent plants of the Canary Islands, Madeira, Cape Verde Islands, Morocco, and Arabia, the forty species of this genus belong in the orpine

Aegopodium podagraria

family CRASSULACEAE. Formerly included in *Sempervivum*, they are still often known by that name in gardens. *Aeonium* differs from sempervivums chiefly in the great majority of its kinds being subshrubs with clearly evident, fairly tall, usually branched stems. Unlike most sempervivums none is hardy in the north; at most they stand very slight frost. The name is adapted from one used by Dioscorides for *A. arboreum*. Because of the abandon with which these plants hybridize in the wild and because of the confusion that exists in the application of names in cultivation, cultivated plants, often of hybrid origin, are frequently misidentified. Ordinarily the hybrids have characteristics intermediate between those of their parents.

Except for biennial *A. glandulosum*, aeoniums are evergreen perennials. Some die after they bloom once, but again excepting *A. glandulosum*, that does not happen until they are a few years old. They have rosettes of alternate, fleshy, stalkless or short-stalked leaves, typically obovate to spatula-shaped or lanceolate, and with rounded undersides. Except for their margins, which may be fringed with hairs or tiny teeth, the leaves are generally hairless. The yellow, or more rarely whitish or pink, mostly starry blooms are in panicles of sometimes large size. They have six to thirteen each sepals, petals, and carpels, and twice as many stamens. The fruits are follicles. Some plants previously included in *Aeonium* belong in *Aichryson*.

Tall aeoniums popular in cultivation include *A. arboreum* and its varieties and hybrids. From 2 to 3 feet in height and few-branched, this native of Morocco is extensively naturalized throughout the Mediterranean region. In dense, flat or slightly hollowed rosettes at the branch tips, its lustrous, broadly-inverted-wedge-shaped leaves, hairless except along their margins, are 2 to 3 inches long. The bright yellow flowers have nine to eleven petals, downy individual stalks, and are in stalked panicles the flowering portions of which are 4 inches or so long and as broad. Variety *A. a. foliis-purpureis* has dark purple leaves. In *A. a. atropurpureum* the leaves are even

Aeonium arboreum atropurpureum

darker. The leaves of *A. a. luteo-variegatum* are mottled with bright yellow. Other variegated forms probably exist. A Canary Island native *A. balsamiferum* is quite similar to *A. arboreum*, but with gray-green, broader, hairless leaves that are balsam-scented. The inner leaves of its loose rosettes are erect and form cuplike centers. This species is a shy bloomer.

Other yellow-flowered, Canary Island natives of the *A. arboreum* relationship are *A. manriqueorum*, *A. holochrysum*, and *A. undulatum*. The **A. manriqueorum** has a short, stout stem, and more or less sprawling, tortuous branches up to 6 feet in length. The rosettes, 5 to 9 inches across,

Aeonium manriqueorum

are of spatula-shaped hair-fringed, shining green leaves, sometimes streaked with brownish-purple. The terminal, ovoid to pyramidal, glandular-hairy flower panicles are 6 to 9 inches long. The flowers, on short-hairy individual stalks, have ten or eleven petals. The panicles of bloom of *A. holochrysum* differ from those of *A. manriqueorum* in not being hairy. Easily distinguished by its 3 to 4 feet or taller stem, branched only toward its base, it is one of the most imposing and handsome aeoniums. Flat rosettes of often markedly wavy-edged, blunt, spatula-shaped leaves 4 to 6 inches long or occasionally longer, and with hair-fringed margins, are characteristic of *A. undulatum*. With their lower parts densely-leafy, the erect, 2- to 3-foot-long flower-bearing stems of this species end in broad, pyramidal panicles 1 foot to 2 feet long and up to 1½ feet wide, of bright yellow blooms that have nine to twelve petals.

Smaller, common in cultivation, and handsome, *A. haworthii* branches freely to form a roundish subshrub 1 foot to 2 feet tall, and 1 foot to 2 feet wide. Its slender branches end in loose rosettes of thick, pointed, broadly-obovate, usually glaucous leaves 1 inch to 2 inches long or

slightly longer. They are red-edged and have forward-pointing, fleshy hairs. Up to 1 foot tall, the erect sparingly leafy, few-branched blooming stems have bell-shaped rather than flat flowers with seven to nine petals. They are pale yellow suffused with rose-pink. This kind is endemic to the Canary Islands. Similar, but with thinner, rather limp, spatula-shaped, glaucous leaves, purplish-edged when old, and greenish or pinkish-white flowers with erect petals, *A. castello-paivae* is also of the Canaries. Much like it, but with green, or in sun reddish, not glaucous, red-edged leaves, and pink flowers, is another Canary Island species, **A. decorum.**

Aeonium decorum

Shining, sticky, very small foliage and clammy young shoots characterize *A. sedifolium* of the Canary Islands. Densely-twiggy and 6 inches to 1 foot tall, it has slender, tortuous branches. Less than ½ inch long and rounded on both surfaces, its obovate, stalkless, toothless, hairless leaves are besprinkled and edged with minute beadlike points, and are marked with reddish lines. The flowers, in forked clusters of up to twelve, have nine to eleven spreading or reflexed petals. They are bright yellow. In aspect much like *A. sedifolium*, but larger, and with less sticky, bead-edged, obovate-spatula-

Aeonium undulatum

Aeonium sedifolium

Aeonium sedifolium

The most remarkable species of the genus, **A. tabulaeforme** is astonishingly symmetrical. Growing in the wild in vertical, shaded rock crevices in hot, lowland areas of the Canary Islands, old specimens have stems up to 10 inches long. More com-

Aeonium tabulaeforme

monly they are much shorter, so that the perfectly flat, platelike rosettes, up to 1 foot in diameter and consisting of up to 200 leaves laid in tight overlapping spirals with remarkable precision, are flat upon the ground. The leaves narrow below and are fringed with white hairs. The 1-foot-long panicles of seven- to nine-petaled pale yellow flowers are borne on stout, erect stems. Resembling *A. tabulaeforme,* but of biennial duration and having the upper sides of its leaves hairy instead of hairless, **A. glandulosum,** of Madeira, has rosettes of balsam-scented leaves up to 1 foot or more in width. Its flower panicles are shorter and broader than those of *A. tabulaeforme.* The straw-yellow flowers have eleven to thirteen petals and are 1 inch in diameter.

Rosettes of foliage up to 3 feet in diameter, bigger than those of any other kind, are typical of **A. canariense,** an inhabitant of the Canary Islands. It has short, thick stems. The rosettes are of velvety, fleshy, loosely arranged, glandular-pubescent leaves 2 to 6 inches wide, the inner being

shaped, thick, finely-hairy, fleshy leaves about ¾ inch long, **A. spathulatum** has blackish branches and finely-hairy young shoots. Its eight- to ten-petaled, yellow flowers are carried in panicles 2 to 4 inches long and wide. It is a native of the Canary Islands. Pink-flowered **A. goochiae,** of the Canary Islands, is a clammy foliaged, much-branched species about 6 inches tall and 1 foot wide. Its stalked, limp, obovate leaves, in flattish rosettes, are about 1 inch long. The flowers are in squat panicles of up to thirty. They have seven or eight petals.

Other sticky-leaved kinds are *A. gluti-nosum* and *A. lindleyi,* the former from Madeira, the latter from the Canaries. Lax and scarcely shrubby, **A. glutinosum** has rosettes of broadly-spatula-shaped leaves, hairless except at their margins, and up to 4 inches long. The panicles are up to 1 foot long and as broad or broader. The bright yellow flowers have nine to ten petals. Similar to *A. goochiae,* but differing in having yellow flowers as extremely fleshy leaves, thicker than those of any other species, **A. lindleyi** is about 1 foot tall. Its leaves are obovate to spatula-shaped, and glandular-pubescent. Its flowers have eight or nine petals.

Aeonium canariense

erect and forming a cup. On downy, leafy stems 1½ to 2 feet in length, the pyramidal flower panicles are nearly as long as these stems. The bell-shaped, pale greenish-yellow blooms have eight to ten petals. Very similar, but smaller and grayer, **A. palmense** is closely related to **A. virgineum,** which is even smaller and more branched. Both have lemon-yellow blooms and are natives of the Canary Islands.

Dying after they bloom, but living more than two and often five to ten years, *A. urbicum, A. hierrense,* and *A. nobile* are also natives of the Canary Islands. The first in bloom, **A. urbicum,** generally about 3 feet tall, but sometimes 6 or 7 feet, has dense rosettes, up to 1 foot or more wide, of hairless, green or glaucous, red-edged leaves, and unbranched stems with panicles up to 2½ feet long of greenish, white, or pinkish, nine-petaled, wide-bell-shaped blooms. The similar **A. hierrense** differs in having pubescent flower stalks not over 2 feet tall. It also has more compact panicles of mostly deeper pink blooms. The dark-red flowered **A. nobile** is distinctive. Even out of bloom this species is readily recognizable by its loose rosettes of thick leaves crowning erect stems up to 1 foot long. Often the leaves, 8 inches to 1 foot long and folded upward to form channeled centers, are obovate and two-thirds as broad as they are long. The branching flower stems are about 1 foot high and end in flat-topped panicles, which can be 2 feet in diameter. This species grows slowly and blooms infrequently.

More closely resembling the hardy sempervivums than any other aeonium, **A. simsii** (syn. *A. caespitosum*) grows in low clusters, with rosettes about 3 inches in diameter of hairy-margined, strap-shaped leaves. It has flower stems that are lateral rather than arising from the centers of the rosettes. Up to about 4 inches long, erect, and clothed with small up-pointing leaves, they end in flattish panicles a little less to a little more than 1 inch across, consisting of bright yellow blooms with seven to nine petals.

A popular nameless hybrid between *A. simsii* and *A spathulatum* is excellent and common in cultivation. Of bushy habit, it is up to 6 inches tall and twice as broad. It branches freely and has terminal rosettes about 2 inches in diameter, of spreading, oblong-lanceolate leaves. Their upper sides are green with a brown center line; beneath they are paler. The erect flower stalks, often from horizontal branches, are glandular-pubescent.

Garden and Landscape Uses. As outdoor plants aeoniums are very satisfactory in Mediterranean-type climates, where summers are warm and dry and winters mild and fairly moist. They are eminently suitable for gardens in California and the Southwest, and are appropriate for rock gardens, banks, rocky places, dry walls, and similar locations. They need very well-drained soil and do well in full sun or part-day shade. As indoor plants they are useful for window gardens and for growing with other succulents in greenhouses, either in pots or ground beds.

Cultivation. The soil must be porous. One of a sandy character is best. For indoor plants it is helpful to mix with it a generous amount of small crocks (pieces of flower pot) or broken brick; some crushed limestone is also helpful. Repotting is done at the beginning of the season of new growth, usually in early fall. Watering is moderate when the plants are in active growth, in most cases from early fall to late spring, but in the case of *A. glandulosum* in summer. Resting plants should be watered sparsely. Constant saturation is disastrous. Occasional applications of dilute liquid fertilizer help specimens that have filled their containers with roots, but must not be given when the plants are dormant. In greenhouses winter night temperatures of 45 to 50°F are adequate, with not more than, at that season, an increase of five to ten degrees by day. On all favorable occasions the greenhouse must be ventilated freely. Cuttings and seeds afford ready means of securing increase. Because of the proclivity of many kinds to hybridize, seeds may not produce plants true to type if other kinds grow near the seed parent and are in bloom at the same time. For further information see Succulents.

AERANGIS. See Angraecum.

AERATION OF THE SOIL. The roots as well as the above-ground parts of plants need oxygen. Plants that grow naturally in water (aquatics) and bogs, like fish and other animals that live in similar environments, obtain their oxygen supply from water. Most plants cannot do this. The oxygen their underground parts require must come from air in the soil. If this is deficient the roots die.

Manipulation and care of the soil includes making sure that it is adequately aerated. The ideal condition for the vast

Aerating a small lawn with a spading fork

majority of plants is that each soil particle or tiny aggregate of particles be surrounded by a film of moisture but with small air spaces between them. Thus the particles or aggregates somewhat resemble in miniature a bunch of grapes dipped in water and withdrawn. If water fills all the interstices air is driven out. If a considerable proportion of the particles are exceedingly fine, separate, and glutinous, as are those of clays in a deflocculated condition they cling together in a pasty mass to the exclusion of air.

Garden practices and operations aimed at improving soil aeration, which are usually less necessary in sandy earths than clayey ones, include in extreme cases installation of land drains. More usually routine manipulation such as plowing, spading, forking, rototilling, cultivating, and hoeing, together with the addition from time to time of compost or other bulky organic material take care of the matter. Liming may also be helpful. Drainage holes, covered with a layer of crocks or other material that promotes the rapid escape of excess water, are important in the bottoms of containers in which plants are grown. Lawns may be aerated by the use of spiked rollers and similar devices or, on a small scale, by jabbing them at intervals of a few inches with the tines of a spading fork.

Additives of a nonleachable, nondegradable nature such as sand, grit, perlite, broken crock, stone chips, coal cinders, and charcoal are also used, more especially in potting soils and earths prepared for special limited areas such as rock gardens than on a more extensive scale.

AERIAL YAM is *Dioscorea bulbifera*.

AERIDACHNIS. This is the name of bigeneric orchids the parents of which are *Aerides* and *Arachnis*.

AERIDES (Aerìd-es). Appropriately, the name of the genus *Aerides* of the orchid family ORCHIDACEAE is derived from the Greek *aer*, air. It directs attention to the manner in which the plants grow. They are epiphytes. They live on trees without taking nourishment from them, or occasionally on rocks. Chiefly tropical and native from Japan to India, the Philippine Islands, and Indonesia, they number forty species.

Much resembling vandas, these generally handsome orchids are without pseudobulbs. The erect stems, which often develop aerial roots, are sheathed at their bases by two-ranked, more or less fleshy, rigid leaves that are often notched at their apexes into a pair of unequal lobes. In most kinds the leaves are strap-shaped, in a few cylindrical. The medium-sized to fairly large blooms, generally white or green and white suffused with magenta or amethyst-purple and spotted with the same hues, have three spreading sepals, the up-

per one smaller than the others and similar to the two lateral petals. The lip, like the lateral sepals attached to the base of the column, is three-lobed with the middle lobe spreading, the side lobes erect. It has a hollow, generally upturned spur. Often strongly fragrant, the blooms, which are usually numerous, are in long, pendulous, cylindrical racemes from the leaf axils. Most cultivated species vary considerably in size of bloom and color of flower. Varieties based on such variations are recognized by specialists.

The most often cultivated species, *A. odorata* is a variable native of wide distribution through much of the natural range of the genus. From 3 to about 5 feet tall, it has strap-shaped leaves 6 to 10 inches long by less than 2 inches wide, notched at their apexes. The arching to drooping racemes of waxy, fragrant, creamy-white, magenta-, purple-, or pink-marked blooms are rarely 2 feet long, usually considerably shorter. Each flower is 1 inch to 1¾ inches across and has a strongly curved spur to the funnel-shaped lip. The very fragrant blooms of *A. quinquevulnera* a native of the Philippines, are similar to those of *A. odorata* except that the middle lobe of the lip is toothed along its margins. They are up to 1 inch across and have green spurs. In *A. q. purpurata* the flowers are burgundy-red. Also a native of the Philippines, *A. lawrenceae* is up to 5 feet tall. Its curved leaves, up to 1 foot long and 2 inches broad, are notched at the tips. The densely-flowered racemes may be 2 feet long. The flowers are fragrant, waxy, and about 1¾ inches across. They are white with magenta to crimson-purple tips to the sepals and petals. The lip has an amethyst-purple middle lobe and a green spur. Orchid fanciers cultivate a number of other species and a few hybrids. One of the finest hybrids, the result of crossing *A. lawrenceae* with *A. fieldingii* is 'Hermon Slade'.

Aerides lawrenceae

In addition, there are hybrids between *Aerides* and *Vanda, Aerides* and *Phalaenopsis,* and *Aerides* and some other genera.

Among species likely to be grown are the following: *A. crassifolia,* of Burma, rarely attains great height. Its closely-spaced leaves are up to 7 inches long, up to 2 inches wide, and notched at their tips. Somewhat loosely arranged, the 1½-inch-wide, fragrant flowers, in racemes up to 2 feet long, are bright rose-purple, often paler in the lower parts of the sepals and petals. The spur is tipped with green. *A. crispa,* of India, up to 5 feet tall, has rather widely-spaced leaves up to 8 inches long by 2 inches wide, with notched tips and a tiny point between the lobes. About 2 inches in diameter, the pineapple-scented blooms are in racemes, often branched, up to 3 feet long. They are white, suffused on the backs of the sepals and petals, and near their tips on the fronts, with magenta. The lip is fringed, its outer one-half deep amethyst-purple, its base and the lateral lobes white streaked with magenta. *A. falcata* differs in being often taller, with longer, narrower leaves, and smaller blooms. It comes from Indochina. *A. f. houlletiana* has yellowish-tan flowers with white lips, and its sepals and petals are tipped with orange-brown. *A. f. leoniae* has larger blooms, their white sepals and petals tipped and dotted near their bases with amethyst-purple. Their lips are white dotted and marked with the same color, the middle lobe darker purple. *A. fieldingii* has a shortish stem crowded with leaves up to 10 inches long by 1¾ inches wide. Mark-

Aerides fieldingii

edly drooping, and up to 2 feet long, the racemes, sometimes few-branched from their bases, are of fragrant blooms 1 inch to 2 inches wide. Their sepals and petals are amethyst-purple suffused with white or—rarely are pure white. Sometimes the bases of the sepals and petals are white dotted with purple. The lip is purple sprinkled with white with a whitish spur. *A. multiflora,* of Indochina to the Himalayas, is generally of moderate height and has curved leaves approximately 9 inches long by 1 inch wide. Longer than the leaves, the arched racemes are crowded with fragrant blooms ¾ to 1 inch across. They are

white with amethyst-purple tips, with a few purple dots on the upper sepal and the petals. The lateral sepals are white stained with purple, and the amethyst-purple lip is darker along its center. The spur is short and straight. *A. vandara,* of northern India, the Himalayas, and China, has slender stems up to several feet in length, and pointed, cylindrical leaves, grooved along the upper side, 6 to 8 inches long. The blooms, solitary or in racemes of two or three, are about 2 inches wide. Translucent white, they have lips usually suffused with yellow.

Garden and Landscape Uses and Cultivation. Aerides are beautiful grown outdoors in the humid tropics and warm subtropics and indoors in greenhouses. They are adapted for growing in hanging baskets and large pots. Their needs are generally those of vandas. They revel in a rather loose, coarse-textured rooting mixture such as one containing chunks of osmunda, tree fern fiber, or fir bark and some chopped crocks and charcoal. They are impatient of stagnant conditions at the roots and of root disturbance. Each year some of the old compost should be carefully picked out and replaced with new, taking great care, as must be done when potting, not to injure the brittle roots. Constant high humidity, without the atmosphere being dank and stagnant, and sufficient shade to prevent the foliage from being scorched, but not more, are required. Excessive shade inhibits flowering. Most aerides require minimum night temperatures of 65 to 70°F with increases of up to fifteen degrees by day. Some from less intensely tropical areas are satisfied with 60°F at night; *A. vandara* can be grown at 55°F, with proportionate increases by day. The rooting medium must be moist throughout the year. Propagation is by removing and potting separately basal offshoots called keikis, by taking the upper portions of stems well furnished with aerial roots and potting them, and by sowing the seeds. For more information see Orchids.

AERIDOCENTRUM. This is the name of orchid hybrids the parents of which are *Aerides* and *Ascocentrum.*

AERIDOFINETIA. This is the name of bigeneric orchids the parents of which are *Aerides* and *Neofinetia.*

AERIDOPSIS. This is the name of bigeneric orchids the parents of which are *Aerides* and *Phalaenopsis.*

AERIDOSTYLIS. This is the name of bigeneric orchids the parents of which are *Aerides* and *Rhynchostylis.*

AERIDOVANDA. This is the name of bigeneric orchids the parents of which are *Aerides* and *Vanda.*

AERUA. See Aerva.

AERVA (Aér-va). The name *Aerva,* sometimes spelled *Aerua,* comes from its Arabic one. Its ten species of herbaceous plants and subshrubs are natives of Africa, tropical Asia, or Indonesia and belong in the amaranth family AMARANTHACEAE. They have alternate, opposite, or whorled (in circles of more than two) leaves, and spikes of tiny bisexual or unisexual blooms. The flowers are white or reddish-brown.

More or less climbing and subshrubby, *A. scandens* has softly-hairy, opposite or alternate, pointed-ovate to lanceolate, green leaves 1½ to 2½ inches long. Its tiny flowers are in cylindrical, white-woolly spikes about 1 inch long. Each has four or five fertile stamens and the same number of sterile ones (staminodes). The most commonly cultivated kind, *A. s. sanguinea* (syns. *A. sanguinea, A. sanguinolenta*) has leaves that are dark red above with paler undersides.

Garden and Landscape Uses and Cultivation. In the tropics and subtropics this species and its variety are cultivated as ornamentals. They may be trimmed to form edgings to paths and beds. They succeed in ordinary soil in sunny places. The red-leaved variety is sometimes grown in greenhouses. It succeeds where the night temperature in winter is about 55°F and that by day is five to fifteen degrees higher. At other seasons more warmth is appropriate. Full sun, except for slight shade in summer, is needed and a fairly humid atmosphere. Aervas grow well in free-draining, fertile soil, kept moderately moist. Their stems should be pinched occasionally to promote bushiness. Propagation is by seeds and cuttings.

AESCHYNANTHUS (Aeschyn-ánthus)—Lipstick Plant. Formerly *Trichosporum,* the tropical Asian and Indonesian genus *Aeschynanthus* belongs to the gesneria family GESNERIACEAE. Consisting of about eighty species, it is the Old World counterpart of the strictly American *Columnea.* Its name derives from the Greek *aischyne,* to be ashamed, and *anthos,* a flower, referring to the red flowers.

Aeschynanthuses are evergreen, woody or herbaceous perennials mostly with vining or drooping stems. In the wild they perch on trees, without taking nourishment from them, and so are epiphytes, or on logs and rocks, where their roots can find a foothold in the accumulations of organic debris. They have slender stems and in twos, threes, or fours, toothless or slightly-toothed, thick, equal-sized leaves. The blooms are solitary or in pairs from the upper leaf axils or in clusters at the shoot ends. They have short-tubed calyxes with long, slender lobes or long calyx tubes with very short, toothlike lobes. The corolla is tubular with the lower, slender portion often cosseted in the calyx. Its usually short lobes (petals) form two lips, the upper lip of two, the lower lip of three lobes. There are four slightly protruding fertile stamens and one staminode (abortive stamen). The style, hairy or hairless, is topped with a broad stigma. A small ringlike disk surrounds the base of the ovary and distinguishes *Aeschynanthus* from *Columnea*, in which the disk is represented by a conspicuous, sometimes two-lobed gland. The fruits of *Aeschynanthus*, like those of *Columnea*, are capsules. Garden varieties and hybrids of *Aeschynanthus* are few, those of *Columnea* many.

Lipstick plant (**A. radicans** syns. *A. boschianus, A. javanicus, A. lobbianus*), a variable native of Java and the Malay Peninsula, has hairless or minutely-hairy, trailing or drooping stems and short-stalked, elliptic to ovate or broad-ovate, paired, sometimes purplish, smooth-edged or toothed, thin or thick, hairless or hairy leaves ¾ inch to 3 inches long by ⅓ to 1¼ inches wide. The flowers usually occur in short-stalked pairs from the leaf axils or clustered near and at the ends of the stems.

Aeschynanthus radicans

They have a green to dark purple, hairless or hairy calyx ¼ inch to 1¼ inches long that embraces the lower part of the corolla. The latter, bright red, 1¾ to 3 inches long, and hairy, is much constricted above its base and then widens gradually. The stalks of the stamens are hairless and the ovary and style are pubescent. Also sometimes called lipstick plant, the closely related **A. pulcher** of Java and the Malay Peninsula differs from *A. radicans* chiefly in its blooms, which except for a fine fringe along the edges of the petals, are hairless.

Flowers in conspicuous clusters of four to twenty at the branch ends are featured by **A. speciosus,** a showy, desirable, robust native of Borneo, Java, and the Malay Peninsula. Immediately below the flowers is a whorl (circle) of four to eight leaves. Lower on the stems the leaves are rather distantly-spaced and mostly in whorls of three or four. They are pointed-ovate-lanceolate, fleshy, 2½ to 4 inches long by 1

Aeschynanthus pulcher

inch to 1¾ inches wide, and have wavy or pleated margins. The flowers, 2½ to 4 inches long, have slightly hairy calyxes divided almost to their bases, a similarly hairy corolla tube that expands gradually in its upper one-half from a slender lower portion. The lower part of the corolla tube is orange-yellow, higher it is orange-red. The petals have a dark blackish-red band separating their scarlet apexes from their orange-yellow bases. Hybrid **A. splendidus,** the parents of which are *A. speciosus* and *A. parasiticus*, is very like *A. speciosus*, but is distinguished by flowers that have

deep maroon blotches without orange-yellow bases and by the tube of the calyx, which is as long as its lobes. It is a very fine ornamental.

Another robust native of Java, **A. longiflorus** differs from *A. speciosus* in its leaves always being in pairs and having flat margins. They are pointed-ovate, lustrous above, paler on their undersides, 2 to 6 inches long and ¾ inch to 2½ inches wide. The flowers, in clusters of two to seven at the branch ends, have dark red calyxes and crimson corollas 2½ to 4 inches in length, their petals marked by a black-edged, yellowish-red blotch.

Beauty of foliage not bloom is the chief appeal of **A. marmoratus** (syn. *A. zebrinus*). Its slender stems are furnished with pairs of slightly-toothed, narrowly-elliptic leaves, 2½ to 4 inches long, their upper sides pale green, with darker, indefinite marbling, their under surfaces paler and marked with red. Solitary from the leaf axils, the 1½-inch-long flowers have sparingly-hairy calyxes cleft nearly to their bases and green corollas splashed with chocolate on their small petals. The stamens, and style at maturity, are much protruded. This species is indigenous to Burma, Thailand, and Malaya.

Other kinds sometimes cultivated include the following: **A. ellipticus,** a native of New Guinea, has opposite, thick, glossy, ovate leaves up to 4½ inches long by one-half as wide. Its blooms, clustered at the

Aeschynanthus splendidus

branch ends, have short, yellow-green, tubular calyxes and 3-inch-long, bright reddish-orange corollas striped with dark red. The stamens are dark red. *A. evrardii,* with opposite, lanceolate, thick, hairless leaves, has blades about ¾ inch long. Its flowers, in the leaf axils and clustered toward the branch ends, have 1-inch-long, hairless calyxes and red corollas 2¾ to 3½ inches in length. *A. micranthus,* of the Himalayan region, is a slender-stemmed trailer with opposite, small, lanceolate leaves and little tubular flowers in twos or threes from the leaf axils that are dark purplish-red with blackish margins to the petals near their

Aeschynanthus micranthus

apexes. *A. obconicus,* of Malaya, has oblong-elliptic to ovate, glossy leaves 2 to 3½ inches long and dark red, fuzzy-hairy flowers nearly 1 inch long in pairs. *A. parasiticus* (syns. *A. grandiflorus, A. parviflorus*) is a straggling trailer, with fleshy, slender-pointed, oblong-lanceolate, toothed leaves up to 4 inches long. Its curved blooms, 1½ to 2 inches long, are deep crimson tipped with orange and very dark, almost black, purple. It is a native of India. *A. tricolor,* a native of Borneo, has slightly-hairy stems and ovate leaves up to 1½ inches long by ½ inch wide. Usually in pairs, the scarlet flowers streaked with black and yellow are about 2 inches long and glandular-hairy.

Garden and Landscape Uses. Except in the humid tropics, these are strictly plants for warm greenhouses and other indoor environments where the atmosphere is not too arid and other conditions approximate those of a greenhouse. They are admirably suited for hanging baskets and other suspended containers that allow their stems to trail and the plants to display their full beauty of foliage and bloom. In tropical gardens they may with good effect be located in crotches of trees and similar perches packed with a loose, humus-type mixture of the sort in which their roots revel.

Cultivation. In suitable environments little difficulty attends growing these attractive plants. In temperatures of 70 to 75°F they root readily from cuttings and from layers. Seeds generally are a less satisfactory means of propagation. Make the cuttings 2 to 4 inches long from firm, but not hard shoots, and remove all except the upper two pairs or circles of leaves. Transfer the rooted cuttings individually to small pots in a very sandy, peaty soil. For later pottings or plantings use a loose potting mix that permits the free passage of water and air and that consists largely of organic material such as coarse leaf mold, peat moss, and bark chips of the kinds used for potting orchids. Add to these one-quarter to one-third part by bulk of good top soil, some coarse sand, a generous dash of dried cow manure and bonemeal, and some crushed charcoal. Pack the mix only moderately firmly about the roots. It is important to encourage the best possible growth during the early stages. To do this, maintain night temperatures of 65 to 70°F rising by day to levels five to fifteen degrees higher depending upon the brightness of the weather. Maintain a humid atmosphere. Water freely from spring to fall and somewhat more cautiously in winter. Do not allow blooms to develop during the first year; pick off flower buds as soon as they appear. Specimens that have filled their receptacles with roots benefit from weekly or biweekly applications of dilute liquid fertilizer from spring to fall. Give as much light as the plants can take without their foliage yellowing or becoming scorched. This will necessitate light shade from spring to late summer or early fall. Recondition old plants each late winter or spring by pruning back straggly shoots and removing as much of the top layer of soil as can be taken without damage to the roots and replacing it with new. The chief pests are mealybugs, scale insects, and red spider mites.

AESCULUS (Aés-culus)—Horse-Chestnut, Buckeye. Of the thirteen species of this genus of the horse-chestnut family HIP-POCASTANACEAE, seven inhabit North America, five Asia, and one southern Europe. They so obviously resemble each other and so differ from other trees and shrubs that even a beginner can at a glance identify them as to genus. And their separation into species is by no means difficult, but numerous hybrids occur and these are less susceptible to easy identification. The name *Aesculus* is an ancient one for an oak or other tree that produced seeds eaten by livestock. First used by Pliny, it is derived from the Latin *esca,* nourishment.

The origin of the name horse-chestnut is not surely known. A likely explanation is that it dates back to the botanist Matthioli, physician to Emperor Maxmilian II. In 1557 he learned from a Flemish doctor in Constantinople of the existence of a tree from the seeds of which the Turks prepared a meal they fed to their horses to assist them to breathe more easily. The Turks called the tree at-kastan (horse-chestnut). Based on this information Matthioli named the tree *Castanea equina,* the Latin equivalent of horse-chestnut. Later a French botanist translated the Latin into Greek and the name of the tree became *Hippocastanum.* Still later, when the great Linnaeus classified the known plants of the world and established the binomial system of nomenclature we use today he retained *hippocastanum* as part of the name he gave the tree introduced from Constantinople and which we now know as the European or common horse-chestnut (*Aesculus hippocastanum*). The native American species of *Aesculus* are commonly called buckeyes. This name derives from the fanciful resemblance that a fruit, with part of its husk removed to reveal the pale brown scar on the rich brown surface of the seed, has to the half-open eye of a deer.

The lumber of horse-chestnuts and buckeyes is of little economic importance. It is light, soft, and not very durable. That of the common horse-chestnut and Japanese horse-chestnut are used to some extent for boxes, inexpensive furniture, spools, and interior trim, that of the Ohio buckeye and the sweet buckeye for paper pulp and utensils. The Indians ground the seeds of the Texas and Ohio buckeyes into meal, which, mixed with wheat flour, they used to stupefy fish. Indians of California boiled and ate the seeds of *A. californica.* From the fruits of the Texas buckeye New Mexican Indians extracted a strong emetic.

The most obvious feature of horse-chestnuts is their deciduous, large, long-stalked leaves of five to nine leaflets that spread from the top of the leafstalk like the fingers of a hand. The leaves are opposite, an arrangement uncommon among trees that attain any considerable size and are hardy in temperate America (the most familiar that conform to this arrangement are the horse-chestnuts, ashes, and maples, a combination easy to remember because the initial letters of their names spell HAM). True, there are a few other hardy deciduous trees with opposite leaves, such as dogwoods, lilacs, and phellodendrons, but they are considerably smaller or of lesser importance than the great three. The winter buds of horse-chestnuts and buckeyes are characteristically large and have several pairs of conspicuous outer scales. The asymmetrical flowers, red, pink, white, or yellow, are in showy, erect, symmetrical, terminal panicles. They have bell-shaped to tubular, four-, or five-toothed calyxes, four or five petals narrowed at the bases to a claw or shaft, five to nine stamens, and one style. The seeds, solitary or in pairs, resemble chestnuts and are contained in large three-chambered capsules.

The common or European horse-chestnut is widely planted in North America, Europe, and other temperate parts of the world. One of the earliest trees to leaf out in spring, this is the famous "chestnut tree" of Paris and of Bushey Park near London. Many thousands of Londoners make the pilgrimage on "Chestnut Sunday" to see the huge trees in bloom. The horse-chestnuts in Bushey Park were planted in 1699 by Sir Christopher Wren. They form an avenue about 1 mile long and 170 feet wide, with five rows of trees on each side spaced 42 feet apart. At one end the horse-chestnuts encircle a large pond and fountain, which provide an impressive terminal focal point to the view. Some of Wren's original trees have died and been replaced, but many remain, and the largest, fully 100 feet in height and branched to the ground, when in bloom afford a spectacular sight worth traveling far to see. There are reliable records of seeds of the common horse-chestnut being imported into America in 1741 and again four years later. In 1763 Peter Collinson of London, replying to a letter from John Bartram of Philadelphia, wrote "But what delights me is, to hear that our horse-chestnut has flowered. I think it much excels the Virginia, if the spikes of flowers are as large with you as with us." Strangely enough, although this tree had been in cultivation for centuries its native habitat was a matter of speculation until 1879 when it was definitely established to be the mountains of northern Greece. It is also native to Albania.

The common horse-chestnut (**A. hippocastanum**) may exceed 100 feet in height, and have a trunk diameter of fully 7 feet. It has massive limbs and a densely-foliaged crown, bell-shaped or forming a round-topped pyramid. Its winter buds are very sticky. The size and disposition of the coarsely-toothed leaves, which are smooth above, but have patches of hair in the axils of the veins beneath, produce a distinct and beautiful pattern, a perfect foil for the erect spires of bloom, up to 1 foot in length, that decorate the ends of every branchlet in late spring. The blooms of the typical species are predominately white, with yellow spots that eventually become red on the uppermost of the five petals. The stamens and style project horizontally, providing a convenient landing strip for bees, which are chiefly responsible for the pollination of horse-chestnuts. The upper flowers of each spire are males, the lower are bisexual. The fruits are globular, spiny, and 2 to 2½ inches in diameter. The common horse-chestnut is hardy into southern Canada. In addition to the type, several varieties are cultivated. Of these, _A. h. albo-variegata_ has leaves variegated

with white, _A. h. baumannii_ has double white flowers, _A. h. digitata_ (syn. _A. h. pumila_) is a dwarf, _A. h. luteo-variegata_ has leaves variegated with yellow, _A. h. pyr-_

Aesculus hippocastanum baumannii (flowers)

Aesculus hippocastanum baumannii

amidalis is narrow and compact, _A. h. umbraculifera_ has a round, compact crown, and _A. h. pendula_ has drooping branches.

The Japanese horse-chestnut (**A. turbinata**), a native of Japan, is less showy than the European and blooms two or three

weeks later. It has sticky winter buds, and warty, but not spiny, pear-shaped fruits about 2 inches in diameter. Its leaves, more regularly toothed than those of the European, have five to seven leaflets, smooth on their upper sides and beneath somewhat glaucous and with tufts of hair in the vein axils. This kind has a maximum height of about 100 feet. Its five-petaled flowers, smaller than those of the common

Aesculus hippocastanum

Aesculus hippocastanum (flowers)

Aesculus hippocastanum

Aesculus hippocastanum (seeds)

horse-chestnut, in 6- to 10 inch-long panicles, are yellowish-white with a red spot. The Japanese horse-chestnut is hardy in southern New England.

The Indian horse-chestnut (**A. indica**), native of the Himalayan region, is hardy in North America in mild parts only. In its native habitat it is up to more than 100 feet tall, in cultivation, it is commonly lower. It has a short, thick trunk from which the bark, in old specimens, peels in strips. Its winter buds are sticky. It has glossy leaves,

Aesculus indica

with usually seven leaflets, hairless on both sides. The center leaflet is much the largest, sometimes as much as 1 foot long. The spires of flowers may be more than 1 foot long. They consist of numerous four-petaled, white blooms, with red and yellow blotches at the bases of the two longer petals. The other petals are tinted pink. The rough, but not spiny, pear-shaped fruits are 2 to 3 inches long. This blooms a month later than the common horse-chestnut.

The sweet or yellow buckeye (**A. octandra** syn. *A. flava*), the largest and one of the best sorts native in North America is indigenous from Pennsylvania to Illinois and Georgia. Not as showy in bloom as the European horse-chestnut, it attains a height of 90 feet, has a rounded top, and leaves of five leaflets, dark green above and paler on their undersides. Like all American species except *A. californica*, its buds are without the sticky, resinous coating that characterizes European and Asian kinds. Normally yellow, the blooms, in panicles 4 to 6 inches long, have four petals of very unequal lengths, with hairy, but not glandular margins, and stamens shorter than the petals. The fruits are smooth.

The Ohio buckeye (**A. glabra**), ranging in the wild from Pennsylvania to Nebraska and Alabama, is the only member of the genus that develops good fall color. Its foliage turns brilliant yellow to orange before it drops. About 30 feet tall, this has leaves with five leaflets. Its greenish-yellow flowers have protruding stamens and four pet-

Aesculus glabra

als of almost equal length, with hairy, but not glandular margins. The flower panicles are 4 to 6 inches long. The fruits are spiny. Variety *A. g. arguta* (syn. *A. arguta*), the Texas buckeye, native from Kansas to Texas, is a shrub 6 to 7 feet tall with leaves of seven to nine leaflets, hairless when mature. Its flowers are pale yellowish-green. Smooth, nearly white bark is characteristic of *A. g. leucodermis*.

The red buckeye (**A. pavia** syns. *A. discolor*, *A. splendens*) only occasionally exceeds 12 feet in height, and sometimes 24 feet. Its leaves have five or seven oblong to oblanceolate leaflets. Its bright red to yellow flowers are in loose panicles up to 10 inches long. Their petals have glandular, but not hairy margins. The fruits are smooth. Native from Virginia southward and to Illinois, Missouri, and Texas, this species is hardy in southern New York.

Native from North Carolina to Tennessee and Georgia, (**A. sylvatica** syn. *A. neglecta*) is a tree up to 60 feet tall with flowers, usually yellow veined with red, in 6-inch-long panicles. Variety *A. s. georgiana* is generally shrubby and not more than 6 feet tall. Native from North Carolina to

Aesculus pavia

Alabama and Florida, this has wider, denser panicles of bloom than typical *A. sylvatica*. Its flowers, usually yellow and red, are sometimes all yellow or all red.

The dwarf or bottle brush buckeye (**A. parviflora**) is a shrub up to 12 feet in height. It spreads by suckers, forming a billowy mound of attractive foliage, and after midsummer bears numerous narrow, cylindrical panicles 8 inches to 1 foot long of white flowers each with four or five petals, and stamens more than twice as long as the petals. The leaves have five to seven nearly stalkless leaflets, finely-toothed, and pubescent beneath. Native of the southeastern United States, the bottle brush buckeye is hardy throughout most of New England. Variety *A. p. serotina* blooms two or three weeks later than the type and has leaves with less hairy undersides.

Aesculus parviflora

The California buckeye (**A. californica**) is a shrub or tree 10 to 40 feet tall. It has a short gray or whitish trunk and a flat-topped head, usually wider than high, of wide-spreading branches. Its leaves of four to seven leaflets are smaller than those of most species. Their leaflets, up to 7 inches long, are smooth except for tiny hairs in the vein axils on their undersides. The fragrant, white or pale pink flowers have four petals and protruding stamens. They are in dense, erect, rather slender panicles up to 8 inches long. The fig-shaped fruits, 2 to 3 inches long, are rough, but not spiny.

Aesculus californica

Aesculus californica (flowers)

Native to California, it is satisfactory in mild climates only. It is the only American species with sticky winter buds.

Hybrid horse-chestnuts and buckeyes are many. Unquestionably the best and perhaps the most beautiful of the entire genus is the red horse-chestnut (*A. carnea*) the parents of which are the European horse-chestnut (*A. hippocastanum*) and the American red buckeye (*A. pavia*). Hardy as far north as southern Canada, this round-headed tree is intermediate between its parents. From its European ancestor it inherits the slight stickiness of its winter buds and its somewhat prickly fruits, from its American parent it derives its flower

Aesculus carnea

Aesculus carnea (flowers)

color and the glands that fringe its petals. Its leaves usually have five leaflets. The red horse-chestnut originated before 1818, but probably not long before. There is no record as to exactly when or where it came into being. An interesting feature about it is, that except for some variance in the depth of color of its flowers, it breeds true from seeds. This is unusual for a hybrid. A few well-marked forms of the red horse-chestnut are cultivated. One with larger trusses of bloom and flowers more brilliantly colored, almost scarlet, is *A. c. briotii*. Another, the damask horse-chestnut (*A. c. plantierensis*), differs in having more prickly fruits, leaves with usually seven leaflets, and whitish flowers flushed with pink, and aging pink. Pendulous branches are characteristic of *A. c. pendula.* Variants with variegated leaves are known. The medium-sized, very variable **A. hybrida** has for parents *A. octandra* and *A. pavia*. Its flowers, in panicles about 6 inches long, range from yellow slightly tinged with pink to red. Their petals are margined with hairs and glands. A shrubby hybrid between *A. pavia* and *A. sylvatica* is **A. mutabilis.** This has panicles of red and yellow flowers 4 to 6 inches in length. Variety *A. m. harbisonii* has bright red flowers in panicles 6 to 8 inches long.

Aesculus carnea plantierensis

Garden and Landscape Uses. For selected locations horse-chestnuts and buckeyes are very desirable, but their planting sites should be chosen with regard for their needs and for the space they will ultimately need. Certainly larger kinds are not suitable for small gardens, and even the shrubby, suckering *A. parviflora* and the low-growing *A. pavia* cannot be displayed to advantage unless they have considerable space in which to spread. To be seen at their best horse-chestnuts and buckeyes should be viewed from some little distance, preferably across an expanse of lawn. The taller ones can be effective overhanging a wall. They are not good street trees because they tend to produce considerable litter and because their large

leaves, fallen, wet, and slippery, can be hazardous. The common horse-chestnut, beautiful though it is, has two disadvantages. In many areas, especially where summers are hot, its foliage in summer is marred by a brown, conspicuous physiological scorching. The other disadvantage is that its fruits are so very attractive to boys that in their eagerness to acquire them they damage the trees by throwing stones and sticks among the branches. Because of this, in exposed locations it is best to confine plantings to the double-flowered sort that does not produce fruits. Branches of the common horse-chestnut, cut in late winter when their great sticky buds are plump with the promise of spring, and stood in water soon develop attractive fresh green foliage and are delightful indoor decorations.

Cultivation. In reasonably deep, porous, fertile, fairly moist, but not wet soils both horse-chestnuts and buckeyes grow well. They transplant easily and need no regular pruning beyond that necessary to shape young specimens and any that may be required later to remove damaged limbs or parts unwanted for other reasons. Propagation is by seeds, which do not retain their vitality long and generally are sown as soon as they are ripe in a cold frame or outdoor bed protected by wire mesh or other means from rodents. Good results are also had by storing the seeds in polyethylene bags in a temperature of 40°F and sowing in spring. Hybrids and varieties, including the double-flowered horse-chestnut, are propagated by grafting in the greenhouse in late winter. Varieties and hybrids of large tree kinds, such as those of *A. hippocastanum,* are grafted on seedlings of that species. For smaller growing kinds *A. octandra* and *A. glabra* are appropriate understocks. Both *A. parviflora* and *A. pavia* can be increased by root cuttings.

Diseases and Pests. A nonparasitic leaf scorch that becomes apparent after midsummer seriously mars the common horse-chestnut in many parts of America. This is apparently associated with the tree's inability to absorb and transport from roots to leaves adequate amounts of water to compensate for that transpired by the foliage. Individual trees seem to vary in their susceptibility. Pruning to reduce the total amount of leaf surface each tree must carry, moderate fertilizing, and deep watering during dry weather may help to reduce the incidence of this unsightly condition. The sorts of this genus are sometimes preyed upon by mealybugs, Japanese beetles, and caterpillars of the tussock moth.

AETHIONEMA (Aethio-nèma) — Stone-Cress. This genus of about seventy species of the mustard family CRUCIFERAE is botanically perplexing. Identifying its kinds can be difficult. That they hybridize freely adds to the confusion. Aethionemas are mostly more or less subshrubby perennials, more rarely annuals, of low growth. They are natives of the Mediterranean region and western Asia that differ in technical details of their ovaries and fruits from the closely related *Thlaspi*. A more easily observed detail is that their petals have slender bases (claws) and are usually three-veined. The generic name is from the Greek *aitho,* scorch, and *nema,* a filament, probably in reference to the appearance of the stamens.

As with other members of the mustard family aethionemas have four petals arranged in the form of a cross (from which feature derives the family name *Cruciferae*), six stamens of which two are shorter than the others, and seeds in pods of a kind botanists call siliques. Aethionemas have many slender branched or non-branching stems and usually stemless, unlobed, toothless, glaucous leaves, alternate or sometimes opposite. The flowers, pink, white, or rarely yellowish, are in racemes that often elongate markedly as the lower blooms fade and seed pods develop. The petals are equal in size. The stalks of the four longer stamens are usually dilated and sometimes toothed or joined. The seed pods, round, ovate, or boat-shaped, are usually notched at their apexes.

A beautiful and variable perennial, *A. grandiflorum* (syn. *A. pulchellum*), a native of Transcaucasia, Anatolia, Iraq, and Iran, often goes under other names. It has branched or unbranched, spreading or erect stems up to 1½ feet long, with leaves evenly spaced along its flowering and non-flowering shoots, and ovate or round, winged seed pods about ⅓ inch long and notched to one-third of their length. The

Aethionema grandiflorum

wings of the seed pods may have smooth edges or be slightly toothed. The leaves of this kind are glaucous gray-green and linear-oblong. The flowers are pink, in loose racemes that lengthen markedly as seed pods form. Closely related to *A. grandiflorum,* but with smaller pale pink blooms

and seed pods strongly toothed at their edges, is *A. diastrophis,* a native of Armenia. Often confused with *A. grandiflorum* and perhaps hybridizing with it, *A. coridifolium* occurs in the wild in Lebanon, Turkey, and Asia Minor. It does not exceed 8 inches in height. It is distinguished from *A. grandiflorum* by its leaves being mostly on the non-flowering shoots and its winged, wavy-edged seed pods being slightly smaller and more shallowly notched. The flowering stems of *A. coridifolium* do not branch. Its pink blooms are in heads that lengthen and loosen as the seed pods develop. This plant is sometimes misnamed *A. jucunda* and *Iberis jucunda.*

Two other perennials with many stems and quite loose racemes of flowers are *A. speciosum* and *A. stylosum.* The former is native of Anatolia, Iraq, and Iran, the latter of Asia Minor. Both are about 1 foot high and have pink, or in the case of the *A. stylosum,* sometimes lilac or white blooms. The former has branchless, glaucous stems and ovate-oblong, blunt leaves often narrowed at their bases. The leaves of the latter are pointed ovate-lanceolate; often they broaden at their bases. The stems of *A. stylosum* are branched or without branches and glaucous. Both kinds have ovate seed pods with protruding styles.

Two medium-sized perennials with flower clusters that do not lengthen markedly as the seed pods develop are *A. iberideum* and *A. schistosum.* The former, a native of Turkey, attains a height of 6 inches and has freely-branched, erect stems, mostly opposite leaves, and compact clusters of white usually fragrant blooms. The stems of *A. schistosum,* also a native of Turkey, are erect and branched or branchless. They are about 5 inches tall and are thickly clothed with linear leaves. The flowers are pink.

Aethionema schistosum

Native of Lebanon and Anti-Lebanon and distinguished by its more or less triangular-heart-shaped leaves, somewhat stem-clasping at their bases, *A. cordatum* (syn. *A. cardiophyllum*) is a rather stiff perennial of shrubby habit, with leafy, branched, or branchless stems. Its white, pale yellow, or pink blooms are in racemes that lengthen markedly as seed pods are formed. It is up to 8 inches tall. Having stems not more than about 5 inches in length branchless *A. armenum,* a native of Anatolia and Transcaucasus, has pointed, linear-oblong leaves and flower racemes, that elongate considerably as seed pods develop, of pink or rarely white flowers. The extraordinarily beautiful *A. warleyense* of compact habit and with deep pink flowers and leaves edged with pink is

Aethionema warleyense

probably a hybrid of this species. Another beauty, *A. oppositifolium* (plants grown as *A. rotundifolium* seemingly belong here), is a native of Lebanon, Turkey, and Transcaucasus. Only about 2 inches tall, its branchless stems are thickly furnished with round or obovate fleshy leaves. The flowers are lilac or pink with purple sepals. The ovate or elliptic seed pods are notched at their rounded or pointed apexes.

Non-perennial species include *A. arabicum,* an annual, and *A. saxatile,* which flowers only once, usually in its second year, and then dies. Compact annual *A. arabicum* (syns. *A. buxbaumii, A. cappadocicum*) has pointed, linear-oblong leaves and branchless stems. Its racemes of pink or white flowers scarcely elongate as seed pods develop. It is up to 5 inches tall. The stems of *A. saxatile* (syns. *A. creticum, A. gracile, A. ovalifolium*) do not branch and have upper leaves that are linear-lanceolate. The lower leaves are somewhat broader. The white or pink flowers are loosely arranged. These sorts are natives of southern Europe and southwest Asia.

Garden Uses. The better stone-cresses are elegant and altogether admirable for rock gardens and, the taller, more robust kinds, such as *A. grandiflorum* and *A. coridifolium,* for fronting flower borders. The discriminating gardener must be ruthlessly selective and ever ready to discard inferior plants. These often appear when aethionemas are raised from seeds. They may represent naturally weedy species, poor forms of acceptable species, or hybrid mongrels of insufficient garden merit. Despite their coming from warm Mediterranean lands and places to the east of there, most stone-cresses are surprisingly hardy. Many winter outdoors satisfactorily in New York City, and probably further north, in a warm, sheltered, sunny location with soil sharply drained.

Cultivation. If plants of good habit with flowers of comparatively large size and pleasing color are available the best way of increasing perennial aethionemas is by cuttings. These are easily rooted in late spring or early summer in a shaded cold frame. The cuttings are made from firm, non-flowering shoots and are planted in sand, vermiculite, or a mixture of sand and peat moss. Seeds must be used to raise the annual *A. arabicum* and *A. saxatile.* The seeds of all kinds germinate very readily. With the exception of those of *A. arabicum,* which are sprinkled thinly in early spring and raked into the soil surface where the plants are to remain, they may be sown in a cold frame or outdoors in May and the young seedlings transplanted individually, as soon as they are big enough to handle, into small pots. They are kept in pots, buried to their rims in a bed of sand or peat moss, in a cold frame until the following spring when they are set out where they are to remain. Stone-cresses do not need a rich soil. They make more seemly growth and probably live longer in a lean medium not too well charged with what are for most plants the good things of life. They are lovers of lime and the incorporation of ground limestone in the soil and, if available, chunks of limestone varying from pea- to walnut-sized pieces, is decidedly helpful. Routine care makes few demands on the gardener's time. In spring stirring the surface soil and replacing its top ½ inch with fresh may be desirable or, if the plants are grown with a mulch of stone chips around them, attention to tidying this at that time may be necessary. Shearing old flower stems after the blooms have faded (unless seeds are to be gathered) is necessary. In late fall a light covering of branches of pines or other suitable evergreens provides all the winter protection necessary.

AFRICAN. The word African is employed as part of the common names of these plants: African-boxwood (*Myrsine africana*), African-cherry-orange (*Citropsis*), African-daisy (*Arctotis stoechadifolia* and *Lonas annua*), African-dog-rose (*Oncoba kraussiana*), African-hemp (*Sparmannia africana*), Afri-

can-holly (*Solanum giganteum*), African-horned-cucumber (*Cucumis metuliferus*), African-mahogany (*Detarium senegalense*), African marigold (*Tagetes*), African milk bush (*Synadenium grantii*), African-millet (*Eleusine coracana* and *Pennisetum americanum*), African oil palm (*Elaeis guineensis*), African-tulip-tree (*Spathodea campanulata*), African-valerian (*Fedia cornucopiae*), African-violet (*Saintpaulia*), blue-African-lily (*Agapanthus*).

AGALINIS (Agal-ìnis). The name *Agalìnis,* derived from the Greek *aga,* remarkable, and the Latin *linum,* flax, alludes to a superficial resemblance of the flowers to those of flax. This entirely New World genus of about sixty temperate region species belonging in the figwort family SCROPHULARIACEAE consists of summer- and fall-blooming annuals, and more rarely perennials. They were formerly named *Gerardia.*

These are graceful plants of airy appearance. Typically, they have slender, erect-branched stems and except for the upper ones, which may be alternate, opposite leaves. Their somewhat asymmetrical, rather penstemon-like, bell- to funnel-shaped flowers, in racemes or solitary at the ends of the branches, have pink, purple, or rarely white corollas, marked sometimes with yellow. The corollas have tubes often swollen on their undersides, and five lobes (petals), the lower three of which are spreading, the others arched, spreading, or slightly recurved. The hairy-stalked stamens are in two pairs of different lengths. The fruits are capsules. Individual blooms last one day only, but a succession provides a fairly long display.

Variable, and by botanists divided into several varieties, *A. purpurea* (syn. *Gerardia purpurea*) is found in the wild from Nova Scotia to Minnesota, South Dakota, Florida, Texas, Mexico, and the West Indies. From less than 1 foot, to 4 feet tall, it is freely, sparsely, or not at all branched, the branches wide spreading or, in *A. p. racemulosa,* erect. The leaves are up to 1½ inches long and up to ⅙ inch wide. Its few to numerous short-stalked blooms are ½ inch to 1½ inches long. Their stalks are shorter than the calyx tubes.

Usually freely branched, *A. tenuifolia* (syn. *Gerardia tenuifolia*) is a variable kind that gives botanists reason for recognizing several varieties. From 1 foot to 2 feet tall, it favors moist soil, and occurs in woodlands and prairies from Maine to Manitoba, North Dakota, Florida, and Texas. It has linear leaves up to 1¼ inches long and up to ⅙ inch wide. Variety *A. t. macrophylla* has broader leaves. The blooms, up to ¾ inch long, are light purple with darker spots. The stalks are longer than the calyx tubes.

Garden and Landscape Uses and Cultivation. These are delightful plants for woodland gardens, but because they are

perhaps partially parasitic on the roots of other plants, are not always easy to establish. Seeds should be sown in early spring in moist, but not wet places, in open woodlands or similar habitats, and the areas kept free of weeds and other intrusive plants.

AGALMYLA (Agálmy-la). Closely related to *Aeschynanthus,* from which it differs in technical details, the genus *Agalmyla* consists of five species of Borneo, Sumatra, and Java. It belongs in the gesneria family GESNERIACEAE. Its name, derived from the Greek *agalma,* ornament, and *hyle,* wood, suggests that these epiphytes (plants that perch on trees, but take no nourishment from them) embellish their hosts.

Agalmylas are evergreen trailers or climbers with rooting stems. Their leaves are opposite, those of each pair markedly different in size, the smaller one early deciduous. The flowers, some unisexual, some bisexual, are in clusters from the leaf axils. They have a deeply-five-lobed calyx, a two-lipped, curved, tubular-trumpet-shaped corolla, two fertile stamens, and one style. The fruits are capsules.

Native to Java, *A. parasitica* (syn. *A. staminea*) has stems about 2 feet long. The largest of each pair of leaves, elliptic to ovate-oblong, 6 inches to 1 foot long by 2½ to 4 inches wide, has toothed margins. The smaller leaf is up to 2 inches long and narrowly-linear-lanceolate. The flowers, up to a little over 2 inches long, are in crowded axillary clusters. Densely-hairy on their outsides and narrowly-trumpet-shaped, they are rich scarlet blotched with dark maroon. They have a long-protruding, purplish style.

Agalmyla parasitica

Garden Uses and Cultivation. Agalmylas serve the same garden uses and need the same conditions and care as *Aeschynanthus.* For more information see Gesneriads.

AGANISIA (Agan-ísia). Three tropical South American and West Indian epiphytic (tree-perching) species of the orchid family OR-

CHIDACEAE constitute *Aganisia*. The name of obvious application is from the Greek *aganos*, gentle, hence desirable.

These orchids have creeping rhizomes and short stems that develop into small pseudobulbs. Each stem or pseudobulb usually carries a single leaf and sometimes two. From the bases of the pseudobulbs arise erect, few-flowered racemes of bloom. The flowers have nearly similar, spreading sepals and petals and a lip with a center lobe that is two- or three-lobed or smooth-edged. The side lobes of the lip are small or absent.

Brazilian **A. cyanea** has egg-shaped pseudobulbs 1½ to 2 inches long and longitudinally-pleated, pointed-broad-elliptic leaves 6 inches to 1 foot in length, up to 5 inches in width and with channeled stalks. The erect flowering stalks, up to about 1 foot long, carry few to several showy blooms 2 to 2½ inches across and have blue to purple-blue sepals and petals and a pale-veined, bluish-purple lip with a fringed shaft or claw. The column is streaked with red or purple.

Garden Uses and Cultivation. A very beautiful plant for inclusion in orchid collections, *A. cyanea* needs decidedly tropical, humid conditions, with shade from bright sun. As a potting medium osmunda fiber or bark chips, kept evenly moist, but not constantly saturated are satisfactory. For more information see Orchids.

AGAPANTHUS (Agap-ánthus)—Blue-African-Lily. Blue-Lily-of-the-Nile. Romantic though it may sound, blue-lily-of-the-Nile, commonly used as a colloquial name for members of this African group, is quite misleading. Blue-African-lily is more appropriate. No species of *Agapanthus* is found wild north of the Limpopo River in southeast Africa, and that is a long way from the Nile. The genus consists of ten species. It belongs in the lily family LILI-ACEAE and has a name that comes from the Greek *agape*, love, and *anthos*, a flower. Blue-African-lilies are old in cultivation. They were first described under the name *Hyacinthus africanus tuberosus* from a plant that bloomed in Europe in 1679. In 1692 an excellent illustration of *A. africanus* was published by Plunkenet who stated that it flowered at Hampton Court Palace gardens in England. Until 1965 the genus was believed to consist of one highly variable species, *A. africanus* (syn. *A. umbellatus*). Careful research among wild populations in South Africa dispelled that belief.

Agapanthuses are beautiful evergreen and deciduous, non-hardy herbaceous perennials with short tuberous rootstocks, and thick, fleshy roots. Their leaves are slightly succulent or leathery, linear or strap-shaped, and arching or spreading. The flower stalks, naked of leaves, are round or slightly flattened. They rise above the foliage and are surmounted with um-

bels of blooms with two bracts at the bases of the clusters. Blue, purple-blue, lavender, or white, the nearly symmetrical blooms have six tepals (a name used for perianth parts when sepals and petals are essentially alike) joined in their lower parts, slightly keeled on their undersides, and grooved on top. There are six stamens of unequal length, and a slender style tipped with a small stigma. The fruits are capsules containing many black, winged seeds. In most species the tepals, or as they are commonly called, and as we shall refer to them, petals, spread quite widely, but in others the blooms are funnel-shaped to cylindrical.

Evergreen agapanthuses form no apparent stems, their leaves arise separately. All except *A. walshii* have blooms with wide-spreading petals. They include the classic and variable **A. africanus.** Its thick, fleshy petals are 1 inch to 2 inches long, and dark blue to purplish. The uncrowded umbels, on stalks 1 foot to 3 feet tall, consist of few to as many as thirty blooms. The two-ranked, more or less erect, channeled leaves are usually not more than 1¼ feet, rarely up to 1¾ feet, in length. They are from a little less than ½ to ¾ inch wide. The varieties believed to belong with this species are *A. a. flore-pleno*, with double flowers, and *A. a. variegatus*, the leaves of which are white with a few longitudinal green stripes.

Aganisia cyanea

Agapanthus africanus

Agapanthus africanus (flowers)

The beautiful *A. praecox* differs from *A. africanus* in having dense umbels of few to many, thinner-textured blooms of pale to medium lilac-blue or sometimes white, on stalks up to 4 feet tall. Typically its petals are 2 to 3½ inches in length, but in *A. p. orientalis* and *A. p. minimus* they are shorter. The first of these varieties forms dense clumps of foliage and has flower stalks 2½ feet long or longer. In *A. p. minimus* the flower stalks are considerably shorter and the clumps of foliage less crowded. The arching, evergreen leaves of *A. praecox* are bright green and reach a maximum of 3 feet in length and 3 inches in width, but in some variants are considerably smaller. A large number of evergreen-foliaged horticultural hybrids, some of them considerably hardier, have been developed from this species in various parts of the world and are commonly cultivated.

The loose, few- to many-flowered umbels of the graceful and very decorative *A. comptonii* top slender stalks up to 4 feet tall. The blue or lavender-blue, narrowly-bell-shaped flowers have petals more than 2 inches long. The leaves of *A. comptonii* are evergreen, narrow, stiffish, and usually less than 2 feet long. The last of the evergreen species, *A. walshii* is rare and distinguished by its 1½-inch-long flowers being tubular, pendulous, and in umbels of up to nineteen on stalks up to 1½ feet long or slightly longer. The leaves are linear, up to 8 inches long and less than ½ inch wide. It is not known to be cultivated.

Deciduous agapanthuses have leaves with their bases overlapping to form apparent stems. Except for *A. inapertus*, they have wide open or funnel-shaped flowers. In *A. inapertus,* however, they are tubular, very pendulous, and blue-violet to dark blue, or rarely white. An identifying feature of this species is that the perianth tubes are as long or longer than the free parts of the petals. This is a very variable kind and botanists recognize several subspecies or varieties. The name *A. weillighii* is applied to vigorous hybrids of *A. inapterus.*

Other deciduous species with drooping or partly pendulous blooms include *A. nutans* and *A. dyeri.* *A. nutans* has nine to a dozen two-ranked, erect or arching, glaucous leaves to each short-stemmed shoot. They are 8 inches to 1½ feet or a little more long by up to 1¾ inches wide. The few- to many-flowered umbels of blue, trumpet-shaped, slightly nodding blooms top stalks up to 3 feet tall. Probably not in cultivation, *A. dyeri* has five to seven leaves, up to a little more than 1 foot long by about ¾ inch wide, to each shoot. The blue blooms, in loose umbels, are on stalks up to 3 feet long. They have narrow throats and spreading petals. Except for its very short corolla tubes this species resembles a form of *A. inapterus.*

The highly variable, deciduous *A. campanulatus* has six to twelve leaves to each

Agapanthus campanulatus

short-stemmed shoot. They are up to about 1½ feet long by ½ to 1 inch broad, and have usually purplish bases. Rarely the flower stalks exceed 3 feet in height; often they are shorter. They have few to many pale to deep blue or white flowers ¾ inch to 1¼ inches long, with wide-spreading, but not recurved petals. In this the flowers differ from those of *A. caulescens* and *A. coddii*, the petals of which curve backward. In *A. campanulatus patens* the leaves are shorter and narrower, and the flowers are in more compact umbels than in *A. campanulatus.* The various plants grown under the name *A. mooreanus* are comparatively hardy hybrids of *A. campanulatus.*

Another variable deciduous species, *A. caulescens* has seven to fifteen glossy, soft green leaves, the longest up to 2 feet by as much as 2 inches wide, to each distinctly stemmed cluster. Its rigid flower stalks may exceed 4 feet in height, and terminate in many-flowered umbels of spreading and slightly drooping blue blooms up to 2 inches long, with widely spreading or slightly recurved petals. Varieties *A. c. angustifolius* and *A. c. gracilis* have much narrower leaves and smaller blooms. The about ten erect, somewhat glaucous leaves of each shoot of *A. coddii* form conspicuous stems with their purplish bases. They are 6 inches to 1½ feet long by ¾ inch to 2 inches wide. The rather crowded umbels

of blue flowers are at the tops of stoutish stems up to 3½ feet tall. The blooms are 1¾ inches long and usually have wide-spreading petals.

Garden and Landscape Uses. Of stately appearance, agapanthuses are greatly esteemed as garden ornamentals and for cultivation in greenhouses. Deciduous kinds are considerably more cold-resistant than evergreen agapanthuses, but none is satisfactorily hardy in the north. In the milder parts of England some survive outdoors, but it is in more salubrious climates, such as those of California and the Southwest, that these fine plants have their greatest usefulness as permanent outdoor furnishings. In such places they are splendid in beds and borders and for planting in irregular sweeps in informal landscapes. Dwarf kinds are appropriate in rock gardens. The flowers are useful for cutting and last well in water.

As pot and tub plants agapanthuses are highly regarded for decorating greenhouses, and more especially for standing on terraces, steps, patios, and near outdoor pools. They associate splendidly with architectural features. Where the climate is too harsh to permit their permanent residence outdoors, it is common practice to use container-accommodated specimens to embellish the outdoors in summer, and to winter them indoors.

Cultivation. Deep, fertile, loamy earth, with, during their growing season, sufficient moisture to prevent it from becoming really dry, but never so much that the roots are in a saturated condition for long periods, best suits agapanthuses. Good drainage is essential. Plants grown permanently outdoors need minimum attention: fertilize at the beginning of each new season of growth, remove faded flowers, and when they become crowded to the extent that blooming deteriorates, lift, divide, and replant in freshly spaded and fertilized soil.

Container-grown specimens are better accommodated in tubs than large pots because the pressure of the expanding roots is likely to break earthenware receptacles. Repotting is done at intervals of a few years in late winter or early spring. At that time, too, old plants may be divided. As an aid in doing this, after the plant has been removed from its pot or tub, with a stream of water from a hose wash away as much as possible of the soil from the old ball. Then carefully separate the mass of growths into pieces of suitable size, each consisting of one or more crowns or shoots. Trim any broken roots, and replant in well-drained pots or tubs big enough to hold the roots comfortably, but not overly large. Work the new soil among the roots without damaging them and make it firm. Finish with the soil surface sufficiently below the rim of the container to allow for future watering. For container agapanthuses the soil should be coarse, porous, loamy, and fertile; one that is suitable for geraniums and chrysanthemums is appropriate.

From spring (about the time tomatoes are put out) until fall frost threatens, agapanthuses may be kept outdoors in full sun or where there is a little part-day shade. If accommodated indoors conditions should approach as closely as possible those natural outdoors at that season. Watering is done generously so that the soil is evenly moist, but not saturated, and specimens that have filled their containers with roots are regularly supplied at about weekly intervals with dilute liquid fertilizer.

Where winters are too severe to leave the plants outdoors they are taken inside before frost damages them and are stored in any light place where the temperature ranges between 40 and 50°F. Warmth, to the extent that new growth is stimulated, is very harmful until well into spring, and watering must be done with great caution during this season of dormancy or semi-dormancy. The soil should be kept nearly dry. If facilities approximating those of a sunny greenhouse are available, in March or April somewhat higher temperatures are in order and more generous watering may be resumed. Propagation is generally by division, but seeds may also be used. Those from garden plants, often of hybrid origin, are likely to give variable offspring.

AGAPETES (Agapèt-es). Including the half-dozen previously named *Pentapterygium* that belong here, the genus *Agapetes* contains eighty species and is represented in the wild from the Himalayas to southeast Asia, and Malaya. It belongs in the heath family ERICACEAE. The name, from the Greek *agapetos*, lovable, alludes to the beauty of these evergreen shrubs.

Many are epiphytes growing in the forks of living and dead trees, on fallen logs, and on rocks, wherever they find moisture and a little organic debris from which they can extract nourishment. They are not parasites; they do not take food directly from the living trees upon which they grow. Their leaves are alternate and leathery. The tubular to bell-shaped flowers are in racemes or clusters, or rarely are solitary. They have five generally short, curved or erect corolla lobes, and ten short-stalked stamens. The fruits are many-seeded berries.

Native to the Himalayas and western China where it grows as an epiphyte in humid forests, *A. serpens* (syn. *Pentapterygium serpens*) has at or just below ground

Agapetes serpens

Agapetes serpens (flowers)

level a large tuberous rootstock. Its slender, arching or drooping stems are up to about 3 feet long, and are furnished for much of their lengths with regularly and closely spaced, spreading, evergreen, lanceolate, nearly stalkless leaves about ½ inch in length, and in two rows in one plane. Like slender Chinese lanterns the numerous stalked, nodding flowers festoon the undersides of the stems. About ¾ inch long, they have five-lobed, five-angled, green calyxes about one-third as long as the corollas. The latter, constricted slightly at their ends, have five short, nearly erect lobes. They are bright red with darker v-shaped markings. Flowering begins in late winter or spring, outdoors in the region of San Francisco about March. Variety *A. s. alba* has white flowers.

Less common, ***A. buxifolia*** (syn. *Thibaudia buxifolia*) is a twiggy shrub up to about 5 feet tall with small, bright green, oblong-elliptic leaves toothed at their apexes, and 1-inch-long, waxy, bright red flowers in clusters. It is native to Bhutan.

Garden and Landscape Uses. Graceful and charming, these shrubs are adapted for outdoor gardens in fairly humid regions where little or no frost is experienced, and for greenhouse cultivation, especially in hanging baskets. Outdoors some shade from bright sun is usually considered advisable, but good results have been reported from the San Francisco region with plants outdoors in full sun.

Cultivation. As with most epiphytes, the roots of these must have perfect drainage; a well-aerated rooting medium, consisting chiefly of decayed organic matter, is essential to success. A mixture of equal amounts of partially rotted pine needles and leaf mold is suitable, and good results have been had in decayed leaves of Douglas-fir alone. In greenhouses fir bark such as is used for orchids, mixed with a little turfy soil, an abundance of coarse leaf mold or peat moss, with some crushed charcoal and a little bonemeal added and, if procurable, some small lumps of dried cow manure, is satisfactory.

Greenhouse temperatures should be 50°F on winter nights with a rise of five to ten degrees more by day permitted, and at other seasons both night and day temperatures a few degrees warmer. Routine care is not demanding. Water to keep the soil always moderately moist and fairly high humidity being the chief needs. On bright days it is beneficial to spray the foliage lightly with water. Repotting or rebasketing is done as soon as flowering is through. Then, too, any pruning needed to contain the plants or improve their shapes is done. Propagation is by cuttings under mist or in a greenhouse propagating bench, and by seeds. The latter are sown on milled sphagnum moss or other medium that assures a moist, airy root run. The seedlings develop sizable tuberous bases before they make appreciable top growth.

AGASTACHE (Agástach-e) — Giant-Hyssop. Of the twenty species of the mint family LABIATAE included in this genus three inhabit eastern North America, sixteen western North America, and one is native of Japan. A few of the Americans are grown in gardens. The name comes from the Greek *agan*, much, and *stachys*, an ear of wheat. It alludes to the clusters of many flowers. Agastaches are herbaceous perennials with square stems, pairs of usually ovate leaves, and cylindrical or tapering spikes or slender panicles of many flowers crowded in whorls (tiers). Often the blooms are accompanied by conspicuous leafy bracts. The asymmetrical flowers have five-toothed calyxes, and corollas with forward-pointing, shallowly-two-lobed, upper lips, and lower lips down-curved and three-lobed. There are four protruding stamens, two curving upward and two downward. The nutlets (usually called seeds) are minutely-downy at one end.

Native to Arizona, New Mexico, and Mexico, **Agastache cana** (syn. *Brittonastrum canum*) is 2 to 3 feet tall, much branched, and has more or less woody stems and foliage with minute hairs that produce a hoary appearance. The leaves have triangular-ovate, coarsely-round-toothed blades 1 inch to 1½ inches long. The rosy-pink, 1-inch-long flowers are in dense spikes 4 to 8 inches in length. The Mexican *A. mexicana* (syns. *Brittonastrum mexicanum, Cedronella mexicana*) differs but slightly from *A. cana*. Its leaves are usually larger, its flower spikes shorter.

Agastache foeniculum

Agastache mexicana

The quite handsome *A. foeniculum*, a native of prairies and dry woods throughout much of the Midwest, is also spontaneous in New England and eastern Canada although not originally native there. It has stems up to 3 feet tall, sometimes branched above. Its short-stalked, ovate to triangular-ovate, coarsely-toothed leaves, up to 4 inches long are hairless above and whitish below because of fine hairs so short that they can scarcely be seen even

through a hand lens. The flowers are blue and in cylindrical spikes. Mostly the spikes are interrupted in their lower parts so that portions of stem show between tiers of flowers. Individual blooms are about ⅓ inch long. The other species considered here have leaves green beneath. One, *A. scrophulariaefolia,* has deep purple blooms and ovate to ovate-lanceolate leaves, smooth or softly-hairy beneath. It is 3 to 4½ feet in height and has spikes of bloom the flowering parts of which are continuous or have their one or two lowest tiers of blooms separated by a visible stem. This species is native in woodlands from Vermont and New York to Ontario, North Carolina, and Kansas. The greenish-yellow flowered *A. nepetoides* resembles *A. scrophulariaefolia*. It grows in open woods from Vermont to Ontario, Nebraska, Georgia, and Arkansas. The more western *A. urticifolia* is native from Montana to British Columbia, Colorado, and California. It attains a height of 3 to 6 feet, has ovate or triangular-ovate, coarsely-toothed, short-stalked, somewhat hairy leaves, 2 to 3½ inches or slightly more or less in length, and very dense spikes of rose-pink or violet flowers. This species favors moist soils.

Garden and Landscape Uses. For providing variety in beds and borders giant-hyssops appeal, although they are by no means as showy as some more familiar perennials. They are also appropriate for native plant gardens and for use in landscapes maintained in an informal semiwild state.

Cultivation. These plants respond to any fairly good soil that is well drained, and thrive in sun or part-day shade. They need no special care, but like most perennials, respond to a spring application of a complete fertilizer. When the clumps become overly large they can be reduced by lifting and splitting them in spring or early fall. Division and seed afford sure and ready means of propagation.

AGATHAEA COELESTIS is *Felicia amelloides*.

AGATHIS (Á-gathis)—Dammar-Pine, Kauri-Pine. Together with *Araucaria* this genus of twenty, tall, evergreen, resinous trees constitutes the araucaria family ARAUCARIACEAE. It differs from *Araucaria* in having its seeds free instead of united to the cone scales. The name *Agathis* is from the Greek *agathis*, a ball of thread. It alludes to the flowers being in clusters. The name dammar-pine is used for the genus, and individual species are often known by other names. The genus is indigenous from the Malay Peninsula to the Philippines, Australia, and New Zealand. Its members require tropical, subtropical, or at least warm-temperate conditions. Some kinds are planted in California, Florida, and Hawaii.

Dammar-pines have horizontal branches that on young trees are frequently in whorls (tiers), but more irregularly disposed on older specimens. Their leaves, opposite or alternate, and commonly more or less in two ranks, are flat, broader than those of araucarias, and are marked with fine parallel veins. They vary considerably in size and shape on the same tree and even on the same branch. The leaves remain alive for many years, sometimes as many as twenty, and when they fall leave small raised scars. Individual trees are usually bisexual. The male catkins, rigid, crowded, and cylindrical, are solitary in the leaf axils. The fruiting cones are compact, globose or egg-shaped, and composed of thick-margined, fan-shaped scales. They disintegrate as soon as the seeds mature.

Dammar-pines are commercially important for their lumber and as sources of valuable copal resins, one of the most notable of which is kauri gum, a product of the kauri-pine (*A. australis*). These resins are employed in the manufacture of varnishes, paints, linoleum, and other products. The best kauri gum is not obtained from living trees, but is dug from bogs where kauri-pine trees grew previously and is called fossil resin, although it is not truly fossilized. Resin, both fresh and fossil, is also a product of the Queensland kauri-pine (*A. robusta*) as well as of *A. celebica, A. dammara, A. palmerstonii,* and other species.

The kauri-pine (*A. australis*) inhabits the North Island of New Zealand and has been called the monarch of New Zealand forests. Under favorable conditions it attains a height of from 120 to 150 feet and a trunk diameter of 7 to 9 feet. It has flaking, bluish-gray, very resinous bark, and narrowly-lanceolate, thick, leathery leaves 1 inch to 3 inches in length and up to ⅓ inch in width; the largest leaves are on young trees. An interesting feature is that young trees usually bear flowers of one sex only, but with age become bisexual. The fruiting cones are up to 3 inches in diameter. The comparatively small and narrow leaves serve to distinguish this species. Kauri-pines are long-lived trees, and specimens said to be 4,000 years old are reported from New Zealand. The Queensland kauri-pine (*A. robusta*), a native of Australia, attains a maximum height of about 150 feet, with a trunk up to 9 feet in diameter that tapers slightly and is commonly free of branches for a considerable distance from its base.

Agathis robusta

It has scaly, thick, brown bark, and a spreading, heavily branched crown. Its leaves, 2 to 5 inches long and ¾ inch to 2 inches wide, are lustrous dark green above and paler on their undersides. The fruiting cones are 4 to 5 inches long and rather less wide.

Other sorts include *A. dammara* (syn. *A. alba*), a variable entity by some authorities treated as several distinct, but related species. Taking the broader view, it is widely distributed through Indonesia, becomes 150 feet tall and has leaves up to 5 inches long and 2 inches broad. Its subglobose fruiting cones are about 4 inches in length. Another, a native of the Fiji Islands, *A. vitiensis* occasionally is 100 feet tall, but usually shorter. It has whitish, peeling bark and leaves up to 5 inches long by 1½ inches wide. Its fruiting cones are 4 to 5 inches long by about three-quarters as wide. The lumber, called dakua wood, is used locally for many purposes, and the Fijians use its resin for glazing pottery and as a source of a black dye (obtained from its smoke) used for coloring cloth and tattooing.

Garden and Landscape Uses. The species most adaptable for cultivation in the warmer parts of the continental United States and Hawaii is the Queensland kauri-pine. The New Zealand kauri-pine is less satisfactory because as a young tree it has a poor habit of growth and sparse foliage. In cultivation the Queensland kauri-pine is often misidentified as its New Zealand relative. These trees are handsome as single specimens or in groups.

Cultivation. These evergreen trees thrive in any well-drained, reasonably fertile soil that is not excessively dry, and need no special attention. They are propagated by seeds sown in sandy peaty soil.

AGATHOSMA (Agath-ósma). Even in botanical gardens not many of the about 140 species of *Agathosma* are cultivated, and still fewer are known to most gardeners. South African evergreen shrubs of more or less heathlike appearance, they belong in the rue family RUTACEAE. Their name, from the Greek *agathos*, pleasant, and *osma*, a smell, alludes to the fragrance of the crushed foliage. The former genus *Barosma* is now included in *Agathosma*.

Agathosmas have small, undivided leaves, opposite, alternate, or in whorls (circles of more than two). Generally in clusters at the shoot ends, but sometimes solitary or few together from the axils of the upper leaves, the usually small flowers have a five-parted calyx, generally five petals, and five each fertile and infertile stamens (staminodes). The fruits are capsules separating into one to five sections (carpels).

From 1½ to 2 feet tall or sometimes taller and much-branched, *A. corymbosa* (syns. *A. ventenatiana*, *A. villosa*, *Diosma purpurea*) has hairy shoots and overlapping, pointed, linear-lanceolate leaves up to ⅓ inch long.

Agathosma corymbosa

In umbel-like clusters ½ to ¾ inch across, the white, lilac, or purple flowers, each with two carpels, are borne in spring.

From 3 to 4 feet tall and freely-branched, *A. pulchella* (syns. *Barosma pulchella*, *Diosma pulchella*) has slender, pubescent shoots with hairless, thick-margined, alternate, glossy, ovate leaves mostly up to ¼ inch long, thickly disposed along them. The purplish-white flowers, ⅓ inch across on slender ½-inch-long stalks, one or two from each leaf axil, form terminal raceme-like sprays. About 2 feet tall and much-branched, *A. ovata* (syn. *Barosma ovata*) has shining, ovate to obovate leaves up to ½ inch long. Its small white to pale mauve

flowers are in clusters from the leaf axils. They mostly have three carpels. A chief source of buchu leaves, from which is extracted a diuretic, *A. betulina* (syn. *Barosma betulina*) is low and freely-branched. It has opposite or alternate, obovate to ovate, toothed leaves ½ to ¾ inch long. The flowers, solitary or in twos or threes on short branchlets from the leaf axils, are pink and have narrowly-ovate petals and five carpels.

Garden and Landscape Uses. Very much easier to grow than the many heaths they somewhat resemble, agathosmas succeed in sunny locations outdoors in essentially frost-free climates such as that of California. They are not choosy as to soil so long as it is nonalkaline and well-drained, but prefer earth of a sandy peaty character. They are adapted for the fronts of shrub plantings and for rock gardens and other sites where low shrubs can be displayed advantageously and are useful as pot plants for cool greenhouses.

Cultivation. Outdoors these plants need no special care. Routinely they are sheared or cut back after the flowers have faded. A mulch of peat moss or other organic material maintained around them is helpful. Propagation is by cuttings of semimature or mature shoots in summer or early fall and by seeds sown in spring in sandy peaty soil in a temperature of 55 to 60°F. Pinching out the tips of the shoots of young plants occasionally, promotes branching.

In greenhouses grow the plants in full sun where the winter night temperature is 45 to 50°F and day temperatures are a few degrees higher. Never allow the atmosphere to be highly humid or stagnant. To avoid this, ventilate the greenhouse freely whenever weather conditions permit. In summer agathosmas benefit from being buried to the rims of their pots in a bed of sand, peat moss, or other suitable material in a sunny place outdoors. Bring them in before fall frost. Prune by cutting the plants back moderately after blooming, and two or three weeks later, when new growth begins repot them. Never allow the soil to become very dry, but avoid keeping it saturated for long periods. Biweekly applications of dilute liquid fertilizer from spring to fall benefit well-rooted specimens.

AGATI GRANDIFLORA is *Sebania grandiflora*.

AGAVE (A-gà-ve)—Century Plant, American-Aloe. Natives of warm-temperate, subtropical and tropical parts of the Americas, the 300 species of agaves are among the most striking elements of arid and semiarid parts of that region. The agaves and cactuses are largely responsible for the uniqueness of American deserts. The ge-

Agaves with palms and araucarias in Florida

nus *Agave* belongs to the amaryllis family AMARYLLIDACEAE, or according to those who favor the division, to the agave family AGAVACEAE. The name, from the Greek *agauos*, admirable, makes reference to the imposing appearance of blooming specimens. Agaves and aloes, the former sometimes called American-aloes, are often confused by those not familiar with them. The two are easily distinguished. The leaves of agaves contain strong fibers and only with great difficulty if at all can be torn across. Those of aloes contain soft pulpy tissue and can be snapped across and broken as easily as a carrot. Also, the ovaries of the flowers of aloes are above the petals (are superior), in agaves they are below the petals (are inferior).

Agaves are evergreen, perennial, nonhardy, often suckering, succulents and semisucculents. Their thick, tough, rigid leaves, often of imposing size, are in rosettes, stemless and sitting directly on the ground or crowning short, trunklike stems. From the centers of the rosettes rise, often to great heights, spikes or panicles of flowers. Some kinds, notably the common century plant, bloom once when many years old, and then die; some bloom annually; others at longer intervals, but without dying afterward. The leaves are undivided, lobeless, narrowly-linear, to sword-shaped, dagger-shaped, oblong-elliptic, or ovate. Usually they are spiny along their margins, often viciously so. Other kinds are without marginal spines, and in some the leaf edges are frayed with loose fibers. Not infrequently the spines are hooked. Some may point backward, others forward, or all in one direction. A long, sharp spine terminates each leaf. The flowers are numerous and more or less funnel-shaped. They have a short perianth tube and six usually erect, narrow petals (more properly tepals) of approximately equal size. There are six slender-stalked, usually long-protruded stamens with the anthers attached by their middles. The short, stout

style is tipped with a headlike three-lobed stigma. The fruits are oblong-cylindrical, woody capsules containing flattened, black seeds. Century plants, the name most commonly used for *A. americana,* but applied also to other agaves, popular belief to the contrary, do not live for 100 years then bloom and die. It is true that many kinds die after flowering and that they take many years to accumulate and store the immense food resources needed to develop a flowering stalk, but this does not require a century. The actual time such agaves live before they bloom depends upon environmental conditions, but probably ten to twenty years is about average.

Commercial interest in agaves is centered chiefly in the cultivation of *A. sisalana* and *A. fourcroydes* as sources of strong fibers known, respectively, as sisal or sisal hemp and henequen. The products of some species are used pharmacologically. Local uses involve a greater number of species for such purposes as making twine, ropes, mats, sacking, brushes, and sandals and as soap substitutes for washing clothes, hides, and animal hair. In Mexico the leaves of some kinds provide feed for animals. The short stems and young flowering shoots are cooked and eaten by Indians. A commercially important use of several agaves is in the production of the alcoholic beverages pulque, mescal, and tequila.

The common century plant (**A. americana**), presumably native to Mexico although its exact nativity is not known, is naturalized in several parts of the world,

Agave americana

notably around the Mediterranean basin, in islands of the Atlantic, and in warm, dry parts of Asia. It was introduced by the Portuguese into the Azores as early as the sixteenth century. This familiar species forms huge, stemless, freely-suckering rosettes of twenty to thirty elegantly disposed, rigid, fleshy leaves 4 to 6 feet long by above their centers up to 8 inches in width. From that point of greatest breadth they narrow gradually to near their bases, where

they again expand, and to their wickedly-sharp-spined apexes. The upper portions of the larger leaves arch and droop gracefully. The leaf edges are shallowly-scalloped and furnished with strong, curved, dark-colored spines. This blooms at long intervals only, the flowering rosettes dying afterward. The stout-stalked, horizontally-branched panicles of bloom attain heights of 20 to 40 feet. Variegated-leaved kinds of the common century plant are popular.

Agave americana in bloom

The leaf margins of *A. a. marginata* are banded with yellowish-white to yellow; those of *A. a. marginata-alba* are banded with white or creamy-white, with the young leaves often suffused with pink. In *A. a.*

Agave americana marginata

medio-picta the leaf variegation is central instead of marginal. A yellow band sometimes streaked with green runs down the center of the leaf. The broadly-yellow-edged, dark green leaves of *A. a. variegata* are twisted in sinuate fashion.

Agave americana medio-picta

Agave franzosinii

As it ages, this kind develops stout trunks up to 5 feet tall. The numerous greenish-yellow flowers are in crowded, cylindrical spikes 10 to 14 feet long that arch gracefully until their tips nearly touch the ground. This species prefers a location shaded from the strongest sun. It thrives best and is most imposing in fertile, reasonably moist soil.

A very beautiful Mexican, **A. victoriae-reginae** has a compact, many-leaved, nearly spherical, stemless rosette without offsets.

Agave americana variegata

They have a terminal spine 2½ to 3 inches long and strong, hooked marginal spines ¾ to 1 inch apart, more widely spaced toward the apex. The panicles of yellow flowers are up to 35 feet in height. It produces offsets.

A species that is safe to plant in public places as well as in home gardens because its spineless leaves present no hazard, **A. attenuata** is handsome in foliage and quite astonishing in bloom. Its rosettes are of smooth, soft green or gray-green, pointed-ovate, wide-spreading, soft-tipped leaves up to 2½ feet long by 8 or 10 inches broad.

Agave victoriae-reginae

Distinguished from typical *A. americana* by its leaves being rigid throughout, not drooping toward their ends, *A. a. expansa* has gray-green leaves with a short, thick terminal spine. It is probably native of Ar-

Agave attenuata

Extremely rigid, the bluntish leaves end in a short spine often with two smaller ones flanking it. The leaves, commonly up to about 6 inches long by 2 inches wide, curve slightly inward, have concave upper surfaces and rounded under ones keeled toward their tips. Their smooth margins are narrowly banded with white, distinctly hornlike tissue. Their upper surfaces are decorated with oblique, narrow white lines. The flowers, usually in threes, are in spikes, crowded above, looser below, that reach to heights of up to 12 feet. Variants with variegated leaves have been described. Similar to *A. victoriae-reginae*, but with fewer, more tapered, triangular leaves with more pronounced, nearly black, three-angled, about ½-inch-long spines flanked by one or two smaller ones, **A. ferdinandi-**

Agave americana expansa

izona. With much the aspect of *A. americana*, but larger, and its whitish-gray to blue-gray leaves up to 8 feet long by at the widest 1¼ feet broad, the beautiful **A. franzosinii** is imposing. Believed to be a native of Mexico, it has leaves that arch or bend over and droop toward their ends.

Agave attenuata in bloom

Agave ferdinandi-regis

regis has rigid, deeply-channeled leaves approximately 6 inches in length; their undersides are prominently keeled. It is native to Mexico.

Leaves frayed into threads at their edges but without marginal teeth are typical of *A. filifera* and *A. parviflora*, both natives of Mexico, and the latter also of Arizona. Stemless or nearly stemless and producing offshoots freely, *A. filifera* is variable. Typically it has beautiful spherical rosettes of numerous slightly upcurved, somewhat channeled, tapered-lanceolate leaves 8 to 10 inches long by about 1¼ inches wide.

Agave filifera

They are marked with two or three white lines on their upper surfaces, their margins are horny, and their apexes are furnished with a spine ½ inch to ¾ inches long. The short-stalked, paired, greenish-yellow flowers are in stout, dense, cylindrical spikes up to about 10 feet tall. Variety *A. f. filamentosa* has proportionately narrower leaves about 1½ feet in length. Variety *A. f. compacta* has leaves that are shorter and proportionately broader than those of the typical species. Its many-leaved rosettes 6 inches or so across, *A. parviflora* rarely develops offsets. Rigid and narrow-lanceolate, its leaves, dark green with their upper surfaces marked with white lines, are about 4 inches long by ½ inch wide. The margins are toothed in their lower parts, shredded into conspicuous white threads above. The loosely-flowered spikes of bloom are 3 to 5 feet tall.

Sisal and henequen are natives of Yucatan. The first, *A. sisalana,* is now widely cultivated as a commercial crop there and in various other parts of the world. It has a stout stem up to 3 feet tall topped by a crowded rosette of rigid, lanceolate-sword-shaped, gray-green leaves 4 to 6 feet long by approximately 3 inches wide, tipped with a short spine. Marginal spines are usually absent, but sometimes weakly developed. Variants with spines are *A. s. armata.* This species and its variety develop offsets. Their panicles, carried to heights of about 20 feet, have green flowers.

Henequen (*A. fourcroydes*) has stems up to 4 feet tall, with offsets from their bases. The rosettes are of rigid, oblanceolate-sword-shaped, somewhat glaucous, gray-green leaves that point in all directions, about 5 feet long by approximately 4 inches wide. They end in a stout, black spine. The leaf margins are armed with spines spaced approximately 1 inch apart. The yellowish-green flowers are in many-branched panicles up to about 20 feet or so tall. Numerous plantlets develop among the flowers.

Other agaves are cultivated, especially in collections of succulents. Some of those more commonly encountered are as follows: *A. angustifolia,* nativity unknown, has a stem up to 1¼ feet tall with offsets from its base. The rosettes are of many scarcely-fleshy, leathery, dull to lustrous, stiff, linear-lanceolate to sword-shaped leaves. Their marginal teeth have slightly curved tips set ½ to ¾ inch apart. The terminal spine is black and a little more than ½ inch long. The flowers are in panicles lifted to heights of 8 or 9 feet. The leaves of *A. a. marginata* are edged with creamy-

Agave angustifolia marginata

white. *A. applanata* forms compact rosettes with few offsets. Its many, erect, rigid, tapering, broadly-linear-lanceolate leaves up to 3 feet long by 4 inches wide

Agave applanata

have marginal spines with strongly-curved tips and a terminal spine nearly 3 inches long. The panicled flowering stalk, 25 to 36 feet in height, has many bracts. Its flowers are greenish-yellow. It is native to southeastern Mexico. *A. atrovirens* of southern Mexico has offset-forming rosettes of up to twenty spreading to erect dark green, oblanceolate leaves 4 to 6 feet long by up to 1 foot wide, more or less incurved toward their apexes, concave on their upper sides with rounded keels be-

Agave atrovirens

neath. The terminal spine is about 2 inches long. The somewhat wavy leaf margins have large teeth 1¼ to 2 inches apart toward their middles, more widely spaced above. The tall flowering stalks have panicles of greenish-yellow blooms. This species is much used for making pulque. *A. bracteosa* is stemless. Its rosettes are of arching, long-tapered, not very fleshy, finely-toothed leaves 1 foot to 1½ feet long, 1 inch to 1½ inches wide, without permanent spines at their apexes. They are gray-green to pale green. The handsome flower spikes rear like giant fluffy candles to a height of about 6 feet. They are about 8 inches in diameter and without branches. It is a native of Mexico. *A. celsii,* probably Mexican, has stemless rosettes of soft green to somewhat glaucous-gray, fleshy, pointed-elliptic leaves 1½ to 2 feet in length by up to 6 inches wide. There is a prominent white spine at the leaf apex, but marginal spines are poorly developed. The spikes, up to approximately 4 feet tall, are of yellow-green flowers in pairs. *A. deserti,* native to California, suckers freely to form dense clumps. Its gray rosettes are without stems. They are of triangular-lanceolate leaves with channeled upper surfaces and up to 1 foot long by about 2 inches wide. The terminal spines are a little over 1 inch long. Marginal spines are spaced about ⅓ inch apart or closer. The flowering panicles have ascending branches. They are 6 to 10 feet tall with yellow flowers. *A. falcata* is Mexican. It has numerous stiff, three-angled leaves.

They are pale gray to purplish or reddish-brown, finely-toothed, linear, up to about 1½ feet long by slightly over ½ inch wide, ending in a 1-inch-long, sharp spine. The slender flower spikes have papery bracts and flowers in mostly paired, short, slender spikes. **A. felgeri,** of Mexico, has rosettes of green to yellow-green, linear to narrowly-lanceolate, straight or sickle-shaped leaves often with a pale center stripe, with a few threadlike filaments along the margins and a weak terminal spine. They are up to 1¼ feet long by a little over ½ inch wide. The spikes of yellowish-green flowers rise to heights of 4 to 10 feet. **A. ferox** is Mexican. It has stemless rosettes of bold aspect up to 6 feet wide. They have twenty to thirty, rigid, fleshy, dark green leaves, more or less recurved toward their apexes. The oldest ones are often prostrate, the others spreading to erect. They are 1 foot to nearly 1½ feet broad at their widest, oblong-spatula-shaped, narrowed to their bases, and abruptly tapered at their apexes. They have concave upper sides and are markedly round-keeled beneath. The shallowly-scalloped margins are furnished with dark, hooked spines ½ to 1 inch long. The stout, conical, terminal spine is 2 to 4 inches long. **A. huachucensis,** of Arizona and Mexico, has stemless, compact, globular, many-leaved, suckering rosettes of light glaucous-gray, incurved, rigid, ovate-lanceolate leaves that taper abruptly at their apexes and are margined with spines spaced approximately ½ inch apart. The leaves, up to 1½ feet long by about one-half as wide, have a 1-inch-long spine at

Agave huachucensis

the apex. The imposing panicles of lemon-yellow flowers attain heights of 12 to 14 feet. **A. kerchovei,** of Mexico, has a usually leaning rosette of somewhat channeled, triangular-tapered, large-spined, gray-green leaves 1½ to 2½ feet long by 3 to 4 inches wide. The dense, flowering stalks are to 18 feet tall. **A. lophantha** is Mexican. It has offset-producing rosettes of very rigid, gray-green, linear to narrow-lanceolate leaves up to 3 feet long by, at their bases,

Agave lophantha

1½ to 2 inches wide. They taper from base to apex, which is terminated by a 1-inch-long, sharp spine. The marginal spines are stout. The paired, greenish-yellow flowers are in spikes up to 15 feet tall. Several varieties of this variable species have been named. **A. margaritae** is Californian. Stemless and suckering, its rosettes are of roundish to oblanceolate leaves about 6 inches long and nearly as broad. They are green with faint glaucous-grayish crossbands. On each margin there are up to eight spines. The stout, dark-colored terminal spine is a little more than 1 inch long. From 9 to 12 feet tall, the panicles have short, yellow flowers. **A. parrasana** is Mexican. It forms attractive rosettes that rarely produce offsets. The thick, ovate leaves are glaucous blue-gray. They are about 1 foot long by approximately one-half as wide and taper rather abruptly to the apex. The terminal spine is about 1 inch long, and the margins are regularly

Agave parrasana

spine-toothed. The flowers are not known. **A. parryi,** native to Arizona and Mexico, has stemless rosettes, which are sometimes solitary and sometimes clustered. They are of gray, oblong leaves 1 foot to 1½ feet long by approximately one-third as wide. Their margins are furnished with prickle-like spines spaced ½ to ¾ inch apart. The terminal spine is ¾ to 1 inch long. In panicles 9 to 15 feet tall, the flow-

ers are pale yellow. **A. patonii** is very beautiful. Native to Mexico, it has symmetrical, stemless rosettes of many light gray leaves rounded at their apexes and furnished with a dark terminal spine 1 inch long or a little longer and marginal spines spaced ¾ to 1 inch apart. The flowers are in panicles. **A. polyacantha,** probably native to Mexico, is a variable species with broad rosettes that branch as they age, usually after flowering, to form clumps. Spreading and ascending, thinnish, broad-lanceolate to elliptic, the leaves taper to a terminal

Agave patonii

spine 3 to 6 inches long. The margins are fringed with small, triangular dark spines. The blooms are in usually paired spikelike racemes along the upper lengths of the 6- to 8-foot-tall flowering stalks. The loose-flowered, sometimes branched, spikes of pale yellow blooms, in clusters of four or fewer, are 2½ to 6 feet tall. **A. scabra** (syn. **A. wislizenii**), native to Mexico, is similar to **A. applanata,** but has thinner, much broader, light gray leaves in stemless rosettes. They are broadly-ovate, up to 6 inches long by 8 to 10 inches wide. Their upper surfaces are concave, their margins spiny. The terminal spine is ½ to ¾ inch long. Yellowish, the long-stalked flowers are in panicles up to 12 feet tall. **A. shawii,** a native of California and Baja California and nearly stemless, has clusters of dense

Agave shawii

rosettes of prickly-margined leaves 1 foot to 1½ feet long. They are ovate to lanceolate-ovate, pointed, up to 4½ inches broad, and have a terminal spine 1 inch to 1¼ inches long. The greenish-yellow blooms are in panicles 9 to 10 feet tall. *A. striata*, of Mexico, has a short stem and a globular head of numerous rigid, narrowly-linear, dark-striped, gray-green, smooth-edged leaves up to 1½ feet long. The green flowers are in spikes 9 to 12 feet tall. Variety *A.*

Agave striata nana

s. nana is smaller. *A. stricta* is Mexican, has rosettes of numerous smooth- to rough-edged, rigid leaves about ¼ inch wide, up to 1¼ feet long, with a sharp terminal spine. The flowers are crowded in spikes 5 to 10 feet tall. Nearly stemless, when old this species branches to form several-headed clusters. *A. toumeyana* is native of Arizona. It has dark green, tapered-narrow-lanceolate leaves with white lines on their upper surfaces. The toothless margins have long, threadlike fibers frayed from them. *A. utahensis,* of the Grand Canyon region of Utah, is stemless. It has stiff, gray-green leaves up to 1 foot long by ¾ to 1 inch wide, ending in a slender spine. The upper surfaces of the leaves are conspicuously convex. The marginal teeth are hooked and white. The yellow flowers are carried in panicles up to heights of 6 to 15 feet.

Garden and Landscape Uses. The architectural qualities of the majority of agaves suggest their most important uses. A few kinds, notably *A. americana* and its varieties, are popular in warm, dry regions as featured specimens in tubs, large urns, and other containers. They are appropriate in such formal surroundings as terraces, steps, and the entrances to buildings, always with care being taken that they be placed where there is no real possibility that their commonly spiny leaves harm passers-by. Occasionally agaves are used in these ways in climates too cold for them to live outdoors permanently. Then, they are kept overwinter in a light frostproof cellar or similar accommodation indoors. In desert and semidesert regions many kinds are grown permanently outdoors as hedges and dividers between properties and parts of properties, as boundary plants, in foundation plantings, in decorative groupings, and as lawn specimens. Smaller agaves are appropriate in dry-climate rock gardens. Many kinds are to be found in greenhouse collections of succulents. Occasionally small specimens are grown in windows.

Cultivation. Once their simple needs are met agaves are among the easiest plants to grow. Most are extremely tenacious and persist even when grossly mistreated. They adapt to a wide variety of soils so long as they are very well drained, preferring fertile ones with a low organic content. They will not survive in wet ground. Like most succulents, agaves flourish in arid atmospheres, yet some adapt surprisingly well to humid environments. Primarily sun-lovers that do well fully exposed in regions of intense sunlight, some kinds appreciate a little shade from the strongest light. Their leaves may bleach or scorch if denied this.

Containers on the small side compared to the sizes of the plants are best for agaves. Potting is needed only at long intervals preferably in spring. When it is done pack the soil firmly. Water with caution. Always allow the soil to become nearly dry and then soak it. In winter very little watering is needed, but water more from spring to fall. Well-rooted specimens benefit from monthly applications of dilute liquid fertilizer from spring to late summer. Indoors winter temperatures may at night be 40 to 50°F with a daytime rise of five to fifteen degrees permitted. At other seasons higher temperatures are in order. Propagation is easy by offsets taken from the bases of the plants, and in some cases by plantlets that develop on the flowering stalks. Seeds germinate readily, but if they come from a place where more than one kind of agave were in bloom at the same time they are likely to produce hybrids, and seeds collected from hybrid plants are likely to produce a variable batch of offspring. Scale insects and mealybugs are the commonest insect pests, root rots and leaf spots the most usual diseases. For more information see Succulents.

AGDESTIS (Ag-déstis). This unusual genus has only one species, so different from its nearest relatives that some botanists allot it a family of its own, the AGDESTIDACEAE. More conservative authorities include it in the pokeweed family PHYTOLACCACEAE. Its anomalous standing gives reason for the name, being derived from that of a mythical hermaphrodite monster.

Native to Mexico and Guatemala, and naturalized in parts of the deep south, *Agdestis clematidea* is a tall vine with red stems that may attain lengths of 40 to 50 feet in one season. It has an immense gray tuber, rocklike in aspect and usually partly above ground. The tubers weigh up to 150 pounds. Alternate and heart-shaped, the stalked leaves are 3 inches or more in diameter. The flowers, abundant in fall, are in terminal panicles of racemes 4 to 7 inches long. In contrast to the ill-scented foliage they are sweetly fragrant. They are without petals and are ½ inch wide. Each bloom has four or rarely five, persistent white sepals that become papery with age, no petals, fifteen to twenty stamens, and a conelike style with three or four recurved stigmas. The fruits are four- or five-winged achenes about ½ inch in diameter.

Garden and Landscape Uses. In the deep south and elsewhere where little or no frost occurs and there is a long, hot growing season, this vine makes a good screen, but because of its malodorous foliage it should not be used on porches, near windows that are to be open, or elsewhere where its odor may cause distress.

Cultivation. Deep, fertile soil that does not lack for moisture produces the best results. Planting is done in spring before new growth begins. Propagation is by seeds, and by small tubers that develop freely about the old ones.

AGERATUM (Agéra-tum). Although *Ageratum* is best known for the many garden varieties of *A. houstonianum* and *A. conyzoides* commonly grown as summer-flowering annuals, it contains a number of delightful wild species well worth cultivating for the same purposes. As the group exists in nature, it consists of sixty species of annuals and perennials, some of a subshrubby character. It belongs in the daisy family COMPOSITAE, and to that section of the family that has flower heads without ray (petal-like) florets. The fruits are seedlike achenes. The name is from the Greek *a*, not, and *geras*, old, and alludes to the fact that the flowers retain their color for a long time. As wildlings, ageratums are natives of the tropical, subtropical, and warm-temperate zones of the Americas.

Cultivated ageratums range in height from about 6 inches to 2 feet. They produce their showy, long-lasting blooms continually from spring through fall and, under suitable conditions, in winter. They have undivided, mostly opposite, stalked, toothed leaves. The flower heads are tassel-like and grouped in roundish-topped clusters. They are blue, white or, more rarely, pink. The involucral bracts (small leaflike organs surrounding the flower head) of *A. houstonianum* are densely-hairy and slightly sticky, those of *A. conyzoides* are scarcely or not at all hairy. Also, the leaves of *A. houstonianum* are usually heart-shaped at their bases; those of *A. conyzoides* are rounded. It seems probable that some of the numerous horticultural varieties represent hybrids between these species. The Mexican *A. corymbosum* is a charming

Ageratum houstonianum

Ageratum houstonianum, dwarf variety

plant about 1½ feet tall, with lanceolate or pointed-oval leaves and blue flowers about ¼ inch across. A native of Florida, *A. littorale,* up to 2 feet tall, has rather sprawling stems, smooth, pointed-ovate leaves, and bright blue flowers.

Garden and Landscape Uses. The chief uses of ageratums are for filling summer beds and borders, and for planting in window boxes, porch boxes, urns, hanging baskets, and other containers. They are also charming for cultivating in pots in greenhouses for winter and spring bloom.

Cultivation. Ageratums are raised from seeds and cuttings. Cuttings gives plants of great uniformity, which is an advantage in formal plantings. But modern seed stocks are so improved that from them, too, plants can be raised that show surprisingly little variation. Cuttings root readily at any time. To have plants of suitable size for summer bedding, they are taken from February to April from stock plants wintered in a greenhouse. They root very quickly. Seeds sown indoors in February or March produce plants suitable for planting outdoors about the time it is safe to set out geraniums, tomatoes, and other frost-tender plants. The seeds germinate in about ten days in a temperature of 60 to 65°F. As soon as the young plants are well up, reduce the night temperature to 50 or 55°F. By day it may be five to ten degrees higher.

When the seedlings have developed their second pair of leaves transplant them to flats or individually to small pots. If flats are used, set the plants about 2 inches apart. The temperature now should be 50°F at night and somewhat warmer by day. Treat rooted cuttings the same way as seedlings. The soil must be porous and fertile, and the containers well drained. After the young plants are 2 or 3 inches tall, pinch out their tips to encourage branching, and repeat this once or twice later if needed. For winter and spring bloom in greenhouses, take cuttings or sow seeds in August or September and grow the plants in fertile, porous soil in full sun in a greenhouse where the winter night temperature is 55°F and the day temperature is five to ten degrees higher. By lengthening the day by the use of artificial light the plants can be encouraged to bloom even in winter. Without this aid they do not flower freely until spring. Specimens in 4- and 5-inch pots are attractive. When their flowering pots are filled with roots they benefit from regular applications of dilute liquid fertilizer.

AGLAOMORPHA (Aglao-mòrpha)—Bear's Paw Fern. The genus *Aglaomorpha* consists of robust, evergreen, tropical ferns of the polypody family POLYPODIACEAE. Natives of southeast Asia, the Philippines, and Taiwan, they are epiphytes, which means that they grow on trees, stumps, or rocks where a little humus has collected. They do not take nourishment from the live trees that serve as hosts. There are four species. The name, from the Greek *aglaia,* splendor, and *morphos,* form, was given in tribute to their impressive appearances. Aglaomorphas have creeping, mostly fleshy rhizomes and pinnately-lobed, usually stalkless leaves. These plants have been cultivated under the names *Drynaria* and *Polypodium.* Species formerly named *A. heraclea* and *A. coronans* are now in the genera *Drynariopsis* and *Pseudodrynaria,* respectively.

Bear's paw fern (*A. meyeniana*) has stout rhizomes shaggy with rusty-brown scales. Its stalkless, pinnate, leathery leaves are of two kinds, sterile and fertile. The lower leaf divisions are blunt, much shorter than those above, and are joined so that the lower part of the leaf somewhat resembles an oak leaf. Above, the leaflets are much longer, separate, but close together, and pointed. Overall the leaves are 2 to 3 feet long with a maximum width of up to 1 foot. Fertile leaves are similar to sterile ones except that their middle leaflets are shorter and the upper ones longer and so slender that they consist of only midribs with narrow wavy edged bands of tissue strung with round clusters of sporebearing organs bordering them.

Garden and Landscape Uses and Cultivation. Aglaomorphas are suitable for large

tropical greenhouses, and for outdoor or lath-house cultivation in the humid tropics and warm subtropics. They may be planted in pans or baskets, or on rafts, stumps, or slabs of wood or bark piled with suitable material into which they can root. This may be osmunda fiber mixed with sphagnum moss, or a mixture of shredded fir bark, sphagnum moss, or peat moss, with a little fibrous loam and charcoal mixed in. So long as the mixture is largely organic and admits the free passage of water and air it is likely to serve satisfactorily. The rhizomes must not be buried, simply pegged to the soil surface. In greenhouses a minimum winter night temperature of 60°F is desirable, but higher by day. Good light with shade from bright sun, and a humid atmosphere, are important. The rooting medium must be always moist, but not saturated for long periods. Propagation is by division and by spores. For other information see Ferns.

AGLAONEMA (Aglao-nèma) — Chinese Evergreen. Several familiar species are among the twenty-one that constitute this genus of the arum family ARACEAE. The group is tropical, and in the wild confined to Indo-Malaysia. Its name comes from the Greek *aglaos,* bright, and *nema,* a thread. It is thought to allude to the glossy stamens.

Aglaonemas are evergreen herbaceous plants, often with much the aspect of *Dieffenbachia.* They have somewhat canelike, decumbent or erect, thick stems ringed with scars marking the places from which leaves have fallen. More rarely they are apparently stemless. The leaves are alternate and have stalks shorter than, or at least not longer than, the blades. The bases of the leafstalks sheathe the stems. The blades are broad-ovate-lanceolate to oblong-lanceolate or lanceolate. Their midribs are thick, their primary side veins rather few. The flowers, as is usual in the arum family, are crowded in spikes called spadices (singular spadix). At the base of each spadix is a leaflike or petal-like bract called a spathe, which in *Aglaonema* is small, green or yellowish, and open to the base. It may equal or exceed the spadix in length. Spadix and spathe together form what is called an inflorescence. This is commonly thought of as a "flower." The inflorescences of *Aglaonema* have stalks shorter than the leafstalks and are solitary or often clustered in the leaf axils. The flowers, of insignificant size, are unisexual. The males, with essentially solitary, thick, cream stamens, are crowded on the upper part of the spadix. The less numerous green females are below. The fruits, at first green, ripen through orange to showy bright red berries.

The Chinese evergreen (*A. modestum*), a native of South China, is probably best known. In the wild it is 2 to 3 feet tall or sometimes taller. Its pointed-ovate leaves, 6 to 10 inches long, are dark green, fairly lustrous, and hairless. Their four or five primary pairs of side veins are not depressed on the upper surfaces, and their stalks are shorter than the blades. The inflorescences, from the leaf axils, are on stalks 1½ to 2½ inches long. They have spadixes about 2 inches long and spathes up to 1 inch longer. The foliage of *A. m. variegatum* is irregularly and conspicuously variegated with creamy-white. In cultivation *A. modestum* has been misidentified as the Malaysian species ***A. simplex.*** The latter has green, ovate-oblong to narrowly-oblong, lustrous leaves of thinner texture than those of *A. modestum,* with six to eight pairs of primary side veins, depressed above and prominent on the undersides.

Aglaonema simplex angustifolia

The leaves are 6 inches to 1 foot long by 2 to 4½ inches wide. Variety *A. s. angustifolium* has very narrow leaves.

Much resembling a dieffenbachia, the popular ***A. commutatum*** of the Philippine Islands is very variable. It has erect, often branched stems up to about 1½ feet tall, and oblongish, thick leaves with blades 4 to 7 inches long, variegated with ashy-gray blotches along the side veins. The inflorescences, on stalks up to 3 inches long, come from the leaf axils. They have greenish-white spadices about 1¼ inches long.

Aglaonema modestum

Aglaonema simplex

Aglaonema commutatum

The berries are bright to dark red to purple. Some botanists are of the opinion that *A. commutatum* may be of hybrid origin, with *A. nitidum, A. marantifolium,* and *A. simplex* involved in its parentage.

Varieties of *A. commutatum* are very numerous. They include *A. c. albo-variegatum,* a sport or mutant with white stems and leafstalks and leaves variegated with silvery-gray, *A. c. elegans* (syn. *A. elegans*), with larger and longer leaves and spathes than the typical kind, *A. c. pseudobracteatum* (syn. *A. pseudobracteatum*), which has white stems marbled with green and long, pointed-lanceolate, dark green leaves, variegated with lighter green and yellow,

Aglaonema modestum (inflorescence)

Aglaonema commutatum pseudobracteatum

Aglaonema commutatum tricolor

From 1 foot to 2 feet tall, **A. pictum** is neat. It has slender, erect stems, and pointed, broad-ovate, bluish-green leaves, irregularly patched with silvery-gray, and with a dull, velvety sheen. It is native to Sumatra. From Sumatra also comes *A. p.*

Aglaonema pictum

with their centers creamy-white, *A. c. treubii* (which is quite distinct from *A. treubii*, a species not in cultivation), a slender kind with bluish-green leaves with marbled stalks and blades variegated with silvery-gray, more narrowly pointed-lanceolate than *A. c. pseudobracteatum* has, *A. c. maculatum* (syn. *A. marantifolium maculatum*), a robust variety with pointed, broadly-lanceolate,

Variety *A. n. curtisii* is similar, but with foliage that is clearly marked with a herringbone of narrow, irregular, silvery-gray bands that angle upward from the midrib.

Aglaonema nitidum curtisii

Not a variety, but with some aspect of *A. nitidum*, the Malayan **A. cuscuaria** has leaves broadest at their bases rather than at their middles. It has pointed-ovate, sparsely-spotted, green leaves. Choice, handsome, and rather rare, **A. rotundum,** a native of Sumatra, has broad, short-stalked, thick, leathery, ovate leaves that are dark green to coppery-green, with pink veins and wine-red undersides.

tricolor (syn. *A. versicolor*), its leaves abundantly mottled with two shades of green and silvery-gray, and with pinkish stalks.

Reputed hybrids are *A.* 'Fransher', its parents supposedly *A. commutatum treubii* and *A. c. tricolor*, and *A.* 'Parrot Jungle', an offspring of *A. n. curtisii* and *A. p. tricolor*. The former hybrid is slender and has white-stalked, green and milky-green, lanceolate leaves variegated with creamy-white. The latter hybrid has pointed-lanceolate leaves of greenish-silvery hue, spotted and more or less margined with green.

Aglaonema commutatum treubii

dark green leaves sparingly feathered with grayish-green, *A. c.* 'Malay Beauty', a sport or mutant of *A. c. pseudobracteatum*, but less variegated, and a heartier grower, *A. c. robustum* (syn. *A. robustum*), a very vigorous kind with leaves up to 1½ feet long, *A. c. tricolor* (syn. *A. marantifolium tricolor*), a variety with pink leafstalks and variegations on the upper and lower surfaces of its broadish, oblong-elliptic leaves.

A familiar species long known as *A. roebelinii* (syn. *Schismatoglottis roebelinii*), **A. crispum** is native to the Philippine Islands. It has leathery, pointed-oblong-ovate, grayish-green leaves attractively and prominently variegated with broad brushings of silvery gray.

Of rigid habit, **A. nitidum** (syn. *A. oblongifolium*) has plain green, pointed-elliptic, leathery leaves. It is a native of Malaya.

Aglaonema rotundum

Aglaonema pictum tricolor

Stemless and low, **A. costatum** of Thailand has glossy, pointed-broad-ovate leaves somewhat heart-shaped at their bases, 3 to 5 inches long, abundantly spotted with white, and with a white midrib. From it, *A. c. foxii* differs in being much more sparsely spotted, and *A. c. virescens* in its broader leaves being only lightly spotted.

Aglaonema costatum

Aglaonema costatum in bloom

A creeper, with much longer leafstalks than *A. costatum*, is **A. brevispathum hospitum,** of Thailand. Its broad-ovate, glossy leaves are usually more or less heavily spotted and blotched with white. In one variant the leaves are without spots, but have a clear white midrib. Somewhat similar in the shape of its long-stalked leaves **A. siamense** has leaves without spots, but with a clear white midrib. It is native to Thailand.

Aglaonema brevispathum hospitum

Garden and Landscape Uses and Cultivation. Aglaonemas are extremely useful ornamentals for outdoor planting in the humid tropics, for tropical greenhouses, and as houseplants. For houseplants the most frequently cultivated are *A. modestum, A commutatum,* and *A. pictum.* The low-growing *A. costatum* and its varieties are excellent terrarium plants. All need about the same conditions and care as dumb canes (*Dieffenbachia*), responding to rich, loamy, porous soil that has a reasonably high humus content and which must always be kept moderately moist. A fairly high to high humidity is requisite, and good light with shade from strong sun. Established specimens benefit greatly from the regular applications of dilute liquid fertilizer. Propagation is by division, terminal and sectional stem cuttings, and air layer-

ing. The Chinese evergreen withstands low atmospheric humidity remarkably well and is an admirable houseplant. Leafy stems without roots are often stood in containers of water as decorations. Under favorable conditions (ordinary room temperatures and fairly good light) these root, grow, and remain attractive for many months, but eventually, unless taken from the water and set in soil, die from lack of nourishment. To forestall this, at the first signs of deterioration, pot them singly in 4-inch, or three together in 5-inch, pots.

AGNIRICTUS. See Stomatium.

AGONIS (Ag-ònis). Confined in the wild to Australia, *Agonis* consists of fifteen species of the myrtle family MYRTACEAE. Its name, derived from the Greek *agon,* a collection, alludes to the numerous seeds. This genus differs from the closely related *Leptospermum* in its flowers being crowded in stalkless, glandular heads.

Evergreen trees and shrubs, agonises have alternate, undivided, frequently crowded leaves, and dense, rounded clusters of small flowers. Each bloom has a five-lobed calyx, five rounded or spoon-shaped petals, and ten to thirty stamens. The fruits are leathery capsules.

A graceful tree up to 40 feet tall that because of its willow-like leaves is called willow-myrtle in its native Western Australia, **A. flexuosa** has drooping branchlets and linear-lanceolate to elliptic, short-stalked, often pendulous leaves 2 to 6 inches long and up to ½ inch wide. The ½-inch-wide, white flowers, with pink bases to their tiny petals, have twenty to thirty stamens; they occur in clusters of up to ten in the leaf axils.

Up to 12 feet or more in height, **A. linearifolia** has pointed, linear or linear-lanceolate leaves up to 1 inch long. Its tiny white flowers, each with ten stamens, are in dense clusters in the leaf axils. It is native to Western Australia.

Also from Western Australia, **A. marginata** is up to 12 feet tall or sometimes taller. This shrub has short-stalked, blunt,

obovate-oblong, three- or five-veined leaves ½ inch to 1¼ inches long, and about one-third as wide as long. The little white flowers with reddish-purple centers, and with twenty to thirty stamens, are in axillary or terminal clusters of up to twenty that are about ¾ inch wide.

Garden and Landscape Uses and Cultivation. Agonises are suited for outdoor planting in salubrious, dry climates such as that of California. They can be grown in cool greenhouses under conditions appropriate for acacias, leptospermums, and suchlike woody plants. They succeed in well-drained fertile soil that has a fair organic content. They should not be allowed to become excessively dry. They need sunny locations. Propagation is by seeds and cuttings.

AGOSERIS (Agó-seris) — Mountain-Dandelion. Nine or ten species, one from South America, the others from western North America, belong here. They are in the daisy family COMPOSITAE and have milky juice and black, chicory-like taproots. The name, from the Greek *aix,* a goat, and *seris,* chicory, alludes to the roots.

Agoserises are annuals and hardy herbaceous perennials. Their leaves are mostly in basal tufts, with few or none on the lower parts of the stems. They are hairy or hairless, with the hairs when present distributed over the entire surface and not confined to the leaf margins and midribs. The flower heads, yellow to orange, and fairly large, are solitary. Like those of chicory and dandelions, they are composed of all strap-shaped flowers. The fruits are beaked, seedlike achenes.

The variable perennial *Agoseris glauca* has mostly basal leaves, linear to oblanceolate, 2 to 10 inches long, hairy or nearly hairless, and toothless or toothed. Its yellow to pinkish or purplish flower heads, 1 inch to 1½ inches across, are on stalks up to about 1 foot long. This species is native to western North America. The plant formerly named *A. cuspidata* is *Nothocalais cuspidata.*

Garden Uses and Cultivation. Agoserises are too dandelion-like in appearance to have much general appeal. Occasionally they are planted in flower beds, naturalistic areas, and rock gardens. They grow with little care in ordinary soil, especially sandy or gravelly. Earth comparatively poor in nutrients is better than too fertile earth if compact specimens that look best in rock gardens are desired. Full sun is needed. Propagation is by seed and by division.

AGRIMONIA (Agrim-ònia) — Agrimony. The genus *Agrimonia* of the rose family ROSACEAE is of little interest to gardeners. It consists of erect, herbaceous perennials, mostly of the northern hemisphere, but represented south of the equator in the

Aesculus hippocastanum (flowers)

Aethionema warleyense

Agave angustifolia marginata

Aglaonema commutatum

Albizia julibrissin

Agave victoriae-reginae

Aglaonema commutatum variety

Alcea rosea

Alchemilla mollis

Allium christophii

Allamanda neriifolia

Aletris farinosa

Allium moly

Allamanda cathartica variety

Agrimonia repens in seed

Andes. There are about twenty species. None is very showy. The name is believed to be a corruption of *Argemone,* as used by Dioscorides.

These plants have stout rhizomes and alternate, pinnately-divided leaves, the largest pairs of leaflets alternating with pairs of tiny ones. At the base of the leaf-stalk are two conspicuous, leafy, usually deeply-toothed, appendages called stipules. The small yellow flowers, in interrupted spikelike racemes, are followed by fruits that are prickly burrs. Occasionally *A. eupatoria,* a native of Europe, Asia, and North Africa, naturalized in North America, is planted in semiwild areas. This kind attains a height of about 3 feet. There are several native American species; generally they are not cultivated. A similar species, but more freely-branched and with larger flowers, the resin-scented *A. repens* (syn. *A. odorata*) is native to Europe, Asia, and North America. Agrimonias are easily raised from seeds, and by division in early spring. They grow in ordinary soil in part-day shade or sun.

AGRIMONY. See Agrimonia. Hemp-agrimony is *Eupatorium cannabinum.*

AGROSTEMMA (Agrostémm-a) — Corn Cockle. The name *Agrostemma* is often applied in gardens to various kinds of *Lychnis,* but in good botanical practice it is re-

stricted to two species of annuals or biennials closely related to *Lychnis* and common natives of Europe and temperate Asia. The genus *Agrostemma* belongs in the pink family CARYOPHYLLACEAE. Its name is derived from the Greek, *agros,* a field, and *stemma,* a crown, and alludes to the natural habitat and to the beauty of the flowers.

The corn cockle is occasionally cultivated. As a native it is a colorful weed, common in grain fields. Some authorities maintain that the biblical phrase (Job 31:40) "Let thistles grow instead of wheat, and cockle instead of barley" refers to this plant, but there is no general agreement on this point and not all Bible translations employ the word "cockle." Some authorities believe that the biblical reference is to grain field weeds in general, which in the Holy Land, include the corn cockle.

The corn cockle (*A. githago*) is a hardy, 3-foot-tall, branching plant covered with silky, whitish hairs, and with undivided, narrow, erect leaves. The spreading petals of its magenta-red, more or less spotted, five-petaled, long-stalked flowers are exceeded in length by the lobes of the leafy calyx. The flowers open early in the morning and close in the afternoon.

Garden Uses and Cultivation. The corn cockle is suitable for inclusion to a modest extent in plantings of annuals, in mixed flower borders, and gardens of Bible plants. Its culture is of the simplest. Seeds are

sown in early spring where the plants are to bloom and are covered with soil to a depth of ¼ inch or less. If they are scattered thinly little thinning out of the resulting plants is needed because to produce a satisfactory effect they must stand closely together; 3 or 4 inches between individuals is enough. No other attention except weeding, watering in dry weather, and possibly light and unobtrusive staking is required. The plants begin blooming in ten to twelve weeks from the time the seeds are sown and continue for a month or more. If the ground near the plants is left undisturbed volunteer seedlings are likely to appear the following year. Corn cockles require a sunny location.

AGROSTIS (Agrós-tis)—Bent Grass, Cloud Grass, Redtop or Whitetop or Fiorin, Hair Grass or Silk Grass. With a wide distribution in temperate regions and at high altitudes in the tropics and subtropics, *Agrostis,* of the grass family GRAMINEAE, comprise 120 annual and perennial species. Several are used for lawns, some as ornamentals. The name is an ancient one for an unidentified grass. It stems from the Greek *agrostis,* a field.

Bent grasses have spreading rhizomes or stolons, or form tufts. Their stems are slender, their leaves narrowly-linear to almost threadlike. The flowers are usually in graceful, freely-branched, crowded or loose, panicles. The spikelets are small, one-flowered, and have usually three stamens.

Annual species cultivated as garden decoratives and for cutting for fresh and dried flower arrangements include *A. elegans* and *A. nebulosa.* Native to the western Mediterranean region, *A. elegans* is tufted and about 1-foot tall. Its very slender leaf blades are up to 4 inches long. Its loose panicles, with up to five branches from their bases, are 4 to 6 inches long. The spikelets are only ¹⁄₃₀ inch long. Cloud grass (*A. nebulosa*), a native of Spain, Portugal, and Morocco, differs from *A. elegans* in being a little taller, and in having spikelets ¹⁄₁₆ inch long in panicles with ten or more branches from their bases.

Creeping bent (*A. stolonifera*) like redtop is sometimes called *A. alba.* It is a variable, closely-matting perennial that spreads by leafy stolons. From 6 inches to 1½ feet tall, it has slender stems, and very narrow leaf blades up to 6 inches long. The usually crowded, narrow panicles, up to 6 inches in length, are of spikelets up to ⅛ inch long. Variety *A. s. palustris* (syn. *A. palustris*) is a rather coarse, taller inhabitant of moist soils. Dwarf forms of *A. stolonifera,* identified as *A. s. compacta* (syn. *A. alba maritima*) and called seaside bents, are vigorous. Used for lawns, they have erect leaves. One of the first superior selections, Washington bent, is still planted. Other named selections are available.

Velvet bent (*A. canina*) and brown bent (*A. c. montana*) are perennials, ½ foot to

2 feet tall or sometimes taller, employed as lawn grasses. Brown bent normally inhabits drier soils than velvet bent, spreads by scaly, subsurface rhizomes, and is more densely tufted. Velvet bent forms a short, dense turf of rooting surface stolons from which arise tufts of slender stems with narrow leaf blades and crowded, contracted, panicles of spikelets up to ⅛ inch long. The panicles are 1 inch to 8 inches in length.

Colonial, Rhode Island, Prince Edward Island, and New Zealand bents are selections of *A. tenuis* (syn. *A. vulgaris*). They are employed as lawn grasses. Special selections such as 'Astoria', 'Exeter', and 'Raritan' are grown. It is probable that 'Highland' bent also belongs here. Native to Europe, and naturalized in North America, *A. tenuis* is a tufted perennial that forms a good turf. From 6 inches to 2 feet tall, it has very slender stems, narrow leaf blades, and usually very open panicles up to 8 inches long of spikelets up to ⅛ inch long. This loosely-tufted species is up to 4 feet tall.

Redtop, whitetop, or fiorin (*A. gigantea*) like creeping bent is sometimes called *A. alba*. It is likely to be confused with *A. stolonifera* and *A. s. palustris*, with which it intergrades. It differs in having loose, very open flower panicles. A loosely-tufted perennial, suitable for pastures, it is not an acceptable turf grass, but is often included in cheap lawn grass seed mixtures.

Hair grass or silk grass (*A. hiemalis*), native over much of North America, is a variable, ornamental perennial 1 foot to 3 feet in height, with slender leaf blades up to 5 inches long and mostly basal or low on the stems. The panicles of bloom, up to 1 foot long, are pyramidal or ovoid.

Garden and Landscape Uses and Cultivation. For the cultivation of turf grass agrostises see Lawn Maintenance. Kinds grown as ornamentals may be grouped in beds or planted in rows for cutting. They are easy to manage in fairly good, moderately moist soil in sunny locations. Seeds of the annuals are sown in spring where the plants are to remain, and the seedlings are thinned to prevent uncomfortable crowding. The perennials are propagated by seed and by division. For more information see Lawns, Their Making and Renovation.

AICHRYSON (Aichrỳ-son). The annual, biennial, occasionally triennial, or longer-lived, soft succulents of *Aichryson* of the orpine family CRASSULACEAE have botanical characteristics midway between those of *Sedum* and *Sempervivum*. They inhabit the Canary Islands, Madeira, and the Azores, and number ten variable species, which are often difficult to distinguish from one another. Their name is the one used by Dioscorides for *A. arboreum*.

Aichrysons have hairy, succulent, erect, branched stems. Except at the ends of the branches, where they are crowded, the alternate, stalkless, flattish, fleshy, hairy leaves are rather distantly spaced. The small, starry, yellow or sometimes red-tinged flowers are in broad, forked clusters. Each has a five- to twelve-parted, green, fleshy, cup-shaped calyx, as many petals as calyx segments, and twice as many stamens as petals.

Perennial, subshrubby kinds include *A. tortuosum* (syn. *Aeonium tortuosum*) and a hybrid of it, *A. domesticum* (syn. *Aeonium domesticum*). These are fairly frequently cultivated, the latter often misidentified as the former. From *A. tortuosum* and the only other subshrubby species, *A. bethencourtianum* (syn. *Aeonium bethencourtianum*), *A. domesticum* differs in being larger and more branched, in its older branches becoming woody, and in having foliage that scarcely looks hairy to the naked eye. About 4 inches tall and woody at its base, *A. tortuosum* has hairy, freely-forking, tortuous stems, crowded toward their ends with stalkless, round-ended, very fleshy, spatula-shaped or obovate leaves about ½ inch long and one-half as wide as long. Their upper surfaces are nearly flat, beneath they are rounded. When grown in full sun under dryish conditions the foliage often becomes reddish or coppery. The branches of the forking flowering shoots terminate in loose clusters of golden yellow, eight-petaled flowers up to ½ inch across. This species is native to the Canary Islands. Similar, but less freely branched, about 6 inches tall, and with bigger, broader, thinner, less hairy leaves, *A. bethencourtianum* has larger flower clusters, and differs in technical details. It is endemic to the Canary Islands.

Attractive hybrid *A. domesticum* is presumed to have as parents *A. tortuosum* and either *A. divaricatum* or *A. punctatum*. Its variety *A. d. variegatum* has leaves broadly, or in one variant narrowly, edged with white. From 6 inches to 1 foot in height, this hybrid has much-forked, tortuous branches, naked of foliage in their lower parts, crowded-leafy near the ends of their branches, and less congestedly so below the clusters of blooms. Its bluntish, spatula-shaped to obovate, sparingly glandular-hairy leaves are ¾ inch long and one-half to two-thirds as wide. The flowers are golden-yellow, have seven or eight petals, and slightly exceed ½ inch in diameter.

An attractive annual or biennial, *A. laxum* (syn. *A. dichotomum*) is softly-glandular-hairy and attains a height of up to 1 foot. A native of the Canary Islands, it has forking, usually reddish branches, and spatula-shaped to roundish leaves with blades up to ½ inch long or a little longer. The pale yellow flowers produce a cloudlike effect. They have nine to twelve petals. A purple-leaved variety, *A. l. foliis-purpureis*, comes true from seeds. Similar, but with more or less horizontal branches and richer yellow, usually eight-petaled flowers, *A. villosum* of the Azores is bushy and usually up to 8 inches tall. The blooms of these annual and biennial kinds remain attractive for two or three weeks. As they fade

Aichryson villosum

the flower clusters assume a greenish appearance as the conspicuous green ovaries increase in size.

Garden and Landscape Uses. In warm, dry, sunny climates such as are characteristic of many parts of the American West these plants can be grown outdoors and are suitable for rock gardens, flower borders, and inclusion in collections of succulents. They need dryish, well-drained soil and full sun. They are attractive in pots in greenhouses and window gardens.

Cultivation. The perennials grow with little trouble in any well-drained soil and are extremely easy to propagate by cuttings and by seeds. Indoors a night temperature in winter of 40 to 50°F is adequate, with a slight increase by day allowed. Watering should be done with such caution that the soil never remains wet for long periods and approaches dryness between applications. In winter the soil is kept drier than in summer.

Seeds of biennial kinds are sown in late summer or early fall to give plants that bloom the following spring. Outdoors, sowing may be done where the plants are to remain and the seedlings thinned to 4 to 6 inches apart. Or seeds may be sown in a pot or seed bed and the young plants transplanted to their flowering sites. In greenhouses seeds of *A. laxum* are sown in pots in late August or early September and the young seedlings, as soon as they are big enough to handle, are transplanted individually to small pots. Later they are planted three together in well-drained, 6-inch pans (shallow pots) in which they will bloom the following May. They are grown throughout in a cool, sunny greenhouse, one that is well ventilated and in which the night temperature in winter is maintained at 50°F, with a rise of five to ten degrees by day permitted. The soil should never be allowed to remain saturated for long periods; it is always permitted to nearly dry out before water is applied. The soil should be coarse and porous. If it is acid the addition of broken or ground limestone is beneficial. For further information see Succulents.

AILANTHUS (Ailánth-us)—Tree-of-Heaven. Although ten species of the Asian and northern Australian genus *Ailanthus* are recognized, only the ubiquitous tree-of-heaven is well known to gardeners. Ailanthuses belong to the quassia family SI-MARUBACEAE. The name is derived from *ailanto,* a native name of *A. moluccana* that means tree of heaven. In China the wood of the tree-of-heaven, although soft, light, comparatively weak, and not durable when exposed to weather, is used for general carpentry and fuel, and wild silkworms are fed on leaves of it as well as those of *A. vilmoriniana.*

This genus consists of large deciduous trees, with alternate, pinnate leaves having an odd number of leaflets. The small greenish flowers have five or six sepals and the same number of petals. The stamens number ten. Male and female flowers are normally on separate trees. Rarely both occur on the same individual. The fruits somewhat resemble those of maples, and like maple keys are technically samaras. Each samara consists of a compressed seed with a large wing attached. In the case of maples the seed is at the end of the wing, but in *Ailanthus* it is near its center. The wing is slightly twisted in the manner of an airplane propeller so that when the samaras are blown from the tree they twist and twirl in the air and are carried for considerable distances. Ailanthuses are usually sparingly branched. Their leaves do not drop entire; instead, individual leaflets fall from the midribs, and the latter often remain after all or most of the leaflets are shed.

The common tree-of-heaven (*A. altissima*) was brought to England from its native China in 1751 and to the United States

Ailanthus altissima

Ailanthus altissima in New York City

in 1784. In Great Britain it has remained a considerate guest, occupying only sites where it is planted and never trespassing beyond, but in the United States it has assumed the prerogatives of the family and of naturalized citizenship. It not uncommonly lives in places few native American trees would tolerate. Chiefly it is a resident of the eastern United States, where it grows spontaneously in all sorts of unlikely places in cities and other man-made environments. It colonizes railroad embankments, vacant lots, ash dumps, and neglected corners of all kinds. Its seedlings spring up between crevices in paving and areaways and at the bases of walls and fences. The tree-of-heaven tolerates a combination of heat, drought, poor soil, and polluted atmosphere better than any other tree. For these virtues it is the ideal city tree, but like so many plants (and people) invested with good qualities, it has others less admirable. Among these, its wood is weak and so the tree is much subject to storm damage, its male flowers have a putrid odor, and pollinated female trees produce vast numbers of seeds that scatter widely and result in seedlings springing up as weeds in both likely and unlikely places. Weighing the good against the bad,

Ailanthus altissima in seed

it may be concluded that the tree-of-heaven is worth planting where choicer trees cannot be expected to grow, but that it cannot be generally recommended for most suburban and country gardens and landscapes, although even there it is possible to use occasional specimens to advantage for the sake of their bold foliage and often brilliantly colored fruits.

The tree-of-heaven at its maximum reaches a height of 100 feet, but even at maturity is frequently lower, and may at-

Ailanthus altissima (fruits)

tain a trunk diameter of 3 feet and sometimes more. Its leaves, up to 2 feet long (considerably longer on young, vigorous seedlings), are similar to those of *Cedrela sinensis* and not unlike those of certain sumacs. It is easily distinguished from both by its leaflets having two to six teeth at their bases each with a prominent gland on the underside. Also, the foliage of the tree-of-heaven, when crushed, has a rather unpleasant odor. Female trees make a really colorful display from late summer onward as their great bunches of fruits change gradually from green to pink to bronzy-red or quite brilliant red. The intensity of the color varies considerably in different individuals, and so for decorative planting it is worthwhile to concentrate on specimens that have the most brightly colored fruits. Variety *A. a. erythrocarpa* has been described as having especially bright red fruits, but they do not appear to be superior to those of selected individuals from almost any batch of seedlings. Another variety, *A. a. pendulifolia*, has large drooping leaves. Purplish leafstalks and larger fruits distinguish *A. a. sutchuenensis*, and *A. a. vilmoriniana* differs from the typical species in its young shoots and leafstalks being pubescent as are the undersides of its leaves. This latter variety is not quite as hardy as *A. altissima*. A native of India, *A. excelsa* is grown in Hawaii. Much more tender to cold than the common tree-of-heaven, it is a tall tree with leaves up to 3 feet long, each with up to twenty-eight slightly sickle-shaped, conspicuously-toothed or -lobed, pubescent leaflets. The small, yellow, five-petaled flowers are in panicles from the leaf axils.

Garden and Landscape Uses and Cultivation. Certain limiting factors to be considered before the tree-of-heaven is selected for landscape planting have been discussed above. If it is chosen, female trees only should be set out, since male specimens when in bloom not only have an objectionable odor, but produce large amounts of wind-carried pollen to which some people are allergic. This pollen causes

nearby female trees to bear viable seeds, which, when they germinate in large numbers, may create a weed problem. The tree-of-heaven thrives in a wide variety of soils from dry to quite wet, from fertile to infertile, and is hardy throughout most of New England. It prospers best in full sun, but stands some shade. It may be pruned to any extent deemed desirable. In Europe it is common practice to cut it to the ground each spring and fertilize it to encourage the development of stout shoots several feet tall that bear enormous leaves of exotic appearance. The tree-of-heaven is easily raised from seeds, but these give rise of course to a mixture of male and female plants and among the females there is likely to be much variation in the quality of the color of their fruits. By far the best plan is to multiply desirable individuals of known decorative value by root cuttings, a simple and reliable procedure.

Diseases and Pests. The tree-of-heaven is susceptible to a wilt disease and a shoestring root rot for neither of which are there effective controls, as well as to the less serious leaf spot and twig blight diseases. The chief insect pests are the larvae of the cynthia moth and the ailanthus webworm.

AIPHANES (Aíph-anes)—Coyure Palm, Palma de Coyer. Forty species of feather-leaved palms of tropical America constitute *Aiphanes* of the palm family PALMAE. They include plants sometimes called *Martinezia*. The name derives from the Greek *aiphnes*, abrupt, and refers to the blunt ends of the leaflets.

These trees have trunks ringed with rows of sharp spines and once-pinnate leaves with wedge-shaped leaflets, irregularly-toothed or jagged at their broad apexes. The leafstalks and other parts are also spiny. The flowers are in long simply-branched clusters with two spathes. The clusters develop among the foliage. The one-seeded, globose fruits, yellow, pink, or red, are about the size of cherries.

One of the commonest species in cultivation is a coyure palm of northern South America, *A. caryotaefolia*, which attains a height of 30 feet or more and has leaves 3 to 6 feet in length. The leaflets are 6 inches to 1¼ feet long and about one-half as broad. The ends are slightly three-lobed and jagged-toothed. The fruits are reddish-yellow. Indigenous to Colombia, *A. lindeniana* has a slender trunk up to 15 feet in height. Its leaflets are as long as those of *A. caryotaefolia*, but very much narrower, and its fruits are red. The palma de coyer of Puerto Rico (*A. acanthophylla*) is endemic there and is one of only two native palms that are spiny, the other being the corozo (*Acrocomia media*). The palma de coyer is up to 40 feet in height and has a straight trunk of nearly even thickness around which from its base often develops

Aiphanes caryotaefolia

a mass of aerial prop or stilt roots. Spines are often nearly absent from the lower parts of old trunks. The leaves, 10 to 12 feet in length, have many blunt, ragged-ended leaflets up to 1½ feet long. The very numerous, glossy, bright red fruits are ½ inch or slightly more in diameter. This kind grows in forests in moist limestone soils. Another West Indian species, *A. corallina,* is the grigri palm of Martinique. About 20 feet tall, it has leaves with blunt-ended, 1-foot-long leaflets and red fruits about ½ inch in diameter.

Garden and Landscape Uses and Cultivation. Because of their prickly character aiphanes are primarily plants for collectors. They are handsome and satisfactory for planting outdoors in southern Florida, Hawaii, and other essentially frost-free, tropical regions where they are afforded reasonably moist conditions and fairly good soil. They are easily grown in containers and prosper when these are rather small relative to the size of the specimens. The containers must be well drained and the soil coarse, fertile, and porous. Water should be applied freely from spring through fall, more moderately in winter, but the soil must never be dry. A humid atmosphere at all times and a minimum winter night temperature of 60°F are favorable. Night temperatures at other seasons should be at least five or ten degrees higher, and at all times day temperatures should be five or ten degrees above those maintained at night. Shade from strong sun is essential indoors. Well-rooted plants respond favorably to biweekly applications of dilute liquid fertilizer. Propagation is by fresh seeds sown in sandy soil at a temperature of 80 to 90°F. For additional information see Palms.

AIR and AIR POLLUTION. In order to live, plants like animals need air. Unlike most animals they have no specialized respiratory organs comparable to lungs yet every one of their living cells above and below ground, or with aquatics under water, must be supplied with air. Like animals, plants respire, take in oxygen, give out carbon dioxide. This is a continuous process, it never completely ceases so long as cells live. Even dormant seeds respire.

But because plants do not maintain body temperatures higher than their surroundings and because they do not expend energy in mobility and activity in the ways that most animals do, the amounts of oxygen they need are very much less. Indeed green plants in a process essentially the reverse of respiration, called photosynthesis, give off during periods of exposure to light (photosynthesis is not operative in darkness) very much greater volumes of oxygen than they need for respiration. The excess comes from the breaking down into its constituent elements of carbon dioxide absorbed from the air. The carbon is retained and used to build the plant body, the oxygen vented into the atmosphere.

Air consists of approximately 78 percent nitrogen, 21 percent oxygen, 0.03 percent carbon dioxide, with traces of other gases. In addition, to be agreeable to plants, it must contain a satisfying amount of moisture (water vapor). Although one of the most essential and important plant nutrients, nitrogen is not fixed (metabolized) directly from the air by ordinary plants. Some, notably many members of the pea family LEGUMINOSAE achieve this indirectly by establishing a symbiotic relationship with nitrogen-fixing bacteria.

To be healthful for plants, air must be free of damaging pollutants or at least must not contain any harmful concentrations. Such pollutants can cause stunting, leaf drop, disfigurement, abnormal growth, and other woes including death.

In some parts of North America the presence of pollutants in the atmosphere is so manifest that certain crops cannot be raised successfully over wide areas, and most vegetation is harmed to a greater or lesser extent. Almost everywhere local invasions of the air by substances toxic to plants, such as escaping manufactured gas and products of industrial processes, may cause trouble. An extreme example may be seen at Ducktown, Tennessee, where fumes from copper smelting so destroyed the vegetation over an area of several square miles that decades later the earth was essentially devoid of plants and deeply gullied by erosion.

Generally, pollution is most severe in urban areas where its causes are most concentrated. It is not a new problem. The filthiness of the atmospheres of such regions as the Black Country of England, the Ruhr Valley of Germany, and Pittsburgh, Pennsylvania, was well established before the beginning of the twentieth century. Some of the causes of this earlier pollution, notably the quantities and types of coal burned and the methods of burning it, have since been modified in favor of a cleaner atmosphere. But other sources of air contamination, particularly automobiles, which have greatly increased in number, have appeared, and by the 1960s a gradually increasing public awareness of the problem reached proportions that resulted in legislative action seeking to control the most flagrant polluters.

Common sources of air pollution beside automobile engines are smelters, industrial plants, electric generators, heating plants, burning refuse, and forest fires. Many of the contaminants occur in smog. A list of some of the commonest harmful chemical air pollutants follows.

Chlorides (often as HCl) are discharged from industrial smokestacks. Concentrations of more than 0.5 parts per million result in damage similar to that caused by sulfur dioxide.

Ethylene (H_2C-CH_2) even in concentrations of less than one part in a million causes stunting, drooping of shoots, leaf drop, leaf and stem distortion, and premature aging of blooms. Especially sensitive are carnations, cattleyas, narcissuses, snapdragons, sweet peas, and tomatoes. Ethylene is a product of burning fuels and of plant metabolism and decomposition. It is present in manufactured gas.

Fluorides when present in the air in gaseous form, but not in ordinary fluoride-treated drinking water, cause the tips or margins or both of leaves to assume a burnt or scorched appearance, often with a distinct reddish-brown or yellowish line between the damaged and living tissues. Young, soft growth is most susceptible. Especially sensitive plants include citrus fruits, corn, grapes, gladioluses, irises, and white pine.

Nitrogen-dioxide in concentrations of two to three parts per million, like sulfur dioxide, results in bleaching of leaf tissues. It is produced by the photochemical oxidation of nitrous monoxide.

Ozone (O_3) is usually associated with peroxyacetyl nitrate (PAN) or smog. It results from a photochemical reaction of nitrogen dioxide and olefin-like particles chiefly from automobile exhausts. Damage typically consists of a disfiguring dark or pale strippling or flecking of the upper surfaces of mature foliage, bleaching or chlorosis, leaf drop, stunting, and killing of tissues. Plants quite sensitive to this pollutant include beans, grapes, grasses, potatoes, spinach, tomatoes, and white pine.

Peroxyacetyl nitrate (PAN) chiefly results from automobile exhausts. It occurs as the result of a photochemical reaction of nitrogen dioxide and volatile hydrocarbons. Its presence in amounts of more than two parts per million manifests itself by the undersides of leaves assuming a glazed appearance and immature leaves becoming bronzed or silvered. The needles of affected conifers turn yellow, grasses become bleached. Leaf drop, stunting, and early maturity also occur. Plants especially susceptible include alders, avocados, beans, elms, endive, *Ficus*, hibiscuses, honey-locusts, maples, mints, peppers, petunias, pines, rhododendrons, salvias, spinach, Swiss chard, and tomatoes.

Sulfur dioxide, one of the commonest and most distressing pollutants, is harmful in concentrations as low as 0.5 part per million. Chiefly the output of industrial smokestacks, especially those venting oil and coal furnaces, it causes the leaf margins and the tissues between the leaf veins of many plants to bleach to a papery-white or straw color. The leaves of grasses develop tannish to white longitudinal streaks. Beginning at their tips, the needles of conifers turn reddish-brown. Particularly sensitive to this pollutant are apples, blackberries, cabbages, crab apples, hawthorns, larches, raspberries, rhubarb, sumacs, tulips, and violets.

The degree of air pollution varies from time to time depending upon such factors as industrial activity, automobile use, and most especially weather. In urban areas in still air contaminants soon build up to intolerable levels. This is especially true when what is known as an inversion occurs, when immobile layers of warm and cold air are superimposed in such a way that smog collects in increasing amounts beneath a barrier layer. Los Angeles, California, is notable as a region where such inversions are frequent.

Resistance to air pollutants, especially photochemical smog, is more characteristic of some plants than others. Even within a kind varieties may differ. For example, petunias with colored blooms are more resistant than white-flowered ones, small-flowered varieties than large-bloomed (grandiflora) types, petunias with small leaves than those with large. Young and old foliage are commonly less damaged by air pollutants than leaves that have recently matured. Plants that grow fast and have soft foliage are more susceptible to harm than slower-growing, firm-leaved ones. The United States Department of Agriculture advises that the following plants have considerable resistance to photochemical smog: acacias, aralias, arbutus, ash (*Fraxinus*), boxwoods, bridal wreath (*Spiraea*), camellias, cedars, (*Cedrus*), *Cistus*, cotoneasters, cypresses (*Cupressus*), dieffenbachias, dracaenas, fatsias, firethorns (*Pyracantha*), lilacs, the maidenhair tree, oaks, philodendrons, pittosporums, *Prunus*, viburnums, and yuccas.

Control of air pollution and the damage it brings can, rarely, be achieved by individual gardeners, and usually only when they themselves can moderate or eliminate a strictly local cause. In a broader measure it is a public problem to be dealt with by a society better educated to the awareness of the damage wrought, not only to plants, but to animals and to man and many of his works, and by appropriate legislation properly enforced.

In the meantime a modicum of relief can be had in badly affected areas by concentrating on plants least susceptible to harm (breeding programs are developing some varieties of beans and other plants with superior resistance to ozone).

Pollution damage can be minimized during periods of heaviest concentrations by slowing growth by reducing the frequency of watering and the amounts of nitrogen fertilizer given. Sprays containing ascorbic acid or other substances have been advocated for reducing smog damage, but according to a 1971 United States Department of Agriculture advice "There are no practical chemical treatments available that can be used on plants to increase their tolerance of the polluted environment."

For information about damage done by manufactured gas used for heating, socalled illuminating gas, see Gas Injury, and House or Indoor Plants.

AIR DRAINAGE. As air cools it becomes heavier and when there is little or no wind flows down slopes and collects in hollows and sometimes in gardens surrounded by walls, fences, or hedges that impede its further movement. Such frost pockets as they are called are more subject to early frosts in fall and late ones in spring than higher land from which cold air can slide to lower levels. For this reason fruit growers usually prefer to plant orchards part way up a slope rather than at its bottom or near its more exposed top. Similarly, in California relatively tender plants such as proteas are most satisfactory where there is good air drainage. Air drainage is important also in limiting the incidence of certain diseases, such as mildews, and black spot of roses, which thrive when the atmosphere is still and humid. When hillside gardens that are to be enclosed are designed, it is well to make provision on the side facing the down slope for one or more openings to permit the outflow of cold air.

AIR-FERN or NEPTUNE-FERN. The novelty commonly sold as air fern, neptune fern, aqua fern, and magic fern and frequently advertized as growing without soil, water, or light, is not a fern, not a plant, and is not alive. It is the skeleton of colonies of the coralline marine animal, a hydroid zoophyte, named *Sertularia argentea* and commonly known as sheep's tailed coralline, squirrel's tail, and in England, white weed. The creature lives in waters off the shores of northeastern North America and northern Europe. Commercial supplies are dredged in English waters and dried and dyed green or magenta, before being packaged for sale.

AIR LAYERING. Air layering is an ancient and under favorable conditions very sure method of plant propagation. Sometimes called Chinese layering and marcottage, it has been practiced in China and other Asian countries from time immemorial. It is employed extensively in warm, humid climates and in greenhouses. It serves equally well the home gardener faced with problems caused by certain houseplants, such as aralias, crotons, dracaenas, fatshederas, fatsias, philodendrons, rubber plants, and schleffleras that have outgrown their allotted space or have become extremely tall and leggy. If faced with such a situation, consider air layering. It is a simple technique.

Propagation by ordinary leafy stem cuttings consists of taking a shoot from a plant, preparing it suitably, and planting it in an appropriate rooting medium in a favorable environment. When it has made new roots the young plant is transferred to a soil of its liking. Air layering is exactly the same in principle. The only difference is that the cutting is caused to make new roots *before* rather than *after* it is removed from the mother plant.

Plants most amenable to increase by air layering or at least kinds with which air layering has been most successful are natives of the tropics and subtropics. When polyethylene plastic film was first introduced as an aid to gardening much interest was generated in the possibility of using it to air layer outdoor trees and shrubs in temperate climates. Some success with this has been recorded, but not as much as hoped. Hardy plants that have been increased in this way include cotoneasters, crab apples, dogwoods, forsythias, *Halesia*, hemlocks, hollies, *Koelreuteria*, rhododendrons, viburnums, wisterias, and zelkovas. Nevertheless the results have been spotty and much less sure than air layering adaptable tropicals, and the technique as applied to outdoor plants in temperate regions is not much used.

To make an air layer, proceed as follows. Decide from where on the main stem or branch you want the new roots to come. This should be at some little distance from the end. If it is too close to the apex it is likely to be so soft that the stem will rot instead of root. If it is too far from the end of the stem it may involve tissues too hard to root readily, or it may give you a layer that when rooted and cut free of its mother plant has too much foliage for its limited amount of roots to care for, with the result that it either dies or its lower leaves drop and leave you with a bare-stemmed specimen. Stimulate root development by injuring the stem and surrounding the wounded part with a constantly moist medium porous enough to admit air freely and agreeable to roots. In the past gardeners often met these requirements by carefully splitting a flower pot lengthwise into two halves, tying these around the injured part of the stem, filling the pot with sandy soil, and keeping it moist by frequent watering. Or sphagnum moss was tied around the wound of a plant kept in a highly humid atmosphere and kept moist by repeated watering. The availability of polyethylene plastic film made possible a less troublesome procedure.

But first about the wounding. You may do this in several ways. In the procedure sometimes called ringing, a cylinder or band of bark about ½ inch wide is removed from around the entire stem. An alternative method is to make one or more ¾-inch to 1½-inch longitudinal slits around the stem, widening each slightly by cutting from its side a sliver of bark. This is often the best method with slender stems. Most commonly the wound is made as a notch ¾ inch to ½ inches long extending into the stem for about one-third of its thickness. Make the notch by slicing in an upward and inward direction. Prevent it from closing and its parts from growing together by inserting a matchstick-like sliver of wood into the notch.

The best material to wrap around the wound is sphagnum moss, fresh or dried, but in the tropics fibers from coconut husks and other sources are used. Some gardeners sprinkle coarse sand among the sphagnum. Dusting the wound with a hormone root-inducing powder may help rapid rooting, but is not essential. Now to complete the job. First soak the sphagnum in water. Then take a couple of good handfuls and squeeze them as hard as possible between the hands. The moss will now be of the right dampness. If sand is to be used sprinkle it among the moss. Next swathe the wounded part of the stem with the moss, taking care if the stem is notched to push the moss well into the notch. Press the moss firmly and mold it into the shape of a football. Then wrap it completely in transparent polyethylene plastic film. Secure the ends of the wrapped "football" to

(b) Push a sliver of wood into the cut

(c) Bind a "football" of moist sphagnum moss securely around the cut

(d) Enclose the moss in transparent polyethylene plastic and tie it tightly at bottom and top

(e) When new roots show clearly, remove the plastic and cut off the rooted top (in the illustration, a dracaena)

(f) Plant the top in a pot in sandy soil

(g) In a suitable environment, the cutback plant will generate new shoots, which when large enough can again be air layered

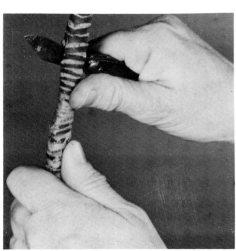

To air layer: (a) Make a upward cut into the stem

the stem by tying securely, or better still with adhesive tape. Make sure that water cannot enter the upper end. Now put the "patient" you have operated on in a warm, light, but not sunny place and await the results. No interim care is needed. The polyethylene prevents the escape of moisture yet permits air to pass through. The above directions apply to plants indoors. There is no difference with outdoor plants except that one cannot control the temperature, and it may be necessary to erect a temporary shade to prevent the polyethylene from acting like an unventilated greenhouse with the result that its contents become overheated.

The time taken for enough roots to develop to make it practicable to remove the layer varies from a few weeks to several months, depending upon the kind of plant, time of the year, temperature, and other variables. Do not take the plastic off until a fair number of young roots are visible. When that time comes, sever the air layer from the mother plant, remove the plastic and plant the propagation immediately in very sandy soil in a well-drained pot only a little bigger than the ball of moss and roots. Special care is now needed. The new plant, now entirely dependent for moisture on its own limited amount of roots, is likely to suffer if subjected to a dry atmosphere, drafts, or direct sun. Keep it for a month or more in a lightly shaded, warm place where the air is humid. In a greenhouse these conditions are usually easily achieved and so, except for the humid atmosphere, are they in homes, offices, stores, and similar places. In such places transparent polyethylene plastic film, perhaps in the guise of a freezer bag or turkey bag as they are sometimes called, can be used to assure that the air immediately surrounding the plant is humid. By enclosing the young plant in a tent of this material you can make sure that it is protected from drying. Do not allow direct sunshine to play on the tent and when roots have taken good hold of the soil remove the covering. When you take rooted air layers from hardy outdoor plants treat them in the same way. A closed or only slightly ventilated cold frame, lightly shaded or not exposed to direct sun, is a suitable place in which to keep newly potted air layers of these plants until their roots are well established in the new soil.

AIR PLANT. This is the common name of *Kalanchoe pinnata.* The term is also used in a different sense to include all epiphytes. See Kalanchoe, and Epiphyte or Air Plant.

AIR-POTATO is *Dioscorea bulbifera.*

AIRA (Aì-ra)—Hair Grass. Nine species of slender annual grasses constitute this genus of the grass family GRAMINEAE. They

Ringing, an alternative way of air layering: (a) Remove a narrow band of bark from all around the stem

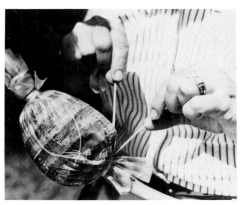

(c) Tie the moss securely in place and encase it in transparent polyethylene plastic tied tightly at the bottom and top

are indigenous to Europe, western Asia, and North Africa. One is cultivated as an ornamental. The name *Aira* is an ancient Greek one for an unidentified weed, probably a grass. The present genus differs from the closely related *Deschampsia* in its members being annuals, and from *Agrostis* in its spikelets having two flowers. The common name hair grass is applied to both *Deschampsia* and *Aira.*

The *Aira* cultivated is *A. elegans* (syn. *A. capillaris*). This grows in loose tufts and has slender stems and leaves. The former are 9 inches to 1½ feet tall, the latter up to 2 inches long and hairlike. The panicles of bloom, 1 inch to 4 inches long and about as broad as long, are loose and have numerous, very slender, spreading branches. The spikelets are less than 1/10 inch long and silvery and have one or two short bristles. This plant is native of the Mediterranean region; it is naturalized in North America.

Garden and Landscape Uses and Cultivation. This is an elegant grass for the fronts of beds and borders and for use, fresh or dried, in flower arrangements. It grows in ordinary garden soils and is especially well suited to sandy ones. It thrives in part-shade. Seeds are sown in early spring where the plants are to remain and the resulting plants thinned to 4 or 5 inches apart.

(b) Wrap moist sphagnum moss around the wounded place

(d) When ample roots have developed cut off the top, remove the plastic, and pot the new plant in sandy soil

AISTOCAULON ROSULATUM is *Aloinopsis rosulata.*

AIZOACEAE—Carpetweed Family. The 130 genera and approximately 1,200 species of this family of dicotyledons are widely distributed, especially in warm regions, and are particularly numerous in South Africa. Chiefly low herbaceous perennials and subshrubs, they have alternate or opposite, usually fleshy leaves and symmetrical flowers often brightly colored, in aspect but not botanical detail resembling the flower heads of daisies. They have inferior or superior ovaries, four or five sepals, many or no petals, and four or five stamens. The fruits are capsules.

Among the best known members of this family are the ice plant and numerous related sorts, including stone plants and windowed plants of South Africa belonging to such genera as *Acrodon, Aloinopsis, Antegibbaeum, Aptenia, Arenifera, Argyroderma, Aridaria, Astridia, Bergeranthus, Berresfordia, Bijlia, Braunsia, Carpanthea, Carpobrotus, Cephalophyllum, Cerochlamys, Chasmatophyllum, Cheiridopsis, Conicosia, Conophyllum, Conophytum, Cylindrophyllum, Dactylopsis, Delosperma, Didymaotus, Dinteranthus, Diplosoma, Disphyma, Dorotheanthus, Dracophilus, Drosanthemum, Eberlanzia, Ebracteola, Erepsia, Faucaria, Fenestraria, Frithia, Gibbaeum, Glottiphyllum, Hereroa,*

Herrea, Herreanthus, Imitaria, Jacobsenia, Juttadinteria, Kensitia, Lampranthus, Lapidaria, Lithops, Machairophyllum, Malephora, Mesembryanthemum, Meyrophytum, Metrophyllum, Monilaria, Muiria, Muirio-gibbaeum, Nananthus, Nelia, Odontophorus, Oophytum, Ophthalmophyllum, Orthopterum, Oscularia, Platythyra, Pleiospilos, Prenia, Psammophora, Psilocaulon, Rabiea, Rhinephyllum, Rhombophyllum, Ruschia, Sceletium, Schwantesia, Semnanthe, Sphalmanthus, Stomatium, Tischleria, Titanopsis, Trichodiadema, and *Vanheerdia.*

AJUGA (A-jùga)—Bugle Weed. A few of the forty to fifty species of this genus of the mint family LABIATAE are popular garden plants. The group includes annuals and low perennial herbaceous plants; only the latter meet much favor among gardeners. The generic name is of doubtful derivation. In the wild ajugas are widely distributed through temperate parts of the world. Some are naturalized in North America.

The leaves of *Ajuga* are usually toothed; sometimes they are deeply-lobed, sometimes without teeth. The flowers, blue, purple, pink, or white, in leafy-bracted spikes, are without stalks, and develop two to many together in the axils of the bracts. The upper parts of the spikes are crowded with the rings of flowers close together, but toward the bases of the spikes the circles of flowers may be interrupted so that sections of stalk show between them. The upper lips of the flowers are represented by three tiny teeth, the lower lips are lobed. There are four protruding stamens, the two upper shorter than the lower. The fruits consist of four joined nutlets, commonly called seeds.

Common bugle weed (*A. reptans*), native to Europe, is a nearly hairless plant, usually 4 to 8 inches tall, that spreads by stems that run at or near the surface of the soil, root, and give rise to new rosettes of foliage, and eventually flowers, along their lengths. The lower leaves often have slightly wavy, but not toothed edges. They are

Ajuga reptans

obovate to oblong-elliptic narrowed below to winged stalks. The upper leaves are stalkless and elliptic or ovate. In the typical species, which is naturalized in parts of North America sometimes as a weed in lawns, the flowers are blue-purple. Those of *A. r. alba* are white, those of *A. r. rubra,* pink. In addition, there are kinds with especially attractively colored leaves. Those of *A. r. atropurpurea* are deep bronze-purple, those of *A. r. variegata* are splashed with creamy-white and pink, those of *A.*

Ajuga reptans variegata

r. multicoloris (syn. *A. r.* 'Rainbow') are even more plentifully pink-marked. Other varieties include 'Jungle Beauty' with large, ovate, green leaves and spikes of blue flowers, 'Jungle Bronze' with extra large, crisped, bronzy leaves and flower spikes up to 10 inches long, and 'Jungle Green' with extra large and roundish green leaves.

Ajuga reptans 'Jungle Beauty'

The blue- or purple-flowered *A. pyramidalis,* a native of Europe, differs in being an erect, hairy plant 6 inches to 1 foot tall that develops prostrate running stems late in the season or not at all. Its ovate to obovate leaves are slightly toothed. The lower ones are stalked, the upper ones stalkless. The flowers are in dense spikes. The dwarf *A. p. metallica-crispa* has leaves

Ajuga pyramidalis

with a metallic-green sheen, and deep blue flowers. Hairy, erect, and 6 to 10 inches tall, *A. genevensis* differs from *A. reptans* in never having trailing, rooting stems and in its elliptic-oblong to obovate leaves being coarsely-toothed. The flowers are blue, pink, or white, the upper ones forming a dense spike, the circles of lower flowers separated by visible portions of flower stalk. Six or more blooms comprise each whorl (circle). This Eurasian is naturalized in North America. Variety *A. g. brockbankii* spreads more and is dwarfer than typical *A. genevensis.* It is, in fact, intermediate between that species and *A. reptans* and quite possibly is a hybrid. Its flowers are dark blue.

Ajuga genevensis

Garden and Landscape Uses. The chief horticultural use of bugle weeds are as groundcovers and edgings and in rock gardens. They are easy plants to grow, the common *A. reptans* and its varieties succeeding in light shade or in sun, provided the soil is fairly moist; the others generally prefer sun or at most part-day shade. For *A. pyramidalis* damp soil is desirable, but *A. genevensis* prefers drier conditions.

Cultivation. Little care is needed to maintain bugle plants. The suppression of weeds, most likely to be troublesome in new plantings, is the chief chore. In dry weather watering may be needed. It is always necessary to prevent piles of fallen leaves accumulating over the plants in fall. Such coverings ensure conditions favorable to the development of diseases that cause ajugas to rot and die. In poor soils a light spring dressing of a complete garden fertilizer promotes good growth. The planting distance for young plants is 6 to 8 inches. Propagation is very easily effected by division or, in the case of the typical species, by seeds. Bugle weeds are very susceptible to the fungus disease called crown-rot, which may destroy large patches.

AKEBIA (Akèb-ia). This eastern Asian genus of the lardizabala family LARDIZABA-LACEAE is usually considered to consist of two species, but some botanists recognize five. Its name is derived from its Japanese name, *akebi*.

Akebias are twining, woody vines, deciduous or evergreen, depending upon the climate. Their chief attractions are their neat growth and good-looking foliage. The long-stalked leaves have distinct leaflets that spread like the fingers of a hand. The blooms are interesting, but not colorful. They are in axillary racemes with the lower ones of each raceme female, and the upper male. The latter are considerably smaller than the females. The showy parts of the flowers consist of three petal-like sepals, but there are no petals. The fruits, rarely produced in cultivation, are technically berries. They contain many small seeds and are edible. In the Orient the stems of akebias are used for basketmaking.

Akebias are hardy in southern New England. The most attractive species is the five-leaf akebia (*Akebia quinata*), which attains a height of 30 feet and has leaves of five obovate to elliptic leaflets 1 inch to 2 inches long and notched at their ends.

Akebia trifoliata showing large female flowers and much smaller males

They are dark green above and glaucous on their undersides. The fragrant, slender-stalked flowers appear with the new leaves in spring. The females are purplish-brown and 1 inch or somewhat over in diameter; the males are rosy-purple and about ½ inch across. The fruits are cylindric-ovate, 3 to 4 inches long, purple with a waxy bloom, and quite decorative. This species is a native of China, Korea, and Japan. The three-leaf akebia (*A. trifoliata*), of China and Japan, is coarser-foliaged than *A. quinata* and does not ordinarily exceed 20 feet in height. Its leaves have three, smooth-edged or toothed, broad-ovate to ovate leaflets up to 3 inches long, notched at their tips and greenish or slightly glaucous on their undersides. The female flowers are deep maroon and about 1 inch across, the males are much smaller and light purple. The fruits, 2½ to 3½ inches long, are pale purple. A variety, *A. t. australis*, be-

lieved to be more tender, has leathery, mostly toothless leaves. Variety *A. t. clematifolia* has thin, toothless leaves. A hybrid between *A. quinata* and *A. trifoliata*, called *A. pentaphylla*, has leaves of three to five leaflets.

Garden and Landscape Uses. Akebias, particularly *A. quinata*, are splendid vines for sun or part-shade where heavy foliage effects are not required and good texture is an advantage. They are excellent for training on fences and walls and provide good backgrounds for flowers planted in front of, but not crowded against them. They are useful for draping pergolas and arbors and for hiding or partly hiding rocks. They may be used as groundcovers. The five-leaf akebia is useful as a climber in cool greenhouses and in porches, patios, and cool, light places indoors.

Cultivation. These vines grow without difficulty in any moderately fertile, well-drained garden soil. They require good light, but not necessarily direct sun, and a reasonable amount of moisture. Pruning to keep the plants shapely should be done, to any extent desirable, in spring. Akebias are easily increased by seeds, cuttings of leafy shoots in summer, hardwood cuttings in fall, by division of the roots, and by layering.

AKEE is *Blighia sapida*.

ALAMO VINE is *Merremia dissecta*.

ALBIZIA (Albíz-ia)—Mimosa, Silk Tree, Woman's-Tongue Tree or Lebbek Tree or Siris Tree. More than one hundred species of tropical and subtropical trees and shrubs belong here, few of which are cultivated. They are in the pea family LEGUMINOSAE

Akebia quinata

Akebia quinata (leaves and flowers)

and range as wildlings chiefly through the warmer parts of Asia, Africa, and Australia; one is a native of Mexico. The name, sometimes spelled *Albizzia*, commemorates F. del Albizzi, an Italian eighteenth-century naturalist.

Most kinds are deciduous. They have alternate, twice-pinnately divided leaves, with one or more glands on the main leaf-stalk and numerous small leaflets. The flowers, in dense, globose heads or cylindrical spikes, are pink, yellowish, or white. The genus belongs in the *Mimosoidae* subfamily of the LEGUMINOSAE and hence the flowers are not the familiar pea-shaped ones characteristic of most temperate zone legumes, but are structured like those of *Acacia* and the powder puff tree (*Calliandra*). The corollas are small, the showy parts of the flower heads are numerous projecting stamens, with those of each tiny bloom separated above but joined below.

The best known kind in eastern North America and the hardiest of the albizias is **A. julibrissin**. This is the mimosa of the south. It is also called silk tree. It is quite distinct from the acacias, which are also called mimosas, and from the botanists' genus *Mimosa*, which is that of the sensitive plant. It thus presents a good example of the lack of precision in the application of common names. The silk tree is very commonly planted from Maryland southward, and in recent years has become popular as far north as New York City. An exceptionally hardy specimen has lived for many years at the Arnold Arboretum, near Boston, Massachusetts. It has been described as *A. j. rosea* and is a smaller tree with brighter pink flowers than the typical kind. The silk tree is native of warm-temperate parts of Asia from Japan to Iran. It attains a height of about 45 feet and spreads widely. The foliage is lacy and graceful, each leaf has eight to twenty-four divisions each with narrow leaflets about ¼ inch long. The slender-stalked pompon-like flower heads are borne in profusion over a period of a month or more in summer. They are 2 to 3 inches wide and vary in

Albizia lebbek, by day its leaves expanded

Albizia lebbek, at night its leaves folded

color on different seedling trees from pale to rosy-pink. The flat, papery, brown pods are 3 to 6 inches in length, rather under 1 inch wide, and after ripening hang for a long time before falling.

Hardly flattering to the ladies is the colloquial name applied throughout the English-speaking tropics and subtropics to *A. lebbek*. The woman's-tongue tree is so called because its long, flat, tan seed pods remain hanging for several months and when dry rattle and chatter with every passing breeze. Also called lebbek tree and siris tree, it attains a height of 50 to 100 feet and forms a broad, umbrella-shaped head of feathery foliage. Individual leaves are large. They consist of four to eight major divisions, each of ten to eighteen leaflets 1 inch to 1½ inches long. Forming globose, tassel-like heads in clusters of three or four, the fragrant blooms have 1-inch-long stamens; they are pale greenish-yellow. The seed pods are 6 inches to 1 foot long and about 1½ inches wide. Under favorable conditions *A. lebbek* grows fast, but not as fast as another of the genus, *A. falcata* of Malaysia, which may attain a height of 50 feet in three years and 100 feet in a decade. A native from North Africa and tropical Asia to northern Australia, the woman's-tongue tree is naturalized in some

other parts of the tropics including the West Indies. Its wood resembles walnut and is excellent for cabinet work and as fuel.

Albizia distachya, young plant

The plume albizia (**A. distachya** syns. *A. lophantha*; *Acacia lophantha*) is a tree or shrub of southwestern Australia that attains a maximum height of about 20 feet.

Albizia julibrissin at The New York Botanical Garden

Albizia julibrissin

Albizia julibrissin showing seed pods

Its leaves have fourteen to twenty-four divisions each with forty to sixty leaflets about ⅓ inch long. The yellowish flowers are in dense cylindrical spikes about 2 inches long and usually in pairs; they are stalked. The pods are 3 inches long by about ½ inch wide.

Garden and Landscape Uses. The woman's-tongue tree is popular as a shade and street tree in many parts of the tropics. In the warmer parts of the United States and in similar climates and in cool conservatories, *A. distachya* is cultivated as an ornamental. It flowers abundantly even when of shrub dimensions. This elegant kind is sometimes grown in pots for use outdoors in summer subtropical beds in regions too cold for it to winter outdoors. The silk tree is a most graceful and beautiful species, well adapted for use on small properties and those of larger dimensions as a lawn tree, for planting near houses and other buildings, and along boundaries. In winter, when devoid of foliage, it has a rather stark appearance.

Cultivation. Albizias have no special peculiarities with regard to soil. Provided the soil is well drained and of fair moisture content they grow without difficulty. They are commonly propagated by seeds, although it would seem desirable to propagate silk trees that produce especially fine colored flowers by other means. Cuttings taken in summer may be rooted under mist, and budding onto seedlings understocks would appear worth trying. They bloom when quite young, however, and an alternative to vegetative propagation is to plant the seedlings in nursery rows and weed out poorly colored ones at their first blooming. Even as far north as New York City self-sown seedlings spring up freely around old specimens. This tree needs full sun. Any pruning, to restrict the plant to size, may be done in spring, but except for the purpose of containment pruning is rarely necessary.

The more tender albizias are easily raised from seeds. If these are not freshly gathered it helps to soak them for twelve hours in tepid water before sowing. Specimens of *A. distachya* cultivated in pots or tubs respond to any ordinary, well-drained potting soil. Repotting is done in late winter or very early spring and then, too, the plants are pruned to shape. Through the summer weekly or biweekly applications of dilute liquid fertilizer are helpful. Watering should be done freely from spring to fall, more moderately in winter. A winter night temperature of 45 to 50°F is adequate. By day the temperature may rise by five or ten degrees.

Diseases and Pests. A very serious wilt disease affects the silk tree. The foliage droops and shrivels and the branches die. Removing and burning infected trees is the only method of control. Supposedly wilt-resistant varieties, some of which have been given such horticultural names as 'Charlotte' and 'Tryon', are sometimes planted. The chief insect pests are webworms, scale insects, and nematodes.

ALBUCA (Al-bùca). There are some fifty species of this African genus of the lily family LILIACEAE. They are bulb plants related to *Urginea* and *Ornithogalum*. Few are cultivated, and none is hardy. The name comes from the Latin *albucus*, asphodel, hence whitish, alluding to the flower color of some kinds.

Albucas differ from *Urginea* in that the perianths of the blooms remain attached after they fade, and from *Ornithogalum* in having markedly flattened instead of spherical or obovoid seeds. They have often large bulbs, and all basal, linear to strap-shaped, or cylindrical leaves. The erect flower stalks end in unbranched racemes of erect or nodding, white, yellow, or greenish blooms. The perianth consists of six segments, commonly called petals, but more correctly tepals. The inner three, shorter than the others, are erect and touch each other at their edges, the others are more or less spreading and usually have green, reddish, or brownish keels along their backs. There are six stamens, often with winged stalks. The obconical or cylindrical style ends in a three-lobed stigma. The fruits are capsules containing black seeds.

The showiest cultivated kind is **Albuca nelsonii**, native to Natal. It has a large bulb, and bright green, strap-shaped leaves up to 3½ feet long by 1¼ to 2¼ inches wide, channeled at their bases. Rising 3 to 5 feet, the flowering stalk carries many 1½-inch-long blooms. They are erect and clear white, with a center stripe of dull red down the back of each petal. The stamens, all fertile, have winged stalks.

Commonest in cultivation, *A. canadensis* (syn. *A. major*, *A. minor*) from the Cape of Good Hope region, has bulbs up to 2 inches in diameter, and erect, linear-lanceolate, channeled leaves up to about 2 feet long. They are glaucous and have whitish longitudinal streaks. The stoutish flower stalk, erect and 2½ to 3 feet tall, carries up to one dozen nodding blooms. They have yellow petals with green keels. The outer petals are 1 inch long, the inner ones are slightly shorter and paler. The stamens, the outer three sterile, have stalks flattened at their bases. The green style ends in a small yellow stigma.

Native of Swaziland, *A. fastigiata* is an attractive kind with tapering sword-shaped leaves 1 to 3 feet long. The up-facing white flowers, with a green stripe or blotch on the outside of each petal, are about 2 inches in diameter. All six stamens are fertile.

Garden and Landscape Uses. Albucas are attractive for flower borders and infor-

Albuca canadensis

Albuca fastigiata

Cultivated alceas are tall, erect, herbaceous perennials, or sometimes biennials, with alternate, rounded, angled or lobed leaves. The flowers differ from those of *Malva* in having false outer calyxes of six or seven bracts, united at their bases, instead of two or three. There are five sepals, five petals, notched at their apexes, and many hairless stamens united into a tube surrounding the pistil.

The hollyhock (**A. rosea** syn. *Althaea rosea*), for long believed to be native to China, is not known in the wild and is now thought to be a hybrid between *A. setosa* of Turkey and *A. pallida* of eastern Europe.

Single-flowered hollyhocks

Alcea rosea

A double-flowered hollyhock

mal gardens in California and places with rather similar climates, and for greenhouses. They are easy to grow, do well in pots and other containers, and where space permits, can be grown in cool sunrooms and window gardens. They need well-drained, fertile soil and sunny locations. Flowering is chiefly in winter and spring.

Cultivation. Planting and repotting is done just before new growth begins in late summer or fall. Established bulbs are best left undisturbed so long as they are doing well. Repotting is needed only at intervals of a few years. From the time new leaf growth begins until the foliage dies naturally after flowering the soil is kept evenly moist. When the bulbs are dormant it should be dry. Well-rooted specimens benefit from dilute liquid fertilizer given at weekly or biweekly intervals during their time of active growth. Indoors, winter night temperatures of 45 to 50°F are adequate. By day an increase of five to fifteen degrees is permissible. On all favorable occasions the greenhouse must be ventilated freely. Propagation is by offsets, bulb cuttings, and seeds.

ALCEA (Al-cèa)—Hollyhock. On the basis that the tube formed by the stamens is five-angled instead of cylindrical, and the blooms are prevailingly decidedly longer, commonly exceedingly 1½ inches in diameter, very short-stalked, and in spike-like racemes, the genus *Alcea* of perhaps sixty species of the mallow family MALVACEAE is segregated from *Althaea*. It is an Old World genus, with its center of distribution in southwest and central Asia. Its most familiar constituent is the hollyhock. The name is a modification of the ancient Greek *alkea*, used for a species of *Malva*.

The fig-leaved hollyhock or Antwerp hollyhock (*A. ficifolia* syn. *Althaea ficifolia*) is also probably of hybrid origin; perhaps *A. rugosa* is one parent. The hollyhock is roughly-hairy, up to 9 feet tall and has rough, rounded to heart-shaped leaves with five to seven angles or shallow lobes. Its single, semidouble, or double blooms are borne in late spring and early summer and may be 3 inches or more in diameter. They come in a wide range of colors, white, cream, pale yellow, pink, and red, to deep almost black-maroon. The figleaf hollyhock differs chiefly in having somewhat shorter stems and deeply seven-lobed, toothed leaves. Its blooms are lemon- to orange-yellow.

Other kinds occasionally cultivated include *A. pallida* (syn. *Althaea pallida*), *A. heldreichii* (syn. *Althaea heldreichii*), and *A. lavateriflora*. The first is a native of eastern Europe and Crete; the second of the Bal-

kans, to the Ukraine; and the third of Turkey and southwest Asia. The chief differences between *A. pallida* and *A. heldreichii* are that **A. heldreichii** is less robust, has somewhat smaller blooms, and the parts of the false outer calyxes of its flowers are scarcely one-half as long as the calyx, whereas in *A. pallida* they are three-quarters or more as long. Hairy and 6 or 7 feet tall, **A. pallida** has rounded-heart-shaped to somewhat triangular, round-toothed and often shallowly-lobed, grayish-hairy leaves. The flowers pink, sometimes yellowish at the bases of the petals, are 2½ to 3 inches wide. The name *Althaea pontica* has been applied to **A. lavateriflora**. This alcea has many to few yellow hairs. It is about 3 feet tall, and has rounded leaves, the lower ones shallowly-lobed, the upper ones very deeply so. The violet flowers have petals yellow at their bases. They are about 3 inches in diameter.

Garden and Landscape Uses and Cultivation. The plants described above have much the same uses and require the same culture as hollyhocks. See Hollyhock.

ALCHEMILLA (Alchem-ílla)—Lady's Mantle. This botanically bewildering genus is represented in gardens by a few kinds grown chiefly for their attractive foliage. Their loose clusters of small greenish or yellow blooms are pleasing, but make no great display. The genus belongs in the rose family ROSACEAE and is widespread throughout temperate and arctic Europe and Asia and in parts of North America. It occurs also in the mountains of tropical America, Africa, and Asia. Botanical confusion exists as to species limitations because these plants develop seeds without pollination. They are what botanists call apomicts. The result is that whole populations develop from a single plant without being involved in any sexual process, and so are genetically extensions of one individual as are plants obtained from cuttings or by division. Each slight variant can be perpetuated as a discrete population, a condition that confuses botanists in their evaluations of species. Several hundreds of such variants have been described and given names; no one really knows how many species there are. Horticulturally only a few are worth considering. These are all natives of Europe and are hardy herbaceous perennials.

The name *Alchemilla* may come from the Arabic name of the plant, *alkemelych*, or perhaps is of modern Latin origin. Both sources refer to the plant's use in alchemy. Its common name, Lady's mantle, was bestowed in the Middle Ages because the pleating and scalloping of the leaves of some kinds suggested the headdress of the Virgin Mary. Because of this it is proper to write Lady's with a capital rather than a small initial.

The genus contains a few annuals, but consists chiefly of low herbaceous perennials. Their leaves are lobed or divided palmately (in maple leaf or handlike fashion) and have large leafy appendages (stipules) at the bases of their stalks. Those of some species exude moisture. The loosely-clustered flowers are small, with calyxes of usually four sepals that persist after the fruits form. There are no petals, one to four stamens, and usually one, but sometimes two to four, pistils. The achenes (fruits) look like and are generally called seeds.

The common Lady's mantle (**A. vulgaris**), native to northern Europe, Asia, and probably Labrador, occurs in the wild as a naturalized inhabitant of eastern Canada and the northeastern United States. It is less beautiful than some other kinds, but is interesting as being the species to which the common name in the Middle Ages was probably most frequently applied. This kind is 1 foot to 2 feet tall and has hairy, pleated, kidney-shaped leaves, 2 to 6 inches wide, that are six- to nine-lobed and toothed and green on their undersides. Its tiny flowers are yellowish-green.

Alchemilla vulgaris

One of the most pleasing kinds is **A. mollis**, a native of the mountains of eastern Europe and Asia Minor. It is sometimes cultivated as *A. major* and *A. vulgaris major*. A vigorous plant up to 2 feet tall with large, slightly-lobed, grayish-green leaves, it is round in outline and densely covered with soft hairs. Its flowers, plentifully produced and held well above the foliage, and yellow tinged with green, are more showy than those of most alchemillas. Seemingly a native of the Caucasus, **A. speciosa** differs from *A. mollis* in having less densely-hairy leaves, lobed almost halfway from their margins to the bases of their blades. The name *A. alpina* as used

by gardeners is conveniently applied to a complex of nearly related plants close to if not identical with true *A. alpina*. The true **A. alpina** is under 1 foot and often not over 6 inches tall and has leaves divided essentially to their bases into five to seven, almost separate segments. They are 1 inch to 2 inches across and have silvery-hairy undersides. Closely related, but more robust, **A. conjuncta** of the European Alps is 1 foot to 1½ feet tall. It differs from *A. alpina* in having its leaf segments more obviously joined for a little distance at their bases.

The species *A. glaucescens*, *A. rigida*, and *A. sericata* differ in not being more than 1 foot tall and having less showy and greener flowers. The shallowly-lobed leaves of **A. glaucescens** have rounded blades and brown bases to their stalks. In **A. rigida** and **A. sericata** (these kinds are very similar and difficult to separate) the leaf blades are kidney-shaped and deeply-lobed, and the bases of the leafstalks are green or pinkish. A strong grower, **A. glabra** is clearly distinguished by the upper sides of its leaves being almost or quite devoid of hairs.

Garden Uses. Lady's mantles are pleasant enough foils and companions for more colorful flowering plants. Their foliage is attractive, especially when, like silvery beads, raindrops or dewdrops rest on their hairy surfaces. In the ancient practice of

Alchemilla mollis

alchemy these were believed to absorb healing and other virtues from the foliage of the Lady's mantle and the liquid was collected and employed in magic brews. The practice of the occult arts being less commonly pursued than formerly, Lady's mantles are hardly likely to appeal as sources of wonder-working potions, but, because of their ancient employments it is legitimate to include them in gardens devoted to plants once thought to be of medicinal significance. The smaller kinds are attractive in rock gardens, the larger ones, at the fronts of borders, where they make attractive clumps and edgings. They need sunny locations and well-drained soil.

Cultivation. Provided with a soil and site as suggested above, Lady's mantles are of the easiest culture. They need no special care and are easily increased by division in spring or early fall and by seeds. Often they self-sow prolifically.

ALDER. This is the common name of the genus *Alnus*. Black-alder is a vernacular name of *Ilex verticillata* and *Viburnum nudum*. Red-alder is *Cunonia capensis*. The name white-alder is applied to *Clethra*.

ALDROVANDA (Aldro-vánda). This rare aquatic is carnivorous. It belongs to the sundew family DROSERACEAE and is native from central Europe to the East Indies and Australia. Its name commemorates Ulysses Aldrovandus, an Italian botanist. There is only one species, **A. vesiculosa**, and a few varieties. They are rootless floating plants with elongated stems up to 10 inches in length, and whorls (circles) of five to ten leaves about ⅓ inch long with four to six long bristles. Each terminates in a nearly separated section of two hemispherical parts, much like those of the Venus's fly trap (*Dionaea*). They trap minute creatures that are subsequently digested. Flowers are rarely produced; they have five sepals, petals, and stamens. As the stem elongates it dies at the rear. In constantly warm water growth is continuous, but in regions of fairly cold winters in fall winter buds that sink and hibernate on the bottom are produced, and the floating plant dies. Variety *A. v. australis* of Australia has large leaves; those of *A. v. verticillata* of India are still larger.

Garden Uses and Cultivation. This carnivore is truly a collector's item of great interest to students of botany and biology. It may be grown in pools or tanks that receive plenty of light, but not direct sun; strong artificial light is adequate. The water should be soft and clear; rain water is best and should contain infusoria and minute crustacea, needed for the plant's nourishment. The plant seems to be best adapted to shallow water among reeds and rushes such as *Typha*, *Juncus*, and *Scirpus*. The addition to the water in tanks, during that part of the year when the plant is in active growth, of such creatures as *Daphnia* and *Cyclops*, is beneficial. Some growers suggest adding a slight amount of sodium chloride (common salt) or calcium chloride.

ALECTRYON (Aléc-tryon)—Titoki. Twenty or fewer species of the soapberry family SAPINDACEAE constitute *Alectryon*, a native of the islands of the Pacific, including Hawaii to New Guinea, Australia, and New Zealand. The name, from the Greek *alektor*, a rooster, is of uncertain application.

Alectryons are evergreen trees with alternate, pinnate leaves with an uneven number of leaflets. Their bisexual or unisexual small flowers are in terminal or axillary panicles. They have four- or five-lobed calyxes hairy on their insides, no petals, and five to eight stamens. The fruits are leathery or woody capsules.

The titoki (**A. excelsum**) is endemic to New Zealand. Approximately 30 feet tall and stout-branched, it has shoots, branches of the flower panicles, and fruits, when young, densely covered with reddish hairs. The leaves, 4 inches to 1¼ feet long, have nine to thirteen toothed or toothless leaflets 2 to 4 inches long and about one-half as broad as long. They are ovate-lanceolate to ovate-oblong, and pointed. The looselybranched flower panicles are up to 1 foot long. The flowers have six to eight stamens with large red anthers. The fruits are about ½ inch long. The wood of this species is esteemed for tool handles and other purposes. The smooth rambutan (**A. subcinereum**) is an Australian species that attains a height of 30 feet and has leaves with usually two to six oblong-lanceolate to lanceolate, hairless leaves 3 to 5 inches long, and loose panicles of flowers. The tiny fruits are almost stalkless.

Garden and Landscape Uses and Cultivation. Not hardy in the north, these are attractive small trees for general purpose landscaping for the south and southwest where little frost occurs. They grow in ordinary garden soils, need no special attention, and are propagated by seeds.

ALERCE. This name is applied to *Fitzroya cupressoides* and *Pilgerodendron uviferum*.

ALETRIS (Ál-etris)—Star-Grass, Colic Root. This genus of the lily family LILIACEAE consists of five species native to the eastern United States and six of eastern Asia. The mealy appearance of their flowers inspired the generic name; it is from the Greek *aletris*, a female slave who ground grain. Perennial herbaceous plants, star-grasses have fibrous roots, basal rosettes of spreading lanceolate leaves, and erect spikelike racemes of small, tubular to bellshaped flowers with six perianth lobes. They are roughened on their outsides with numerous tiny scales, which produce their mealy appearance. There are six short-stalked stamens that do not protrude, and a slightly three-lobed style. The fruits are many-seeded capsules.

A species common in acid, sandy, moist or dry soils from Maine to Florida, Minnesota, Illinois, Arkansas, and Texas, is the white-flowered **Aletris farinosa**. Its narrowly-lanceolate to oblanceolate, pointed leaves are up to 8 inches in length. The flowers are tubular and ⅓ inch long or slightly longer. They are in racemes 1 foot to 3 feet high. The yellow colic root (**A. aurea**) is similar, but with yellow, bellshaped flowers that are usually more loosely arranged. It is found from Maryland to Florida and Texas and favors wet or moist, acid soils. Species of this genus were believed to have medicinal properties and were used by American Indians and others for relief of stomach troubles.

Garden Uses and Cultivation. Although star-grasses are sometimes included in flower borders, their chief horticultural uses are in gardens of native plants and for colonizing in semiwild places. They are not showy enough to warrant wider attention. For their successful cultivation they need a sunny location and damp or wet acid soil; one containing an abundance of peat moss or other decayed organic matter is to their liking. Although star-grasses can be increased by careful division in spring, a much more rapid and generally more satisfactory method of increase is by seeds sown in acid peaty soil kept constantly damp.

ALEURITES (Aleurìt-es)—Candlenut, Tung Oil Tree, Japan Wood Oil Tree. Milkyjuiced trees of the spurge family EUPHORBIACEAE constitute the eastern Asian genus *Aleurites*. The generic name is from the Greek *aleuron*, floury, and alludes to the young foliage being covered with a white scurf that suggests a dusting of flour. The genus consists of about five species. They have alternate, unlobed or three- to fivelobed leaves with long leafstalks and a pair of glands where the stalk joins the blade. Mostly they have flowers of both sexes on the same tree in lax terminal clusters. Each flower has a calyx dividing into two or three parts, five white or pale colored petals, eight to twenty stamens, and a twobranched style. The stiff-husked, globose to egg-shaped fruits contain one to seven hard-shelled seeds.

Commercially important drying oils much used in paints and varnishes, for treating fabrics and other purposes, are obtained from the seeds of *Aleurites*. They are tung oil (from *A. fordii*), Japanese wood oil (from *A. cordata*), candlenut oil (from *A. moluccana*), and oils similar to tung oil (from *A. montana* and *A. trisperma*). The residue of the seeds from which the oil has been expressed is used as fertilizer. Soot obtained by burning tung oil is a basic ingredient of India ink. In China and Japan the oils of

Aleurites are used for illumination. Natives dried the seeds of candlenuts, strung them on strips of the midribs of palm leaves, and burned them like candles for illumination. In Hawaii the fruits of the candlenut tree were used as a source of a black dye, and the oil to treat tapa cloth. The black shells of the seeds are used to some extent for costume jewelry. After baking the seeds may be pounded, mixed with chili peppers and salt, and eaten as a relish. The candlenut tree is the official state tree of Hawaii.

The candlenut, candle-berry, or varnish tree (*Aleurites moluccana*), probably originally a native of Malaya, is widely distributed in the tropics. It is spontaneous in Hawaii and other Pacific islands. Up to 60 feet tall and evergreen, with spreading or drooping branches and twigs with upturned tips, it has triangular, pointed-ovate, or heart-shaped shallowly-three- to five-lobed leaves, up to 8 inches long and often with toothed margins. Their undersides at first are rusty-pubescent beneath, but with age this disappears except from the veins and leafstalks. The younger leaves have a white, frosted appearance, which is particularly evident when the trees are in bloom. The flowers are in 4- to 8-inch-long clusters with the males toward their tops and the females below. Globose to pear-shaped, the dull, green or brown, fruits are 1½ to 2½ inches long; each has one to three black seeds with white kernels. This tree sometimes blooms twice a year. Its seeds, violently purgative and poisonous when raw, are edible when cooked.

The tung oil or China wood oil tree (*A. fordii*) is about 25 feet tall and differs from the candlenut in having the hairs of its pubescence stellate (branched in a starlike manner) rather than unbranched. Its

Aleurites fordii in New Orleans

pointed-ovate leaves are sometimes three-lobed, usually without lobes. The reddish-white flowers are larger than those of the candlenut, appear before the leaves, and have petals 1 inch long or longer. The fruits, top-shaped or approximately glo-

bose, are 2 to 3 inches in diameter. The mu tree (*A. montana*) of China is very similar to the tung oil tree. Its fruits are egg-shaped and have three longitudinal and many transverse ridges.

The Japan wood oil tree (*A. cordata*), a native of northern China, is much cultivated in Japan. It has pointed-ovate, lobed or toothed leaves and flattened, warty fruits containing flattened seeds about as big as castor beans.

Native of the Philippines, the lumbang or banucalad nut (*A. trisperma*) has deciduous leaves less variable in shape than those of other species, being round to heart-shaped, and unlike those of other species, are unlobed except at their bases. The flowers are white to lavendar and the fruits, about 2 inches in diameter, are pointed-globose and contain three poisonous seeds.

Garden and Landscape Uses and Cultivation. All species of *Aleurites* have decorative merit and lend themselves for use as shade trees. They grow best in somewhat acid, loamy soils that are well drained, but they are not fussy as to the earth they grow in and succeed on land too poor and dry for most agricultural crops. The candlenut and the lumbang grow in southern Florida, but it is too warm there for the tung oil to prosper; it needs cooler winters. It does well in northern Florida, Georgia, Louisiana, and Mississippi. The Japan wood oil tree stands only a little frost. These trees are commonly raised from seeds. Cuttings also provide a simple means of propagation. Under favorable conditions the trees grow rapidly.

ALEXANDERS is *Smyrnium olusatrum*. Golden alexanders is *Zizia*.

ALEXANDRIAN-LAUREL. This name is applied to *Calophyllum inophyllum* and *Danae racemosa*.

ALFALFA. Alfalfa or lucerne (*Medicago sativa*) is a clover-like forage crop. Of little or no horticultural importance, it would serve well as a green manure. It belongs to the pea family LEGUMINOSAE and so has the ability to extract from the air free nitrogen. This is stored in nodules on its roots in forms that enrich the soil when the roots decay. Tree alfalfa is *Medicago arborea*.

ALGAE. Algae (singular alga) are mostly aquatic, flowerless plants related to fungi, but usually containing chlorophyll. Of very diverse forms, they range in size from microscopic to certain seaweeds that may be 1,000 feet long. Most plants that live in the oceans are algae and as part of the plankton and in other forms they are the chief ultimate foods of sea creatures including fish.

Algae are not cultivated, but several are exploited commercially. Notable are kinds

used as human food by the Japanese and Chinese, kinds from which pectinic jelling materials used in ice cream and jams are obtained, and kinds that supply agar-agar, used in confectionary and as a medium on which to culture bacteria and fungi. It is speculated that algae will be used by interplanetary travelers to produce oxygen from the carbon-dioxide they exhale and as foods.

Gardeners are chiefly acquainted with algae as the green more or less slimy coatings that clothe the sides, usually the north sides, of tree trunks, and that grow on pots, posts, paths, and other moist surfaces, in ponds, pools, and aquariums, and on compacted, poorly-drained, moist soils, not infrequently those of lawns. In some of these favored places algae are a nuisance or are unsightly and steps to eliminate them are in order. This may be done in aquariums by reducing light intensity, in lawns by improving drainage and soil porosity and by following good cultural practices. Algicides are sold for the purpose of clearing pools and may be used on paths and other surfaces. Or these last can be cleaned of algae by scrubbing vigorously or by incinerating them with a flame gun of the type used for destroying weeds.

ALGARROBO is *Hymenaea courbaril*.

ALGICIDE Preparations used to kill algae are called algicides.

ALISMA (Alís-ma)—Water-Plantain. The name of this widely distributed genus of five species of herbaceous perennials is a Greek one of uncertain derivation. Its members belong in the water-plantain family ALISMATACEAE, all are aquatics or bog plants with erect or floating leaves and loose-branched clusters of bisexual flowers with three sepals, three white or pinkish petals, and six to nine stamens. The fruits are dry and flattened and ribbed along their curved backs.

Favoring ponds, streams, and marshes, *Alisma plantago-aquatica* is indigenous from Nova Scotia to Quebec, New York, Michigan, Wisconsin, Oregon, and California. It has oblong to ovate, conspicuously veined, deciduous leaves, and flowers about ½ inch in diameter in panicles up to 3 feet high. Very similar, but with considerably smaller flowers, *A. subcordatum* is a common native from Vermont and Massachusetts to Minnesota, Florida, and Texas.

Garden Uses and Cultivation. Although not very showy in bloom, these aquatics are suitable for planting in a small way to provide variety at watersides, bogs, and in shallow, still water. They grow without trouble in any fairly good wet soil, preferably one that contains abundant organic matter, and are easily propagated by division in spring and by seeds sown in pots of soil submerged almost to their rims in water.

ALISMATACEAE—Water-Plantain Family. Thirteen genera and ninety species constitute this cosmopolitan monocotyledonous family of wetland and aquatic perennial herbaceous plants. They have erect, floating, or submerged, long-stalked leaves and whorls of symmetrical, bisexual or unisexual flowers in usually much-branched panicles or racemes. The blooms have three petals, and three sepals, six or more stamens. The fruits are clustered achenes. The most familiar cultivated genera are *Alisma, Echinodorus,* and *Sagittaria.*

ALKALINE SOIL. See Acid and Alkaline Soils.

ALKANET. See Anchusa.

ALL-AMERICA SELECTIONS. Founded in 1932, All-America Selections is an organization dedicated to testing new varieties of flowers and vegetables grown from seeds and to making awards of recognition to those considered outstanding. In pursuance of this aim it maintains trial gardens (fifty-five in 1973) in various parts of the United States, Canada, and Mexico and display gardens open to the public (sixty-five in 1973) including two in Hawaii and one each in Alaska, Bermuda, and New Zealand.

Entries are sent every year from many parts of the world by commercial, governmental, and private plant breeders. Upon receipt each is given an identifying code number under which it is grown at the various trial gardens without its source being known to the growers or judges. For comparison each entry is grown alongside what is believed to be its nearest older equivalent. The entries are judged by leading horticulturists, seedsmen, and researchers in the field. In order to score highly a variety must give a good account of itself at most of the test gardens. Gold, silver, and bronze medals are awarded. Many seedsmen indicate in their catalogs which varieties have been winners of All-America Selections awards.

ALLAGOPTERA (Allagóp-tera). Ten species from South America and the Marquesas Islands constitute this genus of the palm family PALMAE. The name may be from the Greek *allage,* alternate or change, and *pteron,* a feather or wing, but its application is uncertain. Previously the genus was named *Diplothemium.*

These bisexual palms are little known in cultivation, but one at least seems to offer horticultural possibilities especially as a plant for seaside planting in tropical and warm subtropical regions. It is *Allagoptera arenaria* (syn. *Diplothemium maritimum*), a native of sandy dunes and strands along

the Brazilian coast and plentiful some few miles south of Rio de Janeiro. This species has underground stems and roots, but no above-ground trunk. Its arching, feather leaves, silvery on their undersides and green above, spread in all directions and are about 3 feet long. The yellow, spikelike flower clusters, rigid and erect, overtop the foliage and have woody spathes yellow on their inner surfaces and green outside. The fruits are small and ovoid.

Garden Uses and Cultivation. It is presumed that this palm is about as hardy as the queen palm (*Arecastrum romanzoffianum*), which withstands a few degrees of frost without succumbing and is a native of the same general region as *A. arenaria,* although it grows in different habitats. Conclusions as to its probable cultural needs and tolerances may be drawn from a consideration of the conditions under which the *Allagoptera* grows naturally. As a wildling it withstands brackish water, salt spray, sea winds, and full sun; it roots in nearly pure sand. For other information see Palms.

ALLAMANDA (Alla-mánda). The name of this genus is sometimes spelled *Allemanda.* Among its members are some of the most familiar and splendid nonhardy garden vines. Their clear yellow trumpet flowers are well known to almost all who have been to Florida, southern California, Hawaii, and other subtropical and tropical parts of the world. The name, as colloquially used, is almost synonymous with golden-yellow-flowered vine. Yet not all allamandas are vines nor do all have yellow blooms. Among cultivated kinds one is a low shrub and one has red-purple,

wine-colored flowers. The plant called wild-allamanda is *Urechites lutea.*

Allamandas are placed by botanists in the dogbane family APOCYNACEAE, and thus is their relationship to *Vinca* and oleanders acknowledged. There are about fifteen species, natives of Brazil and Central America. Their name commemorates an eighteenth-century Leyden (Holland) professor of natural history, Dr. Frederik Allamand.

These are milky-juiced plants with opposite or whorled (in circles of three or more) leaves, and trumpet- to bell-shaped, showy flowers in clusters at the branch ends. Each bloom has a deeply-five-lobed calyx and five spreading corolla lobes (petals). The five stamens are contained within the corolla tube. There is a solitary style. The fruits are large prickly capsules.

The common allamanda (*Allamanda cathartica*) is quite variable. All the cultivated yellow-flowered vining kinds belong to it. A native of Brazil, it is a vigorous climber that raises itself by clambering rather than by attaching itself to supports. Its stems neither twine nor have means of adhering and it produces no tendrils or holdfasts. Its leaves commonly are in threes or fours, sometimes in twos. More or less obovate and tapering at both ends, and with very short stalks, they are 4 to 6 inches in length, wavy-margined, and typically hairless except on the veins beneath. The blooms of the wild species are usually whitish in their throats and 2 to 3 inches in diameter; they have broad-ovate corolla lobes. In variety *A. c. grandiflora* the flowers measure 4 to 4½ inches across and are paler yellow than those of the typical species. This variety grows

Allamanda cathartica hendersonii in a large conservatory

Allamanda cathartica nobilis

compactly and has thin, wiry stems. An especially vigorous, free-blooming kind *A. c. hendersonii* has thick, hairless leaves and flowers 4 to 5 inches in diameter. Its flower buds are brownish on their outsides. Purplish shoots and leaves that are hairy, especially on their undersides, distinguish *A. c. nobilis*, which has fragrant blooms as large as those of *A. c. hendersonii*. Variety *A. c. shottii* has dark-striped throated, very large blooms and a slight pubescence on the young shoots and leafstalks. The flowers of *A. c, williamsii* are up to 3 inches in diameter and have throats stained with reddish-brown that are deeper yellow than the corolla lobes. The shoots and both sides of the leaves are slightly hairy.

The purple-flowered allamanda (*A. violacea*) is much less commonly cultivated than its yellow-flowered relatives. A native

of Brazil, it is a slender vine with ovate leaves up to 6 inches long and usually in circles of four. Its claret-red rather than purple blooms are whitish toward their bases and 2½ inches across. An entirely different vine, *Cryptostegia grandiflora*, is sometimes called purple-allamanda.

The bush allamanda (*A. neriifolia* syn. *A. oenotheraefolia*) is also Brazilian. A shrub rarely exceeding 3 feet in height, it sometimes exhibits a slight tendency to climb. Its elliptic to oblong leaves are in circles of four or five and are 3 to 5 inches long. They are short-stalked and the veins beneath are pubescent. The flowers, 1 inch to 1½ inches across, are rich golden-yellow with their throats striped within with reddish-brown. The base of the corolla tube is greenish and enlarged. A double-flowered variety of this species is sometimes grown.

Allamanda neriifolia, showing fruit

Garden and Landscape Uses. The popular varieties of *A. cathartica* are superb for growing on porches, pillars, archways, pergolas, trellises, fences, and other supports over which they may clamber or to which they can be tied. They withstand a few degrees of frost and are practicable for outdoor cultivation as far north in Florida as Jacksonville. Although they suffer from cold there, well-established specimens recover from brief exposures to as low as 20°F. In even somewhat colder climates it is possible to grow the yellow-flowered allamandas by digging them up each fall, wintering them indoors, and planting them outdoors in spring. The purple-flowered allamanda is tenderer and is recommended only for frost-free or nearly frost-free climates. Its uses are the same as those of the yellow-flowered, vining kinds. The bush allamanda is about as hardy as the varieties of *A. cathartica*. It is useful for shrubberies, foundation plantings, lawn beds, and informal low hedges, and is seen to especially good advantage when associated with the purple-flowered *Thunbergia erecta*. All allamandas are splendid greenhouse and conservatory ornamentals.

Although the bush allamanda will stand part-shade it does better in full sun; for the others maximum exposure is essential. Another requirement is rich, well-drained soil that is never excessively wet, but is sufficiently moist through the growing season to promote vigorous growth.

Cultivation. The bush allamanda is the only one that produces seeds regularly. It is readily propagated from seeds, but is more commonly grown, like *A. cathartica* and its varieties, from cuttings. Both kinds root quickly and easily. The cuttings may be terminal ones made from short new shoots, preferably with a heel (sliver of older stem) attached at the base, or by sections, consisting of two or three nodes (joints), of firm shoots of the previous year's growth. Either type may be rooted in sand, vermiculite, perlite, or other propagating medium held at 70 to 80°F at any time of the year, but spring is usually the preferred season. Cuttings may even be rooted with their bases in water to which a few pieces of charcoal have been added to keep it sweet. Because *A. violacea* is often difficult to propagate from cuttings and because it does not grow as thriftily on its own roots as when grafted onto *A. cathartica*, it is most usually propagated that way. The variety *A. c. hendersonii* is especially well suited for use as an understock. Grafting is usually done in greenhouses in winter or early spring.

Both outdoors and in, allamandas give little trouble to the gardener. They should be pruned annually to keep them from becoming overcrowded. In warm climates where they bloom more or less throughout the year the time to attend to this is immediately after a main flush of bloom has

Allamanda neriifolia

exhausted itself. In places where a more pronounced winter brings a bloomless season of partial rest the end of this and the imminence of a new growing period signals pruning time. Under greenhouse cultivation pruning is done in late winter. It consists of thinning out old, crowded, and weak shoots and shortening those that remain. The lateral growths are cut back to within one or two joints of their bases.

Allamandas are gross feeders and should be fertilized liberally when in active growth. Then, too, they should be watered adequately. Specimens grown in greenhouses are kept "on the dry side," but never completely dry, during the winter. At that time the atmosphere should be less humid than it is from spring to fall. In greenhouses and conservatories these plants are at their best in ground beds, but excellent specimens can be obtained in large pots and tubs. When grown in containers repotting or top dressing should be done early in the year before much new growth is made. However they are grown, it is necessary to tie the shoots to supports, and this should be done before they become too firm. A winter night temperature of 55°F is adequate. At other seasons the night temperature may be 60 to 70°F and higher when the outside temperature exceeds this. At all seasons day temperatures may, with advantage, be five or ten degrees higher than those maintained at night.

ALLEGHENY SAND-MYRTLE is *Leiophyllum buxifolium prostratum.*

ALLEGHENY-SPURGE is *Pachysandra procumbens.*

ALLEGHENY-VINE is *Adlumia fungosa.*

ALLEMANDA. See Allamanda.

ALLIGATOR-PEAR OR AVOCADO. See Avocado, and Persea.

ALLIUM (Ál-lium) — Flowering Onion. Common onions, chives, and garlic are the most familiar members of the genus *Allium* of the lily family LILIACEAE, or if one follows the classification adopted by some botanists of the amaryllis family AMARYLLIDACEAE. Other esculent vegetables are leeks, shallots, and rocambole. All of these are generally found only in vegetable gardens and herb gardens, although chives is sufficiently attractive to warrant planting as an ornamental. Except for chives, they are not dealt with here, but under their common names in other parts of the Encyclopedia. Among the 450 species of this widely distributed northern hemisphere genus are some pesky weeds as well as a considerable number deemed worthy of cultivation. Because of the great confusion that exists in the application of names it is certain that fewer kinds are being grown

than listings and garden catalogs suggest. Gardeners who engage in assembling representative collections of decorative alliums or even seek a few other than those most plentiful and commonly grown must be prepared to receive again and again under names of much more glamorous and unfamiliar kinds such species as *A. cernuum, A. senescens,* and *A. schoenoprasum.* The name derives from the classical latin word for garlic.

The botanical characteristics of *Allium* are simply stated. Its members are bulb plants, some kinds with the bulbs scarcely developed. They include hardy and nonhardy biennials and perennials usually with the foliage all or nearly all basal. The flowering stalks, frequently hollow, support terminal umbels of few to many small or comparatively small blooms. In the bud stage the umbel is enclosed in a membranous spathe that splits later into one to three persistent, withering parts that remain united by their bases. The flowers have six similar perianth parts, usually called petals, but more correctly tepals, that are completely separate or at most are joined only at their bases, six stamens, and a style with a three-parted or entire stigma. The fruits are three-celled capsules containing many seeds. A further identifying feature of most kinds although this occurs in some other related and unrelated plants including *Ipheion uniflorum* and *Tulbaghia fragrans* is the alliaceous (onion-like) odor of the crushed or bruised foliage and bulbs.

Hardy alliums with yellow blooms include quite a few delightful ones. One of the most satisfactory, **A. moly** of southwestern Europe, has clustered bulbs each with one or two pointed, elliptic to lanceolate leaves up to about 1 foot long and ¾ inch to 1½ inches wide or wider. As long or somewhat longer than the leaves, the flowering stalks terminate in many-flowered, approximately 3-inch-wide umbels of bright yellow, up-facing, starry blooms almost 1 inch in diameter. This species does not start into growth until late spring, and

the foliage dies in early summer soon after flowering. It prefers a location in light shade. The quite different **A. flavum,** native of dry, rocky places from southeastern Europe to western Asia, belongs to a group distinguished by the bladdery sheaths that enclose the umbels in the bud stage, being extended as long, slender, pointed tails. In bloom from 9 inches to 1½ feet tall, it has bluish, subcylindrical leaves approximately ¹⁄₁₆ inch wide and about as long as the flowering stalk. The umbels erupt into a fire-cracker-like golden rain of soft to clear yellow blooms about ½ inch long. The stalks of the individual flowers are of varied lengths. The stamens protrude. The outer flowers are pendulous, the center blooms erect. European **A. flavescens** (syn. *A. ammophilum*) has blooms that are more greenish-yellow than those of *A. flavum.* Its markedly taper-pointed, lanceolate leaves, less than ¹⁄₁₀ inch wide, sheath the lower one-thirds of the flowering stalks, which are 2 to 3 feet tall or taller.

Hardy, blue-flowered alliums are not numerous, but include some really delightful sorts. One of the most lovely, **A. caeruleum** (syn. *A. azureum*), grows 1 foot

Allium caeruleum

to 2 feet tall and bears atop its slender flowering stalks dense, nearly spherical heads of small cornflower-blue blooms with darker mid-veins to the petals. Sta-

Allium moly

Allium moly

mens and petals are equal in length. Its leaves, triangular in section and linear, are shorter than the flowering stalks. Of Asian nativity, this was first introduced to gardens in 1830. Coming from western China, **A. cyaneum** has flowers of brilliant blue. Its bulbs are slim, its leaves narrowly-linear or more slender, channeled along their upper sides. The bell-shaped blooms are loosely arranged in erect to nodding, subspherical to spherical umbels of up to twenty. The protruding stamens are distinctly longer than the petals. A species of similar geographical origin, **A. kansuense** differs from *A. cyaneum* in the stamens of its slender-bell-shaped, violet-blue blooms being shorter than the petals and hence not exserted. Its flowering stalks, 6 inches to 1 foot tall, are leafy to about their middles. The leaves are linear, channeled along their undersides. The many-flowered, somewhat nodding, hemispherical umbels are of flowers with petals up to ⅓ inch long. Bright blue to purplish-blue flowers are borne by **A. beesianum**, a high mountain native of western China. This has slender bulbs and linear, long-sheathing leaves, two to four to each flowering stalk. The blooms, their petals ½ to ¾ inch long, are in umbels topping stalks 1 foot tall or a little taller.

White- or nearly white-flowered species include several of good grace and some too smudgy to have garden appeal. In addition to those to be considered now there are white-flowered varieties, mostly greenish or grayish rather than pure, of some pink-, purplish-, and reddish-flowered alliums. They are mentioned under their species. Outstanding among the hardy white-flowered kinds are *A. ramosum* and *A. tuberosum*, the first native from Japan to India, the other central Asia. Both have been known in gardens as *A. odorum* a synonym that correctly applies only to *A. ramosum*. Both have densely-clustered, very slender bulbs, a plenitude of approximately 1-foot-long, linear leaves, and stiffly-erect flowering stalks 1 to 2 feet tall. The many-flowered umbels are of strongly heliotrope-scented, up-looking blooms. Should their pleasing fragrance delude you into thinking that the flowers cannot be those of the onion, crush a leaf or two for olfactory confirmation of their relationship. Blooming in high summer, **A. ramosum** has somewhat hollow leaves and slightly bell-shaped, starry blooms with petals nearly ½ inch in length and stamens one-half as long. Blooming in late summer and early fall, *A. tuberosum* always has solid leaves and smaller flowers with more spreading petals. Called Chinese chives, it is commonly cultivated in the Orient for salad.

Flat, broadly-ovate to elliptic, fleshy, blue-green leaves 6 to 9 inches long, ¼ to ½ inch wide, characterize **A. karataviense**, a native of Turkestan. There are usually

Allium tuberosum

Allium karataviense

two, sometimes three from each bulb and they arch outward so that their tips touch the ground. The flowers, crowded in big, ball-like heads, top stout stalks 4 to 6 inches long. Their whiteness leaves something to be desired, being an uninteresting pinkish-white rather than pure, but the seed heads are interesting and decorative. Not reliably hardy in the North, at least not in the vicinity of New York City unfortunately, **A. neapolitanum** (syn. *A. cow-*

anii) is choice. Its name acclaiming it the onion of Naples, it inhabits fields and other grassy areas and olive groves in southern Europe. Among its charms are the purity of its blooms and freedom from the prevailing smell that is the so-common badge of its clan. A spring-bloomer, it has linear to linear-lanceolate, keeled leaves ½ to ¾ inch wide, and atop three-angled stalks 1 foot to 2 feet tall loose umbels of many somewhat cupped flowers with spreading petals up to ½ inch long. The stamens are shorter than the petals. A native of moist, shady places in southern Europe, **A. triquetrum** is an excellent onion of low stature, unfortunately of questionable hardiness in the vicinity of New York City, but comfortably permanent a few score miles to the south. It has linear

Allium triquetrum

leaves from somewhat under ½ to 1¼ inches broad, keeled on their undersides and channeled above. Its stout flowering stalks, up to 1¼ feet long, are markedly three-angled. Each carries a few- to many-flowered, loose, one-sided, drooping umbel of bell-shaped blooms described as being "as crisp and dead-white as any Narcissus or Snowflake, with smart lines of

Allium neapolitanum

vivid green down the backs of each petal." The petals are approximately ½ inch long. It is fairly well endowed with the characteristic odor of so many of its relatives. Among the most strongly-scented species, **A. ursinum,** a native of moist soils in Europe and Asia, even without bruising, pervades the air with the unmistakable odor of garlic, most strongly after rain. European livestock farmers detest it because the milk, butter, and meat of animals that graze it are unmistakedly garlic-flavored. Yet it is not without decorative pretensions and is deserving of a place in herb gardens on the basis that European peasantry used it, in Britain under the name of ramsons, to flavor food and medicinally. Of curious appearance, *A. ursinum* has usually two stalked, flat, arching and spreading, lily-of-the-valley-like leaves 1 inch to 2 inches wide. The flowers, in flat umbels of up to twenty, carried on three-angled to nearly cylindrical stalks, have white, more or less erect petals less than ½ inch long. Lebanon is home territory to **A. zebdanense.** It has flat, lanceolate to linear leaves shorter than the 1- to 1½-foot-tall flowering stems, the latter leafy in their lower parts. The blooms, in umbels of six to many, have white petals with a red center vein and stamens shorter than the petals. Their individual stalks are as long or longer than the flowers.

Allium zebdanense

Pink, lavender, purple, or red flowers are typical of these not native American species. The color range is that most frequent among alliums. Species usually exhibit some variation in hue. A few of the most commonly available kinds are discussed first then others are presented in alphabetical sequence. Of noble, indeed astonishing aspect, **A. giganteum** is aptly named. Raised on stout, scarcely-ribbed stalks to heights of 3 to 4 feet or more, its ball-like umbels of starry, bright lilac-pink blooms are 4 inches in diameter. The strap-shaped, 1½-foot-long, 2-inch-wide leaves are bluish-green. It is native to the Himalayan region. Two other tall growers of much merit are *A. aflatunense* of China and *A. rosenbachianum* of central Asia. From 2½

Allium giganteum

to 4 feet tall or taller, **A. aflatunense** has dense, rounded umbels of starry, lilac-purple blooms the petals of which have darker mid-veins, the stamens violet-colored anthers. The leaves are bluish, linear-lanceolate to strap-shaped, up to 4 inches wide, smooth-edged, much shorter than the flowering stalks. From 2 to 3 feet tall, **A.**

Allium aflatunense

rosenbachianum has starry, purplish-violet or purplish-lilac flowers in globose umbels up to 6 inches in diameter atop strongly-ribbed stalks. The two, three, or sometimes more leaves are pointed-oblong-lanceolate, bright green, about ½ inch wide, and shorter than the flowering stalks. Huge umbels of bloom of astonishing presence are also displayed by **A. christophii** (syn. *A. albopilosum*), native to Turkestan. It has more or less pointed, strap-shaped to lanceolate leaves up to 1½ feet long by 1¾ inches wide, abundantly clothed with white down on their undersides. The globular, uncrowded umbels almost 1 foot in diameter are of up to eighty starry flowers of a metallic-lilac hue. The slender petals retain their shapes and positions without withering or twisting after flowering, which makes possible the effective use of the dried umbels in flower arrangements.

Allium christophii

The name *A. pulchellum* is applied to two sorts, the true species and a related kind at present identified as *A. p.* 'Van Tubergen', but which may yet prove to be a different species. Native to southern Europe, **A. pulchellum,** 1 foot to 1½ feet in height, much resembles *A. flavum*, except for the color of its blooms. It blooms at the same time as that species and can be planted in proximity to it with telling effect. It has

Allium pulchellum

longish, narrow bulbs and flowering stalks leafy to about their middles. The leaves are slender-linear, approximately as long as the flowering stalks. The flowers, drooping and erect in loose umbels, are red-purple dulled and softened by a light bloom to rosy-lavender, or less commonly are yellowish suffused with pink with a similar bloom. They set seed abundantly. By contrast, *A. p.* 'Van Tubergen' rarely produces seeds. More robust than the typical species, it bears lilac to violet-rose-pink flowers later in the season. Very variable and botanically not well understood, **A. senescens** is commonly grown under a variety of names, some botanical synonyms but most those that properly belong to other species. Native from western Europe to Mongolia and Manchuria, and robust, *A.*

Allium senescens

senescens has short, fleshy rhizomes, clusters of weakly-developed, cylindrical-conic bulbs, and short, flat, sickle-shaped, green or grayish-green leaves ¼ to nearly ½ inch wide. The flowering stalks, sometimes more than 2 feet tall, are two-edged or winged in their upper parts. The wide-bell-shaped, rosy-pink to lilac-pink blooms are in fairly dense, many-flowered umbels. Their stamens protrude. Variety *A. s. glaucum* of eastern Asia is distinguished by its much-twisted, usually blue-glaucous leaves. It is commonly dwarf and has flowering stalks generally winged above.

Other exotic alliums with flowers in the pink, lavender, purple, and red color range are as follows: *A. cyathophorum farreri* (syn. *A. farreri*), a native of western China, has clusters of slender bulbs each with four to six grassy leaves up to 7 inches long, ¼ inch or less wide. The three-angled flowering stalks lift to from 6 inches to about 1 foot one-sided, many-flowered, loose umbels of rosy-purple blooms. The stamens do not protrude, the lower halves of their stalks are united into a tube. *A. insubricum* closely resembles *A. narcissiflorum* and by some is considered a variety of it. Equally as desirable, it differs in having membranous rather than net-coated bulbs, in its foliage being glaucous, and in the

umbels nodding even when the flowers are expanded. *A. narcissiflorum* (syn. *A. pedemontanum*), one of the most attractive ornamental alliums, is a native of Italy. It has distinct rhizomes, and clusters of poorly developed bulbs. The narrowly-linear, flat leaves are green, erect or ascending, about ⅛ inch wide, and shorter than the flowering stalks. In umbels of usually eight or fewer, the bright rose-pink, bell-shaped flowers are about ½ inch long. In the bud stage the umbels nod, but as the flowers open, unlike those of *A. insubricum*, they become erect. *A. oreophilum* is a dwarf inhabitant of the Caucasus and Siberia. Its bulbs produce two or three linear, channeled leaves 4 to 6 inches long and up to ¹⁄₁₆ inch wide. The slender flowering stalks, 2 to 4 inches long, support dense, usually many-flowered umbels of bell-shaped blooms, purplish-red with a darker midvein to each ½-inch-long petal. The stamens are one-half as long as the petals. A

Allium oreophilum

native of Turkestan, *A. ostrowskianum* resembles *A. oreophilum*, but is taller, its flowering stems under favorable conditions up to 1 foot in height. From each bulb come two or three flaccid, gray-green, linear leaves longer than the flowering stalks.

The many-flowered, subspherical umbels are of broadly-bell-shaped, maroon-red flowers with stamens less than one-half the length of the ½-inch-long petals. *A. przewalskianum* seems to be the species often grown as *A. tibeticum*. The latter apparently is not in cultivation. Not exceeding 1 foot in height, *A. przewalskianum*, a Chinese species similar to *A. cyathophorum farreri*, has umbels of more numerous rosy-lilac to deep lavender-colored flowers with protruded instead of included stamens. Like those of *A. cyathophorum farreri*, the lower halves of the stalks of the stamens are joined to form a tube. The bulbs have fibrous-netted rather them membranous coats. *A. sphaerocephalum* is an inhabitant chiefly of sandy, woodland soils in Europe, North Africa, and Asia Minor. Each bulb has three or four nearly cylindrical, hollow leaves sheathing at their bases, up to 2½ feet long. The slender, stiffly-erect flowering stalks 1½ to 2½ feet tall, terminate in dense, many-flowered umbels of widely-bell-shaped, purple-red blooms with petals not more than ¼ inch long and considerably longer stamens. The stalks of individual flowers that compose the umbels of this attractive species are of various lengths.

Allium sphaerocephalum

North American native alliums include a number of species that are quite charming, but the most attractive are mostly inhabitants of the western reaches of the continent. Not widely cultivated, it is not difficult to make a selection from among them agreeable for rock gardens and other purposes.

Eastern species include the distinctive wild-leek (*A. tricoccum*) the American counterpart of the Old World *A. ursinum*, both with an unadmired tendency to become weedy, but acceptable in certain shady, natural, and naturalistic areas. The wild-leek inhabits rich woodlands from Quebec to Minnesota, North Carolina, and Tennessee. In the southern Appalachian Mountains its bulbs, there called ramps, are esteemed as a spring delicacy. In foli-

Allium ostrowskianum

Allium insubricum

age most un-onion-like *A. tricoccum* has stalked, flat lanceolate-elliptic leaves up to 8 inches long by almost one-third as wide. They wither and die before the flowers open. The latter are small, white, up-facing, in 2-inch-wide umbels carried on erect stalks to heights of 6 inches to 2 feet. Wild chives (*A. schoenoprasum sibiricum*), indigenous from Newfoundland to Alaska, Maine, Colorado, and Washington, and in Europe and Asia, is taller, up to 1½ feet, and stouter than cultivated chives (*A. schoenoprasum*), which is an otherwise similar native of Europe. As an ornamental, wild chives is rather less meritorious than common chives. Variable *A. cernuum* favors dry woodlands and prairies from New York to British Columbia, Washington, Oregon, Virginia, Kentucky, Missouri, and Arizona. Forming dense turfs of slender bulbs each with several leaves up to ⅓ inch wide, shorter than the flowering stalks, it has many-flowered, loose, nodding umbels about 2 inches wide on stalks 1 foot to 2 feet tall that have an abrupt bend at their tops. The blooms are purplish- to rosy-pink, or occasionally a rather poor white. The stamens protrude.

The western North American species well worth considering for gardens include those now to be described. There are others. *A. acuminatum*, plentiful in dry soils in the Pacific Northwest, and in California, has usually clustered bulbs each with two or more slender, channeled leaves shorter than the flowering stalks and withering early. From 4 to 8 inches or sometimes longer, the flowering stalks are surmounted by loose umbels of several bell-shaped, pink to rose-purple or white flowers. The ends of their petals spread or recurve. The stamens are about two-thirds as long as the petals. The latter become papery and close against the capsules in the fruiting stage. *A. amplectens* inhabits moist soils of the Pacific Northwest and California. Its mostly clustered bulbs have each two to four channeled to cylindrical, slender, flexuous, early-withering leaves shorter than the flowering stalks. The flowering stalks, 6 inches to 1 foot long or a little longer, terminate in few- to many-flowered, subglobose umbels. The white or pink blooms become papery as they age. They have stamens nearly as long as the petals. *A. campanulatum* is found in the dry woodlands from Nevada to Oregon and California. Its bulbs have usually two, occasionally more channeled leaves generally not more than ¼ inch wide and about as long as the flowering stalks, which mostly do not exceed 6 inches but sometimes attain nearly 1 foot. The blooms are in loose, few- to many-flowered umbels. Most commonly their petals are purplish with a darker purple zone near their bases. Less often they are white. The stamens are shorter than the petals. The latter dry and remain rigid and spreading in the fruiting stage. *A. crenulatum* is a charming native of barren soils on mountain summits in the Pacific Northwest. The bulbs produce two or sometimes one flat, sickle-shaped leaves markedly longer than the two-edged flowering stalk, the latter being about 3 inches long. Pink with darker midveins, the flowers, in globose umbels of several to many, become papery as the seed capsules develop. *A. douglasii*, a variable native of the Pacific Northwest, has solitary or clustered bulbs each with two flat or channeled, more or less sickle-shaped leaves, shorter than the flowering stalk and up to a little more than ½ inch wide. They do not wither early. The pink or occasionally white blooms, in umbels of several to many, have stamens as long as or longer than the petals. The petals dry, are spreading and rigid in fruit. *A. geyeri*, widely distributed in moist soils in western North America, has usually clustered bulbs each with generally three or more channeled leaves up to ¼ inch wide, persistent until maturity and shorter than the flowering stalks, which are 6 inches to 1½ feet tall. Usually pink, rarely white, the blooms are in umbels of few to many. The petals are erect rather than spreading. In *A. g. tenerum* small bulbils replace many or all of the blooms. *A. lemmonii* is a desert species that grows in clayey soils in the Pacific Northwest and in California. Its clustered bulbs have each a pair of thick, flat, more or less sickle-shaped leaves rarely more than ¼ inch wide, remaining green at least until flowering time, finally breaking off at their bases. The flowers have protruded stamens. Their petals are pale pink or white with pink or greenish mid-veins. In spherical umbels of several to many they become papery as seed capsules form. *A. nevadense* of mostly sandy and gravelly, desert soils in the Northwest has bulbs with only one leaf. This leaf is cylindrical and usually twice as long as the rather slender flowering stalk, which is generally under 2 inches in length, but sometimes twice as long. The flowers are whitish or pinkish with deep pink midribs to the petals. They are in loose, rounded umbels of few to many. *A. textile* inhabits dry hills and plains in much of the Pacific Northwest. It has usually clustered bulbs each most commonly with two persistent, channeled leaves usually as long or longer than the flowering stalk and less than ¼ inch in width. The rounded umbels are of several to many white or rarely pink flowers. They top stalks up to 1 foot long or a little longer. The petals have red or reddish-brown mid-veins, and the tips of the inner three spread markedly. *A. unifolium* is curiously ill-named. Each bulb has usually two or three leaves nearly flat and mostly shorter than the flowering stalk. Less hardy

Allium unifolium

than some others of the Pacific Northwest and California, it is one of the largest and most attractive of the region. Pink or rarely white, the starry blooms are in many-flowered, rather loose umbels. Their petals become papery and spreading in the seed stage. This inhabits moist soils.

Garden and Landscape Uses. Flowering onions lend themselves to a variety of purposes, the taller ones for inclusion in perennial beds and borders, for less formal landscaping, and for use as cut flowers, the shorter ones for rock gardens and similar places, and *A. triquetrum* and *A. neapolitanum* for forcing as early-blooming pot plants. Indigenous American species are suitable for native plant gardens. All commonly cultivated kinds are easy to grow, but insufficient experience is reported about many western American species to make absolute judgments about this. Probably most are tractable, especially if environments approaching those they know in the wild are provided. As a group these plants need full sun. Some few do well with some shade. Belonging here is *A. moly* and the kinds such as *A. ursinum* and *A. tricoccum* that in the wild grow in woodlands. Be wary about locating *A. tricoccum*. It may easily proliferate to the extent of becoming a pest. Well-drained, dry or dryish, poorish soils, and warm, sheltered locations are most satisfactory for most kinds. Some few, including the woodlanders, prefer richer soils and more moisture. The prevalence among flowering onions of flower colors cataloged as rosy-mauve, rosy-lavender, rose-purple and other sometimes thinly disguised euphemisms for magenta (which sensitive gardeners of the garden club elite so unfairly deplore) discourages some from acquiring alliums; the alliaceous odor scares off others. Except for one or two kinds no odor is discernible unless the plants are crushed, and why must you do that? As for colors, even the most bluish or pinks, the most violent of the magentas look well in suitable company, associated for instance with soft yellows, creamy-whites, whites, or with gray foliage. If magentas still cause a shudder, reject all offenders among the flowering onions and plant only the not inconsiderable number with white, yellow, and blue blooms.

Cultivation. Early fall and spring or immediately after blooming is over are the best seasons to plant and transplant alliums, although with care most kinds can be moved successfully at any season. Once established these bulb plants need practically no routine care and may be left undisturbed as long as they bloom satisfactorily. If, usually because the bulbs have become too crowded, flower production falls off, dig them up, divide or separate the bulbs or growths, and replant in newly spaded and conditioned ground. Some kinds self-sow with great abandon. To cir-

cumvent this snip off faded flower heads before seeds form. Propagation is by offsets, division, and seeds, less commonly by bulbils.

To force *A. neapolitanum* and *A. triquetrum* for early bloom plant bulbs in early fall in pots or pans (shallow pots) allowing about as much space between the bulbs as their diameters and setting them with their tips just beneath the soil surface. Do not as is done with some hardy bulbs, put the planted containers in the dark or where they will freeze. Keep them throughout in a sunny greenhouse or window where the night temperature will be in the 45 to 50°F range and the temperature by day five to fifteen degrees higher, the escalation being proportionate to the brightness of the weather. Water moderately at first, more freely as root and leaf growth develop. When the receptacles are well filled with roots stimulate mildly with biweekly or weekly applications of dilute liquid fertilizer. When, after flowering is over, the foliage begins to die naturally, increase the periods between waterings and finally stop watering. Store the bulbs through the summer dry in the soil in which they grew. In late August or September shake them free of the old soil and repot.

ALLOPHYTON. See Tetranema.

ALLOPLECTUS (Allo-pléctus). Some seventy species of evergreen, shrubby, and subshrubby species are allotted to the tropical American genus *Alloplectus* of the gesneria family GESNERIACEAE. The group is not very well understood botanically and few of its members are cultivated. Probably readjustments in their classification and naming will in time be made. The name alludes to the calyxes of the flowers appearing as if they were plaited in various directions. It derives from the Greek *allos*, diverse, and *pleco*, to plait.

In their native habitats these plants grow in the ground or perched on trees as epiphytes. Often their stems are more or less clambering or climbing. The leaves are opposite, with the individuals of each pair of the same or different sizes. Generally their undersides are reddish or purplish. The flowers sprout from the leaf axils. They have usually colored calyxes and may be in dense heads or more loosely arranged. The corollas are tubular, constricted at their tops. They have five rounded lobes (petals). There are four stamens, their stalks united. At the back of the ovary is a two-lobed gland. The fruits are berry-like capsules. The plant grown as *A. sanguineus* is *Columnea sanguinea*.

Stout, erect and up to 3 feet tall, **A. capitatus**, of Colombia and Venezuela, has bluntly-four-angled, red-hairy stems and

Allium triquetrum as a pot plant

attractive foliage. Its leaves, those of each pair of equal size, have red-hairy stalks and ovate, sharply-fine-toothed blades 6 to 8 inches long and nearly or quite one-half as wide as long, reddish beneath and with a slender, pale mid-vein. From the upper leaf axils come in stalked, bracted, dense, globular clusters or heads of many, downy flowers with crimson, broad-lobed calyxes and slightly longer yellow, urn-shaped corollas with short, scarcely spreading lobes (petals) up to about ¾ inch long. Much like *A. capitatus*, but its velvety-hairy foliage is more beautiful, the leaves being decorated with a pale green longitudinal central band and with the bases of the lateral veins similarly colored, *A. vittatus* is native to Peru.

Alloplectus teuscheri

Alloplectus vittatus

It attains 2 feet in height, has ovate, hairy leaves with red under surfaces, up to 6 inches long and 3 inches wide. Borne in stalked clusters from the upper leaf axils, the flowers have dark red-purple, hairless calyxes and equaling them in length, tubular, hairy, pale yellow corollas, narrowed at their throats and with brief, spreading petals. Also erect, *A. schlimii* of Colombia and Venezuela has ovate to ovate-oblong, short-hairy, stalked leaves with somewhat heart-shaped bases. Up to 4 inches long, they have scalloped margins fringed with red hairs. The comparatively-long-stalked blooms come several together from the upper leaf axils. They have bright red calyxes with lobes twice as long as the hairy, red-tipped, yellow corollas. The quite distinct *A. teuscheri* (syn. *Hypocyrta teuscheri*) of Ecuador is erect-branched, square-stemmed, and shrubby. It has pointed-ovate, rough-textured leaves up to 6 inches in length, their upper sides olive-green and with silver veins, their lower surfaces dark red. The flowers have red calyxes and 1-inch-long, yellow corollas with petals narrowly edged with red.

Its stems vinelike and straggling, *A. ambiguus* of Puerto Rico has pairs of distinctly unequal-sized, oblong to elliptic, hairy leaves with shallowly-scalloped edges. The bigger one of each pair is up to 1½ inches

long and approximately ¾ inch wide. The flowers, in short-stalked twos or threes from the leaf axils, have green or red calyxes with four few-toothed lobes and one toothless one. The yellow corollas, clothed with red hairs, are nearly 1 inch long. Somewhat bloated toward their middles, they have slightly-spreading lobes (petals)

Alloplectus ambiguus

not quite ¼ inch long. The fruits are spherical white berries. An evergreen or sometimes deciduous trailer with slender, hairy stems often enlarged at the nodes (joints), *A. nummularia* (syn. *Hypocyrta nummularia*) of Mexico and Central America has thinnish, short-stalked ovate to broadly-obovate leaves ¾ inch to 2½ inches long, round-toothed above their middles and often reddish. The solitary, short-stalked, vermilion blooms are nearly or quite ½ inch long by ½ inch wide. They have tiny yellow petals spreading from the violet-tinged neck of the pouched corolla.

Alloplectus nummularia

Garden Uses and Cultivation. These are primarily greenhouse plants, the vining kinds suitable for hanging baskets, the erect ones for pot cultivation. They respond to the environmental conditions and general care that suit *Columnea*, *Nautilocalyx* and other evergreen gesneriads.

ALLSPICE is *Pimenta dioica*. Carolina-allspice is *Calycanthus floridus*.

Alloplectus ambiguus (fruits)

ALLUAUDIA (Alluaùd-ia). The six species of trees and shrubs that compose this genus are endemic to Madagascar. Although not widely grown, they are prized by fanciers of succulents. They are members of the didierea family DIDIEREACEAE. The genus is named in honor of Charles A. Alluaud, a French explorer and naturalist born in 1861.

Alluaudias attain heights of 30 to 50 feet, have succulent trunks and stems with erect or spreading branches, and solitary or paired spines. They may be leafless or have small, roundish, fleshy leaves in pairs below the thorns. The unisexual, four-petaled flowers are in umbel-like clusters. The fruits, enclosed in the persistent calyx, contain a single seed.

A shrub or small tree branching elegantly and up to 20 feet tall, *Alluaudia humbertii* has solitary thorns about 1 inch long and broad-ovate to obcordate, stalkless leaves ¼ to ¾ inch long. The flower

Alluaudia humbertii

clusters are up to 6 inches long. Sometimes 50 feet tall, but often lower, *A. procera* (syn. *Didierea procera*) is sparsely furnished with erect branches that tend to curve inward and have broad-based, conelike spines and obovate to oblong leaves up to 1 inch long and one-half as wide as long. The flower clusters are 4 inches to 1 foot long.

Less well-known are *A. comosa* and *A. montagnacii*. The first is a shrub or tree 6 to 25 feet tall with slender thorns about 1½ inches long, mostly in pairs. Its leaves, obovate to nearly circular, spread from the stems at right angles. *A. montagnacii* differs in its solitary or paired, nearly circular leaves lying almost flat against the stems.

Alluandia comosa

Garden and Landscape Uses and Cultivation. These are essentially plants for collectors. They grow well under conditions similar to those that suit *Fouquieria*.

Alluandia montagnacii

ALMOND. Almonds are primarily a commercial crop of minor interest to amateur gardeners. In the United States their production is chiefly centered in California. Lesser quantities are grown in other states west of the Rocky Mountains. The trees, varieties of *Prunus dulcis*, are deciduous and as hardy as peaches, but because they flower about a month earlier are much more subject to having their flower buds damaged by late frosts.

Soil for almonds must be very well drained. The trees are intolerant of wetness. They thrive best in sandy earths and need full sun. They stand drought better than most fruit trees.

Planting is usually done in winter or early spring. Because almonds are self-sterile and do not set fruit to their own pollen it is necessary for fruit production to interplant compatible varieties.

Space the trees 20 to 30 feet apart each way. Following planting, cut them back to a height of 2 to 2½ feet and remove any branches not well placed to make permanent scaffold limbs. At the end of the first year select from the shoots that have developed three to retain as scaffold branches. Have these spaced as equally as possible around the trunk and 6 to 8 inches apart vertically. Remove all other branches. Cut the retained shoots lightly back, to laterals if such exist. Later pruning consists chiefly of careful thinning to assure a well-spaced framework of branches and prevent overcrowding. If the ground is moderately rich little or no fertilization is needed.

Propagation is by budding superior varieties onto seedlings of almonds, usually bitter almonds, or peaches in August or September. The understocks are raised from seeds that, after being stratified in sand, are planted in nursery rows in February. Peach understocks are favored if the trees are to be grown on irrigated ground, almond understocks for trees to be planted on land without irrigation.

Varieties include hard-shelled and soft-shelled sorts. 'Nonpareil' is most frequently planted. Other popular kinds are 'Davy', 'Drake', 'Ne Plus Ultra', 'Peerless' and 'Texas'.

Pests and Diseases. These and their controls are as for peaches. See Peach.

ALMONDS, ORNAMENTAL. The common flowering almond is *Prunus triloba*, the dwarf flowering almond *P. glandulosa*. The Russian almond is *Prunus tenella*. The tree called tropical- or Indian-almond is *Terminalia catappa*. The red-almond is *Alphitonia excelsa*.

ALNIPHYLLUM (Alni-phýllum). This is a genus of one, or according to some interpretations as many as eight, species of trees and shrubs of southwestern China, Indochina, and Taiwan. Related to *Halesia*, it belongs in the storax family STYRACACEAE. The name, alluding to the similarity of the foliage, is derived from that of the alders (*Alnus*) and the Greek *phyllon*, a leaf.

A slender tree up to 30 feet tall or even taller, *Alniphyllum fortunei* has alternate, short-pointed, ovate to broad-ovate leaves 3½ to 5 inches long by a little over 2 inches broad. They have tiny, rather distantly spaced teeth along their margins, and stalks approximately ½ inch long. The white blooms, about 1 inch wide, are in several- to many-flowered racemes or panicles. They have persistent, bell-shaped, five-toothed calyxes, five spreading petals, five long and, alternating with them, five short stamens, their stalks united for most of their lengths into a deep tube, and one style with an obscurely three-lobed, head-like stigma. The fruits, oblong, wingless, beaked capsules about ¾ inch long, split lengthways into five parts to release the seeds, which are winged at both ends. In these features they differ from *Halesia*, which has nonsplitting fruits and wingless seeds.

Garden and Landscape Uses and Cultivation. This rare species is of good appearance and well suited for planting to add variety and interest to collections. Little information is available about its particular needs. Not hardy in the north, in mild climates it may be expected to prosper in ordinary soils and locations, perhaps grateful for a little shade, such as it receives in its natural habitats. It may be propagated by seeds and probably by grafting onto *Halesia* or other members of the storax family.

ALNUS (Al'-nus)—Alder. This genus of thirty-five deciduous trees and shrubs is closely allied to the birches (*Betula*) from which it differs in its flowers having four rather than two stamens and the scales of its female catkins being five-lobed and persistent instead of three-lobed and early deciduous. The name *Alnus* is the ancient Latin one for the alder. The genus belongs in the birch family BETULACEAE. It must be noted that the name black-alder is used colloquially for *Ilex verticillata*, which is not related to the black alder (*Alnus glutinosa*), and that white-alder is applied as a common name to the unrelated *Clethra*.

Alders are plants of wet soils and cool climates that occur throughout the northern hemisphere and in the Americas cross the equator into the mountains of Ecuador, Bolivia, Peru, and Argentina. Their leaves are alternate and toothed. Their unisexual flowers are without petals. Males and females are on the same plant in catkins.

Alnus glutinosa (female and male catkins)

Male catkins are pendulous, slender, cylindrical, and attractive when they mature in fall, late winter, or early spring. Females are shorter and ovoid or ellipsoid, being in fact small woody cones called strobiles. The strobiles are usually few together in open clusters and are conspicuous throughout the winter when the branches are leafless. They contain small nutlets, the fruits.

The lumber of alders is of minor importance and indifferent quality, yet it has been used by man since before recorded history. Its greatest virtue is that, submerged in water, it lasts practically indefinitely, although if exposed alternately to wet and dry conditions it soon decays. The earliest boats of which there are written records were constructed of alder, and this same wood long served for water pipes, watering troughs, sluice gates, and pumps. According to ancient records the piles upon which the Rialto at Venice and those upon which Amsterdam were built were of alder. Present-day uses of alder lumber include the exploitation of *A. rubra* in

northwestern America for furniture manufacture. Often this wood is stained to imitate mahogany and walnut. High in the Andes where other woods are scarce, local species provide wood for furniture, interior trim, scaffolding and molds used in construction. In Europe alder wood is used for a variety of purposes including the manufacture of boxes and crates and sabots and clogs and the construction of models for scientists and engineers. From this wood, too, charcoal for gunpowder is made. Mexicans employ alder bark for tanning and dyeing; it is also used in medicines. In the wild, alders serve the useful and important purpose of stabilizing and saving from erosion riverbanks and other waterside soils their roots invade. Alders furnish a remarkable example of symbiosis, the living together of two organisms to their mutual benefit. On their roots, nodules usually small, but sometimes as large as oranges, develop. Inside these live immense numbers of microorganisms that have the ability to fix the free nitrogen of the air into protein upon which the alder eventually draws for part of its nitrogen needs. When leaves and other parts of alders decay they enrich the soil by increasing its nitrogen content. In these ways alders function like most legumes. In the Arctic there is often a noticeable gradation in the size of wildflowers that grow around alders. Those located nearest the roots or where fallen leaves have collected are obviously larger than those more distant from these sources of nutritional nitrogen.

The Italian alder (**A. cordata**) is one of the most handsome kinds. A symmetrical, round-headed native of southern Italy and Corsica, it attains a maximum height of about 80 feet and is hardy in southern New England. It has smooth, angled twigs, and broad-ovate to nearly orbicular, glossy leaves up to 4 inches long that are distinctly heart-shaped at their bases and quite hairless except for tufts in the axils of the veins beneath and some hairs on the veins when the foliage is young. Its winter buds are larger than those of most alders and are solitary.

The black alder (**A. glutinosa**), native from Europe to Siberia and North Africa, sometimes occurs as an escape from cultivation in eastern North America. Up to 90 feet in height, it has a dark trunk that may be 3 feet in diameter, and an ovoid or pyramidal crown of dark green foliage that hangs late in the season and drops without changing color. This species has sticky, but not hairy young shoots. Its broad-ovate leaves, up to 4 inches long by about 2⅔ inches wide, taper to wedge-shaped bases and are hairless except for tufts in the vein axils beneath. As a timber tree it is more useful than most alders. It is hardy in New England and adjacent Canada. The black alder is not particularly handsome. For garden planting the following varieties are

Alnus glutinosa in summer

Alnus glutinosa in late winter

usually preferred: *A. g. aurea*, with yellow leaves; *A. g. barbata*, which has leafstalks and the undersides of the leaves pubescent; *A. g. denticulata* with finely-toothed leaves; *A. g. imperialis* with deeply-lobed leaves, the lobes narrow and scarcely-toothed; *A. g. laciniata* with deeply-lobed leaves, that are larger than those of the preceding variety and broader; *A. g. pyramidalis*, which is narrow-pyramidal; *A. g. quercifolia*, with leaves deeply and irregularly-lobed; *A. g. rubrinervia*, handsome with red leafstalks and red-veined leaves; and *A. g. sorbifolia* with small-lobed leaves with the lobes overlapping.

The speckled alder (**A. incana**) is one of the few species of trees indigenous to both North America and Europe. It occurs also in western Asia. Often shrubby, under favorable conditions it reaches a height of 60 feet and has a rounded top of dull, dark green, broad-elliptic to ovate or obovate leaves up to 4 inches long, rounded or wedge-shaped at their bases, and grayish-hairy or glaucous beneath. In fall they drop while still green. The bark of *A. incana* is smooth and light gray. Its twigs are hairy when young. Very variable and one of the hardiest of trees, the speckled alder grows about as far north as trees can exist. Of its varieties *A. i. acuminata* has leaves lobed about halfway to their midribs; *A. i. aurea* has yellowish foliage; *A. i. pendula* has drooping branches; and *A. i. pinnatifida* has small, deeply-lobed leaves.

The red alder (*A. oregona* syn. *A. rubra*) is spontaneous from Alaska to California and Idaho. Favoring moist soils, it has a narrow, pyramidal crown of drooping branches, attains a height of 80 feet, and has nearly smooth, light gray bark. Its twigs, at first covered with fine down, soon become hairless and dark red. The oblong or oblong-ovate leaves up to 5 inches long, are grayish or glaucous beneath, with or without hairs, and are squared or broadly-wedge-shaped at their bases. They have red or yellow veins. This species is planted in Hawaii for reforestation.

The American green alder (*A. crispa* syn. *A. viridis crispa*) is a shrub up to 10 feet in height that occurs as a native from Labrador to North Carolina. It has ovate or broad-elliptic, bright green leaves, up to 3 inches long, rounded or slightly heart-shaped at their bases, glutinous and fragrant when young. A variety, *A. c. mollis*, has the undersides of its leaves and young branches pubescent.

Other alders sometimes cultivated are these: *A. cremastogyne*, a western Chinese sort little known in cultivation is unusual in that its catkins are solitary in the leaf axils and the female catkins are long-stalked. This is characteristic too, of nearly allied *A. lanata* from the same region. *A. cremastogyne* attains a height of 80 feet and has obovate or ovate, finely-toothed leaves up to 5½ inches long. *A. hirsuta*, the Manchurian alder, of northern Japan and northeast Asia, is up to 60 feet high and has broad-ovate leaves up to 6 inches long that are reddish-pubescent beneath. *A. h. sibirica* is similar, but sparingly pubescent on the undersides of the leaves except for the densely-hairy mid-veins. *A. japonica*, the Japanese alder, of Japan and northeast Asia, is up to 80 feet in height and has narrow-elliptic or ovate-lanceolate leaves up to 5 inches long, wedge-shaped at their bases and pale green beneath. *A. lanata* is similar to *A. cremastogyne* in having catkins solitary in the leaf axils and the female catkins long-stalked. It differs in its young leafstalks, flower stalks, and undersides of its leaves having a dense, brown, woolly covering. *A. maritima*, the seaside alder, is one of the few kinds that bloom in fall. Usually a shrub, it sometimes is a tree up to 30 feet in height. It has ovate to obovate leaves up to about 4 inches long, glossy above, paler beneath, and at their bases

wedge-shaped. This kind, which is attractive in bloom, occurs as a native along streams and lakesides in Delaware, Maryland, and Oklahoma. *A. nepalensis* of the Himalayas, has elliptic-lanceolate leaves up to 7 inches long, and cones in lateral clusters. It is planted in Hawaii for reforestation. *A. nitida*, in its native Himalayas 100 feet in height, may have a trunk up to 5 feet in diameter. It blooms in fall, and has handsome, thin-textured, glossy leaves up to 6 inches long and 3 inches wide, wedge-shaped at their bases, and smooth except for tufts of hair in the leaf axils beneath. It is hardy as far north as Long Island, New York. *A. pendula* of Japan is a shrub or tree up to 25 feet tall of graceful habit and with oblong-lanceolate leaves up to 5 inches long. It is hardy in southern New England. *A. rhombifolia*, the white alder of California and Washington, inhabits mountain streamsides, and attains a height of 100 feet. Its young shoots are covered with white scurf, its ovate to nearly round leaves, with long, tapered bases, are very hairy at first and permanently retain down on their undersides. They are 2 to 5 inches long. The flowers appear very early, in January or February in its home territory. *A. rugosa*, the smooth alder, occurs from Maine to Florida and Texas. Up to 25 feet tall and with elliptic or obovate leaves, wedge-shaped at their bases and up to 4 inches long, it has smooth or hairy twigs and is usually a rather coarse shrub. *A. sinuata* is native from Alaska to California. Often shrubby, it is sometimes a tree up to 50 feet tall. When young, its twigs are finely-hairy and glandular. Its bright green, ovate leaves are more or less shallowly-lobed and sharply-toothed. They are glabrous, or hairy only on the midrib beneath. *A. subcordata*, of the Caucasus and Iran, is a handsome, large-leaved alder up to 60 feet in height. Its ovate leaves, rounded or slightly heart-shaped at their bases, are up to 6 inches long and 4 inches wide. It somewhat resembles *A. cordata*, but differs in having young shoots that are downy and leaves that are more hairy and less conspicuously heart-shaped at their bases. It is hardy, in most of New England. *A. tenuifolia*, the mountain alder, is a shrub or tree up to 30 feet tall that ranges from British Columbia to New Mexico and Baja California. Its usually yellowish-green leaves are mostly rounded at their bases and are up to 4 inches long. It is hardy in southern New England. *A. viridis*, the European green alder, is up to 6 feet tall. It is very similar to the American green alder, but smaller in all its parts and less ornamental. As its common name implies this is native to Europe.

Garden and Landscape Uses. The best uses for alders are for planting in wet locations where few other trees or shrubs thrive. By the waterside, specimens of

such kinds as the black alder, the Italian alder, and red alder are quite attractive and ornamental, especially in late winter when their male catkins are mature.

Cultivation. The cultivation of alders presents no difficulties. As already indicated all prosper in and most need, moist soil, but the Italian alder, the speckled alder, and the Japanese alder grow well in any average, reasonably fertile earth not excessively dry. Propagation is easy by seeds, which should be gathered before they are dispersed by fall winds and stored in a cool, dry place. Sown in spring in soil kept uniformly moist they germinate quite rapidly. They may also be rooted from hardwood cuttings taken after leaf fall and planted in moist soil with their tips just showing above the surface. Although these do not root as surely as willows, the proportion that take root under favorable conditions is high. Rare kinds can be increased by grafting in the greenhouse in late winter. Some alders produce suckers that provide a ready means of propagation.

Diseases and Pests. Alders are subject to a leaf curl disease and to leaf rust, powdery mildew, and canker. Their chief insect enemies are aphids, flea-beetles, lacebugs, and psyllids.

ALOCASIA (Alo-càsia). The seventy species of *Alocasia* of the arum family ARACEAE are natives of tropical Asia and Indonesia. They are herbaceous perennials, often large and of striking appearance. Their name is a variant of that of the related genus *Colocasia*, from which alocasias differ technically in the arrangement and greater number of ovules in the ovaries, coupled with the Greek *a*, without.

Alocasias have short, thick, sometimes tuber-like rootstocks, very brief to quite tall, trunklike, thick stems ringed with old leaf scars, and heart-shaped to arrow-shaped, long-stalked leaves with the lower parts of their stalks wrapped around each other. When young, and often later, the leaves are peltate, that is, the leafstalks are attached to the blades some distance in from their margins. As is characteristic of the family, the parts usually called flowers are inflorescences consisting of a spadix and spathe. The significance of these terms can be explained in relation to the familiar calla-lily, the central yellow shaft of which is the spadix, the trumpet-form, white, petal-like part that encircles it, the spathe. In *Alocasia* the spadix is shorter than the persistent spathe. The lower part of the spathe is tubular, the spreading upper part usually boat-shaped. Crowded along most of the spadix, except rarely the uppermost part, are many small unisexual flowers, the males with their stamens united. The lower part of the spadix is occupied by female flowers. Above them come sterile males with staminodes (nonfunctional stamens) instead of stamens, then fertile males above which are more sterile males. The fruits are generally reddish berries.

Much like the taro or elephant's ear (*Colocasia antiquorum*) in general appearance, the tropical Asian *A. macrorrhiza* has a stout, erect stem from a few inches to a few feet tall. From it spread upward and outward, sometimes to a height of 15 feet from the ground, thick, lustrous, heart-shaped, prominently-veined, somewhat wavy-edged, green leaves. They have green stalks 2½ to 4½ feet long, blades nearly as long by up to 2½ feet wide. The spathes are yellowish-green. In *A. m. variegata* the leaves are marked very irregularly with white blotches. In many respects resembling *A. macrorrhiza*, but differing in the blades of its smaller, narrow-triangular leaves being deeply pinnately-lobed, *A. portei* (syn. *Schizocasia portei*) is a native of New Guinea. Its inflorescences, on stalks about 6 inches long, have slender-pointed spathes about 3 inches in length, their bases swollen and spherical. A variant of this, previously called *Schizocasia regnieri*, is distinguished by its yellowish leafstalks and the midribs on the undersides of the blades being conspicuously marked with reddish-brown. A similar giant, this a native of southeast Asia, the Philippine Islands, and Taiwan, *A. odora* has a stout, man-high trunk and broadly-heart-shaped, corrugated, light green leaves with raised midribs and veins. Their green stalks and blades are each 3 feet long, the latter 2½ feet wide. The flowers are fragrant.

Alocasia plumbea (inflorescence)

Alocasia korthalsii

Alocasia cuprea

Alocasia cucullata

Alocasia odora

Its stout stem 3 to 6 feet tall, *A. plumbea* (syn. *A. indica metallica*) of Java in aspect resembles *A. macrorrhiza*. Its glossy leaves are broad-arrow-shaped, prominently-veined, olive-green blades 1 foot to 1¼ feet in length, about one-half as wide, with a metallic-purplish overcast. The spathes are yellowish or, on their insides, sometimes purplish. The foliage of *A. p. variegata* is green with paler midribs and veins. Beneath, the leaves are glaucous. Their stalks are variegated with violet. Native to Malaya, *A. cuprea* has characteristic rich metallic-green, peltate leaves with blades 1

foot to 1½ feet long and one half to two-thirds as wide as their lengths. They have darker, depressed veins and reddish-purple undersides. The spathes have green tubes and green to purple blades. This species has tuberous rhizomes.

Very distinct and attractive, *A. sanderana* of the Philippine Islands is tuberous. Its always peltate, lustrous metallic-green, deeply-pinnately-labeled, arrow-shaped leaves have grayish-white midribs, lateral veins, and margins. Their under surfaces are purple. Variety *A. s. 'Van Houtte'* (syn. *A. s. magnifica*) is smaller, has proportionately broader, slightly-sinuate rather than deeply-lobed leaves, with wider gray-white areas along its midribs and veins. Except that they are not lobed, the heart-shaped-ovate leaves of the short-stemmed Malayan *A. korthalsii* (syn. *A. thibautiana*) are much like those of *A. sanderana*. Their upper sides are grayish-olive-green veined with silvery-gray, their undersides purple. The blades are about 2 feet long by 1½ feet wide. The leafstalk is attached to the blade 2 to 3 inches from its margin.

Other cultivated species include the following: *A. cadierei*, native of Annam, has broad, arrow-shaped to heart-shaped, wavy-edged, rich green leaves with clearly evident gray-green veins. *A. cucullata*, of Bengal and Burma, has prominently-veined leaves up to 1 foot long or longer. They are lustrous dark green, pointed-heart-shaped,

peltate with somewhat cupped, shallowly-lobed bases. *A. longiloba*, of Java, has leaves with brown-striped, pink stalks and bluish-green, pointed-arrow-shaped blades with silvery-gray midribs and veins. The stalks are joined to the blades ½ inch in from their margins. *A. lowii*, of Malaya, has green-stalked, broadly-arrow-shaped, deep metallic-green leaves relieved by silvery veins and light green margins. They have purple under surfaces. The leafstalk joins the blade about 1 inch in from the margin. *A. l. grandis* has broader leaves, dark metallic-brownish-green, with silvery veining. *A. l. veitchii* has leaves less distinctly silvery-veined than those of the last. Their stalks are variegated with pink and green. *A. micholitziana*, native to the

Alocasia micholitziana

Philippine Islands, has a stem up to 1½ feet tall, and arrow-shaped, emerald-green leaves with blades up to 1 foot long that have white midribs and veins. The pale leafstalks are banded with purple. **A. porphyroneura** (syn. *A. princeps*), an almost stemless native of Malaya, has smallish, purplish-veined, wavy-edged, olive-green, arrow-shaped leaves with red-spotted stalks. **A. putzeysii**, native to Java, has crinkled, wavy-edged, dark green, broadly-arrow-shaped leaves with silvery-white midribs, main veins, and margins. The blades are 1 foot to 1½ feet long. **A. regina** hails from Borneo. It has 1-foot-long, pointed-arrow-shaped leaves with long basal lobes and slightly sinuate edges. Dark olive-green with a metallic sheen, they have grayish-maroon undersides with very dark maroon veins. The stalks are spotted with brownish-purple. **A. villeneuvei** has ovate-heart-shaped, light green leaves, the blades with irregular, paler or sometimes reddish spots, the stalks rough and with brown spots. This is native in Borneo. **A. watsoniana** has an erect stem and puckered, peltate, blackish-blue-green leaves with blades 2½ feet long clearly marked with a light gray midrib and main

Alocasia watsoniana

veins. Their undersides and stalks are purple. This is a native of Malaya. **A. wentii** (syn. *A. whinckii*), of New Guinea, has leaves, always peltate, shallowly-lobed at their bases, with stout, light-colored stalks and rich green blades with slightly sinuate margins. **A. zebrina**, of the Philippine Islands, has short stems and large, plain green, arrow-shaped leaves with blades 1 foot to 1½ feet long and slender stalks banded with brown. The spathes are white.

Hybrid alocasias commonly exhibit characteristics intermediate between those of their parents. In addition to the named ones here listed, some others are culti-

vated. Two with *A. longiloba* as one parent are *A. argyraea* and *A. chelsonii*. With *A. pucciana* its other parent, **A. argyraea** has peltate, heart-shaped to broad-arrow-shaped leaves with an overall silvery suffusion. **A. chelsonii** has bronzy-olive-green, pointed-heart-shaped, peltate leaves, with slightly sinuous margins that like the midrib and main veins are clear silvery-gray. The other parent of this sort is *A. cuprea*. Another hybrid of *A. cuprea* is **A. sedenii**. This, its other parent *A. lowii*, has large, peltate, green-stalked, heart-shaped, sinuately-margined, metallic-green leaves with raised veins and purple undersides. With *A. korthalsii* and *A. sanderana* as parents, the beautiful **A. amazonica** has dark green, slightly scalloped-edged, peltate, narrowly-heart-shaped leaves, their midribs, main veins, and margins picked out in white. A hybrid of unknown parentage, **A. vanhoutteana** has large, thick-stalked, heart-shaped, very glossy, puckered leaves, with white midribs, veins, and margins.

Alocasia amazonica

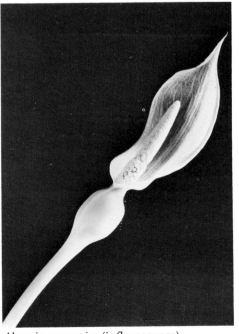

Alocasia amazonica (inflorescence)

Garden and Landscape Uses. Among the most beautiful of tropical foliage plants, alocasias thrive outdoors only in warm, humid climates. They are splendid greenhouse ornamentals, but adapt poorly to dry atmospheres and so are not satisfactory indoor decoratives for houses or other buildings. The tall, large-leaved kinds of noble aspect can be featured with stunning effect in tropical gardens. They, as well as lower kinds, look especially well planted near water and beneath tall trees. They revel in rich, fairly moist soil where there is some shade from strong sun and reasonable shelter from high winds.

Cultivation. Alocasias are propagated by seeds, offsets or sucker shoots, by pieces of rhizome, and by the small tubers developed by some kinds. Given high temperatures and high humidity they are easy to grow. In greenhouses they may be planted in well-drained ground beds or in pots containing generous amounts of drainage material. The soil should be coarse and porous and contain a liberal proportion of organic matter and be kept evenly moist, but not saturated. Slightly drier conditions in winter than in summer are appropriate. Minimum temperature on winter nights should be 60°F. A few degrees higher is better. Day temperatures should be five to fifteen degrees above the night level. At other seasons higher temperatures are in order. Misting the foliage lightly with water on bright days is very beneficial. Repotting is done, when needed, in spring. Specimens that have filled their containers with healthy roots benefit from weekly, spring-to-fall applications of dilute liquid fertilizer. Shade from strong sun is necessary.

ALOE (A'l-o-e)—Aloe. The botanical name of this important group of nonhardy, perennial succulent plants is pronounced in three syllables, its common one, spelled identically, in two. The genus so identified belongs to the lily family LILIACEAE. It consists of approximately 325 species, nearly one-half natives of South Africa, the remainder of tropical Africa and Madagascar except for twelve to fifteen indigenous to Arabia and one to the Atlantic islands. The name *Aloe* is derived from an old Arabian word. For plants sometimes called American-aloe see Agave. The false-aloe is *Manfreda virginica*, the green-aloe *Furcraea foetida*, the water-aloe *Stratiotes aloides*.

Although aloes were cultivated in Egypt, especially in cemeteries, since remote times and were known to peoples of the Mediterranean region at least four centuries before the beginning of the Christian era (the Greeks were familiar as early as that with medicinal aloes brought from the island of Socotra, and aloes were cultivated in pots in Rome and Naples) the three biblical Old Testament references to aloes are not to the plants we know by that name. They allude to a tree, possibly *Aquilaria agallocha*, that produces a fragrant gum. Misinterpretations by translators of the Bible into English are responsible for the error. It is possible, however, that the New Testament allusion to aloes being used to embalm the body of Christ refers to *Aloe barbadensis* or *Aloe perryi*. Aloes are of medicinal value and the products of some aloes are official in the United States Pharmacopeia and in the British Pharmacopoeia. Mediterranean peoples and natives of Africa have long applied split leaves of aloes to wounds and sores, and more recently those of *A. barbadensis*, *A. arborescens*, and *A. mutabilis* have been employed by dermatologists, reportedly successfully, to heal x-ray burns. The chief medicinal products of the genus *Aloe* are Curacao aloes and Cape aloes, the first a product of *A. barbadensis*, the other of *A. ferox*. The national floral emblem of the Republic of South Africa is *A. ferox*.

Aloes, by the botanically unobserving, are sometimes confused with agaves, but the distinctions are definite. The genus *Agave*, which is entirely American, belongs in the amaryllis family AMARYLLIDACEAE. The ovaries of its flowers are below the petals, in *Aloe* the ovaries are above the petals. Leaves of agaves contain strong fibers and cannot be broken easily, those of aloes snap like carrots and contain juicy pulp, but no strong fibers. Agaves are sometimes called American-aloes.

Aloes are small or large, often stemless, but some kinds have tall, stout, freely branched or branchless trunks, others have thin, clambering stems. The leaves, usually in rosettes, are sometimes two-ranked, or may be scattered along the stems. They often have spiny teeth along their margins and, more rarely, on their upper or lower surfaces. The flowers are in racemes, often arranged in large panicles, sometimes umbel-like. Many aloes are showy and strikingly beautiful. The flowering stalks come from the leaf axils or are apparently terminal. They are densely- to more loosely-flowered with the flowers on longish or short individual stalks. Generally tubular, their perianths are more or less three-angled. Sometimes they are curved, often swollen at their bases, and constricted just above. There are six petals, or more correctly tepals, separate or united toward their bases. The three inner may be joined by the lower parts of their backs to the outer ones. There are three stamens and a slender style. The fruits are papery or somewhat woody capsules.

Not only is the number of species of *Aloe* great, but further complicating the correct identification of individual plants, numerous natural and artificial hybrids exist. Some species are distinct enough for easy recognition, but many are not, especially when young or when grown in greenhouses. The kinds described below are among the most commonly cultivated.

Others are grown in botanical collections and by specialists. For convenience they are presented here as tree aloes, kinds with tall, much-branched trunks; single-stemmed aloes (these, mostly tall, may occasionally produce a branch or two, but rarely); shrub aloes, those that are much branched bushes or vines; and stemless aloes, those without stems or at most very short ones. Unless otherwise stated all are natives of South Africa.

Tree aloes with stout trunks and much-branched massive heads include several much esteemed sorts. The tallest and biggest of the genus, **A. bainesii** attains a maximum height of 60 feet. Its trunk at ground level may be 9 feet in diameter. It tapers upward until at a height of 6 feet or more it begins to fork repeatedly and so develops a large, impressive, much-branched, rounded head. Each ultimate branch ends in a rosette of about twenty, sword-shaped, fleshy leaves 2 to 3 feet in length and with sheathing bases. Gray-green to dull green, spreading and recurved, the leaves are 3 to 4 inches wide at their bases. Their undersides are rounded, their margins furnished with dull white, brown-tipped, horny teeth.

Aloe bainesii

The bell-shaped, green-tipped, salmon-pink to rose-pink blooms are 1¼ to 1½ inches long. They are in crowded, cylindrical racemes 8 inches to 1 foot in length, usually three of which are on each 1½- to 2-feet-long flowering stalk. Distinctive, 20 to 30 feet tall **A. dichotoma** has a trunk and branches that fork repeatedly so that old specimens develop very large heads atop trunks up to 4 feet in diameter. In crowded, often slightly spiraled rosettes of about twenty, the glaucous-green, lanceolate-linear leaves are 6 to 9 inches long by up to 2 inches broad at the base. Their edges have small, triangular teeth. The blooms, bright yellow to lemon-yellow, about 1¼

Aloe dichotoma

inches long, are in lax racemes 6 to 8 inches in length. The imposing **A. pillansii** is a tree, beautiful in bloom, up to 30 feet or more high with a broad-based, tapering trunk with a candelabrum of erect, often-forked branches above. The bottom of the trunk attains a diameter of 3 to 6 feet. In

Aloe pillansii

crowded rosettes at the branch ends, the gray-green to brownish-green, pointed-lanceolate, slightly sickle-shaped, spreading leaves are approximately 2 feet long by 4½ inches wide and ½ inch thick at the base. Their upper sides are channeled toward the apexes and flat below. Beneath they are rounded. They have white-edged, toothed margins. Coming from the axils of the lower leaves, the branched panicles of up to fifty cylindrical racemes of blooms are about 1½ feet long. The lemon-yellow to pale yellow flowers, which much resemble those of *A. dichotoma*, are nearly 1½ inches long.

The fan aloe (*A. plicatilis*) is so called because its strap-shaped leaves are in two opposite rows so that the clusters suggest open fans. Native only to mountain regions in the Cape Peninsula in South Africa, this striking, unique species attains heights of 10 to 15 feet. Its trunk forks and reforks, each branch and branchlet ending in a dozen or more flat leaves, their bases overlapping. They are about 1 foot long by 1½ inches wide, usually minutely-toothed in their upper one-thirds. At flowering time a single-stalked, cylindrical, loose raceme of twenty to thirty, 2-inch-long, scarlet flowers, tinged green at their apexes, is borne from each leaf cluster.

Aloe plicatilis

Tree aloes mostly without branches include many handsome kinds. Some have massive terminal rosettes of foliage, in others the leaves are more distantly spaced down the stems. Many kinds retain their dead foliage as skirts around their trunks in much the manner of *Washingtonia* palms. Others have naked trunks. Descriptions of some of the best known of this group now follow: *A. africana* is distinctive, easily rec-

Aloe africana

ognizable by its splendid erect, long-conical racemes of yellow to orange-yellow flowers that stand well up from the rosettes of foliage crowning the usually branchless stems clothed with skirts of withered foliage. The stems are 6 to 12 feet tall. The rosettes are of about thirty dull green to glaucous, spreading to recurved leaves approximately 2 feet long by 4½ inches wide, their upper surfaces flat below, channeled toward their apexes, the lower surfaces rounded. They have a few reddish spines and red-toothed edges. The down-pointing, 2-inch-long flowers, in the bud stage dull red, are in two- to four-branched panicles of densely crowded racemes 1½ to 2 feet long. This species frequently hybridizes with the somewhat similar *A. ferox*, which differs from it in having thicker leaves up to 3 feet long by 6 inches wide and usually scarlet blooms in erect, five- to eight-branched panicles of more cylindrical rather than sharply-tapered racemes. The rosettes consist of up to sixty leaves with spiny to spineless surfaces. *A. marlothii*, from 6 to 18 feet tall, has a trunk terminated by a dense rosette of forty to fifty pointed-lanceolate, dull green to glaucous leaves 3 to 4½ feet long by up to nearly 1 foot wide at their bases.

Aloe marlothii

Their upper sides are flat in their lower parts, deeply channeled toward their apexes. The undersides are rounded. Both are thinly or heavily studded with reddish spines. The leaf margins are furnished with red teeth. The panicles of bloom have many branches that spread nearly horizontally and are 1 foot to 1½ feet long. Along them the orange to yellowish-orange blooms about 1¼ inches long are disposed in crowded, markedly one-sided racemes. *A. thraskii*, native to sandy beaches near the ocean, is a handsome aloe 3 to 12 feet tall, its stems clothed with skirts of withered foliage. Dull green to glaucous, its deeply-channeled, long-tapered, strongly-

Aloe thraskii

recurved leaves are up to 4½ feet long by nearly 1 foot wide at their bases. Their narrowly-red-bordered margins have small, red teeth. The one to few panicles of erect, crowded, broad-cylindrical flower spikes are held well above the rosettes. The 1-inch-long, green-apexed, lemon-yellow to light orange blooms are greenish to orange in the bud stage. Out of bloom this aloe is much like *A. recurvifolia*, but the latter has flowers in branchless, poker-like, narrow, cylindrical spikes instead of candelabra-like panicles. *A. vaombe* of Madagascar is majestic, highly ornamental. It has a single, branchless trunk skirted with old, dead foliage, crowned with a great rosette of thirty to forty leaves. The leaves gradually taper from base to apex. At their widest they are 6 to 8 inches across. They are deeply-channeled above, rounded on their lower surfaces, 2½ to 3 feet long. The lower ones are recurved, those above spreading. In season the rosette is surmounted by up to four many-branched panicles of bloom. The panicles are about 3 feet tall. Each is of about twenty-five erect, closely-flowered racemes of bright crimson blooms a little over 1 inch long.

Some aloes are large shrubs, generally much-branched and bushy or in the case of *A. ciliaris* clambering or vining. The following sorts belong in this group: *A. arborescens* is perhaps the best known of these. In the wild, it is the most widely distributed South African species. It is a native in regions of moderate to high rainfall. From 6 to 9 feet tall and about as wide as high, it has spreading, somewhat downward-arching, tapered, toothed, dull green to gray-green leaves 1½ to 2 feet long by 2 to 3 inches wide at their bases. The tall, erect, generally branchless flower stalks end in conical racemes up to 1 foot long of pendulous, scarlet, 1½-inch-long blooms, those near their tops densely crowded. *A. ciliaris* is very easily identified by, besides its vinelike growth, the much-fringed collars formed by the bases of the leaves, which completely surround the slender stems. In the wild, it clambers over shrubs and has been observed with stems 20 feet long. Distantly-spaced, the dark green leaves are confined to the terminal 1 to 2 feet of the slender branches.

Aloe ciliaris

They spread or recurve, are long-pointed, linear-lanceolate, 4 to 6 inches long by ½ to 1 inch wide. Their upper surfaces are flat or slightly channeled, beneath they are rounded. The strongly-drooping scarlet to scarlet-crimson blooms, a little more than 1 inch long and rarely branched, have yellowish-green mouths. *A. divaricata* of Madagascar is up to 10 feet tall. It usually branches low to form a bush taller than it is broad; it is sometimes single-stemmed. Its rather widely-spaced, sword-shaped, toothed leaves are not in rosettes, but spread, or the lower ones recurve from the upper parts of the stems which they sheath with their bases. They are about 2 feet long by 3 inches wide at their bases. Their upper surfaces are channeled toward their apexes and flat below. Their undersides are rounded. Reddish-scarlet flowers a little more than 1 inch long are in 3-feet-tall candelabra panicles that tower upward from the tops of the plants. *A. mitriformis* is variable. It has slender, sprawling, often prostrate stems 3 to 6 feet in length, which are too weak to stand erect and support the weight of the rosettes of foliage. Fleshy, spreading or incurved, ovate-lanceolate leaves clothe the upturned end portions of the stems forming rosettes up to 1½ feet wide or sometimes wider. Glaucous-green to green, the leaves, except toward their apexes where they are slightly channeled, are flat on their upper surfaces, rounded and slightly keeled beneath. They are up to 8 inches long by 4 to 6 inches wide, prominently toothed along their margins and with a few teeth along the keels. The two- to five-branched panicles of bloom are 1¼ to 2 feet tall. Each branch terminates in a short, flattish to sometimes conical, compact, headlike raceme of crowded, dull scarlet blooms approximately 1½ inches

long. *A. pearsonii*, of very distinctive aspect, inhabits regions where the rainfall seldom exceeds 5 inches a year and summer temperatures may reach 110°F. It branches freely from the base to form bushes 3 to 6 feet tall and as wide as high.

Aloe pearsonii

Rather slender, its stems are furnished for most of their lengths with pointed-ovate to ovate-lanceolate, reflexed leaves 3 to 4 inches long by about 1½ inches wide, in four or five vertical ranks. They are often reddish and have whitish to red teeth along the margins. Their upper surfaces are nearly flat when moisture is available. In times of drought their margins bend upward. Arising from near the tops of the stems, the sparingly-branched flowering stalks are erect. They carry medium-dense racemes of usually yellow, sometimes red, 1-inch-long blooms. *A. ramosissima* forms broad, shrubby clumps up to 6 feet tall or taller and as broad or broader. Its stems repeatedly fork from ground level upward. Crowded in dense, terminal rosettes of ten to fourteen, the glaucous-green leaves, spreading or down-curved, are 6 to 9 inches long, at their bases nearly 1 inch wide and a little more than ¼ inch thick. Their margins are finely-toothed. From 6 to 10 inches long and branched from the base the flowering stalks carry cylindrical racemes of loosely-arranged greenish to canary-yellow, pouch-shaped blooms nearly 1½ inches long. The stamens and style protrude conspicuously.

Aloes with large- to medium-sized rosettes at or near the ground include many splendid, showy kinds. The rosettes may be stemmed or stemless, solitary or in clusters. Here is a selection of the most popular: *A. audhalica*, native to western Arabia, has usually solitary rosettes of up to thirty pointed-triangular, glaucous-green to pinkish-brown, toothed leaves, erect and up to 1½ feet long by 6 inches wide at their bases. Except toward the apexes,

where they are somewhat channeled, the leaves have flat upper surfaces, are rounded beneath. They have narrow, pink margins with brown teeth. Rising to a height of 2½ to 3 feet, the flowering stalk may have up to four branches. The narrowly-conical racemes are of spreading to pendulous, scarlet blooms 1¼ inches long. This species, native at high altitudes, is occasionally exposed to frost in winter. *A. barbadensis*, often misnamed *A. vera*, is called Barbados aloe not because it is native of that island, but because it was much cultivated there.

Aloe barbadensis

Believed to have originated in the Cape Verde Islands, the Canary Islands, and perhaps Madeira it was distributed presumably by man throughout the Mediterranean region and to more distant places in remote times. In the first century A.D. Dioscorides discussed its medicinal virtues, and about 512 A.D. it was shown in color in a manuscript prepared at Constantinople. This is the oldest known picture of an aloe, excluding possibly the rock pictures of African natives. More than 1,000 years elapsed before the next picture of the Barbados aloe that is extant appeared. *A. barbadensis* is stemless, suckers freely, and makes strong clumps of compact rosettes each of about sixteen sometimes reddish-tinged, gray-green, thick, fleshy leaves up to about 1½ feet long and 3 inches wide at the base. They taper gradually from base to apex and have toothed margins. Their upper surfaces are flat except near the apex where they are slightly channeled. Beneath they are rounded. Often without branches, sometimes with one or two, the flowering stalk is 2 to 3 feet tall. Main stalk and branches terminate in tapering, cylindrical, dense racemes of rigid, down-pointing, yellow flowers 1 inch long or slightly longer. *A. broomii* has the distinction of being one of two distinguishable species of aloes depicted in ancient rock paintings by primitive South African natives. It has usually a solitary rosette. More rarely it is divided at the top of its some-

Aloe broomii

times 3 feet long, procumbent stem into two or three rosettes. The rosettes are of ovate-lanceolate, 1-foot-long leaves, terminating in long, dry points. The strongly-toothed, red-edged leaves are 4 inches wide, with flat upper surfaces except toward their more or less channeled apexes. Their undersides are rounded. Usually not branched, the flowering stalk is 3 to 4½ feet in height. Densely-flowered, the strictly erect, poker-like racemes are of crowded pale yellow blooms ¾ to 1 inch long that open in succession from base to top of the raceme in a narrow band that spirals around the raceme. A peculiarity of this kind, which cannot be classed as showy in bloom, is that the flowers even when fully open, except for their protruding stamens and styles are hidden from view by the floral bracts. *A. buettneri*, of tropical Africa, has underground bulblike organs broader than long, up to 4 inches in diameter. Its deciduous leaves, about sixteen to a rosette, average 1½ feet in length. They are tapered in their upper parts to pointed apexes and are somewhat channeled there. They have toothed margins. The flowering stalks, 2 to 2½ feet tall, have three to five erect branches terminating in racemes of greenish-yellow to bright red, pendulous, 1½-inch-long blooms with perianth tubes characteristically markedly swollen at their bases. *A. ecklonis* exhibits considerable

Aloe ecklonis

variation. Its stemless or almost stemless rosettes are solitary or grouped. Each is of up to twenty dull green leaves of varied shapes up to 1¼ feet long. Their upper surfaces are slightly channeled, their undersides somewhat rounded. White teeth fringe their margins. In short, tight, head-like clusters of about forty atop branchless stalks 1½ feet tall, the yellow to orange or red flowers are about 2 inches long. *A. greenii* is very handsome. Its crowded, stemless rosettes multiply rapidly by offsets to form dense clumps. Each has a dozen to sixteen tapered, linear-lanceolate leaves about 1½ feet long by 3½ inches wide, spreading to recurved from their middles outward. Flat to slightly channeled and bright green, they are decorated on both surfaces with longish whitish spots arranged in irregular, zigzagged crossbands. The leaf margins are wavy-toothed. The blooms of this aloe are displayed in slightly loose, cylindrical racemes 6 to 10 inches long at the terminations of the branches of a candelabrum-branched flowering stalk 3 feet tall or a little taller. The flowers are pale to deep flesh-pink, slightly over 1 inch long. *A. inermis*, native to Arabia, is one of the few aloes with toothless leaves. It has slender stems up to 1½ feet long. By suckering it forms clumps, which are sometimes large. The spreading or slightly to strongly recurved leaves are narrow-lanceolate to pointed-sword-shaped, gray-green to olive-green, sometimes with a few white spots. They are mostly 1 foot long or a little longer and 2 to 3 inches broad. Their upper sides, slightly channeled toward their tips, are flat in the lower parts. Beneath, the leaves are rounded. Dull scarlet to yellow flowers a little over 1 inch long are borne in racemes on the many branches of broad, airy panicles that are 2 to 2½ feet in height. *A. myriacantha* is stemless. Its rosettes are up to twelve more or less erect, slender-linear, dull green leaves about 10 inches long by ⅓ inch wide, broader at their bases. Their channeled upper surfaces have a few white spots toward their bases. Beneath they are rounded and more freely white-spotted toward their bases. Minute white teeth are along the margins. The branchless flower stalks, solitary or sometimes in twos, are bracted in their upper parts. Each terminates in a dense, conical head of twenty to thirty about 2-inch-long, reddish-pink, rarely greenish-white blooms. *A. saponaria* is very variable. It may be stemless or have a stem up to about 1½ feet tall. In crowded rosettes of twelve to twenty its leaves are narrow- to broad-lanceolate, up to 1 foot long by 4½ inches wide, with brown-toothed edges. Their upper sides are flat or nearly so, their lower ones rounded. The leaves have numerous whitish, oblong spots mostly in wavy cross-bands. The stout flowering stalks have a few erect branches that hold the

terminal umbel-like, crowded heads of about thirty blooms high above the foliage. The drooping, red, quite long-stalked flowers are 1¼ to 1¾ inches long. *A. secundiflora* is a stemless or very short-stemmed native from Tanzania and Kenya to Ethiopia and the Sudan. Usually solitary, its rosettes are of about twenty mostly ascending and erect leaves about 1½ feet long by up to 6 inches wide at their bases. They are pointed-ovate-lanceolate, toothed, dull green, without spots. Toward their apexes their upper surfaces are channeled, below they are flat. The undersides are flattish toward their bases, rounded above. The wide-branched, loose panicles of decidedly one-sided racemes of flowers are from 3 to 4½ feet high. The blooms are rose-pink to dull red minutely spotted with white. They are nearly 1½ inches long. *A. sinkatana* inhabits extremely arid regions in the Sudan. It has usually clusters, less often solitary rosettes of twenty or rather fewer upward-angled, spreading, sometimes white-spotted leaves 1½ to 2 feet long. From 3- to 4-inch-wide bases they gradually taper to rounded apexes furnished with a few tiny teeth. The upper sides of the leaves are channeled, the lower rounded. The margins are toothed. In short umbel-like heads at the ends of the few branches of a candelabrum-like, erect panicle, the scarlet, orange, or yellow blooms are 1 inch long. *A. striata*, called the coral aloe, is distinct and handsome.

Aloe striata

It is one of the very few aloes with toothless leaves. The procumbent stems of old specimens may be 3 feet long. The usually solitary, massive rosettes are of twelve to twenty spreading, up-curved, broad-lanceolate leaves 1½ feet long by nearly one-half as wide, flat-topped at their bases, with edges somewhat upturned toward their apexes. Glaucous to slightly reddish, they have longitudinal striations and sometimes obscure spots on their upper surfaces. They are narrowly edged with

A hybrid between *Aloe striata* and *Aloe saponaria picta*

pink or red. The flowers are in heads or short conical racemes at the branch ends of the candelabra panicles. Each rosette produces flower panicles on erect stalks to a height of 3 feet. Their lower branches are again branched. Coral-red to peach-red, green-tipped in bud, the nodding flowers are about 1¼ inches long. *A. succotrina* is a name that has been much misapplied. It makes no allusion to the island of Socotra as has often been supposed, but refers to the yellowish color of the sap crystals.

Aloe succotrina

True *A. succotrina* is endemic to the Cape Peninsula. Variable, it has sprawling to more or less erect stems from short to up to 6 feet in length, branchless or fork-branched. The many narrowly-triangular tapered leaves of each rosette bend upward from their nearly horizontal lower parts. They are about 1½ feet long, 3 to 4 inches wide at their bases, ½ to ¾ inch thick at their middles, toothed, dull green or gray-green sometimes with a few white spots. Their upper surfaces are flat becoming slightly channeled toward their apexes. Their undersides are rounded. Rarely

branched, the erect flowering stalk is up to 3 feet tall. It terminates in a dense, conical, crowded raceme of lustrous, green-tipped, red to reddish-salmon flowers 1½ inches long. *A. turkanensis* is a clump-forming native of intensely hot, dry regions in Kenya. It has procumbent, rooting stems and forms dense groups of rosettes each of about twenty-five long-pointed-lanceolate, erect leaves with overlapping bases. Up to 2 feet long, they are about 4 inches wide at their bottoms. Bluish-green, irregularly marked with longish and round whitish spots, they are margined with brown-tipped, whitish teeth. Their lower sides are rounded. Rising to heights of 3 to 4½ feet, the slender flowering stalks have branches angling outward and upward that bear slender, loose, somewhat one-sided racemes of 1-inch-long, dull, pinkish-red blooms. *A. virens*, is an attractive stemless sort with broad clumps of rosettes of narrowly-lanceolate leaves up to about 8 inches long, and with white, fleshy, triangular marginal teeth. Its showy

Aloe virens

red flowers are in erect racemes approximately 2 feet tall. *A. wickensii* is another stemless or nearly stemless species. It has rosettes of up to fifty spreading and erect,

Aloe wickensii

lanceolate-sword-shaped leaves up to 2½ feet long, margined with dark brown to black spines. Up to about 5 feet tall, its stiffly-erect flowering stalks terminate in a comparatively short, crowded spike of 1- to 1¼-inch-long, brownish-tipped, chrome-yellow flowers. *A. wildii*, of tropical East Africa, is stalkless, and has one to few about six-leaved rosettes of two-ranked, rigid, suberect leaves usually not more than 9 inches in length. Linear, they have overlapping bases, are about ⅓ inch broad, slightly channeled above, and rounded on their undersides. Toward their bases they are white-spotted. Their margins are finely-toothed. The flowering stalks, rarely much more than 1 foot tall and often shorter, are without branches. In loose racemes of twelve to sixteen, the drooping, green-tipped, bright orange blooms are about 1¼ inches long.

Miniature aloes include a number of kinds especially appropriate for window planting, and in mild, dry climates, for rock gardens. Those now to be described are of that type. *A. albiflora*, of Madagascar, is charming, and has slender, branchless spikes up to 1 foot tall of white flowers suggestive of those of a *Scilla*. Stemless, it has linear leaves 3 to 4½ inches in length, green with white tubercles. *A. aristata* is stemless and usually forms clusters of up to twelve rosettes of numerous green to grayish- bluish-green, narrow-lanceolate leaves nearly or quite 4 inches long by up to approximately ½ inch wide at their bases. The tip of each ends in a tufted bristle. The top surfaces of the leaves are flat and have scattered, white spots. The undersides are rounded, more densely white-spotted, with a few spines near their apexes. The flowering stalk with usually up to six branches is about 1½ feet tall. The 1½-inch-long flowers on red individual stalks are greenish-brown. *A. bakeri* is an attractive species from Madagascar. It makes clumps of many slender stems 4 to 8 inches long, their upper parts with about twelve spreading to recurved leaves that sheathe the stems with their bases. The leaves are flat to slightly channeled above, with rounded undersides. Green or reddish-tinged, about 3 inches long, they are white-toothed at their margins. From bases ¼ inch wide or a little wider they narrow gradually to pointed apexes. The flowering stems are without branches, slender, and up to 1 foot tall. The dozen or fewer pendulous, 1-inch-long blooms are apricot-yellow in their lower one-thirds shading above to through orange and yellowish to a green-tipped end. *A. brevifolia* forms compact, symmetrical, stemless rosettes of thirty to forty spreading, ascending and erect, coarsely-toothed, triangular-lanceolate, glaucous leaves a little more than 2 inches long by at their bases ¾ inch wide. Their upper surfaces are flat to slightly hollowed, with a few soft spines toward their

Aloe brevifolia

tips. Not branched, the flowering stalks rise to a height of 1¼ feet. Crowded in conical racemes up to 6 inches long, the drooping, light scarlet flowers are slightly greenish at the apexes of the petals. Their anthers protrude. *A. descoingsii*, stemless or nearly so, suckers to form crowded groups. Native to limestone areas in Madagascar, it has pointed-ovate leaves, eight to ten to each rosette, a little more than 1 inch long and at their bases one-half as wide as long. The leaves spread widely or are recurved. They have white-warted upper sides flat toward their bases, channeled for most of their lengths. Their undersides are rounded. The margins are furnished with firm, white teeth. The flowering stalk, not branched and up to 6 inches tall, has at its apex a short raceme of about ten scarlet blooms, about ⅓ inch long. *A. haworthioides* is well named. Out of bloom it surely looks like an attractive haworthia. Native of Madagascar, it has rosettes, solitary or densely clustered, about 2 inches in diameter, of about thirty leaves. They are narrowly-triangular, short-pointed, and covered with white pustules sometimes tipped with white hairs. The leaf margins are fringed with conspicuous, soft to firm, white teeth. Up to 1 foot tall, the slender flowering stalk terminates in a crowded, cylindrical-conical raceme of twenty to thirty up-pointing, white to pale pink blooms up to ⅓ inch long. *A. jucunda* is a charming miniature tropical African aloe that in growth habit suggests a haworthia. It has stalkless or very short-stalked rosettes not more than 4 inches across in dense clusters, 1 foot to 1½ feet wide. Each rosette has about twelve pointed-ovate, spreading or recurved, dull-white- or pale-green-spotted leaves channeled in their upper halves, with rounded undersides. Their margins are sharp-toothed. The flowering stalk, a little more than 1 foot tall and without branches, ends in a loose raceme of about twenty ¾-inch-long, light rose-pink to coral-pink, pendulous blooms. *A. longistyla*, in bloom one of the most beautiful aloes, has usually

solitary, sometimes clusters of two, three, rarely up to ten, stemless rosettes. Each rosette has twenty to thirty erect-incurved, glaucous leaves 4½ to 6 inches long, at the base up to 1½ inches wide. Both surfaces are studded with white spines, the margins with white, horny teeth. The erect, crowded racemes, about 4½ inches long and broad consist of forty to fifty up-curving, pale salmon-pink to rose-red blooms slightly more than 2 inches wide, with greenish-veined, spreading tips to the petals and long-protruded styles. *A. rauhii*, of Madagascar, is stemless or almost stemless. It forms crowded clumps of rosettes each approximately 4 inches in diameter. The leaves are triangular-lanceolate, ½ to ¾ inch wide at their bases. The older ones spread, the younger ones are ascending or erect. Gray-green sometimes suffused with brown, they are decorated with numerous H-shaped spots. The upper surfaces are channeled, the lower ones round. The white, horny leaf margins are furnished with tiny white teeth. Rarely with a short branch, mostly branchless, the nearly 1-foot-tall flowering stalks terminate in a loose raceme of 12- to 18-inch-long nodding blooms, rose-scarlet becoming paler toward their mouths. *A. sladeniana*, stemless, forms clusters of rosettes of overlapping, pointed-lanceolate, channeled leaves that are 2 to 3½ inches long by up to 1½ inches wide. Both surfaces are green speckled with white spots irregularly scattered or more or less in cross-bands. There are a few white teeth along the margins and keel. Branchless or once-forked below its middle, the flowering stalk terminates in one or two loose racemes of drooping, dull pink, greenish-mouthed blooms a little more than 1 inch long. Anthers and stigma protrude slightly. This species rarely forms seeds. *A. variegata*, the partridge breast aloe, is a great favorite, aptly named, and

Aloe variegata

quite easily recognizable. In the wild it is widely distributed in desert and semidesert regions. In South Africa called kanniedood, which means cannot die, it is said that a specimen hung in the air will live and bloom for a year or more. The partridge breast aloe forms dense clumps of stemless, sometimes elongated rosettes up to 8 inches tall or occasionally taller. The crowded, densely-overlapping leaves are in three vertical or spiraled ranks each of three to six. They are triangular-lanceolate, broadly channeled toward their bases, deeply so nearer their apexes. The undersides are rounded below, keeled in their upper parts. From 4 to 6 inches long by up to 2¼ inches wide, the leaves are usually rich green and conspicuously ornamented with white, oblong spots displayed in irregular cross-bands. The leaf edges are horny and round-toothed. Branchless or with one or two branches, the flowering stalks are about 1 foot tall. The spreading to slightly drooping flowers in loose racemes 4 to 8 inches long are approximately 1½ inches in length, flesh pink to dull scarlet.

Garden and Landscape Uses. For warm arid and semiarid regions *Aloe* supplies a wealth of handsome and useful outdoor ornamentals. They come in a vast variety of forms and sizes. Most bloom abundantly and beautifully, but even out of bloom many are quite stunning. The larger aloes associate splendidly with buildings and other architectural features and lend themselves to planting as single specimens and in groups; the smaller ones are ideal for rock gardens and similar places. Bushy aloes make effective informal hedges and screens, climbing *A. ciliaris* does well and can be displayed effectively on a fence or trellis. Aloes have the great advantage over agaves, which in general are of similar forms, of flowering annually, and the blooms of the majority of aloes cultivated are brightly colored and very showy. Those of some kinds are delightful in flower arrangements. By selecting different kinds of aloes in southern California and other favored regions, some can be had in bloom every month of the year.

As pot and tub plants aloes thrive with minimum care and depending upon size can be used to decorate patios and terraces, or be grown in windows. They are commonly included in greenhouse collections of succulents, grown in containers or planted in ground beds.

Cultivation. As with most succulent plants aloes demand a very well-drained soil. So long as water passes very freely through it other characteristics matter less. Sandy, loamy, and clayey earths will grow good aloes. Most do well in soils containing limestone. Reasonable fertility is helpful, but aloes will prosper even in soils quite poor in nutrients. For their best advantage they need full sun, but they tolerate a little part-day shade and in greenhouses some kinds may benefit from mild relief from the full intensity of the sun. These plants live and grow satisfactorily for several to many years in containers without repotting. Because of this, it is important to use suitable soil. One containing a large proportion of organic matter that in time will break down and impede free passage of water and air is unsuitable. Depend upon inorganic additives to keep the rooting medium open and porous. The soil should be mixed with generous amounts of broken brick, coarse cinders, crushed limestone, perlite, or similar stuffs, but very little peat moss, leaf mold, compost, and the like. A generous sprinkling of coarse bonemeal, mixed in, is advantageous. If necessary pot at any time, but if the choice is yours select late winter or spring. Do not use too large containers, and pack the soil firmly. These plants prosper when their roots are fairly crowded. The watering schedule is simple. Soak the soil thoroughly at intervals spaced widely enough that the earth in winter is nearly quite dry, from spring to summer is moderately dry, before application is made. Old specimens that have crowded their containers with roots benefit from monthly applications of dilute liquid fertilizer from spring to fall. Aloes appreciate a dry, airy atmosphere; therefore ventilate greenhouses containing them freely whenever weather permits. Night temperatures in winter of 40 to 50°F are satisfactory with increases of five to fifteen degrees by day. At other seasons both night and day temperatures that are considerably higher are in order. Propagation of aloes is easily achieved by offsets, and of some kinds, by cuttings. Seeds germinate readily, but if of hybrid origin will result in plants not identical with the one from which the seed was taken. For additional information see Succulents.

ALOINOPSIS (Alo-inópsis). Fifteen South African species of the *Mesembryanthemum* group comprise *Aloinopsis* of the carpetweed family AIZOACEAE. They are low, tufted, tuberous-rooted, succulent perennials, velvety-hairy or smooth. Their leaves range from broad-spatula-shaped to linear-lanceolate and club-shaped. The flowers, solitary or in twos or threes, open late in the day or evening. They superficially resemble daisies, but are structured very differently. Unlike daisies, they are single blooms, not heads of many florets each representing a flower. Each have five or six sepals of nearly equal size, many yellow, yellow-striped-with-red, or pink petals and numerous stamens. There are no staminodes (nonfertile stamens). There are six to fourteen stigmas. The fruits are capsules. The name *Aloinopsis,* from the name of the unrelated genus *Aloe,* and the Greek *opsos,* a likeness, is of obvious application.

Not to be confused with *Rabiea jamesii,* which also was once called *Nananthus jamesii,* is *Aloinopsis jamesii* (syn. *Nananthus jamesii*). This has shoots with four to six leaves ½ to ¾ inch long, ⅕ inch wide at their middles and narrowed to both ends. They are roughly-warty and gray-green. Their upper surfaces are slightly hollowed. Beneath, they are keeled toward their apexes, rounded toward their bases. The 1-inch-wide blooms are golden-yellow, with a red center line to each petal. In its homeland *A. rosulata* (syn. *Aistocaulon rosulatum*) frequently grows with only the tips of its leaves showing. The remainder of the plant is buried in the earth. A small, fleshy-rooted succulent, it forms clumps of shoots with opposite, blunt-ended, spatula-shaped, lustrous green leaves, the alternate pairs of which are at right angles to each other. The leaves are up to 1 inch or slightly longer and at their broadest ½ inch or slightly wider. Their upper sides are flat or somewhat hollowed. Beneath, they are rounded and have slight keels toward their ends where their margins are roughened with small whitish warts. The yellow flowers, solitary or up to three together, are 1¼ to 1½ inches in diameter. They have strongly reflexed stamens.

Rosettes of four or six spreading, pointed-ovate leaves, the alternate pairs at right angles to each other, are characteristic of *A. rubrolineata* (syns. *A. dyeri, Nananthus rubrolineatus, Mesembryanthemum rubrolineatum*). The leaves are gray-green, roughly-warted except toward their bases and approximately 1 inch long by up to ¾ inch across at their centers. They narrow somewhat to their bases, more evidently to their apexes. Their upper surfaces are flat, their undersides rounded and toward the tips somewhat keeled. The shining, reddish-yellow flowers are from somewhat less to somewhat more than ½ inch across. The charming, tiny *A. schooneesii* of South Africa has broadly-spatula-shaped leaves ½ inch long or a little longer arranged in somewhat rosette fashion in clusters of eight to ten. Its lustrous yellow-red flowers are approximately ½ inch across. Rosettes of four to six leaves up to ¾ inch long by up to ¼ inch wide are developed by *A. setifera* (syn. *Titanopsis setifera*). Roughly-warted and with bristly teeth, they have flat upper surfaces slightly recurved at their ends. Their undersides are rounded for most of their lengths, keeled toward their apexes. The rich yellow to salmon, yellow-centered flowers are 1 inch to 1½ inches wide.

Garden Uses and Cultivation. These rare and often difficult-to-grow plants are suitable for inclusion in collections of the choicest succulents. They need conditions similar to those suitable for lithops, conophytums, and other choice, small *Mesembryanthemum* relatives of the South African deserts. Even though in the wild their up-

per parts may be partially to nearly completely buried, in cultivation their leafy parts must be above ground. Well-drained pots of porous soil, and a sunny greenhouse where the winter night temperature is 50°F are appropriate. Water moderately from spring to fall, more sparingly in winter. Propagation is by seeds, division, and cuttings. For more information see Succulents.

ALONSOA (Alon-sòa)—Mask Flower. Six species of herbaceous and subshrubby perennials of the Andean region constitute *Alonsoa* of the figwort family SCROPHULARIACEAE. In gardens they are nearly always grown as annuals. The name commemorates Alonzo Zanoni, who was Spanish Secretary at Bogota in about 1798. Mask flowers have four-angled stems, toothed or smooth-margined leaves, opposite or in whorls of three, and terminal racemes of red, orange-red, or rarely white, very asymmetrical flowers twisted on their stems so that they are upside down and have the biggest corolla lobe (petal) uppermost. The stamens number four. There is one style. The fruits are capsules.

The best known species is the elegant and bushy, herbaceous *A. warscewiczii* of

Alonsoa warscewiczii

Peru, which is 2 feet tall or taller. It has slender, reddish stems and ovate-lanceolate, toothed leaves. Its flowers, produced in great abundance, are cinnabar-red to scarlet, with the upper lip four or five times as long as the calyx. Also native to Peru, *A. acutifolia* differs in that its largest flower lobe is only three to four times as long as the calyx. It is a subshrub 2 feet or more tall. It has toothed leaves and red flowers larger than those of *A. warscewiczii.* There is a white-flowered variety, *A. a. candida.* Another Peruvian, *A. incisifolia,* is subshrubby, 1½ to 2 feet tall, and has black-throated, scarlet flowers almost ½ inch across, with the largest lobe of the corolla two to four times as long as the calyx. Its leaves are ovate to ovate-lanceolate and deeply-toothed. A white-flowered variety is known. Another Peruvian sub-shrub, *A. linearis* (syn. *A. linifolia*), is slender, with small scarlet flowers spotted at their bases with black and with the upper lip twice as long as the calyx. Rarely exceeding 1½ feet in height, and often lower, it has pointed, linear leaves either toothed or smooth-edged.

Other kinds that are perhaps sometimes cultivated include *A. mathewsii,* subshrubby and about 1 foot tall with narrow, toothed leaves and scarlet flowers, and a native of Peru; *A. meridionalis* (syn. *A. mutisii*), a native of Colombia, has dull orange flowers and attains a height of about 1 foot; and *A. caulialata*, herbaceous and about 1 foot tall, has slightly-toothed leaves and scarlet flowers and is a native of Peru.

Garden and Landscape Uses. Alonsoas are attractive plants for summer beds, and although they last for two or three days only, their flowers are elegant for cutting. They are dainty and lend themselves for use in arrangements. Alonsoas are also excellent for growing in greenhouses for winter, spring, and summer display in pots.

Cultivation. Alonsoas need well-drained, fertile soil and full sun. For outdoor use good results are had by sowing seed in early spring where the plants are to bloom and thinning out the seedlings to 6 to 8 inches apart, or seeds may be sown indoors about eight weeks before the young plants are to be planted outside, which should be done as soon as all danger of frost has passed. The young plants, when 2 or 3 inches tall, may have the tips of their stems pinched out to encourage branching. To have nice pot specimens that will bloom in the greenhouse, sow seeds from late August to January in a temperature of 55 to 60°F. Transplant the seedlings 2 inches apart in flats. Pinch out their tips when they are about 2 inches tall, and later transfer them individually to 4-inch pots. When these are filled with roots, pot the plants into containers 5 or 6 inches in diameter. They will bloom in these. Tie the stems neatly to slender stakes before they begin to fall over, and as soon as the final pots are well filled with healthy roots apply dilute liquid fertilizer once or twice a week. Alonsoas are most commonly raised from seeds, but they are also easily propagated by cuttings. This is sometimes a convenient way to obtain plants for blooming in winter in the greenhouse. For this purpose cuttings may be taken in late August.

ALOPECURUS (Alopec-ùrus)—Foxtail Grass. Except for the occasional use of colored-foliaged varieties of *Alopecurus pratensis* as ornamentals, this genus of the grass family GRAMINEAE is without horticultural importance. It consists of twenty-five species. One, the meadow foxtail, is cultivated for forage and is a common component of meadows. The genus takes its name from Greek *alopex*, a fox, and *oura*, a tail, and alludes to the flowering spikes.

The group includes both annuals and perennials, natives of temperate parts of the northern hemisphere. From the closely related timothy (*Phleum*) it differs in having softer spikelets that fall when mature.

Meadow foxtail (*A. pratensis*) is a hardy, tufted perennial up to about 3 feet tall. It has rough, flat leaf blades, and crowded, cylindrical, scarcely-tapering, spikelike panicles of flowers, pale green or purplish, soft, and 1 inch to 4 inches long. The one-flowered spikelets are in spirals. Variety *A. p. aureus* has yellowish leaves. In *A. p. aureo-variegatus* the leaves are striped green and yellow.

Alopecurus pratensis aureus

Garden Uses and Cultivation. As novelties for flower beds and borders or in other locations, the colored-leaved varieties have minor merit. They succeed in sun in any moderately good soil that does not lack for moisture and are easily increased by division in spring or fall.

ALOPHIA (Alòph-ia). The genus *Alophia* consists of ten species previously named *Herbertia*. Belonging to the iris family IRIDACEAE, it is native from Texas to Argentina and Chile. Its name is perhaps from the Greek *a*, without, and *lophos*, a mane, and refers to a characteristic of the blooms.

Alophias have corms. Their leaves, narrowly-linear, and folded or pleated, sheath the base of a slender, erect, generally branchless stalk that carries a spathe (bract) from the axil of which come one to six short-lived blooms. Each flower has three spreading or deflexed outer perianth segments (commonly called petals) much larger than the three erect inner ones. The short stalks of the three stamens are united, and as the flowers fade the anthers become spirally twisted. The slender style has three twice- or thrice-cleft branches. The fruits are triangular-oblong capsules.

A spring-bloomer endemic in southern Texas, *Alophia drummondii* (syn. *Herbertia drummondiana*) inhabits grasslands and prairies. From a bulb deep set in the ground are produced leaves approximately equal in length to the 1-foot-long flower stalk that bears a 2-inch-long spathe, and one or two blooms about 2 inches in diameter. Their spreading outer petals are nearly round and pale to deep lavender with a violet-spotted, white base outlined with a halo of violet. The inner petals are violet above and in their lower parts blackish-violet sometimes spotted with white. The erect style branches have each two toothed stigmas. Plants with white flowers are sometimes found.

South American species that are perhaps cultivated include *A. amoena* of Argentina and Uruguay and *A. pulchella* (syn. *Herbertia pulchella*) of Brazil and Chile. Up to 1 foot tall, *A. amoena* has somewhat shorter, linear leaves and solitary or paired, violet flowers with outer petals a little over ½ inch long. About 9 inches in height, *A. pulchella* has narrowly-sword-shaped leaves and blue-purple flowers with outer petals with lilac-dotted, white bases.

Garden and Landscape Uses and Cultivation. Not hardy in the north, the species discussed are of interest for planting in warm-climate regions. They thrive in sandy and clayey soils that are well drained and reasonably fertile, and need full sun. New plants are easily raised from seeds, and more slowly by natural multiplication of the corms.

ALOYSIA (Alòy-sia)—Lemon-Verbena. Most familiar of this group is the old-fashioned and popular lemon-verbena. It is one of more than thirty-five species of *Aloysia,* of the vervain family VERBENACEAE. The genus, native to warm parts of the Americas, is named in honor of Maria Louisa, wife of King Charles IV of Spain. She died in 1819.

Aloysias are sweet-aromatic, nonhardy shrubs with undivided, toothed or toothless leaves opposite or in whorls (circles of more than two). The small, tubular flowers are in spikes or racemes from the leaf axils that often form terminal panicles. The bracts at the bases of the blooms are early deciduous. The calyx is four-toothed, the corolla has two nearly equal lips. There are four stamens in pairs of two lengths. The fruits are two seedlike nutlets enclosed by the persistent calyx.

Lemon-verbena (*A. triphylla* syns. *A. citriodora, Lippia citriodora, L. triphylla*), a native of Chile and Argentina, is an attractive evergreen shrub 10 to 15 feet tall. It has angled young shoots, and foliage that when brushed against or bruised is strongly lemon-scented. Its short-stalked leaves, mostly in worls (circles) of three, or sometimes four, are 2 to 4 inches in length by ½ to nearly 1 inch wide. They are pointed-lanceolate, lightish green, and are glandular on both surfaces. Their edges are toothless or toothed, and fringed with bristly hairs. Not very showy, the tiny, lavender blooms are borne in summer in terminal, slender, downy, spikes 3 to 5 inches long, arranged in panicles.

The bee brush or white brush (*A. gratissima* syn. *Lippia ligustrina*) ranges in the wild from the southwestern United States to southern South America. A slender shrub up to 12 feet tall, it has gray, often spine-tipped branches, and stalkless or nearly stalkless, toothless, narrowly-elliptic to lanceolate-oblong leaves up to 1 inch long, often with clusters of tiny leaves in their axils. The undersides of the leaves are densely pubescent. Strongly vanilla-scented, the little white or lavender-tinged flowers are in spikes ¾ inch to 3 inches long, often arranged in quite large panicles. Variety *A. g. schulzae* has broader, elliptic to obovate leaves up to ¾ inch long by ⅓ inch wide, and frequently with a few large teeth. Another South American species sometimes cultivated, *A. virgata* (syn. *A. urticoides*), is a tall shrub with broad-elliptic, toothed leaves 3 to 5 inches long and nearly one-half as wide as long. They are hairy on their undersides and along the veins above. The tiny vanilla-scented flowers are in panicles of spikes.

Garden and Landscape Uses. Lemon-verbena is prized for its fragrance. An old-time favorite, it was common practice in the past to include a sprig or two in bouquets of flowers, and to float short leafy twigs in finger bowls. Hardy only where there is little or no frost, in places such as southern California, it is excellent for planting where its fresh fragrance can be readily appreciated. Full sun and well-drained soil are to its liking. In less salubrious climates it is raised in pots and tubs, in greenhouses, sunny windows, and such like locations.

Cultivation. For best results container-grown lemon-verbenas must be given cool, airy conditions. A winter night temperature of 40 to 50°F is adequate, with a moderate increase by day. In summer the plants are best outdoors with their containers buried nearly to their rims in a bed of sand, peat moss, or similar material that will ensure the roots being kept uniformly moist and fairly cool. Good loamy soil such as suits geraniums, chrysanthemums, and many other popular pot plants satisfies lemon-verbena. Water to keep it moderately moist, but not soggy from spring to fall, and rather drier in winter. During the growing season give well-rooted specimens regular applications of dilute liquid fertilizer. Pinch out the tips of the shoots to keep the plants bushy and shapely. In late winter or early spring prune to size and shape. At the same time take the plants out of their containers, tease away as much old soil as possible without doing too drastic harm to the roots, and repot in fresh earth. Lemon-verbenas can be trained as standards (specimens with a single trunklike stem topped by a round bushy head) by following procedures used for se-

curing similarly shaped specimens of lantanas, heliotropes, fuchsias, and other plants.

The other species of *Aloysia* described above are less important horticulturally than lemon-verbena. They adapt to warm, dryish areas, such as those in the southwestern United States, and have moderate appeal for landscaping, more especially for naturalistic plantings. Propagation of aloysias is by cuttings and seeds.

ALPHITONIA (Alphit-ònia). This genus of the buckthorn family RHAMNACEAE includes possibly twenty species of Australia, Polynesia, and Malaysia. Perhaps only one, *A. excelsa*, is cultivated in the United States. Called in Australia, bushman's red-ash, red-almond, and silver leaf, and a native of the open forest, it is a handsome, tall tree with a wide-spreading head. Favoring dryish areas, *A. excelsa* has alternate, ovate to lanceolate, leathery, toothless, leaves up to 6 inches long, dark glossy green above and white-hairy beneath. The tiny greenish-white flowers are in branched clusters. The globular fruits are about ½ inch in diameter. The name is from the Greek *alphiton*, pearl barley, and alludes to the appearance of the seeds.

Garden and Landscape Uses and Cultivation. This is an attractive species for planting in mild, relatively dry climates. It has been introduced into California. It favors sandy loamy soil, grows with fair rapidity, and is propagated by seed.

ALPINE. By definition alpines are plants that occur in the wild on mountains, only or chiefly above timberline. Some that with propriety may be included, in the far north inhabit lower altitudes that are there above the limits of tree growth. Gardeners often employ the term loosely to include mountain plants not or rarely found above timberline. Alpine should not be applied, as it sometimes is, to all low plants adaptable for rock gardens. Alpines are mostly restricted in their uses to rock gardens and alpine greenhouses and cold frames.

Alpine is used as an adjective in the common names of many plants, chiefly of mountain and boreal regions, among them alpine-azalea (*Loiseleuria procumbens*), alpine bearberry (*Arctostaphylos alpina*), alpine bells (*Cortusa matthiolii*), alpine catchfly (*Silene alpestris*), alpine currant (*Ribes alpinum*), and alpine-rose (*Rosa pendulina*). The name alpine-rose is sometimes applied to *Rhododendron ferrugineum* and *R. hirsutum*. The alpine wallflower is *Erysimum linifolium*.

ALPINE GARDEN. Rock gardens devoted exclusively or mainly to alpine plants are sometimes called alpine gardens. See Rock and Alpine Gardens.

ALPINE GREENHOUSE or Alpine House. Little known in America, but popular in

Europe, alpine houses are unheated greenhouses devoted to the cultivation of alpine and other small, choice rock garden plants. Unless cooled, they are impracticable in regions of high summer temperatures. Their chief function is to protect early-flowering plants from the inclemencies of weather and to bring the pleasure of abundant bloom well before there is much in the outdoor rock garden. Also, they make it possible to grow kinds of plants not hardy or for other reasons unsuitable for outdoors. Cold frames used for similar purposes are called alpine frames.

ALPINIA (Al-pínia)—Shell Flower or Shell-Ginger, Red-Ginger. A few cultivated ornamentals, popular for outdoor cultivation in the tropics and sometimes grown in greenhouses, are among the 250 species of *Alpinia* of the ginger family ZINGIBERACEAE. The group is native in the tropics of Asia and Polynesia. Its name commemorates Prosper Alpinus, an Italian botanist, who died in 1617. From its cousins, the gingers (*Zingiber*) and the nearly related *Amomum*, this group differs in having its blooms at the ends of tall leafy stems rather than directly from the rhizomes.

Alpinias are usually tall, leafy, stemmed herbaceous plants with lanceolate leaves, the bases of which sheath the stems, in two ranks. The flowers, in racemes or panicles, are usually developed from the ends of the stems, more rarely on branches lower down or on separate stalks directly from the rhizomes, which, in most kinds, have the smell and flavor of ginger. The asymmetrical blooms are curiously formed, having one large conspicuous, bilobed staminode (sterile stamen) that looks like a broad petal. The tubular calyx and corolla are three-parted. There is one fertile stamen. The flowers are partly concealed by floral bracts. The fruits are three-compartmented capsules.

The shell flower or shell-ginger (*A. zerumbet* syn. *A. speciosa*) is one of the most familiar and ornamental of tropical garden plants. Often misnamed *A. nutans*, in Ha-

Alpinia zerumbet

waii its blooms are much used for leis. A native of southeastern Asia, it has stems up to 12 feet tall bearing leaves that may be 2 feet long, 5 inches broad, and that are hairy only along their margins. The blooms are in pubescent, eventually nodding, racemes at the ends of gracefully arching stems. Each looks like a polished seashell. They are irregularly bell-shaped and have waxy white calyxes. The curved petal-like part, 1¼ to 2 inches long, is yellow finely veined with red or brown and like the bracts is tipped with purplish-red.

The red-ginger (*A. purpurata*), native to islands of the Pacific, is another kind popular in Hawaii and other parts of the tropics. Varying in height from 4 to 15 feet, it bears at the terminations of its stems 7-inch to 1-foot-long, usually erect, flower spikes that angle from the stems and have as their showy parts many purplish-red bracts. The 1-inch-long, narrow-lipped, white flowers are not conspicuous. An interesting feature of red-ginger, the seeds often germinate and produce baby plantlets among the bracts before they fall to the ground.

Alpinia purpurata

A handsome variegated-leaved kind, of unknown origin, is *A. sanderae* (syn. *A. vittata*). A common ornamental in the trop-

Alpinia sanderae

ics and grown in greenhouses elsewhere, this plant is sterile and its botanical identification is doubtful; it may be a variety of the Malayan *A. rafflesiana*. It attains a height of 6 feet or so and has leaves up to 8 inches long by up to 1 inch wide, striped obliquely from midrib to margins with white. Similar, but with yellowish variegation, is *A. tricolor.* Native to the Malay

Alpinia rafflesiana

peninsula, *A. rafflesiana* is up to 4½ feet tall. It has arching stems and narrow-elliptic leaves up to 2 feet long by 2 inches wide. The yellow to orange-yellow flowers veined or suffused with crimson have a lip about 1 inch long.

Less common alpinias include several worth cultivating. The small shell-ginger or orchid-ginger (*A. mutica* syn. *Catimbium muticum*) of southeastern Asia is 4 to 5 feet tall and has erect spikes of bloom, the flowers white with orange lips. Unlike those of *A. zerumbet*, the floral bracts of this kind soon drop off and most often the flowers open at one time. Its fruits are an added attraction. In long-persistent clusters they are globose, orange to red, and covered with a felt of hairs. Each is almost ¾ inch in diameter and contains brown seeds.

Garden and Landscape Uses. In the tropics alpinias are among the most useful of decorative herbaceous perennials. They form great leafy clumps of handsome foliage and have attractive flowers useful for cutting as well as garden embellishment. They are fine border plants and the taller ones make effective screens. They grow in sun or part-shade and prefer rich, moist soil. Located on highish ground close to the margin of a pool or a stream, these plants are especially effective. Alpinias are also fine plants for growing, either in ground beds or containers, in shaded, humid, tropical greenhouses; for this purpose the variegated-leaved kinds are especially suitable. When accommodated in containers they are usually lower than when afforded a free root run.

Cultivation. Provided with fertile, moist soil, a humid atmosphere, and high temperatures year round, alpinias thrive indoors or out. Depending upon climate and availability of moisture, they may be evergreen or may become dormant for a short period each year. Propagation is very easy by fresh seeds sown in sandy peaty soil in a temperature of 70°F or more, and by division of the clumps at the beginning of a new growing season. Greenhouse specimens should have a minimum winter night temperature of 60 to 65°F with a rise of ten to fifteen degrees permitted by day; at other seasons both night and day temperatures may with advantage be higher. Coarse, fertile soil and well-drained beds, tubs, or pots are necessary. Water is supplied copiously from spring to fall, more sparingly, but not in niggardly fashion, in winter. From spring to fall weekly applications of dilute liquid fertilizer are helpful to specimens that have filled their containers with healthy roots.

ALSEUOSMIA (Alseu-ósmia). The honeysuckle family CAPRIFOLIACEAE, so plentiful in the northern hemisphere and represented there by such well-known genera as *Abelia, Diervilla, Kolkwitzia, Lonicera, Sambucus, Symphoricarpos, Viburnum,* and *Weigela,* is represented in the native flora of New Zealand only by *Alseuosmia,* an endemic genus of possibly eight species that hybridize freely and are often difficult to identify. One is cultivated in West Coast gardens. The name is from the Greek *alsos,* a grove, and *euosme,* a pleasing fragrance, and alludes to the delightful scent.

Alseuosmias are evergreen shrubs with tufts of minute red hairs in the axils of the veins on the lower sides of the leaves. Their leaves are alternate or nearly opposite. Their drooping, tubular flowers are solitary or clustered in the leaf axils. They have four- or five-toothed calyxes, corollas with four or five spreading lobes, and four or five stamens. Their fruits are many-seeded red berries.

Indigenous to both islands of its homeland, *A. macrophylla* is 4 to 10 feet tall and has elliptic to oblongish leaves 3 to 7 inches in length by 1 inch to 2½ inches wide, sometimes with distantly-spaced, shallow teeth. Its crimson- to cream-colored flowers are solitary, in twos, or threes. They are 1½ inches long, about 1 inch wide, and are succeeded by crimson berries about ⅓ to ½ inch long.

Garden and Landscape Uses and Cultivation. Rare in cultivation, this shrub is adaptable only to areas of little or no frost, such as southern California. It succeeds in ordinary soil without special attention and is propagated by seeds and cuttings.

ALSINE. See Arenaria.

ALSOPHILA. See Cyathea.

ALSTONIA (Al-stònia)—Scholar Tree or Devil Tree. Native from India and Malaya to Australia, the trees and shrubs of this genus of the dogbane family APOCYNACEAE have leaves usually in whorls (circles) of three to eight, but sometimes in twos. There are fifty species. The name commemorates a former professor of botany at Edinburgh, Scotland, Dr. Charles Alston, who died in 1760.

Alstonias are evergreen or deciduous and have milky sap and undivided leaves. Their small, white, fragrant flowers, in terminal panicles, have corollas longer than their spreading, overlapping lobes (petals). The fruits consist of paired pods (follicles). The seeds are flat and hairy.

The scholar tree or devil tree (*Alstonia scholaris*), acquired the less ominous of these designations because its fine-grained wood was used as "slates" for school children and as blackboards. Writing on these was erased by scrubbing the surface with the sand-papery leaves of certain other plants or, alternatively, the wood was coated with pipe clay and impressions made on that. The name devil tree alludes to a belief held in India that this species is the abode of evil spirits. Native medicines are prepared from its bitter bark, and the bark of some other species.

Of pagoda-like outline because of its tiered, horizontal branches, *A. scholaris* is 40 feet tall or taller. Its narrowly-elliptic to narrowly-obovate leaves are 3 to 9 inches in length and one-third as wide as long. In circles of four to eight, they are dark green above and milky white on their undersides. The greenish-white flowers, in umbel-like clusters, are succeeded by very slender, pendulous fruits.

Another species, *A. macrophylla*, in its homelands attains heights of 100 feet or more, has short branches, and oblong-lanceolate or elliptic-lanceolate leaves, more pointed than those of the scholar tree, mostly in circles of three, and slightly paler beneath than on their upper sides. They are 6 inches to 1 foot long. The small white flowers, in terminal and axillary clusters, are followed by stringy clusters of seed pods.

Garden and Landscape Uses and Cultivation. These are interesting trees for general landscaping in frost-free or nearly frost-free climates such as those of southern Florida, southern California, and Hawaii. In moist soils they are evergreen, but they lose their leaves for part of each year in dry ones. They prefer fertile earth. Propagation is by seed.

ALSTROEMERIA (Alstroem-èria). All sixty species of *Alstroemeria* of the amaryllis family AMARYLLIDACEAE are South American. Their name honors Baron Alstroemer, who was a friend of the great Swedish botanist Linnaeus. He died in 1794. These are beautiful, summer-flowering herbaceous perennials not generally hardy north of Washington, D.C., although with protection *A. aurantiaca* survives in southern New England.

Unlike many plants of their family, alstroemerias are without bulbs or tuberous roots; instead, they have masses of fleshy, fibrous roots from which develop erect, leafy, slender stems, some of which are sterile and some of which bear terminal clusters of, or more rarely solitary, rather lily-like flowers. The clusters or umbels may be branched or not. The leaves are narrow and have short, twisted stalks. The blooms are more or less asymmetrical. They have six spreading petals (more correctly tepals) separated to their bases. There is no perianth tube. There are six down-pointing stamens, often unequal in length, and a style with a three-branched stigma. The fruits are capsules that contain spherical seeds.

Orange, yellow, or red flowers predominate in some kinds. The hardiest, *A. aurantiaca* is a robust native of Chile. It is about 3 feet tall and has many lanceolate, shortly-stalked leaves, bright green above, grayish on their undersides, and 3 to 4 inches long. Its showy flowers, in many-branched umbels, are about 1½ inches in length and are typically bright orange-yellow with their upper petals spotted and streaked with purplish-brown. The tips of the three outer, longer petals are green.

Alstroemeria aurantiaca

The stamens are conspicuously down-pointed. In *A. a. aurea* the blooms are yellow with thin lines of red on the upper petals. Variety *A. a. concolor* has plain yellow flowers.

Another Chilean, *A. haemantha*, 2½ to 3 feet tall, has numerous thin, lanceolate leaves, glaucous on their undersides and with a fringe of hairs at their margins. They are 3 to 4 inches long and die at about the time the flowers open. Usually up to a dozen blooms constitute each branched cluster. They are rather narrow, about 2 inches long, and have green-tipped, bright red outer petals and purplish spotted and streaked, reddish-yellow inner ones. The stamens are much shorter than the petals. With flowers ranging from red through pink to white in its horticultural varieties, *A. chilensis* is a sturdy kind 2 to 3 feet in height, with obovate to lanceolate, slightly-glaucous leaves minutely fringed with hairs. The flower clusters have five or six branches each with usually two blooms. Yellow lines mark the two upper inside petals, which are longer and narrower than the others. This sort, not well understood botanically, may represent variants of *A. pulchra*.

The Brazilian *A. pulchella* (syn. *A. psittacina*) is up to 3 feet high and has oblong to oblong-spatula-shaped leaves, those of the non-flowering stems stalked and of the flowering stems fewer and nearly stalkless. The four to six blooms of each cluster are about 1½ inches long and have dark red petals very unequal in size, tipped with green and spotted on their insides with brownish-purple. They are stalked.

Alstroemeria pulchella

Another Brazilian is *A. brasiliensis*. It attains a height of 2 to 4 feet and has lanceolate leaves, 3 to 4 inches long, on its sterile shoots, linear ones on its flowering stems. The reddish-purple blooms, 1½ inches long, are in five-branched umbels, each branch with one to three flowers. The inner petals are spotted with brown and green. Much more tropical, Brazilian *A. caryophyllea* has fragrant, red or red-and-white-striped, long-stalked, markedly two-lipped blooms. It is commonly not more than 1 foot to 1½ feet tall.

Dark red flowers spotted with brown and tipped with green, their upper petals longer than the lower, characterize the Brazilian *A. psittacina*. In clusters of four to six they top stems up to 3 feet tall, with lanceolate leaves up to 3 inches long. The plants grown as *A. brasiliensis* and *A. pulchella* may belong here.

Purple, lavender, pink, and white are the prevailing flower colors of some kinds. Here belongs the handsome Chilean *A. pelegrina*. This species, 1 foot to 2 feet in height, has erect, lanceolate leaves 2 to 3 inches long, and in garden varieties, numerous 2-inch-long lilac or rosy-lilac blooms in much-branched clusters. The inner petals are yellow spotted with purple at their bases, the outer ones blotched with purple-red. In the wild, plants of this species have fewer flowers than cultivated ones.

Alstroemeria pelegrina

The stamens point downward. Much variation in color is exhibited by this sort. In *A. p. alba* the blooms are white, in *A. p. rosea*, rose-pink. The white-flowered variety is sometimes called lily-of-the-Incas.

Another Chilean, **A. pulchra** (syn. *A. tricolor*), some forms of which are incorrectly named *A. chilensis*, is about 1½ feet in height, with linear-lanceolate leaves. The branches of its flower clusters each have two or three white to pink flowers, with broad outer petals tipped with green and the upper petal blotched with yellow, streaked and tipped with purple or red.

St. Martin's flower (*A. ligtu*) is Chilean. More robust than *A. pelegrina*, it is 1½ to

Alstroemeria ligtu

2 feet tall and has narrowly-linear, erect leaves 2 to 3 inches long. Its flower clusters have three to eight branches and twenty to thirty 1½-inch-long, long-stalked blooms. Their obovate outer petals are whitish, pale lavender, or reddish. The upper pair of inner petals are narrower, with their upper parts yellow striped with reddish-purple. The stamens are shorter than the petals.

Garden and Landscape Uses. When seen growing wild along roadsides and in fields of Chile and other parts of South America alstroemerias cannot fail to attract attention and admiration. In effect they rival our familiar daylilies (*Hemerocallis*). Unfortunately, they are much less tolerant of conditions in most parts of North America than are daylilies. They like neither severe winter cold nor blistering summer heat. Most give of their best only where summer heat is tempered and winters are comparatively mild. With a heavy winter covering *A. aurantiaca* may be wintered outdoors in sheltered places, such as at the base of a south wall, at least as far north as New York City, but it can scarcely be regarded there as a good, free-flowering perennial. The other kinds are less hardy. In favorable regions they are splendid flower border plants. They are also satisfactory for growing in pots or benches in greenhouses. Their flowers last for a long time when cut and are beautiful and decorative.

Cultivation. Although in hot climates alstroemerias may benefit from a little shade they are basically sun-lovers and need good light. They must have a well-drained soil. One of a sandy character is most agreeable, but it should not lack fertility. Mix in, before planting, peat moss, good compost, or leaf mold in generous amounts, and some bonemeal to assure success. Earth into which roots can descend deeply is most favorable. It is advisable to set out young pot-grown plants. Divisions resulting from the crude separation of old plants often fail to establish themselves or at best do so with exasperating slowness. The crowns of the plants may be set 6 to 8 inches deep and about 1 foot apart. Early fall is the recommended planting season.

If alstroemerias growing outdoors are doing well it is inadvisable to transplant them. A spring application of a complete garden fertilizer and a mulch of compost, coarse leaf mold, or peat moss at the beginning of summer encourages satisfactory growth. In dry weather liberal amounts of water are needed to keep the plants growing and to check any tendency for the stems and foliage to die prematurely. Unless seeds are needed for propagation faded flowers should be removed promptly. If this is not done seed development uses energy that could be better expended in building stronger roots to support the following year's bloom. Under no circum-

stances (except to a limited extent when cutting flowers) should stems or foliage be removed before they have died naturally. Non-flowering shoots should never be cut until then. To do so limits the plant's ability to build strength.

In areas where their winter hardiness is doubtful a heavy protective covering of leaves, litter, salt hay, branches of evergreens, or other insulation should be put over the plants after the ground has frozen to a depth of an inch or two. An alternative plan is to dig the plants up before winter, surround their roots with damp peat moss or sand, and keep them in a very cool, but frost-proof place until spring when they may be planted in the garden.

As greenhouse plants alstroemerias may be accommodated in large pots, tubs, or in beds or benches in loose, porous soil that contains an abundance of organic material. The receptacles or beds must be well drained. Repotting, or replanting, which should receive attention each year, is done after the roots have been shaken free of old earth, and the stronger separated from the thinner, weaker ones. After potting or planting the soil is well watered and the greenhouse is maintained with a night temperature of 45 to 50°F except for *A. caryophyllea* and *A. psittacina*, which prefer 55 to 60°F, and daytime temperatures, but a few degrees higher. Care must be taken not to keep the soil too moist at first, but it must never completely dry. As roots, stems and foliage develop more frequent applications will be needed, and after the containers are filled with roots occasional waterings with dilute liquid fertilizer are stimulating. After flowering has occurred every effort must be made to keep the foliage active as long as possible and no attempt made to dry the plants off until the natural dying of their leaves signal the approach of their dormant season. During the resting season the roots are left in the pots, which are stood in a cool shady place, and the soil is kept quite dry.

Propagation of alstroemerias is easily accomplished by seeds sown in sandy peaty soil in a temperature of about 60°F, and by careful division of the roots. Root divisions should be set individually in pots just big enough to accommodate them and be grown in those until thoroughly established, before being planted out.

ALTAMIRANOA. See Villadia.

ALTERNANTHERA (Altern-anthèra). The genus *Alternanthera* comprises possibly 200 species of the tropics and subtropics. A few are popular low foliage plants. They belong in the amaranth family AMARANTHACEAE and owe their name to the fact that in most species fertile anthers alternate with barren ones.

Alternantheras are mostly herbaceous perennials, with opposite, stalkless or stalked leaves varying in shape from linear to obovate and sometimes indefinitely toothed. The flowers, minute and chaffy and in terminal or axillary dense clusters, are without significant decorative appeal. The fruits are utricles.

Cultivated alternantheras are all referable to the group formerly named *Telanthera*, distinguished by having five fertile and five alternating sterile stamens joined to form a tube. The varieties are chiefly distinguished by the shapes and colors of their leaves.

Procumbent to erect and up to 1 foot tall or taller, the South American **A. ficoidea** is a bushy species, with long-pointed, broad-lanceolate to elliptic leaves 1 inch to 3 inches long, that are variously blotched and veined with brownish-red, carmine, and orange. The stalkless heads of white flowers are solitary or in twos or threes.

Varieties of *A. ficoidea* include *A. f. amoena*, which is rarely more than 4 to 8 inches tall and has lanceolate to elliptic leaves veined and splashed with red. Variants of this include *A. f. rosea-nana*, with rosy-pink leaves, and *A. f. sessilis*, the leaves of which have very short stalks. Generally taller than *A. f. amoena* and its variants, the subshrubby *A. f. bettzickiana* (syn. *Achyranthes bettzickiana*) has olive-green to red, narrow-spatula-shaped leaves that at first carry some hairs lying flat on their surfaces, but later are smooth. Its flower heads are without stalks, and are solitary or in twos or threes. Variants of this include *A. f. aurea-nana*, which has yellow leaves, and *A. f. brilliantissima*, with bright red leaves. Rather taller

Alternanthera ficoidea aurea-nana

than the others described here, *A. f. versicolor* branches freely and has short-stalked, obovate, crinkled leaves, tipped with short points. They are dark green, coppery, or red, with veinings of purplish-pink and are margined with pink and white.

Sometimes called indoor clover, a designation that alludes to the heads of flowers rather than the foliage, **A. dentata rubiginosa** is a red- to purple-leaved form of a normally green-leaved species that is na-

Alternanthera ficoidea brilliantissima

Alternanthera ficoidea versicolor

tive to the West Indies and Brazil. From the species it does not differ significantly except in the color of its foliage. Erect and bushy and 1 to 2 feet tall, this plant has richly-colored, glossy, pointed-ovate leaves up to 3½ inches long by 2½ inches wide. The white to greenish-white flower heads, on stalks 3 to 6 inches long, are about 1 inch long. The names *A. ramosissima* and *A. ramosissima versicolor* are often incorrectly applied to *A. dentata rubiginosa*.

Garden and Landscape Uses. The chief horticultural value of these plants is for formal summer bedding, especially that of the type called carpet bedding, but *A. dentata rubiginosa* can be employed less formally in summer beds and flower borders with excellent effect. In the tropics alternantheras are useful for permanent edgings, groundcovers, and similar purposes. They also are attractive pot plants for greenhouses and terrariums.

Cultivation. Full sun, well-drained soil not excessively moist, and high temperatures bring out the best in alternantheras. Given these, they grow with great facility. Cuttings, which root with remarkable ease and in a very short time, and division, afford the usual means of multiplication. In temperate regions the practice is to root cuttings in late summer or fall, overwinter

the plants in a greenhouse in a minimum temperature of 55 to 60°F, propagate from these plants during the winter, and grow their progeny on to be set outdoors when the weather is thoroughly settled and warm. It is usual to keep the plants clipped or sheared during the summer to maintain formality while they are in the outdoor garden.

ALTERNATE. This adjective is used to describe leaves, leaflets, or other plant parts disposed singly along a stem, midrib, or other axis and not opposite each other in pairs or greater numbers. Scattered is sometimes used to describe alternate leaves that spread irregularly in many directions rather than being in distinct ranks.

ALTERNATE HOST. Some organisms that damage plants live for parts of their lives, usually a portion of each year, on one kind of plant, the remainder on another, generally botanically unrelated kind. The infected or infested species are both obviously hosts to these organisms and in relation to each other are alternate hosts. Where alternation of hosts is an essential part of the life cycle of a disease or pest, control may be had by eliminating either host from an area sufficiently large to prevent the causative organism gaining access to the plants to be protected. Several rust diseases have life cycles that require two hosts. Examples involve wheat and barberry, white pine and juniper, and cabbage and wild mustard. Insects that favor alternate hosts include the Cooley spruce aphid (spruces and Douglas-fir), mealy plum aphid (plums and grasses or cat-tails), and woolly apple aphid (apples and related plants, and elms).

ALTHAEA (Al-thaèa)—Marsh-Mallow. As presented here this genus consists of a dozen species of the mallow family MALVACEAE. Kinds sometimes included that have the tube formed by the stamens five-angled instead of cylindrical, and very short-stalked flowers ordinarily more than 1½ inches in diameter and in spikelike racemes, are segregated in *Alcea*. There belong the common and fig-leaved hollyhocks. Deciduous shrubs and small trees previously included in *Althaea* and known as shrub-althea and rose-of-Sharon are varieties of *Hibiscus syriacus*.

The genus *Althaea*, inhabiting Europe and temperate western and central Asia, bears a name used by the ancients and derived from the Greek *altheo*, to cure, in reference to its supposed medicinal virtues. Its members are biennials or herbaceous perennials, with distinctly-stalked flowers in racemes or panicles. The blooms have false outer calyxes that differ from those of *Malva* in being of six to nine bracts instead of two or three, united at their bases. They have five petals that may be notched at their apexes, and many stamens, commonly hairy at their bases and united in a tube that surrounds the pistils.

The thick mucilaginous roots of the marsh-mallow are used in confectionary and medicine, and *A. cannabina* produces a useful fiber. To Dioscorides the marsh-mallow was known as Althaia, but he remarks that "some call it Ibiscus." He describes it well as having a roselike flower and a clammy root, white within, and he presents an easily recognizable illustration. Among many virtues the ancient Greek ascribes to it are being good for "wounds, ye Parotides, ye struma, Suppurations, enflamed duggs, ye griefs of ye seats, bruises, flatulent tumors, ye distentions of ye nerves." He further says that sodden with vinegar it "assuageth pains of ye teeth" and recommends a preparation of its seeds as being "good against ye stings of bees and of all small beasts," and as a preventer of "being hurt by poisonous beasts."

The marsh-mallow (*A. officinalis*) is a perennial inhabiting moist soils and coastal marshes through much of Europe and adjacent Asia. From 3 to 6 feet in height, it has triangular-ovate, often somewhat pleated, toothed leaves that may be lobed palmately (in hand-like fashion) up to half-

Althaea officinalis

Althaea officinalis

way to their bases. They are grayish with a dense covering of stellate (star-shaped) hairs. The blooms, 1 inch to 1½ inches in diameter, are pale lilac-pink to rose-pink, with purplish-red anthers. They are in clusters or, more rarely, solitary, in the leaf axils and at the ends of the branches. The fruits have stellate hairs. Kinds previously known as *A. kragujevacensis* and *A. taurinensis* belong in *A. officinalis*. Similar, but sparsely hairy and with the leaves deeply three- and five-cleft into linear-lanceolate to obovate lobes, *A. armeniaca* is another native of wet soils in central and southwest Asia and adjacent Europe. From southern and eastcentral Europe comes *A. cannabina*, a perennial up to 6 feet tall with stellate (starry) hairs. Its leaves are deeply palmately lobed, sometimes to their bases, and the lobes are sometimes again lobed or are toothed. The solitary or clustered flowers with pink petals up to 1 inch long or slightly longer, and purplish-red anthers, are occasionally solitary, but more often are in clusters of two or more on long, branched stalks from the leaf axils. Often they are in terminal panicles. The fruits are hairless.

Garden and Landscape Uses and Cultivation. Because their blooms are smaller and not so obviously in spikelike racemes these are generally less showy plants than cultivated species of the related genus *Alcea*. They may be accommodated in flower borders and used naturalistically in semiwild and informal plantings. The marsh-mallow is of interest for inclusion in collections of plants used by man. The species described grow in moist soils in full sun and are easily propagated by seed.

ALUM ROOT is *Heuchera*.

ALUMINUM PLANT is *Pilea cadierei*.

ALUMINUM SULFATE. This is used to acidify (lower the pH of) soils. Although it acts more rapidly than finely ground sulfur employed for the same purpose the latter is generally preferred. This, because aluminum sulfate used in excess makes the ground toxic to plants and determination of amounts safe to use calls for some special knowledge and experience. On sandy soils an application of ½ pound of aluminum sulfate to 10 square feet may lower the pH from 6 to 5, but up to seven times as much or more may be needed to accomplish the same result with a heavy clay soil. After the aluminum sulfate is thoroughly mixed with the soil, allow it to stand two weeks or more, during which soakings with rain or irrigation occur, before planting. For more information see Acid and Alkaline Soils.

ALYOGYNE (Alyo-gỳne). There are six species of *Alyogyne* of the mallow family MALVACEAE, natives of Australia. The name,

of no obvious application, is derived from the Greek *allo*, other or another, and *gyne*, female.

These plants are closely related to *Gossypium*, the genus to which cotton belongs. They differ chiefly in their seeds being only partially clothed with short hairs, instead of completely covered with much longer ones. From related *Hibiscus*, which they resemble, they differ in their flowers having styles thickened at their tops and grooved or lobed.

Shrubs or subshrubs, alyogynes have alternate, lobeless to deeply-lobed leaves. Solitary from the leaf axils the flowers have a false calyx or collar or up to twelve small bracts below the five-lobed calyx. There are five petals united briefly at their bases and in bud twisted spirally, many stamens joined below into a tube surrounding the pistil, and a style tipped with a five-lobed or five-branched stigma.

An attractive native of Western Australia, *A. hakeaefolia* (syn. *Cienfuegosia hakeaefolia*) is 3 to 9 feet tall. Except for a few stellate (star-shaped) hairs on its leaves and calyxes and hairs on the backs of its petals, it is hairless. It has linear, nearly cylindrical leaves not more than ¹⁄₂₅ inch wide, and sometimes pinnately- or three-lobed. The flowers have purple petals 1½ to 2½ inches long with a dark red-purple blotch at the base of each. The ovoid capsules contain many short-hairy seeds.

In Australia called desert-rose, a name it shares with *Hibiscus farragei*, the beautiful *A. huegelii* (syn. *Hibiscus huegelii*) is a

Alyogyne huegelii

dry-climate shrub 3 to 6 feet tall. It has thickish, rough-hairy leaves ¾ inch to 3 inches long, green on both surfaces, and cut to their middle or beyond into three or five lobes or segments. The flowers have broadly-wedge-shaped, lilac to reddish-purple, 2- to 3-inch-long petals dark-spotted toward their bases. They exceed the stamens in length.

Garden and Landscape Uses and Cultivation. Suitable for California and places with similar mild climates, the sorts described are attractive general purpose flowering shrubs having the same uses and needing the same care as hibiscuses. They succeed in ordinary soils in sun and are readily increased by seeds and cuttings.

ALYSSOIDES (Alys-sòides)—Bladderpod. This is the current designation for a group of plants once named *Vesicaria* and sometimes included in *Alyssum*. It belongs in the mustard family CRUCIFERAE and has much the aspect of its close relative, *Alyssum*, a circumstance recognized in its name, which comes from that of the more familiar genus and the Greek *oides*, resembling. From *Alyssum*, the four species of *Alyssoides* are readily distinguished by their bloated, bladder-like seed pods. For the decorative effect of these pods, as well as for their yellow flowers, one or two kinds of *Alyssoides* are occasionally cultivated.

Bladderpods are hardy herbaceous perennials that grow as natives on cliffs, rocks, and walls in central and southern Europe. They are more or less woody at their bases, much- or little-branched, and have two-branched or stellate (star-shaped) hairs. The flowers have four sepals, four petals that spread to form a cross, two short and four long stamens, and a long style. Each compartment of the seed pod contains four to eight, usually winged, seeds.

A variable species, **A. utriculata** (syn. *Vesicaria utriculata*), of the European Alps, has much the general appearance of *Auriniai saxatile*. It branches freely from the base and is about 1½ feet high. Its leaves are green, those of non-flowering branches stalked, in crowded rosettes, and spatula-shaped, those of the flowering branches lanceolate and stalkless. The flowers, ¾ inch wide, are succeeded by pods about ½ inch long. Differing in technical details only, *A. graeca* (syn. *Vesicaria graeca*) is a native of Italy and the Balkans.

Garden and Landscape Uses and Cultivation. Well-drained, not too fertile soil and full sun are favorable to these plants, which are attractive for the fronts of flower borders, rock gardens, dry walls, and such like places. They are easily raised from seeds, and from early summer cuttings planted in sand, vermiculite, or perlite in a humid atmosphere in a shaded greenhouse or cold frame, or under mist.

ALYSSUM (Alýs-sum)—Madwort. Botanically this is a difficult genus. Its limits are not easy to define and there has been considerable difference of opinion regarding recognition of species within it. Problems concerning cultivated kinds are complicated by their misidentification in gardens. Seeds and plants are very usually offered and grown under names not rightly theirs. Sometimes plants of other genera are named *Alyssum*. The familiar sweet-alyssum, fre-

quently called *A. maritimum*, is *Lobularia maritima*, the plant formerly named *A. saxatile* is *Aurinia saxatilis*. Other plants sometimes grown as *Alyssum* belong in *Alyssoides, Aurinia, Berteroa,* and *Schivereckia.*

Of the mustard family CRUCIFERAE, the genus *Alyssum* comprises 160 species. It ranges from the Mediterranean region to Siberia, with many of its species favoring dry, rocky, and stoney ground, and cliffs. Most are too weedy to attract gardeners, some are decidedly ornamental, a few are alpine gems. Not many are well known. Some that are not are worth seeking.

Alyssums include annuals, herbaceous perennials, and subshrubs with branched or star-shaped hairs. Their leaves are alternate, undivided, but sometimes toothed, often in loose rosettes. The flowers, in terminal racemes that lengthen as they pass into seed, have four sepals alternating with four petals arranged to form a cross, and six stamens, two shorter than the others. The fruits are flat, short-oblong to nearly circular pods, with one or two seeds in each of two compartments. The name comes from the Greek *a*, not, and *lyssa*, madness or rage, and alludes to ancient beliefs that infusions of these plants were specifics against rabies, and that they assuaged anger. The kinds discussed are all perennials.

Vigorous sprawling kinds include **A. diffusum**, which has trailing shoots, gray-green, pointed leaves, more or less lax flowering stems 4 to 10 inches long, and straw-colored flowers. It is indigenous from Spain to Italy. From it **A. montanum**, a kind

Alyssum montanum

that occurs through much of Europe, differs in having gray-white to nearly white, narrower and blunter leaves, and usually bright yellow blooms. It forms dense mats

2 to 10 inches in height. Variety *A. m. gmelinii*, of eastern Europe, is of denser, more erect habit, and has longer, rigid flower stems. Also with stiffer and more erect flower stems than *A. montanum* is **A. atlanticum** of southwestern Europe and North Africa. Its foliage is grayish or silvery, and its blooms are bigger than those of *A. montanum*. A variable species of eastern Europe, **A. repens** has erect stems, from woody bases, up to 2 feet high. The leaves are greenish, lanceolate to oblanceolate, and pointed. The orange-yellow flowers, in long racemes, are on stems beset with spreading hairs. **A. scardicum**, native to the Balkans, is a loose, green to gray-green, mat-forming plant up to 10 inches tall. Its upper leaves are linear, its basal ones elliptic-oblanceolate, its blooms bright yellow. Differing chiefly in having broader leaves and paler flowers, **A. wulfenianum** is indigenous to the European Alps.

Tall and erect, **A. borzaeanum** is native to southeastern Europe and western Turkey and **A. markgrafii** in the Balkans. Attaining a height of 6 inches to 1 foot or more, **A. borzaeanum** has grayish-white, obovate to rounded leaves, and bright yellow blooms in large clusters. About 1 foot tall, **A. markgrafii** has narrow-linear or spatula-shaped leaves and crowded clusters of bright yellow flowers. Erect **A. murale** (syn. *A. argenteum*), of southern Europe, is up to 1½ feet tall and has leaves greenish above and grayish beneath, the upper larger than the basal ones. The deep yellow flowers are in loose, rather lax, flattish racemes.

With usually sprawling, but sometimes erect stems **A. serpyllifolium** may be 3

Alyssum serpyllifolium

inches to 1 foot tall. It has many crowded, non-flowering rosettes of foliage on shoots that grow, as do the flowering stems, from a woody base. Its minute, folded, spatula-shaped leaves are silvery, the densely clustered flowers small and pale yellow. This is native to southwestern Europe and North Africa. Differing chiefly in having the upper surfaces of its leaves greenish and the lower silvery, and in its larger, deeper yellow flowers, *A. bertolonii* grows in Italy and the western Balkans. From the eastern Balkans and western Turkey, *A. stribrnyi* is woody at its base and attains a height of up to 10 inches, and 2 feet in width. Its stems and leaves are conspicuously silvery, its flowers large and orange-yellow. With few non-flowering shoots, *A. tortuosum* is 3 inches to 1¼ feet high or higher, and has twisted and often lax flower stems with grayish-green, oblanceolate to lanceolate leaves and broad, branched clusters of bright yellow flowers.

Dwarf alyssums, ordinarily up to 6 inches in height, include *A. alpestre,* a mounded plant with silvery, hoary leaves closely arranged on slender stems up to 4 inches tall, and pale yellow flowers profusely borne. It comes from the European alps. Two to 6 inches tall, *A. cuneifolium,* is mounded, and has the gray to almost white leaves of its flowerless shoots in rosettes, and its lax flowering stems long and with soft yellow blooms. It is native to the mountains of southern Europe. About the same size, *A. moellendorfianum,* of Yugoslavia, is very attractive. Its roundish leaves, on the non-flowering shoots in rosettes, are silvery or gray, and its yellow blooms are in crowded, short racemes. Prostrate and at its biggest 6 inches tall and as wide, *A. ovirense* has trailing stems, rounded to spatula-shaped, fleshy, green or gray-green leaves, on the sterile stems in rosettes, and bright yellow flowers.

A subshrub up to 2 feet tall forming rounded cushions, *A. spinosum* (syn. *Ptil-*

Alyssum spinosum

otrichum spinosum), a native of the Pyrenees, has much interlaced whitish branches and branched spines. Its leaves are silvery, those of the non-flowering shoots obovate-spatula-shaped, those of the flowering shoots linear-lanceolate. The small, white to purplish flowers borne freely in compact clusters are succeeded by flat, roundish seed pods. The blooms of *A. s. roseum* are pale pink or lilac. Similar, but looser and

without spines, is *A. lapeyrousianum* (syn. *Ptilotrichum lapeyrousianum*), of the Pyrenees. It has white flowers about twice as big as those of *A. spinosum,* and larger seed pods. It has silvery foliage and is up to 1¼ feet tall. Quite distinct and less hardy than the last two species described, *A. purpureum* (syn. *Ptilotrichum purpureum*) is a native of the Spanish Sierra Nevada. Forming compact cushions 1 inch to 4 inches in height, it has slender, silvery-white leaves and purple blooms. Its seed pods are oblongish and sharply-pointed.

Garden and Landscape Uses. All the alyssums described above, and all those ordinarily cultivated are perennials. Commonly they retain their foliage through the winter and are hardy in the north. They are generally reliable, easy-to-handle plants well adapted for rock gardens and dry walls and, the more vigorous growers, for the fronts of flower beds, edgings, and planting on banks, and as groundcovers.

Cultivation. Two requirements for the successful cultivation of alyssums are thoroughly well-drained soil and full sun. Excessive fertility is not desirable; it encourages lush growth at the expense of neatness of habit and profuse bloom. Soil largely mineral in content rather than one fat with organic matter gives the best results. The tiny alpine kinds are best accommodated in rock garden moraines. Planting is done in spring or early fall, the distance between plants varying from 6 inches to 1 foot or even more depending upon the growth habit of the kind. Routine care is not exacting. After blooming the plants should be sheared to promote neatness and compactness. Watering in times of drought to prevent the leaves wilting, but no more, is beneficial. In very cold climates a light covering of salt hay, branches of evergreens, or similar protection may be put in place after the ground has frozen to a depth of 1 inch to 2 inches and should be left until new spring growth is about to begin. At that time a light application of a slow-acting, complete fertilizer is helpful if the soil is rather poor.

Propagation is easy by seed. Cuttings, taken in early summer and planted in a bed of sand, vermiculite, or perlite, in a cold frame or cool greenhouse where the atmosphere is humid and shade from sun is provided, or inserted under mist, root readily.

ALYXIA (Alýx-ia). The genus *Alyxia* of the dogbane family APOCYNACEAE, consists of eighty species of evergreen woody shrubs, natives of tropical Asia, the Pacific Islands, Australia, and Madagascar. Its name is the native one of an Indian species. Alyxias have glossy leaves, opposite or in whorls (circles of three or more), and usually fragrant flowers each with a cylindrical corolla tube, often swollen above its middle or narrowed at its throat. There are usually

five spreading, twisted corolla lobes (petals) and as many stamens. There is one style. The fruits are fleshy berries.

The native maile (*A. olivaeformis*) is greatly esteemed in Hawaii. Its stems and foliage are used for leis and other decorative purposes. A straggling or climbing shrub with twining stems, it has sweet-scented bark and vanilla-scented, short-stalked, pointed-ovate leaves, 1 inch to 2 inches in length. The leaves are opposite or in whorls of three or four. The corollas of the tiny, yellowish flowers have tubes about ¹⁄₁₆ inch long and four or five short petals. They are in groups of three or four in the leaf axils. The fruits are fleshy, black, and consist of two or more single-seeded sections. They are ½ inch long or longer.

Two Australian species, *A. buxifolia* and *A. ruscifolia,* are suitable for outdoor planting in southern California and places with similar climates. A low, stiff shrub with opposite, ovate-oblong to nearly circular leaves up to 1 inch long, *A. buxifolia* has few-flowered terminal clusters of stalkless flowers each not much more than ¼ inch across. Its fruits are orange berries. A tall shrub, *A. ruscifolia* has leaves in whorls of three or four. They are narrow-lanceolate to broadly-ovate-elliptic. Its small white flowers are in terminal clusters.

Alyxia ruscifolia

Garden and Landscape Uses and Cultivation. The maile has good-looking foliage and is well worth growing as an ornamental evergreen in the humid tropics and in tropical greenhouses. It responds to fertile, well-drained soil kept always reasonably moist and, in greenhouses, to a minimum winter night temperature of 60°F. It is propagated by seeds, cuttings, and layering.

AMARACUS. Plants previously named *Amaracus* are included in *Origanum.*

AMARANTH is *Amaranthus.* Globe-amaranth is *Gomphrena globosa.*

AMARANTHACEAE — Amaranth Family. This family of dicotyledons comprises sixty-five genera, about 850 species of tropical, sub-tropical, and temperate regions. Most are annuals or herbaceous perennials, often of weedy aspect. A few are shrubby. They have opposite or alternate, undivided leaves and minute to small, unisexual or bisexual flowers associated with dry scales and sometimes massed in showy inflorescences. The blooms have a two- to five-parted perianth and one to five stamens. The fruits are technically achenes or utricles, or may be berry-like. Genera most familiar to gardeners include *Aerva*, *Alternanthera*, *Amaranthus*, *Celosia*, *Deeringia*, *Gomphrena*, *Iresine*, *Nototrichium*, and *Ptilotus*.

AMARANTHUS (Amarán-thus)—Love-Lies-Bleeding, Prince's Feather, Joseph's Coat. Only a few of the sixty vigorous and often coarse annuals that constitute *Amaranthus* of the amaranth family AMARANTHACEAE are important ornamentals. The name of the genus is from the Greek *amarantos*, unfading, in allusion to the lasting qualities of the flower parts. Amaranths are mostly natives of tropical, subtropical, and warm-temperate regions and occur in many parts of the world. Most are too weedy to be garden plants, but among those cultivated are such popular kinds as love-lies-bleeding, prince's feather, and Joseph's coat. As tampala, a green-leaved form of *A. tricolor* is grown for food, either cooked or for use as salad greens, and so, in the Orient and the tropics, are redroot (*A. retroflexus*) and *A. mangostanus*. The seeds of some, including *A. caudatus*, *A. grandiflorus*, and *A. retroflexus*, are used in various parts of the world as food.

Plants of this genus, which is related to *Celosia*, are erect or spreading and have alternate, stalked, lobeless leaves and minute flowers in dense, often spike-like, and in some kinds large and showy, clusters. The flowers are without petals, but have three to five persistent sepals, three chaffy bracts, and two to five stamens and two or three stigmas. The fruits are small and bladder-like, technically utricles.

Love-lies-bleeding or tassel flower (*A. caudatus*) is a variable species probably originally native to South America. From 3 to 6 feet tall, it has a stout, erect, branching stem and, typically, ovate, long-stemmed, green leaves, but cultivated varieties sometimes have blood red or reddish-purple foliage. The flowers are in very long, pendulous, leafless, tassel-like spikes and are normally red. Variety *A. c. albiflorus* has whitish flowers. The prince's feather (*A. hybridus erythrostachys*) usually has reddish-purple foliage. Its leaves are pointed-oblong-lanceolate and it has heavy flower panicles of many spikes, the center one much longer than the others. The flower clusters are arching or drooping, crimson

Amaranthus caudatus

or brownish-red. The species *A. hybridus* has green foliage and is of little or no ornamental value. Native to tropical America, it is widely naturalized in fields and waste places in North America.

The gaily-colored foliage plants that include the kind known as Joseph's coat are varieties of the very variable *A. tricolor*, a native of the tropics. They are erect, mostly freely-branched, 1 foot to 4 feet tall. Their leaves, or some of them in cultivated forms, are highly colored. Their flowers are red and are in small, spherical clusters in the leaf axils, or in the upper parts of the plant form narrow, panicle-like clusters. They are not showy. The variety called Joseph's coat (*A. tricolor splendens*) has leaves irregularly splashed with several colors including green, yellow, orange, carmine, crimson, and purple. Other horticultural varieties that have upper leaves of brilliant clear carmine-pinks and reds are offered under such names as 'Molten Fire' and 'Early Splendor'.

Garden Uses. For supplying brilliant foliage color through summer and fall no annuals excel the garden varieties of *A. tricolor*. This is especially true of those such as 'Molten Fire' that have terminal heads of strikingly colored leaves. Such kinds, as well as Joseph's coat, are invaluable for creating tropical and subtropical effects of

Amaranthus hybridus erythrostachys

rare splendor. They may be used to equally good purpose in porch and window boxes as in beds and borders, and they remain in their full glory until frost cuts them down. They need full sun and porous, moderately fertile soil. Kinds grown chiefly for their flowers, such as love-lies-bleeding and prince's feather, are almost as tropically exotic in appearance. They brinng a feeling of lushness and luxuriance to any planting of which they are a part and remain decorative for a long time. These flowers are useful for cutting and can be dried and used as "everlastings." To prepare them for this last use they are cut as soon as they are fully open, tied in small, loose bunches, and suspended upside down in a dry, airy place, out of direct sun, until they are quite dry.

Cultivation. Amaranths are tropicals. They make little growth until settled warm weather arrives, therefore, in the north, it is advantageous to sow the seeds, especially those of *A. tricolor* and its varieties, indoors some eight weeks before the weather is expected to be warm enough to transplant the young plants to their outdoor stations, which may be done about the time it is safe to set out tomatoes. Where longer growing seasons prevail than in the north outdoor sowing is entirely satisfactory, and this practice can be followed in the north, too, but the summer display is later than if the plants are given an early start. When grown indoors the seeds should be germinated in a temperature of 70°F and the plants grown in a 60°F minimum temperature. Until planting out time they may be carried in flats, with the plants spaced 3 inches apart, or individually in small pots. In the garden they may be spaced 1½ to 3 feet apart according to the vigor of the variety.

AMARCRINUM (Amar-crìnum). This hybrid genus of attractive bulb plants of the amaryllis family AMARYLLIDACEAE has also been named *Crindonna* and *Crinodonna*. All hybrids between *Crinum* and *Amaryllis* (not to be confused with plants popularly called amaryllises, which belong in the genus *Hippeastrum*) are now correctly identified as *Amarcrinum*, a name formed by combining parts of the generic names of the parents. By an interesting coincidence similar hybrids between *Amaryllis belladonna* and *Crinum moorei* were raised in the early part of the twentieth century in Italy and California. The Italian production, the first to be named, was in 1921 designated *Crinodonna corsii*, the American *Amarcrinum howardii*. Because the first of these combines a portion of the generic name of one plant with part of the specific epithet of another it is not botanically acceptable, and the generic name given the American plant is the correct one.

A beautiful ornamental not hardy in the north, *A. memoria-corsii* (syns. *A. howar-*

dii, Crinodonna corsii) forms clumps of long-necked bulbs 3 to 4 inches in diameter. Its evergreen, recurved leaves are strap-shaped, up to 2 feet long by 1½ to 3 inches wide. The umbels of three to twelve trumpet-shaped, lily-like, soft rose-pink blooms, 3 to 4 inches across, carried on stout stalks to heights of 2 or 3 feet, have short perianth tubes. Their stamens point downward.

Amarcrinum memoria-corsii

Garden and Landscape Uses. Flowering in late summer and fall, amarcrinums are effective for locating permanently outdoors in climates where little or no frost is experienced and for tubs and other large containers on patios, terraces, steps, and in similar locations. They are satisfactory in greenhouses and sunrooms.

Cultivation. Deep, rich, well-drained soil is required, with generous supplies of water from spring to fall and much less in winter. In summer, container specimens in the north may be stood outdoors in light shade, but they must be brought indoors before frost. Winter temperatures of about 45 to 50°F at night with a few degrees increase by day are satisfactory. Applications of dilute liquid fertilizer made at weekly intervals from spring to fall are of great benefit to well-rooted container specimens. Propagation is by removing offset bulbs in spring.

AMARINE (Amarìn-e). The name of this bigeneric hybrid group is derived from the names of its two parent genera *Amaryllis* and *Nerine*, both of the amaryllis family AMARYLLIDACEAE. The typical kind is *Amarine tubergenii* raised by C. G. Van Tubergen of Holland from crosses made about 1940 and exhibited in London, England, in 1967. Its parents are *Nerine bowdenii* and *Amaryllis belladonna*, both natives of South Africa. Similar hybrids or presumed hy-

brids were raised in England some thirty-five years earlier and named *Nerine fletcheri*. The hybrid has also been known, but neither name was botanically validated, as *Nerinodonna* and *Brunserine*. Amarines have flowers intermediate between those of the parents. In size and shape they resemble those of the belladonna-lily (*Amaryllis belladonna*), but they are slenderer and have narrower and more recurved petals with slightly wavy margins. The blooms range from brilliant magenta-pink to soft pink and deep carmine. The leaves are larger than those of *Nerine bowdenii*, resembling those of *Amaryllis belladonna*, but unlike those of the latter, and like those of the former, they persist through the flowering season.

Garden Uses and Cultivation. This bigeneric hybrid should prove a useful and interesting addition to the many fine tender bulbs cultivated for ornamental blooms. No extensive experience with growing them is yet recorded, but it may confidently be supposed that they will respond to the care that suits nerines. The best time for planting the bulbs is July or early August, when they are dormant.

AMARYGIA (Amarý-gia). This is the name of hybrids between *Amaryllis* and *Brunsvigia*. It replaces *Brunsdonna*, which is botanically unacceptable because it combines part of the generic name of one parent with part of the specific one of another. The newer name is a combination of parts of the generic names of both parents. Successful crosses between these genera have been made on several occasions, sometimes with one and sometimes with the other as the female parent. Generally the most successful matings have been those in which *Amaryllis* was the seed parent. Amarygias are intermediate between their parents.

Deep rose-pink flowers usually suffused with carmine, but varying to some extent as to color in different seedling strains are typical of **A. parkeri** (syns. *Amaryllis parkeri, Brunsdonna parkeri*). The violet-pink-flowered sort raised in Holland named *A. thunbergii* probably belongs here.

Similar to *A. parkeri*, but its flowers shorter and with broader petals, **A. bidwellii** is sometimes grown as *A. multiflora*. Variety *A. b. alba* (syn. *A. multiflora alba*) has pure white, fragrant flowers with wavy-edged petals and chartreuse throats. It was raised in Australia.

Garden and Landscape Uses and Cultivation. These are as for the parent genera *Amaryllis* and *Brunsvigia*, both of the amaryllis family AMARYLLIDACEAE.

AMARYLLIDACEAE — Amaryllis Family. One of the most horticulturally important families of monocotyledons, this comprises eighty-five genera, approximately 1,100 species. Widely distributed, particu-

Amarygia bidwellii alba

larly in the tropics and subtropics, amaryllids, as members of this family are called, are bulb plants or have rhizomes and mostly fleshy roots. Some are evergreen, most are deciduous, many that are natives of arid lands produce their leaves after seasonal rains. Frequently showy, the blooms are generally solitary or in umbels or heads atop leafless stalks. Symmetrical or asymmetrical, they have six tepals (usually called petals), six stamens, an inferior ovary, and one style. Sometimes, as in *Eucharis* and *Narcissus*, there is a center crown or corona. The fruits are capsules or berries.

This family contains a number of important drug and fiber plants, but unlike the lily family, none of considerable importance as foods. It is rich in showy ornamentals. Among cultivated amaryllids are *Agave, Alstroemeria, Amarcrinum, Amarine, Amarygia, Amaryllis, Ammocharis, Anigozanthos, Beschorneria, Bomarea, Boophone, Brunsvigia, Calostemma, Chlidanthus, Clivia, Crinum, Curculigo, Cyanella, Cybistetes, Cyrtanthus, Doryanthes, Eucharis, Eucrosia, Eurycles, Eustephia, Furcraea, Galanthus, Habranthus, Haemanthus, Hippeastrum, Hyline, Hymenocallis, Hypoxis, Ixiolirion, Leptochiton, Leucojum, Lycoris, Manfreda, Narcissus, Nerine, Pamianthe, Pancratium, Paramongaia, Petronymphe, Phaedranassa, Phycella, Polianthes, Rhodohypoxis, Sprekelia, Stenomesson, Tecophilaea, Urceolina, Vagaria, Vallota, Worsleya,* and *Zephyranthes.*

AMARYLLIS (Amarýll-is)—Belladonna-Lily. For long the name *Amaryllis*, has been a botanical football. At one time or another it has been applied to bulb plants now included in several genera. For example, the plant often called *A. hallii* is *Lycoris squamigera*. In recent years much controversy, largely expressed in wordy battles in technical journals, has raged as to whether the name *Amaryllis* correctly belongs to a single South African species, that some prefer to call *Callicore rosea,* or to the group of South American plants for which amaryllis is used as a common name and which many botanists call *Hippeastrum.* The former view seems to prevail and is followed here. For information about the beautiful red-, pink-, and white-flowered amaryllises commonly grown as pot plants, chiefly for winter and spring blooming, and outdoors in the deep south, consult Hippeastrum. The name amaryllis is a feminine name used by early Greek authors.

As treated here, *Amaryllis* consists of one variable species, the belladonna-lily (***Amaryllis belladonna***), of South Africa. It belongs in the amaryllis family AMARYLLI-DACEAE and has egg-shaped, fibrous-coated bulbs 2 to 4 inches in diameter, and deciduous, dull green foliage that develops in late summer after the flowers. Its leaves are strap-shaped and 1½ to 2½ feet long. The lily-like flowers are fragrant, up to 3½ inches long, and few together in umbels (clusters) atop solid stems 1½ to 2 feet tall or even taller. The blooms have short tubes and are slightly asymmetrically funnel-shaped. There are six wavy perianth lobes (petals) that flare at their ends and range in color from deep purplish-pink to white, six stamens, and a slightly-three-lobed stigma. The fruits are capsules containing nearly spherical fleshy seeds. From *Hippeastrum* the belladonna-lily differs in having solid flower stems and globose rather than flat seeds. Varieties varying in the size and color of their blooms have identifying names such as *A. b. blanda,* with large white blooms that become tinged with pink as they age, *A. b. rosea,* with pink flowers, and *A. b. maxima,* with large pink flowers. As a parent, *A. belladonna* has been crossed with *Brunsvigia josephinae* to produce the bigeneric hybrid *Amarygia,* and with *Crinum moorei* to give the bigeneric *Amarcrinum* (syn. *Crinodonna*).

Garden and Landscape Uses. The belladonna-lily is attractive for planting in beds and borders where winters are moderately mild. At The New York Botanical Garden it survived for several years against the foot of a south-facing wall and bloomed, with the protection of a heavy winter covering of salt hay, but it certainly cannot be counted as hardy so far north. Washington, D.C. represents more normally its northern limit of hardiness. Its flowers are excellent for cutting and last well in water.

Cultivation. The bulbs are planted in June or July before their blooms or leaves develop. They should be set with their apexes 4 to 6 inches beneath the surface, in a well-drained location where there is a depth of 9 inches to 1 foot of nourishing, porous soil beneath them. Once planted, it is better not to disturb the bulbs unless quite necessary for the purpose of propagation or other good reason. An annual application of a complete garden fertilizer of rather low nitrogen content, made about midsummer, promotes growth; the excessive use of nitrogen can be harmful. Propagation is simply accomplished by offsets, bulb-cuttings, and seeds.

Belladonna-lilies can be successfully grown in containers, large pots, or tubs. The best results are had when three bulbs or more occupy a receptacle. Good drainage and rich soil are necessary and, during winter, a frost-free, light location such as a cool greenhouse where the minimum night temperature is 40 to 50°F. Repotting is necessary at intervals of several years only. From the time in summer when new growth begins until the foliage dies naturally frequent applications of dilute liquid fertilizer should be given to specimens that have occupied their pots or tubs for a year or more.

AMARYLLIS, BLUE-. The plant known by this name is *Worsleya rayneri.*

AMASONIA (Amas-ònia). Eight species of subshrubs of the vervain family VERBENA-CEAE constitute *Amasonia.* They are natives of tropical South America and Trinidad. The name probably commemorates George Anson, a famous traveler in America, who died in 1762, and not, as is often stated, some unknown traveler in America named Thomas Amason.

Amasonias have alternate, undivided, usually toothed leaves, the upper ones small. The yellow flowers are in clusters, racemes, or panicles. They have colored, bell-shaped, five-cleft calyxes and tubular, more or less two-lipped, five-lobed corollas, the lobes spreading or turned back, and short. There are two pairs of stamens, and a style with a two-lobed stigma. The fruits are drupelike (structured like plums).

Native to Guiana, *A. calycina* (syn. *A. punicea*) is upright, sometimes slightly branched, and has irregularly-toothed, narrow, oblong-lanceolate to elliptic-lanceolate leaves up to 1 foot long. The flower spikes, clothed with red-purple hairs, have pale yellow or cream blooms. They come from the axils of showy, red bracts. The latter give to the spikes much the appearance of those of the scarlet sage (*Salvia splendens*).

Garden and Landscape Uses and Cultivation. The species described is of use as an outdoor ornamental in the humid tropics and warm subtropics, and may occasionally be grown in greenhouses. It grows without difficulty in fertile, well-drained soil. In greenhouses a winter night temperature of 60 to 65°F is satisfactory, with a five to fifteen degree rise by day allowed. A humid atmosphere, and good light, with

Amaryllis belladonna

shade from strong sun are needed. Water to keep the roots comfortably moist, but not sodden. The plants are pruned to shape and repotted in spring. Propagation is by cuttings and seeds.

AMATEUR GARDENER. The distinction between an amateur and a professional or commercial gardener is not always clear. In general it is based on motivation. If profit is the chief or an important reason for horticultural effort the practitioner is not an amateur. Amateurs garden as a hobby because of their interest in the activity, for pleasure, and healthful exercise.

The question as to who is and who is not an amateur sometimes arises when the acceptance of entries in restricted classes at flower shows is under consideration. Perhaps the aspiring entrant in an amateur class sells a few plants from time to time or undertakes an occasional landscape commission for a fee. Do such activities label him or her professional? Rational interpretation suggests they do not. Only if engagement in such activities is substantial and fairly continuous should amateur status be denied. The decision must be that of the flower show committee or the exhibition committee. A question is sometimes raised when the exhibitor, an amateur, employs the services of a professional gardener, perhaps on a full-time basis. Good sense seems then to dictate that if the employee has substantial training and experience as a gardener and is employed for an appreciable part of his time the entries should be in professional classes, but this rule should certainly not preclude an amateur from making use of hired labor of a less skilled kind than one would generally term professional. Again, the interpretation, which should be made as clear as possible in the schedule of the show, must be that of the flower show committee.

AMATUNGULA is *Carissa grandiflora*.

AMAZON-LILY is *Eucharis grandiflora*.

AMBARELLA is *Spondias cytherea*.

AMBERBOA (Amber-bòa). Closely allied to *Centaurea* and sometimes known as *Volutaria* and *Volutarella*, the genus *Amberboa*, of the Mediterranean region, contains two annuals occasionally cultivated in flower gardens. The name of the genus, which belongs in the daisy family COMPOSITAE, is derived from a Turkish name for the sweet sultan (*Centaurea moschata*).

Amberboas have alternate, pinnate or deeply-pinnately-cut leaves, and purple, blue, or white heads of all tubular florets the outer ones of which are large, sterile, and petal-like. They are useful as cut flowers as well as for the embellishment of flower beds and borders. The cultivated kinds are *A. maroccana* with white blooms and *A. muricata* with pink or purple ones. The former is a native of Morocco, the latter of Morocco and Spain. Growing to a height of 2½ feet or more, *A. maroccana* has rather narrow, often rather deeply-toothed or lobed, narrow-pointed leaves, and dense flower heads up to ½ inch long, and in panicles. Normally not exceeding 2 feet in height, *A. muricata* has lanceolate leaves and faintly fragrant heads of flowers carried high above its foliage. The slender, spreading ray florets give a starry appearance to the blooms, which are up to 2 inches in diameter. The pink-flowered phase, sometimes called *A. m. rosea*, is the more attractive.

Cultivation. Seeds may be sown in early spring outdoors where the plants are to bloom and the seedlings thinned, or they may be sown indoors about eight weeks before plants are to be set in the garden, which may be done as soon as the weather is warm and settled. In either case they should be given a sunny location and ordinary, well-drained garden soil, and the plants should be spaced about 9 inches apart. A temperature of 55 to 60°F is appropriate for starting seeds indoors, and the seedlings, spaced 2 inches apart in flats, are grown in full sun in a greenhouse in a night temperature of 50°F and five or ten degrees more by day. These plants bloom for a long period in summer.

AMBURANA (Ambur-àna). One species of this genus of the pea family LEGUMINOSAE was distributed by the Fairchild Tropical Garden, Miami, Florida, in 1971 for trial. The genus, of two or three species of trees, is endemic to tropical South America. In its homeland it provides useful lumber and oils used in perfumery and medicine. The name is derived from a native one of South America.

Amburanas have pinnate leaves, without terminal leaflets, of eleven to fifteen alternate leaflets. They have racemes of yellowish-white, pea-shaped flowers with tubular, five-toothed calyxes and, remarkable for the family, a single petal. The petal is broadly-heart-shaped. There are ten free stamens, and a short style. The fruits are one-seeded pods.

Described as a large, drought-resistant tree, **Amburana caerensis** is expected to attain a height of 35 or 40 feet in Florida. Its leaves have leaflets 2½ inches long by 1 inch wide. The blooms come in spring. Little is known about the requirements of this species in cultivation, but it is expected to require a sunny location and well-drained soil. Propagation is by seed.

AMELANCHIER (Amelán-chier) — Shadblow, Shad Bush, June Berry, Saskatoon, Service Berry. Except for one species endemic to Europe and another to Asia all amelanchiers are native Americans. There are about twenty species, but the group is taxonomically perplexing and botanists are by no means agreed as to the proper disposition of its components. There are many hybrids. Belonging in the rose family ROSACEAE, the genus is most closely related to apples, mountain-ashes, pears, and quince. It has been hybridized with the first two. The name is derived from a provincial French vernacular one, *amelancier*, for the European kind.

Amelanchiers are thornless, deciduous shrubs and small trees. They have alternate, undivided, toothed, oblong to roundish leaves, and flowers most commonly in short, leafy racemes of eight to fourteen. Rarely they are solitary or in twos or threes. The blooms, which appear in early spring, either with or before the foliage, are white or creamy-white. Each has a five-parted, bell-shaped, persistent calyx, five narrow petals, ten to twenty short stamens, and usually five, rarely two or three, styles. The fruits are fleshy, berry-like, and usually dark blue to black. Rarely they are pink or cream. They vary in length from less to somewhat more than ½ inch. Technically they are pomes, that is they are structured like the fruits of apples, pears, and mountain-ashes. They ripen in summer and are eagerly eaten by many kinds of birds.

Most kinds are palatable to humans, and especially in the prairie states and adjacent Canada, they formed a welcome addition to the diets of Indians, early travelers, and settlers. They were mixed with buffalo flesh and fat to make pemmican. The Indian name of the fruit was mis-sask-qua-too-min, changed by white men to saskatoon, and *A. alnifolia* is still known as saskatoon. The Canadian city Saskatoon received its name because of the abundance of this fruit nearby. Interest in the saskatoon as a cultivated crop is increasing, and its fruits are used for pies, jellies, and wines.

The finest flowered ornamental is the natural hybrid *A. grandiflora*. Its parents are believed to be *A. laevis* and either *A. arborea* or *A. canadensis*. Up to 25 feet tall

Amelanchier grandiflora

and hardy as far north as southern Canada, it has spreading branches and pendulous racemes of pure white blooms about 1 inch across. Its foliage when young is purplish and in fall assumes attractive hues of yellow and orange. The edible fruits are purple-black. Variety *A. g. rubescens* has pink-tinged blooms and purple-pink flower buds.

A desirable ornamental species, **A. laevis** attains a maximum height of 45 feet,

Amelanchier laevis (fruits)

but often does not exceed the dimensions of a tall shrub. Its native range extends from Newfoundland to Minnesota, Georgia, Alabama, Iowa, and Indiana. It has spreading branches and sharply-toothed, elliptic to ovate, short-pointed leaves up to 3 inches long. They are hairless or almost so, and when they first unfold they are purplish. In loose, pendulous racemes, the flowers are fully open when the leaves are about half grown. The narrow petals are ½ to ¾ inch long, the fruits purple-red to black. From the last **A. arborea** differs in having leaves that when young are hairy on their undersides, and flowers open well before the leaves are half grown. It is a shrub or tree up to 30 feet in height with spreading branches, and finely toothed, oblong-obovate leaves. Its flowers, in drooping racemes, have narrow petals about ½ inch long. The fruits are dark red-purple. This species ranges from Maine to Minnesota, Florida, Louisiana, and Oklahoma.

An alder-like, clump-forming shrub or small tree that mostly inhabits wet woods and swamps from Newfoundland to Mississippi, **A. canadensis** attains a maximum height of about 25 feet. It has elliptic to elliptic-oblong leaves up to 3 inches in length that are toothed, often obscurely. When young they are densely-white-hairy beneath. They are hairy also on their upper surfaces. The flowers, in short, erect, densely-hairy racemes, appear with the leaves and have petals about ⅓ inch long.

Amelanchier canadensis

Amelanchier canadensis (flowers)

Amelanchier canadensis (fruits)

They are succeeded by dark purple to black fruits.

Native from Alaska to California and eastward to Michigan, **A. florida** is an extremely hardy shrub 4 to 15 feet tall, with erect, slender branches and elliptic to elliptic-oblong leaves 1 inch to 2 inches in length, coarsely-toothed near their tips, and when young more or less hairy, especially beneath, but hairless later. They become rich yellow in fall. The flowers,

with petals ½ inch long or longer, are in erect racemes 1½ to 3 inches long. The fruits are purplish-black.

The saskatoon (**A. alnifolia**) is one of the most variable species. Growing naturally over an extensive region of the prairies of the northern United States and Canada, it merges in the east with *A. canadensis* and in the west with *A. florida*. It varies in height from 2½ to 25 feet and is upright-spreading to nearly columnar. Its blunt leaves are densely-pubescent beneath when young. The creamy-white flowers, in short, erect spikes of up to fourteen, open before the leaves come and are very numerous. The fruits, sometimes ⅝ inch across, are usually purple-black, but on individual bushes may be pink or cream. Such maverick bushes are self-sterile, they produce fruit only if purple-fruited individuals are nearby to pollinate them. Of this species, several horticultural varieties with superior fruits have been named and at least one, *A. a.* 'Altaglow', for its merits as an ornamental. This is a columnar tree up to 20 feet tall with cream fruits, and foliage that in fall changes to rich shades of purple, red, reddish-brown, and yellow.

Another very variable and hardy species, **A. sanguinea** extends over a wide territory from Quebec to Michigan, Minnesota, Iowa, and New York, and in the mountains of North Carolina. Several botanical varieties have been described in-

Amelanchier sanguinea

Amelanchier sanguinea (flowers)

cluding *A. s. grandiflora*, from central New York, which must not be confused with the hybrid *A. grandiflora*. A straggly, usually clump-forming shrub up to 10 feet tall, *A. sanguinea* has oblong to rounded, toothed leaves up to 3 inches long, at first hairy, later hairless on their undersides. Its comparatively long-stalked flowers, in loose racemes, open when the leaves are half developed. In variety *A. s. grandiflora*, the petals are from less than ½ to sometimes more than ¾ inch long.

A low-growing, colony-forming species, *A. stolonifera* is from 6 inches to 4½ feet tall and spreads by suckers. At flowering time its leaves are half grown and densely-white-hairy on their under surfaces. Later they lose the hairs. They are broad-elliptic to roundish-oblong, 1 inch to 2 inches long, and toothed in their upper parts. The flowers are in dense, erect racemes ¾ inch to 1½ inches long. They have petals about ⅓ inch long. The juicy fruits are purple-black. This species inhabits dryish soils from Newfoundland to Ontario, Minnesota, Michigan, and Virginia.

Exotic amelanchiers, not natives of North America, include the service berry or snowy-mespilis (*A. ovalis* syn. *A. vulgaris*) of Europe and *A. asiatica* of Japan and Korea. A variety of the latter, *A. a. sinica* comes from China. A distinctive characteristic of the European service berry (*A. ovalis*) is that the five styles of its flowers are not joined at their bases, as are those of the other kinds described, and are not longer than the calyx tube. Hardy through New England, this upright or spreading, rather stiff-branched shrub is 1½ to 8 feet tall, and has broad-elliptic to obovate, toothed leaves 1 inch to nearly 2 inches long. When young they are densely-white-hairy beneath. The flowers are few together in hairy, erect racemes. Often they are 1½ inches in diameter. The fruits, at first red, ripen to blue-black. The Asian species (*A. asiatica*) and its variety, distinguished by having smaller leaves and being less hairy, are similar to *A. canadensis*, but have blooms with ovaries with very woolly tops. Their leaves are ovate to elliptic-oblong and toothed, those of the species all along the margins, those of the variety usually above their middles only. The flowers are in pendulous racemes. The fruits are blue-black. This species is hardy in New England.

Garden and Landscape Uses. Amelanchiers are pleasant, non-assertive trees and shrubs especially well adapted for informal and naturalized plantings. They possess an airy grace and meld with other woody plants without discordance. They are quite lovely in bloom, but unfortunately, their displays are brief, for the flowers last for but a very few days. Their fruits attract birds, and in fall the foliage of most kinds colors well. Although amelanchiers cannot compete with flowering cherries or crab

apples in the richness of their floral offerings they are surely worthy of representation in many gardens and as a group are extremely hardy. They are especially suitable for fringing woodlands, but also may be used effectively as free-standing specimens.

Cultivation. Amelanchiers are among the easiest of woody plants to grow. They need very little routine attention beyond cutting out any dead, crowded, and weak shoots. This is best done in late winter. A mulch maintained around them is advantageous, but by no means necessary. Propagation is by summer cuttings under mist, hardwood cuttings taken in fall, root cuttings, layering, and in some cases by suckers, in addition to seeds. The seeds should be freed from their surrounding pulp and sown in a cold frame or outdoor seed bed immediately they are ripe, or be mixed with damp peat moss and stored for three to four months in a temperature of about 38°F and then be sown in flats in a cool greenhouse.

AMELASORBUS (Amela-sórbus). This, a bigeneric hybrid between *Amelanchier florida* and *Sorbus scopulina*, derives its name from those of its parent genera.

A robust shrub, *Amelasorbus jackii* has elliptic leaves 1½ to 2¼ or rarely up to 4 inches long, deeply-lobed or divided into leaflets below their middle and coarsely-toothed above. At first they are pubescent, but they soon become hairless. The flowers, intermediate between those of the parents, are in panicled clusters up to 2 inches long, have oblong petals ⅓ inch long, and usually five styles. The dark red fruits, up to ⅓ inch in diameter, have a slight bluish, waxy coating.

Garden Uses and Cultivation. This plant is grown as a botanical or horticultural curiosity. It responds to the same treatment as its parents and is hardy in southern New England.

AMELLUS (Amél-lus). The genus *Amellus* consists of about fifteen species of South African annuals and herbaceous perennials of the daisy family COMPOSITAE. Its name is one used by Virgil for a plant that grew by the river Mella.

The sorts of this genus have opposite lower leaves, alternate upper ones. Their solitary, stalked, daisy-like flower heads have bisexual disk florets, fertile, female ray florets. The fruits are seedlike achenes.

The annual *A. annuus* (syn. *A. strigosus willdenovii*) is prostrate or diffuse, has hairy, oblongish leaves up to 2 inches long, usually with a single tooth on each side, and solitary flower heads borne in great profusion. The heads, about 1¼ inches across and with yellow centers and blue- or violet-colored rays, expand fully only in warm sunny weather. At other times the rays are rolled under.

A freely-branched subshrub up to 1½ feet tall, *A. asteroides* (syn. *A. lychnitis*) has linear to oblanceolate, toothless leaves up to 1½ inches long and blue or less commonly white flower heads almost or quite ½ inch in diameter.

The annual described is suitable for the fronts of flower beds and similar places. It succeeds where summers are relatively cool in sandy, well-drained soil in full sun and may be raised from seeds sown in early spring outdoors where the plants are to bloom, or indoors earlier. Outdoors, the seedlings are thinned to about 4 inches apart, and the same spacing is satisfactory for plants set out from indoor sowings, which may be done as soon in spring as the weather is warm and settled. Sow indoors in a temperature of 60 to 65°F about eight weeks before planting out time. Transplant the seedlings 2 inches apart in flats and grow them in a sunny greenhouse in a night temperature of 50°F with a daytime rise of five to ten degrees. Summer care is minimal. Unobtrusive staking may be necessary. After the first flush of flowers is over cut the plants back lightly to encourage second blooming. The flowers are not useful for cutting.

The perennial described is suitable for rock gardens and the fronts of shrub borders in mild, frost-free or nearly frost-free climates. It prospers in well-drained soil of ordinary fertility in sunny locations. Propagation is by seeds and by cuttings of semifirm shoots.

AMERICAN. The word American forms part of the common names of these plants: American-aloe (*Agave*), American columbo (*Frasera carolinensis*), American-cowslip (*Dodecatheon*), American-ipecac (*Gillenia stipulata*), American-pennyroyal (*Hedeoma pulegioides*), American-spikenard (*Aralia racemosa*), and American wormseed (*Chenopodium ambrosioides*).

AMETHYSTEA (Amethýs-tea). One fragrant-foliaged annual, native from Persia to Manchuria, is the only species of this genus of the mint family LABIATAE. Its name is derived from the Greek, *amethystos*, amethyst, from the color of the blooms of *Amethystea caerulea*. An erect, hairless, slender-stemmed plant about 2 feet tall with purplish stems, and opposite leaves each of three ovate-lanceolate, coarsely-toothed leaflets up to 3 inches long, this has tiny sky-blue flowers in dense, terminal or axillary clusters; their styles are longer than their stamens. The fruits are of four small seedlike nutlets.

Garden Uses and Cultivation. This quite charming plant may be grown in flower beds and borders, and in pots for late winter or spring blooming in greenhouses. It succeeds outdoors in any ordinary, well-drained garden soil in sunny locations, and in greenhouses in a night temperature of about 50°F with a few degrees increase permitted during the day. For greenhouse decoration seeds should be sown in September or October. Three plants in a 6-inch pot make a satisfactory display. Outdoors, seeds are sown in early spring and covered up to a depth of ¼ inch. The young plants are thinned to 6 inches apart. No care is required other than that necessary to keep down weeds and, if the weather is very dry, watering. Blooming begins in twelve to fourteen weeks from seed sowing.

AMHERSTIA (Am-hérstia). Often proclaimed the queen of flowering tropical trees, and surely one of the most beautiful, *Amherstia nobilis,* the only species of its genus, is not as commonly planted in the American tropics as in some other parts of the world. It certainly should be tried wherever there is prospect of success. Unfortunately, this species does not thrive everywhere it might be expected to, in Hawaii for example. A member of the pea family LEGUMINOSAE, this genus is named after the Countess Amherst, wife of a nineteenth-century Governor of Burma, and her daughter Lady Sarah Amherst, both of whom were much interested in the botany of India.

At its best **A. nobilis** may be 40 to 60 feet high, but is often lower. It is upright and

Amherstia nobilis

evergreen. Its pinnate leaves, 2 to 3 feet in length, are composed of four to nine pairs of leaflets without a terminal one. They are whitish on their undersides. When young they are pinkish-copper and, like those of the chocolate tree and mango, hang as limply as wet seaweed. Gradually they change to rich bronze, stiffen, and finally become green and horizontal. The remarkable flowers are in long pendulous racemes. They are on stalks 3½ to 4 inches long with two large bright-red, petal-like bracts at their middles. The blooms have four recurved sepals and three petals, the central one much larger than the others.

They are red, and pink flecked with red, spectacularly marked at their apexes with golden-yellow. There are nine stamens, five longer than the others. The style is long and threadlike. The fruits are flat, beaked pods about 7 inches long by 1 inch to 1½ inches wide.

Garden and Landscape Uses and Cultivation. High temperatures and high humidity are necessary for the successful cultivation of *Amherstia.* It needs a deep fertile soil and succeeds best in sheltered locations at low altitudes. It is not recommended as a seaside or street tree. Propagation is attended by some difficulties. Seeds probably give the surest results, but in many places where the tree succeeds they are rarely or never produced. Air layering is perhaps the commonest way of securing increase. Some success is reported with cuttings. In their young stages amherstias appear to be delicate and often fail then.

AMIANTHIUM (Amiánth-ium)—Fly Poison. The only species of *Amianthium* of the lily family LILIACEAE is a native of open woods from New York to Florida and Arkansas. Its name comes from the Greek *amiantos,* without spots, and *anthos,* a flower, and alludes to the glandless corolla.

The fly poison (*A. muscaetoxicum*) is a deciduous, bulbous herbaceous perennial,

Amiathium muscaetoxicum

with chiefly basal foliage consisting of linear leaves up to 1½ feet long and up to 1 inch wide. The erect stems, 1 foot to 4 feet tall, have a few much smaller leaves. Each stem terminates in a dense, conical or cylindrical, many-flowered raceme of creamy-white, bisexual flowers, 2 to 5 inches long. The individual blooms are ⅓ inch across and have six spreading, persistent petals

(more correctly tepals), and six stamens with flattened filaments (stalks). The ovary is deeply-three-lobed. The capsules contain seeds with fleshy, red coats. The bulbs and other parts of *Amianthium* contain a toxic substance. The bulbs have been used for making fly poison. From nearly related *Zygadenus* this plant is distinguished by its sepals and petals being without glands and from *Stenanthium* by its stamens being much shorter than the petals.

Garden Uses and Cultivation. The fly poison is very attractive for lightly shaded places in fertile, reasonably moist soil that contains a fair abundance of organic matter. It blooms in summer and is best propagated by fresh seeds sown in sandy peaty soil.

AMICIA (Am-ícia). The eight species of *Amicia* of the pea family LEGUMINOSAE are natives of Mexico. The name honors the Italian botanist and physician Giovanni Battista Amici, who died in 1863. Amicias are shrubs with pliable, subvining branches. Their alternate, pinnate leaves generally have large, deciduous appendages (stipules) at their bases and usually four obovate of reverse-heart-shaped leaflets. The pea-shaped, yellow flowers, in racemes from the leaf axils, have calyxes with the two upper lobes markedly bigger than the other three. The standard or banner petal is rounded to obovate-oblong, narrows to a slender shaft or claw at its base, and is notched at the apex. The wings are obovate or short and narrow. The keel is incurved. There are ten stamens joined into a sheath, and a slender style. The linear fruits are pods jointed between the seeds.

Occasionally planted in California and elsewhere in mild, dry climates, **A. zygomeris** is a shrub 3 to 8 feet high. Its leaves,

Amicia zygomeris

generally of four or six pairs of reverse-heart-shaped leaflets up to 2 inches long and nearly as broad as their lengths, have glandular dots clearly visible on their undersides. At the bottoms of the leafstalks are a pair of quickly deciduous, red-veined stipules. The pale yellow flowers, often marked with purple on their keels, are 1 inch to 1¼ inches long. They are in long, slender, stalked racemes, with each slender-stalked bloom arising from the axil of a conspicuous, nearly circular, red-veined bract. The seed pods are of two joints.

Garden and Landscape Uses and Cultivation. The species described is drought-resistant, and may be used as a shrub or a semiclimber to give variety to landscape plantings. It thrives in ordinary soils, and stands part-shade. Propagation is by seed.

AMMI (Ám-mi). An Old World group of ten species of herbaceous plants of the carrot family UMBELLIFERAE, the genus *Ammi* has an ancient Greek name. Its members have thick roots, and one- to three-times-pinnate or pinnately-divided, ferny leaves. The small, white or yellowish flowers are without sepals or have five tiny ones. They have five petals, five stamens, and two styles, and are in umbels of many smaller umbels, with an involucre (collar) of leafy bracts at the base of the main umbel. The fruits are slightly flattened and seedlike.

Native to the Mediterranean region, *A. majus* is a rather glaucous annual 1 foot to 3 feet tall, very variable in habit of growth and leaf dissection. Its lower leaves are pinnate, with elliptic to lanceolate, toothed leaflets. The upper leaves are twice- or thrice-pinnate into slender lobes or leaflets and are of ferny appearance. Characteristic is the involucre of conspicuous bracts beneath the main umbel of flowers. These are deeply-pinnately-lobed into three or five slender segments.

Ammi majus

Garden Uses and Cultivation. Sometimes grown in flower beds and less formal areas and for cutting to mix with more substantial blooms to give lightness to flower arrangements and bouquets, the species described here is easily raised from seeds sown in spring where the plants are to remain. The seedlings are thinned to prevent crowding. Sun or a little part-day shade,

and fertile reasonably moist soil are sufficient for satisfactory results. For spring blooming in pots in cool, sunny greenhouses, sow seeds in September and treat the young plants in the manner recommended for clarkias. Plants grown in this way may be 5 to 6 feet tall.

AMMOBIUM (Ammòb-ium)—Winged Everlasting. Only one species of this group of two Australian perennial herbaceous plants is generally cultivated. The genus belongs in the daisy family COMPOSITAE. Its name is from the Greek *ammos*, sand, and *bios*, to live, and refers to the preferred habitats of this genus. Ammobiums have yellow, rayless flower heads surrounded by collars of dry, silvery bracts and chaffy scales. The florets that compose the heads are bisexual. The fruits are seedlike achenes.

The winged everlasting (***Ammobium alatum***) is a white-woolly plant about 3 feet tall, with winged or sometimes only angled stems and branches and mostly basal oval leaves that taper to the stems, and fewer, smaller, distantly-spaced, lanceolate stem leaves. The flower heads have petal-like, chaffy bracts and are about 1 inch in diameter. The variety *A. a. grandiflorum* has flower heads 2 inches across and is superior as a garden plant.

Ammobium alatum

Garden Uses and Cultivation. The winged everlasting is generally cultivated as an annual or a biennial. Satisfactory results are had if seeds are sown outdoors in early spring where the plants are to bloom and the seedlings are thinned to 1 foot apart. In regions of mild winters September sowing outdoors is practicable. This species succeeds in ordinary, well-drained soil in sunny locations. To preserve its flowers as everlastings cut them with long stems just before they reach maturity, tie

them in small bundles and hang them upside down in a cool, shady place until they are quite dry.

AMMOCHARIS (Ammóch-aris). Very little known in cultivation, this African genus of five bulbous species belongs in the amaryllis family AMARYLLIDACEAE. Its name is derived from the Greek *ammos*, sand, and *charis*, beauty, and refers to habitat and appearance. The genus *Ammocharis* is related to *Crinum* from which it differs in the peculiar behavior of its leaves, which elongate at their bases for several years even though they die back to the tops of the bulbs during each period of dormancy. The leaves are in two ranks. They usually lie flat on the ground and have withered ends. Generally they are more or less sickle-shaped. The flowers have six similar petals or more correctly tepals, six stamens, and one style. The fruits are capsules containing fleshy seeds that often germinate before they are shed from the capsule.

A native of the slopes of Mount Elgon, East Africa, *A. heterostyla* has bulbs about 4 inches in diameter. Its glaucous-green, narrow-linear leaves, up to 1¼ feet long and with finely-toothed margins, lie flat on the ground in two opposite fans; their tips are withered. In terminal umbels atop short, erect stalks are carried the long, slender-tubed, starry flowers, with six narrow, spreading, slightly recurved petals. When fresh they are creamy-white with pinkish corolla tubes; as they age they become uniformly pinkish. The stamens protrude slightly. The style is included in the corolla tube. The flowers are sweetly fragrant. Another species, *A. coranica* (syn. *A. falcata*) may be cultivated. This has a bulb up to 8 inches in diameter from which sprout eight or nine deciduous, strap-shaped leaves that curve outward and toward the ground and are usually about 1½ feet long by 1½ inches wide, but may be considerably larger. Reclining on the earth at the ends of flattened stalks that come from beneath the foliage, and 6 inches to 1 foot long, the globular heads of about twenty rosy-crimson or more rarely pink or white flowers are about 6 inches in diameter.

Garden Uses and Cultivation. These rare plants are collectors' items. Very little experience has been had with them in North America. The East, African species has been grown in California and bloomed freely when planted outdoors, but not in pots in a greenhouse. The bulbs that bloomed outdoors were overwintered inside. Full sun, and porous, fertile, very well-drained soil, fairly moist when the plants are in foliage, but at other times dry, probably provide environmental conditions best suited for the ammocharises. They reproduce by offsets and from fresh seeds. Plants raised from seeds may take four or five years before they first bloom. Bulb cuttings would almost surely provide yet another means of increase.

AMOLE is *Chlorogalum pomeridianum*.

AMMONIUM NITRATE. Containing 32.5 to 34 percent nitrogen, ammonium nitrate or nitrate of ammonia is a highly soluble, quickly available, acid fertilizer that unless properly granulated and packed in moisture-proof bags cakes badly. If stored where ventilation is poor it may burn or even explode. It is applied at from ¼ to ½ ounce to 10 square feet.

AMMONIUM SULFATE Also called sulfate of ammonia, this is an excellent inorganic fertilizer. It contains about 20.6 percent nitrogen that becomes available to plants fairly soon after application although not as rapidly as that of sodium nitrate (nitrate of soda) or urea. Ammonium sulfate has an acid reaction so that, except for acid soil plants, ground on which it is used should be adequately limed beforehand. It is applied in spring and summer at rates of ½ to 1 ounce to 10 square feet.

AMMOPHILA (Ammó-phila)—Beach Grass or Marram Grass. Although of no particular ornamental merit, species of this genus of the grass family GRAMINEAE are planted locally as sand binders, especially along sea coasts. They are hardy, coarse perennials with extensive creeping, deep-penetrating, subterranean rhizomes, long, tough, stiff leaves that are flat in their lower parts, but have their margins rolled inward for most of their length, and taper to slender points; their dense, slender, spikelike flower heads are composed of many one-flowered compressed spikelets. The name is from the Greek *ammos*, sand, and *philos*, loving, and refers to the natural habitats of these grasses.

The genus consists of one or two European and one American species. It is closely related to *Calamagrostis*. The most extensively planted kind is the common European beach grass or marram grass (*Ammophila arenaria*). This kind attains a height of 3 to 6 feet and has leaves up to 2 feet long. Its dense, straw-colored flower panicles are up to 10 inches long. The spikelets are about ½ inch long and compressed. The American species (*A. breviligulata*) is very similar to *A. arenaria*. Native to dry sandy shores and dunes along the sea coast from Newfoundland to North Carolina and along the shores of the Great Lakes, it differs in having the tongue-like projection called a ligule that occurs where leaf blade and leaf sheath join not more than ⅛ inch long; in *A. arenaria* the ligule is ½ inch long or longer.

Landscape Uses and Cultivation. The only landscape use for these beach grasses is in conservation projects designed to sta-

Ammophila arenaria planted to hold a bank

bilize dunes and other loose or moving sands. For this they are invaluable. They have the ability to continue growing even when covered with wind-blown or water-deposited sand and to push their stems through the surface and develop new foliage. Propagation is most usually by division although seeds may be used. The divisions or young plants are set out at about 2 feet apart.

AMOMIS CARYOPHYLLATA is *Pimenta racemosa*, the bay rum tree.

AMOMUM (Amòm-um). One of the more than 100 species of this tropical genus of the ginger family ZINGIBERACEAE is cultivated as a foliage plant. From ginger (*Zingiber*) this group differs in technical details of its anthers and their connections. It is indigenous to tropical Asia and Indonesia, and bears a name thought to be of Arabic origin.

The cultivated *Amomum compactum* (syns. *A. kepulaga*, *A. cardamomum*), must not be confused with the true cardamom (*Elettaria cardamomum*), which belongs in the same family and is of somewhat similar appearance. The seeds of the *Amomum* are used to some extent in the same ways as cardamom seeds, but are inferior. The leaves of *A. compactum* of Java, are hairless, those of *Elettaria cardamomum* are finely pubescent on their undersides. Also, the flowers of the former are in dense, canelike spikes, those of the latter in distantly flowered, loose spikes or panicles.

Attaining a height of 3 to 7 feet, *A. compactum* has creeping rhizomes and many erect, leafy, cane-like stems with stalkless, linear-lanceolate, evergreen leaves up to 10 inches long by 3 inches wide, with long-pointed apexes. When crushed they have a pronounced ginger-like odor. The flower stems arise from the creeping rhizomes, and are 2 to 4 inches in length. They have pointed-ovate bracts from among which the blooms protrude. Each flower has a tubular, three-lobed calyx and a slender corolla tube ¾ inch in length. The showy part of the bloom is an obovate spreading, three-lobed lip about ¾ inch long, which is actually a modified, nonfunctional stamen (staminode) rather than the petal it appears to be. There is one fertile stamen. Because the flowers are produced near the ground, they are ordinarily hidden by the foliage.

Garden and Landscape Uses and Cultivation. In the tropics *A. compactum* is a useful, handsome outdoor herbaceous foliage plant that thrives in shade. It is excellent in tropical greenhouses and also stands room conditions remarkably well. It is one of the most long-lasting plants for use in indoor window boxes where light is comparatively poor. The cultural needs and propagation methods are the same as for *Alpinia*.

AMOMYRTUS (Amo-myrtus). Two Chilean species of the myrtle family MYRTACEAE constitute *Amomyrtus*. Alluding to the type of soil in which these plants grow as natives and their botanical relationship, the name comes from the Greek *amos*, sand, and the name of the genus *Myrtus*.

These evergreen shrubs or small trees have opposite, undivided leaves and flowers in racemes of few to several. They have five each calyx lobes and petals, and many stamens. The fruits are berries.

An attractive ornamental, **A. luma** (syns. *Myrtus luma, M. lechlerana*) is a large shrub or tree up to 30 feet tall and of dense habit. Suggesting those of the evergreen blueberry (*Vaccinium ovatum*), its glossy, ovate to broad-oval leaves, when young of a beautiful coppery hue, are ¾ inch to 1¼ inches long. In racemes of up to ten from the upper leaf axils, the fragrant, ¼-inch-wide flowers are white. They are succeeded by edible berries about as large that change color as they ripen from reddish to black. From *Luma apiculata* with which it is sometimes confused, *A. luma* differs in having smaller flowers with five rather than four petals.

Garden and Landscape Uses and Cultivation. The species described is a handsome ornamental not hardy in the north, but suitable for mild climates. It thrives in sun or part-day shade in ordinary well-drained soils and is easily propagated by cuttings and seeds.

AMORPHA (Amór-pha) — False-Indigo, Bastard-Indigo, Lead Plant. False-indigos number twenty species of the pea family LEGUMINOSAE. The genus occurs in the wild from Canada to Mexico. Its members are deciduous shrubs and subshrubs, the kinds dealt with here are hardy in the north, some extremely so. The name, from the Greek *amorphos*, misshapen, alludes to the flowers lacking wing and keel petals.

False-indigos have foliage dotted with tiny glands. Their alternate, pinnate leaves have small, toothless leaflets, including a terminal one. The blue-violet to whitish flowers, in dense, often clustered terminal spikes are small. They have five-lobed calyxes and a corolla of one petal wrapped around the ten protruding stamens, of which one is separate and nine are united at their bases. The fruits are short, one- or two-seeded pods.

Lead plant (**Amorpha canescens**), one of the most attractive kinds, is wild from Michigan to Saskatchewan, Indiana, Texas, and New Mexico. From 3 to 4 feet tall, it has densely-gray-hairy shoots and foliage. Its leaves, 2 to 4½ inches long, have fifteen to forty-five elliptic to elliptic-oblong leaflets up to ¾ inch long. The short-stalked, clustered spikes of bloom, 1½ to 6 inches long, make an attractive showing in early summer. The flowers are blue with contrasting orange-colored anthers. Not as hardy as the typical species, *A. c. glabrata* is much less hairy.

Bastard-indigo (*A. fruticosa*) is a variable species of which there are a number of geographical varieties. It is wild through

Amorpha fruticosa

much of eastern and central North America from New England to Saskatchewan, Florida, New Mexico, and Texas. Up to 20 feet tall, it has hairless or slightly-hairy shoots, and finely-hairy or nearly-hairless foliage. Its purplish-blue flowers are in clustered spikes 3 to 6 inches long. The seed pods are 3 to 4 inches long, and curved. Variety *A. f. albiflora* has white flowers, *A. f. coerulea* pale blue. The leaves of *A. f. crispa* have curled edges. The branches of *A. f. pendula* are arching or drooping.

Nearly or quite hairless, **A. nana** is very hardy. Native of dry prairies from Manitoba to Saskatchewan, Iowa, and New Mexico, it attains heights of 1 foot to 3 feet, and has leaves up to 4 inches long, of thirteen to nineteen elliptic to oblong leaflets. Its flowers, usually in solitary spikes 2 to 4 inches long, and reminiscent of those of some hebes, are purple. The pods are tiny.

Garden and Landscape Uses and Cultivation. The lead plant is the most attractive amorpha for gardens. For its gray foliage and colorful flowers it is worth planting in shrub beds and other places where its tendency to grow out of bounds will not cause distress or can be controlled. It does well in sunny locations where the soil is well drained, and prospers in drier, less fertile earths than most shrubs. Less showy in bloom and its foliage less unusual, *A. nana* has similar uses. Bastard-indigo is less easy to accommodate in most garden landscapes. It grows very vigorously, and with age often becomes rather gawky. Also, the numerous volunteer seedlings it often gives rise to can be a nuisance. The employment of this is best restricted to extensive landscapes where it succeeds well in dryish soils in sun. Amorphas are propagated by seeds, suckers, layers, and by hardwood and leafy summer cuttings.

AMORPHOPHALLUS (Amorpho-phállus)— Devil's-Tongue or Snake-Palm, Krubi. This genus of the arum family ARACEAE is chiefly notable for the krubi (*Amorphophallus titanum*), frequently, but incorrectly re-

ferred to as the largest flower in the world. It also includes a kind not uncommonly cultivated in North America previously named *Hydrosme rivieri*, but now known as *A. rivieri*, that on occasions of its blooming is quite often featured and pictured in newspaper stories. The name, alluding to the inflorescence, is from the Greek *amorphos*, shapeless, and *phallos*, a penis.

Restricted in the wild to tropical Asia and Africa, *Amorphophallus* comprises about 100 deciduous, mostly tuberous, herbaceous perennials. Often the tubers are large, and sometimes immense. From each comes each year usually a single leaf with an upright stalk and a spreading blade of three primary divisions pinnately cleft and recleft into many small leaflike lobes. The flowers come when the plant is leafless. What is commonly called the "flower" is an inflorescence, a combination of many small flowers and attendant parts. It is built on the plan usual in the arum family, of the jack-in-the-pulpit (*Arisaema triphyllum*) and calla-lily (*Zantedeschia aethiopica*), and consists of a central shaft or spike called a spadix, bearing many little flowers, from the base of which comes a large, modified leaf called a spathe. In the jack-in-the-pulpit, the spike-like organ that represents the preacher, and in the calla-lily the central yellow organ, are the spadices (plural of spadix). Jack's hooded pulpit and the white, petal-like trumpet of the calla-lily are spathes. In *Amorphophallus* the spadix has female flowers toward its base, male flowers above, and usually above them a flowerless terminal appendix. The spathe does not form a hood over the spadix. When fully mature the female flowers are receptive to pollination; then the blooms of some kinds emit a penetrating foul, nauseous odor that in the wild attracts carrion insects, which are the pollinating agents. The fruits are berries.

The devil's-tongue or snake-palm (*A. rivieri* syn. *Hydrosme rivieri*), native of Cochin-

Amorphophallus rivieri

China, is handsome in foliage, curiously so in bloom. Unfortunately the stink of its flowers at maturity is such that it is necessary to remove the offending plant from human proximity for a few days. The most commonly cultivated kind, the devil's-tongue has a flattish tuber up to about 10 inches across. Its leaf has a white-mottled, brownish-green stalk 2 to 4 feet tall, and a divided, much-cleft, umbrella-like blade 2 to 4 feet wide. The inflorescence ("flower") is at the top of a stout stalk 2 to 3 feet long. Its wavy-edged spathe, up to 1 foot long, on its outside green spotted with brown and white, is purplish toward its margins. The inside, like the spadix, is a dull, dark, plum-purple.

Species less commonly cultivated include *A. bulbifer.* This native of India has a subspherical tuber 2 to 4 inches wide.

Amorphophallus bulbifer

From 2 to 3 feet tall, its olive-green leaf-stalk, spotted and streaked with paler markings, supports a blade up to 2 feet or more in diameter that has along its ribs small, potato-like tubers. The inflorescence ("flower"), topping a stalk approximately 1 foot long, has a green and pink spadix with a flowerless, flesh-colored terminal part up to 3 inches long, and a spathe, on its outside spotted toward the base with pink and red, and yellowish-green toward the top on its inside. Native to Indonesia and New Guinea, the teve or daga (*A. campanulatus*) has flattish tubers up to 10 inches in diameter. Its leaves, rarely two from a tuber, have pale-spotted, dark green stalks up to 3 feet long, and blades almost as wide. The inflorescences ("flowers") are on stalks 3 to 6 inches in

length. They have wavy-margined green spathes, purplish on their outsides. The spadix, about 10 inches long, is dark purple. The West African *A. eichleri* has a smallish tuber. Its leaf has a 1-foot-long, green stalk and a blade about 1½ feet wide. The inflorescence ("flower"), at the apex of a short stalk, has a wavy-margined spathe 3 to 4 inches long, greenish on the outside, purplish at its base, and with longitudinal crisped ridges inside. The spadix ends in a pinkish flowerless portion about 3 inches long.

Amorphophallus eichleri

Although few if any of those who read these words are ever likely to have the opportunity of, or the responsibility for, growing the krubi (*A. titanum*), the author

Amorphophallus titanum flowering at The New York Botanical Garden in 1937

of this Encyclopedia feels that his experience in successfully bringing to bloom three of the perhaps half-dozen that have ever flowered in temperate regions should be recorded. The first of the three bloomed

at Kew Gardens, England in 1926, the others at the New York Botanical Garden, one in 1937, the other in 1939. The Kew specimen and the first New York Botanical one were grown in large tubs of rich soil raised a few inches above the level of a pool, in full sun in a highly humid, very tropical conservatory housing the giant water-lily (*Victoria amazonica*). The other was planted in a ground bed under similar conditions of high temperature and humidity, but with shade from strong sun. The first to bloom at the New York Botanical Garden produced the largest inflorescence of any recorded, and its progress was best documented. When received from Sumatra in 1932 the corm weighed sixty pounds. In each of three succeeding years it produced a solitary, successively larger leaf, the biggest over 6 feet tall and having a much-divided, umbrella-like blade with a spread of more than 10 feet. Following the dying of each leaf a few weeks' dormancy occurred, after which a new leaf appeared. During the dormant periods the soil was kept dry, but through the growing season generous supplies of water and regular applications of dilute liquid fertilizer were given. By fall 1936 the tuber had become too big for its 30-inch-square tub and it was carefully replanted in one 3 feet square. The estimated weight of the tuber then was more than 100 pounds. In 1937 new growth began in early April and by May 27th was 3½ feet tall. At that time it was evident that an inflorescence rather than a leaf was developing. From then on growth was rapid until, on June 8th, the spadix attained its maximum height of 8 feet 5 inches. The afternoon of the previous day the spathe began to open into an enormous, upturned fluted bell, dark green merging to purple above outside, and almost black-purple within. It attained its

A tuber of *Amorphophallus titanum* at The New York Botanical Garden in 1937

maximum dimensions of 4½ feet long and 4 feet 1½ inches in diameter the following evening. The inflorescence remained in good condition until June 10th. At the height of its development it emitted a strong, unpleasant odor, but not comparable in intensity to the disgusting stench of the Kew specimen of 1926. After blooming, the tuber, measuring 6 feet in circumference, weighed 113½ pounds. Although attempts were made to induce seed production by hand pollinating, and to achieve increase, after it began to disintegrate, by removing portions for propagation, these attempts failed. A botanist familiar with this remarkable plant in the wild said that after blooming the tuber sends out long runners at the ends of which young tubers develop, but this did not happen to the specimen planted in a ground bed at the New York Botanical Garden. Like all other cultivated specimens it died after flowering.

Garden and Landscape Uses. These plants are usually grown as curiosities, which is all that their inflorescences, striking in appearance though they often are, can be considered. Their foliage, however, is highly ornamental and for it amorphophalluses are worth growing in gardens in the tropics and in tropical greenhouses. In temperate climates *A. rivieri* can be planted outdoors for summer foliage effects. It is dug up in fall and the tuber stored dry over winter in a temperature of 55 to 60°F.

Cultivation. Amorphophalluses revel in coarse, rich soil that contains an abundance of organic matter and is kept moist from the time leaf growth appears until the foliage starts to die naturally. When that occurs, gradually longer intervals are allowed between soakings, and finally, water is withheld completely, and the tubers kept dry and dormant until the next season of growth begins. Well-rooted specimens in leaf benefit from frequent applications of dilute liquid fertilizer. For their best comfort these plants need high temperatures and humidities. Because roots originate from the tops of the tubers it is important to plant them in containers so that they are covered with at least 2 or 3 inches of soil. Outdoors the tubers should be set considerably deeper. Pots or tubs of generous size in proportion to the size of the tubers are needed, and repotting into fresh soil should be done at the beginning of each new growing season. Because offsets are rarely produced, seeds afford the most practical means of propagation. To ensure the development of fertile seeds the female blooms must be hand pollinated.

AMPELODESMA (Ampelo-désma). Sometimes the name of this genus is spelled *Ampelodesmos.* Derived, apparently from the Greek *ampelos,* a vine, and *desmos,* a chain, its application is not obvious. The genus consists of one perennial species of the grass family GRAMINEAE, a native of the Mediterranean region. A robust plant forming large, dense clumps of stiff, erect stems 6 to 9 feet tall, ***Ampelodesma mauritanicus*** (syn. *A. tenax*) has long, narrow, wiry, rough-edged leaves curved at their bases, and loose, one-sided flower panicles 8 inches to 1½ feet long with drooping branches and crowded spikelets each of two to five flowers.

Garden and Landscape Uses and Cultivation. In a mild climate, such as that of California, this grass is sometimes planted as an ornamental in sunny beds and borders. It is propagated by seed and division and thrives in any fairly good garden soil.

AMPELOPSIS (Ampel-ópsis). Closely related to *Vitis* and *Parthenocissus,* the genus *Ampelopsis* belongs in the grape family VITACEAE. It differs from *Vitis* in having nonshredding bark, in the pith of its stems being white, and in its flowers having petals that fall separately. It is distinguished from *Cissus* by its blooms having usually five- instead of four-parted calyxes, and from *Parthenocissus* in having branched tendrils without disks at their tips and in its flowers having the ovary encircled by a prominent disk. There are about twenty-five species, natives of North America and Asia. The name is from the Greek *ampelos,* a vine, and *opsis,* resembling.

Ampelopsises are deciduous, alternate-leaved vines with tendrils opposite the leaves. The latter are long-stalked and undivided or separated into leaflets. The small, greenish, bisexual flowers are in long-stalked clusters opposite the leaves or terminal. The flowers have as many stamens as petals. The fruits are pea-sized berries containing one to four seeds.

The pepper vine (***A. arborea***), commonly planted in gardens in the warmer parts of the United States, is not hardy in the north. Native from Virginia to Florida, Texas, and Mexico, this bushy, more or less climbing sort has twice-pinnate, finely-divided leaves 3 to 9 inches long, with usually-ovate leaflets that are deeply notched and from ½ inch to 1½ inches long. The leafstalks and veins on the undersides of the leaves are hairy. The calyx and corolla are often four-parted and the fruits are very dark purple. This species is sometimes without tendrils or has very small ones. Another species with leaves pinnate or twice-pinnate, is the western Chinese ***A. megalophylla,*** a vigorous vine distinguished by its very large winter buds and leaves. The latter, consisting of several to numerous segments or leaflets, are 6 inches to 1¼ feet long and have pointed-ovate to ovate-oblong, toothed leaflets up to 5 inches long and rounded to somewhat heart-shaped at their bases. The flowers and blue-black fruits are in loose clusters. This kind is hardy about as far north as Philadelphia. Yet a third *Ampelopsis* with divided leaves, ***A. aconitifolia*** is a slender vine native of northern China with nearly-round leaves 2 to 4 inches in diameter separated into five conspicuously toothed leaflets sometimes further divided or cleft,

Ampelopsis aconitifolia

that spread palmately (like the fingers of a hand) and on their undersides are paler than above and sometimes hairy on the veins. The small fruits are orange to bluish. Variety *A. a. glabra* differs in having leaves of usually three-lobed, toothed leaflets.

Kinds with leaves lobed or toothed, but not divided into separate leaflets include the popular porcelain berry (***A. brevipedunculata*** syn. *A. heterophylla amurensis*).

Ampelopsis brevipedunculata in fruit

This vigorous vine becomes woody below and has slender young stems that, like the leafstalks and the main veins on the bottoms of the leaves, are hairy. The somewhat three-lobed, ovate-heart-shaped leaves are clearly toothed and 2 to 4 inches in diameter. They have a wide basal opening. The fruits are very attractive. Small and in rather dense clusters they are glossy and porcelain-like; at first pale lilac they change as they ripen to verdigris-green. Occasionally they are pale yellow. The berries are ¼ inch in diameter, and the clusters at one time may contain individuals of all the colors mentioned. The porcelain berry is native to northeastern Asia. An extraordinarily pretty variety is *A. b. elegans* (syns. *A. variegata, A. tricolor*), which has leaves beautifully marbled with green and white and sometimes pink. In *A. b. maximowiczii* (syn. *A. heterophylla*) the leaves are deeply-three- or five-lobed and almost or quite hairless. The leaves of *A. b. citrulloides* are even more deeply cut and have slender lobes the center one of which narrows sharply at the base and at or above its middle and the lateral ones of which are often again lobed. This species and its varieties are hardy near New York City and perhaps further north.

Resembling the wine grape (*Vitis*) in its leafage, *A. humulifolia* is a climbing, woody vine, a native of northern China and hardy in southern New England. Its handsome lustrous green leaves have whitish or pale under surfaces, are broadovate, 3 to 4½ inches across, three- to five-lobed, and coarsely toothed; beneath they may be hairy or hairless. The pale yellow to pale blue fruits are usually not freely produced.

Other kinds include these: *A. bodinieri* (*syn. A. micans*) is similar to *A. humulifolia*, but usually has lobeless leaves and dark blue or violet fruits. It is a native of China. Its variety *A. b. cinerea* often has deeply three- or five-lobed leaves, grayish below or on both surfaces. *A. cordata* is a tall climber, with pointed, round-ovate, scarcely three-lobed leaves, green beneath, and with greenish or bluish fruits. It is native from Virginia to Florida, and Mexico. *A. delavayana* is a vigorous vine with usually three-lobed or divided leaves but sometimes lobeless toothed leaves and dark blue berries. It is a native of China. *A. japonica*, native to Japan and China, has tuberous roots and lustrous leaves with three to five pinnate or pinnately-lobed leaflets with the midribs of the leaves with wide wings. The berries are blue. *A. orientalis*, of southwest Asia, has pinnate or twice-pinnate leaves with sharp-toothed leaflets. Its berries are red.

Other plants commonly called *Ampelopsis* by gardeners belong in *Cissus* and *Parthenocissus*. Examples are *Cissus striata*, the Virginia creeper (*Parthenocissus quinquifolia*), and the Boston-ivy (*P. tricuspidata*).

Garden and Landscape Uses. Unlike *Parthenocissus*, which is related, members of this group do not attach themselves by adherent pads at their tendril ends and so must be given supports other than a flat surface such as a wall. To climb they need wires, a lattice, or other supports around which their tendrils can twine. They are attractive for pergolas, arches, and screening and are chiefly esteemed for their foliage and, *A. brevipedunculata* and its varieties, for their attractive berries, unique as to color among hardy vines. Ordinary garden soil is agreeable to these plants. They prosper in sun or part-shade. Because ampelopsises grow vigorously they should be allowed generous space. In pots and tubs *A. b. elegans* is especially delightful.

Cultivation. Little attention is needed. Once established these vines pretty much take care of themselves, except for any pruning necessary to keep them tidy and orderly. This is best done in spring. Propagation is very easy by leafy cuttings inserted in summer in a greenhouse or cold frame propagating bed or under mist, and by hardwood cuttings taken about the time the leaves drop in fall. Seeds germinate readily if sown in sandy, peaty soil in a cool greenhouse, cold frame, or outdoors where they will not be disturbed.

When grown in pots, tubs, or other containers the altogether charming *A. brevipedunculata elegans* needs a fertile, loamy, well-drained soil. The plants should be repotted or top dressed each late winter or early spring. At that time, too, shoots of the previous year of specimens that have an established framework of older branches are pruned back close to their bases. If this is done regularly the plants do not increase appreciably in size beyond that determined by the extent of the branches that form a permanent skeleton that was determined as to size during the early years of the plant's life. Specimens so small that they can be permanently accommodated in 5- or 6-inch pots are quite practicable or they may be grown as bigger specimens in larger containers. They may also be trained as standards, that is in tree-form with a single stem or trunk 3 to 6 feet high with a rounded head of branches at the top. When trained in this way the main stem must be staked securely. Container-grown specimens should be watered freely from spring to fall, but kept dry or nearly dry in winter. Occasional summer applications of dilute liquid fertilizer are helpful. In winter they may be accommodated in a cool greenhouse, protected cold frame, or other place where the temperature does not go so low that the soil freezes solidly.

AMPHIBLEMMA (Amphí-blemma). Of the eleven species of tropical West African *Amphiblemma* of the melastoma family MELASTOMATACEAE, only one seems to be cultivated and that rarely. The group consists of herbaceous plants and low shrubs and is named with reference to botanical ambiguities of its flowers, from the Greek *amphi*, both, and *blemma*, an eye. The genus has opposite, stalked, pointed-ovate, toothed leaves, with five to nine prominent longitudinal veins linked by parallel cross ones. The attractive pink flowers, in branching clusters, have five-toothed calyxes, five petals, and ten markedly unequal stamens. The fruits are turban-shaped capsules splitting at the top in five places and containing many small seeds.

The kind cultivated, *A. cymosum* (syn. *Melastoma corymbosum*), is nearly hairless, and has erect stems and long-stalked, five- to seven-veined, pointed-ovate, finely-toothed leaves up to 7 inches long by almost 5 inches wide. Their upper surfaces are a beautiful, satiny, olive-green; beneath they are paler. The bright pink-magenta flowers are borne in terminal clusters over a long period in summer.

Garden Uses and Cultivation. Except in the humid tropics this is strictly a greenhouse plant. It is very easily propa-

Amphiblemma cymosum

gated from cuttings and may be raised from seeds. Usually, new plants are started in spring. For best success this *Amphiblemma* needs, when grown in greenhouses, some shade from strong sun, a humid atmosphere, and a minimum winter temperature of 55 to 60°F. By day an increase of five to fifteen degrees is in order, and in summer considerably higher temperatures are acceptable. The soil should be fertile, coarse, and contain an abundance of peat moss, leaf mold, or other decayed organic matter, but must be porous. Good drainage is essential. Water to keep the earth always moderately moist, slightly drier in winter than at other times. When well rooted in the containers in which they are to bloom, which may be 5- or 6-inch pots, the plants benefit from weekly applications of dilute liquid fertilizer. In their early life they should have the tips of their shoots pinched out once or twice to encourage branching. Neat staking and tying are needed.

AMPHICARPAEA (Amphi-càrpaea)—Hog-Peanut. Horticulturally unimportant, *Amphicarpaea* of the pea family LEGUMINOSAE consists of six species of eastern Asia and one native of North America. The latter is occasionally cultivated. The name, which refers to the two kinds of fruits produced, is from the Greek *amphi*, both, and *karpos*, fruit. The group consists of twining perennial herbaceous plants with pinnate leaves of three leaflets, and axillary racemes or panicles of small purplish to whitish pea-like flowers that are succeeded by usually three-seeded pods. In addition to these evident blooms the plants develop near the bottoms of their stems, or even underground, flowers without petals that give rise to small single-seeded pods.

The hog-peanut (**A. bracteata** syn. *A. monoica*) native from Nova Scotia and Que-

Amphicarpaea bracteata

bec to Manitoba, Montana, Florida, and Texas, is very variable. It has pubescent stems up to about 3 feet in length and long-stalked leaves of blunt or pointed, ovate or rhombic-ovate, more or less hairy leaflets, the largest 1 inch to 4 inches long.

Its pale purple to whitish flowers, about ½ inch long, are in fairly long-stalked clusters from many of the leaf axils. The curved pods are pubescent all over or are hairless except near their edges at their bases. They contain three or four mottled seeds.

Garden Uses and Cultivation. This is a quite elegant twining vine of limited horticultural use for shaded locations and in native plant gardens where the soil is fairly moist. It is easily raised from seeds.

AMPHICOME. The plants previously known by this name are now included in the genus *Incarvillea*.

AMPHILOPHIUM (Amphi-lòphium). Eight species of the bignonia family BIGNONIACEAE constitute *Amphilophium*. They are natives of warm parts of the Americas. The name, from the Greek *amphi*, both, and *lophos*, a crest, is of uncertain application.

Amphilophiums are woody vines with opposite leaves of three leaflets or the terminal leaflet replaced by a tendril, and terminal panicles of purple blooms. The flowers have a bell-shaped calyx bearing two or three interior lobelike appendages and a two-lipped corolla with a cylindrical tube and longer spreading lobes (petals), two of which form one lip, three the other. There are four stamens and one style. The fruits are thick, flattened, smooth or nearly smooth, oblong-elliptic pods containing prominently winged seeds.

A vigorous vine with stems many feet long, and like the foliage, with short, fine

hairs, **A. paniculatum**, of Central and South America, has leaves with broad-ovate to somewhat heart-shaped leaflets 3 to 6 inches long. About 1¼ inches in length, the flowers, white in bud, purple when expanded, are in loose panicles 6 to 10 inches long. The football-shaped fruits are 2 to 4 inches in length.

Garden and Landscape Uses and Cultivation. This is useful in the tropics and warm subtropics for arbors and other supports that call for a strong-growing vine. It succeeds in sun in ordinary soil, and needs no particular care other than pruning, which is best done after flowering to contain it to shape and size. Increase is by cuttings, layering, and seeds.

AMRA is *Spondias pinnata*.

AMSONIA (Am-sònia). Of the twenty-five species of the American and Japanese genus *Amsonia* few are cultivated. The genus consists of erect herbaceous perennials of the dogbane family APOCYNACEAE. Its name commemorates an eighteenth-century American physician, Charles Amson. Amsonias have alternate or scattered leaves and terminal clusters of starry blue flowers. The blooms have deeply-five-parted calyxes and slender-tubed corollas, hairy in their throats, and with five spreading slender lobes (petals). The five stamens are included in the corolla tube. There is one style. The fruits are long slender pods.

The most commonly cultivated species is **A. tabernaemontana,** an inhabitant of

Amsonia tabernaemontana

wet woodlands and river banks from New Jersey to Illinois, Missouri, Louisiana, Oklahoma, and Texas, and naturalized as far north as Massachusetts. This is 1 foot to 3 feet tall and has narrow-lanceolate to broadly-elliptic leaves 3 to 6 inches long and sometimes finely-hairy beneath. The calyxes of its soft slaty-blue blooms are hairless. The flowers are about ⅓ inch across and are in flattish or pyramidal clusters. Their corolla tubes are hairy on their undersides. A variant with narrower leaves, usually without hairs on their undersides and glaucous there, and with fewer flowered clusters is *A. t. salicifolia.*

Another kind sometimes cultivated is *A. ciliata,* which differs from *A. tabernaemontana* in having narrow-linear leaves and the outsides of the corolla tubes hairless. This is native to dry open woods from North Carolina to Missouri, Florida, and Texas. Occasionally up to 5 feet tall, its stems are so crowded with foliage that the leaves may give the impression of being opposite or whorled (in circles of three or more). They are without stalks. The purplish-blue flowers are slightly more than ½ inch across. In *A. c. filifolia* the leaves are narrower. Variety *A. c. texana* has slightly longer flowers.

Garden and Landscape Uses. Amsonias are excellent hardy garden plants for early summer flowering in borders and native plant gardens. Theirs is a quiet beauty. For brilliance of bloom they certainly cannot compete with peonies, poppies, or phloxes, but they make good foils and complements for more gaudy companions, are neat in habit, and have the appearance of quality. A point in their favor is that they do well in part-shade. A soil moderately fertile, moist for *A. tabernaemontana,* drier for *A. ciliata,* suits these plants.

Cultivation. Once established, clumps can remain undisturbed for several years. Until they begin to show signs of deterioration there is no need to lift, divide, or replant them. Spring or early fall are the best times to transplant. When planting, it must be remembered that the clump will eventually need a space 2 to 3 feet in diameter. Propagation is by division, summer cuttings, and seeds. All are reliable and comparatively easy to grow.

ANACAMPSEROS (Ana-cámpseros). How many of the about seventy species of this genus of small fleshy plants have been introduced to cultivation is not known, but a few are not uncommon, and others are likely to be found in special collections of succulents. With one exception, *A. australiana,* a native of Australia, the species are South African. The genus belongs in the purslane family PORTULACACEAE. Its name is from the Greek *anakampto,* to accomplish the return of, and *eros,* love. The plant is regarded as a talisman of love by some African tribes.

Species of *Anacampseros* are low, branching perennials, often with thickish roots. They have very fleshy, often cobwebby-hairy, more or less ovate, alternate leaves from the axils of which bristly hairs often arise. These represent leaf appendages called stipules. In some kinds the leaves are arranged spirally. The flower stalks, usually slightly coiled and bearing two to four blooms, are from the ends of the shoots. The blooms either do not open or do so for a very short time, often for only an hour or two, and only in sun. They have two sepals and five quickly deciduous petals. The fruits are capsules.

A favorite is *A. telephiastrum,* which forms mats of freely-branched, stout stems ending in rosettes of green or brown-tinted, pointed, broad-ovate to roundish leaves about ¾ inch long and wide, with only a few bristly hairs not longer than the leaves. The deep rose-pink flowers, solitary or in clusters of up to four, are 1 inch to 1½ inches in diameter and have thick, fleshy stalks up to 6 inches long. Another fairly common species, *A. rufescens* (syn. *A. arachnoides grandiflora*), is likely to be mis-

Anacampseros rufescens

Anacampseros rufescens

named *A. arachnoides* in gardens. It has thickened roots and makes a dense mat of creeping or erect, much-branched stems 2 to 3 inches in height. Along these the thick, tapered, ovate-lanceolate leaves,

some ¾ inch long and one-half as wide, are spiraled. Their undersides are brownish-red. There are many bristly, often wavy, hairs almost as long as the leaves. On stalks up to 4 inches long two to four pink blooms 1¼ to 1½ inches in diameter are borne.

The short-stemmed *A. lanceolata* has much the aspect of *A. telephiastrum,* but its

Anacampseros lanceolata

narrower leaves have curly hairs that exceed them in length sprouting from their axils. The rosettes are of spine-tipped, green to reddish leaves ¾ to 1 inch long by up to ⅓ inch wide. Solitary or in two or three on stalks 3 to 4 inches long, the deep pink flowers are 1 inch or somewhat more in diameter. Quite different, *A. tomentosa* has thick roots and obovate, overlapping leaves with squarish ends. They are less than ½ inch in length and somewhat narrower than long. Their undersides are densely-felted with soft white hairs. The bristles are few. A few pink flowers, 1¼ inches across, are carried on 2- to 2½-inch-long stems.

Representative of a group that have papery, silvery-white stipules as appendages to the leaves instead of mere bristles, is the charming *A. papyracea.* So large and conspicuous are its blunt stipules that they completely hide the tiny leaves. They point toward the tips of the shoots, overlap, and hug the stems so that each shoot looks like a whitish grub or worm. It is claimed by some that this is a form of mimicry, that the resemblance of the shoots to bird excrement, deceives foraging creatures. This species has thickened roots and a short stem with many branches or shoots, mostly prostrate and about 2 inches long by ⅓ inch in diameter. The solitary, stalkless blooms are greenish-white to pale yellow. Having much the aspect of *A. papyracea* but smaller, its branchlets rarely more than ½ inch long, *A. buderana* is attractive. Its minute leaves are hidden by silvery-white stipules that lie flat against them.

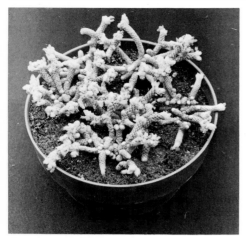

Anacampseros buderana

Another kind with silvery, papery stipules, but in this case only half concealing the leaves. *A. rhodesica* is scarcely more than 1 inch high. It has numerous branches and spirally-arranged, roundish-ovate, shortly-tapered leaves up to 1 inch long, less than ¹⁄₁₀ inch wide, and curving outward at their tips. The solitary, terminal blooms are white to pale pink.

Garden Uses and Cultivation. These plants are best accommodated in greenhouse collections of succulents. Only in warm, dry climates will they succeed outdoors. They are easy to grow in very porous, fertile soil and are readily propagated by seeds, cuttings, and leaf cuttings. For information regarding more detailed care see Succulents.

ANACARDIACEAE—Cashew Family. This family of dicotyledons consists of sixty genera, approximately 600 species. The trees, shrubs, and few vines that compose it are chiefly natives of the tropics or subtropics, but some are found in warm-temperate and colder regions; among the best known are poison-ivy and poison-oak. The ability to produce severe dermatitis characteristic of these handsome pests is possessed to a greater or lesser degree by many members of the family including mangoes and the species of *Rhus* from which Chinese and Japanese lacquer is procured.

Members of the *Anacardiaceae* have alternate, undivided or divided leaves and panicles of mixed, small unisexual and bisexual flowers each typically with five each sepals and petals, five or more stamens, and one to six styles. The fruits are technically drupes or nuts. Cultivated members of this family include *Anacardium, Cotinus, Harpephyllum, Lithraea, Mangifera, Pachycormus, Pistacia, Pleiogynium, Rhodosphaera, Rhus, Schinus,* and *Spondias.*

ANACARDIUM (Ana-cárdium)—Cashew. Cashew nuts are obtained from one member of *Anarcadium* of the cashew family ANACARDIACEAE. The group consists of fif-

teen species of trees and shrubs of the American tropics. It is related to the mango and poison-ivy. The name is derived from the Greek *ana,* similar, and *kardia,* the heart, and alludes to the shape of the cashew apples.

The only cultivated kind is the cashew (*A. occidentale*). Widely planted in the tropics, it has become naturalized and reproduces by self-sown seeds in many parts of the world far from its original home. It is an evergreen tree of spreading, irregular form, up to 40 feet in height, with milky sap. Its thick leaves are oblong-oval to obovate, 4 to 8 inches long, with lateral veins at nearly right angles to the midrib.

Anacardium occidentale

Anacardium occidentale

Like others of the genus, its leaves are alternate and the plants bear unisexual flowers of both sexes as well as bisexual ones. The flowers are ¹⁄₃ inch in diameter, fragrant, and have five calyx lobes, five narrow petals, and eight to ten stamens; they are yellowish-pink and are in loose, terminal panicles 6 to 10 inches long. Most remarkable are the fruits, using the word in its generally accepted, non-botanical sense. These consist of a large, fleshy part called the cashew apple, really an enlarged portion of the stalk to which the flower parts are attached, and, at its apex, the kid-

ney-shaped cashew nut, about ³⁄₄ inch long, which botanically is the fruit. Both cashew apples and cashew nuts are edible. The former are apple-shaped, bright red or yellow when ripe, 2 to 4 inches long and 1½ to 3 inches in diameter. Fragrant, very juicy, and somewhat astringent, they are usually cooked, but may be eaten raw. They are made into jams and jellies, and are used as pie fillings and in refreshing ades. From them is made a good wine and a very intoxicating liquor.

Raw cashew nuts are poisonous in the way poison-ivy is. Their shells contain a non-volatile oil that causes severe dermatitis in sensitive people. This is released only if they are broken; unbruised fruits may be handled with impunity. The roasting process to which they are submitted before marketing the cashew nuts for human consumption, destroys the poison. An oil expressed from the seeds is an excellent lubricant and is used in varnishes and inks and for other purposes.

Garden and Landscape Uses. The cashew is sometimes grown in sheltered spots in southern Florida, but it is not common there. It is planted in Hawaii. This tree succeeds in earth too poor in fertility for many crops. It has some value as a small shade tree, decorative when bearing ripe fruits, but is planted chiefly as a fruit tree.

Cultivation. Cashews grown under favorable circumstances begin to bear when four or five years old and from then on with but little attention crop annually. Despite their ability to grow in poor, dry soils, they respond to fertilization, and to irrigation during dry periods. When young they are very sensitive to cold and in the continental United States should be protected during their early years. Propagation is commonly by seeds, which germinate in a month or less in a temperature of 70°F or above, and by air layering.

ANACHARIS. See Elodea.

ANACUA is *Ehretia anacua.*

ANACYCLUS (Anacỳc-lus). This group of twenty-five species of annuals and herbaceous perennials is indigenous from the Mediterranean region to the Orient. It belongs in the daisy family COMPOSITAE. The name is from the Greek *a,* without, *anthos,* a flower, and *kyklos,* a circle. It alludes to a characteristic of the flower heads. The kinds of *Anacyclus* have pinnately-cleft leaves and solitary, daisy-like flower heads, with yellow centers and white, yellow, or purplish ray florets. They somewhat resemble those of chamomile. The fruits are achenes.

Two annual species are grown, *A. officinarum* of southern Europe and *A. radiatus* of the Mediterranean region. The former attains a height of 1 foot or more, the latter possibly twice that. With white-rayed flower heads about 1 inch in diameter, and finely-cut, feathery foliage, *A. officinarum* is fairly showy in bloom. The undersides of its ray florets are stained with purple. The flower heads of *A. radiatus* are bright yellow, 1½ inches in diameter. Its leaves are deeply-incised. Variety *A. r. purpureum* has blooms attractively and strikingly striped with maroon.

Anacyclus officinarum

The best known perennial, *A. depressus* is native to Morocco. It has usually prostrate, sometimes ascending stems, and leaves once-, twice-, or thrice-pinnately-cleft. The flower heads, up to 2 inches in diameter, have white, dark red, or white-margined, red ray florets, purplish or reddish-purple on their undersides. Other

Anacyclus depressus

perennials are *A. atlanticus,* softly-hairy, prostrate, and with leaves two- or three-times-pinnately-divided and flower heads about ⅜ inch across, and *A. pyrethrum,* a prostrate species with twice-pinnately-divided leaves and flower heads with white rays that are purplish beneath. These perennial sorts may not be reliably hardy in climates colder than that of Long Island, New York.

Garden Uses and Cultivation. These plants are sun-lovers. They need porous soil. The perennials are best adapted for growing under scree or moraine conditions in rock gardens. The annuals are also suitable for rock gardens and for summer beds and borders. Their flowers are useful for cutting. All are easily raised from seeds, which in the case of the perennials, may be sown in spring in pots in a cold frame or cool greenhouse. The perennials can also be increased by cuttings in summer and by division in spring. Seeds of annual kinds are sown outdoors where the plants are to bloom as soon in spring as the ground can be worked. The young plants are thinned to from 1 foot to 1½ feet apart. Alternatively, seeds may be sown earlier indoors and the young plants transplanted to the garden at the spacing suggested after all danger of frost has passed. If the latter method is adopted the seeds should be sown about eight weeks before the plants are to be transferred to the garden, in a temperature of 60 to 65°F. The seedlings are transplanted 2 inches apart in flats or singly in 3-inch pots and are grown in a sunny greenhouse with a night temperature of 50°F and a day temperature between 50 and 55°F until they are hardened off in preparation for planting in the garden. Hardening is done by standing the plants outdoors in a sheltered location or in a cold frame for a week or two.

ANAGALLIS (Anagá-llis)—Pimpernel. Several charming garden plants are included in *Anagallis*, which comprises twenty-eight species of the primrose family PRIM-ULACEAE. The genus, of wide distribution in the wild, is most numerous as to species in western Europe and Africa. The name is from the Greek *anagelao*, to laugh, or to give delight.

Pimpernels include annuals, biennials, and herbaceous perennials, all low-growing, mostly with angled stems. Their leaves are opposite, alternate, or in threes. The flowers, mostly slender-stalked and solitary, have deeply-five-parted calyxes with spreading lobes. The corollas, wheel-shaped to shallowly-bell-shaped, are deeply-cleft into five obovate to linear lobes (petals). There are five stamens, with usually pubescent stalks, and one style.

Varieties of the annual scarlet pimpernel or poor man's weatherglass (**A. arvensis**) are pleasing. The best known are *A. a. caerulea*, with rich dark blue flowers; *A. a. latifolia*, with broader leaves and bright blue flowers; and *A. a. phoenicea*, which has deep red blooms. These variants are low, spreading plants with pointed-ovate leaves up to ¾ inch long, and blooms ¼ inch or slightly more in diameter. The scarlet pimpernel, native of Europe and Asia, is sparingly naturalized in North America. It is called poor man's weatherglass because its blooms close under dark skies. Indigenous to the Mediterranean region, *A. monellii* (syn. *A. linifolia*) is an attractive biennial or

Anagallis arvensis

Anagallis arvensis

perennial that can also be cultivated as an annual. Under favorable conditions it attains a height of 1 foot to 1½ feet and has flowers ¾ inch in diameter. Its leaves, linear to narrowly-lanceolate or ovate, are about 1 inch long. This is a variable native of dryish soils and open locations. Its flowers range from blue with reddish undersides to the petals to pink or purplish. A species not usually exceeding 6 inches in height, *A. tenella* of moist soils in the Mediterranean region and western Europe, has round-ovate leaves about ½ inch long, and small, red, bell-shaped flowers on stalks that are longer than those of *A. arvensis*.

Garden Uses. Pimpernels are excellent for edging flower beds and may be used with discretion to provide summer bloom in rock gardens. Because of their lush growth and because they do not look like high mountain plants, they are not suitable neighbors for choice alpines, however. They are attractive when grown in pots for decorating greenhouses in winter and spring. They need full sun.

Cultivation. Few plants are easier to grow. They thrive in any ordinary garden soil, the varieties of *A. arvensis* and *A. monellii* favoring sandy, well-drained ones, *A. tenella* doing best under somewhat damper conditions. Seeds may be sown directly outdoors in early spring and the resulting plants thinned to about 6 inches apart, or plants raised from seeds sown indoors earlier and grown on in flats or small pots can be set out at the same spacing as soon as danger from frost has passed. The seeds take about eighteen days to germinate in a temperature of 60 to 65°F. To have pot plants for flowering in winter and spring, seeds are sown in August or September and the resulting plants accommodated through the winter in a sunny greenhouse where the minimum temperature is 55 to 60°F. Good specimens may be had in 5- or 6-inch pots. When the final pots are well filled with roots regular applications of dilute liquid fertilizer help to maintain vigor and good foliage color. Perennial kinds are easy to propagate by cuttings and division as well as from seeds.

ANANAS (An-ánas)—Pineapple. The pineapple is one of five species of a genus endemic to the American tropics. Like most important food plants it has been transported by man to regions distant from its homeland, and is now cultivated in vast numbers in Hawaii, Puerto Rico, and other tropical areas. The genus *Ananas* belongs in the pineapple family BROMELIACEAE. To the same group belongs Spanish-moss (*Tillandsia usneoides*). It and the pineapple are unlikely looking close relatives.

The majority of the 1,400 species of bromeliads (members of the BROMELIACEAE) are epiphytes that perch on trees and shrubs, but do not extract nourishment from them. One of the minority, *Ananas* lives in a more ordinary manner with its roots in the ground. Its name is a modification of a South American aboriginal one.

Plants of *Ananas* have rosettes of rigid, wide-spreading, sword-shaped, usually spiny-toothed leaves, from the centers of which arise stout, generally elongated, leafy stems topped by a dense tuft of short leaves (the crown of the pineapple fruit). Below the crown the crowded, stalkless flowers develop. They are bisexual and reddish or violet. They have three short sepals and three petals, separated to their bases, but forming a tube-like flower. The stamens number three. The slender style is three-branched. The fruits are compound. They are formed by the more or less complete fusing of the greatly enlarged soft fleshy stem and the true fruits (which are technically berries) and adjacent parts embedded in it. The berries are arranged spirally and appear in the fruits of cultivated pineapples as six-sided, exterior segments. After fruiting, the stem and basal rosette of leaves dies and is replaced by sucker shoots from the bottom of the plant.

The pineapple (*A. comosus* syn. *A. sativus*) is regularly cultivated for its fruit only in favorable places in the tropics, but in the nineteenth century it was grown in

special greenhouses on the estates of wealthy amateurs in England. It was there that the superior type that is the basis of a vast agricultural enterprise in Hawaii and elsewhere in the tropics was developed.

Ananas comosus

Ananas comosus (flower)

Ananas comosus (fruit)

Until the English raised these improved, larger-fruited, seedless varieties, pineapples were very much less desirable fruits. Even before Europeans discovered America, however, the Indians made use of the small-fruited, seedy, wild types for food. These were observed on the island of Guadeloupe by Columbus in 1493 and

within a few years were introduced by the Spanish and Portuguese to Africa and later to India and Indonesia.

The wild species is rarely grown. Its superior varieties cultivated for their fruits, each with an identifying name, are grouped as *A. c. sativus*. In addition, there are highly ornamental variegated-leaved varieties. Of these, *A. c. variegatus* has leaves bordered with creamy bands, and *A. c. porteanus* leaves of olive-green, with a central stripe of yellow. A spineless-leaved variety, *A. c. lucidus*, is described. The leaves of pineapples may number thirty to fifty to a rosette and be 3 to 5 feet long by 1½ to 2 inches wide or wider. The stems that bear the fruits are 3 to 4 feet tall. In the wild species the flowers are about 1 inch long and the fruits often not more than 6 inches long.

Ananas comosus variegatus

Other kinds are also sometimes cultivated for ornament. The species **A. bracteatus** differs from *A. comosus* in having floral bracts that are conspicuous, strongly saw-toothed, and usually brightly colored; they completely hide the tops of the ovaries. Its large fruits are edible and nearly seedless. Variety *A. b. albus* has white floral bracts and fruits with many seeds. In *A. b. tricolor* (syn. *A. b. striatus*) the handsome leaves have coppery green centers and margins of creamy-yellow with red spines.

The species **A. ananassoides** has long, spiny leaves up to 1 inch wide that curve backward, and a slender stem that bears a few reddish-purple flowers succeeded by a seedy, miniature pineapple up to 6 inches in length. A smaller edition of the last, **A. a. nanus,** is attractive for growing in pots. Its fruit does not exceed 3 inches in length and is nearly or quite seedless.

Garden and Landscape Uses. In the tropics variegated-leaved pineapples are interesting low ornamentals. Elsewhere they, and as conversation pieces sometimes the green-leaved kinds, are cultivated in greenhouses devoted to tropical plants, and more rarely as houseplants.

Alpines, in containers

Amaranthus tricolor splendens

Anacampseros rufescens

Alstroemeria aurantiaca

Alpinia purpurata

Amaranthus tricolor 'Molten Fire'

Pineapple (*Ananas comosus* variety)

Ananas comosus variegatus

Anemone apennina alba

Anemone coronaria, with other foliage

Anemone coronaria

Anemonella thalictroides

Anemone pulsatilla

Ananas ananassoides nanus

Cultivation. The prime requirements for the successful cultivation of pineapples are fertile, well-drained soil with adequate moisture, high temperatures, and a humid atmosphere. Because most homes lack sufficient humidity, specimens grown as houseplants rarely succeed. In greenhouses a minimum winter night temperature of 65 to 70°F is most favorable, but they will stand a few degrees lower. By day in winter and at night at other seasons temperatures five to fifteen degrees, in high summer even more, above the winter minimum are advantageous. Propagation is by suckers from the base of the plant and by using the leafy crowns of the fruits as cuttings. For more information see Bromeliads or Bromels.

ANAPALINA (Anap-alìna). Members of this genus of seven species of the iris family IRIDACEAE have been incorrectly named *Antholyza*, a designation correctly reserved for related plants. Anapalinas are all South Africans. The name, derived from the Greek *anapalin*, in the reversed order, alludes to the bracts being shorter than the bracteoles.

Anapalinas have globose or subglobose corms (bulblike organs solid throughout, instead of consisting of superimposed layers or of overlapping scales). They have branchless stems and a few firm, narrowly-sword-shaped basal leaves that often are dying by the time the flowers are produced. There may or may not be stem leaves. The flowers, arranged spirally in dense spikes, are asymmetrical. They have perianths with slender, curved tubes, widening above, and longer than the six narrow and unequal lobes (petals). The latter become recurved as the blooms mature. There are three long-stalked stamens, and a style with three short branches. The fruits are more or less ellipsoid capsules containing angled seeds.

An inhabitant of stony and sandy, grassy slopes, **Anapalina nervosa** (syns. *A. revoluta, Antholyza revoluta, Antholyza nervosa*) is 1 foot to 1½ feet tall. It has four or five rigid, conspicuously four-veined, pointed basal leaves, and minute brown stem leaves or none. The dark salmon-pink or sometimes red blooms have perianths with tubes about 1¼ inches long, and blunt lobes of which the top one is almost 1 inch, and the others about ½ inch long.

Garden and Landscape Uses and Cultivation. For grouping in flower beds for summer bloom *A. nervosa* is useful. Not hardy in the north, it can be treated like gladioluses, taken up in fall and the corms stored over winter in a temperature of 40 to 50°F, and planted outdoors in spring. In regions where frost does not penetrate deeply enough to reach the corms they may remain in the ground permanently. The corms are set at a depth of 4 or 5 inches and 3 or 4 inches apart. Where the growing season is short they may be started early indoors in pots in a cool greenhouse and transplanted to the garden after the last frost. Propagation is by offsets and by seeds.

ANAPHALIS (Anáph-alis)—Pearly Everlasting. This chiefly eastern Asian genus of the daisy family COMPOSITAE is also represented in the wild in Europe and North America. It consists of thirty-five species. Its name is believed to be one applied by the ancient Greeks to some similar plant. The kinds described here are hardy.

Pearly everlastings are herbaceous perennials, similar to, but taller than antennarias, with stems and foliage clothed with white- or silvery-woolly hairs. They have alternate, undivided, toothless leaves, the basal ones not markedly bigger than the stem ones and often early deciduous. At the tops of leafy stems the several to many flower heads are displayed in branched, often ample clusters. Individually rather small, the flower heads are predominantly unisexual, with the sexes on separate plants, but female heads may have a few male florets at their centers. The florets are all of the disk kind (the type that compose the centers of the flower heads of daisies). There are no petal-like ray florets. Female florets have two-branched styles. The styles of male florets are generally undivided. The involucres (collars of bracts at the backs of the flower heads) are of several rows of dry, chaffy, usually white bracts.

The common pearly everlasting *A. margaritacea* is native of much of northern North America and also of Europe and eastern Asia. Quite variable, it is found wild on banks and in fields and other chiefly dry and open locations, especially in sandy and gravelly soils. It has erect, branched or branchless stems 1 foot to 3 feet tall, white-woolly or becoming somewhat rusty-colored with age. From 3 to 5 inches long, the linear or narrowly-lanceolate leaves have rolled-under margins. Sometimes their upper surfaces are green and may be hairless, but more often are furnished, although much less abundantly

Anaphalis margaritacea

than the undersides, with white hairs. The many gray-white to pearly-white flower heads, ¼ to ⅓ inch wide or a little wider, are in flattish or rounded, crowded clusters. The variant sometimes cultivated as *A. yedoensis* is *A. m. yedoensis*.

Anaphalis margaritacea yedoensis

Its ample clusters of larger flower heads more showy than those of the common pearly everlasting, *A. triplinervis* of the Himalayas is a more desirable garden plant. From 1½ to 3 feet tall, its stems are clothed with obovate to elliptic-oblong leaves 3 to 8 inches in length and up to ¾ inch wide.

Anaphalis triplinervis

Their undersides are thickly covered with white, woolly hairs, their upper surfaces are less hairy. The pale gray-white flower heads are ½ to ¾ inch in diameter.

Garden and Landscape Uses. Pearly everlastings are suitable for flower beds and less formal areas, and the common kind for inclusion in native plant gardens. They provide attractive, but not brilliant displays of bloom in late summer and fall. The flowers are useful for cutting and are easily prepared for dried arrangements. This is done by cutting them before they attain their fullest opening and before the whiteness of the stems and foliage begins to dim, tying the stems in small bundles, and hanging them in a cool, airy, shaded place. It is common practice to color the dried flowers by dipping them in dyes.

Cultivation. Pearly everlastings thrive with little care in sunny locations where the soil is thoroughly well drained and tends to be dryish rather than wet. They are easily increased by division in early spring, and can be raised from seeds. Dividing in fall is likely to result in winter losses. On poor soils these plants benefit from a spring application of a complete garden fertilizer, but this is unnecessary where the soil is reasonably fertile. Old plants that show signs of deterioration should be dug up, divided, and replanted in fall or spring. This may be needed every third or fourth year.

ANARRHINUM (Anarrhìn-um). One of this group of a dozen species is cultivated. The genus *Anarrhinum* is a native of the Mediterranean region and includes biennials and herbaceous perennials. It belongs in the figwort family SCROPHULARIACEAE. The name comes from the Greek *an*, without, and *rhinion*, a snout. It alludes to the absence of a large spur to the flowers. The spur may be minute or lacking.

Closely related to snapdragons (*Antirrhinum*) and toadflaxes (*Linaria*), this genus differs in its flowers not having palates in their throats. The plants have alternate, mostly-toothed basal leaves in rosettes. The leaves on the flowering stems are palmately (hand-like) split into three to seven narrow divisions that may or may not be toothed. The small, two-lipped, asymmetrical flowers are in slender racemes or panicles. They have five-lobed calyxes, tubular, two-lipped corollas with the upper lip two-lobed, the lower three-lobed. There are four nonprotruding stamens and one style. The fruits are capsules.

Cultivated *A. bellidifolium* is doubtfully hardy in climates more severe than that of New York City. It is a biennial about 2 feet tall, with spatula-shaped, deeply-toothed basal leaves up to 3 inches in length and stem leaves of three to seven linear segments. The flowers, about ⅛ inch long, are in long erect racemes. They are blue, blue with a white fringe, or white, and have a

short recurved spur. This is a quite pretty, but by no means extravagantly showy species.

Garden Uses and Cultivation. The chief use of this plant is to introduce variety into flower beds and borders. It blooms in early summer. To secure good plants, seeds are sown outdoors or in a cold frame in July or August, and the seedlings transplanted about 4 inches apart to sunny nursery beds or cold frames where they make their first season's growth and remain through the winter until they are transplanted in early spring to their flowering quarters. Their final spacing may be about 9 inches between individuals. In severe climates the frames in which the plants are overwintered should be protected by mats in very cold weather. This plant sets seed freely and this should be collected and sown to provide new stock. Old plants, except any needed for seed production, are discarded after they are through blooming. Anarrhinums grow best in full sun in porous soil. Their blooms are without merit as cut flowers.

ANASTATICA (Anastát-ica)—Rose-of-Jericho or Resurrection Plant. This genus of one species has a certain interest because of the unusual, but not unique, method by which its seeds are distributed, because when dead it is hydroscopic, and because it is very likely the "rolling thing before the whirlwind" and "the rose plant in Jericho" to which reference is made in the Bible. It is a small annual of the mustard family CRUCIFERAE, native to sandy deserts of the Near East and North Africa. Its name is derived from the Greek *anastasis*, resurrection. The common name resurrection plant is also applied to the completely different *Selaginella lepidophylla*, native to the Americas.

Without ornamental merit, ***Anastatica hierochuntica*** is a gray annual 3 or 4 inches in height. Its branches radiate from the top of a deep taproot. It has oblong-spoon-shaped, toothed leaves, and tiny white flowers followed by hairy seed pods. After the plant matures it breaks free of its roots, its branches dry and curve inward to form a light skeleton of a ball, and it is rolled along the desert floor by the wind. In this way, like American tumbleweeds, it is carried considerable distances and disperses its seeds as it rolls. Most curious is the hydroscopic property the plant exhibits after it is dead. Then, when dry, the branches are curled into a loose ball, upon moistening they spread out, but curl inward again upon drying. This opening and closing, which can be repeated indefinitely by alternating the availability of moisture, is the reason for the common name resurrection plant.

Garden Uses and Cultivation. Although without decorative merit this is a fascinating little plant to grow because of its inter-

esting behavior and associations. Its needs are of the simplest. It is well accommodated in porous, well-drained, not-too-fertile soil in full sun and is especially adapted for dry slopes. Its seeds, sown where the plants are to grow or started early indoors in a temperature of about 65°F, sprout quickly. In the garden the plants should be spaced 3 to 4 inches apart.

ANCHOMANES (Anchomá-nes). Ten species of the arum family ARACEAE constitute *Anchomanes*, a tropical African genus closely related to *Amorphophallus*. Its name was used by Dodonaeus for a related plant. Members of this group are tuberous, herbaceous perennials. As is characteristic of the family, the flowers are tiny and crowded in spikes (spadixes) from the bases of which sprout a more or less petal-like bract (spathe). Spadix and spathe constitute the inflorescence. In *Anchomanes* this is calla-lily-like in form. The fruits are berry-like.

Sometimes cultivated, *A. difformis* has a large tuber from which develops an in-

Anchomanes difformis (inflorescence)

florescence in spring or early summer. The stalk of this is prickly and up to 2½ feet long. The flowering part consists of a cream spadix about 9 inches long partially enclosed in a dark brownish-purple, hooded spathe. When in bloom the plant is leafless, but immediately after the flowers fade a solitary leaf develops. Its stalk, 3 to 7 feet long, is prickly. The divisions of its three-parted, up-to-3 feet long blade are deeply-pinnately-lobed. The leaf dies in fall and the tuber remains dormant through the winter. Summer- or fall-flowering *A. wel-*

witchii has a leaf with three primary divisions each bipinnately divided into sharp-pointed, broad-angled leaflets. Its inflorescence, topping an erect stalk a foot or more tall, has a club-shaped spadix and an erect yellow-green spathe the base of which is spiny and encloses the lower part of the spadix and the upper part of which looks like a reflector behind a candle flame.

Anchomanes welwitchii

Garden Uses and Cultivation. This handsome aroid is a collectors' item suitable for growing in tropical greenhouses and, in the tropics, outdoors. It requires rich, porous soil, constantly moist from when growth begins in spring until the foliage has died down naturally in fall. During the dormant period the soil of specimens grown in greenhouses should be kept dry. Repotting is done in spring just before the new growth starts. Specimens that have filled their containers with healthy roots benefit from fertilizing regularly throughout the summer. During winter the tubers are kept in the soil in which they grew in a temperature of 55 to 60°F. Throughout the growing season humid, tropical conditions are necessary, with the greenhouse temperature never dropping below 70°F and the humidity always high. Shade from strong direct sun is needed. Propagation is by seed.

ANCHOR PLANT is *Colletia cruciata.*

ANCHUSA (Anch-ùsa). A few kinds of this genus of fifty species of annuals, biennials, and herbaceous perennials of Europe, western Asia, North Africa, and South Africa are old-time and present-day garden favorites. They belong to the borage family BORAGINACEAE and have a name, the "ch" of which should be pronounced as "k," derived from the Greek *anchousa*, a paint for the skin. It alludes to an ancient use of these or related plants. Plants once included in *Anchusa* and still sometimes grown under that name are *Brunnera macrophylla* and *Pentaglottis sempervirens.*

Anchusas are hairy, often bristly so. They have alternate, undivided leaves. Their small flowers are ranked along coiled, elongating branches of the panicles. Their persistent calyxes are cleft into five lobes or parts. The trumpet- or funnel-shaped corollas have five rounded lobes (petals). Their throats are nearly closed by erect, blunt scales. There are five stamens. The fruits are of four seedlike nutlets, but quite often only one matures.

The most popular perennial anchusas are garden varieties of **A. azurea** (syn. *A. italica*). In the wild this native of the Mediterranean region is 3 to 5 feet tall. It has somewhat lustrous, oblongish to lanceolate leaves that may exceed 1½ feet in length, which have winged stalks or are essentially stalkless. Borne in summer, the bright blue to purple-blue flowers, ½ to ¾ inch in diameter, are in large panicles. Cultivated varieties of *A. azurea* have even bigger panicles, of flowers up to 1 inch wide or wider in various shades of blue.

Anchusa azurea

A lower perennial, rarely more than 2 feet tall, **A. barrelieri** has yellow-throated, rich blue, ¼-inch-wide flowers, with corolla lobes (petals) considerably longer than the corolla tube. Its oblong-lanceolate to spatula-shaped leaves, the lower ones long-stalked, those above stalkless, are up to about 6 inches long, and sometimes have wavy or toothed margins. This kind is native of Europe and Asia Minor. About as tall as the last, and perennial or some-

times biennial, **A. officinalis** comes from Europe and western Asia and is naturalized in New England. It has lanceolate leaves up to 6 inches long by 1 inch wide, the clustered basal ones stalked, those higher on the stems stalkless. The flowers have blue or purple-blue, or in *A. o. incarnata* pink, corollas up to ¼ inch across and with lobes (petals) much shorter than the tube.

Anchusa officinalis

Dwarf **A. caespitosa** of Crete is nearly stemless. It has basal tufts of many narrowly-linear leaves 2 to 4 inches long. Short-stalked, the bright blue, ½-inch-wide flowers are in few-flowered clusters usually nestled among the foliage. Sometimes mistakenly identified as the above, **A. angustissima** of Asia Minor differs in having leaf-bearing stems up to more than 1 foot tall, broader leaves, and flowers with sharp-pointed instead of blunt calyx lobes (sepals). These two species are perennials.

Anchusa caespitosa

South African *A. capensis,* a biennial less hardy than the other kinds discussed here, is often grown as an annual. From 1 foot to 1½ feet tall, it has slender, lanceolate to linear leaves up to 6 inches long, and narrowed to their bases. The flowers, about ¼ inch in diameter, are blue with white throats and are edged with red. Those of *A. c. alba* are white. The calyx lobes are shorter than the calyx tube.

Garden and Landscape Uses. The taller anchusas are admirable flower garden plants. Their predominantly rich blue blooms bring to beds, borders, and flower arrangements hues duplicated by few summer flowers except delphiniums, and when well grown the finest varieties of anchusa almost rival delphiniums in their landscape effect. They supply useful flowers for cutting, and are attractive to bees. Anchusas of low stature, such as *A. caespitosa,* are suitable for rock gardens.

Cultivation. Perennial anchusas for their best performance need deep, fertile, well-drained soil and full sun. They are hearty feeders that respond to a spring application and another later in the season of a complete garden fertilizer. Because of their robust habit and lush, slightly-coarse growth tall kinds need ample room. It is fatal to crowd them among other strong-growing plants. Allow at least 1¼ to 1½ feet between individuals. Although anchusas demand excellent soil drainage they will not stand dryness. Generous watering is needed in dry weather. To prevent storm damage it is usually desirable to support tall anchusas with discreetly placed stakes to which their stems are tied. As soon as the first flush of bloom is over cut the stems back to below the flowers. This often induces a second blooming. Perennial anchusas are easy to raise from seeds sown in a cold frame or outdoors in late spring, but choice, named varieties cannot be so propagated. Division in early spring, or better still, cuttings made in late summer of short sections of thick roots are the surest means of increasing such plants. Plant the root cuttings in sandy soil in a cold frame or protected place outdoors. Often, the best results are had with perennial anchusas when new plants are raised yearly and the old ones are discarded at the end of their first blooming season. Neither *A. caespitosa* nor *A. angustissima* are as tolerant of hot humid summers as the taller kinds. They are most likely to succeed in climates such as those of the Pacific Northwest.

Where winters are mild *A. capensis* can be grown as a biennial for blooming in spring. To achieve this, seeds are sown outdoors in summer. The seedlings are transplanted to nursery beds to complete their first season's growth, and in fall or the following spring are transferred to their flowering stations. This can also be treated as an annual, either by sowing seeds in early spring outdoors where the plants are to remain, and thinning the seedlings to 5 or 6 inches apart, or by sowing earlier indoors, transplanting to small pots or flats, and about six weeks after sowing, when danger of frost is passed, setting the young plants in the garden. Because *A. capensis* does not withstand hot, humid weather well, where summers are apt to bring such, it is advisable to start the plants early indoors so that they bloom before distressing weather arrives. When that happens the plants fail.

In greenhouses, *A. capensis* makes good late winter and spring displays in pots, or grown in benches or ground beds supply useful cut flowers. For these purposes sow seeds in September. Transplant the seedlings individually to small pots, and later from these to containers 4 or 5 inches in diameter, or space them 4 to 6 inches apart in benches or beds. They grow satisfactorily in ordinary well-drained soil, and need full sun. The night temperature should be between 45 and 50°F, that by day five to fifteen degrees higher depending upon the brightness of the weather. Ventilate the greenhouse freely on all favorable occasions.

ANCISTROCACTUS (Ancistro-cáctus)—Fishhook Cactus. Belonging to the cactus family CACTACEAE, this genus of four species inhabits the southwestern United States and Mexico. It differs from *Coryphantha* in the ovaries of its flowers being scaly, and from *Thelocactus, Mamillopsis,* and other close relatives, in having at least one spine at each areole (specialized portion of cactus stems from which spines develop) that is hooked. The name, alluding to the hooked central spines, is from the Greek *ancistros,* a fishhook, and cactus. These are small, spherical or sometimes low-cylindrical plants, with conspicuous protrusions from the plant body called tubercles, each ending in an areole. The flowers are short and comparatively small and are at the tops of the plant bodies. The juicy, green, thin-skinned fruits are approximately oblong.

An inhabitant of southern Texas and adjacent Mexico, the fishhook cactus (***Ancistrocactus scheeri*** syn. *Echinocactus scheeri*) has spherical to stout club-shaped plant bodies about 2 inches in height. They are usually solitary and generally have thirteen indistinct, spiraled rows of prominent conical tubercles. Each tubercle ends in an areole with fifteen to eighteen pale yellow to white, spreading radial spines and three or four long central ones of which one is strongly hooked. The greenish-yellow blooms are about 1 inch long. Another native of Texas, the fishhook cactus (***A. brevihamatus*** syn. *Echinocactus brevihamatus*) is similar to the last, but up to 4 inches tall and 3 inches in diameter. Its plant bodies are spherical to egg-shaped with the narrow end toward the ground. Similar to the *A. scheeri,* it differs, in addition to being bigger, in having the upper sides of its tubercles grooved for their entire lengths rather than one-half their lengths, in usually having only a dozen radial spines from each areole, and in its blooms being pink and about 1½ inches in length.

There arises from each areole of the Mexican *A. megarhizus* usually four central spines of which one is much larger than the others and is markedly hooked, and twenty or more radial spines, pale yellow when young, whitish when old, and arranged in comblike fashion. This species has globular plant bodies, solitary or in groups of up to four. They are up to 3 inches in diameter. Its flowers are not described.

Garden and Landscape Uses and Cultivation. These are the same as for other small desert cactuses and are explained under Cactuses.

ANDIRA (An-dìra)—Angelin Tree or Cabbage-Tree or Partridge Wood. The most important of this genus of thirty-five species of tropical American and West African evergreen trees is the angelin tree, cabbage-tree, or partridge wood (*Andira inermis*) of tropical America, the West Indies, and tropical West Africa. Its hard, heavy, strong, durable lumber is used locally for heavy construction, fashioned into small articles such as canes and umbrella handles, and used in turnery. Its bark and seeds have been employed medicinally.

Andiras have alternate leaves with an uneven number of leaflets, fragrant, pealike flowers in terminal panicles, and nutlike, one-seeded fruits that do not split to release their seeds. The flowers have toothless or nearly toothless calyxes, ten stamens of which usually one is free and the others united, and a short style. The genus belongs in the pea family LEGUMINOSAE. Its name is Brazilian.

The angelin tree (*A. inermis*) is variable and in the wild attains a height of 100 feet, but in cultivation is often not more than 50 feet tall. It has ill-smelling, ragged bark, and leaves with four or more pairs of oblong leaflets up to 2½ inches long. The small flowers, lilac, pale rose-pink, or red in 1-foot-long panicles, are succeeded by ovoid, woody pods 1 inch to 1½ inches long, each with a large seed.

Garden and Landscape Uses and Cultivation. The angelin tree is suitable only for humid tropical regions. It succeeds best in deep, fertile, moist soil, and transplants readily. It is usually increased by seeds, which germinate irregularly over a period of several months. Cuttings and air layering afford alternative means of increase.

ANDRACHNE (An-dráchne). The genus *Andrachne* of the spurge family EUPHORBIACEAE is distributed in the wild from North and South America and the West Indies to the Cape Verde Islands, the Mediterranean region and eastward, in Africa, and Australia. It consists of twenty-five species. Its name is a Greek one, *andrachne,* in ancient times applied to purslane and to the strawberry tree (*Arbutus unedo*).

Andrachnes are shrubs and herbaceous perennials with alternate leaves and from the leaf axils small, unisexual flowers, with both sexes on the same plant. They have five or rarely six sepals, usually as many petals, and the males as many stamens as sepals. The three styles are deeply-two-lobed. The female blooms are solitary, the males in clusters. The fruits are three-compartmented, six-seeded capsules.

Ranging in the wild from Missouri to Arkansas and Texas, *A. phyllanthoides* is an erect, deciduous shrub up to 3 feet tall, with downy, angled young shoots. Its elliptic to obovate leaves, sometimes downy on their undersides, ⅜ to ¾ inch long, have stalks only about ¹⁄₁₆ inch in length. The pale yellowish-green, starry flowers are about ¼ inch in diameter, the subspherical fruits slightly bigger. A native of the Caucasus, *A. colchica* is a dense, deciduous, twiggy, 3 foot-tall shrub differing from the last in having slenderer, hairless shoots. Its leaves are without down, and have ½-inch-long stalks and blades about ¾ inch long by approximately one-half as wide. The flowers and subspherical fruits are about ¼ inch wide.

Garden and Landscape Uses and Cultivation. Although neat in habit, andrachnes, of small ornamental merit, are unlikely to interest other than the botanically-minded. The species described are easy to grow in sunny locations in ordinary soils and are hardy in the vicinity of New York City. They can be increased by seeds and by summer cuttings.

ANDROMEDA (Andróm-eda)—Bog-Rosemary. The plants commonly known as *Andromeda* in gardens belong to the related genus *Pieris*. Others, *Chamaedaphne, Enkianthus, Gaultheria, Leucothoe,* and *Lyonia,* are also sometimes called *Andromeda*. True *Andromeda* has only two species and even these are considered to be merely variants of one by some botanists. It belongs in the heath family ERICACEAE. Its name is that of a maiden of Greek mythology. It inhabits northern latitudes around the world.

Andromedas are low, evergreen, creeping shrubs with wiry stems and alternate, short-stalked, narrow, toothless, leathery leaves. They have pinkish or white, urn-shaped, nodding flowers in compact terminal clusters. The five short perianth segments (petals) are recurved, and there are ten stamens. The fruits are dry capsules with many seeds.

Bog-rosemary (*A. polifolia*), native to cold northern bogs in North America, Europe, and Asia, is about 1 foot high. It has oblong to linear leaves up to 1½ inches long, with rolled-under margins. They are green above and without pubescence, often glaucous beneath. The flowers, which come in late spring or early summer, are ¼ inch long. Of this variable plant gardeners have selected and propagated desirable individuals that are identified by tacking such varietal designations as *angustifolia, compacta, minima,* and *nana* onto the end of the specific *A. polifolia*. The larger **A. glaucophylla** differs in size and in having leaves white-pubescent on their undersides. It reaches a height of 2 feet or slightly more and its linear to oblong leaves are up to 2½ inches long. It is an inhabitant of bogs and watersides from Greenland to Newfoundland, Minnesota, and Indiana and, in the mountains, to West Virginia. Hybrids, to which the name *A. jamesiana* is applied, exist between *A. polifolia* and *A. glaucophylla.*

Andromeda polifolia compacta

Garden Uses and Cultivation. These are quite charming items for those interested in the unusual and for inclusion in collections of native American plants. As may be gathered from a consideration of their native habitats they are extremely hardy to cold, but they withstand hot summers less successfully. They are best accommodated in bog gardens, rock gardens, and by watersides. Their soil must be decidedly acid. One of a sandy peaty character that is perpetually moist is best. If irrigation is required care should be taken that the water is free of lime. Some shade from strong summer sun is needed, but it must not be dense. Propagation can be by seeds sown on a finely sifted surface of sandy peaty soil or milled sphagnum moss in pots in a shaded cold frame or cool greenhouse. The seeds are very small and are merely pressed into the surface without being covered except for a sheet of shaded glass laid across the top of the pot. The pot is then stood in a saucer kept filled with water so that the soil surface is kept moist by capillarity. An alternative method of propagation is by cuttings of firm terminal shoots taken in summer and planted in a mixture of sand and peat moss in a propagating frame, preferably under mist. Division of older specimens can also be practiced. Established plants benefit from being kept mulched with peat moss or sphagnum moss.

Andrachne colchica

ANDROSACE (Andrósa-ce) — Rock-Jasmine. Temperate North America, Asia, and Europe are the home regions of these chiefly mountain plants. Androsaces, which belong to the primrose family PRIMULACEAE, include many intriguing species, some easy, some extremely challenging to grow, as well as a number too weedy in appearance to interest gardeners. There are about 100 species. The name comes from the Greek *androsakes,* applied to an unknown maritime plant.

Rock-jasmines are very closely related to primroses (*Primula*) and *Douglasia*. The significant botanical differences are that their flowers have corolla tubes shorter instead of longer than the calyxes, and the throats of the blooms are constricted. They include many tufted and rosette-forming species as well as others with leafy stems and of looser, more open, growth. The flowers, solitary, or in umbels with a number of leafy bracts at their bases, have five-toothed calyxes, corollas with five lobes (petals), five stamens, and one style. The fruits are capsules. Unless otherwise stated, all of the kinds now to be described are perennials.

Easiest to cultivate and entirely delightful are *Androsace primuloides,* more compact *A. p. chumbyi,* and *A. sarmentosa.* The first two are natives of the western Himalayas, the other ranges from the Himalayas to western China. These pretty plants take to lowland gardens with considerably more enthusiasm than most alpines. They have rosettes of foliage that send out, in strawberry-like fashion, slender, interlacing surface runners 1 inch to 6 inches long, at the ends of which new rosettes develop and root into any hospitable earth. The umbels of pink flowers terminate slim, erect stalks that come from the leaf axils of new rosettes of foliage that develop in spring above the old ones.

Variable *A. primuloides* has oblanceolate, toothless leaves mostly from up to ½ inch long or slightly longer, with a few of the upper ones considerably bigger. They are clothed with whitish hairs, as are the 2- to 4-inch-long flower stalks. The bracts at the bases of the umbels are lanceolate, of unequal breadths, and from ⅕ to ¾ inch long. Pink, and ⅓ inch wide or wider, the flowers have individual stalks shorter or longer, but not more than one-and-one-half times as long as the bracts. Their calyxes are lobed to about one-half their lengths. In contrast to those of *A. primuloides* and its variety, the floral bracts of *A. sarmentosa* are essentially of one size, about ¼ inch long, and are pointed-linear instead of broadly-lanceolate. Also, the stalks of the individual flowers of *A. sarmentosa* are two-and-one-half to three times as long as the bracts, and the calyxes of the flowers are lobed to about one-third their lengths. The plant sometimes called *A. s. watkinsii* is *A. sarmentosa.*

Similar to, but smaller than the andro-

Androsace sarmentosa

saces discussed above, perennial *A. sempervivoides* has rosettes scarcely ¾ inch wide, of closely overlapping, ovate-spatula-shaped, green leaves about ¼ inch long, and hairless except for eyelashed margins. Its runners are up to 2 inches long. Less than ¼ inch wide, the pink flowers are in little umbels carried on glandular stalks to a height of 1 inch or 2 inches. It is a native of Kashmir and Tibet.

The type species of the *Chamaejasme* group of *Androsace,* to which the kinds described above belong, *A. chamaejasme* is a rosette-forming perennial of mountains throughout the northern hemisphere, including North America. Its lanceolate, silky-hairy leaves are rather less than ½ inch long. Its blooms, white with yellow eyes that deepen to crimson, are ¼ to ½ inch wide, and in two- to eight-flowered umbels topping hairy stalks up to 5 inches tall. Variety *A. c. carinata,* native to the Rocky Mountains and Cascade Mountains, has leaves keeled beneath. Generally resembling *A. chamaejasme,* but smaller, choicer, and more temperamental, *A. villosa* is a high mountain perennial of Europe and Asia. Its rosettes of linear-lanceolate to

ovate-lanceolate leaves are thickly clothed with silvery hairs. They develop short runners. Rather less than ½ inch wide, the white to pink blooms have yellow to reddish eyes and are in short-stalked to stalkless umbels. This kind is reported to be partial to limestone soils, but in gardens grows satisfactorily in other gritty soils. A native of the European Alps, *A. obtusifolia* is another perennial relative of *A. chamaejasme.* Without runners, it is a taller, looser, smaller-flowered, greener-leaved representative of the group, not as pretty as *A. chamaejasme,* and usually with off-white flowers.

Very different from rosette androsaces is the late-blooming, Himalayan *A. lanuginosa.* Fairly accommodating to life in gardens, this silvery-hairy gem of a perennial has trailing, but not rooting leafy stems, and from the leaf axils on 3 to 4 inch long stems, umbels of pale lilac-pink blooms, each flower ⅓ inch wide or wider, and with a yellow center. The leaves are ovate-lanceolate and up to ¾ inch long. In variety *A. l. leichtlinii* the flowers are white with yellow eyes that change to red.

Responsive to cultivation, *A. lactea* is a charming, rosette perennial of the European Alps that forms mats several inches

Androsace lanuginosa leichtlinii

Androsace villosa

wide. Its thin, linear to linear-lanceolate, glossy green leaves are up to ¾ inch long, and fringed with hairs. The pure white flowers, less than ½ inch wide, and with yellow throats, occasionally are solitary, more often in umbels of up to four, on stems 2 to 4 inches tall.

Androsace lactea

Another accommodating perennial, **A. carnea** inhabits the Pyrenees and European Alps. Very variable, it has linear, toothed, more or less erect leaves with marginal hairs, in rosettes 1½ inches wide. On stalks from the leaf axils up to 3 inches long, the umbels are of eight or fewer pink or, in variety *A. c. alba* white, blooms with

Androsace strigillosa

yellow throats. Variety *A. c. halleri* has bold rosettes of lustrous, hairless, out-curved leaves 1 inch long or longer, and deeper pink, yellow-throated flowers. The rosettes of *A. c. brigantiaca* are less crowded, and its leaves are broader than those of *A. carnea*. The flowers are usually white. The very distinct *A. c. laggeri* forms mosslike mounds of stems with spreading or uppointing, slender leaves about ½ inch long. These kinds accommodate to limestone, neutral, or slightly acid soils, and do best in screes.

Quite distinct **A. strigillosa,** which not infrequently passes in gardens under the

Androsace foliosa

name that rightly belongs to another species, *A. foliosa*, is reasonably cooperative. It does not have runners. Its erect, firm-tipped leaves are narrowly-oblong to obovate, more or less thickly beset with stiff hairs, and are 1½ to 3 inches long. Its small, lilac-mauve blooms are few together in umbels topping stalks 6 to 8 inches in height. This native of the Himalayas is not one of the most attractive androsaces. Also Himalayan, *A. foliosa* is without runners. Its leaves, all basal, are elliptic to obovate, 2 to 3 inches long and hairy on both sides. The yellow-eyed, pink flowers, in umbels of many, are ½-inch in diameter.

Annual or sometimes biennial androsaces in the main are so inferior to the better perennials that they are without ornamental worth. Two that may be given places in gardens are *A. lactiflora* (syn. *A. coronopifolia*) and *A. macrantha*. The first comes from the Siberian-Mongolian border, the other from Asia Minor. Said to attain heights of up to 1 foot in the wild, but as known in cultivation much shorter, **A. lactiflora** has rosettes of glossy, linear-lanceolate, toothed leaves 1½ to 2 inches long from which arise many stems bearing ample clusters of ½-inch wide white blooms. Rarely more than 2 inches tall, **A. macrantha** has rosettes of oblong-lanceolate, toothed leaves less than ¾ inch long, and white flowers larger than those of *A. lactiflora* in umbels of up to ten at the tops of 2-inch-long stalks.

Garden Uses. The garden employments of these delightful plants are to a large extent dependent upon the attention they receive from rock garden enthusiasts, who find them admirable and often challenging to grow outdoors and in alpine greenhouses and cold frames. Easy-to-manage exceptions are *A. sarmentosa* and its kin. These hearty representatives of the race, incidentally among the best for rock gar-

dens, adapt willingly to less specialized sites than do most androsaces, and can be grown in dry walls and as low groundcovers in small areas. They thrive in lowland gardens in the East and, unlike many of their relatives, are not unduly disturbed by hot, humid summers.

Cultivation. The most important soil need of androsaces is that drainage be perfect. They will not thrive where there is any suspicion of stagnancy or where air and moisture cannot pass freely through their rooting medium. Sandy earth, not too rich, and very generously laced with stone chips of limestone for some kinds, of sandstone or other rock for others, comes near the ideal, but more difficult kinds are likely to respond best to scree conditions (see Scree under Rock and Alpine Gardens). The soil bed should be deep, and from spring to fall moderately moist. A little shade during the hottest part of the day is appreciated by most androsaces, especially where summers are very hot. In cooler climes shade is less essential. The more difficult species are plants to toy and experiment with until locations and treatment best suited to their needs in particular gardens are found. They are easily raised from seeds, and many kinds by offsets and cuttings.

ANDROSTEPHIUM (Andro-stèphium). This genus of three species of the lily family LILIACEAE is endemic to the southwestern United States. Its name is derived from the Greek *andros*, male, and *stephanos*, a crown, in allusion to the filaments (stalks) of the stamens being joined. These plants have corms (often improperly called bulbs) that, like those of crocuses, are covered with fibrous tunics. Their all-basal leaves are linear and channeled. The funnel-shaped flowers are in umbels atop erect stalks, each bloom with an unjointed individual stalk. The perianth segments (commonly called petals) are joined into a tube below with erect, cleft lobes between the anthers. There are six stamens that have their lower parts united into a tube. The fruits are bluntly-three-angled capsules containing black seeds. The tubular crown or corona with bifid lobes between the anthers distinguishes *Androstephium* from the related *Brodiaea*.

The most likely to be cultivated is **A. caeruleum,** a pretty spring-blooming native of Kansas to Texas. Up to 8 inches in height, it has four to six very narrow leaves and lilac to violet flowers with spreading perianth segments. The corona is about one-half as long as the perianth segments.

Garden Uses and Cultivation. These plants are best adapted for rock gardens and similar locations. They should be planted in groups with the corms about 6 inches beneath the surface. Well-drained sandy soil suits them. They are less well adapted to eastern North America than to the drier climates of the West Coast.

ANDRYALA (Andrý-ala). To the daisy family COMPOSITAE belong the twenty-five species of *Andryala*, natives of the Mediterranean region. The name is of uncertain derivation.

Andryalas are milky-juiced herbaceous perennials and subshrubs. Their alternate leaves have smooth, toothed, or lobed margins. Like those of dandelions, their flower heads are of petal-like, strap-shaped florets. The fruits are seed-like achenes.

An attractive alpine subshrub of Spain, *A. agardhii* is 3 to 6 inches tall. It has crowded basal rosettes of stalked, lanceolate to oblanceolate or spatula-shaped leaves, 1 inch to 3 inches long by up to a little more than ½ inch wide, densely felted with yellowish or white hairs. The few distantly-spaced leaves of the stalks bearing the solitary flower heads are much smaller and pointed-linear. Solitary and about ¾ inch across, the flower heads are carried well above the foliage.

Garden Uses and Cultivation. Suitable for sunny rock gardens, *A. agardhii* thrives in gritty, well-drained soil. It is hardy, but unlikely to prosper where summers are hot and humid. Propagation is by seed.

ANEMARRHENA (Anema-rrhèna). Although scarcely worthy of consideration as an ornamental, the only species of this genus of the lily family LILIACEAE, because of its use in Japan and China for medical purposes, is an appropriate occupant of herb and medicinal gardens and is possibly of interest to collectors of rare and unusual plants. Its generic name is perhaps from the Greek *anemonos*, wind, and *arrhen*, male, but is of uncertain application. The specific epithet of *A. asphodeloides* suggests its similarity to its close relative, the asphodel (*Asphodelus*). A native of northern China, this deciduous, herbaceous perennial is up to 3½ feet high, has mostly basal, tapering, grass-like leaves up to 2½ feet long and ⅜ inch wide and an erect flower stem rising well above the foliage. Its rootstock is a woody rhizome. The faintly fragrant flowers, about ⅓ inch long, are dull purple on their outsides and buff-colored within. In warm sunny weather they open at dusk and close the following morning, but on cool, dull days they remain open.

Garden Uses and Cultivation. Appropriate uses in gardens are discussed above. The plant is hardy in New England and is easily raised from seeds. It grows without difficulty in ordinary garden soil in full sun.

ANEMIA (Anè-mia)—Flowering Fern. Formerly spelled *Aneimia*, the genus *Anemia* of the schizea fern family SCHIZAEACEAE comprises ninety tropical and subtropical species of ferns, mostly natives of the Americas, with two indigenous to the United States. The name, from the Greek *aneimon*, naked, and *heima*, clothing, alludes to the spore clusters being uncovered.

Anemias have creeping or ascending rootstocks and one- to three-times-pinnate or pinnately-cleft leaves (fronds) of two types, fertile or spore-bearing, and sterile or not spore-bearing. The lowermost pair of leaflets of fertile fronds are considerably lengthened, often overtopping the rest of the leaf. They are slender, and on the backs of their very narrow segments there develops two rows of spore cases. This is the feature responsible for the colloquial name flowering fern, the spore-bearing portions of the fertile fronds suggesting panicles of tiny blooms.

Native in coral rock and sandy soils in Florida and extending to tropical South America, *A. adiantifolia* is up to 3 feet tall, with creeping rootstocks. Its long-stalked, thrice-pinnate leaves have broad-based, triangular blades up to 1 foot long with shallowly-lobed, usually obovate to wedge-shaped ultimate segments. The spore-bearing panicles, which originate well below the lowest leaflets, are erect, tan or brown. The other species indigenous to the United States, *A. mexicana*, is native in dry soil in Texas and adjacent Mexico. It has creeping rhizomes and pinnate leaves up to 2 feet tall or taller, with four to six pairs of short-stalked, toothed, ovate-lanceolate side leaflets and a larger terminal leaflet. The spore-bearing panicles, longer than the rest of the leaf, originate well below the lowest regular leaflets.

Native from Mexico to South America and Cuba, *A. phyllitidis* has once-pinnate leaves with blades up to 1 foot in length with four to twelve pairs of lanceolate, round-toothed, stalkless leaflets, the spore-bearing ones 4 inches to 1 foot long and originating level with the lowest pair of regular leaflets. The Brazilian *A. rotundifolia* has once-pinnate, narrow leaves up to more than 1 foot long, with oblongish to lozenge-shaped or rounded leaflets that slightly diminish in size from base to apex. The fertile leaflets originate well below the sterile ones.

Garden Uses and Cultivation. These are for choice fern collections and for growing by fanciers of ferns. Indoors they do best in pots or pans (shallow pots) in warm, humid places with shade from strong sun. Well-drained soil rich in organic matter and kept damp suits anemias. Propagation is by division and spores.

ANEMONE (Anemó-ne)—Windflower. For the name of this genus the pronunciation *Anémo-ne* is more commonly used than more correct, classical *Anemò-ne*. The group it identifies comprises about 120 species of the buttercup family RANUNCULACEAE, mostly of north-temperate and arctic regions of both eastern and western hemispheres. Many kinds inhabit high places in high mountains. Besides a selection of natural species, lovely, highly-developed horticultural varieties and hybrids of some kinds are popular. The name *Anemone* probably is derived from a word of Semitic origin alluding to the blood red flowers of

Anemia phyllitidis

A. coronaria. By some authorities the pasque flowers are segregated from *Anemone* to constitute the genus *Pulsatilla,* but that is not done here. The shrubby plant called tree-anemone is *Carpenteria californica.* The rue-anemone is *Anemonella thalictroides.*

Anemones are hardy and nonhardy herbaceous perennials many of which bloom very early, others not until fall. They range in size from diminutive to well-branched plants 2 to 5 feet tall or taller. Some have tuberous roots, some have rhizomes. Mostly basal, their leaves are sometimes divided into separate leaflets, more often are coarsely- to finely-palmately (in hand-fashion) -lobed or -cleft and toothed. The erect stems have, close to or some considerable distance down from the bloom, an involucral-like ruff of two or three leaves usually smaller than the basal ones. Anemone flowers are without petals. The white or brightly colored parts that look like petals are petal-like sepals. The numerous stamens are shorter than the sepals. The many pistils each mature into a seedlike fruit (achene). In the sorts by some authorities placed in the segregate genus *Pulsatilla,* the styles are feathery and elongate dramatically as the blooms pass into the fruiting stage. These possess nectar-secreting staminodes (abortive stamens).

Florists' anemones, popular as cut flowers and in the Pacific Northwest as garden plants, are horticultural derivatives of the poppy anemone (*A. coronaria*), *A. hortensis,* and *A. pavonina.* Not hardy in the north, in regions of milder winters and in greenhouses and cold frames these are among the most gorgeous of spring flowers. They have small, very irregular, knobby tuberous roots of most unpromising appearance when dry. It is scarcely believable that from such apparently lifeless scraps can come, and in such short time, the magnificent blooms that these plants bear. Florists' anemones attain heights of 1 foot or more, have finely-divided, somewhat parsley-like foliage, and long-stalked flowers 2 to 3 inches across. They come in white and in a wide variety of brilliant hues except yellow and orange. The best known strains are the St. Brigid and the de Caen. The former have semidouble to double flowers with several rows of lanceolate, petal-like sepals. The blooms of the de Caen strain have a single row of broad-obovate, petal-like sepals. Other good strains are the St. Bavo and the Creagh Castle. Excellent varieties are 'His Excellency', single crimson-scarlet flowers with white centers; 'Mr. Fokker', single blue blooms; 'Sylphide', single mauve flowers; 'The Admiral', deep pink semidouble flowers; 'The Bride', single white flowers; and 'The Governor', scarlet double blooms.

Japanese anemones are great favorites for fall display, worthy companions for chrysanthemums and Michaelmas daisies or perennial asters. They are admirable as ornamentals in gardens and as cut flowers. The first known of these garden varieties developed in Japan and China, were introduced to Europe from Shanghai by Robert Fortune in 1844. They were first named *A.*

japonica, which name had previously been used for a semidouble variety of *A. hupehensis,* now identified as *A. h. japonica,* and cultivated in Japan and China. Three years after being brought to England they were hybridized there with *A. vitifolia* to produce offspring now designated *A. hybrida* (syn. *A. elegans*). Garden Japanese anemones, available in a number of named va-

Anemone hybrida

rieties and with flowers white and in various shades of pink, are varieties of *A. hybrida.* They are considerably taller, usually 3 to 5 feet in height, than *A. hupehensis* of China and its variety, *A. h. japonica,* which do not exceed 2 feet. Also, their flowers usually have a few more than the five or six petal-like sepals of *A. hupehensis* and fewer (usually many fewer) than the twenty or more characteristic of *A. h. japonica.* Japanese anemones are hardy herbaceous perennials. They have sturdy, freely-branched stems and long-stalked leaves of three ovate, lobed or toothed leaflets sparsely-hairy on their undersides. The flowers, beautiful, plentifully produced, and up to 3 inches in diameter, are white, pale pink, rose-pink, or purplish-pink. There are single, semidouble, and double varieties. Among the most popular are 'Margarette', with double pink blooms; 'Profusion', its flowers deep rose-pink; and 'September Charm', which has delicate pink flowers shaded with rose pink. Yellow-centered, white flowers are borne by *A. h. alba.*

Anemones of the pasque flower relationship, segregated by some authorities as the separate genus *Pulsatilla,* include a number of species of considerable horticultural merit. They are chiefly inhabitants of meadows at subalpine and lower altitudes rather than high alpines. Typically, they have very long and deep woody roots, attractive ferny foliage, which may or may not be well developed at flowering time, and plumy heads of seeds that are almost or quite as decorative as the blooms. The

Florists' anemones

sorts now to be considered all belong in this group.

The common European pasque flower (**A. pulsatilla** syns. *Pulsatilla vulgaris, P. amoena*) blooms in spring before attaining its mature height of 9 inches to 1¼ feet and before its foliage is developed. Softly-hairy throughout, this charming sort has its chief leaves thrice-pinnately-divided and 4 to 6 inches long. Those that form the ruffs beneath the flowers are about 1 inch long. The blooms, solitary and up-facing, are typically blue to lavender or reddish-purple and 2 to 2½ inches across. Those of *A. p. alba* are white; those of *A. p. albicyanea* bluish-white; those of *A. p. mallenderi* dark purple; and those of *A. p. rubra* reddish-purple. Native from central Europe to the Ukraine, *A. p. grandis* has leaves less finely cut than the typical species, which become hairless as they age.

Anemone pulsatilla

Another pasque flower, **A. patens** (syn. *Pulsatilla patens*), of northern Europe, has leaves of three slender-lobed divisions, hairy most especially on their undersides. The solitary blue-violet to purple, yellow, or white flowers with blue-violet sepals hairy on their backs, 2 to 3 inches across, are nearly erect. They appear early, before the foliage.

The American pasque flower (**A. nuttalliana** syn. *Pulsatilla nuttalliana*), native from Nebraska to Utah, Washington, and Alaska, differs from the European kind in recondite botanical detail and more obviously in developing a goodly amount of foliage before its flowers open. The middle division of the three of each leaf in this sort has a little individual stalk, which is lacking in the leaves of the European pasque flower.

Other sorts of the pasque flower group include these: **A. albana** (syn. *Pulsatilla albana*), a native from Asia Minor to central Asia, is 4 to 6 inches tall, has twice-pinnately-lobed, white-hairy leaves and nodding, more or less bell-shaped, solitary flowers up to 3 inches across, purple and silky-hairy on their outsides, milky-white to pale yellow within. The blooms of *A. a.*

georgica of the Caucasus are violet-rose-colored. **A. alpina** (syn. *Pulsatilla alpina*), 4 inches to 1¼ feet tall and native to the mountains of Europe, is one of the finest of the race. It has ferny leaves, the lower ones thrice-divided, the upper ones twice-divided. The solitary, up-facing flowers, 2 to 3 inches wide and with six milky-white to pale blue sepals (commonly called petals), are tinted purple on their backs. The blooms of *A. a. sulphurea* (syn. *A. sulphurea*) are sulfur-yellow, about 2 inches across. **A. halleri** (syn. *Pulsatilla halleri*) is excellent.

Anemone alpina sulphurea

Native to the European Alps and 4 inches to 1 foot tall, this silky-hairy sort has long-triangular leaves cleft into slender segments. Its lilac-purple to violet-purple, or much more rarely white or pink, flowers face nearly upward, and are 2½ to 3 inches wide. **A. occidentalis** (syn. *Pulsatilla occidentalis*) is the North American equivalent of *A. alpina*. Native from Montana to British Columbia and California, it is sometimes 2 feet tall when fully developed, though considerably shorter at blooming time. Its silky-hairy leaves are thrice-parted with the divisions twice-pinnately-cleft into linear segments. The flowers are solitary, have five to eight, 1-inch-long, white or purplish sepals, hairy on their backs. Native from northern Europe to Siberia **A. pratensis** (syn. *Pulsatilla pratensis*), is silky-hairy, up to 1 foot tall. Its leaves are pinnately-cleft into narrow segments. The solitary, urn- to bell-shaped blooms, nodding rather than erect, have six sepals with tips that spread or curl backward, are from pale to dark violet in color. Those of *A. p. nigricans* are black-violet. **A. vernalis** (syn. *Pulsatilla vernalis*) is a European high alpine of glorious merit. From 2 to 6 inches tall and clothed with golden-bronze hairs, it has evergreen, pinnate leaves 1 inch to 2 inches long of three- to five-lobed segments. The 2-inch-wide flowers when open face upward, have six white sepals about 1 inch long that become purplish as they age, or the sepals may be from pink to rich purple.

Anemone vernalis

Wood anemones include American and European sorts. The former differs from the latter chiefly in its frailer appearance and in having more slender stems and smaller blooms. Native in humid woodlands from Quebec to Manitoba, Georgia, and Iowa, the American wood anemone (**A. quinquaefolia**) is 4 to 8 inches tall. It has a single, long-stalked basal leaf of three or seemingly five cleft leaflets and a whorl of smaller, but otherwise similar leaves on the stem. The long-stalked, up-facing, white flowers, sometimes tinged red on their undersides, have usually five spreading, petal-like sepals. They are usually less than 1 inch wide. The lovely European wood anemone, (**A. nemorosa**), showier than its American relative, is as hardy, and easy to grow. It has one or two, long-stalked, three- or apparently five-parted basal leaves, the divisions or lobes deeply-cleft. Up to 1 foot high, but much more commonly not exceeding 6 inches in height, the stems have leaves similar to, but smaller than the basal ones and with flattened stalks. The 1½- to 2-inch wide, somewhat cupped, drooping blooms have usually six or seven, sometimes five, rarely up to twelve, petal-like sepals, hairless on their outsides, typically white suffused with pink or purple, less commonly blue or purple. Their anthers are deep yellow. A splendid variety is *A. n. allenii*, the sturdiest and largest-flowered. This has pale lavender-blue blooms, rosy-lilac on their outsides. The flowers of *A. n. robinsoniana* are clear, light lavender-blue. Those of *A. n. 'Royal Blue'* are of a bright deeper blue. Yet others have been named *A. n. 'Blue Beauty'*, its pale blue flowers silvery on their undersides, and *A. n. 'Blue Bonnet'*, with large blooms of soft blue. The double-flowered *A. n. alba-plena* has white blooms with six petal-like sepals and their centers filled with a powder puff of modified petal-like stamens.

The yellow wood anemone (**A. ranunculoides**) is aptly named (*ranunculoides* means resembling a buttercup). Native of Europe where it grows in dampish, often limestone soils, this charming spring-bloomer thrives with abandon, but without being aggressive in gardens in eastern North America and is deserving of being more widely grown. It has brown rhizomes, stems 4 inches to rarely 1 foot tall, usually one deeply-palmately-divided, toothed basal leaf, and similar, but smaller, stem leaves. The blooms, usually two, less often one or more than two on a stem, are up to ¾ inch in diameter. Variety *A. r. wockeana* is smaller, has shorter rhizomes, and forms dense patches. The rare *A. r. pleniflora* has double blooms.

Commonly accepted as two species, but perhaps more realistically regarded as variants of one, *A. apennina* of Southern Europe and *A. blanda* of southeastern Europe are choice. Mountain relatives of the European wood anemone, these beauties differ from it in their flowers, daisy-like in aspect, but not in structure, having eight to fourteen, usually blue, petal-like sepals pubescent on their outsides, and pale yellow to white anthers. These have tuberous rhizomes and stems about 6 inches tall.

Anemone blanda

Anemone blanda

The leaves are deeply-lobed with the lobes cleft or toothed. Those of *A. apennina* are hairy on their undersides, those of *A. blanda* hairless. The flowers of the former

tend to have fewer sepals than those of *A. blanda* and in the fruiting stage remain erect instead of nodding.

The snowdrop anemone (*A. sylvestris*) inhabits central and eastern Europe and extends into Sweden and northern France.

Anemone sylvestris

Its slightly drooping, usually solitary, pure white, fragrant flowers from 1½ to nearly 3 inches across, have mostly five broad-ovate sepals and yellow anthers. The fruits are densely-woolly. From 9 inches to 1½ feet tall, this pretty species spreads freely by running rootstocks. Its three- to five-parted leaves, hairy on their undersides, basal and stem ones similar except that the latter are smaller and have shorter stalks, are deeply-lobed. Selections with especially large blooms have been named *A. s. grandiflora* (syn. *A. s. macrantha*). A double-flowered variety is *A. s. flore-pleno*.

Anemone sylvestris grandiflora

Other anemones cultivated to a greater or lesser extent include these: *A. baldensis* native to mountains in Europe is a choice alpine up to about 4½ inches high in bloom, though taller later. Its stalked,

basal leaves are three-times thrice-divided into toothed segments, its stem leaves similar, but smaller. Its usually solitary, white blooms, 1 inch to 1½ inches wide, have eight to ten petal-like sepals. *A. canadensis,* native of damp soils from Quebec to

Anemone canadensis

British Columbia, Maryland, Missouri, and New Mexico, is 1 foot to 2½ feet tall, with slender rhizomes. Its several, long-stalked basal leaves have deeply-three-parted blades, rounded in outline and with their primary divisions further divided or cleft, and smaller, stalkless, but otherwise similar stem leaves. The slender-stalked, up-facing blooms are white, 1 inch to 1½ inches wide. *A. caroliniana,* 4 inches to 1¼ feet tall, is a native of dry soils from Wisconsin and South Dakota to Georgia, Louisiana, and Texas. It has short, tuber-like rhizomes and long-stalked, three-parted, basal leaves, their divisions deeply and irregularly slashed into pointed segments. The stem leaves, below the middle of the stem, are similar to the basal ones, but stalkless and smaller. The white to rose-pink or purple, solitary blooms have ten to twenty petal-like sepals, are from less than ½ inch to nearly 1 inch across. *A. coronaria,* the poppy anemone of the Mediterranean region, is one of the parents of the florists' hybrid anemones. It has tuberous roots, basal leaves twice divided into three, their divisions deeply-lobed. The stem leaves are slashed into slender segments. From 1½ to 2½ inches across, the solitary red, blue, or white blooms have five to eight elliptic, petal-like sepals, and blue anthers. It is 6 inches to 1½ feet tall. *A. fulgens,* a natural, more or less intermediate, red-flowered hybrid between *A. coronaria* and *A. pavonina* shows considerable variation when raised from seeds. *A. hortensis* of the central Mediterranean region resembles *A. coronaria,* but its basal leaves are lobed rather than divided to their bases and the linear-lanceolate stem leaves are generally not divided. The light purplish blooms have twelve to nineteen petal-like sepals. **A. multifida,** an inhabitant of southern South America, is represented in the flora of North America by *A. m. hudsoniana* and *A. m. richardsiana,* the former ranging from Newfoundland to Alaska, Maine, and Oregon, the latter, which differs in having larger flowers, native to Quebec. From 6 inches to 2 feet tall, these have long-stalked, deeply-three-parted basal leaves with the divisions cleft into slender divisions or lobes and similar, stalkless, smaller stem leaves. The long-stalked, usually solitary blooms ½ to 1 inch across, have five to ten white, yellowish, or red petal-like sepals. These kinds in the wild favor limy soils. **A. narcissiflora** of the mountains of southern and central Europe and of the Urals is a variable species 9 inches to 1½ feet tall. Its long-stalked basal leaves are divided into three to five lobes with pointed-linear segments. The stem leaves are stalkless, three- to five-cleft.

Anemone narcissiflora

White or cream, sometimes pinkish or purplish on their outsides, the flowers have five or six obovate petal-like sepals. **A. pavonina,** native from southwest France to Turkey, a parent of the florists' tuberous anemones, is tuberous-rooted. Unlike *A. coronaria,* to which it is related, its stalkless stem leaves are scarcely or not divided. From *A. hortensis,* which it much resembles, it differs in its flowers having usually eight or nine, more rarely seven or up to twelve broader, scarlet, purple, or pink, petal-like sepals often yellowish toward their bases. **A. virginiana** inhabits dry and open woodlands from Quebec to North Dakota, Georgia, Alabama, and Arkansas. From 1 foot to 2½ feet tall, it has long-stalked basal and stem leaves, rounded in outline, deeply divided into three or five coarsely-toothed segments. The flowers have white to greenish-white petal-like segments, are usually up to ¾ inch across, but variants sometimes identified as *A. v. leucosepala* have pure white blooms up to nearly 1½ inches across. **A. vitifolia,** of the Himalayan region and China, is about 2 feet tall. It has large, long-stalked five-lobed leaves, white-woolly on their undersides and never divided into separate leaflets. The flowers, usually have five petal-like sepals, hairy on their outsides. It is less hardy than *A. hupehensis* and *A. hybrida* which in habit it resembles.

Garden and Landscape Uses. The anemone clan provides choice materials for discriminating gardeners. The florists' tuberous kinds, unfortunately not hardy in the north, are superb for garden embellishment in the Pacific Northwest and other parts suitable for their cultivation and are grown in considerable quantities in greenhouses for cut blooms. They need cool temperatures indoors so where winters are not excessively severe cold frames or slightly heated frames can substitute for greenhouses. The ancestral species of florists' anemones are suitable for mild-climate rock gardens. Like the florists' anemones, these revel in full sun. Japanese anemones are primarily for flower beds and borders and for supplying cut blooms. They prefer deep, fertile, moist, but not wet soil and a location where just a little middle-of-the-day shade tempers the full intensity of summer sun. The same environments suit *A. hupehensis* and *A. vitifolia* and these have the same garden uses as hybrid Japanese anemones. The taller native Americans *A. canadensis,* *A. multifida,* and *A. virginiana* are suitable for native plant gardens and more or less naturalistic areas. They do well in lightly-shaded places in fairly-rich, not-too-dry soils approximating those they favor in the wild. Wood anemones are delightful for colonizing beneath trees and shrubs and in rock gardens where there is just a little shade and where the soil is fairly loose and has a high organic content. They delight in leaf mold and woods' earth, damp, but not wet, and in dappled shade. The snowdrop anemone and *A. narcissiflora* also need partial shade and a woodland-type soil. They can be given homes in naturalistic areas among deep-rooting trees or shrubs or in rock gardens. And rock gardens and similar intimate landscapes are obviously the most suitable accommodations for mountain species and other dwarf anemones.

Cultivation. With such a large and varied assemblage, coming from such diverse native habitats as anemones, cultural needs are likely to vary considerably. And with anemones they do. Florists' anemones and the species from which they have been bred (*A. coronaria,* *A. hortensis,* and *A. pavonina*) are treated similarly. In mild climates give them sunny locations and for preference sandy soil, or at least not a sticky clayey one or gumbo. Enrich it by incorporating generous amounts of good compost, peat moss, or similar organic material. Plant the tubers in early fall about

Florists' anemones as cut flowers with vaccinium foliage

2 inches deep, 8 to 10 inches apart. Where winters tend to be cold, mulch after planting with 3 or 4 inches or more of peat moss and remove this when danger of damaging cold is past. In spring after flowering, the foliage gradually dies. When this is completed you may dig the tubers and store them packed in peat moss or vermiculite in a dry, reasonably cool place until the fall planting season, or if you prefer, leave them in the ground undisturbed, without watering during the summer dormant period, for more than one year, until crowding with its consequent threat of reduced floral display indicates the need for lifting, separating, and replanting the tubers in freshly worked and conditioned soil.

In the north good results can be had with these anemones by planting in fall in cold frames kept well protected against hard freezing but ventilated freely whenever weather permits. Greenhouse cultivation is also very practical in benches, ground beds, or pans (shallow pots). Use sandy, fertile soil containing an abundance of peat moss or other organic conditioner. Purchased tubers may be planted as soon as they can be obtained in fall as advised for outdoor planting, but the best results are usually had from seeds sown in May and the resulting plants grown on indoors without resting or check until after they bloom the following spring. If you follow this plan transplant the seedlings as soon as they are big enough to handle to flats or small pots and from those, before they become crowded, to benches or ground beds spacing them 5 to 6 inches apart, or to successively larger containers until they occupy pans or pots 6 to 8 inches in diameter. Shade lightly from the fiercest summer sun. The most important factor is the maintenance of a cool environment. Fall to spring night temperatures of 40 to 45 or at most 50°F are adequate. By day let these increase by five, ten, in brilliant sunny weather toward spring even fifteen degrees, but whenever the weather outdoors permits ventilate the greenhouse freely. Water moderately in fall and winter; water newly planted tubers sparingly until they have made foliage, freely as spring approaches. When flower buds begin to show nourish the plants moderately with dilute liquid fertilizer.

Hardy anemones that bloom in spring and disappear from view after flowering, the wood anemones and the alpine kinds grown in rock gardens, respond to well-drained, gritty soils containing appreciable amounts of organic matter and, especially for wood anemones, of fairly loose texture. Except for the wood anemones, these others are grateful for a generous admixture with the soil of chips of limestone or crushed oyster shells. Locations subject to sweeping winds are not to their liking. Sites affording shelter and a little dappled shade are preferred. Plant as soon after the

foliage has died as possible or in fall at depths of 2 to 3 inches, spaced 3 to 4 inches apart. Lift and replant only when growth becomes obviously too crowded. Late spring or early summer just before the foliage completely dies down is the best time for this. Propagation of these anemones is by offsets and division at the time the foliage dies and by seeds sown in summer or early fall in sandy, woodland-type earth.

Japanese anemones and other herbaceous perennials that retain their foliage until killed by fall frosts require somewhat different conditions and care. Their overall treatment is that of the run of hardy garden perennials. In cold regions plant them in spring, in areas where winters are not excessively severe in spring or fall. Space them about 2 feet apart. It is beneficial to maintain a mulch around them at all times. Lifting, dividing, and replanting is likely to be needed every third or fourth year. Propagation is easy by division and root cuttings, and of kinds that produce fertile seeds by sowing those as soon as ripe in a shaded cold frame. To raise plants from root cuttings dig up a plant in spring, cut its thicker roots into 2-inch-long pieces, strew them over a bed of soil in a cold frame and cover with sandy earth to a depth of 1 inch. When sufficient leaf growth has developed, pot individually in small pots, winter in a cold frame, and plant out in spring.

ANEMONELLA (Anemonél-la) — Rue-Anemone. The only species *Anemonella thalictroides* is native of woodlands from

Anemonella thalictroides

New Hampshire to Minnesota, Kansas, and Florida. It differs from nearly related *Anemone* in that its flowers have knob-like stigmas without styles. The rue-anemone belongs in the buttercup family RANUNCULACEAE; its name is a diminutive of *Anemone*. Occasionally up to 9 inches tall, it is slender-stemmed, hairless, and has a small cluster of tuberous roots. Its long-

stalked basal leaves are twice- or thrice-divided into broad-ovate, three-toothed leaflets. Its flower stems carry, just below the blooms, a collar of two or three stalkless, thrice-divided leaves, the leaflets of which are three-notched at their ends. The flowers have no petals; the parts that resemble petals are sepals. They number five to ten, are white to pale purplish-pink, and spread to form a bloom up to 1 inch or slightly less across. Plants with double flowers are not infrequent. The common name refers to the similarity the foliage has to that of the meadow-rue (*Thalictrum*).

Double-flowered *Anemonella thalictroides*

Double-flowered *Anemonella thalictroides*

Garden Uses and Cultivation. Despite its delicate appearance, the rue-anemone is easy to satisfy in gardens. It is best adapted for woodland environments, shaded rock gardens, and such like places where it is not called upon to compete with more vigorous neighbors. It prospers around the bases of old trees, nestling with charming effect against larger roots that protrude above ground and finding sustenance in the leaf compost that accumulates near them. Earth that is not over-dry suits it best, but it is remarkably tolerant of a fairly wide range of soil conditions. The rue-anemone is easily raised from seeds and transplants readily.

ANEMONOPSIS (Anemon-ópsis). One herbaceous perennial, *Anemonopsis macrophylla*, a rare native of mountain woods in Japan, is the only species of this genus of the buttercup family RANUNCULACEAE. Its name is derived from that of the genus *Anemone* and the Greek *opsis*, resembling. It alludes to likenesses between these genera. About 2½ feet in height, **A. macrophylla** has much the appearance of *Anemone japonica*, but is smaller. Its quite large, coarsely-toothed hairless leaves are twice- or thrice-divided. The long-stalked, nodding flowers are in loose raceme-like panicles. They have seven to ten lilac or light purple petal-like parts that are really sepals; the three outer ones are purple on their outsides. The true petals are about ten. They are linear-oblong, about one-third as long as the sepals, and rather thick. There are numerous stamens and a long slender style. The fruits are follicles (dry and capsule-like).

Garden and Landscape Uses and Cultivation. This plant is appropriate for beds and borders and for semiformal plantings. It flourishes in part-shade in porous soil that contains abundant organic matter and that does not dry excessively. It is propagated by division in spring and by seeds. It is hardy.

ANEMOPAEGMA (Anemo-paégma). Tropical South America is home to the thirty species of *Anemopaegma* of the bignonia family BIGNONIACEAE. They are evergreen flowering vines, many of great beauty. Unfortunately, few have ever been cultivated, and only one is at all well known. The genus takes its name from the Greek *anemos*, the wind, and *paigma*, sport.

Anemopaegmas have opposite leaves of technically three or five leaflets, but quite commonly the terminal one is represented by a tendril so that there are only two or four obvious leaflets; sometimes the terminal leaflet is entirely absent. The blooms, usually in axillary racemes, are yellow, white, or rarely purplish. They have cup-like, sometimes shallowly-toothed, calyxes and tubular, very slightly two-lipped corollas with five spreading lobes. There are four stamens, included in the corolla. The tendrils are not branched. The fruits are capsules.

Native to Brazil, **A. chamberlaynii** (syn. *Bignonia chamberlaynii*) is a vigorous vine that superficially resembles an allamanda, but differs obviously in its leaves having two leaflets or more. In gardens *Doxantha unguis-cati* is frequently misnamed *Bignonia chamberlaynii*. The leaves are leathery and hairless and consist of three leaflets, two leaflets and a tendril, or sometimes a pair of leaflets. The leaflets are elliptic to

Anemopaegma chamberlaynii

ovate and pointed. The light yellow, trumpet-shaped flowers, approximately 2½ inches long, have rather short corolla lobes (petals). They are in pendulous racemes and are slightly ill-scented.

Garden Uses and Cultivation. These are the same as for *Clytostoma*, and *Allamanda*.

ANEMOPSIS (Anem-ópsis)—Yerba Mansa. One species of the lizard's tail family SAURURACEAE comprises this genus. The name is derived from that of another genus, *Anemone*, and the Greek *opsis*, resembling; it alludes to the appearance of the flowers. Native from California to Nevada, Texas, and Mexico, the yerba mansa (**Anemopsis californica** syn. *Houttuynia californica*) in-

Anemopsis californica

habits wet and especially wet-alkaline soils. It has aromatic creeping rhizomes and woolly-pubescent stems 4 inches to 1½ feet tall or a little taller. Except for a solitary, broad-ovate, clasping stem leaf with one to three smaller ones in its axil, the leaves are basal, elliptic-oblong, 1¾ to 6 inches long, and with stalks about the same length. The conical spikes of minute, inconspicuous flowers, each arising from a collar of white petal-like bracts, are ⅓ inch to 1¾ inches long. The plant is used in Mexico to relieve colds and indigestion and to purify the blood. Beads, fashioned from the rhizomes, are strung into necklaces by the Indians.

Garden Uses and Cultivation. A rather unusual plant, *Anemopsis* is suitable for bogs, wet places by watersides, and shallow, still water. It can be accommodated in suitable places in the garden or in tubs or other containers in pools. It thrives best in non-acid soil, with a generous proportion of organic matter. Propagation is by division in spring or by seeds sown while fresh in pots of soil stood almost to their rims in water.

ANETHUM (An-èthum)—Dill. The one well-known and widely grown species of this genus of two of the carrot family UMBELLIFERAE is dill. The genus *Anethum* is an

Old World one. Its name is a modification of the ancient Greek one, *anethon,* for dill. Anethums are strongly aromatic annuals or biennials with branching, hairless stems, and leaves pinnately three or four times cut into narrow-linear or threadlike segments. The short-stalked, tiny yellow flowers are in quite large umbels. The ribbed fruits, usually called seeds, are elliptic and flattened.

Dill (*A. graveolens*), which freely naturalizes waste places throughout much of North America, is usually 2 to 4 feet tall or sometimes taller. Its fennel-like foliage has leaflets about ¾ inch long. The umbels may be 6 inches across. Their flowers are succeeded by seeds about ⅙ inch long. The seeds, for which the plant is grown commercially, are used for flavoring foods and in medicines. Their best known employment is in the preparation of dill pickles, for which whole seed heads as well as leaves are used.

Garden Uses and Cultivation. Dill is a must for herb gardens and is also appropriate for vegetable gardens if fresh leaves (which are much superior to dried) and seeds are wanted for flavoring. Its cultivation is very simple. A well-drained, porous soil and a warm, sunny location give the best results. Dill is quite hardy, but is killed by the extreme cold weather of the far north. Usually seeds are not produced until the beginning of the plant's second year, but early sowings may crop at the end of the first summer. For the best results seeds are sown in spring in rows 2 to 3 feet apart and the young seedlings are thinned to allow about 1 foot to 1¼ feet between individuals in the rows. When grown chiefly for foliage closer spacing may be employed. Subsequent care consists of keeping down weeds. The seed heads are harvested whole by cutting them, with a small portion of stalk attached, before they are fully mature.

ANGELICA (Angél-ica). A genus of about fifty species, *Angelica* has an unusual natural distribution, being indigenous to all continents of the northern hemisphere and New Zealand. The only species of importance to gardeners is an Old World one used as an herb. The group belongs in the carrot family UMBELLIFERAE. Its name is from the Latin *angelus,* an angel, and alludes to what were considered the angelic healing properties supposed to be possessed by the cultivated kind. To reiterate and reinforce the implication of the generic name the great Swedish botanist Linnaeus applied to the familiar herb the specific name *Angelica archangelica,* and that is its designation today. Angelica is also a common name of *Polyscias filicifolia.*

Angelicas are perennial or rarely biennial, deciduous, hardy herbaceous plants of stout habit and bold appearance. Usually they die after flowering and producing

Angelica archangelica

one crop of seeds, but this generally does not occur until the plants are three years old or older; if the flower stalks are harvested regularly before seeds form the plant is likely to persist for many years. Their leaves mostly have long stalks and are pinnately-divided, but they gradually become smaller and less complex toward the tops of the plants and the uppermost are often without blades. Mostly the small flowers are white or greenish-white and are in compound umbels. The ovate, flattened fruits, usually called seeds, are ribbed, with the lateral ribs broadly winged. The cultivated *Angelica* is a vigorous, erect biennial or perennial, 5 to 7 feet tall and hairless except for its flower heads. Its leaves are twice- or thrice-divided into nine, irregularly-toothed or lobed leaflets 2 to 3 inches long. The largest are up to 3-feet long. The umbels of the small whitish flowers are 3 to 6 inches in diameter. The fruits (seeds) are ⅓ inch long.

During its long association with man many medicinal virtues have been ascribed to *Angelica.* In 1629 the herbalist Parkinson in "Paradise in Sole" accounted it as most worthy of all medicinal plants. It is not so regarded now.

Garden and Other Uses. The garden cultivation of *Angelica* is pretty much confined to herb gardens. Its chief modern home use is for its stems, which are candied and used in confectionary; they should be cut for this purpose in June or early July. Its seeds are used for flavoring gin, vermouth, chartreuse, and other liqueurs, and its leaves in preparing hop bitters.

Cultivation. By far the best method of propagation is by seed; division and the removal of offshoots are less satisfactory. Seeds should be sown in the late summer or early fall of the season in which they ripen; they do not retain their capacity to germinate for long. They may be sown in a seed bed and transplanted the following

spring either to their final location or to a nursery bed where they are spaced 1½ feet between individuals. If the latter plan is adopted they are set out permanently the following fall. A final spacing of 3 feet is satisfactory. Angelicas give of their best in deep, fertile, fairly moist soil and appreciate light shade, although they will grow in full sun if the soil is kept moist. They prosper by watersides where the banks are well above the water level if their roots can reach moist strata.

ANGELICA TREE. See Aralia.

ANGELIN TREE is *Andira inermis.*

ANGELONIA (Angel-ònia). The name *Angelonia* is a modification of angelon, a South American colloquial name for *A. salicariaefolia.* The genus it identifies consists of about thirty nonhardy species of mostly herbaceous perennials and more or less shrubby plants, but includes some annuals. It belongs in the figwort family SCROPHULARIACEAE and ranges in the wild from Mexico to Brazil and the West Indies.

Angelonias much resemble alonsoas, to which they are closely related botanically, but differ in their flowers not being inverted and in having swollen lower lips. Also, the flowers are blue, purple, or white, whereas those of *Alonsoa* are characteristically red, or rarely white. The leaves of *Angelonia* are opposite, or the upper ones alternate. The flowers are in racemes or are solitary in the leaf axils. They have five-parted or five-toothed calyxes and corollas with little or no tube, but a one-sided swollen or pouched throat, with two projecting teeth at its base. The corolla has two lips, the upper two-, the lower three-lobed. There are four short-stalked stamens in pairs. The fruits are capsules, spherical or football-shaped.

The best known kind *A. salicariaefolia,* of the West Indies and northern South

Angelonia salicariaefolia

Angelonia salicariaefolia

America, is the plant cultivated as *A. grandiflora* in gardens. Some 2 feet in height, it is a sticky-hairy perennial with erect stems and nearly stalkless, toothed, lanceolate to linear-oblong leaves some 3 inches long. The violet-blue, slender-stalked flowers, ¾ inch across, are in racemes with many leafy bracts. Variety *A. s. alba* has white flowers. The perennial *A. angustifolia,* of Mexico and the West Indies, has more slender leaves and is neither hairy nor sticky. Its deep violet flowers are in long racemes.

Garden and Landscape Uses. Angelonias, even the perennials, are usually grown in other than tropical and subtropical regions as annuals. They are pretty and elegant, but less colorful than many popular annuals. Furthermore, they come into bloom rather late in the season, about August, and remain in flower usually for one month to six weeks. They are useful as fillers to be planted in beds and borders to succeed fleeting annuals such as early clarkias and larkspurs that have passed out of bloom. For such use angelonias are carried in pots until they are set in the borders. As pot plants they are useful as greenhouse and conservatory ornamentals.

Cultivation. Propagation is by seeds sown in a temperature of 70 to 75°F in February or March or by cuttings taken in March or April from stock plants wintered in a greenhouse. Cuttings root readily in sand, vermiculite, or perlite in a tempera-

ture of 65 to 70°F. However started, the young plants are potted individually in sandy soil in small pots and as soon as they have recovered from the shock of transplanting are transferred to a sunny location in an airy, but humid greenhouse where the night temperature is 60°F and the day temperatures range, according to the sunniness of the day, from five to fifteen degrees higher. When the plants are about 4 inches tall their tips are pinched out to encourage branching and this is repeated when the branches are 4 inches long. As root growth makes necessary the plants are transferred to successively bigger pots until they occupy containers 5 or 6 inches in diameter. Rich, but porous soil is used and good drainage provided. Water is given in amounts to keep the soil always evenly moist. In summer, plants in greenhouses need light shade. As an alternative to pot culture up to the time of blooming, the plants may be set in the garden as soon as the weather is really warm and settled, about the time it is safe to plant begonias and geraniums or some two weeks after the first planting of corn. A spacing of 8 inches is satisfactory. The soil should be fertile, contain a decent proportion of organic matter, such as compost, humus, rotted manure, or leaf mold, and be moistish rather than dry.

ANGEL'S TEARS is *Narcissus triandrus*.

ANGEL'S TRUMPET. See Brugmansia, and Datura.

ANGIOPTERIS (Angi-ópteris). Some botanists recognize more than 100 species of large ferns in this genus of the marattia family MARATTIACEAE; others regard them as all variants of one. The genus is native to the southern hemisphere and the warmer parts of Asia. It has massive stems or short trunks and twice- or thrice-pinnate leaves with boat-shaped, sporebearing organs in marginal rows on the undersides. The name is derived from the Greek *aggeion*, a vessel, and *pteron*, a wing.

Only one species, *Angiopteris evecta*, is ordinarily cultivated. It is native from Japan to Australia and Madagascar, and develops a fleshy stem up to 2 feet wide and 2 to 6 feet tall. The mostly twice-pinnate, evergreen leaves are 6 to 15 feet long. Their final segments or leaflets are 4 inches to 1 foot long, ½ inch to 1½ inches wide, and are sometimes slightly toothed.

Garden and Landscape Uses. The big, impressive, and somewhat coarse *A. evecta* is adapted for outdoor cultivation in the tropics and subtropics and for cultivating in warm conservatories and large greenhouses.

Cultivation. Coarse, fertile soil that contains an abundance of organic matter and is constantly moist is most suitable. When grown in pots or tubs it is well to keep the

containers standing in 2 or 3 inches of water. Shade from strong sun, a humid atmosphere, and, indoors, a minimum night temperature of 55°F afford satisfactory conditions for growth. Well-rooted specimens benefit from regular applications of dilute liquid fertilizer. Because the spores produced by cultivated specimens are not fertile propagation is done vegetatively. It is effected by taking fleshy scales from the bases of the leaf stalks, placing them on a layer of sand, covering them with sphagnum moss, and keeping them in a humid atmosphere in a temperature of 70 to 80°F or by waiting until the scales develop young plants spontaneously and then removing them and potting them separately. If scales are started in spring young plants are had by summer or fall. For further information see Ferns.

ANGLE POD. See Gonolobus.

ANGOPHORA (An-góphora)—Gum-Myrtle. Ten evergreen eastern Australian trees and shrubs related to *Eucalyptus* constitute *Angophora* of the myrtle family MYRTACEAE. The name is from the Greek *angos*, a vessel, and *phero*, to bear, and alludes to the shape of the fruits. This genus differs from *Eucalyptus* in having opposite leaves, flowers having five instead of four sepals and petals, and in the petals being completely separate and not joined. The leaves are neither lobed nor toothed. The white flowers, the showy parts of which are the many spreading stamens, are in terminal clusters.

One species, *A. costata* (syn. *A. lanceolata*), is occasionally planted in warm parts of the United States including California and Hawaii. In Australia it is known as the smooth-barked-apple, red-barked-apple, and brown-apple. It is decidedly ornamental, attains a height of 50 to 80 feet, and has a short trunk and a large, irregularly branched, rather open head. The bark sheds from the trunk and branches. The leaves, up to 5 inches long by 1 inch wide, are lanceolate; when mature they are bright green, when young red. This species is prominent in public parks and elsewhere in and near Sydney.

Garden and Landscape Uses and Cultivation. This tree has about the same landscape values and needs the same culture as *Eucalyptus*.

ANGRAECOPSIS (Angrae-cópsis). The genus *Angraecopsis* of the orchid family ORCHIDACEAE consists of fifteen species in Africa, Madagascar, and the Mascarine Islands. Its name, from that of related *Angraecum* and the Greek *opsis*, like, suggests a resemblance. This genus is most closely related to *Mystacidium* from which it differs in its flowers having unequal sepals and usually a three-lobed lip, and in other details.

Angraecopsises are small, short-stemmed plants with a few curved, oblique leaves and longish, slender raceme-like inflorescences of small to almost minute, spidery flowers. The pair of lateral sepals project forward and are longer than the other. The petals are triangular. Most usually the lip is three-lobed, but in a few sorts is nearly lobeless. The spur is narrow-mouthed.

Flowers with the largest spurs of any species of the genus are produced by *A. tenerrima* of East Africa. The leathery, strap-shaped leaves are 3 to 8 inches long. The white to yellowish flowers, about ¾ inch across, have a lip with side lobes from very slightly shorter to a little longer than the middle lobe and somewhat lobed at their apexes. The spur is 2 to 2½ inches long. The only other species with flowers with really long spurs is *A. gracillima,* also

Angraecopsis gracillima

of East Africa. This differs from *A. tenerrima* in the side lobes of the lips of its yellowish flowers being shorter, often much shorter, than the middle lobe and in not being notched at their apexes. The spur is 1 inch to 1¾ inches long. Also, the leaves of this rarely exceed ½ inch, whereas those of *A. tenerrima* are ½ to 1 inch broad. The West African *A. ischnopus* has leaves up to 2 inches long and less than ½ inch wide. The petals of its yellowish, ¼-inch-wide flowers are broader than long. The side lobes of the lip slightly exceed the center lobe. The spur is about ½ inch in length, slender and longer than the lip.

Garden Uses and Cultivation. These are collectors' orchids. They respond to care and cultivation appropriate for tropical angraecums. For more information see Orchids.

ANGRAECUM (An-graècum). Some 250 species of the orchid family ORCHIDACEAE are included in *Angraecum*, a genus related to *Phalaenopsis* and *Vanda* and represented in the native floras of tropical Africa, South Africa, Madagascar, the Comoro Islands, the Seychelles Islands, the Mascarine Islands, and the Philippine Islands. The

name is a Latinized form of *angurek*, a Malayan name for epiphytic plants.

Angraecums perch on trees, but unlike parasites take no nourishment from their hosts. They are epiphytes. As a group they exhibit considerable diversity. Some species previously included in *Angraecum* are relegated to other genera by modern botanists; these genera include *Eurychone, Macroplectrum, Mystacidium,* and *Neofinetia.* Commonly angraecums have short to long leafy stems, with the leaves fleshy and in two rows in one plane. The blooms, small to large (the largest-flowered orchids of Africa and Madagascar belong here), are mostly white to green or white and green. Less often they are yellow. They are nearly always in racemes, which may be short or long, rarely they are solitary. Their sepals, petals, and lip usually spread widely to produce a starry effect. The lip, often much bigger than the sepals and petals, is with or without small side lobes, often has a short-pointed or tail-like apex, and is spurred. The spur in some kinds is extraordinarily long.

Pendulous or vining slender stems 3 to 4 feet long or longer and sparsely-branched are characteristic of *A. eichleranum* of tropical West Africa. Its thinnish, leathery, rather distantly-spaced leaves are oblong-elliptic, 3 to 5 inches long by some 2 inches wide. Their tips are notched. Usually solitary, occasionally in twos or rarely threes, the 3- to 3½-inch-wide blooms are thick-textured and strongly fragrant. They have narrow, yellow-green to green spreading sepals and petals and a broad, cupped white lip, apple-green in its throat, with a prominently-projecting point at its apex and a spur nearly 2 inches long.

Angraecum eichleranum

Somewhat resembling *A. eichleranum* to which it is closely related, *A. infundibulare* inhabits humid tropical forests of East Africa. A vining species of *Vanilla*-like habit, it has root-producing stems that in the wild cling to tree trunks and may attain lengths up to 30 feet. The fleshy leaves,

evident only near the tops of such long stems, are alternate and in two rows. They are oblong and notched at their apexes. Its handsome, long-lasting blooms are fragrant, up to 3½ inches or perhaps sometimes more in diameter. They have spreading, slender, greenish or yellowish-green sepals and petals and a broad-ovate, white lip with a projecting point at the apex. The spur of the lip, up to 1¾ inches long, is bent at its middle.

Native to Madagascar, *A. modestum* (syn. *Aerangis modesta*) has a densely-leafy stem up to 8 inches in length from which aerial roots sprout freely. Its two-ranked, narrow-obovate to narrow-obovate-oblong leaves are 3 to 7 inches long by 2 inches wide. Pure white except for their light orange-red stalks, the 1- to 1½-inch-wide flowers, two-ranked and faced in the same direction, are in arching racemes of twelve to twenty. Their spurs are 2 to 3 inches long.

A brilliant red column is a feature of the otherwise white flowers of *A. rhodostichum* (syn. *Aerangis rhodosticha*) of Africa. The short stems, usually drooping, have about eight slightly-sickle-shaped, narrowly-strap-shaped leaves up to 6 inches long, with two-lobed apexes. The 1-inch-wide flowers, from six to twenty-four in each raceme, are in two ranks. They have green-tipped, curved spurs a little more than 1 inch long.

Angraecum rhodostichum

The cylindrical leaves characteristic of *A. scottianum* of the Comoro Islands are much like those of *Vanda teres.* In the wild angraecums with foliage of this type favor sunnier habitats than do flat-leaved species. The present sort grows where it is exposed to afternoon sun and where temperatures and atmospheric humidity are always high. It usually has several straggling or hanging stems generally up to 2 feet long, with the foliage confined to their upturned apexes. The leaves are 3 to 4 inches long, grooved along their upper sides. From the upper leaf axils come short racemes of two to four fragrant, white, waxy blooms or sometimes the flowers are solitary. Always displayed with the lip upward and the 4- to 6-inch-long slender spur hanging like a tail, they are about 2½ inches wide. The sepals and petals are slender and recurved. The concave lip, broader than long, has a short point at the apex. Its 4- to 5-inch-long spur is pale reddish-brown.

Robust and 3 to 5 feet tall or taller, *A. superbum* (syn. *A. eburneum*), of Madagascar, branches from its base to form large clumps. Its closely-set, rigid, strap-shaped leaves, their lower parts folded inward, may be 2 feet long or longer by 2 inches wide. They are notched at their tips. The erect to horizontal, several- to many-bloomed racemes are sometimes 4 feet in length. The long-lasting flowers, 3 to 4 inches across and very fragrant, have narrow, greenish-white to bright green, spreading sepals and petals, a large, broad, white lip, and a 3 inch-long green spur.

Angraecum superbum

Because the blooms are carried in an inverted position the lip is uppermost. In *A. s. virens* the center of the lip is greenish.

The yellow-flowered *A. citratum*, of Madagascar, has very short stems and few broad-elliptic to obovate leaves. Its ¾-inch-

Angraecum citratum

wide flowers, in arching or pendulous racemes 1 foot to 1¾ feet long, yellow to creamy-white, have a long, slender spur. A small species from the Comoro Islands, *A. hildebrandtii,* has somewhat recurved, oblong-strap-shaped leaves, unequally two-lobed at the apex, and slender, pendulous racemes long in comparison to the size of the plant, of tiny orange-yellow flowers each with a slender spur.

Angraecum hildebrandtii

Garden Uses and Cultivation. Angraecums include a number of interesting and handsome sorts of merit for orchid collections and for growing with other tropical plants. In general they are not beyond the abilities of a reasonably skilled amateur to manage and to have bloom successfully. Details of culture vary somewhat according to kind. Most respond to decidedly tropical conditions, with winter night temperatures of 60 to 65°F, and appropriate increases by day. Some succeed in slightly cooler temperatures. Angraecums are reported not to grow well in the bark chips such as suit many orchids. Satisfactory rooting mixtures for most are osmunda fiber and shredded tree fern fiber. Some growers advocate a mixture of tree fern fiber and sphagnum moss. Some sorts thrive in hanging baskets, and vining types do well attached to slabs of tree fern trunk. Good drainage is important. Shade from bright sun and fairly high atmospheric humidity, but not a dank, oppressive atmosphere are needed. Give water generously whenever the plants are in growth, which with most kinds is more or less throughout the year. Mild applications of fertilizer benefit well-established specimens. For more information see Orchids.

ANGULOA (Angu-lòa)—Tulip Orchid. Cradle Orchid. Handsome, easily grown orchids to the number of about ten species and a number of natural and artificial hybrids constitute *Anguloa*. Hybrids between *Anguloa* and closely related *Lycaste* are named *Angulocaste*. Anguloas are natives of the Andes, mostly at high elevations. They belong to the orchid family ORCHIDACEAE. Their name commemorates the Spanish naturalist Don Francisco de Angulo, who died about 1790. The vernacular tulip orchid directs attention to the cupped forms of the blooms of some kinds.

Anguloas are mostly evergreen or partially evergreen, terrestrial (growing in the ground) or epiphytic (perching on trees) plants. They have more or less egg-shaped pseudobulbs sheathed by the leaf bases, each with two to four large, broadly-lanceolate, longitudinally-pleated, short-stalked leaves. The fleshy, cup-shaped to nearly globose blooms are solitary atop stalks that come from the bottoms of the pseudobulbs, and are conspicuously furnished with bracts. The sepals partially envelop the petals. The lip, small, fleshy, and three-lobed, is jointed, and can readily be rocked back and forth, a characteristic that along with the shape of the bloom gives reason for the name cradle orchid.

Its clustered pseudobulbs 5 to 6 inches long, *A. clowesii,* of Colombia, has leaves 1½ to 2 feet long, and in early summer, on stalks that may be 1 foot long, many thick, waxy, subspherical, bright yellow, fragrant blooms up to 3 inches long. They have freely movable, boat-shaped, cream to orange-yellow lips with erect side lobes. Smaller, but with otherwise similar pseudobulbs and foliage, *A. ruckeri* (syn. *A. ruckeri*) has shorter-stalked, very fragrant, variously-colored flowers that most commonly are greenish-brown on their outsides and yellow thickly spotted with red within, but may be nearly white to almost blood-red. It is native to Colombia.

The flowers of *A. uniflora* (syn. *A. virginalis*) are more open than those of other kinds described here and have a not very pleasing scent. About 4 inches long, they most commonly are white or creamy-white dotted or stained on their insides with pink, but sometimes are pure white, or are more definitely and distinctly spotted. Their stalks are 6 to 9 inches in length. The 4- to 7-inch-long pseudobulbs are ribbed, the leaves up to 2 feet long or longer. It is a native of Colombia, Ecuador, and Peru.

Garden Uses and Cultivation. Anguloas are best treated as cool or intermediate house orchids. They grow satisfactorily in well-drained pots in a mixture of one part fertile loam, one-half as much chopped osmunda fiber, and smaller proportions of fresh sphagnum moss and shredded leaves, or they may be planted in fir or redwood bark or similar rooting medium generally favorable to orchids. A humid atmosphere and bright light, tamed only sufficiently by shading to prevent scorching of the foliage, are necessary. During the periods of active growth abundant water, and for well-rooted specimens regular fertilizing, promote well-being. As soon as the new pseudobulbs are fully matured a rest period is initiated and is respected for several weeks, until the roots show signs of becoming active. When resting, water is applied only occasionally, just often enough to sustain the leaves that usually remain, and the plants are kept in a drier atmosphere where the temperature is 50°F or slightly higher. For additional information see Orchids.

ANGULOCASTE. This is the name of orchid hybrids the parents of which are *Anguloa* and *Lycaste*.

ANIA. See Ascotainia.

ANIGOZANTHOS (Anigo-zánthos)—Kangaroo Paws. Limited in the wild to Western Australia, this genus of ten or fewer species is one of many curious elements in Australia's unique flora. It belongs in the amaryllis family AMARYLLIDACEAE and has a name derived from the Greek *anoigo*, to expand, and *anthos*, a flower, in allusion to the corolla being split.

In their mode of growth these plants suggest irises. They have extensive, branching rhizomes that root from their undersides. From above they develop upright and recurved, leathery, parallel-veined, narrowly strap-shaped or sword-shaped leaves. The erect, branched flower stalks, usually with two or three leaves, carry the asymmetrical flowers in one-sided spikes or racemes. The blooms are tubular, have six spreading perianth lobes (petals), and are split down one side nearly to their bases. They have six stamens and one style. The fruits are capsules.

The red-and-green kangaroo paws (*Anigozanthos manglesii*), the official floral emblem of Western Australia, is handsome, about 3 feet in height, has flower stalks covered with velvety, bright crimson wool, and 3-inch-long blooms, similarly clothed, that are bright green with red bases. The style protrudes. Hardier and more robust, the yellow kangaroo paws (*A. flavidus*) in bloom may attain a height of 6 to 8 feet, but is often lower. In color its flowers range, on different plants, from yellow to light green or reddish and are about 1¼ inches long. They are less showy than those of *A. manglesii*. A smaller, less well-known species, the green kangaroo paws (*A. viridis*), has vivid green blooms.

Garden and Landscape Uses and Cultivation. In dryish, warm-temperate climates where little or no frost occurs kangaroo paws are welcome additions to flower borders, for locating at the fronts of shrub plantings, and for similar uses. They prop-

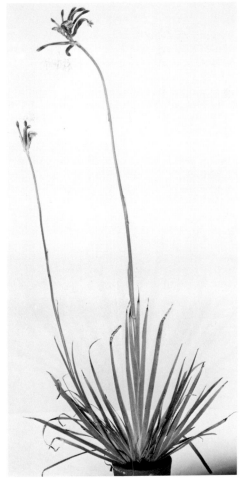

Anigozanthos manglesii

agate readily from seed, and can be increased by division just before new growth begins. They grow well in fertile, sandy peaty soil. During their season of growth they need generous supplies of water.

In sunny greenhouses kangaroo paws succeed in winter night temperatures of 50 to 55°F with an increase of five to ten or fifteen degrees by day. They may be accommodated in deep pans (shallow pots)

Anigozanthos flavidus

or ground beds, in fertile, well-drained soil. Watering from spring through fall should be generous, much scantier supplies are needed in winter. Regular applications of dilute liquid fertilizer from spring to fall benefit well-rooted specimens. Repotting needs attention each spring.

ANIMATED OAT is *Avena sterilis*.

ANISACANTHUS (Anisac-ánthus) — Desert-Honeysuckle or Chuparosa. Fifteen species are recognized as constituting *Anisacanthus* of the acanthus family ACANTHACEAE. They are natives of the southwestern United States and Mexico. The name is from the Greek *anisos*, asymmetrical, and *akanthos*, a thorn. Chuparosa is also a name of *Justicia californica*.

These are shrubs with opposite or clustered, undivided, toothless, linear to lanceolate leaves. Their flowers are in one-sided, terminal, often loose spikes or racemes, or are solitary or in clusters from the leaf axils. They have five-lobed calyxes, tubular, cylindrical, to funnel-shaped, two-lipped, usually red corollas, with the rear lip not lobed and the forward one deeply-cleft into three lobes. There are two stamens as long or longer than the corolla tube and a slender style tipped with a two-lobed stigma. The fruits are capsules containing two to four seeds.

Desert-honeysuckle or chuparosa (*A. thurberi*), native to New Mexico, Arizona, and northern Mexico, is chiefly found in canyons and washes. It is browsed by cattle and sheep, especially in times of drought. From 2 to 8 feet high, it has white branches, and clustered, short-stalked, lanceolate to ovate-lanceolate leaves 1 inch to 2½ inches long. The flowers, solitary or in leafy clusters of up to five, from the leaf axils along the stems, are mostly brick-red, sometimes yellow or orange. They are 1 inch to 1¼ inches long. They do indeed in general appearance suggest the blooms of honeysuckles.

Anigozanthos flavidus

Native to Texas and New Mexico, where it favors rocky banks and flood plains, *A. wrightii* is 2 to 4 feet tall. Its short-stalked leaves are lanceolate to broadly-lanceolate, ½ inch to 2 inches long, and usually more or less hairy. The flowers, 1¼ to 1½ inches long, and solitary or paired in one-sided, narrow spikes terminating fairly long leafy branchlets, have corollas with slender tubes and narrowly-ovate lobes (petals).

Garden and Landscape Uses and Cultivation. These are attractive shrubs for warm, dry climates. They succeed in ordinary soils in full sun and are increased by seeds and cuttings. Pruning to shape and to restrict their size may be done as soon as flowering is through. Propagation is by seeds and cuttings.

ANISE is *Pimpinella anisum*. Star-anise is *Illicium verum*.

ANISODONTEA (Aniso-dóntea). This exclusively South African genus of the mallow family MALVACEAE accommodates some species previously included in *Sphaeralcea* and *Malvastrum*. With the removal of the African species from those genera, the first consists of only American natives, the latter of American species plus two that occur also widely elsewhere, but these are believed to owe their Old World distribution to human activities since Columbus's discovery of America. There are nineteen species of *Anisodontea*. None is hardy. The name, from the Greek *anisos*, unequal, and *odontion*, a little tooth, presumably alludes to the little irregular projections on the carpels of some species.

Anisodonteas are prostrate or erect subshrubs or shrubs, usually hairy, sometimes nearly hairless. They have generally stalked, rarely nearly stalkless, variously lobed or sometimes lobeless, alternate leaves, and mallow-like flowers, solitary, in pairs, or groups of several from the leaf axils or the axils of bracts. Three or sometimes four or five bracts form an involucre below the three- to five-lobed calyx. There are typically five, rarely more, or less, white to magenta-pink, essentially-obovate petals, usually deeper colored or with darker veins toward their bases. The petals spread widely or form a cupped bloom. The lower parts of the many stamens are united in a column surrounding the style. The pistil is of a single circle of five to about five times as many carpels, equaled in number by the style branches that overtop the stamens. The fruits are the matured, dry carpels.

A subshrub 3 to 4 feet tall, *A. capensis* (syn. *Malvastrum capense*) is conspicuously or sparsely clothed with stellate (star-shaped) hairs. Its shallowly- to deeply-three- or occasionally five-lobed, toothed leaves have blades about 1 inch long and almost 1 inch wide. The almost 1-inch-wide flowers, solitary, or in twos or threes from the axils of small bracts, have stalks

up to 1 inch long. They have five-lobed calyxes and are displayed in slender, erect racemes. Their petals, pale magenta deepening at their bases to darker magenta, spread widely. Each carpel usually contains one seed. Plants cultivated as *A. capensis* may be *A. scabrosa* (syn. *Malvastrum scabrosum*), a very variable species differing in technical details from *A. capensis*, particularly in its brownish to black, instead of pale tan to reddish-brown carpels that generally have deep grooves instead of inconspicuous grooves between adjacent ones. Believed to be a hybrid *A. hypomandarum* (syn. *Malvastrum hypomandarum*), is a slender-branched shrub up to 10 feet tall, its parts clothed with a mixture of stellate, branched, and branchless hairs. Variable, its toothed leaves, in outline ovate, 1 inch to 1½ inches long, are commonly three-, but sometimes five-lobed. The flowers, one to three from the bract axils, have stalks usually longer than the leaves. They are 1 inch to nearly 1½ inches wide, white or light pink, streaked with magenta at the bases of the petals. There are one or rarely two seeds to each carpel.

Garden and Landscape Uses and Cultivation. The kinds described above are attractive ornamentals for outdoor cultivation in mild, dryish climates. They respond to well-drained soils and sunny locations, are increased by seeds and cuttings, and are suitable for flower beds and informal landscapes.

ANISOSTICHUS. See Bignonia.

ANISOTOME (Anisóto-me). This botanically complex genus of about twenty species, the majority endemic to New Zealand, and a few Australian, is of little horticultural import. It belongs in the carrot family UMBELLIFERAE and comprises tufted, rhizomatous, herbaceous plants. The name is from the Greek *anisos*, unequal, and *tome*, cut, in allusion to the unequal segments of the leaves.

Anisotomes have pinnately-divided leaves and small, generally unisexual, white, pinkish, or reddish flowers in umbels of smaller umbels. The flowers have five tiny calyx teeth or none, five petals, and five incurved stamens. There are two styles. The fruits are seedlike.

Robust and 6 feet tall or taller, *Anisotome latifolia* (syn. *Ligusticum latifolium*) is a perennial with deep taproots and stout, grooved stems. Its leathery, lustrous leaves are twice- or sometimes thrice-pinnate. On stalks 6 inches to 1 foot long or longer, the leaf blades are ovate-oblong to oblong, and are from 6 inches to 2 feet long by 2 to 10 inches wide. They have five to fifteen primary divisions. The numerous little flowers are in umbels 2½ to 3½ inches in diameter, aggregated in clusters about 8 inches wide. They are white to reddish-mauve.

Garden Uses and Cultivation. Not hardy in regions of harsh winters, the species described is sometimes grown in flower beds and in semiwild, informal areas in mild climates. It succeeds in sun, in ordinary soil, and is propagated by division at the beginning of the growing season, and by seed.

ANNATTO is *Bixa orellana*.

ANNONA (Ann-òna)—Cherimoya, Sweetsop, Soursop, Bullock's Heart, or Custard-Apple, Ilama, Pond-Apple. Several of the 120 species of *Annona* of the annona family ANNONACEAE are cultivated in the tropics and warm subtropics for their edible sugary fruits, various kinds of which are known by the names listed above. Their botanical name is a Latinized form of a native one. The genus consists of deciduous and evergreen trees and shrubs mostly natives of tropical South America, but some of Africa and Asia.

Annonas have thinnish, leathery foliage and solitary or clustered white or yellow flowers. The latter usually have a tubular calyx of three sepals, generally six petals in two circles, but sometimes only one circle of three, and numerous stamens with fleshy filaments (stalks). The pistils are numerous and the fruits large and fleshy. Actually each fruit is an aggregation of many small fruits embedded in and united with part of the stem that bears it; they are structured something like blackberries. The leaves of some kinds are aromatic when crushed. As fruits, the cherimoya, sweetsop, and soursop rank highest. The bullock's heart and white annona are less delicious. The fruits of the mountain soursop are decidedly inferior and those of the pond-apple inedible. Mature cherimoyas are eaten raw as are those of the sweetsop and soursop. The fruits of the bullock's heart and white annona, are delicious in drinks, ices, and custards.

The cherimoya (*A. cherimola*) has fruits with custard-like flesh. The tastiest of the annona fruits, they are described as having a flavor midway between that of pineapples and bananas. They vary from ovoid to nearly spherical, are 3 to 8 inches at their greatest diameter, and are smooth or covered with small knobs. Yellowish or pale green, they weigh up to a pound, and their white flesh is embedded with dark brown to black, wrinkled seeds. The cherimoya is shrubby or spreading and up to 25 feet tall. Its young shoots are hairy, and it has deciduous, broadly-elliptic, ovate or obovate leaves, velvety hairy on their undersides, and usually not more than 6 inches, but sometimes up to 9 inches in length. The brownish, fragrant flowers have tiny inner petals and much larger outer ones. It is a native of the Peruvian Andes.

The soursop or guanabana (*A. muricata*), an evergreen native of tropical

America, up to 30 feet tall, has horizontal or down-curved branches and glossy, obovate to elliptic leaves with broad wedge-shaped bases. They may be 1 foot long, but usually are not much more than one-half that length and often are less. Their undersides are rusty-hairy, at least at first, and have little pockets in the axils of the veins, a feature shared only with *A. montana*. The outer petals of the 1- to 2-inch-long, solitary flowers are yellow or yellow-green, the inner ones, approximately the same size, are yellow or red. The fruits, which are up to 1 foot long and weight 3 to 8 pounds, are shaped like pineapples without terminal tufts of foliage. The divisions are marked faintly and from the center of each protrudes a soft, curved spine. Their slightly acid, white, cottony flesh contains black seeds about 1 inch in length. Very similar to the soursop, and like it having little pockets in the axils of the veins on the undersides of the leaves, the mountain soursop (*A. montana*) is a native of the West Indies. Its fruits are more or less spherical, not more than 6 inches in diameter, have straight spines, and contain whitish or yellowish pulp and tan-colored seeds.

The sweetsop or sugar-apple (*A. squamosa*) is a deciduous native of the West Indies and Central America, up to 20 feet in height, with long, slender branches that angle sharply upward from the trunk but may bend downward at their ends. Its short-stalked elliptic to slightly-ovate, dull green leaves are hairy when young as are the young shoots and leafstalks; they have mostly rounded bases. The flowers, solitary or up to four together, yellowish-green and about 1 inch long, are succeeded by heart-shaped to ovoid fruits 2 to 5 inches long and about as broad, composed, like pine cones, of loose, easily separated parts. They generally have a frosted appearance. Their custard-like flesh is yellowish-white.

The custard-apple or bullock's heart (*A. reticulata*) also passes by the name cherimoya in some places, although that name more properly should be reserved for *A. cherimola*. A partially evergreen to deciduous native of tropical America, it attains a height of up to 25 feet and has lanceolate to oblong-lanceolate, long-pointed, short-stalked leaves 5 to 10 inches long, and yellowish flowers about 1 inch long. This species often has a leaning trunk. Its more or less heart-shaped tan or reddish-brown fruits, up to 5 inches long and weighing up to 1 to 2 pounds, are marked with a reticulation of impressed lines and have rather lumpy surfaces. They are not readily separated into parts. Their flesh is creamy-white.

The white annona or ilama (*A. diversifolia*) ranges as a native from Mexico to Central America and is up to 25 feet in height. It has aromatic, furrowed bark and

leaves, and shoots, that except immediately around the leaf scars, are hairless. The leaves, oblanceolate to broad-elliptic, and wedge-shaped or rounded at their bases, are 3½ to 8 inches long. The maroon or yellowish blooms are followed by heart-shaped to nearly-spherical, somewhat lumpy fruits about 6 inches long and contain cream or pinkish flesh and light brown seeds about 1 inch long.

The pond-apple (*A. glabra*) is a 40-foot evergreen native of tropical America that extends its range into southern Florida; it also is native to West Africa. This species has ovate leaves up to 7 inches long, and yellowish-brown, fragrant flowers. Its ovoid, yellowish fruits, up to 4 inches long, have no merit as edibles. This species is used as an understock for grafting.

The atemoya is a very good hybrid between the sugar-apple and the cherimoya. A tree of spreading open habit, the atemoya is intermediate between its parents. It bears high quality fruits more resembling those of the cherimoya than those of the sugar-apple. Some pruning is needed to keep the tree shapely. This hybrid must be propagated by grafting, budding, or cuttings.

Garden and Landscape Uses and Cultivation. Annonas are cultivated primarily for their fruits, but also are of ornamental value. They were the first fruit trees to be introduced to Florida and are still popular there as well as in other warm regions. In Florida the most generally successful kind is the sweetsop, which will grow as far north as St. Petersburg. The most tender to cold is the soursop, which is grown in southern Florida and in many places in the tropics. The cherimoya thrives best at high altitudes in the tropics and subtropics where summer humidity is not too oppressive. It is not too successful in Florida, but is grown to a limited extent in southern California successfully. The other kinds are intermediate in their preferences regarding climate. These trees generally prosper best in somewhat clayey soils, but adapt to a variety of conditions. With the exception of the pond-apple they are intolerant of poorly drained locations. Propagation is by seed, or less commonly by grafting or budding most usually onto understocks of *A. cherimola* or *A. squamosa*. Less commonly cuttings of firm shoots planted in a greenhouse propagating bed with mild bottom heat is employed.

ANNONACEAE—Annona Family. Mostly tropical and chiefly natives of the Old World, 120 genera and approximately 2,100 species constitute this family of dicotyledons. With one exception all are trees or shrubs. They have alternate, undivided leaves and usually bisexual, solitary or clustered flowers. The blooms have three sepals and six similar petals, many or rarely few stamens. The fruits, those of

some kinds edible and highly esteemed, are usually aggregations of many berries, but sometimes are capsules. Among the most important genera are *Annona, Artabotrys, Asimina, Cananga,* and *Rollinia*.

ANNUAL POINSETTIA is *Euphorbia heterophylla*.

ANNUAL RINGS. Trunks and branches of trees of dicotyledonous families, which include the vast majority of deciduous and evergreen kinds, increase in diameter as a result of the growth of successive layers of woody tissue around their perimeters. When cut across, these show as a series of concentric rings familiar to anyone who has looked at the end of a piece of lumber. Because one ring is normally laid down each year these rings are called annual rings. By counting annual rings the age of trees can be determined or closely approximated, this last because rarely, in unusual seasons, if growth ceases because of a dry spell and is resumed later two rings may develop in one year. Annual rings are studied as indicators of past climatic conditions. When moisture is plentiful the rings are thicker than in seasons of sparse rainfall.

ANNUALS. Strictly speaking annuals are plants that naturally complete their entire life cycle from seed to flowering, seed production, and inevitable death within one growing season. Typical examples are celosias, clarkias, sweet peas, and zinnias. Most begin life in spring, and die before winter. Some, called winter annuals, germinate in fall, in the wild, remain as small seedlings through winter, and resume growth in spring. They differ from biennials in not making substantial growth and not building up considerable reserves of stored food before winter.

Flower border of annuals

Besides true annuals, gardeners usually include in their use of the term a considerable number of other plants that for con-

Annuals in ornamental urn

Window box with petunias

venience they grow as annuals. Ageratums, petunias, snapdragons, verbenas, wax begonias, and many other favorites belong here. These, if not subjected to frost and if kept growing in suitable environments, are perennials.

Hardy and half-hardy are terms applied to annuals by gardeners in regions of severe winters and comparatively short spring-to-fall growing seasons. The terms are imprecise, but convenient. Hardy annuals are those satisfactory when sown outdoors as soon in spring as the ground can be brought into condition. They are not harmed by light frosts and make satisfactory growth at fairly low temperatures. Half-hardy annuals are sorts that because they are tender to frost need fairly warm growing conditions, or because they grow too slowly in their young stages to come into bloom quickly enough for outside sowings to be generally useful, are started early indoors and set in the garden as quite sizable young plants after the weather is warm and settled. There is no sharp distinction between hardy and half-hardy annuals. The terms apply to methods of cultivation rather than to types of plants. Many annuals can be grown either way. In mild climates the terms hardy and half-hardy are without significance.

Bowl planted with petunias and geraniums

Narrow edging of Madagascar-periwinkle

Planting annuals from flats: (a) About two weeks before planting slice the soil in the flat into blocks each containing one plant to reduce the shock of transplanting

(b) Tap end of flat sharply on ground to make space for fingers

(c) Insert fingers under plants to lift them out

(d) Separate plants with minimum disturbance to roots

(e) Make hole of ample size to accommodate roots

(f) Position plant and firm soil around it

(g) Water well with a fine spray

The chief uses of annuals are in flower beds and borders, for furnishing window and porch boxes, tubs, urns, hanging baskets, and other decorative containers, and as cut flowers. A few kinds are suitable for rock gardens, dry walls, and chinks between paving stones. Many are excellent for growing in greenhouses in beds or benches as cut flowers, and as pot plants.

As outdoor plants annuals give the quickest returns on minimum investments that gardens provide. They bloom the year you plant them. You sow the seeds, care for the crop, enjoy the flowers, and discard the plants all within the space of a few months or even weeks. And next year you begin all over again. It is as simple as that.

Annuals are musts for the short-term garden. If you rent rather than own and do not want to spend too much on the gar-

den, annuals are for you. If you want to improve your soil over a period of years by turning it each fall and adding humus, grow annuals. If you seek variety among cut flowers or want to brighten the garden during the summer try zinnias, marigolds, petunias, and other annual flowers.

No plants are easier to grow once their simple requirements are understood. Almost all need plenty of sun; a few stand light shade. All grow well in a freely-drained fertile soil that would produce good vegetables. Some succeed in poorer soil.

Give annuals room to develop. Keep them free of weeds, pests, and diseases, water and stake them when necessary and they will reward you grandly.

It is important to select the kind of annuals best adapted to your purpose. Do

Popular flower annuals and plants grown as annuals: (a) Love-lies-bleeding

(b) China-aster

(c) Madagascar-periwinkle

(d) Spider flower

(e) Flowering tobacco

(f) Petunias

(g) African marigold

(h) Zinnia

Popular foliage annuals and plants grown as annuals: (a) Coleus

(b) Dusty miller *(Senecia cineraria)*

(c) Summer-cypress underplanted with wax begonias

not sow larkspurs or gaillardias, if what you want is an all-summer display because they bloom lavishly, but briefly in early summer and die when the first real hot weather comes. Yet they are splendid as early summer cut flowers. On the other hand globe-amaranths and begonias bloom all summer and are fine for garden display, but are of little use for cutting. And so it goes.

Sowing dates are important and differ considerably in different parts of North America depending upon climate. In the south and the west and wherever mild, practically frost-free winters prevail sowing in fall for winter and very early spring bloom is practiced with many annuals. In the north spring is the time to sow most annuals, although where the soil is porous and well drained a few of the hardiest will succeed if sown outdoors in fall. Spring sowings include those of long-season kinds started early indoors and others sown directly in the open. Time the sowings of those you start indoors so that the plants are just ready to put out when the weather is warm enough to permit this. Do not let them get crowded and starved while

awaiting transplanting. Avoid sowing so late, however, that your plants are undersized at setting-out time. Amateurs commonly make indoor sowings too early.

On the other hand they are apt to delay outdoor sowing too long. The seeds of many annuals should be gotten into the ground on the first occasion in spring when the soil is workable. With others wait until danger from frost has passed. And in still other instances successive sowings to ensure an extended season of bloom are desirable.

From the time annuals sown directly outdoors break through the ground give attention to surface cultivation. Keep down all weeds and maintain the top inch of soil in a loose condition. Never cultivate deeper than this. If you do you will injure delicate feeding roots. Stir the soil each time rain packs it, not immediately after the rain ends, but as soon as the soil has dried to the extent that it does not stick to shoes and cultivator.

You must thin the young plants too. Whether you sowed the seeds broadcast or in drills the seeds will (or should) come up more thickly than the mature plants are to

be. There are maybe four times as many seedlings as you need in the area, or even more. Remove the surplus before they harm their neighbors by crowding.

If possible choose cloudy weather for thinning out. Do not remove all the plants at one time. Spread the operation over three or four weeks. At the first thinning pull out the weakest seedlings of those that are beginning to crowd. When the plants left begin to touch, thin again, once more take out the weakest (so far as you can make such a selection) and still leave those standing correctly spaced.

The ultimate spacing will depend upon the kind of annual you are thinning. A very approximate rule suggests that the plants should be spaced finally at distances equal to one-half their height. This is not exact because some kinds spread naturally more than others. But it serves fairly well as a guide.

You may have sown some annuals of easily transplantable kinds such as asters or stocks in a seedbed outdoors with the idea of moving them to their flowering quarters when big enough. This is a good plan if the place where they are to bloom

Annual vines: (a) Cup-and-saucer vine

(b) Balsam-apple

(c) Canary bird vine

is not ready at sowing time. Dig such plants up and transfer them when their second pair of leaves are well developed. Do not break the roots.

Cloudy weather is best for planting, but you will not always be able to wait for this. Under exceptional conditions when you transplant in bright hot weather you may have to shade the plants temporarily after they are moved. Usually this is not necessary. Water the plants thoroughly to settle the soil about their roots.

If plants are overgrown and "leggy," in most cases they will be improved if you pinch them back. Pinching back consists of cutting or nipping off between the thumbnail and forefinger the tips of the growing shoots. This is successful only with such plants as petunias, snapdragons, and verbenas that form side branches.

After the plants are set out keep the surface soil cultivated regularly as advised for annuals sown directly outdoors.

Tall-growing plants will need support of some kind. Staking should be done neatly and securely and well before the plants grow crooked or have been damaged in any way.

Unless you intend to collect your own seed keep all faded flowers picked. This prolongs the blooming season. Seed production seriously drains the plant's energy.

Shade, light not heavy or for part of the day only, is tolerated by a few annuals. None prosper in heavy shade. Among the most amenable to some shade are balsams (*Impatiens*), browallias, *Calceolaria mexicana*, exacums, flowering tobacco (*Nicotiana*), lobelias, patience plant (*Impatiens*), wax begonias, and wishbone flower (*Torenia*).

In greenhouses many annuals are eminently satisfactory as cut flowers and as pot plants. A few of the best are blue lace flower (*Trachymene*), calendulas, calceolarias, candytuft (*Iberis*), celosias, China-asters (*Callistephus*), cinerarias (*Senecio*), clarkias, cornflowers (*Centaurea*), gomphrenas, larkspurs (*Consolida*), linarias, love-in-a-mist (*Nigella*), lupines (*Lupinus*), marigolds, mignonette (*Reseda*), monkey flower (*Mimulus*), nemesias, painted tongue (*Salpiglossis*), patience plants (*Impatiens*), Schizanthuses, snapdragons, statice (*Limonium*), stocks (*Matthiola*), sweet peas (*Lathyrus*), and wishbone flower (*Torenia*).

The kinds of annuals are very many. In the lists that follow the vining sorts have been separated and an attempt has been made to divide the others into two groups: those that where summers are hot can be depended upon to give a long season of bloom and those that under such conditions flower for a comparatively brief time. The separation may not be completely satisfactory because other conditions such as type of soil and whether or not they receive ample water influence the continuance of bloom. Then again, some kinds,

calendulas for example, may struggle along through hot weather and produce some inferior flowers without making a very satisfactory display. So the lists may serve as suggestions rather than absolutes, to be used for guidance, not to be depended upon under all circumstances. In addition to the annuals listed here are a number of grasses. For these see Grasses, Ornamental.

These annuals generally can be relied upon to give a long season of bloom: ageratums, angel's trumpet (*Datura*), balsams (*Impatiens*), basket flower (*Centaurea*), browallias, calandrinias, *Calceolaria mexicana*, calendulas, California-poppies (*Eschscholzia*), carnations (*Dianthus*), cigar flower (*Cuphea*), cockscomb (*Celosia*), cosmoses, dwarf dahlias, dwarf-morning-glory (*Convolvulus*), evening stock (*Matthiola*), exacums, flowering tobacco (*Nicotiana*), four o'clocks (*Mirabilis*), gamolepis, geraniums (*Pelargonium*), globe-amaranths (*Gomphrena*), gloriosa-daisy (*Rudbeckia*), heliotropes (*Heliotropium*), ice plant (*Mesembryanthemum*), Indian pinks (*Dianthus chinensis*), lobelias, love-lies-bleeding (*Amaranthus*), Madagascar-periwinkle (*Catharanthus*), marigolds, African and French (*Tagetes*), Mexican tulip-poppy (*Hunnemannia*), nasturtiums (*Tropaeolum*), nierembergias, patience plant or sultana (*Impatiens*), petunias, phlox (*Phlox drummondii*), portulacas, prickly-poppies (*Argemone*), prince's feather (*Polygonum*), salvias, *Sanvitalia procumbens*, snapdragon (*Antirrhinum*), spider flower (*Cleome*), star-of-Texas (*Xanthisma*), sunflowers (*Helianthus*), sweet-alyssum (*Lobularia*), Tahoka-daisy (*Machaeranthera*), tassel flower (*Emilia*), tithonias, unicorn plant (*Proboscidea*), verbenas, wax begonias, winged everlasting (*Ammobium*), wishbone flower (*Torenia*), and zinnias.

Where summers are hot these annuals generally bloom for a comparatively short period only: African-daisies (*Arctotis*), amberboas, anchusas, annual chrysanthemums, anodas, *Asperula orientalis*, baby's breath (*Gypsophila*), blazing star (*Mentzelia*), blue lace flower (*Trachymene*), calliopsis (*Coreopsis*), candytuft (*Iberis*), Cape-marigold (*Dimorphotheca*), China-asters (*Callistephus*), Chinese-forget-me-not (*Cynoglossum*), clarkias (including godetias), collinsias, collomias, cornflowers (*Centaurea*), cream cups (*Platystemon*), *Cynoglossum amabile*, flax (*Linum*), gaillardias, gilias, heliophila, horned-poppy (*Glaucium*), immortelle (*Xeranthemum*), kingfisher-daisy (*Felicia*), larkspurs (*Consolida*), lavateras, leptosynes (*Coreopsis*), linarias, lobelias, love-in-a-mist (*Nigella*), lupines (*Lupinus*), malopes, mask flower (*Alonsoa*), meadow foam (*Limnanthes*), mignonette (*Reseda*), monkey flower (*Mimulus*), nemesias, nemophilas, phacelias, pheasant's eye (*Adonis*), pimpernel (*Angallis*), poppies (*Papaver*), rose-of-heaven (*Lychnis*), salpiglossis, sand-verbena (*Arbonia*), saponarias, scabious

(*Scabiosa*), schizanthus, *Schizopetalon walkeri*, silenes, statice (*Limonium*), stocks (*Malcomia* and *Matthiola*), strawflowers (*Helichrysum*), Swan-River-daisy (*Brachycome*), Swan River everlasting (*Helipterum*), sweet sultan (*Centaurea*), tidy tips (*Layia*), *Tolpis barbata*, twinspur (*Diascia*), ursinias, venidiums, vipers' bugloss (*Echium*), and Virginia-stock (*Malcomia*).

Annuals grown for their foliage effects include these: annual poinsettia (*Euphorbia*), bronze hibiscus (*Hibiscus*), castor-bean (*Ricinus*), coleus, dusty millers (*Centaurea* and *Senecio*), Joseph's coat (*Amaranthus*), ornamental or flowering kale (*Brassica*), perillas, snow-on-the-mountain (*Euphorbia*), summer-cypress (*Kochia*), and variegated corn (*Zea*).

Annual vines include these: balloon vine (*Cardiospermum*), balsam-apple (*Momordica*), balsam-pear (*Momordica*), black-eyed-Susan-vine (*Thunbergia*), canary bird vine (*Tropaeolum*), cardinal climber (*Ipomoea*), cup-and-saucer vine (*Cobaea*), cypress-vine (*Ipomoea*), gourds (*Cucurbita, Lagenaria,* and *Luffa*), hyacinth-bean (*Dolichos*), Japanese hop (*Humulus*), maurandyas, moonflower (*Ipomoea*), morning glory (*Ipomoea*), nasturtium (*Tropaeolum*), scarlet runner bean (*Phaseolus*), and sweet peas (*Lathyrus*).

ANODA (Anò-da). These mostly subtropical plants of the mallow family MALVACEAE are annuals or are grown as such, although in their native regions some kinds are herbaceous perennials. There are about fifteen species. The name is derived from the Greek *a*, without, and *nodus*, a joint (the plants lack the node on the flower stems that is present in the related genus *Sida*).

Anodas have alternate, often lobed leaves, and solitary pink, lilac, purple, or rarely yellow flowers in the leaf axils that have five-parted calyxes, five each petals and sepals, and styles with head-like stigmas. Unlike those of nearly related *Malvastrum*, the flowers of *Anoda* do not have collars of leafy bracts (involucres) behind them. They differ from *Malva* in having stigmas that are club-shaped or knob-ended. The fruits are dry, seed-like carpels.

The most commonly cultivated anoda, **A. cristata** (syns. *A. acerifolia, A. hastata, A. lavateroides, A. triangularis*), of Central America, attains 2½ feet in height. Its leaves are lobed or lobeless, triangular-lanceolate to halberd-shaped, toothed or smooth-margined, hairless to conspicuously hairy. The long-stalked blooms ½ inch to 2 inches across are rose-pink to lavender or white. Popular varieties are *A. c.* 'Opal Cup', with bluish-pink blooms, and *A. c.* 'Snowdrop', with pure white flowers. Native of Arizona, New Mexico, and Mexico, **A. wrightii** is 1 foot to 2 feet tall and densely-hairy. Scarcely-lobed, its ovate to oblong leaves, have heart-shaped bases. The flowers, about ¾ inch wide, are yel-

Anoda wrightii

low-orange, with the bases of the petals pale violet to purple.

Garden Uses. Anodas are splendid additions to summer flower beds and borders. Beginning about midsummer, they bloom for a long period. They may also be grown in greenhouses for late winter and spring flowering and be used as decorative pot plants for the embellishment of greenhouses and conservatories. Their blooms are not suitable for use as cut flowers.

Cultivation. Most anodas need fertile soil and respond best to a medium-heavy loam, but *A. cristata* thrives in rather poor earth. Seeds may be sown outdoors as early in spring as the ground is workable and the seedlings thinned or transplanted about the time they are producing their second pairs of leaves. They transplant without difficulty. If possible transplanting should be done in dull, moist weather. Space between individuals should be varied according to the needs of the different kinds, about 1 foot for *A. wrightii*, 1 foot to 1½ feet for *A. cristata* and its varieties.

Instead of seeding outdoors an early start may be had by setting out young plants from flats as soon as the weather is warm and settled. The plants are raised from a sowing made in a greenhouse seven or eight weeks before they are to be transplanted to the garden. The seedlings are transplanted 2 inches apart in flats and grown to planting out size in a sunny

greenhouse where the night temperature is 50°F and the daytime temperature is five to ten degrees higher. Summer care of anodas is minimal. Control of weeds and removal of faded blooms to prevent seed formation (unless seeds are to be collected) are the chief chores and, of course, watering in dry weather. Little or no staking is ordinarily required.

To have plants in bloom in greenhouses in late winter and spring seeds are sown from September to January in a temperature of 60 to 65°F and the seedlings are transplanted individually to 2½-inch pots. When their pots become filled with roots the plants are transferred to bigger pots until the size in which they are to bloom is attained. The final pots may be 6 to 10 inches in diameter depending upon the vigor of the species and the date of the sowing. Early sowings give much larger plants than those made later in the fall. Anodas are vigorous rooters and gross feeders and must not be permitted to become pot bound until in their final containers. The soil should be coarse, porous, and fertile. When the roots have permeated the soil in the pots in which the plants are to flower, weekly applications of dilute liquid fertilizer are highly beneficial. Greenhouse-grown anodas need full sun, airy conditions, and a night temperature of 50°F with daytime temperatures five or ten degrees warmer. Very high hu-

midity is to be avoided. The greenhouse should be ventilated freely on all favorable occasions. Although anodas will not tolerate a compact soil that remains constantly wet, they do need abundant supplies of moisture and soon wilt, to the detriment of continued satisfactory growth, if they do not receive this.

Diseases and Pests. Rust disease sometimes can be troublesome and the plants may be infested with aphids and red spider mites.

ANOECTOCHILUS (Anoecto-chìlus). Twenty-five rare species of the orchid family ORCHIDACEAE constitute *Anoectochilus*. Formerly certain orchids now assigned to other genera, including *Dossinia* and *Ludisia*, belonged here. Natives of tropical Asia, Polynesia, and Australia, and extremely rare in cultivation, these orchids grow chiefly in the ground, much less often on rocks or in accumulations of moss and debris at the bases of trees. The name, from the Greek *anoiktos,* open, and *cheilos,* a lip, refers to the form of the flowers. They are colloquially called jewel orchids.

Jewel orchids, the name is used also for some other sorts previously included in this genus, are admired chiefly for their splendidly colored foliage. Typically they have creeping, branched rhizomes and short, fleshy, erect, jointed, few-leaved stems. The leaves are pointed-elliptic to pointed-ovate. The small flowers are in erect terminal spikes.

Kinds sometimes cultivated include these: *A. regalis,* of Ceylon has pointed-broad-elliptic, velvety, green leaves about 2 inches long by 1½ inches wide, wonderfully netted with gold veins. Its flowers are greenish-white and white. *A. roxburghii,* of India, has velvety, elliptic leaves 2½ inches long by 1½ inches wide, green netted with silver. Its pinkish flowers have white lips. *A. sikkimensis,* of Sikkim, has leaves 2½ inches long by 1½ inches wide decorated with a tracery of gold veins. Its flowers are olive-green and white.

Garden Uses and Cultivation. Challenging to grow, these orchids need a loose, porous rooting medium that contains abundant organic material, and drains rapidly. It is kept evenly moist. A mix of approximately equal parts by bulk of osmunda or tree fern fiber, sphagnum moss, coarse leaf mold, and perlite is likely to satisfy. Temperatures of 70 to 80°F and higher and atmospheric humidity of 80 percent or higher are needed for best results. Shade from direct sun is essential. Repotting should not be done oftener than absolutely necessary. Anoectochiluses much resent root disturbance. Propagation is by careful division. For more information see Orchids.

ANOECTONARIA. This is the name of bigeneric orchid hybrids the parents of which are *Anoectochilus* and *Haemaria*.

ANOGRAMMA (Ano-grámma). Natives of temperate regions of the northern and southern hemispheres, the seven rather poorly defined species of *Anogramma* belong in the pteris family PTERIDACEAE. They are included in *Pityrogramma* by some authorities. The name, presumably derived from the Greek *ano,* upward, and *gramma,* writing, is not of obvious application.

These are small, short-lived ferns of tufted habit with poorly-developed rhizomes, and fronds (leaves) that at maturity are three times pinnate or sometimes more. The clusters of spore capsules, located along the veins, are without coverings (indusia).

A delightful native of Mexico, *A. chaerophylla* grows in heavy shade in moist habitats. Its slender-stalked fronds, 3 to 7 inches tall, have lacy, triangular-ovate blades thrice-pinnately-divided into tiny forked or toothed ultimate segments.

Garden Uses and Cultivation. Easy to grow, the species described is perhaps best adapted to cultivation in terrariums. Afforded well-drained soil containing considerable organic matter such as leaf mold or peat moss, and shade from direct sun, this fern prospers where the night temperature in winter is about 55°F and the air is humid. Its soil should be kept damp, not constantly wet. Propagation is very easy by spores.

ANOMATHECA is *Lapeirousia.*

ANOPTERIS (An-ópteris). One species of fern, native from Jamaica to Brazil, is the sole representative of *Anopteris* of the pteris family PTERIDACEAE. Its name, from the Greek *ano,* upward, and *pteris,* a fern, alludes to its habit of growth. It differs from *Pteris* in having fertile leaves somewhat different from the sterile ones.

Of delicate appearance, *A. hexagona* (syn. *A. heterophylla; Pteris heterophylla*) has short, erect rhizomes, and clusters of two- or three-times-pinnate, hairless fronds (leaves) 6 inches to 2 feet long and 3 inches to 1 foot wide. The final divisions of the sterile leaves are oblong and deeply-sharp-toothed; those of fertile ones are smaller, narrower, toothed at their apexes, and have nearly continuous clusters of spore capsules along their margins.

Garden Uses and Cultivation. Hardy outdoors only in the tropics and warm subtropics, this fern is adaptable for planting in shaded locations and in lath houses. It is also cultivated in greenhouses, where it responds to the conditions and care satisfactory for *Pteris.* For more information see Pteris, and Ferns.

ANOPTERUS (Anóp-terus). Australia and Tasmania are homes to the two evergreen small trees and shrubs that constitute this genus of the saxifrage family SAXIFRAGACEAE. Neither is hardy in the north. The

name, given in recognition of the seeds being winged at the top, comes from the Greek *ano,* above, and *pteron,* a wing.

Anopteruses are hairless, and have alternate, leathery leaves, and terminal racemes of white flowers. The blooms have persistent, short-tubular calyxes with six to nine lobes, and as many stamens and petals as there are lobes to the calyx. The fruits are capsules.

The beautiful *Anopterus glandulosus* is native at high elevations in Tasmania where it becomes a tree 20 to 40 feet in height; in cultivation it is usually a shrub. Its narrowly-obovate or oblanceolate, glandular-toothed leaves, crowded at the ends of the shoots, are 2 to 6 inches long. The cupped, campanula-like, white or pink-tinged flowers, ⅝ inch in diameter, and generally with six petals, are in erect terminal racemes up to 6 inches long. The slender, erect seed capsules are about ½ inch long.

Garden Uses and Cultivation. This choice species is suitable for the Pacific Northwest and other regions of cool summers and mild winters. It needs well-drained, sandy peaty soil containing abundant humus, which never becomes excessively dry. A mulch of peat moss or other suitable organic material maintained about the plant is helpful. Any pruning needed to keep the plant shapely should be done in late spring as soon as blooming is through. Propagation is by seeds or by summer cuttings, which root readily in a propagating

bed in a cold frame or greenhouse, or under mist.

ANOTA (An-òta). The four or five species of *Anota* belong to the orchid family ORCHIDACEAE. They are natives of Burma and Malaya and the Philippine Islands. The name from the Greek *an,* without, and *otos,* an ear, alludes to the column being without ears.

Anotas are tree-perching (epiphytic) plants with leafy stems and racemes of flowers with long-elliptic sepals and petals and a spurred lip with two conspicuous raised veins and lobed at its apex.

Very handsome *A. violacea* (syns. *Rhynchostylis violacea, Saccolabium violaceum*), of Burma, has leaves up to 1 foot long by 3 inches wide on a stout stem ordinarily not more than 4 inches long. Up to 1 foot in length, the gracefully pendent racemes are 3 inches in diameter and consist of numerous, closely-arranged, fragrant blooms a little over 1 inch wide. They are cream-colored, attractively spotted with bright rosy-purple. The three-lobed lip is amethyst-purple with darker veinings. The blooms remain in good condition for a long period. Burmese *A. densiflora* (syns. *Rhynchostylis densiflora, Saccolabium giganteum*) has stems up to 8 inches long and 1-foot-long, 1½- to 2-inch-wide leaves. The racemes, their blooms more densely crowded than those of *R. violacea,* are up to 1¼ feet long. The 1-inch-wide flowers have white

Anota densiflora

sepals and petals spotted at their bases with purple, and a white-based, violet-purple lip.

Garden Uses and Cultivation. These are as for *Rhynchostylis*. For further information see Orchids.

ANREDERA (Anréd-era). This is the botanically accepted name of a group of five or more species of the basella family BASELLACEAE, previously known as *Boussingaultia*. The new designation is a commemorative one.

Occurring in the wild from the southern United States to the West Indies, Argentina, and Galapagos Islands, *Anredera* consists of tuberous-rooted, herbaceous perennial vines with much-branched stems, and undivided, more or less fleshy, ovate, heart-shaped or elliptic, toothless leaves. The tiny bisexual or unisexual, stalked flowers are in terminal and axillary, spike-like racemes. They have two sepals, five persistent petals, five stamens, and a three-lobed or three-cleft style. The fruits are small, spherical, and enclosed by the persistent perianths.

The Madeira vine or mignonette vine (*A. cordifolia* syns. *Boussingaultia gracilis, B. g. pseudo-baselloides*), native to Argentina, is naturalized in the southern United States. This was, and still often is, misidentified as *Boussingaultia baselloides,* which name properly belonged, before its transfer to *Anredera*, to a native of Mexico and Ecuador, probably not cultivated.

A popular garden plant, *A. cordifolia* grows very rapidly. Its annual stems are 10 to 20 feet long, its heart-shaped, slightly fleshy leaves 1 inch to 4 inches long. The white, delightfully fragrant flowers, in slender, branched or branchless racemes up to 1 foot long, are borne profusely in late summer and fall. So far as is known this species does not produce fruits. Small tubers develop freely in its leaf axils.

Garden and Landscape Uses. The Madeira vine is commonly cultivated to clothe porches, pergolas, arbors, and suchlike structures that afford support for its twining stems. It thrives in ordinary well-drained soil, in sun or part-day shade.

Cultivation. This species is frost-tender, but even though its tops are killed it persists over winter if its roots are not frozen. Where danger of this exists, it is usual to dig the plants up in fall, store the roots over winter in a cool place, and replant in spring after there is no longer danger of frost. Propagation is by division of the roots, and by the small tubers that grow in the leaf axils.

ANSELLIA (Ansél-lia)—Leopard Orchid. The pattern of the markings of the blooms give reason for the vernacular name of the one or two very variable species of this genus of the orchid family ORCHIDACEAE. The botanical name commemorates the African explorer John Ansell, who died in 1847.

Endemic to tropical and South Africa, *Ansellia africana* is an evergreen, tree-perching (epiphytic) species that develops clusters of erect, narrow, stemlike pseudobulbs, nearly cylindrical or sometimes thickened at their middle or toward their top. They are up to 2 feet long or longer, and carry along their upper parts approximately six arching, linear, or narrowly-strap-shaped leaves up to 1 foot long by 1¼ inches wide. In loosely, many-flowered, erect, terminal, mostly branched spikes from 1 foot to 3 feet in length, the long-lasting, lightly fragrant blooms are borne in spring and summer. They are about 2 inches wide, and have spreading, similar sepals and petals, ranging in color from bright yellow to nearly green, spotted or cross-banded with light or dark chocolate-brown. The lip, yellowish to yellow with light or dark brown veins, is three-lobed, with the erect side lobes partly enclosing the column.

Garden Uses and Cultivation. The better forms of *Ansellia*, some the result of deliberate crossing of parental stocks to obtain superior horticultural varieties, are very worth while. Among the easiest of tropical orchids to grow, if afforded high temperatures and humidity, they succeed when potted in osmunda fiber, a compost of equal parts chopped tree fern and tree bark, or other rooting mediums favored for epiphytic orchids. Good light with some shade from strong sun is needed. Watering and fertilizing of well-rooted specimens should be given when the plants are in active growth. At other times water is given a little less freely, the atmosphere kept a little drier, and fertilizer is withheld. For further information see Orchids.

ANSIDIUM. This is the name of orchid hybrids the parents which are *Ansellia* and *Cymbidium*.

ANT TREE and LONG JOHN ANT TREE. See Triplaris.

ANTEGIBBAEUM (Antegib-baèum). This genus of one species of the carpetweed family AIZOACEAE is so nearly related to *Gibbaeum* that some botanists include it there. A small succulent plant, it is sought by collectors of the rare and unusual. The name, from the Latin *ante*, before, and the name of the genus *Gibbaeum*, alludes to the relationship.

Native to South Africa, **Antegibbaeum fissoides** (syns. *Gibbaeum fissoides, G. nelii*) is a clump-forming species. Each grayish-green to reddish plant body consists of paired leaves separated at least two-thirds to their bases. The leaves of each pair, up to about 2¼ inches long, are of slightly different lengths. Their upper or inside surfaces are flattish, beneath they are rounded. The showy, almost stalkless, terminal flowers, 2 inches in diameter, are reddish to purple, with darker mid-veins to the petals. The fruits are capsules.

Garden Uses and Cultivation. These are as for Gibbaeum.

ANTELOPE BRUSH. See Purshia.

ANTENNARIA (Anten-nària)—Ladies'-Tobacco, Pussy Toes. This genus of perhaps 100 species of modest mien belongs in the daisy family COMPOSITAE. With the exception of Africa, it is indigenous to most temperate and many subtropical regions. The name, from the Latin *antenna*, the

Ansellia africana

yard of a sailing ship, calls attention to the pappus (hairs accompanying the florets and fruits) fancifully suggesting the antennae of an insect.

Antennarias are low, more or less evergreen, herbaceous perennials with stems, foliage, and clustered flower heads woolly. Their leaves are mostly basal, those on the stems alternate. The small flower heads, without petal-like ray florets, are of all disk florets (the type that form the eyes of daisies). They are backed by an involucre (collar) of several rows of bracts, the inner ones membranous and white or colored. The fruits are seedlike achenes.

A common native from Newfoundland to Alberta, Virginia, and Arizona, *Antennaria neglecta* is very variable. It includes *A. canadensis, A. campestris,* and *A. neodioica,* by some botanists accepted as species, and is closely related to and hybridizes with *A. plantaginifolia.* The oblanceolate to spatula-shaped leaves of *A. neglecta* are markedly less woolly above than on their lower sides. They are up to ¾ inch wide and have one chief vein, or are sometimes obscurely three-veined. The flower stalks, up to 1 foot tall, bear clusters of white flower heads. Its botanical name by no means inappropriate (*plantaginifolia* means with foliage like that of a plantain), ladies'-tobacco (*A. plantaginifolia*) has leaves considerably bigger than those of the other kinds here considered, the largest up to 2 inches long or a little longer by ¾ inch wide or wider, the basal ones ovate to obovate, with three or five conspicuous veins. Their upper sides are nearly hairless, their undersides are white-hairy. The stem leaves are mostly lanceolate or linear. The whitish to cream-colored flower heads are clustered at the tops of stems 4 inches to more than 1 foot tall.

Its flower heads with pink, or sometimes cream-colored bracts, and its foliage white-hairy on both surfaces, *A. rosea* is one of the more attractive kinds. In the wild it ranges from Ontario to California and Alaska. This forms creeping mats and has flower stems up to heights of 8 inches to 1 foot or more. Its oblanceolate leaves are ½ to ¾ inch long. Another kind with leaves white-woolly on both sides is *A. parvifolia* (syn. *A. aprica*). Mat-forming, and with flowering stems usually not more than 6 inches tall, it occurs wild in dry soils in open places from Minnesota to Manitoba, British Columbia, Nevada, and Arizona. Its leaves, oblanceolate to spatula-shaped, and up to a little more than 1 inch long, often assume purplish tints in winter. The flower heads have white or more seldom old-rose-colored involucres.

Other sorts sometimes cultivated include these: *A. alpina,* of North America, Europe, and Asia, is mat-forming, and 2 to 5 inches tall, has rosettes of oblanceolate leaves ½ to ¾ inch long, densely-gray-hairy on their undersides, becoming green and hairless above. The stem leaves are linear. The cream flower heads are mostly in threes. The especially lovely *A. a. media,* of western North America, has leaves densely-white-hairy on both surfaces. *A. dioica* is another matting kind. Its leaves are green and nearly hairless on their upper surfaces, white-hairy beneath. Those of the rosettes are spatula-shaped and up to 1 inch long. The stem leaves are linear. The white or pinkish flower heads are in groups of up to a dozen. Variety *A. d. tomentosa* (syn. *A. tomentosa*) is markedly white-hairy. *A. lanata,* of western North America, has basal tufts of erect oblanceolate leaves 3 to 4 inches long, and smaller, narrower stem leaves, all felted with gray hair. The whitish flower heads up to 1¼ inches wide are several together atop stalks 4 to 9 inches tall.

Garden and Landscape Uses and Cultivation. Although not in great favor horticulturally, antennarias can serve very well in selected places as groundcovers, in rock gardens, and for similar purposes. To be at their best they must have poorish soil, dry rather than moist, and full sun. Also, gardeners should be prepared to go to some little trouble to select the most desirable forms of the species. This may involve some searching in the wild, or raising a goodly number of seedlings from among when they have attained flowering size, one can select the most appealing. Since not all antennarias produce seeds this last method is not always possible. Except that very silvery-leaved, high mountain and desert sorts do not always adapt well to hot, humid summers, antennarias give little trouble. Once established in suitable locations they pretty well look out for themselves. It is desirable to remove faded flower heads. Division in spring or fall, and cuttings inserted in a bed of sand, sandy soil, or some similar medium in early summer, and when procurable, seeds, afford easy means of propagation.

ANTHEMIS (Án-themis) — Golden-Marguerite. Some 200 species of the daisy family COMPOSITAE constitute *Anthemis.* They are natives from the Mediterranean region to Iran, and include annuals, biennials, and herbaceous perennials. Their name is the Greek one of camomile.

Anthemises have stems and foliage that when bruised are strongly scented. The leaves are from one- to three-times-pinnately-divided, often finely so. Daisy-like in form, that is, consisting of many florets, the central ones of the disk type, the surrounding petal-like ones of the ray type, the flower heads terminate slender stalks. The collars behind them are of several rows of overlapping, papery-edged bracts. The disk florets are yellow, the rays yellow or white. The angled or ribbed, seedlike fruits are achenes. Formerly named *A. nobilis,* the camomile or chamomile is now *Chamaemelum nobile.*

The golden-marguerite (*A. tinctoria*) is the most popular perennial anthemis. Bushy, with erect, angular stems sometimes prostrate in their lower parts, it is 1½ to 2½ feet tall. The pinnate leaves,

Antennaria rosea

Anthemis tinctoria

more or less downy on their undersides, have as primary divisions segments pinnately-cleft into toothed, ovate or oblong lobes. Golden-yellow, the flower heads are 1 inch to 1½ inches in diameter. The outer bracts of the involucre are pointed. The achenes are four-angled. Horticultural varieties with larger flower heads and often more finely-divided foliage are favored. Among the best are *A. t. kelwayi*, its flower heads with pale yellow rays, 'Grallagh Gold', with rich yellow heads of flowers, and 'Mrs. E. C. Buxton', with lemon-yellow flower heads. The golden-marguerite, native of Europe and Asia, is naturalized in North America.

Rich orange ray florets and yellow disks are characteristic of the 1- to 2-inch-wide flower heads of **A. sancti-johannis**, a variable native of the Balkans. It is 2 to 3 feet in height, erect, perennial, and more or less furnished with soft, gray hairs. The leaves, the lower ones up to 5 inches long, the upper smaller, are two- or three-times-pinnately-divided into oblong segments ending in firm white points. The involucral bracts are edged with dark brown. The achenes are four-angled. Native to the Caucasus, and up to 1 foot tall or taller, **A. marschalliana** (syn. *A. biebersteiniana*) has silvery-hairy stems and leaves, the latter twice-pinnate. The 1-inch-wide flower heads have yellow rays.

Anthemis marschalliana

Cushion-like and with white-rayed flower heads, the variable **A. montana** is 4 to 10 inches tall. Native to Europe and adjacent Asia, its stems and foliage are more or less woolly-hairy. The leaves are twice- or thrice-divided and lobed into linear or lanceolate segments. From 1 inch to 1½ inches wide, the flower heads have narrowly-brown-edged, lanceolate involucral bracts. The achenes are slightly four-angled. White-rayed flower heads are borne by the cushion-forming **A. carpatica,** of eastern Europe. It has leaves pinnately-divided into

Anthemis sancti-johannis

fewer and wider, sometimes three-toothed, segments than those of *A. montana*. The flower heads are 1½ inches wide. About 1 foot tall, **A. cinerea** has gray-hairy stems and foliage. Native to the Balkans, it has ovate, pinnate leaves with the primary divisions pinnately-cleft into blunt, oblong lobes. The white-rayed flower heads are large.

Also with white-rayed flower heads, **A. triumfetti,** of the Mediterranean region, is up to 2½ feet high. Its leaves, hairy on their undersides, are once-pinnately-cleft into oblong, toothed lobes. The flower heads are up to 1½ inches across. Less hardy than most and suited only for mild climates, **A. cupaniana** is somewhat woody toward the bases of its stems. It forms a broad mat 2 to 3 feet wide of silvery-gray foliage 6 inches to nearly 1 foot tall, and has white-rayed flower heads 1½ to 2 inches across on 6-inch-long stalks. It is native to Italy.

Annual and biennial kinds are infrequently cultivated. Those now to be mentioned are natives of Europe. One of the best is annual **A. ruthenica.** Forming a compact mass of feathery foliage and up to about 1½ feet tall, it has white-rayed flower heads about 1½ inches wide. Up to 3 feet in height, **A. altissima** is an annual, with white-rayed flower heads some 2 inches across. It has finely-divided foliage. An annual or a biennial, **A. austriaca** is up to 2 feet tall or taller. It has light green foliage and white-rayed flower heads 1¾ inches wide. The biennial **A. macedonica** is pretty. It forms a dense mass of finely-divided foliage, and produces masses of tiny white-rayed flowers. It is useful for edging.

Garden and Landscape Uses. The plants considered here are easy-to-grow ornamentals, the lower ones suitable for rock gardens and similar places, the taller ones for flower beds and as cut flowers. All are easy to grow and generally hardy.

Cultivation. These are sun-lovers. For their best comfort they need thoroughly well-drained soil, preferably neutral or slightly alkaline. The perennials are very easily increased by division in early fall or spring, and by seed. Once established, they need no special care. The annuals are sown in early spring where they are to remain, and the seedlings thinned to 8 inches to 1 foot apart. They are rather easily damaged by wind and heavy rain and so neat staking is required. The biennials are treated in the same way except that the seeds are sown in late summer to give plants that will bloom the following year.

ANTHER. The part of the stamen in which the pollen develops is called an anther.

ANTHERICUM (Anthér-icum)—St. Bernard's-Lily. The number of species accepted as composing *Anthericum*, of the lily family LILIACEAE, varies according to interpretations of different botanists. A conservative estimate is that it consists of about fifty species, a more liberal one accounts for three hundred species. Accepting the narrower viewpoint, the genus is represented in the native floras of America, Africa, and Europe. The name is from the Greek one, *antherikon*, for the asphodel. Gardeners frequently label plants that belong in *Chlorophytum* and *Paradisea* as anthericums.

Unlike many members of the lily family anthericums do not have bulbs. Their roots are more or less fleshy or tuberous, their leaves are all basal, linear, or grasslike, usually shorter than the leafless flower stalks. The flowers, in loose, terminal racemes, have six wide-spreading perianth segments, commonly called petals, six slender stamens, and a slender style. The fruits are capsules containing three-sided seeds.

The St.-Bernard's-lily (*A. liliago*) is the only kind of any considerable horticultural

Anthericum ramosum

Anthericum liliago

Anthericum ramosum

import. A native of Europe, it is a very fine, hardy, deciduous, herbaceous perennial of satisfyingly easy culture. From its base it produces numerous, slender, gray-green leaves that recurve gracefully and are up to 1 foot long. They form considerable tufts. The many erect, branchless flower stalks rise to a height of about 2 feet and in May are bedecked with starry, pure white blooms, about 1½ inches in diameter, that somewhat resemble those of *Camassia*. The stalks are sufficiently wiry and slender that they are moved by slight breezes and the flowers sway gayly when the air is not still and add life to the garden in a way that those of their stiffer cousins the perennial asphodels (*Asphodelus*), which bloom about the same time, do not. Variety *A. l. major* is a larger plant than the typical species, and *A. l. grandiflorum* has been described as having larger flowers.

Another species, **A. ramosum,** native of southern and western Europe, has branching flower stalks and smaller flowers than those of *A. liliago*. Also, the styles of its flowers are straight rather than curved as are those of the St.-Bernard's-lily. It is less often cultivated. There are other species of *Anthericum*, especially some native to South Africa and some to Mexico, that might well be brought into cultivation. It is not expected that these would prove hardy in the north, but they should be suitable for milder parts of the United States.

Garden and Landscape Uses. The anthericums presently cultivated are grace-

ful, elegant plants for flower borders, the fronts of shrub borders where root competition is not too keen, and for colonizing in relatively carefree and informal parts of gardens. They prosper with minimum attention and may be allowed to "stay put" for long periods without disturbance. At The New York Botanical Garden colonies have flourished for more than twenty years without being replanted and without spreading appreciably. Anthericums are well-behaved plants. They grow well in a variety of earths including those of limestone derivation, and are especially grateful if organic matter in the soil is in fair supply.

Cultivation. Planting is best done in spring. A spacing of 6 to 8 inches between young plants or divisions is satisfactory. No special routine care is needed. An annual spring dressing of a complete fertilizer is helpful and in dry weather watering is desirable. Propagation is simply accomplished by seed or by careful division in early spring.

ANTHOLYZA (Antho-lȳza). Most of the plants that have been cultivated under this name belong in allied genera, including *Anapalina, Chasmanthe,* and *Curtonus.* One

or more species, depending upon the interpretations of different botanists, are admitted in *Antholyza,* a genus of the iris family IRIDACEAE, endemic to Africa. The name, from the Greek *anthos,* a flower, and *lyssa,* rage, was given because of a fancied resemblance between the wide-open lips of the flowers and the gaping mouth of an animal about to bite.

Typical of the genus, and by some considered the only species, **A. ringens** (syn.

Antholyza ringens

Babiana ringens) has corms (bulblike organs not consisting of concentric layers or overlapping scales like the bulbs of onions and lilies, but solid throughout). There is a short underground stem enclosed by the leaf bases, and several longitudinally-corrugated, sword-shaped leaves 4 to 8 inches long and up to ¼ inch wide. The one-sided, dense flower spikes are lateral and up to 1 foot high. The red, asymmetrical blooms, compressed laterally, have curved, funnel-shaped perianth tubes 1¼ to 1½ inches long, and six lobes (petals) of which the uppermost is erect and encloses with its inturned lower margins the stalks of the three stamens and the three-branched style, which are as long or longer than the upper petal. The five lower petals form a projecting lip. The fruits are capsules.

Garden and Landscape Uses and Cultivation. The species described is something of an oddity, suitable for outdoor cultivation in rock gardens in California and other places with frostless or nearly frostless, Mediterranean-type climates, and for pots in greenhouses where the winter night temperature is 45 to 50°F. It needs somewhat sandy, fertile soil, and full sun. Its cultivation is as for *Ixia*.

ANTHRACNOSE. This is a name applied to certain diseases caused by fungi responsible for lesions on stems, leaves, fruits and other parts of particular plants. Among the most common anthracnoses are those of beans, cactuses, grapes, hollyhocks, maples, melons, rubber plants, sycamores

Annuals: Lavender nierembergia; yellow French marigold; red, white, and red-and-white petunias in a small home garden

Annuals: Purple verbena with red and pink petunias. The yellow flowers are cannas

Angraecum superbum

Anemopsis californica

A garden of annuals at New Paltz, New York

Annuals: Yellow African marigolds and lavender ageratum

Annuals: Dwarf dahlias and yellow marigolds

Antirrhinum majus variety

Anthurium scherzeranum

Antirrhinum majus, a butterfly variety

(*Platanus*), and tomatoes. The type of injury varies with the plant affected. Small brown spots on the pods that enlarge to depressed, black circular ones, and dark lesions along the veins on the undersides of the leaves are typical of bean anthracnose. Infected sycamores show first damage to the unfolding foliage. Later, areas of pale brown dead tissue develop along the veins and sometimes over most of the leaf surface. The shoot ends wither and die and cankers may develop lower on the limbs. Rubber plants show anthracnose infection by the apexes and other marginal parts of the leaves becoming yellowish, changing to light and finally dark brown, the destruction moving slowly inward until the whole leaf is destroyed. Rather similar effects can result from fungus leaf spot diseases and from unfavorable environments, especially exposure to hot, dry air.

Leaves of *Platanus* affected by anthracnose

Controls employed to limit damage done by anthracnose diseases vary with the kind of plant and to some extent local conditions. Consult local Cooperative Extension Agents or State Agricultural Experiment Stations for the latest recommended methods of preventing and combating these infections.

ANTHRISCUS (An-thrícus)—Salad Chervil. About a dozen species native of Europe and western Asia belong here, some are naturalized in North America. The best known is the salad chervil (*Anthriscus cerefolium*), which is esteemed as a salad ingredient. For this its parsley-like, aromatic leaves are employed, as they are also for garnishing. They are milder than parsley and have a slight flavor of anise, with just a trace of bitterness. The name is a modification of *anthriskon*, used by the ancient Greeks for some plant in the group to which *Anthriscus* belongs, the carrot family UMBELLIFERAE.

Anthriscus cerefolium

Except for salad chervil *Anthriscus* has no appreciable horticultural importance. It consists of annuals and biennials with branched stems, twice- or thrice-dissected ferny leaves with toothed or more deeply-cut leaflets, and umbels of small white flowers. The distinct beak to each fruit (commonly called a seed) clearly separates these plants from *Chaerophyllum*, to which genus the altogether different turnip-rooted chervil belongs.

Cultivation. Salad chervil succeeds in any ordinary fertile vegetable garden soil in full sun. It is grown chiefly as an early summer and fall crop and is ready to harvest in six to eight weeks from seed sowing. It does not thrive in very hot weather and in many regions must be omitted as a summer crop. It is easy to grow. The seeds are sown in rows about 1½ feet apart and the seedlings thinned to 8 inches to 1 foot apart in the rows. The plant is 1 foot to 2 feet tall.

ANTHURIUM (An-thùrium)—Tail Flower, Flamingo Flower. This is an important group. Some 550 species of tropical American evergreen plants, herbaceous or sometimes with woody stems, compose *Anthurium* of the arum family ARACEAE. They include kinds cultivated for their often brilliantly colored inflorescences, popularly called flowers, and others the chief attraction of which is their handsome foliage. In addition to the natural species, many garden hybrids are grown. The name comes from the Greek *anthos*, a flower, and *oura*, a tail, in allusion to the form of the inflorescences.

Anthuriums differ considerably in their growth habits. Some kinds form tufts or clumps of essentially all basal foliage, others have erect, creeping, or climbing rooting stems. The leaves may be undivided, with or without shallow to deep lobes, or divided into separate leaflets that spread in finger-fashion (palmately) from the top of the leafstalk. Most often they are ovate to heart-shaped, arrow-shaped, or halberd-shaped. As is usual in the arum fam-

ily the tiny true flowers are crowded on a spike called a spadix from the base of which comes a modified leaf called a spathe. Spadix and spathe together constitute what technically is an inflorescence, but in common parlance is referred to as the "flower." In *Anthurium* the spathe does not enclose the spadix. It may be greenish, yellowish, or purplish and more or less leaflike or bright red, pink, white, or combinations of these. It may spread widely or downward and be flat or twisted. The spadix is straight or spiraled. The inflorescences are solitary and terminal on usually long stalks. The true flowers are bisexual. They have four narrow perianth segments, four stamens, and a slightly-two-lobed stigma. The fruits are berries, often attractively colored.

Showy flowers, properly inflorescences, are the chief attractions of the plain-green-leaved *A. andraeanum* and *A. scherzeranum*, their many varieties and hybrids. Native to Colombia, *A. andraeanum* has a short,

Anthurium andraeanum

upright stem, and erect, pointed, broad-oblong to oblong-ovate or oblong-heart-shaped leaves with blades up to 1 foot long on longer stalks. The long-stalked inflorescences have spathes, typically bright scarlet or orange-red, but in some variants pink or white, 4 to 6 inches or even more long and broad-ovate to heart-shaped. The spadix, straight or slightly curved, 3 to 5 inches in length, is yellowish with a white base. In *A. a. album* the spathes are waxy-white with purplish bases and yellow apexes. The spathes of *A. a. giganteum* are exceptionally large and salmon-red. Vigorous *A. a. rhodochlorum* has salmon-red spathes, with green extremities. Spathes up to 1 foot long, with large basal lobes, carmine-red, bordered by brownish-red, edged with green are characteristic of a variant of the last-named, *A. a. schlingii*. Deep red spathes and yellow-tipped, white spadices are borne by *A. a. rubrum*. The strongly spiraled or curled, yellow spadices of its long-stalked inflorescences most conveniently distinguish *A. scherzeranum*

Anthurium scherzeranum

Anthurium clarinervium

long by 10 inches wide, pinkish on their undersides and with cylindrical stalks. Its linear-oblong, green spathes are up to 6 inches long. It is native to Colombia and perhaps Peru. The Colombian *A. magnificum* differs from *A. crystallinum* in its leafstalks being four-angled and winged toward their tops. The leaf blades are 1 foot to 2 feet in length. The laceolate to oblong, green or reddish spathes are 4 to 8 inches long. Similar to the last two, but smaller, *A. clarinervium,* of Mexico, has reddish-

from *A. andraeanum.* Its spathes, 2 to 4 inches long, broadly-ovate to ovate-oblong, are rich scarlet to crimson or, in varieties, salmon-red, rose-pink, white, or white spotted with red or pink. It has a very short stem. Its leaves have slender stalks as long or longer than the rather narrow-lanceolate to elliptic, pointed blades, which are 4 to 8 inches long or longer and up to about 2 inches wide. They have a conspicuous vein near and paralleling the margin. Variety *A. s. nebulosum* differs from the species, in its inflorescences having double, red-spotted, white spathes. In *A. s. rothschildianum* the red spathes are dotted with white.

Hybrids of *A. andraeanum* include several with showy inflorescences. Here belongs *A. carneum,* its other parent *A. nym-*

phaeifolium. Its inflorescences have rose-carmine spathes up to 7 inches long and 6 inches wide, and a pink spadix. Crossing *A. andraeanum* with *A. veitchii* produced *A. chelseaense,* which has ovate leaves, pointed-heart-shaped, carmine-red spathes, white to green spadices. The free-flowering *A. ferrienense,* offspring of *A. andraeanum* mated with *A. ornatum,* is a robust climber with rose-pink, ovate-heart-shaped spathes, and white to pink spadices. Probably a hybrid of *A. andraeanum* and an unrecorded species, *A. mariae* is vigorous. Its large, heart-shaped spathes are glistening white blushed with pink. Its rose-pink spadices point downward.

Heart-shaped leaves with prominent clear white or faintly green veins are characteristic of several anthuriums. One of the best known, the short-stemmed *A. crystallinum,* has leaves with blades up to 1¼ feet

green spathes. Native to Bolivia, *A. grande* has large, pointed-heart-shaped, velvety leaves netted with pale veins. Its olive-green, pale-green-veined leaves more arrow-shaped than those of kinds described above, *A. cordatum* of Brazil has green spathes up to 8 inches long. Its silvery-veined leaves large, its spathe slender and coppery-green *A. hoffmannii* is indigenous to Costa Rica and Panama. Oblong-heart-shaped leaves about 1¼ feet long, dark olive-green relieved by narrow silvery-green veins above, paler on their undersides, are typical of *A. regale,* of the Amazon region and Peru. The silvery-white-veined leaves of Colombian *A. forgetii,* a small relative of *A. crystallinum,* differ from other pale-veined kinds discussed here in being peltate, which means that the leafstalk joins the blade some distance in from its margin. Proportionately much longer than the leaves of other kinds in this grouping, those of Colombian *A. warocqueanum* are up to 3 feet long, are velvety, and have ivory-white veins. This kind is a climber with inflorescences with a 4-inch-long, greenish spathe and an up to 1-foot-long spadix.

Heart-shaped to broad-arrow-shaped plain green leaves without strongly-marked lighter veins are characteristic of the anthuriums now to be described. The heart-shaped to arrow-shaped leaves of *A. berriozabalense* have two long basal lobes that curiously turn toward each other and often overlap. It is a native of Guatemala. Short-stemmed, West Indian *A. cordifolium* (syn.

Anthurium carneum

Anthurium crystallinum

Anthurium warocqueanum

A. caribaeum) has leaves with heart-shaped blades up to 2 feet long and 1 foot wide and rather longer stalks. Its long-stalked inflorescences have a narrow green spathe up to 7 inches long and equaling or exceeding it, a black-purple spadix. Native to Colombia, **A. corrugatum** has heart-shaped to broad-arrow-shaped leaves, with pointed basal lobes. Light green, they have wrinkled or corrugated surfaces. Short-stalked, leathery leaves with heart-shaped bases are typical of **A. grandifolium,** of Vene-

Anthurium grandifolium

zuela and the West Indies. A climber, and a native of Cuba, **A. gymnopus** has very broad, waxy-green leaves with depressed centers and paler veins. The Brazilian **A. longilinguum** has markedly-arrow-shaped, glossy green, leathery leaves, their blades spreading more or less horizontally from the apexes of wiry stalks. The leaves of **A. macdougallii** have long, wiry stalks and spreading, broadly-heart-shaped, somewhat wavy blades. It is a native of southern Mexico. The handsome, lustrous, heart-shaped leaves of hybrid **A. mortefonta-**

nense, which has as parents *A. veitchii* and *A. andraeanum,* are prettily quilted or corrugated. The inflorescences have a creamy-white spathe and pink spadix. A Colombian plant with long-triangular, arrow-shaped leaves with rounded basal lobes *A.* 'Negrito', characteristically has very dark green foliage. From Colombia and Venezuela, *A. polyrrhizum* is a vigorous climber, with slender-stalked, bright green to reddish, broadly-heart-shaped leaves. The Ecuadorean **A. pulchrum** has broad-arrow-shaped, dull green leaves, with widely-spaced, rounded basal lobes. The inflorescences of this robust kind have a light green spathe and red spadix. From Colombia, **A. quindiuense** has wiry-stalked leaves, with ovate-heart-shaped blades. Creeping or climbing **A. radicans,** a Brazilian, has closely-set, short-stalked, pointed-ovate leaves, with short basal lobes. The depressed veins are responsible for their decidedly quilted appearance. They have pale undersides. Broadly-heart-shaped leaves with veins paler than the body of the blade typify **A. robustum,** presumed a hybrid of *A. regale.* Bluish-green, arrow-shaped leaves three times or more as long as wide are characteristic of **A. sanguineum.** Native to Colombia, it has large inflorescences with a rosy-red spathe and green spadix. The large-foliaged **A. spendidum** of Colombia has broadly-ovate-heart-shaped wrinkled leaves, with deeply-impressed veins and a deep, narrow opening between the basal lobes. Their upper surfaces are convex. The inflorescences have a green spathe and pink to reddish spadix. Broadly-arrow-shaped leaves, with a wide gap between the basal lobes, are borne by **A. watermaliense** of Colombia. Wavy-surfaced and lustrous, they have stalks triangular in section. The inflorescences are remarkable for their huge coppery-black spathes. The spadix is brown.

Slender, undivided, plain green leaves without lobes are typical of the kinds now to be considered. A neat native of Costa Rica and Guatemala, the short-stemmed **A. bakeri** has rather short-stalked, strap-

Anthurium bakeri in flower and fruit

shaped leaves 1 foot to 2 feet long, up to about 2 inches wide, with prominent midribs. The narrow, pale green, down-turned spathes are 1 inch to 2 inches long. The bright scarlet fruits are in spikes about 4 inches long. Short-stalked, leathery, pointed-lanceolate leaves in rosettes characterize the Brazilian **A. comtum.** The spathe is pink. Very much like *A. gracile,* Costa Rican **A. friedrichsthalii** has short-stalked, linear leaves up to 1½ feet long by about ½ inch wide. The spathes are reddish-brown. Drooping, narrow, prominently-veined leaves up to 5 feet in length are typical of **A. gladifolium** of Venezuela and Brazil. The spathes are narrow. The emerald-green, linear-elliptic leaves of **A. gracile,** native from Costa Rica to Peru, are much like those of *A. scolopendrinum.* They have raised midribs and rolled-under margins and are about 1 foot long by up to 1 inch wide. The Colombian **A. pendulifolium** has bright green, pendulous leaves up to 4 feet in length. Their midribs are pale. The spathes are purple. The foliage of *A. p. aureovariegatum* is variegated with pale yellow and chartreuse. A native of Costa Rica, **A. pittieri** has long-stalked leaves with elliptic blades up to about 10 inches long by 2¼ inches wide. The spathes are light green. Native to South America, **A. crispimarginatum** forms rosettes of erect, slender-oblanceolate, waved or crisped leaves up to about 2 feet long.

Broader, undivided leaves not heart-shaped at their bases are typical of the kinds now to be described. A native of the West Indies, **A. acaule** forms open rosettes of wavy-edged, oblanceolate leaves up to about 2½ feet long by 10 inches wide. Its inflorescences have narrow spathes, reddish on their upper surfaces. South American **A. affine** has bold rosettes of broad-elliptic, strongly-veined, leathery, wavy-edged leaves. Its spathes are violet. A parent of *A.* 'Anita', the Colombian **A. antrophyoides** has pointed-elliptic to nearly diamond-shaped leaves, their veins depressed, and profusely-produced, white-spathed inflorescences. Long-stalked leaves with broad-elliptic, pale-veined, lustrous blades, and inflorescences with brownish spathes that later become green are typical of **A. caucanum,** native to Colombia and Peru. Variety *A. c. maximum* has larger, nearly-round leaf blades with depressed veins that produce a quilted effect. Up to 4 feet in length, the leaves of South American **A. coriaceum** have short stalks, are erect and gray-green, with a strong midrib. The thick, lustrous, channeled leaves of **A. crassinervium,** native from Mexico to Venezuela and Honduras, are elliptic to oblanceolate, and up to 3 feet long. Sometimes very broad, they are in rosettes. The spathes are red and green. The West Indian **A. cubense** has rosettes of big, wavy-edged, obovate, short-stalked leaves. Panama and Costa Rica are homelands of **A. hacumense,** which has bold rosettes of leathery, broad-oblanceolate leaves about 2 feet long. The showy, bright red fruits are in dense spikes. Lustrous, narrow-lanceolate or oblong-lanceolate leaves with slender stalks and bold midribs are typical of Brazilian *A. harrisii.* Their blades are up to 2 feet long, and may exceed 3 inches in width. The spathes are narrow and green or pink. The 2-feet-long, broad-ovate to broad-oblanceolate leaves of *A. hookeri* are in regular, bird-nest-like rosettes. The spathes are green. This native of the West Indies and northern South America resembles *A. affine.* Venezuelan *A. microphyllum* has leaves with lustrous,

Anthurium microphyllum

fleshy, elliptic blades held at sharp angles to their long stalks. Native to tropical America, *A. oblanceolatum* has rosettes of short-stalked, thick, strongly-veined, broad-oblanceolate leaves. Wavy-edged, pointed, broad-lanceolate-oblong to oblanceolate leaves up to 3 feet long by 1 foot wide and in loose rosettes are characteristic of *A. recusatum* of Cuba. Its spathes are greenish-white. The lanceolate-linear leaves of *A. reticulatum,* of Colombia, are long and drooping. The inflorescences have narrow, green spathes. Neat and vining, *A. scandens,* native from the West Indies to Ecuador, is often not over 1 foot tall. It has

Anthurium scandens in bloom

small, long-stalked, elliptic to lanceolate leaves. Its spathes are green. Its very decorative spikes of white or purple, berry-like fruits remain in good condition for a long time. The leaves of *A. scolopendrinum* are long, slender-stalked, narrowly-strap-shaped, with sunken veins. Native to Central and South America, it bears drooping spikes of bright red, berry-like fruits. Another good-looking, small-foliaged sort, *A. spathulatum* has leaves with elliptic to nearly-round blades and slender, wiry stalks. It is a native of Venezuela. The short-stalked, wavy-margined, oblanceolate leaves of *A. tetragonum,* of Costa Rica, are in loose rosettes. They are 3 or 4 feet in length. Rosettes of short-stalked, wide-spreading, triangular-ovate leaves are typical of *A. venosum,* native to Cuba.

Leaves usually deeply-cleft or divided into separate leaflets, but in a few sorts less deeply-lobed, are characteristic of the sorts now to be considered. A vine native from Mexico to Costa Rica, *A. aemulum* (syn. *A. heptophyllum*) has long-stalked, thin, lustrous leaves divided into five to seven pointed, obovate leaflets that spread in finger-fashion. The spathes are green, the spadixes purple. Another vining kind, *A. angustisectum,* of Colombia, has leaves with drooping blades each of about five lanceolate leaflets up to 1 foot long. The hybrid *A. bullatum,* its parents *A. subsignatum* and *A. crystallinum,* has foliage much like that of the first-named parent except that the center lobe of the leaf is, proportionately to the side lobes, much wider. The leaf blades have three rather shallow lobes. Their veins are sunken, giving a decidedly quilted appearance to the surface.

Anthurium scandens in fruit

A strong-growing vine, *A. clavigerum* inhabits Colombia, Venezuela, and Peru. It has huge, long-stalked leaves, pentagonal in outline and with seven- to eleven-lobed,

Anthurium clavigerum

elliptic leaflets that spread like the fingers of a hand. The spadixes are lavender-colored. The fruits of this magnificent species are purple. *A.* 'Cochabamba', believed to be a native of Bolivia, but not identified as to species, has leaves of about seven very narrow, strap-shaped leaflets that spread in finger fashion from the top of the leafstalk. Vining *A. digitatum,* of Venezuela, Colombia, and Brazil, has long-stalked leaves each with five to eleven oblanceolate leaflets that spread in finger-fashion from the top of the leafstalk. The spathes are green and purple, the spadixes purple.

Anthurium digitatum

A vining Brazilian, *A. enneaphyllum* (syn. *A. variabile*) has long-stalked, leathery leaves divided into about seven pointed, narrowly-linear leaflets about 1 foot long and with a short point at the apex. The spathes are green, the spadixes purple. The West Indian *A. fissum* has thick leaves with blades cleft in hand-fashion, sometimes almost to their bases, sometimes more shallowly into pointed-obovate lobes. The spathes are green and narrowly-linear, the spadixes slender and brownish. The nearly circular leaves of the very short-stemmed *A. fortunatum* (syn. *A. elegans*), of Colombia, are very deeply-lobed, but not cut to their bases into separate leaflets. The seven to eleven narrowly-oblong to oblanceolate lobes, the center one almost twice as long as the others, have wavy margins. The spathes are green, the spadixes brown. *A. holtonianum* has climbing stems 6 feet tall or taller and leaves with stalks up to 3 feet long. The blades are of five to nine spreading, pinnately-lobed leaflets, elliptic to oblanceolate in outline, most up to 1 foot long, the center one about twice as long as the others. One foot or more in length, the spathe is purple, the spadix grayish. The Colombian *A. insigne* is a vine with leaves of three oblanceolate to elliptic leaflets up to 1 foot long. They have raised veins. A Central American, *A. kalbreyeri* (syn. *A. araliifolium*) is a climber with glossy green leaves of five to seven broad, wavy, conspicuously-veined, oblong-elliptic leaflets. The spathes are purplish-green. Native to Mexico, compact *A. lowii* has leaves cleft into conspicuously-veined lobes that are slightly lobed and spread in finger fashion from the top of the leafstalk. The large leaves of the Brazilian *A. panduratum* are of seven or nine deeply-lobed leaflets up to more than 1 foot long that spread from the tip of the leafstalk in the way of fingers. The very long spathes and spadixes are purple. Native to Mexico, *A. pedato-radiatum* has short, erect stems and nearly circular leaves up to 2 feet across and very deeply-cleft, but not divided into separate leaflets. The seven to eleven lobes are narrowly-oblanceolate, the basal ones broader and usually lobes. The spathes are green, up to 10 inches long by 1 inch wide, the spadixes violet. A vigorous vine, *A. pentaphyllum* occasionally belies its name by the glossy, pale-veined elliptic to oblanceolate, pointed leaflets of its long-stalked leaves numbering more than five. The leaflets are up to 1 foot long. Spathes and spadixes are green to purplish. It is native from Colombia to Brazil and Trinidad. From a short trunk *A. podophyllum* sprouts long-stalked leaves, with blades rounded in outline and twice-cleft into slender, spreading, clearly-veined lobes. It is a very handsome native of Mexico. The distinctive *A. signatum* has leaves with a pointed-triangular center lobe and two very large, elephant-ear-like basal ones. The spathes are yellowish-green. It is native to Ecuador and Venezuela. Somewhat like the last, *A. subsignatum* (syn. *A. wrightii*), of Costa Rica, because of the shape of its leaves, is sometimes unflatteringly called cowface. The basal lobes of its trilobed leaves spread at right angles. They are proportionately smaller than those of *A. signatum*. The spathes are green, the spadixes yellow. It is a parent of *A. bullatum*. Another with three-lobed leaves, *A. trifidum* (syn. *A. tri-*

lobum) is native to Colombia. It develops a short stem and has thinnish, leathery leaves, with lanceolate lobes somewhat under 1 foot long. The spathes are purplish, the spadixes purple. A vine of Brazil and Peru, *A. undatum* has thin, glossy leaves similar to those of *A. pentaphyllum*, but with shorter, narrower, unequal leaflets. The spathes are purplish, the spadixes purple. Vining *A. polyschistum*, of Colombia, has leaves with spreading from the tops of long stalks nine to fifteen wavy-edged, pointed-elliptic leaflets up to 8 inches long by ¾ inch wide. A little longer than spadixes, the spathes, narrow, greenish, are 3 to 4 inches long.

Garden and Landscape Uses. This genus furnishes landscapers and greenhouse gardeners with some of the most handsome and useful tropical decoratives. Its members come in a wide variety of sizes and leaf-forms. The foliage of some is strikingly veined with white or pale green. Others produce beautiful, large, often brilliantly-colored inflorescences, usually called flowers. These, which remain in good condition for months, may be succeeded by handsome spikes of berries, which also last well. When cut the flowers last for weeks. They are much used by florists.

In the humid tropics nonclimbing sorts are admirable for massing in places sheltered from wind in the shade of palms and other trees. Some prosper when set as epiphytes to the trunks and branches of trees or planted in accumulations of organic debris on rocks or cliffs. Vining sorts can be used effectively to clothe tree trunks and similar supports.

In greenhouses anthuriums can be displayed to excellent advantage with other plants that appreciate considerable warmth, humidity, and shade. They are among the choicest furnishings for large conservatories. Little *A. scandens* is an excellent terrarium plant.

Cultivation. Given the basic environment conditions just listed, and the type of soil they need, anthuriums make few demands of the cultivator. The rooting medium is important. It must contain abundant organic matter and be very well aerated. Compact earth and soils deficient in humus-forming materials are not to the liking of these plants. Water aplenty is essential to good growth, but stagnancy is abhorred. Provide perfect drainage so that there is never a suspicion of water collecting around the roots to the extent that air is excluded.

Anthurium polyschistum

In greenhouses the minimum winter night temperature should be 60°F. A few degrees higher is advantageous. By day and at other seasons considerably higher temperatures are desirable. At all times the atmosphere should be highly charged with moisture and on warm, bright days spraying the foliage lightly with water is beneficial. Shade from strong sun is essential. Water to keep the rooting medium always pleasantly moist, not sodden. From spring through fall give well-rooted specimens applications of dilute liquid fertilizer at one- or two-week intervals.

A suitable soil consists of one part turfy loam, two to three parts coarse leaf mold and sphagnum moss, one part coarse sand or perlite, a generous dash of dried cow manure, and a sprinkling of crushed charcoal. But the components can be varied so long as the objectives of coarseness, porosity and a high humus content are achieved. To assure a coarse texture the addition of bark chips of the kind used for potting orchids is useful.

Avoid setting the plants too low in their containers. Mound the surface of the rooting mixture so that the plant is on a small hill a few inches or so higher than the rim of the pot or tub and with the base of the mound a little below the rim. With a blunt wooden dibber press the mixture firmly among and around the roots, but do not pound it or bruise or disturb the roots. Repotting is normally needed at intervals of three or four years only. In between many anthuriums develop roots from their lengthening stems that if not packed around with moisture-retaining material will harden, die, and cease to be of any use in supporting the plant. If this happens the new leaves and inflorescences (flowers) deteriorate in size. To prevent this, from time to time mound sphagnum moss around the stems and tie it into position so that emerging roots may travel through this to reach the rooting medium in the pots or tubs. When the stems become too tall and perhaps ungainly sever them at their bases and plant the mass of roots contained in the sphagnum moss in new containers. From the old stumps, which should be kept a little on the dry side, new shoots that can be used to start new plants will arise.

Propagation of some kinds is easily achieved by division and of others by removing sucker shoots, potting them individually, and burying them to the rims of their pots in a propagating case where bottom heat of about 80°F is maintained. This is best done in January or February. When dividing or taking off suckers use great care not to do more damage than absolutely necessary to the thick, fleshy roots. If you do, decay is likely to result. Seeds also afford a ready means of increase. Remove these from their surrounding pulp and sow before they dry out in sphagnum moss or a mixture of peat moss and sand or perlite. Place them for germination in a humid propagating case where the temperature is 75 to 85°F.

Anthuriums are not much troubled by pests or diseases. Scale insects and mealybugs occasionally infest them and they sometimes are infected with a fungus leaf spot disease controllable by copper fungicides.

ANTHYLLIS (Anthýl-lis)—Jupiter's Beard, Kidney-Vetch, Bladder-Vetch. About twenty species compose this genus. Natives of Europe, North Africa, and western Asia, they belong in the pea family Leguminosae. The name is the ancient Greek one for some unidentified plant.

Anthyllises are annuals and evergreen and deciduous herbaceous perennials and subshrubs. They have alternate leaves rarely undivided or with three leaflets, more commonly pinnate, with an uneven number of leaflets, and generally covered with silvery hairs. The pea-shaped flowers are small, in dense, stalked, terminal, cloverlike heads or clusters from the leaf axils. They are purple, yellow, or white, and have ten stamens joined in a tube, or sometimes one is separate in its upper one-half. The tubular calyxes are five-toothed and often become inflated as they age. The standard or banner petal is ovate. The wings are longer than the keel. The fruits are pods with one to several seeds.

Jupiter's beard (*Anthyllis barba-jovis*) is a dense, evergreen shrub up to 3 feet tall with foliage silvery-white-hairy beneath, and green, and less sparsely hairy above. At the ends of short twigs are borne globular heads of pale to bright yellow flowers ¾ to 1 inch across, nestling against a pair of broad, deeply-cleft, silvery bracts. The leaves, 1½ to 2 inches long, have nine to nineteen narrow-elliptic to narrow-obovate leaflets. The pods contain a solitary seed. This attractive species ranges from Spain to Yugoslavia, often favoring rocky places near the sea.

Another pretty shrub, differing from the last in being deciduous, having branches ending in spines, leaves undivided or rarely of three leaflets, and blooms in axillary clusters of up to five or solitary, is *A. hermanniae* of the Mediterranean region. About 1½ feet tall, this crooked-branched kind has leaves with obovate to spatula-shaped leaflets usually under ¾ inch long, and yellow or orange-yellow flowers about ⅓ inch long, followed by one-seeded pods. Among the herbaceous perennial kinds *A. montana* is one of the best. Native of the mountains of central and southern Europe, it is a spreading, mat-forming kind 4 inches to 1 foot in height, with somewhat woody stems, and pinnate leaves mostly on the lower parts of erect flowering shoots. The leaves have seventeen to forty-one narrow-elliptic to narrow-obovate leaflets, hairy

Anthyllis hermanniae

on both surfaces, and ¼ to less than ½ inch long. The pink to purple flowers are in solitary heads that sit closely upon two encircling, deeply-cleft, leafy bracts. The standard petal is much larger than the wings and keel. Botanists recognize three varieties or subspecies of *A. montana* based chiefly on differences in the calyxes. In gardens variants with distinctive flower colors are given such appropriate identifying names as *A. m. carminea*, *A. m. rubra*, and *A. m. atrorubens*.

Kidney-vetch (*A. vulneraria*) is exceedingly variable. About thirty varieties or subspecies are recognized, many of which have at times been accorded the rank of species. Of these *A. v. argyrophylla* is often known as *A. webbiana*, and *A. v. praepropera* as *A. dillenii*. Both have red to purple blooms. The leaves of the former are densely-silvery-hairy on their upper sides. The lower leaves of *A. v. praepropera* have one to three leaflets. Interpreted as a single, variable species, kidney-vetch inhabits most of Europe and North Africa, and is naturalized in North America as far north as Vermont and North Dakota. There are annual, biennial, and herbaceous perennial phases. Commonly inhabiting dry soils, kidney-vetch is 6 inches to 1½ feet tall, and has lower leaves of a single leaflet

Anthyllis montana

or if more than one, the terminal one much the largest. The upper leaves are of few to many leaflets. The yellow, orange, whitish, red-purple, or bicolored flowers are many together in usually paired heads with two broad, deeply-cleft bracts immediately beneath the blooms. One, or rarely two, seeds are in each pod.

A procumbent annual, the bladder-vetch (*A. tetraphylla*) is gray-hairy, spreading, and 6 inches to 1½ feet tall. Its leaves have three to five leaflets, the terminal one obovate and much larger than the others. They are hairy, more so on their under surfaces than above. Pale yellow, tipped with red, the flowers, rarely solitary, more usually two to seven together in stalkless, axillary clusters, are slightly more than ½ inch long, and are succeeded by usually two-seeded pods constricted between the seeds. This is native to the Mediterranean region.

Garden and Landscape Uses and Cultivation. The shrub kinds are not hardy in the north; they are adaptable only for mild, dryish climates. Over-rich soil is not to their liking, they need well-drained, dryish, poorish soil, and full sun. They are attractive for shrub plantings and rock gardens and need no special care. The herbaceous perennials are hardy, and suitable for rock gardens, banks, and similar locations in full sun. They need porous, not excessively fertile soil. The annual *A. tetraphylla* has the same uses as the herbaceous perennials, but is not, of course, permanent. Its seeds are sown in early spring where the plants are to remain and the young plants are thinned to whatever extent is necessary to prevent overcrowding. Propagation of shrubby kinds is by seeds and summer cuttings, of the herbaceous perennials by seeds and division.

ANTIARIS (Anti-àris)—Upas Tree. The deadly upas tree, as it is sometimes called, *Antiaris toxicaria*, is one of the four or five

Antiaris toxicaria

species of a genus that has its home in the tropics of Africa, Madagascar, and Indo-malaysia. It belongs in the mulberry family MORACEAE and bears a name derived from a native one of Java. Evergreen, milky-juiced trees, the upas and other members of its genus have alternate, sometimes toothed leaves, and unisexual, petal-less blooms, the males in dense heads, the females solitary. The calyxes of the male flowers are three- or four-parted, and the short stamens number three or four. The female blooms are without calyxes, but the ovary is enclosed in an involucre (collar of bracts). The styles are two-branched. The fruits are fleshy.

The upas tree achieved its chief fame as the result of extravagant, fantastic, completely untrue statements published about it in the seventeenth century. These are still occasionally resurrected and retold by writers of sensational "plant wonder" articles. The chief tall story is that the tree gives emanations so noxious that neither plants nor animals can live near it, that men and beasts who come close to it die, and that the ground around it is barren of vegetation. All of which is poppycock. It is true that the milky sap of the upas tree is poisonous and was used in arrow poisons, and this may be the basis for the yarns told about it.

The upas tree (*A. toxicaria*) inhabits India, Ceylon, Malaya, southern China, and Java. It may be 150 feet tall or taller and for the first 100 feet or so has comparatively short branches. The tops of tall specimens develop as spreading heads of large branches. The leaves are oblong, and slightly toothed or not. They are up to 8 inches long. The fruits, pear-shaped, red-brown, and about ¾ inch long, are reported to be eaten by children. The inner, fibrous bark of the upas tree and of some other species of its genus is used to make blankets, clothing, and bags.

Garden and Landscape Uses and Cultivation. In warm frost-free and essentially frost-free countries the upas tree is occasionally grown in botanical collections, and because of interest in the myths associated with it. It is without outstanding merit, and prospers in deep soil of ordinary fertility. Propagation is by seeds and cuttings.

ANTIBIOTICS. These are chemical substances produced by certain fungi and microorganisms that in dilute solutions have the capacity of killing or inhibiting the growth of bacteria and certain other microorganisms. Some, notably penicillin and streptomycin, have gained wide and well-deserved acceptance in the treatment of diseases of man and animals. In the main they have proved less effective in controlling plant diseases, the best results with antibiotics in plants having been obtained in treating fire blight, leaf blight of haw-

thorns, and some diseases of lawn grasses. The antibiotics used for these purposes are streptomycin, marketed as Agrimycin, and cyclohexamide, as Acti-dione.

ANTIDESICCANT or antitranspirant. In regions of severe winters where deep freezing interferes with the ability of roots to replace water lost by transpiration from above-ground plant parts, much winter killing, especially of trees and shrubs, may result from drying out (desiccation) of tissues even when temperatures are not low enough to kill them otherwise.

Spraying with an antidesiccant or antitranspirant as such preparations are called is an effective means of checking excessive water loss from trunks, branches, shoots, and foliage. Such preparations made from latex rubber or plastics are sold by garden supply dealers. For winter protection it is usual to spray once at the beginning of severe weather and once or twice more at monthly intervals. Antidesiccants are also advantageous for applying to evergreens immediately before or after transplanting.

ANTIDESMA (Anti-désma)—Bignay. Confined as natives to the tropics of the Old World, 170 species of trees and shrubs of the spurge family EUPHORBIACEAE constitute this genus. Few are cultivated. The name is derived from the Greek *anti*, for, and *desmos*, a band, and alludes to the use of the bark for cordage.

The bignay (*Antidesma bunius*) is cultivated for its fruits, which are eaten raw and made into jellies and wine. This native from India to Australia is an attractive evergreen shrub or tree up to about 30 feet in height in cultivation, but often taller in the wild. It forms a rounded head of drooping branches and has alternate, glossy, somewhat leathery, oblong-elliptic leaves from 4 to 8 inches long and 2 to 3 inches wide. The petal-less, unisexual, green flowers, in terminal or axillary spikes, are segregated according to sex on separate trees. Female trees, even without a nearby male to pollinate them, fruit abundantly. The fruits are red and in currant-like clusters. Less than ½ inch in diameter, each contains a single stone. Another species, *A. dallachyanum,* of Australia, is similar, but smaller. It has smaller leaves and larger fruits, the latter red and slightly more than ½ inch in diameter. Its ovate to elliptic leaves are up to 6 inches long. A Hawaiian native, *A. platyphyllum* is a more upright tree with shorter leaves and smaller fruits than the bignay.

Garden Uses and Cultivation. These good-looking trees with laurel-like foliage are attractive for tropical and warm subtropical climates and can be used with good effect in ornamental plantings. They grow satisfactorily in ordinary soil and need no special attention. Propagation is by seed.

ANTIGONON (Antíg-onon)—Coral Vine, Corallita, Rosa de Montana, Cadena de Amor, Confederate Vine. One of the eight slender vines that compose this genus of the buckwheat family POLYGONACEAE is a great favorite in tropical and subtropical gardens everywhere. Known, among others, by the vernacular names listed above, *Antigonon leptopus* has Mexico as its original home. The other members of the clan are Mexican and Central American. The name is from the Greek *anti*, against, and *gonia*, an angle, probably in reference to the zigzag stems.

Antigonons have jointed, slender stems, alternate, heart-shaped to halberd-shaped, lobeless, untoothed, stalked leaves, and small buckwheat-like flowers in racemes that end in a branching tendril. The blooms are without true petals, but have five showy, papery, petal-like sepals, the two or three outer of which are broader than the inner ones. There are eight stamens and three styles. The fruits are three-angled achenes.

The coral vine (*A. leptopus*) is vigorous and attains a height of 30 to 50 feet. It is

Antigonon leptopus

almost or quite hairless and has thin, pointed, heart-shaped, halberd-shaped, or more or less triangular evergreen leaves mostly 1 inch to 3 inches long, but often longer on the lower part of the plant. The leaves are conspicuously netted with veins. The bright coral-pink to coral-red flowers, in axillary racemes, are succeeded by small, dry triangular fruits. Variety *A. l. album* has white flowers. The Costa Rican *A. guatemalense* (syn. *A. macrocarpum*) differs in having thicker, hairier, somewhat larger leaves, fruits obscurely rather than sharply three-angled, and outer sepals that at fruiting time are round instead of heart-shaped.

Garden and Landscape Uses. Outdoors these are highly decorative vines for covering porches, fences, arbors, and for screening. They grow rapidly and exhibit their festoons of bloom, reminiscent of those of their relative the silver lace vine (*Polygonum aubertii*) of northern gardens, over a very long season. They are untidy, however, in the sense that their dead leaves and twigs must be cleaned off and removed. They need full sun and grow in any ordinary soil; being well suited for rather infertile sandy ones. Antigonons stand some frost. Even if their tops are completely killed they will send up new shoots the following season, provided the roots have not been frozen, and these will bloom the first year. Since large specimens do not transplant well, it is always advisable to set out young pot-grown plants. Antigonons are delightful ornamentals for greenhouses. When trained beneath the roof glass they give light shade beneficial to many kinds of plants that can be grown underneath them.

Cultivation. These vines need well-drained soil not excessively rich in nitrogen; excessive supplies of this element are likely to result in an exuberance of growth, but few flowers. Seeds, which are produced in abundance, form the readiest means of propagation; they germinate quickly if sown in porous soil in a temperature of 55 to 60°F. In Florida and other warm regions self-sown seedlings are likely to spring up around old plants and these, when small, are easily transplanted. Cuttings can also be used as a means of increase; they root readily in sand, vermiculite, or perlite in a humid atmosphere in a temperature of 60°F or above. Quite severe pruning to restrict their size, to prevent them from becoming too thick and tangled, and to remove dead material should be done in winter or spring after blooming is through. At that time the repotting of greenhouse-grown specimens should be undertaken. Watering plants in greenhouses should be freely done from spring to fall, less freely in winter. Atigonons in pots or other containers should be watered with dilute liquid fertilizer at one- to two-weekly intervals from spring to fall.

ANTIRRHINUM (Antirrhìn-um)—Snapdragon. Snapdragons belong in the figwort family SCROPHULARIACEAE. They are natives of the Mediterranean region and western North America and include forty-two species. Their generic name is derived from the Greek *anti*, like, and *rhinos*, a nose. It refers fancifully to the snoutlike shape of the flowers. By far the most important horticultural kinds are the many splendid varieties that have been bred from the common snapdragon. These are cultivated extensively outdoors and in greenhouses. A few other species are grown, mostly in rock gardens and in botanical gardens. The group includes annuals and perennials. Cultivated kinds, including the common snapdragon, are chiefly perennials, but the common snapdragon is usually grown as an annual and discarded at the end of its first blooming season.

The genus *Antirrhinum* is characterized by its lobeless leaves, mostly alternate, but sometimes opposite in the lower parts of

Snapdragons in a border of mixed annuals

Bed of snapdragons

the plant, and its flowers, which are in terminal spikes or are solitary in the axils of the leaves. When in spikes, each bloom arises from the axil of a small leafy bract. The flowers are asymmetrical, tubular, and pouched, but not spurred. In this last respect they differ from nearly related *Linaria*, the flowers of which have distinct spurs. The blooms are constricted to form a two-lipped, closed mouth, the lower lip consisting of three petals, the upper of two. Both lips spread outward. There are four stamens and one style. The fruits are dry capsules containing numerous small seeds that escape through small holes in the capsule wall. The flower structure effectively prevents insects other than bees from entering the blooms in search of nectar. Bees are heavy enough to depress the lower lip, which results in the mouth opening so that the insects can enter the flower. In doing this they effect pollination. There are varieties of common snapdragon called butterfly snapdragons, with nearly symmetrical, open-mouthed flow-

Butterfly snapdragon

ers. Double-flowered sorts are occasionally grown.

Common snapdragon (*A. majus*) as a wildling is an evergreen perennial herba-

Double-flowered snapdragon

ceous plant about 3 feet tall with lanceolate to oblong-lanceolate leaves up to 3 inches long. It has erect, terminal spikes of usually purplish-red to white flowers each about 1½ inches long. This Mediterranean-region species, or forms, reverted from garden varieties of it to become closely similar to the wild species, are naturalized in northern Europe and parts of North America. In Great Britain it is not uncommon to find these growing contentedly on old walls, their roots reveling in the porous lime-sand mortar used between the stones or bricks, and obtaining nourishment from whatever organic debris that has accumulated. This suggests the liking of these plants for somewhat alkaline soils.

Improved garden varieties of the common snapdragon came into existence long ago and a limited number of kinds and colors were popular in grandmother's day, great-grandmother's day, and even earlier, but not until the present century did plant breeders begin to develop the wide range of flower colors and forms or plants of such varying heights as are now available. With these horticultural improvements have come, to at least a minor degree, certain losses. Modern varieties are mostly less hardy to cold than older kinds and possibly, indeed probably, are more susceptible to disease. Because they are grown chiefly as annuals the first-mentioned change is not serious and success is now being had in breeding disease-resistant strains. Certainly few would be willing to forego the gorgeous colors and useful and various plant forms of modern snapdragons in return for the small advantages possessed by old-fashioned kinds.

For convenience snapdragon varieties are divided into three groups, tall, intermediate, and dwarf or Tom Thumb. The

Common snapdragon

tall grow to 2 to 3 feet, the intermediate 1¼ to 1½ feet, and under normal conditions the dwarfs to about 9 inches in height. A wide range of colors is available in each. Almost every hue other than blue is represented. There are especially lovely apricots, salmons, rich crimsons, clear yellows, and pure whites as well as kinds with orange-yellow, flame-colored, and red-purple flowers. Some varieties have rich, deep blackish-red foliage. There are kinds for every taste.

Tom Thumb snapdragon

Other species worth growing include *A. molle* of southern France. This has weak, flopping stems, like the foliage clothed with soft, woolly, but not sticky, hairs. Its broadly-ovate to nearly-round leaves are up to ¾ inch long. The whitish to soft yellow blooms, each 1¼ inches long and softly-hairy on their outsides, are in loose, leafy spikes. A native of Spain, *A. glutinosum* is a sticky-hairy, prostrate plant,

Antirrhinum molle

Garden Uses. Varieties of common snapdragon are among the most gorgeous of annuals. They are admirable for flower beds and borders and for cutting, and can be used effectively in window and porch boxes. Dwarf kinds are useful in rock gardens. As greenhouse plants their chief function is to provide cut flowers, but they can also be grown for use as decorative pot plants. The prostrate and trailing snapdragons such as *A. glutinosum, A. molle,* and *A. sempervirens* are essentially for rock gardens and wall gardens. They are charming plants for such locations. Erect-growing species other than the common snapdragon are of interest mostly to botanical gardeners and collectors of the unusual and may be cultivated in beds or borders. American species are suitable for including in gardens of native plants.

Cultivation. Although perennial where mild winters prevail, the common snapdragon is almost invariably propagated afresh each year and the old plants discarded at the end of their first blooming season. Among other advantages of this practice if the new plants are raised from seeds, is that it minimizes the risk of carrying over certain diseases from year to

with oval leaves and yellowish-white blooms, red-striped on their lips, about 1¼ inches long and in spike-like racemes. From the Pyrenees comes the prostrate, evergreen *A. sempervirens,* a much-branched plant with opposite, ovate to oblong leaves and white flowers that have yellow throats and are spotted with purple. They are less than ¾ inch long. This kind is less hardy than *A. molle.*

Native American snapdragons include *A. coulterianum, A. multiforum* (syn. *A. glandulosum*), and *A. nuttallianum,* all inhabitants of dryish locations in California. The first (*A. coulterianum*), called chaparral snapdragon, is an erect annual 1 foot to 3 feet tall, branchless below and with twisting branchlets above that twine around supports in the manner of tendrils. Its ovate leaves are up to 1¼ inches long. The flowers, about ⅓ inch long, are in spikes. They are white or yellowish with a softly-hairy, yellowish palate at the mouth. Variety *A. c. orcuttianum* has purplish blooms. An annual or short-lived perennial, *A. multiflorum* is 1½ to 4 feet in height and is sticky-hairy in all its parts. Its stalkless, lanceolate leaves are up to 2½ inches long. The rose-pink, ¾-inch-long flowers, which have white or cream-colored palates, are in long, dense, spikelike racemes. A sticky-pubescent annual or biennial, *A. nuttallianum* is up to 3 feet tall. It has twisting branchlets and broad-ovate leaves about 2 inches long. Its violet or purple blooms are in lax, leafy-bracted racemes. They have pale palates veined with violet, which are up to ½ inch long.

Snapdragons in a mixed planting with perennials

Snapdragons for cut flowers in a greenhouse

year. Modern seed strains produce plants so true to type that they afford by far the best and most convenient way of raising new plants. Only when it is desired to perpetuate a particular kind for which seeds are not available, or which are known to be unlikely to breed true, as with double-flowered kinds, should cuttings be employed. Cuttings, made of flowerless shoots 2 or 3 inches long, sliced cleanly across just beneath a node and with the lower leaves removed, root readily. In mild climates they may be planted, spaced about 3 inches apart, in sandy soil in cold frames in late summer or early fall, or they may be set in a propagating bench in a cool greenhouse.

Raising plants from seeds calls for some care. It is not difficult, but precautions must be taken against damping-off of the seedlings, a common trouble, disturbance of the seeds by ants, and the seedlings "drawing" so that they become weak and lanky and hence more subject to damping-off and other diseases. Danger from damping-off is combated by sowing thinly in sterilized soil, milled sphagnum moss, or vermiculite, by maintaining a free circulation of air, by avoiding an oppressively humid atmosphere, and by careful watering so that the young plants do not lie wet for long periods. Ants are extremely fond of snapdragon seeds. They can be foiled by raising the seed containers on small pots, inverted and standing in saucers kept filled with water. The attenuation and weakness of seedlings termed "drawing" results from insufficient light, too high temperatures, or both. Snapdragons are sun-loving and from the time the seedlings break ground should be fully exposed.

Snapdragon seeds are very small and should either be scattered thinly on the surface of the sowing medium and merely be pressed in or barely covered. They germinate well in a temperature of 55 to 60°F. Great care must be taken not to disturb the seeds when watering. It is best to use the immersion method and allow the moisture to seep up from below rather than practice overhead watering. When the seedlings are large enough to handle they are transplanted 2 inches apart into well-drained flats of porous soil and are grown on in a temperature of 45 to 50°F at night with a daytime rise to 55 or 60°F. Alternative methods are to transfer the seedlings from the containers in which they germinated to individual small pots or to hotbeds under the protection of glass sash or suitable plastic coverings.

The time of seed sowing depends on the climate and the treatment to be afforded the young plants. To have plants to set in the garden in spring (snapdragons are comparatively hardy and give of their best when planted out at the earliest date possible after all danger of frost is passed), seeds may be sown indoors about ten weeks before planting out time. After the first transplanting and when the seedlings are about 3 inches tall their tops are pinched out to encourage branching. Where winters are fairly mild excellent results are had by sowing in August or September, transplanting the seedlings 3 inches apart into cold frames in porous soil, and protecting them from severe frost with glazed sash and, if needed, mats, during the winter. Under this system it is most important to ventilate the frames freely whenever the outdoor temperature is above freezing and to harden the plants by taking the sash off for a week or two before planting out time.

Spacing snapdragons outdoors depends on the purpose for which they are being grown and the type. For cut flowers tall varieties are grown in rows spaced 1¼ to 2 feet apart with 9 inches to a foot allowed between plants in the rows. The same kinds planted in groups in flower borders may be about 1 foot apart each way. Intermediate varieties may stand a little closer and 6 to 8 inches apart each way is sufficient for dwarf snapdragons. The soil for these plants should be well drained, fertile, and in good condition. A slightly acid to slightly alkaline soil capable of producing good vegetables is ideal. The location should be sunny.

After-planting care calls for keeping weeds down. Frequent stirring of the surface soil to a depth of about ½ inch, but not so deep that feeding roots are injured, is highly beneficial. A mulch applied when hot weather is imminent conserves moisture and helps to maintain relatively cool soil conditions, which tend to keep the plants thrifty and prolong the blooming season. In dry weather deep watering should be done every few days. Tall varieties are likely to need staking. The best, longest-stemmed cut flowers are obtained by restricting each plant to six to nine stems and removing all side shoots that develop on these while they are quite small. Seed formation is exhausting to the plants; therefore faded flowers should be removed promptly. If this is not done the blooming season is shortened. In hot summer weather snapdragons are likely to take on a rather tired appearance and to bloom sparsely. They can be rejuvenated for later display by cutting them back, applying a light dressing of fertilizer that supplies some readily available nitrogen, and making sure they do not suffer from lack of moisture.

Greenhouse cultivation of snapdragons is not dissimilar to growing them outdoors for cut flowers. They are usually grown in benches or ground beds and varieties especially suitable for the purpose are selected. Some are much better winter bloomers than others. For winter blooming, seeds are sown from May to August in a cold frame or in the coolest part of a greenhouse. The seedlings are treated as previously described for outdoor snapdragons except that they are very lightly shaded from fierce summer sun. The soil in the benches or beds must be porous and fertile. The addition to it of some superphosphate is usually helpful in promoting good root growth, and lime may be used if needed to bring the soil to an almost neutral condition. Plants are usually set in the benches or beds from 2- or 2½-inch pots, but if the areas are vacant equally good results can be had by transplanting directly from the seed pots or flats to the beds or benches.

Spacing between plants depends on the method of cultivation. If the young plants are pinched after they have developed three or four pairs of leaves and each is let develop from two to four stems, 8 inches each way between plants is satisfactory. If they are to be grown single-stemmed without pinching, and this results in blooms two or three weeks earlier, the spacing may be 4 by 4 inches for summer crops and 4 by 6 inches for plants that are to bloom in darker winter days. The time taken from setting the young plants in the beds or benches to blooming varies from seven to nine weeks for summer crops to about twenty-two weeks for winter blooms.

During late fall and winter snapdragons should be grown in a night temperature of 50°F with a rise of five degrees on dull days and ten on sunny days permitted, but in early fall and spring both night and day temperatures may, but not necessarily must be, raised to five or even ten degrees above these minimums. Full sun and airy conditions are essential. The atmosphere must never be oppressively humid and the foliage should not be wetted. Support for the plants is usually supplied by stretching above the bench or bed a grid of wires and strings as is done for carnations. Disbudding or disbranching is practiced by removing, as soon as they are big enough to nip out with finger and thumb, all side shoots that grow from the flowering stems.

Watering is done with restraint during the early stages of the plants' development, but once the available soil has been permeated with healthy roots more generous watering is practiced. A constantly soggy condition inhibits satisfactory root growth, and especially in winter, the soil should be permitted to dry somewhat between waterings.

Snapdragons grown in pots, either as decorative specimens or for cutting, are entirely satisfactory. The general procedure is the same as for bench-grown plants. For cut flowers, tall varieties are used and are grown without pinching, one plant to a 4- or 5-inch pot. The intermediates or dwarfs are usually selected for specimens that are to be displayed as pot plants although if height is needed the tall ones are selected. In either case the young plants are pinched after they have developed three or four pairs of leaves to encourage branching. Unless cut flowers are the objective the pots should be well spaced on the benches so that each plant receives light from all sides and is encouraged to bush out and grow symmetrically.

Diseases and Pests. Rust is one of the most serious diseases of snapdragons. This is kept in check by using rust-resistant varieties, by avoiding wetting the foliage of greenhouse-grown plants and by spraying with fungicides. Other diseases are anthracnose, blight, gray mold, mildews, wilt, root rot, stem rot, crown rot, and leaf spot. Insects that may cause damage are aphids, leaf tiers, caterpillars, mites, stink bugs, and nematodes.

ANTITRANSPIRANT. See Antidesiccant or Antitranspirant.

ANTS. These familiar insects, like termites, bees, and many wasps, live in large colonies of castes each with a specific function. That of males is to impregnate the females, that of the females to bear young, that of the wingless workers to forage for food and to do the work of the colony. After mating males die, females shed their wings and found new colonies of which they are the queens. Unlike termites, with which they are sometimes confused, ants have bodies sharply constricted into head, thorax, and abdomen. Their waists are well defined. Some ants, especially certain tropical species, bite or sting painfully. The food of ants varies. Some kinds live on grease and sugars, others on seeds, grains, and roots. Yet a third group cultivate fungi for food. Others favor honeydew, an excretion of aphids, mealybugs, and scale insects; some prey on other insects.

A chief damage that ants do in gardens is the loosening of soil and disturbing of roots, especially those of young seedlings. They carry aphids from place to place and spread the bacteria and the spores of some diseases. The holes, runways, and mounds

Dusting to control ants, which have deposited on the path small circular piles of fine soil brought from below

made by certain kinds of ants disfigure lawns, paths, and other places. But not all activities of all ants are bad. Some species serve usefully to pollinate flowers and to scavenge and some to reduce populations of harmful insects. Control of ants is mostly by baits and by spraying or dusting the nests.

ANUBIAS (Anùb-ias). Endemic to Africa, *Anubias* of the arum family ARACEAE consists of about fifteen species of nonhardy, evergreen herbaceous perennials. The name is taken from that of Anubias, the ancient Egyptian jackal-headed god.

Plants of this genus have short horizontal rhizomes and lanceolate to elliptic or ovate leaves. The little, sepal-less, unisexual flowers, as usual in the family, are arranged in spikelike fashion along a central core to form a spadix from the base of which springs a bract called a spathe.

Native to tropical West Africa, *A. afzelli* (syn. *A. lanceolata*) attains heights up to 2 feet or somewhat more, has leaves with stalks up to 1¼ feet in length, and elliptic blades up to 1½ feet long and 7 inches

Anubias afzellii

wide. The inflorescences, consisting of spadix and spathe, the former 3 to 4 inches long, the latter up to 2½ inches long, terminate stalks that equal the leafstalks in length.

Garden Uses and Cultivation. The species described is sometimes grown in aquariums and is well suited for cultivation in wet soils outdoors in the tropics and in greenhouses where a minimum night temperature of 60°F, with increases of five to fifteen degrees or more by day are maintained. High humidity and shade from strong sun are essential. Propagation is by division or by freshly collected seeds that are not allowed to dry out before sowing.

APACHE PLUME is *Fallugia paradoxa*.

APERA (Á-pera)—Silky-Bent Grass. Three European and Asian species of annuals of the grass family GRAMINEAE constitute *Apera*. The name is an invented one without particular meaning.

Aperas have leaves with narrow-linear blades and much-branched, loose or compact flower panicles of numerous, small, one-flowered spikelets. The most attractive sort, loose silky-bent grass (*A. spica-venti* syn. *Agrostis spica-venti*) of Europe and northern Asia, is 1 foot to 3 feet tall, has hairless leaves and somewhat nodding, ovate to cylindrical, loose, feathery panicles 4 to 10 inches long. In fall this sort turns an attractive buff or reddish-tan. Dense silky-bent grass (*A. interrupta* syn. *Agrostis interrupta*) is 1 foot to 2 feet tall. Native to Europe and adjacent Russia, it has hairless leaves and erect, dense flower panicles up to 8 inches long. Shortly after blooming it turns an unattractive brown.

Garden and Landscape Uses and Cultivation. The species described supply useful cut flowers for dried arrangements. The first is attractive as a landscape ornamental, the other is not. Aperas are easily grown from seeds sown in spring where the plants are to remain. Thin out the seedlings to prevent overcrowding. These prosper in ordinary soils in sun or part-day shade. For further information see Grasses.

APEX. The summit or tip of a leaf, sepal, petal, or other organ or structure.

APHANAMIXIS (Aphán-amixis). One or two of the twenty-five species of this tropical Asian and Indonesian genus of evergreen trees is cultivated in Hawaii and other parts of the tropics, often under the synonymous name *Amoora*. The group belongs in the mahogany family MELIACEAE and is characterized by having pinnate leaves with an uneven number of leaflets and usually unisexual, tiny flowers with the sexes commonly on separate trees. The blooms have five sepals, three petals, and three to six stamens joined as a tube. The fruits are pods containing one to three seeds enclosed in fleshy coats. They are not edible. The name *Aphanamixis* is from the Greek *aphanes,* obscure, and *mixis,* mingling. Its application is not apparent.

The kind most likely to be cultivated is *A. grandifolia* (syn. *Amoora grandifolia*) of Malacca. It is about 40 feet tall and has leaves 1 foot to 3 feet long composed of five to nine opposite leaflets and a terminal one. The ovate leaflets increase in size from the base of the leaf upward except that the terminal one may be smaller than those that flank it; the largest may be 1 foot long. Small and inconspicuous, the flowers are in axillary spikes. They are followed by pendulous strings of conspicuous, pink to rose-red, globose fruits about 1 inch in diameter that open to reveal the orange-red coats that partly enclose the shiny seeds.

Native to India, Ceylon, and Malaya, *A. polystachya* (syn. *Amoora rohituka*) is a round-crowned tree up to 60 or 70 feet tall, with male and female blooms on separate trees. The former are in terminal branched clusters, the latter in spikes shorter than the leaves. The globular to egg-shaped fruits, 1 inch to 1½ inches in diameter and yellow, open to display seeds with orange to scarlet coverings. The leaves, of nine to fifteen elliptic to ovate, pointed leaflets, are 1 foot to 3 feet long. From the base of the leaf upward the leaflets increase in size except for the terminal one, which is usually smaller. The leaflets are 3 to 9 inches in length.

Garden and Landscape Uses and Cultivation. These trees will succeed only in the humid tropics. They are esteemed for their handsome foliage and colorful fruits. They grow best in fertile, reasonably moist soil and are propagated by seed.

APHANOSTEPHUS (Aphanó-stephus). The eleven species of *Aphanostephus* are North American annuals and biennials of the daisy family COMPOSITAE. Their name derives from the Greek *aphanes,* inconspicuous, and *stephanos,* a crown, and alludes to the comparatively small size of the flower heads. These plants have erect stems, alternate leaves, and solitary daisy-like heads with yellow centers and white, blue, purple, or violet rays. The fruits are achenes.

The kind most likely to be cultivated is *A. skirrobasis,* a native from Florida to Texas, about 1½ feet in height, and with linear to narrowly-spoon-shaped, gray-pubescent leaves up to 2½ inches long, the lower ones lobed or toothed. The flower heads, up to 1 inch in diameter, have white rays and in appearance resemble those of fleabanes (*Erigeron*). Native to the southwestern United States, *A. arkansanus* is 1 foot to 2 feet tall, has oblong-spoon-shaped to broad-lanceolate leaves,

the lower ones usually lobed or toothed, and flower heads 1 inch or more across with whitish rays. The quite distinct *A. ramosissimus,* native to Texas, forms a mat about 4 inches tall and has flowers 1 inch or more across, blue with yellow centers. Its leaves are deeply-divided. Members of this genus are sometimes called lazy-daisy.

Garden Uses and Cultivation. These plants are worth cultivating in flower beds and borders and may be grown for decorating cool greenhouses in late winter and spring. They grow well in full sun in any ordinary, well-drained, garden soil and need no special care. For greenhouse display seeds may be sown in September or October. For outdoor garden use they are sown outdoors in spring or earlier indoors and the plants grown in flats until cold weather is over and it is safe to plant them in the garden. Outdoors, plants of *A. skirrobasis* should stand 9 inches to 1 foot apart. Allow 6 inches between those of *A. ramosissimus.* The latter is an attractive edging plant; the flowers of *A. skirrobasis* are useful for cutting. Under favorable conditions these plants bloom throughout the summer.

APHELANDRA (Aphel-ándra). Tropical and subtropical American evergreen subshrubs and shrubs compose *Aphelandra* of the acanthus family ACANTHACEAE. Many are highly ornamental. The species number 200. The name is from the Greek *apheles,* solitary, and *aner,* a male in allusion to the single-celled anthers.

Aphelandras have usually smooth, less often spiny stems. Their leaves are opposite, undivided, toothless or toothed, and in some species lobed. The strongly-two-lipped, stalkless, tubular flowers are crowded in solitary or clustered, four-sided spikes that stand well above the foliage. They terminate the shoots or come from the leaf axils and are attended by conspicuous and sometimes highly-colored, overlapping, floral bracts. The yellow, orange, pink, or red corollas have generally cylindrical tubes, erect upper lips, and spreading or down-turned lower ones. There are four stamens and a slender, undivided style. The fruits are capsules with, commonly, four seeds.

Especially popular as florists' plants are several varieties of *A. squarrosa* commonly called zebra plants. Native to Brazil, this vigorous, erect species has crowded, pointed-ovate to pointed-elliptic, lustrous, short-stalked, toothless leaves 6 inches to 1 foot long. In cultivated varieties the midrib and veins are white. The pale yellow blooms, about 1½ inches long, are in handsome terminal spikes that are solitary or in threes. The blooms protrude somewhat beyond the orange-yellow bracts. In *A. s. leopoldii* the stems are red and the large, olive-green leaves narrowly-white-veined. The floral bracts are reddish. A

Aphelandra squarrosa 'Louisae'

compact kind, *A. s. louisae* has emerald-green, broadly-white-veined, sometimes slightly-crinkled leaves, and waxy, green-tipped, golden-yellow blooms. A hybrid between the above varieties, *A. s.* 'Fritz Prinsler', is intermediate and very attractive. It has canary-yellow blooms and deep yellow bracts with green markings. This plant is more compact and its white-veined leaves smaller than those of *A. s. leopoldii.* Various selections of these kinds have been given horticultural names such as 'Brockfeld' and 'Dania'.

Another Brazilian native, *A. chamissoniana* has thinner, narrow-elliptic leaves 4

Aphelandra chamissoniana

or 5 inches long, with broader and less defined silvery-white areas bordering the veins. It is a rather weak shrub, with clear yellow blooms about 1½ inches long that come from among long-pointed, green-tipped, toothed, recurved, yellow bracts. The spikes are 3 to 4 inches long by 2 to 3 inches wide.

Especially brilliantly colored flowers are borne by *A. aurantiaca* (syns. *A. fascinator, A. nitens*), of Mexico, and its variety *A. a. roezlii.* From 2 to 4½ feet tall, this species

Aphelandra aurantiaca roezlii

has ovate green leaves 4 to 9 inches long and leaden-gray along the veins, and scarlet flowers flushed with orange along the corolla tubes and in their throats. Their lower lips are three-lobed and spread horizontally. The floral bracts are sharp-toothed. Variety *A. a. roezlii* has somewhat twisted leaves, dark green with silvery areas between the veins, and orange-scarlet blooms.

Beautiful pink blooms are freely produced by vigorous *A. sinclairana,* of Central America. The overall light salmon-pink or coral-pink effect results from a combination of rosy-pink flowers and orangy-coral-pink bracts. The latter are not toothed, but are covered with soft hairs. The spikes, many together at the shoot ends, are very showy. The thin, lustrous green leaves have indented veins.

Aphelandra sinclairana

Other kinds cultivated are *A. bahiensis* (syn. *A. atrovirens*), a low plant with rigid, shining, dark green, ovate-elliptic leaves, the midribs and bases of the side veins lined with white and the under surfaces purple. The flowers are yellow. It is a native of Brazil. *A. fuscopunctata,* of northern South America, has green stems and hairy, ovate leaves, dark green above and paler on their undersides. The flower spikes

have sticky red bracts and light brown flowers with darker spots. *A. ignea* (syn. *Stenandrium igneum*), of Brazil, is a low herbaceous perennial with heart-shaped leaves 2 to 4 inches long and yellow flowers about 1¼ inches in length. *A. tetragona,* from tropical South America and the West Indies, is a loose-growing plant 6 or 7 feet tall with broad-ovate leaves and immense terminal or axillary, clustered spikes of bright scarlet blooms 2 to 3 inches long.

Aphelandra tetragona

Garden Uses. In the tropics aphelandras may be grown in the open, but in North America they are chiefly plants for greenhouses. Some, notably varieties of *A. squarrosa,* are raised commercially as decorative pot plants. Although they remain attractive in bloom and foliage for a considerable time they rarely do well as permanent houseplants. For their well-being they need a moister atmosphere than most homes provide. The flowers last longer, however, if the plants are removed when they begin to bloom to somewhat drier conditions than those of a humid tropical greenhouse.

Cultivation. The soil used for aphelandras should be coarse, nourishing, and contain an abundance of organic matter. It must be freely permeable. The addition of some chopped charcoal to the mixture is helpful. The pots must be well drained. Old plants are started into growth in late winter or early spring. They are pruned by cutting out weak shoots and shortening others to just above the lowest or second node (joint) from the bases of the previous year's shoots. Then the plants are put in a humid greenhouse where the temperature is 70°F or higher. Very light misting with water encourages new growth. When this begins the plants are removed from their containers, the old drainage material is taken out, as much old soil as possible shaken away, and straggly roots are shortened. The plants are then potted into smaller pots than they previously occupied and are returned to a warm, humid greenhouse.

Watering is done rather sparingly at first, but light overhead sprayings are frequent. When the new pots are filled with roots transfer to a larger size is in order and as the amount of foliage increases more frequent watering becomes necessary. When the final pots are filled with roots regular applications of dilute liquid fertilizer are very helpful. Throughout the growing season a minimum night temperature of 65 to 70°F is appropriate, and this may rise from ten to fifteen degrees by day. It is not desirable to pinch out the ends of the shoots. To do so results in smaller spikes of bloom. After blooming the plants are partially rested by keeping them in a dryish, but not dry condition in a temperature of 55°F.

Propagation is easy by seeds, and self-sown seedlings of some kinds are likely to spring up on and under greenhouse benches. The common method of multiplication, however, is by cuttings of young shoots taken in spring. These root with facility in a propagating bench in a tropical greenhouse and provide plants that bloom the following fall. Such first-year specimens commonly carry one flower head and are accommodated in 4- or 5-inch pots as finals. Second-year plants will need larger containers; they develop more heads of bloom. The commonest pests are mealybugs, scale insects, and red spider mites.

APHIDS. Among the more common insect pests of gardens are aphids or plant lice. There are numerous species, some that confine their attentions to one kind of plant, others that infest a wide variety of hosts. Some, such as the Cooley spruce gall aphid and the mealy plum aphid, alternate between different hosts at different seasons of the year. Characteristically aphids are soft-bodied, wingless or winged, crawling creatures, small but easily visible to the naked eye. Often they cluster in colonies along young, tender shoots and on the under surfaces of leaves. Some kinds infest the roots of plants. They are of many colors, black, gray, brown, red, pink, lavender, and yellow. Some kinds, the woolly and gall-producing aphids, are more or less clothed with waxy, cottony threads.

Aphids often have complicated life histories with some generations laying eggs, others consisting of all females that without mating produce live-born young. Yet other kinds of aphids are reproduced only from eggs. Honeydew, a sugary, sticky liquid that mars the appearance of stems and foliage and attracts ants, which feed upon it, is excreted from the anus by all aphids. A disfiguring black fungus often lives on the surface of the dried honeydew.

As a result of infestations by aphids plants lose vigor and become stunted or foliage and other parts may be puckered, curled, or otherwise deformed. Even more serious is the part aphids play in transmitting from plant to plant viral and bacterial diseases such as various mosaics and fire blight. Control of aphids is usually by contact sprays either during the growing season or, in the case of deciduous woody plants, with dormant sprays applied when they are leafless.

APHYLLANTHES (Aphyl-lánthes). The one species of this genus of the lily family LIL-IACEAE, native of the Mediterranean region, is little known horticulturally. It is a tufted, spreading, plant with a vast system of tangled fibrous roots and slender, grayish, rushlike stems that have small membranous leaves only at their bases. The stems are 4 to 10 inches tall and some of them, in early summer, erupt at their tips with solitary or sometimes paired flowers about 1 inch in diameter. The quite lovely blooms have six spreading, ovate perianth lobes (commonly called petals), deep blue or, more rarely, white. The name, from the Greek *aphyllos*, without leaves, and *anthos*, a flower, refers to the appearance of the plant.

Garden Uses and Cultivation. Of interest to the collector of the rare and unusual, *Aphyllanthes monspeliensis* is suitable for rock gardens where winters are mild, and in cool greenhouses where a minimum winter temperature of 40 to 50°F is maintained. It requires sandy peaty, fairly fertile soil and a little shade from strong sun. It dislikes intensely having its roots disturbed and is likely to sulk for a considerable while after transplanting. Propagation is by careful division at the beginning of the spring growing season and by seeds sown as soon as they are ripe in sandy peaty soil.

APICRA. See Astroloba.

APIO is *Arracacia xanthorrhiza*.

APIOS (À-pios)—Groundnut or Potato-Bean or Wild-Bean. One tuberous rooted twining vine is the only one of the ten species of this genus of the pea family LEGUMI-NOSAE likely to be cultivated. Most members of the group are Asian, but the one sometimes planted in gardens, the groundnut, potato-bean, or wild-bean (*Apios americana* syn. *A. tuberosa*), is native to North America, occurring as a wildling in moist woods from Quebec to Minnesota, South Dakota, Florida, and Texas. The name, derived from the Greek *apion*, a pair, refers to the tubers often being two together.

Species of *Apios* have tuberous roots and twining, non-woody stems. Their leaves have an odd number, three to nine, of leaflets arranged pinnately, and their pea-like flowers are in short, often branched, dense clusters. They have a slightly two-lipped calyx, a broad, reflexed standard (upper petal), and an incurved, horse-shoe-shaped

keel to the corolla. Nine stamens are joined, one is separate. The style curves with the keel and by continued growth finally exceeds it in length. The many-seeded, slender pods are straight or slightly curved.

The groundnut (*A. americana*) has deciduous stems that climb to a height of 4

Apios americana

to 8 feet, and slender rhizomes having two tubers or more in series. The tubers are edible. The leaves mostly have five or seven lanceolate to ovate leaflets 1½ to 2½ inches long. Their undersides are covered with short hairs or are hairless. The blunt heads of ½-inch-long purplish brown, fragrant flowers appear in late summer and early fall and are succeeded by pods 2 to 4 inches long, containing a few small seeds. This plant sports a curious and interesting floral mechanism. The tubelike keel of the flower curves upward and is held under tension against a hollow in the standard petal. When an insect alights on it the tension is suddenly released and the keel jerks downward and coils tightly, thus exposing the stamens and stigma, the sexual organs.

Similar to *A. americana*, but much rarer, is the only other American species, *A. priceana*. This native of woodlands in Kentucky and perhaps Tennessee has solitary tubers 4 to 8 inches in diameter. Its greenish-white flowers are pink-tipped.

Garden and Landscape Uses and Cultivation. The horticultural uses of the groundnut are pretty much limited to its inclusion in wild gardens. There, it should be planted only where there is ample space for it to climb over bushes or other sturdy vegetation. Its most agreeable environment is fertile, moist soil in a shaded location. The plant is easily established by transplanting its somewhat potato-like tubers and from seeds. Often self-sown seedlings spring up spontaneously. Once

well established the groundnut may be difficult to eradicate.

APIUM (À-pium). According to some botanists the only one, but by others held to be one of fifteen or twenty species of its genus, *Apium graveolens* is the wild progenitor of cultivated celery and celeriac. A member of the carrot family UMBELLIFERAE, it inhabits wet places, especially marshes near the sea, and, if a broad interpretation of the species is accepted, occurs in temperate parts of Europe, Asia, and Africa. As reverted progeny of cultivated celery this species is naturalized in parts of North America, especially in the Southwest. With characteristically strong-smelling foliage, it is a tap-rooted biennial 2 to 3 feet in height with leaves pinnately-divided into three to seven wedge-shaped leaflets, and compound umbels of small greenish-white flowers. The foliage is coarser than that of cultivated celery and is bitter. In all probability it and other parts of the plants are more or less poisonous. The name *Apium* is an ancient Latin one for several plants of the carrot family UMBELLIFERAE. Except for it being the parent species of two cultivated vegetables, *A. graveolens* holds no interest for gardeners. See the entry entitled Celeriac, Knob Celery, or Turnip-rooted Celery.

APLECTRUM (A-pléctrum)—Putty Root or Adam-and-Eve. Endemic in rich woodlands from Vermont and Saskatchewan, to California, North Carolina, and Arkansas, the delightful little ground orchid called Adam-and-Eve and putty root (*Aplectrum hyemale*) is the only one of its genus. It is a member of the orchid family ORCHIDACEAE. Its botanical name is from the Greek *a*, without, and *plektron*, a spur. It refers to the blooms.

The name Adam-and-Eve refers to the underground bulblike part usually consisting of two globose corms linked by a slender rhizome. Each corm ordinarily lives for two years and in summer sends up a solitary, broad-elliptic leaf that narrows gradually to a short stalk and is 4 to 6 inches long. The following spring an erect, slender, seven- to fifteen-bloomed, leafless flower stalk develops and attains a height of 1 foot to 2 feet. The flowers have oblanceolate sepals and petals, about ½ inch long, and much alike. They are brown with purplish bases. The sepals are widespreading, the petals point forward over the column. The broadly-obovate lip, about ½ inch long, and white with violet markings, has three upcurved lobes and, toward its middle, three slight parallel ridges. Adam-and-Eve differs from the related crane fly orchid (*Tipularia discolor*) in its flowers being without spurs.

Garden Uses and Cultivation. Like many native orchids Adam-and-Eve has not proved very amenable to cultivation. Plants collected from the wild are sometimes transplanted to gardens, but this should be done with great discretion and only from locations where they are plentiful and to sites where there is a very good chance of their surviving. This is most likely if they are provided with conditions closely similar to those under which they grow in the wild.

APLOLEIA (Aplo-lèia). This American genus of wandering-jew-like plants of the spiderwort family COMMELINACEAE was previously known as *Leptocallisia*. It is native to Mexico, Central America, northern South America and the Caribbean region and resembles *Tripogandra*, differing in its loosely-branched clusters of less conspicuous flowers without inner circles of stamens and in other characteristics. The generic name is from the Greek *haploos*, single, and *leios*, smooth and presumably refers to some flowers of *A. monandra* having only one stamen and that without hairs. There are two or three species.

In aspect these plants resemble *Callisia*. They have diffuse or ascending stems with alternate, ovate to lanceolate leaves and much-branched terminal clusters of stalked flowers, with two to three sepals and two to three petals. The stalks of the erect stamens are not hairy. The style is very short. The few-seeded fruits are capsules.

The most decorative kind is *A. multiflora* (syns. *Leptocallisia multiflora, Callisia multiflora, Tradescantia mertensiana*). This native of Mexico and Guatemala has hairless or slightly-hairy stems up to about 1½ feet long, sometimes branched above, and elliptic-lanceolate leaves densely clothed with minute hairs and up to 1¾ inches in length. Its violet-scented white flowers have three petals, are about ⅓ inch in diameter, and have three stamens and a three-lobed stigma. Having a wide natural distribution in Caribbean tropical America and represented in the West Indies and Baja California *A. monandra* (syns. *Leptocallisia monandra, Callisia scopulorum*) has slender stems, often glandular-hairy in their upper parts and 1½ feet long or slightly longer. Its light green, ovate-lanceolate leaves are up to 1½ inches long. The inconspicuous, tiny, translucent-white flowers have two to three sepals, two to three petals, and one to three stamens; flowers on the same plant vary in these respects. The blooms are very short lived, they are open for only a few hours in the morning. The ornamental value of this species is as a foliage plant.

Garden Uses and Cultivation. Satisfied with any ordinary soil, aploleias are easy to cultivate and are suitable for growing several together in pots and hanging baskets in greenhouses and as houseplants, or outdoors in frost-free regions. They are readily raised from seeds and propagated from cuttings and do well in a minimum temperature of 55 to 60°F. The soil should be kept evenly moist. Well-rooted specimens are kept vigorous by weekly or bi-weekly applications of dilute liquid fertilizer. Good light with shade from strong sun is desirable.

APOCYNACEAE—Dogbane Family. The 180 genera and about 1,500 species of *Apocynaceae* are dicotyledons, chiefly tropical but some natives of temperate regions. Most have milky juice. The majority are vines or climbing shrubs some of great size. A few are erect, shrubby, or herbaceous. The leaves are undivided, alternate, opposite, or in whorls of three, commonly with parallel side veins set closely together. The symmetrical flowers have calyxes deeply five- or four-cleft, a corolla funnel-shaped or with a slender tube and five or four petals spreading in wheel fashion, as many stamens, and one style. The fruits are usually paired long pods called follicles. The *Apocynaceae* differs from *Asclepiadaceae* in its flowers being without coronas, in the stalks of the stamens being separate, and in the anthers not being joined to the stigmas. Cultivated genera include *Acokanthera, Adenium, Allamanda, Alstonia, Alyxia, Amsonia, Apocynum, Aspidosperma, Beaumontia, Carissa, Catharanthus, Cerbera, Chonemorpha, Dipladenia, Echites, Forsteronia, Funtumia, Kopsia, Mandevilla, Neobracea, Nerium, Ochrosia, Odontadenia, Parsonsia, Pleiocarpa, Plumeria, Prestonia, Rauvolfia, Rhaboadenia, Rhaza, Stemmadenia, Strophanthus, Tabernaemontana, Thenardia, Thevetia, Trachelospermum, Urechites, Vallaris,* and *Vinca*.

APOCYNUM (Apó-cynum)—Dogbane, Indian-Hemp. The application of the name *Apocynum sibiricum*, which means of Siberia, to a species of this genus, is somewhat misleading because known species are natives of North America and nowhere else. The error does not, however, invalidate the name. According to the rules of botanical nomenclature the oldest name applied in accordance with approved principles stands, irrespective of its geographical appropriateness. Although of minor horticultural importance the group is not without interest because of its usefulness to the original inhabitants of America, the Indians. They discovered in it a source of tough fiber from which they made fishing nets and lines, and twine, as well as employing it for basketmaking. The extraordinary botanical collector David Douglas, after whom the Douglas-fir is named, when he visited California early in the nineteenth century observed these uses and wrote of the nets used by the Indians to catch salmon "The rope of the net is made of a species of willow or of cedar, and the cord of *Apocynum*—a gigantic species peculiar to this country whose fibre affords a great quantity of flax. The flax is collected from the withered stems in autumn." One wonders what local influence could have been responsible for this careful Scot's application of the adjective gigantic to a West Coast *Apocynum*. The tallest kind that grows there scarcely exceeds 2½ feet in height and the species most used, the Indian-hemp (*A. cannabinum*) is accorded by West Coast botanists a height of up to 2 feet. Eastern North American plants of this variable kind are sometimes as tall as 4½ feet but usually shorter.

The genus *Apocynum* belongs in the dogbane family APOCYNACEAE and consists of seven species and a goodly number of often difficult to distinguish natural hybrids. It occurs throughout North America. Its name is modified from an ancient Greek one derived from *apo*, from, and *kyon*, a dog, and used by the Greeks probably for *Marsdenia erecta*. Apocynums are herbaceous perennials with erect, branching stems and mainly opposite lobeless leaves. They contain milky sap and, their bark, tough fibers. The flowers are small with five-lobed calyxes and cylindrical, bell- or urn-shaped, short-tubed, five-cleft corollas with five small appendages on their insides. There are five stamens and a large stalkless stigma. The seed pods (follicles), slender, cylindrical, and usually in pairs, contain numerous silky-hairy seeds. The roots of apocynums are used medicinally.

The spreading dogbane (*A. androsaemifolium*), common in many parts of North America, is somewhat ornamental. It has leaning stems, 1½ to 4 feet long, alternate branches, and somewhat drooping, stalked, oblong-lanceolate to ovate leaves, more or less hairy on their undersides and 1½ to 3 inches long. The fragrant, bell-shaped, pink to nearly white flowers have their insides veined with red. They are ¼ to ⅜ inch long and in terminal and lateral loose clusters. The corolla lobes are spreading or recurved.

The Indian-hemp (*A. cannabinum*) occurs throughout most of North America in open places in dry or humid soils. Its stems are erect and branched and attain a height of 2 to 4½ feet. The leaves, which point upward, are oblong-lanceolate, broadly-elliptic or ovate, hairless, or pubescent on their under surfaces, and shortly-stalked. From white to greenish, the flowers are ⅛ to ¼ inch long and have cylindrical to urn-shaped corollas with spreading or recurved lobes. They are not red-veined on their insides. They are in terminal and lateral loose clusters.

Garden and Landscape Uses and Cultivation. Except as they interest those specializing in plants exploited by the Indians and used medicinally, apocynums have little valid claim on the attention of gardeners. At best they are a rather weedy looking lot, scarce worthy of including even in gardens of native plants except on the bases mentioned. They grow without difficulty in any ordinary soil and are increased by division and seed.

APONOGETONACEAE — Aponogeton Family.

The genus *Aponogeton* is the only one of this monocotyledonous family. Consisting of perennial aquatics with floating or submerged leaves and native of Asia, Africa, and Australia, its characteristics are those of the genus.

APONOGETON

(Apono-gèton)—Water-Hawthorn, Lace Leaf or Lattice Leaf. This, the only genus of the aponogeton family APONOGETONACEAE comprises thirty species of aquatic plants of Asia, Africa, Madagascar, and Australia. None is very hardy although the water-hawthorn survives winters outdoors in the north in well-protected pools. The name *Aponogeton* is derived from *Aquae Aponi,* the ancient name of Abano, and *geiton,* a neighbor. It refers to the plant's habitat.

Aponogetons are mostly perennials with tuberous rhizomes and usually floating leaves with parallel longitudinal veins joined by many cross veins. The flowers are carried above the water surface. The small blooms are in spikes, which in African and Madagascan species are paired, in those from other regions solitary. The flowers have one to three (usually two) petal-like perianth segments, six stamens, or sometimes more, and usually three carpels. Rarely they are unisexual with the sexes on separate plants. The fruits are follicles.

The hardiest kind is the water-hawthorn or Cape pondweed (*A. distachyus*), an

Aponogeton distachyus

easy-to-grow native of South Africa, naturalized in Hawaii. It has lobeless, oblong-lanceolate to strap-shaped leaves 3 to 6 inches long, often blotched and spotted with purple. Its spikes of delightfully fragrant white flowers are at the ends of long leafless stalks. Each spike is 2 to 4 inches long. The flowers, which have one large white petal-like perianth segment, are arranged alternately in two rows. The jet-

black anthers are in striking contrast to the white perianth segment. In cool weather the blooms sometimes assume pinkish hues as they age. Varieties of the water-hawthorn are *A. d. lagrangei,* which has its flowers and undersides of its leaves violet, and *A. d. aldenhamensis,* which has larger flowers and is possibly synonymous with *A. d. grandiflorus.* Similar to *A. distachyus,* but with cream-colored flowers that lack the black stamens of the water-hawthorn, is the somewhat more tender *A. desertorum* (syn. *A. leptostachyus*) also native to South Africa.

A distinct oddity is the lace leaf or lattice leaf *A. madagascariensis* (syns. *A. fenestralis, Ouvirandra fenestralis*), of Madagascar. Its remarkable feature is that the oblong-elliptic leaves consist of nothing but a tessellated lattice work or window-like network of veins, without tissue between. The leaves, 6 inches to 1½ feet long, float just beneath the water surface. The small, but numerous flowers are in spikes about 2 inches long. Each has two white petal-like parts, six stamens, and three carpels. At their bases the flower spikes are united and jointed to the top of a long stalk. Another kind, with longer and narrower leaves, similarly skeletonized but with smaller openings between the veins, is *A. bernerianus,* also native to Madagascar.

Submersed aquatic kinds suitable for aquariums include *A. crispus* of Ceylon and *A. undulatus* of India. The latter is much smaller than the former and its leaves are green rather than olive-green or brown; otherwise the kinds are similar. The leaves of *A. crispus* are translucent and have wavy-edged blades 8 inches to 1 foot long or even longer and 1 inch to 2 inches wide. The flowers, in loose spikes, have two creamy-white perianth segments, six stamens with blackish-purple anthers, and three carpels. Also suitable for aquariums, *A. ulvaceus* from Madagascar has translucent, bright green submersed leaves, 1½ to 3 feet long and 1½ to 4 inches wide, with wavy margins. In addition to these, various submersed aponogetons of hybrid origin are grown in aquariums.

Garden Uses and Cultivation. Most common in gardens is the water-hawthorn, an easy-to-grow kind admirably suited for ponds and pools where the water is 6 inches to 2 feet deep and the location is sunny. Under such circumstances it blooms freely over a long period and constantly delights with the vanilla scent of its blooms. The somewhat more tender *A. desertorum* serves similar purposes, but thrives best in water 4 to 9 inches deep. The submersed aponogetons are plants for aquariums where they aid in keeping the water habitable for fish. The lace leafs (*A. madagascariensis, A. bernerianus*) are essentially plants for the keen aquarist and the collector of choice and rare plants.

Cultivation. Aponogetons are easy to raise from seeds sown in pots or pans of soil covered with ½ inch of sand, and submerged so that the soil surface is 2 or 3 inches under water. The seeds must be stored in water or kept in wet moss from the time of gathering to the time of sowing. In many places the water-hawthorn self-sows freely and new plants arise spontaneously. In some gardens they even become something of a nuisance. To prevent this, spent flowers may be cut off before they form seeds; this can be accomplished with a knife tied or wired to a net, the latter to catch and collect the cut-off blooms. These plants can also be increased by division in spring. The water-hawthorn and *A. desertorum* grow well outdoors or in greenhouses in submerged containers or in mud-bottomed pools and ponds. They prefer a clay-loam soil and will thrive in the kind that suits water-lilies. The best time to plant is spring. The lace leaf (*A. madagascariensis*) is highly temperamental and provides a real challenge to the collector. It may be tried in aquariums, but better results seem to be had in a wooden tub with light coming only from above. A container 2 feet deep and 3 feet in diameter is adequate. Into the bottom, 8 inches of soil is placed and covered with ½ inch of coarse sand or pea-sized gravel. The young plant is set in this. Then water at a temperature of 75°F is run in slowly until its level is 1 inch from the rim. Alternatively, the plants can be grown in large pots or pans (shallow pots) filled with soil surfaced with ½ inch of sand and lowered slowly into the water until the sand is 1 foot to 1½ feet beneath the surface. The lace leaf needs heavy shade and a constant water temperature of 75°F. It is very important that the water be kept free of algae. To keep these leaf-fouling growths down water snails and fish that feed on algae may be employed. It is a good plan to partially change the water at intervals of 1 to 2 weeks by running in additional (at the appropriate temperature) and allowing an overflow of about one-fifth to one-quarter of the total water content of the tub or tank. This seems more advantageous than changing all the water at one time, although that must be done and the algae carefully sponged off the leaves if its growth becomes at all heavy and is otherwise uncontrollable. It is thought that *A. bernerianus* is somewhat easier to grow than *A. madagascariensis,* but this is a moot point. Excellent results with both have been had at The New York Botanical Garden with plants grown in wooden tubs kept near the heating pipes under the bench in a tropical greenhouse.

In aquariums *A. crispus, A. undulatus, A. ulvaceus,* and their hybrids are planted in unwashed sand spread over the floor of the tank. The water temperature should be about 70°F throughout most of the year, but they are greatly benefited by being rested in winter at about 63°F.

APOROCACTUS (Aporo-cáctus)—Rat Tail Cactus. Six species of succulents of the cactus family CACTACEAE constitute *Aporocactus*. All are probably natives of Mexico although the first specimens of the common rat tail cactus, which has never been found wild, were brought to Europe from Peru in 1690. In Mexico the dried flowers of rat tail cactus are used medicinally. The name, meaning that the plants are impenetrable, is from the Greek *aporos*, with no way through.

These cacti have creeping, trailing, clambering, or pendulous, slender stems with seven to twelve ribs, clusters of bristly spines, and often aerial roots. The young stems are green, the older ones grayish. The smallish, day-opening, narrowly-funnel-shaped, somewhat asymmetrical flowers have a corolla tube more or less bent at the base. The face of the bloom is slightly oblique in relation to the tube. Protruding from it is a tight cluster of stamens. The bristly, spherical fruits contain few seeds.

The rat tail cactus (*A. flagelliformis*), common in cultivation, is a free-blooming

Aporocactus flagelliformis

plant popular for hanging baskets and grafting on pieces of *Selenicereus* so that its drooping stems can display their blooms to full advantage. The stems, ½ to ¾ inch in diameter, erect at first then creeping or pendulous, have eight to twelve ribs and closely-spaced clusters of reddish-brown spines. Approximately 3 inches long, 2 to 3 inches across, the crimson flowers have perianths sharply bent just above the ovary, the innermost of their many more or less spreading petals broader than the reflexed outer ones. Its flowers remain open for three or four days. Less than ½ inch in diameter, the red fruits contain yellowish pulp. Crested forms of this species are known. It has been hybridized with *Heliocereus* to produce offspring to which various names have been applied including *A.*

mallisonii, but the correct name of the hybrid is *Heliaporus smithii*. Differing from *A. flagelliformis* in its flowers being straight rather than sharply bent, *A. conzattii* has stems ½ to 1 inch in diameter with eight to ten ribs and closely-spaced clusters of light brown spines. Its red flowers remain open for about two days.

Garden Uses and Cultivation. Interesting and decorative for greenhouses, windows, and in warm, frostless climates for ornamenting porches, balconies, and other outdoor places, these plants need full sun. Indoors in winter a night temperature of 55 to 60°F is most suitable with an increase of several degrees by day. Then keep them dry. From spring to fall water them with moderation. They are subject to infestations by red spider mites. For more information see Cactuses.

APOSTLE PLANT or Twelve Apostles. See Neomarica.

APPLE. This word forms part of the common names of many plants not of the genus *Malus* to which true apples belong. Examples are apple-berry (*Billardiera*), apple mint (*Mentha piperita citrata*), apple-of-Peru (*Nicandra physalodes*), Apple-of-Sodom or Dead-Sea-apple (*Solanum sodomeum*), Argyle-apple (*Eucalyptus cinerea*), balsam-apple (*Momordica balsamina*), bitter-apple (*Citrullus colocynthis*), custard-apple (*Annona reticulata*), elephant-apple (*Dillenia indica*), kangaroo-apple (*Solanum aviculare*), kei-apple (*Dovyalis caffra*), Malay-apple (*Syzygium malaccensis*), mammee-apple (*Mammea americana*), May-apple (*Podophyllum peltatum*), Otaheite-apple (*Spondias cytherea*), pitch-apple (*Clusia rosea*), pond-apple (*Annona glabra*), rose-apple (*Syzygium jambos*), squaw-apple (*Peraphyllum ramosissimum*), star-apple (*Chrysophyllum cainito*), sugar-apple (*Annona squamosa*), thorn-apple (*Datura stramonium*), wood-apple (*Limonia acidissima*).

APPLES. Most important of temperate region fruits, apples are also among the oldest of cultivated ones. Their history under domestication extends back 2,500 years or more. Centuries before the birth of Christ man grew apples. Their wild progenitor (*Malus pumila*) is believed to have originated in the area of southwest Asia between the Caspian and Black seas. There considerable forests of it still exist as wildlings showing very diverse characteristics of growth habits and fruits. Apples were brought to America and planted by the early settlers. Seeds of these, planted by Indians and others and occasionally seeds distributed by birds and other natural agencies, gave rise to many apple trees in favored localities. A somewhat legendary character known as Johnny Appleseed traveled widely in eastern North America and the Ohio Valley, planting ap-

ple seeds wherever he went. The vast majority of seedling trees were of inferior quality. Some few were decidedly superior and many varieties still in favor are selections of seedlings grown nearly a century ago.

Apple tree in bloom

The chief limiting factor to the successful growth of apples is temperature. Coolness they like, but excessive winter cold such as characterizes the Great Plains and certain other regions in North America limits the production to a few inferior, hardy varieties. Too high winter temperatures are also a stumbling block to good apple production. Along the Gulf States and in southern California there is insufficient cold for the trees to prosper. The choicest of the North American apple-growing regions are from Ontario to the Mississippi Valley and Virginia and from California to Washington and adjacent Canada.

Orchard apples

As fruits for home gardens apples are well suited for those willing to give them reasonable attention. Without that, good quality crops cannot be had. Even so, mature specimens, usually remnants of old orchards, are very worth preserving as picturesque elements in the landscape. It is

Old apple trees are often picturesque

these and trees on E M IX are those grafted on E M 26. A height of about 12 feet is attained by trees grafted on understocks E M II and M M III. On understock M M 104 trees attain almost normal size for the variety.

Spur-type trees are fairly recent developments that even when grafted on seedling understocks attain sizes only about three-quarters those of standard-sized apple trees. On dwarfing understocks they are considerably smaller. The reason for their compact habit is that the terminal shoots they produce each season are shorter than those of regular trees and their leaves are closer together. Also, they develop numerous fruiting spurs on two-year-old wood and commonly come into bearing earlier than standard varieties.

Fruiting spurs of apples

scarcely worth while to plant young trees for decorative effects alone. For that, ornamental crab apples are better.

Amateur gardeners are commonly more limited than commercial orchardists in their choice of sites. They must adapt to existing conditions about their homes rather than seek more favorable ones away. It is well therefore to appraise these in relation to the needs of the trees before planting.

Home orchard of apples

Essential for good results is a deep, reasonably fertile soil with satisfactory subsurface drainage. Neither wet lands nor those that dry excessively will do. Given these qualities, the soil may vary from a fairly sandy to a quite clayey loam, with a medium-textured one most acceptable. Very compact clays, gravelly earths, and those consisting largely of coarse sand are to be avoided. If soil drainage is unsatisfactory land drains may be installed to correct this.

Of great importance is good air drainage. Low frost pockets spell trouble. There cold air collects on winter nights to the great detriment of the trees, and in summer stagnant, humid air that favors the development of diseases. Ideal sites are likely to be gentle slopes, sunny and open to free air circulation. Too severe grades may result in soil erosion. Do not plant apple trees where their roots must compete with those of large trees or where they will be shaded.

In choosing varieties rely upon the recommendations of authorities familiar with your area. The local County Cooperative Agent and your State Agricultural Experiment Station are excellent sources of such advice. So are nurseries specializing in fruit tree production. Remember that the same variety grafted on different understocks will give trees of very different ultimate size. For home gardens small trees that take minimum space and are easier to tend in such operations as pruning and fruit picking are often preferred. Trees on East Malling IX (E M IX) understock are dwarfest. They usually do not exceed 6 feet in height. This understock is often specified for apples to be trained as espaliers. Trees approximately 10 feet tall result from grafting on understocks E M VII and Malling-Merton 106. Intermediate between

Spacing must be considered. Crowding results in the trees shading each other to the detriment of all. Normal-sized trees should be at least 35 feet apart. Wider spacing is allowed in commercial orchards. Trees on dwarfing understocks may be set closer and so may spur-type trees. For the latter and those on E M II and III allow no less than 20 feet. Trees on E M VII and M M 106 understocks need a minimum of 15 feet, those of E M IX and E M 26 10 feet.

Another factor to bear in mind when selecting varieties is the desirability or necessity of planting in proximity more than one. In isolated locations in which cross-pollination with other kinds cannot occur many varieties are unfruitful. Some set fruit quite well to their own pollen and are satisfactory when isolated. Check on this before ordering trees.

Obtain planting stock from reliable specialist nurserymen. Place the order well in advance of planting time. Specify the numbers, varieties, and ages of the trees you want, also whether they are wanted for spring or fall delivery.

Upon arrival open the bundles. Inspect the trees for damage and evidences of drying. If in acceptable condition heel them in (plant them closely together in a trench). Do this so that they are sloped about thirty degrees from the horizontal with their tips to the south. This reduces damage from sun scald. Cover the roots well with moist soil.

Soil preparation in advance of planting must be thorough. Apples are long-lived trees. Whatever is done to improve subsurface soil conditions must be accomplished before the trees are installed. Ordinarily this make-ready consists of turning the soil with plow or rototiller to a depth of 8 inches or more and incorporating generous amounts of organic material. Half-rotted stable manure mixed in at the rate of three to six bushels to each 100 square feet is splendid. Unfortunately it is not generally available. For it may be substituted double the amounts of compost, or green manuring may be done. This last is accomplished by plowing under, over a period of a year or two, several successive crops of clover, sweet clover, soybeans, or buckwheat. The objective is to bring the soil into a mellow, friable state such as would be agreeable in a vegetable garden.

In addition to turning and mixing in organics, the soil may be improved in other ways for planting. If it is more than slightly acid apply lime to bring the pH to from 6 to 6.5. Often a dressing of superphosphate worked in is beneficial. Do not use regular garden fertilizers at this stage.

Planting is usually done in early spring, but can be done in fall where winter cold is not too severe. At planting time the above-ground parts must be dormant. Some activity at the roots is favorable. Dig a hole large enough to hold the roots without crowding. Keep the topsoil and subsoil separate. Now fork over the bottom of the hole, mixing with the under soil a generous amount of rotted manure, compost, or peat moss. Tread this firm. Drive a stake, to which the newly planted tree will be tied, before proceeding further. Next throw enough topsoil into the hole so that there will be some under the roots and the tree will be at the correct level (2 to 3 inches deeper than it was in the nursery) when planting is finished.

Before setting the tree trim any broken or jagged-ended roots with a sharp knife or pruning shears. Center the tree in the pit. Spread the roots and fill in topsoil with which has been mixed compost or peat moss. As filling proceeds jiggle the tree up and down a little so that soil falls among the roots. Work it under the roots with the hands so that no voids are left. Pack the soil firm by treading. Tie the trunk securely but not tightly to the stake. Finish the surface as a shallow saucer with a raised rim to hold water.

First-year care consists chiefly of weed control and, if the season is dry, soaking the soil at intervals to a depth of 8 to 10 inches. Shallow cultivation at intervals keeps down weeds and promotes growth. Mulching may be done to minimize the need for both watering and cultivation.

Routine summer care of established trees includes following the spray schedule appropriate for the region. If clean cultivation is practiced regular stirring of the surface soil is necessary. If the orchard is maintained in sod or mulch keep a 2- or 3-feet circle around the base of each tree clear of these. In prolonged droughts deep soakings of the root area at intervals is beneficial. Thinning of the fruits is likely to be necessary at least in some years. This, be-

Thinning: (a) Unless the fruits are thinned out apples may crop so heavily that branches break, the fruits are of inferior size or quality, and the next season's crop is likely to be sparse

(b) Remove surplus fruits while quite small

Apple tree in grass sod

(c) A young tree in fruit

cause the trees often set (develop) more young fruits than the tree can carry to maturity as a high quality crop. In large operations chemical thinning (prevention of too heavy a set) is often partly accomplished by spraying the trees about two weeks after full bloom with NAA (naphthalene acetic acid) or Sevin (an insecticide) in appropriate concentrations. This is supplemented by hand thinning, or manual thinning may be relied upon entirely. The objectives are to have fruits spaced 6 to 8 inches apart and solitary, rather than in pairs or threes. Adequate thinning is of help in counteracting the tendency to biennial cropping, to fruit heavily and lightly in alternate years.

Pruning apples is rarely well understood by amateurs and sometimes looms as a rather formidable task. It need not be if a little thought is given to the objectives. During the first two to four years chief emphasis is on developing well-placed, permanent scaffold branches, the main framework of the tree. If you begin with one-year-old plants (whips) cut them to a height of 3½ to 4 feet at planting time, somewhat lower if they are on strongly dwarfing understocks. Should your trees be two years old at planting time they will have developed side branches. Prune any of these closer to the ground than 2 feet to a length of 6 inches, the others to one-half their length. The next year cut off flush with the trunk the ones previously shortened to 6 inches. Throughout the early years of training prevent the development of V-shaped crotches that may later be subject to breakage. Do this by shortening severely one of any pair of shoots of about equal size and thickness that form a V of a 45 degree or narrower angle. This will encourage the other to become dominant.

Prune to prevent development of V-shaped crotches

And continue to prune in such a way that all parts of the tree receive adequate light, crossed or interlaced branches are not allowed to develop, and any sucker shoots from the trunk or main limbs are removed.

Young apple tree correctly pruned

Early pruning of espalier-trained trees follows much the same pattern, with greater emphasis on retaining only the needed number of well placed branches and tying them into place in the positions they are to occupy permanently. Every winter shorten the leading shoot of each branch to about two-thirds its length and all side shoots (these summer pruned the previous year) to within about 1 inch of their bases. In summer cut the tips out of the new leafy shoots when they have six or seven fully developed leaves and out of the secondary shoots that develop, after their first leaf.

Older, bearing trees are pruned to keep their centers uncrowded and encourage reasonably vigorous, balanced growth. Weak and surplus shoots are cut out, others may be shortened. It is better to prune rather lightly each year than to allow trees to go unpruned for long periods and then cut severely. Late winter is the best time to prune.

Rehabilitation pruning of neglected trees calls for sterner measures. It may be necessary to remove some quite thick branches completely and head back others. Remove crossing and interlacing branches but do not open up the crown in any one year to such an extent that limbs previously heavily shaded will be scalded by the sun as a result of sudden exposure. If necessary spread the operation over two pruning seasons. Such rehabilitation pruning must be fortified by the instigation of an adequate spray program and if needed fertilizing.

Except as picturesque landscape features old trees that are decrepit, that have badly rotted trunks or branches, or that have a considerable proportion of their tops killed by disease or other cause are not worth

Apples trained as espaliers: (a) After winter pruning

(b) In bloom

(c) Flowering profusely

(d) In fruit (early thinning would have prevented this too-heavy concentration of fruits)

Summer pruning an espaliered apple tree

saving. If you want to keep them, treat them as recommended above for neglected trees. Clean out rotted portions of trunks and major branches to live wood and paint exposed surfaces with an asphaltum or other tree-wound paint. It is usually better not to fill the cavities.

Fertilization is often not necessary, but if annual growth is not enough the application of nitrogen in some form or other to the soil is recommended. Any fertilizer that contains nitrogen in fairly readily available form may be used in amounts that supply 1/10 pound of actual nitrogen for each year of age of the tree, but in no case more than a pound to each normal-type tree or 1/2 pound for dwarf trees. Too much nitrogen causes excessive shoot growth especially subject to winter-kill and reduced fruit production.

Fruit production may sometimes be encouraged by scoring the trunks of trees that grow with excessive vigor, but fruit sparingly or not at all. To do this take a sharp knife and make a spiral cut through the bark just below the lowest branch and encircling the trunk about twice, with the overlaps of the cut spaced about 2 inches apart. Bark ringing or girdling is similar to scoring except that a very narrow sliver of bark about 1/8 inch wide is removed. This may be taken from a complete circle around the trunk, but it is better if two half circles are removed from opposite sides of the trunk, about 4 inches apart. Paint the narrow slit with grafting wax or tree-wound paint.

Harvesting calls for a little judgment as to when the fruits have reached optimum development. Only then do they have the finest flavor. The time for picking varies with varieties and other factors. A paling of the green of some varieties and a deepening of the red or yellow colors of others signals apple picking time. As a simple test lift the fruit upward in the hand. If it releases readily from the branch it is ready for taking. It is important to pick early apples promptly and usually, because the

fruits do not all ripen at once, by going over the trees again at suitable intervals. Do not shake fruits from the tree, but for home use it is permissible with early varieties to lay a thick mulch of straw or leaves beneath the branches and wait for them to fall naturally.

Propagation of apples is by grafting or much less frequently budding. The understocks used have a very considerable influence on the growth of the scions grafted upon them. Seedling understocks result in full-sized standard trees. Dwarfing understocks are employed for the production of trees of lesser dimensions. Few amateurs propagate their own apples. Most, wisely, buy their young stock from nurseries specializing in fruit tree production. Individual trees are sometimes grafted with more than one variety. While interesting as novelties, such specimens are not very practicable. Almost invariably in the course of time the strongest-growing variety becomes dominant to the detriment of the others.

Varieties of apples are numerous but only a moderate number are grown in quantity. Names such as 'Baldwin', 'Cortland', 'Delicious', 'Golden Delicious', 'Grimes Golden', 'Jonathan', and 'Northern Spy' have long been familiar. Now newer ones, many sports or mutations from older varieties, are appearing. Here belong such kinds as 'Millerspur', 'Redspur', 'Royal Red', 'Starking Delicious', 'Topred', and others. Available kinds are described and often illustrated in fruit tree suppliers' catalogs and often in publications of State Agricultural Experiment Stations. Write for these last to the station in the state where you intend to plant.

Pests and Diseases. Afflictions of apples are fairly numerous. Unless they are controlled crops are likely to be worthless or almost so. Effective spray programs vary greatly from region to region, and so do to some extent the causal agents. Correct timing of spray applications is extremely important. Follow the recommendations of your County Cooperative Agent or State Agricultural Experiment Station. In addition to pests and diseases caused by organisms, physiological troubles may occur. A condition known as water-core manifests itself by the fruits being unusually hard and the flesh near the core having a glossy appearance. The cause is not known. Recommendations are to avoid excessive thinning of the fruit and to harvest before it becomes over-ripe. Round, or angular, sunken spots, the flesh beneath spongy, brown, and bitter are characteristic of the disease called stippen or bitter pit. Although the signs usually are seen after harvesting the causes occurred earlier. The condition is aggravated by excessive pruning, excessive thinning of the fruits, and heavy applications of nitrogen fertilizer.

Mice, rabbits, and other rodents are capable of seriously damaging apple trees by girdling the trunks by gnawing. Keep mulch materials that provide hiding at least 2 feet away from the trunks. Encircle the bases of the trunks with fine wire mesh with its bottom buried in the ground. Use poison baits (as recommended by the manufacturer) if necessary.

APRICOTS. Among the most delicious and distinctly flavored fruits, apricots like their relatives almonds and peaches belong in the genus *Prunus*. The species from which the finest cultivated varieties have been developed is *P. armeniaca,* not as its name indicates native of Armenia, but of western Asia. Other varieties, known as Russian apricots, are derivatives of smaller *P. mandshurica* of Manchuria and Korea and *P. sibirica* of Siberia, Manchuria, and northern China. These are hardier than *P. armeniaca* varieties. The purple apricot is *P. dasycarpa,* the Japanese apricot, *P. mume.*

The chief center of commercial apricot production in the United States is California. There, production for canning and drying is an important industry. Lesser amounts are grown in other western states and in western Canada.

The common apricot is a handsome, deciduous tree hardier than the peach, but because its flowers open earlier in spring more subject to damage by late frosts. This, coupled with the susceptibility of its fruits to brown rot disease and injury by curculio insects has restricted its popularity in the East to a greater extent than is justified. As home garden crops selected varieties, if a suitable spray program is followed, give highly satisfactory results wherever severe frost does not come after the trees are in bloom. In the Northeast favorable sites are likely to be north-facing and west-facing slopes on elevated land near large bodies of water. Russian varieties crop well in most years in western New York.

A wide range of soil types other than extreme clays or sands suit apricots. It is important that they be well drained. Preparation for planting may be as for peaches or apples.

Choose varieties suited to the region. In the West those derived from *P. armeniaca* are best. Here belong 'Blenheim', the nearly identical 'Royal', and the almost as popular 'Tilton'. For eating fresh 'Moorpark' is superb. Others are 'Perfection' and 'Riland'. Russian apricots, adapted to the East, Midwest, and other cold-climate areas are 'Doty', 'Geneva', 'Henderson', 'M 604', 'Robust', and 'Scout'. Obtain your planting stock, one-year-old trees are usually preferred, from a nursery specializing in fruit trees. If your land is sandy and infested with nematodes specify that the trees be on apricot or nematode-resistant peach understocks.

Spacing between trees may be from 20 to 30 feet with on good soils 25 feet the minimum. Handle the trees upon arrival from the nursery and plant them as recommended for apples. At planting time prune by cutting the main stem back to a height of about 2½ feet and any branches back to two buds.

Pruning during their early years is directed toward establishing a sound framework of well-placed scaffold branches. These may be spaced to form a vase-shaped or a modified leader tree. The latter is usually preferred. To attain this form, at the end of the first growing season select for retention as main scaffold limbs three well-placed shoots pointing in different directions and spaced 6 to 8 inches apart vertically. Remove all other laterals and cut back those kept to different lengths with the one to be the leader left the longest.

The next year cut out all shoots below a height of 4 to 5 feet from the ground, and all at or above that height except about five well-spaced ones retained as secondary scaffolds. Prune these so that the leader is the longest. Additional pruning until bearing age is aimed at continuing the development of a structurally strong tree by removing branches that interfere with the main framework or that crowd unduly.

Pruning bearing trees is done to encourage the production of fruiting spurs. It consists of an annual thinning out of shoots that threaten to crowd and shortening others to well-placed laterals. More severe cutting back is likely to be needed by older trees the rates of growth of which have slowed considerably. With them, harder pruning is done as a stimulus to growth and the production of fruiting spurs that are shorter-lived than those of apples and pears.

General management does not differ significantly from that of apples or peaches. Apricots do not need high levels of nitrogen; they need less than peaches, for example, and so some caution is needed with fertilizing. New 1¼- to 2½-feet-long shoots produced each year indicate satisfactory fertility. Early thinning of fruits, to about 4 inches apart, results in larger ones to harvest. Harvest with care when the color of the fruits indicates ripeness and consequent attainment of highest eating quality. Fruits picked before this stage are inferior, but they must not be left until the flesh becomes too soft to handle.

Propagation is by budding onto understocks of seedling apricots or peaches or of myrobolan plum. Dwarf trees are had by budding on understocks of sand-cherry (*Prunus besseyi*).

Pests and Diseases. These are as for peaches. Information about them and up-to-date recommendations for their control can be had from local Cooperative Extension Agents and from State Agricultural Experiment Stations.

APRIL, GARDENING REMINDERS FOR. In northern gardens this is one of the busiest months of the year—so much to do and so little time available it seems. Now one appreciates the benefits that derive from tasks done in March or earlier in anticipation of the spring rush. If you have been dilatory check the entry in this Encyclopedia titled March, Gardening Reminders For, then lose no time in catching up. Finish the pruning of deciduous trees and shrubs and of roses before new growth begins; any needed cutting of maples and birches, however, is better delayed until they are in full leaf. Such delay will reduce the loss of sap ("bleeding") from the wounds.

(a) Prune deciduous shrubs

(b) And deciduous trees

Complete the removal of winter protection this month, but do not be too anxious to get this over with too early. It is easy for the unwary to be lured by a spell of mild weather treacherously followed a bad spell into exposing protected plants prematurely. Cold nights and more especially sunny, windy days can do great harm to delicate shoots just pushing forth. It is much better to remove heavy coverings of salt hay, branches of evergreens, and the like in two operations than in one. Choose if you can dull, humid, windless days for reducing and removing winter coverings.

Rock gardens are about to enter their season of finest floral display. Before new growth has advanced appreciably lightly scratch the surface soil and spread a 1-inch-thick top dressing of crumbly soil as required for the various plants—for those demanding alkaline conditions a mixture containing crushed limestone, for acid-soil sorts a limeless dressing with abundant peat moss, for woodlanders generous proportions of flaky leaf mold or rich compost in the mixture, and so on.

Perennial and mixed beds and borders call for attention now. This may involve dividing and replanting large clumps of summer- and fall-blooming items that tend to spread rapidly, but it is better to wait until after blooming or until early fall to accomplish this with such spring-bloomers as bleeding hearts (*Dicentra*), columbines (*Aquilegia*), coral bells (*Heuchera*), irises, oriental poppies, peonies, and pyrethrums. If Christmas-roses and other sorts of *Helleborus* are to be divided (it is best to leave them undisturbed as long as possible) this is the time to do it.

Divide many sorts of hardy perennials

After winter covering is removed and before the perennial plants are more than 2 or 3 inches tall spread a complete fertilizer and fork it into the surface shallowly.

Fertilize and fork over perennial borders

Be extremely careful not to break or otherwise damage such plants as balloon flower (*Platycodon*) and rose-mallows (*Hibiscus*) that are notoriously tardy in breaking ground.

Trees and shrubs of nearly all kinds, evergreen and deciduous, and including fruit trees and roses, can in April be planted with high expectation of success, but it is better to delay moving magnolias and tulip trees until May. In general transplanting evergreens can be safely accomplished somewhat later than bare-root or balled and burlapped deciduous trees and shrubs, but even they should be installed in their new quarters before they have made very much new growth. Deciduous trees and shrubs and roses established in containers may be set out safely even after they are in full leaf.

Plant shrubs and trees: (a) Deciduous

(b) Evergreen

Lawn work is now in order. Before the first mowing sweep the grass and either top-dress it with a rich mixture of compost, humus, leaf mold, or peat moss and good topsoil fortified with a complete fertilizer or if that is impracticable apply fertilizer alone. Liming may be desirable but many amateurs overdo this. Do not apply lime unless a soil test or the appearance of such indicator weeds as sorrel suggest need.

Fertilize and top-dress lawns

Apply lime to lawns only if needed

Where clover is abundant liming is unnecessary.

Renovation of lawns may include patching bare spots with sod or by seeding. In either case be sure to first condition the soil by forking, fertilizing, and doing whatever else may be needed to make it agreeable to roots. Lawns on sandy soil may benefit from rolling with a light-weight roller although this is a procedure less followed now than in times past. Aerating lawns on clayey soils by rolling with a spiked roller or other means is often helpful.

Patch bare spots in lawn with new sod

If new lawns are to be made by sowing or sodding delay no longer than absolutely necessary. This is particularly true of seeded lawns. If for any reason you cannot sow at the earliest practicable date it may be wise to content yourself with a temporary lawn of annual rye grass for now and delay sowing the much more expensive permanent mixture until early fall. Rye grass gives quick results and forms a good one-season sward. Spaded or rototilled under in fall, the rye grass sod will greatly benefit the soil by adding organic matter and improving its texture.

Sow seeds by hand or mechanical sower for new lawns

Flower and vegetable seed sowing calls for timely attention. A delay of a week or two often makes significant differences in results. This is particularly true of cool-weather annuals such as African-daisies (*Arctotis*), baby's breath (*Gypsophila*), calendulas, California-poppies, China-asters,

Many kinds of seeds may be sown outdoors in April

chrysanthemums, clarkias, cornflowers, dimorphothecas, and love-in-a-mist (*Nigella*). Early outdoor sowing is also necessary to ensure early crops of a wide variety of vegetables. Delay is necessary only with decidedly warm-weather sorts such as beans (except fava beans), corn, cucumbers, melons, okra, and squash. Keep the surface soil between rows of seedlings stirred shallowly with scuffle hoe or cultivator. This does much to encourage growth as well as destroy weeds.

Greenhouse occupants that resent too strong sun, such as ferns, most other foliage plants, orchids, African-violets and other gesneriads, and begonias, need shading more heavily now than earlier. But do not go overboard. Give no more shade than is necessary to prevent paling or scorching of the foliage. Practically all plants are better with the maximum light they will stand without actual damage to their tissues. Excessive shade results in weak growth, susceptibility to disease, and sparse bloom. Light temporary shade afforded plants such as annual chrysanthemums, azaleas, carnations, clarkias, hyacinths, narcissuses, sweet peas, and tulips after their flowers begin to open prolongs their blooming seasons, as does a relatively cool, airy atmosphere.

Pot cuttings inserted earlier that now have roots about 1 inch long. After potting return them for at least a week or two to an environment similar to that from which they were taken then gradually accustom them to conditions normally required by their kind. Other potting will need attention. Plants such as cyclamens that are grown to maturity within a comparatively few months and then discarded must not be allowed to become seriously pot-bound before the containers in which they are to bloom are attained. Needed potting of most flowering and foliage plants of kinds that are grown as permanent specimens from year to year should be completed before the end of April. Specimens not calling for this attention at this time are likely

to benefit from top dressing with rich soil. Prune to shape any that tend to be straggly.

Carnations for planting later in benches or outdoor beds should now be in 4-inch pots. Pinch the ends out of the shoots occasionally to induce branching, but pinch a few each week rather than all at one time. This will encourage continuous production of blooms rather than alternate gluts and scarcities when flowering time comes.

Propagation and duties attendant upon that most interesting phase of greenhouse work are likely to keep greenhouse gardeners busy now. Practically all plants that can be increased by cuttings and air layering in March can be so propagated in April. Read the Encyclopedia entry March, Gardening Reminders For. Begonias especially are likely to make excellent specimens from April propagations. Now is a good time to take cuttings of dahlias from tubers started in a warm, sunny greenhouse in March. Take a thin sliver of tuber with each cutting.

Sow seeds of greenhouse primulas and, if you want big specimens for blooming next spring of calceolarias and cinerarias.

Cold frames and hotbeds are likely to see maximum use now. As early as weather permits, hardy biennials and perennials raised and wintered in them for spring bedding displays should be transferred to their flowering locations. If a greenhouse is operated plants raised in it for setting in the garden later will soon occupy temporarily all the space vacated. Or hotbeds or frames may be used in place of greenhouses for raising early plants. The management of hotbeds and frames consists chiefly of watering and ventilating. It is important on sunny days to open the sash

before the temperature inside attains injurious levels. Do this without exposing tender plants in active growth or those just brought from a greenhouse to harmfully low temperatures, cold drafts, or sweeping, drying winds. For the same reasons before the sun wanes in late afternoon and a evening chill settles in, the sash must be closed or almost closed.

With plants being hardened in preparation for transplanting to the open garden, gradually ventilate more and more freely until for a week or two before the actual transfer they are left uncovered day and night. Too high or too low temperatures, excessive atmospheric humidity, too much shade, and too-dry soil are all harmful to plants in hotbeds and cold frames. Droplets of moisture on the inside of the sash indicate atmospheric humidity is too high, that more ventilation is needed.

Sow seeds of asters, stocks, and other annuals in hotbeds and cold frames to give plants for setting outdoors later. Plant in cold frames corms of gladioluses and montbretias to produce early crops of flowers for cutting.

Houseplants should now be showing considerable improvement as a result of better light, longer days, and less need for heating of such intensity that the atmosphere is dried excessively. April, May, and sometimes June are good months for buying new plants. In spring newcomers adapt more readily to new conditions than in winter and have the opportunity to become acclimated before fall. Unusual sorts in small sizes are available from specialist house plant nurseries that sell by mail and from good garden centers and even dime stores.

April is an excellent time to repot a great many kinds of houseplants, but do this only if needed. Many sorts, especially if in fairly large containers, may if fertilized regularly be left undisturbed for several years without suffering. Young specimens in small pots of most kinds benefit from potting on. Many amateurs make the mistake of using pots too big for the sizes of the plants. Do not do this. Aesthetically and from a health standpoint pot plants look and grow better in containers that are not too large. If the roots of those to be potted have filled their present pots and are healthy the new pot should not ordinarily be more than 2 inches bigger in diameter across its top than the old one. If the plant is small in relation to its present container it may be repotted into a clean pot of the same size, or if its roots are in poor condition perhaps even into one smaller. Plants such as African-violets, aspidistras, certain begonias, and Boston ferns, that lend themselves to increase by division, can conveniently be propagated now.

Other ways of propagating, by air layering, cuttings, and seeds, give good results in April. Now is the ideal time to

Attend to repotting of indoor plants as needed

To increase stocks of many plants propagate by cuttings

lower that leggy dieffenbachia or dracaena by the first method, to insert cuttings and in some cases leaf cuttings in a terrarium or under an inverted Mason jar or a polyethylene plastic bag stretched over a light framework of wire or wood, of a wide variety of favorites, begonias, coleuses, English ivy and other viny types, fuchsias, geraniums, and grape-ivies to mention only a few. Seeds of African-violets, asparagus-ferns, begonias, browallias, cactuses and other succulents, coleuses, geraniums, grevilleas, and patience plants sprout readily now and the offspring given reasonable care will make sizable plants before fall.

A home-made propagator covered with polyethylene plastic is a great aid to rooting cuttings

Water newly-potted plants with decent restraint. Do not let them suffer for want of moisture, but avoid keeping the soil always saturated. These admonitions apply also to established, well-rooted specimens, but more frequent applications will be needed by them than recently-potted specimens. Nor will these last need fertilizing until their roots have taken full possession of the new earth, but older-established specimens of kinds in active growth in most cases will be improved by moderate fertilizing at regular intervals between now

and fall. This is true of hippeastrums. Do not make the mistake of drying them off after they are through flowering. Next year's bloom depends upon vigorous foliage growth this summer. Keep pots of Easter lilies, hyacinths, narcissuses, and other forced bulbs that you intend to plant in the outdoor garden well watered and occasionally fertilized until all danger of frost is passed, then plant the lilies in the garden after their foliage has died down. Store the others in a dry, airy place for fall planting.

Spraying the foliage of all houseplants except kinds such as African-violets that have hairy leaves and many succulents is highly beneficial. A daily misting helps and a weekly or biweekly forceful spraying of the under and upper sides of the foliage does much to remove grime, discourage insects, and promote growth. The forceful spraying may be done conveniently in the bathtub or outdoors. With specimens too big to be handled this way substitute a once-a-month careful sponging of the leaves with mild soapy water.

Tuberous begonia, caladium, and gloxinia tubers planted in April in a terrarium, glass-covered box, or under a tent of polyethylene plastic sprout readily and if cared for properly will make fine ornamentals for summer and early fall display. All need warmth to start. The caladiums are easiest to manage. Where summers are really hot the begonias are not likely to succeed.

In southern gardens give needed attention to lawns. Read the recommendations regarding this in the Encyclopedia entry March, Gardening Reminders For, and put into immediate practice any not previously acted upon. You may still fertilize. New plantings of sprigs or plugs of centipede, Bermuda, St. Augustine, and *Zoysia* grasses can be made. Mow permanent grasses oversown with rye grass twice a week with the mower blades at a height of 1 inch. New lawns of Bermuda grass may be sown now in the middle and lower South. In the upper South Kentucky blue grass lawns can still be sown but only just; delay no longer.

As soon as they are through blooming do any needed pruning of spring-flowering shrubs such as flowering almonds, flowering quinces, forsythias, jasmines, and spireas. Thin out older and ill-placed branches to facilitate reasonable access of air and sunshine and so stimulate the development of strong shoots for blooming next year.

Sow or plant out now warm-weather annuals such as African and French marigolds, amaranthus, castor-beans, celosias, coleuses, cosmos, dahlias, four o'clocks, geraniums, globe-amaranths, moonflowers, morning glories, petunias, salvias, thunbergias, tithonias, torenias, vincas, and zinnias, but forget all about kinds such as cornflowers, larkspurs, and stocks that

fail in hot weather. As soon as all danger of frost is over sow or plant out warm-weather vegetables such as cucumbers, melons, squash, and tomatoes. Make successional sowings of hardier kinds. Before their berries begin to form mulch strawberries to keep the fruits clean and off the ground with salt hay, straw, pine needles, or other suitable material.

Mulching as a water conservation measure, to keep down weeds and to shade and keep the surface soil relatively cool, and in some cases to supply nutrients, is an admirable and labor-saving practice. For the greatest benefit have the mulch in place before, but not too long before, sustained hot weather comes. Even though it may be a little early to mulch warm-weather crops it is not too soon to locate, if not already at hand, supplies of materials to use as mulches. Among such materials are bagasse, bark chips, buckwheat hulls, compost, ground corn cobs, leaf mold, peat moss, pine needles, and wood chips.

Bulbs for summer flowering may be planted in the upper South as soon as the weather is fairly warm and settled. If not already done they may be planted now in the middle and lower South. For suggestions as to suitable kinds see the Encyclopedia entry titled March, Gardening Reminders For. In the upper South make a planting of gladioluses. Further south make successional ones to those made earlier. In April tropical water-lilies may be planted, about the middle of the month in the middle South, later in the upper South.

Attend to spraying or dusting on a systematic basis but do not do either without good reason. Your State Agricultural Experiment Station and local County Extension Agent are your surest sources of wise counsel about these matters. To check black spot disease of roses once-a-week spraying or dusting with a fungicide is necessary.

In West Coast gardens many different kinds of annuals can be sown with every prospect of success and dahlias may be planted. Earlier setting out is not recommended. It may result in earlier blooms but they will be of inferior quality as compared with those from later plantings.

Proceed with pruning spring-flowering shrubs as soon as the blooms fade and, if it has not already received attention, undertake such lawn conditioning tasks as patching, raking, fertilizing, and when growth makes necessary, mowing. In warm sections it is practicable to plant or sow tender annuals and vegetables but in the Northwest such activity must be delayed until there is no longer danger of frost and settled mild weather has arrived. But all hardier sorts can be sown or planted.

In the Northwest rock gardens and other spring-flowering features of the garden will be at their best. As rock garden plants pass out of bloom check the more vigorous to make certain they are not crowding weaker neighbors. Some sorts lend themselves to increase by division at this time.

As soon as the weather moderates to the extent that frost is no longer to be feared make plantings of such summer-blooming bulb plants as galtonias, gladioluses, ismenes, montbretias, and tigridias. In warmer sections tubers of begonias and gloxinias may be planted outdoors.

In southern California plant in favorable locations avocados, cherimoyas, citrus fruits, guavas, macadamia nut trees, mangoes, passion fruits, and sapotes.

APTENIA (Aptèn-ia)—Dew Plant. One species, native to South Africa and previously included in the genus *Mesembryanthemum*, belongs here. A member of the carpetweed family AIZOACEAE, it has a name derived from the Greek *a*, not, and *pteron*, a wing, that alludes to the wingless valves of the fruits. The dew plant (*Aptenia cordifolia* syn. *Mesembryanthemum cordifolium*) is segregated from *Mesembryanthemum* on the basis of technical differences in the characteristics of its fruits. It occasionally occurs spontaneously as an escape from cultivation in California.

A tender, succulent, prostrate perennial, the dew plant has stems up to 2 feet long, and opposite, flat, stalked, pointed-ovate, slightly fleshy leaves ½ to 1¼ inches long. The purple flowers, about ½ inch in diameter, are daisy-like in appearance, but are structured very differently. Instead of consisting of numerous florets (really in-

dividual flowers) as does the flower head of a daisy, each bloom is a single flower. The flowers of the dew plant, which are solitary in the leaf axils, open only in sun. Their sepals are of very unequal size, the two largest flat, the others awl-shaped. Variety *A. c. variegata* has leaves attractively variegated with creamy-white. The fruits are capsules.

Garden and Landscape Uses. In dryish, frost-free or almost frost-free climates, and in warm desert and semidesert regions, this is an excellent plant for flower beds and borders, for rock gardens, and for similar places. It can also be displayed attractively in window and porch boxes, urns, and other decorative containers. As an indoor plant it is suitable for growing as a pot plant in windows and for including in collections of succulents. It stands dry atmospheric conditions better than many houseplants.

Cultivation. Like most vigorous succulents, *Aptenia* flourishes with minimal care. A few environmental needs must be met. It needs full sun. The soil must be well drained and very porous, but need not be very fertile. When grown in containers a coarse mixture containing an abundance of broken brick, sandstone, tufa rock, or crocks, as well as a generous amount of sand, is most satisfactory. Watering should be done only when the soil becomes quite dryish. Then it should be saturated. Constantly wet soil may result in destruction of the plants by rotting. Propagation is very easy by cuttings, and by seeds sown

in sandy, well-drained soil, and scarcely covered with soil. Seeds soon germinate in a temperature of 60 to 65°F. The chief pests are mealybugs. For additional information see Succulents.

AQUARIUM. Besides giving opportunity to grow and observe plants not otherwise easily viewable, well-maintained aquariums can be handsome room decorations. They need care of course, but are not unduly demanding and can go for long periods with little or no attention. Certainly as far as the plants are concerned they present no "what-shall-we-do-with-them-while-we-are-away-on-vacation" problems associated with other indoor plants.

The most satisfactory aquariums are "balanced" ones, those in which the fish and other animal population is compensatory to amount of vegetation. The plants produce oxygen needed by the animal life. The fish and other creatures, such as snails, give off carbon dioxide that the plants use and their excreta fertilizes the plants. If there are too few plants or too many fish the latter are likely to spend much time gulping for air at the surface. If vegetation is too much in comparison to the other forms of life or if the light is of an intensity that stimulates them to be excessively active in producing oxygen, unsightly algae multiply. The correction is to reduce the amount of light or add more fish or both. A rather delicate balance is to be sought.

The aquarium must be watertight and for the best advantage of adequate size. One that holds 25 gallons or more of water is to be preferred. Excellent and handsome examples are available. They may be illuminated with fluorescent lamps and be heated with thermostatically controlled elements. Both plants and fish have definite temperature requirements, but as those of the latter are generally more critical it is usual to set temperatures agreeable to the fish and select plants adapted to those. The temperature will usually be between 60 and 80°F.

Planting aquariums is largely a matter of personal taste. Those with an artistic bent find it easy to create very beautiful underwater-scapes. Begin by covering the bottom of the container with a layer of coarse sand that has been thoroughly washed to remove all fine particles. Pieces of rock, shells, or other appropriate accessories may be placed to give variety of contour. Next comes the placement of the plants. If, as is usual, the aquarium is to be viewed from one side only, set a fairly dense background of tall plants and in front of it at various interesting spacing others of different forms and sizes. All that is usually necessary is to embed the bases of the plants in the sand but sometimes it may be preferable to set the plant in a small pot of

Aptenia cordifolia

Plants for Aquariums: (a) *Ceratopteris*

(b) *Cryptocoryne*

(c) *Salvinia*

soil and bury this in the sand. In addition to plants anchored in the soil, it is well to have some floating kinds. These give some shade and so help to limit the development of algae and also provide refuge to tiny baby fish from their often cannibalistic parents. If chlorinated water is used be sure to allow it to stand in an open container for a few days before putting it in the aquarium.

Plants appropriate for aquariums include species of *Anacharis, Aponogeton, Cabomba, Ceratophyllum, Cryptocoryne, Myriophyllum, Nitella,* and *Vallisneria.* Among suitable floating kinds are *Azolla, Ceratopteris, Lemna, Pistia, Riccia,* and *Salvinia.*

AQUATICS. This is a group name for plants that grow in water rather than on land. It does not include bog plants although there are certain species that prosper in wet soils or in water, and so are both bog plants and aquatics. Typical and most familiar aquatics are water-lilies. There are many others. Aquatics fall into two main groups, submersed, those that grow entirely under water, except for their flowers rising to or above the surface, and emersed, those of which the foliage is at or above the surface. Examples of submersed kinds are *Callitriche, Elodea,* and *Utricularia.* Emersed kinds may be further classified as floating, to include those such as *Azolla, Eichhornia,* and *Pistia,* which have no need to root into soil, although in very shallow water they sometimes do, and others such as water-lilies (*Nymphaea*), *Pontederia,* and *Thalia,* the roots of which must be anchored in earth bottoms. Horticulturally, aquatics are cultivated in water gardens, ponds, other bodies of water, and in tubs and aquariums. For more information see Aquariums, and Water Gardens.

AQUIFOLIACEAE—Holly Family. Three genera of deciduous and evergreen trees and shrubs of which *Ilex* accounts for the vast majority of the about 500 species, are the only ones of this widely dispersed family of dicotyledons. Family characteristics

are undivided, often leathery, alternate, or much more rarely, opposite leaves without permanent stipules and small, symmetrical, bisexual or unisexual, white or greenish flowers, solitary or in clusters from the leaf axils. These have mostly four to six sepals, petals, and stamens, the latter more or less united at their bases. The ovary is superior, the stigma stalkless. The fruits are berries. Cultivated genera are *Ilex* and *Nemopanthus.*

Typical Aquatics: (a) Water-lilies (*Nymphaea*)

(c) Water-hyacinth (*Eichhornia*)

AQUILEGIA (Aquil-ègia)—Columbine. Columbines are well-known, old-fashioned garden plants the species of which, in cultivation, have engaged in such promiscuous interbreeding that it is often difficult or impossible to relate the progeny to particular wild types. Such are the hybrid columbines of seed catalogs including the choice and lovely long-spurred ones. But even rock gardeners who strive not to improve on wild species, but to grow them

(b) Water-lettuce (*Pistia*)

(d) Water-hawthorn (*Aponogeton*)

as they are found in their mountain homes have trouble with columbines and many a prized specimen proudly and imposingly labeled with the botanical name of some choice species would come under suspicion were its ancestry critically explored. Columbines hybridize readily. Even distantly related species are likely to do so and produce at least some fertile seeds. Because in gardens different kinds are commonly grown in proximity, the likelihood of cross-fertilization is great. As a result, columbine seeds sent out under species names by botanical gardens and others often give plants that turn out to be hybrids rather than pure species.

The genus *Aquilegia* consists of possibly 100 species, perhaps not more than sixty-five or seventy, since botanists interpret the group variously. They are natives of the north temperate zone with a few extensions at high altitudes into Mexico and North Africa. Columbines belong in the buttercup family RANUNCULACEAE and are related not only to buttercups, but also to monkshoods, clematises, Christmas-roses, peonies, and the shrub yellow root (*Xanthorhiza*). Truly, if outward appearances only are considered, botany brings together strange bedfellows. The name *Aquilegia* is of uncertain origin. It has been suggested it comes from the Latin *aquilegus*, a water drawer, alternatively, from the Latin *aquila*, an eagle, from a fanciful resemblance of the spurs of the flowers to those of the bird.

Most columbines are erect, branching plants with several stems arising from a thickened rootstock. The leaves are divided, once, twice, or three times, each time into three, and their stalks have conspicuously broadened bases. The upper leaves when present are smaller and have fewer leaflets than those below. Individual leaflets are wedge-shaped to nearly round, commonly notched, the center one of each group of three into three lobes, the lateral ones into two. The blooms are at the branch ends, erect or nodding. The five more or less spreading sepals have the texture and appearance of petals. Five petals alternate with them. These have an expanded blade and a hollow, backward-projecting basal spur with a nectar gland at its base. Spurs and blades may be prominent or almost lacking depending upon the species. There are numerous stamens, the inner ones sterile. The pistils are usually five. The fruits are follicles.

Old-fashioned flower garden columbines were chiefly varieties and hybrids of *A. vulgaris*. They are still grown to some extent and are characterized by their blooms having comparatively short, stubby spurs or none. From 1½ to approximately 3 feet tall, they have much the aspect of *A. vulgaris*. Their flowers may be single or double and most commonly of various shades of blue or purple or are white, blue and white, or purple and white.

Long-spurred hybrid *aquilegias* in a garden bed

Long-spurred hybrid columbines of which seedsmen offer selected strains are a later horticultural development than the old-fashioned varieties based on *A. vulgaris*. As their name implies their blooms have long spurs. These, not only remarkably long but also slender, are to a large extent responsible for the grace and airy appearance of the blooms, which come in a very wide range of colors and pure white and in combinations. The hues include cream, yellow, blue, lavender, purple, pink, and various shades of red. Long-spurred hybrid columbines are attractive, 1½ to 3 feet tall, and bloom with great freedom. Their ancestry is based on the American species *A. canadensis*, *A. chrysantha*, *A. caerulea*, *A. formosa*, and possibly others.

Native American columbines number about fifteen species. Among the best are these: **A. canadensis,** the only one indige-

Long-spurred hybrid *Aquilegia*

Aquilegia canadensis

nous to eastern North America, ranges from Nova Scotia to Saskatchewan, Florida, and Texas. It favors rocks, ledges, cliffs, and dryish woodlands. From 1 foot to 3 feet tall, it has twice-divided leaves, those on the stem diminishing in size above. The loosely-arranged, nodding blooms up to 1½ inches long, have red sepals, petals with brief yellow blades, and nearly straight, backward-pointing, red spurs ½ to 1 inch in length. The stamens project conspicuously. Variants with yellow and with salmon-pink blooms occur. **A. caerulea** is variable. It inhabits moist slopes and light woodlands through the Rocky Mountains. One of the most beautiful columbines and the state flower of Colorado, it is from 8 inches to 2⅔ feet tall and in its upper parts more or less glandular-hairy. It has rather thin, twice-divided leaves. In its typical form the sepals and spurs are glorious light to deep blue. Those of *A. c. ochroleuca* (syn. *A. c. albiflora*) are white or nearly white. The sepals are up to 1¼ inches long. The petals are white to whitish, ½ to 1 inch long. The somewhat pubescent spurs are straight or curve outward. *A. chrysantha* ranges from the Rocky Mountains to Texas. From 2 to 4 feet tall and freely-branched, it has thinnish, mostly three-times-pinnate leaves commonly densely-downy on their undersides. From 1½ to 3 inches in diameter, the clear yellow flowers are erect. Their pointed, narrow sepals are much longer than the blades of the petals. The down-pointing spurs are slender, tapered, wide-spreading, and 2 to 2½ inches long. Variety *A. c. alba* has white blooms. *A. flavescens*, native from Alberta to British Columbia, Colorado, Utah, and Oregon, is 6 inches to 2 feet in height. It has thinnish, twice-pinnate basal leaves and nodding flowers with spreading to backward-pointing, generally yellow sepals ½ to ¾ inch long. The cream petals have blades ⅓ inch in length and slightly to strongly-curved spurs up to slightly more than ½ inch long. *A. formosa* is the western North American representative of *A. canadensis*. A variable kind of which botanists recognize several varieties it ranges, often at high altitudes, commonly in moist woodlands, from Montana and Utah to California and Alaska. From 9 inches to 1½ feet tall and glaucous in its lower parts, above it is loosely-branched and glandular-pubescent. The basal leaves are twice-divided. The more or less pubescent, nodding blooms have pointed, red, spreading to reflexed sepals ½ to 1 inch long, petals with a yellow blade ⅙ inch long, and nearly straight, red spurs up to ¾ inch long. *A. jonesii* grows along the continental divide and a little to the east of it, favoring crevices in limestone rocks and screes from Wyoming to Alberta. One of the loveliest of dwarf columbines, in bloom it is usually from 1 inch to 3 inches tall. Its solitary erect blooms, enormous in comparison to the size of the plant, are carried above the foliage. They have blue or purple sepals up to ¾ inch long and petals with blue blades about ⅓ inch long. The nearly straight spurs, usually less than ½ inch long, are blue. A somewhat less compact form that grows at lower elevations than the dwarfest plants is recognized as *A. j. elatior*. Up to 6 inches tall, it has small leaves with crowded, leathery-textured, pubescent leaflets. *A. longissima* inhabits streamsides and other wet places in Texas, Arizona, and adjacent Mexico. From 2 to 3 feet in height, it has glandular-pubescent upper parts. Its long-stalked, glaucous leaves are mostly thrice-divided. Erect to horizontal and numerous, the pale yellow flowers have spreading sepals up to 1½ inches long and blades up to 1 inch long. The very slender drooping spurs are 4 to 6 inches in length. The stamens are much protruded. *A. saximontana* of the mountains of Colorado is another alpine gem.

Tufted and 2 to rarely 10 inches tall, it has thinnish, twice-divided green leaves and short-stalked, seminodding blooms often nestled among the foliage. The sepals are blue and less than ½ inch long, the petals yellowish-white shading to blue, approximately ⅓ inch long. The spurs are hooked, blue, and up to ⅓ inch long. *A. skinneri*, native to northern Mexico, is perhaps less hardy than others described here. From 2 to 3 feet tall and glandular-hairy in its upper parts, it has thrice-divided basal leaves. Freely produced, its nodding flowers are 1½ inches across. They have yellowish to greenish sepals ¾ to 1 inch long and much shorter greenish blades to the petals. The spurs, straight and light red, are 1½ to 2 inches long. The stamens conspicuously protrude.

European and Asian species of *Aquilegia* include these: *A. alpina* is a variable native of the Alps and Apennines. From 6 inches to 1 foot or sometimes 2½ feet tall, it has pubescent stems and twice-divided leaves. The nodding flowers, 2 to 3 inches across and bright blue or blue and white, have straight spurs ¾ to 1 inch in length and slightly incurved apexes, longer than the blades of the petals. The stamens do not protrude. *A. flabellata* is a very fine, stout-

Aquilegia flabellata

stemmed Japanese species. It has basal and well-developed stem leaves, twice- or sometimes once-divided, thickish, often purplish-tinged, bluish-gray leaves. On stalks up to 1 foot tall three or fewer nodding, blue-purple blooms have hairy individual stalks. Their sepals are recurved at their apexes. The lilac petals are suffused with yellow at their tips. Varieties are *A. f. alba*, with milk-white blooms; *A. f. nana*, a dwarf, 3-inch-tall plant with large flowers, their sepals blue, petals creamy-yellow; *A. f. nana-alba*, similar to the last, but its flowers white; and *A. f. pumila* (syn. *A. akitensis*), not more than 6 inches tall and

with deep blue blooms. *A. glandulosa* of Siberia differs from *A. sibirica* in the upper parts of its stems being glandular-hairy. Up to 1 foot tall, it has twice-divided leaves. One to three on a stalk, the bright blue flowers are suberect. They are about 1¾ inches wide and have extremely short, incurved spurs. *A. jucunda*, also of Siberia, is smaller than *A. glandulosa*. Its flowers have broader petals that are white. *A. pyrenaica* is a variable native of the Pyrenees by some authorities considered to comprise several species. It does not exceed 1 foot in height, and is often shorter. Its lower leaves are twice-divided, its upper ones less. The flowers are bright blue, sometimes with white petals. They have sepals ¾ to 1¼ inches long, petals approximately one-half as long, and slender, straight or nearly straight spurs about as long as the petals. *A. sibirica* as its name indicates comes from Siberia. From 1 foot to 2 feet tall and free-flowering, it has nearly leafless stems, which characteristic serves to separate it from *A. flabellata* with which it is sometimes confused. The twice-divided basal leaves have large terminal leaflets. The somewhat nodding blooms 2 to 3 inches wide have hairless individual stalks, lilac-blue sepals 1 inch long or longer, and petals of the same color or white about one-half that length. The spurs, very markedly curved or coiled inward, are ¼ to ½ inch long. The stamens do not protrude. *A. vulgaris* is a highly variable spe-

Aquilegia vulgaris

cies usually 1 foot to 2 feet tall, sometimes taller, more or less hairy, but not glandular. The lower leaves are twice-divided, the leaflets hairy on their undersides. The many nodding flowers, commonly blue, more rarely white or reddish, have sepals about 1 inch long, and somewhat shorter petals. The strongly hooked, incurved spurs, ½ to nearly 1 inch long, are terminated by knoblike swellings. There are double-flowered forms of this species, which is native of Europe and adjacent Russia and is naturalized in eastern North America.

Garden and Landscape Uses. The taller columbines, especially the hybrids, are exceedingly useful hardy perennials suitable for growing in flower beds and borders and for supplying cut flowers. Their airy, dancing blooms are displayed to good advantage mostly on slender stalks. They are most satisfactory where they get light part-day shade and are generally easy to grow. Those indigenous to the region can be used with good effects in native plant gardens. The smaller columbines, especially those native at high altitudes such as *A. jonesii* and *A. saximontana,* are often provokingly difficult and test the skills of the most experienced rock gardeners. They are suitable only for rock gardens and alpine greenhouses. Many columbines are relatively short-lived, given to dying out after three or four years. It is well to raise replacements from time to time and to discard old specimens that become unduly woody at their bases and show signs of deterioration in their productivity of foliage and blooms.

Cultivation. Columbines are best in sandy loamy soils that contain an appreciable amount of decayed organic matter. They do not do well in heavy clays unless they drain satisfactorily and the soil has been ameliorated by the addition of good compost, leaf mold, peat moss, or humus, and grit or sand to make it less cohesive. New plants can be raised by carefully dividing old ones in early spring and readily from seeds, always remembering that if the seeds are collected from plants with other kinds of columbines growing near they are likely to give hybrid progeny and that the seeds from hybrids do not generally come true to the parent kinds. Seeds of easy-to-grow kinds sown outdoors or in a cold frame about May give young plants that if transplanted as soon as they are big enough to a nursery, in rows about 1 foot apart with about 6 inches allowed between individuals in the row, make excellent growth by fall and may then or the following early spring be transferred to their permanent quarters. Subsequent care is that needed by the run of herbaceous border perennials. It consists chiefly of keeping the plants free of weeds by cultivating, mulching, or hand weeding; deep watering at intervals in dry weather; cutting off faded blooms unless seeds are needed (this tends to prolong the lives of the plants); and removing the killed back tops in fall. Staking is not ordinarily needed. In cold climates a light winter covering of branches of evergreens, salt hay, or other protective material is helpful. Among the easiest rock garden columbines are *A. alpina* in its dwarfer forms, *A. flabellata nana,* and *A. glandulosa;* the most refractory *A. jonesii,* needs perfectly drained gritty soil and a

cool location with possibly slight shade during the heat of summer days. Ample moisture is needed from spring through early summer, lesser amounts in late summer and fall.

ARABIAN-PRIMROSE is *Arnebia cornuta.*

ARABIS (Árab-is)—Rock-Cress. Many of the hundred or so species of this genus of the mustard family CRUCIFERAE are low weedy annuals and perennials of no horticultural consequence. This is true of most kinds native to North America. Several are really good hardy herbaceous perennials; a few are well known and popular. The geographical distribution of *Arabis* extends widely over the northern hemisphere and into South America. Its name derives from Arabia, the homeland of some species.

Rock-cresses are spreading or erect. Most are hairy. The hairs are forked or have radiating branches that can be seen with the aid of a hand lens. The leaves are lobed or not. The white, pink, or purplish flowers, like those of other members of the CRUCIFERAE, have four sepals, four spreading petals in the form of a cross, four long stamens, two shorter ones, and one style. The fruits are pods, of the type called siliques. They contain one or two rows of seeds.

The commonest rock-cress in gardens is **Arabis caucasica** (syn. *A. albida*), which forms loose mats of grayish-green, hairy foliage; the leaves of the non-flowering shoots are rosettes. Its flower stalks are 6 to 9 inches tall or sometimes taller. The blunt, obovate-oblong basal leaves and the ovate stem leaves, the latter stem-embracing at their bases, are few-toothed. The flowers are white, up to 1 inch in diameter, and have petals that narrow abruptly into slender clawed bases. The racemes of

Arabis caucasica

bloom elongate as seed pods form. The rock-cress, in gardens often misnamed *A. alpina,* is native from the eastern Mediterranean to Iran. Especially fine is the double-flowered *A. c. flore-pleno.* Its blooms, which appear slightly later than those of

Arabis caucasica flore-pleno

Arabis caucasica flore-pleno with, at the left, *Iberis sempervirens,* in a rock garden

the single-flowered kind, last longer; they resemble miniature double-flowered stocks. Admirers of variegated foliage enjoy *A. c. variegata* whose leaves are variegated with pale yellow. Similar, but more compact and with smaller rosettes of greener leaves, more sharply-toothed than those of *A. caucasica*, is true **A. alpina.** Its white flowers, in usually shorter racemes than those of *A. caucasica*, are up to ¾ inch across. This native of Europe, Siberia, Greenland, and eastern Canada, is not common in gardens. It is rarely over 6 inches tall.

Arabis caucasica variegata

Pink or purple blooms characterize **A. aubrietioides,** of the mountains of Asia Minor. A low, densely-compact rock-cress, it has weak stems and hairy, green or gray, toothed leaves, the lower ones bluntly-obovate, those of the flower stems pointed and with heart-shaped, stem-clasping bases. The blooms, up to 1 inch across, are in few-flowered racemes that lengthen as seed pods form. A distinguishing feature is that two of the four sepals differ from the others in being markedly pouched. The chief horticultural impact of *A. aubrietioides* has been as a parent, with *A. caucasica*, of some charming pink-flowered hybrids that generally resemble *A. caucasica* in habit. To these hybrids the group designation **A. arendsii** is applied. The best known is *A. a. rosabella.* The hybrids are often wrongly named *A. rosea* which is a synonym of **A. muralis** and is a quite different tufted species up to 1 foot in height from the Mediterranean region. It has blunt, toothed, sparsely-hairy, obovate-oblong basal leaves that narrow gradually to winged stalks and leaves on its flowering stems heart-shaped, toothed, and somewhat stem-clasping. Its purple-pink blooms are twelve to fifteen together in racemes at first nodding, but that straighten later and stretch considerably as seed pods develop. The flowers are ½ to ¾ inch in diameter.

A native American pink- or purple-pink-flowered rock-cress is pretty **A. blepharophylla** of California. From kinds already

Arabis muralis

discussed it differs in the bases of its flowering stem leaves not clasping the stems. It is also less hardy to severe winter cold. A tufted plant, 3 to 4 inches tall, the leaves of this species are spoon-shaped to oblong-elliptic and are fringed with bristly hairs. The roundish petals narrow sharply at their bases into slender claws. The flowers are fragrant and about 1 inch in diameter.

Quite different in appearance from kinds previously described are *A. procurrens*, native to central and southeast Europe, and *A. ferdinandi-coburgii*, of Macedonia. The former is the commoner in gardens. It has underground stems or stolons and forms mats or tufts of low, shining, emerald-green foliage above which arise, to a height of 6 to 10 inches, erect, frail-looking, few-leaved flower stems. The white blooms, about ¾ inch in diameter, are in loose racemes. The basal leaves of **A. procurrens,**

Arabis procurrens

pointed-obovate and narrowing gradually to winged stalks, are hairy at their edges and on the veins beneath, but have hairless upper sides. They sometimes have one tooth on each side. The bases of the narrowly ovate stem leaves do not embrace the stems. Smaller, less rampant, and grayer is *A. ferdinandi-coburgii*. Its leaves lack the bright luster of *A. procurrens* because both sides are hairy. This is a tidier,

less invasive species. Its white flowers in racemes 3 to 4 inches high, of six to nine blooms, are ¾ inch across.

A few other kinds appeal. The densely-tufted, silky-silvery-foliaged **A. androsacea,** up to 2 inches high, has tiny leaves and little racemes of white flowers. It is an inhabitant of mountains in Asia Minor. Of garden origin, **A. sturii** forms tight cushions, 1 inch to 2 inches high, of glossy dark green leaves and has comparatively large white blooms. Both are only suitable for rock gardens.

Garden and Landscape Uses. The more vigorous, easy-to-grow rock-cresses such as *A. caucasica*, and its varieties and hybrids and *A. procurrens* are staple garden plants in temperate and cold-temperate regions. They are part of the regular stock of every garden center and nursery that sells such spring plants as pansies, primroses, creeping phloxes, and English daisies. Once purchased and planted they are more permanent than pansies and English daisies and, in regions of hot summers, than primroses. Common *A. caucasica*, and its variants and hybrids are grand for grouping at the fronts of borders, for massing on ledges in rock gardens, for embellishing dry walls, for bordering paths, and for interplanting with tulips and other spring bulbs in formal bedding. The blooms of the double-flowered *A. c. flore-pleno* last well when cut and are delightful for mixing with other spring flowers in arrangements. Although less widely adaptable, *A. procurrens* has its special uses. It is seen to best advantage when planted in vertical or nearly vertical crevices in dry walls or in clefts in rock gardens. Then its mats of shining foliage hug their rocky backgrounds and a profusion of slender flower stems extend, not outward, but upward, parallel with the rock surface. This kind is also effective for covering the ground over bulb plants that die down after blooming. The other cultivated rock-cresses are most likely to be found in rock gardens and such like special plantings. For these they are best adapted.

Cultivation. Rock-cresses require well-drained soil and plenty of sun. True, some, such as *A. procurrens*, stand part-day shade but, as the saying goes, they are not crazy about it. Apart from these simple needs they call for little else. The tiny rock garden kinds enjoy really gritty soil. The natural species are very easily raised from seeds sown in spring or early summer or, like hybrids and varieties of them that fail to produce seeds or do not breed true from seeds, can be propagated by division or by cuttings. Division is easy in spring or early fall. Cuttings roots readily about the time flowering is through.

For temporary spring bedding it is usual to raise rock-cresses each year and to discard or plant them elsewhere as soon as they are through blooming or are dug up to make way for summer plants. Plants for bedding are started from seeds or cuttings in late spring or early summer and are grown in nursery beds in rows 1 foot to 1½ feet apart with about 8 inches between individuals until early fall or the following very early spring and then are transplanted to their flowering quarters.

With permanent plantings it is advisable, unless seeds are to be gathered, to remove the faded flowers and, with looser and more rampant kinds, to shear stems and foliage at that time too. This checks any tendancy to straggliness and results in more compact plants.

For forcing into early bloom in greenhouses the single- and double-flowered *A. caucasica* and pink-flowered *A. arendsii* varieties are best. For this purpose plants are raised as described above for spring bedding. In early fall they are potted in a nourishing, porous soil in pots or pans (shallow pots) sufficiently large to accept their roots without undue crowding and then are sunk to the rims of their containers in a bed of peat moss, sand, coal ashes, or some similar material in a cold frame. Until they recover from the shock of having their roots disturbed the cold frame is shaded and given minimum ventilation and the plants are sprayed lightly with water two or three times a day. After ten days or so, and gradually, more ventilation is given and finally the cover of the frame is removed entirely and the plants are grown as "hard" as possible until they are brought into the greenhouse for forcing anytime from late January onward. The only protection needed is that afforded by the frames being covered with sash on cold nights and very cold days. Whenever conditions permit plenty of ventilation should be given. Forcing is done in a sunny greenhouse or even in a sunny window in a cool room where the temperature is 45 to 50°F at night and five to ten or, on bright sunny days, perhaps fifteen degrees higher, by day. Water to keep the soil evenly moist. The stimulus of an occasional application of dilute liquid fertilizer is helpful. After blooming, the plants may be set in the garden or discarded. They cannot be forced a second season.

ARACEAE—Arum Family. Horticulturally very important, this family of monocotyledons consists of some 2,000 species distributed among 115 genera. Widespread throughout the world, its kinds, called aroids, are most abundant in the tropics. They include many sorts including aglaonemas, caladiums, colocasias, dieffenbachias, and philodendrons prized as foliage plants as well as calla-lilies cultivated for their blooms and the genus *Amorphophallus*, which contains the curious, commonly grown snake-palm or devil's-tongue as well as the astonishing huge krubi. A prevailing characteristic is the presence in the sap of crystals of calcium oxalate. These sorts, as with dumb cane (*Dieffenbachia*), cause severe, long-lasting pain if plant parts are chewed or eaten in a raw state. Cooking destroys the harmful effects and makes possible the use of taro (*Colocasia*) and some others as food.

Some sorts have tubers, most grow in shade or part-shade in dampish places. A few, *Cryptocoryne*, *Orontium*, and *Pistia*, are aquatics. The leaves of aroids vary considerably according to kind. They are deciduous or evergreen, divided or not, and frequently heart- or arrow-shaped. Juvenile and mature foliage of the same species is sometimes markedly different.

Typically what are commonly called the flowers of aroids are inflorescences, spikes of blooms with an attendant conspicuous bract, which may be green or colored and petal-like, called a spathe. The true flowers, minute to tiny, are crowded along the spike (called a spadix, plural spadices), the males at the top the females beneath. They are without sepals or petals or have those parts represented by much-reduced scales. There are usually two, four, or eight stamens, rarely one. There is one pistil. The fruits are berries crowded along the spadices. Among genera cultivated are *Acorus*, *Aglaonema*, *Alocasia*, *Amorphophallus*, *Arichomanes*, *Anthurium*, *Ariopsis*, *Arisaema*, *Arisarum*, *Arum*, *Caladium*, *Calla*, *Callopsis*, *Colocasia*, *Cryptocoryne*, *Culcasia*, *Cyrtosperma*, *Dieffenbachia*, *Dracunculus*, *Echidnium*, *Epipremnopsis*, *Epipremnum*, *Helicodiceros*, *Homalomena*, *Lagenandra*, *Lysichiton*, *Monstera*, *Nephthytis*, *Orontium*, *Peltandra*, *Philodendron*, *Pinella*, *Pistia*, *Pleurospa*, *Pothoidium*, *Pothos*, *Raphidophora*, *Remusatia*, *Rhektophyllum*, *Rhodospatha*, *Sauromatum*, *Schismatoglottis*, *Scindapsus*, *Spathicarpa*, *Spathiphyllum*, *Stenospermation*, *Symplocarpus*, *Synandrospadix*, *Syngonium*, *Taccarum*, *Thomsonia*, *Typhonium*, *Typhonodorum*, *Xenophya*, *Zamioculcas*, and *Zantedeschia*.

ARACHIS (Ár-achis)—Peanut or Goober or Groundnut. The familiar peanut, goober, or groundnut is the only cultivated species of this genus of the pea family LEGUMINOSAE. Primarily it is an agricultural crop of vast importance as human and animal food and for commercial uses. Among its products are peanut butter, and peanut oil, the latter used in cooking, the arts, and as fuel. The nuts are much used in candies and other confections.

The genus *Arachis* comprises fifteen species, most of them Brazilian. The name is derived from an old one, *Arachidna*, for a clover with recurving, subterranean, fruiting heads. Its members are low, tropical annuals or herbaceous perennials. They have pinnate leaves, with an even number of leaflets (generally two pairs). Joined to the bases of the leafstalks are prominent appendages called stipules. Pea-shaped, the flowers are solitary or few together in the leaf axils. The upper or standard petal is large and wide and the lateral ones are separate from the sharply-pointed keel. There are nine stamens joined, and usually one separate. As the young seed pods form, their stalks lengthen, and they are buried in the ground where they enlarge and ripen. Despite a popular impression and the common names applied to them, the fruits are not nuts. They are pods analogous to peas and beans, but are unusual in the pea family in that they do not split to release the seeds.

The peanut, goober, or groundnut (*A. hypogaea*) is of somewhat uncertain origin

Arachis hypogaea

although there is small doubt that its homeland is South America. It is naturalized in parts of the United States. The discovery, in the late nineteenth century, of jars containing peanuts in Peruvian graves of great antiquity lends substance to this belief. The plant has long been cultivated throughout much of the tropics and subtropics and many varieties are known. A tap-rooted, somewhat hairy annual 1 foot to 1½ feet tall and branched, **A. hypogaea** has stalked leaves with two pairs of broad-elliptic to obovate leaflets, hairless on the upper side, but more or less hairy beneath, not toothed, and 1½ to 2½ inches long. The orange-veined, yellow flowers, in spikelike, axillary clusters, have slender, four-toothed calyxes. They are about ½ inch wide and have long, silky-hairy styles. The blooms soon fade and then their stalks elongate rapidly up to a length of several inches and bury the developing fruits in the ground there to complete their development into the seed pods that are the familiar peanuts. The fruits have wrinkled shells and are constricted between the usually two or three (sometimes there is only one) seeds. For cultivation see Peanut.

ARACHNANTHE. See Arachnis.

ARACHNIODES (Arachniò-des)—East Indian Holly Fern. This group of ferns of the aspidium family ASPIDIACEAE comprises about thirty species mostly natives of tropical and subtropical Asia, but also represented in Africa, and the warm parts of the Americas; there is one species in Australia. Intermediate between *Dryopteris* and *Polystichum*, the genus *Arachniodes* differs from those sorts in usually having long, creeping rhizomes instead of short, erect ones. The name, from the Greek *arachne*, a spider, alludes to the spidery aspect of the clusters of spore capsules.

The only species at all commonly cultivated, the East Indian holly fern (*A. aris-*

Arachniodes aristata variegata

Arachniodes aristata

tata syns. *Aspidium aristatum, Polystichum aristatum*), of Asia, Australia, and islands of the Pacific, has extensive creeping rhizomes up to ⅓ inch thick or slightly thicker and densely covered with brown scales. The rather distantly-spaced fronds (leaves) have stalks 6 inches to 2 feet long, shaggy toward their bases with chaffy scales. Their triangular-ovate blades are 1 foot to 2 feet long by 6 inches to 1 foot wide. They are pinnately-divided, with the upper divisions once more pinnate and the lower ones, which are larger than those above, twice- or thrice-pinnate. The ultimate segments or lobes are toothed and have conspicuous bristles extending from the veins along the leaf margins. The round clusters of small, but numerous spore capsules have covers (indusia) supported on a central stalk. They are in two rows, one each side of the mid-veins of the segments. A variety with variegated foliage is named *A. a. variegata*.

Garden and Landscape Uses and Cultivation. The sorts described are suitable for shaded, humid locations outdoors in the tropics and warm subtropics and for cultivation in greenhouses. They respond best to coarse, porous, fertile soil that contains generous amounts of organic matter such as rich compost, leaf mold, or peat moss and that is kept moist, but not constantly saturated.

In greenhouses winter temperatures should be 55°F by night and up to ten degrees higher by day. Warmer conditions

are appropriate from spring through fall. A humid atmosphere is at all times desirable, but the foliage should not be wetted. Never permit the soil to become really dry, but take care not to keep it constantly saturated. Allow it to become decidedly dryish before soaking, especially with newly potted specimens before the roots have completely ramified through the soil. Except in the depth of winter, shade from strong sun is necessary. Weekly applications of dilute liquid fertilizer from spring to fall benefit specimens that have filled their containers with roots. Late winter or early spring is the best time to repot. Propagation can be effected then by division. Spores supply an alternative means of increase. For more information see Ferns.

ARACHNIS (Arách-nis). Tropical Asian and Indonesian orchids, many very attractive, constitute *Arachnis* of the orchid family ORCHIDACEAE. They are sometimes known by the synonymous name *Arachnanthe*. Arachnises are chiefly epiphytes (tree-perchers), but sometimes grow on rocks or in the ground, especially in moist places where opportunity is presented for the long, rooting stems that are a feature of many kinds to clamber up bushes and trees. There are about seven species. The name, from the Greek *arachne*, a spider, alludes to the forms of the blooms.

Arachnises are allied to *Vanda*, from which they differ most obviously in the lip of the flower being movable instead of fixed rigidly to the base of the column. Some have vinelike stems many feet in length, in others the stems, crowded with leaves, may be under 1 foot long. The

evergreen foliage persists for several years. The blooms, of curious structure, and interesting shapes, are in racemes or panicles and are generally showy. They come in a wide range of colors, chiefly in tones of yellow, brown, green, and purple.

In growth habit *A. cathcartii* and *A. clarkei*, natives of low elevations in the Himalayan region, are similar. They have usually pendulous, sometimes arching stems up to 6 feet long or longer, foliaged throughout their lengths with thick, leathery leaves cleft at their apexes. Those of *A. cathcartii* are linear-oblong, recurved, and 6 to 8 inches long, those of *A. clarkei* are somewhat longer. The waxy, fragrant flowers of *A. cathcartii*, three to six together in horizontal or drooping racemes up to nearly 1 foot long, are about 3 inches in diameter, and have light yellow, similar concave sepals and petals cross-banded with reddish-brown. The lip has two incurved side lobes, white marked with red, and a thick, kidney-shaped center lobe that is yellow with a red-spotted callus. The column is buff-yellow shaded with brown. The waxy, fragrant blooms of *A. clarkei*, rather smaller than those of *A. cathcartii*, and in somewhat shorter racemes, have chestnut-brown, linear-oblong sepals and slightly narrower, sickle-shaped petals cross-barred with yellow. Nearly as long as the petals, the lip has a roundish, chestnut-brown center lobed with radiating white keels and erect side lobes that are from pale yellow to almost white.

Two similar species of Malaya, Borneo, and nearby places, *A. flos-aeris* and *A. hookeriana* have branching stems up to more than 15 feet in length. The rather widely spaced leaves of the first, cleft at their tips, are up to 7 inches long by 2 inches wide, the more crowded ones of **A. hookeriana** are up to 3½ inches in length. Up to 4 feet long, the pendulous flower stalks of **A. flos-aeris** carry many distantly spaced, musk-scented blooms 4 inches across. Their sepals, the lateral ones incurved, and the down-curving petals, are light yellowish-green with spots and bars of purplish-brown. The lip is light yellow marked with purplish-brown. About 2½ inches across, the fleshy flowers of *A. hookeriana* are eight or fewer together in erect racemes up to 2 feet long. They have finely-purple-spotted sepals and petals that are creamy-white deepening to yellow toward their tips. The whitish or purplish lip is striped with purple. A natural hybrid between *A. flos-aeris* and *A. hookeriana,* named **A. maingayi,** more closely resembles the last named.

Most extraordinary, Bornean **A. lowii** (syn. *Dimorphorchis lowii*) is by some authorities segregated with one other species to form the genus *Dimorphorchis*. It has arching stems up to 10 feet tall or taller, densely foliaged with strap-shaped leaves cleft at their apexes into two unequal lobes. They are up to 3 feet long by slightly more than 2 inches wide. The pendulous, flexible racemes of bloom are 6 to 12 feet in length. The flowers are approximately 3 inches wide, and spaced 3 to 4 inches apart. They have wavy, oblong-lanceolate sepals and petals of a yellowish-green obscured by blotches or reddish-brown. The lip is much shorter than the sepals and petals. It is pointed and somewhat slipper-shaped, chiefly yellow spotted with purple, and with a light yellow, fleshy callus. The two or three basal flowers of the racemes differ from the others in having more fleshy sepals and petals that are yellow spotted with crimson.

Garden Uses and Cultivation. In the humid tropics arachnises are suitable for outdoors. They may also be grown in humid greenhouses where a minimum winter night temperature of about 65°F and warmer conditions by day are maintained. They thrive in well-drained, elevated beds of a loose mix of osmunda or tree fern fiber, leaf mold, loamy soil, and coarse sand, with a little manure added, or may be grown in a similar mix in large pots or tubs. The rooting medium must be moist at all times. Well-rooted specimens benefit from regular mild applications of fertilizer. These are sun-loving orchids. In shade they fail to bloom. For additional information see Orchids.

ARACHNOPSIS. This is the name of bigeneric orchids the parents of which are *Arachnis* and *Phalaenopsis*.

ARACHNOSTYLIS. This is the name of orchid hybrids the parents of which are *Arachnis* and *Rhynchostylis*.

ARAEOCOCCUS (Araeo-cóccus). There are four species of *Araeococcus* of the pineapple family BROMELIACEAE. They inhabit Costa Rica, northern South America, Brazil, and Trinidad. The name, from the Greek *araeo,* few, and *kokkos,* a berry, alludes to the fruits.

Members of this genus are low, mostly epiphytic (tree-perching) evergreen perennials. They have inconspicuous flowers with three sepals joined for one-half their lengths and three separate petals. The six

Araeococcus flagellifolius

Araeococcus flagellifolius (fruits)

Araeococcus flagellifolius planted on cork bark

stamens are shorter than, the style is longer than, the petals. The fruits are berry-like.

A distinctive, clump-forming species of spidery appearance of the upper Amazon region, *A. flagellifolius* earns its specific designation by its long, slender, whip-lash-like, bronzy, toothed leaves, which at their bases broaden like great spoons to an extraordinary extent and overlap to form a bottle- or spindle-shaped plant body. They are about 2 feet long. Their upper parts recurve. The small, pink flowers, in broad, loose, many-branched panicles, are succeeded by black berries. Slender **A. pectinatus,** of Costa Rica, is up to 3 feet tall. It has basal stolons and tufts or clusters of arching, tapering, reddish-bronze, mostly spiny-toothed leaves up to 2½ feet long by ¾ inch wide. The pendulous, wiry, few-branched flowering stems are brilliant red above. The floral bracts are small, green, and ovate. The individually-stalkless flowers are in slender, tail-like spikes.

Garden Uses and Cultivation. Of interest to collectors of bromeliads, the species of *Areococcus* respond to environments and care suitable for billbergias. For additional information see Billbergia, and Bromeliads or Bromels.

ARALIA (A-ràlia)—Devil's Walking Stick or Hercules' Club or Angelica Tree, Wild-Sarsaparilla, American-Spikenard, Udo. In addition to the plants that properly belong here, others named *Acanthopanax, Dizygotheca, Fatsia, Panax, Polyscias, Pseudopanax,* and *Tetrapanax* were previously included in *Aralia* and are still sometimes so called in gardens. In this Encyclopedia they are discussed under their modern designations. As now understood, *Aralia* consists of about thirty-five species of herbaceous perennials, shrubs, or small, slender-trunked trees. It belongs to the aralia family ARALIACEAE and inhabits North America, Asia, and Australia. The significance of the name is unexplained. The plants called false-aralia belong in the genus *Dizygotheca*. The five-leaf-aralia is *Acanthopanax sieboldianus*.

Aralias are deciduous. They have spiny or spineless stems. The alternate leaves, clustered near the tops of the stems, are once or more times pinnately-divided into few or many separate, toothed leaflets. The little whitish, yellowish, or greenish flowers are in umbels arranged in panicles often of large size. They have minutely-lobed or lobeless calyxes, five each petals and stamens, and usually five, but sometimes four or six styles. The fruits are berries tipped with the persistent styles.

Tall shrubs or small trees are *A. spinosa, A. chinensis,* and *A. elata.* Known variously as devil's walking stick, Hercules' club, and American angelica tree, **A. spinosa** in the wild inhabits moist and wet woodlands from Delaware to Indiana, Missouri, Florida, and Texas. Exceptionally, this attains

Aralia spinosa

Aralia spinosa in bloom

stalked, narrowly-ovate to oblong-ovate, coarsely-toothed leaflets, hairy on the veins beneath. The umbels of bloom are in panicles up to 1½ feet long. The berries are black. Another herbaceous perennial sometimes cultivated, **A. cachemirica**, native of Kashmir, is 5 to 10 feet tall, and has leaves once-, twice-, or three-times pinnate. Its leaflets are elliptic and up to 3½ inches long by nearly one-half as wide. The umbels of white flowers are in panicles up to 1 foot long.

Aralia cachemirica

a height of 40 feet, but usually it is lower. Its stems and branches are heavily armed with stout thorns, the leafstalks and midribs often with weaker ones. Clustered near the branch ends and 3 to 4 feet long by one-half as wide or wider, the leaves are once or twice divided into firm-textured, distinctly stalked, ovate leaflets 1¾ to 4 inches long. The whitish flowers are in panicles of umbels 3 to 4 feet long. The berries are black. Similar to the last, but with stems less abundantly thorny, leaves without thorns on their stalks or midribs, and with leaflets nearly stalkless, is the Chinese angelica tree (*A. chinensis*). Usually lower than its maximum height of about 30 feet, this native of China has leaves 2 to 3 feet long and panicles of whitish blooms 1 foot to 2 feet long. The Japanese angelica tree (*A. elata*) differs

ican-spikenard, and the udo. The first, **A. hispida** is wild in usually infertile soils in dry woodlands from Newfoundland to Minnesota, West Virginia, and Indiana. It has thick rhizomes and stems up to 3 feet tall, with bristly spines especially toward their bases. The few leaves have stalks generally shorter than the twice-pinnate blades. They have sharply-toothed, ovate to lanceolate leaflets 1 inch to rarely 4 inches long. The slender-stalked panicles are of few to several loosely arranged umbels. The berries are blue-black. American spikenard (**A. racemosa**) is native in rich woodlands from New Brunswick to Minnesota, North Carolina, and Mexico. From 3 to 6 feet tall and freely branched, this kind has aromatic, fleshy roots and few wide-spreading leaves up to 2½ feet in length that have three primary divisions, each with three or five double-toothed, heart-shaped to nearly round leaflets up to 6 inches long. The numerous greenish flowers, in large panicles, are succeeded by dark purple berries. The udo (**A. cordata** syn. *A. edulis*), of Japan and China, is used as a vegetable in those countries, the edible parts being the blanched young shoots. From 4 to 10 feet high, this is without thorns. Its leaves, three- to five-times pinnate, have 2- to 6-inch-long, short-

Much lower than others here discussed, wild-sarsaparilla (**A. nudicaulis**) is an almost or quite stemless herbaceous perennial that grows wild in damp and dry woodlands from Newfoundland to British Columbia, Georgia, and Colorado. From 6 inches to 1½ feet tall, it has long rhizomes, and leaves with three primary divisions each of three or five, pinnately-arranged, finely-toothed, ovate to ovate-lanceolate leaflets 2 to 6 inches long. The insignificant, greenish flowers are in usually groups of three umbels. The berries are nearly black.

Garden and Landscape Uses. Tree-type aralias are among the boldest foliaged woody plants that can be grown in temperate climates. Of those discussed above, *A. spinosa* and *A. chinensis* are hardy in southern New England, *A. elata* considerably further north. Because of their exotic appearance they need locating with considerable skill in landscape plantings. This is especially true of kinds with variegated foliage. Tree aralias are very useful when subtropical effects are desired. Their fruits are much appreciated by birds. The other aralias considered above are generally hardy in the north, but *A. cachemirica* may be somewhat more tender than the others. They are best adapted for semiwild and informal plantings, and the American ones for inclusion in native plant gardens. The udo is occasionally cultivated as a novelty vegetable.

Cultivation. To be seen at their best, tree-type aralias need fertile, moderately moist soil, and this also suits herbaceous

Aralia elata

from its Chinese counterpart in having narrower leaves with more distantly toothed leaflets and panicles of bloom that have short rather than long central axes and spreading lateral branches. Strikingly variegated varieties are *A. e. aureo-variegata*, the leaves of which are margined with yellow, and *A. e. variegata*, which has white-bordered leaves.

Tall herbaceous perennials, or the first a subshrub, are bristly-sarsaparilla, Amer-

Aralia elata variegata

kinds, although the bristly-sarsaparilla prospers in drier, less nourishing earth. The tree types appreciate full sun, but will grow in part-day shade, the others generally prefer light shade. All, except the variegated-leaved kinds, which are propagated by grafting or budding onto thick pieces of root of green-leaved species, can be raised from seeds, which should be sown as soon as ripe or stratified (mixed with slightly damp peat moss and stored in polyethylene bags) for three to, five months at 40°F before being sown. Increase can also be had by suckers and root cuttings. Herbaceous aralias can be raised from seeds, or by divisions taken from the parent plants in spring.

ARALIACEAE—Aralia or Ginseng Family. Widely distributed through tropical, subtropical, and temperate regions, this family comprises 700 species in fifty-five genera of dicotyledons. Abundant in tropical America and Indomalaysia, its members are mostly trees, shrubs, or woody vines, some, like English ivy, that cling by stem rootlets. Others, including ginseng, are herbaceous perennials.

The leaves in this family are evergreen or deciduous, usually alternate, less often opposite or in whorls. Frequently they are very big, usually emit a noticeable odor when crushed, are undivided, and lobed or lobeless, or they may be variously dissected into few or many leaflets. The little, mostly whitish or greenish flowers are in small to very large umbels or compound umbels (umbels composed of smaller umbels) containing unisexual or a mixture of unisexual and bisexual blooms. The petals are usually five. The calyxes are tiny and four- or five-cleft. There are five stamens, an inferior ovary, and one or more often two or more separate or united styles. The fruits are berries or rarely berry-like drupes, a feature that distinguishes this family from the *Umbelliferae*. Among cultivated genera that belong here are *Acanthopanax, Aralia, Boerlagiodendron, Brassaia, Cussonia, Dendropanax, Dizygotheca, Fatshedera, Fatsia, Hedera, Kalopanax, Meryta, Neopanax, Oplopanax, Oreopanax, Panax, Polyscias, Pseudopanax, Schefflera, Stilbocarpa, Tetrapanax, Tetraplasandra, Trevesia,* and *Tupidanthus.*

ARANDA. This is the name of bigeneric orchids the parents of which are *Arachnis* and *Vanda.*

ARANTHERA. This is the name of bigeneric orchids the parents of which are *Arachnis* and *Renanthera.*

ARAUCARIA (Araucàr-ia). Monkey-Puzzle Tree, Norfolk-Island-Pine, Bunya-Bunya, Hoop-Pine. Together with *Agathis* this genus of eighteen species of evergreen trees constitutes the araucaria family ARAUCARIACEAE. Its name is an adaptation of the

name of the Chilean province of Arauco, where the monkey-puzzle tree grows. Araucarias are believed by some botanists to be the most primitive living conifers, and certainly their ancestry is a long one for they are well represented by fossils as far back as the Cretaceous Period, 60,000,000 years ago. Surely they look somewhat prehistoric, none more so than one of the most familiar and the hardiest of the group, the monkey-puzzle tree (A. araucana). Differing from *Agathis* in details of its fruiting cones, *Araucaria* has its seeds united to the cone scales; in *Agathis* they are free. In the wild *Araucaria* is confined to the southern hemisphere where most of its species have limited areas of distribution. In some cases they are endemic to one or two islands. The genus is represented in the floras of South America, New Caledonia, Norfolk Island, New Zealand, Australia, and New Guinea. All kinds produce good quality lumber, and their seeds are edible. Useful resins are obtained from some. The male flowers are in catkin-like cones.

Because of its popularity as a decorative plant for growing in pots and tubs, the best known kind in North America is the Norfolk-Island-pine (**A. heterophylla**), which as a native occurs only in Norfolk Island in the Pacific. This is also popular for planting outdoors in mild regions such as parts of California, Florida, and Hawaii.

Araucaria heterophylla

It is often incorrectly named *A. excelsa.* When young the Norfolk-Island-pine closely resembles the New Caledonian-pine and the latter is sometimes sold as the former. As they age differences between the two species become more pronounced. Altogether broader, with coarser foliage more loosely arranged on the shoots, *A. heterophylla* attains a maximum height in excess of 200 feet, is beautifully symmetrical, and has light green foliage. Its trunk is up to 7 feet in diameter and its branches radiate from it in whorls of usually five. The secondary branches form two rows and spread horizontally or are more or less drooping. Two kinds of leaves are produced, the ju-

venile, about ½ inch long, are awl-shaped, spreading, and have incurved sharp-pointed ends; the adult leaves are lanceolate to ovate-triangular, overlap each other, and lie closely along the shoots pointing in the direction of the shoot ends. The midribs of the adult leaves, which are ¼ inch long, are, unlike those of the New-Caledonian-pine, obscure. The male catkins are 1½ to 2 inches long, the nearly spherical fruiting cones are 3 to 6 inches in diameter. Of the several varieties the following are the most significant: *A. h. albospica,* with its young branchlets and leaves white; *A. h. gracilis,* a compact grower especially well adapted for pot cultivation; *A. h. leopoldii,* compact with glaucous green foliage; *A. h. muelleri,* an especially vigorous grower; *A. h. virgata,* which has slender, whiplike shoots, with short lateral branches. The kind called 'Silver Star' is probably *A. h. albospicata.*

The New-Caledonian-pine (**A. columnaris** syns. *A. cookii, A. excelsa*) inhabits

Araucaria columnaris, young specimen

Araucaria columnaris, mature specimen

New Caledonia, the nearby Isle of Pines, and the New Hebrides. Columnar, this species under favorable conditions attains a height of 200 feet. It has the interesting habit as it ages of dropping its lower branches and replacing them with new shorter ones with the result that mature trees present themselves as dense green columns capped with broader tops. Very characteristically, as they age their trunks lean at a considerable angle from the vertical. The juvenile leaves of this species are awl-shaped and about ½ inch long, the adult leaves are lanceolate-ovate to triangular, have well-defined midribs, and are about ¼ inch long; they overlap, pointing toward the tips of the shoots. The male catkins are 1½ to 3½ inches long, the fruiting cones, often broader than they are long, are 3 to 4 inches in length.

Australian kinds commonly cultivated in tropical, subtropical, and warm-temperate climates are the bunya-bunya and the hoop-pine or Moreton-Bay-pine. The first, *A. bidwillii* of Queensland, is a highly ornamental tree that more closely resembles the monkey-puzzle tree of South America than it does other species, although it is sufficiently distinct to be easily recognizable. Most noticeably its leaves are more loosely arranged, are less rigid, and at their bases are markedly narrower than those of the monkey-puzzle tree. Adult leaves are up to 2 inches long, sharp-pointed, and mostly in two rows. The bunya-bunya attains a height of 150 feet and a trunk diameter up to 4 feet. It is densely-branched, with the lateral branches drooping. As a young tree it forms a symmetrical pyramid, but with age it develops a more irregular top. Individuals are usually unisexual. The male catkins arise from near the ends of the upper branches and are up to 6 or 7 inches long. The fruiting cones, which may weigh as much as 10 pounds, are spherical or egg-shaped, up to 1 foot long by 9 inches wide, and contain about 150 seeds, which are pear-shaped and 2 to 2½ inches long. The seeds mature in their third year, but crops of ripe ones are produced every year. They are nutritious and form an important part of the diet of the Australian aborigines. The Australian government has reserved a large tract of country in which bunya-bunya trees are preserved for the natives.

The hoop-pine (*A. cunninghamii*) sometimes reaches a height of 200 feet, but usually is lower. It is a native of eastern Australia and New Guinea. Distinguishing features are the horizontal cracks in the bark that form hooplike circles about the trunk and its densely-tufted branchlets and more or less asymmetrical crown. The leaves of young specimens are spirally arranged on the shoots. They are lanceolate or triangular, sharp-pointed, spreading, and up to ¾ inch long. On mature trees the leaves are more crowded, shorter, overlapping, and incurved. The male catkins are 2 to 3 inches long. The egg-shaped fruiting cones are about 4 inches long by 3 inches wide. The wood of this tree is

much esteemed in Australia and is used for a great variety of purposes, especially for veneers and plywood. The hoop-pine has been extensively used for reforestation.

The monkey-puzzle tree or Chilean-pine (*A. araucana* syn. *A. imbricata*) is probably the most grotesque evergreen tree that can

Araucaria araucana in its native Chile

Araucaria araucana in a park in Switzerland

be grown in temperate regions and is the hardiest to cold of all trees that are natives of areas south of the Equator. It is commonly planted in southern England and Ireland and in other parts of Europe where winters are not very severe, and is more rarely grown in North America. In very sheltered places on Long Island, New York, the monkey-puzzle tree just survives outdoors, but to thrive it needs milder winters. This native of both sides of the Andes between latitudes 37 degrees and 40 degrees south occasionally exceeds 150 feet in height and may have a trunk up to 5 feet in diameter 4 feet from the ground. In the open it develops a large crown and pendulous branches, upturned at their ends, that sometimes reach the ground; under forest conditions it has a tall, straight, slightly-tapered trunk, devoid of branches to a considerable height, and a candelabra-

like flattened crown. When given room to develop and good conditions, it forms a symmetrical specimen of decidedly unusual appearance under cultivation. The main branches of the monkey-puzzle tree are in tiers of usually five and spread horizontally with their ends curving upward; the secondary branches are horizontal or

Branches and foliage of *Auraucaria araucana*

more or less pendulous and drop off after a few years. The ovate-lanceolate leaves are all of one type and are lustrous, leathery, rigid and very sharp-pointed. Spirally arranged along the snakelike branches, 1 inch to 2 inches long, they overlap. Individual leaves remain alive and retain their rich dark green color for ten to fifteen years, and stay attached for many more years after they have died and turned brown. Most commonly the trees are unisexual. The male catkins, in the leaf axils, are erect and clustered or solitary. The nearly globular fruiting cones are 5 to 8 inches long or sometimes longer, and are slightly less in width; in shape and size they resemble coconuts. They ripen at the end of their second or third year. Varieties of this interesting tree are *A. a. angustifolia*, with leaves thinner and narrower than those of the typical kind and more slender branchlets, and *A. a. aurea*, with yellow foliage. The latter is uncommon. In its native country the seeds of the monkey-puzzle tree are eaten and its wood is employed for a wide variety of purposes including construction, interior finishing, boat building, box making, and making pulp for paper.

Another South American species, the parana-pine (*A. angustifolia*), is the most important timber tree of Brazil. It is similar to the monkey-puzzle tree, but has softer, more loosely arranged foliage, and it is less hardy. As a native it extends into Argentina, Paraguay, and Uruguay. It attains a height of 120 feet and has a flattened, candelabra-like crown of upturned branches topping a long clear trunk. Its leaves are up to 2¼ inches long by ¼ inch wide. The male catkins, 3 to 4 inches in length, develop from the upper leaf axils. The fruiting cones are almost globular and 5 to 6½ inches in diameter; they contain edible seeds. A variety *A. a. saviana*, has glaucous leaves, narrower than those of the typical species.

Garden and Landscape Uses. Lovers of the emphatically unusual are tempted to plant *A. araucana* in inappropriate locations. This species is so very different in appearance from most temperate and warm-temperate region trees that it is all too easy to achieve incongruous effects by its use, and if planted where it does not really prosper the uncomfortable feelings it stirs in plant lovers who have a sense for rightness and congruity are aggravated. The monkey-puzzle tree is displayed best in formal or semi-formal rather than in naturalistic landscapes; it can be associated fittingly with architectural features. Usually it is a mistake to introduce too many of these trees into the picture; attempts to make attractive avenues of monkey-puzzle trees here have not been conspicuously successful. The collector of unusual plants who likes to have something different can usually satisfy this wish without violating aesthetics by selecting the site for this tree with special care, perhaps in a sheltered corner not crowded among, but partially screened by, other evergreens. Other araucarias are much less difficult to place than the monkey-puzzle tree. They are less different from other vegetation with which they are likely to be associated, first because they more closely resemble many other familiar conifers and second because they are not hardy enough to be planted in cool-temperate regions where the appearance of the prevailing flora is so different from that of the tropics. In places such as Hawaii, Florida, and southern California they can be used to good purpose as solitary specimens, in groups, and as avenue trees. Always they should be allowed ample space for growth.

Cultivation. Araucarias grown outdoors prefer deep, moderately fertile, porous soil, preferably reasonably moist, but are surprisingly tolerant of quite dryish conditions. They are at their best where sheltered from sweeping winds. For outdoor use they are best raised from seeds sown in sandy peaty earth kept moist at all times. It is advisable to grow the young plants under light shade from strong sun. When grown indoors the Norfolk-Island-pine and New-Caledonian-pine prefer fairly cool conditions, but they adapt to the warm, dry atmosphere of homes and offices better than might be expected. Under favorable conditions such as those of a cool, light sunroom or similar location where the air is not excessively dry and the night temperature from fall to spring is 50 to 60°F with not more than a five-degree increase by day, they remain at-

tractive for many years. Many thousands of potted plants of these are raised by nurserymen and florists each year. The best are propagated from cuttings, which, if properly selected, produce compact and symmetrical plants. Plants raised from seeds have their tiers of leaves widely spaced and are much less beautiful than those raised from cuttings. Suitable cuttings are obtained by cutting off the top of a plant (these stock plants may be raised from seeds) just above a tier of leaves and then waiting for upright shoots to develop from the branch axils. These are the only type of shoots that make satisfactory cuttings. Cuttings made from side branches develop into leaning, asymmetrical plants that never make a leading shoot and are useless for ornamental purposes. The cuttings are made in fall and are inserted in a very humid propagating case under mist, in a greenhouse. Stock plants produce a crop of new cuttings each spring and may be kept in 6-inch pots for many years. Each spring some of the top layer of soil is removed and replaced with rich, fertile earth.

When grown in pots and tubs araucarias need good drainage, and soil slightly on the acid side that is nutritious and porous. A generous amount of peat moss and sand mixed with the potting soil as well as some dried sheep manure or cow manure and bonemeal are likely to produce favorable results. Repot in late winter or spring just before new growth begins, but large plants do not need this attention every year. It is very important that the soil is never permitted to become really dry; on the other hand, constant saturation is disastrous. Slight shade from strong summer sun is necessary otherwise the plants assume an unpleasant yellowish hue. Specimens that are well rooted in their containers benefit from weekly or biweekly applications of dilute liquid fertilizer from spring through fall.

Diseases and Pests. Neither diseases nor pests are likely to be very bothersome. Young plants are sometimes affected by a blight that causes the branches to bend at their tips and then to die; early removal and burning of affected parts is recommended; repeated spraying with Bordeaux mixture may be helpful. The chief insect pests are mealybugs, scale insects, and indoors, red spider mites.

ARAUCARIACEAE—Araucaria Family. This family of two genera of gymnosperms totaling thirty-eight species is confined as a native to the southern hemisphere, but is absent from Africa. It consists of large evergreen, resinous trees of symmetrical and sometimes strikingly unusual aspect, the hardiest the monkey-puzzle tree (*Araucaria araucana*).

Trees belonging here have branches in distinct whorls (circles of more than two) and usually deciduous branchlets. The fo-

liage of young specimens generally differs in form from and is bigger than that of mature trees. Frequently the awl-shaped to broadly-ovate leaves are in two ranks. The flowers, vestigial and by nonbotanists scarcely recognizable as such, are unisexual with the sexes usually, but not always on different trees. Males are in large catkin-like cones from the leaf axils or at the ends of short branches. They have numerous stamens. Heads of female flowers are terminal on the shoots. They develop into large cones with one big winged or wingless seed on each cone scale. The genera of this family are *Agathis* and *Araucaria*.

ARAUJIA (Araù-jia). This genus of the milkweed family ASCLEPIADACEAE consists of two or three woody vines of South America. The name is its native South American one. The plants have opposite leaves, and flowers in small clusters in the leaf axils. Their calyxes are large and leafy, and their corollas bell-shaped and with spreading lobes, or narrowly-tubular and with spreading lobes. The only kind common in cultivation is *Araujia sericofera* (syn. *Physianthus albens*), of southern Brazil. This evergreen has pointed-oblong leaves, 2 to 4 inches long and about 1 inch wide, dark green on their upper sides and paler and mealy below. If bruised, stems and foliage and other parts emit copious, ill-smelling white latex. The flowers are white or delicate pink, scentless, and up to 1 inch across. The fruits are follicles.

This warm-climate vine climbs by twisting its stems around any support within reach and often forms considerable tangles by entwining its own stems. If trained as they grow, the young shoots can be encouraged to clothe supports such as wires, but often the vine is left more or less to its own devices and should then be allowed ample room so that it does not infringe on the territory of neighbor plants. Up to 20 feet in height, *A. sericofera* withstands light frost; it does well outdoors in California.

Garden Uses and Cultivation. In regions where it is not hardy it may be grown in a greenhouse (winter night temperature 40 to 50°F), in pots, or in beds. It is also satisfactory for setting temporarily in outdoor beds for summer bloom, the plants being lifted before frost and wintered in a greenhouse or sunroom. Pruning in late winter or spring by cutting the shoots of the previous summer's growth back to within two to four buds of their bases is helpful in curbing undue exuberance and is especially necessary with greenhouse-grown specimens. Plants in containers thrive in any good loamy, well-drained soil. They should be watered freely from spring through fall, more sparingly in winter. Propagation is by seeds sown in spring in porous soil in a temperature of about 60°F and by cuttings in March or April. In warm climates *A. sericofera* frequently reproduces itself from self-sown seeds. Its chief pest is scale insects.

ARBOL DE LAS MANITAS is *Chiranthodendron pentadactylon*.

ARBOR. Arbors are plant-covered features or retreats tall enough to stand beneath or walk under. Usually the plants, vines or less commonly trees trained in more or less espalier fashion, are supported by an openwork structure of wood or metal, more rarely trees are pleached to form arbors without supports. Arbors differ from gazebos, summerhouses, and similar features in that the supporting structure is distinctly subordinate to the plants that clothe it. From arches they differ in being longer, from pergolas in being shorter, but the distinctions are by no means precise nor always clear.

Arbor of climbing roses

Besides affording ideal opportunity to display vines effectively, well-located arbors can be pleasing elements in gardens formal and informal. They may frame a gate, shade a seat, or be free-standing features of some prominence.

Arbor of espaliered apple trees

Because arbors are permanent, with supports in the ground, because when dense vines grown on them are very heavy when wet, and because stresses caused by winds great, sound construction is important. Durability is also necessary. Once they are covered with perennial vines repairing arbors is troublesome. In general rot-resistant wood such as cedar, locust, or redwood is the best material to use. Treat less weather-resistant kinds with a wood preservative other than creosote, which is harmful to plants. Arbors of nonrusting metals are effective supports, but are gen-

Metal frame supporting the apple arbor

erally less aesthetically pleasing than wood.

In constructing an arbor let the supporting members extend well below the frost line. Space them to assure rigidity and stability without achieving an over-massive effect. Install all other parts, rails, beams, latticework, etc., so they add to the stability or afford support for the plant cover. If they do not serve either or preferably both of these functions they are unnecessary embelishments, better not installed.

ARBOR DAY. A day set aside and dedicated to the planting of trees is observed officially as Arbor Day in many states of the United States, and unofficially in some others. It also is officially recognized in the District of Columbia, Guam, and Puerto Rico. In the north the most commonly observed Arbor Day is the last Friday in April. Elsewhere dates more appropriate for tree planting locally are chosen.

The idea that led to the establishment of Arbor Day originated with Julius Sterling Morton, who died in 1902. Morton was once Secretary of the Territory of Nebraska and later Secretary of Agriculture of the United States. The first Arbor Day was observed in Nebraska in 1872 by the planting on that day of more than 1,000,000 trees. Arbor Day is usually celebrated by community-sponsored tree planting in which school children prominently participate.

ARBOR-VITAE. See Thuja, and Platycladus. False-arbor-vitae is *Thujopsis dolabrata*. The Hiba-arbor-vitae is *Thujopsis dolabrata*.

In the Strybing Arboretum and Botanical Gardens, San Francisco, California

ARBORETUM. An arboretum, plural arboretums or arboreta, (from the Latin *arbor*, a tree, *etum*, denoting a place) is in its finest expression a botanical garden or part of a botanical garden devoted to the cultivation, presentation, and study of trees, shrubs, and woody vines. It should be oriented toward scientific research and education. In a broader sense the term is used for any fairly extensive collection of trees and shrubs the emphasis of which is on diversity and identification. More loosely the name arboretum is sometimes used for any area planted with a variety of woody plants.

Arboretums usually contain widely varied collections of plant genera, but sometimes are limited to, or place major emphasis on, one genus or group of closely related genera. They are then sometimes given special names such as salicetum for an arboretum of willows, pinetum for one of pines and other conifers. Ownership and management of arboretums may be by private individuals, universities, colleges, other public institutions, or political bodies such as cities, counties, states, and national governments. Some gardens that have Arboretum as part of their official name, the Los Angeles State and County Arboretum for instance, present and care for a rather wide range of nonwoody as well as woody plants. These partake more of the character of a botanical garden than an arboretum as more strictly interpreted.

The most important arboretum in North America is the Arnold Arboretum, Jamaica Plain, Massachusetts. Others of note are the United States National Arboretum, Washington, D.C., the Morton Arboretum, Lisle, Illinois, the Holden Arboretum, Mentor, Ohio, the Strybing Arboretum and Botanical Gardens, San Francisco, California, and the Fairchild Tropical Garden, Miami, Florida. See also Botanic Gardens and Arboretums.

ARBUTUS (Árb-utus)—Madrone or Madrono, Strawberry Tree. One of the most beloved and characteristic trees of western North America belongs here. The madrone or madrono (*Arbutus menziesii*), of the heath family ERICACEAE, represents a genus that consists of about twenty species, natives of North and South America, the Mediterranean region, the Canary Islands, and western Asia. Its name is the classical Latin one for *A. unedo*. Trailing-arbutus is *Epigaea repens*.

Arbutuses are evergreen trees and shrubs with flaking red, orange-colored, or reddish-brown bark, and alternate, toothed or toothless, usually long-stalked, leathery leaves. The small, urn-shaped or globular flowers are in terminal panicles. They have five-lobed, persistent calyxes, and white, pink, or reddish blooms, with five short, spreading or recurved corolla lobes (petals). The ten stamens, which do not protrude, have usually hairy stalks that widen at their bases. The stigma is slightly five-lobed. The fruits, berry-like, usually mealy, and rugged-surfaced, are edible but not very pleasantly so.

The madrone (*A. menziesii*) in the wild varies much in size depending upon where

Arbutus menziesii

Arbutus menziesii (flowers and foliage)

it is growing. Under ideal forest conditions, it exceeds 100 feet, and is the largest member of the heath family, but in the open is lower, and in poor soils and locations and at high altitudes, may be little more than a tall shrub. It is endemic from California to British Columbia. Where it grows in dense stands it is straight-trunked, but as a solitary specimen it develops a short, often leaning trunk, wide-spreading branches, and is picturesque. On young trees the bark peels to reveal smooth, bright orange-red, polished surfaces, on older specimens the bark is reddish-brown, and scaly or fissured. The young shoots are hairless. The broad-elliptic, lustrous, dark green leaves have blades, toothed on young plants and on particularly vigorous shoots, 2 to 5 inches long by about 1 inch to 2½ inches wide. Their stalks are ½ to 1 inch long. Except when quite young, the leaves are hairless. Their undersides are whitish. In spring the flowers are displayed in erect panicles 3 to 6 inches long

and up to 4 inches wide. They have hairy stalks and white to pink corollas ¼ to ⅓ inch long. The orange-red, nearly globular fruits, approximately ⅓ inch in diameter, are borne in great quantities and are very decorative. They are relished by birds. The flowers of this species supply abundant nectar to bees.

The strawberry tree (*A. unedo*) has the distinction of being one of a small group

Arbutus unedo (fruits and flowers)

of several genera that occurs natively in the Mediterranean region and also in Ireland; it is part of what is called the Iberian element in the Irish flora. Up to 40 feet in height, but generally smaller, it is broad-topped and handsome. It has glandular-hairy young shoots and narrowly-elliptic to obovate, toothed, glossy green leaves with stalks about ¼ inch long and blades 2 to 4 inches in length by ½ inch to 1¾ inches wide. The white or pinkish flowers, about ¼ inch long, come in fall in pendulous, broad panicles 2 to 4 inches long. The raspberry-like, orange-red, spherical fruits, ¾ inch in diameter, ripen a year from the time the flowers appear. Variety *A. u. integerrima* has toothless leaves; the low-growing, *A. u. rubra* (syn. *A. u. croomii*) has deep pink blooms; and the dwarf *A. u. compacta* is a shy bloomer.

Scarcer in cultivation than others, *A. andrachne*, native to southeastern Europe, attains about the same size as the strawberry tree. It has smooth, reddish-brown trunks and branches, and young shoots without hairs. On young specimens and on vigorous shoots the broad-elliptic leaves are toothed. They are shining green above, paler on their under surfaces, and are 2 to 4 inches long and 1 inch to 2 inches wide. They have stalks ½ to 1 inch in length. Produced in spring, the downy, broad panicles of bloom are 2 to 4 inches long. Individual flowers are ¼ inch long, and dull white. Less rough-surfaced than those of the strawberry tree, the spherical, orange-red fruits are ½ inch in diameter.

A good hybrid between *A. unedo* and *A. andrachne* is intermediate between and superior to both parents. It occurs spontaneously in Greece. Named **A. andrachnoides** (syn. *A. hybrida*), it differs from the strawberry tree in having longer-stalked leaves slightly glaucous on their undersides, and from *A. andrachne* in its leaves consistently being toothed. The white flowers appear in late fall or spring. The fruits are smaller than those of the strawberry tree. Several variants of this interesting hybrid have been named in Europe as horticultural varieties.

Garden and Landscape Uses. Not hardy in the north, in less harsh climates such as those of many parts of the Pacific Coast, arbutuses are among the loveliest, most ornamental, and most satisfactory of evergreen flowering trees. They are splendid lawn specimens and can be used to good purpose in many other locations. They are satisfied with sun or part-day shade and prefer to be where they are sheltered from drying winds. They succeed in neutral and acid soil of reasonable fertility that is well-drained, but not dry. The strawberry tree is one of the few members of the heath family that grows in limestone soils.

Cultivation. Except that they do not transplant readily arbutuses are easy to manage. It is advisable to grow young specimens in cans or other containers until they are set in their permanent locations, which, for preference, should be done while they are still small. No systematic pruning is needed. Propagation is best by seed, except for selected varieties which must be increased vegetatively. Increase can also be had by late summer cuttings under mist or in a greenhouse propagating bench, preferably with slight bottom heat, grafting onto seedlings, and by layering.

ARCH. A garden arch is a free-standing structure that usually spans a path, serves as an entrance, frames a view, or in some

Arch with roses

A masonry arch with tall yew trees

other way provides a decorative element in the landscape. Usually constructed of wood, masonry, metal, or combinations of these, arches are commonly planted with climbing plants such as roses and grape vines. An arch, very much shorter than an arbor or pergola, has sides usually not more than a foot or two wide. For suggestions on construction see Arbor.

ARCHONTOPHOENIX (Archontophoè-nix) —King Palm, Piccabeen Palm or Bangalow Palm. Two species of tall feather palms, natives of eastern Australia, constitute *Archontophoenix*. They are beautiful trees, much planted in warm parts of the world for ornament. The group belongs in the palm family PALMAE. Its generic name is from the Greek *archontos*, chief or majestic, and *Phoenix*, the name of another genus of palms. It alludes to their regal appearance. King palms in aspect resemble royal palms (*Roystonea*) and are sometimes mistaken for them by uncritical observers. In gardens the piccabeen palm is often, quite wrongly, called *Seaforthia elegans*, which name is a synonym for the entirely different palm *Ptychosperma elegans*.

King palms are tall, bisexual forest trees with solitary, ringed trunks and pinnate leaves up to 10 feet long or longer with sheathing stalks that form a conspicuous column or crownshaft that looks like an extension of the trunk. The flower clusters arise from the trunk below the crownshaft and have many drooping branches and two spathes of equal size up to 2 feet long. The flowers are usually in groups of three,

the center one female, the others males. The small fruits are enclosed in a shell with a fibrous network inside. At maturity they are red and quite decorative.

The piccabeen or bangalow palm (**A. cunninghamiana**) attains a height of 70 feet and has a trunk not prominently enlarged at its base. Its arching leaves have numerous leaflets, green beneath, and often 2 to 4 inches wide. The flowers are lavender or lilac. The fruits are slightly over ½ inch long. Attaining a height of 90 feet or more, the Alexandra palm or northern bangalow palm (**A. alexandrae**) ranges farther north and hence into warmer country than the piccabeen palm but it seems to be almost or quite as hardy as the other in cultivation. The base of its trunk is conspicuously swollen and the undersides of its leaves, which have narrower leaflets than those of the piccabeen palm, are whitish or ash-colored. The flowers are white or cream, and the fruits are about ½ inch long. A variety called the beatrice or step palm (*A. a. beatricae*) is distinguished by the much-enlarged base of its trunk with pronounced rings that often look like steps, and by its leaves, which spread upward and do not arch over and droop.

Garden and Landscape Uses. Among the most stately of the palm family, these trees are beautiful as single specimens, in groups, and in avenues. They grow well in full sun or light shade in any ordinary garden soil, but best in moist fertile ones and are well adapted for cultivation in conservatories. For outdoor cultivation they are suitable in frost-free or nearly frost-free regions only. They are quite rapid growers, especially in their early years.

Cultivation. King palms are easily propagated by fresh seeds sown in a sandy, peaty soil in a temperature of 75 to 85°F. In greenhouses they need a humid atmosphere, shade from strong summer sun, coarse, well-drained, porous soil, and containers that drain readily. During winter the minimum night temperature should be 55 to 60°F, at other seasons five or ten degrees higher. At all times day temperatures may with advantage be five or ten degrees higher than night temperatures. Water should be given generously from spring through fall, somewhat less generously in winter. Well-rooted specimens respond favorably to biweekly applications of dilute liquid fertilizer from spring through fall. For additional information see Palms.

ARCTERICA. See *Pieris nana.*

ARCTIUM (Árc-tium)—Burdock. Of little horticultural interest, these coarse, rather ill-smelling plants of the daisy family COMPOSITAE are most familiar as weeds of waysides and waste places. They are biennials or short-lived perennials, much branched and with large, coarse, alternate, rarely toothed, or lobed leaves. Their whitish, pinkish, or purplish tubular flowers are in somewhat thistle-like or burlike heads, composed, in addition to the flowers, of an involucre of numerous spiny bracts. The name is probably from the Greek *arktos*, a bear, in reference to the rough burlike flower heads. There are four or five rather similar species one of which is wild only in Asia Minor. The others are widely spread as natives in Europe and northern Asia and abundant elsewhere in temperate regions, including North America, as introduced weeds.

Common burdock (**Arctium minus**) rarely exceeds 5 feet in height and has the stalks

Arctium minus

of its lower leaves usually hollow. The leaf blades are narrow- to broadly-ovate and up to 1½ feet in length. The heads of pur-

plish flowers are mostly short stalked and in raceme-like clusters. The great burdock (**A. lappa**), sometimes taller than the common burdock, differs from it chiefly in having mostly solid leafstalks and long-stalked flower heads in more or less flattish-topped clusters. These species hybridize with each other and with other kinds. From the roots of *A. lappa* and *A. minus* a medicinal drug is obtained, and in Japan *A. lappa* is cultivated for its edible roots. The stalks, taken before the flowers open, and peeled and boiled, are said to be a vegetable similar to asparagus and, uncooked, to make an agreeable salad. In days gone by the stems were candied.

Garden Uses and Cultivation. About the only gardens in which burdocks are likely to be grown are those devoted to herbs and medicinal plants. They thrive in any well-drained soil in sun or even slight shade. Seeds sown in fall or spring germinate readily. The plants should be spaced 2 to 3 feet apart. Recommended spacing for field plantings for drug crops is 6 inches apart in rows 1½ to 3 feet apart.

ARCTOSTAPHYLOS (Arcto-stáphylos)—Bearberry, Manzanita. Manzanita is the name used in western North America for members of the genus *Arctostaphylos.* Of the about fifty species all except one are confined as wild plants to that region. The exception, the bearberry, is circumpolar, being indigenous to northern North America and equivalent latitudes in Europe and Asia. The group belongs to the heath family ERICACEAE. Its name comes from the Greek *arktos*, a bear, and *staphyle*, a bunch of grapes. By some botanists *Xylococcus* is included in *Arctostaphylos.*

Manzanitas are evergreen, creeping or upright shrubs and small trees closely related to *Arbutus*, from which they differ mainly in that the ovules of *Arbutus* are many, those of *Arctostaphylos* solitary, in each cell of the ovary. The leaves of *Arctostaphylos* are alternate, undivided, stalked or stalkless, leathery, and may be toothed or not. Often they are held in a nearly vertical plane. The small, urn-shaped flowers are in terminal racemes or panicles. They are white or pink and have four- or five-lobed, persistent calyxes and corollas with the same number of short, rounded, recurved lobes (petals). There are eight or ten stamens. The fruits are berry-like and have granular pulp or are dry and contain a number of nutlets, commonly called seeds. The latter are sometimes joined into a single stone. A characteristic of some species is that they have large, woody bases or rootstocks called burls. From these, new branches sprout freely after the old ones are destroyed by fires that occasionally ravage the chaparral (dense growth of chiefly evergreen shrubs).

Botanically, *Arctostaphylos* is a confusing group. Not only are many of its species

variable and represented by more than one variety, but many natural hybrids occur. Because of this, identification is sometimes difficult. In recent years much work has been done in California, notably at the Rancho Santa Ana Botanic Garden, in evaluating the horticultural virtues of manzanitas and in selecting and propagating desirable kinds.

The bearberry or kinnikinnick (**A. uva-ursi**), of cool parts of North America, Europe, and Asia, is a prostrate, creeping, evergreen shrub, without basal burls, that forms attractive mats of greenery about 1 yard wide. Its leathery leaves are oblanceolate to oblong-ovate and ½ to 1¼ inches long. Their margins are without teeth. The flowers, up to ¼ inch long, are white or tinged pink. The bright red berries, ¼ to ⅓ inch in diameter, are mealy and inedible. The native American populations of this species differ slightly from the European ones in having twigs with persistent hairs and are distinguished by botanists as *A. u. coactilis* with short hairs and *A. u. adenotricha* with long hairs. Horticultural varieties include 'Point Reyes' and 'Radiant'.

Arctostaphylos uva-ursi

Possibly a hybrid between *A. uva-ursi* and *A. columbiana*, spreading and up to 2 feet tall, **A. media** of Washington has

Arctostaphylos media (fruits)

wedge-shaped-obovate leaves up to 1 inch long, short-hairy on their undersides. In racemes at the shoot ends, the flowers are white to pale pink. Variety *A. c. grandiflora* has bigger blooms.

The alpine-bearberry or black-bearberry (**A. alpina** syn. *Arctous alpina*) is a matted, trailing shrub 4 to about 8 inches tall. It has hairless branchlets and alternate, slender-stalked, pointed to round-ended, oblanceolate to spatula-shaped, toothed, crinkle-surfaced, veiny leaves ½ inch to 1¾ inches long. Thin, and with bristly stalks, at the onset of winter they become bright red then turn brown and die, but remain attached. The greenish-white, sometimes pink-tinged flowers in terminal clusters of two to four, have a five-lobed calyx, an urn-shaped corolla with five tiny, hair-fringed lobes (petals), ten stamens with brown anthers, and a style tipped with a headlike stigma. The fruits are juicy, black-purple berries from ¼ to slightly more than ⅓ inch in diameter. In *A. a. ruber* (syns. *A. ruber*, *Arctous ruber*) the fruits are bright red. This variety grows natively in gravelly limestone soils and on limestone rocks.

Other prostrate and low sorts, mostly not higher than 2 feet and with branches that root into the ground, include several suitable for landscaping. The Ione manzanita (**A. myrtifolia**) has usually whitish branches, bristly-hairy when young, and glossy, light green, elliptic to narrowly-ovate leaves ¼ to slightly over ½ inch long. The flower clusters are few-branched or without branches. The white or pinkish blooms ⅙ inch long have hairy ovaries. They are succeeded by greenish berries that split open and soon drop. Little Sur manzanita (**A. edmundsii**) has hairy twigs and broadly-elliptic to roundish, green

Arctostaphylos edmundsii

leaves ¾ to 1 inch long or slightly longer and nearly hairless except for marginal fringes. The usually branchless flower clusters carry pink blooms ⅕ inch long with hairless ovaries. The berries are brown. The dune manzanita (**A. pumila**) has finely-

Arctostaphylos pumila

Arctostaphylos pumila

pubescent twigs, and dull green, obovate leaves ¾ to 1 inch long, slightly hairy above, more densely so on their undersides. The short flower clusters have white to pink blooms ⅙ long with hairless ovaries. The fruits are brown. The Monterey manzanita (**A. hookeri**), occasionally 4 feet tall, is usually lower. It has hairy shoots, and glossy, hairless, ovate leaves up to 1 inch long. The flowers, few together in compact clusters, the terminal ones are white to pinkish and ⅙ inch long. Their ovaries are without hairs. The fruits are bright red and glossy. Variety *A. h. franciscana* has branches with minute, short hairs and larger flowers than the species. It is a low, prostrate plant. The Sonoma manzanita (**A. densiflora**) has many-flowered clusters of blooms, the terminal ones mostly branched. The flowers are white or pink, ⅕ inch long, and have hairless ovaries. This species has finely-pubescent shoots and blackish branches. The leaves are elliptic to oblongish, glossy, bright green, ¾ inch to 1¼ inches long, and are finely-pubescent on their veins and margins. Horticultural varieties are *A. d.* 'Howard McMinn', a fast-growing, mounding spreader, and *A. d.* 'James West', which is lower. Pinemat manzanita (**A. nevadensis**) is an intricately-branching kind with grayish branches, the older ones

Arctostaphylos densiflora

slightly sticky, and bright green, hairless or slightly short-hairy, oblanceolate to obovate leaves about 1 inch long. The compact, few-branched or not branched flower clusters are erect and have many, generally white, ¼-inch-long blooms with hairless ovaries, followed by brownish-red berries.

Several taller manzanitas find favor among West Coast gardeners and landscapers. The hairy manzanita (**A. columbiana**), native from California to British Columbia, is a strongly-branched, open shrub 3 to 15 feet in height and with reddish-brown to purplish-red bark. Its shoots have long, white hairs. Hairy and gray-green, the elliptic leaves are about 3 inches long. The white flowers are succeeded by fruits red on the side exposed to the sun. A more compact sort known as 'Oregon Hybrid' seems to be a variant. Called island manzanita, **A. insularis,** of spreading growth, attains a height of about 8 feet. Its bright green leaves are elliptic, 1 inch to 2 inches long. The white flowers are succeeded by yellowish-brown fruits. Common manzanita (**A. manzanita**) is sometimes called Parry manzanita although this last name is also applied to *A. parryana*. A picturesque, crooked-branched shrub 6 to 12 or occasionally up to 20 feet tall by 4 to 10 feet wide, common manzanita is ex-

Arctostaphylos nevadensis

Arctostaphylos manzanita

ceedingly variable in leaf color and other details. Some variants probably are hybrids with other species. It has smooth, reddish-brown bark and lustrous or dullish, bluntish to pointed, oblong to broad-elliptic leaves 1 inch to 1½ inches long. The pink to white flowers are in ample, drooping clusters. The fruits are white changing to deep red. The serpentine manzanita (*A. obispoensis*) is of striking appearance. Erect and up to about 9 feet tall or sometimes taller, it has twisted branches clothed with purplish-red bark and distinctly grayish-hairy foliage. The ovate to ovate-oblong leaves are ¾ inch to 1½ inches in length. The white flowers are in mostly erect, short-stalked panicles. The fruits are light orange-brown to red-brown.

Arctostaphylos obispoensis

The graceful Stanford manzanita (*A. stanfordiana*) is upright, 3 to 6 feet tall. It has smoothish, reddish-brown bark and slender, longish branches. The lustrous, bright green, mostly erect, hairless, lanceolate-ovate to oblanceolate leaves are 1¼ to 2¼ inches long. The pinkish blooms, in pendulous, loose flower clusters are succeeded by bright red fruits. Several varieties of this species are cultivated. Clammy or sticky hairs clothe the dark branchlets of *A. s. bakeri*. About 4 feet tall and broader than high, *A. s.* 'Fred Oehler' has pendulous

panicles of pink flowers. Similar to *A. stanfordiana*, but said to be better adapted to garden conditions, *A. s.* 'Louis Edmunds', 5 to 6 feet tall, has drooping panicles of pink blooms. Reddish-purple flowers are characteristic of *A. s.* 'Trinity', which otherwise resembles *A. stanfordiana*.

Two other attractive species are *A. canescens* and *A. glauca*. Called the hoary manzanita, **A. canescens** is up to 6 feet in height. Native from central California to southwestern Oregon, it has light green oblong-elliptic to obovate leaves up to nearly 1½ inches long. Its white to pink flowers have densely hairy ovaries. The big berry manzanita (*C. glauca*) is a native of California and Baja California. Up to 18 feet tall and of erect habit, this sort has hairless, glaucous, elliptic to ovate leaves 1¼ to 1¾ inches long, white or pink flowers, and brownish fruits more than ½ inch in diameter.

Arctostaphylos canescens

Arctostaphylos glauca

Garden and Landscape Uses. Not without reason, although possibly with a slight bias toward a favorite group, manzanitas have been described by a Californian horticulturist as "probably the most valuable horticultural asset we have among the many groups of plants with which we are endowed in our highly diverse flora." As furnishings for dryish, mild-climate gar-

dens and other landscapes manzanitas unquestionably rank highly. Nearly all are of good habit and have attractive, foliage, flowers, and fruits. The prostrate sorts are excellent as groundcovers and for clothing steep banks. The lower, mounding kinds can also be used effectively on banks. Taller, erect manzanitas are serviceable in many ways. They are general purpose evergreen shrubs useful for foundation plantings, backgrounds, screens, and similar purposes. Porous soils that drain rapidly are needed by manzanitas. Low, spreading kinds may tolerate more compact earths, taller ones will not.

Extremely hardy, the bearberry or kinnikinnick is admirable as an evergreen groundcover for sunny locations in sandy soils. It serves well to clothe banks, and can be used to good effect in rock gardens and native plant gardens.

Cultivation. Seeds, cuttings, and with low kinds, layering are methods used for propagating manzanitas. Because field-grown specimens transplant badly grow the young plants in pots or other containers until they are set in their permanent locations. Care of bearberry in the East and other summer-rainfall regions is minimal, involving nothing more than possibly an occasional shearing to make it more compact, but usually even this is unnecessary. In dry-region western gardens the best result with manzanitas is had if they are watered with discretion through the summer. Pinching their young shoots during the season of their development keeps the plants compact.

ARCTOTHECA (Arcto-thèca)—Capeweed or Cape-Dandelion. Four South African and two Australian species are the only members of this genus of the daisy family COMPOSITAE. Some were formerly known by the now superseded name *Cryptostemma*, and *Arctotis* has been used as the name of some. From *Arctotis* arctothecas differ in the ray florets of their flower heads being neuter instead of female. The name, alluding to the sometimes densely-woolly fruits, is from the Greek *arktos*, a bear, and *theke*, a case.

Arctothecas are herbaceous plants with short or prostrate stems and generally pinnately-lobed or toothed leaves. Mostly solitary, but sometimes two or three together, the flower heads have usually yellow, infertile petal-like ray florets and a central eye of tubular, bisexual disk florets with five-lobed corollas. The three- to five-ribbed achenes or seed-like fruits are hairless or densely-hairy.

Capeweed or Cape-dandelion (*Arctotheca calendula*, syns. *Cryptostemma calendulaceum*, *Arctotis calendulacea*) is a variable annual. Native to South Africa, it is naturalized in some parts of the world, including Australia, where it has established itself as a pestiferous weed. From 1 foot to 2 feet tall, *A. calendula* usually has a brief stem with a cluster of basal foliage, and more or less sprawling or erect branches. Its pinnately-shallowly- to deeply-lobed leaves are white-woolly beneath and rough-hairy on their upper sides. The showy flower heads, 1 inch to 2 inches across, have the bracts of the involucre (collar of bracts at the bottom of the flower head) with short, narrow, reflexed apexes. The ray florets are bright yellow, those of the central disk usually darker. The flower heads expand fully only in sunny weather, at night they close. The seedlike fruits are densely clothed with silky hairs.

Arctotheca calendula

Garden and Landscape Uses. In California and other places with Mediterranean-type climates the species described is splendid for flower beds, edgings, rock gardens, and gentle slopes. In less salubrious places it is useful as an early-summer-blooming annual, but deteriorates in hot, humid weather. The blooms are not satisfactory as cut flowers.

Cultivation. This annual prospers in sunny locations in well-drained, moderately-fertile soil. It is raised from seeds sown where the plants are to remain, and the seedlings thinned out to prevent overcrowding. Alternatively, seeds may be started indoors some seven or eight weeks before the anticipated date of the last frost. The seedlings are transplanted to flats or individually into small pots, and grown in a sunny, airy greenhouse where the night temperature is 50°F and by day is five to fifteen degrees higher. A week or two before planting out they are gradually hardened off and are then set where they are to bloom, at spacings of 9 inches to 1 foot apart.

ARCTOTIS (Arc-tòtis)—African-Daisy. The name African-daisy used for one species of this group is also applied to *Lonas*. The genus *Arctotis* consists of about sixty-five species of more or less woolly-hairy annuals and herbaceous and subshrubby perennials, natives of South Africa, that be-

long in the daisy family COMPOSITAE. They have alternate leaves and long-stalked, solitary, daisy-type flower heads, with an involucre (collar of leafy bracts at the back of the flower head) of several rows of bracts. The achenes (usually called seeds) are mostly hairy; in the kinds commonly cultivated there is a tuft of silky hairs at their base. The name, derived from the Greek *arctos*, a bear, and *otos*, an ear, alludes to the earlike scales of the pappus (scales or hairs attached to the achenes). For *A. calendulacea* see *Arctotheca calendula*.

Cultivated kinds are annuals or tender perennials commonly grown as annuals. The popular African-daisy (**Arctotis stoechadifolia**), is a branching, bushy tender perennial 2 to 3 feet tall with leafy, ribbed

Arctotis stoechadifolia

stems and toothed, grayish-green obovate leaves up to 3 inches in length. Its flower heads are about 3 inches across and have pearly-white or white-tinged-with-violet rays and steel blue centers encircled with a narrow band of yellow. The flowers are long-stalked. Variety *A. s. grandis* (syn. *A. grandis*) has larger leaves and flower heads than the typical species and the rays of the latter are grayish-lavender on their undersides.

Two popular, attractive kinds are *A. acaulis* and *A. breviscapa*, both stemless or nearly-stemless plants with all basal foliage and leafless flower stalks. The former is a tender perennial commonly cultivated as an annual, the latter a true annual. Perennial *A. acaulis* develops a rather woody rootstock and has oblong, pinnately-lobed leaves, 6 to 8 inches long, with the terminal lobe usually bigger than the others and their margins slightly-toothed; beneath they are covered with a felt of white hairs and when young are white-hairy above. The hairy stalks, mostly up to 1 foot long, support 2-inch-wide flower heads with purplish-black centers and yellow, orange-yellow to almost blood red rays that are wine-purple on their undersides. Rarely exceeding 6 inches in height in bloom, *A. breviscapa* has slender roots and oblong-

lanceolate leaves up to 6 inches in length that are pinnately-lobed; often the terminal lobe is larger than the others. The leaves are green and hairy on their upper sides, beneath they are white-hairy. Two-inch-wide flower heads with orange-yellow rays, sometimes banded brownish or bluish at their bases, and dark brown centers are on hairy stalks 6 inches to 1½ feet tall. The undersides of the ray florets are coppery-colored. The centers of the flower heads are dark brown. In variety *A. b. aurantiaca* the bright orange-rayed flower heads have metallic blue-purple centers.

The annual *A. hirsuta* (syn. *Venidium hirsutum*) is 1 foot to 1½ feet in height, and has pinnately-lobed, toothed, or sinuous-margined leaves up to 6 inches or so long, and like the stems more or less softly-hairy. The bright, orange-colored flower heads, with a dark base to each ray floret, are much like, but somewhat smaller than, those of *Venidium fastuosum*.

Other cultivated kinds include *A. laevis*, a tender perennial with a rather woody rootstock and all basal leaves. It is 6 to 9 inches tall, has usually deeply-pinnately-lobed, slightly-glandular leaves and flower heads up to 3 inches or more in diameter, with metallic brownish-purple to almost black centers and ray florets brownish-orange suffused with scarlet. A rarer tender perennial, *A. fosteri* develops leafy stems and is 3 feet tall or taller. Its deeply-lobed leaves are densely-white-woolly beneath; the terminal lobe is the largest. The upper leaves are stalkless, the lower ones long-stalked. Four inches or more in diameter, the handsome flower heads have brownish-purple centers and ray florets varying from white to pale pink marked at their bases with yellow and purple; their undersides are red. An annual up to 1 foot tall, with pinnately-lobed leaves up to 1 foot long and 1½ inches wide, *A. gumbletonii* has slender-stemmed flower heads about 3 inches across with orange-red ray florets that are brown at their bases. Its flowers are said to last longer when cut than those of most kinds.

Very beautiful hybrids of mostly unrecorded parentage have been developed and are offered by seedsmen. For convenience these are grouped under the name *A. hybrida*. They vary in height from 9 inches to 3 or 4 feet and have mostly large flowers with a quite remarkable color range, including white, cream, yellow, orange, crimson-red, and purple. These hybrid arctotises are very fine ornamentals.

Garden Uses. Where summers are not excessively hot these are among the finest of flower garden annuals, useful for beds and borders and, the lower ones, for edgings and for brightening rock gardens. For the last use, the species are usually considered more appropriate than hybrids. They are attractive cut flowers but do not last overlong in water and, like so many South

Arctotis hybrida

African daisy-type flowers, have the bad habit of closing at night. They do this in the garden too; in fact on dull days they lack the grace to fully expand. Only in sun or at least bright weather do they show their full beauty. Where hot summers prevail good results can be had early in the summer from plants started early and, after torrid weather has passed, plants that survive (not all are likely to) will bloom again, although not as freely and with smaller flower heads than earlier. Good results may be had by growing arctotises for late winter and spring bloom in greenhouses.

Cultivation. Propagation is usually by seeds, which sprout quite quickly, but the perennials are also easy to increase by cuttings. When sown indoors a temperature of 60 to 70°F for the seeds is satisfactory. Outdoor sowings are made in spring as soon as danger of frost has passed and the ground is easily workable and has warmed somewhat. If sown where they are to bloom the seedlings are thinned, according to the vigor of the species or variety, to from 8 inches to 1 foot or even more, apart. Plants raised from indoor sowings are transplanted, as soon as they are large enough to handle easily, to flats in which they are spaced about 2 inches apart or, better still, individually to small pots. They are grown in full sun in a greenhouse, where the night temperature is 50 to 55°F and the day temperature is a few degrees higher, until a week or two before they are to be transplanted to the garden; then they are removed to a cold frame or sheltered location outdoors to harden somewhat before being set in the ground. A danger to avoid is that of overwatering; the young plants stand dryish conditions better than excessive wetness. Their roots are not very compact and so it is necessary to exercise special care to retain as much soil about them as possible during transplanting. Another detail that requires particular attention is that of setting the plants at the correct depth; it is harmful to plant them appreciably deeper than they were in the flats or pots.

To have plants for winter and spring blooming in greenhouses, seeds are sown in late August or September and the young plants are transplanted to small pots and transferred successively to larger ones as root and top growth necessitate. The size of the final containers may be from 5 to 7 inches depending upon how early the seeds are sown and the vigor of the species or variety. At all stages the pots must be very well drained and the soil porous and fertile. Through the winter great care must be taken not to keep the soil too wet; water may be given more generously when the longer and sunnier days of spring arrive. Then, if the pots are well filled with roots, weekly applications of dilute liquid fertilizer are in order. Throughout the winter and spring a night temperature of 50 to 55°F is sufficient and the day temperature may be five to ten, or on sunny days fifteen, degrees higher.

ARCTOUS. See Arctostaphylos.

ARDISIA (Ardís-ia) — Marlberry. Four hundred species of tropical and subtropical evergreen trees, shrubs, and undershrubs chiefly of Asia, the Americas, and a few from Australia, constitute *Ardisia* of the myrsine family MYRSINACEAE. The generic name is derived from the Greek *ardis*, a point or spear head, in reference to the sharp-pointed anthers.

Ardisias have usually alternate, lobeless, elliptic to oblong-lanceolate leaves, with their margins crisped, waved, or toothed, and usually with glands. The wheel-shaped flowers are in terminal or axillary clusters. Comparatively small, they are bisexual or unisexual. The calyx is five-lobed. There are five, rarely four or six, spreading white or pink petals, five short stamens, and a single style. The fruits are one-seeded, berry-like drupes (fruits structured like plums).

The best known kind is **A. crenata** (syn. *A. crenulata*), a native of woods from Japan to Korea, China, and India. It attains a height of 2 to 3 feet and has one main stem with some lateral flowering and fruiting branches from its upper part. The thick, leathery, short-stalked, oblong-lanceolate, toothed leaves have wavy margins and a gland between each pair of teeth. They are alternate and marked with translucent dots. The numerous fragrant flowers, about ⅓ inch in diameter and white, are in clusters at the ends of the lateral branches. Bright red, the spherical fruits are ¼ to ⅓ inch in diameter. A more robust variety is *A. c. taquetii.* Variety *A. c. alba* has white fruits.

The name **A. crispa** has been mistakenly used for *A. crenata.* It properly belongs to another species, a native of woods in Japan, Taiwan, and China, that differs from *A. crenata* in having the upper parts of its stems and flowering branches minutely-downy when young instead of quite

smooth, and the flower clusters axillary and with long stalks instead of being stalkless and terminal on the branches. Its leaves are lanceolate. This species is up to 1½ feet tall and has short-stalked leaves with wavy, toothed margins with a gland

Ardisia crenata

between every two teeth. They are bright green above, slightly paler on their undersides. The white flowers, ⅓ inch across, are succeeded by red fruits ¼ inch or slightly more in diameter. Another native of the woods of Japan, Taiwan, and China, **A. japonica**, is a low-creeping subshrub minutely-hairy on the upper parts of its stems and flower clusters and cultivated, especially in Japan, in several horticultural varieties. The typical kind has ascending stems up to 1 foot in height, each with a few whorls (tiers) of short-stalked, oblong, deep lustrous green leaves 3 to 5 inches long, up to one-half as wide as they are long, and pointed at both ends. The slender-stalked flower clusters arise from the

Ardisia japonica

axils of leaves or scale-like leaves. The flowers, white and nodding and about ⅓ inch across, are succeeded by red fruits about ¼ inch in diameter. The natural variety *A. j. angusta* has slender leaves. Horticultural varieties of this species include *A. j.* 'Hinotsukasa', with curious, irregular-toothed and malformed leaves conspicuously variegated with creamy-white; *A. j. maculata*, with dark green foliage strikingly marked with creamy white; *A. j. marginata*, a dwarf, slow-growing kind with rich green leaves with creamy-white edges; and *A. j.* 'Matsu-shima', which has pink stems and deep green leaves with creamy-white centers.

The marlberry (*A. escallonioides*), often misidentified as *A. paniculata*, is a native of southern Florida, Mexico, and the West Indies. Up to 20 feet in height, it has oblanceolate to lanceolate-oblong, leathery leaves up to 7 inches long, and many-flowered clusters of small purplish blooms succeeded by glossy, black fruits ⅓ inch across. Another New World species, the Guadeloupe marlberry or mameyuelo, *A. obovata* is a small tree or shrub of Puerto Rico, the Virgin Islands, the Bahamas, and some other West Indian islands. It has obovate or elliptic, thick, leathery, slightly shiny leaves and much-branched, pyramidal, clusters, 3 to 5 inches long and wide, of tiny, closely-packed flowers that are greenish with tiny black dots. These are followed by fruits ¼ inch wide or slightly wider that as they mature change from green to red to nearly black. This species, grown in limestone forests, has hard, heavy wood used for posts. Yet another New World species, *A. hirtella*, introduced in 1960 from British Honduras to the Fairchild Tropical Garden, Miami, Florida, has proved very satisfactory in partially shaded locations. It is a shrub 8 or 9 feet tall with elliptic, 3- to 4-inch-long, shiny leaves with faintly-puckered surfaces and slightly-scalloped edges. Its profuse, ½-inch-wide lavender flowers in flat-topped clusters are succeeded by small red berries.

Called duck's eye and shoe button plant because of the appearance of its fully mature fruits, *A. humilis*, native to southern China, Malaya, Indonesia, and the Philippine Islands, is naturalized in Hawaii. In parts of its native territory it is used as a tonic for ailing elephants. A much-branched shrub up to 12 feet tall, *A. humilis* has glossy, elliptic to obovate leaves 3 to 8 inches long that when they first expand are an attractive pink. Its small, starry, pink flowers, in clusters, are succeeded by ¼-inch, white, spherical berries, red at first, glossy black when ripe.

The East Indian *A. polycephala* is a hairless shrub 6 feet tall or taller, with leathery, oblanceolate leaves 3 to 8 inches long that are bronzy-purple when young, and axillary clusters of small pinkish or whitish flowers in June followed by small berries that change from green to red and finally

Ardisia humilis

Ardisia wallichii

to shining black. The clusters of fruit are especially attractive before they reach full maturity. Then, black, red, and immature rose-pink berries are in evidence at the same time. A small species from India, *A. wallichii* is without hairs except on its youngest stems and leaves. The latter are obovate, minutely-toothed, and 3 to 5 inches long. The red flowers, in axillary clusters, are succeeded by red fruits.

Garden and Landscape Uses. Hardy in sheltered places as far north as Washington, D.C., *A. japonica* and its varieties are useful as groundcovers, for the fronts of shrub beds, and in rock gardens. The other cultivated kinds are tropical and are adapted for outdoor cultivation only in warm, frost-

less climates where they are useful as decorative shrubs and as hedges. They are also suitable for cultivating in tropical greenhouses and conservatories. The most popular, *A. crenata* is highly esteemed as an ornamental pot plant. Its bright red fruits remain in good condition and attractive for several months. With its rich green foliage and bright red berries it is an excellent Christmas plant.

Cultivation. Ardisias are responsive to fertile, fairly moist, but well-drained soil that contains a generous proportion of organic matter. Outdoors they succeed in sun or light shade. In greenhouses they should have full sun from October to March, light shade at other times. Propa-

Ardisia polycephala

gation is easy by seeds freed from the pulp that surrounds them and sown while fresh in sandy, peaty soil in a temperature of 65 to 75°F. They also root readily from cuttings. Air layering, too, provides an easy means of increase. This last-named method produces shorter, stockier plants of *A. crenata* than does seeding. Plants raised from air layers and cuttings also branch and fruit lower than seedlings. Cuttings are rooted in a greenhouse propagating case in bottom heat of 75°F and air temperature five degrees lower. Whether raised from seeds or cuttings, young plants of *A. crenata* are potted individually into 2½-inch pots and later, as growth makes necessary, into 4- to 5-inch containers. Good drainage and a coarse, porous, fertile potting soil are needed. The plants are grown in a night temperature of 60 to 65°F with an increase of five to fifteen degrees by day. The atmosphere must be decidedly humid until the plants develop their flowers, then it is beneficial to keep it somewhat drier and to maintain a good circulation of air to encourage the setting of good crops of fruit. Spraying overhead with water should be discontinued while the plants are in bloom. After ardisias have filled their pots with roots they benefit from regular applications of dilute liquid fertilizer. In fall, after the berries are well formed, the greenhouse temperature should be lowered to 55°F. This will hold the plants in good condition without promoting unwanted new growth. Inspect established plants in late winter or spring before new growth begins and repot or top-dress them according to their needs. Those three years old or older are likely to be rather tall and leggy. The best way of correcting this is to air layer them. After the rooted tops are removed and potted, the stumps, if kept in a warm humid greenhouse and watered sparingly, will soon send out new shoots excellent to take as cuttings. Seedlings of *A. crenata* vary to some extent in the size and quality of their berries and in the profusion with which they are developed. When propagating by cuttings or by air layering use only parent stocks of the highest quality. The most serious pests of ardisias are scale insects.

ARECA (Arè-ca)—Betel Nut Palm. Of the more than fifty species of *Areca* of the palm family PALMAE that inhabit tropical Asia, Indonesia, and northern Australia few are cultivated. The name of the genus is a modification of the Malabar name *areec* for old specimens of these trees. By far the best known, at least by reputation, is the betel nut palm, which supplies seeds used as a masticatory by millions of Asians as well as inhabitants of Indonesia, the Philippine Islands, and other islands of the Pacific and Indian oceans. Westerners familiar with the musical comedy "South Pacific" will recall the words "Bloody Mary's chewing betel nuts" as occurring in one of

the popular songs. The common name is sometimes rendered as betle nut palm.

Betel nuts contain narcotic alkaloids, but the habit of chewing them is not considered harmful. It stimulates the flow of saliva and produces mild stimulation and euphoria. The method of use is to spread the leaves of the betel pepper (*Piper betle*) with a gummy substance called cutch obtained from several different plants and lime (calcium carbonate), to put on this slices of betel nut and sometimes cloves, tamarind, or other flavoring, to roll these together, place them in the mouth, and chew. Westerners are likely to consider the habit revolting because it turns the saliva bright red or brown and results in much expectoration. When persisted in, the teeth become red or brown and finally black. The betel chewing habit is of great antiquity. It was described by Herodotus in 340 B.C.

The betel nut palm (*A. catechu*), probably originally a native of Malaya, but now widely cultivated throughout regions where its nuts are in demand for chewing, is a very slender, single-trunked tree up to 100 feet in height, with a quite small crown of pinnate leaves up to 6 feet long. The leaflets are soft and toothed or notched at their ends, the upper ones often more or less joined. The orange or scarlet fruits, usually not more than 2 inches long, have a fibrous outer coating. The betel nut palm resembles other members of the genus *Areca* in being feather-leaved, bisexual, and having the bases of its leafstalks expanded widely and clasping each other to form a crownshaft that looks like an extension of the trunk, also in that its flowers are in much-branched clusters with the males occupying the terminal portions of the branches and the females the lower parts. The flower clusters appear from beneath the crownshaft. The fruits of arecas, one-seeded, ovoid or oblong, have their bases seated in a leafy cup. In the past many palms now placed in other genera were included in *Areca* and they are sometimes still grown under that name in gardens; thus the plant sometimes called *A. lutescens* is *Chrysalidocarpus lutescens*.

The very different **A. triandra**, native from the Malay Peninsula to India, has clusters of slender stems up to 10 feet tall or sometimes taller, and bright green leaves 3 to 5 feet long. Unlike the male flowers of other species described here these have three instead of six stamens. The fruits are red or orange-red. This palm is frequently misidentified as *A. aliceae*. Another with clustered stems, **A. vestiaria** of the Celebes Islands, is about 12 feet tall. The portions of its leafstalks that sheath the stems are bright orange. The leaf blades have about fourteen leaflets on each side of the midrib. The 1-inch-long fruits are scarlet.

Garden and Landscape Uses. Arecas are attractive ornamentals for the humid tropics and warm subtropics. They succeed outdoors in the warmest parts of Florida

and are easy to grow in ground beds and tubs in conservatories and greenhouses. Those with clustered stems make especially attractive tub specimens, well adapted for employment as indoor ornamentals.

Cultivation. These palms are of easy culture. They respond to humid conditions and well-drained soil that is reasonably moist. Indoors, shade from strong sun is needed, a minimum winter night temperature of 60°F, and a minimum night temperature of 65 to 70°F at other seasons suit. Day temperatures should exceed night by five or ten degrees or more. Well-rooted specimens benefit from biweekly applications of dilute liquid fertilizer from spring through fall. Propagation is by sowing fresh seeds in sandy peaty soil in a temperature of 75 to 80°F. For further information see Palms.

ARECASTRUM (Arecás-trum) — Queen Palm. One variable species closely related to and sometimes included in the genus *Syagrus* belongs here. A native of tropical South America, it is commonly planted in the tropics and in southern Florida and parts of California as an ornamental, often under the untenable name of *Cocos plumosa*. A member of the palm family PALMAE, its name is derived from *Areca*, the name of another genus of palms, and the Latin *astrum*, like. It refers to a similarity in appearance.

The queen palm (**Arecastrum romanzoffianum**), is a handsome species 30 to 60 feet in height, with a single, erect, stout-

Arecastrum romanzoffianum

ish, gray-brown trunk ringed with leaf scars and crowned with a graceful foliage mass of glossy green, pinnate leaves of a hundred leaflets or more, each up to 3 feet long and about 1 inch wide, along each side of its central axis. The leaflets, in groups of two to four, spread from the stalk that bears them in various directions and bend downward near their middle, which accounts for the rather disheveled appearance of the foliage. Except at their bases where they are fringed with fibers the leafstalks are smooth. The large, branched flower clusters, each hooded by a pointed, pleated, woody spathe, 2 to 3 feet long, contain numerous bright yellow blooms. The rather fleshy, orange fruits are about 1 inch in diameter and hang in great clusters. Two varieties are commonly cultivated, *A. r. australe* (often misnamed *Cocos flexuosa* in gardens) and *A. r. botryophorum* (syn. *Cocos botryophora*). The latter is taller, more robust, and has less globose fruits than the former.

Garden and Landscape Uses. The queen palm is an excellent fast-growing, but rather short-lived park and street tree and is pleasing in gardens especially when planted in groups of three or more with the individuals spaced 12 to 15 feet apart. Its loose, open crown is easily stirred by even a slight breeze and its glossy leaflets reflect light as they dance and sway with the wind. In Hawaii its seeds are strung for leis and used as earrings. This palm is also sometimes grown in large conservatories.

Cultivation. This species succeeds in well-drained, dryish, rather poor soils. In excessively moist, rich ones it is rather prone to disease. In greenhouses it succeeds in a minimum winter night temperature of 60°F with a rise of five or ten degrees in the day. At other seasons the minimum night temperature should be 65 to 70°F with a corresponding daytime increase. The soil should be coarse, fertile, and well-drained, and kept moderately moist, but not constantly saturated. Well-rooted specimens benefit from biweekly applications of dilute liquid fertilizer. Shade from strong sun and a humid atmosphere are necessary. Propagation is by fresh seeds sown in sandy, peaty soil in a temperature of 75 to 80°F. For further details see Palms.

AREGELIA. See Neoregelia.

ARENARIA (Aren-a̅ria) — Irish-Moss, Scotch-Moss, Sandwort. By some authorities this genus of the pink family CARYOPHYLLACEAE is treated as three genera, (*Arenaria, Minuartia,* and *Moehringia*), but that is not done here. Considered broadly it consists of 150 species indigenous to temperate parts of the Northern Hemisphere. The name derived from the Latin *arena*, sand, alludes to the type of soil many kinds prefer.

Arenarias include annuals, biennials, and herbaceous perennials, the cultivated ones perennial and generally hardy. They have opposite, stalkless or short-stalked, undivided, toothless leaves mostly narrow but ranging from nearly circular to nearly needle-like. Sometimes solitary, more commonly in few-flowered, branched clusters, the prevailingly-white, very rarely li-

lac-colored to pink flowers have typically five, occasionally four each, sepals and petals, twice as many stamens, and two to five, but most commonly three styles. Rarely the flowers are without petals. The fruits are conical or cylindrical capsules.

Very variable *A. verna* (syn. *Minuartia verna*) is often represented in gardens by an extremely compact variety that makes almost mosslike patches or mounds ½ inch to 2 inches high. This is known in gardens as *A. v. caespitosa*, and as Irish-moss, a name also applied to *Sagina subulata*. A

Arenaria verna caespitosa between paving stones

similar variety with yellowish-green leaves (*A. v. aurea*) is sometimes called Scotch-moss, which name is also applied to *Sagina subulata aurea*. At flowering time these plants are besprinkled with clusters of up to four, little, white, starry blooms that sit directly on the mats of foliage. The species of which these dwarf plants are variants is a more or less loose, cushion-forming perennial with linear-lanceolate to awl-shaped leaves up to ¾ inch long. The flowers, solitary or few to many in loose clusters, have petals one-half to one-and-one-half times as long as the sepals. The range of *A. verna* extends through western, central, and southern Europe to northern Russia.

Corsican sandwort (*A. balearica*) is hardy only about as far north as New York City.

Arenaria balearica

A native of islands in the Mediterranean Sea, it forms dense carpets of very slender, branched stems and blunt, broad-ovate to nearly-circular, short-hairy, thick, glossy leaves with blades $\frac{1}{12}$ to $\frac{1}{6}$ inch long and stalks of equal length. The flowering stems are up to 2 inches tall. The solitary, thread-stalked, white blooms nearly ½ inch across have distinctly one-veined sepals one-half as long as the petals.

Hardier and much more robust, *A. montana* makes attractive mounds 4 to 6 inches high. It has more or less trailing stems 4 inches to 1 foot long or longer, and pointed, oblong-lanceolate to linear, short-hairy, single-veined leaves from a little less than ½ to ¾ inch long or sometimes longer.

Arenaria montana

White and solitary or in clusters of up to eleven, the cupped, white flowers are ¾ inch to 1 inch or more in diameter. It is native of western and southwestern Europe. Unlike the last, *A. grandiflora,* native of dry, stony places chiefly in the mountains of central and southern Europe, forms loose cushions of stems 2 to 6 inches long and bristle-pointed, linear-lanceolate leaves with prominent midribs. The flowers are solitary or in clusters of two, three, or sometimes more. They are white, ¾ to over 1 inch in diameter and have petals one-and-one-half to two-and-one-half times as long as the sepals. The latter have prominent mid-veins. Variety *A. g. incrassata* differs in being more compact and having four-angled instead of circular stems and bigger leaves. Plants cultivated under the name of *A. grandiflora* are often *A. laricifolia* (syns. *Minuartia laricifolia, Alsine laricifolia*). A loose, matting plant, *A. laricifolia* has many branched stems 4 inches to 1 foot long. It is native from Spain through the mountains of central Europe to the Carpathian Mountains. It has rigid, pointed, slightly-sickle-shaped, slender leaves and white flowers solitary or in clusters of up to six. The ½-inch-long petals are one-and-one-half to two times as long as the sepals.

Native to the Pyrenees and other mountains of Spain, *A. tetraquetra* forms dense,

Arenaria tetraquetra

gray-green cushions 2 to 10 inches wide. Its bluntly-ovate leaves up to ⅙ inch long, are hair-fringed at their bases, but otherwise hairless. The starry, white flowers, solitary, terminal, and lifted above the foliage, are ½ to ¾ inch wide. They have four or five sepals and petals, the latter up to one-and-one-half times as long as sepals. Compact and up to 9 inches tall, *A. pungens* inhabits Spain and Morocco. It forms loose cushions of stems and spiny gray-green foliage up to 9 inches tall and wider than tall. The leaves are linear to awl-shaped, ¾ to 1 inch long. Lifted just above the foliage, the ½-inch-wide, five-petaled, white flowers are solitary or in clusters of two or three.

Arenaria pungens

The awl-shaped leaves of *A. juniperina* (syn. *Minuartia juniperina*) are spreading or recurved and like the stems, which are prostrate and have swollen nodes, usually rigid. The flowers, in clusters of four or more, have petals one-and-one-half times as long as the sepals. It inhabits rocky alpine and subalpine places in Greece. Similar *A. glandulosa* (syn. *M. juniperina glandulosa*), of Armenia, has flowers with petals twice as large as those of *A. juniperina*. A choice, cushion-forming alpine 1 inch or 2 inches tall, *A. cherlerioides* (syn. *A. are-*

tioides), of the European Alps, has tiny, overlapping, channeled, ovate leaves and almost stalkless, terminal, white, four-petaled flowers.

Lilac-colored flowers are borne by the charming *A. purpurascens,* of the Pyrenees. One of the most pleasing arenarias, it has ascending stems 2 to 4 inches long, branched and leafy above, with only scale leaves in their lower parts. From slightly more to less than ⅓ inch in length, the strongly-one-veined, closely-set leaves are pointed, elliptic-lanceolate to lanceolate. The starry flowers, in rather tight clusters of up to four or rarely solitary, have three- to five-veined sepals one-half or slightly more as long as the petals.

Arenaria purpurascens

Several species that inhabit high altitudes in western North America should be worth trying. Of these *A. kingii* is occasionally listed by nurserymen. A variable species, it is 4 inches to 1 foot tall and usually finely-pubescent. It inhabits dry sagebrush hills and alpine slopes from Wyoming to Oregon and California. Mostly basal, its erect or ascending leaves are ¾ inch long. The white flowers are in branched, loose clusters terminating slender, few-leaved branches. Very dwarf, *A. k. caespitosa* has solitary flowers, and scarcely exceeds 2 inches in height.

Garden Uses. Many arenarias are alpine, subarctic, or arctic plants not easy to please where summers are hot and humid, but satisfying in cooler climates, and inured to harsh winters. They are well suited for rock gardens and alpine greenhouses and the dwarf varieties of *A. verna* for crevices between paving and as neat groundcovers. Some, such as *A. montana,* look well trailing over low rocks, cascading down a miniature cliff in a rock garden, or planted in a dry wall.

Cultivation. Gritty or sandy, well-drained soil that does not hold water at the surface for long periods and that for most kinds is lean rather than fat with nutrients best suits these plants. The popular *A. v. caespitosa* and *A. v. aurea* appreciate richer soil

that does not dry excessively. They benefit from occasional applications of dilute liquid fertilizer. These kinds will grow in full sun if the location is not too hot, but they prefer just a little shade, as perhaps do most other kinds. In time the varieties of *A. verna* build up into little mounds and produce a hummocky condition not out of place in a rock garden but not conducive to a lawn effect. This mounding can be corrected by cutting narrow strips out of the humps and pressing the remainder down. Propagation of these and certain other arenarias is easy by division. Some kinds can be grown from cuttings, most from seeds. In some regions self-sown seedlings are likely to appear as volunteers.

ARENGA (Arén-ga)—Sugar Palm. Most notable of the eleven species of the Indo-Malayan genus *Arenga* of the palm family PALMAE is the sugar palm. As now understood the genus includes plants previously kept as the separate genus *Didymosperma.* Its name is of uncertain origin.

Arengas are short to tall, bisexual, feather-leaved palms with solitary or several trunks. The leaves usually consist of numerous leaflets or sometimes of lobes cut almost to the midrib of the leaf, but not deeply enough to form separate leaflets. Rarely the leaves are undivided. Each leaflet or lobe is cut squarely across or is jaggedly-notched at the apex as if slashed across with a knife and often is notched at the sides also. In these respects the leaves of *Arenga* resemble those of fishtail palms (*Caryota*). Each leaflet or lobe has many conspicuous parallel veins. The flower clusters, one or more at each node, pendulous, many-branched, are usually of flowers of one sex. The males have numerous stamens.

The sugar palm (*A. pinnata* syn. *A. saccharifera*) grows up to 40 feet in height and

Arenga pinnata in fruit at Fairchild Tropical Garden, Miami, Florida

Arenga pinnata, young specimen

has great, spreading leaves 20 to 30 feet long. After many years it flowers and fruits once and then dies. Its lustrous, dark green leaves, with whitish undersides, consist of one hundred to two hundred leaflets spread at various angles from the rachis (central leaf axis). Its stout trunk is covered, at least on its upper part, with the bases of old leaves intermixed with black, needle-like fibers. The many branches of the massive flower clusters hang like huge tassels of rope. Blooming begins when the tree attains maturity, under favorable conditions at about twelve years, and continues for many months. The first clusters to open originate in the axils of the upper leaves. Successively downward other flower clusters develop from the trunk and when the last one has bloomed and fruited the completely exhausted palm dies. The fruits of the sugar palm, about 2 inches in diameter, resemble small apples. Each contains two or three seeds that remain viable for only one month. The fruits are inedible because they contain crystals of calcium oxalate, the same irritant present in the mother-in-law plant (*Dieffenbachia*) and other members of the arum family ARACEAE. The sugar palm is so called because its sap is the source of palm sugar or jaggery. The sap is also made into toddy or palm wine and is distilled to produce the intoxicating beverage arrack. From the trunk a type of sago is obtained and the trunk fibers are used for caulking and other purposes. In India and some other parts of tropical Asia this palm, a native of Malaya, is cultivated for these products. Native in humid, lowland forests in Taiwan and the Ryukyu Islands, *A. engleri* is a tall tree with a stout trunk and leaves up to 10 feet long consisting of many irregularly-toothed leaflets. The globose fruits are dark when ripe. This kind may be expected to tolerate lower temperatures than *A. pinnata*.

Garden and Landscape Uses. Sugar palms can be grown satisfactorily in southern Florida, Hawaii, and elsewhere where climates are humid and essentially tropical. They are also appropriate for planting in very large tropical conservatories such as those of botanical gardens. Few palms are more imposing once they are sizable, but as young specimens they have little to recommend them as ornamentals. Fortunately, their babyhood is fleeting. In fertile soil, with adequate moisture and atmospheric humidity and high temperatures, they soon soar upward and spread their noble plumage so that by the time they are five or six years old they are effective features in the landscape. They are, perhaps, seen at their best as solitary specimens, but can also be grouped attractively.

Arenga engleri at Huntington Botanical Garden, San Marino, California

Cultivation. For best results sugar palms need rich, constantly moist soil. When denied this they are likely to attain maturity, bloom, fruit, and die when much smaller than their maximum height under more favorable conditions, and to have leaves of less impressive size than under optimum conditions. Even so they can be very beautiful. They are best planted in their permanent locations when small and allowed to develop without hindrance or setback. Propagation is by fresh seeds sown in a sandy, peaty soil in a temperature of 80°F. In greenhouses they should be planted in a deep, well-drained ground bed of coarse fertile soil. They are not well suited for growing in pots or tubs. These, even though of the largest size do not permit the root development needed to support a really fine head. Because of their great height the greenhouse cultivation of sugar palms is practicable only in very large and high conservatories in which a minimum winter night temperature of 60°F is maintained. A humid atmosphere and shade from strong summer sun are necessary. For further information see Palms.

ARENIFERA (Aren-ífera). Formerly known as *Psammophora pillansii*, the only species of this South African genus of the carpetweed family AIZOACEAE is now *Arenifera pillansii*. From *Psammophora* it differs in its epidermis not scaling and in technical details of its fruits. The name is from the Latin *arena*, sand, and *ferre*, to carry, and alludes to wild specimens being coated with sand and dust. This genus is related to Mesembryanthemum.

From 4 to 10 inches tall, *A. pillansii* is an erect subshrub branching freely from its base, and with variously shaped, more or less cylindrical, succulent leaves up to 1 inch long by ⅕ inch in diameter, but some considerably smaller. The leaf surfaces are gummy so that dust and sand adhere to them and provide protective shade from the fierce sun. Bright green when young, as they age the leaves become dryish, roughened, and blue-green. Nearly 1 inch wide, the pale pink flowers are in threes. Like others of their family they have a superficial resemblance to daisies, but are really very different. Each is a single bloom and not, like the flower heads of daisies, compound heads of many florets. The fruits are capsules.

Garden Uses and Cultivation. This kind is for collectors of tender succulents. Its outdoor cultivation is limited to areas with climates similar to that of southern California; it can also be grown in greenhouses. Good drainage, full sun, and a dryish atmosphere are needed. In winter the night temperature should be 40 to 50°F, and by day not more than ten degrees higher. At that season very little water is given; the soil is kept nearly dry. From spring to fall it must be moister, but never wet for long periods. Propagation is by seeds and cuttings. For further information see Succulents.

AREQUIPA (Ar-equìpa). This genus of formidably-spined barrel cactuses bears the name of the Peruvian city near which *Arequipa leucotricha* grows plentifully. It belongs in the cactus family CACTACEAE, and by some botanists is included in *Borzicactus*. It is distinguished from *Echinopsis* by its asymmetrical flowers. Endemic to the mountains of Peru and Chile, *Arequipa* consists of five species. A characteristic of these plants is their long, funnel-shaped blooms with scaly perianth tubes and hairs in the axils of the scales. The flowers arise from the centers of the apexes of the plant bodies.

Popular *A. leucotricha* (syn. *Borzicactus leucotrichus*) has solitary or clustered, rarely-branched, erect or prostrate, spherical or somewhat cylindrical plant bodies with ten to twenty ribs. They may attain lengths of 2 feet. From each areole (pad from which spines develop) there are six to twenty spines, the central ones much longer than the others, which are about 1¼ inches in length. The funnel-shaped, slender-tubed, bright red flowers are 2¼ inches long. The globular fruits are about ¾ inch across. Possibly only a variety of the last, the related *A. rettigii* when young has a rotund plant body; later it is likely to become cylindrical. It is up to 3½ inches in diameter and has about twenty ribs closely set with areoles from which radiate spines that practically conceal the body of the plant. The central spines are 1¾ inches long, the radial ones shorter. From carmine to cinnabar-red, the blooms have bright red styles with yellow stigmas.

Garden and Landscape Uses and Cultivation. These are the same as for most of the smaller terrestrial cactuses. For detailed information see Cactuses.

ARETHUSA (Areth-ùsa)—Dragon's Mouth. Two species, one native of Japan, the other a rare inhabitant of bogs and wet meadows from Newfoundland to Minnesota, North Carolina, and Indiana, are the only representatives of this genus of the orchid family ORCHIDACEAE. Their name is that of the nymph Arethusa. These deciduous perennials have solid bulblike organs and erect flower stalks with one to three loose, sheathing basal bracts, and, after the flower expands, a single grass-like leaf that arises from within the furl of the topmost bract. The blooms are terminal and solitary.

The American dragon's mouth (**Arethusa bulbosa**) is 4 inches to 1 foot tall and bears a leaf up to ⅙ inch wide that when mature is almost as long as the stalk. Two small bracts are associated with the flower, which is up to 2 inches long and has lanceolate, magenta, similar sepals and petals, joined at their bases, and erect or arching over the column. The lip, about as long as the petals, curves upward from its base, then bends outward and downward. It has three crested ridges and is pinkish with spots and streaks of purple and yellow. The column fans out toward its apex and is petal-like.

Garden Uses and Cultivation. Occasionally this orchid is transplanted to gardens, but if this is done it should be with great discrimination so that there is no danger of harmfully reducing native stands. Like most native ground orchids it usually does not take well to transplanting nor does it accommodate to garden conditions. If attempted, a site providing conditions as similar as possible to those under which the species grows naturally should be provided.

ARGANIA (Argàn-ia). Little known in North America, the only species of this genus of the sapodilla family SAPOTACEAE may be occasionally planted in warm parts. Closely related to *Chrysophyllum*, it is an evergreen, often spiny-branched, large shrub or tree, native of Morocco. Its name is a modification of its aboriginal one *argam*.

Usually considerably broader than high, **Argania spinosa** (syn. *A. sideroxylon*) is up to 20 feet tall. It has a thick trunk, spiny branches, and hairless, lobeless and toothless, spatula-shaped to oblong-lanceolate leaves ¾ to 1 inch long, in clusters. In

small groups in the axils of the spines and leaves are the minute, stalkless, greenish-yellow flowers. Their parts are in fives. Technically berries, the fruits are plum-shaped to nearly-round and are 1 inch to 1½ inches in length. In its home territory the fruits are fed to cattle, and from their seeds a substitute for olive oil, called argan oil, is extracted. The wood is hard and long-lasting.

Garden and Landscape Uses and Cultivation. In warm, dry climates this species may be planted for variety and interest. It succeeds in well-drained soil in sun, and is increased by seeds, summer cuttings of firm shoots, and layering.

ARGEMONE (Argemò-ne)—Prickly-Poppy. Argemony. The prickly-poppies are well named in that they look like poppies and are decidedly prickly. The latter characteristic serves as a ready means of distinguishing them from true poppies (*Papaver*) without checking less obvious botanical details. The group consists of ten species, all but one annuals or biennials. The exception is the Mexican *Argemone fruticosa*, a shrub. The genus *Argemone* belongs in the poppy family PAPAVERACEAE. Its name is one used by Pliny for an unknown poppy-like plant, the juice of which was believed to cure cataracts, hence the name, from the Greek *argemon*, cataract of the eye.

The prickly-poppies are sturdy, sometimes somewhat coarse, erect, branched plants, with yellow sap, glaucous blue-green or blue-gray foliage, and large, often quite gorgeous blooms. Their leaves are coarsely-pinnately-lobed, with the margins waved and toothed. The flowers have two or three sepals, with hornlike projections, four to six petals, and many stamens. The three to six stigmas (receptive portions of the pistils) sit directly or almost directly on top of the ovary, and are radiate. In this respect the prickly-poppies differ from true poppies, which have more numerous stigmas united to form a many-rayed, conspicuously expanded, crownlike disk covering the ovary. The seed pods of *Argemone* are prickly or bristly. Argemones are all natives of the New World, being indigenous to the United States, Mexico, Central and South America, and the West Indies.

The crested prickly-poppy (**A. platyceras**) is the most commonly cultivated and one of the most handsome. Its stems, leaves, and other parts are densely-spiny, and it grows from 1 foot to 4 feet in height. The flowers are white or occasionally purple and 2 inches or more in diameter. Variants are *A. p. gigantea*, a more vigorous variety; *A. p. rosea*, with brownish-purple flowers; and the hedgehog prickly-poppy (*A. p. hispida*), which is densely bristly and has yellow spines. This species is a native of North, Central, and South America. An-

Argemone platyceras

other popular and quite beautiful kind is Mexican **A. grandiflora**, which grows up to 3 feet tall, and has white-veined leaves and groups of three to six white flowers each 2 inches or more across. This is one of the less well-armed prickly-poppies. Its stems are sometimes without spines or at most

Argemone grandiflora

have a few weak ones. Those on the leaves and seed pods are comparatively few and poorly developed. A variety, *A. g. lutea*, has yellow flowers. One of the showiest prickly-poppies in bloom is **A. mexicana**,

Argemone mexicana

which has peculiarly scented, yellow or orange flowers 2 to 3 inches in diameter, and prickly seed pods. This native of tropical America is 2 to 3 feet tall or sometimes taller. Mexican *A. ochroleuca,* 1 foot to 3 feet tall, has deeply-lobed, glaucous leaves, with light bluish veins. Its flowers are yellow and 1¼ to 2½ inches across. Native from Wyoming to New Mexico and Texas, 2 to 4 feet tall, *A. polyanthemos* (syn. *A. alba*) has fleshy, glaucous, lobed leaves, their upper surfaces without prickles, white flowers 2½ to 4 inches wide, and sparsely-prickled seed pods.

Argemone ochroleuca

Garden and Landscape Uses. Prickly-poppies are grown to provide displays of bloom that begin a few weeks after sowing and continue well into summer. They are appropriate for flower beds and borders and are especially well adapted to hot, dry, sunny locations. Although individual flowers soon drop, a constant succession is kept. These plants are usually grown as annuals.

Cultivation. As with many members of the poppy family, prickly-poppies are sensitive to transplanting and often do not recover well from that operation. It is best, therefore, to sow the seeds in early spring where the plants are to bloom and to thin out the seedlings to about 9 inches apart. Where summers are short it is practicable to sow indoors about six weeks before it is safe to set the young plants in the garden (after all danger of frost has passed) and carefully transplant the seedlings to small pots or flats in which they grow until planting out time. The soil need not be rich, in fact it is advantageous if it is a little on the lean side, because too high fertility makes for excessively vigorous stem growth and leafage without a corresponding increase in the number or quality of the flowers.

ARGEMONY, or prickly-poppy, is *Argemone.*

ARGYLE-APPLE is *Eucalyptus cinerea.*

ARGYREIA (Argyrè-ia)—Woolly-Morning-Glory or Small-Wood-Rose. Of the more than ninety species of *Argyreia* of the morning glory family CONVOLVULACEAE, one is native of Australia, the others of tropical Asia and Indonesia. Most are vigorous, twining vines. A few are shrubs. They have alternate, undivided leaves, and showy, trumpet-shaped, convolvulus-like, purple or rose-pink flowers. The name derives from the Latin *argyreios,* silvery, and refers to the silvery undersides of the leaves. The tender leaves of *A. populifolia* are eaten in Ceylon. The plant previously named *A. tilaefolia* is *Stictocardia campanulata.*

The best known kind is the woolly-morning-glory or small-wood-rose (*A. nervosa* syn. *A. speciosa*). Native to India, Java, and China, this handsome, woody

Argyreia nervosa

vine grows 25 feet or more in height and has broad, pointed-heart-shaped leaves from 6 inches to 1 foot long, green above and conspicuously silver-white-hairy beneath. Their blades hang vertically. The pink flowers, 2 to 3 inches long and about 2 inches in diameter, are constricted at the

Argyreia nervosa (fruits)

bases and tops of their downy corolla tubes. The fruits are clustered capsules. They are rich brown, pointed, nearly spherical, and each rests on a collar formed by the five persistent, ovate sepals. The sepals are lighter brown than the capsule, concave above, and have undersides that, like the stems, leafstalks, and branches of the flower clusters are covered with a felt of fine gray hairs. The collar is about 1¼ inches in diameter. The capsules, each of which contains up to four downy seeds, do not split open. The dried fruit clusters are attractive, and excellent for flower arrangements. The seeds of this species are, according to a report made in 1965, the best plant source of ergoline substances that include the hallucinogenic drug LSD.

Sometimes cultivated in Florida and other tropical and subtropical places, *A. capitata* (syns. *Lettsomia capitata, L. strigosa*) has stems 10 to 30 feet long and long-stalked, heart-shaped leaves, with blades up to 5 inches long. Stems, leafstalks, and the stalks of the flower clusters are clothed with long, soft, brown hairs, the leaf blades with shorter ones. The pink, red, purple, or white flowers are about 2 inches long.

Garden and Landscape Uses and Cultivation. Hardy only in warm climates, these are good vines for pergolas, trellises, and other supports that accept their twining stems. Outdoors and in greenhouses they can be grown very well on wires stretched up walls, and when so trained provide a good cover of foliage. They are also useful for clothing pillars. Sunny locations and moderately rich, well-drained soil are needed. In greenhouses a winter night temperature of 55°F is satisfactory. Any needed pruning or cutting to keep the vines in bounds is done in spring. Propagation is by seeds and cuttings.

ARGYRODERMA (Argyro-dérma). Silver-skin is the literal translation of the name of this genus, which comes from the Greek *argyros,* silver, and *derma,* skin. And argyrodermas are silver-skinned, or at least of a pale bluish-white hue that suggests silver. Belonging in the *Mesembryanthemum* section of the carpetweed family AIZOACEAE, these fascinating, extremely fleshy, small succulents, are natives of a limited region in the South African desert. They are stemless. Each consists of a solitary plant body or of a small cluster of plant bodies of one or two pairs of leaves. If more than one, the leaf pairs are crosswise to each other. Argyrodermas belong to one of several related genera called stone plants, since when out of bloom they so closely resemble the pieces of stone and pebbles among which they grow that they often are very difficult to find in the wild even by experienced botanists. This close apparent mimicry to inanimate objects adds greatly to the interest of cultivators of "flowering stones" as these plants are sometimes called. They are great conversation pieces.

Argyrodermas are readily identified as such by their stigmas being united into a unique disklike or knoblike organ located at the base of a cup formed by the calyx and one side of the ovary. They are often difficult, however, to identify as to species. There is little doubt that too many have been named and that further studies will result in their numbers being reduced from the fifty now recognized. Distinctions between species are based on technical differences of the flowers. Group characteristics, in addition to the critical one of the stigmas, and the color, number, and arrangement of the leaves, discussed above, are that the leaves are smooth and may be short, spreading, and approximately egg-shaped, or sausage- or finger-shaped with flattish upper surfaces. Their lower sides are usually drawn forward to form chin-like ends to the leaves. The leaves are joined toward their bases. Solitary and stalkless or with brief stalks, the attractive flowers come in late summer or fall. They have two small bracts beneath their calyxes, and are bright rosy-mauve, yellow, or white. Like others of the *Mesembryanthemum* clan, they suggest daisies to casual observers. But they differ markedly from daisies in that each bloom is one flower and not a head composed of many florets. The fruits are capsules containing numerous, small, smooth seeds.

Usually misnamed *A. testiculare*, a species probably not in cultivation, the most commonly grown argyroderma is *A. octophyllum* (syn. *A. lesliei*). This resembles *A. testiculare*, but has yellow instead of

Argyroderma angustipetalum

white blooms. It has two to four leaves, each looking like a egg-shaped, milky-blue-gray stone slashed crosswise by the stroke of a sharp knife or axe. The leaves are up to 1¼ inches long and nearly as wide and thick. Their inner surfaces are flat, their undersides drawn forward and upward into rounded chins. About ¾ inch

across, the blooms, with somewhat spirally-twisted petals, are borne regularly and freely. They come from between the youngest pairs of leaves and sit directly on top of the plant bodies. With widely gaping leaves and golden-yellow, very short-stalked blooms 1 inch to 1¼ inches across, *A. australe* has usually solitary plant bodies. It comes from limestone regions. Differing from *A. australe* in that as it becomes older it usually forms clumps, stalkless or nearly stalkless *A. angustipetalum* has 1¼-inch-wide, yellow flowers. Its plant bodies have much the aspect of those of *A. octophyllum*.

Bright, rosy-purple blooms are borne by *A. roseum* (syn. *A. testiculare roseum*), which except for the color and size, 3 to 3½ inches across, of its flowers looks much like *A. octophyllum*. With similar plant bodies, *A. pearsonii* has stalkless or nearly stalkless flowers with magenta-red outer petals and red-striped, ochre-yellow inner ones.

Nearly erect, approximately cylindrical, finger-like leaves are a feature of *A. braunsii*, which, as it ages, forms clusters of growths each with two or four leaves 2 to 3 inches long. Bluish-green to gray, they are sometimes reddish toward their tips. Flowers are rarely produced by cultivated specimens. Also with finger-like leaves is *A. brevipes*, a kind that forms loose clusters of plant bodies each of two erect leaves 2 to 4 inches long and ⅓ inch or a little more in diameter. The leaf ends are green

Argyroderma octophyllum

or reddish, and the light rosy-purple blooms are about 1½ inches in diameter.

Quite different in appearance from most kinds, *A. schlechteri* has a pair of very thick, short leaves joined nearly to their tips so that the plant body looks much like that of a lithops. The bluish-green leaves are up to ¾ inch long and are nearly as broad and thick as they are long.

Garden Uses and Cultivation. Growing these remarkable, beautiful, and delightful plants need not be restricted to gardeners possessed of greenhouses and high skills. They are among the easiest of the stone plants to grow; they can be accommodated successfully even in sunny window gardens. Because they are tender to frost and impatient of wetness and high atmospheric humidity their cultivation outdoors is appropriate only in desert regions where climatic conditions approximate those of their homeland. Elsewhere they are strictly indoor plants. Although all are quite easy to grow not all flower freely and regularly. The popular *A. octophyllum* does.

Argyrodermas are very easily raised from seeds, and from offsets. Their soil must be porous and it is generally advantageous if it contains crushed limestone. It is of great importance that the containers be very well drained. The most pleasing results are had by setting several plants, spaced at irregular intervals, but mostly fairly closely together, in pans (shallow pots) and then surfacing the soil with pebbles or pieces of stone chosen to resemble as nearly as possible the plants. In this way an illusion of their natural surroundings is achieved. Argyrodermas grow in summer and then should be watered moderately, but not excessively. During their winter resting period they are kept dry, although even then tiny seedlings must be given enough water to keep them from shriveling. For more information see Succulents.

Seedling argyrodermas

ARGYROXIPHIUM (Argyro-xíphium)—Silversword. This exclusively Hawaiian genus is a remarkable component of the daisy family COMPOSITAE. Except in choice

botanical collections it is scarcely cultivated, and in those, but seldom. Yet one or more of its members, called silverswords, are well known, at least by reputation, to botanists and horticulturists, as well as to lay visitors to our fiftieth state. The scientific name comes from the Greek *argyros*, silver, and *xyphion*, a flag, and like its colloquial one, alludes to the foliage.

Contrary to rather common belief, there are six, not one, species. Admittedly, they are rather similar, but botanists detect differences. As young plants they develop into handsome rosettes of linear-lanceolate, incurving leaves. In the more familiar species, the Haleakala silversword (**Argyroxiphium macrocephalum**) and the Hawaii silversword (**A. sandwicense**), these are densely covered with silvery hairs. Some kinds, sometimes called greenswords, have

Argyroxiphium sandwicense

Argyroxiphium sandwicense, young plant

broader leaves, less heavily clothed, and are greener. Notable among these is *A. virescens*. When, after a period of years, the basal rosettes have attained sufficient size, in the case of the Haleakala silversword when they are about 2 feet in diameter,

and enough strength for a quite mighty effort, they thrust upward to heights of 3 to 6 feet stout, sticky-hairy flowering stems, that rarely branch, bearing from the bases to the bottoms of the blooming parts numerous alternate, drooping leaves. As with other members of the daisy family, the miniature flowers (called florets) are grouped in heads surrounded by collars of bracts called involucres. The flower heads are numerous and are in racemes or panicles, but are not especially beautiful. Their centers are yellowish and, like the eyes of daisies, are of disk florets. The short ray florets (those that are strap-shaped and look like petals) are purplish. Following flowering, great quantities of seeds develop. As with the century plant, the effort of blooming and seed production so exhausts the plants that they die.

Silverswords inhabit cinder cones and craters of volcanos at high elevations. Because of depredations by man and ravages by insects and disease they are now much less plentiful than formerly and some kinds may become extinct, which would be sad. An interesting association of the Hawaii silversword is that almost certainly the first botanist to become acquainted with it was David Douglas of Douglas-fir fame. Douglas is buried in Honolulu. He was killed in 1834 in Hawaii by a wild bull in a pit dug to trap animals. It is believed that he was purposely pushed to his death by a former convict.

Garden Uses and Cultivation. Under greenhouse conditions in regions of cool summers silverswords grow with fair ease, but they do not prosper where hot summers are the rule. At Longwood Gardens in Pennsylvania they are successfully cultivated in an air-cooled greenhouse. They need fertile, porous earth and moderate, most certainly not excessive, watering. They prosper where the night temperature in winter is 50 to 55°F with a rise of five to ten degrees by day. Well-rooted specimens appreciate applications of dilute fertilizer. Propagation is by seed.

ARIDARIA (Arid-ària). The genus *Aridaria* of the carpetweed family AIZOACEAE enjoys a wide range through South Africa. It comprises more than ninety species. Its name, alluding to the type of habitats it favors, is derived from the Latin *aridus*, dry. This genus has also been known by the now invalid name *Nycteranthus*.

Aridarias are succulent subshrubs of the *Mesembryanthemum* relationship. They have opposite, fleshy leaves those of each pair not or very slightly united at their bases. They are angled or cylindrical, spreading to more or less forward-pointing. Solitary or in threes, the flowers are somewhat daisy-like in aspect, but not in structure. Each is a single bloom, not a flower head of many florets. They generally have five or six sepals, several circles of petals, many stamens and staminodes (nonfunctional stamens), and four or five stigmas. The fruits are capsules.

Its branches spreading, **A. pentagona** has rather distantly-spaced leaves, opposite or alternate, erect or inclined, pale green to glaucous and up to about 1 inch long by ⅛ inch thick. They are cylindrical or sometimes semicylindrical, with flat or concave upper sides. The orange-colored to golden-brown, solitary flowers are a little over 1 inch wide. Variety *A. p. occidentalis* has considerably larger, light salmon-red blooms. A vigorous, cushiony, freely-branched subshrub, **A. splendens** will in a single season cover one square yard of ground. It has cylindrical, incurved, light green leaves up to 1 inch long, with darker green, pimple-like tubercles. The showy, yellowish-white to white flowers, 1 inch to 1¼ inches wide, are produced in profusion. They have toothed petals. Up to about 1¼ feet high, the sparsely-branched, erect **A. defoliata** (syn. *A. radicans*) has semicylindrical, spreading leaves, slightly glaucous and approximately 1½ inches long by about ⅛ inch wide. At the ends of repeatedly three-forked branches, the white to straw-yellow flowers are about 1¼ inches wide.

Garden and Landscape Uses and Cultivation. Aridarias are well suited for groundcovers, rock gardens, and similar outdoor uses in dry, warm climates, and for greenhouse collections of succulents. They are easy to grow in well-drained soil in sunny locations and can be propagated with great ease from cuttings and seeds. Care must be exercised that they are not over-watered, especially in winter. Indoors, temperatures in winter should be 45 to 50°F at night, a few degrees warmer by day. On all favorable occasions ventilate the greenhouse freely.

ARIKURYROBA (Arikuryrò-ba)—Arikury Palm. Botanists recognize three Brazilian species as constituting *Arikuryroba* of the palm family PALMAE, but only one seems to have entered horticulture. The name is derived from a vernacular Indian one.

Brought to southern Florida early in the twentieth century and cultivated successfully, but not very commonly there, **A. schizophylla** is well suited for humid, tropical climates. A low, slender-trunked species, it has a solitary stem not over about 8 feet tall. Its upper part is clothed with the erect remains of the bases of the stalks of leaves that have fallen, thus creating an illusion that the trunk widens upward. The rather dense, comparatively large crown consists of many gracefully arching pinnate leaves up to 8 feet long by 3 feet wide, with purple or blackish, spiny stalks. There are forty leaflets or more on each side of the central leafstalk which is raised on its upper side into a prominent, pointed ridge. The flower clusters, axillary and shorter than the foliage, develop in winter, and on plants even as young as three or four

years. They have two spathes, the inner of which is 2 to 3 feet long and up to 10 inches wide. There are both male and female flowers in each cluster, the former more numerous, smaller than the females, and mostly on the upper portions of the branches. Hanging in grapelike clusters, the edible fruits, the pulp of which is apricot-flavored, mature some eight to ten months after flowering. Each is ¾ to 1 inch in diameter and at maturity bright orange.

Garden and Landscape Uses. The arikury palm is an attractive ornamental that because of its size is well adapted for small properties where it can be installed advantageously in mixed plantings and used in association with buildings and other architectural features and as a lawn specimen. It is also an excellent decorative plant for growing in containers.

Cultivation. Outdoors this species thrives in any fairly good, well-drained garden soil not excessively dry. It will grow in full sun, but succeeds better where it receives partial shade as from a nearby building or large tree. Old leaves that have died should be cut off as close to the trunk as practicable. In greenhouses the plant can be accommodated in well-drained ground beds or in large pots or tubs. A minimum winter night temperature of 60°F is desirable and a humid atmosphere and shade from bright sun are necessary. Propagation is by seeds, which, cleaned of their surrounding pulp and sown while fresh in a sandy, peaty soil in a temperature of 80°F, germinate in a month or less. For further information see Palms.

ARIL. This is an appendage that partially or completely covers the seeds of certain plants. In *Celastrus, Euonymus,* and some other kinds the arils are often brightly colored.

ARIOCARPUS (Ario-cárpus)—Seven Stars. Coming upon these plants out of bloom anyone unfamiliar with the variety of forms cactuses assume might easily suppose them to be curious rock formations or something akin to petrified sunflowers. At that stage they give no hint of the pretty flowers they develop in due season, ordinarily in fall. Belonging to the cactus family CACTACEAE, and numbering four species, *Ariocarpus* in the wild is confined to the Chihuahuan desert of Mexico, with a brief extension of one species into Texas. It favors limestone and gypsum soils. The name derives from that of the old genus *Aria* (now *Sorbus*), and the Greek *karpos*, a fruit, and alludes to superficial similarities of the fruits. Plants treated in this Encyclopedia as *Roseocactus,* and *Neogomesia* are frequently included in *Ariocarpus.*

Ariocarpuses are low, generally branchless plants, spineless or nearly so. They have a thick rootstock and a top-shaped to nearly spherical stem around which spiral to form a rosette, tough, fleshy appen-

dages called tubercles. These are short, or long and leaflike, and in section are triangular or prismatic. Their upper sides wrinkled, or smooth, in some species have a central, woolly rut, or a little woolly spot (an areole) at or near the apex. The flowers open only by day, and are short-lived. They develop from near the centers of the plants, from the woolly bases of the tubercles, and are bell- to shortly funnel-shaped with many spreading perianth segments (petals), numerous stamens, and five to sixteen stigmas. The small oblong fruits, hidden among the woolly hairs, decay and distribute their seeds without falling from the plants.

Seven stars (**A. retusus** syn. *A. furfuraceus*) is a gray- to blue-green, rounded-topped, quite variable species from 4 to 10 inches in diameter, and woolly at the center. The leaflike tubercles, crowded at the base of the plant, and often wrinkled, are ¾ inch to 1½ inches long, and almost as

Ariocarpus retusus

wide. They have areoles at their apexes, but are without grooves on their upper sides. The flowers, white often more or less marked with magenta, are almost or quite 2 inches across. Differing from *A. retusus* in the tubercles not being basally compressed and in not having areoles at their apexes, **A. trigonus** is 4 inches to 1

Ariocarpus trigonus

foot in diameter, and has triangular tubercles. Its pale yellow to cream flowers are up to 2 inches wide. Their petals sometimes have reddish midribs. The only other species without areoles at the tips of the tubercles is *A. scapharostrus,* a gray-green species up to 3 inches in diameter. Its tubercles are not basally compressed, nor are they grooved. The bright, reddish-purple blooms are up to 1½ inches in diameter.

Garden Uses and Cultivation. In the wild these strange plants grow with most of their bodies buried, and only the upper parts showing at or above the surface. They may be exposed to brilliant sun or be where they receive a little shade from nearby bushes. Outdoors in desert and semidesert regions they may be given much the same conditions in rock gardens and similar places. But in greenhouses in more humid climates they do better if more of the plant bodies are out of the soil and if they receive sufficient shade to break the full intensity of summer sun. They are kept dry in winter and watered with some caution from spring to fall. Some growers recommend that the tops of the plants never be wetted, others permit this. Soil drainage must be perfect. Ariocarpuses find agreeable sandy earth containing a small proportion of leaf mold, and some crushed limestone or gypsum. It is sometimes recommended that the pots in which these plants are grown be stood inside larger ones, with the space between filled with regular cactus soil, which alone is watered, the roots receiving enough moisture by absorption through the walls of the inner clay pot. For more information see Cactuses.

ARIOPSIS (Ari-ópsis). The only species of *Ariopsis* of the arum family ARACEAE has a name directing attention to a relationship and similarity. It derives from that of the genus *Arum,* and the Greek *opsis,* similar to.

A low, tuberous, deciduous herbaceous perennial of Indomalasia, *A. peltata* has somewhat the appearance of a green-leaved caladium. Its tuber is 1 inch to 1½ inches in diameter. Its slender-stalked leaves have stalks 6 to 8 inches long and heart-shaped to ovate blades up to 8 inches long by 6 inches wide and glaucous on their undersides. The leafstalk is attached to the blade at some little distance in from the margin. The inflorescences (commonly called flowers) develop with the new foliage. Slender-stalked, they have an ovate, purple-brown spathe (bract) 6 to 8 inches long by 4 or 5 inches wide. The spadix (spike) is furnished with tiny unisexual flowers, the males with three stamens. It is approximately ½ inch long. The fruits are dry berries.

Garden Uses and Cultivation. This is suitable for inclusion in choice collections of tropical plants. It needs the same culture as Caladiums.

ARISAEMA (Arisaè-ma)—Jack-in-the-Pulpit or Indian-Turnip. These relatives of calla-lilies (*Zantedeschia*) and caladiums number 150 species. The group is widely disseminated in East Africa, Asia, and, in fewer numbers, North America. It belongs in the arum family ARACEAE, and thus arisaemas are aroids. The name is from the Greek *aris,* an arum, and *aima,* blood red, and refers to the red-blotched leaves of some kinds.

Arisaemas are tuberous or rarely rhizomatous herbaceous perennials. The arrangement of their floral parts is similar to that of calla-lilies and other aroids. There is a spadix (central spikelike column) crowded with many small unisexual flowers and a more or less leafy bract called a spathe, which in *Arisaema,* as in many other members of the arum family, surrounds or envelops the spadix, and in most species of *Arisaema* bends to form a hood over it. *Arisaema* is closely related to *Arum,* differing in that its spadix is without sterile flowers. The leaves of *Arisaema,* which appear with the flowers, have slender stalks and the blades are divided into three or more lobes. The fruits are berries.

The two most familiar species in North America are the jack-in-the-pulpit or Indian-turnip (*A. triphyllum*) and the dragon root or green dragon (*A. dracontium*). The former is a frequent inhabitant of moist woods from Nova Scotia to Minnesota, Florida, and Louisiana, the latter favors similar habitats from Quebec to Minnesota, Florida, and Texas and is more abundant in the western part of its range. The jack-in-the-pulpit (*A. triphyllum*) commonly has two leaves, each of three large,

Ariopsis peltala

Arisaema triphyllum

pointed leaflets, that at flowering time in spring are 1 foot to 2 feet tall, but may lengthen considerably later. The flowering stalk is erect and up to 8 inches long. The hooded spathe and spadix have a beautiful sculptured appearance and together form an attractive inflorescence. The inside of the spathe is deep purple or bronzy-purple, with paler longitudinal stripes. On the outside it is greenish marked to a greater or lesser extent with purple. An attractive feature is the spike of bright red berries, each the size of a pea, that succeeds the blooms and, after the spathe has died away are exposed in their full beauty.

The dragon root or green dragon (*A. dracontium*) is entirely different. Its corms (bulbs) are in clusters and there is usually only one leaf, at flowering time 1 foot to 1½ feet tall, but later attaining a height up to 3 feet. Its blade is divided into five to seventeen segments, the longest up to 8 inches in length. The flowering stem is shorter than the leafstalk. The spathe is slender and green and envelops the lower part of the spadix, but the latter, long and tail-like, protrudes for from 2 to 4 inches. The berries are orange-red.

The temperate Asian species are not well known in American gardens and most, perhaps all, are less hardy than the American natives. But some, including *A. japonicum* and the lovely *A. sikokianum*, thrive outdoors in the region of New York City. There are other charming kinds among these Asians and they are certainly worth seeking and trying by keen plant collectors. Among the most noteworthy are *A. candidissimum*, of western China, which has lovely white or pink-tinged spathes; *A. consanguineum*, of eastern Asia, which has spathes of green, white, and purple; *A. flavum*, which has greenish-yellow spathes only about 1 inch long and is native from the Mediterranean region to the Himalayas; *A. griffithii*, of the Himalayas, with rich purple spathes veined with green; *A. japonicum* of Japan, which has green spathes striped with white; *A. ringens*, another Japanese, with green and white striped spathes; and Japanese *A. sikokianum*, the spathes of which are rich wine-red striped with white at their bases on their outsides, but ivory-white on their insides with pale green upper parts penciled with translucent white lines. The spadix, shaped like a druggist's pestle, is white.

Garden Uses and Cultivation. These interesting plants are adapted for woodland gardens, rock gardens, and the American kinds for gardens of native plants. They are not demanding of soil or care. Moistish, but not wet earth well enriched with decayed organic matter such as leaf mold, peat moss, or nourishing humus suits. They are helped by a mulch of similar material and need dappled shade for the best results, but will grow even in deeper shade if the light is fairly good. Planting is best

Arisaema japonicum

Arisaema japonicum

Arisaema sikokianum

done in late summer or early fall about the time their foliage dies. Propagation is by offsets or by seeds sown as soon as ripe and without being allowed to dry after removal from the berries. A sandy, peaty seed soil kept nicely moist, but not constantly saturated is appropriate. Sowing may be done in a cold frame or cool greenhouse.

Diseases. A rust disease, a leaf and stalk blight, and fungus leaf spot diseases sometimes affect these plants.

ARISARUM (Aris-àrum)—Mouse Plant. This genus name, used by Dioscorides, belongs to three species of the arum family ARACEAE, natives of the Mediterranean region. They are deciduous, tuberous-rooted, herbaceous perennials related to the jack-in-the-pulpit (*Arisaema*), but differing in the spathes of the inflorescences not being open down one side to their bases, but being joined at their margins to form closed tubes. Typical of the arum family, the inflorescence (aggregation of flowers and attendant parts) consists of a spadix and spathe, together often referred to as the "flower." The true flowers are tiny and are crowded along the spikelike spadix (the part that corresponds to the yellow column of a calla-lily). On the spadix male flowers are above, females below, with no infertile ones between. The spathe is a bract originating at the base of the spadix; in the calla-lily it is the white petal-like part that forms the trumpet. The fruits are berries.

Mouse plant, a vernacular name for *Arisarum proboscideum,* alludes to the long-tailed, pale gray and green inflorescences, which fancifully resemble the bodies and tails of mice with their heads out of view among the foliage, and their hinder parts and tails among the foliage, and extended. This species has long-stalked, arrow-shaped leaves lustrous dark green, with blades 4 or 5 inches in length. The inflorescences have swollen lower portions (the body of the "mouse") 1 inch to 1½ inches long, and the tail 5 to 6 inches in length. The only opening to the interior of the spathe is a tiny aperture at the end of the tail. Through this, attracted by a juice pleasing to them, pollinating insects enter. Once inside they are unable to turn around and leave so they proceed. Finally they reach the enlarged chamber containing the spadix. Light is admitted through the thin walls of this swollen lower part of the spathe and this stimulates the agitated insect to thrash about in an effort to escape. In doing this pollen is transferred from male to female flowers, fertilization is effected, and then, and then only, the spathe splits to release the visitor.

The common *A. vulgare* is a less extraordinary species, more like a conventional *Arum* or *Arisaema* in aspect. Variable, it is about 1 foot tall, and has long-stalked, heart-shaped to somewhat arrow-shaped leaves with blades 2 to 4½ inches long. The dull purple spathes curve at their tops to form something of a hood; they are 2 inches long or a little longer.

Garden Uses and Cultivation. Arisarums appeal to gardeners interested in the unusual and to the botanically curious rather than those who demand great show from their plants. They are adapted for woodland gardens, shady places in rock gardens, fringes of shrubberies, and similar places. Ground that is moist and that contains abundant organic matter suits them best. They may be transplanted, and propagated by division, when the foliage dies in fall. Increase can also be had by seeds sown as soon as they are ripe in a cold frame. A mulch of leaf mold, peat moss, or compost applied in fall is beneficial. Arisarums are hardy in sheltered locations as far north as New York City. They are easy to grow in pots in cool greenhouses.

ARISTEA (Arís-tea). Perennial herbaceous plants of South Africa, tropical Africa, and Madagascar, not hardy in the north, but some well adapted for gardens in California and similar mild-climate regions constitute *Aristea* of the iris family IRIDACEAE. There are about sixty species. The name, alluding to the rigid leaf tips, comes from the Latin *arista,* a point.

Aristeas have woody rootstocks from which issue fibrous roots and numerous fans of linear to nearly cylindrical, erect leaves. The flowers, rather small and usually blue, are in raceme-like arrangements or sometimes erect heads terminating two-edged, usually branched stalks that sometimes have a few leaves near their bases. Individually they are short-lived, but are produced in succession over fairly long periods. They have short-tubed corollas, with six wide-spreading lobes (petals, or more correctly tepals) that twist spirally when they fade, six short-stalked stamens, and a two-branched or nearly branchless style. The fruits are cylindrical, leathery capsules.

Somewhat suggestive of a giant *Sisyrinchium,* the South African *A. ecklonii* has linear, sinuous leaves 1 foot to 1½ feet long and up to ½ inch wide. Its open panicles of many clusters of three or four bright blue flowers ½ to ¾ inch wide are carried on erect, branched stalks up to 2½ feet tall. The stamens are purple.

The very beautiful South African *A. thyrsiflora* has rigid, ribbed, linear leaves ½ inch wide and shorter than its 3- to 6-feet-long flower stalks. Its nearly stalkless, sweetly-fragrant, clear blue, 1¼-inch-wide flowers with blue-purple stamens and yellow anthers, in 9-inch-long, slender panicles, close at about midday. Plants cultivated under the name of the closely related South African *A. capitata* often belong here.

Garden and Landscape Uses. Aristeas are very useful for sunny flower beds, the fronts of shrub plantings, watersides, and large rock gardens in mild-climate regions where the soil is reasonably fertile and not excessively dry. Their foliage has much the effect of that of narrow-leaved irises, but their blooms are less massive, much smaller, and commonly more daintily displayed. Because their individual flowers are so short-lived they are without merit as cut flowers. Aristeas are sometimes grown in ground beds or in pots or tubs in greenhouses.

Cultivation. It is possible to divide aristeas, but because of their tough, woody rootstocks, this is not easily done and often is not successful. It is generally better to rely upon seeds for propagation. These germinate readily in sandy peaty soil kept moderately moist in a temperature of 60°F. The seedlings should be transplanted individually to small pots and grown in these or larger ones to which they are transferred later until they are set in their permanent places. Old specimens usually do not transplant well from the open ground. Routine care calls for little of the gardener's time. Unless seeds are wanted, spent flower stalks should be removed promptly. A spring application of a general purpose fertilizer is helpful. Regular watering is needed during dry weather.

In greenhouses aristeas are satisfied with winter night temperatures of about 50°F, elevated a few degrees by day. On all favorable occasions the greenhouse must be ventilated freely. Watering should be generous, but not excessive, especially in winter. Specimens in root-filled containers are helped to stay vigorous and healthy by weekly applications of dilute liquid fertilizer from spring through fall. When needed, repotting is done in late winter or early spring.

ARISTOLOCHIA (Aristo-lòchia)—Dutchman's Pipe, Calico Flower, Pelican Flower, Birthwort, Virginia Snakeroot. Most abundant in the tropics, but some few kinds wild in temperate regions including the United States, the 350 species of *Aristolochia* belong to the birthwort family ARISTOLOCHIACEAE. They include herbaceous perennials, and woody plants the majority twining vines. Their often bizarre flowers frequently have forms suggestive of birds. This is recognized by the bestowal upon certain kinds of such vernacular names as pelican flower, goose flower, duck flower, swan flower, rooster flower, and bird's head flower. Most familiar to American gardeners are two North American natives known as Dutchman's pipes. The flowers of many kinds are pollinated by carrion insects. These are entrapped for several hours by some species, before being released to pollinate other blooms. To attract the insects, when ripe for fertilization, the flowers of most kinds emit powerful, often nauseating stenches. The name *Aristolochia,* from the Greek *aristos,* best, and *lochia,* delivery, like the vernacular designation birthwort, was given because of the supposed usefulness of the plants in childbirth, this, according to the propounders of the doctrine of signatures, was indicated by God by the fanciful resemblance of the blooms to a human fetus in the womb.

Aristolochias have opposite leaves and from the leaf axils or stems solitary, clustered, or in short racemes, prevailingly greenish or lurid purple, sometimes blotched or spotted, flowers. These are without petals. Their showy parts are the calyxes. Tubular and asymmetrical, they are shaped more or less like a tobacco pipe or the letter S or are straight and have apexes more or less three-lobed or with a single extended lobe. There are generally six stamens, their anthers joined to the stigma, which tips a short style. The fruits are angled capsules.

Dutchman's pipe and pipe vine are names applied to two somewhat look-alike, but distinct species native to eastern North America. To distinguish them with greater precision *A. durior* (syns. *A. macrophylla, A. sipho*) may be called smooth Dutchman's pipe, *A. tomentosa* hairy Dutchman's pipe. A fast-growing, woody vine up to 30 feet tall, native from Pennsylvania to Minnesota, Georgia, and Kansas, **A. durior** has nearly hairless stems and rounded to

Aristolochia durior

broadly-kidney-shaped, dark green leaves 6 inches to more than 1 foot wide that become hairless as they mature. The greenish-yellow flowers, about 1 inch across their faces, and on their outsides hairless, indeed suggest the traditional tobacco pipe of the Dutch. They are U-shaped, with a distinct pouch or bulge immediately above the ovary representing the bowl of the pipe and from it a more slender upturned stem reaching to the mouth of the smoker, formed of the partially cupped, spreading part of the corolla, lobed to form three obscure petals. The seed capsules are 2 to 3 inches long. Its stems as tall as those of the smooth Dutchman's pipe but woolly-hairy, hairy Dutchman's pipe (*A. tomentosa*) is wild from North Carolina to Illinois, Florida, and Missouri. Its round-ovate leaves, heart-shaped at their bases and hairy on both surfaces, are 3 to 6 inches wide. The flowers, about ¾ inch across their faces,

are greenish-yellow with a purple mouth. Their three definite corolla lobes or petals slant backward. The seed capsules are 1 inch long. Very similar to the hairy Dutchman's pipe, *A. californica* grows in woodlands and at streamsides in California. It is western North America's representative of the Dutchman's pipes of the East. It differs chiefly in the tubular part of its bloom being inflated to nearly the same thickness throughout instead of inflated at the base and constricted toward the face of the flower. This has hairy shoots and leaves rough-hairy above and pubescent on their undersides. They are heart-shaped to somewhat fiddle-shaped and 2 to 4½ inches long. Closely related to the smooth Dutchman's pipe, but with its young shoots and undersides of the leaves hairy, *A. manshuriensis* of Manchuria and Korea has purple-flushed, yellow flowers, about 1¼ inches across their faces.

Calico flower (**A. elegans** syn. *A. littoralis*) probably a native of South America,

Aristolochia elegans

is naturalized in many warm regions including Florida. It is an attractive, free-flowering, nonhardy vine, with slender stems and long-stalked leaves with conspicuous appendages (stipules) at their bases. Their blades are kidney-heart-shaped and 2½ to 4 inches across. The solitary flowers, suspended on long, slender stalks from young shoots, are not ill-scented. They have greenish-yellow tubes about 1½ inches long. Their saucer-shaped faces

with heart-shaped bases are 3 to 4 inches across, on their outsides whitish veined with reddish-purple, on their insides richly mottled with deep purple-brown on a nearly hidden cream background.

Magnificant in bloom, the variety of the pelican flower (*A. grandiflora* syn. *A. gigas*) named *A. g. sturtevantii* differs from the species in having even bigger blooms with tails sometimes 3 feet long. Native from tropical Mexico to Panama and the West Indies, **A. grandiflora** is a vine with pointed-heart-shaped leaves 3 to 6 inches across,

Aristolochia grandiflora

downy at first, but at maturity hairless. The solitary, long-stalked flowers have inflated tubes and spreading, wavy-edged, heart-shaped-ovate faces up to about 1 foot long by 8 inches wide, beautifully veined and blotched with rich purple, and with a pendulous, slender tail 1 foot long or longer. The throats of the blooms are livid purple. When first open the blooms stink, but after the first twenty-four hours the odor fades away. Its flowers sometimes larger than those of *A. grandiflora*, but without tails, rarely cultivated **A. gigantea** is native to Panama. Less malodorous than those of the pelican flower, but nevertheless ill-scented, the solitary blooms of **A. brasiliensis** (syns. *A. labiata, A. galeata*), which is sometimes called rooster flower, are mottled with red, yellow, green, and purple or may be nearly all purple. The lower portion of the flower tube is much inflated and at its base has a slender, curved spur. From the apex of the inflated part come a pair of lips, the lower 4 to 6 inches long, rigid, narrowly-lanceolate, and sharply-angled downward; the upper, almost round, 6 inches or more in width and in length, is ruffled and pendant. This species is native to southeastern Brazil.

An easily observable difference between the rather similar *A. ringens* and *A. brasiliensis* is that in **A. ringens** the upper lip of the flower is narrower, about 2 inches wide, obovate-spatula-shaped, and instead of drooping is carried straight forward parallel with the longer, forward-pointing, 6- to 8-inch-long lower lip. A native of the Caribbean region, it is naturalized in Florida. Brazilian **A. labiosa** (syn. *A. cymbifera labiosa*) has solitary, ill-scented flowers with the larger of their two lips 4 inches wide, cream, veined purple, and two-lobed. The throat is purple.

Aristolochia labiosa

Native to Panama, **A. veraguensis** (syn. *A. argyroneura*) is a stout vine, with pointed-heart-shaped leaves 4 to 7 inches long and nearly as wide as long. They are clearly variegated with white veins. The maroon and red flowers, their faces about 1¼

inches long by less than ½ inch wide, come in branched clusters from the bases of the main stems. In growth and foliage characteristics, **A. leucaneura** resembles *A. veraguensis*, and it is quite possible both are the same species, but because flowers of *A. leucaneura* have not been described it is impossible to be certain of this. If they are, under the law of priority, the correct name is *A. leucaneura*.

A nonhardy shrub or small tree, its branches scarcely or not twining, **A. tricaudata** of Mexico is pleasing. Its wrin-

Aristolochia tricaudata

kled-surfaced, pointed-oblong leaves, 5 to 8 inches long, are fringed with hairs. The solitary maroon-red flowers, dark purple inside, come from the older parts of the branches, even down to the ground. They have a bent, short tube and a concave face of three lobes that extend as tails up to 4 inches long.

Virginia snakeroot (**A. serpentaria**) gained its common name because of its unsubstantiated reputation as a cure for snake bite. A herbaceous perennial, up to 2 feet tall, it has slender, erect, sparsely-foliaged stems. The pointed, heart-shaped-oblong, slender-stalked leaves have blades 1½ to 4½ inches long by about one-half as wide. The strongly-curved flowers, usually low on the stems are chocolate to dark purple, and from a little less to somewhat more than ½ inch long. The spreading face of the bloom is bluntly three-lobed. It grows in rich woodlands, often in limestone soils from Connecticut to Illinois, Florida, and Texas. European **A. clematitis** is naturalized from New York to Ohio and Maryland. Erect and hairless, it has many slender stems 1½ to 4½ feet tall, and triangular-heart-shaped to kidney-shaped leaves. The greenish-yellow flowers, a little more than 1 inch in diameter, are in clusters from the leaf axils. Unlike those of other kinds discussed here, they have straight, rather funnel-shaped tubes, with six lobes that extend as tails.

Garden and Landscape Uses. The common Dutchman's pipe (*A. durior*), its southern and western counterparts, *A. to-*

Aristolochia veraguensis

Aristolochia clematitis

mentosa and *A. californica*, respectively, are highly satisfactory screening vines for porches and other places offering suitable support for their twining stems. They can also be used effectively to cover tree trunks, large rocks, trellises, low walls, and the like. The smooth Dutchman's pipe is hardy through most of New England, the hairy Dutchman's pipe as far north as southern New England. The Californian species is considerably more tender. Generous supplies of water are needed from spring to fall, less frequent soakings in winter. Container specimens respond to weekly or biweekly applications of dilute liquid fertilizer from spring to fall. Virginia snakeroot is suitable for native plant gardens and medicinal gardens, and for colonizing in semiwild areas. The other hardy herbaceous perennial discussed above *A. clematitis* can be used similarly to the last except that it should not be included in collections of strictly native plants. It is also suitable, for interest rather than much in the way of display, for including in perennial beds.

Of the nonhardy species, *A. caudata* is suitable for planting outdoors in warm, frost-free climates and as an item of interest for growing in large conservatories. Most popular of the nonhardy vines is *A. elegans*, a graceful kind for outdoors in warm climates and for greenhouses. The other tender climbers are admirable conversation pieces for tropical gardens and tropical greenhouses.

Cultivation. Little difficulty attends the cultivation of aristolochias. They revel in fertile soils not deficient in organic matter and not excessively dry. In greenhouses the best results are usually had in ground beds, but it is by no means impossible to achieve success in large pots or tubs. A minimum winter night temperature of 60°F, with a daytime increase of five to fifteen degrees, depending upon the brightness of the weather, is satisfactory. Some kinds, including *A. elegans* and *A. tricaudata*, get along well in temperatures five degrees lower. Any pruning needed to contain or shape the plants is done in late winter or early spring. Seeds provide a ready means of propagating aristolochias. Summer cutting, planted in a greenhouse propagating bench, preferably with slight bottom heat, may also be used. Those with tuberous roots, such as the Virginia snakeroot and *A. clematitis*, can be multiplied rapidly from pieces of root.

ARISTOLOCHIACEAE—Birthwort Family. This family of dicotyledons is composed of five genera and approximately 400 species of mostly twining, woody vines, but including also nonvining herbaceous plants. Natives mainly but not exclusively of warm regions excluding Australia, its sorts have alternate, stalked, often heart-shaped leaves and small to large flowers with a frequently curiously bent, tubular, corolla-

like calyx of bizarre appearance, with an upper portion that may flare outward, no petals, six or more stamens, sometimes united with the style. The fruits are capsules. Genera cultivated are *Aristolochia* and *Asarum*.

ARISTOTELIA (Aristot-èlia)—New Zealand Wineberry. The great Greek philosopher Aristotle is commemorated by the name of this genus of five species of tender trees and shrubs of the elaeocarpus family ELAEOCARPACEAE. All species of *Aristotelia* are natives of the southern hemisphere. They have opposite or nearly opposite leaves and small, usually unisexual, flowers in axillary racemes or clusters. The blooms have four or five sepals and the same number of sometimes toothed or three-lobed petals. The fruits are small berries. Those of the New Zealand wineberry and of *A. chilensis* are made into wine.

The New Zealand wineberry (*A. racemosa* syn. *A. serrata*) is a deciduous shrub or tree 6 to 30 feet high with broad-elliptic to ovate, sharply-toothed leaves 3 to 4 inches long and red-brown on their undersides. The flowers, in large panicles, are rose-pink to deep claret-red. Its currant-like berries are red. This kind, common throughout New Zealand, is one of the first plants to recolonize burnt-over land and abandoned clearings. The only other New Zealand species *A. fruticosa* is a deciduous shrub 3 to 6 feet in height, with leathery, linear, lanceolate, elliptic, or oblong, crenate-margined, toothed, or sometimes lobed leaves, and flowers in small clusters or solitary. This extraordinary much-branched shrub exhibits tremendous variability in leaf form; the leaves of young specimens are sometimes pinnately-lobed. It is a mountain species. A natural hybrid, intermediate between the two New Zealand species, is *A. colensoi*.

The only other kind likely to be cultivated is the Chilean *A. chilensis* (syn. *A. macqui*), an evergreen shrub up to 15 feet tall, with opposite and alternate, ovate to oblong, shallowly-toothed leaves 2 to 4 inches long. They are dark glossy green. The tiny greenish-white flowers are few together in axillary and terminal clusters. The small berries change from purple to black as they ripen. Variety *A. c. variegata*, with variegated foliage, is said to be less hardy to cold than the green-leaved type.

Garden and Landscape Uses and Cultivation. These shrubs and small trees are attractive plants for mild climates. In North America they are best suited for the West Coast. They are not hardy in the north. They are easy to grow and find any ordinary soil agreeable. They are increased by cuttings and seeds.

ARMATOCEREUS (Armato-cèreus). Restricted in the wild to fairly high altitudes in Ecuador and Peru, *Armatocereus* of the

cactus family CACTACEAE is included by conservative botanists in *Lemaireocereus* or in *Cereus*. It comprises eleven species of night-blooming, columnar, thicket-forming cactuses. The name, alluding to the spiny character of the plants, is derived from the Greek *armata*, bearing weapons, and the name of the related genus *Cereus*.

Armatocereuses have spiny, ribbed, more or less distinctly jointed stems. Their narrowly-funnel-shaped, short-petaled blooms have the lower parts of their perianth tubes furnished with densely-felted areoles (cushion-like, specialized areas on the stems of cactuses from which spines and flowers develop). The petals spread or are more or less erect. The spiny, spherical to ovoid fruits contain black seeds.

Most frequent in cultivation, *A. cartwrightianus* (syn. *Lemaireocereus cartwrightianus*) has a short trunk and many erect, jointed, green branches 3½ to 6 inches in diameter with seven to eight ribs. The closely spaced spine clusters sprout from brownish-woolly areoles. Each has twelve to twenty softish, reddish-white spines ½ to ¾ inch long, the fewer central ones nearly twice as long as the radials or on old stems considerably longer. The flowers are about 3 inches in length, white with reddish outsides.

Other kinds sometimes grown include *A. laetus* (syn. *Lemaireocereus laetus*) up to 18 feet tall. It forms a massive much-branched, blue-gray, but not glaucous head or clump. The stems have four to eight prominent ribs and spine clusters ¾ to a little over 1 inch apart, the spines usually up to 1¼ inches long and sometimes much longer. From 3 to 3½ inches in length, the white flowers are succeeded by green fruits that split down one side when ripe. Dense thickets are formed by *A. humilis* (syn. *Lemaireocereus humilis*). Its stems, rather weak and sprawling to erect, are 3 to 12 feet long by about 1½ inches thick. They have three or four, sometimes five or six, ribs with clusters of five to eight spines, brown at first, later white, up to ¾ inch long. The greenish-white flowers are between 2 and 2½ inches long. The very spiny, globular fruits are about 1¼ inches in diameter.

Garden Uses and Cultivation. Armatocereuses are suitable for inclusion in outdoor collections of succulents in dry regions where little or no frost occurs. They grow with little trouble in environments that suit the majority of columnar *Cereus*-type cactuses. For more information see Cactuses.

ARMERIA (Ar-mèria)—Thrift, Sea-Pink. The thrifts or armerias are, in general, a hardy race of evergreen herbaceous perennials or sometimes subshrubs, with all but a few capable of living outdoors in New York City. They include a number of attractive species and varieties suitable for flower gardens and rock gardens and are easily grown. The genus *Armeria* belongs in the plumbago family PLUMBAGINACEAE and is kin to the sea-lavenders (*Limonium*) and *Plumbago*. In the wild, it is found throughout most of the northern hemisphere, and from northern Chile to the southern tip of South America. The name is an old Latin one. There are eighty species.

Armerias are tufted or mat-forming plants with dense basal rosettes of linear, narrow-lanceolate to narrow-oblanceolate leaves and small flowers crowded in dense, globular heads atop stalks 1 inch to 2½ feet tall. In color they vary from white to pink, red, and deep magenta-purple. Some of the intermediate hues are washy or otherwise unpleasant, but the clearer and purer ones are charming. The flower heads are composed of seven to fifteen very short spikes, each with a bract at its base, of few flowers each arising from the axil of a sometimes vestigial bract or bractlet. At the bottom of the head is an involucre (collar) of bracts without flowers in their axils. The flowers have five-toothed, pleated calyxes, five petals joined at their bases, five stamens, and the same number of separate or united styles. The fruits, technically utricles, are enclosed in the calyxes.

Possibly one of the most variable plant species in cultivation, *A. maritima* includes more than twenty botanical vari-

Armeria maritima laucheana

Botanically much like the last, but dwarfer and compact, *A. juniperifolia* (syn. *A. caespitosa*) has equally slender, linear leaves, not more than ¾ inch long and triangular in section. They are rigid and sharp-pointed so that the foliage feels prickly. From 1 inch to 2 inches long, the flower stalks carry heads, less than ½ inch wide, of rosy-pink blooms. It is native to the mountains of Spain. Variety *A. j. splendens* (syn. *A. caespitosa splendens*) has flat leaves and nodding flower heads on longer stalks. A hybrid between *A. maritima* and a variety of *A. juniperifolia* named *A. sundermannii* has leaves up to 1 inch long, and flower heads bigger than those of *A. juniperifolia*, and not nodding. From southwestern Eu-

rope, *A. juncea* differs from other armerias described here in having rosettes of two types of leaves, the few outer ones more than ⅛ inch wide and 1½ to 2 inches long, the many more wiry inner ones twice as long and one-half as wide. The slender, ½-inch-wide heads are of pink or white flowers and bracts.

Taller, more vigorous thrifts are *A. pseudarmeria* (syn. *A. cephalotes*), *A. gaditana*, and *A. plantaginea*, the first a native of Portugal, the second of that country and Spain, and the other of southcentral Europe. All attain heights up to 2½ feet, and have oblanceolate leaves. Except the very youngest, those of *A. pseudarmeria* are limp and spread near the ground. Hairless and often glaucous, they are five- to seven-veined, and generally ½ to ¾ inch wide. The bright pink flower heads are 1 inch to 1¾ inches in diameter. Variety *A. p. rubra* (syn. *A. cephalotes rubra*) has deeper pink blooms. A variant with white flowers is known. Closely related to *A. pseudarmeria*, but less hardy, *A. gaditana* has flower heads up to 2 inches wide. They differ in technical details from those of *A. pseudarmeria*. The most easily observed difference between *A. plantaginea* and *A. pseudarmeria* is that the leaves of the former rarely exceed ¼ inch in width.

Garden Uses and Cultivation. Armerias are among the easiest plants to grow. The lower ones serve well in rock gardens, in

Armeria maritima

eties that integrate so completely that conservative botanists do not feel justified in recognizing them as separate species. They occur naturally in North America, Europe, and Asia. Characteristically they are 4 inches to 1½ feet tall and have linear leaves more than 1 inch long by not more than ⅛ inch wide. The stalks of the flower heads are downy or hairless. The heads are ½ to 1 inch wide and have at their bases a collar or papery bracts. Flower color varies from white through lavender-pink to deep pink. An especially good horticultural variety is *A. m. laucheana*, which has rich rose-red blooms. Others with bright pink flowers have been given names such as 'Royal Rose' and 'Unique.'

Armeria juniperifolia

A well-fruited apple tree in a home garden

Apples ready for harvesting

Aquilegia jonesii

Araucaria heterophylla

Aquilegia long-spurred hybrid

Arbutus unedo (fruits)

Arctotis hybrida

Ardisia crenata

Arethusa bulbosa

Argemone polyanthemos

Arisaema sikokianum, inflorescence

Arrojadoa rhodantha

groups at the fronts of flower borders, for edgings to paths, and similar purposes, the taller ones are useful for grouping in flower beds and have limited value as cut flowers. All do well near the sea. They need sunny locations and well-drained, not over-rich, preferably sandy soil. They may be raised from seeds sown in spring or early summer in a cold frame or protected place outdoors. The young seedlings grow slowly. When big enough to handle comfortably they are transplanted into a cold frame or outdoor nursery bed where they remain until big enough to be set in their permanent locations. Seedlings often show considerable variation in quality of bloom, and so it is usual to increase the better forms and varieties by division. This may be done in early fall or early spring. The divisions may be planted where they are to remain or, especially if they consist of small pieces, may be potted individually in small pots of sandy peaty soil and plunged (buried to their rims) in a bed of sand, peat moss, or similar material in a cold frame until they are well rooted and are ready for transfer to their permanent locations. For three or four weeks following potting, the cold frame should not be ventilated more than absolutely necessary, keeping in mind that the temperature inside must not rise to harmful levels or the humidity to the extent that the inside of the glass is covered with condensed moisture.

Routine care of armerias is minimal. It includes cutting off faded flower heads, and in spring applying a dressing of fertilizer. In cold climates the protection of a winter covering of branches of evergreens is helpful.

ARMODACHNIS. This is the name of bigeneric orchids the parents of which are *Armodorum* and *Arachnis*.

ARMORACIA (Armor-àcia)—Horse-Radish. Only one species of this genus is cultivated and that ordinarily in the vegetable garden. It is the horse-radish (*Armoracia rusticana*). But an attractive variegated-leaved variety, *A. r. variegata*, exists and is sufficiently decorative to be worth considering as a garden ornamental. The genus *Armoracia* consists of four species of herbaceous perennials of the mustard family CRUCIFERAE. Except for one endemic to North America, they are natives of Europe and temperate Asia. One of the foreign kinds, again the horse-radish, has established itself in waste places in North America as a naturalized and often pernicious weed. Interestingly, the endemic American species, the lake-cress (*A. aquatica*), is an aquatic or bog plant. It is not cultivated. The generic name is the ancient Latin one for the horse-radish.

Plants belonging to *Armoracia* are hairless. Except for the aquatic species, when not in bloom, they have much the aspect of coarse docks (*Rumex*), but are not closely related to that all too familiar race. When in bloom, they are obviously crucifers (members of the mustard family). Their small, white flowers, in large terminal clusters, have four sepals, four petals and six stamens. The petals narrow at their bases into claws. The two outer stamens are distinctly shorter than the other four. Almost always these outer stamens, and usually the inner ones as well, have associated with them minute glands. The fruits are inflated capsules, ovoid to ellipsoid, with at their tips, the persistant long slender style ending in a conspicuous stigma.

The horse-radish (*A. rusticana*) is a coarse, deciduous plant up to 3 feet in

Armoracia rusticana

height. Its thick, fanged roots go deeply into the soil. Its leaves are produced in abundance. The lower ones have long stalks and oblong more or less lobed or toothed blades up to 1 foot in length, with heart-shaped bases. The upper ones are smaller, lanceolate, and have shorter stalks or none. There are several flower racemes, terminal and from the upper leaf axils. This plant apparently never sets viable seeds. Variety *A. r. variegata* has its foliage conspicuously blotched with creamy-white, some shoots and leaves to such an extent

Armoracia rusticana variegata

that they are entirely or mostly devoid of green.

Garden Uses and Cultivation. The variegated-leaved horse-radish grows best in fairly moist deep soil in full sun. It may be used in clumps in semiformal areas to provide accent points of interest. It is seen at its best when it is isolated among grass or other comparatively-fine-leaved foliage. No trouble attends its cultivation. Any tendency to spread beyond its allotted bounds must be curbed by digging offending portions, including every scrap of unwanted roots, out ruthlessly. Propagation is by division and root-cuttings. For the cultivation of horse-radish see Horse-radish.

ARMYWORMS. These, the larvae of caterpillars of night-flying moths, belong to the same group as cutworms, differing from the latter in that they are gregarious rather than solitary. They proceed in armies, devouring as they go practically all vegetation in their paths. Some species are serious pests damaging a wide variety of crops. One is sometimes called the asparagus-fern caterpillar, another the southern grassworm and corn budworm, yet a third the sweet potato caterpillar or cotton cutworm. Armyworms are eaten by birds, skunks, and toads and are parasitized by other insects. Populations of common armyworms reach epidemic levels every few years. Controls consist of strewing poison baits across the line of advancement and of spraying and dusting with materials approved by Cooperative Extension Agents and other authorities. Surface cultivation of the soil, by exposing the pupae of the fall armyworm to birds and other natural enemies, is helpful.

ARNEBIA (Arn-èbia)—Arabian-Primrose. The name *Arnebia* is derived from an Arabian one. The group it denotes consists of about two dozen species of annuals and perennial herbaceous plants. Belonging to the borage family BORAGINACEAE, it inhabits a region centered around the Mediterranean and extending to the Himalayas and tropical Africa. The plant previously named *A. echioides* is *Echioides longiflorum*.

Arnebias are erect or more or less sprawling, rough-hairy plants, with alternate, undivided leaves and racemes or branched clusters of nearly stalkless yellow or violet flowers. The blooms are tubular and have five calyx lobes and the same number of spreading corolla lobes (petals). There are five stamens that do not protrude and a usually two-lobed style. The fruits consist of four dry nutlets, usually called seeds. An interesting feature of some species is that when their blooms first open each petal is marked at its base with a prominent black spot that fades and finally disappears as the flower ages.

The Arabian-primrose (*A. cornuta*) is an annual 1 foot to 1½ feet tall. It has stalkless, lanceolate leaves, the upper ones pointed, the lower ones blunt, and leafy racemes of rich yellow flowers, each with spots that gradually vanish.

Garden Uses and Cultivation. This plant is useful for the fronts of flower borders and rock gardens and is easily satisfied with fertile, well-drained, reasonably moist soil and a sunny location. The Arabian-primrose is grown from seeds sown in early spring where the plants are to remain, or in a greenhouse earlier in a temperature of 60 to 65°F. Young plants started inside are transplanted 2 inches apart in flats and are kept growing in a temperature of 55 to 60°F until they are ready to be hardened (by standing them for a week or two in a cold frame or sheltered place outdoors) prior to planting them in the garden. This may be done about the time the first corn is sown. A spacing of 6 inches between individuals is satisfactory. Seedlings resulting from outdoor sowings are thinned similarly.

ARNICA (Arn-ica). Even by botanists, *Arnica* of the daisy family COMPOSITAE is not always easy to identify as to species, and the difficulties it presents to others interested in the correct naming of plants are often more perplexing. Because of this, arnicas in cultivation are frequently misnamed. The genus consists of more than thirty species, all but two natives of North America, the vast majority endemic there. Four species inhabit Europe and Asia as well as North America. The origin of the name is obscure.

Arnicas are herbaceous perennials, with clustered basal, and opposite stem leaves and long-stalked, usually daisy-like heads of yellow flowers. The ray florets are female and fertile, the disk ones bisexual and fertile. Rarely the heads are without rays. The fruits are bristly achenes.

A tincture called arnica prepared from the dried flowers and roots of certain sorts, although rarely prescribed by physicians, is recognized in the Dispensatory of the United States and is popular for home medication especially as an ingredient of embrocations for treating bruises and strains. The species used as sources of the tincture are *A. montana*, *A. cordifolia*, *A. fulgens*, and perhaps others.

The kind most commonly cultivated is European *A. montana.* This has erect stems, 1 foot to 2 feet high and sometimes sparsely-branched, and stalkless, oblong, lobeless, short-hairy, toothed leaves, the basal ones up to 5 inches long, those above shorter. Its flower heads, solitary or two or three together, are 2 to 3 inches wide. The hairs attached to the ovaries are tan or straw-colored. This is the only species native to Europe occurring south of the Arctic Circle. It is an attractive ornamental. Native to northern Europe and northern North America, *A. alpina* is a pubescent plant up

Arnica montana

to 1¼ feet in height, with lanceolate to spoon-shaped leaves up to 4 inches long. Its usually solitary flower heads are about 2 inches in diameter; the hairs attached to the ovaries are white or straw-colored.

Strictly American species of horticultural appeal are the comparatively tall *A. cordifolia, A. fulgens,* and *A. latifolia* and the lower growing *A. lessingii* and *A. unalaschcensis*. Native of woods and open places from Michigan to Alaska, New Mexico, and California, *A. cordifolia* is ½ foot to 2 feet tall, has hairy stems, long-stalked, sparsely-hairy, heart-shaped, toothed leaves, mostly on non-flowering short shoots, and bright yellow flower heads in ones to fours, 1¾ to 3¼ inches across. The hairs on the ovaries are white. Inhabiting moist soils from Alaska to California and the Rocky Mountains, *A. latifolia* has long-stalked, toothed, ovate to lanceolate leaves and flower heads up to 3 inches across with white or straw-colored hairs to its ovaries. Like *A. latifolia* 1 to 2 feet tall, *A. fulgens,* which is closely related to *A. alpina,* can be distinguished from that species by the dense tufts of tan hairs in the axils of the persistent old leaf bases that clothe its rooting rhizomes. Its flower heads are 1¼ to 1¾ inches in diameter.

Lower-growing kinds of merit are *A. lessingii* and *A. unalaschcensis*. They have solitary flower heads. Those of *A. lessingii* are nodding, are about 1½ inches across, and have deeply-notched or three-toothed ray florets. A native of Alaska, it is up to 1 foot tall. Rarely exceeding 6 inches in height, *A. unalaschcensis,* as its rather unwieldy name reveals, has its home in Unalaska. It is a somewhat hairy species, with oblong leaves that are white-hairy beneath. Its disk florets are light brown, and its ray florets are strongly three-toothed at their apexes.

Garden Uses. Although by no means the most ornamental of herbaceous perennials, the showier tall kinds of *Arnica,* such as *A. montana, A. cordifolia, A. latifolia,* and *A. fulgens* are suitable for perennial borders. These and other tall kinds are also appropriate for less formal, naturalistic

plantings as well as, except *A. montana,* for inclusion in gardens of native plants. The lower growing kinds are quite admirable in rock gardens.

Cultivation. Arnicas are not fussy about soil as long as it is well drained and not excessively dry. In rock gardens a lean, gritty medium that does not supply so much nitrogen that the plants fail to remain low and compact is desirable. Some shade is tolerated and indeed is beneficial to *A. cordifolia* and *A. latifolia*. Others prosper in full sun or with just a suggestion of shade to reduce the most burning glare of summer sun. Propagation is by division in early fall or spring, by cuttings (often these may be taken with a few roots already started) inserted in a cold frame in summer, and by seeds sown in sandy, peaty soil from late winter to late spring.

AROID. Just as orchid is an inclusive name for all plants of the botanical family ORCHIDACEAE and bromeliad is for all plants of the BROMELIACEAE, so is aroid for all plants of the ARACEAE. The group comprises more than 100 genera, and approximately 2,000 species. More than 90 percent of its species are tropical. A few are indigenous to the United States. Except as ornamentals, few are of use to man. The most notable exceptions are dasheens and taros, the tubers of which are staple foods through vast areas of southeastern Asia, Malasia, and islands of the Pacific, and from which Hawaiians prepare poi. The fruits of the ceriman (*Monstera*) are esteemed for eating.

Horticulturally the aroid family is important. Among its most familiar sorts are many popular indoor plants, such as anthuriums, dieffenbachias, philodendrons, and monsteras. Calla-lilies, elephant's ear, and caladiums are aroids as are jack-in-the-pulpit and skunk cabbage. The family includes a few aquatics, notably *Cryptocoryne* and the water-lettuce (*Pistia*), the latter the only free-floating representative of the family. Most of its kinds favor damp or wet, shady habitats. Its tropical species include high-climbing vines, which are inhabitants of rain forests. These often have as young plants juvenile foliage distinctly different from that of mature specimens.

Aroids vary much in appearance. They are predominantly herbaceous, but some develop more or less woody stems. Deciduous or evergreen, they have leaves of widely different patterns and sizes. Sometimes, like most other monocotyledons, these leaves are parallel-veined, but more commonly they are net-veined and the unwary might be misled into mistaking them for leaves of dicotyledons.

A great many aroids contain crystals of calcium oxalate as well as certain toxic proteins in such quantities that chewing on their stems, leaves, or other parts is a highly disagreeable, distressing, or even

Tropical aroids at The New York Botanical Garden in the 1940's

dangerous experience. The crystals become embedded in the tongue and other soft parts to the mouth causing a burning sensation, great pain, and swelling that in extreme cases is said to temporarily deprive the victim of speech. The colloquial name the dumb cane (*Dieffenbachia*) relates to this. The noxious properties are destroyed by heat and so dasheen and taro are edible when scraped, washed, and cooked.

As with all families of flowering plants, the determining characteristics of aroids as a group are to be sought in their flowers and their arrangements rather than in their habits of growth or foliage, although these may supply strong hints to the observant plantsman. The feature of aroids popularly called a "flower," the pristine calla-lily, the flame-red banner and spike of familiar anthuriums, the pulpit with jack inside of jack-in-the-pulpit are not single blooms. They are assemblages of many tiny flowers and attendant parts. Botanically they are inflorescences. Each consists of a spadix (spike) and from its base a bract or spathe. On, and sometimes partly embedded in the spadix, are borne small or minute unisexual or bisexual blooms. If the former, both sexes are usually in the same inflorescence, with the females occupying the lower part and the males above them. The flowers are often ill-smelling and in some cases, certain species of *Amorphophallus* for

example, have a vile, putrid odor. If unisexual, they are usually without perianths (sepals and petals). These are usually present in bisexual ones and consist of four or six segments. The stamens number two, four, or eight or are rarely solitary, as is the style. The spathe encloses, partly encloses, or spreads or droops from the bottom of the spadix. Often large and white or highly colored, but sometimes green or purplish and small, the spathes form the trumpets of calla-lilies, the banners of anthuriums, and the pulpits of jack-in-the-pulpits. The fruits of aroids are berries, often brightly colored and showy.

Genera belonging to the aroid family, *Araceae*, discussed in this Encyclopedia include these: *Acorus, Aglaonema, Alocasia, Amorphophallus, Anthurium, Arisaema, Arum, Caladium, Calla, Colocasia, Cryptocoryne, Dieffenbachia, Dracunculus, Helicodiceros, Homalomena, Lysichitum, Monstera, Orontium, Peltandra, Philodendron, Pistia, Remusatia, Rhektophyllum, Sauromatum, Schismatoglottis, Scindapsus, Spathicarpa, Spathiphyllum, Symplocarpus, Syngonium, Thomsonia, Xanthosoma,* and *Zantedeschia.*

AROMATIC PLANTS. Many plants are esteemed for their aroma, usually the result of essential oils they contain. Some are exploited commercially, numerous others are prized by gardeners for their fragrances and as flavorings.

Among aromatic plants of commercial importance are camphor, cinnamon, cloves, coffee, ginger, junipers, lavender, mint, nutmeg, pepper, sage, and sweet bay. There are many others, their products employed in perfumery, as flavorings, and those of a few such as camphor, red cedar, and West-Indian-Cedar to discourage insects.

The aromatic essense sometimes pervades all or most of the plant, in other cases it is restricted to particular parts such as flowers or seeds. The sorts that have special appeal to gardeners most commonly have aromatic foliage that releases its fragrance when brushed against or rubbed lightly between the fingers. Popular sorts, in addition to those previously mentioned, include a great many grown in herb gardens. Here belong balm, costmary, feverfew, horehound, hyssop, lemon-verbena, marjoram, mints, nepetas, pennyroyal, pinks, rosemary, rue, sassafras, scented-geraniums, southernwood, wormwood and other artemisias, spicebush, tansy, and thymes.

ARONIA (Aròn-ia)—Chokeberry. This group of three prevailingly eastern (one species extends to Texas) American native deciduous shrubs is very closely related to the pears (*Pyrus*) and mountain-ashes (*Sorbus*). Hybrids between the latter and *Aronia* are named *Sorbaronia,* those between *Aronia* and pears, *Sorbopyrus*. Chokeberries differ from mountain-ashes in that their leaves are not divided into separate leaflets or lobed, and from pears in that their flowers are in compound (branched) clusters and are not solitary or in simple umbel-like clusters or racemes. The genus *Aronia* belongs in the rose family ROSACEAE. Its name is a modification of *Aria,* an old name of *Sorbus aria*.

Chokeberries have alternate, elliptic to obovate leaves with glandular, toothed margins and the midribs above with glands. Their flowers are white and have five spreading-roundish or broadly-ovate petals and about twenty stamens; they are in clusters at the ends of the shoots and short side branches. The berry-like fruits are really pomes, that is to say they are structures like apples and pears rather than true berries.

The red chokeberry (**A. arbutifolia**) is distinguished by its red fruits, which remain for a long time. Erect, freely branching, and up to 10 feet tall, this shrub has abruptly short-stalked, short-pointed leaves, 1 inch to 3 inches long and grayish-pubescent on their undersides. The stems of the flower clusters are also hairy. The white or reddish-tinged flowers, up to ½ inch in diameter, are succeeded by pear-shaped to nearly round fruits, about ¼ inch long and dull to bright red. The red chokeberry is native from Massachusetts to Minnesota,

Aronia arbutifolia (fruits)

Aronia arbutifolia (flowers)

Florida, and Texas. Variety *A. a. macrocarpa* has larger fruits than the typical species, *A. a. pumila* is a lower shrub with smaller leaves and darker red fruits. The purple chokeberry (**A. prunifolia**) differs in having slightly larger, nearly spherical, purple-black fruits, and sepals with no or few glands. The fruits are persistent. This species is indigenous from Nova Scotia to Indiana and Florida. From both of the above the black chokeberry (**A. melancarpa**) is distinguished by the lower surfaces of its leaves and the stalks of its flower clusters being hairless or nearly so and by its black fruits, which usually do not remain for long. It is a lower shrub, 1½ to 4 feet in height with somewhat glandular calyx lobes. The fruits are round and about ⅓ inch in diameter. It is native from Nova Scotia to Michigan and Florida. Variety *A. m. grandifolia* is larger in all its parts and is up to 10 feet tall; its leaves are obovate. Another vigorous variety, attaining the same height, is *A. m. elata* with oblong-obovate, pointed leaves; its flowers and fruits are larger than in the typical species.

Garden and Landscape Uses. Chokeberries are good quality ornamental shrubs for naturalizing and for planting under more formal conditions. They are decidedly attractive in bloom and in fruit, and in fall their foliage assumes a fine reddish color. They are abundantly hardy and thrive in full sun or with some part-day shade. They are excellent for planting along the fringes of woodland. As a group they are lovers of moist ground, but the black chokeberry stands drier conditions than the others.

Cultivation. These shrubs are not demanding in the attention they need, in fact, they thrive with very little. No regular pruning is required, but an occasional cutting-out to keep them shapely may be desirable; this may be done in late winter or spring. They are increased by suckers, layers, and by summer cuttings under mist, also by seeds freed of surrounding pulp and sown in fall in cold frames or protected beds outdoors or stratified through the winter and sown in spring.

ARPOPHYLLUM (Arpo-phýllum)—Hyacinth Orchid. As now interpreted, *Arpophyllum* of the orchid family ORCHIDACEAE consists of two tropical species from Mexico, Central and South America, and the West Indies. They are evergreen and grow as epiphytes perched on trees, on rocks, or in the ground. Their name, alluding to the foliage, is derived from the Greek *arpe*, a scimitar, and *phyllon*, a leaf.

Arpophyllums are related to *Epidendrum*. They vary greatly in size and have creeping rhizomes and slender, stemlike pseudobulbs mostly enveloped by several sheathing white bracts. Each pseudobulb ends in a solitary, generally erect, leathery or fleshy, linear-strap-shaped leaf. Brightly colored, the small, stalkless blooms are in long, cylindrical spikes. They have similar sepals and petals, and a slightly-three-lobed, concave lip, joined to the base of the erect column.

Native from Mexico to Colombia and Jamaica, **A. spicatum** (syn. *A. giganteum*), the

Arpophyllum spicatum

more robust species, is sometimes nearly 4 feet in height and has pseudobulbs with smooth sheaths. Its rigid, thick leaves are 1 foot to 2 feet long and not more than 1½ inches broad. The flowers, ½ inch wide or a little wider, and rose-red, pink, or purple-pink, are many together in rather

crowded racemes. They come in spring. Smaller, often not more than 1 foot tall, **A. alpinum** (syn. *A. medium*) has pseudobulbs with warty sheaths. Its purplish-pink flowers, often with a paler lip, are a little larger than those of *A. spicatum*. It is endemic to Mexico, Guatemala, and Honduras.

Garden Uses and Cultivation. These beautiful orchids are suitable for intermediate-temperature greenhouses, and respond to conditions favorable to cattleyas and tropical epidendrums. Light shade from strong sun is necessary, but as much light as they will stand without damage to the foliage is beneficial. Since arpophyllums are very impatient of stagnant conditions, free drainage is very essential. They may be grown in a mixture of chopped tree fern fiber and sphagnum moss or other rooting mediums suitable for epiphytic orchids, which should be kept moist at all times. Well-rooted specimens respond favorably to periodic light applications of fertilizer. Fairly humid, but not dank atmospheric conditions are required. For further information see Orchids.

ARRABIDAEA. See Saritaea.

ARRACACIA (Arra-càcia)—Apio. The more than fifty species of this genus of the carrot family UMBELLIFERAE are natives from Mexico to Peru, but only one has claim to our attention. It is the apio (**Arracacia xanthorrhiza** syn. *A. esculenta*), cultivated at high altitudes in Puerto Rico and elsewhere in the tropics for its edible roots. The name is derived from the Spanish one for some species.

Arracacias are herbaceous perennials with pinnately-divided leaves, and little flowers, white to deep purple, in umbels that themselves are in umbels. The flowers have five-lobed calyxes, and five each petals and stamens. The fruits are flattened and seedlike. The apio is stout-stemmed, has large, twice-pinnate or deeply-pinnately-lobed leaves, with broad, coarsely-toothed leaflets, and white flowers. Its starchy roots are thick and branched. The apio is a native of northern South America.

Garden Uses and Cultivation. In North America this plant may occasionally be planted in the most tropical parts as a curiosity. It is easy to grow in deep, fertile soil.

ARRHENANTHERUM (Arrhen-anthèrum)—Oat Grass. The six species of *Arrhenantherum* of the grass family GRAMINEAE inhabit the Mediterranean region. The name, alluding to the male flowers having awns (bristles), comes from the Greek *arren*, male, and *anther*, a bristle.

These are flat-leaved grasses with narrow panicles of two-flowered spikelets, the lower floret a male, the upper bisexual.

The tall oat grass (**A. elatius**), native of Europe, grown as a meadow grass and nat-

uralized in North America, is 2 to 5 feet tall and has slender stems and soft leaves less than ¼ inch wide. Its usually interrupted, lustrous, narrow flower panicles, 6 inches to 1¼ feet long, are light green or purplish. Variety **A. e. variegatum** (syn. *A. bulbosum variegatum*) has leaves longitudinally striped with white, **A. e. bulbosum** (syns. *A. bulbosum, A. tuberosum*) has clusters or strings of small tubers at the ground surface.

Arrhenatherum elatius variegatum

Garden and Landscape Uses and Cultivation. The variegated-leaved variety is an attractive ornamental, easy to grow in sunny locations in ordinary, well-drained garden soil. Propagation of the species is by seeds, of the varieties by division.

ARROJADOA (Arro-jadòa). This name honors Dr. Miguel Arrojado Lisboa, a twentieth-century Brazilian botanist. It is that of a genus of two species of the cactus family CACTACEAE, natives of eastern Brazil.

Arrojadoas are low, freely-branching plants with slender, cylindrical, many-ribbed stems bristling with closely-set clusters of spines springing from tiny areoles. The flowers come from a patch, technically a pseudocephalium, of red or pink bristly-hairs and spines located at the top of each stem and branch. The blooms are narrowly-funnel-shaped to cylindrical, with short, spreading petals. The stamens do not protrude. New stem growth pushes through the center of the pseudocephalium leaving it as a collar encircling the stem. This gives to these plants the peculiarity of the older parts of the branches being encircled at irregular intervals with bands of bristles. Some botanists include these plants in *Cephalocereus*. Their fruits are berry-like.

From 3 to 6 feet in length and ¾ inch to 1½ inches in diameter, the short-jointed stems of **A. rhodantha** are at first erect, later spreading or clambering. They have ten to thirteen low ribs, with closely-set clusters of spines of nearly equal size that change from brown to white as they age.

Arrojadoa rhodantha

Clustered near the branch ends, the flowers are pink and nearly 1½ inches long. The oblong to obovate, red fruits are about ¾ inch long. In contrast, *A. penicillata* has stems from less to somewhat more than ½ inch in diameter. They mostly have ten low ribs and clusters of spines, with the central ones conspicuously longer, up to ¾ inch to 1¼ inches, than the others. The deep pink blooms are a little over 1 inch long. The nearly spherical fruits are purplish, a little over ½ inch long.

Garden Uses and Cultivation. These easy-to-grow plants are of interest for including in collections of succulents. Guidelines to their needs may be inferred from the fact that in the wild they grow in leafy soils in lightly shaded woodlands. For additional information see Cactuses.

ARROW-ARUM. See Peltandra.

ARROWHEAD. See Sagittaria.

ARROWROOT. West Indian arrowroot is *Maranta arundinacea.* East Indian arrowroot is obtained from *Tacca leontopetaloides* and *Curcuma angustifolia.*

ARROWWOOD is a common name of *Viburnum acerifolium* and *V. dentatum.*

ARTABOTRYS (Artá-botrys) — Climbing-ylang-ylang or Tail-grape. More or less climbing evergreen shrubs of the tropics of the Old World comprise *Artabotrys* of the annona family ANNONACEAE. There are more than 100 species. They have remarkably fragrant flowers and climb by means of curiously modified flower stalks, which develop opposite the leaves, curve around available supports, and that after the blooms fall, harden into hooks that hold up the shoots. The name comes from the Greek *artao*, to support, and *botrys*, grapes, and refers to the fruits.

These shrubs have alternate leaves, and solitary or clustered flowers, with three-parted calyxes, six petals in two rows, many stamens, and few to many pistils. The corolla is constricted above the stamens. The fruits look like clusters of small plums or olives attached to the hardened receptacles (ends of the flower stalks).

Climbing-ylang-ylang or tail-grape (*A. hexapetalus* syns. *A. odoratissimus*, *A. uncinatus*) is prized for the delicious fragrance of its greenish-yellow blooms. This vigorous climber has short-stalked, oblong to broadly-lanceolate leaves 3 to 6 inches long, with glossy upper surfaces. The blooms, solitary or paired, have hairless petals 1½ to 2 inches in length. The fragrant, smooth, pointed, yellow fruits are 1 inch to 1¼ inches long. It is native from China to India and the Philippine Islands.

Garden and Landscape Uses and Cultivation. In southern Florida, Hawaii, and other frost-free or nearly frost-free, warm regions, this popular and easily grown species is suited for planting in patios and other intimate areas where its perfume can be enjoyed. It grows without difficulty in a variety of soils and is easily propagated by seeds. A certain amount of pruning and guiding of the shoots to keep the plants to size and shape is likely to be needed. An application of a complete fertilizer at about the time new growth begins is of benefit.

ARTEMISIA (Artem-ísia)—Wormwood, Southernwood, Tarragon, Sage Brush. Chiefly natives of the northern hemisphere and most abundant in dryish and arid regions, the 400 species of *Artemisia* are included in the daisy family COMPOSITAE. In addition to kinds more or less commonly cultivated they include the sage brushes of western North America and a pestiferous kind sometimes called chrysanthemum-weed, but better identified as mugwort (*A. vulgaris*), a native of Europe naturalized in North America. The herb tarragon is *A. dracunculus.* The liqueur genipi is flavored with *A. genipi*, absinthe with *A. absinthium.* The vermifuge santonica is *A. cina.* From it the drug santonin is prepared. The name refers to Artemis of mythology, Greek goddess of chastity. The vernacular name wormwood alludes to the use of some kinds as vermifuges.

Artemisias are annuals or herbaceous perennials or, usually low, shrubs, with alternate, smooth-edged, toothed, lobed, or often finely-dissected leaves. Their typically small, but numerous flower heads are without ray florets (the petal-like ones that in daisy-type flowers encircle the central eye). Yellow to whitish, usually nodding, they are in panicles. The fruits are seedlike achenes. Vast desert and semi-desert areas in western North America are dominated by two sage brushes, *A. tridentata* and *A. arbuscula.* These dusty-gray-foliaged, evergreen shrubs, *A. tridentata* up to 12 feet tall, *A. arbuscula* very much lower, are rarely cultivated except perhaps in collections of native plants.

Artemisia tridentata

Common wormwood or absinthium (*A. absinthium*) is a hardy, spreading, freely-branched, subshrubby, fragrant perennial 2 to 4 feet tall. Native to Europe, but widely naturalized in North America, it has white-silky-hairy shoots and foliage.

Artemisia absinthium

The lower leaves are long-stalked, rounded-ovate, 1½ to 4 inches long, two- or three-times deeply-pinnately-divided. Upward, the leaves become progressively shorter-stalked, smaller and less divided. The many flower heads, ⅛ inch across, are in leafy panicles. Russian wormwood (*A. gmelinii* syn. *A. sacrorum*), of northern Asia, is a gray-hairy subshrub up to 5 feet tall. It has long-stalked leaves deeply-pinnately-lobed, the lobes cleft in comblike fashion into many segments. The chief axis of the leaf is winged. Nodding and in panicles of slender racemes, the flower heads are about ⅛ inch across. Their involucres are more or less hairy, but not white-hairy. The summer-fir (*A. g. viridis*) is a perennial frequently grown as an annual. Pyramidal, it attains heights up to 10 feet. Its finely-dissected foliage is green. Roman wormwood (*A. pontica*) is a hardy native of Europe sparingly naturalized in North America. A subshrub 1 foot to 4 feet tall, it spreads by creeping rhizomes. Mostly ½

Artemisia pontica

inch to 2 inches long and more or less gray-hairy on both surfaces, the broad-ovate to broad-triangular leaves are two- or three-times deeply-pinnately-lobed into slender segments. At the base of the leafstalk there is usually a pair of stipule-like lobes or appendages. The nodding, spherical, whitish-yellow flower heads, about ⅛ inch across, have white-hairy involucres. They are in long, loose, slender panicles.

Beach wormwood or old woman (*A. stellerana*) is also called dusty miller, a name it shares with a number of other plants that have white-felted stems and foliage, including species of *Centaurea*, *Lychnis*, and *Senecio*. Beach wormwood, native of sandy beaches from Kamchatka to Japan, is well established as a naturalized native in similar habitats from Quebec to Virginia and occasionally inland. Not aromatic, it spreads by creeping rhizomes. Felted on both surfaces with white hairs, the obovate, few-lobed leaves, the lobes sometimes slightly again lobed, are 1 inch to 4 inches long and up to 2 inches wide. The yellow flower heads, in narrow, often crowded spikelike panicles, are ¼ inch in diameter.

Artemisia stellerana

Sweet wormwood (*A. annua*), unlike the wormwoods described above, is an annual. Native to Asia and naturalized in North America, it is sweetly fragrant, hairless, 1 foot to 5 feet tall, and usually much-branched. From 1 inch to 4 inches long, its broad, feathery leaves are mostly two- or three-times pinnately-cleft into sharp-toothed, linear or lanceolate segments. The short-stalked, often nodding flower heads, ½₂ inch across and yellow, are in loose, broad panicles.

Southernwood, old man, or lad's love (*A. abrotanum*) is an old-fashioned favorite. Its parts deliciously aromatic when brushed against, this native of Europe is sparingly naturalized at roadsides and waste areas in North America. A hardy, much-branched subshrub or shrub 1½ to 5 feet tall, it has hairy or hairless shoots. Its leaves, 1½ to 2½ inches long, green and nearly or quite hairless above, have thinly-

Artemisia abrotanum

hairy undersides. They are once- to three-times pinnately-cleft into slender, linear to almost threadlike, ascending segments. The rather large, loose panicles are of yellowish flower heads ⅕ inch across, with more or less pubescent involucres.

Silver king artemisia is even more at-

Artemisia ludoviciana

tractive than *A. ludoviciana* of which it is the variety *A. l. albula*. The species is a rhizomatous, aromatic, hardy herbaceous perennial native in dryish soils from Illinois to British Columbia and Mexico. From 1 foot to 4 feet tall, it has erect stems not branched below the flowering parts. The narrow- to broadly-lanceolate, toothless or irregularly-toothed, sometimes deeply-lobed leaves are 1¼ to 4½ inches long. They are persistently white-hairy beneath. Their upper surfaces, more or less white-hairy at first, usually soon lose most of their pubescence. The flower heads are in broad or narrow panicles. Beautiful *A. l. albula* (syn. *A. albula*) is a hardy perennial, with silvery-white stems and foliage. Native from Colorado to Texas and Mexico, it is erect, 1½ to 4 feet tall. The leaves on its lower parts are ovate to obovate, ½ inch to 2 inches long, and usually have three to five lanceolate lobes. The upper leaves, lin-

Artemisia ludoviciana albula

Artemisia ludoviciana albula (foliage)

Artemisia ludoviciana albula (flowers in bud)

ear or nearly so, are toothed or toothless. The whitish flower heads, about ¹⁄₁₆ inch across, are in loose panicles. From 1 foot to 3 feet tall and perhaps not hardy in the north, *A. pycnocephala* is a subshrubby perennial that spreads by rhizomes. It has linear to lanceolate, oblong, or elliptic leaves 1¼ to 4 inches long, smooth-edged or with a few teeth or lobes, white-hairy beneath and sometimes above. The broad or narrow panicles are of little erect or nodding, usually densely-hairy flower heads. This kind is native in dry soils from Ontario to California, Arkansas, and New Mexico.

Artemisia pycnocephala

White mugwort (*A. lactiflora*) is another erect, hardy herbaceous perennial. Up to about 5 feet in height, this native of China much resembles *A. vulgaris,* but unlike that pest does not ordinarily become established as a weed. It is distinguishable from *A. vulgaris* by the absence of hairs on the undersides of its leaves. Except on its stems and the chief veins of the leaves, white mugwort is hairless. Its leaves, dark green above, pale yellowish-green beneath, are pinnate or pinnately-cleft into toothed, broad-lanceolate or again-cleft leaflets or lobes. Approximately ¹⁄₁₆ inch wide, the whitish flower heads are in large, loose panicles.

Tarragon, or estragon (*A. dracunculus*), is a native of temperate regions of all continents of the northern hemisphere. In North America it is spontaneous from Illinois to Manitoba, British Columbia, Texas, and Mexico. This nearly odorless to strongly-scented hardy herbaceous perennial attains heights of 2 to 4 feet. Usually hairless, sometimes somewhat hairy, it has narrow-linear to lanceolate-linear, rarely three-cleft leaves ¾ inch to 3½ inches long. The nearly globular flower heads, in large, loose panicles, are greenish-white, up to ⅛ inch wide.

One of the most beautiful artemisias, unfortunately not hardy north of Washington, D.C., *A. arborescens* is a shrubby, aromatic native of maritime cliffs and similar

Artemisia arborescens

habitats in the Mediterranean region. It attains heights of 1½ to 3 feet, is bushy, and forms a filigree of finely-divided silvery-white-hairy stems and foliage. The leaves are broad-ovate and up to 4 inches long. The lower ones are stalked and three-times cleft, those above short-stalked or stalkless and once- or twice-cleft. The ultimate segments are linear and slender. Globular, yellow, and up to ¼ inch wide, the flower heads, erect at maturity, are in

somewhat one-sided racemes. The involucres are white-woolly. Except that its stems and leaves are green and smell strongly of camphor, *A. camphorata* of southern Europe resembles *A. arborescens.*

Lower kinds include *A. frigida,* with a natural range extending from Minnesota to Alaska and Texas, and in Siberia. From 1 foot to 1½ feet tall, its stems erect or spreading, this kind has silvery-silky-hairy shoots and leaves, the latter ½ inch to 1½ inches long and three- or four-times pinnately-cleft into short, linear segments. The lower leaves are stalked, the upper stalkless. The yellow flower heads, ⅕ inch wide, are in racemes arranged in narrow, leafy panicles. Native of coastal areas and high mountains in Japan, lovely, creeping *A. schmidtiana,* 1 foot to 2 feet tall, has filigree-like, silvery-white, silky-hairy foliage. The leaves, twice-pinnately-cleft into pointed, linear-lanceolate segments, are 1¼ to 1¾ inches long. The flower heads, about ⅙ inch wide, are in pyramidal panicles. A dwarf variety is identified as *A. s. nana.* Its home in the mountains of Europe,

Artemisia schmidtiana nana

A. genipi (syn. *A. spicata*) is a tufted, hardy perennial 4 to 6 inches tall, with silvery-hairy stems and foliage. The lower leaves

Artemisia frigida

are stalked and of often three-lobed leaflets. The upper leaves are stalkless and less lobed. The spherical flower heads, ⅕ inch or less in diameter and with woolly involucres, are in loose, one-sided spikes. Native to the Alps of Europe, *A. glacialis* is a tufted hardy herbaceous perennial 2 to 6 inches tall. Its silvery-silky-hairy leaves are stalked and one- to three-times palmately-cleft (in hand fashion) into short, linear-lanceolate segments. The yellow flower heads are in small, dense clusters. Another native of the European alps, *A. laxa* (syn. *A. mutellina*) differs from the last in its small yellow flower heads being in loose, leafy racemes. This kind is a tufted, hardy perennial, 4 to 8 inches in height, with silvery-hairy stems and foliage. Its long-stalked leaves are palmately-cleft into pointed, linear-lanceolate, toothed or toothless segments.

Garden and Landscape Uses. Artemisias serve a wide variety of purposes. Tarragon is esteemed as a culinary herb and for making tarragon vinegar. It and others, notably common wormwood, Russian wormwood, Roman wormwood, sweet wormwood, and southernwood are proper in herb gardens. Southernwood is also delightful for the fronts of beds and borders and for locating near pathways where its foliage can be casually brushed or stroked in passing. Toward the rear of flower borders silver king artemisia and mugwort can be displayed to excellent advantage. The first and other silvery-leaved kinds, such as the beach wormwood, *A. frigida*, and *A. schmidtiana*, are especially pleasing when used in conjunction with plants that have

blue, lavender, purple, pink, red, yellow, or orange flowers. Beach wormwood is one of the most satisfactory plants for seaside gardens. For rock gardens, *A. frigida*, *A. schmidtiana nana*, *A. glacialis*, and *A. laxa* are appropriate. Beautiful *A. arborescens* can be displayed with good effect in like manner, in mild climates as a perennial, elsewhere by planting it out for summer show and wintering it indoors like geraniums are managed.

Cultivation. Artemisias are sun-lovers adaptable to a variety of soils, even those low in fertility, and especially dryish and dry ones. Wet soils are not to their liking. High mountain kinds such as *A. glacialis* and *A. laxa* are likely to suffer during spells of very hot, humid weather, but usually recover with its passing. Artemisias are easily propagated by division and cuttings and many kinds by seeds. Garden tarragon rarely, perhaps never, produces seeds. Its cultivation is dealt with under Tarragon.

ARTHROCEREUS (Arthro-cèreus). Four species of Brazilian cactuses of the cactus family CACTACEAE belong here. Their name is from the Greek, *arthron*, a joint, and *Cereus*, another genus of cactuses; it alludes to the stems of some kinds. These are small, commonly prostrate plants related to *Monvillea* and *Trichocereus*, but distinct in being dwarfer and having more slender-tubed flowers, hairier on their outsides, and borne mostly from close to the ends of the stems. The stems are erect and club-shaped or are jointed and consist of spherical or football-shaped segments. They are spiny. Large in comparison to the plant's

size, the white or pink, funnel-shaped blooms are open only at night and are 2½ to 4 inches long. Egg-shaped to spherical, and yellowish, the fruits contain brown seeds embedded in white pulp.

Much-branched, prostrate, lustrous green stems are a distinguishing feature of **Arthrocereus microsphaericus.** Their segments have eight to eleven shallow ribs and are the size of an olive or somewhat bigger. Many bristle-like spines, the centrals brown, the radials white, spring from each of the closely-set areoles. The very pleasantly fragrant blooms, 4 inches long or longer, have pointed perianth segments (petals). The inner ones are white, the outer green. There are a few short, white stamens and a long style, with an eight-lobed stigma. The fruits are spherical. The stems of *A. rondonianus* are semi-upright and cylindrical or somewhat club-shaped. Light green, and 1½ feet tall or slightly taller by 1 inch to 1½ inches in diameter, they have fourteen to eighteen shallow, blunt ribs. Forty to fifty bright yellow spines or bristles sprout from each areole. One or two of the central ones may be 2¾ inches long; the others are very much shorter. The blooms, 3 to 4 inches long, are lilac-pink with short, purple stamens. Their slender tubes have scales, dark hairs, and a few bristles on their outsides.

Garden and Landscape Uses and Cultivation. These cactuses need part-shade. The first species discussed usually gives best results when grafted on a strong-growing understock. For general suggestions regarding cultivation and uses see Cactuses.

ARTHROPODIUM (Arthro-pòdium)—Rock-Lily or Renga-Lily. Confined in the wild to New Zealand, Australia, and New Caledonia, the genus *Arthropodium* of the lily family LILIACEAE consists of eight species of evergreen herbaceous plants with grass-like leaves and loose panicles or racemes of small white or purplish blooms. Its name is derived from the Greek *arthron*, a joint, and *pous*, a foot, and alludes to the stalks of the flowers being jointed.

Arthropodiums are rather similar to *Anthericum*. They are tufted plants with fibrous roots, little or no stem, and leaves that sheath each other at their bases. The flowers are solitary or few together in the axils of small papery bracts. They have six spreading, perianth parts (commonly called petals, but more correctly tepals) that do not drop when they fade, and six stamens with hairy stalks. The latter distinguishes *Arthropodium* from *Anthericum*. The fruits are capsules containing a few angular black seeds.

Two New Zealand natives are quite commonly cultivated in California and similar mild regions and sometimes in cool greenhouses and conservatories. They are *A. candidum* and *A. cirrhatum*. Not more than 1 foot tall, **A. candidum** has branched flower stems and soft leaves up to 9 inches long by ⅛ inch wide. Its white flowers have recurved petals and are about ½ inch in diameter. Called in New Zealand rock-lily and renga-lily, **A. cirrhatum** attains a height of 1 foot to 3 feet and has spreading leaves 1 foot to 2 feet in length and up to 2½ inches wide. Its many white flowers, up to 1 inch in diameter, are in much-branched, broad panicles. The stalks of their stamens have a two-lobed, tendril-like appendage.

Arthropodium cirrhatum

Arthropodium cirrhatum

Two species from Australia, *A. panicu-latum* and *A. pendulum*, less hardy than the New Zealanders, are satisfactory outdoors in nearly frost-free regions. About 3 feet tall, *A. paniculatum* has narrowly-lanceo-late leaves and clusters of white flowers in interrupted racemes. The flowers of *A. pendulum* are white and face downward. They are carried on branching stems.

Garden and Landscape Uses and Culti-vation. As outdoor plants in mild climates arthropodiums are appropriate for beds

and borders and for grouping in front of plantings of shrubs. The low *A. candidum* is an attractive rock garden plant. In green-houses they grow well in ground beds and in pots and tubs. They like well-drained, fertile, sandy soil that contains an abun-dance of peat moss or other organic mat-ter. Full sun is desirable. A winter night temperature of 45 to 50°F is satisfactory, with a rise of a few degrees by day per-mitted. On all appropriate occasions the greenhouse should be ventilated freely. These plants do not thrive under dank, humid conditions. They are watered mod-erately at all seasons, but the soil is kept rather drier in winter than at other times. From spring to fall regular applications of dilute liquid fertilizer are helpful to well-established specimens. Propagation is by careful division in early spring, and by seeds sown in sandy peaty soil in a tem-perature of about 60°F.

ARTHROPTERIS (Arthróp-teris). The ge-nus *Arthropteris* of the davallia family DAV-ALLIACEAE comprises about twenty species of the Old World tropics, Australia, and New Zealand. The name derives from the Greek, *arthron*, a joint, and *pteris*, a fern.

Occurring natively as tree-perchers (epi-phytes), or some species growing in the ground, these ferns have long vining or creeping, scaly rhizomes and pinnate fronds (leaves), with much the aspect of those of *Nephrolepis*, to which this genus is allied. The clusters of spore capsules are on the backs of the leaflets in single rows one each side of the midrib. They may be na-ked or covered by a round to kidney-shaped indusium.

Native to Australia, Norfolk Island, New Zealand, and New Caledonia, *A. tenella* (syn. *Polypodium tenellum*) has sparingly-branched, slender rhizomes up to about 3 feet long, and short-stalked fronds with ovate- to lanceolate-oblong blades 4 inches to 1 foot long or sometimes longer and 2 to 4 or rarely up to 6 inches broad. Their rather distantly spaced leaflets, alternate, linear to narrow-lanceolate, and usually pointed, are 1½ to 3½ inches long. The clusters of spore capsules are without or have only vestigial covers.

Garden Uses and Cultivation. These are as for *Nephrolepis*. For more information see Ferns.

ARTHROSTEMA (Arthro-stéma). Native from Mexico to tropical South America and the West Indies, *Arthrostema*, a genus of three or four species, belongs in the me-lastoma family MELASTOMATACEAE. Its name, derived from the Greek *arthron*, a joint, and *stema*, a stamen, alludes to the apparently jointed stamens.

The sorts of this genus are nonhardy herbaceous perennials, sometimes some-what woody toward their bases, and thin, stalked, ovate to ovate-lanceolate, toothed

leaves, with three or five chief veins. In loosely-branched clusters or panicles, the flowers have a calyx with four short lobes, four petals, eight unequal stamens, and one style. The fruits are capsules.

Native from Mexico to Bolivia, and of Cuba and Jamaica, *A. ciliatum* (syn. *A. fragile*) is 3 to 10 feet tall, has sprawling to more or less vining, sparingly bristly-hairy, fleshy stems and rather distantly spaced, pointed-ovate, finely-bristle-toothed leaves with longish, slender stalks and blades 1 inch to 3 inches long, with five chief veins. The flowers, red and pink in bud, open bright purplish-pink. From 1½ to 2 inches across, they are in loose clusters or pani-cles.

Garden and Landscape Uses and Culti-vation. The species described is sometimes grown in warm climates. Little is recorded of its needs, but it seemingly adapts to or-dinary soils not excessively dry, preferring those with a fairly high organic content, and to light shade. Increase is easy from seeds and cuttings.

ARTICHOKE. A choice and favorite vege-table, the artichoke or globe artichoke (*Cynara scolymus*) is a tall, somewhat this-tle-like, perennial herbaceous plant com-pletely different from Jerusalem and Chinese artichokes. The part of the plant that is eaten is the immature flower head.

Globe artichoke

In North America the chief center of com-mercial production is California, but arti-chokes can be grown elsewhere in home gardens. They are somewhat tender and although the plants may survive if well protected they do not produce satisfactor-ily where harsh winters prevail. Seeds do not give plants true to type. A large pro-portion of seedlings are of inferior quality. Suckers are the usual and most satisfactory means of establishing plantings. They are produced in abundance. Cut them back and plant them in spring at least 6 feet apart each way in deep, fertile soil in a

Globe artichoke

sunny location. Cultivate to keep down weeds, and irrigate or water regularly during dry weather. Artichokes are gross feeders, fertilize them generously. Harvest the heads in fall and winter before they become hard and tough. Do not let them reach the blooming stage. After harvesting cut off all old stems. For the best results renew plantings every three or four years. This crop is subject to aphids, caterpillars, and leaf spot diseases. Consult local Co-operative Extension Agents regarding control measures.

ARTICHOKE, CHINESE OR JAPANESE. Scarcely known as a vegetable in North America, and little known in the Western world, *Stachys affinis*, variously known as Chinese artichoke, Japanese artichoke, chorogi, knotroot, and crosnes, is worth trying as a novelty. The edible parts are underground tubers, arranged in long strings of curious shape. These artichokes are simple to grow. Plant tubers in early spring in rows about 1½ feet apart with 6 inches between the tubers in the rows. Except for cultivating to control weeds no particular care is needed. By fall the crop is ready for harvesting, and can be handled in the same way as Jerusalem artichokes. The tubers should not be kept long out of the soil. Exposure to air causes them to darken.

ARTICHOKE, JERUSALEM. This is very different from the common artichoke. It is in fact a sunflower (*Helianthus tuberosus*), and far from having any connection with Jerusalem, is a native North American. It was one of the very few plants cultivated for food by North American Indians. The popular name has been thought to be a corruption of its Italian one girasole. An alternative suggestion is that it is a corruption of artichoke van Ter Neusen, the last being a place in Holland where it was grown. It was called artichoke because the consistency and flavor of the cooked tubers was thought to resemble those of artichokes. The edible parts are nutritious,

underground, potato-like tubers. As a vegetable, it is less popular in America than in Europe. Because the tubers contain inulin rather than starch Jerusalem artichokes have been recommended as food for diabetics.

Jerusalem artichokes are extremely easy to grow. They thrive in sunny locations in any reasonably fertile garden soil. Because of their vigorous growth (their stems may be 12 feet tall) locate them where they will not shade other vegetables. Plant the tubers, either whole or cut into pieces, in spring or fall, in rows 3½ to 4 feet apart with 1½ to 2 feet between the tubers in the rows. Cover them with about 2 inches of soil. The crop is harvested in fall. Then, the tubers may be dug and stored in slightly-damp soil, peat moss, or sand in a cool or cold (unlike Irish potatoes, Jerusalem artichokes are improved rather than harmed by freezing) place until needed for use. Or you can leave the crop in the ground and dig and use it in spring. When harvesting remove all tubers. Any that remain will become nuisance weeds among other crops sown or planted in the same place.

ARTIFICIAL LIGHT GARDENING. See Indoor Light Gardening.

ARTILLERY PLANT is *Pilea microphylla*.

ARTOCARPUS (Arto-cárpus)—Breadfruit, Breadnut, Jackfruit or Jakfruit, Marang. Captain William Bligh's famous expedition in the H. M. S. Bounty (1787–88) had as its objective the collection and transportation of a species of *Artocarpus* from Tahiti to the West Indies. The attempt failed because the crew mutinied, but a later expedition in the ship *Providence* under Bligh's command, which sailed from England in 1792, succeeded and 1,200 breadfuit (*Artocarpus altilis*) were brought to the New World. Actually this did not represent the first introduction of the species to the Americas. Ten years before Bligh's successful voyage the French had brought in a seed-bearing kind called breadnut. Bligh's cargo was of the much more valuable seedless type, the breadfruit. The British Government hoped that the breadfruit would provide abundant cheap food for slaves, but it did not prove as practicable for this purpose in the West Indies as the banana, which the negroes preferred and which was more productive. Yet the breadfruit grew well in its new home and is now common in Caribbean lands as well as in other parts of the humid tropics.

The genus *Artocarpus* belongs in the mulberry family MORACEAE and consists of nearly fifty species of trees all natives of southeastern Asia and the Pacific islands. Its name is derived from the Greek *artos*, bread, and *karpos*, fruit, and refers to the breadlike quality of the breadfruit when

baked. Artocarpuses contain milky sap and have alternate, divided, lobed, or unlobed stiff leaves of large size. Their tiny flowers are unisexual and very numerous. Each tree bears both sexes, the males in stout, club-shaped spikes, the females in dense spherical to oblong heads with much of the flower embedded in the thick stalk on which it is borne.

The breadfruit (**A. altilis** syns. *A. communis*; *A. incisa*) is a handsome tree 40 to

Artocarpus altilis

60 feet in height. It has a wide-spreading head, densely foliaged with thick, lustrous, deeply-pinnately three- to nine-lobed, leathery leaves. The leaves are broadly-ovate in outline and up to 2 feet long or longer. Their undersurfaces and the veins on the upper leaf surfaces are more or less pubescent. The spikes of male flowers, up to 1 foot long, are yellow and down-curved or drooping. The female spikes ripen into greenish to yellowish ellipsoid to nearly globular compound fruits 4 to 8 inches long. The fruits have few or no seeds.

Cultivated since prehistoric times, the breadfruit probably is derived from a species native to the Malay Archipelago and was transported to the islands of the Pacific, including Hawaii, by early man. All known varieties probably originated in cultivation. The first accurate description of this fruit was given to the Western World at the end of the seventeenth century when it was observed on the island of Guam, but seafarers, undoubtedly, had encountered it well before then. The breadfruit exists in many varieties. Its fruits are made ready for eating by boiling, baking, and frying. They are nutritious and when cooked have a somewhat bread-like texture.

The breadnut is a seed-bearing race of *Artocarpus altilis* and probably closely resembles or is identical with the wild progenitor of the breadfruit. Its seeds are eaten, but it is much less important as a food plant than the breadfruit. The flesh of breadnut fruits is of no significant value as food, but their chestnut-like seeds are highly regarded for eating after they have been boiled or roasted.

The jackfruit or jakfruit (*A. heterophyllus* syn. *A. integrifolia*) is a stately evergreen tree, native of India, and now widely dispersed throughout the humid tropics.

Artocarpus heterophyllus

Attaining heights of 50 to 70 feet, it has stiff, glossy, usually lobeless, elliptic to obovate leaves, 4 to 8 inches long. In contrast to the breadfruit, its flowers and huge fruits are developed from the trunk and major limbs of the tree rather than from young branches. Its flowers are similar to those of the breadfruit, but its fruits are much bigger. Normally they weigh twenty to forty pounds and are reported to sometimes attain twice this latter weight, but that may be something of an exaggeration. They vary from egg-shaped to irregularly-oblong and may attain a length of 2 feet or more. Their rind, pale green ripening to greenish-yellow or brownish, is beset with short hard points. Inside, the fruit is divided into numerous small compartments each containing a seed enclosed in soft aromatic flesh flavored somewhat like that of a banana, but stronger, and rather repulsively scented. These fruits are among the largest produced by any plant.

Pliny and Theophrastus knew of the jackfruit and mentioned it in their writings. The mid-fourteenth-century traveler and writer Marignolli described it as "something marvellous to see, being as big as a great lamb or a child of three years old. It has a hard rind like that of our pine cones, so that you have to cut it open with a hatchet; inside it has a pulp of surpassing flavor, with the sweetness of honey, and of the best Italian melon; and this also contains 500 chestnuts of like flavor, which are capital eating when roasted." Modern taste scarcely agrees with Marignolli's enthusiastic tribute. Although of some importance as a food in some tropical countries, it is generally regarded as much inferior to

the breadfruit and does not find favor with Europeans or Americans. The flesh of jackfruits is eaten raw or preserved in syrup, the seeds after boiling or roasting.

The marang (*A. odoratissimus*), native of Borneo and the Philippines, has fruits

Artocarpus heterophyllus (fruit)

superior to those of the jackfruit and breadnut, which they somewhat resemble, but are only about 6 inches in length. They have a thick skin densely covered with short, soft, yellowish-green spines, and pleasantly-flavored, aromatic, juicy flesh, which is eaten raw. A medium-sized tree of quite handsome appearance, the marang has large, dark green leaves that are unlobed or three-lobed.

Garden and Landscape Uses. The breadfruit and breadnut are strictly plants of the humid tropics and cannot be expected to grow outdoors in any part of the continental United States. In Hawaii and other places where they prosper they are attractive, handsome ornamentals as well as producers of edible fruits. They have the added distinction of being "conversation pieces" to display to visitors from more temperate climes. The jackfruit is also a good ornamental and, because of its fruiting habit and the great size of its fruits, even more of a curiosity. Although essentially tropical, it is hardier than the breadfruit and may be grown in southern Florida, although the trees there do not attain large size and their fruits are of comparatively poor quality. The marang is probably no hardier than the breadfruit and is unsuited for growing outdoors in the continental United States. In greenhouses devoted to the cultivation of plants useful to man these species are sometimes grown for their interest, but are not known to fruit when so cultivated.

Cultivation. High temperatures and high humidity are the chief needs of these plants. Given these, they thrive in any ordinary soil that does not lack for moisture,

but is well drained. In greenhouses a minimum winter night temperature of 60 to 70°F is satisfactory, and daytime temperatures may be allowed to reach 80°F or, in summer, even higher. They grow well in well-drained pots, tubs, or ground beds in coarse, fertile soil. Some shade from strong summer sun is necessary for plants grown in greenhouses. Any pruning required should be done in late winter or early spring, and then, too, needed potting or top dressing should receive attention. The soil must be kept evenly moist, and well-established specimens supplied with regular applications of dilute liquid fertilizer from spring through fall.

Propagation of the breadnut, jackfruit, and marang is easily accomplished by seeds sown in a temperature of 75 to 80°F. The seeds do not retain their germinating powers for many weeks and should be sown as soon after they ripen as practicable. The breadfruit is increased by rooted shoots that develop spontaneously from the roots or may be induced by cutting or wounding some of the stouter roots that develop at or near the ground surface. Root-cuttings and air-layering afford alternative methods of increase.

ARUM (Ar-um)—Cuckoo Pint or Lords-and-Ladies, Black-Calla. The name *Arum* is of ancient linage and at various times has been used for several quite different plants. Botanically its application is now limited to about fifteen species of the arum family ARACEAE, closely related to the jack-in-the-pulpit (*Arisaema*). They are natives of Europe, North Africa, and Asia. A simple difference between arums and arisaemas is that the former have arrow-shaped, but not deeply-lobed or dissected leaves, whereas the leaves of the latter are either very deeply-lobed or consist of separate leaflets. Besides being the name of the genus discussed here, the word arum is used as part of the common names of the arrow-arum (*Peltandra*), dragon-arum (*Dracunculus*), ivy arum (*Scindapsus*), twist-arum (*Helicodiceros*), and water-arum (*Calla*).

Arums are tuberous, deciduous, herbaceous plants, with erect, stalked leaves, and flowering stalks that terminate in a typical calla-lily-like "flower" that is not an individual bloom, but an inflorescence (cluster of flowers and attendant parts). In *Arum*, as in other members of the family, an inflorescence consists of a spadix or congested spike of tiny blooms (typified by the erect yellow central column in the center of a calla-lily) and from its base a spathe (a bract either green or petal-like, represented in the calla-lily by the white, yellow, or pink, trumpet-shaped organ). In *Arum* the upper part of the spadix is without flowers. Below this, in descending succession, are concentrations of sterile male flowers, fertile males, fertile females, and sterile females. The lower, flower-bearing section of the usually purple spadix is contained below a more or less marked narrowing of the spathe. Through the neck of the constriction the cylindrical, tail-like, sterile portion of the spadix protrudes, giving reason for the fanciful name cuckoo pint applied to one species. The fruits are berries. For the plant once named *A. viviparum* see Remusatia.

The cuckoo pint, or lords-and-ladies (*A. maculatum*), is a variable native of Europe and North Africa. Up to 1 foot high or higher, it has long-stalked, arrow-shaped, usually dark-spotted, glossy leaves with blades 3½ to 8 inches long, the basal lobes spreading or not. They appear in spring with the blooms. The inflorescence, with its stalk, is about as long as the leaves. Its spathe, yellowish-green margined and usually spotted with purple, is 6 to 10 inches long. That of *A. m. immaculatum* is without spots. The bright red berries are poisonous.

The black-calla (*A. palaestinum* syn. *A. sanctum*), an interesting spring-blooming native of Syria and Israel, occurs in the vicinity of Jerusalem. Its leaves have blades 6 inches to 1 foot long or longer, arrow-shaped with flaring basal lobes, and stalks longer than those of the inflorescences. The 6- to 10-inch-long spathes, green more or less blotched or spotted with purple on the outside and rich black-purple inside, are 3 to 5 inches wide. The spadix, its upper part deep purple, is much shorter than the spathe.

Arum italicum

Arum palaestinum

Native to western Europe and North Africa, the very variable *A. italicum* blooms later than the cuckoo pint. Its inflorescence has a short yellow spadix and a much longer, greenish-white spathe the upper part of which flops over when the flowers fade. It is larger and more robust than the cuckoo pint. Its leaves, triangular-arrow-shaped, have spreading lower lobes. In *A. i. albispathum* the spathe is white. The leaves of *A. i. marmoratum* are marbled with yellow.

Arum italicum, in fruit

Autumn-flowering and its fully grown leaves with heart-shaped bases, *A. pictum*, of the Mediterranean region, produces its oblong-ovate leaves in spring and blooms when it is leafless. The leaves have stalks and blades each up to 10 inches long. The inflorescence is on a stalk about 4 inches long. Its spathe has a swollen green lower part and is violet above. The black-purple spadix protrudes. The berries are red.

Other sorts sometimes cultivated are *A. creticum*, *A. hygrophilum*, and *A. orientale*. Native to Crete, *A. creticum* has leaves with a stalk up to 9 inches long and an arrow-shaped blade 4 to 5 inches in length and approximately 3 inches wide. The inflorescence on a stalk 9 inches to 1¼ feet long, has a short tubed, slender-pointed, whitish spathe 3 to 6 inches long. An inhabitant of Cyprus, Israel, and Turkey, *A. hygrophilum* is much like *A. palaestinum*,

but has narrower leaves and an inflorescence with a spathe 4 to 5 inches long by 1½ to 3 inches wide, cream above, green toward its base, and with narrow, purple margins. The spadix is purple. Variable *A.*

Arum hygrophilum

orientale resembles *A. pictum*. Wild from Greece to Russia and about 1 foot tall, it has arrow-shaped leaves with rather widely-spreading basal lobes and a stalk two to three times as long as the blade. The inflorescence has a tube white on its inside and an ovate to elliptic-oblong blade twice as long as the tube and black-purple or sometimes greenish or purple-flushed spathe and, about one half as long as the spathe, a blackish-purple spadix.

Garden and Landscape Uses. The cuckoo pint and *A. italicum* are reasonably hardy and can be expected to survive in sheltered places outdoors at least as far north as

Arum orientale

ica. It grows 4 to 7 feet tall and has erect, branched stems and abundant handsome foliage. The leaves are large and twice- or thrice-divided into many pointed, sharply-double-toothed, ovate to lanceolate leaflets 1 inch to 4 inches long; they may be hairless or somewhat pubescent. The multitude of tiny flowers, each about ⅛ inch across and creamy-white, forms showy plumelike panicles of rather widely spaced spikelike branches. The panicles rise well above the foliage. The flowers are unisexual, the individual plants male or female. Because of the many stamens, male plants are the showier in bloom. Each flower has a five-lobed calyx and five petals. The males have numerous stamens, the females usually three pistils (in *Spiraea* there are five). Variety *A. d. kneiffii* is 3 to 4 feet tall and has more finely divided foliage.

Aruncus dioicus

Aruncus dioicus

New York City; the others described are somewhat less cold-tolerant. Arums appeal chiefly to gardeners interested in the curious and unusual. They need to be accommodated in deep, dampish woodland soil in light shade and are appropriate for rock gardens, open woodlands, and for planting beneath deep-rooting trees and shrubs. When cultivated in pots, they and other sorts make unusual and interesting cool greenhouse plants.

Cultivation. The tubers must be planted deep enough to allow for the development of roots from their upper sides. An annual mulch of leaf mold, peat moss, or good compost is highly beneficial, and in cold climates, winter protection in the way of a thick cover of leaves, salt hay, branches of evergreens, or other suitable material may be needed. Care must be taken that the soil is moist at all times when foliage is in evidence.

When grown in pots or pans (shallow pots) good drainage is necessary. A fertile soil containing generous amounts of peat moss or leaf mold is used. Potting and re-potting is done in fall or winter before new growth begins. Cool temperatures, 40 to 50°F at night and a few degrees more by day, are appropriate for most; for *A. palaestinum* they may be slightly higher.

When in active growth potted specimens benefit from applications of dilute liquid fertilizer. As the leaves die naturally watering is gradually reduced and finally withheld altogether and the soil kept dry until the beginning of the next growing period. Propagation is by offset tubers and by fresh seeds sown without drying in sandy peaty soil kept evenly moist, but not constantly wet.

ARUNCUS (Arún-cus)—Goat's Beard. Only one of the two or three species of this northern hemisphere genus of the rose family ROSACEAE is at all commonly cultivated, and it often under the name of the allied genus *Spiraea*. Goat's beards differ from *Spiraea* in being herbaceous (nonwoody) perennials, rather than shrubs, and in having leaves of many separate leaflets. They greatly resemble astilbes of the saxifrage family SAXIFRAGACEAE, but are very much larger; also, their stamens are numerous rather than as many as or twice as many as the petals. The name *Aruncus* is one used by Pliny.

The cultivated goat's beard (**A. dioicus** syns. *A. sylvester*, *Spiraea aruncus*) is a good-looking, summer-blooming native of rich, moist woods in temperate parts of Europe, Asia, and Western North Amer-

Garden and Landscape Uses. Of easy cultivation, the goat's beard is attractive for partly shaded places where the soil is fertile and not deficient in moisture. It is hardy and well suited for flower beds and for grouping toward the fronts of shrub borders and the fringes of woodlands. It is a good background plant for small gardens and its blooms may be cut and used indoors. It looks well beside water, set on ground 1 foot or so higher than its surface.

Cultivation. Given the type of soil and situation indicated in the previous paragraph as being to its liking, the goat's beard presents no special problems to the gardener. It is propagated by division in spring or early fall and by seeds sown in May in a moistish spot outdoors, or in pots or flats indoors earlier. The seeds germinate readily.

ARUNDINA (Arún-dina)—Bamboo Orchid. Although not native to Hawaii, the bamboo orchid (*Arundina graminifolia* syn. *A. bambusifolia*) is naturalized there. The original range of this variable, evergreen species, the sole member of its genus, of the orchid family ORCHIDACEAE extends from southern China and Malaysia to the Himalayas, Indonesia, and some islands of the Pacific. Its name, a diminutive of that of the reed *Arundo*, alludes to the appearance of its stems. The vernacular name bamboo orchid also makes reference to the clumps of the closely-set, branchless, tall, reedy stems, clothed with alternate, grass-like leaves.

From 5 to 10 feet in height, and growing in the ground rather than like many orchids perched on trees, *A. graminifolia* has along the greater length of its stems, two-ranked, stem-clasping, pointed-linear leaves up to 1 foot long, and rarely more than 1½ inches wide. The fragrant flowers are several together in loose, terminal racemes, with only one or two in each open at once. They look much like small cattleyas. Their rosy-lilac sepals and petals spread widely, and the blooms are 2 to 3 inches wide. The sepals are conspicuously narrower than the petals, the two lateral ones angling sharply downward so that they are behind the handsome lip. The latter encloses the column with its tubular base. Toward its apex it flares widely, and is bright rosy-purple. Its paler throat has a yellow patch, and is veined with purple. Variety *A. g. alba* is pure white with a yellow throat.

Garden and Landscape Uses and Cultivation. In the humid tropics and warm subtropics this orchid is a delightful outdoor ornamental. It blooms nearly continuously, and can be used effectively in clumps and for screening. Perfect soil drainage is essential. A coarse, porous rooting mixture composed of fertile topsoil, with which has been mixed, in generous quantities, shredded leaves and osmunda fiber, and a liberal dressing of dried manure or slow-acting fertilizer, preferably an organic one, suffices. A warm, sunny location is needed. Watering is done to prevent the soil from ever being really dry. When planting, it is important not to set the roots so deeply that the bottoms of the stems are buried. Staking is usually needed to keep the plants from toppling. Routine care, besides watering, involves fertilizing at regular intervals throughout the almost continuous growing season.

In greenhouses the bamboo orchid is generally less free-flowering than in the open. It may be accommodated in large, well-drained pots or tubs in a soil mixture similar to that suggested for outdoors, possibly with small lumps of charcoal added. A humid greenhouse with a minimum night temperature of 60°F and warmer by day affords suitable growing conditions through most of the year. In summer the plants benefit from being stood in a sunny location outdoors. For more information see Orchids.

ARUNDINARIA (Arun-dinària). Approximately 150 species of bamboos of the grass family GRAMINEAE constitute *Arundinaria*. In addition, some botanists include about 100 species that other botanists segregate as *Pleioblastus*. The segregation is accepted in this Encyclopedia. Included are the only bamboos indigenous to the United States. The genus contains some of the hardiest bamboos, several sufficiently cold resistant to winter outdoors in sheltered places as far north as southern New York. Most, however, are subtropical or tropical. The name derives from the Latin *arundo*, a reed, and alludes to the appearance of their stems. Some species previously included in *Arundinaria* belong in *Chimonobambusa*.

Arundinarias are graceful. They have cylindrical, straight canes with many branches from each node. Their rhizomes are slender and the clumps compact or with their canes widely spaced, according to kind. The flowers differ from those of *Bambusa* in having three instead of six stamens.

Native American kinds are the Southern cane or cane-reed (*A. gigantea* syn. *A. macrosperma*), which forms natural cane brakes mostly along river banks from Virginia and Kentucky southward, and the small-cane or switch-cane (*A. g. tecta*), native to swamps and moist soils from Maryland to Indiana and southward. A form of this last, common in western North Carolina, is unusual among bamboos in that it is not evergreen, but drops its foliage in fall and remains bare of leaves until spring. Attaining heights of 15 to 25 feet, *A. gigantea* forms dense stands. Its dull yellowish stems have nonpersistent leaf sheaths and numerous short branches with leaves 4 inches to over 1 foot long and up to 1½ inches wide. Its rhizomes spread freely. As its name implies, the small-cane is less vigorous and this is true also of its variety. These have slender stems 2 to 12 feet in height with leaves up to 6 inches lng by 1 inch wide. The foliage of the deciduous variety turns yellow before it drops. The small-cane, except for size, is similar to the Southern cane but the sheaths persisting on the canes and the upper sides of the leaves, as well as the undersides, are decidedly pubescent instead of being nearly

hairless. Its foliage provides cattle fodder in its native haunts.

Of Asian species, the Tonkin bamboo (*A. amabilis*) is one of the most important. It is esteemed as the source of fine quality canes of many and varied uses. Its origin is doubtful, since it is known only in cultivation, but it must be regarded as essentially subtropical. Even so, at Savannah, Georgia, it produces stems 30 feet in height and has withstood, without damage, temperatures as low as 17°F. The Tonkin bamboo forms open clumps, with the very erect canes spaced distantly. It characteristically has three branches from each node of the center portions of the canes, and none from the lower nodes. The leaves are dark green above, paler beneath. The Simon bamboo (*A. simonii* syn. *Pleioblastus simonii*) is a vigorous, relatively hardy native of China and Japan that attains a height 20 feet or more and has numerous branches from the nodes of its erect, olive-green to dull green canes. Its cane sheaths are very persistent. The leaves, up to 1 foot long by 1¼ inches wide, taper to a long point and are markedly tessellated. They are bright green above, and beneath are deep green on one side and grayish-green on the other. The young shoots are edible. The rhizomes of this species are running, but it is not an invasive plant. It can be used effectively as a screen or hedge. A variety, *A. s. variegata* (syn. *A. s.* 'Silverstripe'), has leaves variegated with white. It often reverts to the green form. The plant sometimes called *A. s. chino* is *A. chino*.

A Japanese native and one of the hardiest kinds, but less decorative than many arundinarias, *A. chino* (syn. *Pleioblastus chino*) has dark green canes usually with purplish blotches. About 7 feet tall, they have rather persistent cane sheaths. Toward the middles of the canes the branches are solitary, but are likely to be multiple above and below. The long-pointed leaves, up to 10 inches long by 1 inch wide and clearly tessellated, are in plumelike clusters. They are dark green above, dull grayish-green beneath. The rootstocks spread rather widely and under favorable soil conditions may tend to be invasive. Another running Japanese sort, *A. disticha* (syns. *A. argenteostriata disticha*, *Bambusa disticha*), known only in cultivation and called dwarf fern-leaf bamboo, is 2 to 2½ feet tall. It has slender, zigzagged canes and bristly-edged leaves, bright green above, slightly glaucous on their undersides, and distinctly arranged in two rows. It is useful as a groundcover.

Native at high altitudes in Sikkim and Bhutan, where it blooms annually, a characteristic not maintained in cultivation, *A. aristata* (syn. *Thamnocalamus aristatus*) has brownish-green canes up to 15 feet tall or taller with many reddish branches and branchlets. The cane sheaths are not persistent. Up to 5 inches long by ½ inch broad, the leaves taper to points curiously twisted at their ends. Bright green above, gray-green on their under surfaces, they are moderately tessellated and all along the margins are fringed with fine bristles. This handsome bamboo, very satisfactory as a tub specimen, is probably not hardy north of Washington, D.C. Compact clumps of canes that under highly favorable conditions attain a height of 60 feet, but are often only one half as tall are characteristic of *A. falconeri* (syn. *Thamnocalamus falconeri*) of Nepal. The peripheral canes of the clumps of this arch gracefully outward, are green with brownish-purple marks at the nodes, and become dull yellow with brownish-purple joints at maturity. The cane sheaths are soon deciduous. The leaves, mostly about 4 inches long by ½ inch broad, but terminal ones sometimes considerably larger, show no tessellation; they are bright green on their upper surfaces, paler beneath. This species, most satisfactory in partial shade, is hardy about as far north as Washington, D.C. It is a good tub plant.

Chinese *A. hindsii* (syn. *Pleoblastus hindsii*), cultivated for centuries in Japan, but not native there, is a spreading, moderately-invasive plant that kept under reasonable control makes a good screen or hedge. One of the hardier species, it attains a height of about 12 feet and has dark olive-green canes, the older ones with many branches from each node. The branches form heavy clusters toward the tops of the canes. The leaves, tapered to long points, are thick and have one margin edged with fine hairs, the other partially so. Very variable in size, they are up to 9 inches long by 1 inch wide. They are conspicuously tessellated and dark green above, dull grayish-green beneath. It stands considerable shade. It has been cultivated as *Bambusa gracilis*.

Perhaps the finest of the variegated-leaved bamboos is *A. viridistriata* (syns. *A. auricoma, Pleoblastus viridistriatus*). A hardy kind of doubtful provenance, it at-

tains a height of 4 to 6 feet and has dark purplish-green stems. Its cane branches are solitary or paired, and the leaves, variable in size and up to 8 inches long by 1¾ inches wide, are mostly conspicuously striped with green and brilliant yellow in proportions varying from leaf to leaf. Often some leaves are completely golden. The leaves are pubescent beneath. Although it has running rhizomes, this species is not unduly invasive and is easy to keep under control. Another attractive variegated kind, with white rather than yellow leaf variegation, Japanese *A. variegata* (syns. *A. fortunei, Pleoblastus variegatus*) sometimes attains 4 feet; sometimes it is lower. This hardy sort is attractive for growing in containers as well as in gardens. Its canes are slender and pale green with usually solitary, but occasionally paired branches. Its leaves, commonly up to 6 inches long by ¾ inch wide, sometimes attain a length of 8 inches and a width of 1 inch. Short-pointed, and dark green conspicuously tessellated and striped with white fading to pale green, they have one margin fringed with fine hairs, the other partially so. This bamboo has running rhizomes that tend to be invasive. Also with variegated foliage, *A. argenteostriata* (syn. *Bambusa argenteostriata*) is known only in cultivation but a green-leaved variant, *A. a. communis*, which is wild in Japan, doubtless represents the stock from which this was derived. The canes of this species and its variety, up to 9 feet long and ½ inch thick, have nodes densely-hairy at first, later nearly hairless. The pointed-lanceolate leaves up to 1 foot long and 1¼ inches wide are in groups of three to thirteen.

Among the smallest and hardiest bamboos is *A. pumila* (syn. *Pleoblastus pumi-*

Arundinaria pumila

lus), of Japan. Up to 2½ feet in height, it is useful as a groundcover. Its dull purple canes with a whitish deposit beneath the nodes are very slender and have quite persistent sheaths that have a circle of hairs at the base, a characteristic that serves to distinguish it from *A. vagans*. The branches are solitary or sometimes occur

in pairs. Up to 7 inches long by ¾ inch wide, the leaves are pubescent on both surfaces and are clearly tessellated. The margins are fringed with hairs. Above, the leaves are dark green. Their under surfaces are duller. This species spreads rapidly and should not be planted where space is limited. Even lower than *A. pumila* is *A. pygmaea* (syn. *Pleoblastus pygmaeus*), the dwarfest of the hardy bamboos. In its native Japan it inhabits forest floors and thus can stand a fair amount of shade. Up to 1 foot in height, its canes, bright green becoming purplish at their tips, are extremely slender and solid rather than hollow. The branches are usually solitary, but sometimes occur in pairs. The leaves are up to 5 inches long by up to 1 inch wide. The species occurs in two forms, one with pubescent leaves, the other with hairless foliage. It is a vigorous spreader that should not be planted close to delicate plants it is likely to smother. A third low-growing, hardy species is *A. vagans* (syn. *Pleoblastus viridistriatus vagans*). A native of Japan that attains a height of up to 3½ feet, it is a vigorous grower and rampant spreader with green canes and persistent leaf sheaths that are without the rings of hairs at the bases of the leaf sheaths characteristic of *A. pumila*. The plant called *A. japonica* is *Pseudosasa japonica*.

Garden and Landscape Uses and Cultivation. For information on these subjects see Bamboos.

ARUNDO (Arún-do)—Giant Reed. Only one of the dozen species of these very tall grasses of the Old World is commonly cultivated, the giant reed, a native of the Mediterranean region now naturalized in many warm countries. The genus *Arundo* belongs in the grass family GRAMINEAE. Its name is an ancient Latin one for this plant. Arundos have broad, flat leaves and huge terminal plumes of minute flowers that in the cultivated kinds are highly decorative.

The giant reed has a long history. It was well known to the ancients and is frequently depicted in their arts such as those that decorated the temples of Egypt. A reproduction of its flower cluster was the Egyptian hieroglyphic for the equivalent of the letter A, and some believe that our modern letter can be traced to that source. This grass grows plentifully and luxuriantly along the banks of the Nile, along the shores of the Dead Sea, and is common elsewhere in the Bible lands. Because of this, authorities believe that many references to reeds in the Bible are to this plant, but in other instances different plants, such as *Typha* and *Phragmites*, are undoubtedly indicated.

The stems of the giant reed are used for various purposes, such as reeds of bagpipes, clarinets, and organs, and for making screens, lattices, mats, and fishing poles, as well as for light construction.

Arundinaria viridistriata

The giant reed (*A. donax*) sends erect stems up to a height of 20 feet from knotty rootstocks. The gray-green, alternate leaves are regularly spaced in two opposite ranks that spread in the same plane. They are 1 foot to 2 feet long by 1 inch to 3 inches wide and are without hairs except for a tuft

Arundo donax

near the base of the blade. The erect or slightly drooping, rather narrow panicles of bloom are 1 foot to 2 feet in length and have numerous slender branches. The variety *A. d. versicolor* (syn. *A. d. variegata*) is rather less vigorous and less hardy. Its leaves are beautifully striped with creamy-yellow or white. A native of New Zealand, *A. conspicua* is tenderer than *A. donax*, ordinarily does not exceed 8 feet in height, and has slenderer stems and narrower leaves that are 2 to 4 feet long. The yellowish-white or silvery drooping flower panicles remain attractive over a long period.

Arundo donax variegata

Garden Uses and Cultivation. Arundos are grasses of noble appearance, and well-placed clumps are striking features in landscapes. They are distinctly subtropical and luxuriant in aspect and serve well as lawn specimens and in places near pools or other bodies of water where the banks are sufficiently high to ensure that the main

body of their roots are in drained ground. Full sun and deep, porous, fertile soil assure the best results. They do not prosper in sticky, clayey soils. Propagation is by division of the clumps, or by placing a stem in a receptacle of water and leaving it to develop new little plants, which it will do from every joint, in a short time.

ASARABACCA is *Asarum europaeum*.

ASARINA (Asar-ìna). The genus *Asarina* consists of possibly sixteen species of perennial herbaceous plants closely related to snapdragons (*Antirrhinum*), but with twining or prostrate stems and lobed or coarsely-toothed leaves. The leafstalks of the climbing kinds coil themselves around supports in tendril-like fashion. Asarinas are mostly natives of Mexico, the southwestern United States, and the West Indies. One is indigenous to Europe. The group belongs in the figwort family SCROPHULARIACEAE. Its name, a Spanish vernacular one for a snapdragon (*Antirrhinum*), calls attention to the resemblance of *Asarina* to *Antirrhinum*.

Asarinas have alternate, stalked leaves, and two-lipped, pouched, foxglove-like flowers that in some species have mouths closed with a palate like those of snapdragons, but in others are more open. They have four fertile stamens, the stalks of which bear two rows of nail-like glands. The fruits are capsules.

An inhabitant of desert and semidesert regions, usually in limestone soils, from California to Texas and Mexico, *A. antirrhiniflora* (syn. *Maurandya antirrhiniflora*) is a hairless vine with slender, much-branched stems about 6 feet long, and triangular, toothless, arrow-shaped, halberd-shaped or five-lobed leaves with blades and stalks each up to about 1 inch long. Its solitary, axillary blooms, up to 1¾ inches in length, are on slender stalks ¾ to 1 inch long. The lobes of their lips are purple to rose-pink with a yellowish palate. The tube of the corolla is whitish.

A native of Spain and Portugal, *A. procumbens* (syn. *Antirrhinum asarina*) is a

Asarina procumbens

trailing, sticky-hairy, soft, gray-green perennial. It has frail, succulent stems and opposite, broadly-heart-shaped, more or less five-lobed leaves with round-toothed margins. The 1½-inch-long flowers, solitary from the leaf axils, are white, creamy-white, or pinkish, with red-striped lips.

Other species cultivated are Mexican. Popular *A. barclaiana* (syn. *Maurandya bar-*

Asarina barclaiana

claiana) has deep purple, funnel-shaped flowers, downy on their outsides, 1½ inch to 3 inches long, with long-pointed, sticky-hairy sepals and flaring petals. Its toothless, angular-pointed or halberd-shaped leaves have blades about 1 inch long and long, twining stalks. Often misidentified as *A. scandens*, the species correctly named *A. erubescens* (syn. *Maurandya erubescens*) is glandular-hairy. It has triangular, toothed leaves about 3 inches long, and rose-red flowers of about the same length with one-sided, swollen corolla tubes, and broad, leafy sepals up to 1 inch long. From it *A. scandens* differs in not being hairy, in having arrow-shaped leaves usually not more than 1½ inches long and purple blooms 1 inch long. The sepals of *A. scandens* are lanceolate and about one-half as long as the corolla tube. Sometimes confused with *A. erubescens*, but differing in having flowers

Asarina procumbens

Asarina erubescens

not hairy on their outsides and corolla tubes straight rather than swollen at one side, is *A. lophospermum* (syn. *Maurandya lophospermum*).

Garden and Landscape Uses. In mild climates where little or no frost is experienced, asarinas can be grown as outdoor perennials, but elsewhere they must be cultivated as greenhouse plants or be grown outdoors in summer and overwintered in a cool greenhouse. Alternatively, they can be started early indoors from seeds and treated as annuals. This is a popular method. Asarinas are attractive for late summer and fall display outdoors and for blooming in greenhouses in fall and winter. The climbers can be used to adorn trellises and other supports where vines of some delicacy and not woody growth are desired. Sunny locations are desirable for these plants.

Cultivation. Asarinas need deep, well-drained, porous soil of medium fertility. They respond to neutral and somewhat alkaline soils. If the earth is acid, it is helpful to mix into it a dressing of lime. Propagation is usually by seeds, which germinate satisfactorily in a temperature of 60 to 65°F. Cuttings root readily and may be taken from greenhouse plants in winter or, in mild climates, from outdoor specimens in summer. They can be rooted in sand, vermiculite, or perlite, under mist or in a humid propagating frame. To have plants that will bloom outdoors the first year, sow seeds indoors in January or February. Pot the young plants individually in 2½-inch pots and keep them in a sunny greenhouse in a night temperature of 55 to 60°F until a week or two before they are to be planted outdoors, at the time it is safe to plant tomatoes. Before planting harden the plants by standing them for a week or two in a cold frame or sheltered place outdoors. In greenhouses day temperatures five to fifteen degrees above those maintained at night are appropriate. From the 2½-inch pots the plants are transferred to 4-inch pots. Outdoor spacing of 1 foot to 1½ feet between individuals is satisfactory.

For fall and winter blooming in greenhouses sow seeds in April or May. Pot the seedlings individually into containers 3 inches in diameter and successively into bigger ones until they occupy 8-inch pots. Let the soil be fertile and porous. A little ground limestone or lime mixed with it is beneficial. The kinds grown indoors are vines that coil their leafstalks around suitable supports. Provide such by sticking two or three bamboo canes into each pot to lead the stems to a system of strong twine or wires stretched a few inches beneath the roof glass or to a trellis against a wall or other surface. Asarinas need generous amounts of water and, after the final pots are filled with roots, weekly applications of dilute liquid fertilizer. Very slight shade from strongest summer sun is all that is necessary. Throughout the summer the greenhouse is ventilated freely, at other seasons sufficiently to keep the day temperature not more than five to fifteen degrees above the night temperature of 55 to 60°F. The atmosphere should be fairly humid at all times.

ASARUM (Ásar-um)—Wild-Ginger, Canada Snakeroot. This genus of seventy stemless, deciduous and evergreen, herbaceous plants is not a relative of the true ginger (*Zingiber*) of the ginger family ZINGIBERACEAE, but belongs in the birthwort family ARISTOLOCHIACEAE. Its name is a modification of an ancient Greek one, *asaron*, for *Asarum europaeum*. Called wild-ginger because of the aromatic, ginger-like odor of the bruised rhizomes and leaves, these plants are natives of temperate and subtropical parts of the northern hemisphere, occurring most abundantly in eastern and southeastern Asia, including Japan. The name heart leaf is sometimes used colloquially for these asarums.

Wild-gingers have elongating rhizomes the branches of which each year produce one to three, but in most kinds two, leaves and a short-stalked, reddish-brown flower. The blooms have minute petals or none. Their most apparent feature is a deeply-three-lobed calyx, which at its base is tubular. There are twelve stamens, and six styles, which may be joined or separate. Because the dull-colored blooms are hidden by the foliage they make no effective display. The chief ornamental feature of wild-ginger is the foliage. The fruits are fleshy capsules.

The American Indians employed the roots of *A. canadense* and *A. arifolium* to alleviate stomach pains. The roots of *A. canadense* have been used medicinally as a spring tonic, carminative, and stimulant, but are no longer official in the United States Pharmacopoeia. They have also been used as a substitute for the spice ginger.

A familiar species is the Canada snakeroot (*A. canadense*), native to rich woods from Quebec to Ontario, Minnesota, North

Asarum canadense

Carolina, Alabama, and Arkansas. Somewhat variable, it has more or less pubescent rhizomes and broad heart-shaped deciduous leaves 5 or 6 inches across, on stalks up to 1 foot long. Its flowers are ¾ inch to 1¼ inches long and have spreading or reflexed calyx lobes. Two excellent western North American evergreen species are *A. caudatum* and *A. hartwegii*. The former is remarkable because its blooms have calyx lobes ending in long tails.

Confined as a native to the deep shade of forests in California, *A. caudatum* has heart-shaped to kidney-shaped leaves, pubescent below and on the veins above, about 6 inches in diameter and with stalks up to 7 inches long. Its flowers have united styles as long as the stamens. Ranging as a wild species from California to Oregon, *A. hartwegii*, one of the handsomest wild-gingers, has heart-shaped to kidney-shaped, dark green leaves beautifully marbled with silver. They are hairless or sometimes pubescent on the veins above and more or less hairy on their undersides. Up to 5 inches across, they have stalks up to 8 inches long. The flowers have styles that are nearly separate and are shorter than the stamens.

Six evergreen species native to the southeastern United States that have the styles of their flowers completely separate and prolonged beyond the stigma to form two horns are by some authorities designated as the separate genus *Hexastylis*. Among the loveliest of these, *A. shuttleworthii* (syn. *Hexastylis shuttleworthii*) is a variable species in which the 2- to 3-inch-wide leaves, on stalks up to 8 inches long, may be plain green, but are often prettily mottled with silver-gray. The urn-shaped, short-stalked flowers, with spreading lobes, are 1½ to 2 inches long. This kind is native to rich woods from Virginia and West Virginia to Alabama. Closely resembling *A. shuttleworthii* in foliage and appearance, *A. virginicum* (syn. *Hexastylis virginica*) has flowers not more than 1 inch long; they have spreading lobes. The leaves of this species are up to 4 inches across and have stalks about 7 inches long, they are usually mottled with silver-gray. This kind inhabits moist and dry woods from Virginia to West Virginia, Kentucky, Georgia, and Alabama. Favoring similar habitats from Virginia and Kentucky to Florida and Louisiana, *A. arifolium* (syn. *Hexastylis arifolia*) has triangular-arrow-shaped leaves up to 6 inches long and short-stemmed flowers ¾ inch to 1¼ inches long. The tube of the bloom is markedly narrowed near its top, the corolla lobes are spreading.

The European wild-ginger or asarabacca (*A. europaeum*), with glossy, rich green, evergreen foliage, is one of the finest kinds. Its heart-shaped, slightly-wavy leaves, about 3 inches wide, have 5- to 6-inch-long stalks. The flowers are about ½ inch long, and drooping.

Asarum europaeum

Garden Uses. The wild-gingers are admirable for shaded places where the soil is rich and fairly moist. They lend themselves well for use as underplantings in open woods, beneath trees, and among shrubbery and can be used effectively in rock gardens, native plant gardens, and informal areas. The European wild-ginger and other evergreen kinds are choice, handsome, easy-to-satisfy groundcovers that should be planted much more commonly as a change from pachysandra, running myrtle (*Vinca minor*), and English ivy. The evergreen wild-gingers are hardy in New York City and perhaps in even harsher climates; under such conditions, however, *A. caudatum* loses its foliage (is deciduous), and in exceptionally hard winters *A. europaeum* and *A. hartwegii* may do so late in the season.

Cultivation. Asarums are easily raised from seeds sown in a cold frame or outdoors where they will not be disturbed, in sandy soil containing an abundance of leaf mold or peat moss. Sowing may be done as soon as the seeds ripen, or in the fall. Self-sown seedlings often appear beneath established plants, and they can be trans-

planted. They accommodate well to this. The seedlings are grown for a year or two in nursery beds before being set in their permanent quarters at planting distances of 9 inches to 1 foot. These plants can also be increased by division in early fall or spring. Clumps of wild-ginger increase in size slowly, and unless rapid propagation by division is desired, they can remain undisturbed for many years. Seasonal care gives little trouble. Watering in dry weather and weeding may need occasional attention, although in deeply-shaded places where the soil is naturally moist even these chores may not be needed. A top dressing of leaf mold, screened compost, or peat moss, and a light dressing of a complete fertilizer each spring promotes vigor and well-being.

ASCARINA (Ascár-ina). This genus belongs in the chloranthus family CHLORANTHACEAE, a small group related to the pepper family PIPERACEAE. It is endemic to New Zealand and islands of the Pacific including New Caledonia and Tahiti. Only one of its eight species is likely to be cultivated. Ascarinas are aromatic trees and shrubs, with opposite leaves and racemes or spikes of tiny unisexual flowers. The one-seeded fruits are berry-like. Its name, from the Greek *askaris,* a worm, alludes to the anthers being wormlike.

Native to New Zealand, *Ascarina lucida* is a shrub or a tree up to 25 feet tall with handsome, short-stalked, glossy, dark green, fragrant leaves that are oblong-elliptic, coarsely-toothed, and about 2 inches long. The branched flower spikes droop and are 2 or 3 inches long.

Garden and Landscape Uses and Cultivation. This sort, the chief attraction of which is its foliage, is planted to some extent in California and similar mild regions. It thrives in ordinary soil in sun and is propagated by seeds and cuttings.

ASCENDING. As used in describing branches and other plant parts this means angled upward, but not vertical.

ASCLEPIADACEAE—Milkweed Family. Many plants of horticultural importance belong here. Familiar examples are hoyas, milkweeds, and stephanotises. Also included are stapelias and a number of related genera of equally unusual appearance. Some 2,000 species representing 130 genera of dicotyledons belong here.

Asclepiads (the embracing name for members of the family) are most abundant as to genera and species in the tropics, subtropics, and warm-temperate regions, but are represented, especially by milkweeds (*Asclepias*), elsewhere. Many are desert plants. Most have milky sap. Included are herbaceous plants, shrubs, and twining vines, some with tubers. Their leaves are opposite, whorled (in circles of three

or more), or rarely alternate. They are undivided, seldom lobed or toothed. The leaves of desert species frequently drop early or are vestigial and nonfunctional. The symmetrical flowers in branched, often umbel-like clusters or sometimes raceme-like inflorescences have a calyx of five lobes or sepals, a five-lobed corolla, and five stamens usually joined into a column and with their anthers united with the stigma. There are two styles. A very usual feature is a central corona or crown developed from the corolla or stamens. The fruits are paired, podlike follicles, one of which may fail to develop fully, containing many seeds generally furnished with long, silky hairs. Genera cultivated include *Araujia, Asclepias, Brachystelma, Calotropis, Caralluma, Ceropegia, Chlorocodon, Cryptolepis, Cryptostegia, Cynanchum, Diplocyatha, Dischidia, Dregia, Duvalia, Echidnopsis, Edithcolea, Fockea, Frerea, Gonolobus, Hoodia, Hoodiopsis, Hoya, Huernia, Huerniopsis, Luckoffia, Marsdenia, Matelea, Morrenia, Oxypetalum, Pachycarpus, Pachypodium, Pechtinaria, Periploca, Piaranthus, Raphionacme, Sarcostemma, Stapelia, Stephanotis, Stultitia, Tavaresia,* and *Trichocaulon.*

ASCLEPIAS (Asclèp-ias)—Butterfly Weed or Pleurisy Root, Milkweed, Blood Flower. This, the genus of the milkweeds or silkweeds, consists of herbaceous perennials of North, Central, and South America. Of the more than 100 species, many are hardy. Dedicated to Asklepios, the Greek god of medicine, *Asclepias* is the type genus of the milkweed family ASCLEPIADACEAE.

Most kinds of *Asclepias* have milky juice. Their leaves are sometimes alternate or opposite, more commonly in whorls (circles of three or more). Their smallish blooms are in umbels, terminal or from the leaf axils. Individual flowers have deeply-five-cleft, wheel-shaped corollas the lobes of which when the flower becomes mature spread backward and conceal the usually small, five-toothed calyxes. There is a corona or crown of five hoods, erect or spreading, straight or curved, variable in shape and structure, each with or without a horn protruding from near its base. The stalks of the five stamens, which have winged anthers, are united to form a tube adherent to and surrounding the five-lobed or five-angled stigma. The fruits are generally erect, more or less spindle-shaped, podlike follicles containing flat seeds, each with a tuft of silky hairs.

Butterfly weed or pleurisy root (*A. tuberosa*), one of the most beautiful American wild flowers, is distinct from most other kinds in having nonmilky sap. Varying considerably in habit of growth, foliage, and flower color, in the wild it ranges from Ontario to Minnesota, Colorado, Florida, and Arizona. From 1 foot to 3 feet in height, its stems are branchless or are freely-branched in their upper parts. The

Asclepias tuberosa

stalkless or very short-stalked leaves are 2 to 4 inches long, alternate, or those of the branches opposite. They are linear, lanceolate, or oblanceolate and pubescent. Varying in color from rich orange-red to yellow, the ¼-inch-wide flowers are in short-stalked umbels 1½ to 2 inches across, solitary and terminal, or more numerous and from the leaf axils of the branches. The erect seed pods, on down-pointing stalks, are 3½ to 5 inches long.

Swamp milkweed (*A. incarnata*) is a common, bold-appearing inhabitant of wet

Asclepias incarnata

soils from Nova Scotia to Manitoba, Florida, and New Mexico. Its stems, except sometimes the branches, are hairless and up to 4½ feet tall. The leaves, opposite or in threes, are oblong or linear-oblong, usually pointed, hairless, or sometimes sparsely-hairy along the veins, and 3 to 6 inches long. The rose-pink to purplish-red or rarely white flowers, many together in stalked umbels, are ¼ inch wide. Slightly pubescent, the erect seed pods, on erect stalks, are 2 to 3½ inches in length. Variety *A. i. pulchra* (syn. *A. pulchra*) has somewhat broader leaves that, like its stems, are densely-hairy.

Common milkweed (*A. syriaca*) grows in fields, meadows, prairies, and at roadsides from New Brunswick to Saskatchewan, Georgia, and Kansas. Up to 5 feet tall, it has mostly branchless hairy stems, and thick, elliptic, ovate, or oblong, short-stalked leaves, softly pubescent on their undersides, up to 4 inches long and approximately 2 inches wide. About ¼ inch wide, the greenish to purplish-white flowers are in stalked umbels. The seed pods, on down-pointing stalks, are erect, 3 to 5 inches long, and covered with small, conical, warty projections.

Asclepias syriaca

Blood flower (*A. currassavica*) is not hardy in the north. Native to tropical America and naturalized in the southern United States, this highly ornamental species is up to 3 feet tall. Except for the upper parts of its stems sometimes being minutely-pubescent, it is hairless. Its glossy, short-stalked, narrowly-oblong to oblong-lanceolate, usually pointed leaves are 2 to 6 inches in length. The brilliantly-colored flowers, in terminal or axillary umbels, have rich red-purple to crimson corollas and bright orange, ovate hoods. The erect seed pods, on erect stalks, are sometimes minutely-downy. They are 1½ to 4 inches long.

Asclepias curassavica

The plants formerly segregated as *Asclepiodora* are now incorporated in *Asclepias*. As a result the sort previously named *Asclepiodora decumbens* becomes *Asclepias asperula capricornu*. Native to Texas, it often occurs on clayey and limestone soils. From a stout rootstock it sends sprawling to erect stems up to about 1½ feet long. Its lanceolate to linear, thick leaves are up to 6 inches long. Stalkless or nearly so, the umbels are about 2 inches wide. Their flowers, pale yellowish-green, with greenish-cream hoods that, unlike those of kinds discussed above, spread horizontally rather than being erect, and are without horns. The species *A. asperula* differs from its variety in having narrower leaves, and more obviously stalked umbels of flowers with purple, spreading hoods.

Garden and Landscape Uses. Except for the butterfly weed and blood flower, asclepiases are rarely cultivated other than in native plant gardens and naturalistic areas. For such places they are well adapted and grow without difficulty and with little care under conditions similar to those they favor in the wild. In environments to their liking they often increase rapidly from self-sown seeds, and may then create something of a problem. Butterfly weed is magnificent in naturalistic surroundings and as a highly colorful addition to perennial beds. In the deep south, blood flower can be planted as a perennial in flower beds or be naturalized in more informal areas. It can also be grown and used to good effect as an annual. When so managed, it makes a colorful summer display even in the north and is also attractive in pots in greenhouses and sunny windows. As cut flowers, milkweeds last well if the ends of their stems are seared immediately after they are cut and are then plunged in water. Stems with seed pods attached are useful in dried arrangements.

Cultivation. Milkweeds generally succeed in ordinary soils in full sun. Butterfly weed prospers in comparatively sterile, dryish, sandy, and gravelly ones in the wild, but does not object to richer diets. Because of their deep roots, milkweeds do not transplant readily. The best results are had by raising plants from seeds or root-cuttings and containing them in individual pots until they are planted where they are to stay. This method of handling the young plants is as applicable to the blood flower when grown as an annual as to other kinds. In greenhouses and in windows, blood flower may bloom in 4-, 5-, or 6-inch pots. It needs porous, fertile soil, full sun, and a minimum night temperature of 60°F with an increase of up to fifteen or more degrees by day.

ASCLEPIODORA. See Asclepias.

ASCOCENDA (Asco-cénda). This is the name, a combination of parts of those of

269

ASCOTAINIA

Ascocenda

the parent genera, of hybrids between *Ascocentrum* and *Vanda* of the orchid family ORCHIDACEAE. Ascocendas are beautiful, easy-to-grow orchids with spikes of bright pink, purple, or red flowers ranging in size, according to variety, from about 1 inch to 1¼ inches. They have much the aspect of vandas, but are smaller and of neater growth. They succeed under conditions that suit vandas or cattleyas. For further information see Orchids.

ASCOCENTRUM (Asco-céntrum). The cultivated representatives of this group were previously included in *Saccolabium*. They are still often grown under that name. Belonging to the orchid family ORCHIDACEAE, the genus *Ascocentrum* consists of five species native from southern China and Taiwan to the Himalayas, Philippine Islands, and Indonesia. Its name comes from the Greek *askos*, a bag, and *kentron*, a spur. It alludes to the large spur hanging from the lip. There are hybrids between this and several other orchid genera.

Ascocentrums are epiphytes (tree-perchers that take no nourishment from their hosts). More rarely they perch on rocks. Low and compact, they are without pseudobulbs. Their erect stems, with linear to strap-shaped leaves, often develop aerial roots. The rather small, brightly-colored flowers are in erect, cylindrical racemes from the leaf axils. They have three spreading sepals and two similar petals, joined to the base of the column, and a three-lobed lip, the side lobes erect and usually small, with a conical spur or pouch at its base. The blooms remain attractive for a long time.

One of the best known, *A. ampullaceum* (syn. *Saccolabium ampullaceum*), is a native of Burma and the Himalayas. Rarely its stems are 10 inches tall, more often lower. The leaves are keeled, leathery, narrowly-strap-shaped, deeply-cleft and toothed at their apexes. They are 5 to 6 inches long and up to ¾ inch wide. The short-stalked, dense racemes, up to 6 inches long, consist of deep rose-pink to rose-carmine blooms,

½ to ¾ inch in diameter, with an often paler, recurved, narrow-oblong lip that has a slender spur longer than the blade, with two rounded protuberances at its mouth. The column is white with a yellow anther. Flowers ¾ inch across, ranging from orange-yellow to orange or nearly scarlet, with a short column with a purple anther form the up to 5-inch-long racemes of *A. miniatum*. This native from Malaya to the Himalayas, Java, and Borneo has stems ordinarily not more than 4 inches long. The stiff, fleshy, strongly-keeled,

Ascocentrum ampullaceum

Ascocentrum miniatum

channeled, linear leaves, 3 to 8 inches in length, and generally not more than ½ inch wide, are often cleft at their tips. The blooms have linear-oblong, reflexed lips. The slender spur is longer than the blade of the lip and has a tiny lobe at each side of its mouth. Resembling the last, *A. curvifolium* (syn. *Saccolabium curvifolium*), of the Himalayas, has stems usually not more than 6 inches tall. Its stiff, fleshy, down-curved, channeled leaves are 7 to 10 inches long by about 1 inch wide. They have a pair of sharp teeth at their apexes. The crowded racemes, up to 6 inches long or sometimes longer, are of flowers approximately ½ inch wide that vary in color from cinnabar-red to vermilion and purplish-

orange-scarlet. Their lips have an orange keel and a pair of small protuberances at their bases. Native to Borneo, *A. hendersonianum* (syn. *Saccolabium hendersonianum*) has stems 3 inches tall or sometimes taller with usually not more than five narrow-strap-shaped, keeled leaves. The racemes of up to thirty blooms are erect and up to 6 inches long. About 1 inch in diameter, the delicately fragrant, rose-pink to magenta-pink flowers have lips and spurs usually paler than the sepals and petals. The lobes of the lip are represented by small teeth.

Garden Uses and Cultivation. Ascocentrums are charming in orchid collections, blooming over a long period, and of sizes easily accommodated in small greenhouses. They are easy to manage, requiring the same conditions and care as tropical vandas. For more information see Vanda, and Orchids.

ASCOFINETIA. This is the name of bigeneric orchid hybrids the parents of which are *Ascocentrum* and *Neofinetia*.

Ascofinetia 'Peaches'

ASCONOPSIS. This is the name of orchid hybrids the parents of which are *Ascocentrum* and *Phalaenopsis*.

ASCORACHNIS. This is the name of orchid hybrids the parents of which are *Arachnis* and *Ascocentrum*.

ASCOTAINIA (Asco-tàinia). The eleven species of *Ascotainia*, or *Ania*, as perferred by some botanists, are members of the orchid family ORCHIDACEAE. They grow in the ground or occasionally on moss-covered, moist rocks, and are wild from the Malay Peninsula to the Himalayas, and Indonesia and the Philippine Islands. The name is derived from *Tainia*, that of another genus of orchids.

Ascotainias have flask-shaped pseudobulbs, each with a solitary, pleated leaf. Their flowers are in racemes that sprout from the rhizomes. They have narrow sepals and similar petals, an erect, sometimes three-lobed lip, usually with three to five keels, and a rather long column.

Native to China and Burma, *A. viridifusca* (syn. *Tainia viridifusca*) has leaves up to 1½ feet long by 3 inches wide. Its brownish-olive-green flowers, with a yellowish-white lip, are on stalks 1½ feet long or longer.

Garden Uses and Cultivation. Ascotainias are of minor horticultural importance. They succeed under conditions that suit cattleyas, in well-drained pots in a mixture of equal parts fibrous loam, osmunda or tree fern fiber, coarse leaf mold, and coarse sand, with the addition of some crushed charcoal. Annual repotting is recommended. Throughout the season of growth water copiously. After the new pseudobulbs have matured give a rest period of about one month during which time somewhat lower temperatures and less atmospheric humidity are appropriate and no more water is given than necessary to prevent shriveling. For more information see Orchids.

ASCOVANDORITIS. This is the name of hybrid orchids the parents of which include *Ascocentrum*, *Doritis*, and *Vanda*.

ASEXUAL OR VEGETATIVE PROPAGATION. Reproduction by seeds and spores involves the fertilization of a female reproductive cell or gamete by a male reproductive one and hence is dependent upon the sexual transmission of the characteristics of both parents. All other methods of plant multiplication, such as the use of cuttings, division, and grafting, are without sexual involvement, and thus asexual or vegetative. Except for rare mutations, plants raised asexually, or vegetatively as it is called, are genetically identical with their parent stocks.

ASH. This is the common name of members of the genus *Fraxinus*. Other plants that have the word ash as part of their vernacular names are the Australian-mountain-ash (*Eucalyptus regnans*), Bushman's-red-ash (*Alphitonia*), mountain-ash (*Sorbus*), prickly-ash (*Zanthoxylum americanum*), scrub-ash (*Acronychia*), and wafer-ash (*Ptelea trifoliata*).

ASHES. Coal ashes, or more properly coal cinders, and wood ashes are useful in gardens. See Coal Cinders, and Wood Ashes.

ASIMINA (Asím-ina)—Pawpaw. The only hardy representative of the large, almost completely tropical and subtropical annona family ANNONACEAE is the pawpaw or papaw (*Asimina triloba*), which ranges in the wild from New York to Nebraska, Florida, and Texas. It and seven other species, all North American, constitute the genus, the name of which is a modification of the Indian one *assimin* or *rassimin* for the pawpaw. In the tropics, a quite different plant,

the papaya (*Carica papaya*) is often called pawpaw.

Asiminas are deciduous or rarely evergreen shrubs, or less commonly small trees, with alternate, lobeless and toothless, feather-veined, usually sizable leaves. When crushed, their foliage has a rather disagreeable scent. Their nodding, short-stalked blooms are solitary or in clusters of few from the shoots of the previous year's growth. They have three sepals that soon drop, six petals, the inner three generally erect and smaller than the spreading outer ones, numerous stamens, and three to fifteen carpels with recurved styles. The pulpy fruits, technically berries, are ovate to oblongish.

The pawpaw (*A. triloba*) attains a maximum height of about 40 feet, but usually is smaller, and often is only a tall shrub. Its shoots are pubescent when young, later hairless. The short-pointed, obovate-oblong, drooping, deciduous leaves have blades 6 inches to 1 foot long, and stalks 2 to 4 inches in length. They turn bright yellow in fall. The lurid purple flowers, 1½ inches wide or somewhat wider, have sepals greenish on their outsides. Ellipsoid to oblongish, the edible, creamy-textured, aromatic, sometimes disagreeably resin-flavored fruits are 3 to 7 inches long and up to 2 inches thick. They are greenish-yellow ripening to brown. Usually they drop before they are fully mature and must be stored or exposed to light frosts to ripen to edibility.

Garden and Landscape Uses and Cultivation. The pawpaw and other species of *Asimina* are attractive ornamentals. Their chief decorative appeal is their bold foliage. The pawpaw is also grown occasionally for its fruits. For best results rich, moist soil and a fairly open location are needed. Asiminas do not transplant easily. Best results are had by moving young, small specimens rather than bigger, older ones. Once established, no special care is needed. Propagation is chiefly by seeds sown in fall, or stratified and sown in spring, more rarely by root-cuttings, and by layers.

ASOKA is *Saraca indica*.

ASPARAGUS. This word forms part of the common name of some plants other than those of the genus *Asparagus* treated in the next entry. The asparagus-bean is *Vigna sesquipedalis*, asparagus-lettuce *Lactuca sativa asparagina*, asparagus-pea *Psophocarpus tetragonolobus*.

ASPARAGUS (Aspára-gus)—Asparagus-fern, Smilax. In addition to the popular vegetable, this genus of herbaceous perennials, shrubs, and woody vines, of perhaps 300 species of Europe, Asia, Africa, and Australia, contains other plants of ornamental importance. It belongs in the lily family LILIACEAE and is characterized by having, in appearance resembling leaves, leaflike organs believed to be cladodes.

Asimina triloba (flowers)

Morphologically, cladodes are short branches that function as leaves. The true leaves in *Asparagus* are represented by scalelike bracts. In this discussion the cladodes will be called leaves. The flowers of *Asparagus* are tiny, generally bisexual, occasionally unisexual. They have six perianth segments, commonly called petals, but more correctly tepals, six stamens, and a style often with a three-parted stigma. The fruits are usually fleshy berries containing one to several seeds. Many kinds have tuberous roots. Their name is an ancient one used by Theophrastus.

The asparagus used as a vegetable is derived from *A. officinalis,* native of the seacoasts of Europe and temperate Asia. A hardy herbaceous perennial, in its cultivated forms usually 3 to 6 feet tall, but often lower in the wild, it has nonprickly stems, branched in their upper parts, that die to the ground in winter. Because of its numerous threadlike leaves it is graceful and feathery, and when in fruit is quite decorative. The flowers, usually in groups of up to four, are greenish. Those of female plants are followed by bright red berries.

A few other hardy or nearly hardy kinds are grown to a limited extent for ornament. Among them is *A. acutifolius,* of the Mediterranean region. It attains a height of about 5 feet, has branching stems, and awl-shaped, spine-tipped leaves in clusters of up to one dozen. Its flowers, solitary or in pairs from the leaf axils, are yellow. The berries are red. Native of eastern Asia, *A. filicinus* is a climbing or straggling, spineless, branching plant, with branchlets in one plane much like those of *A. setaceus.* Its flowers are green, axillary, and in clusters of up to five. From Japan and China comes *A. schoberioides,* which has tuberous roots and is up to 3 feet tall. Its linear, three-angled leaves point upward and are in clusters of three or four. Its abundant small berries are red. Ranging in the wild from Iran to Siberia, *A. verticillatus* is a climbing species 10 to 15 feet in height, with somewhat woody, branching stems with short spines, and hairlike leaves, in

Asparagus densiflorus

Asparagus verticillatus

clusters of up to ten, that are about 2 inches long. Its flowers are solitary or in clusters of two to three. Its one- to three-seeded berries are red and about ¼ inch across.

The most important ornamental asparaguses are *A. densiflorus* (syns. *A. sprengeri;* *A. myriocladus; A. sarmentosus*), *A. setaceus* (syn. *A. plumosus*), and *A. asparagoides* (syn. *A. medeoloides*), all natives of South Africa and none hardy in the north. A lax or scrambling evergreen with finely-grooved stems with many short branchlets, but usually without major branches, *A. densiflorus* is 1 foot to 2 feet long, or sometimes longer, and generally has weak, hooked prickles. It is tuberous rooted, and has often slightly sickle-shaped, slender-linear, flat or sometimes three-angled leaves, in wild specimens usually not more than ¾ inch long, but which in cultivated forms may be longer. Usually they are solitary, sometimes in clusters of three or more. The white or delicate pink blooms, borne in loose racemes 1 inch to 3 inches long in late spring or early summer, are very fragrant. Up to ½ inch in diameter, the long-lasting, one-seeded berries are coral-red. This is a variable species. The plant known in gardens as *A. myersii,* not *A. meyeri* as often spelled, is *A. densiflorus* 'Myers'. The shoots of this form broad-cylindrical plumes, more densely packed with leaves than those of the typical species. They suggest bushy, green tails. In *A. d. variegatus* the leaves are variegated with white.

Asparagus-fern is the common name of *A. setaceus.* It is not, of course, a fern, but its flat branches are certainly fernlike in appearance. This evergreen has nontuber-

Asparagus densiflorus 'Myers'

ous roots and tall, slender, usually thornless, twining, grooved stems, with comparatively short, horizontal leafy branches that again branch to form what appear to be flat, triangular, pinnate fronds, with their numerous hairlike leaves, less than ½ inch long and in clusters of eight to twenty, in one plane. The creamy flowers, usually solitary, but sometimes in twos or threes, come in fall and are succeeded by one- to three-seeded red to purplish berries ¼ inch in diameter. In its native land *A. setaceus* is chiefly a forest plant. Several horticultural varieties of it have been named, the most important of which are *A. s. compactus* (syn. *A. plumosus compactus*), and *A. s. nanus* (syn. *A. plumosus nanus*), dwarf kinds well adapted for use as pot plants. A presumed variety of curious, dense, erect growth is cultivated as *A. plumosus pyramidalis.*

Asparagus setaceus compactus

Smilax is the common designation of **A. asparagoides.** It is quite different from plants of the genus *Smilax*. It has tuberous roots and slender, twining, nonwoody stems up to 10 feet long, without prickles, and in the wild of annual duration. The many branches are similar to the main stems. The solitary, stalkless, flat leaves, broadly-ovate to lanceolate and ½ inch to 2½ inches long, have about seven prominent veins. They usually spread horizontally. The slender-stalked flowers, solitary or in pairs from the leaf axils, are succeeded by red berries containing up to eight seeds. A horticultural variety named *A. a. myrtifolius*, elegant and small-leaved, is sometimes called baby smilax.

Asparagus asparagoides

Other South African kinds grown as ornamentals include **A. africanus** (syns. *A. cooperi, A. dependens*), which is without tubers. Its smooth or somewhat grooved, slightly zigzagged, hairless or pubescent stems usually have spreading or downcurved spines, and spreading or reflexed branches that branch freely and are frondlike. The rigid, hairlike leaves, mostly not over ½ inch long, are in groups of up to twenty. The flowers, in clusters of two to twenty from the leaf axils or sometimes terminal, are succeeded by red, one-seeded berries about ¼ inch in diameter. From *A. setaceus*, to which it is closely allied, *A. africanus* is distinguished by having axillary rather than terminal flowers. Tuberous roots and weak straggling or climbing stems up to 3 feet long, or in cultivation longer, and of annual duration, are characteristics of South African **A. crispus** (syn. *A. decumbens*). The angled, zigzagged branches are many and drooping. The slender leaves, chiefly in threes, but in twos where branches arise, are rather soft, flat or three-angled and under ½ inch long. Solitary, in the leaf axils, the fragrant flowers are followed by white or pinkish berries ½ inch in diameter, with three to nine seeds.

Up to 6 feet in height, or in cultivated plants taller, and with often zigzagged, spiny, woody stems, **A. laricinus** is a shrubby, spiny kind, without tubers, and much branched. Its firm, slender, awl-shaped leaves, in clusters of fifteen to sixty, are up to 1¼ inches long. The flowers are in terminal or axillary clusters of up to eight. The berries are red, about ¼ inch in diameter, and contain one to three seeds. Rather similar, **A. retrofractus** is a dense shrub or weak scrambler up to 6 feet high or sometimes higher, with zigzagged stems and spreading or reflexed branches similar to the stems. The stems, but not the branches, sometimes have reflexed spines. In clusters in which the individuals are of varying lengths, the threadlike leaves are up to a little over 1 inch long. In terminal and axillary clusters of usually two to six are borne the flowers. The orange fruits, ⅕ inch in diameter, are one- to three-seeded. Both *A. laracinus* and *A. retrofractus* are natives of South Africa.

Tuberous-rooted and with slender, scrambling or climbing, perennial, tortuous, but not zigzagged stems up to about 6 feet tall that branch freely, South African **A. scandens** has wide-spreading to upright branches. Its flat, linear-lanceolate, sickle-shaped leaves in threes, with one of each trio decidedly longer than the others, up to ¾ inch in length, are all in one plane. The leaves have a single conspicuous vein. The white or rarely pinkish flowers, usually solitary, are from the leaf axils. The fruits are one-seeded, red berries less than ¼ inch in diameter. The plant previously called *A. s. deflexus* and now named **A. ramosissimus** differs in having its leaves in more than one plane. A herbaceous perennial up to 3 feet tall, it has deflexed branches, with angled or flattened leaves up to a little more than ½ inch long, in clusters of three, and solitary blooms. The one- or two-seeded, red berries are about ⅓ inch in diameter. Less ornamental than many kinds, but distinct and sometimes useful because of its very upright growth, **A. virgatus** occurs in South Africa and northward especially at the margins of forests. It has essentially spineless stems 3 feet tall or sometimes taller with upright branches without branchlets. They have not very abundant, usually straight leaves up to 1 inch long and in clusters of up to seven. Terminal and axillary, the yellowish-green flowers are in groups of up to six. The one-seeded berries, ⅕ inch across, are red.

Two species indigenous to both Africa and Asia are *A. racemosus* (syn. *A. tetragonus*) and *A. falcatus*. A woody climber with grooved, spiny stems up to 12 feet or so long, **A. racemosus** often has solitary, spreading or erect branchlets. Its numerous very slender, angled leaves, up to ¾ inch long, are in groups of three to eight. White or pinkish, the flowers are in axillary or terminal clusters. The wrinkled, red berries have a solitary seed. This species ranges from South Africa northward, and eastward to India. A very vigorous forest climber or scrambler with long, tortuous, much-branched, spiny stems, **A. falcatus** occurs in the wild from South Africa to India and Ceylon. Its dark green leaves are flat, straight or sickle-shaped, have prominent mid-veins and are up to 4 inches long by ⅓ inch wide. In branched or branchless clusters the fragrant, creamy or white flowers develop terminally and from the leaf axils. About ⅕ inch across, the one- or two-seeded berries are red. Variety *A. f. ternifolius* has smaller leaves and branching flower clusters.

A central African native that enjoys higher temperatures than the South African species, *A. drepanophyllus* (syn. *A. duchesnei*) is a tall climber, with sickle-shaped, linear leaves up to 3 inches in length and arranged in frondlike, ferny fashion. Its greenish flowers are in erect racemes. The berries are red and about ½ inch across.

Somewhat resembling butcher's broom (*Ruscus aculeatus*) in aspect, *A. madagascariensis* is 1 foot tall or taller. An erect, much-branched shrub, it has pointed, lanceolate, dark green leaves in threes and usually in one plane so that the branchlets look rather like pinnate leaves. The creamy-white flowers are terminal and usually in clusters of four. The three-lobed, red berries are freely produced. This kind enjoys somewhat warmer conditions than the South African species. It is a native of Malagasy (Madagascar).

Asparagus madagascariensis

Garden and Landscape Uses. The hardy edible asparagus is dealt with in the next entry. Here we are concerned with kinds grown primarily for decoration, most of which are not hardy in the north. Ornamental asparaguses are highly esteemed for greenhouse embellishment, in dryish, frost-free or essentially frost-free climates for outdoor planting, and for cultivation in lath houses. The foliage of many, but most especially that of the asparagus-fern (*A. setaceus*) and *A. densiflorus,* is regarded with much favor for mixing with cut flowers, and for other florists' purposes. For such uses it equals or surpasses the best ferns. These plants like fertile, but not over-wet soil. Good drainage is essential. They are mostly at their best where they

receive light shade, although some will stand full sun, particularly if the soil is not unreasonably dry. The taller growers are excellent for clothing pillars and other supports, the dwarfer kinds are good pot plants for greenhouses and cool room window gardens, and some, such as *A. setaceus, A. densiflorus,* and *A. d.* 'Myers', are handsome furnishings for hanging baskets.

Cultivation. It is possible to propagate asparaguses by careful division and in some cases by cuttings, but seeds usually provide the most convenient and best source of new plants. These resemble small, hard peas, and it is advantageous to soak them in tepid water, or better still to file a tiny slit through the outer coat of each, before sowing. This promotes rapid even germination. Indoor sowing is in well-drained pots or flats in sandy soil kept moderately moist. A temperature of 60 to 70°F is satisfactory. As soon as the seedlings are large enough to conveniently handle, they are set individually in 2½-inch pots and are later transferred to larger containers or possibly are planted in ground beds, greenhouse benches, or hanging baskets. Seeds of hardy kinds are sown in nursery beds outdoors in spring.

Indoors most asparaguses prosper where the night temperature from fall to spring is 50 to 55°F and daytime levels are five to fifteen degrees higher depending upon the intensity of the light, warmer conditions being appropriate on sunny days. Species from tropical regions appreciate somewhat warmer conditions than those native to South Africa and other more temperate regions. In bright weather they benefit from being sprayed lightly with water, provided their foliage dries before nightfall. The soil should be watered moderately from spring to fall, less copiously in winter. Excessive dryness results in the leaves yellowing and falling. This can result too, especially in winter, from too-wet soil.

Asparaguses are long-suffering and stand much neglect without dying, but unless reasonably well cared for they become poor miserable ghosts of what they otherwise would be. They are gross feeders. To encourage really good results specimens with their roots crowded in containers should be given applications of dilute liquid fertilizer weekly or biweekly from spring to fall, less frequently in winter. Those in greenhouse benches and ground beds need less frequent, but nevertheless regular attention in the matter of fertilizing. Each late winter or early spring the repotting or top dressing of container-grown specimens should be given attention. The twining stems of smilax (*A. asparagoides*) need support. It is usual to allow them to grow up strong thin threads or string stretched vertically and tautly, and to cut these with the stems when they are needed as floral decorations.

Hardy kinds give little trouble and may remain undisturbed for many years. In the fall their stems are cut to the ground after frost, and after the ground has frozen to a depth of an inch or two a protective mulch, to be removed in spring, may be applied. A spring dressing of a complete garden fertilizer is helpful.

Pests and Diseases. The chief pests of ornamental asparaguses are mealy bugs, scale insects, thrips, and red spider mites. They are also fed upon by caterpillars, beetle grubs, cutworms, and fleahoppers. Crown rot, root rot, and a blight that causes the branches to dry and drop are the diseases to which they are subject.

ASPARAGUS, EDIBLE. A much esteemed spring crop, the vegetable asparagus is the earliest to be harvested from the open garden. It represents a horticultural development, designated *A. o. altilis,* of *Asparagus officinalis* of the lily family LILIACEAE, a native of sea coasts of Europe and temperate Asia and naturalized in North America. Asparagus, unlike the majority of vegetable crops, is a hardy perennial. Well established and properly managed, a bed will produce satisfactorily for ten to twenty years. In view of this long occupancy of the land, it is obvious that very thorough initial preparation of the soil is necessary.

Asparagus gives of its best only in deep, well-drained, fertile, cool earth in sunny, warm, sheltered locations. Prepare the ground for spring planting by deep spading, rototilling, or plowing in fall. Mix in very liberal amounts of manure, compost, or other humus-forming material and a dressing of complete garden fertilizer. Anything short of very thorough soil preparation is likely to be wasted effort. The thin, tough shoots asparagus produces on shallow soils deficient in organic content and fertility little resemble the fat, juicy, tender products harvested from rich, deep soils. The best planting stock is strong one-year-old roots. Those two or three years old are less satisfactory. You may purchase the plants or raise your own. Even though the last procedure may delay your first harvest by a year, it is often preferable. To raise plants, sow seeds, after soaking them in water for twenty-four hours, in drills 1½ to 2 feet apart. After germination, encourage growth by frequent shallow surface cultivation of the soil and later perhaps by mulching. Water copiously at regular intervals in dry weather. Thin the seedlings to 3 to 4 inches apart. The following early spring transplant them to their permanent quarters.

Set the young plants, selecting only strong ones, 1½ to 2 feet apart in rows 3 to 5 feet apart. This is more satisfactory than the once popular much closer spacing in beds 5 or 6 feet wide. Plant in trenches or furrows 8 to 10 inches deep, spreading the roots carefully so that they are not bunched and hilling a little soil under the center of the crown so that the roots point slightly downward. Cover with not more than 2 or 3 inches of soil. Fill in more soil as the plants grow. Do not harvest any shoots the first year, few or none the second. In the third year after planting begin normal harvesting.

Routine care includes keeping down weeds by shallow surface cultivation between the rows, taking care not to injure the young shoots or the large, ferny tops later, or by mulching, and by hand pulling between the rows. Watering liberally during dry weather is important. Asparagus is a greedy crop. Generous fertilization is needed for tip-top results. This can be done by spreading, in fall or spring, a 3-inch layer of rotted manure or compost followed by a spring application of a quickly available nitrogenous fertilizer such as nitrate of soda or urea, and an application in summer as soon as harvesting is finished of a complete garden fertilizer. Do not cut the ferny tops down until after fall frost. As long as they are green and active, they are strengthening the roots for next year's growth. In very cold climates it is well not to remove the tops until spring. Left standing they serve to entrap snow. This forms a protective mulch that limits the depth of frost penetration into the soil.

Harvesting requires some care. The trick is to sever the shoots when 5 to 8 inches long 1 inch to 2 inches below the surface and to do this without damaging other shoots that have not yet reached the surface. A special asparagus knife is handy for this purpose. If you use an ordinary

Harvesting, with an asparagus knife

knife be sure to slide its blade down the side of the shoot and to make the cut at a downward angle, not horizontally. All shoots of suitable thickness may be taken as they reach suitable size until the end of June. Cease cutting them then so that enough foliage will mature to build up reserves of food in the roots to assure a good crop the following year.

The most satisfactory variety for most gardeners is 'Mary Washington'. This produces early crops of heavy stalks and is resistant to rust disease. A few other varieties are offered, including 'Martha Washington', 'Waltham Washington', and 'Viking' ('Mary Washington Improved'), the last two claimed to be especially rust-resistant. The chief troubles with this crop are asparagus beetle and a rust disease caused by a fungus. The first chews the tips of the spears and causes black spotting. Control may be had by dusting with rotenone or by following other recommendations of your Cooperative Extension Agent. Rust disease discolors the aboveground parts. It is helpful to cut and burn all infected stems and foliage in late summer before winter resting spores are formed. Plant only rust-resistant varieties.

ASPARAGUS-PEA. Two quite different plants of the pea family LEGUMINOSAE are known by this name. They are not peas, although their seed pods look a little like those of that familiar vegetable, nor are they related to asparagus. Both have square, winged pods that when young are cooked and eaten like snap beans.

The asparagus-pea or winged-pea of temperate regions *Lotus tetragonolobus* is rarely grown as a novelty vegetable. It is raised by sowing seeds in spring in fertile soil of a kind that may be expected to produce good vegetables. Sow in rows 2 to 3 feet apart and thin the plants to 1 foot to 1½ feet apart in the rows. Keep down weeds by cultivating or mulching, and water generously in dry weather. Pick the pods before they are fully grown and cook them whole by boiling.

The asparagus-pea, winged-bean, or Goa-bean of the tropics *Psophocarpus tetragonolobus* is cultivated in warm countries for its edible pods and for its young shoots, which are used as a potherb. Its roots are also eaten. It is a robust annual that does best in fertile soil, and thrives especially well in regions of high rainfall. This vegetable is grown like pole beans. The seeds are planted in lands of seasonal rainfall at the beginning of the rainy season and again later. The plants need much water and in dry periods must be irrigated freely. Staking is as for pole beans. The young pods are usually sliced and boiled. As a novelty, this asparagus-pea is occasionally grown in the United States, usually by raising young plants early indoors under conditions that suit tomatoes and planting them outdoors in fertile soil in a warm, sunny location after the weather has become settled.

ASPASIA (As-pàsia). Evergreen epiphytes (plants that perch on trees without taking nourishment from them) of the American tropics make up this genus of ten species. They belong to the orchid family ORCHIDACEAE.

Attractive hybrids between *Aspasia* and *Oncidium* are called *Oncidasia* (syn. *Aspa-*

Aspasia epidendroides principissa

Aspasia lunata

pink or red-marked lip changes as it ages from nearly white to light yellow. It is yellow at its base. Very lovely **A. lunata** has flattened, ovate pseudobulbs about 2 inches long, with one or two-strap-shaped leaves up to 8 inches in length. Its solitary or paired blooms, 2 to 2½ inches wide, have very slender sepals and petals that are green, spotted and barred with brown. The broad, showy, white lip has a violet base. This kind is native to Brazil. Similar to *A. epidendroides* but smaller, **A. variegata,** of Brazil, Guiana, and Trinidad, has leaves approximately 6 inches long. Its blooms, usually three or fewer on each flowering stalk, are 2 to 3 inches wide. The sepals and petals are green cross-banded with brown or purple-brown. The three-lobed lip, white dotted with purple, has a yellow blotch at its base.

Garden Uses and Cultivation. Comparatively inexperienced orchid growers succeed with this rewarding genus. Its members grow with little trouble in pots or pans (shallow pots) or attached to slabs of tree fern and suspended. In containers they grow satisfactorily in osmunda and tree fern fibers and in the various barks used for potting orchids. Warm, humid conditions such as are provided in an intermediate- or warm-temperature greenhouse are to their liking. Except for a period of partial rest of about one month's duration following flowering, water should be given

sium). The name, derived from the Greek *aspasmos,* to cling, alludes to the lip being joined to the column.

Aspasias in habit resemble certain brassias. They have two-edged, often stalked pseudobulbs surmounted by one or two arching leaves, and in the axils of basal leaves or bracts, rather short, erect racemes of blooms. The flowers have narrow, spreading sepals and petals, and quite large, showy lips that, unlike those of related *Trichopilia,* are not rolled around the column.

Its pseudobulbs stalked and sheathed at their bottoms with large bracts or basal leaves, and a pair of leaves at their apexes up to nearly 6 inches long, **A. epidendroides** (syn. *A. fragrans*) is a native in Central America and Colombia. The largest of its broadly-lanceolate leaves may be 1 foot long by 2 inches wide. They are often much smaller. The flowers, few to several in erect racemes, with their stalks, are up to 10 inches in length. The blooms are 1½ to 2 inches across. They have greenish sepals banded with brown or brownish-lavender, and pale lavender to greenish-brown petals. The white lip, yellow at its base, is clearly marked with lilac or lavender. Similar in growth, but less vigorous, *A. e. principissa* (syn. *A. principissa*) has flowers 2 to 3 inches wide that have light green, or yellowish-green sepals and petals striped lengthwise with light brown. The mauve-

Aspasia variegata

liberally, and well-rooted specimens are encouraged with regular light applications of fertilizer. Bright light, with sufficient shade to prevent a very strong sun from scorching the foliage is desirable. For additional information see Orchids.

ASPASIUM. This is the name of bigeneric orchids the parents of which are *Aspasia* and *Oncidium.*

ASPEN. See Populus.

ASPERULA (Aspéru-la)—Woodruff. This genus of 200 species has a rather unusual natural distribution, being indigenous to Europe, Asia, and Australia. Australian kinds differ from the others in the plants being unisexual. In part because of this, some botanists believe they should be segregated as a separate genus. Woodruffs belong in the madder family RUBIACEAE. The name *Asperula* is a diminutive of the Latin *asper*, rough. It refers to the leaves.

These are low annuals, herbaceous perennials, or rarely small subshrubs, with usually square stems, and leaves and leaflike stipules in whorls (tiers). Their flowers, in terminal and axillary clusters, are small and usually have four sepals, petals, and stamens. The fruits are leathery, rarely fleshy berries. The genus is closely related to *Galium* from which it differs in having funnel-form flowers. The cultivated sorts are attractive, hardy perennials and annuals. The sweet woodruff or waldmeister, formerly *A. odorata* is *Galium odoratum.*

A blue-flowered annual, well adapted for rock gardens and the fronts of flower borders, *A. orientalis* (syn. *A. azurea-setosa*), of Asia Minor to the Caucasus, in cool climates blooms from early summer to fall, but where summers are hot it is likely to die when torrid weather arrives. This pretty sort branches freely and is up to about 1 foot tall. It has lanceolate leaves in whorls of eight, up to 1 inch long and with rough edges. The flowers, about 3/8 inch in length, are in headlike clusters.

Rather less well known, perennial *A. hexaphylla,* native of dry places in southern Europe, has hairless leaves not more than 1/8 inch long, in whorls of six. It attains heights of 1½ to 2½ feet and spreads as widely. It has pink or white flowers in pretty sprays or panicles. They are useful for cutting to mix with other blooms in arrangements. Native to Europe and Asia, *A. cynanchica* has leaves in whorls of four. Its stems, 1 foot long or longer, are erect or sprawling. Its pink, lavender-pink, or white flowers are in branched clusters. A native of Sicily, *A. gussonii* (syn. *A. suberosa*) is a pretty, low, compact alpine, with slender stems, tiny leaves in whorls of four, and pleasing pinkish flowers in almost stalkless clusters at the ends of its stems.

Additional kinds include the following: *A. arcadiensis* of Greece, tufted, gray-

Asperula gussonii

woolly, and 3 to 4 inches tall, has narrow-linear leaves and few-flowered clusters of pink blooms not downy on their outsides. Difficult to cultivate, this sort is choice. *A. hirta* spreads by underground runners and forms 3-inch-high mats of stems and foliage. Its leaves are in whorls of six and four. The flowers of this native of the Pyrenees are white to pink. *A. lutea,* of Greece and Crete, has yellow flowers with black anthers and linear, bristle-tipped leaves in whorls of four. *A. nitida,* of Greece, forms a compact cushion of erect stems and, in whorls of four, linear leaves ending in white points. Its pink flowers are few together in clusters. *A. setosa,* of Asia Minor, is an annual similar to *A. orientalis* except that its flowers are lighter blue. *A. taurina,* of southern Europe, has erect stems up to

Asperula taurina

1 foot tall, ovate-lanceolate leaves in whorls of four, and white flowers in axillary clusters. Dyer's woodruff (*A. tinctoria*), of dry locations in Europe, attains a height of 1 foot to 2 feet and has purplish, lax stems and leaves in whorls of six and four, and the uppermost opposite. Its flower buds are red. The open flowers, in three-branched clusters, are white.

Garden Uses and Cultivation. The more robust woodruffs such as *A. hexaphylla, A. cynanchica*, and *A. taurina* are suitable for lightly-shaded flower beds and rock gar-

dens where the soil is well-drained but not dry. Other perennial sorts need much the same conditions, but not all, especially those from high altitudes, are as easy to satisfy. For them a very gritty soil and fairly cool summers are important. The perennials can be propagated by seeds and by division in spring or early fall. Annual *A. orientalis* does well in sunny or lightly-shaded locations. Sow seeds of it in spring outdoors where the plants are to bloom and thin out the seedlings to 3 to 4 inches apart.

ASPHODEL. This is the common name of *Asphodeline* and *Asphodelus.* For bog-asphodel see Narthecium, for false-asphodel, Tofieldia.

ASPHODELINE (Asphodelin-e)—Jacob's Rod. Fifteen or perhaps more species of Mediterranean region plants of the lily family LILIACEAE are contained in *Asphodeline,* the name of which is a modification of that of the closely related *Asphodelus.* From the last, the Jacob's rods (*Asphodeline*) are distinguished by their leafy stems, and their flowers having stamens of two lengths alternating with each other. Other relatives are *Paradisea* and *Eremurus.* Jacob's rods differ from paradiseas in their blooms being spaced equally around the stalks and from asphodeluses in the stalks (filaments) of their stamens broadening at their bases and their anthers not being erect. The common name asphodel, often applied indiscriminately to both *Asphodeline* and *Asphodelus,* is perhaps better reserved for the latter, Jacob's rod for the former.

Jacob's rods are hardy, deciduous, herbaceous perennials, with more or less rhizomatous roots and stiff, vertical, leafy stems the upper parts of which display in spikelike fashion numerous flowers with six spreading petals (properly tepals), stamens or three stamens and three staminodes (nonfertile stamens), and an undivided style. The blooms, yellow or white, open in the afternoon, and have usually withered before morning. Only in dull weather do individual flowers keep open for twenty-four hours.

Asphodelines, at least some sorts, have been familiar to civilized man since early historic times. The Greeks in their mythology associated *Asphodeline lutea,* with death, very likely because of the pale color of its foliage and flowers, and planted it near graves in the belief that its seeds would provide food for the departed on their journey to Heaven or Hades. Homer refers to the asphodel meadows of the dead. The most commonly cultivated kind in America is *A. lutea,* the asphodel of the ancients. It is 3 to 4 feet in height and has thick, fleshy roots and fragrant yellow flowers along the upper parts of its branchless stems, leafy throughout their lengths. In this last *A. lutea* differs from *A. liburnica,* which has the upper parts of its stem,

Asphodeline lutea

also branchless, naked of foliage. The latter species rarely exceeds 2 feet in height, and its yellow flowers have a green midrib on the back side of each flower segment. Easily distinguished from the above by its white flowers striped with green on their undersides is **A. taurica.** Its stems are leafy throughout and usually branchless.

Asphodeline liburnica

Garden Uses. Jacob's rods may be grown in mixed borders of hardy herbaceous perennials, but are seen to best advantage in informal groups in less sophisticated, more naturalistic surroundings. They stand a little shade, but prefer full sun. Any ordinary garden soil is satisfactory.

Cultivation. Once they are established practically no care is needed. An annual spring application of a complete fertilizer encourages strong growth, and in periods of drought watering is beneficial. After killing frost the stems are cut off at ground level and removed. Propagation is easily achieved by division in spring or early fall. Seeds sprout readily if sown in a cool greenhouse in spring or in a cold frame or bed outdoors protected from disturbance. The seed soil should be porous, well drained and sandy.

ASPHODELUS (Asphódel-us)—Asphodel. At one time this genus and *Asphodeline* were united as *Asphodelus,* but more critical study suggested the need for recognizing them as separate genera. The flower stems of *Asphodelus* are devoid of leaves, their stamens are all of the same length, and their flowers are white or pink, but not yellow. The common name asphodel is better reserved for *Asphodelus* and the name Jacob's rod applied to *Asphodeline.* Almost certainly the asphodel of antiquity was the plant now named *Asphodeline lutea.* Belonging in the lily family LILIACEAE, *Asphodelus* comprises ten to fifteen species (the number varying according to interpretations by individual botanists) and ranges in the wild from the Mediterranean region to the Himalayas. Most kinds are deciduous herbaceous perennials, a few annuals. They have funnel-shaped flowers, with six perianth segments (commonly called petals but more correctly tepals). The name is an ancient Greek one of unknown significance.

Perennial asphodels with thick, fleshy or tuberous roots include **A. delphinensis,** which is treated by some authorities as a distinct species and by others is included in *A. albus* or considered to be only a variety of that species and named *A. a. delphinensis.* It differs from *A. albus* in its larger flowers and fruits. Native to southern Europe, **A. albus** is about 3 feet in height and has white, or sometimes pale pink flowers up to ¾ inch long and seed capsules up to ⅖ inch long. The flower stems of both the above are branchless or have only a few short branches from their bases. Differing in having freely-branched

Asphodelus albus

flower stems are **A. microcarpus,** which occurs as a native from the Canary Islands to Asia Minor, and **A. cerasiferus** (syn. *A. ramosus*), of the western Mediterranean region. Both have white flowers. The former attains a height of about 3 feet, the latter, the tallest of the asphodels, 4 to 5 feet. The fruits of *A. microcarpus* rarely exceed ½ inch in length and usually are considerably smaller; those of *A. cerasiferus* are over ½

Asphodelus cerasiferus

inch long. Also, the flowers of the latter are larger than those of *A. microcarpus,* being ¾ to 1 inch long. Quite distinct from any of the above and less hardy is the North African **A. acaulis.** Unlike other asphodels this kind does not have evident flower stems. Its flowers are in clusters low down in the center of the plant; they are white or pink, the individual flowers up to 1½ inches long.

Short-lived kinds with fibrous rather than tuberous roots and hollow stems are *A. fistulosus,* which is usually biennial, but sometimes persists for three or four seasons, and *A. tenuifolius,* an annual. Some authorities consider the latter to be merely a variety of the former; they are very similar. Attaining a height of 2 to 2½ feet, native from the Canary Islands through southern North Africa and southern Europe and Asia Minor, *A. fistulosus* has rosettes of twelve to thirty narrow-linear leaves up to 1 foot in length and panicles of white or light pink flowers. More slender, sometimes taller, and with smaller flowers and fruits, *A. tenuifolius,* indigenous from southern Europe and North Af-

Asphodelus fistulosus

rica to India and Mauritius, has a wider natural distribution than any other asphodel.

Garden Uses and Cultivation. These plants serve the same purposes and need the same conditions and care as asphodelines. The annual *A. tenuifolius* must, of course, be raised afresh from seeds each year and so should the biennial *A. fistulosus*. Seeds of the latter should be sown in May or June for blooming the following year, seeds of the former in early spring.

ASPIDIACEAE—Tectaria or Aspidium Family. By some authorities included in the *Polypodiaceae,* the assortment of some 3,000 species grouped in the fern family ASPIDIACEAE contains many familiar to gardeners. Of cosmopolitan natural distribution, the group consists of chiefly terrestrial plants and a few that perch on trees as epiphytes.

Ferns of this family have creeping to upright rhizomes rarely more or less vining or rarely developed as short trunks. The fronds (leaves) are all similar, or sometimes the fertile and sterile ones differ. They are undivided or one or more times pinnate. The generally round, less often elongate clusters of spore capsules typically are on or at the ends of veins and have kidney- to shield-shaped covers (indusia). Less commonly they are spread along the veins and are without indusia. Genera belonging in the *Aspidiaceae* include *Arachniodes, Athyrium, Bolbitis, Ctenitis, Cyrtomium, Cystopteris, Didymochlaena, Diplazium, Dryopteris, Elaphoglossum, Gymnocarpium, Matteuccia, Onoclea, Phanerophlebia, Polystichum, Quercifilix, Rumohra, Tectaria, Thelypteris,* and *Woodsia.*

ASPIDISTRA (Aspid-ístra)—Cast Iron Plant. Although botanists recognize about eight species in this genus of the lily family LILIACEAE, only one is familiar to gardeners. It is the cast iron plant (*Aspidistra elatior*). Once one of the commonest of window plants, vying with the Boston fern as a badge of respectability in Victorian parlors, it has been largely superseded by a variety of tropicals and is less popular than formerly. Nevertheless, it is worth a place amongst house plants and for planting outdoors in suitable climates.

The genus *Aspidistra,* which is represented in the native floras of Japan, Taiwan, Vietnam, China, and the eastern Himalayas, is unusual in the lily family because the parts of the flowers of most of its species are in fours or eights instead of threes or sixes. In this it is not unique. The same is true of *Paris.* Most gardeners have never seen *Aspidistra* in bloom. In cultivation flowering is rather rare, but strong old specimens do sometimes have flowers, dingy productions at soil level that neither by color nor scent attract attention.

Aspidistras are stemless plants, with horizontal rhizomes from which arise

Aspidistra elatior

Aspidistra elatior, outdoors in California

closely arranged, erect or curving, parallel-veined, evergreen leaves that commonly narrow at their bases to channeled, slightly winged stalks. Their flowers have mushroom-shaped stigmas, a feature perhaps responsible for the generic name, derived from the Greek *aspidiseon,* a small, circular shield.

Native to Japan, **A. elatior,** has tough, leathery leaves over, usually much over 1½ inches wide, oblong-lanceolate, and up to 2 feet long. Its flowers, ⅖ inch long or longer, have eight petal-like parts and a stigma with purplish ridges. Variety *A. e. variegata* has leaves handsomely variegated with stripes of creamy-white. A variety known in horticulture as *A. e. minor* has dark leaves with small whitish spots. In cultivation, *A. elatior* often passes as *A. lurida,* but true **A. lurida,** a native of China, differs in that its leaves arise two or three

together from a single basal sheath, whereas the sheaths of *A. elatior* produce solitary leaves. The flowers of *A. lurida* are unspotted deep purple. Another Chinese species, **A. typica,** is distinguished by its dirty whitish flowers speckled with purple-red having six petal-like parts. Very much rarer, and distinct from *A. elatior,* is the narrow-leaved **A. minutiflora,** of southern China. This kind has recurving leaves up to 1½ feet long by less than 1 inch wide. Its flowers are up to ⅕ inch long.

Garden Uses. The implication of the name cast iron plant for *A. elatior* is well deserved. Few indoor plants can withstand as much neglect. Widely varying temperatures, poor light, arid air, sporadic watering, indifferent soil, lack of fertility, and even combinations of these adverse factors usually fail to kill this hardy liliad.

Aspidistra elatior variegata

Aspidistra minutiflora

True, when the going is really rough the plants are likely to look unhappy and bedragged, but hang on to life they usually do. Only bad drainage, with repeated overwatering, to the extent that the soil is constantly saturated and the roots are rotted, brings certain death; even then aspidistras expire slowly.

From the above it must not be inferred that poor treatment is recommended for aspidistras. They respond handsomely to congenial environments and care. They are useful ornamentals when grown in containers and are excellent groundcovers in shade in large conservatories and outdoors in subtropical climates. The common *A. elatior* is much hardier than generally supposed. Even in New York City it has wintered outdoors at the base of a sheltering wall, but it cannot, of course, be considered hardy there.

Cultivation. For their best growth, aspidistras should have well-drained, fertile, loamy soil, be grown in a not excessively dry atmosphere, and not be exposed to cold drafts or other adverse conditions. The temperature range in which they succeed is a wide one, but not unexpectedly, they make faster growth in the higher range here suggested than under cooler conditions. They will stand temperatures both lower and higher than those here given. A winter night temperature of 50 to 70°F is satisfactory; daytime temperatures may be somewhat higher than those held at night. Watering should be done to keep the soil always evenly moist, but not constantly saturated. Specimens that have filled their containers with healthy roots benefit from monthly applications of dilute liquid fertilizer. Too liberal fertilization, however, may induce the variegated-leaved variety to revert or partially revert to the plain green-leaved type. Repotting is normally needed at long intervals only. Specimens will often remain vigorous and healthy for several years without this attention. Spring is the best time to repot, and that is the time, too, to propagate aspidistras, which is done by dividing the plants and potting the rooted pieces separately.

Pests. The most common pest of aspidistras is red spider mite, which is especially likely to be troublesome if the atmosphere is hot and arid. Thrips and scale insects also sometimes infest these plants.

ASPIDIUM. See Arachniodes, and Dryopteris.

ASPIDOSPERMA (Aspido-spérma)—White Quebracho. Consisting of about 50 species of the dogbane family APOCYNACEAE, the genus *Aspidosperma* inhabits chiefly dryish parts of tropical America. Its name derives from the Greek *aspidos*, a shield, and *sperma*, a seed. Quebracho bark, used commercially for tanning and as a source of drugs employed in treating bronchitis, asthma, and emphysema, is obtained from the white quebracho.

Aspidospermas are trees usually with milky or reddish sap. Their leaves are undivided and mostly alternate. Many together in clusters shorter than the leaves, the small flowers have five each sepals, petals, and stamens and a pistil of two carpels. The fruits, solitary or in pairs, are woody, podlike follicles containing winged seeds.

The white quebracho (*A. quebracho-blanco*) is a medium-sized to large stiffly-branched, white-barked, evergreen tree of Argentina, Paraguay, and Brazil. It has lustrous, leathery, ovate-lanceolate, bristle-tipped leaves 1¼ to 3 inches long by ⅓ to 1 inch wide, and white blooms. The ovoid fruits are about 3 inches long. The hard white wood is used locally as lumber and is excellent fuel. This kind must not be confused with the red quebracho (*Schinopsis lorentzii*), which also is a source of tanning material, but belongs to a different family.

Native to Brazil, Argentina and Bolivia, evergreen *A. australe*, up to 60 feet in height, has longish-stalked leaves, with ovate to elliptic or narrow-oblong blades 3 to 4½ inches long. The flowers are greenish to yellowish, the fruits flattened and deeply-boat-shaped to nearly circular.

Garden and Landscape Uses and Cultivation. In parts of California and in other warm regions the species described are planted to some extent for shade and ornament. They succeed in ordinary soil and are propagated by seeds.

ASPIDOTIS (Aspid-òtis)—Pod Fern. Closely related to *Cheilanthes*, the fern genus *Aspidotis* of the pteris family PTERIDACEAE consists of three species native in North America, one in Africa. The name, from the Greek *aspis*, a shield, presumably alludes to the coverings of the spore clusters.

These are small, evergreen, rock- and cliff-inhabiting plants. They have short, scaly rhizomes and nearly similar fertile and sterile fronds, two- to four-times pinnate. The edges of the leaf segments turn

under to serve as continuous or discontinuous covers for clusters of spore capsules.

Widely distributed as a native in western North America and from Quebec to Ontario, the pod fern (*A. densa* syns. *Pellaea densa, Cheilanthes densa, C. siliquosa, Onchium densum*) has slender, ascending, scaly rhizomes. Its clustered fronds include rarely produced sterile ones and larger, abundantly developed fertile ones. The largest fronds are up to 10 inches long. They have a purplish stalk considerably longer than the triangular, thrice-pinnate blade. There are five to eight pairs of subopposite primary divisions each of six or fewer pairs of secondary divisions of one to three pairs of narrowly-elliptic-lanceolate segments scarcely ¼ inch long. The few large clusters of spore capsules are covered by recurved, toothed portions of the leaf margin. Except that their sharply-toothed segments are broader and without clusters of spore capsules the sterile fronds are similar to the fertile ones.

Californian *A. californica* (syn. *Cheilanthes californica*) grows in its native state in moist or dry places and in rock crevices. It has densely-tufted, broad-ovate-triangular to pentagonal, hairless fronds up to nearly 1 foot tall, four times pinnate or pinnately-lobed, the ultimate segments lanceolate and toothed. The spore cluster coverings are confined to single veinlets.

Garden and Landscape Uses and Cultivation. These are as for *Cheilanthes*. For additional information see Ferns.

ASPLENIACEAE—Spleenwort Family. This family of ferns, by some authorities included in the *Polypodiaceae*, contains about 660 species distributed in nine genera of which *Asplenium* is the only one of more than five species. Its members grow chiefly on cliffs or rocks or in the ground or less frequently perch on trees (are epiphytes). They have creeping or suberect rhizomes and small to huge, usually firm-textured fronds, undivided and lobeless or once or more times cleft or pinnate. The long, narrow clusters of spore capsules lie along the veinlets and have covers (indusia) similar in shape to the clusters joined to the veinlets. Genera cultivated are *Asplenium, Camptosorus, Ceterach*, and *Phyllitis*.

ASPLENIUM (Asplèn-ium)—Spleenwort, Bird's Nest Fern. This group of 650 hardy, subtropical and tropical ferns of the spleenwort family ASPLENIACEAE is represented in the native floras of many parts of the world including North America. Most of its members are evergreen, a few are popular cultivated plants. Some species previously included in *Asplenium* belong in the related genus *Athyrium*. The name is derived from the Greek *a*, without, and *splen*, spleen. Like the English name spleenwort, it alludes to virtues certain species were supposed to have for curing diseases of the spleen.

Spleenworts vary greatly. Their fronds (leaves) may be undivided or deeply-incised, or they may have separate leaflets. The distinguishing feature is the presence of sori (singular, sorus) or spore-containing structures. These, on the undersides of the fronds, are linear and usually straight, or more rarely slightly curved; they are placed obliquely in herringbone fashion between the midrib and margin of a frond or leaflet. Spleenworts are distinguished from *Athyrium* by their sori not being bent into a V or J shape, from *Onychium* by the sori not being in pairs, and from the hart's tongue fern (*Phyllitis scolopendrium*) in their leaf bases not being heart-shaped.

Hardy spleenworts include several natives of North America, few of which are cultivated to any considerable extent. The maidenhair spleenwort (*A. trichomanes*) is one of the most desirable. It inhabits northern Europe and northern Asia as well as America, favoring rich woods and especially limestone rocks. This evergreen fern has rich green necklaces of narrow-linear, once-pinnate leaves up to 6 inches long by ½ to ¾ inch wide; the more or less oval leaflets rarely exceed ¼ inch in length and are often smaller. The ebony spleenwort (*A. platyneuron*) is similar, but larger. Its fronds are 8 inches to 1½ feet long or somewhat longer. Its leaflets are up to 1 inch in length. This kind has both fertile (spore-bearing) and sterile fronds; those of the maidenhair spleenwort are all fertile.

Asplenium nidus

tropical Asia and Polynesia, is popular as a pot plant and in small sizes is frequently used in dish gardens and terrariums. When fully grown its fronds may be 4 feet long by 8 inches wide. Very different, but equally as accommodating to pot cultivation is the mother spleenwort (*A. bulbiferum*). Native of Australia, New Zealand, and Malaya, this species has arching fronds up to 4 feet long by 1 foot wide, twice- or thrice-pinnately-divided. The leaflets are lobed or divided and up to 1½ inches long. A curious and interesting feature is the profuse development of little bulbous plantlets on the upper surfaces of mature leaves. The variety *A. b. laxum* is distinguished by its drooping fronds and narrower leaflets. Similar to the mother

spleenwort and having the same habit of developing baby plants on its leaves, is *A. daucifolium* (syn. *A. viviparum*), of Madagascar, Mauritius, and Réunion. This is a stiffer and rather less luxurient species than *A. bulbiferum*.

Other aspleniums in cultivation include these: *A. adiantum-nigrum*, the black spleenwort, is a hardy, variable species, of wide natural distribution. Its tufted, once-to thrice-pinnate fronds 6 inches to 1½ feet long by 2 to 4 inches wide, sometimes develop plantlets at their apexes. They have twelve to twenty leaflets on each side of the midrib, the lowermost 1½ to 2 inches wide. *A. auritum*, of tropical America, has tufts of fronds with once-pinnate blades up to 1 foot long by 4 inches wide, with

Asplenium bulbiferum, young specimen

Asplenium trichomanes

The bird's nest fern (*A. nidus* syn. *A. nidus-avis*), one of the most familiar of the genus, differs markedly from all other cultivated spleenworts. Its paddle-shaped leaves spread upward and outward to form a green funnel, the "bird's nest" of the originators of its colloquial name. In its native state organic debris such as forest leaves collect in the funnel and remain moist and into this the fern roots. The bird's nest fern is an epiphyte; it grows, like many orchids, on trees, but does not take nourishment from the host as do parasites. This handsome kind, a native of

Asplenium bulbiferum, with plantlets

Artemisia pycnocephala, with red-flowered Heuchera

Artemisia schmidtiana nana

Artemisia stellerana

Asclepias tuberosa

Artocarpus altilis (breadfruit)

Aruncus dioicus

Ascocenda variety

Asarum caudatum

Aster (Michaelmas-daisy), garden variety

Asphodeline lutea

Astrophytum capricorne

Astilbe, garden variety

Astilbe, garden variety

ten to fifteen 2- to 3-inch-long, ½-inch-wide, toothed or lobed leaflets on each side of the midrib. The clusters of spore capsules are in two rows angling upward from the mid-veins of the leaflets. *A. belangeri* is an elegant native of Malaya, Indonesia, and China, with narrowly-oblong to lanceolate, lacy fronds up to 2½ feet long and up to 4 inches wide. They are twice-pinnate, with the final divisions ¼ inch long. Buds or plantlets are sometimes borne along the midribs. *A. falcatum,* the willow spleenwort, is indigenous from Madagascar to Malaya and New Zealand. This kind has linear-oblong fronds up to 3 feet long by 8 inches wide. They are once-pinnate, with the leaflets irregularly toothed or lobed and again finely-toothed. *A. flaccidum,* of Australia, New Zealand, and South Africa, in cultivation is frequently misnamed *A. mayi* or *A. majus.* It has short creeping to erect rhizomes and drooping to recurved fronds with winged midribs. The leaf blades and their deeply-lobed leaflets vary considerably in shape and size. The former are commonly 1 foot to 3 feet long by 4 to 8 inches wide. The leaflets are narrow, with narrow, widely-spaced ultimate segments. *A. formosum,* a widespread native of the tropics, has tufted, short-stalked, linear fronds 1 foot to 1½ feet long, about 1 inch wide, with on each side of the midrib twenty to forty ½-inch-long leaflets the upper margins of which are deeply-double-toothed, their lower edges toothed toward their apexes. The linear clusters of spore capsules are one to four on each side of the mid-vein. *A. friesiorum* of tropical Africa has arching or spreading, lanceolate, pinnate fronds up to 1 foot or more long by 8 inches wide. They have black or nearly black stalks and midribs and coarsely toothed or double-toothed leaflets. *A. marinum,* the Euro-

Asplenium friesiorum

pean sea spleenwort, is highly variable and typically has tufted, oblong-lanceolate to linear fronds 6 inches to 1½ feet long, 2 to 4 inches wide, with toothed leaflets, the lower ones often triangular. *A. ruta-muraria* is a delightful, dainty, hardy min-

iature, native of usually limestone soils and shaded or sunny, often exposed cliffs in north-temperate regions. It has tufts of fronds 2 to 6 inches long, with triangular blades of a few leaflets again two- or three-times pinnate into rather few-toothed ultimate segments. *A. septentrionale* is an inhabitant of temperate parts of the northern hemisphere. It forms dense, grasslike tufts of toothed fronds undivided or cleft from their tops into two or three slender, alternate 2 to 6 inches long and once- or twice-pinnate, with ultimate segments that are lobeless or cleft wedge-shaped lobes. The elongated clusters of spore capsules cover much or all of the under surfaces of the fronds. *A. squamulatum* of Malaya has rosettes of somewhat wavy, thick, leathery, narrow-elliptic leaves 8 inches to 1½ feet long by 2 to 3 inches wide, with scurfy undersides. *A. stuhlmannii* of East Africa is an attractive species with short-stalked pinnate leaves 8 inches to 1¼ feet long by 2 to 3 inches wide. Its thin, leathery leaflets, three- to five-lobed at their apexes, are triangular-ovate.

Asplenium squamulatum

Asplenium stuhlmannii

Garden and Landscape Uses. The maidenhair and ebony spleenworts and some other hardy kinds are choice subjects for

shady rock gardens, native plant gardens, and woodlands. The others may be grown in the open in shaded locations in southern California, southern Florida, and Hawaii as well as indoors there and elsewhere. The bird's nest fern and the mother spleenwort especially are good houseplants. All the tender kinds discussed are attractive for greenhouses and conservatories.

Cultivation. The maidenhair and ebony spleenworts are not the easiest plants to establish and maintain in gardens. The former grows best in limestone soil packed in crevices between chunks of limestone rock; the latter responds to woodland soil of approximately neutral acid-alkaline reaction. For both, the soil should be moist, but the ebony spleenwort stands occasional dry spells better than does the other.

The tender kinds prosper in any coarse, porous soil enriched liberally with organic matter such as partially decayed leaf mold, coarse peat moss, or rich compost. If dried cow or horse manure is obtainable its addition to the soil in proportions up to one-tenth part by bulk is helpful, and a liberal scattering of bonemeal is in order. Planting or potting is best done in late winter or spring just as new growth begins. A mulch maintained around specimens planted in ground beds is helpful. Discretion must be used in watering. The objective is to keep the earth always moist, but not so constantly saturated that the foliage turns yellow; it is especially important to guard against this in winter. Well-rooted specimens are helped to remain in good condition by dilute liquid fertilizer applied weekly or biweekly from spring through fall. Appropriate greenhouse temperatures are winter minimums of 55 to 60°F, but the mother spleenwort will stand considerably lower temperatures provided it does not actually freeze. By day the temperature may be five or ten degrees higher and in the warm part of the year both day and night temperature will be above those recommended for winter. Every effort should be made to maintain a genial humidity. Although these ferns persist in drier atmospheres than many kinds, they really flourish only when the atmosphere is moist. Shade from strong sun is needed. Propagation is by spores, division, and in the kinds that produce plantlets on their fronds, by pegging mature leaves that have these well developed, onto the surface of sandy peaty soil and keeping them in a humid, warm place until they have rooted sufficiently to separate them and pot them individually.

Pests. The chief pests are snails, slugs, scale insects, mealy bugs, and leaf nematodes.

ASPLUNDIA (As-plúndia). Related to and formerly included in *Carludovica,* the genus *Asplundia* comprises eighty-two species of the cyclanthus family CYCLANTHACEAE.

Confined in the wild to Central America, the West Indies, and tropical South America, it is little known horticulturally. The name commemorates the twentieth-century Swedish botanist Dr. Erik Asplund.

Asplundias include stemless or stemmed herbaceous and shrubby plants, as well as vines that climb by rooting stems. They have pleated, palmlike leaves, with stalks not more than twice as long as the blades. The latter are basically divided into two lobes, which in older leaves may further split irregularly. The flowers are similar in form and arrangement to those of *Carludovica*, but the spadixes are usually shorter. The fruits are berries.

A root-climbing vine up to 30 feet tall, with branched stems and leaves congregated at the branch ends, **A. rigida** (syn. *Carludovica plumerii*) has leaves with stalks usually 6 inches to 1 foot long, and blades cleft for rather more than one-half their 1- to 2-foot length into narrowly- to rarely broadly-lanceolate lobes. The flowers are on pendulous spadixes that have at their bases five or six white, greenish-white, or rarely red spathes (bracts). This kind is native to moist forests, often growing near waterfalls in the West Indies and Trinidad.

Garden and Landscape Uses and Cultivation. In the humid tropics and warm subtropics, *A. rigida* is occasionally planted to climb up palms and other trees. It succeeds in shady locations in forest-type soil. Propagation is by seeds, cuttings, and air-layering.

ASSAI is *Euterpe oleracea*.

ASTELIA (Astèl-ia). The name of this group of twenty-five species is derived from the Greek *a*, without, and *stele*, a pillar, and refers to some species being epiphytic and relying upon trees to hold them well above the ground. Of particular interest to botanists, because of the curious natural distributions this and closely allied genera enjoy, the genus *Astelia* belongs in the lily family LILIACEAE. The headquarters of the genera involved is New Zealand, but they are represented in Australia, islands of the Pacific including Hawaii, and the Indian Ocean island of Réunion, as well as South America. This may support the theory that these land masses were once joined.

Astelias are large, clump-forming, evergreen herbaceous plants, with mostly basal, swordlike leaves and large, spreading panicles of numerous, small, unisexual flowers, the sexes on separate plants. The blooms have six spreading or reflexed perianth lobes (petals), the males, six stamens, and the females six staminodes (aborted stamens) and an ovary. The fruits are small, yellow, red, or purple-black berries.

Most astelias are epiphytes. They grow high in trees, but do not take nourishment from them; they accept lodging only. In this they resemble orchids and bromeliads, and as with these groups, not all of the species are epiphytes—a minority grow in the ground. A curious habit of some astelias is that they climb trees. New Zealand forests are composed chiefly of evergreens and because of this little light penetrates. Starting as seedlings at ground level, young specimens of these "climbing" astelias embrace the trunks of trees and, by extending themselves always upward and dying behind as they go, eventually reach a level where there is sufficient light to favor the production of flowers and fruits. As the leafy masses ascend, they trail dead rope-like stems behind them. Other astelias spend their entire lives in crotches high above the ground, having developed there from seeds. From below they look like immense birds' nests. The sweet berries of these plants are eaten by the Maoris.

Planted for ornament in California and other mild regions, **A. nervosa**, of New

Astelia nervosa

Zealand, includes plants previously segregated as *A. cockaynei*. Unlike most, this sort is not epiphytic, it grows with its roots in the ground. In the wild often forming large colonies, *A. nervosa* has rigid, arching leaves 2 to 5 feet long or sometimes longer by ¾ inch to almost 2 inches wide. They are densely clothed with scales that form a smooth surface or a shaggy fur completely hiding the green of the tissues beneath. The greenish-tan to deep maroon flowers, with petals up to ¼ inch long, are in panicles of twelve or fewer racemes. The berries are orange to red, and ¼ inch or a little over in diameter.

Garden and Landscape Uses and Cultivation. The species described here grows in sunny locations in ordinary soil, preferring one of a sandy peaty nature. It may be used as bold, grasslike clumps by watersides and elsewhere where such features can be effectively displayed. Propagation is by seeds and division.

ASTER. The genus *Aster* is treated in the next entry. Plants called China-asters belong in *Callistephus*. The name golden-aster is applied to *Chrysopsis* and *Heterotheca*. Stokes'-aster is *Stokesia laevis*. Olearias are called tree-asters.

ASTER (Aś-ter)—Michaelmas-Daisy, Goldilocks. China-asters do not belong here. They are treated under their generic name, *Callistephus*. We are here concerned only with the genus *Aster*, which includes the plants commonly in Britain and sometimes in the United States and Canada called Michaelmas-daisies. Most of the about 500 species are natives of the Americas. Others occur in Europe, Asia, and South Africa. The name, alluding to the form of the flower heads, is from the Latin *aster*, a star. The genus belongs in the daisy family COMPOSITAE. The closely related *Solidago* and *Erigeron* do not differ from *Aster* in any firm botanical characteristics. The prevailingly yellow flower heads form the chief identifying feature of *Solidago*, the commonly earlier season of bloom and some unstable characteristics of *Erigeron*. For some plants previously named *Aster* see Felicia, and Heteropappus.

Asters are chiefly herbaceous perennials, sometimes somewhat woody at their bases. A very few not known to be cultivated and not described here are annuals. They have alternate, undivided leaves and usually clustered, rarely solitary, nearly always daisy-form flower heads, the ray or petal-like florets in a wide variety of hues excepting clear yellow and orange. Blues, purples, violets, and whites predominate, with good pinks and reds available in horticultural varieties. The centers of the flower heads, of yellow disk florets sometimes changing to purple or rose-purple, are generally surrounded by one or two rows of ray florets (rarely, rays are wanting), the whole backed by an involucre (collar) of several rows of more or less leafy bracts usually of different sizes that overlap like shingles. The fruits are seedlike achenes.

Michaelmas-daisies of gardens are chiefly horticulturally selected forms of European *A. amellus* and of the American species *A. cordifolius*, *A. drummondii*, *A. dumosus*, *A. ericoides*, *A. laevis*, *A. lateriflorus*, *A. novae-angliae*, *A. novi-belgii*, *A. simplex*, and *A. vimineus*, bred for their more desirable habits of growth, improved size and color of flower heads, and other characteristics esteemed by gardeners. Except for these botanically unimportant details, the plants generally retain the basic characteristics of the species. A lesser number of Michaelmas-daisy varieties, perhaps of hybrid origin, exhibit characteristics intermediate between those of their presumed parents.

Michaelmas-daisy, garden variety

Michaelmas-daisies of gardens are identified by horticultural names rather than botanical ones, although in catalogs they are sometimes grouped with reference to their typical species, for instance as amellus varieties, novae-angliae varieties, and novi-belgii varieties.

Here are presented in alphabetical sequence descriptions of the chief species from which garden varieties of Michaelmas-daisies have been derived: *A. amellus*,

Aster amellus

1½ to 2 feet tall, has rough stems and foliage. Its leaves are oblong-lanceolate, its solitary to many flower heads are purple, 1½ to 2 inches in diameter. This sort is native of Italy. *A. cordifolius*, native in woodlands from Nova Scotia to Minnesota, Georgia, and Missouri, is a variable species up to 5 feet tall. It has more or less minutely-hairy to rough-hairy, thinnish,

Aster cordifolius

sharply-toothed, narrow- to broad-heart-shaped, pointed leaves up to 4½ inches long by 3½ inches wide, with scarcely-winged stalks. The lower ones are long-stalked, those above progressively shorter-stalked. In loose panicles, the about ¾-inch-wide, blue, purple, or rarely white flower heads have mostly eight to twenty ray florets. The usually partly purple bracts of their involucres are narrow, blunt to short-pointed. *A. drummondii* is native from Ohio to Minnesota, Louisiana, and Texas. Favoring clearings and open woodlands, it is 1½ to 4 feet tall. Its firm-textured, shallowly-toothed leaves, roughish above, densely-pubescent on their undersides, toward the base of the plant are long-stalked, broad- to narrow-heart-shaped, up to 6 inches long by 3 inches

wide. Those higher on the stems have progressively shorter, mostly broadly-winged stalks, less heart-shaped to rounded bases. The many flower heads, ½ to ¾ inch wide, have ten to twenty bright blue ray florets in panicles of fairly dense clusters. They have strongly-pointed involucral bracts usually without purple coloring. *A. dumosus* is a variable native of dryish or moist, often sandy soils from Massachusetts to Kentucky, Florida, and Louisiana, also the northcentral states and adjacent Canada. From 1 foot to 3 feet tall, it has usually branched stems somewhat hairy in their upper portions, and stalkless, linear, lanceolate-linear, to narrowly-elliptic leaves, roughened with brief hairs on their upper surfaces, hairless beneath, up to 4½ inches long by ⅜ inch wide. The flower heads, on longish, leafy individual stalks, have twelve to thirty short, bluish, pale lavender, or sometimes white rays. They are about ½ inch wide and are in large, very loose panicles. Several dwarf horticultural varieties including 'Lady Maddocks' and 'Niobe' are derivatives of this species. *A. ericoides*, the heath aster, native in dry, open places from Maine to Manitoba, Pennsylvania, Missouri, and Texas has erect to sprawling, much-branched, slender stems 1 foot to 3 feet tall. Its stalkless, toothless, rigid leaves, those on the lower parts usually early deciduous, are numerous, linear, rarely 2¼ inches long by ¼ inch wide, and usually smaller. Generally white, less commonly blue or pink, the dainty, approximately ½-inch-wide flower heads are arranged somewhat one-sidedly along the wide-spreading slender branches of the loose panicles. *A. laevis* occurs na-

Aster laevis

tively in open, dry places from Maine to British Columbia and Georgia, Alabama, and New Mexico. From 1 foot to 3½ feet tall, the usually branchless stems, except sometimes among the flowers, are hairless and often slightly glaucous. Very variable in shape, the thick, mostly toothed leaves clasp the stems with their bases. The basal leaves often have winged stalks. In open, panicle-like clusters the several to many flower heads each with fifteen to twenty-five light blue, purple, lavender, or white ray florets, are ¾ inch to 1¼ inches in diameter. *A. lateriflorus,* of Quebec to Minnesota, Florida, and Texas, inhabits open woodlands, dry, open areas, and beaches. From 1 foot to 4 feet tall, this kind has curly-haired or practically hairless stems. Its toothed or toothless leaves, short-stiff-hairy to hairless on their upper sides, underneath are seemingly without hairs except along the midribs. They are broadly-linear to lanceolate-elliptic, up to 6 inches long by a little over 1 inch wide. The foliage on the lower part of the stems is soon deciduous. The flower heads have nine to fourteen white or purple-tinged ray florets. They are along the slender, wide-spreading, raceme-like branches of loose panicles. *A. novae-angliae,* the New England aster, is a showy inhabitant of moist,

Aster novae-angliae

Aster novae-angliae

usually open places from Massachusetts and Vermont to Alberta, Wyoming, and New Mexico. From 2 to 6 feet in height, stoutish-stemmed and conspicuously hairy

at least in its upper parts, this strong-rooting kind has toothless, lanceolate leaves up to about 4½ inches long by nearly 1 inch wide. Stalkless and crowded, they clasp the stems with eared bases. Their upper sides are rough-hairy, their undersides more softly so. The glandular-stalked flower heads, 1 inch to 2 inches wide, are in loose, rather short, leafy clusters at the branch ends. Their involucres are glandular. They have usually forty-five to more than twice as many generally bright, rosy-purple to reddish-purple ray florets. Old and well-known horticultural varieties of this are 'Harrington's Pink' and 'Survivor'. *A. novi-belgii,* the New York aster, inhabits moist soils including salt marshes from Newfoundland to Georgia and perhaps Alabama, chiefly in coastal regions. Very variable, usually stout-stemmed, and 1 foot to 5 feet tall, this kind has stems hairy or hairless except below the flower heads, but not glandular. Its stalkless, toothed or toothless, usually thickish leaves, lanceolate to lanceolate-linear or elliptic, have more or less stem-clasping bases. They are up to 7 inches long by 1 inch wide, hairless except along their margins. In open, usually leafy clusters, the approximately 1-inch-wide flower heads have twenty to fifty blue or less often rose-pink or white ray florets. The New York aster is a parent of probably the majority of horticultural varieties of Michaelmas-daisies. *A. simplex* (syn. *A. paniculatus*) lives in moist soils from Nova Scotia to North Dakota, Virginia, and Texas. Variable, it forms colonies of stout stems up to 5 feet in height, usually somewhat hairy in their upper parts. Nearly always toothed, the lanceolate to linear leaves are hairless or sometimes slightly rough with very short hairs on their upper sides. They are stalkless or have sometimes slightly stem-clasping tapered bases and are up to 6 inches long by nearly 1½ inches wide. The flower heads, each with twenty to forty white or more rarely lavender or blue ray florets, are in long, leafy, panicle-like clusters. They are approximately ¾ inch in diameter. *A. vimineus* grows mostly near the coast from Maine to Florida and Louisiana and along the basin of the Mississippi River. From 2 to 6 feet in height, its stems are hairless to more or less finely-hairy. Up to 4½ inches long by under ½ inch wide, those of the branches are much smaller than the lower ones, the leaves are linear to narrowly-lanceolate, pointed, and hairless except sometimes for very short, rough hairs on their upper surfaces. In loose panicles, the flower heads are arranged more or less one-sidedly along long, wide-spreading branches. They have fifteen to thirty short, white or rarely purplish ray florets and are ⅓ inch wide.

Native North American asters of many kinds other than those described above may be brought into cultivation from time

to time especially in native plant gardens and naturalistic areas. These are well described in wild flower books and floras of the regions. Among the best are the following: *A. divaricatus,* the white wood aster, native in woodlands from Quebec to Georgia and Tennessee, 2 to 2½ feet tall, has long-stalked, ovate-lanceolate leaves and loose, rounded clusters of 1-inch-wide, white-rayed flower heads with fewer than twelve white ray florets. *A. grandiflorus,* native from Virginia to North Carolina and perhaps to Florida, often in pine woods, and up to 2½ feet tall, has oblong to linear leaves. Its flower heads, with up to forty-five violet ray florets, are up to 2 inches wide. *A. linariifolius* ranges from Quebec to Florida, Wisconsin, and Texas. About 2 feet tall and very leafy, it has linear, toothless leaves and solitary or in clusters of several, 1-inch-wide flower heads with ten to twenty violet or sometimes white ray florets. *A. macrophyllus,* native in woodlands from southern Canada to Georgia and Wisconsin, about 3 feet tall, has large heart-shaped leaves and broad clusters of numerous 1-inch-wide flower heads, with nine to twenty lavender ray florets. *A. patens* occurs wild from New Hampshire to Missouri, Florida, and Texas. Its leaves, their bases stem-clasping, are ovate-oblong and toothless. The few to many flower heads, each terminating a branch of the cluster, are 1 inch wide. They have fifteen to twenty-five blue or rarely pink ray florets and are in very loose, branched clusters. *A. puniceus,* sometimes 8 feet tall, grows in wet soils from Newfoundland to

Aster puniceus

Alabama. Its stalkless or nearly stalkless, stem-clasping, lanceolate to elliptic-oblong leaves are toothed or toothless. Few to many, the flower heads are up to 1½ inches wide. They have thirty to sixty purple, more rarely pink or white, ray florets. *A. spectabilis,* native from Massachusetts to South Carolina, is up to 3 feet tall. It has toothless, or nearly toothless elliptic leaves. The flower heads, about 1½ inches across and blue-violet, are in roundish clusters of

Aster spectabilis

Aster spectabilis

few to many. **A. tradescantii,** native of shores and stream banks from Nova Scotia to Michigan and New York, is up to 2 feet tall. It has shallowly-toothed or toothless, linear to lanceolate-elliptic leaves, the lower stalked, those above stalkless. The rather few flower heads, about ½ inch wide, have fifteen to thirty white ray florets.

Goldilocks (**A. linosyris** syns. *Crinitaria vulgaris, Linosyris vulgaris*), is a native of

Hybrid between *Aster linosyris* and *A. sedifolius*

Aster linosyris

Europe and temperate Asia. It has wiry, erect stems 1 foot to 2 feet tall, much-branched at their tops. Its small, linear, toothless leaves are numerous. The very numerous flower heads are small and pale yellow. Normally they are rayless, being composed of all disk florets, but sometimes ray florets develop. A hybrid between *A. linosyris* and European *A. sedifolius* has flower heads always with a few ray florets.

Other Asian species in cultivation include **A. tataricus** of Japan, China, and Siberia, and naturalized to some extent in

North America. This very late bloomer is 6 to 7 feet tall. Its lanceolate to ovate-lanceolate, coarsely-toothed leaves are up to 2 feet long by 6 inches wide. The lower foliage is long-stalked, upward from the base the leaves gradually diminish in size and become shorter-stalked or stalkless. The bluish or purplish, approximately 1-inch-wide flower heads each with fifteen to twenty ray florets are in large, flat-topped clusters. Native to the Himalayan region, late spring-flowering **A. diplostephioides** is hairy and 6 inches to 1½ feet tall. It has toothless or few-toothed, obovate to oblanceolate leaves up to about 4 inches long by 1 inch wide, the lower stalked the upper stalkless. Solitary and 2 to 3 inches in diameter, the flower heads

Aster diplostephioides

Aster tongolensis

Aster frikartii

have blackish-purple-tipped, reddish-orange disk florets and blue or violet-blue ray florets. Sometimes confused with the last, *A. tongolensis* (syn. *A. subcaeruleus*) is native from western China to India. Up to 1 foot high, it has somewhat hairy, oblong-spatula-shaped to oblong-lanceolate, toothless leaves up to 5 inches long and solitary flower heads up to 2 inches across with yellow centers and blue ray florets. Another closely related Chinese, *A. farreri* differs chiefly in its narrower, linear-lanceolate leaves. Its flowers are sometimes 3 inches in diameter. Also similar is *A. yunnanensis*, of western China. This kind has obovate leaves, the lower ones deciduous, and flower heads solitary, or in twos or threes, about 2½ inches across. They have broad, light blue-mauve ray florets.

A mountain plant of Europe and the Rocky Mountains, *A. alpinus* is from 6 inches to 1 foot tall. It has toothless, spatula-shaped basal leaves tapering to winged stalks, and stalkless, linear-lanceolate upper leaves. The solitary flower heads, about 1 inch to 2 inches wide, are displayed in late spring. They have blue or violet ray florets. The flower heads of *A. a. albus* have white rays, those of *A. a. rubra* red. From 9 inches to 1 foot tall or taller, *A. bellidiastrum*, of mountains in southern Europe, has rosettes of stalked, broad-ovate leaves and solitary, white-rayed flower heads 1 inch or a little more wide atop long

Aster alpinus albus

leafless stalks. Himalayan *A. thomsonii*, of importance as a parent of popular *A. frikartii*, is 1 foot to 3 feet tall. It has stem-clasping, slender-pointed, broadly-ovate leaves up to 4 inches long and relatively few, long-stalked flower heads 1½ to 2½ inches in diameter. They have pale lilac ray florets. Hybrid *A. frikartii*, the parents of which are *A. amellus* and *A. thomsonii*, is one of the most satisfactory garden plants. This kind is 2 to 2½ feet tall. Over a long season it displays many yellow-eyed flower heads with light blue ray florets. They are up to 3 inches across. The leaves are oblong. Choice varieties are 'Wonder of Staffa' and 'Jungfrau'.

Garden and Landscape Uses. Many native wild asters of North America are charming for naturalizing in semiwild places, such as, depending upon kind, woodland gardens, open meadowlike areas, the fringes of woodlands, and by watersides. If you elect to do this, remember that many species are variable and that it is worth while seeking individual plants with particularly good habits, flower sizes, and colors for transplanting to the garden. Michaelmas-daisies derived from some of these, the available kinds listed under horticultural names and described with fulsome praise and often illustrated, sometimes in color, in the catalogs of dealers in hardy plants, are admirable for adding fall color to sunny garden beds and borders and for supplying welcome cut blooms. They do well in city gardens. They come in varieties from those that form dense cushions only a few inches high to others 2 to 4 feet tall or taller, some compact, others with loose, graceful sprays of bloom. These are admirable companions for early-flowering chrysanthemums, but do not last in bloom as long as those popular perennials. It should be noted that Michaelmas-daisies of the amellus group, those that have *A. amellus* as one parent, do not do well in most parts of North America. Much like Michaelmas-daisies, but blooming early and remaining in flower for a much longer season, *A. frikartii* and its varieties are splendid perennial border plants and also afford flowers for cutting.

Low asters with solitary flower heads, *A. alpinus*, *A. bellidiastrum* (not reliably hardy in cold climates without winter protection), *A. diplostephioides*, *A. farreri*, and *A. yunnanensis*, adapt well to rock gardens and the fronts of flower beds.

Cultivation. Except for a few native North American kinds that favor wet soils, asters need well-drained ones. Some prosper under dryish conditions, the great majority where the soil is moist enough for the majority of flower garden plants. For Michaelmas-daisies and related kinds, let the ground be reasonably fertile, but not so rich that gross growth with attendant lanky, weak stems is encouraged. The low rock garden species are best with somewhat leaner, but not excessively dry soil.

Best results with most Michaelmas-daisies and their parent species are had when they are divided and replanted annually or every other year. Other kinds require this attention when reduction in vigor of growth or increasing sparseness of bloom suggest the need. Division is done in spring or fall, except that fall division or transplanting is not recommended for amellus varieties. Select for replanting small rooted portions from the vigorous outsides of the clumps. If as many as possible new plants are needed from a limited stock of old ones pot the latter or plant them in deep flats in fall, put them in a cold frame, and in late January or February bring them into a sunny greenhouse where the night temperature is about 50°F. A succession of new shoots will soon grow. As soon as they are 2 to 3 inches high cut them off with as many roots attached as possible and plant individually in small pots in sandy soil. Grow them under cool, sunny conditions but not exposed to frost, until it is safe to plant them outdoors. By pinching out the tips of the young plants as soon as they have recovered from the potting operation, branching is encouraged. This is generally desirable, but if you want the largest, most magnificent trusses of the finest blooms, say for a flower show, do not pinch tall varieties. Allow each to develop only one stem and keep this tied to a stake to avoid breakage from the time the young plant is set out in richer-than-usual soil in a sunny garden bed.

Summer care consists of controlling weeds by surface cultivation or mulching, of watering in dry weather, avoiding as much as possible wetting the foliage because this favors mildew, of staking neatly and not obviously, and of cutting off all flowers as soon as they have faded. If this last is not done seeds are likely to ripen, fall to the ground and give rise to inferior plants undistinguishable, until they flower, from the choicer parent variety.

ASTERAGO LUTEA is *Solidaster luteus*.

ASTERANTHERA (Aster-ánthera). An inhabitant of cool, humid forests in Chile where it creeps or climbs over tree trunks, *Asteranthera ovata* is the only representative of its genus. It belongs in the gesneria family GESNERIACEAE and has a name, alluding to the anthers of its four stamens being joined to form a star, from the Latin *aster*, a star, and *anthera*, an anther.

Under cultivation *A. ovata* is usually more compact than in the wild. It becomes a shrublet up to 1 foot tall, with opposite, ovate-elliptic to nearly round, few-toothed, blunt leaves, more or less furnished with white hairs. The leaves of individual pairs are frequently unequal in size. They range

from less than ½ inch to 1½ inches in length and are approximately one-half as wide as long. On stalks longer than the leaves, with a pair of little bracts near their middles, the raspberry-red blooms are borne singly or in twos from the leaf axils. They have five-lobed calyxes, and narrowly-funnel-shaped corollas slightly under 1½ inches in length. The face of the bloom is oblique to the tube and consists of two lips, the lower markedly three-lobed and striped with yellow. The fruits are berry-like.

Garden Uses and Cultivation. A pretty plant for inclusion in collections of gesneriads (plants of the gesneria family), *Asteranthera* is uncommon in cultivation. It may be expected to succeed under the treatment recommended for *Sarmienta* and, like it, may be displayed in hanging baskets. Success with this plant outdoors is reported from mild regions in England and it probably would survive in parts of the Pacific Northwest. For more information see Gesneriads.

ASTERISCUS (Astér-iscus). Native of the Mediterranean region, the Cape Verde Islands, and Canary Islands, *Asteriscus* of the daisy family COMPOSITAE was formerly named *Odontospermum*. It comprises fifteen species. The name, referring to the form of the flower head, is derived from the Greek *aster*, a star.

These plants have opposite, lobeless, toothless or rarely deeply-toothed leaves, and solitary or clustered flower heads of the daisy type, each with a central eye of disk florets encircled by spreading, petal-like ray florets. The seedlike fruits are achenes.

A beautiful shrub 2 to 4 feet tall, with silvery-silky-hairy foliage and golden-yellow flower heads, *A. sericeus* (syn. *Odontospermum sericeum*), is a native of the Canary Islands. Broad and much-branched, it has linear, wedge- to spoon-shaped leaves. In summer, its stalkless, terminal and axillary flower heads, 2 to 3 inches in diameter, are borne with great freedom.

A herbaceous perennial, woody toward its base, *A. maritimus* (syn. *Odontosper-*

Asteriscus maritimus

mum maritima) inhabits rocky places near the Mediterranean Sea. Forming tufts 2 to 10 inches tall, it has oblanceolate to spoon-shaped, usually roughly-hairy leaves. Its flower heads, much resembling single calendulas, are bright orange-yellow, and about 1½ inches across. They have approximately thirty ray florets, finely-toothed at their ends.

Garden and Landscape Uses. A fine ornamental, *A. sericeus* is suitable for beds, borders, and rock gardens in a dryish climate, such as that of California, and for growing in containers to embellish patios, terraces, steps, and similar places. In climates too cold for it to survive outdoors the year around, specimens in pots or tubs are sometimes wintered in sunny, cool greenhouses and are stood outdoors in summer. Hardier than the last, but not sufficiently so to winter outdoors in the north, *A. maritimus* is best suited for rock gardens and similar intimate plantings.

Cultivation. These plants need sunny locations, and porous, well-drained, dryish rather than wet soil. Propagation is by seeds and by summer cuttings of firm, but not hard, woody shoots planted in a bed of sand or perlite in a greenhouse or cold frame. The sand or perlite must be kept just moist, not saturated.

ASTILBE (Astíl-be)—Spirea. Although very different in appearance from the genus *Spiraea*, the kinds of which are appropriately commonly called spireas, the same vernacular name is often given to astilbes. A ready distinction is that *Spiraea* consists exclusively of shrubs, *Astilbe* of herbaceous perennials.

Astilbes look much more like goat's beard (*Aruncus*) than *Spiraea*. They differ from *Aruncus* in their flowers having ten, eight, or rarely fewer stamens, and two or three more or less united or sometimes separate pistils. In *Aruncus* there are numerous stamens and several to many separate pistils. The name *Astilbe* comes from the Greek *a*, without, and *stilbe*, luster. It alludes to the foliage of some kinds. There are about twenty-five species of *Astilbe*, of which one, or doubtfully two, are indigenous to the United States. The others inhabit temperate Asia. They belong to the saxifrage family SAXIFRAGACEAE.

The astilbes that are cultivated are hardy, deciduous, leafy plants forming clumps of slender stems with more or less hairy, largely basal foliage above which rise graceful, showy, feathery panicles of tiny white, pink, or red flowers. Usually the leaves are large, and two-, three-, or four-times divided into toothed leaflets, so that they are of a ferny appearance. Less commonly they are comparatively small, lobed or toothed, but not divided into separate leaflets. The flowers are bisexual or unisexual, individual plants carrying one or both types. The calyx is small and generally three- or four-parted. There are three, four, or rarely no petals, and ten or fewer stamens. The fruits are follicles.

Species 1 foot to 3 feet tall, with ample masses of ferny, divided leafage, are *A. japonica* and *A. thunbergii*, of Japan, and

Astilbe japonica

Chinese *A. chinensis*. These have showy, pyramidal, erect panicles of white flowers. The basal leaves of the first are twice divided into three. They are of thickish texture and have lanceolate to oblanceolate leaflets 1½ to 3 inches long, the terminal ones narrowed at their bases. The tiny flowers have stalks longer than the bracts from the axils of which they sprout. Very variable *A. thunbergii* differs from *A. chinensis* in its basal leaves being thrice divided into three, and in the foliage, in its typical phase, but not in all its variants, being thinner. The leaflets are round-ovate to narrowly-ovate or rarely lanceolate, with their bases rounded or heart-shaped, or the terminal ones up to 4 inches long and rarely narrowed at their bases. The plant, introduced from Japan and cultivated as *A. astilboides*, apparently belongs with *A. thunbergii*. From *A. japonica* and *A. thunbergii*, in both of which the stalks of the flower panicles are glandular pubescent, *A. chinensis* differs in having corresponding stalks thickly clothed with brown hairs. The petals of *A. japonica* are broad and blunt, those of *A. thunbergii* very slender. Variety *A. chinensis davidii* (syn. *A. davidii*) has purple-pink flowers in narrower panicles than those of *A. chinensis*. Variety *A. c. pumila* is dwarfer and more compact. A variegated-leaved variety of *A. japonica* is sometimes cultivated.

Its ovate-heart-shaped leaves undivided, but palmately (in handlike fashion) three- or five-lobed, and coarsely-toothed, *A. simplicifolia* is a native of Japan. From 6 inches to 1 foot tall, it has leaves about 3 inches long. The white flowers are in arching, loose panicles. A hybrid between this and a variety of *A. arendsii*, called *A. simplicifolia rosea*, has leaves with usually three leaflets. Its flowers are rose-pink.

Astilbe chinensis pumila

Astilbe simplicifolia

American *A. biternata* closely resembles goat's beard (*Aruncus sylvester*). The differences are explained earlier in this entry. Native to moist mountain woodlands from Virginia to Georgia and Kentucky, this kind is 3 to 6 feet tall and glandular-pu-

bescent in its upper parts. It has leaves divided two or three times into sharply-toothed leaflets. The ample panicles are of yellowish-white flowers, the females often without petals.

Hybrid astilbes are more common in gardens than species. These carry varietal names such as 'Avalanche' and 'Deutschland', with white flowers; 'Betty Cuperus', tall, flowers pink; 'Europa', also pink-flowered; 'Peach Blossom', with light pink blooms; and 'Fanal' and 'Red Sentinel', with bright red flowers. Most numerous of the hybrids are the fine varieties grouped as *A. arendsii*. These are the result of *A. chinensis davidii* having been interbred with other species. Their blooms vary in color from almost white through pink to crimson. Another hybrid complex, *A. lemoinei* has as a parent *A. astilboides*. Its feathery panicles of white blooms have pink or pinkish stalks. Beautiful pink-flowered hybrids between *A. chinensis* and *A. japonica* are identified as *A. rosea*.

Garden and Landscape Uses. Among the easiest to grow and the most satisfactory hardy, herbaceous perennials, astilbes are adapted for planting naturalistically in open woodlands and at watersides and for more formal beds and borders. They are beautiful as single specimens, in small groups, and in large sweeps and drifts. Dwarf kinds can with good grace be admitted to rock gardens. The flowers, fresh or dried, are attractive for arrangements. Astilbes force well and make good-looking flowering pot plants when so grown. Their needs are simple: fairly moist, but not wet soil well fortified with compost, leaf mold, peat moss, or other decayed organic matter, and light shade from the strongest sun. Although they will grow in full sun, neither the foliage nor the flowers there are as beautiful as those of plants located in part-shade. In exposed places the flow-

Astilbe arendsii

ers often do not open fully, and the foliage is likely to develop poorly and to scorch.

Cultivation. Astilbes are usually increased by division, a very simple operation best done in early fall or spring. The divisions are planted 1 foot to 2 feet apart, except those of the dwarfer kinds, which are set more closely. Plants can also be raised from seeds sown in spring in a greenhouse or cold frame. Transplanted a couple of times and kept growing throughout the summer, the seedlings bloom in their second year. Routine care of established plants calls for little attention. Removal of faded flower panicles and of the foliage after it dies in fall are necessary measures of tidiness. Watering may be needed in dry weather. The maintenance of a mulch is desirable.

To force plants into bloom early, plant strong clumps of roots in fall or winter in sandy, fertile soil in pots a little larger than the clumps. If planted in fall, stand the pots in a cold frame with leaves, sawdust, peat moss, or some similar material packed between them. If potting is delayed until winter, dig the roots from the garden in fall and store them packed in slightly damp earth, sand, or peat moss in a temperature of 30 to 40°F until early the following year. Then pot them. Begin forcing by bringing the potted plants into a light greenhouse where the night temperature is 50 to 65°F, and temperatures by day are somewhat higher. Water liberally. Growth soon begins, much faster of course at higher than lower temperatures. As leafage increases so does the plant's water needs. It is a good plan to stand the pots in saucers or trays containing 2 or 3 inches of water, thus assuring a constant water supply to the roots. After the flower buds begin to show color the night temperature should not be above 60°F, and five degrees lower is better. After blooming is over, if the plants are kept well watered they will continue to grow, and after all danger of frost is over, may be planted outdoors, where they soon recover and become established. The same plants are not suitable for forcing in successive years.

ASTRAGALUS (Astrág-alus)—Milk-Vetch. Although this vast genus of prevailingly horticulturally unattractive plants includes among its possibly 2,000 species a small proportion that are decidedly ornamental, it is not well known in gardens. The reasons are several. They include the unavailability of many kinds, and the sheer cussedness of the responses to cultivation of some of the most desirable. Belonging to the pea family LEGUMINOSAE, *Astragalus* is native to all continents except Australia. Many of its members inhabit hot, arid and semiarid regions, others favor more gentle environments. The name, an ancient one, from the Greek *astragalos*, an ankle bone or a die, may allude to the rattling of the seeds in the pod. Some milk-vetches supply useful forage. Others, called locoweeds in North America, accumulate selenium in their tissues in such amounts that when eaten by livestock they cause the distressing symptoms of loco disease and even death. From *A. gummifer*, a shrubby species of southeastern Europe and western Asia, gum tragacanth, used medicinally and for printing calico and for other industrial purposes, is obtained.

Milk-vetches include annuals, herbaceous perennials, and subshrubs. They usually have pinnate leaves, with or without a terminal leaflet. In some the midribs of the leaves end in a spine. The flowers, structured like those of peas, are in heads or racemes from the leaf axils. The calyxes have five equal or unequal teeth. The wing petals are joined to the keel. There are generally ten stamens of which nine are united, and one is free. More rarely there are only five stamens, all united. The fruits are pods containing one to many seeds.

Tall perennials worthy of consideration as garden plants include *A. centralpinus, A. alopecuroides* (syn. *A. narbonensis*), and *A. galegiformis*. In cultivation *A. centralpinus,* often misidentified as *A. alopecuroides,* is native to southern Europe. It has stout, hairy stems 1½ to 4 feet tall, and leaves with twenty to thirty pairs of elliptic to ovate-lanceolate leaflets, and a terminal one. The golden-yellow flowers, in egg-shaped, stalkless racemes, have standard or banner petals ½ to ¾ inch long. The corollas are persistent and the calyxes become inflated as the fruits form. The seed pods are hairy. Rarer in cultivation, *A. alopecuroides* differs from the last in having smaller leaves, with twelve to fifteen pairs of leaflets, and very crowded spherical to cylindrical racemes of somewhat larger,

Astragalus alopecuroides

pale yellow blooms, with calyx teeth shorter rather than longer than the calyx tube. It is a native of Spain and France. Native to western Asia, *A. galegiformis* is distinct from the two species described above in having smaller yellow flowers in slender, longer-stalked, loose racemes. They have nonpersistent corollas and calyxes that do not become inflated as the hairless seed pods develop. This kind is 1½ to 4 feet tall and has leaves with eleven to sixteen pairs, and a terminal one of elliptic to lanceolate-oblong leaflets.

Japanese *A. shinanensis* is a mountain perennial similar to *A. frigidus*. Tufted and sparsely-branched, and 1 foot to 2 feet tall, it has short-stalked leaves with narrow leaflets, hairy on their lower sides, hairless above. The stalked racemes are of ten or fewer yellow or white blooms. The leaves of *A. frigidus,* which attains heights up to 2 feet and is perennial, have oblong to broad-elliptic leaflets 1 inch to 2 inches long and short, long-stalked, crowded racemes of several to many yellowish flowers. This species is native of Europe.

Two easy-to-grow lower perennials are the prairie-plum or ground-plum (*A. crassicarpus*), native from southern Canada to Arkansas and Texas, and *A. sempervirens* of the mountains of Europe. The prairie-plum is up to 1 foot tall or somewhat taller. It has green or grayish hairy leaves 1½ to 6 inches long, with usually fifteen to thirty-three elliptic leaflets. The flowers are purple, lilac, greenish-white, or cream, with purple- or pink-tipped keels. The seed pods, ¾ to 1 inch long, somewhat resemble plums. With procumbent or ascending stems up to somewhat more than 1 foot in length, *A. sempervirens* has spine-tipped leaves up to 3 inches long and four to ten pairs of linear-oblanceolate leaflets. The short-stalked racemes are of three to eight white to purple or more rarely yellow flowers. The seed pods are densely-hairy.

Other low perennials that may be cultivated are *A. onobrychis, A. danicus,* and *A. agrestis.* The first two are natives of Europe and adjacent Asia. With procumbent and ascending stems, woody at their bases and up to 2 feet in length, *A. onobrychis* has leaves of eight to fifteen pairs of hairy, elliptic-lanceolate leaflets. Usually violet, but sometimes white or yellowish, the flowers are in fairly dense egg-shaped to cylindrical racemes terminating stems longer than the leaves. The seed pods are conspicuously hairy. Up to 1 foot tall, *A. danicus* has slender stems, not woody at their bases, and leaves of four to thirteen pairs of oblong-ovate to oblong leaflets lightly-hairy on both surfaces. On stalks longer than the leaves, the small purplish to bluish-violet flowers are in spherical to cylindrical racemes. The egg-shaped seed pods are clothed with silky-white hairs. Not exceeding 9 inches in height, and native from New Mexico to the Yukon, perennial *A. agrestis* (syn. *A. goniatus*) has stems up to 8 inches long, often shorter, and slightly hairy leaves, with nine to twenty-one small leaflets. The purple to whitish flowers are in ovoid-cylindrical heads of up to twelve.

A permanent and satisfactory rock garden perennial, *A. monspessulanus* is highly variable. About 9 inches tall, it has trailing stems. Its leaves have usually ten to twenty pairs of leaflets, hairless above, sparsely-hairy on their undersides. The egg-shaped to cylindrical racemes of up to thirty vinous-purple, red, pink, or rarely whitish blooms, are on stalks longer than the leaves. The slightly- to much-curved seed pods are sparsely-hairy to nearly hairless. This kind is native to Europe and adjoining Asia.

The most handsome milk-vetch, perennial *A. coccineus,* is an inhabitant of deserts in western North America. It has stems not exceeding 4 inches in length and densely-white-hairy leaves 2 to 4 inches long of seven to fifteen obovate to broad-elliptic leaflets. The up-pointing, scarlet flowers, 1¼ to 1¾ inches long, have white-woolly-hairy calyxes. They are in loose racemes or heads of usually four to ten. The seed pods are covered with a silky coat of brownish hairs. Native from southern Canada to Oklahoma and New Mexico, *A. missouriensis* is a perennial with several weak stems up to 4 inches long that, like the foliage, are densely gray-hairy. The leaves, 2 to 4 inches long, have nine to fifteen leaflets. The short racemes are of up to twelve ½- to ¾-inch-long, rose-purple blooms. The seed pods are straight and about ¾ inch in length. Variable *A. gilviflorus* is a silvery-hairy, tufted, cushiony perennial about 4 inches tall. Native to dry parts of western North America, it has long-stalked leaves of only three rather narrow leaflets up to ¾ inch long, and from the leaf axils glistening white flowers standing erectly among the foliage. The blooms last for only a few days. When in flower this kind is very beautiful, but later it takes on an untidy appearance.

Garden and Landscape Uses and Cultivation. Cultivated astragaluses, according to their heights, are suitable for flower beds and rock gardens. They need full sun, and mostly are best satisfied with porous soil of medium fertility. In addition to the kinds described above there are many natives of desert, semidesert, and alpine regions that are attractive, but have proven difficult or impossible to tame as residents of gardens. In part this is perhaps due to the absence of mycorrhizal organisms with which their roots are associated in the wild. As a group they do not transplant readily, and it is better to set young pot-grown specimens where they are to remain. Propagation is by seed.

ASTRANTIA (As-trántia)—Masterwort. These hardy herbaceous perennials are not much grown in American gardens, perhaps because they are less colorful and less showy than many more familiar summer decoratives. They are more popular in Europe, possibly because they are natives of that continent and adjacent Asia. Be that as it may, they are easy enough to grow in gardens in temperate North America and add a distinctive, if not brilliant touch to garden plantings.

Astrantias are in the carrot family UMBELLIFERAE, but in aspect are different from more familiar members of that group. A casual observer might not be unwilling to believe that they were members of the daisy family COMPOSITAE because the colored involucres (collars of leafy bracts beneath the flower clusters) suggest the ray florets of a daisy, and the tight central umbel of tiny flowers its eye. The generic name is seemingly a corruption of *magistrantia* from the Latin *magister*, a master, or possibly comes from the Greek, *aster*, a star, in reference to the form of the flower heads.

Masterworts number ten or fewer species of Europe and western Asia. Their main foliage is basal and consists of palmately-lobed or divided leaves. The flowering stems are erect and branched. Each flower head consists of an umbel that sits upon an involucre of many spreading bracts. The fruits are dry and seedlike.

The principal cultivated kinds are *A. major, A. biebersteinii, A. bavarica,* and *A. carniolica.* Attaining a height of 2 to 3 feet, *A. major* has three-, five-, or occasionally seven-parted, basal leaves with their middle lobes separate and free for at least two-

Astrantia major

Astrantia major

thirds of their length. Its involucre bracts, more or less joined at their bases, and usually lanceolate are as long as or longer than the umbels of blooms. It is native to central and eastern Europe. Variety *A. m. folius-variegatus* has leaves partly edged with white. Differing in rarely exceeding 1 foot in height and in its leaves having smaller, blunter, basal lobes, *A. biebersteinii* is a native of the Caucasus. In *A. bavarica* the leaves are cleft into five lobes with the center one free almost or quite to its base. The narrowly-lanceolate bracts of the in-

Astrantia biebersteinii

Astrantia carniolica

volucre of this native of the European Alps are longer than its umbels of flowers. From the last named, *A. carniolica,* also a native of the European Alps, differs in its leaf lobes being ovate and the middle ones joined in their lower parts to the lateral lobes.

Other kinds occasionally grown are *A. maxima,* of western Asia, which is similar to *A. major,* but has the bracts of the flower heads fringed with hairlike teeth; *A. minor,* a European kind, slender and with usually seven-parted basal leaves with lanceolate to obovate lobes free or separate almost or quite to their bases and floral bracts longer than the umbels of bloom; and *A. pauciflora,* which is much like the last named but has basal leaves of usually five or six linear-lanceolate lobes. This kind is native to Italy.

Garden and Landscape Uses. Masterworts are at their best in lightly shaded places where the soil is fertile and fairly moist. They are especially suitable for planting in open woodlands where some sun reaches them and at streamsides where the soil is well above water level, but they may also be made content in a bed or border of mixed perennials.

Cultivation. Planting is done in spring or early fall, individuals being spaced 1 foot or so apart. No special routine care is needed other than plentiful watering if there is danger of the soil becoming really dry. Propagation is easy by division in spring and by seeds started in a cold frame in spring or summer, or earlier indoors, in sandy peaty soil kept evenly moist.

ASTRIDIA (Astríd-ia). The name of this genus of about ten species of South African succulents of the *Mesembryanthemum* association honors Mrs. Astrid Schwantes. Its members belong in the carpetweed family AIZOACEAE. They are not hardy. Low subshrubs, they have branches with opposite leaves slightly joined at their bases, with portions of stem showing between alternate pairs, which spread at right angles to each other. The flowers, which have the daisy-like aspect characteristic of the *Mesembryanthemum* group, are not, as are daisies, heads composed of numerous florets, but single blooms. They are solitary or few together on short stalks.

Compact and about 1 foot in height, *Astridia velutina* has finely-pubescent, grayish-white, very fleshy, somewhat crescent-shaped leaves, with a few translucent dots. They are three-angled and about 1¼ inches long by ⅙ inch wide at their bases and slightly narrower toward their tips. The solitary white or pink blooms are 1¼ inches across. Variety *A. v. lutata* has dull yellowish leaves, 1 inch to 2 inches in length, and whitish to yellowish flowers.

Garden Uses and Cultivation. Choice items for collections of nonhardy succulents, astridias require similar treatment to *Bergeranthus* and other small, very succulent *Mesembryanthemum* relatives. They need a long summer resting period during which they are kept dry. Beginning in fall they are watered moderately. Very well-drained soil and full sun are needed. Although propagation is simply accomplished by seeds and cuttings, success in maintaining these plants in cultivation has often proved difficult. For additional information see Succulents.

ASTROCARYUM (Astrocàr-yum)—Black Palm, Coquillo Palm. This genus of about fifty species of handsome, unisexual, feather-leaved palms is not frequently cultivated. Occasionally specimens are included in specialist collections. In their native lands some sorts are exploited as sources of oils and fibers. The name is from the Greek *astron,* a star, and *karyon,* a nut. It alludes to the starlike patterns of radiating black lines that mark the seeds. The genus *Astrocaryum* belongs in the palm family PALMAE and is native from Mexico to Brazil. One species, *A. aureum,* is endemic to Trinidad.

Astrocaryums are spiny. They have one or more trunks of considerable height or are trunkless. Characteristically, their leaves, leafstalks, and other parts are more or less prickly, and the leaflets are pointed or obliquely blunt-ended. The undersides of the leaves, paler than the upper sides, are often silvery-white. The blooms are in dense spikes at the ends of the branches of the flower clusters. The one-seeded, red or orange fruits are ovoid to globular. There are two spathes the lower of which is membranous and soon falls, the upper woody and persistent.

The black palm (*A. standleyanum*), of Panama and Costa Rica, one of the most conspicuous palms of the forest there, has a solitary trunk up to 40 feet in height with rings of down-pointed spines 4 to 6 inches long. The arching and drooping leaves, up to 12 feet long, form a compact crown. The leaflets are up to 3 feet long by 1½ to 6 inches wide. The flowers are fragrant and in dense cylindrical clusters up to 2 feet long. The females are succeeded by large clusters of 1½- to 2-inch-long oblong, not spiny, orange fruits each containing a very hard, large seed marked with longitudinal black stripes and radiating black lines from each of three pits. The black palm is so called from the color of its extremely hard wood, which is used for walking canes.

The coquillo palm (*A. alatum*), of Costa Rica and Panama, has solitary trunks up to about 25 feet high, without spines, but with spiny leaf bases attached. The leaflets of the pinnate leaves are joined together in groups. The midribs and stalks are armed with formidable spines. The fruits are also densely-spiny. The murumuru palm (*A. murumuru*), of Brazil, has a trunk 6 to 18 feet in height, armed with long black spines. Its pear-shaped fruits hang in dense clusters and are covered with reddish pulp, which is relished by animals. The seed kernels contain oil, which is extracted commercially for making soap. Another Brazilian species, the tucum palm (*A. vulgare*), grows to a height of about 30 feet and has a very spiny trunk. Its fruits are covered with yellow-orange pulp, which is eaten by animals and is used to some extent for cattle feed. From the kernels of its seeds is extracted an oil used for making shampoos and soaps and suitable for cooking oils,

salad oils, shortenings, and other purposes.

Garden and Landscape Uses and Cultivation. The highly spiny character of the members of this genus is probably responsible for their limited acceptance by gardeners and horticulturists. Only in frost-free or nearly frost-free, humid, tropical climates can they be expected to live outdoors. They are appropriate for southern Florida and Hawaii. They can also be cultivated in greenhouses. When grown in containers these should be rather small in relation to the size of the plants. Astrocaryums require the same cultural care as *Aiphanes.* For additional information see Palms.

ASTROLOBA (Astro-lòba). This is the name of the plants previously called *Apicra.* The group belongs in the lily family LILIACEAE and looks much like *Haworthia* and *Aloe.* Its name is from the Greek *astron,* a star, and *lobos,* a lobe, and refers to the flowers. Unlike the blooms of haworthias, those of astrolobas are symmetrical. The plants differ from aloes in not having bitter sap.

The genus *Astroloba* is entirely South African and consists of a dozen or more species of small, very often somewhat horny, succulent plants with thick, spine-tipped leaves arranged spirally or in vertical rows and crowded on short, usually erect, stems. The undersides of the leaves are often ridged or keeled, with the angle of the keel to one side of the center of the leaf. The small whitish blooms, commonly striped with green, are tubular and have six short, spreading perianth lobes (petals) and the same number of stamens. It is possible that any or all of the species may be cultivated in collections of fanciers of succulents, but most are rare.

The one most frequently grown is *A. pentagona* (syn. *Apicra pentagona*). Its stems are up to 1 foot in height and the plant branches from the base. The leaves, in five vertical or slightly spiraled rows, are triangular-lanceolate and 1¼ to 1¾ inches long by up to ¾ inch wide. They point upward and have flat or hollowed upper sides and lower ones keeled and besprinkled with white pustules. Sometimes the flower stems, which may be 1½ feet tall, are branched. The greenish blooms are ½ inch long. This species is variable, and several minor variants have been given varietal names. Here belong *A. p. spiralis, A. p. spirella,* and *A. p. torulosa.* Another interesting kind is *A. aspera* (syn. *Apicra aspera*), which has triangular leaves that taper suddenly near their tips and are arranged spirally in three or four rows. They are ½ to ¾ inch long and wide, and rounded and warty on their backs. The stems, up to 6 inches high, at first erect, later become horizontal. The branchless racemes of pinkish or greenish flowers, each bloom ⅜ inch long, rise to a height of 1 foot. About 3 inches in diameter, *A.*

Astroloba skinneri

skinneri has sharp-pointed, triangular leaves with concave uppersides and keeled undersides displaying many whitish pustules.

The leaves of **A. deltoidea** (syn. *Apicra deltoidea*) are in five, slightly twisted rows on stems up to 10 inches long and erect or more or less procumbent. They are pointed, broadly-triangular, and about 1 inch long, with flat upper surfaces and the older leaves spreading. The undersides of the leaves are roundish and keeled. Two varieties, *A. d. intermedia* and *A. d. turgida*, have more definitely spiraled leaves and are somewhat larger and more vigorous. The plant previously named *A. rubriflora* is now *Poellnitzia rubriflora*.

Garden and Landscape Uses and Cultivation. Astrolobas belong in collections of succulents, outdoors in warm, dry climates, and in greenhouses. They are also satisfactory window garden plants and require the same care as aloes, haworthias, and gasterias. This is detailed under Succulents.

ASTROPHYTUM (Astró-phytum)—Bishop's Cap Cactus, Star Cactus, Sea Urchin Cactus or Sand Dollar Cactus. At one time included in *Echinocactus*, six species of Mexican cactuses of the cactus family Cactaceae are now segregated as *Astrophytum*. The name refers to their plant bodies being more or less star-shaped when viewed from above. It is from the Greek *astron*, a star, and *phyton*, a plant. All are fascinating. They have flattened, globular, short-cylindrical, or miter-shaped plant bodies with a few widely spaced, prominent ribs and areoles (places on cactuses from which spines, hairs, and flowers arise) that may or may not have spines. Their large blooms are yellow or yellow with reddish centers.

The bishop's cap cactus (**A. myriostigma**) is imaginatively named. It suggests, more especially the variety *A. m. quadricostatum*, an ecclesiastical headpiece. It is spineless and has usually five, rarely only four, and sometimes up to eight, pronounced angles lined on their edges with closely arranged woolly areoles. There is a hairless form, but commonly the entire

Astrophytum myriostigma

plant, roughly spherical and becoming somewhat elongated with advanced age, and 4 to 8 inches in diameter, is clothed with minute, starry, scalelike hairs. These produce a light gray appearance that make the plant look as though it were carved from stone. The flowers, 1¾ to 2 inches wide and as long, are yellow or yellow with reddish bases to their satiny perianth lobes (petals). They develop from the tops of the plants. This species is a free bloomer. It is variable and many varieties are recognized. Chief among these is *A. m. coahuilense*, which tends to be conical with a slightly raised center and rounded ribs, and is very gray with scales. Its blooms are yellow with red centers, its fruits purplish.

Astrophytum myriostigma potosinum

In *A. m. potosinum* the center of the plant is slightly sunken. It has only a moderate number of scales and so is greenish-gray. There are occasionally more than five, sometimes rounded, ribs, and the comparatively small blooms are usually without red centers. This kind may develop an elongated plant body. Because it has only

four ribs *A. m. quadricostatum* (syn. *A. m. tetragona*) most closely resembles a bishop's miter. Its plant body is broad, its ribs rounded, and it has comparatively small flowers unblotched with red. Usually with five, but sometimes up to ten sharp ribs that spiral slightly around the plant body, the variable *A. m. tulense* has large flowers that may or may not have central red blotches. This kind often becomes somewhat elongated. In addition to the varieties there are hybrids between *A. myriostigma* and *A. ornatum*. These have short spines.

Very handsome and spiny, the star cactus (**A. ornatum**) becomes cylindrical with

Astrophytum ornatum

age and may be more than 1 foot in height and 6 inches or more in diameter. It has eight sharp ribs fringed with areoles furnished with clusters of five to eleven formidable, mostly straight, sharp spines up to 1½ inches long, and flowers at first sulfur-yellow, but later becoming brown. The silky blooms are clear yellow. Their inner perianth lobes (petals) are toothed. They are 3 to nearly 4 inches in diameter. Usually this species does not bloom until of fairly advanced age. A beautiful variety, *A. o. mirbellii*, is covered with silvery-white scales and has golden-yellow spines. In *A.*

Astrophytum ornatum mirbellii

o. glabrescens, the scales are few and the spines yellow or brownish. Hybrids, less spiny than this species, occurring between it and *A. myriostigma,* are usually more free-flowering.

Somewhat more challenging to grow than the kinds previously mentioned, and more difficult to raise, is **A. capricorne.**

Astrophytum capricorne

When young it is spherical, but later club-shaped. It is 4 to 8 inches tall, about 4 inches in diameter, and has about eight ribs edged with brown-woolly areoles. Its plant body is freely besprinkled with white scales. A distinguishing feature is the contorted, angular spines 1½ to 4 inches long, and gray, black, or reddish. From close to the apex of the plant the blooms, almost or quite 3 inches across, arise. Their outer perianth segments (petals) are reddish, their inner ones lemon-yellow with red bases. The stamens and pistils are yellow. In *A. c. aureum* the spines on the younger, upper part of the plant are yellow. Smaller than the typical species and with smaller blooms, is *A. c. minus.* It has shorter, dark gray or black spines twisted in all directions. The flowers of *A. c. crassispinum* (syn. *A. c. majus*) have no red and all parts of the plant are bigger than in the typical species. The spines are up-curved and gray. Another larger variety, *A. c. niveum,* is so thickly covered with white scales that the plant body is practically concealed. Its gray spines mostly curve upward. Much less plentifully furnished with white scales than the typical kind, *A. c. senile* is bigger and has spines that twist in all directions. At first black, they become gray with age. They are nearly cylindrical.

Sometimes called the sea urchin or sand dollar cactus (it has much the look of a sea urchin), **A. asterias** is very low, only slightly domed, and is marked by deep grooves into eight segments shaped like those of a sliced pie. The plant is spineless, but has a row of woolly, circular areoles spaced centrally between each pair of grooves.

Astrophytum asterias

The plant body is 2 to 3 inches in diameter, and in season it produces yellow blooms 1¼ to 1¾ inches wide with reddish centers. The few-seeded fruits are egg-shaped and are clothed with scales.

Garden and Landscape Uses and Cultivation. Astrophytums should be in every cactus collection no matter how modest. They are not difficult to grow and are very beautiful. Propagation is almost exclusively by seeds because they very seldom make offsets and are not susceptible to increase by cuttings. Sometimes they are grafted onto columnar cactuses. Soil containing lime in the form of crushed limestone, broken oyster shells, or tuffa rock is particularly to their liking, and they respond favorably to a moderate content of humus, leaf mold, or old rotted manure. These plants need the general care detailed for most terrestrial cactuses under Cactuses.

ASYNEUMA (Asyn-eùma). Closely allied to *Phyteuma* and something of a botanical way station between that group and *Campanula,* the genus *Asyneuma* has flowers in loose, spikelike panicles, instead of dense heads. It belongs to the bellflower family CAMPANULACEAE and comprises fifty species of mostly hardy, herbaceous perennials and biennials. One is native to eastern Asia, the others to terrain extending from the Mediterranean region to the Caucasus. The name is of uncertain derivation. Except for the arrangement of the blooms, the botanical description given under Phyteuma applies to *Asyneuma.*

Asyneumas are neither wildly exciting nor widely cultivated. Occasionally *A. canescens* (syn. *Phyteuma canescens*) and *A. limonifolium* (syn. *Phyteuma limonifolium*) are planted by botanically-minded gardeners. Erect, its rigid stems often branchless, **A. limonifolium** is 6 inches to 2 feet tall. Its lanceolate, toothed or toothless, long-stalked leaves are basal. The little violet-colored flowers, individually stalkless or nearly so, are solitary or in twos or threes in the axils of bracts along the upper parts

of the stems. This kind is an inhabitant of rocky places in the mountains of Europe. Canescent, meaning gray-hairy, correctly describes the stems and foliage of southern European **A. canescens.** It has erect, slender stems about 1½ feet tall, sometimes branched below, and clothed with linear to lanceolate, toothed, stalkless leaves up to a little over 1 inch long. The upper parts of the stems are furnished with small pale violet blooms, one to three from each bract axil.

Garden and Landscape Uses and Cultivation. These are as for tall kinds of *Phyteuma.*

ASYSTASIA (Asys-tàsia). The plant known in gardens as *Asystasia bella* is *Mackaya bella.* It differs from *Asystasia* in having two instead of four fertile stamens. Only one of the forty species of *Asystasia* is at all commonly cultivated, *A. gangetica* (syn. *A. coromandeliana*), native from Malaya to Africa, and naturalized in the West Indies. The genus belongs in the acanthus family ACANTHACEAE. It consists of shrubs and herbaceous perennials with opposite, lobeless, sometimes toothed leaves and tubular flowers in terminal clusters. The floral bracts, unlike those in many genera of the acanthus family, are small and inconsequential. The calyx is divided to its base. The corolla has five nearly symmetrical corolla lobes and a tube that expands conspicuously above its middle. There are four stamens. The fruits are dry capsules. The name *Asystasia* is of unknown derivation.

The cultivated **A. gangetica** is native from Malaya to Africa, and naturalized in

Asystasia gangetica

the West Indies. It is hardy only in the tropics and warm subtropics. It is a clambering or trailing shrub that if left unattended may attain a few feet in height or form billowy masses of spreading stems and light green foliage. The stems root freely wherever they touch the ground. The leaves, thin-textured and 1 inch to 4 inches long, are pointed-ovate. The yellowish, white, or purplish flowers are in one-sided loose racemes up to 6 inches in length. They are pubescent, bell-shaped, 1½ inches long, 1 inch across the mouth, and have a curved corolla tube and broad, spreading corolla lobes.

Garden and Landscape Uses. The best purposes served by this species are as a dense groundcover and as a facing or filler shrub among other kinds where there is space for it to develop and display its wide, billowy character. It grows and blooms well in partial shade as well as sun. It is used in southern Florida.

Cultivation. Of easy culture, *A. gangetica* thrives in any ordinary soil. It needs pruning hard once or twice annually to keep it neat and forestall straggliness; this is especially important when it is employed as a groundcover. Propagation is very easy by seeds, cuttings, or by taking up rooted pieces of established plants and transplanting them.

ATALANTIA (Atal-ántia). Trees and shrubs of *Citrus*-like appearance and relationship constitute *Atalantia* of the rue family RUTACEAE. The genus, native from India to China and Australia, comprises eighteen species. Its name is that of one of the Hesperides of mythology.

Atalantias have solitary sharp spines or may be nearly spineless. Their more or less leathery, strongly net-veined, short-stalked leaves have one leaflet or blade. The flowers, in axillary or rarely terminal clusters or panicles, are small. They have three- to five-lobed or sometimes lobeless calyxes that split irregularly as the flowers expand. There are usually five, sometimes fewer petals and twice as many stamens more or less united into a tube. The subglobular, thin-skinned, yellowish-green fruits resemble miniature oranges.

A usually spiny tree 15 to 30 feet tall, of Indochina, *A. citrioides* has ovate, toothless leaves up to 4 inches long by 1½ inches wide, notched at their apexes. The fragrant flowers, from the leaf axils, have three- or four-lobed calyxes, and four or five ovate petals that bend strongly backward. The stamens, united for about two-thirds of their lengths from their bases, are almost as long as the petals. The fruits are ¾ inch in diameter. The species once named *A. stenocarpa* is *Murraya stenocarpa*. The plant sometimes named *A. buxifolia* is *Severinia buxifolia*.

Garden and Landscape Uses and Cultivation. The species described here is occasionally planted for its interest. It prospers under conditions that suit oranges and is propagated by seeds and cuttings.

ATAMASCO-LILY. See Zephyranthes.

ATEMOYA. See Annona.

ATHAMANTA (Atham-ánta). Restricted in the wild to the Mediterranean region and temperate Asia, this genus of the carrot family UMBELLIFERAE comprises fifteen species of herbaceous plants, most of little or no horticultural merit. The name comes from that of Mt. Athamas in Sicily, where some species grow.

These plants have leaves two- to five-times pinnately-divided into narrow segments and small white or rarely yellow flowers in umbels, with five notched or two-lobed petals. The seedlike fruits are pubescent and have short beaks.

A quite variable perennial up to 1½ feet in height, **Athamanta turbith** (syn. *A. matthiolii*) has hairless or sparsely-hairy, dark green leaves two to four times pinnately-divided into threadlike or narrowly-linear segments up to 1½ inches long. The minute white flowers are in umbels of smaller umbels.

Garden Uses and Cultivation. Occasionally grown in rock gardens and informal areas, this species responds to well-drained ordinary soil and full sun. It is hardy, and is increased by seeds, and by division in spring.

ATHANASIA (Athan-àsia). Of minor horticultural importance, *Athanasia* of the daisy family COMPOSITAE consists of approximately fifty species of mostly aromatic shrubs or subshrubs, natives of Africa, chiefly South Africa, and Madagascar. Its name, relating to the long-persistent, dry bracts of the flower heads, comes from the Greek *a*, not, and *thanatos*, death.

Athanasias have alternate, often much-crowded, undivided, smooth-edged, or pinnately-lobed or toothed, hairy or hairless leaves. The flower heads, without ray florets (petal-like ones like those that surround the central eyes of daisies), are bisexual, five-lobed, tubular, and of the disk type (similar to those that form the eyes of daisies). The involucre or collar of bracts at the back of the flower head is cylindrical, egg-shaped, or subspherical. The fruits are seedlike, ribbed achenes.

Native of South Africa, *A. parviflora* is a densely-foliaged, much-branched shrub 3 to 6 feet tall, with stems and foliage scantily-hairy at first. The leaves, 2½ to 4 inches long, are deeply divided into very slender, linear lobes. Its tiny flower heads, each of three or four florets, and sulfur-yellow, are crowded many together in much-branched, flat-topped clusters 3 to 4 inches across.

Garden and Landscape Uses and Cultivation. In mild, dryish regions such as California athanasias can be grown outdoors. They are satisfied with ordinary, well-drained, dryish soil, and are propagated by seeds and cuttings. The species described can be used at the fronts of shrub beds, on banks, and in rock gardens.

ATHROTAXIS (Athrotáx-is)—Tasmanian-Cedar, King-William-Pine. This Tasmanian genus of the taxodium family TAXODIACEAE

Athanasia parviflora

contains only three species, rare in cultivation, occasionally grown in mild, moist regions including parts of the Pacific Coast. The name, from the Greek *athros*, crowded, and *taxis*, arrangement, alludes to the disposition of the cone scales.

Tasmanian-cedars are densely-branched evergreens most closely related to *Cryptomeria* and like that genus with the ultimate divisions of their branchlets deciduous. The small, crowded, overlapping, scalelike leaves, of even shape and size, are arranged spirally. The trees are bisexual, with solitary cones resembling those of *Cryptomeria japonica*, the females terminal, the males catkin-like and with spirally-arranged scales. The cones ripen the first season.

Shapely and pyramidal when young, but frequently assuming a somewhat irregular and untidy appearance as they age, these trees have fibrous bark, slightly furrowed, that peels in shreds. In their homeland the wood of Tasmanian-cedars is used for interior finishing and cabinet work. Light in weight, straight-grained, and easy to work, when newly cut it is pale red, but the color lightens with exposure. From fossil records it is clear that *Athrotaxis* was once more widely distributed in the wild than at present. Fossils of it from the Eocene period have been found in Great Britain.

King-William-pine (*A. selaginoides*) is the largest of the genus. At its maximum it attains 100 feet in height, with a trunk 3 feet in diameter. Its sharp-pointed, leathery, lanceolate leaves, keeled on their undersides and with opaque margins and ¼ to ½ inch in length, curve inward and overlap loosely. The cones are ½ to ¾ inch long and about as wide. From the last, *A. laxifolia* differs in having leaves up to ⅓ inch long that spread slightly and have translucent margins. This kind does not usually exceed 45 feet in height, but specimens nearly 60 feet tall are recorded as growing in England. The third species *A. cupressoides* has leaves pressed much more closely to the stems than the others and not more than about ⅛ inch long. Their margins are translucent. It attains a height of up to 45 feet.

Garden and Landscape Uses. These trees are essentially for collectors of unusual conifers. They are not likely to become plentiful enough to be available for general landscaping.

Cultivation. Tasmanian-cedars succeed best in a porous, sandy, loamy soil that is neutral or slightly acid and does not lack for moisture. It is helpful to keep the ground about them mulched. They may be propagated by seeds sown in sandy peaty soil or by cuttings under mist, taken in late spring or summer. Success has been had by grafting on understocks of *Cryptomeria japonica*. For additional information see Conifers.

ATHYRIUM (Athý-rium)—Lady Fern, Glade Fern. Only a few of the possibly 600 species of this cosmopolitan genus of mostly tropical ferns of the aspidium family Aspidiaceae are cultivated. Those discussed below are hardy. The name, from the Greek *a*, without, and *thyreos*, a shield, alludes to the spore-bearing organs. Although it is better to reserve the name for species of *Asplenium*, some athyriums, because they were previously included in that genus, are often called spleenworts. Athyriums closely resemble aspleniums. They differ in having usually curved, most commonly oblong to narrowly-oblong clusters of spore cases that generally straddle a vein. For other ferns sometimes named *Athyrium* see Diplazium.

Lady fern (*Athyrium filix-femina* syn. *Asplenium filix-femina*) is a highly variable species native from far north in America, Europe, and Asia to the tropics, and by botanists divided into a number of geographical races. In addition, there are many horticultural varieties. The lady fern has stout, creeping or partially erect rhizomes clothed with abundant, persistent scales. The hairless or minutely-glandular, clustered, bright green fronds, up to 3 feet long, have lanceolate, to ovate-lanceolate, pinnate blades up to 1 foot wide or a little wider. The leaves have twenty to thirty pairs of major divisions and a terminal one; the divisions are pinnate or deeply-pinnately-lobed. The short spore-case clusters are more or less hooked or horseshoe-shaped. The following variants are natives of North America. Variety *A. f. asplenioides* has leafstalks often as long as the blades. In *A. f. angustum* (syn. *A. f. michauxii*) they are usually one-half as long and in *A. f. cyclosorum* about one-third as long. There are several horticultural varieties including dwarf *A. f. minutissima* and *A. f. medusae*, the leaves of which are divided in parsley-like fashion.

Silvery glade fern or silvery spleenwort (*A. thelypteroides* syns. *Asplenium acrostichoides*, *A. thelypteroides*) has leaves somewhat like those of the New York fern (*Thelypteris noveboracensis*). They are not clustered, have stalks shorter than the blades, and are 1½ to 3 feet long or a little longer. Mature leaves have distinctly silvery undersides. The blades, slightly re-

Athyrium filix-femina minutissima

Athyrium filix-femina medusae

Athyrium filix-femina

Athyrium filix-femina augustum

duced in width toward their bases, and pointed at their apexes, are 5 to 8½ inches wide. They have fifteen to twenty pairs of major divisions and a terminal one that are linear-lanceolate, and deeply-pinnately-lobed. The spore-case clusters are long and slender. In the typical species the final segments are scarcely toothed, in *A. t. acrostichoides* they are markedly toothed. This fern occurs in moist, rich woodlands and along roadsides from Nova Scotia to Ontario, Iowa, Georgia, and Louisiana and in eastern Asia.

Glade fern or narrow-leaved spleenwort (**A. pycnocarpon** syns. *Asplenium pycnocarpon, A. angustifolium*) differs from others discussed here in having pinnate leaves with leaflets neither divided nor lobed, and only shallowly toothed. Its rhizomes creep widely. The lanceolate, nearly hairless leaves, scattered rather than clustered, are 2 to 4 feet long, 4 to 8 inches wide, narrowed slightly at their bases, and pointed at their apexes. They have a terminal, and twenty to thirty pairs of lateral leaflets. The clusters of spore cases are elongated. This native of cool woodlands occurs from Quebec to Ontario, Minnesota, Georgia, Alabama, and Louisiana.

A northern species, **A. distentifolium** (syn. *A. alpestre*), inhabits alpine regions and rocky places in Newfoundland and Quebec, and from the Rocky Mountains to California and Alaska. It also occurs in Europe and Asia. It has short, not obviously creeping, rhizomes, and leaves 1 foot to 3 feet tall in clusters. Their lanceolate blades are up to 3 feet long by one-half to one-third as broad. They have twenty to twenty-five pairs of major divisions and a terminal one. These are deeply-lobed, with the margins of the lobes toothed. The groups of spore cases are circular.

Beautiful soft gray-green foliage stained with wine-purple along the midribs is a pleasing feature of the Japanese painted fern (**A. goeringianum pictum** syn. *A. nipponicum pictum*). Native to shaded places in Japan and Taiwan, the typical species has plain green foliage. Like its variety it

Athyrium goeringianum

Athyrium goeringianum pictum

is hardy and deciduous. Its mostly spreading, tapering fronds, 1 foot to 2 feet long, are broadly-lanceolate and pinnate, with the major divisions again pinnate, and toothed. The elongated groups of spore cases are in herringbone pattern. Both the species and the variety, which is smaller and less vigorous, prosper in gardens, and often reproduce spontaneously from spores.

Garden and Landscape Uses and Cultivation. Athyriums are pleasing and easy to grow. They are suitable for woodland gardens, borders, semiwild places, and except exotic kinds, native plant gardens. The silvery glade fern does well by watersides. Japanese painted fern is one of the loveliest ferns for rock gardens. All grow well in slightly acid to neutral, woodland soils of fairly loose texture; for *A. pycnocarpon*, some crushed limestone mixed in may be advantageous. Light or part-day shade is preferred, but these ferns grow in full sun provided the soil does not become unduly dry. Watering copiously in dry weather is of much help in keeping the foliage green into late summer and fall. Propagation is by spores and division. For additional information see Ferns.

ATMOSPHERE. Technically this is the envelope of air that surrounds the earth. Gardeners employ the word in a slightly different sense to describe microclimates in greenhouses. They speak of a growing atmosphere when temperature and relative humidity are favorable to stimulating growth, of a buoyant atmosphere when the air circulates freely, of a close atmosphere when it is decidedly humid and there is little air circulation. See also Air and Air Pollution.

ATRAGENE See Clematis.

ATRAPHAXIS (Atra-pháxis). The twenty-five species of this genus, which is indigenous from the Mediterranean region to the Himalayas and Siberia, belong in the buckwheat family POLYGONACEAE and are mostly small, often spiny, deciduous shrubs

and subshrubs, chiefly of arid soils. The name *Atraphaxis* is derived from *atraphaxys*, the ancient Greek name for orach (*Atriplex hortensis*).

Atraphaxises mostly have small, short-stalked, alternate leaves with a pair of sheathing, membranous appendages (stipules) joined for most of their lengths at their bases. Their small, white to pink flowers, in short terminal racemes, are without petals, but have four or five more or less petal-like sepals, the inner two or three of which are persistent. These enlarge and enclose the achenes (little nuts) that are the fruits. There are six to eight stamens joined at their bases, and two or three stigmas.

Extremely hardy, **A. frutescens** (syn. *A. lanceolata*) is up to 2½ feet tall. Only rarely are its shoots spine-tipped. From ⅓ inch to 1¼ inches long, its pointed, linear-oblong to elliptic, glaucous, gray-green leaves have wavy or bluntly-toothed margins. The greenish-white to pinkish flowers, ⅓ inch in diameter, have five sepals, the inner ones never more than slightly longer than the three-angled fruits, and eight stamens. This kind is native from southern Europe to the steppes and semideserts of central Asia. From it **A. spinosa** differs in its ⅓-inch-wide flowers having four pink sepals with white margins, the two inner of which enlarge to enclose its two-edged, rather than triangular, fruits. This species branches freely; many of the branches are leafless toward their ends, and spine-tipped. Inhabiting the steppes and semideserts of southern Russia and southeast Europe, *A. spinosa* is 1 foot to 2½ feet tall, of sprawling habit, and usually broader than high.

Native of southeastern Europe and western Asia, **A. billardieri** is 1 foot to 2½ feet tall, and usually semiprostrate. Its shoots, sometimes spiny at their ends, bear fine-pointed, smooth, green, narrowly-elliptic to lanceolate, toothless leaves up to ⅓ inch long. The blooms, ¼ inch wide, are in globular clusters at the ends of short, leafy shoots. They have five sepals, the two outer small and reflexed, the others pink, about twice as long as the three-angled fruits they eventually enclose.

Most ornamental of the group and differing markedly from other cultivated kinds in its superior height, larger foliage, and bigger flowers, **A. muschketowii** is a loose, rather straggling shrub up to 8 feet tall. Its very short-stalked, light green leaves, 1 inch to 3 inches in length and ¼ to ¾ inch wide, are elliptic with crisped margins. In leafy racemes 1 inch to 2 inches long, the slender-stalked, white flowers, nearly ½ inch in diameter, are borne in late spring. This species, a native of central Asia, is hardy in southern New England. About as hardy, **A. caucasica** (syn. *A. buxifolia*) occurs from Transcaucasia to Turkestan. Up to 2½ feet tall, and with rather short, sometimes slightly spine-tipped branches, it has very short-stalked, dull green, wavy-edged, broad-obovate or elliptic leaves usually not over ¾ inch long. Its pinkish-white blooms, with five sepals and eight stamens, and ⅓ inch across, appear in early summer in racemes 1 inch to 1½ inches long. The three persistent sepals enlarge, deepen in color, and ultimately enclose the fruits.

Garden and Landscape Uses. Although these hardy, late spring- and summer-blooming plants cannot be rated among the finest of hardy, flowering shrubs, they are of sufficient merit to warrant being planted more frequently. They are especially well adapted for dry soils, and sunny exposed locations, and can be used effectively on banks and in rock gardens. Their calyxes, which are the showy parts of the flower and fruit clusters, remain colorful and attractive for long periods.

Cultivation. Except that they do not transplant well when large, and so are better grown in pots until they are set in their permanent locations, these plants need no special care. No regular pruning is necessary; any to keep the plants shapely may be done in spring just before new growth starts. Seeds afford a ready means of propagation and are best sown in spring, either in a cool greenhouse or outdoors. It is important that the seed soil be very porous, and not be kept too wet, otherwise the seedlings are likely to rot. Summer cuttings may be rooted in a propagating bed in a greenhouse or cold frame. Layering is a slower but sure method of obtaining increase.

ATRIPLEX (Átrip-lex)—Saltbush, Orach. The common name saltbush refers to the fact that these plants often grow in saline soils. They belong in the goosefoot family CHENOPODIACEAE and include about 200 shrubs and herbaceous plants of temperate and subtropical regions. Few are horticulturally interesting. Some are troublesome weeds. Their leaves are usually alternate, rarely opposite. Often they are covered with whitish meal or scurf. Their greenish flowers are small or minute and have little or no display value; mostly they are unisexual and are in clusters that may or may not branch. The name is the ancient Latin one for orach.

Orach (*Atriplex hortensis*) is cultivated as a minor edible green and, its colored-leaved variety, for garden ornament. This species, native of Asia, is commonly naturalized on the Pacific Coast and less abundantly elsewhere in the United States. It is a stout, erect annual up to 6 feet tall. Green, yellowish-green, or tinged red, it has opposite, more or less triangular-ovate and toothed lower leaves 2 to 7 inches long, and smaller, alternate, lanceolate-oblong upper ones. The plants are unisexual, the flowers in terminal panicles of ax-

Atriplex hortensis atrosanguinea

illary spikes. In variety *A. h. atrosanguinea* the stems and foliage are rich purplish-red.

Shrubby kinds include the quail brush (*A. lentiformis*). This occurs natively in saline soils in southern California. Up to 10 feet tall, unisexual or bisexual, it has silvery-gray, ovate-oblong leaves mostly up to 2 inches long. Hardiest of the shrubby species is *A. canescens*; it survives in southern New England and is native from South Dakota and Oregon to Texas and Baja California. Up to 4½ feet in height, it has whitish stems and nearly stalkless, linear-lanceolate to oblongish, grayish-green leaves 1 inch to 2 inches in length. The flowers are usually unisexual in terminal spikes or panicles of clusters. Up to 6 feet tall, and native of southern Europe, *A. halimus* is less hardy than *A. canescens* and differs from that species in having broader, rhomboid-ovate leaves that are white-scurfy and up to 2½ inches long.

Atriplex halimus

The desert-holly (*A. hymenelytra*) is a beautiful and conspicuous inhabitant of the Mojave and Colorado deserts and southward into Mexico. It favors dry, alkaline habitats and forms characteristic rounded bushes up to about 3 feet high. Its mostly opposite, broadly-elliptic to ovate

leaves, irregularly- and sharply-toothed, are silvery-white and ½ inch to 1¾ inches long. Male and female blooms are on separate plants, the males in short, dense, leafy panicles, the females in short, dense spikes. In many regions the collection of this plant from the wild is forbidden by law.

Garden and Landscape Uses. Orach is used as a vegetable or potherb. The richly colored, amaranthus-like *A. h. atrosanguinea* makes a splendid background in flower beds and borders. It combines especially well with pinks, delicate lavenders, and whites. Petunias of those colors planted near it show to excellent advantage. For sunny, windswept, and seaside locations in a dry, mild climate, such as that of California, the quail brush is a good ornamental shrub; it is favored as a hedge plant. The desert-holly is well worth attempting in well-drained soil in warm, dry regions. Established plants cannot be transplanted with any prospect of success, therefore, even if it were legal, it would be futile to dig them from the wild. Seeds afford the most promising way of securing young plants.

Cultivation. Orach, both the kind raised for eating and its ornamental variety, are grown from seeds sown in spring where the plants are to remain. The young plants are thinned to allow adequate space for them to develop. Alternatively, seeds of the ornamental kind can be sown indoors eight weeks or so before it is safe to set plants in the garden. Until then they are grown in flats or small pots. They require about the same care as petunias. Ordinary garden soil and a sunny location suits these plants. The other kinds are raised chiefly from seeds and from cuttings. They need no particular care except whatever shearing or pruning is needed to keep them shapely. This is best done in spring.

ATROPA (At-ròpa)—Deadly Nightshade or Belladonna. The common name of this member of the nightshade family SOLANACEAE is well merited. It is poisonous in all its parts and much too deadly to be admitted to ordinary gardens. Only where it is necessary for drug production, scientific research, or teaching should it be grown, and then under strict safeguards. Death can come too easily to a child or other person as a result of eating its attractive sweet berries for this plant to be treated casually. Dogs and cats are very susceptible to the poison, but some other animals including hogs, goats, sheep, horses, donkeys, and rabbits appear to be immune and birds eat the berries without harm. One point must be made clear, the slender vine with clusters of bright purple, yellow-centered, starry flowers and bunches of brilliant red berries that inhabits hedgerows and waste places in many parts of North America and is often mistakenly called deadly nightshade is not the plant to which we refer. That is the woody nightshade or European bittersweet (*Solanum dulcamara*), a plant of much less sinister attributes.

Despite, or because of, its deadly properties *Atropa belladonna* is an extremely useful plant. It is the source of medicinal belladonna and of the drug atropine used in ophthalmology to dilate the pupils of the eye. The ladies of ancient Rome, it is said, were aware of this quality and employed the plant to enhance the brilliancy of their eyes. It is believed that the name belladonna, beautiful lady, refers to this practice.

On historical occasions the deadly nightshade has served less worthily, at least from the point of view of its victims. Plutarch records that in the Parthian wars it was used to poison the soldiers of Marcus Antonius and it is related that a Danish army that invaded Scotland were poisoned by the soldiers of Macbeth who, during a truce, plied them with a deadly brew containing belladonna that so incapacitated them that they were easily slaughtered by the Scots.

The genus *Atropa*, its name, significantly, is a modification of *Atropos*, one of the Fates who cut the thread of human life, consists of four species of temperate parts of the Old World. Its best known kind, the deadly nightshade (*A. belladonna*), is a

Atropa belladonna in flower

Atropa belladonna in fruit

hardy perennial deciduous herbaceous plant with thick roots from which develop yearly stout, branched, erect stems that do not vine, but stand sturdily without support. They are 3 to 4 feet tall or occasionally taller, and like the foliage, are usually without hairs although their younger parts may be somewhat pubescent. The dullish green leaves vary considerably in size on the same plant. They are pointed-ovate, without teeth, 3 to 10 inches long, and at their bases gradually narrow to short stalks. Those on the lower part of the plant are alternate, the upper ones are in pairs with the pairs alternating on opposite sides of the stem and one member of each considerably bigger than the other. When crushed the fresh foliage has an unpleasant scent. The bell-shaped, solitary flowers, arising from the leaf axils, are dingy purple, purplish-green, or dull greenish. They are about 1 inch in length and have five shallow, slightly reflexed lobes. The five-parted persistent calyx remains with the fruit, which is a berry at first green, but shining black when ripe, and ½ to 1 inch in diameter. The berries contain inky juice and several small seeds.

Garden Uses and Cultivation. The deadly nightshade has no legitimate garden or landscape uses except as mentioned in the opening paragraph of this entry. When grown for scientific, instructional, or medicinal uses it is best treated as a biennial or short-lived perennial. It grows exceedingly well in limy earths, but thrives in any that are not excessively acid. For the best results the soil should be reasonably moist. Part-shade suits it well. Plants are raised from seeds, from terminal leafy cuttings, and from root-cuttings. They germinate slowly. It is important that the seedbed be kept constantly moist. The plants do not attain their full size until their second year. They require a spacing of 2 to 3 feet between individuals. They are hardy at New York City and probably further north.

ATTALEA (Attalè-a)—Piassava Palm. Some forty New World species are included in *Attalea*, but few are in cultivation and considerable confusion exists as to their identification and in their differentiation from closely similar *Orbignya* and *Scheelea*. They belong in the palm family PALMAE. The name is from the Greek *attalus*, magnificent, and alludes to the imposing appearance of these fan-leaved trees, or according to some authorities, it commemorates Attalos, king of Pergamum.

Commonly attaleas have erect, spineless, ringed trunks surmounted by a huge tuftlike crown of upswept, arching and erect leaves. They are unisexual or bisexual according to species, the heavy flower clusters originating among the leaves. The clusters have very big woody spathes, and the female flowers are succeeded by nutlike fruits 2 to 3 inches long covered on their outsides with a fibrous coating. Male

flowers usually have more than six stamens.

From the piassava palm (*A. funifera*) of Brazil is obtained piassava fiber much esteemed for brush making, especially for the brushes of street-sweeping machines and other heavy duty sweepers. The long, bristle-like fibers produced on the swollen bases of the leafstalks are chopped off with axes. From the seeds of this palm a useful oil is obtained. The piassava palm has a trunk up to 30 feet in height and leaves about as long. The leaflets, in groups of three to five, are narrow-linear, spreading, and numerous. The fruits are about 4 inches long. The cohune palm, often called *A. cohune*, is *Orbignya cohune*.

Garden and Landscape Uses and Cultivation. These palms are suitable for outdoor cultivation only in humid tropical or essentially tropical lands. In the United States they may be grown outdoors only in southern Florida and Hawaii. They are primarily palms for collectors. Some kinds are suitable for growing in displays of plants useful to man, such as those maintained in some large conservatories. They require the same culture as *Areca*. For additional information see Palms.

AUBERGINE. See Eggplant.

AUBRIETA (Aubrièt-a). Although often rendered *Aubrietia*, the original and correct spelling of the name is as given. The genus so identified belongs in the mustard family CRUCIFERAE and is closely allied to *Arabis* and *Alyssum*. Its name honors a famous French botanical artist, Claude Aubriet, who died in 1743.

There are twelve to fifteen species, natives of the mountains from the central Mediterranean region to Iran. They are low, hardy, herbaceous, more or less trailing or mat-forming, evergreen perennials. Their stems and foliage have forked or several-branched (stellate) hairs. Their ovate to oblong leaves may be coarsely-toothed or smooth-margined. The flowers in the wild characteristically purplish-rose to violet, or more rarely white, are, in some garden varieties, good pinks. They are in few-flowered racemes and, proportionate to the plants, are large. Typical of the mustard family, the blooms have four spreading petals in the form of a cross, four long and two short stamens, and seed pods of the kind called siliques that are oblong to spherical and contain two rows of seeds.

Aubrietas are much less well known in American than in European gardens, and almost all cultivated are seedlings of the horticultural group generally referred to *Aubrieta deltoidea*. In Europe many fine selections of this complex have been named and are propagated vegetatively by cuttings and division, but this is not generally done in America. Almost surely, not all plants referred to *A. deltoidea* are straight derivatives of that species. Most, if not all, are of hybrid origin and probably should be grouped under the name *A. cultorum*, but since their ancestry is not well understood and since *A. deltoidea* is the cognomen most applied to them it is so employed here. The other species of *Aubrieta* have no great merit as garden plants and are likely to appeal only to purists among alpine gardeners who are impelled to grow every high mountain denizen.

The species **A. deltoidea** occurs in the wild from Sicily to Asia Minor and has

Aubrieta deltoidea

quite long, branching stems and short-stalked spoon-shaped to obovate or rhomboid-shaped leaves, with a few large teeth. Its flowers are rosy-lilac to purple and are succeeded by pods usually less than ½ inch long, with branchless bristly hairs as well as branched, starlike ones. Native to Greece, *A. d. graeca*, is distinguished by its larger leaves and flowers, the latter with light to dark lilac or occasionally white, broad petals. Garden varieties (and hybrids) conform pretty well to the above description. They vary chiefly in compactness of growth, size and color of blooms, and other details of importance to gardeners. One has mostly double flowers and several have variegated or yellow foliage. Catalogs of dealers should be consulted for

Aubrieta deltoidea, a variegated-leaved variety

available varieties, always with the full understanding that from seeds, at the best, they come only approximately true.

Garden Uses. As permanent plants aubrietas serve well in rock gardens, dry walls, and as edgings to flower borders. Where summers are hot they suffer more than do their near relatives, the rock cress (*Arabis albida*) and the basket-of-gold (*Aurinia saxatilis*). Under such circumstances it is often wisest to treat them as biennials, raising new plants each year and discarding them after they are through blooming. This, too, is the way to handle aubrietas for temporary spring bedding (for which purpose they are excellent) with tulips, hyacinths, and other bulbs or in combination with such favorites as pansies, English daisies, and polyanthus primroses. For permanent plantings in regions of hot summers, locations tempered by a little shade in the heat of the day are advantageous, but drip from trees and heavy shade are likely to be disastrous. Basically these plants are sun-lovers.

Cultivation. Sandy, well-drained soil, with a generous content of compost, humus, peat moss, or other organic amendment, suits aubrietas. They are repelled by clayey earths, those poorly aerated, and those that lie wet for long periods. Planting is done in early fall or spring; smallish to moderately-sized plants recover from this operation and generally are more satisfactory than over-large ones. Aubrietas for permanent effects benefit from shearing as soon as the blooming season is over, and from top dressing each spring with soil mixed with a complete fertilizer. A good time to take cuttings is about when flowering is through. They can be rooted in cold frames. Careful division in spring or early fall offers another way of increase.

Raising aubrietas from seeds is easily accomplished. They are sown in May in well-drained pots, pans (shallow pots), or cold frames, in light sandy soil. As soon as the seedlings are big enough to handle comfortably they are transplanted to outdoor nursery beds or, where harsh winters prevail, to cold frames. In frames they are spaced 6 inches apart, outdoors in rows 1 foot apart with one-half that distance between plants in the rows. Summer care consists of keeping weeds down and watering in dry weather. In fall or the following spring the plants are transferred to their flowering quarters. In very cold climates a light winter covering of branches of evergreens or salt hay may be helpful.

AUCUBA (Au-cùba)—Spotted-Laurel or Gold Dust Tree. Variegated-leaved varieties of *Aucuba japonica* are probably the commonest evergreens of English city and suburban gardens. They survive the grime of the worst industrial regions, withstanding neglect and ill-treatment with equanimity. They are reliable standbys for screening under the most difficult condi-

tions. Because of this, in English city parks they are often massed around public conveniences. As may be imagined, the English do not regard them as choice. In America they are less known than they deserve to be for they are handsome shrubs and undoubtedly the British, who are great lovers of plants, would esteem them more were they rarer or more difficult to grow.

The genus *Aucuba* consists of perhaps three species of eastern and central Asia belonging to the dogwood family CORNACEAE. Some botanists do not accept the variants within this genus as separate species, but regard them as merely subspecies or varieties of one species. The name is a modification of its Japanese name, *Aokiba*.

Aucubas are thick-branched, evergreen shrubs with opposite leaves and small reddish-purple flowers in terminal clusters, the sexes on separate plants. There are four sepals and petals to each flower and the males have four stamens. After pollination the female flowers develop one-seeded, berry-like fruits. The only species known to be cultivated is **A. japonica**, which in the wild ranges from Japan to the

Aucuba japonica

Himalayas as an undershrub in woodlands. It is from 6 to 15 feet in height and has ovate to oblong or sometimes oblong-lanceolate, leathery, glossy leaves 3 to 8 inches long, 1½ to 3 inches wide, and usually coarsely-toothed above their middles. The scarlet, or rarely yellow or white, fruits are oblong-ovoid and are ½ inch long or slightly longer. There are several variants of this species. One of the commonest is the spotted-laurel or gold dust tree (*A. j. variegata* syn. *A. j. maculata*), a vigorous bush as tall as the typical species, with foliage profusely spotted with yellow. Variety *A. j. crotonifolia* has broader and thinner leaves than *A. j. variegata*, lighter green and more freely-blotched and marbled with yellow or ivory-white. Variety *A. j. dentata* has leaves smaller than those of the typical kind, and with one or two large

Aucuba japonica variegata

Aucuba japonica variegata

Aucuba japonica variegata (female flowers and fruits)

Aucuba japonica crotonifolia

teeth on each side. The fruits of *A. j. fructo-albo* are yellowish-white. The leaves of *A. j. goldeana* are large and golden-yellow, with an irregular green band around the margins. In *A. j. longifolia* (syn. *A. j. salicifolia*) the leaves are narrower than in the typical species and up to 5 inches long. Large and especially broad leaves characterize *A. j. macrophylla*. The leaves of *A. j. picta* are without spots, but have a broad marginal band of yellow or sometimes are almost entirely yellow. Serrated leaf margins are characteristic of *A. j. serratifolia*. Aucubas are not generally hardy north of Washington, D.C., but even in New York City they survive in sheltered locations and are quite handsome if not exposed to strong sun or cutting winds. If, there, in exceptionally cold winters they are killed back they soon renew themselves with new shoots from below.

Garden and Landscape Uses. Because they form dense bushes and have handsome foliage *A. japonica* and its varieties are excellent for screens and backgrounds and for including in plantings of mixed shrubs. They are especially well suited for shady locations, indeed in most places in America their foliage "burns" in strong summer sun, although in the less intense light of England they stand full exposure. Other virtues are their tolerance of city conditions and ability to compete successfully with the demanding roots of other shrubs and trees. They grow well at the seaside. Aucubas are not particular as to soil, flourishing in any of good to fair or even poor quality. As landscape plants the green-leaved kinds, although less popular than those with variegated foliage, have much to recommend them. They are less insistent in the landscape and do not compete as blatantly for the eye of the observer; they are better foils for flowers. All are splendid for tubs, planters, and other containers and so accommodated are excellent for decorating terraces, patios, and fairly cool rooms indoors. The fruits are highly decorative in fall. To be sure of having an abundance of these a small proportion of male bushes must be planted among mostly female plants.

Cultivation. So easy to grow are these plants that there is little to say about their cultivation. They respond to any pruning thought necessary. If grown indoors or in greenhouses, temperatures in winter not much above 60°F or below freezing are most appropriate. Container-grown specimens need generous supplies of water from spring through fall, less abundant amounts in winter; when well rooted they benefit from occasional applications of dilute liquid fertilizer. New plants are raised with great ease from cuttings. Under favorable conditions fairly large branches, 1 foot to 2 feet long, treated as cuttings root without difficulty. Seeds sown in a temperature of about 60°F may give rise to variable progeny.

Aucuba japonica serratifolia

AUDOUINIA (Audouín-ia). One South African evergreen shrub of heathlike aspect is the only member of this genus. It belongs in the brunia family BRUNIACEAE and was named to commemorate a professor of natural history at Paris, France, J. V. Audouin, who died in 1841.

From 2 to 3 feet tall, *Audouinia capitata* (syn. *Diosma capitata*) has slender, erect, few-branched stems clothed with spirally-arranged, three-angled, linear leaves that hug the shoots and overlap like shingles on a roof. They are from ⅙ inch to twice that in length. The pinkish-lilac to crimson flowers are arranged in dense, terminal, spikelike heads, ½ inch to 2 inches long and ¾ to 1 inch wide. Flowers at the centers of the spikes open first, followed in succession, by those above and below them. Each bloom is ¼ inch long and has a five-toothed calyx, five spatula-shaped petals, and five stamens.

Garden and Landscape Uses and Cultivation. This charming shrub is adapted for outdoor cultivation in beds and rock gardens in mild regions such as California, and in pots in cool greenhouses. It prefers sandy peaty soil, well drained and with moderate moisture, and full sun. After blooming the plants may be sheared lightly to keep them compact. Increase is had by cuttings of moderately firm shoots taken in summer, and by seeds sown in sandy peaty soil kept evenly moist in a temperature of 55 to 60°F. Young plants are pinched occasionally to promote branching.

Greenhouses in which audouinias are grown must be ventilated freely whenever weather permits. A winter night temperature of 45 to 50°F, with an increase of five to ten degrees by day, is adequate. In spring, after blooming, the plants are pruned lightly to moderately, and two or three weeks later, just as new growth begins, are repotted. In summer they do best in a sunny place outdoors with their pots buried to their rims in a bed of sand, peat moss, or other material to keep them evenly moist and cool. They are brought inside before fall frost. The soil of these plants should be kept always moderately moist, never wet for long periods.

AUGUST, GARDENING REMINDERS FOR. Routine maintenance such as occupied much of last month (see July, Gardening Reminders For) makes similar demands on gardeners' time through August. Hot, often dry weather is likely to prevail over much of North America, but toward the end of August lower night temperatures in the north are likely to bring some relief to alpines, cool-weather annuals, and other sorts not happy with excessive heat. Plants that revel in tropical weather are now at their best and continue to grow lustily. So, unfortunately, do weeds. Warm-weather pests and diseases multiply and prosper.

Chief among routine tasks are frequent surface cultivations, and where necessary hand pulling or other methods of destroying weeds, deep watering at intervals short enough to prevent distress from lack of moisture, and prompt preventive or remedial action against pests and diseases that threaten the garden. Attend to fertilizing as needed. Keep lawns cut to a height of approximately 2 inches.

If the weather is dry water lawns and other areas as needed

If you have not already sent in your orders for bulbs to plant this fall delay no longer. Except for tulips and irises, practically all hardy bulbs are best when set in the ground as early as the dealer can supply them, which in many cases means as soon as he receives supplies from Holland.

Plant as soon as bulbs are available:
(a) Colchicums

Cultivate frequently to control weeds

(b) Madonna lilies

It is of especial importance to plant colchicums (often called autumn-crocuses) and true crocuses that bloom in fall (these are not as well known as their merits deserve), early. That is true too of Madonna lilies, bulbs of which should be available this month.

In the north, early August presents the last call to sow for spring display seeds of pansies, forget-me-nots, and English daisies. All perform better if sown sooner, but give creditable results from early August seedings.

Do not delay in sowing seeds of: (a) Pansies

(b) Forget-me-nots

(c) English daisies

Other August sowings to be made are successional ones of vegetable garden crops that can be expected to attain harvesting size before winter. In many sections of the north, carrots, corn salad, endive, lettuce, peas, radishes, snap beans, and spinach will prove successful. The harvesting season of carrots, lettuce, and corn salad can be extended considerably by protecting them later from severest cold. Transplant seedlings of lettuce from sowings made outdoors now to cold frames. Sow corn salad directly in cold frames. Alternatively, make sowings where later the plants can be protected in situ with polyethylene plastic film supported by metal hoops or a light wooden framework straddling the rows. Splendid carrots can be had all winter if August sowings are left in the ground and protected after the soil has frozen to a depth of an inch or two with a thick covering of leaves, straw, or similar material. If you are raising celery that is to be blanched begin the process this month either by wrapping with heavy paper or mounding with soil.

Harvesting vegetables, cut flowers, and herbs for drying are important tasks. Beginner gardeners are likely to make the mistake of allowing vegetables to attain too great a size before sending them to the kitchen. Let eating quality, not mere size, be the criterion. There is no virtue in oversize eggplants, kohlrabis, squash, or turnips, in beans that have attained that lumpy, gouty appearance that proclaims departed youth, or in okra pods more than 2 to 3 inches long. On the other hand, tomatoes and melons fully vine-ripened are superior. Do not harvest onions for storage until their tops have turned completely brown and their skins are well ripened. To promote this, when the tops begin to die push them over with a rake so that they lie flat on the ground. In the cut flower garden keep blooms picked regularly whether your need for them is great or not. Allowing them to go to seed discourages the production of more blooms. For the same reason as well as for neatness, keep faded flowers picked from ornamental plantings.

Some transplanting and planting needs attention in August. Seedlings of June-sown biennials and perennials such as coreopsis, delphiniums, hollyhocks, sweet williams, and others will need transferring to nursery beds or cold frames to grow to sizes suitable for setting in their flowering quarters in fall or spring. Pansies from July or early August seedings will need similar attention. Set out strawberry plants, preferably pot-grown ones, in sunny, deeply-spaded beds of fertile soil.

Evergreens can be transplanted as soon as the season's growth is firm and relatively mature. This is generally achieved by mid-August. After that the earlier moving is done the longer the plants have before winter to reestablish their root systems. Immediately after planting and if the weather is dry periodically, soak the soil of newly planted evergreens very thoroughly. A mulch about them will do much

Transplant seedlings of biennials and perennials from sowings made earlier

to conserve soil moisture. Spraying their tops with an antidesiccant or daily with water is of great aid.

Complete dividing and replanting Japanese and Siberian irises as soon as possible and toward the end of the month or in early September attend to peonies that are to be so treated. It is better not to disturb peonies unless quite necessary. The irises are better for dividing and transplanting every few years. This is a good time to dig up, divide, and transplant tall summer phloxes. Choice kinds are easily increased by root cuttings now.

Lawn-sowing time is at hand. If not done earlier delay no longer preparing the ground. Seeding can with advantage be done from the last week in August to mid-September. The great advantage of an early start is that after contouring, grading, fertilizing, and other conditioning work is completed the ground may be left fallow for three or four weeks or more to settle and to give weed seeds a chance to germinate. By cultivating the surface shallowly periodically or by using an appropriate weed killer during the fallow period the weeds are destroyed and a clean bed assured for the lawn grass seed.

Soil improvement by increasing its organic content engages the attention of all true gardeners. Two means of accomplishing this are available now. One is to continue unrelentingly to collect and store makings for compost piles, the other is to sow cover crops of winter rye in areas in vegetable gardens and cut flower gardens from which crops have been harvested, as well as on other land that would otherwise lie bare until spring. All that is necessary is to rake the seeds into the surface. The young plants take up nutrients that would otherwise be lost to the soil by leaching. When the grass is turned under in late winter or spring these nutrients are returned to the earth together with substantial amounts of humus-making organic material.

In greenhouses a new phase of activity begins in August. Great preparations need be made for winter and spring displays. Cool-weather plants, such as calceolarias, cinerarias, cyclamens, and primulas, that have sulked through the dog days of summer perk considerably with the coming, as September approaches, of cooler nights. Soon they may need transferring to bigger pots.

In need of potting and starting into new growth now are calla-lilies and Martha Washington geraniums that have been dormant for several weeks. Prune the geraniums quite severely at potting time. It is not too early to plant or pot freesias for earliest blooms. Bulbs from cold storage of *Lilium speciosum* and other available sorts potted at two-week intervals from the start of August until mid-September will assure a succession of blooms.

Pot calla-lilies in August

Seeds of many flowering annuals sown now will give splendid plants for supplying cut blooms and for use as ornamental pot specimens in winter and spring. Sowings of the same kinds made in September or October result in smaller, but often very useful plants. Kinds to sow now include those mentioned in the Encyclopedia entry "July, Gardening Reminders For," and additionally, clarkias, linarias, lupines, nasturtiums, ursineas, and venidiums. Other seeds to sow in August include calceolarias, cinerarias, and cyclamens. From early-in-the-month seeding cinerarias make nice 5- or 6-inch-pot specimens for March

(b) Cyclamens

In the greenhouse sow seeds of:
(a) Cinerarias

(c) Calceolarias

blooming. Cyclamens from seed sown late in the month will flower in fifteen to eighteen months in 6-inch pots. Calceolarias seeded about the same time should be nice 5-inch-pot specimens in flower for Easter.

Pinch the tips out of the shoots of carnations for the last time early in August and of chrysanthemums grown for fall blooming about the middle of the month. Transfer to final pots *Buddleia asiatica, B. farquhari, Erlangea tomentosa,* and stevias (*Piqueria*) that are to bloom in winter in a cool greenhouse. After potting put them outdoors in a sunny place with their pots buried nearly to their rims in sand, soil, sawdust, peat moss, or similar material. Keep them neatly staked and tied. Toward the end of the month pot Christmas begonias into the containers in which they are to bloom.

Regularly fertilize plants, except any in a dormant or partially-resting stage, that have filled their pots with roots. Let little and often be the rule rather than stronger concentrations at longer intervals. Weekly applications of dilute liquid fertilizer give satisfactory results with most sorts.

Cold frames afford great opportunity to propagate a wide selection of plants from cuttings made and inserted in August.

Here belong such evergreens as boxwoods, hollies, lavender, sage, santolinas, thyme, and yews. Among groundcovers, English ivy, evergreen euonymuses, pachysandra, and vinca are easily increased from August cuttings. Responsive to the same treatment are a goodly variety of rock garden plants, such as arabises, arenarias, aubretias, campanulas, dianthuses, galiums, helianthemums, iberises, phloxes, sedums, and veronicas. Frames used for propagation must be shaded and the atmosphere inside kept highly humid until rooting takes place. Little or no ventilation is needed until then, at which time the young plants are gradually accustomed to a freer circulation of air. If you have a mist propagation setup, outdoors or in a greenhouse, the kinds of plants suggested for propagation in cold frames can be rooted as easily or even more expeditiously. An advantage of the cold frame method is that the rooted cuttings can stay put until spring. Those under mist need potting as soon as they have rooted and then transferring to a cold frame or other suitable accommodation for overwintering.

Care of cold frames other than those sheltering new propagations calls for little

attention in August. Before the end of the month and before they become leggy through crowding, pansy seedlings from July sowings will be ready for transplanting into them. Keep the surface soil between earlier-sown, frame-grown biennials, such as Canterbury bells, sweet williams, and wallflowers, lightly stirred to repress weeds and encourage growth. Water as needed to keep the soil in a moderately moist condition.

Houseplants in August should mostly be at their healthiest. Give attention to those summering outdoors. If their pots are plunged (buried to their rims) in a bed of sand or similar material or in the ground, lift them out occasionally, rub off any roots emerging from the drainage holes in the pots, and replace them. Plants so plunged need less frequent watering than if they were standing on the top of the ground, on a terrace, on steps or similar places, but still they must not be neglected.

Do not fail to attend to fertilizing and watch for early evidence of insect infestations. Practically all houseplants that have filled their containers with roots benefit from weekly or biweekly applications of dilute liquid fertilizer at this time. Aphids, mealy bugs, red spider mites, thrips, scale

August cuttings of many plants root readily in a cold frame, among them:
(a) Boxwood

(b) Sage

(c) Pachysandra

(d) Helianthemum

(e) Iberis

(f) Phlox

insects, and other pests prosper in hot weather. Spray whenever necessary to keep them under control. This can be done with greater ease and more effectively outdoors than in. If you attend as thoroughly as you should to pest control your plants will be clean and healthy to enter the fall and winter.

Attractive specimens for winter and early spring flowering in pots in sunny windows can be had by sowing outdoors now seeds of calendulas, dwarf marigolds, nasturtiums, sweet alyssum, and other quick-growing annuals. Transplant the seedlings as soon as they are big enough to handle to a sunny outdoor bed and in four or five weeks, before frost and before they are too big, lift them carefully, pot them, water well, and shade them for a few days before moving them to indoor locations.

Take cuttings in August of abutilons, ageratums, coleuses, English ivy, fuchsias, geraniums, heliotropes, impatiens, iresenes, and wax begonias to give small plants that will be useful ornamentals by spring.

In the south timely attention to watering is highly important. In particular, do not allow azaleas or camellias to want for moisture. Mulching is a good way of conserving water as well as of keeping the soil cool. Water lawns thoroughly in dry weather but refrain from fertilizing them at this time. Mow to a height of 1½ to 2 inches.

Fertilize dahlias to keep them moving and disbud those being grown for large exhibition-type blooms. Spray or dust as needed to check black spot disease of roses and other troubles best controlled in these ways.

Much seeding now needs attention. Sow for fall crops beets, cabbages, carrots, collards, cow-peas, kale, kohlrabi, lettuce, radishes, rutabagas, snap beans, spinach, and turnips. In the lower south sow also cucumbers, eggplants, okra, peppers, squash, sweet corn, and tomatoes. Among annuals to sow in the lower south are asters, calendulas, cosmos, gypsophilas, larkspurs, marigolds, nasturtiums, nemophilas, petunias, portulacas, salvias, sweet alyssum, sweet peas, and zinnias.

Perennials that can be conveniently raised from seeds give good results if sown about the middle of August. Sorts that can be expected to give satisfaction include aquilegias, coreopsises, gaillardias, geums, gypsophilas, hollyhocks, platycodons, pyrethrums, Shasta-daisies, and veronicas. Sow in a cold frame or lightly shaded place outdoors where the soil can be kept moist.

Planting and transplanting bearded and Louisiana irises is best done in August as are, toward the end of the month in the upper south, peonies. In the lower south, hippeastrums or amaryllises as they are commonly called can be planted now when they are in a semi-dormant condition.

Other bulbs to plant are leucojums, lycorises, Madonna lilies, ornithogalums, oxalises, sternbergias, and zephyranthes, and in the lower south calla-lilies and Easter lilies.

Propagation by cuttings of a wide variety of evergreens is practicable now in a cold frame, glass-covered box, under a Mason jar, or even in a sheltered place outdoors. Shade from direct sun, a moist rooting medium, and a humid atmosphere are requisite. The same sorts of cuttings succeed in full sun if planted under mist. Satisfactory kinds include abelias, azaleas, barberries, boxwoods, camellias, cherry-laurels, euonymuses, hollies, osmanthuses, photinias, privets, skimmias, and sweet bay (*Laurus nobilis*).

In West Coast gardens much of August's work is routine concerned with supplying water, controlling weeds, and taking preventative or death-dealing action against diseases and pests. All this calls for constant watchfulness, early and correct diagnoses, and prompt action.

Many plants including camellias, fuchsias, gardenias, and rhododendrons benefit from daily misting their foliage with water. Take care that these and others known to appreciate moist soil do not suffer from your failure to apply water when needed. Give carnations their last pinch toward the end of the month.

If seeds were not sown late last month to give plants to set out in beds in October to bloom in spring get busy with seed sowing at a fairly early opportunity. Consult the entry "July, Gardening Reminders For," for suggestions. Be sure to keep the seed beds shaded and moist. Toward the end of the month sow early-flowering sweet peas. Other seeds that can be sown now except in regions of extreme heat, where it is better to wait until next month, are those of hardy perennials. Sow, too, cabbage for spring use and other quick-growing vegetables such as snap beans and lettuce for harvesting in fall. Set out young plants of savoy cabbage to provide fall and winter greens.

In the Northwest, transplant seedling biennials from seed beds to nursery beds before the end of the month. Prepare for planting bulbs in anticipation of their arrival from the dealer. Early planting is especially important with colchicums, cyclamens, fritillarias, lycorises, Madonna lilies, sternbergias, and trilliums. As soon as the crops have been harvested, prune blackberries, boysenberries, and youngberries.

AULU is *Sapindus oahuensis*.

AUREOLARIA (Aureo-lària)—False-Foxglove. These quite lovely plants of eastern North America and Mexico are partial parasites. They have green leaves and so are able to elaborate nutrients, as do plants of more independent habit, from the ele-

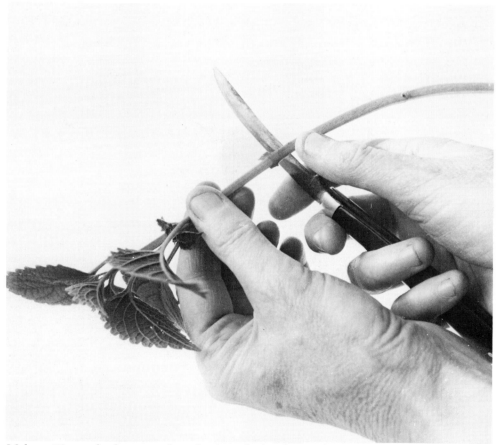

Make cuttings of coleuses and a selection of other houseplants

ments of earth and air. But false-foxgloves are not content with the nourishment they secure in that way. They supplement the food of their own manufacture by tapping the roots of oaks for sustenance. Because of this parasite-host relationship they are often difficult to establish in cultivation. There are about ten species, annuals, biennials, and herbaceous perennials. They belong in the figwort family SCROPHULARIACEAE. The name *Aureolaria* is derived from the Latin *aureolus*, golden, in allusion to the color of the blooms. At one time the group was included in the nearly related genus *Gerardia*. Flower color and technical differences separate the two.

False-foxgloves are erect, branched, and have lobed or lobeless leaves, the principal ones opposite, the smaller, upper ones usually alternate. The large, showy, upfacing, yellow, stalked, asymmetrical flowers are solitary in the axils of the upper leaves. They have narrowly-bell-shaped corolla tubes and five rounded, spreading corolla lobes. Among the several kinds that occur in the United States are *A. flava*, a perennial 3 to 6 feet tall, with hairless, somewhat glaucous stems. Native from Maine to Ontario, Wisconsin, Florida, and Louisiana, this kind has ovate-lanceolate leaves up to 6 inches long, the lower ones deeply-lobed, and 1½- to 2-inch-long orange-yellow flowers. Another perennial, *A. virginica* ranges in the wild from Massachusetts to Ontario, Michigan, Florida, and Alabama. Its lower leaves usually have one or two pairs of blunt lobes. The flowers are up to 1½ inches long. This species is about 3 feet tall. The annual *A. pedicularia* has lanceolate to narrowly-triangular, deeply-pinnately-lobed leaves. It is finely-hairy with some of the hairs, especially those of calyx tubes and flower stalks, glandular. The flowers are 1 inch to 1½ inches long. This kind attains a height of up to 3 feet.

Garden and Landscape Uses and Cultivation. Aureolarias are lovely plants for decorating woodlands, but because of their parasitic proclivities are often difficult to establish where they do not grow naturally. Where they do, every effort should be made to encourage and preserve them by maintaining the degree of shade that seems to suit them and by restricting the growth of any other plants that threaten to take over their territory. Their establishment elsewhere may be attempted by setting out plants gathered from the wild and transferred with good balls of soil attached to their roots, and by sowing seeds in likely places. Sites for such attempts should be within the spread of the roots of oak trees and under conditions as close as possible to those under which aureolarias are observed to grow naturally.

AURICULA. This is the common name of *Primula auricula* and its varieties. These for-

Primula auricula

merly achieved great popularity especially in Great Britain as fanciers' or specialists' flowers. Today they chiefly interest rock gardeners. See Primula.

AURINIA (Aur-ínia)—Basket-of-Gold. Formerly included in *Alyssum* and by some botanists still treated as a section of that genus, *Aurinia* consists of seven species of the mustard family CRUCIFERAE. Its name, alluding to the color of the blooms of *A. saxatile*, comes from the Latin *aureus*, golden.

Aurinias, natives of central and southern Europe and Turkey, are low biennials and herbaceous perennials, with tufted rosettes of wavy-edged, toothed, or pinnately-lobed leaves with grooved stalks and stem leaves considerably smaller than the basal ones. The yellow or white flowers, in racemes or panicled clusters, have

four each sepals and petals, four long and two short stamens, and one style. The fruits are flattened or somewhat inflated pods. The plants that remain in *Alyssum* differ from aurinias in having stem and basal leaves of approximately the same size, rarely more than 1 inch long, with lobeless, toothless, not wavy margins and cylindrical stalks, and the basal ones being in looser rosettes.

Basket-of-gold or golden tuft (*A. saxatilis* syn. *Alyssum saxatile*), native to southern and central Europe, is undoubtedly the most familiar species. In gardens throughout temperate North America in early spring, it paints splendid splashes of welcome gold, complementing hyacinths, tulips, pansies, and a host of other bright seasonal blooms. This is a grateful plant, prospering with slight attention and persisting for many years. It comes in several forms. From a somewhat woody base, basket-of-gold develops tussocked masses of more or less lax stems and slightly hoary foliage. Its lower leaves are numerous, oblanceolate to obovate-oblong and, with their stalk, 2 to 5 inches in length. Their edges are scallop-toothed or toothless. The leaves on the flowering stems are similar to the lower ones, but smaller. Brilliant golden-yellow blooms are so profusely borne that they almost smother the foliage. The seed pods are more or less circular. The typical kind is 1 foot to 2 feet tall. From it *A. s. compactum* differs in being much lower and, as its name indicates, more compact. In *A. s. citrinum* (syns. *A. s. sulphureum*; *A. s. luteum*) the blooms are a lovely soft sulfur-yellow. The double-flow-

Aurinia saxatilis

ered *A. s. plenum* has flowers with more than four petals that are intensely brilliant yellow. Foliage variegated with soft yellow characterizes *A. s. variegatum*.

Less common in cultivation, *A. corymbosa* (syn. *Alyssum corymbosum*) and *A. petraea* (syn. *Alyssum edentulum*) are natives of southeast Europe. A perennial 9 inches to 1½ feet tall, **A. corymbosa** has usually toothed, spoon-shaped to lanceolate, more or less hairy leaves and in branched clusters yellow flowers up to ½ inch across, and with the tips of their petals notched. A biennial or a short-lived perennial, with whitish-hairy stems and foliage, **A. petraea** from 6 inches to 2 feet high and more or less hairy, has toothed or wavy-edged, obovate-oblong basal leaves and racemes of up to ½-inch-wide yellow flowers.

Garden and Landscape Uses. The cultivated sorts of this genus are useful for the fronts of flower beds, rock gardens, dry walls, and similar situations, and *A. saxatilis* and its varieties for spring bedding. The dainty flowers are useful for cutting for use in arrangements. For the best results all need a sunny location and well-drained, not excessively rich soil.

Cultivation. Among the easiest garden plants to grow, the species of aurinias are usually raised from seeds sown outdoors or in a cold frame in spring or earlier indoors. Double-flowered and variegated-leaved varieties of the basket-of-gold cannot be propagated from seeds; instead, in spring or early summer take cuttings of nonflowering shoots and insert them in a shaded cold frame or greenhouse where a humid atmosphere is maintained.

When basket-of-gold is raised as a biennial for temporary spring displays sow seed in May or early June and transplant the seedlings to nursery beds in rows 1 foot to 1½ feet apart with about 9 inches allowed between individuals in the rows. Transplant the resulting plants to their flowering quarters in early fall or early spring.

AUSTRALIAN. Plants with Australian as part of their common names include these: Australian-beech (*Eucalyptus polyanthemos*), Australian black-pine (*Podocarpus amarus*), Australian bluebell-creeper (*Sollya heterophylla*), Australian brown-pine (*Podocarpus elatus*), Australian brush-cherry (*Syzygium paniculatum*), Australian carrot wood (*Cupaniopsis anacardioides*), Australian climbing-lily (*Luzuriaga*), Australian desert-kumquat or Australian desert-lime (*Eremocitrus*), Australian finger-lime (*Microcitrus australasica*), Australian-fuchsia (*Correa*), Australian-honeysuckle (*Banksia* and *Lambertia*), Australian-lilac (*Prostanthera lasianthos*), Australian love creeper (*Comesperma volubile*), Australian mint-bush (*Prostanthera*), Australian-mountain-ash (*Eucalyptus regnans*), Australian nut-palm (*Cycas media*), Australian-pea (*Dolichos liguosus*), Australian-pine (*Casuarina*), Aus-

Aurinia saxatilis is a good bedding plant for spring display: (a) Lifting plants from a nursery bed

(b) Planting them where they are to bloom

tralian pitcher plant (*Cephalotus*), Australian-red-cedar (*Cedrela australis*), Australian-rosemary (*Westringia fruticosa*), Australian salt bush (*Rhagodia nutans*), Australian tea tree (*Leptospermum laevigatum*), Australian tulipwood tree (*Harpullia pendula*), Australian-willow (*Geijera parviflora*), and Australian-yellow-wood (*Rhodosphaera rhodanthema*).

AUSTROCACTUS (Austro-cáctus). Uncommon in cultivation, *Austrocactus* consists of about eight South American species of the cactus family CACTACEAE. Its name derives from the Latin *auster*, south, and cactus.

Austrocactuses have rather soft-fleshed, cylindrical stems with clusters of stout spines with strongly-hooked centrals. The funnel-shaped flowers, borne near the tops of the stems, remain open during the day. The fruits are spiny.

Chilean *A. hibernus* has prostrate stems about 1¼ inches in diameter and 4 inches long with upturned tips. They have seven or eight ribs and spine clusters of five to eight very slender radials up to ⅜ inch long and one to four centrals about 1¼ inches long. The white to rose-pink flowers are about 2 inches long.

Occasionally cultivated, *A. patagonicus*, of Argentina, has stems 8 inches to 1½ feet tall by 2 to 3¼ inches wide. They have nine to twelve ribs. The spine clusters are of six to ten radials about ¾ inch long, and one to four centrals up to 1 inch long. The flowers are pink, about 2 inches across.

Garden and Landscape Uses and Cultivation. Austrocactuses are for collectors of choice succulents. Reputed to be somewhat difficult to grow, they may be expected to accommodate best to conditions that suit temperate-region cactuses. Sandy, slightly acid soil with a low organic content is suggested for these plants. For further information see Cactuses.

AUSTROCEDRUS (Austro-cédrus)—Chilean-Cedar. Formerly called *Libocedrus chilensis*, a single species of evergreen coniferous tree of southern Chile and Argentina constitutes *Austrocedrus*. Little known in North America, it belongs in the cypress family CUPRESSACEAE. Its name is derived from the Latin *auster*, south, and *Cedrus*, the name of the true cedars. It implies a resemblance.

Chilean-cedar (*A. chilensis*) is up to about 80 feet tall and attractive in cultivation. Until quite old it is narrow, then it broadens. Its branchlets are in flattened sprays held horizontally. They have overlapping, scalelike leaves in pairs that form four rows along the shoots. Alternate pairs are markedly unequal in size. The larger ones, up to ³⁄₁₆ inch in length, have their tips turned inward. Male cones are tiny. Female cones, solitary at the tips of short branchlets, have four scales, the upper two

Austrocedrus chilensis (center)

of which are fertile and usually produce two seeds each. The wood of the Chilean-cedar, long-lasting and durable, is used for interior trim and other purposes. Good natural stands of this species exist near Bariloche, Argentina.

Garden and Landscape Uses and Cultivation. This choice conifer is unlikely to be found in cultivation except in special collections of rare and unusual plants. It is less hardy than the incense-cedar (*Calocedrus decurrens*) and will grow only in regions of comparatively mild winters. It succeeds outdoors in sheltered places in southern England, and in North America would probably be best adapted to parts of the Pacific Northwest. A humid atmosphere is required for its best growth. Where it succeeds it may be expected to respond to approximately the same cultural conditions and to serve the same ornamental purposes as the incense-cedar. For further general information see Conifers.

AUSTROCEPHALOCEREUS (Austro-céphalo-cereus). Modern botanists tend to include the three species of *Austrocephalocereus* in closely related *Cephalocereus*. This at least has the virtue of shortening the rather formidable name by a couple of syllables. Many cactus fanciers and dealers, however, retain the group as a separate entity and so, without prejudice to the opinions of those who think otherwise, it

is dealt with in that way here. Belonging in the cactus family CACTACEAE and being limited in the wild to South America, *Austrocephalocereus* has a name that indicates this distribution. It derives from the Latin *australis*, southern, and the name of the genus *Cephalocereus*.

These cactuses differ only in minor technical details from *Cephalocereus*. According to species they range up to 15 feet in height and branch freely or scantily, mostly from near their bases. The ribbed, cylindrical stems of older specimens develop on one side near their tops a densely-hairy patch called a pseudocephalium from which come the flowers; their lower parts are more or less embedded in the hair. The globose to club-shaped fruits contain rough-surfaced seeds.

A choice item for collectors, *A. dybowskii* (syn. *Cephalocereus dybowskii*), of Bolivia and Brazil, branches freely. It is up to 12 feet tall. Its stems, 3 to 3½ inches in diameter, have twenty or more low ribs. They are densely clothed with white, yellowish, or grayish hairs that hide the radials of the spine clusters each of which has in addition to numerous needle-like radials two or three longer centrals of similar form about 1¼ inches long. The pseudocephalium is about 2 feet in length. The flowers are white, approximately 1½ inches long. Globose and about 1 inch in diameter, the fruits are pink.

Garden and Landscape Uses and Cultivation. These are as for *Cephalocereus.* For more information see Cephalocereus, and Cactuses.

AUSTROCYLINDROPUNTIA (Austro-cylindropúntia). South American cholla-type cactuses of eighteen species perhaps more are accommodated in *Austrocylindropuntia* of the cactus family CACTACEAE. The genus, a split from *Opuntia,* by conservative botanists is included there. The separation is based chiefly on its spines having sheathes, which are absent in North American opuntias. The name, in allusion to the geographical range of the genus, comes from the Latin *australis,* southern, and *Cylindropuntia,* the name those who split *Opuntia* into several genera apply to North American cylindrical-stemmed sorts.

Because in North America cylindropuntias are generally treated under *Opuntia* that is done in this Encyclopedia. Admittedly this does not reflect botanical logic if *Austrocylindropuntia* and other segregates of *Opuntia* are described separately, but nevertheless it seems a horticultural convenience until such times as further botanical studies resolve the present uncertainty of generic limits.

Sorts cultivated include these: *A. clavarioides* (syn. *Opuntia clavarioides*) is a low, straggling bush, native to Chile, with stems with smooth cylindrical segments sometimes thickened conically or in fan-shaped fashion at their tops. They have closely-set areoles with stars of four to ten hairlike, white spines. The greenish-brown, sparingly-produced flowers are about 2 inches wide. Curiously cristate, A. c. 'Niggerhand' is common in cultivation. *A. cylindrica* (syn. *Opuntia cylindrica*), of Peru and Ecuador, grows 8 to 12 feet tall and has sparse branches with cylindrical segments with neatly patterned, flat, lozenge-shaped tubercles. Mostly in groups of two or three, sometimes up to six, the whitish spines are less than ½ inch long. Sometimes they are absent. The deep pink to red flowers 1 inch in diameter are followed by yellow-green fruits about 2 inches long. A crested variety is cultivated. *A. pachypus* (syn. *Opuntia pachypus*), about 3 feet tall, has stems 1½ to 2 inches thick. The areoles have yellow glochids and awl-shaped, down-pointing spines ¼ to ¾ inch long in clusters of twenty to thirty. The scarlet flowers are approximately 1½ inches in diameter. It is a native of Peru. *A. salmiana* (syn. *Opuntia salmiana*), of Argentina and southern Brazil, branches from the base. It is 3 to 6 feet tall, with slender, often purplish, sometimes somewhat vining, smooth stems approximately ½ inch in diameter. They have areoles with yellow glochids and usually but not always a few white spines up to ¾ inch long. From ¾ to 1 inch across, the flowers are pink to red in bud, when open pale yellow with red-

Austrocylindropuntia salmiana

dish outsides. The fruits are club-shaped and red. A white-flowered variety is *A. s. albiflora,* and *A. s. spegazzinii* has green stems, smaller blooms, and bluish-green fruits. *A. subulata* (syns. *Opuntia subulata, Pereskia subulata*), of Peru, is a freely-branched bush 5 to 12 feet tall, sometimes with a single trunk up to 4 inches wide and with stems up to 2¾ inches thick with more or less lozenge-shaped tubercles. The cylindrical leaves, 2 to 4½ inches in length and spread at right angles to the stems, are persistent on the young parts. One, two, or rarely more spines 2½ to 3 inches long sprout from each areole, or sometimes there are none. The flowers are reddish or orange- or greenish-yellow. The oblong, leafy fruits are 2 to 4 inches long. *A. teres* (syn. *Opuntia teres,* a name that has also been applied to *A. vestita*), of Bolivia, forms clumps 1 foot wide or wider of approximately ½-inch-wide stems the easily detachable segments of which may be short and almost spherical or up to about 8 inches in length. Cylindrical leaves up to ¾ inch long are developed on their younger parts. The conspicuous areoles bear white glochids, a few long hairs, and five or six needle-like, brownish spines ¾ to 1 inch long. The ¾-inch-wide blooms are deep red. The reddish fruits are approximately globular. *A. verschaffeltii* (syn. *Opuntia verschaffeltii*), of Bolivia, grows in dense,

much-branched clumps up to 1 foot high. It has slightly-warted stems from a little less to a little more than ½ inch in width of short, nearly spherical to cylindrical, easily detachable segments, or in cultivated specimens, of longer, cylindrical ones. On their young parts leaves up to 1¼ inches long remain for a considerable time. The areoles have yellow glochids and frequently one to three slender, twisted, bristle-like, yellowish spines up to 1¼ inches long. Spines are often absent. About ¾ inch in diameter, the flowers are deep orange to red. The spines of *A. v. longispina* are about 2 inches long and spread widely. *A. vestita* (syn. *Opuntia vestita*), of Bolivia, has erect to sprawling, sparsely-branched, irregularly-warted stems with cylindrical segments up to nearly 1 foot in length by approximately 1 inch in diameter. The cylindrical leaves, which persist for some time on their younger parts, are less than ½ inch long. The areoles have white glochids, many long white hairs that nearly hide the stems, and two to eight awl-shaped spines up to ¾ inch long. The dark red blooms are ¾ to 1¼ inches across. The ellipsoid fruits are about ½ inch long and red and woolly. *A. v. major* has thicker stems and leaves 1½ to 2 inches long; *A. v. chuquisacana* has spines in clusters of about twenty. A cristate variety is also cultivated.

Garden and Landscape Uses and Cultivation. These are essentially as for *Opuntia*. Some growers suggest that certain sorts, including *A. clavarioides* and *A. vestita*, are better if located where they receive a little shade from the strongest sun. These and other low kinds are frequently grafted on strong-growing opuntias. For more information see Cactuses.

AUTUMN COLOR. The leaves of many temperate-region trees and shrubs, more particularly those of deciduous kinds, change color quite markedly in fall. Those that assume the most brilliant and dramatic hues are greatly esteemed for this and garden planners should give thought to including them in plantings.

Such changes are natural to the senescence that begins well before the leaves fall and generally well in advance of killing frost. They are intensified by periods of sunny, warm days and cool nights, such as are common in eastern North America at that season to a very much greater degree than is true of northern Europe. Many native eastern North American trees and shrubs color brilliantly in fall. Few Europeans do. But climate is not the only factor involved. Inheritance plays a large part as to whether the foliage of particular kinds colors in fall. Planted side by side in any climate where they thrive the American sugar maple colors brilliantly, the Norway maple not at all. The tulip tree native to North America changes its garb to golden-yellow in fall whether growing in its homeland or in much less sunny and much cooler England. And the characteristic persists in the seedling offspring of such trees growing in foreign climes.

The chemistry of autumn coloration is concerned with the unequal rate at which senescence comes to different parts of the leaf. Pigments of the carotenoid series, persisting after the green chlorophyll is depleted and in some cases augmented by the presence of tannins, account for the yellowish to brilliant yellows characteristic of aspens, birches, ginkgos, and tulip trees. Red or purplish anthocyanins resulting from accumulations of sugars in the leaves due to photosynthesis persisting after their translocation from the leaves to other parts ceases are chiefly responsible for the dull reddish to brilliant reds and purples of many oaks, maples, and other sorts. The presence of tannins is also often of significance here as well.

The brilliance of autumn color differs considerably in any one region from year to year and often there are marked differences in the intensity of the color of individuals of the same species growing under similar circumstances. The only regions of the world where a large proportion of native trees and shrubs color magnificently in fall are eastern North America, temperate eastern Asia, and a very much smaller area in southern South America. All are predominantly regions of deciduous forest.

When selecting trees and shrubs for autumn color your choices will naturally be made from among kinds noted for fine displays. It may even be worthwhile to visit nurseries in fall and pick individuals that show the most intense hues. This is especially true of sorts propagated from seeds. Those raised from vegetative propagations have an inherited factor to color to the same degree as the mother plant. All propagations from one individual by cuttings, layers, grafts, and suchlike asexual means will under similar circumstances color identically.

When siting trees and shrubs for fall foliage display remember the finest results are had only in full sun. Early morning shade is unlikely to seriously diminish the effect, but full exposure from noon on or earlier is essential for the best effects. Ground that is well drained and dryish in fall tends to encourage better coloration than moist soil, but one must go carefully here because planting in places too dry for the optimum or at least acceptable needs of individual kinds can result in unsatisfactory growth and even in the foliage withering to brown instead of coloring as it should.

Red, or in some, red and yellow, is the predominant autumn color of the foliage of these: maples (*Acer circinatum, A. ginnala, A. mandshuricum, A. palmatum, A. rubrum, A. saccharum, A. spicatum, A. tataricum*), service berries (*Amelanchier grandiflora, A. laevis*), red chokeberry (*Aronia arbutifolia*), barberries (*Berberis,* many kinds), hornbeam (*Carpinus caroliniana*), dogwoods (*Cornus alba sibirica, C. florida, C. mas, C. officinalis*) smoke bushes (*Cotinus coggygria, C. obovatus*), hawthorns (*Crataegus crus-galli, C. lavallei, C. nitida, C. phaenopyrum*), *Enkianthus campanulatus, E. perulatus, Euonymus alatus, Fothergilla* (all kinds), *Franklinia,* sweet gum (*Liquidambar styraciflua*), sour gum (*Nyssa sylvatica*), sourwood (*Oxydendrum arboreum*), *Parrotia persica,* Virginia creeper (*Parthenocissus quinquefolia*), Boston-ivy (*Parthenocissus tricuspidata*), *Prunus maximowiczii, P. sargentii,* pears (*Pyrus calleryana, P. ussuriensis*), oaks (*Quercus borealis, Q. coccinea, Q. palustris, Q. rubra, Q. velutina*), azaleas (*Rhododendron calendulaceum, R. schlippenbachii, R. vaseyi*), sumacs (*Rhus aromatica, R. copallina, R. typhina*), roses (*Rosa rugosa, R. setigera, R. virginiana*), *Sassafras albidum,* mountain-ashes (*Sorbus americana, S. aucuparia, S. discolor*), *Spiraea prunifolia, Stewartia koreana,* blueberries (*Vaccinium,* several kinds), *Viburnum dentatum, V. lantana,* and *V. prunifolium.*

Wine-red to purplish tones are characteristic autumn colors of these: white ash (*Fraxinus americana*), *Forsythia viridissima,* oak-leaved hydrangea (*Hydrangea quercifolia*), *Stephanandra incisa,* and dockmackie (*Viburnum acerifolium*).

Yellow autumn foliage is characteristic of these: maples (*Acer pensylvanicum, A. platanoides, A. saccharinum*), *Actinidia arguta,* pawpaw (*Asimina triloba*), birches (*Betula,* most kinds), bittersweets (*Celastrus*), redbud (*Cercis canadensis*), yellow-wood (*Cladrastis lutea*), sweet pepperbush (*Clethra alternifolia*), *Ginkgo,* witch-hazels (*Hamamelis japonica, H. mollis, H. vernalis, H. virginiana*), larches (*Larix decidua, L. laricina*), spicebush (*Lindera benzoin*), aspens and poplars (*Populus alba, P. grandidentata, P. nigra italica, P. tremuloides*), *Prinsepia sinensis,* and golden-larch (*Pseudolarix amabilis*).

Bronzy-yellow to bronze to brown tones are typical of the autumn foliage of these: bottle brush buckeye (*Aesculus parviflora*), hickories (*Carya*), beeches (*Fagus grandifolia, F. sylvatica*), star magnolia (*Magnolia stellata*), and shingle oak (*Quercus imbricaria*).

AUTUMN-CROCUS See Colchicum.

AUTUMN SNOWFLAKE is *Leucojum autumnale.*

AUXINS. These include a group of hormones occurring naturally in plants that in minute quantities are involved in various physiological processes such as root formation, stem growth, suppression of lateral buds, and fruit development. The chief natural plant auxin is indole-3-acetic acid. Related synthetic substances including indolebutyric acid and naphthalene-acetic acid have similar auxin properties. These hormones are employed horticulturally to stimulate root development in cuttings. See Hormones.

AVALANCHE-LILY. See Erythronium.

AVENA (Av-èna)—Oat, Animated Oat. The common oat, one of the most important of the world's grains, is *Avena sativa.* Although sometimes cut and used in decorations, especially at harvest celebrations and Thanksgiving, it is not regarded as a horticultural plant. Close relatives, the animated oat, (*A. sterilis*) and the wild oat (*A. fatua*), are. The genus consists of ten to fifteen annual and biennial species of the grass family GRAMINEAE. The name is the ancient Latin one for oat. In addition to the common oat, a few other species are cultivated in a more limited way as food grains. An old garden practice, which may not entirely be without merit, was to make a slit in bases of cuttings and insert an oat seed in the incision before the cutting was planted. Hormones generated by the germinating seed conceivably could stimulate the cutting to root.

The stems of avenas are solitary or in tufts and usually erect. The leaves are flat and linear. The flower panicles are loose and have large, pendulous spikelets of two to six flowers. Except in some cultivated varieties, they have awns (bristles). The genus is native to temperate regions of the Old World and New World. The plant known in gardens as *A. candida* is *Helictotrichon sempervirens*.

The animated oat (*A. sterilis*) is a single-stemmed or tufted annual or biennial, of the Mediterranean region, with more or less erect stems up to 3 feet tall. The leaves may be 1 foot long by ½ inch wide and the flower panicles 1 foot long by 8 inches wide. The spikelets, 1½ to 1¾ inches long, have twisted awns 2 to 3 inches long. The wild oat (*A. fatua*) often passes in gardens as the animated oat. It differs chiefly in its spikelets and their awns being considerably shorter, the former not exceeding 1 inch, and the latter not more than 1¾ inches. This species, native of Europe and temperate Asia, is naturalized in North America. It is probably the progenitor of the cultivated oat *A. sativa*.

Garden and Landscape Uses and Cultivation. The ornamental oats may be grown in patches in flower beds and supply useful cutting material for use in fresh and dried arrangements. They grow satisfactorily in sun in ordinary garden soil. Seeds are sown in spring where the plants are to remain and the seedlings thinned to about 4 inches apart.

AVENS. See Geum. For mountain-avens see Dryas.

AVERRHOA (Aver-rhòa)—Carambola, Bilimbi. At first sight these evergreen trees seem far removed in relationship from the oxalises of window gardens and the pesky, yellow-flowered weed of the same genus that infests lawns and greenhouses, yet they are sisters under the skin or whatever equates with such in the plant world. All belong to the OXALIDACEAE, the wood sorrel family. As a matter of fact, *Oxalis* and *Averrhoa* are the only two genera of the family commonly cultivated.

Two tropical Asian species cultivated for their edible fruits constitute *Averrhoa*. Both have alternate, pinnate leaves, with odd numbers of alternate or somewhat opposite, toothless leaflets and tiny, fragrant flowers in short clusters. There are five sepals and petals, the latter white, red, or purple, and ten stamens five of which are longer than the remainder. The large furrowed or lobed fruits are fleshy and drooping. The name *Averrhoa* commemorates Averhoes, an Arabian philosopher, who in Spain translated the works of Aristotle into Arabic. He died in 1217.

The carambola (*A. carambola*) is 20 to 25 feet tall and erect and symmetrical and has a trunk usually branched low down. Its young shoots and leafstalks are hairy or nearly hairless. Each leaf, 6 to 10 inches long, has up to thirteen short-stalked, ovate to elliptic leaflets 2 to 4 inches long. An interesting feature is that the leaves, especially the young ones, are sensitive to

Averrhoa carambola

the touch in much the same way as those of the sensitive plant (*Mimosa pudica*), although not as markedly so. The pinkish, reddish, or white flowers, with ¼-inch-long petals, are in clusters in the leaf axils; only five of their ten stamens have anthers. The thin-skinned, yellow to orange, egg-shaped fruits, 3 to 4½ inches in length, have three to five prominent, pointed, longitudinal ridges so that in cross section they are deeply-star-shaped. Their acid to sweet juicy pulp contains a few small, slightly flattened, ovoid seeds. When ripe the fruits have a quince-like fragrance. This species is native of the Malayan region. Under favorable conditions it bears two or three crops of fruit a year.

The bilimbi or cucumber tree (*A. bilimbi*) is quite different. In the tropics it may attain a height of 50 feet or more, but does not exceed 25 feet in Florida. It has hairy shoots and leaves, the latter resembling those of sumac (*Rhus*), with twenty-five or more pointed, oblong-lanceolate leaflets 2 to 3½ inches long. The flowers are on short spurs on the older parts of the branches and trunk and have red-purple flowers, their stamens all furnished with anthers. The almost cylindrical, slightly-five-angled, greenish-yellow, gherkin-like fruits are 2 to 4 inches long and waxy and translucent when ripe. They are borne in drooping clusters and contain very sour juicy pulp and a few flattened seeds. This species, known only in cultivation, undoubtedly originated in India or Malaya.

Garden and Landscape Uses and Cultivation. The carambola and bilimbi, suitable for outdoors in essentially frost-free climates, are grown in southern Florida, southern California, and Hawaii. The carambola is the hardier. Although not without decorative value, the chief objective of growing them is their edible fruits. Those

of the carambola, of which there are sour and sweet varieties, are eaten raw and their juice is used in drinks. Their unripe fruits are made into jelly. Bilimbi fruits are used for conserves and pickles and are candied. Deep, fertile soil and a humid tropical climate is most agreeable to these trees. They are propagated by seeds and, superior forms, by budding.

AVIGNON BERRY is *Rhamnus infectoria*.

AVOCADO. Avocados or alligator-pears are the edible fruits of *Persea americana*, an evergreen tree of the laurel family LAURACEAE. They are cultivated in tropical and subtropical regions, in the continental United States in Florida and California, for their fruits and as ornamentals. Home-raised seedlings are frequently grown as houseplants.

Avocados are classified as three races with many varieties of each and hybrids between them. Those of the Guatemalan race survive, according to variety, temperatures down to 28 or 25°F. Their fruits are of medium size, with thickish, pebbled skins, which, when mature, are green or purple. Their oil content ranges from approximately twelve to over twenty-five percent. Avocados of the Mexican race are recognizable by the distinct odor of anise given off by their crushed shoots and foliage. This odor is absent in other kinds. Mexican avocados withstand temperatures as low as 24 to 20°F and have comparatively small, thin-skinned, green- or purple-skinned fruits with high oil contents. The West Indian race of avocados are more cold-sensitive. Temperatures below 30 to 28°F result in severe injury. Their fruits have thin, smooth, green or purple skins and oil contents in the range of four to seven percent. Cultivation of the West Indian race in the United States is practically confined to southern Florida. California plantings are almost exclusively of the Guatemalan race. This race is also extensively grown in Florida. The Mexican race, although hardiest, is least popular.

For their successful growth avocados need an open, sunny location and well-drained, but not dry soil. Deep, fertile earth is best. Routine management of established trees normally includes the application of a nitrogenous fertilizer yearly. In Florida a fertilizer supplying zinc or other trace elements may be needed. Consult a Cooperative Extension Agent or the State Agricultural Experiment Station about this. Avocado trees need little or no pruning.

Avocados are vigorous trees that spread widely and develop branches that often bend downward under their own weight. Depending upon the known vigor of the variety and with consideration of the fertility of the soil, allow 25 to 40 feet between individual trees. It is important that the tops of the trees are not shaded.

A young avocado tree in California

Flowers of avocado

For fruit production plant only named varieties known or believed to do well in your locality. Seedlings rarely bear abundant crops and their fruits are generally of inferior quality. Poor cropping is largely attributable to a complicated pattern in the sequence of production of male and female blooms. Commercial varieties, with the exception of 'Collison', are self-fertile and set fruits satisfactorily even when not interplanted with another variety.

of inferior varieties may be "top worked" by bark grafting onto them scions of superior ones. The grafts are coated with

grafting wax and enclosed in paper bags until union is complete. Cuttings may be rooted, but not very readily, under mist or in a greenhouse propagating bench. Seeds germinate readily but plants raised from them are mostly useful only as understocks for grafting or as ornamentals.

As houseplants young avocados are interesting and attractive. They are easily raised from seeds. All that is necessary is to remove the single large seed from the center of an avocado fruit and plant it, either vertically with its pointed end up or horizontally, in a well-drained, 4- or 5-inch pot containing a porous, fertile soil. The top of the seed may just show above the soil surface. In a temperature of 60 to 70°F or thereabouts, if the soil is kept moderately moist, but not constantly saturated, growth soon begins and a decorative, leafy plant develops that under favorable conditions will be attractive for several years.

Avocado fruit

Harvest the fruits by clipping. If they are pulled from the tree, wounds inviting to disease organisms result. Not until they are taken from the tree do the fruits soften to usable condition. If harvested at the correct time (a little experience is needed to recognize this especially with those green at maturity), softening will take place in a week or less at room temperature. The fruits store well for several weeks at temperatures between 42 and 50°F.

Propagation of choice varieties is by patch budding or by side grafting onto seedling understocks. In California, seedlings of the Mexican race are commonly employed. In Florida those of Guatemalan and West Indian sorts are used. Old trees

To raise a houseplant: (a) Plant an avocado seed in pot with top of seed just showing

(b) Seed sprouting

(c) The young seedling

(d) An older plant

Aubrieta deltoidea variety

Aucuba japonica (fruits)

Aucuba japonica variegata

Golden-yellow *Aurinia saxatilis* with blue grape-hyacinth and lavender *Phlox divaricata*

Azalea variety, in California

Azaleas, with palms, at the Huntington Botanical Gardens, San Marino, California

An effective planting of Kurume azaleas

Azalea (*Rhododendron obtusum* 'Hinodegiri')

Azalea (*Rhododendron kaempferi* variety)

Azalea (*Rhododendron japonicum* variety)

Azalea (*Rhododendron japonicum* hybrids)

Seeds may also be started into growth in water, but unless the young plants are transferred to soil within a few weeks or months they deteriorate. To start a seed in water, stand it, pointed end up, with its base in the neck of a jar containing water and, if available, a few pieces of charcoal. The water should just touch the bottom of the seed and should be kept at that level by replenishment when necessary. If the neck of the jar is so big that the seed slips into the container prevent this by sticking three stout toothpicks or similar slivers of wood horizontally into the sides of the seed, resting these on the rim of the jar.

Avocado plants grown in pots indoors prosper in sun or good light without direct sun, but not in poorly lighted locations. When they have filled their containers with healthy roots repot them into larger ones, preferably in spring. At other times of the year, well-rooted specimens benefit from being given dilute liquid fertilizer once or twice a month or a slow-release fertilizer at longer intervals. Watering should be done to assure that the soil will never become really dry nor remain soggy and waterlogged for long periods.

After a few years pot-grown avocado plants frequently develop spotted and blotched leaves and a general unhealthy appearance. It is scarcely worthwhile attempting to nurse such specimens back to health. It is easier and simpler to raise new plants from seeds.

Pests and Diseases. Besides the physiological deterioration discussed above that frequently affects avocados grown as houseplants, avocados are subject to other troubles. Among pests, mites, scale insects, and thrips are most prevalent. Diseases include a root rot that afflicts trees in poorly-drained and wet soils and verticillium wilt, most common in lands on which crops of the gourd and nightshade families have been grown. A virus disease called sun-blotch causes one side of the fruits to appear sunburned. Do not use scions from affected trees for budding or grafting.

AWL-SHAPED. This term is used to describe leaves and other plant parts that are narrow to slender, round or approximately so in section, and taper from their bases to pointed apexes.

AXE WEED is *Securigera securidaca.*

AXIL, AXILLARY. The angle that the upper side of a branch, leaf, vein, or flower stalk makes with the axis from which it arises is called an axil. The word is often used to describe the origin or location of growth and leaf buds, of spines, tufts of hair, glands, and other developments. If located in such an angle they are axillary.

AYLOSTERA (Aylos-tèra). Some botanists retain the species considered here in the related genus *Rebutia,* others treat them separately on the grounds that their flowers have bristly ovaries and their stamens and styles are joined to the perianth tube. They are charming plants with decidedly beautiful flowers. *Aylostera* consists of eight species of small cactuses of South America, belonging in the cactus family CACTACEAE. The name is from the Greek *aylos,* a tube, and *stereos,* rigid, and alludes to the flowers.

Native to high altitudes in Bolivia, *A. fiebrigii* has one or, when old, more plant bodies, at their largest about 3 inches high and 2½ inches across. They are approximately spherical or shortly cylindrical, with somewhat depressed tops. Their surfaces are covered with cone-shaped lumps (tubercles) arranged spirally in seventeen or eighteen rows and tipped with whitish areoles (pads from which spines originate). From each areole sprout twenty-five to forty bristly white spines, the two to five largest ¾ inch long and tipped with tan, the others about one-half as long. Brilliant orange-red flowers are plentifully produced in a ring around the plant body. They are 1¼ to 1½ inches long, have many spreading perianth segments (petals), white stamens, and a six-lobed, pale yellow stigma. Similar, but having eleven to thirteen rows of tubercles and commonly only about twelve ¼-inch-long spines from each areole, *A. deminuta* has deep orange-red blooms about 1¼ inches long, with pink stamens and an eight-lobed, white stigma. This kind is indigenous to Argentina. Similar, but with longer brown spines and bright orange-red blooms is *A. pseudodeminuta,* also of Argentina.

Aylostera deminuta

Three other attractive Argentinians are *A. pseudominuscula, A. spegazziniana,* and *A. spinosissima.* These are high altitude species. The first, *A. pseudominuscula,* has clusters of spherical to somewhat cylindrical, reddish-tinged, dark green plant bodies 1½ inches in diameter. Its brown-tipped, yellowish spines are less than ¼ inch long. The brilliant orange-red blooms, 1¼ inches in diameter, have white to yellowish sta-

mens and pistils. The clustered, cylindrical plant bodies of *A. spegazziniana* are up to 3 inches long by 2½ inches wide, each with fifteen to twenty-five rows of spiraled, rather irregularly spaced tubercles. Brown-woolly hairs sprout from each of these along with one to three dark brown central spines and twelve to fifteen translucent, dark-tipped, subsidiary ones. Approximately 1½ inches long by 1½ inches wide, the fiery red blooms have white stamens. Somewhat smaller, and forming cushions of many growths, *A. spinosissima* differs from the last in having bristly spines, the radial, subsidiary ones white, the central five or six ones yellowish with brown ends, from the areoles of its crowded tubercles. Its light red or orange-red flowers, about ¾ inch in diameter, have yellowish-green perianth tubes and white stamens and pistils.

Aylostera pseudominuscula

Larger than other sorts here considered is *A. kupperiana,* a native of Bolivia. Its depressed spherical plant bodies, 4 inches tall by nearly as wide, have about twenty rows of pointed tubercles and from each areole approximately the same number of pale brown to dark gray radial spines and three to four longer, dark-tipped central ones. The brilliant orange-red blooms are about 3½ inches across.

Garden and Landscape Uses and Cultivation. These are the same as for the great majority of small terrestrial cactuses and are explained under Cactuses.

AYO is *Tetrastigma harmandii.*

AZADIRACHTA (Azadir-áchta)—Neem Tree or Margosa Tree. Visitors to India and Ceylon are very likely to see the native neem or margosa tree (*Azadirachta indica* syn. *Melia azadirachta*). Although common throughout the drier parts of those countries and planted extensively for shade, it is little known in the Americas. Belonging to a genus of two species, the neem is a member of the mahogany family MELI-

ACEAE. Its generic name is adapted from its ancient Persian one, *azad-dazakht*.

Evergreen, or for a brief period each year deciduous, *A. indica* attains a height of about 50 feet and has pinnate leaves 6 inches to well over 1 foot long, with an equal or unequal number of leaflets. These number eight to eighteen. They are short-stalked, 1 inch to 4 inches long, ½ inch to 1½ inches wide, pointed, lopsidedly-lanceolate to sickle-shaped, and toothed. The leaves are crowded near the ends of the branches. Sweetly scented and in panicles from the leaf axils, the flowers are about ½ inch across and have five sepals and five white petals. The yellow fruits are elliptic to oblong, thinly-fleshed, and one-seeded. They are ½ to ¾ inch long.

The neem tree serves the people of the lands where it is common in many ways other than as an ornamental. Its durable wood is put to a variety of uses including the manufacture of furniture and agricultural implements, and in ship building. Because the tree is sacred its wood is also used for making religious articles. From this tree is obtained an antiseptic, bitter resin used in soaps, medicines, lotions, and toothpaste. Margosa oil, expressed from the seeds, is medicinal and is used to some extent as an illuminant. For the latter purpose it has the disadvantage of smoking excessively. Neem twigs are used as toothbrushes.

Garden and Landscape Uses and Cultivation. This is a decidedly tropical species adapted to fairly dryish conditions. It succeeds in a variety of soils and is usually propagated by seeds.

AZALEAMUM. This quite inappropriate name has been used commercially for a group of compact, bushy, hardy perennial chrysanthemums that produce a profusion of rather small blooms. They are not even remotely related to azaleas. The name is without botanical standing.

AZALEAS (Az-àlea). Wild-honeysuckle, Pinxterbloom, Rhodora. Botanically azaleas are rhododendrons, but because in gardens they are ordinarily considered separately they are so considered here. For a description of the genus and its history in cultivation see Rhododendron.

Until 1834, azaleas were by botanists segregated from rhododendrons on the basis that known kinds were deciduous and had flowers with five stamens. Such plants they named *Azalea*. The designation *Rhododendron* was reserved for evergreen shrubs the blooms of which had ten stamens. But exploration of parts of Asia that were previously little known botanically brought to light species intermediate in these characteristics and the distinction was abandoned. Azaleas were integrated with *Rhododendron* and are now a subgenus or series of that genus. There are still bot-

Azaleas have many uses: (a) Planted informally in light woodland

(b) In a corner of a formal garden

(c) Forced for indoor display

anists who believe that azaleas and rhododendrons should be separated and perhaps they eventually will be for botanical opinion is notoriously unstable. In the meantime, as one distinguished horticultural authority on azaleas writes "The amateur gardener won't care a hoot about all

this pother and will, we expect, ignore it." And so gardeners continue to call plants that *look like* azaleas azaleas, those that *look like* rhododendrons rhododendrons. And so shall we, with the single concession to botanical purity that in giving names the abbreviation R. (for *Rhododendron*) will be used instead of A. (which would be correct if *Azalea* were recognized as a genus).

Azaleas are deciduous and evergreen shrubs or in natural stands occasionally small trees from kinds about 6 inches tall to those that are 15 feet tall or taller. Typically they are from almost to more than as broad as high and are much-branched. Their undivided leaves range from tiny to quite large, but never as large as those of large-leaved rhododendrons.

The foliage of most azaleas is attractive, that of some, such as the royal azalea, very beautiful. The leaves of many kinds assume bright autumn colors. But the chief glory of azaleas is their flowers. These come in the widest possible range of hues and pure whites. There are creams, yellows from the palest to the deepest golden, brilliant oranges, scarlets, crimsons, and deep blood-reds. There are azaleas with lavender and those with purple and magenta blooms. Varieties with flowers blotched or spotted with colors other than the base one are not uncommon. There are kinds with hose-in-hose, semidouble, and double blooms. The flowers of some are fragrant. There are azaleas to suit every taste.

Kinds of azaleas are many. No less than approximately seventy species occur as natives of the northern hemisphere, in North America, Europe, and Asia. None is native south of the equator. North America is rich in species. But even more important horticulturally than natural species, although they, and especially the native Americans, include many splendid kinds, is the wealth of truly magnificent hybrids developed in the Orient, Europe, New Zealand, and in the twentieth century, especially in the United States. In the treatment that follows American species are presented first, then exotic species, and finally hybrids.

Azaleas indigenous to North America number seventeen species, all except the western azalea whose provenance is California and Oregon native within a region that extends from Newfoundland to Ontario, Florida, and Texas. All are deciduous. Chiefly these plants inhabit open woodlands and streamsides, less commonly swampy areas. All favor acid soils well endowed with organic matter. All exhibit variation, sometimes considerable, in such matters as habit or style of plant and flower color, so it behooves the discriminating planter to exercise some care to secure the best forms.

Color of bloom varies from species to species, and often within a species there is a very considerable range. In some cases, individual blooms display more than one hue. Broadly, these azaleas may be grouped as with kinds with red, orange-red, or yellow flowers, those with pink flowers, and those with blooms that are white or nearly white. The first assemblage comprises *R. austrinum, R. bakeri, R. calendulaceum, R. occidentale, R. prunifolium,* and *R. speciosum.* The pink-flowered group consists of *R. canadense* (here "pink" is stretched a little for the blooms are really rose-purple to lavender), *R. canescens, R. nudiflorum, R. roseum,* and *R. vaseyi.* White-flowered sorts are *R. alabamense, R. arborescens, R. atlanticum, R. oblongifolium,* and *R. serrulatum.* Here in alphabetical sequence of their botanical names are descriptions of the native azaleas of North America.

The Alabama azalea (**R. alabamense** syn. *Azalea atlantica*) 1½ to 3 feet tall and native of dry woodlands in Alabama, spreads by stolons, has elliptic, obovate, or obovate-oblong leaves 1½ to 2½ inches long, almost or quite hairless above, somewhat glaucous and with short hairs on their undersides. Produced at the same time as the leaves, the lemon-fragrant, white, or less commonly pink flowers have a yellow blotch and are 1½ to 2 inches wide. In clusters of six to ten, they have corolla tubes ¾ to 1 inch long, about one-half the length of the stamens. Unfortunately not hardy in the north, this is a very beautiful species.

Native chiefly along mountain streams from New York and Pennsylvania to Georgia and Alabama, **R. arborescens** is hardy at low elevations throughout most of New England. Up to 10 feet tall or rarely taller, this kind has hairless branchlets and obovate to elliptic or oblong-lanceolate, blunt or pointed leaves, 1½ to 3½ inches long, hairless except along their edges and on the midribs of their undersides. They color well in fall. Appearing later than the leaves, the deliciously fragrant, white or pinkish flowers in clusters of up to six are 1 inch long or a little longer, hairy on their insides, glandular-hairy outside, and have petals shorter than the corolla tubes. The stamens and usually hairless style are at least twice as long as the corolla tube. This needs damp soil, and to flower satisfactorily not too much shade.

The coast azalea (**R. atlanticum**), native from Delaware and southern Pennsylvania to South Carolina and hardy to southern New York, is unusual in that it spreads by stolons or runners at or immediately below ground level. Rarely exceeding 1½ feet in height, this kind has mostly obovate to oblong-ovate, often glaucous, grayish leaves, hairless except on the veins on their undersides, and 1¼ to 2½ inches long. In fall they color attractively. The rose-fragrant, white flowers, usually tinted with pink or purple and in clusters of up to ten are about 1½ inches wide, come before the leaves and much earlier than those of somewhat similar *R. viscosum.* Their outsides are glandular-hairy. The stamens and style are much protruded. The coast azalea, one of the most attractive American species, propagates readily from cuttings.

The Florida azalea (**R. austrinum** syn. *Azalea austrina*) inhabits river banks from Georgia to Florida and Alabama and is hardy about as far north as Philadelphia. Up to about 10 feet in height, it has elliptic to obovate or oblong leaves with both surfaces finely-hairy. Appearing before or with the leaves, the smallish, fragrant, yellow to orange blooms, frequently with a few purplish stripes on their outsides, have corollas with cylindrical tubes longer than the lobes (petals). Cuttings of this azalea are fairly easy to root.

The Cumberland azalea (**R. bakeri** syn. *R. cumberlandense*) is very like the flame azalea and has been treated by some authorities as a variety of that species. Native to oak woods on the Cumberland plateau and in the mountains of West Virginia and Kentucky, Tennessee, North Carolina, and Georgia, it is hardy in southern New England. It differs from *R. calendulaceum* chiefly in flowering some three weeks later, after its foliage is well developed. Mostly the flowers are red or orange, but yellow-flowered forms also occur.

The flame azalea (**R. calendulaceum** syn. *Azalea calendulacea*), most splendid of American azaleas and one of the parent species of the Ghent and Exbury hybrids, is native from Pennsylvania to Ohio, Georgia, and Kentucky. Hardy in southern New England, it equals in beauty the finest hybrids. From 5 to 10 or rarely 15 feet tall, it has broad-elliptic to elliptic-oblong or obovate-oblong, pointed leaves 1½ to 3½ inches long, when young finely-hairy on their upper surfaces, more densely so on their undersides. Appearing soon after the leaves in clusters of mostly five to seven, the very showy blooms are yellow to brilliant orange or scarlet or sometimes salmon-pink with an orange blotch on the upper corolla lobe. Their outsides are glandular-hairy. Their corollas have tubes about as long as their lobes (petals). The stamens, longer than the petals and style, protrude conspicuously from the mouth of the corolla.

Rhododendron (Azalea) calendulaceum

Rhodora (**R. canadense** syn. *Rhodora canadensis*) occurs as a wildling in moist woodlands and swamps and along river banks from Newfoundland and Labrador to New York and Pennsylvania. Much-branched and up to 3 feet tall, this kind blooms well before its foliage appears. The dull, bluish leaves are elliptic to oblongish, ¾ inch to 2 inches long or occasionally slightly longer. They have rolled-back, hair-fringed mar-

Rhododendron (Azalea) arborescens

Rhododendron (Azalea) periclymenoides

Rhododendron (Azalea) canadense

Rhododendron (Azalea) periclymenoides

gins, and usually hairy mid-veins. The rose-purple to lavender flowers, in clusters of three to seven, are ½ to ¾ inch long and distinctly two-lipped. The upper lip has three short lobes, the lower two much deeper, narrow ones. There are ten stamens as long as the corolla and a slightly longer style. The flowers of *R. c. albiflorum* are white.

The Florida pinxter (*R. canescens* syn. *Azalea canescens*), ranging as a wildling along stream banks at low altitudes from North Carolina to Tennessee, Florida, Texas, and Arkansas, is hardy into southern New England. From 10 to 15 feet tall or taller, this, the southern counterpart of *R. nudiflorum*, is generally less beautiful than that, having flowers of an off-white or hoar-pink color. Variety *R. c. candidum*, with pure white flowers, is superior.

The Oconee azalea (*R. flammeum* syn. *R. speciosum*), native to sand hills and woodlands from Georgia to South Carolina, is hardy in sheltered locations about as far north as Philadelphia. From 2 to 6 feet tall, it has elliptic to obovate or oblong leaves, with bristly hairs on their upper surfaces and undersides softly-hairy to nearly hairless. Expanding with the foliage, the excellent scarlet to bright or dark red flowers, each with a yellow blotch and 1½ to 2 inches across, have slender corolla tubes ¾ to 1 inch in length and longer than the lobes (petals), finely-hairy, but not glandular on their outsides. The stamens and slightly longer style are much protruded.

Native from Arkansas and Oklahoma to Texas, *R. oblongifolium* (syn. *Azalea oblongifolia*) is very like *R. viscosum*, but blooms earlier. Of secondary horticultural importance, this inhabitant of stream banks and sandy woodlands is 5 to 6 feet tall and has white flowers about 1¼ inches in diameter.

The western azalea (*R. occidentale* syn. *Azalea occidentalis*) inhabits stream banks and other moist soils from California to Oregon. Rather loosely branched and 3 to 10 feet tall or occasionally taller, it has thinnish, elliptic to oblong-lanceolate leaves 1¼ to 3¼ inches long with sometimes scattered hairs and with stiff hairs along their margins. They color well in fall. The deliciously-scented flowers, in clusters of six to twelve or fewer and pinkish or white, usually have a yellow blotch on the upper petal. They expand with or later than the leaves. Funnel-shaped, and 1½ to 2 inches long, they have five protruding stamens. This does not prosper in eastern North America. It has been much used in hybridizing.

The pinxterbloom or wild-honeysuckle (*R. periclymenoides* syns. *R. nudiflorum*, *Azalea nudiflora*), native in dry woodlands from Massachusetts to Ohio and North Carolina, 3 to 6 feet or occasionally 9 feet tall, bears well in advance of its foliage cloyingly sweetly fragrant blooms. Its pointed leaves, elliptic to obovate to oblong-obovate, and hairless except along their margins and a few bristly hairs along the midrib, are 1¼ to 3½ inches long. Typ-

ically pale pink or white, but sometimes purple or plum-red, the funnel-shaped flowers in clusters of six to twelve are about 1½ inches wide and have corolla lobes (petals) shorter than the corolla tube, which is hairy outside and in. The long-protruding stamens are shorter than the style. Much variation in quality of bloom exists between individuals.

The plum-leaf azalea (*R. prunifolium* syn. *Azalea prunifolia*) is a late-blooming native of moist woodlands and along streams from Georgia to Alabama. Up to 10 feet tall, it has elliptic to oblong, pointed leaves 1½ to 4½ inches long. In clusters of four or five the apricot- to orange-red or red flowers, 1½ to 2 inches wide and sometimes sparingly hairy on their outsides, have much protruding stamens and a longer style. Not reliably hardy north of Philadelphia, Pennsylvania, this species roots more easily from cuttings than any other kind with red to orange blooms.

Native on hilltops and mountains from New Hampshire and Quebec to Illinois, Virginia, and Missouri, *R. roseum* (syns. *R. prinophyllum, Azalea rosea*) closely resembles *R. periclymenoides* from which it is distinguished by the undersides of its leaves being densely-hairy and its clear rose-pink flowers being glandular on the outsides of their corollas and having a spicy, clovelike fragrance. This kind has proven difficult to propagate from cuttings.

The southern swamp azalea (**R. serrulatum** syn. *Azalea serrulata*), native from Georgia to Florida and Louisiana and not reliably hardy in the north, is a close ally of *R. viscosum* from which it differs most obviously in having red-brown twigs and toothed leaves. Under favorable conditions it attains heights of 12 to 20 feet, but its white to creamy-white flowers, which come late in the azalea season, are comparatively small.

The pinkshell azalea (**R. vaseyi** syn. *Azalea vaseyi*), a native of the Blue Ridge mountains in North Carolina, and a botanical ally of the rhodora, is hardy throughout most of New England. One of the most attractive American azaleas, this delights with its light pink flowers in spring, its colorful light red foliage in fall. From 5 to 15 feet in height, it has pointed, elliptic to elliptic-oblong leaves 2 to 4½ inches long, fringed with hairs along their margins and mid-veins. In fall they change to bronzy-red. Appearing before the leaves in clusters of five to eight, the two-lipped flowers, 1 inch to 1¼ inches long and spotted with orange on their upper lips, have mostly seven, sometimes fewer stamens, the longest longer than the corolla, and a

longer style. The flowers of *R. v. album* are white as are those of the excellent horticultural variety 'White Find'.

The swamp azalea or swamp-honeysuckle (**R. viscosum** syn. *Azalea viscosa*) inhabits swamps from Maine to South Carolina. Up to 10 or less often 15 feet tall and the latest native American azalea to bloom, this kind spreads by stolons. It has ovate to elliptic-ovate or oblong-oblanceolate leaves ¾ inch to 2¼ inches long, hairless except for the midrib on the under surface and sometimes with a few bristly hairs on the upper surface. The clove-scented flow-

Rhododendron (Azalea) vaseyi

Rhododendron (Azalea) viscosum

ers, which expand after the foliage is fully developed, are in loose clusters of four to nine. They have white or pink-tinged corollas with slender tubes ¾ to 1 inch long, glandular-hairy on their outsides. The corolla lobes (petals) are about two-thirds as long as the tube and nearly as long as the protruding stamens. The latter are exceeded in length by the style.

Exotic species, azaleas not native to North America, include several that have served as important parents in the development of hybrid groups as well as others. The majority are natives of eastern Asia, but *R. luteum* is indigenous to eastern Europe and the Caucasus. There are deciduous, semievergreen, and evergreen sorts, kinds hardy in the north, and others satisfactory only in less severe climates.

The following, in alphabetical sequence, are the exotic species of the *Azalea* subgenus of *Rhododendron* most commonly cultivated with, in addition, two species not belonging in that group, but because they have the aspect of azaleas generally considered as such by gardeners. These are *R. dauricum* and *R. mucronulatum*, the only members of the *Dauricum* series of *Rhododendron*, which in many ways are intermediates between the subgenus *Azalea* and *Rhododendron* in its more restricted sense.

R. albrechtii (syn. *Azalea albrechtii*) is a beautiful deciduous Japanese mountain species 3 to 4½ feet tall, or sometimes taller, and hardy in southern New England. Its thinnish leaves, which turn yellow in fall, are in circles of about five at the branch ends. They are obovate to oblanceolate, more or less pointed, and 1½ to 4 inches long. Their upper sides are sparingly-hairy, their undersides gray-hairy. In groups of five or fewer, the 2-inch-wide flowers, which appear before or with the leaves, have ten stamens of varying lengths the longest equaling the corolla, are shallowly-bell-shaped. They are red to rose-red without a trace of objectionable purple.

R. dauricum (syn. *Azalea daurica*) is native from Japan, Korea, and China to the Altai mountains and hardy through most

Rhododendron (Azalea) vaseyi

of New England. Very much resembling *R. mucronulatum*, by some botanists considered a variety of *R. dauricum*, but as an ornamental inferior to the latter, it differs chiefly in being more compact and twiggy, its smaller leaves, up to 1¼ inches long, being blunt and with short, sharp tips instead of pointed. Typically they are deciduous, but in variety *R. d. sempervirens*, are more or less evergreen. Despite its azalea-like aspect, this very early bloomer does not belong in the subgenus *Azalea*. The hybrid group known as "P.J.M. hybrids" resulted from crossing *R. d. sempervirens* with *R. carolinianum*. These are evergreens.

R. indicum (syns. *Azalea indica, A. macrantha*) must not be confused with the hybrid Indian azaleas grown in greenhouses or with the plant grown as *Azalea indica alba* (really a variety of *R. mucronatum*) in the south. Native of Japan and semievergreen, *R. indicum* is hardy about as far north as New York City. With a variable kind of dense growth, it is 4 to 6 feet tall, and has elliptic-lanceolate to oblanceolate or lan-

ceolate, sparingly-hairy, slightly-toothed leaves ¾ inch to 1½ inches long, slightly glossy and dark green above, paler on their undersides. In pairs or solitary, the broad-funnel-shaped flowers 2 to 3 inches in diameter are bright red to scarlet and have five stamens about as long as the corolla. Much dwarfer *R. i. balsaminaeflorum* has leaves up to 1 inch long and double salmon-red blooms. Other varieties include 'Jean Haerens', with double rose-carmine flowers; 'Paul Schame', the blooms of which are double and salmon-pink; 'Lambertus C. Bobbink', with bright red flowers; and 'Niobe', which has big double white blooms.

R. japonicum (syn. *Azalea japonica*), native of Japan and hardy in southern New England, is highly decorative and generally well adapted for cultivation in eastern North America. Up to about 6 feet tall and deciduous, this kind has obovate to obovate-oblong, hair-fringed leaves 1½ to 4 inches long. Its fragrant, funnel-shaped flowers in clusters of six to twelve gener-

ally appear before the foliage. They are 2 inches wide or a little wider, orange-red to salmon-red or brick-red, and have stamens shorter than their corollas. The blooms of *R. j. aureum* are yellow.

R. kaempferi (syns. *R. obtusum kaempferi, Azalea kaempferi*) is a Japanese species of special beauty. Called the torch azalea, it is a much-branched deciduous or in mild climates semievergreen shrub 3 to 6 feet tall or sometimes taller. It has thinnish, elliptic to oblong or broadly-ovate leaves 1 inch to 2¼ inches long, bristly-hairy on both surfaces and with rust-colored hairs on the stalks and midribs. In fall they become orange and scarlet. Two to four together or less often solitary, and opening before or with the coming of the new leaves, the shallowly-bell-shaped, brilliant orange-red to brick-red to salmon-apricot or less commonly biscuit-white or purple flowers are borne in great profusion.

Rhododendron (Azalea) kaempferi

R. luteum (syns. *R. flavum, Azalea pontica*), a deciduous sort, is native to eastern Europe and the Caucasus. It was a prominent parent of the Ghent hybrids. Usually 4 to 8 feet tall, but sometimes taller, it has oblong to oblong-lanceolate leaves 2 to 4 inches long that in fall change to bright shades of orange, crimson, and purple. The bright yellow, funnel-shaped, richly-fragrant flowers 1½ to 2 inches across and sticky on their outsides, are in rounded clusters of seven to twelve. Not reliably top-hardy north of Philadelphia, but root-hardy in colder climates, this sort was formerly much used as an understock upon which to graft Ghent and Mollis hybrids.

R. mucronatum (syns. *R. ledifolium, Azalea mucronata, A. ledifolia*), called snow azalea, is frequently misnamed *A. indica alba*. Of Japanese origin, but unknown in the wild, it is probably of hybrid ancestry. Hardy in southern New England, this lovely early-bloomer occasionally but rarely exceeds 6 feet in height and often is lower and com-

Rhododendron (Azalea) 'Lambertus C. Bobbink'

Rhododendron (Azalea) kaempferi

thystinum, with pale lilac-purple blooms, *R. m. narcissiflorum*, with double white flowers, and *R. m. plenum*, with double rose-purple blooms.

R. mucronulatum (syns. *R. dauricum mucronulatum*, *Azalea mucronulata*), of Japan, Korea, and China, belies its appearance by not belonging to the subgenus *Azalea* of rhododendron even though it is deciduous. From 4 to 6 feet tall, it blooms early, before or with forsythias, and well before the appearance of its foliage. The thin, elliptic-lanceolate to lanceolate, pointed, loosely-scaly leaves are 1¼ to 3 inches long and in fall change to yellow and bronzy-red. The light to intensely rosy-purple

Rhododendron (Azalea) mucronulatum

pact. It is evergreen or partially so. The leaves produced early in the season are elliptic-lanceolate, 1¼ to 2¼ inches long, and clothed on both surfaces with grayish to reddish hairs. Leaves that develop later are smaller, blunt-oblong-lanceolate, and of firmer texture. Solitary or in twos or

Rhododendron (Azalea) luteum

threes, the freely-produced, fragrant, white flowers have broad-funnel-shaped corollas about 2 inches in diameter and usually ten, or sometimes eight or nine, stamens. Variety *R. m.* 'Sekidera' has 3-inch-wide flowers flushed, blotched, or striped with violet-red. Other varieties are *R. m. ame-*

Rhododendron (Azalea) mucronatum 'Sekidera'

Rhododendron (Azalea) mucronulatum

Rhododendron (Azalea) obtusum

of New York City. Low, creeping, and generally prostrate, it forms mats up to 1 foot or more in diameter. Its leaves, oblanceolate, elliptic, or elliptic-ovate, are up to 1 inch long. The broadly-funnel-shaped, brick-red flowers, 1½ inches in diameter, with ten stamens, are in clusters of two or three. The most commonly cultivated variety, 'Mariko' is possibly not the true species, but a hybrid that originated in Japan.

R. obtusum (syn. *Azalea obtusa*) is believed by Japanese botanists to be of hybrid origin, with *R. kaempferi* and several other species involved in its parentage. It is a parent of many Kurume azaleas. Much-branched and partially evergreen, this kind forms a dense mound up to about 3 feet high, or it is sometimes prostrate. Its leaves, from less than ½ to 1 inch long, are elliptic to elliptic-lanceolate or obovate, dark green and lustrous on their upper surfaces, paler beneath. Except on the midribs of their undersides they are hairless. The flowers, solitary, in twos, or in threes, are funnel-shaped, 1 inch to 1½ inches wide, and orange-red to bright red. They have five stamens. Variety *R. o. album* has white blooms. Those of *R. o. amoenum* are intensely brilliant magenta-purple and have two corollas, one inside the other. Much like the last, *R. o.* 'Hinodegiri' has flowers of brilliant madder-red. These last two varieties are somewhat hardier than the typical kind, which in sheltered locations persists about as far north as New York City.

blooms in tight clusters of six or fewer are funnel- to bell-shaped and up to 1½ inches in diameter. Variety 'Cornell Pink' is particularly fine because its flowers are clear pink without suspicion of purple. Other pink-flowered variants have been identified as *R. m. roseum*. This species and its variety are hardy throughout most of New England. Intermediate hybrids between this and closely related *R. dauricum* are common.

R. nakaharai, endemic to Taiwan and rare in cultivation, is hardy in the vicinity

R. pentaphyllum of Japan is hardy in southern New England. Handsome in bloom and up to 10 feet or sometimes 20 feet tall, this blooms very early and has deciduous foliage that turns orange to crimson in fall. Mostly in circles of five at the branch ends, the pointed leaves are elliptic to elliptic-lanceolate, finely-toothed, and hairless except along the margins and the midrib. Appearing before the foliage, the shallowly-bell-shaped, clear rose-pink flowers in pairs or solitary are nearly or quite 2 inches wide.

R. quinquefolium (syn. *Azalea quinquefolia*), of mountains in Japan and hardy in southern New England, is 4 to 20 feet tall and has thin ovate to ovate-elliptic or rhombic-elliptic, blunt, deciduous leaves in clusters of five at the twig ends. They have short, whitish hairs especially on the midribs of both surfaces. The flowers, solitary, in twos, or in threes and 1¾ inches across, are white except for a few green spots at their bases. They have ten stamens, hairy toward their bases. From closely related *R. pentaphyllum* this is distinguishable by the color of its blooms.

R. reticulatum (syn. *Azalea reticulata*) is a deciduous native of mountains in Japan and hardy in southern New England. It has broadly-ovate to rhombic-ovate leaves 1½ to 3½ inches long, pointed, and more or less hairy especially on the stalks and midribs. Solitary or in pairs, the rose-purple to magenta, bell-shaped flowers are up to 1½ inches in diameter and have ten or perhaps sometimes fewer hairless stamens and a hairless style. The blooms of *R. r. albiflorum* are white.

R. schlippenbachii (syn. *Azalea schlippenbachii*), called royal azalea, is one of the glories of the azalea tribe. Native to Korea and Manchuria, this kind is hardy throughout most of New England. From 9 to 15 feet tall and deciduous, it has short-stalked, obovate to broad-obovate leaves 2 to 4 inches long, usually in clusters of five at the twig ends. When mature they are hairless except on the veins of their undersides. In fall they change to yellow,

Rhododendron (Azalea) nakaharai

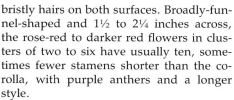

Rhododendron (Azalea) schlippenbachii

bristly hairs on both surfaces. Broadly-funnel-shaped and 1½ to 2¼ inches across, the rose-red to darker red flowers in clusters of two to six have usually ten, sometimes fewer stamens shorter than the corolla, with purple anthers and a longer style.

R. tsusiophyllum (syns. *R. tanakae, R. tsusiophyllum tanakae*) is a rare, but not showy native of mountains in Japan. Prostrate or nearly so and much-branched, it is up to 1½ feet tall and has rather thick, nearly stalkless, elliptic to narrow-elliptic leaves less than ½ inch long. Solitary or in twos or threes, the shallowly four- or five-lobed flowers ⅓ inch or a little more in diameter are white, with five stamens. This kind is hardy in the vicinity of New York City.

Rhododendron (Azalea) tsusiophyllum

Handsome foliage of *Rhododendron (Azalea) schlippenbachii*

tivated in milder climates and in greenhouses in many varieties. Evergreen or partially so and up to 10 feet tall, it has pointed, dull green, elliptic-ovate to lanceolate leaves ¾ inch to 2 inches long with

orange, and crimson. The slightly-fragrant, light pink to rose-pink flowers in clusters of three to six expand with the leaves. They are shallowly-funnel-shaped, 2¼ to 3¼ inches wide, with ten stamens of unequal lengths, the longest as long as the corolla. A rare, white-flowered variant is in cultivation.

R. simsii, of China and Taiwan, in gardens frequently misnamed *R. indicum*, is one parent of the Indian hybrid group of azaleas. Not hardy in the north, it is cul-

Rhododendron (Azalea) simsii

Rhododendron (Azalea) yedoense

R. yedoense, the Yodogawa azalea and long cultivated in Japan, is probably a horticultural selection of the natural species *R. poukhanense* (syns. *R. y. poukhanense, Azalea poukhanense*) native to Japan and Korea. Hardy in southern New England the Yodogawa azalea is deciduous with double purple flowers. The species of which it presumably is a variety *R. poukhanense,* a native of Japan and Korea, is somewhat hardier than the Yodogawa azalea. Up to 6 feet tall, it is compact and more or less spreading. It has oblanceolate to ovate-lanceolate or lanceolate, deciduous or semideciduous leaves up to 3½ inches long that in fall become orange or crimson. Expanding before or with the leaves and in clusters of two or more, its slightly-fragrant, broadly-funnel-shaped, lilac-rose to lilac-purple flowers are 2 inches wide, with ten stamens. They expand before or with the leaves.

Hybrid azaleas are available in immense variety and constitute the greater proportion of these shrubs in landscape plantings and nursery offerings. There are deciduous and evergreen kinds, sorts that are hardy, others that are suitable only for mild climates and greenhouses. They are grouped according to the parental species from which they have been derived. In aspect the varieties in each group have a general resemblance, but may differ consid-

erably in size and color of blooms and to some extent in style of plant, time of flowering, and other details. The great majority are clones, horticultural varieties that can be perpetuated only by cuttings, grafting, or other means of vegetative propagation. Very few, such as certain mollis hybrids, breed surprisingly true from seeds and are reproduced that way. We shall now review in alphabetical sequence the most important hybrid groups. Varieties within the groups will not be listed. In most cases they are very numerous and it seems better that prospective growers should make their choices after studying catalogs of specialist nurseries or, better still, after visiting collections in botanical gardens, display gardens, nurseries, and similar places during the blooming season.

Gable hybrids were developed by Joseph B. Gable of Stewartstown, Pennsylvania. Except near the northernmost limits of their hardiness in southern New England, they are evergreen. First distributed in 1927, their heritage is chiefly *R. kaempferi* hybridized with *R. poukhanense,* but other species are involved. These useful plants, much esteemed in the Northeast and Midwest, vary considerably in habit of growth according to variety and come in a goodly range of flower colors and forms. Their hues chiefly are from orange-red to purple and white. The flowers are 1½ to 2¼

inches wide, mostly single, in a few varieties hose-in-hose, semidouble, or double.

Ghent hybrids, or as they are known in Holland, pontica azaleas, are a complex race, the outcome of crosses made in Belgium in the 1820s between *R. calendulaceum* and *R. periclymenoides* and in England between *R. calendulaceum* and *R. viscosum* and between *R. viscosum* and *R. luteum.* Other crosses made about that period were between *R. viscosum* and possibly *R. molle.* Thus the genes of American species were combined with those of a western Asian and probably a Chinese one to give rise by subsequent crossing and recrossing to the grand race called Ghent azaleas.

Deciduous, tall, erect, and very hardy, Ghent azaleas (**R. gandavense**) usually have fragrant flowers 1½ to 2¼ inches across, with long corolla tubes. They come in single- and double-flowered varieties. Their colors range from white to pale yellow to violet-red often blotched or shaded with another hue. There are many varieties.

Rhododendron (Azalea) gandavense variety

Rhododendron (Azalea) gandavense variety

Glenn Dale hybrids, first made available to gardeners in 1940, exist in a vast number of varieties, far too many some authorities believe. They are of widely diverse growth habits, flower forms, colors, and other characteristics. Some have blooms 4½ inches across. These fine plants were bred by B. Y. Morrison, a famous horticulturist of the U.S. Department of Agriculture. His objectives, largely achieved, were to create a class of evergreen azaleas as spectacular and varied as the Southern Indian azaleas as far as size and floral colors go, but hardy enough to be reliable in the Middle Atlantic States, and to bloom in the "off" season between the flowering of early and late flowering varieties then available in that region. As parents Morrison employed a great many species and hybrids including the southern Indian varieties *R. kaempferi*, *R. mucronatum*, and *R. yedoense*. Some of the Glenn Dale hybrids have proved hardy enough to survive in climates colder than those for which they were developed, but the majority cannot be relied upon much north of Washington, D.C. A few survive in sheltered locations in Boston, Massachusetts.

Rhododendron (Azalea) Glenn Dale hybrid 'Witchery'

Indian hybrid azaleas and indicas are singularly inappropriate names for a race of large-flowered, evergreen, chiefly hybrid kinds that came into being before 1860 and were developed chiefly in Belgium and England, to a lesser extent in France and Germany, and somewhat later in the southern United States. They are neither Indian nor derived from species native to India, nor did *R. indicum*, itself native of Japan, play more than a minor part in their ancestry. Their chief progenitors were *R. mucronatum*, *R. pulchrum*, and *R. simsii*.

This group is subdivided into the Belgian Indian hybrids and the southern Indian hybrids or indicas. The former, developed primarily for greenhouse forcing, have mostly double or semidouble, often frilled blooms of great loveliness. They are not hardy in the north and not, it is

thought, in the south where exposed to freezing, but full information about all varieties is not available and some may prove more resistant to cold than generally supposed. Flower colors include white, pink, red, and various combinations. The blooms are of exquisite forms.

Rhododendron (Azalea) Belgian Indian hybrid

Southern Indian azaleas or indicas are survivors and offsprings of survivors of early Belgian Indian hybrids brought to the United States from the middle of the nineteenth century on. They were probably first taken to the south by David Landreth, a Philadelphia seedsman or by Prosper Julius Alphonse, a nurseryman of Plainfield, New Jersey, who later established Fruitland Nurseries in Augusta, Georgia.

There are two chief groups of southern Indian azaleas. Some are tall, loosely-branched, relatively fast-growing, and generally early to flower. Others are squatter, low to medium in height, slower-growing, and mostly later-flowering. The blooms are 2 to 3½ inches in diameter. They come in a considerable variety of colors. Those of most varieties are single. There are a few doubles. But, not all Indian azaleas are hybrids. Some of those grown outdoors in the south are just varieties of *R. mucronatum*, *R. simsii*, and *R. pulchrum*. It is important to distinguish between these azaleas and the Japanese species *R. indicum*, which has had little if any part in the parentage of the Indian hybrids.

Kaempferi or Malvatica hybrids originated in Holland about the time of World War I and have been added to since. Their genetic inheritance results from hybridizing *R. kaempferi* with a horticultural selection with big purple flowers named 'Malvatica', itself probably a hybrid, possibly between Kurume azalea 'Hinodegiri' and *R. mucronatum*. Kaempferi hybrids have upright branches and attain heights of 8 to 9 feet. The blooms, 1½ to 2½ inches across, are mostly single, sometimes hose-

in-hose. They come in colors from warm orange-reds to purple as well as white. Azaleas of this group are superior in hardiness to most of the Kurume hybrids, but cannot be relied upon in climates much colder than that of southern New England.

Knap Hill hybrids include a great array of varieties made available to gardeners after World War II, but based on a breeding program that began in England as long ago as 1870. The parental stocks were *R. molle*, *R. arborescens*, and reportedly, although some authorities doubt this, *R. calendulaceum*. Three breeders in England and one in New Zealand played the most prominent parts in raising Knap Hill hybrids, among them Lionel de Rothschild at his Exbury estate near Southampton, England. His introductions have been widely disseminated as Exbury hybrids.

Deciduous and showing obvious relationship to the Ghent and mollis groups, Knap Hill hybrids are mostly erect, but some varieties are low and spreading. They have blooms 2 to 3 inches wide with long, slender corolla tubes and shallow faces. The clusters, rounded or flattish and of eighteen to thirty flowers, are remarkable for their large size. Mostly they are displayed in late midseason. Flower colors include almost white, cream, yellow, orange, pink, rose-pink, and vivid red. Some kinds are fragrant. These azaleas are about as hardy as the mollis hybrids.

Mollis hybrids (**R. kosteranum**) are taxonomically a formidably complex race. It is probable that some few varieties commonly assigned here are variants of Japanese *R. japonicum* without hybrid admixture of other species. Be that as it may, the group is considered in the main to represent hybrids between *R. japonicum* and *R. molle*, with in some cases, infusions of genes from the eastern American swamp azalea. Development of the mollis hybrids began in Holland before 1873 with the selection and naming of varieties of *R. japonicum*. By the 1880s these had been hybridized in Belgium with *R. molle* to begin the hybrid swarm we now have. Subsequent breeding and selection, chiefly in Holland, has resulted in numerous beautiful varieties.

Somewhat less hardy than Ghent hybrids, mollis hybrids are mostly late midseason bloomers. They are deciduous, erect, and rather stiffly-branched. Their flowers, about 2½ inches across and always single, are on average bigger than those of Ghents and are shallower, having shorter corolla tubes. They come in clusters of seven to thirteen, in a considerable and very lovely range of colors, notably lemon and deeper yellows, orange, rose-pink, red, and less commonly white. Characteristically they have a rather pleasing musky odor.

Kurume hybrids are among the best known azaleas. They were brought prominently to the attention of the Western

Rhododendron (Azalea) mollis hybrid

Rhododendron (Azalea) mollis hybrid

Rhododendron (Azalea) kurume hybrid

World as a result of being seen in great numbers in Japan in 1914 by "Chinese Wilson" (E. H. Wilson, famous plant explorer of the Arnold Arboretum of Harvard University). The following year they were exhibited for the first time outside Japan by a Japanese nurseryman who displayed a dozen varieties at the Panama-Pacific Exposition in San Francisco. These plants were purchased, propagated, and distributed by Domoto Brothers of California, who soon arranged for additional varieties to be imported from Japan. In 1917,

at E. H. Wilson's suggestion, John S. Ames of North Easton, Massachusetts imported plants from Japan. The next year Wilson visited Kurume for the first time and selected fifty varieties for dispatch to the Arnold Arboretum. These became known as Wilson's Fifty. Later additional importations were made by the U. S. Department of Agriculture. Many Kurume azaleas are known both by their Japanese names and English names, a cause for some confusion. Thus 'Hinodegiri' is 'Red Hussar', 'Ho-o' is 'Apple Blossom', and 'Kirin' is 'Daybreak'. The last has also been called 'Coral Bells' and 'Pink Beauty'. The need for inquiry to be initiated and discretion used before acquiring Kurume varieties on a name basis is indicated.

For more than a century before the introduction of the first Kurumes to the United States, Japanese nurserymen and gardeners of Kurume on the island of Kyushi had been selecting azaleas native to the sacred mountain Kirishima and elsewhere and hybridizing them to produce the Kurume hybrids. As early as 1906, the well-known Yokahama Nursery Company of Japan cataloged in their offerings in English Kurumes trained in umbrella fashion, first as *Azalea indicum*, later as *Azalea indicum* 'Kurume', and subsequently as *Azalea obtusum* 'Kurume'. Despite these early offerings there appears to be no record of Kurume azaleas making an appreciable impact on Western World gardeners before Wilson's 1914 trip to Japan or of having reached America or Europe before 1915.

Kurume hybrids are evergreens believed to have resulted from cross-breeding chiefly species native to Kirishima and two other mountains near Kogashima in southern Kyushu. The species are *R. kaempferi* and *R. kiusianum*. Another, possibly not a true species, named *R. obtusum* may also be involved.

In height Kurumes vary considerably according to variety, mostly from medium to tall. Characteristically they are much-branched, dense, and small-foliaged. Their flowers, produced in such profusion that they frequently completely hide the foliage, come in a range of hues from many shades of pink to scarlet, vivid magenta, purple, and white. Less commonly the blooms are flecked or variegated with a second color. From ½ inch to 1½ inches across, they are single or of the hose-in-hose form. As a group they are not hardy in the north, but a few including 'Hinodegiri' prosper in the vicinity of New York City.

Pericat hybrids, introduced to gardeners by their raiser, Alphonse Pericat of Collindale, Pennsylvania, in the early 1930s and later by others are of unrecorded ancestry. Possibly they are the result of crossing Belgian Indian hybrids with hybrid Kurumes. These would seem promising parents to a hybridizer seeking, as Pericat was, to de-

Rhododendron (Azalea) pericat hybrid 'Orchid'

velop superior plants for greenhouse forcing.

Many of their varieties among the most beautiful azaleas, the pericats have excellent growth habits and display freely their well-formed, beautifully-colored carmine to purple, single, hose-in-hose, and semi-double, often frilled blooms. The plants are densely-branched, mostly of medium height, but some are low and some taller. Most are of spreading habit, a few upright. Pericat azaleas are hardy outdoors at Washington, D.C. and in sheltered locations somewhat further north.

Other hybrid groups are cultivated to a lesser degree or in more restricted geographical areas. Among the better known are the Brook's hybrids, evergreens bred in California for resistance to hot weather, compactness, and large flowers. These are of diverse parentage, their ancestry involving southern Indian hybrids, Kurume hybrids, *R. mucronatum*, and others. Mossholder-Bristow (syn. Gold Cup) hybrids, raised in California from Belgian Indian and Rutherfordianum hybrids are evergreens intermediate between those groups and suitable for outdoors in mild climates and for forcing. Occidentale hybrids are deciduous azaleas produced in England and Holland at the end of the nineteenth century by crossing *R. occidentale* with mollis hybrids, and in the United States later by mating *R. occidentale* with *R. bakeri* and *R. prunifolium*. The American productions are also called Frisbie-Occidentale hybrids.

Rustica Flore-pleno hybrids (**R. mixtum**) are evergreens developed in Belgium near the end of the nineteenth century possibly as a result of crossing double-flowered Ghent azaleas with *R. japonicum*. They are tall, erect plants with double flowers 1¼ to 2¼ inches across that in color range from white tinged with pink or marked with yellow to pink, old rose, red, and yellow. Rutherfordianum hybrids are evergreen intermediates between their parents, Belgian Indian and Kurume hybrids. They were developed in the United States as greenhouse forcing azaleas. They are bushy plants mostly not exceeding 4 feet in height, but sometimes more, with good-looking foliage. Their flowers, often frilled, are 2 to 3 inches wide, single, hose-in-hose, semidouble or double, in white, pink, orange, and red, often blotched with hues different from the basic color. Satsuki hybrids (syn. Chugai hybrids) are Japanese developments of unrecorded parentage probably involving Belgian Indian hybrids. They are a handsome race of low evergreens adaptable for cultivation in pots and in mild climates outdoors. In Japan they are popular as bonsai. They are given to sporting and having flowers of different colors on the same plant. Typically the blooms are variegated and are combinations of white, pink, purple, and red. Their petals may be fringed or wavy. Some varieties are noted for having exceptionally large blooms.

Garden and Landscape Uses. Among the choicest and most admired of flowering shrubs, azaleas are greatly esteemed for outdoor landscaping. All kinds are easily forced into early bloom in greenhouses and some, especially certain hybrid groups, are important florists' pot plants, grown in vast numbers, for the Easter trade. Small-leaved sorts are favorites for training as bonsai.

As members of the heath family ERICA-CEAE, azaleas hate alkaline and saline soils. Although it is possible to grow them in limestone and alkali regions in specially prepared beds, this is an exercise for the enthusiast who simply *must* have azaleas rather than for the average gardener. It is always much easier and surer landscaping practice to depend upon plants suited to the soil than to attempt drastic changes there. The ground for azaleas should be mildly to quite strongly acid. A pH of from 6.5 to 5 or even 4.5 suits.

Partial shade such as comes from day-long filtered sunlight in open woodlands, or part-day shade from trees, cliffs, or buildings, with three or four hours' exposure to full sun daily, suits azaleas. If the soil is not deficient in moisture they can also be grown without shade. The plants then are lower, more compact, and often more floriferous. But for their best comfort and most graceful development some shade is desirable. Only then does the full beauty of the plants become apparent.

Informal and semiformal landscapes afford the finest opportunity for displaying azaleas. In open glades, at the fringes of woodlands, and along woodland paths they are superb. They can also be employed effectively in shrub beds, as backgrounds to flower borders, in foundation plantings, and in other ways. Except in Japanese and other strictly stylized gardens do not clip azaleas into formal shapes. Allowed to develop naturally they are so much more beautiful. Their loveliness is destroyed rather than accentuated by shearing.

Mixing and matching colors in azalea plantings calls for taste and skill. Probably no group of shrubs is more susceptible to being used to produce disastrous, screaming, polychromatic effects than this. Among the many kinds are those with flowers of magentas, purples, reds, oranges, and other hues that in juxtaposition bring shudders to the color-sensitive. Yet carefully selected and blended, these same azaleas can produce quite lovely effects.

Clashing colors among themselves are not all that are to be avoided. Other nearby colors must be evaluated. A particularly horrible, but by no means unusual use of azaleas is the placement of kinds with blooms of strident magenta and related hues in front of red brick houses. All in all, azaleas are at their best among greenery, that of deciduous trees and shrubs, of ferns, and of other leafy plants. Whites such as are supplied by dogwoods and spireas are always safe and the sensitive gardener will achieve other pleasing color combinations. Fortunately, correcting an occasional misjudgment is not too difficult because azaleas transplant satisfactorily even when in bloom. But it is better to avoid this. If in great doubt select and install the original planting at blooming time. In that way you will be sure of the color combinations you will have in future years.

Spacing azaleas calls for thought and decision. Many at maturity are large, wide bushes, but grow slowly and take many years to attain full size. If planted far enough apart to allow for mature development, the planting looks skimpy for many years. As alternatives there are two choices, to plant thickly enough to achieve agreeable effects early and to thin out and transplant the surplus when they begin to grow, or to follow the same spacing procedure and allow the plants to grow together without thinning. Whichever you decide upon at first, the latter plan will usually be followed. Experience shows that good intentions are rarely carried out. If they are, the transplanting must be done before the bushes crowd to such an extent that they are bare at their sides and bases and unshapely. But fairly, not unreasonably, crowded azaleas make good shows even though the full beauty of individual specimens is sacrificed.

Cultivation. Azaleas are mostly long-lived. In congenial environments they reward annually and dependably with magnificent floral displays for many decades. One environmental factor of great importance is the physical condition of the soil. If the ground is so compact that it does not permit the free passage of air it is quite unsuitable for azaleas. See that the earth is crumbly and contains abundant organic matter. Except for the few kinds that grow naturally in wet and swampy places, sub-surface drainage must be adequate to en-

Azalea trained as bonsai

sure that free-standing water (the water table) is not closer than about 3 feet from the surface. Azaleas appreciate moisture, but not constantly "wet feet." It is courting disaster to set them in basin-like holes not greatly bigger than the root balls in heavy, pasty, clay soils or where water will at times stand around their roots for long periods.

Initial preparation of the soil is important. Except where the ground is naturally suited to the needs of these shrubs, as in some woodland regions in eastern North America and elsewhere, attend to making it so in advance of planting. The ideal for which to strive is a satisfactorily-drained subsoil overlaid with at least 1 foot of friable (crumbly) topsoil containing a high proportion of organic matter and at least slightly acid.

If drainage problems exist correct these first. In many places deep spading or turning over and breaking up the soil in equivalent fashion by mechanical means plus mixing in large amounts of organic materials is all that is necessary. In extreme situations, where the water table is too close to the surface, the installation of land drains connected with a suitable outlet is the only solution.

Raise the organic content of soils not already high in this, which means most of those encountered by gardeners, by adding very generous amounts of compost, leaf mold, peat moss, or partially-decayed sawdust. Take care that this is mixed very thoroughly throughout the soil, that it is not left in lumps or clumps embedded in a less agreeable matrix.

Planting is best done from early fall to late spring, but not in the north in winter. In milder climates as long as the ground is not frozen winter transplanting is practicable. Do not move deciduous azaleas while they are in leaf. Evergreens can be transplanted successfully at any time except during hot, dry spells in summer and when the ground is frozen.

Balled and burlapped or container-grown specimens are usually preferred, but in small sizes, say two- or three-year-old plants, bare-root azaleas are entirely satisfactory. See to it that the roots are not allowed to dry. If there is any evidence that some drying has occurred in shipping soak the root ball or roots for fifteen minutes and allow them to drain before planting. If purchased plants have dried to the extent that on arrival the twigs show signs of shriveling reject the shipment.

Dig holes sensibly bigger than the root spread and of sufficient depth that, when installed, the newly-set specimens will be at the same depth, neither lower nor higher than they were previously. Fork into the bottoms of the holes additional organic material. Tread the bottom firm, then set the plant in place. Fill soil around, and with bare-root plants among, the roots and pack it moderately firmly. Finish the surface as a shallow saucer formed by having a raised circular rim or low dyke of soil of the diameter of the root spread, this to make watering easier and more effective. Water thoroughly as soon as planting is completed and spread a generous layer of mulch around the plants extending at least to somewhat beyond the spread of the roots.

Routine care is not demanding. It does need attention. Of first importance is the maintenance of an organic mulch. Beneath trees this may be supplied by natural leaf drop. Very likely it will be necessary to distribute this evenly from time to time by raking out heavy accumulations and spreading them in barer places. It is often desirable to supplement natural leaf drop by spreading compost, peat moss, partly-decayed sawdust, wood chips, bagasse, ground corncobs, or other suitable material. Where there is no natural mulch, reliance must be upon such applied ones. Let the layer of mulch be loose and about 3 inches thick. Add to its surface annually to compensate for the mulch that decays below. If at the time of its application the mulch material is not fairly well decomposed, "half-rotted" to use a gardener's term, apply at the same time a fertilizer high in fairly available nitrogen. This may be supplied by spreading a mixture of one part sulfate of ammonia and three parts cottonseed meal or equivalent organic nitrogenous fertilizer at the rate of 2 pounds to 100 square feet, or a commercial fertilizer of a type prepared for rhododendrons and other acid soil plants may be used instead in amounts recommended by the manufacturer.

Other cultural care includes deep watering at weekly or biweekly intervals during dry weather. It is advantageous to pick off faded flowers, taking care not to harm the young new shoots then developing. Spraying to control lace bugs, petal blight, and other troubles is highly necessary in some areas. Under no circumstances cultivate the surface soil near azaleas. The roots, close to the surface, are easily destroyed by hoes and cultivators.

Pruning, except for highly exceptional reason (such as formal training practiced in Japanese gardens), needs little attention. Fullest beauty is achieved when the bushes are allowed to develop naturally. The chief reasons for pruning are to remove dead and injured branches, to limit the size where excessive growth would be undesirable, and sometimes to thicken up a plant by inducing more vigorous new growth from low down. This last type of pruning is usually needed by Ghent, mollis, and Knap Hill hybrids.

As indoor plants azaleas usually do much better in greenhouses than in dwellings. Not that it is impossible to grow them for periods of many years in houses, it is just that the environment must not differ too much from that of a greenhouse. A cool sunroom, glassed-in porch, or large window in a room kept not too warm may do, but the chance of success in the average city apartment is nil. Gift plants of the kinds grown by florists and received in bloom are best enjoyed for as long as they can be kept attractive then either discarded or kept until all danger of frost has passed and, if a hardy kind, subsequently planted outdoors. Only if you can find a suitable environment indoors will they live and bloom in succeeding years.

The kinds chiefly forced into early bloom in greenhouses are the Kurume and Pericat hybrids and to a lesser extent the Belgian Indian and Rutherford hybrids, but all other kinds can be forced into bloom early indoors and when so managed are very lovely. Many of these, the mollis and Ghent hybrids, for example, do not ship well and so have little appeal to commercial florists. For early forcing select kinds that normally bloom reasonably early outdoors, not late-blooming sorts such as the Satsuki hybrids.

Azaleas to be forced are better if they have been established in pots since at least the spring previously and have been carried through the summer and early fall outdoors or in a lath house, or under similar conditions. But if care is taken not to seriously harm the roots, plants can be lifted in fall from outdoor beds or from beds in cold frames or greenhouses and be potted for spring forcing.

Before freezing weather comes house the plants in a light but not sunny place where the temperature runs between 40 and 50°F and the air is fairly humid. A frost-proof deep pit frame, a greenhouse, or a cool cellar or attic will do.

To have plants in bloom ahead of their normal seasons, after a period of rest or semidormancy (during which time the soil must not be allowed to dry), move them into a warmer place. Although florists bring some of the earliest varieties into bloom for Christmas, it is generally not advisable to begin forcing until early January. From then on start additional plants into growth at intervals of about three weeks to assure a succession. For late blooming indoors the plants may be kept in storage until the higher temperatures normal to spring arrive and growth begins naturally.

Whether growth starts naturally or is forced, the plants should be put where they have good light and be watered regularly. They then need a reasonably humid atmosphere, and specimens that have filled their containers with roots benefit from weekly applications of dilute liquid fertilizer. Until the flower buds begin to open, misting the foliage, or with deciduous varieties the stems, with water sufficiently early in the day that it dries before nightfall is beneficial. Satisfactory forcing temperatures are 55 to 65°F at night, five to ten degrees higher by day. The higher range naturally brings the plants into bloom more rapidly than lower levels, but specimens brought along gradually under comparatively cool conditions have firmer foliage and blooms that last longer. Under warm conditions, azaleas come into bloom in about one month to five weeks from when forcing begins.

Treatment after flowering largely determines the plant's ability to bloom the following year. As soon as the blooms fade pick them off. Turn plants out of their pots, examine the roots, and if repotting is deemed desirable attend to this. If not, with a pointed stick prick away a little of the surface soil and replace with a new, fertile mixture. Established specimens in large containers need repotting only every few years.

Specimens to be repotted are prepared by first soaking the soil with water and allowing it to drain for an hour or two or overnight. Then remove the plants from the pots, take away the old crocks, and loosen the surface of the root-balls by picking away with a pencil-thick, pointed stick a little of the old soil. Crock (put drainage in) a pot not more than 1 inch bigger all around than the one the plant previously occupied and not overbig in comparison to the size of the specimen.

The best soil is a porous mix of good topsoil, peat moss, and sand or perlite, in approximately equal parts. If the soil lacks natural fiber use greater amounts of the other ingredients. Add one-tenth part by bulk of dried cow manure and a generous dash of bonemeal. Other nourishing mixes may be substituted with equal success if they are porous, contain considerable organic material, and are acid.

Pack the soil moderately firmly. Water thoroughly with a spray fine enough not to disturb the new soil, and return the plants to a greenhouse or approximately similar environment where the night temperature is about 55°F, that by day several degrees higher. Keep the air humid (in dwellings this can be done near the plants by covering them with a polyethylene plastic bag). For the first three or four weeks after potting mist the foliage with water once or twice on all bright days. Keep the soil moist, but take care that it is not saturated for long periods.

After the weather is warm and settled, about the time it is safe to plant out tomatoes, put the plants outdoors in a slightly shaded place with their pots buried to their rims in a bed of sand, sawdust, wood chips, or other material that will keep the roots cool and evenly moist.

Summer care consists of watering regularly and, after the pots are filled with roots, applying at about two-weekly intervals dilute liquid fertilizer.

Propagation of azaleas is by seeds, cuttings, layering, division, and grafting. Species breed relatively true from seeds; except in a few instances varieties and hybrids do not. By far the most satisfactory me-

Repotting azaleas: (a) Prick away a little of the old soil from the outside of the root ball

(b) Transfer to a well-drained pot and pack fresh soil around the roots

Propagating azaleas by cuttings: (a) Shoots suitable to take for cuttings

(b) Cuttings prepared for planting

(c) Planted cuttings covered with bell-jar, in lieu of a cold frame or greenhouse

dium upon which to sow seeds is sphagnum moss. Other mediums containing high proportions of peat moss or finely sifted leaf mold and sand may also be used successfully, but because of the greater danger of damping off of seedlings they are often less reliable.

Cuttings provide a ready means of increasing most evergreen azaleas. They can also be used to multiply deciduous kinds, but these usually root less easily. Take them from midsummer to early fall. Make them of firm, but not hard shoots of the current season's growth. Those that come from below the old flowers are much to be preferred to strong shoots from lower down. Let the cuttings be 2 to 3 inches long and for preference have at their bases a thin heel of older wood. Plant them in a greenhouse or cold frame, preferably with a little bottom heat supplied to the rooting medium, in a mixture of peat moss and sand or peat moss and perlite. If the cuttings are to be rooted under mist use only sand. With cuttings of deciduous azaleas it is helpful to dip their ends in a root-inducing hormone before planting them, a procedure that may prove helpful with evergreen kinds also.

Layering is a rather slow, but very certain method of increasing all kinds of azaleas. Self-layering not uncommonly occurs. Although not usually used as a means of multiplication, division in early fall of own-root, but not grafted azaleas can sometimes be done. Grafting is less practiced now than formerly, but it is still done

(in greenhouses in summer) to produce standard (tree-form) specimens of Belgian Indian and Rutherfordianum hybrids. The understocks used are varieties of *R. pulchrum phoeniceum*.

Pests and Diseases. These are fairly numerous and some are decidedly serious. In some cases standard controls used for the

Grafting Belgian Indian Azaleas: (a) Slice stems of scion and decapitated understock with corresponding long sloping cuts

(b) Fit cut surfaces of scion and understock together

(c) Tie with soft string

(d) The finished graft

(e) Keep newly grafted plants in a warm humid propagating case until union between scion and understock is effected

same troubles on other plants are efficacious. In other cases, as with petal blight, special procedures are recommended. Consult State Agricultural Experiment Stations and local Cooperative Extension Agents. Among troublesome pests are aphids, black vine and other weevils, borers, leaf miners, mites, nematodes, scale insects, and whiteflies. The chief diseases are botrytis blotch, canker, damping off (seedlings), dieback, galls of various kinds, leaf spots, petal blight, and root rots.

Chlorosis (lack of development of or loss of chlorophyll resulting in yellowing of the foliage with the veins remaining green) is a common trouble with azaleas. Its cause is a deficiency of iron, rarely because the soil is lacking in that element, but because it is present in unavailable form, usually as a result of the soil being too alkaline or being poorly aerated or waterlogged. In addition to correcting the cause, use as directed by the manufacturer iron chelates as foliar sprays or as applications to the ground. Chlorosis may also result from inadequate aeration resulting from poor drainage and excessive compactness of the soil.

AZARA (Az-àra). Generally hardy only in climates as mild as that of California, these cultivated shrubs or small trees of South America and Juan Fernandez are handsome evergreens with fragrant blooms. They belong in the flacourtia family FLACOURTIACEAE. There are ten species. Their name commemorates J. N. Azara, a Spanish patron of botany.

Azaras have alternate, short-stalked, leathery, toothed or toothless leaves with usually one of the basal appendages (stipules) large and leaflike. The tiny petalless flowers are in stalked racemes or clusters from the leaf axils. They have four to six sepals, usually many but sometimes only five or ten stamens, five glands between the stamens and sepals, and a single long style. The fruits are many-seeded berries.

The hardiest species, it survives outdoors in Washington, D.C., is *Azara microphylla* of Chile. Of elegant aspect, this kind often is not more than 3 to 12 feet tall, but under favorable circumstances may become a tree 30 feet in height. It has glossy, dark green, obovate leaves, more or less toothed at their margins and ½ to 1 inch long. Their basal appendages are about one-half as long as the leaves. The vanilla-scented, greenish flowers, few in a cluster, have five stamens. They appear in late winter or spring. The fruits are red or orange. Variety *A. m. variegata* has irregular bands of creamy-white bordering its leaves.

Hardy only where little or no frost is experienced, *A. lanceolata* is up to 20 feet tall and has downy shoots and bright green, lanceolate to narrow-ovate, toothed

leaves ¾ inch to 2½ inches long. Its tiny, pale yellow, fragrant flowers are succeeded by lavender to white berries. This kind is indigenous to Chile. Two other Chileans, not hardy in the north, are *A. dentata* and *A. serrata*. Sometimes confused in cultivation, they are easily distinguished. The leaves of *A. dentata* are densely-felted on their undersides, those of *A. serrata* are hairless or nearly so. Also, the fragrant blooms of *A. dentata* are in short, branched clusters, those of *A. serrata* in spherical umbels at the ends of slender stalks up to 1½ inches long. Both are yellow-flowered, evergreen shrubs 8 to 10 feet tall or sometimes taller, with downy shoots. They have toothed, ovate to elliptic leaves, those of *A. dentata* up to 1½ inches long, those of *A. serrata* attaining a maximum of about 2 inches.

Azara dentata

Garden and Landscape Uses. In climates where they can be grown outdoors these are beautiful general-purpose shrubs for partially shaded locations where the soil is fertile, well-drained and not excessively dry. They are occasionally grown in greenhouses and conservatories.

Cultivation. Azaras present no particular problems to gardeners. Any pruning needed to control their size or shape is done as soon as they are through blooming. New plants are obtained from cuttings inserted in late summer or early fall in a greenhouse propagating bench, preferably with slight bottom heat, or under mist, or by seeds sown in sandy peaty soil in a temperature of about 60°F. In greenhouses they thrive where the winter night temperature is 40 to 50°F and the day temperatures at that season are but a few degrees higher. Porous, fertile soil containing a generous proportion of organic matter suits them.

AZAROLE is *Crataegus azarolus*.

AZOLLA (Az-ólla)—Mosquito Fern. That these tiny floating plants, which are capable of completely carpeting the surface

of still water, are ferns rather than conventional flowering plants may come as something of a surprise. They belong in the salvinia family SALVINIACEAE and are natives of the Americas. There are six species. Two are grown in pools in greenhouses and conservatories, in aquariums, and occasionally outdoors in mild climates. The name *Azolla* is of uncertain derivation.

Azollas are velvety-looking mossy plants with branched rhizomes, minute twice-lobed leaves, and slender branchless roots that hang in the water. Two species are probably in cultivation, but they are so similar that they cannot be surely told apart without the aid of a high-power microscope; for the purposes of the gardener they may be regarded as one. Usually less than ⅓ inch wide, the moss-green to bluish-green *A. caroliniana* is indigenous from Massachusetts and New York to Florida and Louisiana and perhaps even further westward, and in the West Indies. When grown in sun the plants often turn reddish. Often larger, up to slightly more than ½ inch in width, is *A. mexicana,* a native of the western United States and southward to Bolivia and in Wisconsin, Illinois, and Missouri. Another native of western North America, *A. filiculoides* has rhizomes up to 2 inches long and densely-overlapping leaves approximately ½ inch long.

Garden Uses and Cultivation. The uses of these plants have been indicated. They need no special care and multiply rapidly by natural division, under favorable conditions at an almost alarming rate. They are best confined to aquaria and small pools where their spread can be controlled by removing their unwanted increase with a fishnet or by other suitable means.

AZORELLA (Azor-élla). Natives of the Andes, Antarctic islands, and New Zealand, the seventy or more species of *Azorella* are little known in gardens. Like the "vegetable sheep" (*Raoulia*) of New Zealand, to which, however, they are not botanically related, in the wild, azorellas form tight mounds or cushions, up to 1½ feet high and twice as broad, and so compact and firm that a man may stand on them without damaging them. They belong to the carrot family UMBELLIFERAE. The name is from the Greek *a*, without, and *zoraleos*, scaliness, but its application is not clear.

Azorellas have small, evergreen, lobed or lobeless leaves. Their flowering habit is peculiar, but not uncommon among plants subjected to more or less constant strong winds. The tiny blooms appear in small umbels at the surface of the plant; the next season new branches develop from the old umbels and produce flowers, and this process is repeated.

Under suitable garden conditions, *A. glebaria* (syns. *A. trifurcata, Bolax trifurcata*) of southernmost South America grows

Azorella glebaria

freely and forms attractive green, billowy, cushions of small, hairless, three-lobed leaves. Its flowers are in umbels of four. Native to Ecuador, *A. peduncularis* also has three-lobed, hairless leaves. Each of its umbels consists of only a single bloom.

Garden Uses and Cultivation. Very definitely plants for the keen collector of alpines and likely to succeed only where summers are decidedly cool and humid and winters mild, azorellas need gritty, well-drained soil and full sun. They are adapted for growing in fanciers' green-houses devoted to the cultivation of alpines. They are propagated by division and seeds.

AZTEC-LILY. See Sprekelia.

AZTEKIUM (Aztèk-ium). The one curious species that constitutes this genus of the cactus family CACTACEAE inhabits the precipitous slate cliffs in Nuevo Leon in Mexico. Its name refers to its appearance, which suggest designs of Aztec sculptures perhaps inspired by this plant.

Eventually forming clumps, but for a long time solitary, the plant bodies of *Aztekium ritteri* are under 1½ inches tall and 2 inches in diameter. Their depressed apexes contain masses of white, woolly hairs and short, soon-deciduous spines. The plants have seven to eleven deep ribs, intriguingly folded and furrowed and bearing areoles (places from which spines arise) having off-white wool. The blooms, in clusters from the crowns of the plants and about ¾ inch in diameter, are white with pinkish tips to their petals, which spread to show stamens tipped with golden anthers.

Garden Uses and Cultivation. This is decidedly a collector's item. It grows very slowly and is a few years old before it develops its characteristic appearance. It is usually raised from offsets and seeds. If grafted, it becomes greener and loses something of its distinctive charm. For additional information see Cactuses.

AZUREOCEREUS (Azureo-cèreus). Closely related to *Browningia* and by some botanists included there, *Azureocereus* of the cactus family CACTACEAE comprises two tree-form, candelabrum-branched species, natives of high altitudes in Peru. The name, from the French *azur*, blue, and *Cereus*, the name of an allied genus, alludes to the color of the stems of one kind.

These are long-spined, erect plants up to about 30 feet in height. They have short-cylindrical, white flowers. Most often cultivated, *A. hertlingianus* has stems that in older plants are azure-blue, which have eighteen or more shallow, rounded ribs. The stems of younger specimens are green and have fewer ribs. The spines are brown and in clusters of ten to thirteen, two or three of which are stiff, awl-shaped centrals up to 3 inches long. From this species *A. viridis* differs in having dark green stems with strongly-notched ribs.

Garden and Landscape Uses and Cultivation. These easy-to-grow plants have the uses and respond to the conditions suitable for *Cereus*. For additional information see Cactuses.

B

BABIANA (Bab-iàna). Because the bulblike parts of these plants are a favorite food of baboons, in South Africa they became known by the Dutch name for those animals bobbejane. This was anglicized to babianer, from which *Babiana* is derived. With the exception of one endemic to the island of Socotra near the Indian Ocean entrance to the Red Sea, all sixty-one species are restricted in the wild to South and Southwest Africa. They belong in the iris family IRIDACEAE and are allied to *Freesia, Ixia, Tritonia,* and *Gladiolus.*

Babianas have corms, bulblike organs that are solid like those of gladiolus instead of consisting of concentric layers or overlapping scales as do true bulbs, such as those of tulips, onions, and lilies. The corms have matted, fibrous outer coats, generally extending to ground level as a thin neck surrounding the subterranean parts of the stems. In the wild the corms are commonly at depths of 4 to 5 inches and sometimes more than 1 foot deep. Most species extend their stems above ground, sometimes to a height of 1 foot, but commonly less. The leafstalks may or may not extend above ground. The leaves are various. In kinds commonly cultivated they are lanceolate to sword-shaped, conspicuously pleated lengthways, and in fans. There are others with very much-waved or conspicuously spirally-curled foliage, one, *B. brachystachys,* has slender, cylindrical leaves, and some have the ends of the short leaves so abruptly and raggedly squared off that they give the appearance of having been browsed. In most babianas the stems and foliage are hairy, and each plant ordinarily has five to seven leaves, more rarely as few as three or as many as ten. The flowers, in some kinds fragrant, are white, cream, yellow, pink, red, lavender, blue, or violet, or sometimes combinations of these. The nearly-symmetrical to markedly-asymmetrical, slender-tubed perianths have six parts, commonly called petals but more properly tepals, three stamens, and a three-branched style. The fruits are capsules with few to several small seeds. The plant previously named *B. ringens* is *Antholyza ringens.*

A popular species, **B. plicata** (syn. *B. disticha*), about 6 inches tall, inhabits mountain slopes. It has corms ¾ inch to 1¼ inches across and fans of lanceolate to sword-shaped, corrugated, pubescent leaves 3½ to 4½ inches long and about ¾ inch wide. The four to ten asymmetrical blooms, two-ranked and fairly close together, have tubes ¾ to 1 inch long and petals of slightly varying sizes. They are fragrant, and pale blue to violet, or sometimes white, usually with a yellow area with two purple dots at the base of each lateral petal. Varying to such an extent that botanists distinguish several varieties, **B. stricta** differs from the last in having nearly symmetrical blooms. It has corms

Babiana stricta

up to 1 inch across and is up to 1 foot tall. Its usually six to eight lanceolate to sword-shaped, pubescent, pleated leaves, up to 4½ inches long by ¼ to ½ inch broad, form wide-spreading fans. Mostly rather short, the spikes, atop usually erect stalks longer than the foliage, carry four to eight, scentless or slightly fragrant flowers disposed spirally. They range from blue-mauve to purple and have tubes up to ¾ inch long. The wide-spreading petals are ¾ to 1 inch long. Variety *B. s. sulphurea* (syn. *B. sul-*

phurea) has usually lax stems and sulfur-yellow blooms with purple-black anthers. In *B. s. regia,* the stems ordinarily are lax, and the flowers are dark purple-blue, nearly always with a deep, central ring of dark blood-red. In *B. s. grandiflora,* the mauve-blue to pinkish mauve blooms have tubes up to 1¼ inches, and petals up to 1¼ inches long.

Wine cups, **B. rubrocyanea** (syn. *B. stricta rubrocyanea*), differs from *B. stricta* in hav-

Babiana rubrocyanea

ing large, flattened stigmas with round-toothed margins, and more obviously, in the lower thirds of its petals being brilliant red, in startling contrast to the bright blue-purple of their upper parts. This strikingly beautiful species has nearly symmetrical blooms with perianth tubes about ¾ inch long and petals from ¾ to 1 inch in length. The lower parts of the petals curve upward, above they spread widely. Of unusual aspect, **A. tubiflora** has longitudinally-pleated leaves up to 10 inches long and, in racemes of six or fewer, very long-tubed white flowers usually spotted with red on their outsides.

Offered in catalogs under the name *B. hybrida* and probably selections or hybrids of *B. stricta,* are a number of superior hor-

Babiana tubiflora

ticultural varieties. Here belong 'Blue Gem', with dark blue blooms, magenta-flowered 'Lady Carey', 'Purple Star', with flowers of dark red, 'Tubergen's Blue', with blooms of clear blue, 'White King', which has white flowers with blue anthers, and 'Zwanenburg Glory', with alternate petals of violet-blue and white.

Garden and Landscape Uses. In California and other nearly frost-free, sunny places that have dry summers, and climates that approximate the climate of South Africa, babianas are excellent spring-blooming plants for rock gardens and flower beds. They are also delightful for pots and pans (shallow pots) in cool greenhouses. Outdoors they prosper in well-drained, sandy, fertile soil, in full sun or with a little part-day shade.

Cultivation. Planting or potting is done in August or September. Outdoors the corms are set 4 to 6 inches deep and about 3 inches apart. In containers they are planted with a distance between individuals equal to once or twice their diameters, and are covered with soil to a depth of about 1 inch. The greenhouse must be cool and sunny. Night temperatures of 40 to 50°F are adequate and, when outside temperatures permit, by day, they should not exceed night temperatures by more than five to ten degrees. The greenhouse must be freely ventilated on all favorable occasions, and never excessively humid. Water at first with caution, more freely when roots are well developed. Beginning in late winter applications of mild liquid fertilizer are made weekly or biweekly. After flowering, when the foliage begins to die naturally, intervals between waterings are lengthened, and finally the soil is allowed to dry completely. Then the corms are stored, either in the soil in which they grew or in bags or trays, in a cool, shaded, dry place until time for replanting. Propagation is easy by natural multiplication of corms, and by seeds.

Pests and Diseases. Red spider mites and aphids are sometimes troublesome. Virus diseases, for which there are no known cures, sometimes stunt the foliage and cause a yellowed, unhealthy appearance.

BABY BLUE EYES is *Nemophila menziesii.*

BABY'S BREATH. See Gypsophila. For false-baby's breath see Galium.

BABY'S TEARS is *Soleirolia soleirolii.*

BACCHARIS (Bác-charis)—Groundsel Bush. Shrubby members of the daisy family COMPOSITAE are not numerous among cultivated plants, but they occur in *Baccharis,* a genus endemic to the Americas that includes 300 species or more of deciduous and evergreen shrubs, subshrubs, and herbaceous perennials. Its name is from that of the Greek god Bacchus and was originally applied to some other plant. The group has alternate leaves and panicles or clusters of small, unisexual heads of white or yellowish flowers, the female ones succeeded by fruits (achenes) furnished with many long hairlike bristles. The flower heads are composed of all disk florets. The sexes are on separate plants.

The groundsel bush (*B. halimifolia*) inhabits beaches and coastal marshes from Massachusetts to Florida and Texas. Up to 10 feet in height, it is a rounded, deciduous, freely-branched, hairless shrub, with thick obovate to elliptic, short-stalked leaves 1 inch to 3 inches long and mostly coarsely-toothed, but the upper leaves toothless. In late summer the little, thistle-like flower heads are borne many together in large, terminal, stalked panicles that become quite showy in fruit.

Baccharis halimifolia

Forming dense mats up to about 6 inches tall, *B. pilularis* is an attractive and horticulturally desirable native of dry soils in windswept, exposed places of coastal California. Its older branches are markedly woody, its younger ones slender and leafy. The thick, somewhat resinous, evergreen leaves are blunt, ovate to obovate, usually with a few coarse teeth in their upper

Baccharis pilularis on a bank

parts, and mostly less than ½ inch long. They have one main vein. The many little flower heads are in small axillary and terminal clusters. A variety of this species, the coyote brush or chaparral-broom (*B. p. consanguinea*), is an erect or rounded shrub 3 to 12 feet tall. Intermediates between the typical species and the variety occur.

Garden and Landscape Uses. The chief use of the groundsel bush (*B. halimifolia*) is for landscaping close to the sea. It is extremely resistant to salt water spray and succeeds in wet and saline soils. Useful in such locations for general planting, it is suitable for massing and is especially effective when used rather informally. It is hardy through coastal New England. Much more tender to cold and generally suitable for planting only in rather arid regions of mild winters, such as parts of California and other places in the west, *B. pilularis* is a very good groundcover suitable for clothing sunny banks and other broad areas. For this purpose especially compact forms of the species are desirable. This species and its variety succeed under quite arid conditions.

Cultivation. No particular difficulties attend the cultivation of these shrubs if they are provided with conditions similar to those under which they grow naturally. They are readily propagated by cuttings and by seeds. The low-growing *B. pilularis* when used as a groundcover responds well to shearing annually or more frequently.

BACHELOR'S BUTTON. This is a common name for *Bellis perennis* and *Centaurea cyanus.* Yellow bachelor's button is *Ranunculus repens pleniflorus.*

BACKEBERGIA (Back-ebèrgia). The name of this genus of the cactus family CACTACEAE commemorates the German student and botanical author Carl Backeberg. He died in 1966.

By conservative botanists considered to belong in *Cephalocereus,* the only species *Backebergia militaris* (syns. *Pachycereus chrysomallus, Pilocereus chrysomallus, Cereus chrysomallus, C. militaris*) is a treelike Mexican. Slow-growing and branching freely from near the ground, it attains a height of up to 40 feet. Its numerous crowded branches, erect and glaucous-green, are up to 9 inches in diameter. They have twelve to fifteen lumpy ribs. The spine clusters, each of three or fewer central spines about 1¼ inches long and eight to ten radial spines up to ¾ inch in length, are all brownish to grayish. A helmet-like growth of long, yellowish-brown, woolly hairs caps the end of the flowering branch and from this the broadly-bell-shaped flowers sprout. Opening at night, the blooms are 2½ to 3 inches long. They have a large central mass of stamens, petals with a short portion of their apexes spreading. The spiny fruits contain big black seeds.

Garden Uses and Cultivation. This is an easily-grown item for inclusion in cactus collections. For more information see Cactuses.

BACKHOUSIA (Back-hoùsia). Related to *Metrosideros*, the seven species of Australian trees and shrubs that compose this genus belong in the myrtle family MYRTACEAE. Their name honors the English nurseryman James Backhouse, who died in 1869.

Backhousias are evergreens with opposite leaves and small white flowers in terminal and axillary clusters. The blooms have four-lobed calyxes, four petals, and a conspicuous cluster of many stamens. The fruits are capsules surrounded by the persistent calyx.

The sweet-verbena-myrtle of Queensland (**B. citriodora**) is 20 to 25 feet tall and has narrow-pointed, lanceolate, to ovate-lanceolate, leathery leaves 2½ to 5 inches long and ½ inch to 1¾ inches wide. Its slender-stalked flowers are in crowded umbel-like clusters 1½ to 2 inches across. All parts of the plant give a strong lemon scent when bruised. This species is the source of a commercial aromatic oil.

Garden and Landscape Uses and Cultivation. The kind described is appropriate for warm, frost-free and nearly frost-free climates and may be used effectively as a single specimen or in groups in shrub borders and other plantings. It prospers in well-drained, porous, sandy peaty soil and is propagated by seeds and cuttings.

BACKYARD GARDENS. Small areas at the rears of dwellings can be landscaped as backyard gardens. Such developments bring something of a rural charm to city and small suburban lots. Because ordinarily they are enclosed, backyard gardens serve as outdoor living rooms. They can add a new dimension to family life, affording additional space for relaxing and entertaining and opportunity for amateur gardeners to pursue their interest and exercise their skills without too much or too arduous work.

Features in backyard gardens: (a) A rose arch

(b) A sitting area

(c) A flower bed

(d) A border of herbs

(e) A pleasing statue

(f) Clipped hedges

(g) A birdbath

(h) A cold frame

To create a backyard garden begin by considering the site. Do not be discouraged if it looks unpromising. With a little imagination, sound preparatory work, and the expenditure of a modest amount of money even apparently hopeless areas can be transformed. In planning a backyard garden accept the limitations of the site, take advantage of its opportunities.

The soil must be first appraised. Dig into it in various spots. Determine the depth of the upper, darker-colored part, the topsoil. Note if it is hard and compact, clayey, gravelly, sandy, wet, or excessively dry in places. Observe the condition of any vegetation it presently supports, especially grass and weeds. If these luxuriate it is a good sign. But even if the soil is poor and unsuitable for horticultural achievement take heart, even the worst earths can be improved and brought into condition to grow plants. But more of that later.

Other features of the site must be considered. What is the size and shape of the plot? Is it level or sloping, shady or sunny? Or is part in shade and part in sun? Is it adequately screened to afford the privacy you need? Are tree roots a problem? Having made this initial survey, pass on to the next phase.

Planning a backyard garden calls for some thought. Design it to scale on paper first. Paper lined into small squares (graph paper) is handy for this. Begin by marking in the boundaries and existing features that are to remain, such as trees or shrubbery, paved areas or permanent paths. Then, on the site, not indoors away from it, begin your planning.

Let simplicity prevail. Overelaborate detail spoils many backyard gardens. Unless you have a compulsion for such things (and even if you have, attempt to restrain it) forego gazing globes, ceramic and plastic gnomes, unrealistic-looking waterfalls, and all such garden-center-type "ornaments." This does not preclude the careful placement of a well-designed sundial, birdbath, wall fountain, or other feature that will serve as a point of interest and is in good taste. But such things should not be overdone.

A sense of enclosure is important. This may be had by surrounding the garden with a wall, fence, or hedge. Usually the house itself will be one boundary. The cost of masonry walls in most cases prohibits their installation as surrounds for gardens, even small ones, but in cities it is not uncommon for older houses to have walled backyards. Wooden fences, and they come in many types, are ideal walls for backyard gardens. Hedges are appropriate, but they have the disadvantages of their roots invading what are usually limited planting areas and of needing more attention than nonliving screens. If the garden is shady paint the wall or fence white, very light tan, or gray, or some other pale, neutral color that reflects light. In any case plan to have a few vines or espaliers on the wall or fence. The foliage patterns and flowers of these add much interest.

An impression of greater size, important if the garden is small, is created if the center of the area is left open, uncluttered with flower beds, pools, or other features. Lawn, paving, or groundcovers are appropriate for such places. Beneath trees and elsewhere in heavy shade where grass will not thrive use only groundcovers or paving. A trick occasionally used to create the effect of greater length and distance is that of false perspective. This is achieved by having the side boundaries of the garden and the edges of paths, flower beds, and the like slightly and gradually approach each other as they recede instead of being parallel, but this is only successful where no strong parallel lines, such as dominant ones of neighboring buildings, are in view at the same time.

A paved area or patio is needed if the garden is to be much used for sitting or entertaining. A paved path or paths is usually desirable. Brick, stone, or simulated stone made of cement are satisfactory surfaces, and others are available. If the paved area is raised a little above the remainder of the garden as a terrace (a feature especially appropriate on sloping land), it helps to tie together house and garden and tends to give an impression of greater space. Unless the paved area is shaded by a tree or building it may be desirable to arrange an awning to serve similarly. Beware of creating a chopped-up feeling by having too many paved places and avoid purposeless twists and curves in paths. Remember, the keynote throughout must be simplicity.

Water properly introduced is always attractive. Still, it provides reflections and opportunity to display water-lilies, other aquatics, and fish; flowing, it adds movement and sometimes sound. Several hours' sunlight each day is necessary for aquatics to thrive. In shady gardens, limit water features to fountains.

Planting areas may be borders and beds or containers (see Container Gardening). Arrange them simply rather than fussily. In small backyard gardens borders along the boundaries are usually enough. Use plants with decent restraint. A few well-placed, choice evergreens, and some deciduous shrubs, uncrowded and with opportunity to display their natural beauty, or if sheared or formally pruned effects are preferred, their man-aided beauty, are much better than an overcrowded hodgepodge. For flowers, dependence may be chiefly upon hardy perennials including bulbs, or more continuous bloom can be had in sunny places by using annuals and biennials more freely. Selections must of course be made from the kinds of plants known to prosper in the region. Frequently a combination of perennials, annuals, and biennials is preferable. In making selections give due consideration to the plants need for sun or shade.

Making the garden follows planning. Begin by bringing the soil into as agreeable condition as possible. In extreme cases, this may involve importing topsoil, but it usually does not. Spade the ground where plants are to grow to a depth of at least 8 inches. Mix in abundant amounts of decayed organic material such as peat moss, commercial humus, or compost and a dressing of a complete, slow-acting fertilizer. If the ground is acid, as it often is in cities, liming will be needed for all except acid-soil plants. It is helpful to have a soil test made to determine the need for this. Should poor subsurface drainage, causing wetness of the soil, be a problem it must be alleviated. Often relief may be had by breaking up the hard subsoil with a fork but sometimes the installation of land drains (see Drainage and Draining) is necessary. Following thorough preparation of the soil, planting may be done at seasons appropriate to the different kinds of plants. This and their aftercare is as for other types of gardens. For additional information see City Gardening.

BACOPA (Bac-òpa)—Water-Hyssop. Tropical America is home to the majority of the 100 members of this genus of the figwort family SCROPHULARIACEAE, others are natives elsewhere in tropical, subtropical, and warm-temperate lands including parts of North America. They are small aquatic and subaquatic herbaceous plants, with opposite, lobeless leaves and inconspicuous white or blue flowers, solitary or paired in the leaf axils. The blooms have five sepals very uneven in width, and sometimes in length, and tubular or bell-shaped, nearly symmetrical corollas with five slightly spreading lobes. There are usually four, but sometimes only two or three stamens, and two stigmas. The fruits are capsules. The generic name is a latinized variant of one used by South American Indians.

Kinds cultivated are *Bacopa caroliniana*, often under the name *B. amplexicaulis*, and *B. monnieri*. They may be distinguished by their foliage. The leaves of **B. caroliniana** have three to five veins spreading outward from their bases, those of the latter only one. Their stems creep or float and are sparsely branched and 1 foot or so in length. The leaves of *B. caroliniana* are egg-shaped and up to 1 inch long, the oblanceolate to obovate ones of **B. monnieri** sometimes slightly exceed ½ inch in length, but are often smaller. The flowers of both species are bell-shaped, those of *B. caroliniana* blue, those of the other almost or quite white. Both kinds are native from Virginia to Florida and Texas, and *B. monnieri* is also abundant in the tropics. They

Bacopa caroliniana

inhabit shallow water and muddy and wet-sandy shores.

Garden Uses and Cultivation. Bacopas are planted in bog gardens, shallow-water pools, and aquariums. They are well suited for the latter purpose. They produce their flowers above water in summer. Bacopas succeed in mud or, in aquariums, in un-washed river sand made nutritious by the addition of clay or loam. They prosper when the water temperature is 60 to 70°F, *B. monnieri* seemingly preferring higher temperatures than *B. caroliniana.* Propagation is easy by cuttings.

BACTERIA. According to a widely held scientific theory bacteria (singular, bacterium) are the most primitive group of living organisms. From them, it is postulated, all other living things have evolved. Often classified as plants, there are good reasons for regarding them as neither plants nor animals, but as a group apart. How many kinds there are can only be estimated. They certainly number in excess of 1,000 species widely distributed in the ground, fresh water, seawater, on floating dust particles in the air, and on and in the bodies of plants, animals, and man. They are microscopic. It may take as many as 25,000 laid side by side to equal 1 inch.

Bacopa monnieri

Bacteria multiply by fission, by one bacterium splitting to become two, two to become four, and so on. Under favorable circumstances they do this with extraordinary speed, as often as once every hour. If all survived, the progeny of a single bacterium splitting at this rate would at the end of twenty-four hours number in excess of thirty-three million. Some population explosion! Certain bacteria also reproduce by tough-skinned spores, which are able to survive for long periods under adverse conditions.

Bacteria are classified according to shape. Spherical ones are called cocci, those with rod-shaped bodies bacilli, those with corkscrew-like or spiraled bodies spirilla. The singulars of these terms are coccus, bacillus, and spirillum, respectively. Most bacteria consist of a single cell, a few of more than one cell. Usually they are without, but a few contain, chlorophyll. Some have propulsive organs that enable them to swim through water and films of moisture.

Bacteria are forces for evil, and immense good. The bad attributes of some kinds are more commonly recognized than the good attributes of others. Human discomforts and diseases including boils, septic sore throat, and anthrax are caused by bacteria, so are many other diseases of man, animals, and plants. One kind of bacterium produces the deadly poison that causes botulism. Whereas bacterial diseases of animals and man are chiefly caused by species of the coccus group of bacteria, those of plants are mainly caused by bacteria of the bacillus group. These plant diseases fall into three main groups, blights, wilts, and rots and leaf spots. Familiar examples are fire blight, carnation wilt, and iris root rot, respectively. The bacteria that cause these enter the plant tissues through wounds made by insects, tools, and breakage. They seem not able to penetrate the unbroken skin of plants. Prevention includes avoidance of unnecessary breakage or cuttage, sterilization of tools used on infected plants, control of disease-spreading insects, and general sanitation. Some success has been had by using the antibiotic streptomycin, but generally the best procedure for home gardeners is to destroy infected plants or to at least cut out and destroy affected parts.

Two classes of bacteria are of immense and favorable importance to gardeners. The first consists of those kinds that aid in converting organic matter into humus and break down humus into less complex substances including ammonia. The ammonia is then converted by other bacteria into nitrites and the nitrites by yet others into nitrates, in which form the nitrogen contained in original organic matter becomes available as a plant nutrient. The various kinds of bacteria responsible for this process of decay are of prime importance in what is known as the nitrogen cycle, the

system by which the element nitrogen is cycled and recycled between plants, animals, and the atmosphere. The other class of bacteria of special importance to gardeners comprises those that inhabit nodules on roots of plants of the pea family LEGUMINOSAE and have the ability to fix the free nitrogen of the air for the benefit of the host plant. When such plants are turned under as green manures they add to the amount of nitrogen in the soil.

BACTRIS (Bác-tris)—Peach Palm. This botanically bewildering group of possibly 200 species of tropical American palms is little known in cultivation in North America, but a few of its species are grown in special collections. The name is from the Greek *baktron*, a cane, in allusion to the use made of the young stems as walking canes. The genus belongs in the palm family PALMAE. Species of *Bactris* are mostly low and very prickly. Many are highly decorative, but their spininess limits their popularity as ornamentals. In South America the fruits of the peach palm provide a highly nutritious article of diet. They are prepared for eating by being boiled in salted water. Its wood, called chonta, is used locally for building, and for bows and arrows.

The genus *Bactris* includes solitary- and multiple-stemmed palms with leaves concentrated at the tops of the trunks or scattered along them. Portions of the trunks without leaves are ringed with prominent leaf scars. In some species the leaves are undivided except for a deep terminal notch that gives to each a fishtail shape. In others they are pinnately-divided into equal or unequal leaflets. The flower clusters arise among the foliage and grow out through the prickly basal sheathing part of the leaf-stalk after rupturing it. They have two spathes, the main upper, larger one boat-shaped and woody or woven, and usually not falling until the fruits drop, the lower smaller. These palms have pale yellow or greenish flowers with male and female blooms in the same clusters. They are followed by usually small, ovoid or globular, one-seeded fruits.

The peach palm (**B. gasipaes** syn. *Guilielma gasipaes*) has solitary or multiple trunks up to 60 feet in height ringed with black spines 1 inch long. Its curving leaves about 6 feet in length are dark green above, paler beneath. They consist of numerous slender leaflets about 1½ feet long, minutely prickly or bristly at their margins. The reddish to orange, ovoid fruits, nearly 2 inches long, are in dense clusters. This kind is native from Central America to Peru.

A very prickly, feather-leaved palm up to 12 feet tall, **B. guineensis** (syn. *B. minor*) forms dense clumps of slender stems encircled by rows of 2-inch-long black spines. The leaves, about 3 feet in length, have twenty to thirty somewhat irregularly-spaced, grayish-green leaflets on each side of the midrib. The stems of the flower and fruit clusters are mostly hidden within the spiny, hooded sheaths. The fruits are purplish-black and rotund. This species is a native of wet soils in Colombia and Central America. A native of Central America and northern South America, *B. major* attains a height of 25 feet and has many crowded stems that at their bases lose their spines as they age. The leaves are 6 to 8 feet in length with thirty leaflets or more on each side of the midrib. The flower clusters have prickly sheaths. The elliptic-ovoid fruits, up to 2 inches long, are purplish.

Garden and Landscape Uses and Cultivation. In the continental United States, only in southern Florida is it practicable to grow *Bactris* outdoors. Experience with its cultivation is limited, but it is known that in the wild some species favor wet soils, some grow on beaches and others in forests.

Probably most would succeed in any ordinary, not excessively dry garden soil in sun or light shade. In greenhouses they require a minimum winter temperature of 60°F, somewhat higher temperatures by day and at other times of the year. A humid atmosphere and shade from strong sun are needed as also is a fertile, well-drained soil kept always reasonably moist. The regular application of dilute liquid fertilizer to well-rooted specimens from spring through fall is helpful. Propagation is by seeds sown in sandy, peaty soil in a temperature of 70 to 80°F and by careful division of kinds with multiple stems. For other information see Palms.

BACURUBA is *Schizolobium parahybum*.

BADU. See Xanthosoma.

BAEA. See Boea.

BAECKEA (Baéck-ea)—Heath-Myrtle. Except for one indigenous to China and Malaya and one to Borneo all of the nearly seventy species of *Baeckea* are confined in the wild to Australia and New Caledonia. They belong in the myrtle family MYRTACEAE. The genus is named in honor of Abraham Baeck, a Swedish physician friend of Linnaeus and the discoverer of the first known species.

Baeckeas are heathlike, evergreen shrubs and small trees related to *Melaleuca*. The group, little known in North America, is occasionally cultivated in mild, frost-free parts of the West.

Baeckeas have much the appearance of *Leptospermum*, but their leaves are opposite and their flowers generally have fewer stamens. The leaves are small and without lobes or teeth. The blooms are solitary or in small clusters. The fruits are capsules containing very small seeds.

An erect, loosely-branched shrub or rarely a small tree, *B. virgata* has linear-lanceolate or narrow-oblong, dark green leaves up to 1 inch long. Its white flowers, in loose clusters from the axils of the upper leaves, are small and dainty. They have petals about ⅛ inch long, and five to fifteen stamens. This kind is native to Australia. Also Australian, *B. camphorata* attains a height 3 to 4 feet or sometimes more. It has oblong leaves about ¼ inch long freely dotted with tiny glands, and solitary, white flowers in twos or threes, with petals about ⅛ inch long.

Garden and Landscape Uses and Cultivation. The species described, planted in California, serve in the same way as leptospermums as general purpose flowering shrubs. Branches cut when in bloom are splendid for indoor decoration. These plants prosper in well-drained soil that contains a reasonable amount of organic matter, in full sun. Light pruning immediately after flowering should be done to thin out worn-out, thin, and crowded shoots and to achieve any shaping thought desirable. Seeds germinate readily and cuttings 2 or 3 inches long made of firm, but not woody shoots root with facility. In greenhouses care that suits leptospermums is appropriate for baeckeas.

BAEL FRUIT. See Aegle.

BAERIA. See Lasthenia.

BAGASSE. See Mulching and Mulches.

BAGWORMS. These are the larvae (caterpillars) of certain kinds of moths. They differ from other caterpillars in that they construct and carry with them small individual, tentlike bags made of a very strong silklike material exuded by the insect. The wingless, practically legless females rarely leave their bags.

Bagworms on arbor-vitae

Only one species, ranging from Massachusetts to Florida, Texas, and Oklahoma is common. It infests a wide variety of evergreen and deciduous trees sometimes in such numbers that they are killed. The bag of this species is spindle-shaped, 1 inch to 2 inches long, covered with fragments of leaf, bark, and similar debris gleaned from the tree on which the insect is feeding. From the eggs contained in bags overwintered attached to host trees caterpillars hatch in late spring. These feed and develop their own individual bags, which increase in size and assume their characteristic shapes as the creature grows to its mature size of ¾ to 1 inch long. Dark brown to black, the caterpillars have white or yellowish heads and black-spotted thoraxes. The bags are attached to the twigs where they remain suspended. In late summer the caterpillars pupate; subsequently the male moth, black and furry, mates with the maggot-like female who then lays up to 1,000 eggs inside her bag and dies. The eggs give rise to the next season's bagworms.

Control of light infestations is best accomplished by hand picking in winter or early spring. Heavier infestations are controlled by spraying with malathion or other approved insecticide.

BAILEYA (Bàiley-a)—Desert-Marigold. This genus of densely-white-woolly annuals, biennials, and herbaceous perennials of western North America inhabits dry and desert regions and belongs to the daisy family COMPOSITAE. It consists of four species. Its name commemorates Jacob Whitman Bailey, an American microscopist, who died in 1857. These plants have alternate leaves, and solitary, long-stalked, yellow, daisy-like flower heads that become papery as they age and are attractive when dried. The upper leaves are lobeless, the lower ones pinnately-cleft. The fruits are seedlike achenes.

The chief cultivated kind is *Baileya multiradiata*, native from California to Utah, Texas, and Mexico. In the wild a biennial or perennial, this showy plant grows rapidly to a height of about 1½ feet and has many branching stems. Its leaves are linear-oblong to spatula-shaped, the lower ones usually forming a persistent rosette. The upper halves of the stems are leafless. The flower heads are about 1½ to 2 inches across. Almost identical with *B. multiradiata*, and perhaps confused with it in cultivation, is *B. pleniradiata*, an annual or occasionally longer-lived species indigenous from Colorado to Utah, California, Texas, and Mexico. It is common in the Mojave Desert. This kind differs from *B. multiradiata* chiefly in its basal leaves soon withering and its stems being leafy above their middles.

Garden and Landscape Uses. These are quite pretty plants for flower gardens, and for use in native plant gardens in their home regions. Their blooms are moderately useful for cutting to be used fresh and for drying as everlastings. For this last purpose they should be harvested just before they reach maximum development, tied into small bundles, and hung upside down in a dry, airy, shady place until they are quite dry.

Cultivation. The kinds described, including *B. multiradiata*, are grown as annuals. Seeds may be sown in early spring where the plants are to bloom or may be started indoors in a temperature of 60 to 65°F about six weeks before the young plants are to be set in the garden, which is done as soon as all danger from frost has passed. Plants raised from indoor sowings are first transplanted either individually to small pots or about 2 inches apart in well-drained flats. They are grown in a sunny greenhouse where the temperature is about 50°F by night and five to ten degrees higher during the day. Watering must be done carefully to avoid keeping the soil constantly sodden. Dryish conditions suit these plants best. In the garden they need porous, well-drained soil and full sun. Appropriate spacing outdoors is 6 or 7 inches apart. Seedlings from seeds sown in the open should be thinned while yet small to this distance. Baileyas do not stand hot, very humid weather well.

BAILLONIA. See Diostea.

BAKED APPLE BERRY is *Rubus chamaemorus*.

BALD-CYPRESS. See Taxodium.

BALDMONEY. See Meum.

BALLED AND BURLAPPED. The term balled and burlapped and its abbreviation b and b frequently used in nursery catalogs is descriptive of plants dug for transplanting with their roots retained in a compact mass or ball of the soil in which they grew. The ball is wrapped in burlap and tightly laced with stout string or rope to hold it together and to prevent breakage during transportation.

The great advantage of balling and burlapping is that it holds the roots, including many fine feeding ones, in close contact with the soil and by shielding them from sun and wind prevents them drying and

Balled and burlapped shrub

dying. All evergreens except very small ones should be balled and burlapped for transplanting and so should deciduous trees and shrubs of kinds known to be difficult to move "bare-root" as well as any of such large sizes that they are unlikely to survive bare-root transplanting without serious harm.

When purchasing balled and burlapped stock make certain the balls are of undisturbed, unbroken earth in which the roots grew. The practice of "manufacturing" balls is followed by some nurseries, more especially those that sell through garden centers and similar outlets. Manufactured balls are made by packing earth around bare-root or partly bare-root specimens and tying it, pudding fashion, in burlap to simulate a ball. This is helpful to about the extent that heeling in is, but it does not take the place of balling and burlapping. It is reprehensible if, as is sometimes done, specimens so prepared are sold as balled and burlapped. A manufactured ball is not as firm as a natural one. If the burlap is removed the soil falls away.

BALLOON FLOWER is *Platycodon grandiflorus*.

BALLOON VINE is *Cardiospermum halicacabum*.

BALLOTA (Bal-lòta)—Black-Hoarhound. These Old World, pubescent, perennial herbaceous plants and subshrubs related to *Stachys* belong in the mint family LABIATAE and number thirty-five species. The name is from *ballote*, the ancient Greek name for *Ballota nigra*. They are mostly natives of the Mediterranean region. They differ from hoarhound (*Marrubium*) in that their stamens protrude rather than being included in the tube of the corolla. They are of very minor horticultural interest.

The black-hoarhound (*B. nigra*), native of the Mediterranean region and western Asia, is recognized as comprised of two varieties, *B. n. foetida* and *B. n. ruderalis*, both naturalized in waste places in North America. They differ in minor characteristics of their calyxes. This species is 1 foot to 2½ feet tall and has square stems and opposite, short-stalked ovate to broad-ovate leaves 1½ to 3 inches long, the uppermost comparatively short, narrow, and bract-like. When bruised, stems and foliage are rather unpleasantly scented. The strongly two-lipped flowers, slightly more than ½ inch long, have a long, hairy, upper lip hooded over the stamens and a broader, flatter, three-lobed lower one of about the same length. Purplish-pink, the blooms are in loose, short-stalked clusters of four to eight from the axils of small upper leaves. Each has four stamens in pairs of unequal lengths, and a branched style. The fruits are four small nutlets. A kind not known to be in cultivation, but which because of its white-woolly foliage should be

worth considering, is *B. pseudodictamnus*, a native of Crete, which is about 2 feet tall and has purple-spotted white flowers. It is probably less hardy than *B. nigra*.

Garden Uses and Cultivation. The black-hoarhound may occasionally be introduced in gardens, but is scarcely ornamental enough to make much appeal. It is of the easiest cultivation in any ordinary soil and may be propagated by seeds, or division in spring or fall.

BALM. This is the common name of the genus *Melissa*, which includes the sweet herb *M. officinalis*, sometimes called bee-balm and sometimes lemon balm. Somewhat confusedly the name bee-balm is also used for *Monarda didyma* and lemon bee-balm for *M. citriodora*. Other "balms" are bastard-balm (*Melittis melissophyllum*), Canary-balm (*Cedronella canariensis*), horse-balm (*Collinsonia*), Molucca-balm (*Molucella laevis*), and spotted bee-balm (*Monarda punctata*).

BALM-OF-GILEAD. See *Cedronella canariensis* and *Populus gileadensis*.

BALSA is *Ochroma pyramidale*.

BALSAM. Common garden balsam is *Impatiens balsamina*. The balsam-apple is *Momordica balsamina*. The balsam-of-Peru tree and Tolu balsam trees belong in the genus *Myroxylon*. The balsam-pear is *Momordica charantia*. Balsam root is *Balsamorhiza*.

BALSAMINACEAE—Balsam Family. Four genera totaling some 500 species constitute this family of annuals, biennials, and herbaceous perennials. Natives of North America, Europe, Asia, and Africa, they characteristically have watery, sappy stems and alternate, undivided leaves. Their asymmetrical flowers have calyxes of five sepals, one petal-like and prolonged as a spur and two often of reduced size or aborted. There are five petals, the four lateral joined in pairs, and five stamens with anthers that adhere and cover the ovary. The fruits are capsules that when ripe rupture explosively to distribute the seeds. The only genus of this family of dicotyledons in cultivation is *Impatiens*.

BALSAMORHIZA (Balsamo-rhìza)—Balsam Root. Endemic to western North America, this genus contains about a dozen species. It belongs to the daisy family COMPOSITAE and has a name derived from the Greek *balsamon*, balsam, and *rhiza*, a root. It alludes, as does the colloquial name balsam root, to the resinous character of the roots.

Balsamorhizas are herbaceous perennials with deep, woody taproots, carrot-like and usually topped by a single rosette of foliage, or very large and crowned with a cluster of short branches each ending in a rosette of foliage. The leaves, except for often one or more very small ones on the flower stalks, are all basal. In juvenile plants they are elliptic, undivided, lobeless, and toothless. The leaves of older specimens vary considerably according to species. Large and suggesting miniature sunflowers, the usually yellow flower heads are solitary, or more rarely, few together on branched stalks. The disk florets (those of the centers of the flower heads) are bisexual, the spreading, petal-like ones, female. The fruits are seedlike achenes. In the wild, species that grow adjacent to each other hybridize freely, and this causes botanical perplexities. In gardens hybridization is likely to occur when different kinds grow near together. The Indians peeled and ate the roots of these plants.

Balsamorhizas with large taproots surmounted by a crown of short branches each ending in a cluster of foliage include *Balsamorhiza deltoidea*, *B. sagittata*, and *B. macrophylla*. The first two when mature have long-stalked leaves with triangular, ovate, or arrow-shaped blades up to 1 foot long by one-half or more wide. Those of **B. deltoidea** are green, often round-toothed, inconspicuously hairy, and frequently glandular. Toothless, and conspicuously felted with silvery hairs, especially on their undersides when young, the leaves of **B. sagittata** lose much of their pubescence as they age. The flower heads of *B. deltoidea*, topping stems 8 inches to 3 feet tall, are solitary or clustered, with the lateral ones smaller than the terminal head. The latter are usually 2½ to 3 inches across. The always solitary flower heads of *B. sagittata* top stems up to 2½ feet tall. They have mostly thirteen to twenty-one ray florets and are up to 3 inches or sometimes more in diameter. The pinnate, more or less long-hairy leaves of **B. macrophylla** are 1 foot to 2 feet long and glandular at least on their undersides. The broad leaflets, sometimes lobed, are 2 to 4½ inches long. Carried on stalks 1 foot to 3 feet tall, the flower heads are 3 to 4 inches or sometimes more in diameter.

Carrot-like roots usually topped with a single rosette of deeply, once- or twice-pinnately-lobed leaves up to 1¼ feet long are characteristic of **B. hirsuta, B. hookeri,** and **B. incana.** The two first are of similar aspect, but differ in technical details of their solitary flower heads. Their leaves are so finely divided that they are distinctly fernlike or carrot-foliage-like in appearance. They have flower heads 2 to 3 inches wide, with usually ten to sixteen ray florets, topping stalks up to 1¼ feet tall. Abundant silky hairs give a distinctly silvery appearance to *B. incana*. Its leaves are much less finely-cleft or divided than those of *B. hirsuta* and *B. hookeri*. The divisions sometimes have a few lobes or teeth. The flower stalks, 6 inches to 2½ feet tall, are terminated by solitary heads, rather paler yellow than those of most kinds of balsam roots, and 3 to 4 inches across.

Garden and Landscape Uses and Cultivation. These handsome Americans are better adapted to semiarid regions than to wetter ones. They are capable of withstanding considerable cold, but wet soil, especially in winter, is not to their liking. They are not well adapted to eastern gardens. Where they thrive they are fine for flower beds and informal plantings. They need deep, porous, fertile soil and full sun. Because of their deep roots they do not transplant well, and specimens dug from the wild are not likely to live. The best plan is to raise plants from seeds and grow them in pots until they are big enough to be set in their permanent locations.

BAMBOO. The common names of a selection of true bamboos are given at the conclusion of the next entry, Bamboos. The word bamboo also forms part of the names of a few plants that are not bamboos. They include the following: bamboo fern (*Coniogramme japonica*), bamboo orchid (*Arundina*), Chinese sacred- or heavenly-bamboo (*Nandina domestica*), and Mexican-bamboo (*Polygonum cuspidatum*).

BAMBOOS. That there are grasses that grow as tall as a ten-story building and have stems up to 1 foot in diameter sur-

Hardy bamboos at New York City

prises most non-botanical people, yet such exist among the bamboos, and bamboos are grasses just as surely as are corn, wheat, oats, Kentucky blue grass, and crab grass. From other grasses bamboos differ in certain characteristics, but lines of demarcation are not always sharp and there is no one diagnostic feature that can be relied upon to separate them from other members of the grass family GRAMINEAE. Because of this they are usually considered to form a tribe of the grass family, although some botanists do segregate them

Tropical bamboo in a greenhouse

Bamboos are delightful at watersides

as a separate family the BAMBUSACEAE. The most obvious traits of bamboos are their woody, persistent, branched stems and their well-developed systems of branching underground rhizomes. There are additional ways in which they differ from other grasses, such as the presence of distinct leafstalks and details of the structure of their flowers, but these are less noticeable to noncritical observers.

Bamboos include about forty-five genera, the number differing according to the interpretations of individual botanists, and conservative authorities recognizing fewer than do students of the group who lean toward splitting genera on the basis of relatively minor variations. These grasses occur as natives in many parts of the world, including the United States, but none is indigenous in Europe or adjacent Asia to the west, north, or northwest of China and Tibet. The great centers of distribution are southeastern Asia, China, Japan, and Madagascar. In lands where they are abundant, these plants are employed usefully for many purposes, and their products enter commerce and are exported to other regions. In America and Europe, gardeners have long used bamboo canes as supports for plants, and fine fishing poles are made from them. Bamboos are used as carpet rods, and furniture, screens, and curtains are manufactured from them. In the Orient they serve many other purposes. They are used extensively for buildings, bridges, and fences, and from them are made musical instruments as well as many articles of domestic use. The young shoots of some kinds are eaten as vegetables, and the mature stems are pulped for paper. The use of bamboos by man reaches back beyond the dawn of recorded history. Of special interest is a reference made in the journal of Marco Polo; he recorded that since at least 200 B.C. the Chinese drilled wells for oil to depths of up to 3,500 feet by using bronze drills rotated inside bamboo stems. The canes formed the casings of the wells. In parts of South America, the native *Guadua angustifolia* (not known to be in cultivation in North America) is used for numerous purposes and is highly esteemed. It is employed extensively for building even in such large cities as Guayaquil and Lima and is also used for scaffolding, fences, bridges, poles for electric lines, and flooring.

Botanically and horticulturally bamboos are fascinating. To the gardener they offer numerous possibilities, to the botanist many puzzles. There is still much to learn about them. The below-ground portion of a bamboo plant consists of repeatedly-branched rhizomes and fibrous roots. The rhizomes are short, thick, and somewhat like tubers, or long and slender, according to species. The former grow in compact masses that spread slowly, the latter often range widely and spread much more rapidly. From the rhizomes arise the jointed, hollow stems, which are flinty hard on their outsides at maturity. These stems, or canes, are usually erect or arching but a few kinds, little known in cultivation, are scrambling vines. In almost all bamboos, branches develop from the joints of the stems, alternately on opposite sides. The number of branches varies according to kind, and usually each branch is divided or is twice-divided into persistent branchlets that carry the leaves.

Nearly all bamboos are evergreen, but the individual leaves are not long-lived and new ones develop at the ends of the branchlets before the old ones fall. The leaves are pointed-linear or pointed-lanceolate and are attached by a short leafstalk to a sheath that surrounds the stem. The leaf breaks away easily from the sheath, which, together with the presence of a leafstalk, helps to distinguish bamboos from all other grasses. The chief veins of the leaf, longitudinal and parallel, are connected by finer cross-veins, which in some species are so conspicuous that they give a distinctly tessellated or windowed appearance to the leaf surface. The tessellation is usually more conspicuous in relatively hardy bamboos than in tropical kinds and can be most easily observed by viewing a leaf against the light.

The flowering habits of bamboos are extremely diverse and in many cases not yet well understood. Some kinds, though not many, bloom annually or more or less constantly, depending upon climatic conditions. Most follow a cycle of blooming at intervals of several to many years, and once the blooming phase is attained may bloom for one year only or may continue to produce flowers for several years. Yet other bamboos have never been known to bloom. After they flower and fruit many species die, others are so weakened that the flowering canes perish after fruits are produced and for a time no new canes develop, but they recover later, and yet others, mostly low-growing, small kinds, continue to live and bloom without any apparent setback. It is possible that some kinds of bamboos follow a cycle characteristic for their species of blooming at intervals ranging from one to three, seven, fifteen, thirty, sixty, or, even one-hundred and twenty years, but there are no scientific records available to prove that the flowering cycles are of such exact and determinate length and observations of some kinds prove the reverse to be true. It has been stated that when a bamboo blooms all individuals of the same species throughout the world flower at the same time. This is not so. But because cultivated plants often do not represent separate seedlings, but are clones or divisions of one original individual that has been widely distributed in gardens, they are likely to bloom simultaneously. In other words, it seems likely that any given seedling and its vegetatively-reproduced offspring follow a built-in or genetically triggered pattern of flowering, but that other seedlings of the same species may bloom at other times.

As with other grasses, the individual flowers of bamboos are small and decoratively unimportant, but in the aggregate they are graceful and often decidedly ornamental; they are in spikes, racemes, or panicles that in general appearance may suggest those of wheat or oats. The fruits are single-seeded and vary in size and shape from having the appearance of an oversized wheat grain to that of a chestnut or a small pear. They are edible and in India have more than once been proven highly important in alleviating local famines.

The commercial exploitation of bamboos includes the use of their young shoots as edibles. For centuries these have been held in high esteem in the Orient. They play a prominent part in Chinese and Japanese cookery and large quantities are exported; the chief kinds used are *Phyllostachys pubescens* and *P. viridis* but other kinds are also edible. The young shoots of many bamboos contain cyanogens in such amounts that cattle have been killed by eating them, but these are destroyed by boiling and pose no threat to people who consume them as cooked vegetables.

Bamboo canes are much in demand by gardeners as plant supports. One of the prime sources is *Arundinaria amabilis*, which supplies the canes called tonkins. This species is also used for rug poles, hop poles, split and glued fishing rods, and other purposes; it has held first place in world trade in bamboos for over one-half a century, until political considerations interfered with its export from continental China. Experience in England suggests that the canes of *A. anceps*, *A. simonii*, *Chimonobambusa falcata*, *Pseudosasa japonica*, *Sinarundinaria nitida*, and *Yushania niitakayamensis*, all comparatively hardy, are of good quality for garden plant supports. To secure good quality canes it is important that they not be cut until they are mature, but before they are dead and brittle, and that they are properly cured. The canes should be three years old when harvested and, because it is often difficult to judge cane age correctly by visual inspection, it is helpful to mark each current year's shoots with an identifying dab of paint, a different color for each year's crop. The canes are severed just below the lowest node and are trimmed of their branches and of their slender, immature tops. To cure, the newly harvested canes are laid horizontally on well-ventilated racks that support them without allowing them to bend, or on dry floors in an airy shed. There they remain for six months to one year during which time they are turned occasionally to facilitate even drying.

As sources of material for paper pulp, bamboos are important. *Dendrocalamus strictus* is much used in India, *Phyllostachys pubescens* in China and Japan, and *Bambusa vulgaris* in trials carried out in the western hemisphere. In the Himalayan region and also in North America, the foliage of native species provides good cattle fodder.

Garden and Landscape Uses. Although most bamboos inhabit tropical, subtropical, and warm-temperate regions several are sufficiently hardy to live outdoors in sheltered locations as far north as southern New York. In the southern United States, many more can be successfully grown in the open. In addition to their usefulness for outdoor landscaping, many bamboos are well adapted for cultivating in containers to decorate conservatories, sunrooms, porches, patios, and similar places. Bamboos are not as popular with gardeners as their merits warrant; with advantage they could be planted more frequently. They are airy, graceful plants that delight us with the beauty of the lines of their stems as well as with the handsome appearance of their evergreen foliage. These qualities are much appreciated by the Japanese and Chinese as is attested by the frequency with which bamboos are depicted in their paintings and other works of art.

As garden plants bamboos that form compact clumps without rampant and invasive rhizomes that send up new shoots at considerable distances from the mother plant are best; vigorous, rapidly spreading kinds should be admitted only where there is ample space for them to colonize and good reason for allowing them to do so. The less rampant kinds are excellent as single specimen clumps isolated from other tall plantings by lawn or low groundcovers, or when set among, but not crowded against, evergreen shrubs such as rhododendrons, azaleas, and camellias. They are admirable for planting by the shores of ponds, lakes, and streams. Many are ideal for screening, and the dwarf kinds make excellent groundcovers.

Bamboos are not well suited for exposed locations where they are subjected to drying winds. They need shelter from such disturbance and a placid, humid atmosphere;

this is especially true toward the northern limits of their hardiness. They are displayed to best effect against backgrounds of dark green and evergreens such as cedars (*Cedrus*), pines, Douglas-firs, hollies, camellias, and *Magnolia grandiflora* can be used to provide shelter and effective foils.

The soil for bamboos should be deep, rich, and fairly moist, but they do not prosper in waterlogged earth. When planted at watersides the surface of the soil should be 1 foot or so above water level. Gentle slopes leading to ponds, lakes, and streams are often ideal planting sites. Bamboos prosper in sun or light shade. Toward the northern limits of their tolerance of winter cold, the leaves are likely to suffer some damage at that season, especially if they are located where at all exposed to wind, but with the arrival of spring a new crop of fresh green foliage develops.

Cultivation. It is scarcely possible to stress too much the importance of adequate soil preparation. If the earth is not naturally porous, fertile, and rich with organic matter it must be made so to a minimum depth of 1 foot, and deeper is better. Assurance that sufficient moisture will be available is important as is soil porosity and subsurface drainage to prevent saturation of the soil and stagnation around the roots. Soil preparation normally consists of spading deeply and thoroughly incorporating with both topsoil and subsoil very generous amounts of rotted manure, compost, leaf mold, peat moss, or humus. If the soil is clayey, the addition of broken brick and coarse sand, or other non-organic additives that will improve porosity, as well as the organics recommended above is good practice. Alternatively, the clayey soil may be dug out to a depth of a foot or two, the subsoil improved, and new topsoil replaced. If the water table (the level beneath the surface where the spaces between the soil particles are filled with water) is within 1½ feet of the surface, it will be necessary to install drains to lower it or, if this is not practicable as it often is not by the waterside, to raise the level of the ground by adding soil and creating broad, gently sloping mounds of considerable area that will accommodate the roots of the bamboos even after they have reached their maximum spread. Such grading can provide pleasing, naturalistic contours that improve the appearance of the terrain.

Planting is best done at the beginning of the season of active growth, which may be early or late spring or summer according to geographical location and depending upon when new growth is initiated. It is a mistake to set plants out while the ground is yet too cold to encourage root growth and rapid reestablishment of the plant's connection with the soil; on the other hand, waiting until the new shoots have several inches of growth can greatly

reduce the chances of success. The plants should be planted as deep, or very slightly deeper, than they were previously; this can be gauged by the soil marks on the bases of the canes and by the change of color from green to creamy-white of the younger canes at that level. Usually the main mass of rhizomes should be covered to a depth of 3 or 4 inches. It is important to spread the roots evenly, to sift soil among the rhizomes so that no air pockets are left, and to pack it firmly but not excessively hard. As soon as planting is finished the area should be thoroughly watered and mulched with a 3-inch layer of compost, leaf mold, peat moss, bagasse, wood chips, or other suitable organic material. If the plants are taken from pots or other containers, there is no need to cut back their tops, but if they are divisions of plants that have been separated from the parent clump with the inevitable loss of roots and root disturbance that accompanies that operation, it is advisable to reduce the danger of excessive loss of moisture by transpiration by cutting back the old canes to within 2 to 4 feet of the ground. This should be done before or immediately after the division is separated from the parent plant. Great care must be taken that the newly set out plants do not suffer for lack of water at any time during their first season.

Established bamboos need minimum care. They are gross feeders and should be fertilized with a complete garden fertilizer each spring. An organic mulch should be spread over the ground around them to supply nutrients and to conserve moisture in the soil and, in northern latitudes, to reduce frost penetration. It is advisable to apply the mulch before the advent of hot summer weather and, where winter protection is needed, to renew it, if necessary, in late fall.

Care should be taken not to fork or hoe among or close to bamboos unless it is desired to limit their spread, otherwise the rhizomes may be damaged and young shoots broken. Clumps that have reached the maximum size desired can be kept in bounds by keeping the lawn around them closely mowed, or by occasionally rototilling or forking deeply around them. Dwarf sorts with slender rhizomes, such as *Arundinaria pygmaea*, can be controlled by slicing around them to cut through the rhizomes with a sharp spade, and digging out and removing the unwanted portions of the clumps.

Pruning consists of cutting out close to the ground all dead and broken or crooked canes. From time to time dead leaves that drop and lodge among the branches should be shaken free; they may be left on the ground to form additional mulch.

Container-grown bamboos are easy to manage provided the gardener remembers their abhorrence of dryness at the roots, their need for a fairly humid atmosphere and shelter from drying winds, and their gross feeding habits. They may be accommodated in large pots, wooden tubs, or other receptacles that assure good drainage and reasonable root room and remain attractive for years without repotting provided they are fed generously. This means that during the entire season when new canes are developing well-rooted specimens should be given dilute liquid fertilizer twice a week and at other times at weekly intervals. If it is possible to do so without damaging new shoots, some of the surface soil may be removed each spring and replaced with fresh rich earth. On the rare occasions when repotting of large specimens becomes necessary, it is often desirable to reduce the bulk of the root mass by lopping off the basal portion of the root ball; this, because like palms and certain other plants, some bamboos tend to lift themselves up in their containers by massive growth at the base of the root ball. Soil for container-grown bamboos should be coarse, fertile, and contain an abundance of organic matter. If the loam used is heavy (clayey), it is well to mix in up to one-eighth part by bulk of bricks broken to sizes ranging with that of peanuts to walnuts; this does much to ensure porosity and good drainage. When cultivated indoors, bamboos that are natives of warm-temperate and subtropical regions do well if the minimum night temperature in winter is 45 to 50°F, those from more tropical climes need 55 to 65°F minimum. In all cases the night temperatures at other seasons should be higher, and day temperatures at all times may exceed those maintained at night by five or ten degrees.

Propagation of bamboos is chiefly by vegetative means. In most cases seeds are too rarely available for them to be a dependable means of increase. Divisions consisting of sizable pieces of an old clump are most commonly used when extra-rapid increase is not necessary, smaller clump divisions are employed when faster multiplication is the objective, and more rarely, cuttings of various types are employed. The divisions may be taken from the perimeters of established clumps with a spade without disturbing the old plants, but if more than one is to be taken it is advisable to dig up the entire clump, lay it flat on the ground, and cut it into suitably-sized pieces with a machete or other appropriate tool with minimal damage to rhizomes or young shoots. When small clump divisions are made they should, for preference, be of one- and two-year-old canes attached to young soots; older material gives very much less satisfactory results. Clump divisions may be as small as a single cane with an attached piece of rhizome and a young shoot, but such small divisions have a lower survival rate than those consisting of at least one one-year- and one two-year-old shoot with a young shoot attached.

Cuttings made from one-year-old, or even younger rhizomes give success with some bamboos, such as species of *Phyllostachys*, and many kinds of *Arundinaria*, but with some others they are not satisfactory. It is important that the cuttings be taken in spring before new shoot growth begins. Each cutting should consist of several joints and may be 8 inches to 1 foot long. The cuttings, which must not be permitted to dry, are planted in sandy, peaty soil in a slanting position so that their tops just show at ground level and their bases are about 6 inches below the surface or they may be set horizontally and covered to a depth of 5 to 6 inches. If the rhizome cuttings are small, it is advisable to plant them in deep boxes that can be taken into a cool greenhouse before the onset of winter. Treated in this way they continue to grow instead of becoming dormant and attain planting-out size sooner than if they were started in an outdoor bed.

Stem cuttings, consisting of sections of cane having two or three nodes taken from the center portions of stout one-year- or two-year-old canes and cut at the base and top by sawing halfway between nodes, offers a method of increase occasionally used, especially in the Orient, but results reported by Western propagators indicate indifferent success. Each stem cutting must have a leafy branch or branches from at least one node; any others arising from the opposite side of the cane and pointing in the opposite direction are removed. The hollow ends of the cutting are packed with damp sterilized soil, and the cutting is then planted in a pot or box containing sterilized sandy, peaty soil so that the cane is covered to about twice its depth and the leafy branches protrude above the surface. The planted cuttings are kept in a humid, warm greenhouse until rooting takes place, which should be in two or three months.

Layering affords a simple method of propagating some bamboos. Two methods are followed. In the first an entire one- or two-year-old cane is bent down, without detaching it from the mother plant, and pegged securely into a shallow trench dug in the ground and radiating from the clump. It is then covered with sandy, peaty earth, which is kept uniformly moist until well-rooted plantlets develop along its length. Mound layering is the second method used. To achieve this several or all the canes of a clump are cut down so that only one or two nodes with their attendant branches of each remain. The stumps are covered with sandy, peaty earth kept in position by a low fence surrounding the clump and kept evenly moist until newly-rooted plantlets have developed.

Seeds of bamboos germinate readily if planted shortly after they ripen. It is advisable to sow in sterilized sandy, peaty soil in well-drained containers in a temperature of about 70°F. The seeds are covered to about their own thickness with sifted soil and at no time is the soil permitted to dry. Fresh seed is likely to germinate in three or four weeks; seeds that have been partly dried and stored for a time may take up to three months before the young plants break ground.

Diseases and Pests. Bamboos are little troubled by diseases in cool climates, but in the southern United States and other warm regions they are sometimes afflicted with fungal and bacterial leaf spots, smut, and occasionally a rust disease. These are controlled by spraying with Bordeaux mixture or other fungicides. Insect enemies are aphids and cottony scales. Imported canes sometimes harbor eggs or larvae of the bamboo borer, which feeds on the inside of the canes reducing the tissues to a powder. Baking the canes in a temperature of 180°F or boiling them kills this pest.

Bamboos discussed in separate entries in this Encyclopedia under their generic names are: *Arundinaria, Bambusa, Cephalostachyum, Chimonobambusa, Chusquea, Dendrocalamus, Phyllostachys, Pseudosasa, Sasa, Semiarundinaria, Shibatea, Sinarundinaria, Thamnocalamus,* and *Yushania.*

Common names used for bamboos include these: black bamboo (*Phyllostachys nigra*), Buddha or Buddha's belly bamboo (*Bambusa ventricosa*), Chinese goddess bamboo (*Bambusa glaucescens riviereorum*), feathery bamboo (*Bambusa vulgaris*), female bamboo (*Pseudosasa japonica*), giant bamboo (*Dendrocalamus giganteus*), giant timber bamboo (*Phyllostachys bambusoides*), golden bamboo (*Phyllostachys aurea*), male bamboo (*Dendrocalamus strictus*), punting-pole bamboo (*Bambusa tuldoides*), Simon bamboo (*Arundinaria simonii*), square-stemmed bamboo (*Chimonobambusa quadrangularis*), and tonkin bamboo (*Arundinaria amabilis*).

BAMBURANTA. See Ctenanthe, and Hybophrynium.

BAMBUSA (Bambù-sa)—Bamboo. Of the grass family GRAMINEAE, this genus has seventy species, natives of the warmer parts of Asia, Africa, and the Americas. Many are gigantic, a few not in cultivation are climbers. They are not hardy in the north, but some bambusas withstand light freezes and can be grown outdoors in California and Florida. The name *Bambusa* is a modification of a native one of India.

Bambusas have cylindrical, generally-hollow, jointed stems and usually persistent leaf sheaths. They differ from *Arundinaria* in their flowers having six instead of three stamens. Most commonly cultivated, often misidentified as *B. multiplex,* is *B. glaucescens* (syn. *B. nana*) and its varieties. The typical species, a native of southern China, is 12 to 30 feet tall and has numerous erect green stems, 1 inch thick or thicker. Its linear-lanceolate leaves are up to about 6 inches in length, green above and silvery-green on their undersides. The clumps spread slowly and make screens and hedges. Temperatures of 17°F have not killed *B. glaucescens.* Variety *B. g.* 'Alphonse Karr' is distinguished by its canes being bright yellow striped with brilliant green and its leaf sheaths being striped with yellow and white. Green canes up to 20 feet tall and many small green leaves in pairs are typical of *B. g.* 'Fernleaf'. The Chinese goddess bamboo (*B. g. riviereorum*), usually 5 to 10 feet tall, has foliage like that of *B. g.* 'Fernleaf'. It is probably the hardiest of the *B. glaucescens* varieties as well as the dwarfest. Its canes are solid and about ½ inch thick. Variety *B. g.* 'Silverstripe' is perhaps slightly hardier than *B. glaucescens* and differs in having slender white stripes on its canes. About as hardy is *B. g.* 'Stripestem Fernleaf', which is similar in appearance to *B. g.* 'Fernleaf', but its 1-inch-wide canes are yellow or pale red with, when they are young, irregular green stripes. It attains a height of about 10 feet. Variety *B. g.* 'Willowy' has green canes, solid in their lower parts, and with very slender branches. Its leaves are numerous, very slender, and about 4½ inches long. Mature canes usually are arching or drooping.

Feathery *B. vulgaris,* known only in cultivation, undoubtedly originated in tropical Asia and is now widely planted in warm countries. It is extremely susceptible to cold and may be killed to the ground by exposure to 32°F. Thriving in the tropics, it is common in Puerto Rico, Jamaica, and other places in the Americas. It attains heights of up to 60 feet, forms a rather tight clump, and has stems 4 to 5 inches in diameter and green leaves 6 to 9 inches long. Otherwise similar, *B. v. vittata* has leaves striped green and yellow. The cu-

Bambusa vulgaris vittata

rious *B. v.* 'Wamin' is distinguished by the basal nodes of the canes being much closer together than in the typical species and in being swollen just above each node.

The Buddha or Buddha's belly bamboo (*B. ventricosa*) received its common names in recognition of the great swellings between the nodes that characterize its stem. These are especially prominent on plants grown in containers. A native of China, under outdoor conditions in warm climates, it grows 50 feet tall. The punting-pole bamboo (*B. tuldoides*) provides stout canes used in China to push junks and other craft along rivers. Its stems are very straight and sometimes exceed 50 feet in height. Its broad leaves, 6 inches long, are green on both sides. This kind is a native of China.

Bambusa tuldoides

A tropical Indian species, *B. arundinacea* sometimes is 100 feet tall and has branches that, especially on the lower parts of its canes, are decidedly thorny. This imposing bamboo produces dense clumps of stems that at first are glossy green, but become yellow with maturity. Its nearly hairless leaves are up to 8 inches in length and ½ inch or slightly more in width. Flowers are produced at intervals of many years. After blooming and fruiting the plant dies. The edible fruits (seeds) have provided valuable sources of nourishment in times of famine in India. This was the first bamboo to be described scientifically, in 1789. Another tall Indian species, *B. tulda,* has gray-green canes up to about 70 feet high. These often spontaneously develop aerial roots from their lower parts, and their leaves, which may exceed 1 foot in length, are about 1½ inches wide. The leaves are green above and paler and usually hairy on their lower sides.

Native to China, *B. eutuldoides* forms groves of widely-spaced stems up to 30 feet tall and about 1 inch in diameter that are green with paler longitudinal striping. Its leaves are glaucous beneath and about 5½ inches long. Also Chinese, *B. gracillima* is a slow-growing, dainty kind up to 6 feet in height, with slender, solid stems

about ¼ inch in diameter that are green when young and orange at maturity and have leaves up to ¾ inch long on slender branchlets. Indigenous to China and Taiwan, *B. oldhamii* is 60 feet tall with stems that may exceed 3 inches in diameter. Its leaves, dull green above and more lustrous beneath, are about 7 inches long. Southern Chinese *B. textilis,* up to 50 feet or more in height, has stems 2 inches in diameter, with six to ten branches from each node. The leaves, 6 to 8 inches long and about 1 inch wide, are used in China for making mats and baskets. This species has survived temperatures as low as 13°F. The plant grown as *B. gracilis* is *Arundinaria hindsii.*

Garden and Landscape Uses and Cultivation. For information on these subjects see Bamboos.

BANANA. The familiar fruits known by this name belong in *Musa.* The Abyssinian banana is *Ensete ventricosum,* the banana-shrub *Michelia figo,* the banana plant *Nymphoides aquatica.*

BANEBERRY. See Actaea.

BANGALAY is *Eucalyptus botryoides.*

BANJINE is *Pimelea spectabilis.*

BANKS AND STEEP SLOPES. Features of this nature, sometimes bounding lots, sometimes marking different levels within gardens, often present special problems. Give particular thought how best to handle them. They cannot be left bare. They must be planted, eliminated, or modified by grading and terracing. Here we will not consider the latter possibilities, only how to plant them. The objectives are to hold the soil and to secure good appearance and ease of upkeep. Cost must also be considered. Two classes of difficulties arise, those concerned with installation of the planting and those concerned with upkeep. The latter are recurrent. We shall consider them first, because even though it be possible to establish a bank cover of a particular kind there is little point in doing so if maintenance is likely to be prohibitive.

Let us examine the possibilities of lawn grass first. It is least expensive to establish. Dollar for dollar, you can cover more square feet with it than with other types of planting. Also, it is quick. There are no long months of waiting for the soil to be covered if you make even a fairly successful attempt at planting grass. But its upkeep may cost more than other kinds of vegetation suitable for planting on banks.

On slopes of reasonable grade, even long slopes, the maintenance of turf is not greatly more difficult than on the level. But if the grade, for long distances, is steeper than 1 foot of drop for 4 feet of horizontal it adds greatly to the effort needed. Steeper

Bank of grass turf

transplanting them when they are one year old. Yarrow is a strong-rooted perennial that spreads quite rapidly by underground stems. When not mowed it grows to a height of 1 foot to 3 feet and has flattish heads of small white or pink flowers. Its foliage is green, finely-cut, fernlike, and aromatic.

If you want to establish a bank of yarrow either raise the plants you need from seeds or seek plants in lawns and other places where they may occur, dig them up in spring or early fall, split them into small pieces with roots attached and plant them directly on the slope or, if you want to work up a large stock quickly set them in rows in a nursery bed or vegetable patch for a year, then split them again.

Low groundcovers of various kinds can be used to cover banks successfully. They are rather expensive to buy in the first place, but many can be increased at home without much trouble, although it may take some time to obtain a large stock.

If the bank is shaded, English ivy, pachysandra, and creeping myrtle are especially

Bank of English ivy

slopes, up to 1-foot drop for 2 horizontal, are practical for terrace slopes where special care is given, and it is even possible to maintain short slopes that can be mowed with a hand mower operated from the top as steep as 1-foot drop for 1 horizontal, but this is not generally advisable.

The troubles in keeping good grass on steep slopes are due to a number of causes, some obvious, others less so. There is the difficulty of mowing. If the gradient is really steep you are very apt to damage the turf if you mow across the slope. This, because the weight of the mower bears down on the low side of the machine and, especially if the ground is moist and a little soft, may cause it to cut into the surface. Mowing up and down slopes of any considerable length is tiring, to say the least.

On short, steep, terrace-supporting slopes mowing must be done by standing at the top and pulling the machine up and down. If the bank is too long for this it may be necessary to tie a rope to a hand mower to which weights have been attached to keep it from bouncing and then, standing at the top of the slope to pull it up and let it run down, then pull it up again and so on until the whole slope is cut. This is not inviting. Be well advised, do not have grass banks that can be handled only in that way.

Sheet erosion of surface soil inevitably takes place on sloping ground. Not even a healthy growth of turf can stop this entirely. Although the grass breaks the full force of the falling rain the water collects on the surface and trickles downward, washing with it the finer surface soil and exposing the roots. This is highly detri-

mental. Combat erosion by top-dressing the lawn each spring, and again in early fall, with finely sifted soil.

A common difficulty where considerable gradient exists is that much of the rain is not absorbed by the soil but is lost by run-off. For this reason slopes need more frequent watering in dry weather than level areas, and they often dry before flatter places and so need watering earlier in a dry spell. This is especially true if they face south or west or points in between. They must then withstand the hottest summer sun. Surface soil and water are not all that are lost from steep lawns, nutrients are carried away quickly. A generous fertilizing program must be followed to ensure success.

There are other ways of treating steep slopes besides planting them with grass. If you want the effect of a lawn with less trouble try planting yarrow (*Achillea millefolium*). This hard-wearing, ferny-leaved plant needs mowing just as grass does, but much of the other care that grass must have can be forgotten, no watering in dry weather, little or no fertilizing and, unless erosion is severe, no top-dressing. It does not seem to be troubled by disease or pest. Although it sounds like the answer to a lawn maker's dream, it is only that for dry sunny places where the soil is well drained.

Yarrow is not commonly sold by nurseries but seeds can be collected from plants common at roadsides and in waste places in many parts of North America or from garden plants. Plants are easily raised by sowing the seed thinly in spring in rows in a nursery or vegetable garden plot and

Bank of pachysandra

(a) Bank of creeping myrtle

(b) Creeping myrtle (flowers)

juniper (*J. h. douglasii*), the blue rug juniper (*J. h. wiltonii*), and prostrate varieties of *J. chinensis*, *J. communis*, and *J. sabina*.

Two trailing or low roses, the memorial rose (*Rosa wichuraiana*) and 'Max Graf', can be used to hold banks. The former has

(a) Bank of *Rosa wichuraiana*

suitable. All are low, evergreen, and neat. A little taller and more vigorous is the very excellent *Euonymus fortunei coloratus*, sometimes called purple-leaf winter creeper. Other possibilities are evergreen and non-

Bank of purple-leaf winter creeper

evergreen ferns. The hay-scented fern is one of the best of the latter. The Christmas fern is a first-rate evergreen kind. The barrenworts (*Epimedium*) make splendid low bank covers for partial shade. They are not evergreen, but hold their foliage long and flower delightfully in spring. Lily-of-the-valley and *Ajuga reptans* are other good winter-leaf-losing groundcovers of value for part-shaded banks that are not excessively dry. Where winters are not too severe the dwarf lilyturf (*Ophiopogon japonicus*) and the big blue lilyturf (*Liriope platyphylla*) are excellent covers for shaded banks. The lilyturfs are evergreen.

For sunny locations there are excellent possibilities. Sedums of many kinds can be used. Among the best are *S. acre*, *S. album*, *S. hybridum*, *S. rupestre*, *S. sexangulare*, and *S. stoloniferum*. These take hold with great ease, withstand dryness extraordinarily well, and are evergreen. If the soil is acid and freely drained, bearberry (*Arctostaphylos uva-ursi*) can make a magnificent evergreen bank cover. Only small, pot-grown

Bank of dwarf lilyturf

specimens should be set out. It is hopeless to uproot plants from the wild and attempt to establish them in the garden. The moss-pink (*Phlox subulata*) is green throughout the year and blooms profusely—white, pink, lilac, or red—in spring. As a bank cover for full sun this plant is good. Several kinds of creeping or trailing junipers are grand bank covers for full sun. They thrive in full sun and in poor soils, if they are well drained. They are evergreen. Among the best junipers are *Juniperus horizontalis*, *J. h.* 'Bar Harbor', the Waukegan

Bank of *Sedum acre*

(b) *Rosa wichuraiana* (flowers)

white, the latter pink, single blooms. For the best effect these should be sheared back each year immediately after the flowers fade. By this means they are kept to a height of 1½ feet. The crown-vetch (*Coronilla varia*) is vigorous and beautiful in flower, thrives on dry, sunny banks, spreads rapidly, and dies to the ground each winter. For a really choice bank planting try blue plumbago (*Ceratostigma plumbaginoides*). This mat-former thrives in sun or part-shade. It grows 6 to 10 inches tall and for a long period in late summer and fall is covered with conspicuous, dark cobalt-blue flowers. Its foliage is bronzy. It dies to the ground in winter.

Azalea (*Rhododendron mollis* hybrid)

Azalea (*Rhododendron nudiflorum*)

Azalea (*Rhododendron viscosum*)

Azalea (*Rhododendron luteum*)

Azalea (*Rhododendron mucronatum* 'Sekidera')

Azalea (*Rhododendron canadense*)   Azalea, Southern Indian hybrid variety

Babiana stricta variety

Babiana stricta variety   *Babiana rubrocyanea*

Several shrubs, both evergreen and deciduous, are well adapted for holding banks. Some may be grown without pruning, other than occasional removal of dead or misplaced branches, or may be sheared regularly to a table-top flatness parallel with the bank. The severity of the latter treatment has much to recommend it in formal areas. It necessitates a little work, but clipping (especially with electric hedge shears) once or twice a season is much less arduous than maintaining grass. Drooping or weeping shrubs, such as *Forsythia suspensa*, winter-flowering jasmine (*Jasminum nudiflorum*), and a variety of yew (*Taxus baccata repandens*) are excellent for planting on banks and need no regular pruning.

Of shrubs suitable for clipping formally so that their tops form a plane parallel with the bank itself some of the best are Japanese barberry and its purple-leaved variety, yews, especially *Taxus cuspidata nana* (often sold as *Taxus brevifolia*), *Stephanandra incisa* and privet. Any kind of privet may be used. Especially suitable is *Ligustrum vulgare lodense.*

Other good shrubs for planting banks are sweet-fern (*Comptonia*), which needs an acid soil and cutting back every few years. *Cotoneaster horizontalis*, fragrant sumac (*Rhus aromatica*), which is a harmless relative of poison ivy that colors magnificently in fall and must be cut back every two or three years, and coralberry or Indian-currant (*Symphoricarpos orbiculatus*), which stands moderate shade.

Getting bank plantings started presents special difficulty because of the danger of erosion before the roots take hold. A variety of helpful tricks may be used. Let us consider the grassed bank types first.

If anything, soil preparation is more important than for level areas. You simply cannot maintain satisfactory turf on infertile slopes so attend to that. If the grade is not too severe and you select a time when torrential downpours are unlikely you can probably start a lawn by sowing in the ordinary way. Distribute the seed more thickly than usual, up to 10 pounds to each 1,000 square feet. As an added precaution first sow the slope with wheat, oats, or winter rye, using about as much as of the lawn grass seed; then immediately scatter the grass seed. After sowing rake it in lightly and pat it firm with the back of a spade, or use a roller up and down the slope if this is practicable. The wheat, oats, or rye germinate quickly and are strong rooting. They help greatly to hold the soil until the other grasses are established and then are soon killed by repeated mowing. On steep slopes fescue grasses are likely to succeed where Kentucky blue-grass and creeping bent fail. They should form 30 to 60 percent of the seed mixture used.

Another great aid in checking erosion before the grass is established is to cover the new planting with an open-weave net fabric, sold especially for the purpose by dealers in horticultural supplies. This is pegged securely in place and may be allowed to remain and rot or may be taken up when the grass is 2½ inches tall.

Instead of net you may use cheesecloth or burlap, but these must be removed as soon as the shoots are ½ inch long. This necessitates watching the young grass carefully. Do not use burlap that is too heavy. Twenty gauge or 7½ ounce grade is satisfactory. Lap the strips slightly and fasten them down with large nails spaced about 3 inches apart. Choose a cloudy day, if possible, for removing the burlap, or at least do it late in the afternoon, so that tender shoots are not suddenly exposed to scorching sun. Following removal of the burlap a good watering with a fine spray offsets ill effects to a considerable degree. Pick up all nails. They can seriously damage the blades of a mower.

Another good way to get grass quickly established on a bank is to pregerminate it. Mix the seed with seven or eight parts its bulk of just-moist soil and leave it in a garage or similar place for five to eight days, until the seed just begins to sprout. Examine the heap daily and do not delay sowing when you see tiny sprouts appearing. Keep the heap covered with a piece of moist burlap or similar material to prevent drying and ensure darkness. Sow the mixture of soil and germinating seeds as you would seed alone, but thicker so that the seed itself is distributed at the required density. Rake it in, pat it down, and water with a fine spray that will not cause washing. Within two or three days the bank will have greened over.

On long slopes erosion can be greatly retarded by laying 1-foot-wide strips of sod every 6 to 10 feet and seeding between them. Do not lay the strips horizontally across the slope, but at a 20 to 30 degree angle with the horizontal so that water that collects is deflected and gradually drains away without making gullys. If sod is not available, you may use boards, sinking them into the soil on edge or pegging them into that position, but boards are less satisfactory than strips of sod. Yet another method sometimes used is to cover the newly sowed bank with a 1-inch-thick layer of straw or salt hay, which is carefully removed as soon as the young grass can be seen through it.

Banks can also be planted with plugs or sprigs of Zoysia, Bermuda, St. Augustine, and other grasses that spread rapidly by means of runners. It is well to set the sprigs or plugs closer together than when planting on the level.

If, despite all precautions, part of the seed washes away before the grass plants take hold, repair the damage immediately by filling gullys with soil, sowing seed, and fixing net, muslin, or burlap over the area.

When other methods fail a bank can always be grassed by laying turf. A few special precautions should be taken. The turf should be laid either early in fall or early in spring. If the sod is put down too late in the season it will not root sufficiently to prevent it from heaving badly as a result of frost action. This is particularly likely to happen if the soil is clayey. When laying turf on slopes, at least some of the turfs should be pegged to prevent slippage, which is likely to occur after heavy rains.

When planting shrubs and groundcovers on banks it is not always necessary to loosen and prepare the soil all over. If the plants are to be fairly widely spaced, say 1 foot or more between individuals, separate holes for each can be readied. These must be big enough to accommodate the roots, with a little room to spare. Loosen and fertilize the bottoms of the holes. Use enriched soil to pack about the roots.

Do not finish the surface around newly set plants even with the slope, instead let the ground on the high side of each plant be lower than grade and build up the lower side to form a water-retaining ridge or dyke. In other words, set each plant on a saucer-like platform of soil let into the hill.

A mulch or coarse compost, straw, salt hay, or similar material spread over the disturbed soil reduces the danger of erosion. If such a covering will not remain in position without aid you may fasten down straw or salt hay by driving wooden pegs into the bank and interlacing strings between them to form a network that holds down the mulch.

On long steep slopes, a good way of checking erosion is to fix logs, or boards set on edge, across the slope at intervals

Bank with logs fixed to check erosion

of a few feet and drive stakes along their lower sides to hold them securely. These may remain in place for a year or two or until they rot.

Another method that is effective is to "rip-rap" the bank with broken flagstones or concrete slabs and then plant between these. The flags or slopes should be set flat

inches long. Another tree kind, **B. integrifolia,** is 10 to 40 feet tall. It has lobeless, scarcely or not toothed leaves. They are oblong to lanceolate or oblanceolate, very silvery-hairy beneath, and up to 8 inches

Bank rip-rapped to check erosion

Banksia integrifolia

in the bank with very wide joints between them. When the planting matures the stones are completely hidden.

Early spring is by far the best time to plant shrubs and groundcovers. At that season new roots soon penetrate loose soil and fix it. As always with banks, providing moisture is of supreme importance in getting a planting well started. If the soil is at all dry, and there is no immediate prospect of rain, soak the new planting thoroughly with a fine spray, adjusted so that the water is not deposited at a faster rate than the ground can absorb it. Repeat this during the first season whenever the soil is in danger of drying out.

BANKSIA (Bánk-sia)—Australian-Honeysuckle. Banksias are peculiar to Australia. There are fifty species, evergreen trees and shrubs of the protea family PROTEACEAE. The name commemorates Sir Joseph Banks, distinguished English botanist and patron of science, who died in 1820. Contrary to the implication of the common name, these plants are not related to honeysuckle (*Lonicera*).

Banksias have alternate, firm-textured leaves of diverse shapes according to species, on their undersides clothed with whitish to reddish-brown hairs. Their margins are often spiny or conspicuously toothed. The flowers are in dense, terminal spikes, domes, spheres, or cylinders that suggest ears of corn or large bottle brushes, and that become conelike as they pass into fruit. The individual blooms are stalkless and in pairs in the axils of bracts. Usually they are yellow or yellowish, but in some species pink or red. They are without pet-

als, but have a tubular, petal-like perianth of four segments joined in their lower parts. There are four stamens and a long style that protrudes from a slit in the perianth tube until its apex, where the stigma is located, is released. The flowers secrete abundant nectar, which is eagerly sought by birds. Some species of *Banksia* are trees up to 40 feet tall or taller, at the other extreme are kinds so low that their spikes of flowers, attached to subterranean stems, thrust their way out directly from the earth at some distance from the foliaged portion of the plant. The fruits are capsules (pod-like seed containers) interspersed and more or less united with twiglike parts to form woody cones. The strong, handsome wood of certain banksias is used for window frames, boats, and furniture.

Tree kinds include the bull banksia (**B. grandis**), which may be 40 or 50 feet tall, but is usually considerably lower. This has pinnate leaves about 1 foot long, with broad, triangular to ovate, 1-inch-long, stalkless leaflets, that at their bases touch the leaflets at each side of them. The leaflets are pale and pubescent on their under surfaces. The longest are at the middles of the leaves. In spikes 8 inches to 1 foot in length, and up to 5 inches in diameter, the flowers are light greenish-yellow. In Australia this banksia is used as a street tree. Another tall tree, up to 50 or 60 feet high in wet soils in its native Australia, **B. verticillata** has whorls (circles of more than two) of four to six narrow, oblong-lanceolate leaves up to 8 inches long. They may be toothed or not. Their margins are recurved, their undersides white-hairy. The narrow spikes of yellow blooms may be 8

long by 1 inch wide. The greenish-yellow flower spikes are 3 to 6 inches long. Yet a third tree banksia is **B. littoralis.** This achieves a height of 30 feet, has usually toothed, linear leaves up to 8 inches long, white-hairy on their undersides. The flower spikes are up to 10 inches long. From 12 to 25 feet tall or sometimes taller, **B. menziesii** has woolly-hairy shoots, and toothed leaves 6 inches to 1 foot long and up to 1 inch wide, reddish-hairy underneath. The red-orange flowers are in thick spikes up to 5 inches long. A tree up to 30 feet in height, **B. serrata** has coarsely and regularly sharp-saw-toothed, narrowly-oblong-lanceolate to oblong-oblanceolate leaves, pubescent on their undersides, and 3 to 6 inches long by 1 inch wide. Its reddish-

Banksia serrata

brown flowers are in spikes up to 6 inches long. This is a coastal species.

The orange banksia (*B. prionotes*) is one of the finest. In Australia, it is planted as a street tree. Upright, and 12 to 30 feet tall, it has narrow leaves 8 inches to 1 foot long and about ¾ inch wide. They are pinnately-cleft into triangular deep teeth or lobes. The domes of orange flowers, white-woolly in the bud stage, are 3 to 5 inches long. The flowers open from below upward, and before they attain full maturity, the lower parts of the spikes are bright orange and their upper portions white. Other tree banksias well worth planting for ornament include *B. brownii*, a tree up to about 20 feet tall, but often lower and shrubby, with narrow, toothed leaves, snow-white on their under surfaces, about 4 inches long, and divided into numerous narrow segments. Growing from the old wood some distance from the branch ends, the delicate maroon-red flower spikes are about 8 inches long by about 5 inches wide. Silvery-foliaged *B. marginata*, which may reach 25 feet in height, is a splendid kind for coastal regions. It has 1- to 3-inch-long, narrow, smooth-edged leaves with squared or notched apexes. Comparatively small, the heads of flowers are pale yellow and 2 to 5 inches long. This kind is especially beautiful when its pink young growths are unfolding.

Shrubby banksias include many of distinction. Among taller ones are those now to be considered. From 6 to 15 feet tall, *B. coccinea* has stalkless, roundish-obovate, coarsely-prickle-toothed, grayish leaves about 2½ inches long by nearly as wide. The strongly-vertically-ribbed flower heads, 3 inches long by 2½ inches across, are squatty-cylindrical. Their blooms have white bases and scarlet tips. The heath banksia (*B. ericifolia*), as tall as the last, differs greatly from it in having narrowly-linear leaves rarely more than ½ inch long. Its amber-yellow candles of bloom are 6 inches to 1 foot in length by about 2 inches in diameter. Of like dimensions, *B. marginata*, sometimes called silver banksia, has smooth-margined, narrowly-oblong-oblanceolate leaves, blunt or notched at their apexes, with silvery undersides. They are up to 2 inches long. The greenish-yellow blooms are in heads 2 to 5 inches long. Another kind qualified for inclusion here is *B. spinulosa* (with which belongs plants previously identified as *B. collina*). Up to 10 feet in height, this has slender, 2- to 4-inch-long leaves finely toothed along their entire margins or near their apexes only. The heads of flowers, 3 to 6 inches in length, are deep yellow to brownish, with black tips to the pistils. Commonly 5 to 8 feet in height, but reported to occasionally attain the dimensions of a small tree, *B. occidentalis* is an inhabitant of moist and wet soils. Its narrowly-linear leaves, with white undersides, rolled-under edges, and

usually two- or three-pronged apexes, are up to 4 inches long. The deep red flowers, yellow at their bases, are in conelike or cylindrical heads 3 to 6 inches long. The oak-leaf banksia (*B. quercifolia*) is 3 to 6 feet tall. As its vernacular name implies, its round-lobed, gray-green leaves suggest those of an oak. They are 2 to 4 inches in length, and when young are thickly clothed with a felt of brown hairs. A variety with lobeless leaves is known. The heads of deep orange-red flowers are 3 to 4 inches long. This kind favors moist and wet soils. Another that appreciates moist soil, *B. baxteri*, is up to 8 feet tall. Its 4-inch-long leaves have broadly-triangular leaflets about

Banksia baxteri

1 inch long, paler on their undersides than above. The nearly spherical flower heads are about 3 inches in diameter. A fine shrub 10 feet or so tall, *B. speciosa* has pinnate leaves up to about 1 foot long, with alternate and opposite, triangular to rounded leaflets about ½ inch long, white-hairy on their undersides, and with their broad bases touching those of the leaflets on either side of them. The greenish-yellow flower spikes are about 5 inches long by two-thirds as wide. A shapely shrub about 6 feet tall, *B. praemorsa* is well

Banksia praemorsa

adapted for coastal regions. Its cylindrical heads of flowers, often 8 to 10 inches in length, are greenish-yellow. The leaves are oblongish, 1½ inches long by one-third as broad, their undersides minutely-hairy.

Low banksias include several of special worth. Here belongs *B. caleyi*, a 3-foot-tall shrub of tidy appearance, with oblong-lanceolate, more or less oaklike leaves, lobed or prickle-toothed at their margins, and 3 to 6 inches long. The yellow and scarlet flower heads are broad-ovate to nearly spherical. Distinct *B. nutans*, about 3 feet tall, grows in the wild in well-drained, sandy soils. Its narrowly-linear leaves, up to 1 inch long, are crowded in heathlike fashion along the stems. They are ¼ to ½ inch long and have smooth, rolled-under edges. The usually nodding heads of orange blooms are 2 to 2½ inches in diameter. Another with pendulous flower heads is variable *B. sphaerocarpa*. This attains heights of 3 to 6 feet, and has crowded, blue-green, narrowly-linear leaves 1 inch to 3 inches long. Their undented margins are rolled under. In spherical heads about 3 inches in diameter, borne chiefly toward the centers of the bushes, the blooms are yellow. The leaves of prostrate *B. repens* resemble those of a coarsely-lobed fern frond. They are up to 1 foot long and deeply-pinnately-lobed and toothed. The yellow flowers are in heads 3 to 4 inches long that develop from the upturned ends of the up to 2-foot-long branches.

Garden and Landscape Uses. Banksias occur wild in climates of the Mediterranean type, that is where winters are mild and comparatively moist and summers hot and dry. Such conditions are duplicated in many parts of California, and it is there and in like places that the best success with these astonishing protea relatives is to be expected. Mostly of bold appearance, banksias provide strong design elements in the landscape, and many are just sufficiently bizarre in appearance to attract more than passing attention. They by no means succeed everywhere, however, and must be considered choice collection and conversation pieces for those who appreciate the unusual and enjoy meeting the challenge of growing harder-to-manage-than-most plants. Banksias have long blooming seasons. Their cut flower heads are splendid floral decorations and last, in good condition, in water for an amazingly long time. Coastal regions may be more favorable to their growth than places far from salt water.

Cultivation. Not a great deal of experience with growing banksias in North America has been reliably reported. As a group they prefer well-drained, somewhat acid, dry or dryish soils, and open sunny locations, but some succeed under moister conditions. Pruning should be limited to that necessary to maintain shapeliness, and may often be accomplished by cutting the flower heads, with suitable lengths of stem attached, for use in indoor arrangements. Banksias often prove difficult to raise from seeds. Their needs are similar to those of proteas. Cuttings may be rooted, although not always readily, in a greenhouse propagating bed or under mist.

BANUCALAD NUT is *Aleurites trisperma*.

BANYAN TREE is *Ficus benghalensis*. The tree called Chinese banyan is *F. retusa*.

BAOBAB. See Adansonia.

BAPHIA (Báph-ia). Shrubs and trees of Africa and Madagascar compose this genus of the pea family LEGUMINOSAE. There are fifty species or more. None is hardy. The name, from the Greek *baphe*, a dye, has reference to the use of camwood (*Baphia nitida*) as the source of a red dye.

Baphias have undivided leaves, and in axillary clusters or axillary and terminal racemes that in some kinds are paniced, white or yellow pealike blooms. The flowers have short-toothed calyxes split down one side or into two reflexed lobes, a round standard or banner petal, obliquely-oblong or obovate wing petals, and a blunt, slightly incurved keel. The ten stamens are not united. The fruits are leathery pods.

A leathery-leaved, upright shrub about 8 feet tall, **B. racemosa** of Africa has oblong leaves about 3 inches long, and large, leafy panicles of white flowers with purple-veined standard petals. The pods, each usually two-seeded, are about 2 inches long.

Garden and Landscape Uses and Cultivation. As an ornamental the species described is suitable for mild, nearly, or quite frost-free regions. It succeds in ordinary well-drained soil in sunny locations and is propagated by seeds and by leafy cuttings planted in a greenhouse propagating bench or under mist.

BAPTISIA (Bap-tísia)—False-Indigo, Wild-Indigo. Both their common names and the botanical one, the latter derived from the Greek *baptizein*, to dye, allude to certain species of *Baptisia* having been used as substitutes for indigo. The genus belongs in the pea family LEGUMINOSAE. It consists of thirty-five species of hardy, upright, lupine-like, herbaceous perennials, natives of North America.

Baptisias are hairless or pubescent. Their branching stems, bearing short-stalked leaves usually of three leaflets, more rarely are undivided. At the bases of the leaf-stalks there may or may not be appendages (stipules). The pea-like flowers, in terminal and lateral racemes, are blue, violet, yellow, or white. The two-lipped blooms usually have the sides of the nearly circular standard or banner petal, which does not exceed the wing petals in length and may be notched or not, reflexed. The keel is straight. The calyx has five teeth, or the two upper are sometimes united. There are ten separate stamens, and a slightly incurved style tipped with a small stigma. The fruits are oblongish, nearly spherical, many-seeded pods, each ending in a curved beak.

Indigo-blue-flowered **B. australis** is the most ornamental species. Native of moist soils from Pennsylvania to Indiana, North Carolina, and Tennessee, it is naturalized further north. From 3 to 6 feet tall and hairless, it has thickish stems, and blue-green leaves, with stipules at their bases, of obovate leaflets 1½ to 3 inches long. The 1-inch-long flowers, in long, erect, terminal racemes, are succeeded by bladdery seed pods 1 inch to 1½ inches long. A variant, *B. a. minor*, has leaves and flowers and is native from Missouri to Nebraska, Arkansas, and Texas. A hybrid of this and *B. leucophaea*, **B. bicolor**, has flowers with blue standards and cream-colored wings and keels.

Baptisia australis

Bright yellow blooms, few together in very numerous, sparsely flowered, terminal racemes, are borne by freely-branching **B. tinctoria.** This native of poor, dry, acid soils from Maine to Ontario, Michigan, Minnesota, Florida, and Tennessee, is 2 to 3 feet tall, and bushy. The blue-green leaves have obovate leaflets, usually under, sometimes over ¾ inch long, and early deciduous stipules. Commonly under ½ inch long, the flowers are succeeded by ellipsoid to nearly spherical, inflated seed pods up to ½ inch long. A hybrid between this species and *B. leucantha*, **B. deamii,** has yellow standard petals splotched with purple.

White-flowered **B. leucantha** ranges in moistish soils in upland woodlands and prairies from Michigan and Ohio to Nebraska and Texas. Widely-branched and 3 to 6 feet tall, this glaucous, hairless kind has leaves with shortly persistent stipules and narrowly-obovate to oblanceolate, wavy leaflets 1 inch to 2¼ inches in length. The blooms, their standard petals sometimes tinged purple, are about 1 inch in length and are in racemes 8 inches long or longer. The ovoid to oblongish seed pods are 1 inch to 1½ inches long.

Other baptisias sometimes cultivated include *B. alba, B. leucophaea,* and *B. cinerea* (syn. *B. villosa*). Native of dry, sandy woodlands from Virginia to Florida, **B. alba** is 3 to 5 feet tall and much branched. Hairless or nearly so, it has leaves with minute, early deciduous stipules, short, slender stalks, and oblanceolate to oblong-oblanceolate leaflets up to 1½ inches long by ½ inch wide. The flowers, up to ¾ inch long, and white with sometimes a bluish tinge on the standard petal, are succeeded by cylindrical, brown seed pods up to 1½ inches long. Similar in flower color to the last, but its blooms ¾ to 1 inch long, and in downward-arching racemes, **B. leucophaea** has thicker, black seed pods. This kind inhabits light upland woods and prairies from Michigan to Nebraska, Kentucky, and Texas. From 1½ to 2½ feet in height and downy throughout, it has short-stalked leaves, with persistent stipules and oblanceolate leaflets up to 3½ inches in length. The ellipsoid seed pods are up to 2 inches long. Favoring dry, sandy soils, and indigenous from Virginia to South Carolina, **B. cinerea** is up to 2 feet tall, more or less downy, and develops few wide-spreading branches. The somewhat leathery leaves have more or less persistent stipules and elliptic to oblanceolate leaflets 1½ to 3½ inches long. Yellow, and ¾ to 1 inch long, the flowers, in mostly single racemes, are followed by ellipsoid seed pods 1 inch long or a little longer.

Garden and Landscape Uses and Cultivation. Baptisias are suitable for perennial beds and for colonizing in informal and naturalistic areas. They are easy to grow, responding satisfactorily to soils that suit the majority of hardy herbaceous perennials and preferring full sun. Some, notably *B. tinctoria, B. alba,* and *B. cinerea*, stand dry conditions well. Their care is minimal. An annual spring application of a complete fertilizer encourages good growth. In exposed places staking may be needed. Unless seeds are wanted, faded flowers should be removed. At intervals of a few years, when the plants begin to show indications of deterioration, they should be lifted, divided, and reset in newly spaded and fertilized ground. This is best done in early fall or spring. New plants are secured by division and from seeds sown in cold frames or protected places outdoors.

BARBACENIA. See Vellozia.

BARBADOS. This geographical designation forms part of the name of some plants. The Barbados-cherry is *Malpighia glabra,* the Barbados flower fence *Caesalpinia pul-*

cherrima, the Barbados-gooseberry *Pereskia aculeata*, the Barbados nut *Jatropha curcas*.

BARBAREA (Barba-rèa)—Winter Cress, Upland Cress. About twenty species of damp and wet places in Europe and Asia constitute this group of the mustard family CRUCIFERAE. Some are naturalized in North America; some are cultivated as salad plants. Because in olden times they were called herb of St. Barbara their botanical name commemorates that fourth-century saint. Barbareas are biennial or sometimes perennial herbaceous plants, hairless or hairy, with pinnately-divided or -cleft leaves, those on the flower stalks with their bases embracing the stems. The flowers are yellow, with four sepals, four petals spreading to form a cross, six stamens of which two are shorter than the others, and a single style. They are in terminal racemes. The petals are clawed, that is their basal portion is much narrower than the upper part. The fruits are four-angled pods with a single row of seeds in each compartment.

Sometimes a nuisance weed, *B. vulgaris* is widely naturalized in North America. A biennial or perennial up to 2½ feet tall, it has basal leaves with a large terminal lobe and one to four pairs of smaller lateral ones. The stem leaves become progressively smaller, and have shorter stalks and fewer lobes, upward. The flowers, about ⅓ inch wide, are in crowded racemes. The slender pods are ½ inch to 1½ inches long. Sometimes cultivated as ornamentals, variety *B. v. flore-pleno*, called double yellow-rocket, has double flowers, and *B. v. variegata*, foliage variegated with yellow.

Early or Belle Isle cress (*B. verna* syn. *B. praecox*) is a biennial native of southwest Europe commonly naturalized in North America from Newfoundland to Washington, Florida, and California. Hairless or nearly so, it attains a height of up to 2½ feet and has stalked basal leaves, with a large terminal lobe and six to ten pairs of lateral lobes. Progressively upward, the stem leaves have shorter stalks and fewer lobes. The flowers, in crowded racemes, are about ¼ inch wide, the slender pods 1 inch to 2½ inches long.

Grown as an ornamental, *B. rupicola*, a native of Corsica and Sardinia, is a hairless perennial 1 foot tall or slightly taller. It has lower leaves without lobes or with a terminal lobe and one or two pairs of lateral lobes. Its upper leaves are pinnately-lobed. The flowers are ½ inch or more in diameter. The slender seed pods are 1 inch to 2½ inches long or occasionally longer.

Garden Uses and Cultivation. Early or Belle Isle cress is a salad plant. For details of its cultivation see Cress. The kinds cultivated as ornamentals are suitable for rock gardens and the fronts of flower borders. They grow with little or no trouble in ordinary soil that is moderately moist. They need full sun. Propagation, except in the case of the double-flowered and variegated-leaved kinds of *B. vulgaris*, which are increased by division or cuttings, is by seed or division.

BARBERRY. See Berberis, and Mahonia.

BARE-ROOT. As a descriptive term this means a plant dug for transplanting without taking a mass of soil with its roots. It differs from "dug with a ball" and "balled and burlapped." Obviously digging bare-root lightens the task of handling and reduces weight for shipping, but the technique is not applicable to all plants or under all circumstances. In the main its use is limited to deciduous sorts during their seasons of leaflessness and to very young and small evergreens.

A bare-root transplant

The chief precautions to be taken when moving plants bare-root are to preserve as many of the roots as possible and to keep them uniformly moist, usually by keeping them covered with wet burlap, hay, straw, moss, or similar material for any extended period they are out of the ground or by heeling them in (planting them temporarily closely together).

Pruning to reduce the above-ground parts, staking to prevent movement by winds or storms, mulching to conserve soil moisture, and appropriate attention to watering until the root system has repaired itself and the plant has recovered from the shock of moving are all likely to be important to success in bare-root transplanting.

BARK RINGING. See Girdling, or Ring Barking.

BARKLYA (Bárk-lya)—Queensland Gold Blossom Tree. One species endemic to Queensland and New South Wales is the only member of this genus of the pea family LEGUMINOSAE. Its name commemorates Sir Henry Barkly, one-time Governor-General of Cape Colony, South Africa, who died in 1898. The Queensland gold blossom tree (*Barklya syringifolia*) is 40 to 60 feet tall. It has alternate, undivided, heart-shaped leaves 2 to 4 inches long. Its small golden-yellow or bright orange-yellow flowers are in dense, many-flowered, terminal and axillary racemes up to 9 inches in length. The fruits are pods 2 to 3 inches long.

Garden Uses and Cultivation. This attractive tree, highly ornamental in bloom, needs moist, fertile soil and full sun. It has been introduced to southern California and may be expected to adapt to conditions there and to other warm, dryish climates that suit a variety of Australian plants. Propagation is by seeds and by cuttings of firm young shoots in a greenhouse propagating bench.

BARLERIA (Bar-lèria)—Philippine-Violet. Chiefly denizens of the Old World tropics, the 230 species of *Barleria* of the acanthus family ACANTHACEAE include shrubs and herbaceous plants, some with showy flowers, some spiny. Hairy or hairless, they have opposite, undivided, toothless leaves, and white, yellow, or blue flowers solitary or in clusters from the leaf axils, or in terminal, bracted spikes. The asymmetrical blooms have four-parted calyxes, with the outer pair of sepals bigger than the inner, tubular corollas that are narrow below and expanded above, and with five spreading lobes (petals) of nearly equal size. There are four stamens in two pairs, and a style scarcely or not divided. The fruits are ovoid or cylindrical capsules. The name commemorates the French botanist Jacques Barrelier, who died in 1673.

The inappropriately-named Philippine-violet (*B. cristata*) is a native of India. A shrub 2 to 4 feet tall, its shoots are yellow-hairy. The short-stalked, pointed-elliptic leaves, 1 inch to 3½ inches long, are scratchy-hairy. The flowers, commonly pale violet, but sometimes white or delicate pink, and nearly or quite stalkless, come from the leaf axils. They are about 2 inches long, and are accompanied by a pair of pale green or whitish, conspicuously-veined, spiny-toothed bracts ¾ inch long. Another Indian, *B. involucrata* is a subshrub with pointed-elliptic leaves up to 5 inches long that have scattered hairs on their upper surfaces and the veins beneath. The flowers, solitary or few together from the leaf axils, are about 2½ inches across and have at their bases two conspicuous, green leafy bracts.

White-flowered *B. albostellata*, a native of southern Africa, is a subshrub with gray-hairy stems and short-stalked, ovate leaves with blades up to 3½ inches long by 2½ inches wide. The 2½ inch-wide flowers are in clusters of few accompanied by dull purple bracts.

Barleria strigosa

Barleria involucrata

in crowded, one-sided spikes up to 3 inches long.

Garden and Landscape Uses and Cultivation. In the tropics, barlerias are useful general-purpose shrubs that succeed with minimal care in ordinary soils in part-shade or sun. The Philippine-violet is effective as a hedge plant as well as for other decorative employments. Barlerias may be

Barleria albostellata

Yellow-flowered **B. lupulina** (syn. *B. prionitis*) of Mauritius carries its blooms in spikes 2 to 3 inches long. The flowers, 1½ inches long, grow from the axils of overlapping, ovate bracts. This is a broad shrub with, on the stems, at the base of each leaf a pair of long, down-pointed, needle-like spines. Its pointed narrow leaves, with yellow or red mid-veins, are 1½ to 4½ inches in length. Called porcupine shrub in Hawaii, it has become an unwanted weed there. Indian **B. strigosa** has ovate, rather leathery, somewhat bristly leaves. Its blue flowers, about 2 inches long, are

Barleria lupulina

pruned to size or shape as need or fancy dictates. They are very readily increased from seeds and cuttings. Occasionally they are cultivated in warm greenhouses where they succeed in environments that suit plants such as begonias and African-violets. Ordinary, porous soil kept always moderately moist suits. Pinching out the tips of the shoots of young specimens is done to encourage branching. Some shade from strong summer sun and a fairly moist atmosphere are needed.

BARLEY is *Hordeum vulgare.*

BAROSMA. See Agathosma.

BARREL TREE is *Brachychiton rupestris.*

BARREN-STRAWBERRY. See Waldsteinia.

BARRENWORT. See Epimedium.

BARRINGTONIA (Barring-tònia). The tropics of the Old World is home to this group of 100 species of evergreen trees of the lecythis family LECYTHIDACEAE. Its name commemorates the Honorable Daines Barrington, a British naturalist, who died in 1800. One species, *B. asiatica* (syn. *B. speciosa*), a native of India and islands of the western Pacific, is cultivated in the tropics and has been introduced to cultivation in southern Florida and southern California. Attaining 50 to 70 feet in height, this evergreen magnolia-like tree has glossy, blunt, obovate, toothless leaves 9 inches to 1¼ feet long, approximately one-half as wide, and more or less crowded toward the ends of its branches. The fragrant flowers, in erect racemes, are 5 to 7 inches across, with the central cluster of many, white, pink-tipped, stamens nearly as wide. The crimson style is as long as the stamens. There are four petals. Heart-shaped, strongly four-angled, and 3 to 4 inches long, the fruits contain a single poisonous seed about 2 inches in length surrounded by a light brown, fibrous, spongy, waterproof husk. They are buoyant and capable of floating in seawater for long periods without impairing the ability of the seeds to grow. Because of this, they have traveled long distances across the ocean and established the species on the coasts of many islands in the Pacific. The flowers open at night and last but a few hours. At dusk they resemble the buds of large white tulips. Later the petals gradually unfold, bending backward and spreading widely to reveal the pompon of stamens. By morning the petals have fallen and all that remains is the pink stigma, arising from a hollow disk, and the two green sepals. Having a similar natural distribution, *B. racemosa* is a smaller tree with smaller, narrower, pointed leaves, spikes of white, pink-tinged flowers and egg-shaped fruits about 2 inches long.

Garden and Landscape Uses and Cultivation. Excellent shade trees, barringtonias are especially well adapted for landscaping near the sea. They are resistant to wind and salt spray and flourish in strong sun. They are best propagated by seed.

BARTONIA. See Mentzelia.

BARTRAM'S IXEA. See Sphenostigma.

BARTSCHELLA (Barts-chélla). Baja California is the home of the only species of *Bartschella*, a cactus distinguished from *Mammillaria* and other closely related kinds by its fruits, which open by splitting along a horizontal circling line. Named in honor of Dr. Paul Bartsch, it belongs in the cactus family CACTACEAE.

A clump-forming species up to 4 inches high, *B. schumannii* has plant bodies woolly at their apexes and about 2 inches in diameter. They are covered with large, four-angled tubercles. When young the stems are globular. Later they become cylindrical. The tubercles, tipped with areoles (spine-producing areas), at first are woolly, but later hairless. Each areole has about twelve spines of which usually one, but sometimes two or three, are central ones, white with brown ends and one is strongly hooked at its extremity. About 1½ inches in diameter, the carmine flowers have pink margins to their perianth lobes (petals), numerous erect stamens shorter than the slender, pale style, and a six-lobed, green stigma.

Garden and Landscape Uses and Cultivation. These are the same as for most small cactuses of the *Mammillaria* type, but *Bartschella* is rather more finicky and difficult to satisfy than many. It is a collector's item. For further information consult Cactuses.

BASELLA (Basél-la)—Malabar Nightshade. Six species, two African, three Madagascan, and one widely distributed in the tropics constitute *Basella* of the basella family BASELLACEAE. They are related to the Madeira vine or mignonette vine (*Anredera cordifolia*). Two kinds are cultivated for ornament, and their young shoots and leaves are used in the tropics as edible greens or potherbs. The name of the genus is a latinized form of a native Malabar one.

Basellas are somewhat fleshy annuals and biennials. They have smooth, alternate leaves, ovate to ovate-lanceolate, and little flowers in spikelike clusters at the ends of thickened stalks. The flowers have two sepals, five each petals and stamens, and usually three styles. The fleshy fruits are enclosed by the persistent corollas. The cultivated kinds are vigorous, twining vines and so similar that some botanists consider them a single species. Moderately tall *B. alba* has ovate to ovate-lanceolate leaves up to about 6 inches long and noticeably

less wide. Its spikes of whitish flowers are borne in loose clusters. Leaves as broad or broader than long and red flowers in smaller clusters of shorter spikes characterize *B. a. rubra*. The stems of this are purplish or green and in some horticultural variants the leaves are attractively marked with green, white, and pink. The fleshy fruits of both kinds are about ¼ inch in diameter.

Garden and Landscape Uses. Basellas are interesting ornamentals, grown as annuals for screening porches, covering fences, hiding walls, and other purposes for which temporary, quick-growing vines are appropriate. They revel in full sun and succeed in any ordinary, fertile garden soil.

Cultivation. In the south where long, warm growing seasons are experienced, Malabar nightshade may be grown from seeds sown in the open in early spring, but elsewhere it should be started early indoors and grown in pots in a sunny greenhouse in a night temperature of 55 to 60°F and day temperatures five to fifteen degrees higher. The plants may be set in the garden when it is safe to plant tomatoes. To have them available then, sow seeds about eight weeks earlier in a temperature of 65 to 70°F. Grow the young plants in about the same or a little lower temperature. Full sun, a fairly humid atmosphere, and generous supplies of water, if the soil is thoroughly drained, encourage good growth.

BASELLACEAE—Basella Family. Twenty-five American, Asian, and African species of four genera of dicotyledons are accommodated here. They are hairless herbaceous perennials with tubers or rhizomes from which twining stems grow. The generally fleshy, undivided leaves are alternate. Small and symmetrical, the bisexual or unisexual flowers are in racemes, spikes, or panicles. They have usually persistent calyx of five, sometimes partly united, often petal-like sepals, no petals, five stamens, and one style with three or rarely one stigma. The fruits are small berries or drupes. Genera cultivated are *Anredera, Basella,* and *Ullucus.*

BASIC SLAG. This by-product of steel making, sometimes called Thomas slag, is a phosphatic fertilizer, because of its high calcium content alkaline and especially suitable for clayey soils. It should not be used for acid-soil plants. It contains from 2 to 16 percent available phosphoric acid, which is released slowly over a long period. Apply basic slag before the ground freezes in fall at 4 to 8 ounces to 10 square feet.

BASIL. Common or sweet basil (*Ocimum basilicum*) is a herb, the leaves of which are used fresh and dried for flavoring a great

Sweet basil

variety of meat and fish dishes, spaghetti, vegetables, salads, soups, vinegars, and beverages. Its handsome, purple-leaved variety is also planted in flower beds, window boxes, and other places for ornament. Bush basil is a dwarfer, more compact kind with the same virtues and uses. There is also a curly-leaved basil, and one lemon-scented. These herbs have been esteemed since the times of ancient Greece, and in all likelihood from much earlier times. Holy basil (*O. sanctum*), a sacred plant of the Hindu religion, is sometimes included in herb gardens. It requires the same culture as common basil.

Basils grow without difficulty in ordinary gardens. They are treated as annuals. Full sun and thoroughly well-drained, not over-rich soil best suit them. Sow the seeds early indoors to give plants for transplanting outdoors when the weather has warmed five or six weeks later, or sow directly outdoors in spring. As a guide, remember that fully grown plants need at least 1 foot between individuals. Germination takes place within a few days. As soon as the seedlings are big enough to handle easily, transplant those indoors to flats, or individually to small pots. Thin young plants from outdoor sowings to suitable spacings, discarding the thinnings or transplanting them. Except for controlling weeds, little attention is needed. When flowers de-

Purple-leaved sweet basil

velop, cut the plants back to a height of 6 inches. This stimulates an abundance of young growth. Later, another cutting back may be desirable.

As well as its adaptability for herb gardens, flower gardens, and vegetable gardens, basil lends itself obligingly to cultivation outdoors in summer in pots, window and porch boxes, and other containers, and may be grown in pots in greenhouses and sunny windows in winter. For this last purpose plants may be grown from the seedling stage in pots, or in early fall plants from the garden may be cut back,

dug with large balls of soil, and potted. If this is done, they should be well watered and shaded for a week or two to help them recover from the transplanting operation. A night temperature indoors of about 55°F, increased by day by five to fifteen degrees, suits. Allow the soil to become slightly dryish, but not dry, between waterings. Occasional applications of dilute liquid fertilizer are helpful after the pots are filled with roots. For descriptions of common basil and its varieties, and information about other species see Ocimum. The plant called wild-basil is *Clinopodium vulgare*.

BASKET. As part of their common names for the word basket enters into those of these plants: basket flower (*Centaurea americana* and *Hymenocallis narcissiflora*), basket-grass (*Optismenus compositus*), and basket-of-gold (*Aurinia saxatilis*).

BASKETS, HANGING. See Hanging Baskets, Pots, and Planters.

BASSWOOD. See Tilia.

BASTARD. As part of the colloquial names of some plants, bastard generally signifies false. Bastard-balm is *Melittis melissophyllum*, bastard-indigo *Amorpha fruticosa*, bastard-mahogany *Eucalyptus botryoides*, and bastard-teak *Butea monosperma*.

BAT FLOWER. See Tacca.

BATEMANNIA (Bate-mánnia). Sometimes called *Batemania*, this genus of the orchid family ORCHIDACEAE was named in honor of James Bateman, a distinguished fancier who grew and wrote about orchids. He died in 1897.

The two or perhaps more species of *Batemannia* are compact, tree-perching (epiphytic) evergreens, related to *Bifrenaria*, but differing in having a pair of leaves instead of one from the apex of each pseudobulb, and in the loose racemes of flowers being nodding or drooping. A hybrid between *Batemannia colleyi* and *Zygopetalum crinitum* is *Zygobatemania mastersii*.

The pseudobulbs of **B. colleyi**, native of northern South America and Trinidad, are in crowded clusters. They are 2 to 3 inches long, four-angled, and approximately ovoid. The lustrous, leathery leaves, oblong-elliptic to lanceolate, narrowed to their bases, are 6 to 10 inches long by 3 inches wide. Four to seven together in up to 8-inch-long, loose racemes, the long-lasting, fragrant, fleshy flowers are 2 to 3 inches wide. The dorsal or back petal and sepals are nearly similar in size and color. Elliptic-oblong, and often greenish at their tips, they vary from dark wine-purple to brownish-red shaded with brown. The narrowly-oblong, sickle-shaped side sepals, folded along their inner margins, are purple flushed with brown, and margined

Batemannia colleyi

and tipped with green. The white three-lobed lip, which hugs the red-spotted, white column, is stained red at its base. The blooms come in fall and winter.

Smaller-flowered *B. armillata,* of Colombia, has ovoid pseudobulbs about 2 inches long, flattened laterally. Its broadish leaves are up to 8 inches long. Borne in summer, the fragrant, 2-inch-wide, waxy blooms are three to six together in loose racemes. They have greenish-white sepals, petals, and lip, the last suffused with brown, and three-lobed.

Garden Uses and Cultivation. These are as for *Bifrenaria.* For additional details see Orchids.

BATEOSTYLIS. This is the name of orchid hybrids the parents of which are *Batemannia* and *Otostylis.*

BATOKO-PLUM is *Flacourtia indica.*

BAUERA (Bau-èra). By some botanists the three species of the Australian genus *Bauera* are segregated in their own family, the BAUERACEAE, but traditionally they have been considered as belonging to the saxifrage family SAXIFRAGACEAE. They exhibit some characteristics of the loosestrife family LYTHRACEAE. Their name commemorates the German brothers Ferdinand and Franz Bauer, botanical artists of the sixteenth–seventeenth century.

Baueras are small, evergreen, heathlike shrubs of moist or wet soils. They have many slender or spreading stems with opposite leaves, the latter of three leaflets arranged so that each pair of leaves gives the superficial impression of being a circle of six slender leaves. The flowers, which resemble those of *Boronia,* are white to pink,

have calyxes of four to ten segments and as many petals and stamens as there are calyx segments. The fruits are capsules of two compartments containing several seeds.

Called river-rose and dog-rose in Australia, *B. rubioides* is most commonly cultivated. This is a spreading or erect, light-green-foliaged, graceful shrub up to 6 feet tall or taller. Its dainty flowers spread their several pink, or rarely white, petals widely and are freely produced. They are up to ¾ inch across, with yellow anthers. Other species are *B. capitata,* erect and with flowers up to ¾ inch across, in terminal heads, and *B. sessiliflora,* which has stalkless, magenta-pink blooms with dark anthers, in the leaf axils.

Garden Uses and Cultivation. These are plants for sandy, peaty, moist soils and for outdoor cultivation in frost-free or nearly frost-free, warm-temperate climates only. They are adaptable to cultivation in greenhouses in which the winter night temperature is 50°F and the day temperature at that season but a few degrees higher. When outside temperatures permit, the greenhouse should be ventilated freely. They need a sunny location and are easier to grow as pot plants than many Australian shrubs. Care must be taken that the soil is never allowed to become really dry. Propagation is by seeds and by cuttings of firm, but not hard shoots in spring or early summer. In their early stages the plants should be pinched occasionally to induce branching. Plants over one year old are trimmed to shape and repotted in spring in a fertile, peaty soil sufficiently porous to be watered frequently without becoming compact or soggy.

BAUHINIA (Bau-hínia)—Orchid Tree or Mountain-Ebony, Butterfly Flower or Jerusalem-Date, St. Thomas Tree. Widely distributed as natives of the tropics and

Bauera rubioides (flowers)

Bauera rubioides

subtropics of the eastern and western hemispheres, the possibly 250 species of *Bauhinia* belong to the pea family LEGUMINOSAE, but their flowers are not pea-like. They include evergreen and deciduous trees, shrubs, and woody climbers, some thorny. The name, commemorating the sixteenth–seventeenth century Swiss botanist brothers Jean and Gaspard Bauhin, was applied because the paired leaf lobes or leaflets suggested a brotherly relationship.

Bauhinia leaves sometimes have two leaflets, but more commonly are undivided, but deeply-cleft into two lobes, so that in shape they suggest the hoof print of an ox, a deer, a goat, a horse, or some other animal, according to the fancy of the observer. Less often they are without division or cleft. The white, pink, red, purple, or variegated blooms are in terminal or rarely axillary racemes or clusters. They have tubular, sometimes five-toothed, often split calyxes, those of a number of commonly cultivated kinds spathelike. There are five petals, ten or fewer stamens, some often represented by staminodes (nonfunctional stamens). The fruits are pods. In the Orient, the leaves and pods of *B. variegata* are eaten as a vegetable.

The orchid tree or mountain-ebony (**B. variegata**), native to India, southeast Asia, and China, is a favorite ornamental in

Bauhinia variegata (fruits)

southern Florida, Hawaii, and other warm regions. Medium-sized, stiff-branched, and deciduous, this kind has deeply-heart-shaped, nine- to eleven-veined leaves 4 to 6 inches across, cleft to about one-third of their lengths. In few-flowered clusters on short lateral branches the blooms, usually displayed when the trees are losing leaves or are leafless, have spathelike calyxes up to 1 inch long, and overlapping, wide-spreading, obovate petals up to 2 inches long and 1 inch wide or wider. They vary

in color from reddish-purple or magenta, becoming bluish as they age, to pale purple or lavender, with one petal stained darker. There are five fertile stamens, and a pistil nearly equaling the stamens in length. The seed pods are up to 1 foot long. Especially lovely is pure white-flowered *B. v. candida* (syn. *B. v. alboflava*).

Similar to *B. variegata* in foliage, and native of the same geographical region, **B. purpurea** is a less-rigidly-branched tree up to about 30 feet in height. Its fragrant blooms, borne in Florida in fall and early winter before the leaves drop, are in many-flowered clusters near the branch ends. They usually have spathelike calyxes rarely split into two parts or more, and narrowly-oblanceolate, long-clawed petals up to 3 inches long, but often shorter. They vary from palest pink through deeper shades to old rose, carmine, purple, and lavender. There are three or rarely four fertile stamens. The pods are 6 inches to 1 foot long.

Bauhinia purpurea

The butterfly flower or Jerusalem-date (**B. monandra**) is a deciduous shrub or medium-sized tree with spreading branches and foliage that closely resembles that of *B. variegata* and *B. purpurea*. The leaves, 4 to 6 inches across, are cleft nearly or quite to their middles into blunt, roundish lobes. The few-flowered, compressed racemes are borne in abundance in Florida from April to November. The blooms have 1-inch-long, spathelike calyxes. The corollas, about 4 inches wide, have obovate petals, narrowed to long basal claws. They are pale pink to rose-purple bespattered with tiny purple or wine-red spots. The upper petal is conspicuously darker, more brightly colored, and more distinctly spotted or streaked. There is one fertile stamen and staminodes of much reduced size. The seed pods are 6 inches to 1 foot long. This kind is native of tropical Asia.

The Hong Kong orchid-tree (**B. blakeana**) is perhaps the most handsome bau-

hinia. An evergreen, all cultivated specimens are descendants of a few trees discovered in Hong Kong and preserved and propagated there by missionaries. It has not been found in the wild and is believed to be of hybrid origin. The Hong Kong orchid-tree has fragrant, rich rose-purple to rose-crimson flowers 5 to 6 inches wide, borne in abundance over a long fall-to-spring season. They have 1-inch-long, spathelike calyxes, five pink fertile stamens, and two to five staminodes. Except for the number of its fertile stamens this species is very similar to *B. variegata*.

Red bauhinia (**B. punctata** syn. *B. galpinii*) is a wide-spreading, sprawling shrub

Bauhinia punctata

or semiclimber 8 to 10 feet tall that bears an abundance of bright brick-red, nasturtium-like flowers with five equal, slender-clawed, broad-bladed petals about 1½ inches long. The blooms, in Florida borne from May to October, are in clusters of six to ten. They are succeeded by pods up to 5 inches long. This native of tropical and southern Africa, withstands a few degrees of frost. It is popular in southern California and Florida. White-flowered **B. acuminata**

Bauhinia acuminata

of India is also a summer-blooming shrub. About 10 feet tall, it has leaves cleft for about one-third of their length, and showy blooms about 4 inches in diameter that have all ten stamens fertile and are in racemes.

Yellow bauhinia or St. Thomas tree (*B. tomentosa*) is an attractive shrub or small tree up to 15 feet in height, but often considerably lower. Native to India, China, and Africa, and naturalized in the West Indies, it has slender, more or less pendulous branches that, like the undersides of the leaves and the seed pods, are occasionally somewhat hairy. The leaves, 1½ to 3 inches long and about as broad as long, are cleft about one-third way into a pair of ovate lobes. The bell-shaped flowers, solitary or in twos or threes on short stalks from the leaf axils, and 1 inch to 2½ inches long, never open widely. They have a spathelike calyx, and yellow to light lemon-yellow petals, one of which is usually marked with a reddish, chocolate, or almost black spot. With age the flowers become dull purple, red, or brown. The seed pods are 3 to 6 inches long. This species is sometimes misidentified as *B. natalensis*, and its variant with whitish blooms as *B. picta*.

Bauhinia tomentosa

Thorny *B. forficata*, a native of South America, is a night-blooming, deciduous shrub or tree up to 20 feet tall with nine- to eleven-veined leaves up to 4 inches long by 3½ inches wide, and cleft halfway into two narrow lobes. The narrow-petaled, white or cream flowers, solitary or in twos, threes, or fours from the leaf axils, have petals 2 to 3½ inches long. They have all ten stamens fertile. The pods are up to 1 foot long. The plant cultivated as *B. candida*, and sometimes misnamed *B. corniulata*, is grown in California and probably Florida, and survives outdoors at Hous-

ton, Texas. It is a variant of *B. forficata*. Superior to *B. forficata*, very thorny *B. aculeata* (syn. *B. mollicella*), native from Mexico to northern South America, is a broad shrub or tree that attains a height of up to 20 feet. It has softly-hairy leaves cleft to about one-quarter of their length and, in clusters of up to five or sometimes solitary, handsome white flowers usually 3 to 4 inches across that become cream-colored as they age. They have all ten stamens fertile. A nonthorny shrub or small tree with white flowers that usually become pink as they age, *B. divaricata* is a variable native of the West Indies, Colombia, and Mexico to Nicaragua. Hardier than most bauhinias, it has leaves of various sizes that are commonly cleft for about one-third of their length. The blooms, in short, elongating panicles are borne through much of the year. They have one fertile stamen.

A beautiful tendril-bearing vine, phanera (*B. corymbosa*) is a variable native of eastern Asia. It has hairy shoots and leaves 1 inch to 2 inches long cleft nearly to their heart-shaped bases into a pair of three-veined, oval leaflets. The leafstalks and veins on the undersides of the blades are furnished with reddish hairs. The numerous, 1-inch-wide, pale pink flowers, each with three fertile stamens, are in loose panicles. They are succeeded by dark, purplish-brown seed pods about 6 inches long. Another tendril-bearing, more or less vining species, *B. binata* is native to southeastern Asia and the Molucca Islands. From the kinds discussed above it differs in its leaves having two entirely separate, small ovate leaflets. The flowers, in crowded axillary and terminal panicles, are about 2 inches across and white. They have ten stamens that usually become red as the flower ages. In Florida the blooms are borne from April to June. Another species with leaves of two separate leaflets, *B. saigonensis*, of Indochina, has red-veined, lavender-pink blooms in elongating racemes. They are about 1½ inches in diameter and, in Florida, are borne from April to November. Summer-blooming, and with white fragrant flowers about 1½ inches wide, the turtle vine (*B. glabra* syn. *B. cumanensis*), grown in Hawaii, is native from Mexico to the West Indies and South America. Its stems are flat and twisted. This bauhinia has two kinds of leaves, those of the young shoots cleft almost to their bases, others cleft to about their middles. A vigorous vine sometimes 100 feet high, Himalayan *B. vahlii* has leaves up to 1 foot long and wide, cleft to one-third of their length. Its yellowish, 2- to 2½-inch-wide flowers have three fertile stamens.

Garden and Landscape Uses. Throughout the tropics and warm subtropics bauhinias are prized as ornamentals useful for gardens, parks, roadsides, and other landscapes. They are planted in Florida in

Bauhinia vahlii

warm regions along the Gulf Coast, in California, and in Hawaii. The tree types are delightful as lawn specimens and for grouping with other trees and shrubs. The shrub kinds can be used similarly, and are suitable for espaliering against walls. Yellow-flowered *B. tomentosa* is effective as a sheared hedge. The vines are suitable for clothing pergolas and other supports. All thrive in sunny locations in ordinary soils.

Cultivation. Bauhinias are propagated by seeds, layering, and grafting. Cuttings often do not root easily. Maintenance care is minimal, about all usually needed being any pruning considered desirable to shape the plants or limit their size. This is best done as soon as flowering is through. Annual or more frequent fertilizing helps specimens growing in poor soil.

BAY. This is used as part of the common names of various plants. Bull bay is the name of *Magnolia grandiflora* and *Persea borbonia*. The latter is also known as red bay. The loblolly-bay is *Gordonia lasianthus*. Rose bay is *Rhododendron maximum*, mountain rose bay *R. catawbiense*. Swamp-bay is *Magnolia virginiana*. This last is also sometimes called sweet bay, which is also a common name of *Laurus nobilis*.

BAY RUM TREE is *Pimenta racemosa*.

BAYBERRY. See Myrica.

BEACH. A number of plants have included in their common names the word beach. It generally alludes to their seaside habitats. Beach grass is *Ammophila*, beach-heather *Hudsonia*, beach-pea *Lathyrus maritimus*, beach plum *Prunus maritima*. The beach-wallflower is *Erysimum suffrutescens*, the beach wormwood *Artemisia stelleriana*.

BEAD PLANT is *Nertera granadensis*.

BEAD TREE. See Melia, and Ormosia.